Chambers Associate

The Student's Guide to Law Firms

2017 - 2018

CHAMBERS
AND PARTNERS

www.chambers-associate.com

Publisher: Michael Chambers
Editor: Antony Cooke
Deputy Editor: Phil Roe
Writers: Alexis Self, Amalia Neenan, Anna Winter, David Brooks, Eleanor Veryard, Emma Bradding, George Murray, Harry Cerasale, Isaac Martin, Joshua Collier, Katie Read, Katya Gorska, Liv Klingert, Michael Bird, Natalie Bertram, Paul Rance, Rebecca Chircop, Ruaidhri Dowd, Sam Morris, Sarah Fairman, Tania Wimpenny, Thomas Lewis
Production: Jasper John, David Nobakht
Business Development Director: Brad Sirott
Sales Manager: Darren Saunders
Advertising Manager: Saskia van Emden

Published by Chambers and Partners Publishing
(a division of Orbach & Chambers Ltd)
39-41 Parker Street, London WC2B 5PQ
Tel: +44 (020) 7606 8844   Fax: +44 (020) 7831 5662
www.chambers-associate.com

Our thanks to the many associates, recruiters and partners who assisted us in our research.
ISBN: 978-0-85514-637-5

Contents

Chambers Associate 2017-18

"WHEN I was interviewing for firms to work for as law student, I was somewhat overwhelmed by the number, and how similar they all are." This was a Gibson Dunn associate interviewing with us this year. He articulated a problem almost every law student faces: that the market is, at first glance, quite homogeneous and inconveniently huge. When firms benchmark each other so rigorously on salaries, hours, perks or diversity policy, drawing up a shortlist of firms is not easy. And then we're told getting a job is really about finding the 'right fit'. But while you're scouring firm websites to detect any sign of character traits, you find their main messages are frustratingly similar: 'unwavering client service'; 'practice breadth and strength'; 'global opportunities'; 'collegiality'.

This is just the surface, of course – all law firms are genuinely different. To get a sense of a firm's personality, we'd recommend talking to the lawyers working there. It's this kind of personal interaction that we capture in our interview-based research: we find out what lies beyond the branding. Our researchers ask the questions a student might shy away from; our lawyer sources speak more freely than if they were representing the firm publicly.

There is a lot at stake at this stage in your career. You should know what you want – or don't want – from this high-pressured profession. You should proceed knowing you're targeting firms that are *good enough* for you. For this reason we've worked hard to develop our data and comparison tools, which are worth checking out on the website. Online we've also added advice on how to get into each firm, as told by the hiring partners and associates. We've expanded our practice area guides too: lawyers specializing in climate change, wealth management, media law, life sciences, privacy law and many more sectors have pitched in to help us appreciate how they spend their days and the stories affecting their profession. The overall result is a more comprehensive guide that takes you through the difficult decisions, equips you for interviews, and helps you proceed with confidence.

The *Chambers Associate* team
June 2017

Our Editorial Team

Antony Cooke
Editor

Antony Cooke
Editor of *Chambers Associate* and *Chambers Student Guide*. Graduated from Durham University in Russian & French. Taught English at St. Petersburg State University. Previously worked at Michelin as a European project manager, and at PricewaterhouseCoopers as an associate in investment management. Fluent in Russian and French.

antonyc@chambersandpartners.com

Phil Roe
Deputy Editor

Phil Roe
Deputy editor of *Chambers Associate*. Joined Chambers & Partners in 2007 from a global executive search firm, where he advised private equity clients. Has written extensively for both *Chambers Associate* and the *Student Guide*. Graduated with an MA in English from Oxford University, and is a theater critic for London-based newspapers in his free time.

philr@chambersandpartners.com

Our Editorial Team *continued*

Sam Morris
Deputy editor. Sam graduated from the University of Leiden, The Netherlands with a first in Political Science in 2008 and from the London School of Economics with an MSc in Comparative Politics in 2009. He has worked for the Dutch Ministry of Foreign Affairs. Speaks Dutch and German.

Paul Rance
Assistant editor. Graduated from Exeter University with a first in English Literature and also spent a year abroad at the University of Toronto to read Canadian literature. He completed his MA in English at UCL in 2010.

Amalia Neenan
Graduated in 2014 with a degree in law from the University of Kent. Studied the Bar Professional Training Course at City University London and is also an ADR Group Accredited Civil & Commercial Mediator.

Anna Winter
Senior Researcher. Anna graduated with a BA in English Literature from Balliol College, Oxford. She took journalism qualifications following internships at *The Observer* and the *New Statesman* magazine.

Eleanor Veryard
Graduated in 2011 with a bachelor's degree in History before completing a master's in Early Modern History at the University of Sheffield, UK. Previously worked as editor-in-chief of a monthly student magazine and as a teaching assistant.

Harry Cerasale
Graduated in 2015 with a BA in History from the University of Nottingham. Has previously worked as an English teacher in Vietnam and Cambodia.

Michael Bird
Graduated from Royal Holloway, University of London with a BA in History. Prior to Chambers, Michael worked for US-based entertainment websites, and continues to review music in his spare time.

Natalie Bertram
Graduated in 2016 from the University of Exeter with a BA Hons in English Literature. Freelances as a proof reader in her free time.

Tom Lewis
Graduated in 2015 with a BA in History from the University of Sheffield.

What is *Chambers Associate*?

Welcome to *Chambers Associate* 2017-18

NOW in its ninth edition and growing year on year, *Chambers Associate* gives law students an unparalleled view into the working lives of associates at the nation's leading law firms. We're the only US legal career guide to conduct in-depth telephone interviews with thousands of junior associates on the topics that matter to juniors, like the work they do day to day, the social life (if there is one), pro bono, diversity, how hard they work you, how much money you make, personal development, and much more. We grant our interviewees anonymity so they can speak to us honestly and truthfully. We also talk to firm chairs, managing partners and hiring partners to understand who and how they recruit from law school, and the directions their firms are headed.

The qualitative approach

Chambers Associate reviews firms on a qualitative basis. We also draw on *Chambers USA*, our vast annual directory of US law firms based on client reviews. In each Inside View you will see a reference to *Chambers USA* rankings, which gives you a snapshot of a firm's practice area strengths, as rated by its clients. *Chambers USA*'s rankings cover key practice areas across all US states. For the full listing with commentary, visit the Chambers and Partners website.

About Chambers and Partners

Since 1990, Chambers and Partners has published the world's most trusted and comprehensive guides to the legal profession. Titles include *Chambers USA, Chambers UK, Chambers Asia-Pacific, Chambers Canada, Chambers Europe, Chambers Latin America, Chambers Global,* and *Chambers High Net Worth.* Clients and lawyers around the globe consider Chambers to be the authority on the world's leading law firms and lawyers.

For 20 years we've also published the market-leading career guide for law students in the UK, the *Chambers Student Guide.*

All Chambers publications are freely accessible online at www.chambersandpartners.com.

The Associate Satisfaction survey

In the 2017 survey, associates gave a rating for the factors that contribute toward their happiness. We compiled the results. Here are the top 40 firms.

Most satisfied associates 2017

1	Seward & Kissel
2	Finnegan
3	Morrison & Foerster
4	Clifford Chance
5	Perkins Coie
6	Gibson Dunn
7	Weil
8	Cooley
9	Kramer Levin
10	Cravath
11	Latham & Watkins
12	Proskauer
13	Thompson & Knight
14	Jenner & Block
15	Cozen O'Connor
16	Goodwin Procter
17	McDermott Will & Emery
18	Milbank
19	Crowell
20	Waller
21	Skadden
22	Winston & Strawn
23	Fried Frank
24	King & Spalding
25	Debevoise
26	Holland & Knight
27	Paul, Weiss
28	Hogan Lovells
29	Choate
30	DLA Piper
31	Kirkland & Ellis
32	Irell & Manella
33	Simpson Thacher
34	Axinn
35	Mintz Levin
36	Orrick
37	Gibbons
38	Patterson Belknapp
39	Paul Hastings
40	Arnold & Porter Kaye Scholer

LEADING the chart for associate satisfaction is Seward & Kissel, an unassuming New York firm specializing in shipping finance and hedge funds. Most striking about Seward's achievement is that the firm has done nothing particularly showy to get to the top of the table. In fact its formula for satisfaction is a no-brainer: associates got a kick out of the work and enjoyed being with their colleagues. Our sources were attracted to a place with a *"boutique firm feel that still does high-speed work. I think it's our biggest selling point."*

Our research last year showed that niche practices make associates happier. This is true of Seward & Kissel, IP specialists Finnegan in second place, and our third place firm MoFo – a much broader firm but with the IP/tech slant providing the intrigue for associates. And throughout this top 40, the pull of the niche practice area stands out, from advertising litigators Kramer Levin to heathcare experts Waller.

"Its reputation made me want to come here," declared a Finnegan associate. *"Year after year it's ranked as one of the top IP firms in the world."* Prestige is just a perception, of course, but to see the value in your work is the point from which prestige originates – and how valued or valuable you feel affects your satisfaction. To explore this, let's look at the firm in 10th place: Cravath. When we interviewed associates, the firm's formidable reputation was a *"source of pride"* to its juniors, who explained that this factor alone motivated them – *"absolutely no one here shies away from working extremely hard."* The famous Cravath business model endows junior associates with considerable self-worth: *"I was amazed at the level of responsibility,"* recounted one source.

Perhaps surprisingly, some of the most fearsome names in BigLaw pepper this top 40 – Skadden, Gibson Dunn, Latham, Clifford Chance, Milbank, Debevoise, Kirkland, Simpson Thacher – all global leaders where you might expect associate satisfaction to play second fiddle to results and billing. But associates at Gibson Dunn helped us understand how high pressure and happiness can coexist: *"Everyone here is so smart and has something to teach you all the time. The people and the work keep me on my toes, but at the same time it's a warm place – ego is checked at the door!"*

Associates among these high-achieving firms generally felt their firms bucked the BigLaw stereotypes: *"In the law there's a lot of competition, and often a dog eat dog attitude, but I've never felt it within the firm,"* reflected one from Gibson Dunn. *"There are some competitive, intense* people here but their energies are directed toward other side!"

> "I'm respected as a human being and not just an hours generator. If I have to work on weekends it is not because I feel it is expected of me, but because it is required."
>
> – Perkins Coie associate

Throughout this guide you'll see how a firm's structure, or the way it generates income, has a direct impact on its culture. Take Clifford Chance (in at 4th) as an example: *"We're not trying to be a typical New York firm,"* insisted a junior. *"We're intentionally operating a different model: here the partners are not directly competing against one another and all of the groups share profits."* This model at the British firm appears to build *"a strong sense of community. We share the work and we get along – no one gets jealous."* Finnegan associates found a similar environment: *"I feel really comfortable here. We have a team mentality and everyone wants each other to succeed."*

All associates acknowledge the pressures of BigLaw, but those at MoFo felt the firm had found a balance: *"We're serious when we need to be, but the firm in general tends to be laid back and feels very human."* At Perkins Coie *"there aren't any petty tyrants,"* reported associates. *"I'm respected as a human being and not just an hours genera-*

tor. *If I have to work on weekends it is not because I feel it is expected of me, but because it is required. Whenever it's tough there's an appreciation for the work we do."*

"We have a very open and accepting environment where people feel comfortable and make an effort to be inclusive," a Perkins Coie lawyer surmised. *"Junior and mid-level associates constantly put pressure on management to do more than they're doing."* Empowering your associates clearly pays off at this firm, which also scores highly for its attitude to diversity. Similarly, Chicagoan Jenner & Block is famous for the premium it puts on pro bono and diversity – *"the only thing not tolerated is intolerance!"* – joked associates, who raved about their firm during our calls with them.

From all these firms we learn that culture is everything. If a law firm is happy in its own skin, the junior associates are too. If a firm recognizes that humans are its only commodity, humanity defines its culture – a trait common to all the firms in this table.

Methodology
To compile these results we asked associates to rate how happy they were, how stressed they were, how much their firm is worth to them on their resumes, how long they intend to stay, how strongly they'd recommend their firm, and whether the salary justified the dedication required. The firms listed are those demonstrating strong performance.

> '**Throughout this guide you'll see how a firm's structure, or the way it generates income, has a direct impact on its culture.'**

The benefits and lifestyle survey

How well do firms treat their junior lawyers? In the high pressured world of BigLaw, can lawyers find some balance in their lives?

Benefits and lifestyle: The best firms 2017

1	Clifford Chance
2	Gibson Dunn
3	Patterson Belknapp
4	Kramer Levin
5	Morrison & Foerster
6	Proskauer
7	Cahill
8	Goodwin Procter
9	Harris Wiltshire
10	Winston & Strawn
11	Cooley
12	Finnegan
13	Willkie Farr
14	Weil
15	Orrick
16	Crowell
17	Hogan Lovells
18	Latham & Watkins
19	Jenner & Block
20	Munger Tolles & Olson
21	Cozen O'Connor
22	Linklaters
23	Milbank
24	Debevoise
25	Arnold & Porter Kaye Scholer
26	Axinn
27	McDermott Will & Emery
28	Waller
29	Simpson Thacher
30	Cravath
31	Stroock & Stroock
32	Irell & Manella
33	Shearman & Sterling
34	Kirkland & Ellis
35	Thompson & Knight
36	Seward & Kissel
37	Mintz Levin
38	Perkins Coie
39	DLA Piper
40	Fried Frank

MONEY or work/life balance? That's the conundrum law firm applicants usually face. But the trade-off isn't clear cut. You can expect to work long hours wherever you end up. Surprisingly, as this table shows, there are plenty of big name firms where associates smile about their lifestyle as much as their bonus. Top of the list is Clifford Chance, where the daily grind is (one junior told us frankly) *"like that Rihanna song: work, work, work, work, work!"* Nevertheless, and winningly, *"there's a strong sense of community. We share the work and we get along."* Clifforders also loved not being chained to their desks when work is less manic: *"We're not trying to be a typical New York firm."*

Flexibility around daily work hours and vacation time was the deal-clincher for associates at high-performing firms in this survey – treating juniors like adults, in other words. Among our top five, Kramer Levin scored least well for the bonus (although better than many firms), but outperformed others in the family-friendliness and vacation stakes. *"I would say coming into the firm it was a concern, because I have kids,"* reported one Kramer parent, but happily *"nobody has any problems if I leave at 6pm. I've found people to be very respectful of holidays and vacations."* Another chimed: *"It's very pleasant and humane – not a harsh, cut-throat place at all."* Winston & Strawn (10th place) performed particularly well on both the bonus and its willingness to accommodate lawyers with families: the firm *"would be a great option for having kids and making this job work,"* according to someone here.

At Gibson Dunn (2nd), *"things really ebb and flow – sometimes I can come in at 10am and leave at 5pm with an hour for lunch, but if a case is going crazy then I'll be up late."* Crucially, *"everyone is very supportive. The mindset is that we're in this together."* Cahill associates were thrilled about their famously above-market bonuses. Although they also praised generous caregiver policies, taking time off can sometimes be tricky: *"That's the negative side of the free market – getting work on your plate is easy but when you need to get it off it can be really hard."* But like other highly ranked firms in this table, Cahill's work culture shines through: *"One of the biggest reasons that I love my job is the people who work here."*

Our conclusion? A healthy work lifestyle and healthier pay check are not mutually exclusive. True associate happiness, it would seem, flows from a supportive – if demanding – firm culture.

Methodology

We asked associates to rate the bonus they receive against market, the whole benefits package, and their firms' attitudes to flexible working, taking vacation, and raising a family. The firms listed are those demonstrating strong performance.

The pro bono survey

Want to learn the craft of the lawyer fast? Then take on early pro bono cases. We asked associates to rate how well their firms supported this.

The best firms for pro bono 2017

1	Jenner & Block
2	Munger Tolles & Olson
3	Morrison & Foerster
4	Orrick
5	Kramer Levin
6	Arnold & Porter Kaye Scholer
7	Finnegan
8	Gibbons
9	Gibson Dunn
10	Paul, Weiss
11	Hogan Lovells
12	Patterson Belknapp
13	Harris Wiltshire
14	Willkie Farr
15	Morgan Lewis
16	Irell & Manella
17	Crowell
18	Goodwin Procter
19	Fried Frank
20	Latham & Watkins
21	Debevoise
22	Dechert
23	Mintz Levin
24	Skadden
25	Perkins Coie
26	Paul Hastings
27	Weil
28	Proskauer
29	Nutter
30	Winston & Strawn
31	Cooley
32	McDermott Will & Emery
33	Simpson Thacher
34	Hunton & Williams
35	Kirkland & Ellis
36	Stroock & Stroock
37	Milbank
38	Duane Morris
39	Davis Polk
40	DLA Piper

A SENSE of ownership and not worrying about that tiresome clock were common themes at firms that scored highly for pro bono. *"Jenner is awesome about letting you do whatever you want,"* reported an associate at our first-placed firm. Another Jennerite stressed that *"pro bono is very much part of the culture. Partners see pro bono as a time for associates to gain substantive experience."* This is a mindset found at other high-ranking firms including Gibbons (8th place), where *"for a young associate, pro bono is a great way to get onto a deposition, own a case, or stand on your feet."* We should also point out that Jenner's willingness to take on high profile cases – even as far as the Supreme Court, like for gay marriage – also provoked excitement among associates.

At second-placed Munger, *"people have no problems with me doing ridiculous amounts of pro bono"* and *"it's embedded in the culture of the firm."* Similarly, over at MoFo, in third place, *"right away you're staffed on pro bono matters and it's taken very seriously."* At Orrick (4th), one junior associate *"told the pro bono partner I was interested in women's rights, so he gave me cases I'd be interested in."* Respondents at all these firms and more agreed with the Harris, Wiltshire & Grannis (13th) attorney who told us: *"Pro bono hours are treated the same"* as billable hours. They also agreed with the Latham (20th) interviewee who concluded that pro bono is *"a really good way to run your own files."* The best firms for pro bono let their associates run with cases that interest them, and make clear that this kind of work is just as important as assignments for paying clients.

Methodology

We asked associates to give a rating for how interesting the pro bono work is, how much it has helped them further their careers, how dedicated their firm is to pro bono, and whether they feel any pressure from partners NOT to do pro bono. The firms listed are those demonstrating strong performance.

The diversity survey

Associates rate their own firms' diversity efforts.

Diversity: The best firms 2017

1	Debevoise
2	Mintz Levin
3	Cooley
4	Nixon Peabody
5	Paul, Weiss
6	Waller
7	Weil
8	Harris Wiltshire
9	Proskauer
10	Perkins Coie
11	Finnegan
12	Morrison & Foerster
13	Haynes and Boone
14	Clifford Chance
15	Jenner & Block
16	McDermott Will & Emery
17	Goodwin Procter
18	Kramer Levin
19	Orrick
20	Cozen O'Connor
21	Paul Hastings
22	Latham & Watkins
23	Gibbons
24	Crowell
25	Vinson & Elkins
26	Skadden
27	Cravath
28	Gibson Dunn
29	Shearman & Sterling
30	Fried Frank
31	Simpson Thacher
32	Willkie Farr
33	Munger Tolles & Olson
34	Hogan Lovells
35	Patterson Belknapp
36	Cahill
37	Arnold & Porter Kaye Scholer
38	Kirkland & Ellis
39	Duane Morris
40	Baker & McKenzie

THE most striking thing about BigLaw diversity is that even the firms who do it well could do better. Associates gave Debevoise the highest marks for diversity in our survey because *"at the junior and mid levels you can see that there's a lot of progress,"* yet, tellingly, *"any higher and I think it's unbalanced."* Nevertheless, Debevoise attorneys sang the praises of numerous initiatives to make things better, not least an annual firm dinner where *"everyone gets together and the firm talks about where it currently stands on diversity, and where our emphasis is going to be placed in the future."*

Acknowledging and doing something about the diversity problem is a characteristic shared by other firms who performed well in our survey. *"You can't fault the firm for not trying,"* was the verdict of juniors at second-placed Mintz Levin. They too pointed to a yearly diversity event (*"people from all the offices gather for it"*), plus initiatives like affinity groups and a diversity scholarship, as evidence that their firm is trying hard. Likewise at Cooley (3rd place), *"they're making an effort but it's tough. The recruiting pool isn't particularly large and that's a big problem. It's certainly a high priority for the firm."*

Further down our rankings, Perkins Coie (10th) holds not one but two firmwide diversity retreats, one for women and one for minorities. During our calls, interviewees here were *"really looking forward to the women's retreat. I've heard it's everyone's favorite as it focuses more on networking than training and has lots of interesting speakers."* Many firms these days, including Perkins, have a dedicated diversity officer, usually either a partner or full-time staff member. Many also partner with external organizations. Goodwin Procter (17th), for example, is one of many firms in this guide that has established ties with the Leadership Council on Legal Diversity. All of the firms that scored highly for diversity plow significant resources and time into this issue.

Methodology

We asked associates to rate their firm on its efforts to recruit diverse associates, the firm's inclusivity training, the mentoring from diverse role models, how diverse staffing is on teams, and efforts to retain diverse lawyers. The firms listed are those demonstrating strong performance.

Law firm comparison data

How do you choose the right firm?

The menu of firms to choose between is bewildering. Researching them all would be a waste of time. Increase your prospect of getting a job by choosing the firm that suits you.

Step 1: work out what matters in your life – not what others expect of you

Consider how you respond to stress, work/life balance, how much autonomy you can handle, what subject matter gets you going, how you build and rely on personal relationships, and whether prestige motivates you. Will you become a pillar of your local business community or a jet-setting deal-maker? Do you thrive in disorder or need to control everything? Are you buttoned-up or dress down? Aggressive or collaborative?

Step 2: refine your search

Shortlist cities and regions. Then pick some practice areas you think you'd thrive in – firms will be looking for someone with focus and passion. The practice area reviews in this guide will make sense of your options. The chambers-associate.com search will round down the firms you should look at.

Step 3: read the introductions

Open the Inside View and read the first few paragraphs. Does it sound like your bag? Remember your wish list from Step 1 and have a look at our reviews of the firm culture, in particular. Bookmark all the firms that stand out.

Step 4: compare your shortlist

Use the comparison function on chambers-associate.com to compare your firms on every factor that counts: salary, pro bono, billables, diversity stats, size of firm, Chambers rankings, international offices, maternity allowance…

www.chambers-associate.com

Hours and Compensation Survey

Firm	1st year salary	2nd year salary	Billable hour requirement/ target	Average billable hours per associate 2016	Average pro bono hours per at-torney	Billable pro bono hours	Total pro bono hours across US offices in 2016
Adam Leitman Bailey	$150,000	U	U	U	U	U	U
Akin Gump Strauss Hauer & Feld	$180,000	$190,000	None	U	100	Unlimited	83,761
Allen & Overy	$180,000	$190,000	2,000 target	1,602	31	50	5,611
Alston & Bird	$155,000 - $180,000	$160,000 - $190,000	2,000 target	U	64	150	49,514
Arnold & Porter Kaye Scholer	$180,000	U	2,000 target	U	93	U	92,873
Axinn, Veltrop & Harkrider	$170,000 - $180,000	$175,000 - $190,000	1,800	1,840	30	100	1,999
Baker Botts	$180,000	U	2,000	U	80	Unlimited	33,932
Baker McKenzie	$145,000 - $180,000	U	2,000	U	U	U	U
Bracewell	$180,000	$190,000	2,000 target	U	U	100	9,258
Brown Rudnick	$180,000	$190,000	1,900 required	U	59	U	9,159
Brownstein Hyatt Farber Schreck	$135,000	$140,000	1,900 required	1,733	49	100	12,749
Cadwalader, Wickersham & Taft	$180,000	$190,000	2,000 target	1,665	24	200	8,186
Cahill Gordon & Reindel	$180,000	$190,000	None	U	37	Unlimited	11,989
Choate Hall & Stewart	$180,000	$190,000	2,000	U	35	Unlimited	4,115
Cleary Gottlieb Steen & Hamilton	$180,000	$190,000	None	U	80	Unlimited	56,647
Clifford Chance	$180,000	$190,000	None	U	U	Unlimited	U
Cooley	$180,000	$190,000	1,950 target	1,921	57	Unlimited	43,858
Cozen O'Connor	$125,000 - $160,000	U	1,600 - 2,000	1,809	30	75	16,442
Cravath, Swaine & Moore	$180,000	$190,000	None	U	52	Unlimited	25,874
Crowell & Moring	$180,000	$190,000	2,000	1,800	78	50	35,855
Curtis, Mallet-Prev-ost, Colt & Mosle	$180,000	$190,000	2,000 target	1,621	26	Unlimited	3,456
Davis Polk & Wardwell	$180,000	$190,000	None	U	45	Unlimited	40,676
Debevoise & Plimpton	$180,000	$190,000	None	U	132.5	Unlimited	66,268
Dechert	180,000	190,000	1,950 target	U	103	Unlimited	77,671
DLA Piper	$160,000 - $180,000	U	2,000 target	1,827	85	U	117,108
Duane Morris	$140,000 - $165,000	Undisclosed	1,950	U	49	100	31,725
Dykema Gossett	$120,000 - $150,000	U	1,950	U	U	40	U

U = undisclosed

Hours and Compensation Survey *continued*

Firm	1st year salary	2nd year salary	Billable hour requirement/ target	Average billable hours per associate 2016	Average pro bono hours per at-torney	Billable pro bono hours	Total pro bono hours across US offices in 2016
Epstein Becker & Green	$130,000 - $140,000	U	1,950	1,750	21	100	5,500
Finnegan, Hen-derson, Farabow, Garrett & Dunner	$180,000	$190,000	2,000 target	1,897	93.3	100	11,732
Fish & Richardson	$180,000	$190,000	1,900	1,886	56	200	19,253
Fitzpatrick, Cella, Harper & Scinto	$180,000	U	2,160 target	U	28	Unlimited	3,710
Foley & Lardner	$140,000 - $180,000	$150,000 - $195,000	1,900	1,823	56	100	46,656
Fox Rothschild	$115,000 - $160,000	U	1850 (1,900 in litigation)	1,793	10.3	50	7,870
Freshfields Bruckhaus Deringer	$180,000	$190,000	None	U	70	Unlimited	11,743
Fried, Frank, Harris, Shriver & Jacobson	$180,000	$190,000	2,000 target		74.3	300	32,983
Gibbons	U	$135,000	1,980	1,741	70	50	13,109
Gibson, Dunn & Crutcher	$180,000	$190,000	None	U	131	Unlimited	152,912
Goodwin	$180,000	$190,000	1,950	U	67	Unlimited	59,877
Goulston & Storrs	$180,000	$190,000	2,000 target	1,950	U	Unlimited	11,843
Greenberg Traurig	$110,000 - $180,000	U	None	U	16	Unlimited	25,603
Hangley Aronchick Segal Pudlin & Schiller	$135,000	Varies	None	U	U	None	U
Harris, Wiltshire & Grannis	$178,500	$189,500	None	1,485	42.7	Unlimited	2,235
Haynes and Boone	$180, 000	$190, 000	1,800-2,000	1,645	45.1	100	12,915
Hogan Lovells	$180,000 (varies by city)	$190,000 (varies by city)	2,000 target	U	85	Varies	87,864
Holland & Knight	$180,000	$190,000	1900 required	U	65	100	65,908
Hughes Hubbard & Reed	$180,000	$190,000	1,950 target	1,900	140	200	50,000 +
Hunton & Williams	$160,000 - $180,000		2,000 target	1,839	55	50	37,285
Irell & Manella	$180,000	$190,000	2,000 target	1,830	147	Unlimited	18,086
Jackson Walker	$180,000	U	1,950	1,814	16	Count as non-billable hours	6,253
Jenner & Block	$180,000	$190,000	2,100 target	U	141	Unlimited	75,419
Jones Day	$160,000 - $180,000		2,000 target	U		Unlimited ap-proval	108,334
K&L Gates	$140,000 - $180,000	Undisclosed	1,950 target	U	44	Unlimited	53,620
Kasowitz Benson Torres	$180,000	$190,000	2,150 target	U	38	Unlimited	9,903

U = undisclosed

Hours and Compensation Survey *continued*

Firm	1st year salary	2nd year salary	Billable hour requirement/ target	Average billable hours per associate 2016	Average pro bono hours per attorney	Billable pro bono hours	Total pro bono hours across US offices in 2016
Katten Muchin Rosenman	$180,000	$190,000	2,000 required	U	40	100	25,919
Kilpatrick Townsend & Stockton	$120,000 - $180,000	$135,000 - $195,000	1,400 0r 1,900	1,794	56	50	38,099
King & Spalding	$155,000 - $180,000	U	None	1,949	32.7	100	26,094
Kirkland & Ellis	$180,000	$190,000	None	U	67	Unlimited	109,481
Kramer Levin Naftalis & Frankel	$180,000	$190,000	1,950 target	1,743	66	Unlimited	19,633
Latham & Watkins	$180,000	U	1,900 target	U	94	Unlimited	164,628
Linklaters	$180,000	$190,000	None	U	34	Unlimited	4,236
Mayer Brown	$180,000	$190,000	2,000 required	U	60	200	52,608
McDermott Will & Emery	$180,000	$190,000	2,000 target	U	46	100	46,993
Milbank, Tweed, Hadley & McCloy	$180,000	$190,000	None	U	101	Unlimited	49,855
Mintz Levin Cohn Ferris Glovsky and Popeo PC	$180,000	$190,000	2,000 target	U	31	Unlimited if billable target met	14,716
Morgan, Lewis & Bockius	$165,000 - $180,000	$170,000 - $190,000	None	U	57.5	Unlimited	99,404
Morrison & Foerster	$180,000	$190,000	U	U	123	Unlimited	86,000
Munger, Tolles & Olson	$180,000	$190,000	None	1,652	145.7	Unlimited	28,273
Nixon Peabody	$160,000	$165,000	1,850 required	1,761	47	60	33,754
Norton Rose Fulbright	$180,000 (CA, NY, DC, TX)	$190,000 (CA, NY, DC, TX)	None	U	U	100	U
Nutter McClennen & Fish	$160,000	U	1,900	1,686	46.4	Unlimited	6,106
O'Melveny & Myers	$180,000	$190,000	None	U	104	Unlimited	60,914
Orrick, Herrington & Sutcliffe	$165,000 - $180,000	$175,000 - $190,000	2,000 target	1,727	137	Unlimited	84,420
Patterson Belknap Webb & Tyler	$180,000	$190,000	2,150 target	U	135	Once 1,850 billables met	23,749
Paul Hastings	$180,000	$190,000	2,000 target		109	Unlimited	84,672
Paul, Weiss, Rifkind, Wharton & Garrison	$180,000	$190,000	None	U	74	Unlimited	74,167
Perkins Coie	$105,000 - $180,000	$110,000 - $190,000	1,850 - 1,950	1,967	51	Unlimited	52,075
Pillsbury Winthrop Shaw Pittman	$180,000	$190,000	1,950	U	64.8	Unlimited	36,696
Proskauer Rose	$125,000 - $180,000	$130,000 - $190,000	None	U	58.5	Unlimited	422,287
Reed Smith	$130,000 - $180,000	U	1,900 required	U	56	120	54,384

U = undisclosed

Hours and Compensation Survey *continued*

Firm	1st year salary	2nd year salary	Billable hour requirement/ target	Average billable hours per associate 2016	Average pro bono hours per attorney	Billable pro bono hours	Total pro bono hours across US offices in 2016
Ropes & Gray	$180,000	$190,000	None	U	103	Unlimited	112,039
Schiff Hardin	$180,000	U	2,000 required	1,978	53	Unlimited	16,943
Schulte Roth & Zabel	$180,000	$190,000	2,000		37	200	12,583
Sedgwick	Varies	Varies	1,950 required	U	U	25	U
Seward & Kissel	$180,000	$190,000	2,000 target	1,665	39	Unlimited	8,820
Shearman & Sterling	$180,000	$190,000	None	U	85	Unlimited	37,416
Sheppard, Mullin, Richter & Hampton	$180,000	$190,000	1,950 target	1,791	39	Unlimited	29,630
Sidley Austin	$180,000	$190,000	2,000 target	U	67	Unlimited	120,473
Simpson Thacher & Bartlett	$180,000	$190,000	None	U	62	Unlimited	47,492
Skadden, Arps, Slate, Meagher & Flom & Affiliates	$180,000	$190,000	1,800 required	U	97	Unlimited	152,616
Snell & Wilmer	$115,000 - $160,000	U	1,800 - 1,950 target	1,670	34	Unlimited	14,085
Squire Patton Boggs	$135,000- $180,000	U	1,900 required	U	U	100	18,825
Sterne, Kessler, Goldstein & Fox	$165,000 - $180,000	$175,000 - $190,000	1,900 - 2,000 target	1,909	6.4	Varies	1,000
Stroock & Stroock & Lavan	$180,000	$190,000	2,000 target	U	55	200	17,971
Sullivan & Cromwell	$180,000	$190,000	None	U	56	Unlimited	36,406
Thompson & Knight	$180,000	$190,000	1,900 target	2,052	27	Unlimited (with approval)	3,254
Vedder Price	$180,000	$185,000 - $190,000	2,000 target	U	U	60	U
Venable	$180,000	$190,000	1,900 required	U	43	50	29,254
Vinson & Elkins	$180,000	$190,000	2,000 target	U	41.5	Unlimited	23,260
Waller	$115,000	$126,000	1,800	1,743	12	0	2,412
Weil, Gotshal & Manges	$180,000	$190,000	None	U	52	Unlimited	36,800
White & Case	$174,000 - $180,000	$180,000 - $190,000	2,000 target	U	70	200	46,054
Wiley Rein	$180,000	$190,000	1,950	1,924	43	50	11,576
Willkie Farr & Gallagher	$180,000	$190,000	None	U	67	Unlimited	30,663
WilmerHale	$180,000	$190,000	2,000	1,799	99	Unlimited	99,198
Wilson Sonsini Goodrich & Rosati	$180,000	$190,000	None	1,790	76	Unlimited	48,871
Winston & Strawn	$180,000	$190,000	2,000	U	83	100	63,167

U = undisclosed

Firms by Size

Firm	Partners	Associates	Domestic office
Adam Leitman Bailey, P.C.	7	18	1
Akin Gump Strauss Hauer & Feld	268	356	11
Allen & Overy	48	115	2
Alston & Bird	345	366	9
Arnold & Porter Kaye Scholer	319	479	9
Axinn, Veltrop & Harkrider	24	33	3
Baker Botts	238	345	7
Baker McKenzie	344	342	7
Bracewell	169	197	8
Brown Rudnick	85	74	6
Brownstein Hyatt Farber Schreck,	131	79	11
Cadwalader, Wickersham & Taft	71	172	3
Cahill Gordon & Reindel	66	187	2
Choate Hall & Stewart	64	88	1
Cleary Gottlieb Steen & Hamilton	106	442	2
Clifford Chance US	74	200	2
Cooley	300	600	10
Cozen O'Connor	403	147	22
Cravath, Swaine & Moore	78	386	1
Crowell & Moring	167	141	5
Curtis, Mallet-Prevost, Colt & Mosle	58	71	3
Davis Polk & Wardwell	762 lawyers	Not given	3
Debevoise & Plimpton	106	319	2
Dechert	216	400	13
DLA Piper (US)	616	522	28
Duane Morris	397	324	20
Dykema Gossett	276	141	14
Epstein Becker & Green	127	118	13
Finnegan, Henderson, Farabow, Garrett & Dunner	120	144	5
Fish & Richardson	181	165	11
Fitzpatrick, Cella, Harper & Scinto			3
Foley & Lardner	411	457	17
Fox Rothschild	470	224	22
Freshfields Bruckhaus Deringer	36	120	2
Fried, Frank, Harris, Shriver & Jacobson	Not given	Not given	2
Gibbons P.C.	140	65	5
Gibson, Dunn & Crutcher	318	786	10
Goodwin	311	435	6
Goulston & Storrs	113	8	3
Greenberg Traurig	968	1,017	29
Hangley Aronchick Segal Pudlin & Schiller	Not given	Not given	4
Harris, Wiltshire & Grannis	32	20	2
Haynes and Boone	225	311	12

International offices	Revenue 2016 ($ millions)	Intake size 2017	Number of summers 2017
0	U	1	3
9	980	43	76
42	1,970	18	20
2	730.6	44	53
4	944.7	48	64
0	U	4	9
7	846.5	52	96
70	2,640	34	51
2	277	26	30
2	191	6	10
0	173	7	7
2	452	32	26
1	382.6	42	33
0	218.5	15	19
14	1,272	91	160
31	2,056	33	29
2	974	U	56
2	376	12	23
1	U	105	123
2	U	U	U
14	151.5	9	9
7	1,180	143	132
7	735	U	U
15	911.6	68	46
67	2,470	32	49
8	454.3	16	16
0	218.9	10	18
24	U	12	12
5	309.8	19	30
1	407.7	26	36
0	U	6	10
3	671	47	60
0	U	24	25
24	1,944	19	19
3	556	52	70
0	102.4	9	No summer program
10	1,607	93	122
4	912	50	60
0	167	6	7
9	1,378	49	44
0	U	U	No summer program
0	U	3	2
3	375	39	33

U = undisclosed

Law firm comparison data

Firms by Size *continued*

Firm	Partners	Associates	Domestic office
Hogan Lovells	397	489	13
Holland & Knight	621	338	24
Hughes Hubbard & Reed	Not given	Not given	6
Hunton & Williams	264	303	14
Irell & Manella	45	55	2
Jackson Walker	243	99	7
Jenner & Block	213	221	4
Jones Day	954	1,381	18
K&L Gates	629	489	24
Kasowitz Benson Torres	90	125	9
Katten Muchin Rosenman	309	256	11
Kilpatrick Townsend & Stockton	251	233	15
King & Spalding	326	311	9
Kirkland & Ellis	744	860	7
Kramer Levin Naftalis & Frankel	98	205	2
Latham & Watkins	468	1,062	11
Linklaters	43	163	2
Mayer Brown	401	417	7
McDermott Will & Emery	474	220	10
Milbank, Tweed, Hadley & McCloy	112	338	3
Mintz Levin Cohn Ferris Glovsky and Popeo	255	190	7
Morgan, Lewis & Bockius	644	847	17
Morrison & Foerster	247	360	9
Munger, Tolles & Olson	85	96	3
Nixon Peabody	325	224	12
Norton Rose Fulbright	296	419	11
Nutter McClennen & Fish	75	53	2
O'Melveny & Myers	184	419	7
Orrick, Herrington & Sutcliffe	287	379	12
Patterson Belknap Webb & Tyler	51	117	1
Paul Hastings	246	461	10
Paul, Weiss, Rifkind, Wharton & Garrison	129	550	3
Perkins Coie	519	411	16
Pillsbury Winthrop Shaw Pittman	344	199	13
Proskauer Rose	217	384	8
Reed Smith	514	449	12
Ropes & Gray	253	779	6
Schiff Hardin	147	87	6
Schulte Roth & Zabel	89	253	2
Sedgwick	110	158	14
Seward & Kissel	57	104	2
Shearman & Sterling	Not given	Not given	4
Sheppard, Mullin, Richter & Hampton	336	287	10

International offices	Revenue 2016 ($ millions)	Intake size 2017	Number of summers 2017
36	1925	72	127
3	802.9	39	26
2	394	22	23
5	U	29	31
0	U	11	12
0	246.7	17	28
1	457.6	35	47
26	1,977	112	214
22	1,179.1	64	65
0	U	8	9
2	553.8	24	35
3	411.3	17	27
10	1,058	30	51
5	2,651	172	247
1	352	11	17
20	2,823	181	199
27	1,692	13	26
13	1,260	55	60
8	908.7	26	41
9	855.6	67	86
2	372.5	11	15
13	1,860	52	75
8	979.3	62	104
0	U	24	19
4	458	18	20
46	1,686	36	45
0	U	3	8
8	725	33	70
14	929.1	44	66
0	185.5	5	No summer program
11	1,074.5	105	84
5	1,222	118	134
3	781	43	57
5	557	37	38
5	852.4	8	86
15	1,075	42	57
5	1,486	152	145
0	U	10	14
1	U	32	38
2	170.3	4	No summer program
0	U	16	11
16	912	64	61
5	607.2	28	34

Firms by Size *continued*

Firm	Partners	Associates	Domestic office
Sidley Austin	586	988	10
Simpson Thacher & Bartlett	152	605	5
Skadden, Arps, Slate, Meagher & Flom	297	896	8
Snell & Wilmer	210	147	8
Squire Patton Boggs	250	257	17
Sterne, Kessler, Goldstein & Fox	49	87	1
Stroock & Stroock & Lavan	88	204	4
Sullivan & Cromwell	137	454	4
Thompson & Knight	152	81	6
Vedder Price	158	111	5
Venable	295	250	9
Vinson & Elkins	210	316	8
Waller	116	107	4
Weil, Gotshal & Manges	198	517	8
White & Case	203	450	6
Wiley Rein	113	62	1
Willkie Farr & Gallagher	140	338	3
WilmerHale	255	568	7
Wilson Sonsini Goodrich & Rosati	203	464	11
Winston & Strawn	356	447	10

International offices	Revenue 2016 ($ millions)	Intake size 2017	Number of summers 2017
10	1,928	105	127
6	1,302	97	127
14	2,495	188	236
1	U	24	24
29	983.1	15	31
0	U	12	8
0	270.7	14	14
8	1,360	93	133
5	213.4	6	12
2	239.8	12	13
0	498.5	33	35
7	653.9	36	95
0	U	5	12
11	1,267	84	137
34	1,631	6	109
0	U	8	9
6	691	51	62
5	1,130	65	77
4	755	47	56
7	822.8	61	71

U = undisclosed

To rank law firms on all the above data and more, head to the 'Law firms A-Z' list on chambers-associate.com

Work/life and Benefits Survey

Firm	Vacation	Paid maternity	Paid paternity
Adam Leitman Bailey	2 weeks	12 weeks	U
Akin Gump Strauss Hauer & Feld	4 weeks	18 weeks	4 weeks
Allen & Overy	20 days	18 weeks	4 weeks
Alston & Bird	Flexible	18 weeks maximum	18 weeks minmum
Arnold & Porter Kaye Scholer	Unlimited	18 weeks	6 weeks
Axinn, Veltrop & Harkrider	4 weeks	20 weeks	4 weeks
Baker Botts	3 weeks	18 weeks	4 weeks
Baker McKenzie	Unlimited	18 weeks maximum	18 weeks maximum
Bracewell	Unlimited	18 weeks	2 weeks
Brown Rudnick	4 weeks	18 weeks	4 weeks
Brownstein Hyatt Farber Schreck,	3 weeks	3 months	3 weeks
Cadwalader, Wickersham & Taft	Unlimited	18 weeks	4 weeks
Cahill Gordon & Reindel	4 weeks	18 weeks	4 weeks
Choate Hall & Stewart	4 weeks	12 weeks	12 weeks
Cleary Gottlieb Steen & Hamilton	4 weeks	18 weeks	5 weeks
Clifford Chance US	4 weeks	18 weeks	4 weeks
Cooley	4 weeks	20 weeks	10 weeks
Cozen O'Connor	Unlimited	8 weeks maximum	4 weeks minimum
Cravath, Swaine & Moore	4 weeks	20 weeks maximum	4 weeks minimum
Crowell & Moring	Unlimited	18 weeks	4 weeks
Curtis, Mallet-Prevost, Colt & Mosle	4 weeks	12 weeks	2 weeks
Davis Polk & Wardwell	4 weeks	18 weeks maximum	10 weeks maximum
Debevoise & Plimpton	4 weeks	18 weeks	4 weeks minimum
Dechert	4 weeks	18 weeks	4 weeks
DLA Piper (US)	Discretionary	18 weeks	4 weeks
Duane Morris	4 weeks	16 weeks	4 weeks
Dykema Gossett	Unlimited	12 weeks	6 weeks
Epstein Becker & Green	4 weeks	12 weeks	12 weeks
Finnegan, Henderson, Farabow	Unlimited	18 weeks	12 weeks
Fish & Richardson	Unrestricted	16 weeks	12 weeks
Fitzpatrick, Cella, Harper & Scinto	4 weeks	12 weeks	2 weeks
Foley & Lardner	Discretionary	18 weeks	4 weeks minimum
Fox Rothschild	4 weeks	12 weeks	2 weeks
Freshfields Bruckhaus Deringer	20 days	12 weeks	4 weeks
Fried, Frank, Harris, Shriver & Jacobson	4 weeks	18 weeks	10 weeks
Gibbons	3 weeks	12 weeks	12 weeks
Gibson, Dunn & Crutcher	Unlimited	18 weeks	10 weeks
Goodwin	4 weeks	18 weeks	4 weeks (18 if primary caregiver)
Goulston & Storrs	4 weeks	Yes	Yes

Law firm comparison data

Adoption/surrogacy fees	Flexible work arrangements	Retirement plan	Medical and dental plans
U	U	✓	✓
Yes	Yes	401K	✓
No	Yes	401K	✓
Yes, up to $10,000	Yes	401K	✓
Yes, $10,000	Yes	401K	✓
No	Yes	401K	✓
No	U	401K	✓
Yes	Yes	✓	✓
No	Yes	401K	✓
No	Yes	401K	✓
No	Yes	✓	✓
Yes	Yes	✓	✓
No	Yes	401K	✓
No	Yes	401K	✓
No	Yes	✓ Tax Opportunity Plan for Saving	✓
No	U	401K	✓
No	Yes	401K	✓
No	Yes	401K	✓
No	Yes	401K	✓
No	Yes	401K	✓
No	Yes	401K	✓
18 weeks maximum	Yes	401K	✓
No	Yes	401K	✓
No	Yes	401K	✓
No	Yes	401K	✓
No	Yes	401K	✓
No	Yes	401K	✓
No	Yes	401K	✓
No	Yes	401K	✓
No	Yes	401K	✓
No	Yes	401K	✓
$5,000	Yes	401K	✓
No	Yes	401K	✓
No	Yes	401K	✓
Yes	Yes	401K	✓
No	Yes	401K	✓
No	Yes	401K	✓
$5,000 per adoption	Case by case	401K	✓
No	Yes	✓	✓

U = undisclosed

Work/life and Benefits Survey *continued*

Firm	Vacation	Paid maternity	Paid paternity
Greenberg Traurig	Discretionary	18 weeks	Discretionary
Hangley Aronchick Segal Pudlin & Schiller	4 weeks	Short-term disability policy	4 weeks
Harris, Wiltshire & Grannis	Case-by-case	17 weeks	3 weeks
Haynes and Boone	10 days minimum	12 weeks	4 weeks
Hogan Lovells	Unlimited	20 weeks	Up to 12 weeks
Holland & Knight	4 weeks	16 weeks	6 weeks
Hughes Hubbard & Reed	4 weeks	18 weeks	4 weeks
Hunton & Williams	4 weeks	18 weeks	2 weeks
Irell & Manella	Unlimited	18 weeks	4 weeks
Jackson Walker	Unlimited	12 weeks	U
Jenner & Block	3 weeks	18 weeks	6 weeks minimum
Jones Day	4 weeks	18 weeks	6 weeks
K&L Gates	3 weeks minimum	12 weeks	6 weeks
Kasowitz Benson Torres	4 weeks	12 weeks	None
Katten Muchin Rosenman	Unlimited	14 weeks	14 weeks
Kilpatrick Townsend & Stockton	20 days	12 weeks minimum	6 weeks
King & Spalding	4 weeks	18 weeks	6 weeks minmum
Kirkland & Ellis	Unlimited	18 weeks	10 weeks
Kramer Levin Naftalis & Frankel	4 weeks	20 weeks	4 weeks
Latham & Watkins	No cap	18 weeks	4 weeks
Linklaters	22 days	18 weeks	4 weeks of secondary caregiver
Mayer Brown	Unlimited	18 weeks	6 weeks
McDermott Will & Emery	Unlimited	18 weeks maximum	18 weeks maximum
Milbank, Tweed, Hadley & McCloy	4 weeks	18 weeks	4 weeks minimum
Mintz Levin Cohn Ferris Glovsky and Popeo	4 weeks	12 weeks	8 weeks
Morgan, Lewis & Bockius	4 weeks	16 weeks	4 weeks minimum
Morrison & Foerster	4 weeks	20 weeks	6 weeks
Munger, Tolles & Olson	Unlimited	18 weeks	6 weeks
Nixon Peabody	Discretionary	16 weeks	4 weeks
Norton Rose Fulbright	Discretionary	14 weeks	4 weeks
Nutter McClennen & Fish	4 weeks	12 weeks minimum	12 weeks minimum
O'Melveny & Myers	3 weeks minimum	18 weeks	6 weeks
Orrick, Herrington & Sutcliffe	Unlimited	22 weeks	3 weeks minimum
Patterson Belknap Webb & Tyler	4 weeks	18 weeks	4 weeks
Paul Hastings	4 weeks	18 weeks	10 weeks
Paul, Weiss, Rifkind, Wharton & Garrison	4 weeks	18 weeks	4 weeks
Perkins Coie	Discretionary	18 weeks	4 weeks
Pillsbury Winthrop Shaw Pittman	4 weeks	18 weeks	12 weeks minimum
Proskauer Rose	4 weeks	18 weeks	4 weeks
Reed Smith	3 weeks minimum	16 weeks	10 weeks
Ropes & Gray	4 weeks	14 weeks minimum	4 weeks

Adoption/surrogacy fees	Flexible work arrangements	Retirement plan	Medical and dental plans
No	Yes	401K	✓
No	Yes	401K	✓
No	Yes	401(k): 13% matching	✓
No	Yes	✓	✓
lifetime allowance	Yes	✓	✓
No	Yes	401K	✓
No	Yes	401K	✓
Yes	Yes	401K	✓
No	Yes	401K	✓
Yes	Yes	401K	✓
No	Yes	401K	✓
No	Yes	401K	✓
No	Yes	401K	✓
No	Yes	401K	✓
No	Yes	401K	✓
No	Yes	✓	✓
No	Yes	401K	✓
No	Yes	401K	✓
No	Yes	401K	✓
No	Yes	401K	✓
No	Yes	401K	✓
No	Yes	✓	✓
No	Yes	401K	✓
No	Yes	401K	✓
No	Yes, FWA program	401K	✓
Yes	Yes	401K	✓
No	Yes	401K	✓
No	Yes	401K	✓
Yes	Yes	401K	✓
Yes	Yes	401K	✓
No	Yes	401K	✓
No	Yes	401K	✓
No	Yes	401K	✓
No	No	401K	✓
No	No	401K	✓
No	Yes	401K	✓
Yes	Yes	✓	✓
No	Yes	401K	✓
Yes	Yes	401K	✓
No	Yes	401K	✓
No	Yes	401K	✓

U = undisclosed

Work/life and Benefits Survey *continued*

Firm	Vacation	Paid maternity	Paid paternity
Schiff Hardin	4 weeks	18 weeks maximum	18 weeks maximum
Schulte Roth & Zabel	5 weeks	18 weeks	2 weeks
Sedgwick	4 weeks	16 weeks	3 weeks
Seward & Kissel	4 weeks	12 weeks	2 weeks
Shearman & Sterling	4 weeks	18 weeks	4 weeks
Sheppard, Mullin, Richter & Hampton	Unlimited	18 weeks	4 weeks
Sidley Austin	U	U	U
Simpson Thacher & Bartlett	4 weeks	18 weeks	4 weeks if secondary caregiver
Skadden, Arps, Slate, Meagher & Flom	4 weeks	18 weeks	4 weeks minimum
Snell & Wilmer	Unlimited	12 weeks	12 weeks
Squire Patton Boggs	6 weeks	18 weeks	3 weeks
Sterne, Kessler, Goldstein & Fox	Unlimited	12 weeks	2 weeks
Stroock & Stroock & Lavan	4 weeks	18 weeks	4 weeks
Sullivan & Cromwell	4 weeks	18 weeks	4 weeks
Thompson & Knight	Unlimited	18 weeks	4 weeks
Vedder Price	3 weeks	16 weeks	8 weeks maximum
Venable	4 weeks	18 weeks	4 weeks
Vinson & Elkins	15 days minimum	18 weeks maximum	18 weeks maximum
Waller	2 weeks minimum	12 weeks	0
Weil, Gotshal & Manges	4 weeks	18 weeks	10 weeks
White & Case	Unlimited	18 weeks minimum	4 weeks
Wiley Rein	4 weeks	18 weeks	4 weeks
Willkie Farr & Gallagher	4 weeks	18 weeks	4 weeks
WilmerHale	4 weeks	18 weeks	4 weeks
Wilson Sonsini Goodrich & Rosati	Discretionary	18 weeks	10 weeks
Winston & Strawn	Unlimited	20 weeks	20 weeks

Adoption/surrogacy fees	Flexible work arrangements	Retirement plan	Medical and dental plans
Yes	Yes	401K	✓
No	Yes	✓	✓
No	Yes	401K	✓
No	Yes	401K	✓
No	Yes	401K	✓
No	Yes	401K	✓
U	U	U	U
No	Yes	401K	✓
No	Yes	401K	✓
No	Yes	401K	✓
No	Yes	401K	✓
No	Yes	401K	✓
No	Yes	401K	✓
Yes, up to $7,500	Yes	✓	✓
No	Yes	401K	✓
No	Yes, case-by-case	401K	✓
No	Yes	✓	✓
No	Yes	401K	✓
No	Yes	401K	✓
No	Yes	401K	✓
Yes	Yes	401K	✓
No	Yes	401K	✓
No	Yes	401K	✓
No	Yes	401K	✓
No	Yes	401K	✓
No	Yes	401K	✓

U = undisclosed

Diversity

Firm	% female partners	% female associates	% white partners	% white associates	% Black/ African American partners	% Black/ African American associates
Adam Leitman Bailey	25	30	U	U	U	U
Akin Gump Strauss Hauer & Feld	20.2	44	86.9	72.7	2.2	3.3
Allen & Overy	18.4	44.7	89.8	70.7	0	2.3
Alston & Bird	22.8	45.6	92.2	71.1	2.5	8
Arnold & Porter Kaye Scholer	20	49.8	89.1	76.8	2.2	5.2
Axinn, Veltrop & Harkrider	12.5	33	100	61	0	3
Baker Botts	17.2	42.4	76.9	91.1	2.1	2.4
Baker McKenzie	28	50	88.4	73	0.6	5
Bracewell	21	45	92	83	3	3
Brown Rudnick	16	42	U	U	U	U
Brownstein Hyatt Farber Schreck	29	42	94	85	2	4
Cadwalader, Wickersham & Taft	22.5	39.7	90.1	71.9	1.4	4.1
Cahill Gordon & Reindel	18	45	91	79	3	3
Choate Hall & Stewart	19	55	97	84	1.5	1
Cleary Gottlieb Steen & Hamilton	17.4	49.7	89	64.1	2.8	9
Clifford Chance	11	47	82	64	0	2
Cooley	22	56.5	87.4	75.6	1.4	3.1
Cozen O'Connor	24	47	93	84	2.5	3
Cravath, Swaine & Moore	21	39	93	75	1	4
Crowell & Moring	24	55	90	67	4	9
Curtis, Mallet-Prevost	10.5	38.5	81	71	3.5	3
Davis Polk & Wardwell	19	43	88	67	1	5
Debevoise & Plimpton	20.8	53	89.6	65.8	0.9	7.5
Dechert	14.1	42.7	92	75.4	2.4	3.3
DLA Piper (US)	20.6	43.2	86.5	73.4	2.2	4.1
Duane Morris	23.4	39.4	90.5	80.6	2.5	3.1
Dykema Gossett PLLC	23	54	90	80	3	7
Epstein Becker & Green PC	28	53	88	82	1	4
Finnegan	26	44	88	66	3	6
Fish & Richardson PC	17	33	87	69	1	5
Fitzpatrick, Cella, Harper & Scinto	16	45	92	74	0	1.5
Foley & Lardner	19.4	43.7	91.9	74.4	0.7	4.4
Fox Rothschild	23.4	41.9	93.7	81.4	1.1	3.3
Freshfields Bruckhaus Deringer	27	48	92	77	3	4
Fried, Frank	15	43	97	76	0	6
Gibbons	20	43	92	94	3	1
Gibson, Dunn & Crutcher	16.6	45.2	89.9	76.6	1.6	2.3
Goodwin	23	49	93	76	1	4
Goulston & Storrs	21	56	99	75	0	9
Greenberg Traurig	22.4	47.2	87.8	77.1	U	U

% Hispanic/ Latin American partners	% Hispanic/ Latin American associates	% Asian partners	% Asian associates	% LGBT partners	% LGBT associates	% Mixed/ other partners	% Mixed/ other associates
U	U	U	U	U	U	U	U
3.7	2.8	6.72	8.9	0.7	1.5	0.4	1.9
0	4.1	10.2	13.4	10.2	4.9	0	2.3
1.1	6	3.1	9.5	3.1	3.4	1.1	5.4
1.9	4.2	5.3	11	3.1	5	1.6	2.9
0	0	0	30	4	6	0	6
4.6	2.4	11.8	3.1	3	4	4.6	1
4	4	5	14	0.8	2	2	4
3	5	1	3	0.5	2	0	3
U	U	U	U	U	U	U	U
0	1	2	4	U	U	2	6
2.8	4.1	4.2	15.2	4.2	2.3	1.4	4.6
0	6	4.5	12	6	3	1.5	0
1.5	8	0	7	4	4	0	0
3.7	8.8	3.7	13.3	4.6	5.6	0.9	4.7
4	9	3	17	1	3.5	11	8
2.9	2.7	6.9	12.9	1.8	2.7	1.1	4.5
2.5	4	1	5	1	3.5	1	4
1	4	5	13	4	4	0	4
2 *	5	4	17	2	2	1	2
12	14.5	1.75	10	5	1.5	1.75	1.5
4	5	7	21	2	8	0	2
3.8	8.8	4.7	15.7	4.7	6.3	0.9	2.2
2.8	3.8	2.4	15.5	2.8	1.6	0.5	2
2.7	1.8	4.8	14.6	1.3	1.8	1.7	5.8
2.5	3.7	4.5	6.2	1.5	1.5	1.7	3.7
5	5	1	4	0	1	1	3
2	1	6	10	2	3	3	3
0	3	9	24	2	2	0	1
2	2	8	21	2	4	2	2
0	1.5	6	18	0	1	2	5
4	6.6	2.9	13.3	1.4	5.5	0	0
1.3	3.7	2.3	7.9	0.6	2.8	1.7	3.7
5	8	0	11	U	U	0	0
1	4	2	10	1	6	0	4
3	5	2	0	2	5	0	0
1.3	4.2	6	13.5	2.2	6.2	1.3	3.4
2	3	3	14	2	4	1	3
0	7	1	9	3	4	0	0
U	U	U	U	1.7	1.1	U	U

U = undisclosed

33

Diversity *continued*

Firm	% female partners	% female associates	% white partners	% white associates	% Black/ African American partners	% Black/ African American associates
Hangley Aronchick	29	40	U	U	U	U
Harris, Wiltshire & Grannis	24	46	83	61	3	8
Haynes and Boone	22	40	88	69	1	4
Hogan Lovells	25	50	90	73	1	6
Holland & Knight	22	49	88	74	2	6
Hughes Hubbard & Reed	23	49	91	69	1	11
Hunton & Williams	18	49.5	90.8	82.8	2.8	3
Irell & Manella	9	40	82	82	2	0
Jackson Walker	21.8	48	86	73	3.5	7
Jenner & Block	28.8	44.9	90.9	79	2.1	3.4
Jones Day	36.4	48	90.9	92	0	0
K&L Gates	24	46	89	83	2	3
Kasowitz Benson Torres	20	40.8	87.8	80.8	1.1	7.2
Katten Muchin Rosenman	22.5	47.1	93.2	80.2	1.4	4
Kilpatrick Townsend & Stockton	25.2	40.5	92	73.2	2.5	5.5
King & Spalding	23.5	46.5	91	82.3	2.4	4.8
Kirkland & Ellis	22.8	36	88.6	76.8	1.5	2.4
Kramer Levin Naftalis & Frankel	13.3	40.1	91.9	77.9	2	1.2
Latham & Watkins	21	41	92	81	1	4
Linklaters	14	43	86	59	2	2
Mayer Brown	19.7	41.8	90.8	75	1.2	3
McDermott Will & Emery	29.7	52.7	82.9	61.4	1.7	4
Milbank, Tweed, Hadley & McCloy	15.2	40.5	88.4	70.4	1.8	5
Mintz Levin	25	48	91	79	2	5
Morgan, Lewis & Bockius	22.1	51.3	91.9	75.6	1.7	4.2
Morrison & Foerster	23.5	46.2	83.7	68.2	2.4	3.2
Munger, Tolles & Olson	22.4	40.6	82.4	74	0	4.2
Nixon Peabody	25	48.2	90.4	74.6	1.5	5.4
Norton Rose Fulbright	20.9	47.8	91.8	73.1	1	4.8
Nutter McClennen & Fish	28	55	97	81	0	7.5
O'Melveny & Myers	19.1	45.1	89.4	75.8	2.1	1.9
Orrick, Herrington & Sutcliffe	21.9	46.1	78.5	59.6	2.8	2.5
Patterson Belknap Webb & Tyler	17.6	51	90	75	2	2
Paul Hastings	22	42.6	88.7	65.7	2.9	3.7
Paul, Weiss	22	40	87	78	3	5
Perkins Coie	25	48	88	75	2	3
Pillsbury Winthrop Shaw Pittman	22.4	47.9	87	67.8	1.2	3.4
Proskauer Rose	15.4	48.9	93.2	76.8	2.3	2.3
Reed Smith	23.2	49.1	88.6	79.2	1.4	3.1
Ropes & Gray	25	47	84	70	2	4

% Hispanic/ Latin American partners	% Hispanic/ Latin American associates	% Asian partners	% Asian associates	% LGBT partners	% LGBT associates	% Mixed/ other partners	% Mixed/ other associates
U	U	U	U	U	U	U	U
0	0	7	31	10	0	7	0
6	7	4	17	2	2	1	3
4	7	3	11	1.7	4	0.5	4
7	11	2	7	2	1	1	2
3	8	4	9	2	5	1	3
3.2	5	2.8	6.9	0.7	1.7	0.4	2.3
2	0	14	13	2	4	0	5
7	9	2.5	7	1	2	1	4
2.5	4.9	3	9.8	4.2	12.7	1.7	2.9
3	0	0	0			6.1	8
2	3	5	7	2	3	2	4
6.7	4.8	1.1	3.2	1.1	4.8	3.3	4
1.1	4	3.9	11	2.1	4.4	0.4	0.9
0.8	3.2	4.6	13.6	U	U	0	4.6
3	4.2	3.3	6.3	1	3.2	0.3	2.5
3	5.5	5.7	13.2	2.6	4.8	1.3	2.1
0	4.7	6.1	13.4	3.1	3.5	0	2.9
3	6	6	15	3	5	1	1
5	6	2	7	7	6	2	7
3.7	4	2.7	13	2.4	3.3	1.7	5
2.5	4.5	6.8	9.5	2.3	2.7	0.01	1.8
5.4	7.6	3.6	12.9	2.7	3.8	0.9	4.1
3	3	4	11	3	3	0	2
1.1	4.2	4.8	13.5	2.5	4.4	0.5	2.4
4	5.3	10	19.1	2	4.5	0	4.2
3.5	5.2	11.8	11.5	2.4	8.3	0	6.3
2.5	5.4	4	10.7	3.4	5.4	1.5	4
3.4	4.9	3.4	12.9	U	U	0.3	4.3
3	4	0	7.5	1	4	0	0
0.5	5.3	8	14.4	2.7	5.8	0	2.6
1.7	4.8	8	14.4	2.4	6.2	9	18.7
2	3	6	12.5	9.8	6.7	2	7.5
3.3	3.7	4.9	23.3	2	2.4	0.4	3.7
2	2	7	12	6	6	2	3
3	5	4	13	2	3	3	4
2.7	4.2	7.6	20.8	4	5	0.9	2.5
2.7	4.8	2.3	13.6	1.8	3	0	2.5
2.9	2.7	4.6	9.1	U	U	1.3	1.9
1	3	5	12	2	5	U	4

U = undisclosed

Diversity *continued*

Firm	% female partners	% female associates	% white partners	% white associates	% Black/ African American partners	% Black/ African American associates
Schiff Hardin	26.8	47.7	86.7	75	3.9	3.4
Schulte Roth & Zabel	13	42	87	74	2	1
Sedgwick	32	44	82	74	4	3
Seward & Kissel	8.8	46.6	93	83.5	0	2.9
Shearman & Sterling	18	41	90	68	3	5
Sheppard, Mullin, Richter	17	48	89	61	2	4
Sidley Austin	24.6	47.3	89.2	72.1	1.7	4.3
Simpson Thacher & Bartlett	20	43	90	72	2	3
Skadden	21.9	46.6	92.1	70.7	1.4	5.9
Snell & Wilmer	15.3	37.9	91	86	0	1
Squire Patton Boggs	21.2	50.6	85.6	79.4	4.4	2.3
Sterne, Kessler	21.4	24.3	77.8	72.9	3.7	2.9
Stroock & Stroock & Lavan	17	35	93	77	0	5
Sullivan & Cromwell	20	40	91	76	2	3
Thompson & Knight	26	48	94	83	1	6
Vedder Price	18	41	92	78	1	6
Venable	U	U	U	U	U	U
Vinson & Elkins	15	38	90	79	1	4
Waller	16	34	97	86	1.2	6
Weil, Gotshal & Manges	23	49	86	75	3	4
White & Case	19	50	80	60	2	5
Wiley Rein	26	52	89	73	3	8
Willkie Farr & Gallagher	14.3	43.8	92.1	75.7	1.4	4.4
WilmerHale	24.7	49.5	89	76.8	2.7	5.2
Wilson Sonsini Goodrich & Rosati	24	44	77.5	66.8	1.4	2.25
Winston & Strawn	22	45	91	76	2	5

% Hispanic/ Latin American partners	% Hispanic/ Latin American associates	% Asian partners	% Asian associates	% LGBT partners	% LGBT associates	% Mixed/ other partners	% Mixed/ other associates
2.2	2.3	4.4	11.4	2.2	1.1	1.7	2.3
2	3	3	14	2	4	1	3
7	16	2	13	4	1	4	3
1.8	1.9	5.3	10.7	0	0	0	1
2	5	6	19	1	4	0	2
2	5	4	15	3	2	3	15
1.7	6.4	6.5	14.9	U	U	0.9	2.3
3	3	5	17	3	5	0	5
3.1	5.4	3.4	13.5	1.3	4.8	0	4.5
4	3	1	6	1	0	3	2
3.6	5.1	5.2	10.1	U	U	1.2	3.1
5.6	1.4	13	22.9	1.9	2.9	0	0
3.5	7	3.5	7	1	3.5	0	4
4	4	3	14	7	6	1	2
2	2	0	5	U	3	3	5
3	3	4	10	2	2	0	3
U	U	U	U	U	U	U	U
4	4	2	9	3	2	3	2
0	1.2	1.8	7	0	0	0	0
3	5	4	14	1	3	0	2
6	12	10	17	4	2	1	6
3	5	5	13	3	2	0	1
2.9	5.9	2.1	10.4	4.3	2.4	1.4	3.6
0.8	3	6.7	13.4	0.8	5	0.8	1.4
6.6	2.25	14	24.2	1.4	2.9	0.5	4.5
3	5	3	9	1	5	1	5

U = undisclosed

Law firm comparison data

Becoming a Lawyer

What type of law firm suits you?

Researching every firm to find the right fit for you would be madness. So here's how to start a shortlist.

Wall Street firms

BY revenue, New York accounts for a large chunk of the nation's legal market (while the State is home to just 6% of the population). The city's most elite firms will be found in the borough of Manhattan, either near Wall Street or in Midtown. While they can range in size from under 200 to over 2,000 lawyers, all will house teams of attorneys working on high-value cases and deals for high financiers and big business, which are regularly reported on in the pages of the *Wall Street Journal*. A big pull with these firms is the prestige, but it does come at a cost: young lawyers work long hours, so "*from Monday to Friday, they own you.*" New York is also the country's most internationally oriented market, and even though some Wall Street firms may not have legions of lawyers stationed in Chicago, Charlotte or Shanghai, their work can span the nation and the globe. Culture-wise they can be stuffy and hierarchical, even for law firms.

Global firms

Law firms have been 'international' for years. White & Case made the trip from New York to open an office in Paris in 1926, a full year before Charles Lindbergh made the same journey in the Spirit of St. Louis. However, an increasing number of firms are now more than 'international' – they are global. They figure that, in today's world, you need a foothold in every market to have a competitive advantage.

A few early movers like Baker McKenzie have grown organically from small beginnings in other countries, but the current trend is to become global by bolting together two or more large international firms. For example, Dentons (the world's largest law firm by lawyer headcount) is the product of America's Sonnenschein Nath & Rosenthal, the UK's Denton Wilde Sapte, Canada's Fraser Milner Casgrain and the French-founded Salans. This amalgamation means Dentons now operates from a mind-boggling 136 offices in 57 countries across Europe,

On chambers-associate.com...

- We look at the life of a lawyer in all the major legal markets across the US.
- The top 30 best firms for travel opportunities

Canada, the UK, the USA, the Middle East, Asia-Pacific, Central and East Asia, and Africa.

Having flooded the Western world with offices, the global firms are now targeting emerging markets: sending delegations to charm the Chinese and Russians, beginning to open offices in Africa and South America, and keeping a close eye on India (currently off limits to foreign firms, but there are talks that the Indian legal market will soon be liberalized – so watch this space).

The work junior associates undertake is not hugely different from their peers at Wall Street firms. What is different is the strategy these firms employ to achieve their goals. This naturally has a knock-on effect on the culture. Like Wall Street firms, the work will have an international flavor.

Multi-site firms

Clients like their lawyers close at hand, so as they've grown, many firms have established networks of offices across the country. At some multi-site firms, offices work together on nationwide matters, while at others each office focuses on matters in its locality. The size of the deals will often compete with the biggest international firms, as do the salaries.

Many of these firms maintain offices abroad (though they generally have less reach than the global firms mentioned above) which have differing levels of integration with the USA (and many multi-site firms are merging with overseas counterparts to move into the 'global' category). A major benefit of a multi-site firm is that as an associate you can move cities while remaining with the same employer.

Regional firms

There can be quite a difference in the culture, working style and practice remit of firms based in different regions. Many firms take pride in the fact they are Californian, Midwestern or Bostonian. All populous states – from New Jersey and Pennsylvania to Arizona and Minnesota – have their own sophisticated legal markets, with a group of leading firms working on complex transactions and cases.

Becoming a Lawyer

Certain regions are known for certain types of work: banking and finance in New York; government/regulatory in DC; technology and media in California; energy in Texas; private equity in Boston, etc. Many West Coast firms look toward Asia for business, while Florida firms often work in Latin America. Each region has its own set of traits and it is worth thinking about them. When researching a firm, find out about the local market in which it operates. Typically, these firms are seen as less high-stress than the New York elite, and that's reflected in the salary – which is still good, nevertheless.

Boutiques and specialists

Boutiques are firms that practice in a single area of law – litigation or IP, for example. Some are very small; others have hundreds of lawyers. These firms offer a great opportunity for those who know what they want to do and want to work with like-minded people, but they are not a good option if you are unsure what area of law you want to work in. Specialist firms may offer additional practice areas to support their main agenda.

Outside BigLaw: small firms

Only a fraction of the nation's 50,000 plus law firms employ more than 50 lawyers. The others are smaller businesses doing all kinds of legal work often with a local focus, in towns and cities from Portland, Maine to Portland, Oregon, and from Anchorage to Key West. We discuss the opportunities offered by small firms in our small firms feature elsewhere in this guide.

"Regardless of what your first job is as a lawyer, be prepared to work hard. Take the job no one else wants to do, learn the job, excel in the job, enjoy working and connecting with others involved, then move on to the next job no one wants and repeat all of the above."

- Linda Klein, president of the American Bar Association

Becoming a Lawyer

Trends in the recruitment market

We caught up with James Leipold, executive director of NALP, to learn about the state of recruitment in law.

Chambers Associate: 2015 saw the first significant upturn in legal recruitment since the dark days of 2007/8. Has this upturn continued?
James Leipold: What we see in the data reflects a leveling or flattening-out of the market at the high-end. We saw the recession, this big pull-back that lasted a few years, then two years (2014, 2015) of significant growth. What we saw this year was a leveling out – the numbers were flat. Some firms pulled forward, some pulled back, but it was a flat environment. I think the reasons for that are obvious. First, the demand for law firm legal services continues to be flat to soft, and there are lots of reasons for that. Corporate legal departments continue to change the way they seek to solve legal problems and purchase legal services. They're looking for cuts across the board and the continuously rising cost of outside law firms continues to be a challenge. I think over the longer arc law firms in the US will still have to find ways to be more efficient.

"For the first time AI is really beginning to occupy people's thinking in the profession."

Second, we are seeing rapid technological changes and for the first time AI is really beginning to occupy people's thinking in the profession. Law firm leaders are asking things like: What is the right bodycount of people needed to balance financial and professional efficiency? How many lawyers do you need to run a law firm these days? At the same time, some clients that seek BigLaw services have concluded that they don't want to be paying for junior lawyers, and quite frankly, technology has automated some of the things that junior lawyers used to do.

CA: What will the Trump administration mean for the legal profession?
JL: I think compliance work will continue to grow and the data certainly reflects that with regards to hiring. I think what's happening politically, especially with regards to deregulation, is an anomaly. I think talk of a deregulatory thrust is largely overstated. We live in a highly-regulated global economy. Even if US federal regulations take a dip, corporations operate in many jurisdictions and have to comply with many regulatory frameworks – I think that will continue regardless. There may be specific industries: environment, finance, healthcare, that will see the most change. It might be different regulations – but it won't be none. The world will continue to be highly regulated and the changes that may come with this administration are not going to reduce the overall regulatory burden. Rules change, the way that people do business has to change. I don't see that as a downward pressure at all.

CA: Despite all the initiatives, why does diversity remain so poor in BigLaw?
JL: Industry-wide, law firms continue to make very slow incremental growth towards greater diversity. The direction of growth tends to be positive but the fact is that during the recession junior lawyers were the ones to suffer the most in terms of layoffs and they are disproportionately more diverse than their senior counterparts. So it's taken a while to redress that imbalance. Law firms have for the most part bounced back, and diversity numbers have eclipsed what they were before the recession. Minority females in particular continue to be the least well represented. And there are some wrinkles in the recent upturn – the recouped losses have almost exclusively been with Asian associates. African American numbers have actually gone down and are actually lower than they were before the recession. It's a real problem in this country and everyone realizes it's an important thing that needs changing.

"Our secondary school system has fundamentally failed African Americans."

That's why it's such a hard question. Law firms are putting a lot of resources and a lot of good faith into solving the problem and yet, power structures being what they are, and the BigLaw culture being what it is – it's hard to make meaningful gains. As well as all this, clients continue to put pressure on firms to improve figures.

We know from the outset that African Americans enter private practice at the lowest rate of any other group. The reasons are complicated. Our secondary school system has fundamentally failed African Americans. And there continues to be discrimination, so some folks are at a disadvantage from the very start.

That said, minorities are over-represented in law firms at entry-level, so it's retention that's the big problem. People go in-house, because corporations are environments that have often have more inclusive workplaces. BigLaw is tough. I think it's a complicated thing – it's not that they're failing in the profession, but that this particular pathway is not yielding the right numbers.

CA: In terms of salaries, is the law becoming a two-tiered profession – with BigLaw, and then everybody else?
JL: I would say that it's been a two-tiered profession really since 2001, and that distance continues to grow. We have seen salary growth in other areas but the basic bi-modal salary distribution continues to be the norm.

We see more than half the class making $45-65k and then a trough and then another large group, as many as a quarter of the class, making $160-180k without very many salaries in the middle. But we are seeing accounting firms and corporate compliance jobs, and some of these new paths come in with salaries in that valley, between $90,000 and $120,000, so over the longer arc we may see something of the restoration of the bell curve. But with regards to the first-year increase this year [to $180,000], I think it made sense – the salaries had been flat for more than seven years so it made sense that they went up.

"The cost of living in places like New York, DC and San Francisco continues to be huge. And this, coupled with mountains of debt, means that though junior associates can live comfortably, they are by no means 'rich'."

We do our associate survey every two years and it was clear with the most recent survey that not every large law firm office went up to $180k, but many did. Arguably, from an economic standpoint, the bimodal salary distribution suggest that BigLaw pays too much for entry-level talent. But then again, the cost of living in places like New York, DC and San Francisco continues to be huge. And this, coupled with mountains of debt, means that though junior associates can live comfortably, they are by no means 'rich'. Conversely, if you are getting $65k in a major market and you have $180,000 in student loan debt, you are in a difficult position. But that debt position is being moderated as well.

Because interest in law school has gone down so quickly – applications are down something like 40% over a five-year period – one of the things that has happened is that people are paying less for their degrees. There are still schools that are able to set their price, largely at the top

and bottom of the pecking order, but everyone else is discounting tuition significantly. In the long term that's a disaster for the law school business model, but because of supply and demand, the net cost for students has gone down.

There was a recent article by Bill Henderson writing about Harvard's decision to switch to the GRE for recruitment. He argues that the change is about more than just looking for additional applicants. He argues that with the changes in the way that law is practiced and will be practiced, law schools need different sorts of students, and he sees Harvard leading the way. The article explains that undergraduates with a tech background are more likely to take the GRE than the LSE. It's incredibly insightful, you should give it a read.

CA: Do you think there'll be a rethink in terms of salaries e.g. pay less and require fewer billables?
JL: The fact is that law firms still aren't going to pay their partnership track associates less. But they are creating new entry points in terms of staff attorney roles with lower billables. Sometimes it's practice-specific, but we are seeing some real growth even at big brand name law firms – people are coming in at $100k instead of $180k on lower billables. Sometimes stars will emerge from this system, and they will cross over to an associate track and bill out at the higher rate, but it's rare.

We are likely to see the proliferation of these differentiated roles. It doesn't really make sense that everyone makes the same money anymore – there needs to be some diversification. Law firms are becoming more like corporations with more career paths and more differentiated roles and I think that will continue.

CA: Will remote working/telecommuting become the norm in the near future?
JL: I think it will be a big factor everywhere. We have had a big announcement recently by a few firms about allowing associates to work up to two days a week remotely. I think this staffing model is kind of built to allow work from anywhere, and I think it will continue to evolve.

Firms are really rethinking their office footprints – law firms' two big costs are the human bodies and real estate. Having trimmed headcount during the recession, they are now rethinking their space, looking to more shared spaces and smaller offices with an eye to the way young people do their work.

"You're not going to get work from a partner if they don't know you."

Of course, a counter balancing threat is the increased security risks that come with remote working. Data privacy

Becoming a Lawyer

and security are two of the greatest risks facing law firms. I went to the ILTA conference recently and it was really a topic of great concern – how far can you extend the law firm's metaphorical fire wall?

With regards to working remotely, the problem for your career is that you're not going to get work from a partner if they don't know you. However, we have a generation of young lawyers who want to leave work when they need to leave to tend to family obligations, maybe leave at 5:00 and spend time with their kids and then plug back in later in the evening after the kids are in bed and work some more. It's not so much that they don't want to come in, just that they don't want to come in and stay until nine.

CA: Do you have any advice for our student readers?
JL: That's a really hard question. Look, law firms still hire in very traditional and some would say ancient ways. Despite all I've just said, it's still a credential and prestige-driven market. Despite all the thinking law firms do around hiring, most often it still depends on what school you went to, your GPA and whether you were on the journal. Those credentials are the given. Then, maybe the next most important thing is that you're a fully-formed adult. Law firms do want candidates with some maturity, and some experience. If a candidate has never worked before it's tough. To the extent that this generation has a weakness, it's that they're sometimes more comfortable communicating digitally. To succeed at a law firm you have to be able to communicate well face to face. Students should mock interview more than they do. Law firms want to hire adults that they can put in a room with other adults. When people fail despite their credentials, it's usually a failure with regards to adulthood in the interview setting.

Making the most of summer and term time work is important while you get your legal education, so that you at least get as much of that professional work exposure as you can. Someone who interacts with dignity, gravitas and warmth is someone who has that background. Can they work with you? Can you fit in? Law firms are businesses and students are being hired to be part of that business. They are being hired to help the firm make money. Sometimes students don't realize that. Students should try to think of it through the lens of the partners they will work for. How can they add value to the law firm?

Becoming a Lawyer

"To the extent that this generation has a weakness, it's that they're sometimes more comfortable communicating digitally."

Job Fairs

Below is a selection of some of the best law career fairs around the country. Dates and deadlines can change, so check in advance with ones you want to attend (and that you meet the entry criteria).

	Fair	Location	Focus
2017			
July	Bay Area Diversity Career Fair	San Francisco	Bay Area employers
	Los Angeles Off-Campus Recruitment Program	Los Angeles, CA	Regional and national law firms
	Miami Off-Campus recruitment program	Miami, FL	Regional and national law firms
	National Black Prosecutors Association Job Fair	Cleveland, OH	Prosecution at local, state and federal level
	San Francisco Off-Campus Recruitment Program	San Francisco, CA	Regional and national law firms
	Philadelphia Walk-Around Recruitment Program	Philadelphia, PA	Regional and national law firms
	Southeastern IP Job Fair	Atlanta, GA	IP law in the Southeast
	Southeastern Minority Job Fair	Marietta, GA	Minority law students
	Washington DC Off-Campus Recruitment Program	Washington, DC	Regional and national law firms
August	Cook County Bar Association Minority Student Fair	Chicago, IL	Minority students in the region
	Chicago Walk-Around Recruitment Fair	Chicago, IL	Chicago law firms
	Loyola Patent Law Interview Program	Chicago, IL	Patent law
	Indianapolis Bar Association Diversity Job Fair	Indianapolis, IN	Diverse law students in the Midwest
	National LGBT Bar Association (Lavender Law Career Fair)	San Francisco, CA	Corporate, non-profit, government
	Northwest Minority Job Fair	Seattle, WA	Corporate law, public sector
September	Hispanic National Bar Association Annual Convention & Career Fair	Kansas City, MO	Hispanic law students
October	Equal Justice Works Public Service Career Fair	Arlington, VA	Public interest
2018			
January	Nashville Bar Association Damali Booker First Year Minority Clerkship Job Fair	Nashville, TN	Minority law students
	NYU International Student Interview Program	New York, NY	Foreign trained lawyers
February	Midwest Public Interest Law Career Conference	Chicago, IL	Public interest
	Northwest Public Service Career Fair	Seattle, WA; Portland, OR	Government, non-profit
	NYU Public Interest Legal Career Fair	New York, NY	Government, non-profit
	UCLA LL.M. Interview Program (formerly West Coast International LLM Job Fair)	Los Angeles, CA	Foreign trained lawyers
January/ February	Nashville Bar Association Damali Booker First Year Minority Clerkship Job Fair	Nashville, TN	Minority law students
February	Midwest Public Interest Law Career Conference	Chicago, IL	Public interest
	Northwest Public Service Career Fair	Seattle, WA; Portland, OR	Government, non-profit
	NYU Public Interest Legal Career Fair	New York, NY	Government, non-profit
	UCLA LL.M. Interview Program (formerly West Coast International LLM Job Fair)	Los Angeles, CA	Foreign trained lawyers

Who? 1Ls, 2Ls, 3Ls...	Website
2Ls and above	www.sfbar.org/
2Ls and 3Ls from participating schools	http://www.thelawconsortium.org/los-angeles.html
2Ls and 3Ls from participating schools	https://law.utexas.edu/career/interview-programs/event-type/off-campus-fairs/
Not specified	http://blackprosecutors.org/annual-conference
2Ls and 3Ls from participating schools	https://law.utexas.edu/career/interview-programs/event-type/off-campus-fairs/
2Ls and 3Ls from participating schools	http://www.thelawconsortium.org/philadelphia.html
Students from participating schools	http://sipjf.law.gsu.edu/
2Ls, 3Ls, recent graduates	http://www.semjf.org/
2Ls and 3Ls from participating schools	http://www.thelawconsortium.org/washington-dc.html
2Ls, 3Ls	http://ccbaminorityjobfair.org/
2Ls and 3Ls from participating schools	https://law.wisc.edu/career/jobfairs.html
2Ls, 3Ls	http://www.luc.edu/law/career/patent_students.html
Full-time 2Ls, part-time 2Ls and 3Ls	http://www.ibadiversityjobfair.org/
Not specified	http://lgbtbar.org/annual/career-fair/
All law students	http://www.nwmjf.org/
2Ls, 3Ls	http://hnba.com/2017-annual-convention/
2Ls, 3Ls	http://www.equaljusticeworks.org/law-school/conference-and-careerfair
1Ls	https://www.nashvillebar.org/
Foreign-trained LLM students at sponsor schools	http://www.law.nyu.edu/isip
Open to all law students	http://www.mpilcc.org/
Law students and alumni of NW Consortium schools	https://law.lclark.edu/student_groups/public_service_career_fairs/
Students from participating schools	http://pilcfair.law.nyu.edu/
Foreign trained LLM students at sponsor schools	https://law.ucla.edu/careers/employers/attend-a-job-fair-or-event/ucla-llm-interview-program/
1Ls	http://www.nashvillebar.org/Committee/Diversity/1LJobFair.html
Open to all law students	http://www.mpilcc.org/
Law students and alumni	https://law.lclark.edu/student_groups/public_service_career_fairs/
Students from participating schools	http://pilcfair.law.nyu.edu/
Foreign trained LLM students at sponsor schools	https://law.ucla.edu/careers/employers/attend-a-job-fair-or-event/ucla-llm-interview-program/

Becoming a Lawyer

On-campus interviews

We interview the interviewers to help guide you through the OCIs...

The process

HIRING at most top firms follows a similar highly structured pattern: interviews on campus, followed by interviews back at the firms, then (hopefully) a summer associateship. Many components of this process are laid down by NALP's guidelines, and by law schools. Recruitment varies from school to school and from firm to firm, but here we will attempt to give you a rough overview of how the OCI process works, plus tips on how to get through it successfully.

We speak to many dozens of law firm recruiters each year during our research for this guide. Among other things, they tell us what they look for in prospective hires and what questions they're likely to ask during interviews. A number of consistent themes emerge about what they are looking for during these interviews, which we present below with some quotes from hiring partners themselves. Firms' recruiting strategies do differ, of course, and you can find out more about the particular requirements of each in the Get Hired section of our Inside View features.

Bidding

OCIs are aimed at students at the start of their 2L year for summer positions the following summer, between their 2L and 3L years. Although they occur under the banner of 'fall recruiting', OCIs are increasingly held earlier in the year, starting in August and September. Besides BigLaw firms, smaller firms, public interest organizations and government agencies (like the Federal Public Defender's Office, the IRS and Immigration and Customs Enforcement) also recruit on campus. While commercial law firms pay to attend, government and public organizations usually don't.

Students can bid on a certain number of employers (often between 20 and 50), ranking their preferences for firms and office locations. A preset system determines who they interview with: some schools allow employers to select a proportion of the students they interview; others use a lottery system which is entirely based on students' preferences. Bidding deadlines are usually in July.

On chambers-associate.com...

- Good legal writing

Most schools request that students submit a writing sample alongside their resume when bidding for firms at OCI. This is typically a paper written on a legal subject. Good writing skills are essential for junior associates, as drafting is a big part of their staple diet. The writing sample is more important to some firms than to others. "*This firm is really, really serious about the quality of the writing sample,*" one BigLaw associate emphasized to us. "*People with excellent credentials get turned away because their writing isn't top-notch.*"

Besides OCIs, some firms also interview at job fairs with a regional focus (like the Midwest Job Fair) or are focused on a specific minority (like the NBLSA Job Fair and the Lavender Law Fair), or have a specific industry focus, like the Loyola Patent Law Interview Program. Smaller firms often take applicants through a mix of direct applications and OCIs, as they don't have the resources to visit a large number of campuses. A few firms bypass the OCI process entirely. Quinn Emanuel's recruitment 'parties' are the most high-profile example, letting students mingle with the firm's associates and partners at an informal drinks event before submitting resumes.

Resumes

Firms see students' resumes before the interview. A resume should be no longer than a page long, unless you have at least five years' work experience prior to law school, which means you probably don't have space for that paper route you did in 10th grade. It also goes without saying that typos are to be avoided at all costs; even one mistake can make the difference between the 'yes' pile and the rejects, so do enlist someone to proofread your resume. Think carefully about coming up with a clear, punchy layout (there's helpful advice from Harvard here). Keep your resume continually up-to-date, and refine it constantly. Put your strengths somewhere where they can be clearly seen, targeting the five-second glance by a rushed recruiter. And, crucially, think carefully about how to tailor your resume to the jobs you want. It's not enough to say you're passionate about law. Give real and specific evidence which is targeted to the kind of firms you're applying to.

Often a resume will tick the right boxes, but recruiters will want to use the interview to find out if you really live up to your billing. Make sure you have plenty more to say about all the activities, experiences and hobbies you've listed. One interviewer explains that candidates are *"likely to be asked detailed questions about items on their resumes. Their capacity to speak to those topics thoughtfully, compellingly and with some imaginative insight is very important."*

The interview

Most students interview with between ten and 30 firms (assuming they can get that many interviews). OCIs usually last 20 minutes and are conducted by a mix of partners and associates. Some firms have a dedicated group of attorneys (often the hiring committee) which interviews on campus; others let a wider range of attorneys participate. Sometimes interviewers are trained by firms on how to interview and how to present the firm during OCIs. (Take a look at an OCI manual leaked to ATL – abovethelaw.com/2011/09/an-inside-look-at-sullivan-cromwells-recruiting-process/ – to get an idea of how big firms might prep their interviewers.)

Whatever's on your resume, it's how you come across during the OCI which matters most to firms. That doesn't just mean your personality – you need to be able to communicate how and why your past experiences make you right for the firm. The interview process itself is a test of character: interviewers will look at the way you speak, answer questions and make an argument to judge whether you have the qualities they are looking for. For example, many recruiters ask about candidates' undergraduate dissertations. They do this to see how well you still recall your main argument, and how well you can summarize your argument briefly for a lay audience. Of course, this ability to think on your feet is itself an essential quality for any attorney. Pay attention to which of its offices a firm is recruiting for on your campus. Some firms recruit for all their offices on all campuses; others allow specific offices to target specific campuses.

Callback interviews

Firms often have a maximum number of students from any school who they will 'call back' for a second interview. 'Callback interviews' usually take place in October. They involve a half-day or whole day spent on-site at one of the firm's offices. Students are usually interviewed by four to six attorneys – a mix of partners and associates. Often there will also be a lunch or coffee event with junior associates.

Be aware that you are being assessed during the whole day, not just during the interviews themselves. Treat lunches and coffee dates as part of the interview process; there's no need to be formal, but you should always keep in mind that you are being judged – showing an interest in your interviewers' work and the firm in general is a good bet. *"Candidates feel more comfortable during lunches with junior associates, so these interviews will often be more illuminating than the office ones. The associates fill out assessment forms in the same way that partners do,"* a BigLaw hiring partner tells us. How you greet and talk to support staff and recruiters when you first arrive can be important too. Hiring committees usually take into consideration the views of staff and junior associates who have met with candidates.

A 'standard' callback interview will see some interviewers ask about your resume, while others might talk about hobbies, sports and academics to find out more about your skills and personality. *"My interviewer put down my resume and said: 'Let's just have a conversation,'"* one junior associate recalled. *"Then we talked about what I liked and disliked about law school, the firm and my connection to the city."* Most firms allow interviewers a lot of free rein in what they ask. *"Different interviewers will put different weights on certain aspects of a student,"* another recruiter pointed out. Some firms employ so-called behavioral interviewing techniques. This ranges from asking questions directly about skills and competencies ('give an example of when you worked in a team') to structured assessments.

For example, Philadelphia's Pepper Hamilton uses an interactive scenario in which interviewers and candidates work though a legal issue. The aim is to *"see how comfortable the candidate is in a working situation, how they work in a team and how they might counsel a client."* We reckon that this type of interviewing will become increasingly common in future.

If a student is unsure whether to join the firm (or vice versa) they might return to the firm for a 'second look' and meet with a few more attorneys. Candidates are often asked if they want to meet attorneys from certain practice areas during the callback or 'second look'. Make use of this opportunity: asking to meet people from certain departments – even if you're not sure which you want to join – will show you're engaged with the firm's work. A short while after the callback students will hear whether the firm wants to offer them a position as a summer associate. Students have 28 days to accept the offer.

Becoming a Lawyer

On chambers-associate.com...

- What's your greatest weakness? How to handle this annoying interview question

Some top interview tips from hiring partners

"I like to engage students about what their passions are – say what they wrote their thesis on – to see their fluency with language and whether they have a clear world view, sophistication and maturity."

"In interviews we use simple techniques to draw out aspects of someone's personality: when looking at leadership we might ask about past experiences where candidates were put into a leadership role. What was that experience like? Could they describe it in detail? How did you rise to the occasion? And so on."

"We ask about their connection to the city they're interviewing in, about their outside interests and long-term plans, and what they like and don't like about law school."

"One stock question I ask is: what is not on your resume that we should know about you? I like to know what's behind the resume. That's not just personality-related. I want them to go a little deeper so I can find out about their skills as a person. A wonderful response to that question is if someone relates it to a challenge they have overcome or a time when they have shown good judgment."

"The worst answer I have ever had to a question was the person who told me about working on a group project at college where no-one pulled their weight, so they did all the work. They were really proud of it, but it tells me they might not work well in a team."

"Show a serious interest in what the firm does, and what the people you are speaking to do."

"The biggest thing you could do wrong at OCI is not be able to keep up an intelligent conversation for 20 minutes or not have any questions."

"During interviews candidates should have good questions about the firm. Not just questions to which the answers are on our website, but things that show they have done their homework."

"Prepare. It takes more time than some students set aside for it. Practicing to get over the jitters is good, but what's more important is thinking through what you've done in your life to understand what skills you have that can contribute to being a lawyer. When we sense that somebody's done enough thinking about themselves to know which part of their experience to talk about at an interview, we're prone to think they're analytical and will be able to perform the tasks required of them."

"Identify a couple of areas of real interest and educate yourself about those areas, both through law school courses and practice experience. In that way you can distinguish yourself from the mass."

Examples of questions

Here are some examples of OCI and callback interview questions reported by juniors and recruiters:

Why do you want to be a lawyer?

Why are you applying to this firm?

What is it you have heard or read about this firm that made you interested?

What areas of practice are you interested in and why?

Describe to me the central argument of your undergraduate thesis.

What did you enjoy about law school?

Where do you see yourself five or ten years down the road?

What mistakes have you made in your past?

If I called one of your referees now, how would they describe you?

How would your law journal colleagues who worked with you describe you?

Describe a time when you didn't succeed and what you learned from it.

Describe a time you showed leadership. How did you rise to the occasion?

How much time would you spend polishing a draft to get the little points right?

Can you describe a particularly challenging circumstance in your life?

What motivates you?

Are you a team player?

Can you describe a situation where you handled a difficult customer?

Tell me about a time you worked in a team that was dysfunctional.

Tell me about a time you helped successfully produce a certain work product.

Tell me about a time you had to juggle several responsibilities.

Tell me about a time you faced a setback or failure and what you did.

What adversities have you faced in past employment?

Summers

At many BigLaw firms, getting on the summer program is tantamount to getting an associate job. Historically, many firms used the summer program as a final step in the recruitment process: a tough few months' work at the firm would weed out the weaklings, and firms would only give job offers to a certain proportion of each summer class. Some firms still use the old model, but since the recession an increasing number only hire summers who they intend to take on as first-years. Firms now pride themselves on their 100% offer rates – you'd really have to screw up during the summer not to get an offer (the economy aside...).

Summer programs traditionally involved a lot of wining, dining and schmoozing of participating students. This trend, too, is declining. First, a recession-induced squeeze on firms' budgets means less cash to spend on perks for summers. Second, it used to be fairly important for firms to impress (top) students to stop them seeking jobs elsewhere. With the job market as tough as it is, this is barely necessary any more.

Firms now pride themselves on offering students a summer experience which reflects the life of a junior associate.

Recruitment outside OCIs

Aside from OCIs, firms recruit from some schools by allowing students to submit their resumes via a central pool. This is known as a 'resume drop'.

Some firms also accept direct write-in applications outside OCIs. As one recruiter put it: *"If someone writes in to us and they're not from a top-50 school, but they came top of their class and were editor-in-chief of a law journal, that will certainly get our attention."* Networking is also very important if you want to get an associate job outside OCIs. Getting in touch with attorneys at the firm you are interested in either directly or via alumni events is the very least you should do. *"Our attorneys are very involved with their alma maters,"* a hiring partner told us. Networking is also increasingly important if you are applying via OCIs. *"Students need to work hard at networking as more job opportunities are spread by word of mouth than before."*

Some firms like recruiting candidates who have completed an LL.M., especially overseas. Usually though, an LL.M. will do nothing to help your chances of getting a job as an associate.

For more tips from the hiring partners, visit our website, where you'll find interviews with each HP.

Becoming a Lawyer

Callbacks may feel a little less formal than OCIs but may be even more probing:

"We leave it up to the lawyer conducting the callback interview, but there are a number of things we look at. It's a holistic process so we're interested in their experiences and record of success. The interviews are not scheduled for a specific length; they're free-form and organic so some might be an hour long and others only 15 minutes. Partner and associate interviewers will ask what seems important to them based on an applicant's resume and the conversation as it develops."

– Karin DeMasi, litigation hiring partner at Cravath

Summer programs

The halcyon days of extravagant spending might be over, but BigLaw summer associate programs remain a decent mix of solid work experience and social jamborees...

SUMMER associate programs are an integral part of BigLaw recruiting. Attrition rates are high across the profession, so firms run annual programs – usually lasting from six to 12 weeks – to ensure a steady influx of first-years join the ranks each year. A summer stint effectively serves as a prolonged interview, with clear benefits for applicants and recruiting attorneys alike: the former receive a taste of associate life, the latter get an up-close and personal view of potential colleagues in action. Provided all goes well, summers receive an offer to return as a full-time first-year associate upon completion of their law degree.

Recent years have seen summer classes composed primarily of 2Ls. Many firms hire a handful of 1Ls each year, often via scholarships or competitions – the summer of 2014 saw more 1L hires than any year since 2008, according to NALP. However, the chances of nabbing a spot as a 3L are slim, and many law students concentrate on applications during the summer following their 1L year, when on-campus recruiting kicks off. Class sizes took a serious hit during the economic downturn. There has been some recovery, but competition remains fierce so it's vital your grades and extracurriculars are up to scratch. Check out our feature on trends in the recruitment market for more details on class sizes and employment figures. For information about when and how to apply for summer spots, see our feature on the OCI process.

"I felt really integrated into my practice group when I saw that my work product was incorporated into the matters at hand."

The summer associate experience has historically been somewhat artificial, many firms offering made-up tasks that bear only mild resemblance to actual responsibilities. However, the recession prompted an increased reliance on summers at many a cash-strapped firm, and offering 'real' work soon became a necessity. That continues today – most associate interviewees now report a relatively *"authentic"* experience as summers. You'll likely get the chance to try out work across a variety of practice groups, which *"can be really helpful if you don't have a clear idea of what to go into,"* sources agreed. Some firms, like Willkie and King & Spalding, have formal ro-

tation systems in place to ensure summers experience a broad mix of assignments. At the end of the program, candidates typically submit a preference for a particular practice group. That's then taken into consideration at the offers stage.

"I felt really integrated into my practice group when I saw that my work product was incorporated into the matters at hand," one shared. *"When I returned as a first-year, I was able to pick up one project that was still ongoing and see it through to the end."* Another said: *"Firms now realize the value of allowing summers to get their hands dirty with real tasks; that approach demonstrates how you will actually react under certain circumstances and prepares you for the transition into being a first-year."* Indeed, one BigLaw hiring partner confirms *"throwing people into the mix seems to work out best for everyone involved."*

Typical summer duties include small research tasks, drafting memos and attending negotiations or depositions to observe their seniors. *"We make the effort to get people on the phone to listen to the back and forth of arguing a case, and in client meetings so they can witness the kind of behavior that gets things done,"* one hiring partner tells us. When not 'learning by doing', students attend summer-specific training, and are often able to opt into CLE classes alongside fully fledged associates. As well as general introductions to different practices, summer training sessions cover topics as varied as advocacy, due diligence, depositions, legal writing and business development.

In keeping with the post-recession trend of cutbacks across the legal sector, the culture of lavish wining and dining – a summer staple implemented with the intent of wooing top hires – has slowed down to some extent. *"Anyone summering now will find things aren't as flashy as they used to be,"* sources reported. Is this a sore spot? *"Not at all; if anything it helps prepare you for the working world,"* one associate said, looking back on their time as a summer. *"They're not trying to seduce you into thinking associate life is something it isn't – it's not all karaoke, free bars and boat trips down the Hudson River."*

"They're not trying to seduce you into thinking associate life is something it isn't."

Still, socializing remains important to the experience, with lunches, sports events, wine-tastings and theater trips among the standard perks. *"You can still get tickets to a Yankees game, but they won't be behind home plate,"* one source summed up. In any case, attorneys of all levels look forward to summer since *"that's when the majority of the year's social events take place."* Some of the more exciting traditions we've heard about include trips to Disneyland and a destination hike at Quinn Emanuel, cooking classes and Shakespeare in the Park at Debevoise, and mixology courses and sunset sails at Willkie. *"I'd be a summer forever if I could!"* one insider enthused.

Savvy summers will see these events as more than a chance to chill out – they're golden opportunities to meet and mingle. Indeed, a hiring partner at a top international firm says: *"I don't care how busy you are or how tired you are, you need to get out there and go to as many events as possible! It's as good a chance to meet and talk to people as you'll get during office hours and the more contacts you're able to make the better."*

Some firms have programs that let summers spend time in multiple offices, or even outside organizations with which the firm has ties. Certain large international outfits like Linklaters and Debevoise allow associates to spend part of their summer in an overseas office. *"Having that opportunity helped me make valuable connections with my international colleagues and offered a good insight into how the firm operates abroad,"* said one source who'd split their time between London and New York. Others – including Vinson & Elkins and Simpson Thatcher – offer the chance to spend several weeks working with a local public interest organization. Some run mini client secondments for summer associates – Cleary, for example, offers a two-week stint at an investment bank. Check out our features on all these firms for more info.

When it comes to landing an offer, a good impression is imperative – a summer stint is akin to an audition. Whether you're responding to a partner's request or schmoozing at an event, engage appropriately and keep to your best behavior to show you're taking the opportunity seriously. As one BigLaw hiring partner shares, *"being enthusiastic about the work is just as important as demonstrating you're capable of doing it as far as I'm concerned."* Other interviewees advised summers to *"maintain a positive attitude"* and *"show a genuine interest in what's going on at the firm and where it's heading."* That said, *"there's certainly room to relax"* during the program, sources assured us, *"just don't go overboard with the booze!"* Indeed, the point of offering opportunities for candidates to let their hair down is to assess their personalities, *"including how they interact outside a work context,"* one hiring partner reveals. *"It's a good glimpse into people's attitudes and what it'll be like interacting with them on a day-to-day basis."*

"I'd be a summer forever if I could!"

Since the recession, offer rates from summer programs have been high. A tightened grip on financials prompted many firms to limit summer hiring to those they intend to keep on for good, and the ability to claim a 100% offer rate has become a badge of pride on the recruiting side. The latest NALP report shows that more than 95.3% of summer associates in 2015 received offers, a figure up considerably from the 69.3% reported in 2009. *"We always aim to keep everyone, and it's rare when we don't end up with offers across the board,"* one hiring partner tells us. *"When that happens, it's because we haven't done our job perfectly and it turns out someone doesn't really fit in or didn't pan out in terms of our expectations."*

Clerkships

Clerking for a judge is a great way to kick-start your career as a litigator...

What is a law clerk?

A JUDICIAL clerk (or 'elbow clerk') works as a judge's assistant and typically starts after graduating law school. These clerkships normally involve working alongside a single judge. Responsibilities vary from judge to judge, but all clerks engage in research and do copious amounts of writing. Most appointments last one or two years – judges indicate the duration of the commitment at the outset. Whether you want to work in BigLaw or for a smaller outfit, the skills, connections and insights picked up while clerking are invaluable.

Why clerk?

"It's an absolutely amazing experience. If everyone could do it, there would be a lot of better lawyers," one former district court clerk told us. *"It's absolutely hands down the best way to start a legal career,"* says Melissa Lennon, recent judicial section chair at NALP. *"The training you get – really intense research and writing – is incredibly valuable."* According to retired Judge Joel Pisano of the District Court of New Jersey, *"clerking offers an opportunity to be in on the decision-making process, to understand how the courts work, to be mentored by a sitting judge and to be introduced to the members of the Bar."* Clerks learn how judges react to different briefs and styles of advocacy, and are exposed to a wide range of legal issues.

The educational value of clerkships cannot be overstated, as clerks learn directly from the arbiters of the law. A judge might ask a clerk to write a memorandum or even a first draft of a judicial opinion. *"Certainly, I was writing opinions,"* said an associate who had clerked with the District Court of Maryland. *"My writing got a lot better over the course of a year, because of the benefit of having a judge who sees you every day, guides you and shapes your writing style."* Clerks may get an insight into legal administration too. One source had clerked with a judge who sat on the Judicial Conference of the United States – a body concerned with US Courts administration – and had taken on duties related to the Conference.

The judge/clerk relationship often extends beyond the clerkship term. *"Previous clerks are always encouraged to call if they want to chat or need advice,"* according to Judge Pisano. For some this relationship is career-changing as their judge mentors them on the next step in their career. *"I didn't have a good idea of the legal scene so I asked the judge what he recommended,"* one former clerk told us. *"The firm I'm at now is the first one he recommended."*

Clerks also build up a valuable network among members of the Bar, other clerks and judges. This comes in handy when practicing in the same state or district as the judge.

Different courts provide windows into different types of law. For someone who wants to be a criminal litigator, clerking in a state trial court would provide maximum exposure to criminal prosecution. Bankruptcy judges are part of the district court system and have special purview over bankruptcy filings. *"If you are interested in transactional law or corporate governance, working for the Delaware Court of Chancery is significantly advantageous,"* says Melissa Lennon. *"Delaware is the home of corporate law in the US: many groundbreaking corporate and governance issues are decided there."* Equally, those interested in green issues could look into clerking at the environmental division of the Vermont Superior Court (Vermont is one of the few states where courts have specialized environmental divisions).

Types of clerkship
Federal courts

A stint at the US Supreme Court is the most sought-after, hard-to-land position on the clerking circuit. Read our feature on SCOTUS clerkships. While these clerks can practically pick a firm of their choice after this clerkship, several choose to go into academia instead (see endnote 1).

There are 13 federal courts of appeals. Federal circuit court clerks do a lot of research: assessing opposing briefs, going over the trial records, and interpreting application of the law. Many appellate court judges are known as 'feeder judges' as they have a history of having their former clerks hired by the Supreme Court.

There are 94 federal districts in the USA, and federal district courts offer clerkships with either a district judge or a magistrate judge. Federal district clerks have a more varied role than their appellate counterparts as they work in the general trial courts of the US federal system. In addition to the extensive research and writing appellate clerks undertake, district clerks coordinate with attorneys, help resolve discovery-related motions, prepare judges for settlement conferences and attend trial-related hearings.

Budding litigators should note that this is the perfect opportunity to pick up useful skills. Clerking with a magistrate judge is slightly more limited in scope as their remit is constrained by what federal district judges assign them. They do handle a wide range of work: warrants, bail hearings, arraignments, pretrial motions and civil matters related to multiparty litigation. Magistrates also write reports and recommendations to the district judge. Prospective clerks should make sure to find out what matters are referred to a magistrate judge before applying.

There are also opportunities to clerk for federal judges in subject matter-specific special courts. The Court of International Trade is one example; it has jurisdiction over international trade and customs with nine judges who often hire two clerks each (see endnote 2). Each judicial district is also home to a bankruptcy court. Clerks here are exposed to complex commercial cases, including claims made against debtors. The US Tax Court adjudicates tax disputes and arranges settlement payments to the IRS: the court comprises 19 judges, appointed for 15 years each. Other special courts include the US Court of Appeals for Veterans Claims and the US Court of Federal Claims.

State courts
Courts of last resort contribute to the development of state common law and interpret state statute, having a significant impact on state law. Clerks here have similar tasks and responsibilities to federal appellate law clerks. These clerkships are the most competitive to obtain at state level. To be considered for one, high academic standing and some journal experience are essential.

Some states have intermediary appellate courts, which operate along the lines of the federal courts of appeals – resolving appeals arising from the state's lower courts.

Many civil and criminal matters are dealt with at first instance by state trial courts. This grouping includes both general and limited jurisdiction trial courts such as city, county and probate courts. Law students looking to become criminal lawyers might be better off clerking in a state trial court than in federal court. Clerks here gain significant insight into the workings of the local Bar, state procedures and state law while assisting in trial procedures, research and drafting. This is also useful for those wishing to become public prosecutors in the region. NALP provides a detailed guide on clerkships in select state courts.

On chambers-associate.com...

- How to speak judge: an insider's guide to getting, and surviving, your clerkship

Staff attorneys
Some courts hire 'staff attorneys': clerks who work for a group of judges instead of just one. Also known as pool clerks or court attorneys, these positions can be found in both federal and state courts. The core responsibilities of staff attorneys are more limited than those of other clerks and include reviewing appeals, preparing memos and assisting in case management.

Clerkship application
Federal and state clerkships don't abide by the same deadlines. State clerkship deadlines vary from court to court and state to state. Research local deadlines to find out more.

The majority of federal appellate judges hire clerks in the fall of their 3L year. To find out more check out OSCAR, the Online System for Clerkship Application and Review, at oscar.uscourts.gov. This online system allows judges to post vacancies, and students to apply online. OSCAR used to follow a 'Hiring Plan' application schedule, but this has changed as of 2013. Now, rising second-year law students can begin researching clerkship openings on June 1, and can begin submitting applications on August 1. Judges will receive applications immediately and can offer available clerkships at any time. 2L and 3L students and alumni can access OSCAR all through the year. In 2013, 72% of federal judges held OSCAR accounts.

Different judges have different preferences for how they like students to apply. You may be able to find out how the judge you are interested in clerking with recruits by contacting their chambers. Judges usually look for a good writing sample and good personal references. Sometimes schools recommend candidates to judges. Getting a (good) clerkship can often be all about networking, recommendations and connections.

Traditional practice for interviewees has been to accept the first offer they get, as many judges expect an immediate answer. "The crucial thing is never tell a judge, 'I don't want to work with you'," one source advised. At the time of writing, base salaries for federal clerks ranged from $52,329 to $74,584, depending on experience level. Salaries for state clerks vary.

Choosing a judge
Once you've chosen which judges you may want to clerk with, finding out more can be a murky process. Unfortunately there is no guide that will list the quirks of each judge, although it is extremely important to collect every last bit of information you can before applying. "The only place where that information exists is in the halls of law schools," says Melissa Lennon. "If you're lucky enough to

get an interview with a judge, you need to talk to as many people as possible who have clerked or interviewed with that judge. Figure out what the judge is like and how they run their chambers."

There are also blogs and forums where former clerks discuss their judges, their interviews and clerkships. Some clerks have been known to scoff at attempts to gather information this way but, along with networking, doing a few Google searches is a good way to find out more about a judge.

Talking to former clerks is really the best resource; we spoke with a few associates who had clerked and learned a lot. *"Some judges – like Judge Easterbrook – you just don't apply to,"* said one source. *"He and other judges on the Seventh Circuit only take people who are recommended by certain schools."* Court of Appeals Judge Danny Boggs is known as the trivia judge – he administers a general knowledge test to prospective applicants and three of his former clerks have appeared on Who Wants to Be a Millionaire (see endnote 3). One associate had interviewed with a judge who asked them all about college basketball during the interview. *"They don't just look at your academic performance,"* said one former clerk. *"They know they will be working closely with you and want to find out if they can get along with you on a personal level."*

Should you apply?

A federal law clerk should have completed their JD and be a US citizen. Following that, there are no set academic requirements. Students who secure the most coveted clerkships are often from a highly ranked law school, were in the top quarter of their class, have worked on a law journal and have glowing academic references. Given the importance of personal recommendations, it's never too early to start forming connections with the right faculty members.

If you don't have the best grades or you're not at one of the top schools, take heart from these words from Melissa Lennon: *"It's a big country and there are opportunities for federal clerkships for candidates from different schools, not just the top 20. Judges have loyalty to their own schools."* Federal judges post around 1000 open clerkship positions to OSCAR each year (see endnote 4). Given the 480 clerkship positions offered by just the New Jersey Courts for 2017-18 (see endnote 5), it would be a fair estimate that aggregate state and federal clerkships outnumber top-grade applicants, although that doesn't mean that all of those positions are open to all applicants. State judges often have strong ties to the local community, so a strong letter of recommendation from a local school could have more clout than an Ivy League recommendation. *"As with many job applications, showing you have a local link helps,"* one former clerk advised.

If you're desperate for a clerkship but don't have the right grades, journal experience or law school pedigree, try making up with practical experience: intern at a regional firm, work in-house, do pro bono work or work part-time at a small firm (these experiences can also help provide you with the writing samples which judges so love). If you haven't worked on a law journal, highlighting courses in research and writing that you've aced can help too.

Many state and federal courts offer externships to law students, often during 1L or 2L summers. It can be tough to land one of these: you will need the right combination of grades, gumption and connections. Recommendations from these externships can be key to securing a coveted clerkship later on.

Endnotes

1 www.legalauthority.com/articles/70010/Clerkships

2 indylaw.indiana.edu/career/judicialclerkship.htm

3 www.newyorker.com/archive/2001/05/14/010514ta_
  TALK_DEPT_OF_TRIVIA

4 http://news.uscourts.gov/federal-law-clerk-hiring-
  plan-discontinued

5 www.judiciary.state.nj.us/lawclerks/

Becoming a Lawyer

SCOTUS clerkships

Clerking at the Supreme Court, as told by the lucky few who've been there, done that, got the judicial robe...

CLERKING at the Supreme Court of the United States is the holy grail, the most prestigious gig any law grad can get. Only 36 SCOTUS clerkships come up for grabs each year. Only the brightest and very, very best need apply. Over a thousand who consider themselves in this category (and have letters of introduction from distinguished law professors and others to back them up) do so every year. And you don't go to the Supreme Court straight from law school – usually all successful candidates have previously clerked at federal appellate level, and wowed their judges there.

"Nothing else short of being a judge will replicate this experience," one former SCOTUS clerk tells us of their year with a Justice. *"You see directly how things work, which completely changes the way you see cases."*

How do I apply?

At some point during your federal clerkship, bundle your resume, cover letter, transcript, writing sample and letters of recommendation (most Justices require at least three) and ping them to the Court. The Justices decide their own hiring schedules, so keep an eye out for announcements well in advance. *"If you've managed to get a clerkship on the circuit court, you've got some idea that you have both the grades and the recommendations to make you competitive,"* an ex-SCOTUS clerk counsels, encouragingly. A stellar reference from your judge, *"based on the couple months work you've already done for them,"* is essential. *"Many circuit judges have a great record of sending clerks to the Supreme Court."* Aside from this, the application is relatively labor-free – *"it's as brief as a resume and a cover letter."*

Your circuit court judge can help in other ways too: *"Often he can put you in touch with the SCOTUS Justice's previous clerks so you can talk with them about their experiences."* There's a lot to learn, as interviewing style varies as much as the Justices' personalities. Overall, it's important to *"be familiar with their cases and their judicial philosophy by getting your hands on as much of their writing as you can, and by reading their most high-profile cases. You also need to be familiar with all the pending cases the Court is hearing, to demonstrate you have a clear interest in that Court."*

The ex-clerks we spoke to found their interview more relaxed than anticipated. *"It tested whether you can hold an interesting conversation – very different to testing your legal reasoning skills!"* You've made it this far, so they take your legal genius as a given: *"Each Justice interviews ten to 15 people who have extremely good qualifications. They're already confident in you, so their main task is to see if they connect with you on a personal level."* Hopefully this shouldn't be too tricky as the people who recommended you *"already have a relationship with the Justice and have thought about personality and ideological fit – after all, they're sending you to live with someone for a year."* The importance of recommendations from others during the hiring process cannot be overstated: it's *"not just old guys in smoky rooms making the decisions."*

The Chief Justice is authorized to hire five clerks, the eight Associate Justices four and retired Justices one apiece.

So what do SCOTUS clerks actually do?

Something similar to what federal court clerks do. Primarily, their role is to sift through the thousands of petitions and mark the cases worthy of being granted time. *"It's the most basic task, and the constant thing that you do – during the summer it's practically your only task."* The petitions that lawyers write very cleverly argue why their cases should be granted; the clerk's job is *"to screen out those that are legitimate and write bench memos on what we think about the case."* On top of this, there's *"preparing your Justice for argument and conference. You learn very quickly how to handle yourself beyond just thinking 'wow, these people are brilliant!' You learn critical thinking and the big picture, and a sense of professionalism where it would be easy to strongly disagree with folks."*

As term progresses, clerks move *"to the fun part."* Assisting with opinion-drafting is a process that can vary between Justices. *"Sometimes the Justice just wants to talk through an issue, so having a personality that won't be a distraction here is really beneficial,"* says one former clerk. Another enjoyed the close interaction when producing documents: *"We helped a lot with the drafting but ultimately every word that appeared in writing was the Justice's. The best learning experience was going back and forth on a piece of writing and seeing it changing."*

And what do I get out of it?

Being at the heart of such a profound process gives you tremendous insights, something that BigLaw recognizes by offering eye-popping SCOTUS clerkship bonuses. *"Reading and attending oral arguments is the best imaginable lesson by example you can have on being a good lawyer,"* a former clerk says. *"The practice of law has always been an apprenticeship – you learn best by example. You're privileged to see how your Justice writes out an argument, but you also see what kind of things persuade them. That alone is so beneficial in terms of your own perspective and in terms of knowing what persuades judges for when you go into private practice yourself."*

"Even if you didn't learn how to write or earn a dime during the year, it would be worth it to see a branch of government working." Equally – and altruistically – *"you're performing a public service. The issue at the heart of everything is 'what's the right answer, and how can we put it out there in the most persuasive way?'"*

"The level of aggression varies, but generally there's a two-week period where you get taken to lunch by everyone. It's a fairly ego-boosting process."

After their year at the elbow of a Supreme Court Justice, the 36 are in incredibly high demand. *"You get letters from firms as soon as you start,"* explains one. *"It's up to you and your Justice when you start to interview at firms – usually it's in June or July. The level of aggression varies, but generally there's a two-week period where you get taken to lunch by everyone. It's a fairly ego-boosting process, as they're all so nice to you!"*

Ultimately, most *"assume they'll go into BigLaw – there are loads of student loans to pay off, and the signing bonuses available go some way to making a dent in them."* But not everyone's head is turned by gold: *"It can be a real dilemma for some clerks, who'd prefer to go to a public interest group or go be a professor."*

And what of those bonuses? The latest round of SCOTUS clerks received golden hellos of $280,000 or more from their BigLaw firms (in addition to an approx $185,000 base salary) on arrival as third-year associates.

OK I'm sold. What should I do now to have a shot at a SCOTUS clerkship?

Get top grades, a place on Law Review, and glowing references from your law professors. Then you have a chance of a clerkship at federal appellate level. *"There are three ways to develop these relationships,"* explained one ex-clerk. *"The first is by taking regular classes with particular professors. The second is to get onto particular clinics – some schools have Supreme Court Litigation clinics where professors supervise students in brief writing. The professors are very experienced Supreme Court advocates – by virtue of that, they're very well known to the Justices and are impressive in their own right. These clinics are competitive to get into. The third route is to become a research assistant for a professor who has a relationship with the Supreme Court Justices."*

Depending on their particular school, our sources became aware of clerkships around their second year. *"For me it was more a by-product of the underlying material of law,"* says one. *"The professors at my school were clerkship-focused though, and they managed to convey how important they can be."*

The necessity of excellent personal recommendations means the process *"can be idiosyncratic and slightly opaque, but the overall feeling is that there is some sort of meritocracy in play. The same things students do to make themselves competitive also allow you to meet the recommendation people and have them like you."* Our sources concurred that *"you've got to have a very strong paper record before recommenders will help you."* The ex-clerks we spoke to had *"jumped through every hoop necessary,"* but not just out of a sense of duty. *"I did those things for years because I enjoyed them,"* says one. *"People you meet on Law Review come back and talk about the experience they've had and you learn a lot from it. These things may appear resume-focused, but they're also a lot of fun!"*

All of our interviewees now work at Jones Day.

"You see directly how things work, which completely changes the way you see cases."

The Big Interview: Robert Shapiro, OJ's defense lawyer

Robert Shapiro (born 1942; JD Loyola Law School 1968) is best known for forming part of OJ Simpson's successful defense team in the notorious 1995 case. His involvement was recently depicted in the TV miniseries *American Crime Story: The People v. O.J. Simpson*, where John Travolta played him. Following the death of his son, he founded The Brent Shapiro Foundation to raise drug and alcohol awareness, and he's also founded a number of companies, including LegalZoom.com and Shoedazzle.com. Now a senior partner at Los Angeles-based Glaser Weil Fink Jacobs Howard Avchen & Shapiro, he's made the jump from criminal to civil law.

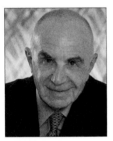

Becoming a Lawyer

Why did you decide to become a lawyer?

I never wanted to be a lawyer. I was a finance major at UCLA looking forward to a career in investment banking and/or business. In 1965 it was the height of the Vietnam War and I was classified 1-A Fit and ready to go. Everyone in that category was immediately drafted upon graduation. There was an exception if you enrolled in graduate school and agreed to be drafted to the age of 35. Thus my legal education began for that purpose.

Starting out, what did you expect from a career in the law?

After winning the moot court competition, I was encouraged to become a trial lawyer. I joined the Los Angeles County District Attorney's office and knew that trial law was in my future.

Has it lived up to your expectations?

I have been fortunate to have represented numerous high-profile individuals that exceeded all my expectations as a young lawyer.

How did you get into the areas of law you are known for today? By design? Chance? Both?

On the criminal side as a prosecutor for the Los Angeles County District Attorney's Office; on the civil side as a name partner in the litigation section of Glaser Weil – both by design.

What do you consider to have been your big break?

My first big case came shortly after leaving the District Attorney's office when I was contacted by Linda Lovelace, the porno star of the seventies, to represent her on the allegations of possession of cocaine for sale in Las Vegas. I was successful in her defense and it was the first nationally publicized case that I was involved in. Getting that case gave me enormous public awareness and virtually launched my career.

> *"Being in a courtroom before a jury gives me the most pleasure as a lawyer."*

What differences do you see today in today's legal market compared to when you started?

When I began practicing law, it was easy to become a sole practitioner. There was only one Public Defender's office and when conflicts arose, judges would appoint lawyers like myself who had just left the District Attorney's office. This not only gave me time to hone my skills as a trial lawyer but allowed me to be in court every day for the first seven years I was a lawyer. Today those opportunities don't exist because of multiple alternate public defenders.

What achievement are you most proud of?

The achievement I'm most proud of is starting The Brent Shapiro Foundation for drug prevention upon the untimely death of our son at the age of 25 due to a combination of alcohol and drugs where he was not given immediate emergency care. He died by aspiration. Today we have over 1,000 kids between the ages of 11 and 16 in our after-school Brent's Club who have agreed to random drug testing. The program has after-school tutoring, athletics and field trips to sporting events, college campus tours and business exposure. Our club members are rewarded after every successful drug test leading to a college scholarship if they graduate as a sober high school student.

What do you consider your greatest failure or regret?

Greatest regret was not following through learning how to play piano. My father was a professional piano player and I never had the knack for it although my mother kept telling me one day you'll regret not being able to play piano – she was right.

What have you enjoyed most during your career in the legal profession?

Being in a courtroom before a jury gives me the most pleasure as a lawyer whether it be in a criminal case or civil case.

What are your thoughts on the portrayal of high-profile cases on TV? Is it a good thing?

I am generally disappointed with the television portrayals of high-profile cases. I favor cameras in the courtroom where the cameras are not used for any purpose other than focusing on the witness while testifying.

"I was greatly disappointed in the cartoonish portrayal of me by Mr. Travolta."

What was your opinion of the recent TV series *American Crime Story: The People v. O.J. Simpson?* What did you think of John Travolta's portrayal of you?

I did not watch the American Crime Story after the first episode. I was greatly disappointed in the cartoonish portrayal of me by Mr. Travolta. I was also disappointed to learn from those who reviewed the entire series that there were numerous inaccuracies and things that were simply made up that never happened. I found it interesting that all the lawyers that were portrayed by actors were nominated for both Golden Globe and Screen Actors Guild Awards. The only person not to win either was Mr. Travolta. He would have been much better served if he had met and consulted with me.

What's the greatest challenge about representing famous individuals?

When representing high-profile individuals, the greatest challenge is keeping them from trying to tell their side of the story outside of the courtroom. I'm a firm believer in that if anyone is to speak regarding a case, the lawyer is the only one for that function.

What were your reasons behind your switch from criminal defense to civil litigation?

I felt I had done everything a lawyer could do trying every type of criminal case from simple misdemeanors to capital murder cases, including cases in the military court. I'm always looking for challenges and civil litigation was something that I wanted to do with my talents. I find it much easier than criminal law.

What law would you change, abolish or create?

I would abolish the death penalty and remove from consideration any jail time for personal possession of any drug. I also would have marijuana reclassified from a Schedule 1 drug to Schedule 5 drug.

Who is your legal hero?

My legal hero is Edward Bennett Williams who was able to excel in both criminal and civil law as well as business.

What career would you have in your second life?

In my second life I'd like to be a boxer.

What slogan would you like to be remembered by?

"Every person deserves the best defense."

What advice would you give to students trying to enter the areas of law in which you are expert?

The practice of criminal law is becoming exceedingly more difficult especially for people who practice as a private practitioner. I would recommend for anybody graduating law school to take the time to get a Masters degree in business. For those who want to pursue a career in criminal law, the best experience is with a public agency. For a prosecutor, I recommend the District Attorney's office because they handle so many varied types of cases, and for the defense side, the State Public Defender's office.

"I would abolish the death penalty and remove from consideration any jail time for personal possession of any drug."

Alternative careers: government

For graduates pursuing a legal career outside of BigLaw, the government offers myriad job opportunities on the federal, state and local levels.

AS NYU Law's former assistant dean for Public Service Deb Ellis points out: *"Working in an entry-level government job offers the opportunity to assume responsibility early in one's career for significant matters, thereby quickly developing one's skills as a lawyer, while also earning an excellent salary and benefits."*

While salaries for government attorneys are admittedly lower than those working at private firms – indeed, an entry-level attorney working for the federal government can expect a starting salary of around $50,000, less than a third of what BigLaw first-year associates make – there are nevertheless many benefits to choosing a government position. These include:

Geographical flexibility – Aspiring government attorneys face fewer geographical limitations than their BigLaw counterparts, who are typically restricted to major cities: state and local governments hire attorneys across all cities in the USA, and the federal government employs around 90% of its workforce outside of Washington, DC.

Loan repayment assistance – *"A major concern of graduates in this economy is finding a position that allows them to manage their debt and still live comfortably,"* a careers adviser at Cardozo School of Law tells us. Fortunately, a number of federal agencies offer student loan repayment schemes to assist recent graduates with their debt, and many law schools have similar financial assistance programs for aspiring public interest lawyers.

Early responsibility – *"One great part of working for the government is that you get substantive work from day one,"* a recent law graduate working for the Department of Labor reflected. Indeed, attorneys in both the federal and state/local government tend to manage their own caseloads from the start of their career rather than answering to a strict hierarchical chain.

Wide variety of work – *"There is a whole slew of practice areas graduates can pursue in the government,"* a careers adviser from the University of Chicago Law School rightly points out. Indeed, federal and state/local government attorneys work in all branches of the government as well as independent agencies performing all types of legal work, including litigation, advisory and regulatory work.

Tangible results – Because government legal employees tend to deal with concrete policies rather than abstract transactions, they're often able to see first-hand the effects of their work within the community, particularly those in the local sector. *"The rewards are more intrinsic,"* explains Laura Mangini, former editor-in-chief of the University of Connecticut's Public Interest Law Journal. *"You come home feeling like you've done something good, like you've helped someone."*

Career flexibility – *"Many government attorneys stay in their jobs a long time, but those who decide to leave have developed valuable transferable skills,"* Deb Ellis tells us. With the variety of skills gained from a legal stint with the government – among them, research, communication and analytical skills – attorneys are equipped to work in a variety of jobs, from in-house or BigLaw associate positions to legal writing and teaching jobs.

Legal jobs with the government are available within two main divisions: the federal government and state/local governments. Some departments and agencies to consider in each include:

The federal route

The federal government employs attorneys in each of its three branches – executive, legislative and judicial – as well as its independent agencies, which include the Federal Reserve System and the National Labor Relations Board. Of these divisions, the executive branch and independent agencies take on the greatest number of attorneys: in 2015, there were over 120,000 employees with full-time, permanent legal positions.

However, in January 2017 President Trump signed an executive order instituting a 90 day federal hiring freeze, while the Office of Management (OMB) and Office of Personal Management (OPM) look at longer-term plans to reduce the size of the federal workforce. It's not clear where future cuts are likely to fall or which agencies or positions are most likely to be affected in the future. A few programs, like the Presidential Management Fellows Program, and positions are exempt from the freeze, so we recommend you check with the individual agency or program you are interested in applying to.

Entry-level positions to consider include those that specifically require a JD – such as attorneys or law clerks for the Department of Justice (DOJ), Department of Homeland Security and Department of the Treasury (all of which have a particularly high number of jobs available each year) – as well as those for which a law degree is not required but highly recommended, such as paralegals, contact representatives, policy analysts, hearing and appeals specialists, estate tax examiners and labor relations specialists.

Contrary to popular belief, pursuing a legal career with the federal government does not restrict you to the courtroom; federal attorneys do everything from drafting legislation to handling depositions to advising on congressional inquiries. Some different areas of work include:

Litigation – Many federal litigators work for the DOJ, handling lawsuits and depositions; others are employed by agencies with independent litigating authorities, such as the Department of Labor, and typically handle drafting and other paperwork.

Advisory – Those interested in an advisory position can act as counselors or attorney advisers, providing advice and analysis for agencies like the Food and Drug Administration.

Regulatory – Regulatory agencies like the Environmental Protection Agency regularly hire lawyers to assist with the implementation of federal rules and regulations.

Public policy – Attorneys engage with public policy work in agencies like the Department of Commerce and Department of State, reinforcing the passage and interpretation of government legislation. There are several routes to landing a legal position with the federal government. While direct hiring is always an option – as all branches of government hire attorneys and other legal staff on a regular basis – there are also a number of programs designed to recruit recent graduates for which law students are eligible:

Recent Graduate Program – Under this program, which came into effect in late 2011, recent graduates are placed on a one-year career development scheme with a federal agency with the possibility of converting to a permanent position upon completion. Such jobs can include legal positions, though not typically attorney positions.

Honors Programs – The most common route for a federal agency attorney position, honors programs are tailored to specific agencies and generally entail a two-year fellowship with an agency, after which the majority of candidates are offered permanent positions. Some agencies with specific honors programs include the DOJ, the FCC and Department of Homeland Security.

Presidential Management Fellows Program – Open to law, masters and doctoral graduates, this program places successful candidates in two-year management or policy positions that have the potential to result in permanent appointments. Again, positions can be legal-based but do not typically include attorney appointments.

Federal positions are highly sought after, so competition can get stiff for places. Having some type of work experience is essential when it comes to proving you're up to the task, whether it's a summer interning for a public interest organization or a full-blown fellowship with the federal government. *"Government employers view work experience like internships as extended job interviews,"* Deb Ellis tells us, pointing out that *"many graduates who land coveted government jobs have interned at a government agency."* Most law school careers development offices can offer advice on how to pursue relevant stints of work experience, some of which include externships with state of US attorneys, clinical programs with the Supreme Court, summer internships with government organizations and post-graduate fellowships with federal bigwigs.

Some federal legal careers to consider in the long run include:

- Public defender
- Military attorney
- Appellate judge
- General attorney
- Trial attorney

The state/local route

Like the federal government, state governments are divided into three branches, all of which routinely recruit law graduates. The structures of local governments vary by community and work together with their respective state government to implement rules and regulations and maintain a balanced justice system. Thanks to a number of economic factors – including the impending retirement of the baby-boomer generation, the members of which occupy a significant portion of public sector jobs in the USA – the Department of Labor predicts that em-

The Big Interview on chambers-associate.com...

- Campaign lawyers and chief legal advisers to Obama, Romney, the Clintons, George W and even Reagan interviewed with us. They offer some pretty valuable career tips and insights.

ployment within state and local governments will rise by 4.2% between 2012 and 2022.

Entry-level jobs of interest to law graduates include honors attorneys – who typically work for city law departments or the state Attorney General's (AG) office – and in-house positions as legal counsel or general staff for various city and state agencies and departments, such as the Governor's Office, Mayor's Office and City Council.

Like their federal counterparts, state and local government attorneys practice a wide variety of law, including:

Administrative law – Many attorneys working for state agencies represent their agency in administrative proceedings and advise agency administrators and professional staff.

Environmental law – Environmental departments within AG offices employ attorneys to advise on state environmental policies and regulate initiatives.

Fraud – One of the main duties of attorneys in state AG offices is to protect citizens from various injustices, which often brings them into contact with fraud cases.

Civil rights law – Most state AG offices have a designated Civil Rights Division where attorneys handle civil rights-related litigation.

Labor law – City law department attorneys tend to practice in this area, among others, and most state AG offices have a Business and Labor Bureau that employs lawyers to handle employment matters.

The path to attaining a state or local government legal position varies depending on the sector: while both are willing to hire directly based on work experience, there are more opportunities to land a position with a local government straight after law school – particularly if you aim for a sizable office like the New York City Law Department, which hired 55 entry-level attorneys in 2014. There are also a few other avenues for entry-level candidates looking to get a foot in the door:

Summer internships – Many state and local agencies and offices have summer intern programs for law students, which they rely on for a certain portion of new recruits. The NYC Law Department, for example, runs a nine-week scheme for 50 interns each year, many of whom are offered permanent employment upon the completion of two summers.

Fellowships/honors programs – Because state and local agencies and offices prefer to hire those with several years of work experience, most offer paid fellowships or

honors programs from which they recruit each year. The schemes range from one to three years in length and give candidates a chance to explore legal work within a particular area of the government.

Firm route

While it's a less common route than either of the aforementioned paths, there is the option of pursuing local government work through a private law firm that specializes in public sector law. Some municipalities contract out their legal work to private firms, so working as a public sector associate for a few years can provide you with enough work experience to apply directly for a legal position in local government work from there.

There's little central coordination when it comes to the hiring process within state and local governments, so it's up to students to research the recruitment process for each office and agency they're interested in and apply directly. "*Some entry-level positions are harder to find and attain than others – the key is persistence,*" advises a source from Duke's Career and Professional Development Center. A tangible interest in government-related work is a crucial factor in the hiring process, so students should look to their law school's CDO for opportunities to get involved with activities that will boost their credentials, such as judicial clerkships, legal externships, courses in public interest law and participation in government-related student groups.

Some state and local government legal careers to consider in the long run include:

- State attorney general
- State solicitor
- Honors attorney
- Policy director
- Legislator

Resources and advice

One of the best places for aspiring government employees to begin their job hunt is their law school's careers development office. CDOs at most law schools have a wing dedicated to assisting students with pursuits in public interest law and can advise on everything from summer clerkships to permanent attorney positions. The public interest departments at the following schools provide some especially useful resources:

NYU – As NYU alum Brandon Egren points out: "*NYU is known as a law school with a big public interest focus – that was definitely visible during my time there.*" In addition to hosting the largest public interest law fair in the USA, which a number of government agencies attend each year, the Public Interest Law Center is the brains behind the PSJD (formerly PSLawNet), an *"incredibly useful"* website that details internships and employment opportunities with government agencies, public interest organizations and private law firms with expansive public interest practices.

Cardozo – Each year, the law school's Center for Public Service Law awards selected postgraduate fellows $2,4000 to participate in eight-week legal placements in public sector offices such as the District Attorney's Office. *"We have a very organized system with routine programs focused solely on helping students attain jobs in the public interest field, including government and judicial placements,"* a source in the law school's Office of Careers Services tells us.

Duke – The law school's career center publishes a career planning manual that outlines various career paths outside of BigLaw, including those with government agencies, and provides advice on interviewing, networking and preparing job applications. According to an insider, the school *"also tries to organize visits from various government departments and holds a reception so that representatives can mingle with students and alumni."*

Yale – Yale's CDO maintains a comprehensive database of job listings for students to access, including opportunities in the public interest sector, and also organizes an annual Public Interest Student Career Fair and co-sponsors the Hyperlink reference not valid.. Additionally, the law school has one of the country's most extensive programs for summer public interest work.

Harvard – The law school publishes an annual directory entitled Serving the Public that details public service job opportunities for both students and graduates, including those in the government. The Bernard Koteen Office of Public Interest Advising also provides access to an online job search database and specialty guides that outline the application process for various types of public interest positions.

Our sources agreed that the avenue to a job with the government takes more focus and drive than most careers. As one points out: *"These jobs are by no means seen as a back-up plan; there are a lot of people who really want to work in the government, so you really have to be focused if you want to succeed. It's imperative to show commitment to all your work throughout law school."* Deb Ellis agrees, urging interested students to *"use your time in law school to develop the skills that will prepare you for a government career. It's helpful to take relevant courses, participate in clinics and develop excellent written and oral communication skills."*

Work experience is also key: *"The best thing you can do for yourself is actually work in government by interning because there is no substitute for having experience in the office where you want to work,"* Ellis continues. Finally: *"It's important that students are broad in their thinking when it comes to a job with the government,"* says another insider. *"The DOJ and FCC are obvious places to start because they each hire a lot of lawyers, but beyond that there are a lot of agencies hiring that students don't even think of, like the Federal Aviation Association. Think creatively and leave the DOJ aside! Some agencies are really focused on their mission and have a whole slew of practice areas available – you just have to look."*

Some good places to start include:

- www.psjd.org – comprehensive guide to career opportunities in the federal and state/local government
- www.usajobs.gov – search directory for job vacancies in the federal government
- www.law.yale.edu/academics/publicinterestemployers.htm – list of employers in the federal and state/local government
- http://gogovernment.org – provides an overview of legal job opportunities in the federal government

Alternative careers: in-house counsel

Trading BigLaw's late nights and client demands for a more predictable life in a company does have its appeal, but applicants can expect to face hurdles in their pursuit – not least the lack of entry-level job opportunities.

Experience counts...

IN-HOUSE counsel are hired by a corporation's law department to handle a range of legal issues affecting the company, among them employment, policy, tax and regulatory matters. More prevalently, they play a managerial role, overseeing work that's been outsourced to attorneys at independent firms. Depending on the size of the corporation and the nature of its work, in-house attorneys may be either specialists in a certain field or general commercial practitioners; either way, there tend to be fewer litigators working in-house than transactional attorneys since most companies prefer to outsource litigious matters to lawyers at private firms, particularly at the entry level. *"When it comes to litigation, they really want people with experience,"* a prominent law school careers dean informs us. *"There are many more opportunities for entry-level corporate work in-house."*

Because corporate law departments employ significantly fewer attorneys than BigLaw firms, recent graduates have traditionally been at a disadvantage when it comes to getting hired: as another law school bigwig points out, corporate law departments *"generally prefer to hire more experienced attorneys rather than graduates straight out of law school."* Indeed, new in-house counsel positions are usually reserved for seasoned recruits with around five-plus years of legal experience, so opportunities to land an in-house position directly after law school remain scarce.

But there are some opportunities...

However, things are starting to look up for graduates as corporations look for alternative ways to minimize costs on the legal front. Fed up with the rising cost of outsourcing work to inexperienced junior associates at BigLaw firms – whose average hourly rate is approaching $300 – a growing number of companies are opting for the more cost-effective route of hiring their own lawyers fresh out of law school and training them in-house. As a result, job opportunities for in-house counsel are anticipated to grow over the next few years.

Among the pioneers of this trend are corporate giants such as Hewlett-Packard and IBM (in some years), which run formal in-house training programs with the aim of whipping recent graduates into in-house shape. *"Most in-house positions don't orient themselves to entry level, but could be an excellent opportunity when they do,"* our source continues. *"New lawyers can learn about both business and law, which is great training for a corporate lawyer, and the company gets to mold candidates in a way that allows them to understand the business better and achieve greater value for the company in the long run."*

Of the few in-house training programs available to recent graduates, Hewlett-Packard's New Attorney Program is arguably the most developed. According to a post by HP's Vice President of Operations on the In-house Access blog, the curriculum incorporates company-specific training, topical bootcamp sessions, skills-based classes on areas like drafting and negotiation, a formal mentoring system and even a sort of reverse secondment wherein some attorneys work for a brief period at a BigLaw firm.

NOT the norm...

Despite their unanimous praise for the aforementioned training schemes, our interviewees were quick to point out that such programs are hardly the norm. *"The reality is that the number of companies recruiting in-house counsel directly out of law school is extremely small, though the number could grow in the coming years,"* a careers dean reveals. *"By and large, people generally have to go to a big firm for a few years before moving in-house."*

Whether they have the potential to become so in the future is anyone's guess, as the dean points out: *"These companies are trying, but no-one's sure whether others will follow suit. It very much depends on things like the economy and whether they can maintain the capacity to bring young people on and train them."* Indeed, considering the volatile state of the economy coupled with the fact that the concept of training lawyers in-house is still relatively nascent, it's difficult to predict whether efforts to increase entry-level opportunities will pan out in the long run.

In-house in the summer

Fortunately, there appears to be a current spike in interest surrounding in-house careers that suggests the programs are safe for now. *"We're seeing more students attaining in-house summer positions,"* reveals another top law school careers adviser. *"And also more seeking fellowships with university general counsels,"* which offer the opportunity to serve for a summer or sometimes an entire year as part of a university's in-house counsel. *"Direct in-house hiring from law school is still a rare thing, but it would be nice to see opportunities increase to give law students another option."*

Advantages and disadvantages...

Indeed, while entry-level in-house opportunities are certainly limited, the advantages to a law career outside of a firm are undeniable. Benefits include:

- Cross-training in several areas of law – unlike BigLaw associates, who typically specialize very early on in their careers, in-house attorneys work as generalists, so they're able to gain experience in many areas of law, including IP, commercial litigation, real estate, M&A and antitrust, to name a few.
- Improved work/life balance – without the tough billing targets of corporate BigLaw, an in-house career lends itself to a more balanced lifestyle than that of a corporate associate. In-house counsel generally have a better sense of upcoming projects, which lessens the chance of unexpected all-nighters or canceled vacations and allows for a more predictable schedule overall.
- Increased business involvement – in many ways, the role of an in-house attorney mirrors that of a BigLaw associate: they draft documents, advise their clients and even get involved with pro bono activities; however, they have the added benefit of working in the same environment as their client, so they're able to gain an insider's point of view on how the company operates by attending business meetings and networking events. They're often also presented with unique benefits, such as stock options – all of which extends their role from that of a mere adviser to an actual stakeholder in the business.
- Unique career opportunities – the most common career path for those looking to advance in the in-house world is to ascend the ranks and become a general counsel, the chief lawyer of a corporation's law department. In-house attorneys also have the option of using their corporate experience as a springboard for pursuing a business-related position such as a corporate strategist or business development director.

However, every rose has its thorn, and in-house work is no exception. Among the disadvantages of pursuing a career in-house are:

- Lower compensation – while in-house counsel are regarded as well paid, they almost certainly receive less than their BigLaw counterparts. In 2016 In-house first year attorneys earn between $82,000 and $125,000 depending on the size of the company. Moreover, in-house attorneys rarely benefit from a lockstep compensation model or the gross salary inflation typical of private firms.
- Little chance to specialize – because in-house counsel are in charge of tackling all of a company's legal issues, they become well versed in a number of areas rather than experts in a single one. As such, there's little opportunity to specialize in a particular area of interest in the same manner that firm associates can.
- Limited mobility – an in-house experience can be sufficient preparation for moving into a non-legal career, but many find a transition back into BigLaw more difficult. The option is definitely there, but attorneys usually have to wait until they reach a rather senior position, such as a general counsel, before they become a commodity of interest to a private firm.
- Small working environment – corporate law departments are significantly smaller than BigLaw firms and thus lack some of the perks of a bigger workplace such as ample support staff and buffers between juniors and seniors. A small workforce also means the turnover is not as high as at a big firm, so competition for landing a position at any level is guaranteed to be fierce – even companies with graduate training programs only take on between three and six new attorneys per year.

Ultimately, an in-house career can be immensely fulfilling, but there are some serious caveats to consider before diving in, particularly at the entry level. Students who decide this career move is for them should try to get as much work experience as possible during law school in order to beef up their resumes – summer internships at big corporations like Procter & Gamble are regularly available and can do you big favors when it comes to honing workplace skills and business know-how. Relevant extracurricular activities, like writing for a business journal, won't go amiss either since they demonstrate a sustained interest in the corporate world.

However, should the elusive entry-level opportunity pass you by, all is not lost – our interviewees strongly discouraged students from discounting the option of working for a few years at a firm before moving in-house. One emphasized: *"Most corporations really want people to go out and work at a firm or a government agency before they try to move in-house. A few years down the line, you'll have gained enough experience to actually have substantive value for the company. It often works out best for everybody."*

For more information on going in-house, check out some of the following resources:

- https://www.goinhouse.com/ – legal job directory: listings for in-house counsel positions.
- www.inhouseblog.com – award-winning blog run by former general counsel: features advice, information and FAQs about the in-house industry.
- www.acc.com– official site for the Association of Corporate Counsel: features articles, a job database and other legal resources for private-sector attorneys based on practice area and region.
- www.inhouseaccess.com– blog published by ACC: provides news updates and op-eds about events affecting the in-house community.

The best way to fast-track into a plum in-house role is to gain sector expertise in private practice. Each law firm review in this guide assesses the quality of the training on offer.

Alternative careers: public interest law

Pursuing a legal career in the public interest arena can be a rewarding but challenging path to take.

STUDENTS at law school often arrive in their first year with a surge of enthusiasm to use their legal knowledge for a good cause, and to help bridge the justice gap between wealthy Americans and low-income individuals. However, the reality is that by their third year, many students end up taking the path of least resistance – the path towards BigLaw.

BigLaw does make sense: for students with large debts to pay off, the offer of a job with a prestigious firm is more than tempting. These offers are usually made in September, while an offer from a nonprofit may not arrive until the following March, or later. Students are often put in an extremely difficult situation, to decide between the security of a sizable salary and a job opportunity that may never materialize.

In-house opportunities are not as prevalent as they were before the economic crisis. To put it simply, many of these organizations do not have the resources to spend on training, internships and fellowships, which form the entry routes into this field of work.

We can't dress it up: pursuing this type of career is difficult and highly competitive, but not impossible. The students who ardently keep on the public interest track tend not to view it as a fall-back option. This is critical, as many public interest employers want to see that a student has a commitment and passion for their cause – a true interest in their mission. This kind of work can't be taken lightly, as it often involves handling people's lives in crisis situations – you could be negotiating child custody for an incarcerated mother, or dealing with people who have had their homes taken away from them. A single-minded focus throughout law school can therefore stand students in good stead with a potential employer.

Get involved from the get-go

While at law school, taking part in legal clinics, joining law clubs which delve into a specific area like family or environment, and pursuing pro bono projects are all essential starting points for a 1L student. Pro bono projects don't have to take up too much time, and can prove a sustained interest in this aspect of law. Using every summer wisely is also a sensible idea. Securing an internship for a nonprofit is tough, but funding opportunities are available, and many law schools will raise money to give grants to students looking to spend their summer in

this way – look out for Dean Summer Service Grants, or check to see whether the school injects any money from its endowment funds to finance these summer schemes. Attending careers fairs and regularly checking websites like idealist.org can also help to get an idea of the scope of available opportunities.

As a 2L, begin to lead fundraising efforts, take more of a leadership role in the campus clinics, and also consider doing an externship with a specific organization. Externships provide students with academic credit during term-time, and can be full or part-time. They're often overseen by a faculty member, and equip students with the experiential learning required to apply for positions post-law school. Some law schools also push 2Ls to apply for any available fellowships, for example those which are facilitated by Skadden and Equal Justice Works. Students first make contact with a nonprofit to develop a project, and then apply for funding through those who advertise the fellowship.

There's a reason why all of this experiential learning is so important. Due to the inability of nonprofits to provide training, it's expected that lawyers who join in-house can hit the ground running. This is not like BigLaw, where you may be tucked away doing doc review or writing up a sophisticated memo for days on end: you have to be on your game to work for a nonprofit. There are often no resources or senior figures to fall back on – you're it, and the organization will expect you to be able to potentially go to court immediately, and handle a high level of responsibility. This does feed into a problem: nonprofits won't hire anyone unless they've passed their Bar exam, which can be difficult for those who are fresh out of law school.

Luckily, some law schools do have some resources to make use of, including 'Bridge Fellowships', which are offered to those who have left law school without a job. These monetary fellowships allow postgrads to take up a position in a nonprofit, pass the Bar, and demonstrate their value to the organization in question, so that they can potentially be first in line should a job opportunity arise. The fellowships also allow nonprofits to be like BigLaw firms, in the sense that they get a chance to sample candidates before making a decision to employ them.

Paying back student debt is another issue to consider, and a prominent reason for law grads to opt for BigLaw.

However, the College Cost Reduction and Access Act of 2007 has made it easier for law students to repay their loans, paving a more viable path towards a career in public interest law. Postgrads can now take out federal guaranteed debt, instead of private debt, meaning that small amounts can be paid back based on income. Law schools also have various repayment programs, and in some cases help to stump up the dollars to pay up to half of a postgrad's monthly debt. A further incentive is federal loan forgiveness, whereby the government writes off any outstanding debt after an individual has worked for a nonprofit for ten years. However, salaries are markedly lower than in private practice, and if your first nonprofit job lands you $60,000 a year, you'll be doing well.

There's no doubt that working in this field is daunting, and the ostensible dearth of opportunities can lead students to remain wary of doing so. Opting for a career as a public interest attorney requires resilience and a pretty high tolerance for what feels like risk, especially when an offer from a BigLaw firm hovers on the horizon. The good news is that if your BigLaw firm is a NALP employer (which they typically are), you can ask them to hold the offer until March, when the offer from a nonprofit may be extended. The law firm isn't obligated to do so, and it also runs the risk of demonstrating that your heart's not set on the private sector, but it is an option nonetheless.

As a general rule, it's probably better to have your heart set on one or the other, and not to try to straddle both, as nonprofits want to see a high level of dedication, just as law firms do. Furthermore, it's a tough road, and you'll be on it for the long haul. It's not all doom and gloom though: you may not be earning a six-figure salary, but many who carve out a career in this field find it to be the most meaningful and intrinsically rewarding way to utilize their expertise and spend their lives.

Becoming a Lawyer

The Big Interview: Mark Geragos, celebrity lawyer

Mark Geragos (born 1957; JD Loyola Law School 1982) is a renowned criminal defense lawyer of clients including Chris Brown, Kesha, Puff Daddy, Winona Ryder, Michael Jackson, and Susan McDougal, one of the defendants in the Clintons' Whitewater scandal in the 1990s. He is one of two attorneys to be named 'Lawyer of the Year' in both criminal and civil arenas (the other being OJ Simpson's defence lawyer, Johnnie Cochran). He is principal of his law firm, Geragos & Geragos, and has appeared as a legal commentator on TV shows including *Larry King Live*, the *Today Show*, and *Good Morning America*. ABC's 2016 legal drama Notorious was inspired by the relationship between Geragos and Wendy Walker, producer of *Larry King Live*.

Why did you decide to become a lawyer?
Up until the age of 13, my father and hero, "Pops," was a hard-charging homicide prosecutor for the Los Angeles County District Attorney's Office. During his stint as a D.A., I would tag along with him to court and watch him in action. The one defining case, which ultimately shaped my entire future, was that of an 18-year-old young man who was a defendant charged with being in a place where marijuana was smoked. Unbelievably to me, this teenager was sentenced to 16 months in prison not for possessing or using drugs, but just for being present in the room! This experience, besides cementing the idea that I could never be a prosecutor, motivated my desire to represent and zealously defend the underdog.

Starting out, what did you expect from a career in law?
Having grown up watching Perry Mason and reading about Atticus Finch, I grew up believing that defense work was the most noble of callings. But unfortunately the times, and the perception of a defense lawyer, have changed. Not a day goes by now that I do not get asked *"how do you represent someone you know is guilty?"* After jokingly responding that *"when the first client admits their guilt I will cross that bridge,"* I usually launch into a diatribe about how we all fight for our clients by any legal means possible because we know that otherwise, the power of the Government goes unchecked. I remind people of the work of the Innocence Project which has brought much needed attention to the scores of people who are falsely convicted by our "justice" system. And I ask them if they would want a zealous advocate by their side if they or someone they love was accused of a crime.

"We all fight for our clients by any legal means possible because we know that otherwise, the power of the Government goes unchecked."

Has it lived up to your expectations?
Absolutely. I've always enjoyed fighting for the underdog and helping those who face overwhelming odds in their quest for justice. That is why for the first 20 years of my career, I focused my practice on criminal defense. However, about a decade ago, I made the decision to transition my practice to fight not just against overreaching prosecutors but also against overreaching governmental entities and corporations, such as Big Pharma and insurance companies. I have found that I personally get the same satisfaction from defending an indigent defendant against out-of-control prosecutors as I do fighting for injured and wronged individuals and non-profits who have been harmed by moneyed interests.

What was your big break?
In 1998 and 1999, I won back-to-back state and federal acquittals for Whitewater figure and former business partner of President Clinton, Susan McDougal, on charges of contempt and obstruction of justice. That's what really put me on the map.

What achievement are you most proud of?
Starting in 2001, my firm commenced class action work fighting on behalf of Armenian families and organizations to assert what many thought to be long lost claims arising out of the Armenian Genocide. These cases presented plaintiffs with a multitude of legal challenges of both a procedural and substantive nature, including jurisdictional issues related to some of the international companies, preclusion under the foreign affairs doctrine, and affirmative challenges based on the statute of limita-

Becoming a Lawyer

tions. The cases were met by many, and in particular the national and international defendant corporations, with skepticism about how claims 90 years old could succeed. But through tireless efforts and extraordinary legal work, the initial two cases resulted in highly successful settlements totaling nearly $40 million for Genocide family survivors and charitable organizations throughout the world. The settlement of these cases were groundbreaking in that they represent the oldest resolved cases in US history and are the first recorded cases addressing issues involving the Armenian Genocide.

What differences do you see in today's legal market compared to when you started?

Thirty-five years ago when I entered law school, the 'be all and end all' of virtually everyone in my class was the brass ring of being a big-firm hire. My daughter Teny, who just graduated Loyola Law School in June, has told me nothing has changed in the decades since. However, I think students are now more receptive to starting off on a small firm path in order to get more experience and develop a name for themselves.

What has been your most interesting experience as a criminal defense/trial lawyer?

I've been blessed to have a lot more than one. Literally every trial I'm in seems to be the most interesting.

What, in your opinion, are the highs and lows of criminal defense?

There is nothing quite like the high of helping someone get justice against all odds and knowing that you have really made a difference in your client's life and future. But there is also nothing quite like the low of dealing with the injustices of an imperfect system and especially of having a client convicted of a crime which you don't believe he committed.

Who is your legal hero?

Undoubtedly my father Pops who was and always will be my hero.

What law would you change, abolish, or create?

Given the detrimental impact modern media and saturation coverage is having on criminal trials in this country, and given the demonstrably ineffective remedies available to courts, I believe that the United States should adopt a system modeled after the British Contempt of Court Act of 1981 which allows courts to effectively curb the dissemination of prejudicial information by the news media by authorizing civil or criminal punishments against journalists who publish stories that present a danger of compromising the fairness of a trial. A properly crafted statute would effectively remove the media's incentive to publish material that could endanger an accused's right to a fair and impartial trial.

What advice would you give to students trying to enter the legal profession today?

I always tell students that want to be trial lawyers that the best thing they can do is to find an attorney they admire and go to court and watch them in various trials. I also advise students to volunteer at a firm they want to be a part of (yes that means for no money) and make themselves invaluable there so they ultimately get hired.

"I also advise students to volunteer at a firm they want to be a part of (yes that means for no money) and make themselves invaluable there so they ultimately get hired."

Pro bono

Doing your bit for society, or advancing your legal skills – whichever way you look at it, pro bono does a world of good.

IT'S SHORT for 'pro bono publico', which, you won't need telling, means 'for the public good'. Pro bono is essentially voluntary work carried out by legal professionals – drawing on their legal nous to help out those who couldn't otherwise afford legal advice. The work offers up limitless opportunities, from advising struggling artists on the technicalities of IP law, to helping draw up new legal constitutions for war-torn African states.

Why do firms do it?

In a profession that is wedded to the billable hour, it seems even shark-like partners have a soft side. The late Esther Lardent, ex president and CEO of the Pro Bono Institute, stated when we chatted a few years ago: *"I think that larger law firms do pro bono for the same reason that many individual lawyers do pro bono. There's a sense that there are problems only lawyers can address – it's a special responsibility."* She continued: *"Fundamentally, this really is a question of passion and a desire to serve."* She certainly embodied that passion (look her up for more info on her fantastic work), but it turns out that giving back to the community is also a pretty smart business move:

1. A top-quality pro bono program attracts top-quality attorneys. Those who enter the profession with dreams of changing the world are more likely to join a firm that lets them run with these projects than one that denies them the chance. Increased pro bono opportunities can seal the deal for gold-standard candidates. Pro bono also serves as an incentive for more senior attorneys or partners to stick around.

2. Pro bono has come to play a central role in training for young attorneys. Juniors tend to be afforded heaps of responsibility on these matters, often taking the lead and liaising with the client directly rather than shuffling papers in the background. Not only is it an effective method of on-the-job training, but it saves both time and money on more formalized programs.

Litigation powerhouse Jenner & Block accumulated a whopping average of 175.2 pro bono hours per attorney in 2013 and remains impressive with a 140 hour aver-

age in 2016. Gabriel Fuentes and Jeffrey Koppy, the firm's previous and current pro bono chairmen, explain: *"A very big factor in a firm's decision to do pro bono is that it's a great training tool for younger associates, particularly for litigators. Given the type of work that firms like Jenner do – very high-end, with millions or billions of dollars involved in any matter – cases often settle before they go to trial. Sometimes the stakes are so high that the youngest associates don't get the participation they might want."* This is where pro bono comes into its own. *"The program allows younger attorneys to make decisions about strategy, and learn how to conduct themselves in court under our supervision. They learn all those essential elements of litigation that young attorneys need in order to develop into successful older attorneys and partners."*

> "A very big factor in a firm's decision to do pro bono is that it's a great training tool for younger associates, particularly for litigators."

3. The work is also a tremendous morale booster. Few things in BigLaw will seem as worthwhile as getting an innocent man off death row, or reuniting an asylum seeker with their family. It's known as *"pro bono glue,"* Esther Lardent explained. *"In terms of goodwill, branding, and the retention of attorneys, large firms have the ability to use pro bono as a rallying force and a source of cross-office collaboration."*

4. A healthy pro bono caseload is a PR officer's dream. Even juniors admit that *"the website looks better when you can show that pro bono is widely available."* Then there's the fact that publicity regarding a pro bono case is cheaper and much more credible than a paid advertisement. It gets the firm's name out into the community, beyond legal circles. Studies have shown that clients are more likely to part with their money if firms are perceived to be involved with worthwhile causes. In this way, pro bono is a nifty exercise in branding.

For a prime example, look no further than Gibson Dunn. The firm's renowned litigator Ted Olson teamed up with David Boies, his opposing counsel in *Bush v Gore*, to challenge Prop 8, a California state constitutional amendment banning same-sex marriage. His work on the lawsuit earned him a place among Time 100's greatest thinkers, and an ABA Medal (the highest award of

On chambers-associate.com...
• 10 pro bono organizations you should know about.

Becoming a Lawyer

the American Bar Association). The case caused such a furore it was even turned into a play, 8, which saw Olson played by John Lithgow and Martin Sheen, and Boies by Morgan Freeman and George Clooney. Not bad publicity for a bit of pro bono work.

So, from a business perspective, pro bono makes sense. Why, then, do some firms do so much more than others? According to our figures, in 2016 attorneys at Munger, Tolles & Olson stacked up an impressive average of 145.7 pro bono hours each, followed closely by Jenner & Block with 140.97, and Orrick with a stunning 137. Compare this to Sterne Kessler (6.4 hours average in 2016), and Waller (12), and you'll be asking yourself some questions.

In 2012, nearly 50% of lawyers in the Am Law 100 did 20 or more hours of pro bono work, compared to just over 30% in the second hundred.

Like so many things in business, this often comes down to the bottom line: there's a clear correlation between gross revenue and the amount of pro bono that a firm racks up. Take Haynes and Boone, for instance. This firm's revenue has steady increased, climbing year by year. Between 2013 and 2016 their revenue has ballooned by 20.5%. Its pro bono contribution has taken a similar gradient, increasing from an average of 22.2 hours per attorney in 2013 to 45.1 in 2016. In fact, every year firms in the *Am Law 100* far outdo those lower down the rankings in terms of pro bono. In 2012, nearly 50% of lawyers in the *Am Law 100* did 20 or more hours of pro bono work, compared to just over 30% in the second hundred.

This is largely down to a lack of resources. Your Sullivan & Cromwells (56 hours) and Ropes & Grays (103 hours) can afford to hire a full-time pro bono coordinator or put together a robust pro bono committee. Many of these law firms have also fostered longstanding relationships with public service organizations. At smaller firms, full-time partners are likely to be juggling pro bono coordination tasks with their already hefty workload, which has a knock-on effect on the program's ultimate impact.

The ratio of associates to partners also plays a part, as does geography. If your biggest office is in Phoenix, Arizona – like Snell & Wilmer (34.3 hours average in 2016) – fewer pro bono opportunities are likely to present themselves compared to a firm based in New York or DC like Shearman & Sterling (85 hours in 2016).

Why do attorneys do it?
After a hard week of training, networking and racking up an obscene amount of billable hours, why spend your time rifling through immigration documents when you could be eating chocolate mousse in front of New Girl? As one associate put it, *"there are two kinds of time: time you're billing hours that count, and time you could be spending on the couch."*

Well, for starters, doing pro bono work just feels good. One junior associate told us: *"It's really nice to step outside of what you're doing for the big clients and help people who wouldn't otherwise be able to afford it."* Plus, on a more cynical note: *"It's often a more interesting topic of conversation at a party than what financing transaction you just closed."*

Secondly, as we've already mentioned, pro bono projects provide some of the best on-the-job training you're likely to receive as an attorney. Another massive bonus is that juniors can actually seek out the type of skills and experience they want to gain, and make a beeline for those cases.

The integral issue of billable hours complicates things. Every firm has a different policy when it comes to pro bono work. Some count time spent on pro bono in exactly the same way as paid client hours (Cleary, Jones Day). Most only count a certain number of pro bono hours as billable (Haynes and Boone, Gibbons). A select few only begin to count pro bono once juniors have reached their billable hour target (Venable, Epstein Becker & Green), while others don't count time spent on pro bono at all (Hangley Aronchick Segal Pudlin & Schiller, although they do say that a minimum of 50 hours is *"expected"*). Of course, within these broad categories fall myriad variations, but all in all, the billable hour/pro bono equilibrium is well worth taking into consideration when choosing the firm to kick-start your career.

State requirements
In 1969, the ABA adopted the Code of Professional Responsibility, which stated: *"Every lawyer, regardless of professional prominence or professional workload, should find time to participate in serving the disadvantaged."* This still stands today, as does the aspirational goal that every lawyer in the USA should spend at least 50 hours a year working on pro bono matters. In most states, however, these rules aren't enforced (apart from Florida, Hawaii, Illinois, Maryland, Mississippi, Nevada and New Mexico). They recognize that attorneys may not be dead on 50 hours each year, but suggest that over the entire course of their career it should pretty much balance out. Some states choose their own aspirational pro bono goal. Virginia, for instance, requires attorneys to dedicate 2% of their professional time to pro bono. In Oregon, the target is 80 hours.

One of the biggest talking points in the pro bono world recently has been New York's adoption of a new hours requirement. On May 1, 2012, New York's then-Chief Judge Jonathan Lippman announced that all applicants for admission to the New York Bar from January 2015 would be required to have completed 50 hours of pro bono. Go online to read more about the impact of this.

What sort of pro bono work is on offer?

The opportunities for pro bono work may well be endless; some firms have an enormous list of options, and strongly encourage associates to bring in their own projects from outside. Others are more limited in their range, working closely with a couple of organizations or insisting that juniors only take on pro bono work that complements their practice area. A lack of pro bono options is a regular grumble among our transactional-focused associates.

That said, in the past few years we've spoken to associates involved in a whole range of fascinating projects, like assisting with Hurricane Sandy relief efforts, volunteering for a presidential election protection helpline to combat corruption, and helping survivors of sex trafficking have their convictions for prostitution overturned (to name but a few).

But it is true that certain types of pro bono matters are likely to crop up more than most. In 2012, firms in the Am Law 200 spent the most time on death penalty cases, with over 64,000 hours clocked up in total. Matters surrounding civil rights (56,481), prisoners' rights (33,699), criminal defense (26,072) and veterans (21,639) make up the rest of the top five.

Current issues in pro bono

After the recession, the 'justice gap' – the divide between the legal needs of low-income people and the ability of civil legal mechanisms to meet these needs – visibly grew. Already bending under pressure, the system came under additional strain. The Legal Services Corporation (LSC), the largest single funder of civil legal services in the USA, has for several years been reporting on the depressingly low percentages of low-income people with civil legal problems who are actually able to obtain the necessary legal assistance. The March 2013 sequestration didn't help matters.

It's perhaps no surprise then that Jonathan Lippman took arguably drastic measures a few years back and implemented a scheme whereby all applicants to the New York bar must have carried out a minimum of 50 hours of legal pro bono work. The new rule has been active since January 2015, and it was estimated that it would add 500,000 hours of voluntary legal assistance in the area.

One of the hottest pro bono matters recently has been The Clemency Project: an initiative in which lawyers have helped non-violent offenders, who would have likely received a substantially lower sentence had they been convicted today, obtain clemency. During his time in office, President Obama granted clemency to 1,927 individuals. In one case, Hunton & Williams obtained clemency for William Ortiz, commuting his 50-year sentence for non-violent, low-level drug offenses.

Immigration and asylum cases have also been on the rise, and this will likely continue in the foreseeable future. The true effects of President Trump's executive order on immigration are yet to be fully seen. In the meantime, Jones Day associates have got involved with the Unaccompanied Minors project. Families who cross the US borders *"end up subject to removal or deportation with no access to legal representation."* The project aims to help children who have been separated from their families gain Special Immigrant Juvenile Status. Check out our website for more on recent pro bono matters.

Becoming a Lawyer

The Big Interview: Evan Wolfson, 'Freedom to Marry' lawyer

Evan Wolfson (born 1957; JD Harvard Law School 1983) is the pioneering LGBT activist and lawyer whose Freedom to Marry organization (freedomtomarry.org) drove the successful strategy that culminated in the Supreme Court gay marriage victory in 2015. Wolfson's pivotal role in this story is told in a recent feature-length documentary, *The Freedom to Marry* (freedomtomarrymovie.com). Author of a landmark book on marriage equality, *Why Marriage Matters* (2004), he recently joined Dentons and has also taken up a teaching role at Georgetown Law Center.

Why did you decide to become a lawyer?

I was always passionate about politics and government, and most especially history – and always wanted to make a difference. And since I was the kind of kid who loved to argue and was pretty articulate, people I always said I should become a lawyer. To me, while I loved watching courtroom dramas and very much enjoyed advocacy, being a lawyer was a way of doing other things I cared most about.

Starting out, what did you expect from a career in the law? Has it lived up to your expectations?

I pretty early on concluded that being a lawyer opened up many doors, and ideally brought a way of thinking and expressing oneself strategically, a set of skills, and a credential that could be applied to many challenges and approaches. And that has been the case for me. While I have done my share of "typical lawyering" – litigating as a prosecutor and as gay rights and civil rights advocate, I think the work I did leveraging my bundle of skills and credibility as a lawyer to the work of winning in the court of public opinion alongside the courts of law, organizing and guiding a campaign and a movement, has been where I've left my biggest mark.

Why did you chose the career path that you did? What was your big break?

In retrospect, the big break was choosing to write my 1983 law school thesis on why gay people should have, and should fight for, the freedom to marry – and pouring into that call to action not just what I had learned in law school, but my love of history, insights from my service in the Peace Corps, and my intuition that to win a change in the law, we had to change hearts and minds, engaging values and claiming a vocabulary of transformation. That distillation of all I had learned up to that point in my life wound up, one way or another, shaping pretty much the course of my career since.

What's your advice to students grappling with whether to join BigLaw or do public interest law?

Go with your passion.

> **"The big break was choosing to write my 1983 law school thesis on why gay people should have, and should fight for, the freedom to marry."**

What differences do you see in today's legal market compared to when you started?

I think the opportunities both for public interest and more "typical" firm jobs have grown, and the people from different backgrounds and communities, more and more, are rising in the profession and its various forms, including women, people of color, and LGBT people (overlapping categories). Law firms are more willing to take on "controversial" cases that we couldn't get them to do back when I was starting. I know from the firm where I am now serving as a part-time Senior Counsel, Dentons (the world's largest law firm), that there is a strong and genuine commitment to diversity and inclusion. We need to keep building on this progress.

What achievement are you most proud of?

Winning the freedom to marry in the United States (and helping win marriage for same-sex couples in 22 countries on 6 continents – 1 billion people – so far), and thereby providing inspiration and lessons on effecting change for more movements, causes, and countries going forward.

What has been your biggest failure or regret?

Right now, it's hard to think of anything I regret more than how threatened our Republic is and how much damage the current regime will inflict on the US and people around the world – indeed, on liberal democracy – before we get our country back on track, as we must.

What have you enjoyed most during your career in the legal profession?

Leading a dazzling team at Freedom to Marry and being part of a wonderful group of activists, most of whom I count as my friends, as we worked to engage non-gay people, fulfil the Constitution, and take gay people from a despised and oppressed minority to victory in claiming the central language and legal institution of love, freedom, equality, dignity, and family.

And enjoyed least?

Some of the frustrations inherent in waking up every day for 32 years fighting and/or pushing. It does kind of warp your personality a bit.

What law would you change, abolish or create?

Aside from abolishing the Electoral College and gerrymandering, I'd like to see full federal civil rights protections, meaningfully enforced, for LGBT and other people, including the right to vote and to make reproductive choices. I'd like to see single-payer health care, strong labor laws, a more progressive tax code, and national service.

Who is your legal hero?

Abraham Lincoln is one. Dan Foley, my Hawaii co-counsel, another. And then my friends at the ACLU, GLAD, Lambda Legal, and the National Center for Lesbian Rights – the pillar legal groups of our movement.

What career would you have in your second life?

Sinatra's.

What is your role at Georgetown?

I have a two-year (for now) appointment as a Distinguished Visitor from Practice. It involves some teaching – for example, a course on law and social movements that I put together with my friend, Prof. Nan Hunter, and another course I will teach with my friend, Paul Smith [ex-Jenner & Block appellate and Supreme Court chair], who just joined the faculty as well. And the affiliation with such a prestigious school gives me the platform from which to take on projects across the country and

around the world, in which I advise and assist those who want to learn the lessons from our successful campaign.

Can you tell us a bit about the *Freedom to Marry* documentary?

Filmmaker Eddie Rosenstein goes behind the scenes with our campaign team and those of key partners, including GLAD and NCLR, to tell the story not just of how we ascended the summit to win the freedom to marry at the Supreme Court in 2015, but how we achieved the transformation in hearts and minds over decades of struggle and across all of the "methodologies of social change" – to use Dr. King's phrase – in order to be able to win in court and change the law.

Even though I of course know the ending, he did a brilliant job at making it suspenseful and I still cry every time I watch it (as do the audiences I've been in). And what makes me happiest is that the film is being seen as a source of inspiration and instruction for other movements; showings have been hosted by immigration, gun control, environmental, and other organizations, as well as in countries as diverse as Australia, the Czech Republic, Israel, Japan, and Taiwan.

What are your LGBTQ-related hopes and fears for the coming years under President Trump?

I hope that our movement, aligned with others in overlapping causes and communities, defends American values and blocks attacks including the effort to put a hostile justice on the Supreme Court and hostile judges on the lower courts, and to carve out licenses to discriminate from the gains we have won, using the false banner of "religious freedom."

Finally, what advice would you give to students – gay and straight – trying to enter the legal profession today?

Think about what you want to achieve in the world, believe you can do it, and arm yourself with the skills, opportunities, and partners to move forward. And hurry up. We need you.

"I hope that our movement, aligned with others in overlapping causes and communities, defends American values and blocks attacks."

Becoming a Lawyer

Diversity in the law

The 1,315,000 licensed lawyers in the US are split 64% men and 36% women

Women make up only 18% of law firm equity partners

Lawyers of color make up only 8% of law firm equity partners; ethnic minorities represent 27.6% of the US population

On average, female lawyers make 89.7% of male lawyers' salary

100% of firms reported that their highest paid US partner was male

On average, women make up 22% of firms' highest governance committees – 6% higher than in 2006

As of 2010, 88% of all lawyers in the US are white

Representation of Black/African-American attorneys still remains below its 2009 high of 4.66%, now at 4.11%

At partnership level, minority women continue to be the most under-represented at 2.76%

Currently, three out of the eight Justices serving on the Supreme Court are women

The overall percentage of openly LGBT lawyers increased from 2.34% in 2015 to 2.48% in 2016

Sources: Chambers Research, NALP, NAWL, ABA Journal, EEOC

The Big Interview: Linda Klein, ABA president

Linda Klein (JD Washington & Lee University 1983) is the current president of the American Bar Association and senior managing shareholder at Baker, Donelson, Bearman, Caldwell & Berkowitz. After becoming the first woman to serve as president of the State Bar of Georgia in 1997, she continued to spearhead female representation at the top of the profession, first as managing partner of Gambrell & Stolz from 2001, then by leading the firm's 2007 merger with Baker Donelson, becoming the newly merged firm's Georgia managing shareholder. Linda Klein served as chair of the ABA's House of Delegates from 2010-2012; four years later she became the organization's president.

When did you decide to become a lawyer? Why?

I knew early on that I wanted to be a lawyer. My grandfather told me stories about life during the depression. He taught me the value that all people should be treated with dignity. He taught me that lawyers protected people who needed help. So I never gave much thought to another profession. I wanted to help people so I pursued law school, a law career and joined the bar.

Starting out, what did you expect from a career in the law? Has it lived up to your expectations?

As a lawyer I have made wonderful friends in my fellow members of the bar, done some interesting and challenging work, and helped my community. Being a lawyer has exceeded the expectations I had when was in law school.

How did you get into the areas of law you are known for today? By design? Chance? Both?

I took opportunities that were offered. I took cases that other lawyers avoided, and I succeeded by working hard and digging deep. I found that the harder I worked the luckier I got. These cases led to others.

What differences do you see in today's legal market compared to when you started?

There were fewer women and people of color in the law profession when I started. I was the only woman in the law firm where I started and knew I had to succeed or I would be the last. For over 25 years now, close to half of law school graduates have been women, entering the workforce at the same rate as men. Today, for the first time, women are the majority of those entering law schools. And there are more women and more people of color in the profession today, so we've come a long way.

But much work remains to be done before our profession is as equitable and fair as it should be. For example, women in law firms receive 77.4% of the compensation of men, one of the widest gaps among industries in the US. The imbalance is even more dramatic for women of color. The American Bar Association is working to close those gaps and open our profession to diversity and inclusion, and elimination of bias is Goal III of the ABA, part of the bedrock that underpins our organization.

> *"Women in law firms receive 77.4% of the compensation of men, one of the widest gaps among industries in the US. The imbalance is even more dramatic for women of color. The American Bar Association is working to close those gaps."*

Another significant change in the profession is the rise of technology. When I began practice the profession was just learning to use online legal research. No lawyers had computers on their desks. The "computer" was a word processor that did not spell check.

What achievement/s are you most proud of?

I accepted my first pro bono case three months after becoming a lawyer. It changed my outlook on life and the profession. My client was a disabled widow trying to collect life insurance benefits from her late husband's policy. She was so disabled, she never knew I was helping her get the money she needed at the end of her life. But I knew, and it was a powerful feeling to help someone in need.

I am also very proud of our work in Georgia to help the indigent victims of domestic violence get the legal assistance they need. Back in 1997 as I was becoming

Becoming a Lawyer

president of the State Bar of Georgia, federal budget cuts threatened the existence of Georgia Legal Services. So I decided that the Georgia Bar needed to work with other organizations to make Georgia one of the first states in the nation to provide state funding for legal representation for our poorest neighbors. The focus was on the indigent victims of domestic violence.

We got the money [$2 million]. In fact, every year since then, the General Assembly has provided funding.

What have you enjoyed most during your career in the legal profession?

I enjoy every day. Each new day presents a new challenge. Of course some days are better than others, but I love what I do. Helping clients is certainly exciting and interesting. And, lawyers are some of the best people I know, so I enjoy working with other lawyers on client matters and on bar service activities.

And enjoyed the least?

Having to explain to clients and the public why underfunding our justice system causes delays in resolving their problems.

Why should students get involved in the ABA?

Everything in life, and every job, is built on good relationships and connections, and for law students there is no better connection than being part of the ABA, one of the world's largest professional associations. And ABA membership for law students is free. That membership offers career-building opportunities and gives law students tools and resources to help them succeed in school and beyond, and provides access to benefits, perks and discounts they can't get anywhere else.

For $25, the ABA offers law students a Premium Membership, which includes free resumé review, $250 off BARBRI bar review courses, a free copy of the annotated version of ABA Model Rules of Professional Conduct, discounts on study guides and more. Membership connects law students with some of our more than 3,500 entities and helps them use the ABA to blaze their legal path.

> ### "There is never a wrong time to defend the Constitution and the rule of law, but this is a particularly important time."

Who is your legal hero?

My friend, former Georgia Chief Justice Carol Hunstein. She overcame incredible obstacles early in life to even be able to go to college and then more obstacles to have the opportunity to attend law school. She does everything with integrity. She is the epitome of a fair and impartial judge.

What career would you have in your second life?

I might have chosen the field of education. My sister, Marla, is a teacher and a very good one who is making a difference in peoples' lives.

What are your hopes and fears in the coming years?

America's rule of law is the gold standard for the world and American lawyers are its guardians. Right now, programs we [the ABA] value are facing challenges. We know there is a threat to eliminate federal funding for Legal Services Corporation, which ensures that everyone has equal access to justice under the law. We need adequate funding for the Legal Services Corporation because LSC provides hope and help to hundreds of thousands of Americans every year. It is a bipartisan necessity.

It is vital, too, that our judiciary remains independent and free from political pressure — independent from party politics, independent from the other branches of government. This is a defining moment for our profession and our nation. We will be actively involved to protect due process and legal representation.

We also must insist on fundamental respect for our laws and the people they protect. There is never a wrong time to defend the Constitution and the rule of law, but this is a particularly important time. American lawyers will defend the Constitution.

What advice would you give students trying to enter the legal profession today?

Regardless of what your first job is as a lawyer, be prepared to work hard. Take the job no one else wants to do, learn the job, excel in the job, enjoy working and connecting with others involved, then move on to the next job no one wants and repeat all of the above. You will develop contacts that will last throughout your career and you will earn the reputation of being a person willing to take on the toughest or worst job and doing it well. Better jobs will follow because all leaders want someone on their team who excels in whatever they do. Soon, you will be the leader. And take pro bono cases. Do good. It will remind you of why you became a lawyer in the first place. You will love the pro bono work you do.

> ### "Take the job no one else wants to do, learn the job, excel in the job [...] and repeat all of the above."

Ten pro bono organizations you should know about...

Interested in pro bono? Every year associates at law firms across the country tell us about the pro bono work they get involved in. Several organizations crop up again and again. Here's a round-up of ten of them...

- **Her Justice** – formerly called InMotion, Her Justice helps women in New York City who are experiencing poverty and, often, domestic abuse. Lawyers provide advice on immigration, orders of protection, and divorces, among many other things.

- **Volunteer Lawyers for the Arts** – founded in 1969, New York-based VLA provides legal representation to low-income individual artists and non-profit arts organizations. Partner firms include Akin Gump, Fitzpatrick, Gibson Dunn, Axinn, Hangley, Davis Polk, and Cravath.

- **My Sister's Place** – this non-profit provides residential shelters and a range of support services (including legal) to victims of domestic violence, and their children. Supporters include Bracewell & Giuliani, Hogan Lovells, King & Spalding, Pillsbury, and White & Case.

- **Human Rights First** – founded in 1978, Human Rights First works with people at home and abroad whose human rights are at risk: for example, refugees, victims of crimes against humanity, and people who have been discriminated against. Offices are in Washington, DC, New York and Houston. As well as pro bono opportunities for lawyers, the organization offers summer and semester internships to law students. Firms include Akin Gump, Debevoise, Cravath, Kramer Levin, Latham & Watkins, Skadden and Weil Gotshal.

- **The Bronx Defenders** – provides criminal defense, family defense, civil legal services, advocacy and other support to indigent residents of the Bronx.

- **The Innocence Project** – was founded in 1992 by Barry Scheck and Peter Neufeld at Cardozo Law to exonerate prisoners who DNA testing could prove innocent. Offering litigation services and public policy recommendations, to date it has helped clear over 300 people, including 18 on death row. Lawyers offer their services pro bono from firms including Winston & Strawn, Paul, Weiss, WilmerHale, Schiff Hardin, Weil Gotshal, Skadden and Fried Frank.

- **Ladder Up** – helps low-income people in the Chicago area file tax returns and claim tax credits. Also offers financial assistance workshops and advice on financial aid for college. Partner firms include Baker & McKenzie, Kirkland & Ellis, Paul Hastings, and Reed Smith.

- **Kids in Need of Defense (KIND)** – co-founded by Angelina Jolie, DC-headquartered KIND provides legal representation to unaccompanied refugee and immigrant children in their deportation proceedings. In 2014, almost 68,000 children came to the US alone. Outside DC, KIND has offices in Baltimore, Boston, Houston, Los Angeles, Newark, New York and Seattle.

- **Immigration Equality** – provides free legal services to LGBT and HIV-positive immigrants. Has a network of lawyers who act pro bono, and also offers internship opportunities to law, grad and undergrad students. Partner firms include Linklaters, O›Melveny & Myers and Jenner & Block.

- **Transgender Legal Defense & Education Fund (TLDEF)** – promotes transgender civil rights in areas including employment discrimination, equal access to health care, and helping with legal name changes. Supporters include Reed Smith, Linklaters, Kirkland & Ellis, Davis Polk, Gibson Dunn, Kaye Scholer and Sullivan & Cromwell.

"In terms of goodwill, branding, and the retention of attorneys, large firms have the ability to use pro bono as a rallying force and a source of cross-office collaboration."

- **Esther Lardent, president and CEO of the Pro Bono Institute**

Becoming a Lawyer

The Big Interview: Blake Liggio, BigLaw transgender pioneer

Blake Liggio (JD Northeastern 2009) is one of the first transgender partners at an *Am Law 100* firm. He began the process of transitioning in his third-year as a law student at Northeastern, and returned to Goodwin Procter in 2010 as a first-year associate, having paralegaled at the firm in 2004 and summered here in 2008. He became a partner in 2016.

When did you decide to become a lawyer? Why?
I have always enjoyed problem-solving and once I was ready to choose a career path, I knew this was the right one for me.

Starting out, what did you expect from a career in the law? Has it lived up to your expectations?
I expected to learn new things every day and to help people. So far, the career has definitely met these expectations.

Can you tell us a little about why you chose the career path that you did? What was your big break?
First, I knew that I did not want to be a litigator, so transactional law was an attractive option for me. I was lucky to become involved very early in my career at Goodwin with various M&A matters and was immediately drawn to the fast pace and substance of that type of work.

In terms of one big break, I don't really view my path in that way. I view the job as more of a marathon run than a sprint, and so I took the approach of focusing on improving my skills each day by getting involved with as many opportunities as possible and learning as much as I could along the way.

What differences do you see in today's legal market compared to when you started?
I started my career right after the financial crisis, so I was grateful to have a job coming out of law school. Following the crisis, I think that the legal services industry has adapted in order to remain relevant with clients by focusing on specialized areas and developing more client-centric approaches in terms of cost demands and other strategies around efficiency.

Corporations also evolved out of the lessons of that time in terms of understanding the need for innovation, and one of the areas of focus has been around the values of diversity. There has also been an increased commitment to diversity initiatives in law firms, in many instances driven by the demands of clients. As companies have developed knowledge about the benefits of diversity within their own organizations, some have also focused on the diversity profiles within the organizations that they engage as external advisors.

> *"I think a central challenge to openly transgender people in any career is overcoming negative conceptions about who we are and stigmas typically associated with transgender identity."*

What are the biggest challenges you have faced in your legal career as a transgender person?
I think a central challenge to openly transgender people in any career is overcoming negative conceptions about who we are and stigmas typically associated with transgender identity. Most people have not met or come to know a transgender person and this is part of the challenge for us. Unfortunately without context, people tend to develop ideas about things that they do not know, and in our case those ideas tend to be negative.

I think that any openly transgender person starting a career is likely to enter their organization with the burden of having to overcome certain misconceptions about who we are and what we will bring to work. That being said, our presence within organizations that have not seen us before is an opportunity to educate people that we are not earth-shattering and that we are there to do our jobs, just like everyone else.

What achievement are you most proud of?
I am most proud of my family; my two kids and my wife.

What has been your biggest failure or regret?
Based on my personal experiences, specifically gaining acceptance around my own identity as a transgender person, I don't really believe in regret or failure. I look back

on certain events and recognize that as they happened, I might have felt regret or failure, but as I moved on and time passed, I revisit those events and they always have taught me something more about myself or maybe out of a failure, how to later achieve success.

What have you enjoyed most during your career in the legal profession?
There is rarely a day when I am not faced with a new challenge.

And enjoyed least?
Feeling like there are not enough hours in the day.

What law would you change, abolish or create?
I would change (abolish) any state and local law with negative impact on LGBT people, whether in the area of relationship recognition, parenting, non-discrimination, school safety, health benefits or restricting transgender people from modifying name and gender information on identity documentation.

Who is your legal hero?
Sandra Day O'Connor.

"I look back and recognize that being trained as a lawyer helped me with certain elements of my transition, like navigating the legal requirements around name change and knowing how to effectively advocate for myself."

What career would you have in your second life?
I am an avid rare sneaker collector so would want to be the owner of a rare sneaker shop.

How can BigLaw firms improve diversity, and what notable initiatives does Goodwin have?
I think the next step for BigLaw firms is to take the diversity initiatives that they have developed in concept in recent years and to continue to translate those initiatives into real changes in their workforce and workplaces. Firms have taken significant steps forward to create policies embracing diversity and the next step is to focus on being mindful of all of the practical changes that can translate policies and initiatives into real on-the-ground changes within organizations.

At Goodwin, we have an Inclusion Advisory Committee, a Committee on Racial and Ethnic Diversity, an LGBT Pride Initiative and a Women's Initiative. We also have a professional development team who have done a great job of translating the work that we do within these various initiatives to progress within the firm whether through mentoring opportunities, training, internal feedback programs or internal and external events focused on diversity issues. The efforts to advance from talking about these issues to implementing real changes is where Goodwin has succeeded in moving its diversity efforts forward.

What advice would you give to students and young lawyers who are simultaneously going through the gender transition process while trying to forge a career in the law?
My advice would be to remember that while it is certainly a challenge to be setting out on two significant journeys, beginning your career and transition, it is possible to do it and you will experience great satisfaction and growth along both paths.

Based on my own experience, I look back and recognize that being trained as a lawyer helped me with certain elements of my transition, like navigating the legal requirements around name change and knowing how to effectively advocate for myself whether regarding health care benefits, employment or other day-to-day challenges that transgender people face.

Finally, what advice would you give to students trying to enter the legal profession today?
First, I would be thoughtful in making the decision to pursue a legal career and also try to take the time to determine what type of lawyer you want to be. There are so many different types of lawyers, and there is no shortage of stories about people who start their careers as lawyers and end up making a change to another profession. Going to law school and becoming a lawyer is a big commitment so I think it is a good idea, whether through internships or post-undergraduate work, to be certain that a legal career is a good fit.

If you do decide to enter the legal profession, my advice would be to work hard and to be humble. I think the learning curve is steep at the entry level, but if you have the attitude that you have a lot to learn, and work hard to do it, you will succeed. I would also try to find a good mentor and don't hesitate to use them. Having someone to discuss your professional goals with who has the benefit of experience that you don't have, is a valuable resource.

"The learning curve is steep at the entry level, but if you have the attitude that you have a lot to learn, and work hard to do it, you will succeed."

Becoming a Lawyer

Practice Areas

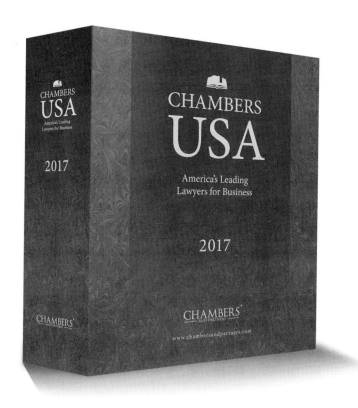

Chambers USA 2017 available now

America's leading lawyers for business

"The gold standard" *The New York Times*

Chambers and Partners has dedicated 26 years to researching and ranking the world's best commercial lawyers. Its guides are relied upon by clients and General Counsel for their accuracy and objectivity. *Chambers USA* is the culmination of thousands of interviews with lawyers and clients carried out by the largest research team of its kind.

Antitrust

In a nutshell

Antitrust attorneys advise clients on whether their business practices comply with regulations domestically and abroad so that markets function effectively on the basis of fair and open competition. In doing so, they undertake a broad range of different legal activities, including litigation, government investigations, merger advice and counseling.

Within litigation, generally there are cases alleging improper single company conduct and those alleging anti-competitive agreements or collusion among two or more entities. The former refers to claims against a single entity for monopolistic conduct, such as predatory pricing or abuse of monopoly power. The latter refers to an agreement or conspiracy among two or more entities that could include conduct such as boycotting, bid-rigging, price-fixing and dividing markets or customers. Many of these cases are brought by a class of affected customers or consumers. Both types are private and civil.

Government investigation, or enforcement, can be brought as a civil or criminal proceeding. Civil enforcement involves investigating companies for certain conduct, asking them to change their behavior, and sometimes fining them. Criminal investigations revolve primarily around cartels and price-fixing, and carry steep criminal penalties.

Merger advice (often called merger control) is another big piece of antitrust work, whereby attorneys shepherd their client through major regulations associated with M&A transactions, which generally result in a greater market share, the likely elimination of competitors and a greater risk of monopolistic conduct. Counseling involves providing clients with advice about their current and future business practices, such as co-marketing or distribution.

What lawyers do

Civil litigation on the defense side

- Receive complaint and file for motion to dismiss. This can often go through several rounds, as the claimant amends the complaint.
- If working on a class action, attorneys conduct 'class' discovery, during which they work with experts to attempt defeating class action certification. They will depose the experts and file and defend their reports.
- If class certification is granted, or if the case was never a class action to begin with, lawyers conduct 'merits'

discovery. This requires producing all the relevant documents and conducting depositions about liability and damages.
- Apply for summary judgment. If summary judgment is denied, attorneys prepare for trial, which involves determining what evidence and depositions to use and whether they will be admitted, drawing up the exhibit list, and deciding what sort of discovery or motions to push for.
- Go to trial. Handle post-trial steps.
- Attorneys for plaintiff conduct due diligence before filing a complaint, oppose motions to dismiss, defend class action certification and oppose summary judgment.

Civil government investigation

- Receive Civil Investigative Demand (CID) from the Federal Trade Commission or Department of Justice, requesting documents. State attorneys general can also initiate investigations.
- Negotiate with the government to narrow the categories of violations, limit the bounds of discovery and win more time.
- Produce the requested documents, ensuring those provided comply with the government's demand. Jay Srinivasan of Gibson Dunn describes this portion as capable of being a *"massive implementation effort"* in larger cases.
- Negotiate and maybe give interviews to the government while waiting for its decision. Depending on the three possible outcomes, attorneys close the investigation, negotiate, or defend the client in court or before an administrative law judge.

Criminal government investigation

- Receive grand jury subpoena or FBI warrant.
- Conduct investigation into possible wrongdoing.
- Produce materials requested by the subpoena or warrant.
- If evidence suggests possible wrongdoing, counsel client on strategies to defend against a possible charge or advise on possible plea arrangements.
- Client decides whether to fight or plea. If the latter, negotiate plea agreement (including scope of charge and fine amount).
- Enter into a plea agreement.
- If negotiations fail and the client does not enter into plea, or chooses to fight the charge, attorneys will go to trial.

Rankings in *Chambers USA*

Top ranked

Alston & Bird	Morgan Lewis
Cleary	Norton Rose Fulbright
Davis Polk	O'Melveny & Myers
Dechert	Ropes & Gray
Gibson Dunn	Sidley Austin
Jones Day	Simpson Thacher
Kirkland & Ellis	Skadden
Latham	White & Case
Mayer Brown	Wilmer Hale

Highly recommended

Allen & Overy	Munger
Arnold & Porter	Orrick
Axinn	Paul Hastings
Baker Botts	Paul, Weiss
Choate	Pepper Hamilton
Cooley	Reed Smith
Cravath	Shearman
Crowell	Sheppard
Freshfields	Simpson Thacher
Haynes and Boone	Sullivan
Hogan Lovells	Thompson & Knight
Hunton	Vinson
King & Spalding	Weil
Linklaters	Willkie
McDermott Will & Emery	Wilson Sonsini Goodrich
MoFo	Winston

For more detail on ranking tiers and locations, visit
www.chambersandpartners.com

Mergers

- If the merger meets one or more of the government's enumerated thresholds, attorneys file a Hart-Scott-Rodino form (HSR), indicating the intent to merge.
- Conduct due diligence and spot issues.
- Determine the likelihood that the merger will be challenged, reviewed or investigated.
- Depending on the government's response to the HSR, lawyers wait, go ahead with the merger, agree to a consent decree, or defend the client in an injunctive trial or administrative hearing.

Practice Areas

Life in Antitrust Law, by Allen & Overy's DC lawyers

Practice Areas

HIGH stakes litigation, cross-border enforcement, international deal work: an antitrust associate in Washington, DC can be expected to advocate on behalf of clients in all these scenarios. Because it involves issues that are high priority for many companies, it attracts high quality practitioners. The field contains litigation, regulatory and transactional elements, and most practices involve all three elements. It also is often international in nature. It therefore offers a broad variety of growth opportunities within a single subject matter. The counseling elements also allow for opportunity to learn the inner workings of a client and see how business decisions at the highest level are made.

Fundamentally, the practice of antitrust lives at the intersection of litigation, transactional, and regulatory work. In speaking with law students around the country, I have found that most students are familiar with transactional and litigation practices at law firms, but know less about the regulatory aspect of law. Attorneys in a regulatory practice have exposure to all the components of a litigation and transactional practice, such as advising, analyzing, and litigating, and constantly use the skills gained in one area to benefit a client in another area.

Our work generally includes advising top-tier business on the best means of navigating antitrust regimes around the globe; guiding complex mergers and acquisitions through the approval processes in the US, Europe and beyond; and defending clients in high-stakes civil and criminal litigation, enforcement, and investigations. Our work allows us to partner with companies in a wide range of industries, including banking and financial services, pharmaceuticals and healthcare, transportation, technology, oil and gas, agricultural products, and more.

The law students who do know something about antitrust are sometimes intimidated because they see it as a numbers-based practice. Students may hear terms such as "market concentration" and "volume of affected commerce" and shy away from the subject for fear that they will get bogged down by the numbers they sought to avoid by coming to law school. These students should rest easy, though: An understanding of broad economic principles is far more important than the numbers themselves, and to master those principles all you need is a willingness to learn and to be challenged. Moreover, the beautiful thing about the antitrust field is that it is constantly changing and new challenges are guaranteed, so no one will ever master it.

Associates who practice antitrust will have the chance to work with – and across from – some of the best and most respected law firms in the world. Many great lawyers began as antitrust associates, drawn no doubt by the exciting challenges offered by the practice. Given the relatively small size of the antitrust bar, associates are virtually guaranteed the chance to work with truly exceptional attorneys. Because the nature of the practice often requires practitioners to work cooperatively on behalf of different clients across different matters, attorneys in this bar tend to treat one another with respect and courtesy. This tight-knit community also provides for a very cordial and warm working environment, a benefit that cannot be stressed enough.

Finally, the field of antitrust allows associates to work on issues that are on the front page of newspapers around the world and will remain center stage. Yet at the core of these large and daunting challenges are often issues which effect ordinary Americans every day. The chance to work in a field that brings together this high-level advocacy with results that impact millions of people across the country and around the globe is another one of the reasons associates that start in the field tend to remain.

Recent Trends

The number of countries that are actively pursuing antitrust violations has increased dramatically in the past 25 years. There are well over 100 countries worldwide which now have active regulatory regimes. The rise in global enforcement in an ever-shrinking world means multinational corporations and individuals face greater and new challenges they have never faced before. The US is one of the global leaders in antitrust enforcement, having issued almost $4 billion in fines in sanctions over the past twelve months while regimes in South Korea, Brazil, and across the European continent continue strict enforcement.

Antitrust at A&O

This global trend towards more enforcement means it is an exciting time to be an antitrust attorney at a global firm like A&O. Clients expect us to be experts on global, cross-border issues because they seek legal and practical advice which will impact their business all over the world. We seek to solve multijurisdictional problems by relying on our experiences to help our clients to navigate government investigations and civil litigation. This requires us to have more than a commercial litigation or corporate background and to be able to provide help outside the confines of legal issues.

It is important to note that A&O's antitrust practice places an emphasis on working together as one global team. Our global competition team is comprised of over 100 attorneys, and we all work together to provide the sort of seamless global advice our globalized clients need. We routinely coordinate work and advice across the network, often requiring associates in the US to work with colleagues in Brussels, London, Poland, or Australia. A&O also brings antitrust associates together as a team for trainings in London and for off-sites around the world.

There is no typical day-to-day as an Antitrust associate here at A&O. One day an associate could be drafting briefs, preparing proffers, and interviewing witnesses, while the next could consist of analyzing whether a proposed business arrangement will be approved in ten countries around the world. In addition, we are expected to be contributing team members from day one and are staffed on some of the biggest, most impactful matters from the start. Associates work closely with both clients and partners and are regularly relied upon to provide advice. Associates are asked to draft deposition outlines, defend depositions, review potential mergers and contracts, and provide regulatory counseling regarding the Federal Trade Commission and Department of Justice.

The practice itself in DC has grown substantially in the past two years and continues to grow. We are a young practice group, looking for team members who want to try things they have not done before and make an impact

right away. Given its small size and growth, we are also expected to understand the business and to help with client relationships. Although team members may be pushed outside their comfort zones in order to deliver for a client, this work is done alongside seasoned practitioners that are able to give the support and advice all new attorneys need. Associates are valued as members of a team, not cogs in a wheel.

We work with some of the best practitioners in the world and while the learning curve is steep, we learn by doing with great support and collaboration from across the network. We have all been tasked with building the practice, growing our expertise, and meeting people in the industry. The team is consistently given opportunities to lead and learn.

I came to Allen & Overy because I wanted to be part of a global team of lawyers that works on sophisticated matters. I wanted to be the person in the room who both co-workers and clients alike look to for advice and counsel. In the past two years, I have been given exactly that opportunity. I have taken six depositions and second-chaired another six, helped navigate deals for clients from China and Europe, drafted motions and interviewed witnesses, and taken part in planning sessions for the best ways to navigate complex civil litigation.

I urge students looking for the right future fit to consider the type of practice area and team in analyzing firms. Practicing in the A&O antitrust group provides the unique combination of gaining legal and business expertise in transactional, litigation, and regulatory fields.

Practice Areas

Authors

John Roberti

John is a partner in the firm's D.C. Investigations and Litigation practice who focuses his practice on civil antitrust litigation and investigations. He provides strategic guidance to clie nts on all issues that relate to antitrust, and represents companies in court and before the agencies in their most important matters. John received his J.D. from New York University and his B.A. from Brown University.

Mathew Boucher

Matt is an associate in the antitrust practice group and a member of the firm's D.C. Investigations and Litigation practice. His practice deals with a broad range of antitrust and competition issues, ranging from large-scale criminal and civil litigation to providing guidance in antitrust clearance for mergers and acquisitions. Matt received his J.D. from the University of Michigan and his B.A. from Northwestern University.

ALLEN & OVERY

When M&A meets Antitrust Law: Freshfields' lawyers tell us how it all works

Chambers Global places Freshfields among the top two firms in the world for antitrust, and among the top four firms worldwide for M&A. We interviewed associates from the firm's DC and New York offices to learn how these two teams spend their days and work together...

Chambers Associate: **What is corporate law?**

Camille Ranadive [corporate associate, New York]: We do a lot of cross-border public and private M&A, private equity transactions, venture capital deals and joint-venture arrangements. Then there's general corporate governance: dealing with boards and board appointees, and advising on board decisions. Our work essentially involves working on documentation to achieve a client's goal: that might be deciding to purchase a company or selling assets or a business division.

Paul Humphreys [corporate senior associate, New York]: Corporate and M&A are overlapping and the terms get used interchangeably. Corporate, I think of as encompassing everything from M&A, to capital markets to fund formation to more run-of-the-mill corporate maintenance, like record keeping, updating minutes, and corporate secretarial-type activities. M&A, I think of as buying and selling businesses or investing in businesses, and that can be public or private transactions. Our practice is primarily M&A and capital markets.

CA: What is antitrust law?

Justin Stewart-Teitelbaum [antitrust senior associate, Washington, DC]: Antitrust law is a legal analysis of competition. There are two high-level areas of practice: the conduct side – legal assessment or litigation over business conduct which could be deemed anticompetitive – and M&A approval: regulators in the US and around the world assess planned mergers to determine if their consummation might result in competition issues. The two key US enforcers are the Federal Trade Commission (FTC) and Department of Justice (DOJ).

Ilana Kattan [antitrust associate, Washington DC]: Put simply, the antitrust laws aim to preserve competition. Antitrust lawyers advise clients on a wide range of issues, including on mergers, agreements with competitors, and monopolization. We advise clients in the M&A context, in regulatory investigations and litigation, and in private litigation. We also provide advice to clients on antitrust compliance.

"You need to really understand the mechanics of the market you're analyzing: the product, players, how it functions."

CA: What kind of work is involved day to day?

CR: Today I am supervising a due diligence project. The firm's legal services center employs trained attorneys who do a lot of due diligence for us, and then we review it. Additionally I'll be doing due diligence myself and updating diligence reports. Thankfully there's also a lot beyond diligence. I'll be working on documentation to add board members to an incentive program and reviewing stock purchase agreement precedents. A lot my time is devoted to phone calls with other offices and clients.

JST: One thing I enjoy about antitrust law is that it's highly fact-intensive – you need to understand the mechanics of the market you're analyzing: the product, players, how it functions, the regulatory framework. You're really digging into what underpins the market. In addition to the legal and factual analysis, I liaise with clients to pursue transaction clearance and work directly with the regulatory agencies – it's their job to review the merger and our job to explain why the transaction should not be considered to present competition concerns.

PH: I manage deal teams, which usually consist of one or two junior associates, maybe a mid-level associate and a partner, depending on the size of the transaction. At Freshfields 99% of what we do is cross-border, so often teams are not just based in the US. As a senior associate I draft, negotiate and solve outstanding issues. The partner takes a senior leadership role and would deal with any tricky relationship issues or very difficult negotiation points.

"One of the great things about corporate practice is that it's very people focused."

CA: What is the difference between junior-level work and partner-level work?

CR: We all work together all the time, on an hourly basis, not just daily. We're constantly in each others' offices. One of the great things about corporate practice is that it's very people focused – you don't just bury your head in research and not surface for hours. As a junior, you're expected to really get into the details: if you're doing diligence on a company, you need to understand everything about them and tell the partner everything they need to know about that company. They can then condense that into a client-friendly version.

PH: Juniors do a lot of diligence work – reviewing contracts and other key documents – and draft red-flag reports for the client, which highlight problematic legal and commercial issues and recommend what to do about them. Juniors also manage the global diligence team, which for our global practice usually means teams in some locations where we rely on outside counsel. Junior associates do not only do due diligence. At Freshfields, they will be involved in preparing first drafts of transaction documents. We also involve our junior associates in the firm's business development efforts, so you may find a junior preparing a presentation for a client. Our partners often involve the juniors who have done the work in the presentation to the client as well.

JST: As you move up in seniority you become more focused on the tactical and strategic implications of issues arising from diligence. For example, junior attorneys often conduct factual research and analysis and become experts on an area of the matter or the market. Then as a team we'll set the strategic course of action.

"Our roles fit together like puzzle pieces."

CA: How do the antitrust and corporate teams work together?

PH: Almost all transactions we work on in the US involve antitrust filings, as the threshold for making a filing is very low compared to the size of transactions on which we work – so our antitrust people are almost always involved.

JST: The corporate team is very aware that antitrust filings and review are often an important aspect of getting a transaction closed – thus we liaise closely on various aspects during transaction consideration and after signing, often we'll look at the antitrust considerations of a transaction before even discussing various other parts.

CR: As soon as we're aware of an M&A deal we get the antitrust team involved to understand what competition issues might arise in order to give a realistic deal timeline to the client. The worst thing to do would be to assume there are no competition issues and that it's going to be a quick deal process, only to find out you have to do an HSR [Hart–Scott–Rodino] Act filing – that can delay a deal by months, if not years.

IK: Our roles fit together like puzzle pieces. The corporate team organizes the strategy for large M&A deals and shepherds the process from origination of the deal to closing and beyond. The antitrust team works closely with the corporate team, assessing the antitrust risks of the deal and obtaining antitrust approvals for the deal.

PH: The antitrust team also provides training for the M&A team on potential antitrust issues that can arise during a transaction.

"We are getting a lot of questions about how certain political events will affect antitrust enforcement."

CA: What would you say about the future of M&A and antitrust practice?

JST: The proliferation of antitrust law and regulatory agencies around the world means the field will continue to grow. As more jurisdictions come into play and more antitrust laws are introduced, trying to comply with them all can be complex. There may also be an increase in private antitrust litigation, in particular outside of the US.

CR: We at Freshfields see M&A becoming increasingly global and cross border. US companies are realizing that they have to expand beyond the US to stay competitive and relevant. It'll be interesting to see what the next few years bring with Brexit and the new presidential administration in the US, but we have a positive outlook that M&A will continue to grow. 2016 didn't quite keep up with booming 2015, but it almost did. As clients become more global, they need law firms that have a global presence and we have offices around the world that work together on a daily basis.

IK: We are getting a lot of questions about how certain political events will affect antitrust enforcement. For example, how will Brexit affect competition law in Europe? How will antitrust enforcement change under the Trump administration? Despite this uncertainty – or in some cases, because of this uncertainty – companies have been proposing a large number of deals over the past couple of years that raise significant and complex antitrust issues. This merger wave likely will continue.

Practice Areas

PH: The regulatory landscape changed a lot for our clients after the financial crisis. Now with the Trump administration many of those new regulations may be removed. That theoretically paves the way for more consolidation and merger activity. But while things are in limbo, everyone may remain in a wait-and-see mode. In particular, in-bound M&A from places like China may wane until the Trump administration's policies are better understood.

The Obama administration was very active in looking at M&A deals from an antitrust perspective – they were willing to fight against deals they believed were anticompetitive and some fell apart. That may change under the Trump administration. There is a lot of talk about renegotiating trade deals – that will affect what foreign investment will look like for cross-border businesses and what type of investments non-US buyers are able to make. Another key trend for businesses in developed economies is the replacement of individual labor with intelligent machines. That will impact productivity but also change the labor force, as workers no longer need to be qualified just to put stuff together but rather to be someone who, for example, develops software. It'll be interesting to see how that drives consolidation, and how it creates opportunities for businesses.

"Summer associates are able to spend two weeks in a foreign office after their time with us in the US."

CA: What particular opportunities are available to antitrust and corporate juniors at Freshfields?

JST: There's definitely the opportunity for international travel – the work we do has a lot of travel built in. Summer associates are able to spend two weeks in a foreign office after their time with us in the US. Training also happens internationally – once or twice a year there is an antitrust training conference somewhere abroad. I have also been on a secondment to London and that has made me feel very close to the people in our team around the world. I know them, they know me, and we work together very closely. The commitment to trainings and secondment to other offices shows the firm's commitment to its unified network approach.

CR: It's good to go abroad and be there on the ground, as you just can't get as much done over the phone or by email as you can when you're in the room. Often juniors are the ones to travel to foreign offices for closings etc.

IK: One of the best things about Freshfields is the firm's focus on training. Several times a year, the junior associates in our antitrust team travel to Brussels from around the world to attend training on particular antitrust topics. These trainings not only allow for associates in the US to have a handle on the approach to antitrust issues outside the US, but also allow associates to get to know their colleagues on a personal level. These relationships continue to be developed as associates become more senior, with trainings scheduled each year for mid-level associates and senior associates.

CA: What's unique about Freshfields' antitrust and M&A teams?

CR: Our corporate team is small – it has about 20 associates and just a handful of partners, so it's very intimate. We all know each other very well and work with everyone closely. But at the same time we have the resources of a large global law firm, so it's the best of both worlds.

JST: Freshfields is considered to have the best antitrust practice in world, but the team doesn't feel overly big or impersonal – either locally or globally. For example, the Washington team is not particularly large compared to many other US antitrust practices – the team is close knit.

PH: We don't think of our international network in the sense that we would say 'oh, we have 15 people in Milan, who handle Italian law issues.' I think of Milan as a partner named Luigi Verga, who I've worked with on cross-border deals on multiple occasions. We don't just outsource non-US issues to a "network" office. We are one global firm, and we work incredibly hard to encourage internal networking and to build actual relationships with colleagues around the globe.

We want our clients' experience with the firm to be the same in Italy as it is in New York. We achieve this through things like global conferences, which start with 'Career Milestones' training for associates in their first and second year, and sector group conferences as you go along. The end result is that we know the individuals with whom we work, and we actually like working with one another. This is a huge benefit for clients as it improves efficiency and ensures the global team – not just the lead partner and lead associate – is committed to helping the client achieve its goals.

It is not uncommon for associates from our offices outside the US to visit the New York office on a vacation or personal trip to the US to meet in person someone with whom they have worked. I just don't think that is so common at other firms, and I believe that is a real testament to the culture of collegiality across borders that we strive to build and maintain.

CA: What's your advice for law students wanting to succeed in these areas?

JST: In terms of seeking positions at law firms, I recommend that you demonstrate your interest in each specific firm. That doesn't just mean knowing how many offices or associates we have, but also understanding the type of work we do. We don't expect you to be an expert on it during the interview process, but make sure you've done your homework – and if you want to know something then make sure you ask a question. Also, in the interview, try to showcase your interests and personality rather than simply reciting talking points.

CR: Take law school classes that are practical: I took seminars on 'the art of the deal' and general M&A which really gave me exposure to what corporate work is and made me familiar with certain terms. M&A seminars given by practitioners are most useful, as they give you a taste of what corporate practice is really like.

Learn more about life at Freshfields on p.**309**

Authors

Camille Ranadive is a corporate associate in New York.

Camille Ranadive

Ilana Kattan is an antitrust associate in DC.

Ilana Kattan

Paul Humphreys is a senior associate focusing on cross-border public and private M&A, private equity transactions, venture capital and general corporate governance.

Paul Humphreys

Justin Stewart-Teitelbaum is a senior associate in DC whose practice areas include representing clients in investigations of mergers and acquisitions before the Federal Trade Commission (FTC) and the Antitrust Division at the Department of Justice (DOJ).

Justin
Stewart-Teitelbaum

Practice Areas

 Freshfields Bruckhaus Deringer

Cartels, Pharmaceuticals & Class Action: insights from the antitrust experts at White & Case

Legal Trends: Cartels

Criminal and civil cartel litigations in the United States are usually brought under Section 1 of the Sherman Act (15 U.S.C. §1), which prohibits agreements between competitors on price, output, market or customer allocation, and bid-rigging. The US Department of Justice (DOJ) is charged with criminal enforcement, while private parties can bring civil actions.

The DOJ recently has intensified its investigations of possible international cartels. This is important for global businesses because companies found liable are exposed to large criminal penalties, and their executives may face prosecution.

A key, evolving issue is the extraterritorial reach of the Sherman Act, which is limited by the Foreign Trade Antitrust Improvements Act (FTAIA) (15 U.S.C. §6a). Under the FTAIA, the Sherman Act applies to conduct outside the United States only if that conduct is in US import commerce or has a direct, substantial and reasonably foreseeable effect on US domestic commerce, which proximately caused a plaintiff's injury. The Seventh Circuit has indicated that the FTAIA may apply differently in criminal and civil cases. *Motorola Mobility, LLC v. AU Optronics*, 775 F.3d 816 (7th Cir. 2015).

Legal Trends: Pharmaceuticals and Health Insurance

The pharmaceutical industry has seen an onslaught of antitrust cases involving Section 1 claims that defendants agreed to restrain trade, as well as claims that defendants engaged in monopolization or attempted monopolization under Section 2 of the Sherman Act (15 U.S.C. § 2). Pharmaceutical antitrust litigation theories include "product hopping" and "reverse payments," among others.

In "product hopping" cases, plaintiffs challenge brand manufacturers' introduction of new versions of existing drugs and discontinuation of older versions, which plaintiffs claim thwarts generic competition. Only two appellate courts have weighed in on such claims to date, with only the Third Circuit doing so after full discovery on the merits. *Mylan Pharmaceuticals Inc. v. Warner Chilcott PLC*, 838 F.3d 421 (3d Cir. 2016) (affirming district court's grant of summary judgment for defendants, holding that launch of new acne drug was not exclusionary conduct); *New York v. Actavis plc*, 787 F.3d 638 (2d Cir. 2015) (affirming district court preliminary injunction preventing defendants from limiting distribution of older Alzheimer's drug).

In "reverse payment" or "pay for delay" cases, plaintiffs challenge patent infringement settlements between a brand manufacturer and a generic competitor, arguing that they constitute payments by the brand to delay generic competition. The Supreme Court established a rule of reason framework for analyzing reverse payment settlements in *FTC v. Actavis, Inc.*, 133 S. Ct. 2223 (2013). Post-*Actavis*, efforts by lower courts to apply the framework have sometimes resulted in diverging holdings.

In the health insurance industry, 2016 saw two high-profile actions by the DOJ to block mergers under Section 7 of the Clayton Act (15 U.S.C. § 18). In both cases, the defendants argued that the mergers would create efficiencies outweighing any alleged harm from the loss of competition post-merger. While the defendants in the Aetna-Humana and Anthem-Cigna mergers lost at trial, the Anthem-Cigna case has been appealed, giving the DC Circuit an opportunity to clarify when the efficiencies defense applies and what evidentiary showings will establish it.

Legal Trends: Class Actions

Civil antitrust actions frequently involve class action claims by direct and indirect purchasers. Damages in private actions typically are measured by the "overcharge" resulting from the alleged anticompetitive conduct. Damages are trebled if liability is proven, meaning that damages in such cases can be substantial.

Purchasers at different levels of the distribution chain may have standing to bring claims for the same alleged behavior, which can create problems with multiple recoveries when such purchasers claim they suffered injury from the same overcharge. Direct purchasers argue that they absorbed any overcharges from the alleged anticompetitive conduct, while indirect purchasers argue that the direct purchasers passed on any overcharges.

Courts have recently weighed in on whether plaintiffs seeking class certification must show that class members are ascertainable prior to certification. In *Carrera v. Bayer Corp.*, 727 F.3d 300 (3d Cir. 2013), the Third Circuit held that ascertainability is a standalone, threshold requirement, meaning class plaintiffs must offer a "reliable

Practice Areas

and administratively feasible mechanism" for identifying class members. In *Mullins v. Direct Digital, LLC*, 795 F.3d 654 (7th Cir. 2015), the Seventh Circuit disagreed, instead finding that ascertainability is subsumed by the assessment of whether a class action is a superior means of resolving the dispute. The Ninth Circuit followed Mullins earlier this year in *Briseno v. ConAgra Foods, Inc.*, 844 F.3d 1121 (9th Cir. 2017). The evolution of the ascertainability doctrine may affect whether civil litigants can certify large classes of consumers that allegedly purchased price-fixed goods, where plaintiffs often seek to certify the largest classes possible in order to increase potential damages and generate leverage during settlement negotiations.

What an up-and-coming lawyer in this area can expect

- Representing clients in connection with complex and often headline-grabbing investigations and litigations
- Advocating for clients at meetings with the DOJ and foreign regulators
- Advising clients on developing compliance programs

and policies
- Preparing and representing witnesses in providing testimony in grand jury investigations, civil depositions, and trials
- Drafting motions to dismiss, summary judgment motions, and various substantive non-dispositive motions
- Working with experts to assess overcharge claims, class certification issues, relevant antitrust markets, and other issues

White & Case LLP's Antitrust Practice

White & Case has experience in all aspects of civil and criminal antitrust investigations and litigation. With more than 190 antitrust lawyers in 24 offices in 15 countries, White & Case offers our clients an integrated team with deep competition law capabilities, providing a coordinated approach to global competitive issues. White & Case is recognized by *Global Competition Review* as one of the world's elite competition practices. In 2017, *Chambers USA* also awarded White & Case in the US a Band 1 Ranking for its Antitrust: Cartel work.

Authors

J. Mark Gidley

J. Mark Gidley chairs the Firm's Global Antitrust practice. His practice focuses on mergers, acquisitions and cartel cases, frequently with a transnational focus. In December 2014, Mark was named one of the inaugural Litigation Trailblazers by *The National Law Journal*. (University of Kansas (BS) and Columbia University (JD))

Martin M. Toto

Martin M. Toto is a partner in the Firm's Global Antitrust practice, concentrating in US antitrust law and complex commercial litigation. He has served as trial counsel and successfully defended clients in several recent price-fixing and monopolization trials. Martin also has advised companies on virtually all aspects of antitrust law. (Lehigh University (BS) and New York University (JD))

Jack Pace

Jack Pace is a partner in White & Case's Global Antitrust practice and Executive Partner of the Firm's New York office. He represents clients in complex litigation matters, particularly class actions, involving claims under the antitrust, RICO, consumer

protection and other laws. (Fordham University (BA and JD))

Michael Hamburger

Michael E. Hamburger is an associate in the Firm's Global Antitrust practice. He represents clients in civil and criminal antitrust cases, and has significant experience defending clients at trial and on appeal. (Lafayette College (BA) and Fordham University (JD))

Kristen Shaughnessy

Kristen O'Shaughnessy is an associate in the Firm's Global Antitrust practice. She represents clients in civil antitrust cases, and has significant experience representing clients in the pharmaceutical industry. (Northwestern University (BS) and Georgetown University (JD))

Practice Areas

WHITE & CASE

Appellate Law

"There can be nothing more thrilling than distilling an entire appeal down to oral argument an appellate lawyer will make."

In a nutshell

In simple terms, appellate law is a stage of dispute resolution. More specifically, it involves handling cases on appeal, but the best appellate practices think of it more broadly and consider sophisticated legal analysis, strategy and issue identification – even at the trial level – to be part of their core function.

Appellate lawyers, though all experts in appellate advocacy per se, often come to specialize in different areas. This includes the likes of antitrust, state and federal taxation, corporate law, punitive damages, telecommunications, labor & employment, environment, and intellectual property. *"To be a good appellate lawyer is to have a set of skills that cross-cut substantive areas in the law,"* according to **Kathleen Sullivan** of **Quinn Emmanuel.**

They will also often have a court-specific focus, developing expertise in state appellate courts, federal courts of appeal, state supreme courts, or the US Supreme Court.

What lawyers do

- Evaluate the issues in the case.
- Review motions filed by lawyers in trial court, because they tend to identify the important issues.
- Read the trial transcript.
- Work with trial lawyers to understand the facts of the case.
- Conduct legal research to assess the strength of the issues raised at trial.
- Write an 'issues memo' after the research and analysis, and consult with the client and trial lawyers to identify the most promising issues.
- Write the brief. This process takes time.
- Share the brief with the client and trial counsel; incorporate their comments and reactions.
- Continue to refine the brief until it must be filed.
- Present the oral argument.
- Manage post-hearing steps.

Realities of the job

- Oral argument *"is an incredibly adrenalin-fueled experience,"* says **Evan Tager** of **Mayer Brown**. *"It adds spice to your ordinary research and writing routine."* Practicing appellate lawyers often note this as one their favorite parts of the job, with Kathleen Sullivan noting:

"There can be nothing more thrilling than distilling an entire appeal down to oral argument an appellate lawyer will make."

- It is, however, a relatively small part of the case. The strength of the appeal rests on the shoulders of the brief, though most clients still hire appellate lawyers based on their oral argument capabilities. The recent changes in federal rules of procedure have increased the need for this asset. As Kathleen Sullivan notes, *"it can take longer to write a shorter brief. It is a skill to argue in a more succinct and attention-grabbing way,"* one which must be developed by aspiring appellate lawyers.
- Prior to an oral argument, appellate lawyers should go through one or more moot court sessions in preparation for the real thing. *"Appellate judges appreciate the extra preparation,"* explains **Stephen Shapiro** of **Mayer Brown**.
- *"The reality is that appellate work is far more people-centric than most assume,"* **Carter Phillips** of **Sidley Austin** says. *"You're going in as part of a much broader team, and if you're successful it's because you have the right skills to work effectively with others."*
- Appellate law is a highly intellectual area that involves cutting-edge legal issues. Phillips adds: *"Those who practice appellate law tend to have remarkably strong credentials coming out of law school."* According to **Kannon Shanmugam** of **Williams & Connolly**, the role of an appellate lawyers is to *"research legal questions, but also policy arguments. It is important to develop these skills early in your career."*
- Associates must enjoy spending countless hours doing research and crafting written statements. This work decreases with seniority.
- *"If you like to play with language, prose and sentence structure, if you consider writing to be an art, then appellate law is a great opportunity to immerse yourself in that,"* says Tager.
- There is no law stating that you have to do a clerkship in order to become an appellate lawyer, but *"it's much easier and a natural progression for those who have,"* Phillips tells us. Working in government in an appellate division can also be beneficial. Kannon Shanmugam elaborates: *"A clerkship is important, I don't think it's a requirement, but having done an appellate clerkship is useful to understand how appellate courts operate and their internal mechanisms and structures."*
- Courts around the country are constantly issuing de-

cisions that appellate lawyers need to keep up with, though practitioners can generally limit their focus to decisions made in the courts or areas of law that apply to their practice.

- *"It's useful to develop a wider array of litigation skills in the first year or two,"* according to Phillips. **Seth Waxman** of **WilmerHale** confirms: *"I could never have been the kind of appellate lawyer that I am without putting together cases from scratch, learning how to establish facts in a trial record and developing a facility for never doing the same kind of substantive case twice."*

- Another key difference between appellate law and litigation is the considerable shift toward answering questions as opposed to asking them. This is done by *"meeting the obvious questions head on in a brief, or being prepared to quickly and thoughtfully provide answers to questions that judges ask during oral advocacy,"* says Waxman. Kannon Shanmugam notes: *"Appellate litigation tends to be more purely law focused; there is not so much of a focus on the development of the record."*

- Judges are human. They have predispositions and find it difficult not to view a case through the lens of their biases, often frustrating even the best-laid plans – although this is less of an issue in the Supreme Court compared to the lower court levels.

Current issues

- Appellate lawyers are being brought onto cases at increasingly earlier stages such as immediately after jury verdicts or even when winning a case starts to look unlikely. Some clients are even requesting that an appellate lawyer be staffed from the get-go, with the purpose of keeping an eye on potential appeal strategies. Specialized appellate lawyers have also become increasingly common in recent years.

- The Federal Rules of Procedure for appellate case have been amended as of December 2016. Amongst the revisions was a decrease in the word limit for briefs. In an area of law rewarding concision, the impetus for succinct and effective prose will increase.

- Numerous new 'pro se' or 'pro bono' appellate programs have been developed throughout the country over recent years, to tackle the influx of self-represented civil litigants in appellate courts and to improve efficiency in this regard. Public Counsel operates two clinics to assist pro se litigants: the Appellate Self-Help Clinic and the Federal Pro Se Clinic.

- In Texas, a trend has been observed: the state's leaders are increasingly turning to appellate litigators to fill top government legal positions. Former Texas Assistant Solicitor General Jimmy Blacklock was appointed general counsel to the incoming governor, while another alum of the Texas Solicitor General's office, Brantley Starr, was appointed the new Deputy Attorney General for Legal Counsel. These big-shot appellate litiga-

tors were appointed because of their ability to handle the thorniest of legal issues: an ability which had been honed thanks to the complex issues generated within the Appellate Bar. Whether this trend will surface in other states remains to be seen, but it indicates something about the potential career progression of a successful appellate lawyer, and the value of handling intricate appellate cases.

Advice from the appellate law gurus

Carter Phillips, partner and chair of the firm's executive committee, **Sidley Austin**:

"If you're coming out of law school, get a clerkship with an appellate judge because there's no better way to understand the process than to spend a year on that side of the ledger. After that, the critical mass of the practice is in Washington DC, so you should start out there if you really want to be an appellate lawyer."

"It's also good to spend time in government, as it's a great proving ground for developing appellate skills. And if you can land a spot in the Solicitor General's office, you will have the opportunity to argue before the US Supreme Court – and that's pretty heady stuff."

Stephen Shapiro, partner and founder of appellate group, **Mayer Brown**:

*"The road to success in appellate law starts in law school, where interested students should work on a law review and take part in the moot court program. Most important, a neophyte appellate lawyer should read and listen to as many of the best briefs and oral arguments as possible."**

"Young appellate lawyers learn a great deal from the edits of senior lawyers working on their draft briefs. They should keep those edited briefs in their files for future reference; I still have some edited drafts from my mentor, Judge Frank Easterbrook."

Seth Waxman, chair of the appellate and Supreme Court litigation practice group, **WilmerHale**:

"You certainly need to have a real affinity for quiet solitary work. It's not the life of the academic, but some aspects are much more solitary than many other types of law practice. I always have my door open and I spend a lot of my day wandering in and out of colleagues' offices, as I tend to work better in a collegial setting. But at the end of the day, when you're talking about writing or preparing a brief, or preparing to argue a case, there is no substitute for spending a long time on your own with the door closed and focusing your mind in a concentrated way. To be fulfilled

and successful as an appellate lawyer you have to have an appreciation for quite a different way of working."

*Editor's note: sample briefs and arguments are available at www.appellate.net

Rankings in *Chambers USA*

Top ranked

Gibson Dunn	WilmerHale
Sidley Austin	

Highly recommended

Akin Gump	Latham
Arnold & Porter	Mayer Brown
Hogan Lovells	MoFo
Jenner	O'Melveny
Jones Day	Orrick
King & Spalding	Vinson
Kirkland	

For more detail on ranking tiers and locations, visit www.chambersandpartners.com

"Trial practice is not for everyone, but if you find your way to the first chair remember my most important trial motto: KISS (keep it simple stupid), followed by one of my favorite courtroom rules: when you're winning the argument with the Court, stop speaking. Sometimes the more you argue, the more you might convince the Court that it was wrong in initially agreeing with you."

- star litigator and *Chambers USA* lifetime achievement award winner Elkan Abramowitz

Practice Areas

Banking & Finance

In a nutshell

Banking and finance lawyers deal with the lending and borrowing of money, and the management of financial liabilities. Their task is to help structure their clients' transactions, to protect their clients' best legal and commercial interests, and to negotiate and document the contractual relationship between lenders and borrowers. It's a hugely technical, ever-evolving and jargon-heavy area of law. For anything banks do with capital raising or financial instruments, see Capital Markets.

> *"This area allows you to push yourself and increase the percentage of time spent doing things that are new, interesting, challenging and occasionally frightening."*
>
> – James Florack, Davis Polk

Straightforward bank lending: a bank or other financial institution lends money to a borrower on documented repayment terms. Bank loans may be bilateral (made by one bank to the borrower) or syndicated (arranged by one or more financial institutions and made by a group of lenders).

Acquisition finance: a loan made to a corporate borrower or private equity sponsor for the purpose of acquiring another company. This includes **leveraged finance**, where the borrower finances the cost of an acquisition by borrowing most of the purchase price without committing a lot of its own capital (as typically done in leveraged buyouts).

Real estate finance: a loan made to enable a borrower to acquire a property or finance the development of land, commonly secured by way of a mortgage on the acquired land/buildings. **Project finance:** the financing of long-term infrastructure (eg roads or power plants) and public services projects (eg hospitals) where the amounts borrowed to complete the project are paid back with the cash flow generated by the project. **Asset finance:** this enables the purchase and operation of large assets such as ships, aircraft and machinery. The lender normally takes security over the assets in question. **Islamic finance:** Muslim borrowers, lenders and investors must abide by Shari'a law, which prohibits the collection and payment of interest on a loan. Islamic finance specialists ensure that finance deals are structured in a Shari'a-compliant manner.

Financial services regulation: lawyers advise financial and other businesses on everything that they might need to know about the legal limits of their financial and investment activities. They focus especially on new and complex federal and state regulations. Major clients are usually banks, hedge funds, private equity firms, broker-dealers and insurance firms. Post-recession there has been a multifold increase in the volume of legislation governing the financial sector.

What lawyers do

Bank lending

- Meet with clients to establish their specific requirements and the commercial context of a deal.
- Carry out due diligence – an investigation exercise to verify the accuracy of information passed from the borrower to the lender or from the underwriter of securities to potential investors. This can involve on-site meetings with the company's management, discussions with the company's auditors and outside counsel, and review of material agreements and other documents.
- Negotiate with the opposite party to agree the terms of the deal and record them accurately in the facility documentation. Lenders' lawyers usually produce initial documents (often based on a standard form or an agreed precedent) and borrowers' lawyers try to negotiate more favorable terms for their clients. Lawyers on both sides must know when to compromise and when to hold out.

> *"We work at the intersection of law and markets, so lawyers in our field not only need an understanding of the law, but an inquisitive mind and an interest in real-world economic and political developments."*
>
> – Robert Tortoriello, financial services senior counsel, Cleary Gottlieb

- Assist with the structuring of complicated or groundbreaking financing models, and ensure innovative solutions comply with all relevant laws.
- Gather all parties to complete the transaction, ensuring all agreed terms are reflected in the loan documents, all documents have been properly signed and delivered and all conditions to closing have been met.
- In a secured loan (most bank loans to below investment-

Practice Areas

101

grade borrowers require collateral), ensure that the agreed-upon collateral has been properly granted and that all filings, registrations and other procedures necessary to 'perfect' the security have been or will be made.

Financial services regulation

- Receive calls from banks and other financial institutions that seek guidance as to how business initiatives can be implemented most effectively in US markets, in full compliance with the letter and policy of US law.
- Sit down with the client – speaking to individuals at a very senior level – to find out what the client's business plan and intentions are.
- Analyze the implications of implementing that plan based on what current or future regulation looks like, or can be expected to look like, and what the legal, compliance, reputational, strategic, cross-border and related risks of that plan might be.
- Give advice on what changes may need to be made to the business initiative to achieve regulatory compliance and minimize risk.
- Regulatory lawyers are not just involved with compliance counseling: they also advise on enforcement and internal and external investigations; the restructuring and disposition of bank assets; the organization of bank units and subsidiaries; acquisitions, investments, strategic alliances and joint ventures; capital raising initiative and the creation and distribution of bank securities and deposit and other financial instruments; the structuring of 'living wills' and recovery and resolution plans; and the implementation and evaluation of bank marketing, cross-selling and similar initiatives.

Realities of the job

- Some firms act for investment or commercial banks on highly complex and often cross-border financings, whereas the work of others generally involves more mainstream domestic finance deals.
- A good working knowledge of the bankruptcy laws is critical for lawyers practicing in the area of leveraged finance. Banking lawyers advise for the worst-case scenario, which is often a bankruptcy filing by the borrower. Understanding how the rules change once that filing is made is critically important, even for lawyers who never expect to set foot in a bankruptcy courtroom.
- Lawyers need to appreciate the internal policies and sensitivities of their clients in order to deliver pertinent advice and warn of the legal (and reputational) risks involved in the transactions. Deals may involve the movement of money across borders and through different currencies and financial products. International deals have an additional layer of difficulty: political changes in transitional economies can render a previously sound investment risky.

- Banking clients are ultra-demanding and the hours can be long. On the plus side, clients will be smart and dynamic. It is possible to build up long-term relationships with investment bank clients, even as a junior associate.
- Working on deals can be exciting. The team and the other side are all working to a common goal, often under significant time and other pressures. Deal closings bring adrenalin highs and a sense of satisfaction.
- You need to become absorbed in the finance world. Start reading *The Wall Street Journal*, the various deal-related trade publications or other good business-oriented websites.
- Regulatory lawyers need to remain constantly aware of the latest political developments (potentially) affecting regulations. *"We are not management consultants, but our role involves a huge amount of market-based business analysis. Lawyers who want to work in this area need to become very knowledge-focused. Staying on top of the latest news in all the areas involved is a great ongoing challenge of the job,"* says **Robert Tortoriello**, a senior counsel in **Cleary Gottlieb**'s financial institutions practice.
- Regulatory lawyers operate on shifting sands. *"Abnormal is the new normal,"* says Robert Tortoriello. *"It is a constantly evolving practice. At present lawyers are advising on the 'likely' implications of the 'likely' regulatory framework that will emerge from the ongoing legislative process, which has come forth from proposed regulations."*

Current issues

- The new Trump administration seeks to strip away the Dodd-Frank Act and replace it with pro-growth policies. It's not entirely clear what form the new legislation will take but both financial institutions and lawyers will be keeping a close eye on the changes. Tax reforms are another area likely to change under the new administration; lower taxes for businesses, for example, could see an increase in investments in the US.
- Regulators are increasingly turning their attention to cybersecurity concerns. The New York State Department of Financial Services (DFS) released a proposal to require DFS regulated financial institutions to establish a cybersecurity program, appoint a chief information security officer and comply with requirements such as annual risk assessments and regular vulnerability testing.
- Fintech may only make up a small share of the market but it's rapidly growing. While these start-ups can compete directly with banks in areas such as wealth management, loans or payment products, larger financial institutions are being to explore the opportunities fintech platforms can provide, in areas such as mobile banking apps or services.

Rankings in *Chambers USA*

Top ranked

Alston & Bird	Mintz Levin
Bracewell	Proskauer
Cahill	Reed Smith
Cravath	Ropes & Gray
Davis Polk	Sidley
Foley & Lardner	Simpson
Goodwin	Skadden
Greenberg	Squire Patton Boggs
Jones Day	Waller
King & Spalding	White & Case
Latham	

Highly recommended

Baker Botts	Morgan Lewis
Choate	MoFo
Cleary	Norton Rose Fulbright
Debevoise	Nutter
Duane Morris	Orrick
Fried Frank	Paul Hastings
Gibson	Paul, Weiss
Goulston	Shearman
Haynes and Boone	Sheppard
Holland & Knight	Thompson & Knight
Hunton	Vedder
Katten	Vinson
Kirkland	Weil
Mayer Brown	Willkie
McDermott Will & Emery	WilmerHale
Millbank, Tweed, Hadley	Winston

For more detail on ranking tiers and locations, visit
www.chambersandpartners.com

- Interest in blockchain (the database technology which underpins digital currency bitcoin) continues to increase. The security of the blockchain, its transparency – anyone using the system can view trades – and irreversible nature of blockchain transactions have all proved attractive to financial institutions. Although the practice is yet to go mainstream, banks continue to experiment with the tech and how it can be applied to benefit their businesses.
- The UK's exit from the EU could have major implications for overseas banks based in London if their access to the wider continent is cut off or the UK's banking industry undergoes a regulatory overhaul. Several US firms, particularly those with a base in London, have been quick to capitalize on the opportunity to provide financial regulatory advice to clients investing in both the UK and European Union. Some experts predict that Brexit could even allow US banks to extend their market share opportunity over their European counterparts.

Advice from the banking and finance gurus

Marc Hanrahan, partner and leader of the leveraged finance group, Milbank:

"It's a demanding area. People often work all night and into the next day."

"Since the economic troubles began, there's an increased emphasis on identifying and controlling risk. Issues that might not have been paid much attention five years ago are given tremendous focus now. Clients respect our contribution to transactions today. Lawyers are seen as less of an impediment and businesses know that they can't just disregard what we say."

James Florack, partner and co-head of the global credit group, Davis Polk:

"This area allows you to push yourself and increase the percentage of time spent doing things that are new, interesting, challenging and occasionally frightening. You'll be confronted with a puzzle, like a logic puzzle, and you have to find a way out of it that doesn't compromise your client – the bank – or indeed the bank's clients. You need an ability to solve problems creatively."

"It's important to realize that while we're running a business, the client is also running a business. If you solve a problem in a way that impacts negatively on the client's client – the borrower – you may end up reducing the usefulness of the financing and, as a result, corrode the overall relationship among the parties."

"Confidence in your intellectual ability, discipline and patience are necessary to work in this area. An even temperament is important because transactions aren't always negotiated in perfect conditions – they might be going on against the backdrop of a larger M&A transaction or under time constraints."

Robert Tortoriello, financial services senior counsel, Cleary Gottlieb:

"We work at the intersection of law and markets, so lawyers in our field not only need an understanding of the law, but an inquisitive mind and an interest in real-world economic and political developments. So if you aren't prepared to learn how to read a balance sheet, or work with care through the footnotes in a financial statement that describe a derivative, you will not be successful in this field."

Practice Areas

Life as a Banking Lawyer, by White & Case

Business Climate and Recent Trends

Since its development in the 1980s, the syndicated loan market has become the primary source of loan financing for corporate borrowers.

In 2016, global syndicated lending reached US$4.0 trillion (9,302 deals). US loans accounted for 58 percent of the global loan volume, totaling US$2.1 trillion.

The syndicated loan market can be divided into two sections: the market for investment-grade borrowers and the market for non-investment-grade borrowers (the leveraged loan market). Investment-grade transactions involve large, highly creditworthy borrowers and although the amounts involved can be very large, the deals are generally more straightforward and unsecured, with the funds provided mainly by commercial banks. Leveraged loan transactions involve borrowers with lower credit ratings. They are riskier and more complex and typically involve taking a security interest in the assets of the borrower as well as more extensive and more heavily negotiated documentation provisions.

The market is highly dynamic, with deal terms and structures rapidly evolving in response to economic conditions, fluctuations in interest rates, the ebb and flow of the M&A market and changes in business sentiment. A variety of forces shaped US market activity in 2016. Regulations (particularly the Leveraged Lending Guidance and the CLO capital requirements under Basel III), macro-economic conditions, the presidential election, increased competition between financial institutions and non-traditional lending sources, and higher purchase price multiples in M&A transactions all served to influence the US loan market.

The large supply of capital has resulted in strong competition among lenders and has allowed companies and financial sponsors to push for lower interest rates and more borrower-friendly terms (such as those seen in so-called "covenant-lite" transactions). In addition, in recent years, large financial sponsors who are active consumers of debt products with significant market power have had a strong influence on documentation principles and loan terms.

Debt financing is incurred by companies for a variety of purposes, such as financing acquisitions, refinancing maturing or more expensive debt, financing dividends paid to equity owners, financing working capital and for general corporate purposes. Loans for general corporate purposes dominated the market in 2016, accounting for a 69% share, with proceeds totaling US$ 1.5 trillion. Acquisition finance and working capital financings followed, capturing 17% and 5% of the market, respectively.

Global economic trends also have significant impact—macroeconomic uncertainty and regulatory constraints in the European and Asian markets in recent years have resulted in a dramatic increase in the number of European and Asian borrowers accessing the US loan market in transactions that utilize New York-law governed documents.

With regulators increasingly focused on banks' underwriting standards and the impact the performance of high-risk loans could have on the banks' "stress test" results, regulatory scrutiny and the challenges that banks face as a result are likely to remain the key focal points for market players in 2017. In particular, it is anticipated that a shift towards "non-regulated" alternative capital providers as a source of financing for riskier credits will continue as a consequence of the regulatory clampdown.

What an up-and-coming attorney in this area can expect

- Representing a mix of banks, financial institutions, private equity firms, hedge funds, top-tier financial sponsors and corporate borrowers in connection with a variety of complex and often headline-grabbing financing transactions
- Structuring, negotiating and documenting complex financing arrangements for clients in a vast array of industries and across multiple jurisdictions
- Counseling clients on changes in current market trends and regulatory changes and remaining at the forefront of developing innovative financing solutions, structures and techniques
- Leading deal teams across a global network of offices to address local law issues in complex cross-border transactions and liaising with counsel in focused areas of legal experience to provide one-stop solutions for clients
- Working directly with clients and senior lawyers to provide top-quality service and technical advice in a high-performance and collaborative environment
- Access to extensive training and professional development resources

White & Case LLP's Bank Finance Practice

White & Case has a market-leading Global Bank Finance Practice that focuses on advising financial institutions, private equity funds and corporations in connection with a broad range of financing transactions, including leveraged buyouts, dividend recapitalizations, asset-based lending transactions, real estate, structured, trade and investment-grade financings, workouts, restructurings, and debtor-in-possession and exit financings. Our group comprises more than 350 lawyers with established teams in all the major financial markets globally, including New York, London, Frankfurt, Paris, Hong Kong, Tokyo and Singapore, and in many regional financial centers. The international strength of our Global Bank Finance Practice is reflected not only in White & Case's recognition for its banking work in *Chambers Global 2017*, but also in more than a dozen Chambers individual market and regional rankings, including rankings for USA Nationwide, Europe-wide, Latin America, United Kingdom, Germany, France and Asia.

Authors

Eric Leicht

Eric Leicht, a partner in White & Case LLP's New York office, is head of the firm's Americas Bank Finance Practice. Eric represents major commercial and investment banks, as lead agents, arrangers and borrowers, in a variety of lending transactions, with an emphasis on acquisition and leveraged financings.

Binoy Dharia

Binoy Dharia is a partner in the Bank Finance Practice of White & Case LLP. Based in the firm's New York office, Binoy represents lenders, private equity funds and corporate borrowers in connection with a wide range of domestic and international secured and unsecured lending transactions, including leveraged and investment-grade acquisition financings, general syndicated financings, asset-based financings and exit financings.

Practice Areas

WHITE & CASE

Leveraged Finance:
an introduction, by Allen & Overy's specialists

Practice Overview

Leveraged Finance is an exciting specialty within the broader Banking & Finance practice area. Leverage refers to strategic use of debt capital (i.e., loans and bonds) to achieve higher returns on investment at lower risk to the borrower and its equity holders. A leveraged borrower is one carrying a high debt load relative to its cash flows, to the benefit of equity holders who invest less of their own money to acquire or develop the business.

Leveraged Finance attorneys negotiate, document and advise clients on loan agreements, bond indentures and related contracts entered into to finance specific strategic transactions (e.g., leveraged buyouts ("LBOs"), mergers and acquisitions and capital expenditures) and related activities.

Attorneys in this practice area represent numerous principal players: investment banks, who arrange and commit to provide these financings; private equity financial sponsors, who utilize these financings to purchase target companies or recapitalize portfolio companies; corporate borrowers, who require debt financing for strategic investments and acquisitions or for working capital; and other syndicated debt market participants (e.g., investment funds, alternative lenders, business development companies ('BDCs') and asset managers), who hold the debt until it is traded or repaid.

Leveraged Finance is a uniquely dynamic and multi-faceted practice area. Attorneys in this specialty are exposed to companies in all stages of the corporate life cycle. At times when M&A activity is booming, leveraged finance attorneys find themselves in very high demand, as financial sponsors compete to acquire target companies and investment banks and alternative lenders compete to provide the debt commitments to back those acquisitions. When markets turn, borrowers and their creditors seek counsel from leveraged finance attorneys with respect to the ongoing requirements (or "covenants") under their debt documents and, when compliance with those terms proves too challenging, amendments, restructurings and bankruptcy-related advice. As a result, the skills of high quality leveraged finance lawyers will always be in demand, regardless of the economic climate.

Practitioners in this area are often well-rounded and well-versed in numerous legal areas, including general corporate law, laws related to mergers and acquisitions and shareholders' rights, contract law, government regulation, secured transactions and the Uniform Commercial Code, and bankruptcy law, to name a few. Additionally, while strong leveraged finance lawyers develop detailed contract drafting and negotiation capabilities, their skill set often extends beyond an understanding of law and contracts and into the advisory realm, being regularly called upon to opine on current market trends and strategic financing alternatives. This allows leveraged finance lawyers to blend the legal perspective with a business understanding of the financial markets.

Allen & Overy is uniquely placed in the global leveraged finance market. As of the beginning of 2017, there are over 50 leveraged finance partners, 250 banking partners, and 1,000 other banking and finance (including capital markets) practitioners in our firm worldwide. Due to the size and scope of the finance offering at A&O, attorneys in our leveraged finance practice have a breadth of transactional experience that is difficult to replicate at other firms without the scale that A&O offers. With 44 offices in 31 countries, A&O provides its associates a unique opportunity to work on some of the most complex and interesting financings, often requiring A&O's expertise across multiple jurisdictions.

Recent Market Developments

Leveraged loans and high yield bonds have long been active and robust asset classes given the returns they generate for lenders and other investors despite relatively low historical default rates. The Leveraged Finance industry is dynamic, with the creation of new investment vehicles, the implementation of new regulations, the globalization of the capital markets and other developments and trends creating opportunities for new market entrants and product offering expansion by existing market participants. In the late 2000s, leveraged debt issuance soared with the increase in popularity of private equity investment. Financing for such transactions was usually provided by the traditional investment banks (often referred to as 'bulge bracket' institutions) who agreed to commit to lend to private equity sponsors in return for a fee, with the ultimate goal of selling (or 'syndicating') the resulting debt instruments to other lenders or investors in the secondary market.

Following the Lehman Brothers bankruptcy in 2008 and the ensuing global financial crisis, as banks faced increased regulatory pressure, including capital require-

Practice Areas

ments and limits on the amount and terms of loans made to highly leveraged borrowers, new market entrants in the form of alternative lender funds, BDCs, and even direct lending arms of private equity firms, emerged. Because many of these new lenders are technically not regulated banking institutions, and therefore not subject to the same government restrictions, they are able to compete aggressively with traditional banks for market share. This increase in competition contributes to the greater negotiating power that borrowers and equity sponsors have enjoyed in the current market climate. It also expands the corporate debt marketplace generally as the new capital sources introduce additional products to distinguish themselves from traditional banks, and existing players innovate to retain market share. In light of this changing landscape and the evolution of the capital markets, including the convergence of historically distinct geographical markets, there has never been a more exciting time to be an attorney in the Leveraged Finance space.

Role of an Associate

Leveraged Finance is a team sport. Transactions require collaboration, and every member of the deal team is indispensable and necessary for the success of the transaction. At A&O, we staff strategically to ensure significant and direct interaction between partners and associates, and among associates of differing seniority levels. Associates are challenged early and often to take on as much responsibility and client contact as they desire. As a result, junior associates in our group tend to have drafting and negotiation responsibilities earlier than in other transactional practice areas.

In particular, Leveraged Finance associates:

- draft and review commitment letters, fee letters, term sheets and definitive documentation (credit and security agreements), with significant substantive responsibility early in their careers;
- negotiate legal terms directly with opposing counsel, and facilitate the negotiation of commercial terms between principal parties;

- analyze market precedents for latest developments and advise clients as to whether a particular proposal is consistent with *"market"* terms (i.e., what similarly situated lenders or investors are currently accepting in comparable circumstances);
- stay in close and direct contact with clients and other attorneys (including local counsel in other jurisdictions), managing communications in order to ensure the transaction is running smoothly;
- coordinate with various other practice areas across the firm, including tax, environmental, regulatory, sanctions, employee benefits, intellectual property and litigation, among others;
- on cross-border matters, coordinate with counsel in our foreign offices or our local counsel in other jurisdictions, to ensure global consistency and coordination of terms and documentation;
- manage all aspects of the transaction process, from overseeing due diligence to maintaining the master agenda and steering the team toward a coordinated and timely closing; and
- importantly, develop their own direct relationships with clients, both on- and off-deal, which at A&O is encouraged from an associate's earliest days.

About A&O

Allen & Overy has a market-leading global Leveraged Finance practice that advises the world's foremost financial institutions, investment funds, corporations and financial sponsors across all types of debt financings. We provide a full service offering for senior, second-lien, mezzanine and PIK debt, cash flow and asset based financings, bridge-to-bond financings, bank/bond financings, high-yield debt offerings, debt buy-backs and leveraged leases and regularly advise clients on complex debt restructurings, workouts, debtor-in-possession financings and exit financings.

Our practice comprises a devoted and highly experienced group of partners, counsel and associates, both in the US and globally. We dramatically expanded our New York team in 2016, further augmenting our existing US banking and finance capability, which is fully integrated into A&O's unmatched international platform.

Practice Areas

Authors

Judah Frogel
Partner

Rajani Gupta
Partner

Todd Koretzky
Partner

ALLEN & OVERY

Bankruptcy/Restructuring

In a nutshell

The essential task of bankruptcy and restructuring lawyers is to avoid a client's bankruptcy. The term 'bankruptcy' itself is a technical term that refers to when financially distressed companies, unable to restructure on their own, file for Chapter 11 to undergo a court-supervised restructuring.

In order to avoid this scenario, a company must successfully *"restructure its debt to keep the company together and retain its value,"* head of **Davis Polk**'s insolvency and restructuring practice **Don Bernstein** explains. But the path to financial viability – through court or not – can be convoluted. The legal know-how required and the multitude and variety of actors involved make bankruptcy and restructuring a rather complex practice.

Bankruptcy and restructuring attorneys must be adept at **transactional** work and **litigation** across a range of areas like M&A, securities, banking, labor and employment, environment, tax and IP.

Troubled companies will first attempt out-of-court restructuring, or corporate reorganization, in which they try to reach an agreement with their creditors. This has become an increasingly important stage. *"Traditional Chapter 11 cases can be expensive, inefficient and harmful to the business,"* according to **Jay Goffman**, global head of **Skadden**'s corporate restructuring group. *"This means it's important to advise companies on how to avoid Chapter 11 or shorten their time in Chapter 11 and similar insolvency proceedings, rather than convincing them to do it."*

"Bankruptcy is the last bastion of the generalist."

Chapter 11 provides for a **court-supervised restructuring** and, crucially, protection from creditors, who are barred from seeking to retrieve their money until the company is restructured. A notable feature of Chapter 11 work is the growing prevalence of 'distressed M&A', which describes the selling of parts – or the whole – of the ailing company. Such sales are done under the provisions of Section 363 of the Bankruptcy Code and often referred to as '363 deals'. Deals can also take place outside of court, but it is less common; buyers often prefer the safety of court-sanctioned sales.

The number of parties involved in a restructuring can be vast. They come from all walks of a company's life and often have competing interests. Acting for the **debtor** is

a challenge on its own, because then *"everyone's problem is your problem. You have to deal with every creditor and ensure the pie is allocated fairly,"* Bernstein explains.

Representing **creditors** is often simply about trying to recover as much as you can from a debtor, but there are many different types of creditors to choose from. 'Secured' creditors include commercial and investment banks, insurance companies and hedge funds, while 'unsecured' creditors include bondholders and vendors, or 'trade creditors' (eg, auto parts suppliers). In Chapter 11, there are official committees of unsecured creditors and debtor in possession (DIP) lenders, while out-of-court proceedings will have bondholder committees.

Other parties involved may include strategic buyers and private equity firms and hedge funds interested in acquiring distressed assets. They engage in the purchase, sale and trading of debt claims. This has become one of the biggest administrative components of Chapter 11 cases. A special committee set up by the board to oversee the restructuring may also be involved and, in instances of 'gross mismanagement' by the company, a trustee is appointed to handle matters.

What lawyers do

Out-of-court restructuring for debtor

- Analyze the situation in order to determine the feasibility of staying out of bankruptcy. What's the problem? What caused it? How big is it? Will it result in a default that is uncontrollable? Who's in the creditor body? Are they secured or unsecured? What's the litigation status? What's the liquidity status? Are there sufficient funds to stay in business while being restructured?
- Work with financial advisers to create a model of how the crisis will be dealt with.
- Negotiate with creditors and try convincing them that the problem is best solved out of bankruptcy.
- If negotiations are successful, work out payment plans for each creditor.
- If not successful, file for Chapter 11.

Court-supervised restructuring for debtor

- Initiate a Chapter 11 case to pursue restructuring within the protective provisions of the Bankruptcy Code (usually known as 'filing for Chapter 11').
- Prevent stigmatization of employees and business operations. Create a detailed communication plan to

include regulators, shareholders, employees, vendors and clients. *"Entry into Chapter 11 should be made as smooth and unruffled as possible,"* says **Davis Polk**'s insolvency and restructuring group co-head **Marshall Huebner**.

- Secure financing. *"Without liquidity to pay the bills, all is for naught,"* Huebner explains.
- Once liquidity is secured, work with the management team and financial advisers to decide what's core and non-core to the business. Establish the company's new vision.
- Build creditor consensus around the chosen exit strategy. This can be a lengthy process and require delicate negotiations.
- If creditors think they are being economically harmed, there could be extensive litigation.
- Document and effectuate the eventual agreement.

Realities of the job

- *"You need to be psychologically ready to handle the stress and strain inherent in being involved in a practice in which, by definition, there are huge amounts of failure,"* says **James Sprayregen** of **Kirkland & Ellis**.
- **Jonathan Henes** of **Kirkland & Ellis** sets out the skills needed by junior associates: *"In the early years the focus needs to be on strong writing skills and learning how to be a strong oral advocate whether in negotiations or in court. As you get more senior, you need to also focus on the commercial aspects of the restructuring and become a counselor to clients."*
- Henes highlights the attraction of the bankruptcy practice as being *"helping companies go from a place of trauma to a place of strength – that is a powerful thing."*
- This area is renowned for being particularly suited to those keen to get involved in the client side of things. Henes explains that you need *"good judgment to thrive because these are hard situations not just intellectually but emotionally. You need to be focused on the human aspect of it all."*
- The extent to which transactional work and litigation cross paths during a restructuring cannot be overstated. *"There is a transactional aspect even when in court. You litigate by day and negotiate by night,"* Bernstein describes.
- The nature of cases can vary enormously. Sprayregen adds: *"Our work involves dozens of industries and that really does give you the opportunity to learn a lot."*
- Debtors face innumerable difficulties. They have no political muscle, whereas creditors do – and flex it. Though bankruptcy laws are constantly amended, they continue to favor creditors.
- In order to lead such a diverse group of parties to a consensus, debtor attorneys must possess strategic, tactical and managerial skills.
- Steering clients clear of Chapter 11 through out-of-

court restructuring often requires a creative and innovative approach.

- The current Chapter 11 was passed in 1978, but it comes from Chapter X, which was passed in the 1930s. *"The Bankruptcy Code has its roots in the Great Depression,"* Bernstein says.
- Chapter 15 is the provision for cross-border bankruptcies that dictates proceedings in the USA when the main proceeding is in another country. Designed to ensure that all creditors and debtors are treated fairly irrespective of jurisdiction, it may also involve Chapter 11 proceedings if the debtor's assets are sufficiently complex.
- Restructuring is a lengthy process that requires a considerable amount of work before an outcome can be reached. *"There are so many different stakeholders and other components, and you spend a lot of time on the process itself – which I didn't expect as a young associate,"* Sprayregen tells us.
- Bankruptcy and restructuring is considered a countercyclical practice. When the market is healthy, bankruptcy attorneys may find themselves working on more diverse corporate matters.
- Negotiating terms for debtors in possession is a complicated balancing act. Attorneys must assess liens or security interests, prioritize creditors, determine the value of secured properties and argue for or against continued possession of secured properties in order to remain operating to better pay off creditors.
- Lenders' needs have to be attended to carefully, Huebner explains, because *"very frequently if lenders have a vested interest in a company, they're the ones who will get wiped out; more typical than not they become Chapter 11 financiers."* As such financiers, lenders tend to impose very difficult and sometimes onerous terms on the debtor to stimulate sales and liquidations.
- Sprayregen notes that, *"ultimately, the most successful cases will be the ones that are the least problematic. Those cases are less interesting from the media's perspective, but that's when you really see success."*
- **Ira Dizengoff** of **Akin Gump** describes how bankruptcy is a very fast-paced area of the law: *"The nature of the companies that undergo reorganizations means you will see more cross-border restructuring which adds to the complexity. You are at the cutting edge and it moves quickly – there is never a dull moment."*

> *"You need to be psychologically ready to handle the stress and strain inherent in being involved in a practice in which, by definition, there are huge amounts of failure."*

Practice Areas

Current issues

- While the recession brought about a significant rise in bankruptcy filings in the USA, this has since been decreasing. The American Bankruptcy Institute calculates that total bankruptcies remain on track for under 800,000 in 2016 which sets it at the second-lowest totally since BAPCPA [Bankruptcy Abuse Prevention and Consumer Protection Act] was implemented in 2005.

- There is, however, a general trend of commercial filings marginally increasing over recent years with total US commercial bankruptcy filings increasing by 26% in November 2016 compared to November 2015 making it the thirteenth consecutive month with an increase.

- With e-commerce booming a trend of large retail liquidations is set to increase. The American retail landscape is significantly overstored and this pressure is causing the trend of liquidation, rather than reorganization, for large retail debtors to take hold.

- The number of oil and gas company bankruptcies continues to dramatically increase. Haynes and Boone has tracked 105 North American oil and gas producers that have filed for bankruptcy since the beginning of 2015 through to the end of 2016. These bankruptcies, including Chapter 7, Chapter 11, Chapter 15, and Canadian cases, involve approximately $67.9 billion in cumulative secured and unsecured debt. Following the decision by OPEC members and other countries to cut production it is predicted that the oil price will marginally increase in 2017 but the future for many oil and gas producers still remains uncertain.

- Following the appointment of Donald Trump and his policy agenda involving big tax cuts and new infrastructure spending, higher interest are likely to be on the way. A higher interest rate environment leads of variable rates in loans and therefore to more bankruptcies and more restructuring.

- Traditional Chapter 11 bankruptcy is already an expensive and lengthy process, which companies try to avoid, but recently it's been rumored to have become even more costly. The Wall Street Journal reviewed numerous bankruptcy filings to report on rising legal fees at top US firms, discovering that partner rates are reaching $1,500 per hour. Bankruptcy is known to be expensive because the stakes are so high and the work lawyers do is of vital importance to clients in dire straits.

- In the news recently: American Apparel has had a turbulent couple of years following a number of scandals and has now filed for bankruptcy for the second time. The retailer has received approval in court to use the rest of its $30 million bankruptcy loan after the retailer resolved issues with its unsecured creditors.

Rankings in *Chambers USA*

Top ranked

Akin Gump	King & Spalding
Alston & Bird	Kirkland & Ellis
Arnold & Porter	Milbank, Tweed, Hadley
Brown Rudnick	Mintz Levin
Davis Polk & Wardwell	Norton Rose Fulbright
Greenberg Traurig	Paul, Weiss
Haynes and Boone	Perkins Coie
Hunton & Williams	Reed Smith
Jones Day	Vinson & Elkins
K&L Gates	

Highly recommended

Baker Botts	Latham & Watkins
Bracewell	Mayer Brown
Choate Hall & Stewart	Morgan, Lewis & Bockius
Cleary Gottlieb	MoFo
Debevoise & Plimpton	O'Melveny & Myers
Dechert	Orrick
DLA Piper	Paul Hastings
Duane Morris	Proskauer Rose
Dykema Gossett	Ropes & Gray
Foley & Lardner	Schulte Roth & Zabel
Fox Rothschild	Sheppard, Mullin, Richter
Gibbons	Sidley Austin
Gibson, Dunn & Crutcher	Simpson Thacher
Goodwin	Skadden
Goulston & Storrs	Squire Patton Boggs
Hangley Aronchick Segal	Stroock & Stroock
Holland & Knight	Thompson & Knight
Hughes Hubbard & Reed	Vedder Price
Irell & Manella	Venable
Jackson Walker	Weil
Jenner & Block	White & Case
Kasowitz Benson Torres	Willkie Farr & Gallagher
Katten Muchin	WilmerHale
Kilpatrick Townsend	Winston & Strawn
Kramer Levin Naftalis	

For more detail on ranking tiers and locations, visit www.chambersandpartners.com

"It's definitely a 'learn on the job' type of practice. In essence, you get an MBA on the job."

Capital Markets

In a nutshell

Capital markets lawyers feel all the highs and lows of market forces more than any other practitioner, and when the Great Recession hit the practice went under too. However, the vast sums exchanged and the technicality of the transactions mean that it will always remain an important area for BigLaw firms. Essentially, the world's capital markets are trading floors (either real or virtual) on which cash-hungry businesses obtain funding by selling a share of their business (equity) or receiving a loan (debt) from lenders.

These 'markets' are used by companies with unique financing needs which traditional bank loans cannot satisfy. They offer more freedom to companies than obtaining cash via bank loans, which tie both parties into the term of the loan. Capital markets allow for companies to obtain massive sums with more flexibility; they also offer up limitless investment opportunities. Large financial institutions offer customized services to companies seeking funding on the capital markets. These services include advice on debt and equity offerings, on securitization and on the creation of derivatives. Debt (bonds), equity (stocks) and derivatives are all types of security, and capital markets law is sometimes referred to as 'securities law'.

> *"The range of capital raising companies pursue is almost endless, and is limited only by human creativity."*

Attorneys advise companies ('issuers') and investment banks ('underwriters') on these complex capital markets transactions. Issuer and underwriter will both engage a separate law firm. The issuer's attorneys will sometimes help their client analyze which type of security to issue. This decision depends on the nature of the company, the desired duration of the loan, who the buyers are likely to be, and market demand. If an issuer is new to the market, they may begin by seeking their lawyers' advice on the processes involved, before approaching an underwriter.

Equity capital markets

Within equity, there are initial public offerings (IPOs) and follow-on offerings of common and preferred stock. An IPO is a transformational event for a company. *"The IPO is the 'ne plus ultra' of capital markets work,"* says **Josh Bonnie**, capital markets partner at **Simpson Thacher**. *"The decision of whether or not to become a public company is incredibly commercial and requires a great deal of strategy. It's unlikely the client will have IPO experience,*

so they will be reliant on their attorneys." The New York Stock Exchange and NASDAQ are the major exchanges in the US and most American public companies will be listed on one of them. Companies can list on multiple exchanges around the world.

Debt capital markets

This covers many types of debt instrument, but generally speaking it deals with a borrower raising capital by selling tradable bonds to investors, who expect the full amount lent to be paid back to them with interest. Bonds (also called 'notes') come in all shapes and sizes, from investment grade to high-yield ('junk') bonds. The terms of the bond – including the interest rate (or 'coupon') and maturity date – are decided on by the underwriter and issuer.

Why would a company issue bonds rather than take out a bank loan? As mentioned above, the terms of a bank loan can be restrictive to both parties: bank debt can prevent companies from making equity or debt issuances or from acquiring other companies until the loan is paid off. The terms of a bilateral loan tie both parties in, so a bank can't transfer risk or sell this debt with the same flexibility that the bonds market allows. Bonds are tradable; risk and its rewards can be sold on and spread across numerous lenders (bondholders), meaning that a company can raise much larger sums that can only be matched by arranging a syndicated loan (a group of banks chipping in on the principal), but without the same bank loan obligations that syndications entail. Plus bondholders can be anyone, not just a bank.

Structured finance and securitization

This can get gloriously complex, but its aims are simple: to increase liquidity and structure risk, which in turn offers up extra funding for borrowers. Securitization is the core of the process, which takes a lowly untradable piece of debt, such as a mortgage, vehicle loan or a credit card receivable, bundles it together with debt of the same class, and sells the bundle of debt on to investors, such as pension funds, hungry for the cash flows that come with the debt.

To securitize debt a bank will first set up a special-purpose entity (SPE) to isolate the debt risk from the bank's main operations, and separate the legal rights to the debt, enabling it to be transferred to new holders. Within the SPE are the bundled loans which enable the SPE to issue bonds, where the interest on the bundled debt forms the cash flows or bond yields. Mortgage securities like residential mortgage-backed securities (RMBS) and commercial mortgage-backed securities (CMBS) are among the most common in the market, but *"the range of capital raising companies pursue is almost endless, and is limited only by human creativity,"* says **Josh Bonnie** of **Simpson Thacher**. Collateralized debt obligations (CDOs) are a unique structure in that they group a variety of types of debt and credit risk, where different classes are called 'tranches', and the higher the tranche's risk, the greater the yield.

Securitization shouldered much of the blame for the credit crunch and the ensuing global economic havoc. Complicated structures led to a murky tangle of debt obligations, grouping different debt classes and exploiting credit enhancement. All was rosy until the housing bubble burst, mortgages defaulted and the ugly truth emerged. Don't let this put you off; there still is and will be demand for structured finance lawyers, but the order of the day is caution. For a leisurely introduction to the topic, watch *The Big Short*.

Derivatives

At its most basic, a derivative is a financial instrument used by banks and businesses to hedge risks to which they are exposed due to factors outside of their control. They can also be used for speculative purposes by betting on the fluctuation of just about anything, from currency exchange rates to the number of sunny days in a particular region. The value of a derivative at any given time is derived from the value of an underlying asset, security or index. Futures, forwards, options and swaps are the most common types of derivatives. **Forwards** are agreements between two parties that one will buy a certain product from the other for a fixed price at a fixed date in the future. Hedging against future price risks and speculation over the price movement of the underlying assets are the big attractions. **Futures** are standardized forwards, which can be traded on the futures market. **Options** are optional futures, where a buyer has the right but not the obligation to purchase or sell a product at a certain date in the future for a certain price. **Swaps** are agreements between two parties to exchange assets at a fixed rate, for example to protect against fluctuations in currency exchange rates.

What lawyers do

IPO or other equity offering

- Work with the client and its accounting firm to prepare and file a registration statement with the Securities and Exchange Commission (SEC).
- Do due diligence on the issuer company and draft a prospectus (as part of the registration statement) that provides a welter of information about the company and its finances, as well as past financial statements.

- Help the accountants draft a comfort letter, assuring the financial soundness of the issuer.
- File with the SEC and wait 30 days before getting initial comments from them.
- Undergo multiple rounds of commentary back and forth with the SEC. This can take one or two months.
- Negotiate approval of a listing on the stock exchange. This involves the submission of documentation, certifications and letters that prove the client satisfies the listing requirements.
- Finalize the underwriting agreement and other documentation.

Debt offering

- Plan out the deal with issuer and underwriter. A timeline is drawn up and tasks are allocated between the different parties.
- Draft a prospectus for SEC registration or a Rule 144A offering memorandum.
- Conduct due diligence on the issuer to examine its creditworthiness, make the disclosure accurate and highlight any associated risks.
- Deliver to the underwriters at closing a legal opinion and a disclosure letter on the offering based on due diligence.
- Draft the indenture: a document describing the bond's interest rate, maturity date, convertibility and so on.
- Draft the purchase (or 'underwriting') agreement.

Securitization

- Work with the underwriter and issuer to draw up the structure of a security, and help the parties negotiate the terms of that structure. *"We will literally sit down with all the parties and draw boxes, charts and arrows on a whiteboard in order to come up with new ideas,"* explains **John Arnholz**, structured finance transactions partner at **Morgan, Lewis & Bockius**
- Draft the disclosure document and the prospectus or private placement memorandum. *"It is a descriptive piece – almost like a magazine article,"* says John Arnholz. *"It covers all the risks and other characteristics of owning a security."*
- Draft the purchase agreement documenting the transaction. *"This involves a lot of negotiation back and forth between issuer, underwriter, trustees, service providers and insurers,"* says John Arnholz.

Derivatives

- Be approached by a financial institution client (e.g. a hedge fund) with an idea to create a new derivatives product.
- Communicate back and forth with the client discussing legal issues and risks related to various possible

Practice Areas

structures for the product.

- Home in on a specific structure for the product.
- Prepare a memo explaining the problems, issues and legal risks associated with the derivative's agreed-upon structure, as well as suggesting ways to resolve or mitigate those problems and issues.
- If all has gone well, and if the new structure has sufficient prospects for legal and commercial success, lawyers will draft new documentation describing the make-up of the derivative.

Realities of the job

- Notwithstanding the differences mentioned in the descriptions above, there are big similarities between the work of lawyers on debt, equity and other securities transactions.
- The nature of lawyers' involvement in a capital markets transaction depends on its novelty. *"If someone is doing a securitization or designing a derivatives product they must address those issues which are novel,"* says **Josh Cohn**, head of US derivatives and structured products at **Mayer Brown**. *"If you are working on a product based on a preexisting structure, you may be asked to look at certain details like new swaps arrangements."*
- Junior lawyers usually practice in all areas of capital markets law, sometimes combining this with other corporate work too. Some top firms have specialist departments for each capital markets subgroup. Partners often specialize in debt, equity, securitization or derivatives work, but they may continue to dabble in other areas too. Junior associates should therefore aim to get involved with as many different types of transactions as possible to maximize experience and develop preferences.

> *"It may sound odd, but companies do have their own personality, so it's akin to meeting a new person each time."*

- Clients in the world of finance are incredibly demanding and attorneys usually work very long hours. On the plus side, clients are also smart, sophisticated and dynamic. Large law firms usually have strong and close relationships with investment bank clients, meaning that juniors can get frequent client contact. *"I love working with companies' management teams and with bankers,"* says **Arthur Robinson**, head of the capital markets practice at **Simpson Thacher**. *"On each deal I do I 'meet' a new company and learn about the business from the inside from the CEO and CFO. It may sound odd, but companies do have their own personality, so it's akin to meeting a new person each time."*
- The content and organization of prospectuses tends to be fairly standard, but lawyers consider working on

them a rewarding exercise because a good deal of creative writing is required to communicate a company's narrative.

- The purchase agreement is a lengthy contract in which the underwriter agrees to buy the securities and resell them to investors.

- As soon as a company undergoes an IPO, it will be subject to all the rules and requirements of a public company, so the necessary organizational structure must be in place before the IPO.
- Follow-on offerings of common equity are much simpler than an IPO because most of the basic disclosure has already been drafted and will only need to be updated.
- Underwriters' counsel draft most documents related to a bond issue. An issuer's lawyers will comment on them and negotiate changes.
- Due diligence is conducted by both underwriter's and issuer's counsel, but is most important to the underwriter. A due diligence investigation may help in establishing a 'due diligence defense' in any future investor lawsuits claiming a violation of securities laws.
- A debt offering can be registered with the SEC or unregistered under Rule 144A of the 1933 Securities Act. In the latter case bonds can only be bought by certain large registered institutional buyers.
- Issuers' and underwriters' counsel work together with a team of bankers, accountants, insurers and an issuer's management to get securities issued. *"There is a very collaborative atmosphere,"* says **Bill Whelan**, corporate partner at **Cravath, Swaine & Moore**. *"The team has the common goal of getting the deal done. There are moments when we have disagreements, but rarely does it get acrimonious."* If teams get on particularly well, deals may end with a closing dinner or drinks event.
- The bond market is huge and influential. It is generally considered to have a large influence on the health of the US and global economy.
- Market conditions are very important to the success of capital market deals – more important even than the willingness of the parties to get the deal done. *"The one negative in this area of practice is that the markets are always unpredictable,"* says Bill Whelan of Cravath, Swaine & Moore. *"You can invest a lot of time in getting a deal organized, but market conditions can mean it falls through."*
- Practitioners recommend that those interested in the field should take law school classes in securities regulation, corporate finance and the Uniform Commercial Code (UCC). Knowledge of bankruptcy, property and tax law is useful too, as is gaining an understanding of the basic principles of accounting. Reading the financial press – starting with The Wall Street Journal – is a must.

Current issues

- Global IPOs fell 16% by number and 33% by capital raised in 2016, according to EY Global IPO Trends. There were fewer deals and fewer megadeals – attributed to political uncertainty of US presidential election, the UK's Brexit vote, Middle East conflicts and the EU migrant crisis, among other world events.
- Many IPO candidates decided to wait until 2017, and the result is a busy start to the year.
- In the US there were 105 deals in 2016 – the lowest number since 2009 (in 2015 there were 170 and 275 in 2014). Proceeds raised were $18.8 billion in 2015 compared to $30 billion in 2015 (and $85.3 billion in 2014). Source: Renaissance Capital US IPO Market
- The Dow Jones Industrial Average has risen by approximately 10% since the election of Donald Trump and hit a record 21,000 points in March 2017. The increase has been attributed in part to a 'Trump bump', including anticipated regulatory cuts like the rolling back of Dodd-Frank.
- March 2017 saw the headline-grabbing $24 billion IPO of Snapchat, one of several high profile expected tech IPOs in 2017 (other hotly anticipated IPOs include Uber and Airbnb).
- A big development in Europe, meanwhile, is the European Commission's proposed 'Capital Markets Union' (CMU) – which aims to remove barriers to investment in Europe. The UK's Brexit has put a spanner in the works somewhat, although the CMU appears to be going ahead.
- The Federal Reserve raised interest rates to 1% in March 2017 and expects to raise them to 1.5% during the year, to 2% in 2018 and 3% in 2019. Rates had been at 0% from 2008 until December 2015. Rates before the economic crisis were 4%-5%.
- According to the Goldman Sachs outlook report for 2017, global growth will be at the top end of the 3%-3.5% range experienced in the last five years, thanks to an improving US economy and emerging markets.
- Economists predict an upward trend in inflation rates in the USA, Europe and Japan in the coming months. This could mean that inflation-linked securities might become an essential part of investment portfolios.
- *"Securities law is changing dramatically,"* John Arnholz of Morgan, Lewis & Bockius comments. *"In the old days, rules about securities weren't written down. They were based on lore. Many regulations in the industry are new. That means old hands like me have a smaller advantage over new people entering the field than we used to. Industrious young associates can learn about new regulations and outsmart the partners!"*
- John Arnholz adds that *"for young associates eager to get client contact, no practice area provides more of an opportunity to work directly with clients."*

Rankings in *Chambers USA*

Top ranked

Akin Gump	King & Spalding
Alston & Bird	Kirkland & Ellis
Arnold & Porter	Milbank, Tweed, Hadley
Brown Rudnick	Mintz Levin
Davis Polk & Wardwell	Norton Rose Fulbright
Greenberg Traurig	Paul, Weiss
Haynes and Boone	Perkins Coie
Hunton & Williams	Reed Smith
Jones Day	Vinson & Elkins
K&L Gates	

Highly recommended

Baker Botts	Latham & Watkins
Bracewell	Mayer Brown
Choate Hall & Stewart	Morgan, Lewis & Bockius
Cleary Gottlieb	MoFo
Debevoise & Plimpton	O'Melveny & Myers
Dechert	Orrick
DLA Piper	Paul Hastings
Duane Morris	Proskauer Rose
Dykema Gossett	Ropes & Gray
Foley & Lardner	Schulte Roth & Zabel
Fox Rothschild	Sheppard, Mullin, Richter
Gibbons.	Sidley Austin
Gibson, Dunn & Crutcher	Simpson Thacher
Goodwin	Skadden
Goulston & Storrs	Squire Patton Boggs
Hangley Aronchick Segal	Stroock & Stroock
Holland & Knight	Thompson & Knight
Hughes Hubbard & Reed	Vedder Price
Irell & Manella	Venable
Jackson Walker	Weil
Jenner & Block	White & Case
Kasowitz Benson Torres	Willkie Farr & Gallagher
Katten Muchin	WilmerHale
Kilpatrick Townsend	Winston & Strawn
Kramer Levin Naftalis	

For more detail on ranking tiers and locations, visit www.chambersandpartners.com

Life in Corporate Finance, by Cahill Gordon & Reindel

Legal trends and business climate

Whether a company is a startup, needs acquisition financing, is looking to raise capital in an IPO or private equity transaction, is the subject of a leveraged buyout by a private equity fund, or simply wants to refinance existing debt at lower interest rates, the financing needs of companies of all sizes and across all sectors will involve the input of legal specialists in corporate finance.

Many of the most complex, interesting, and creative financing situations involve companies with lower credit ratings, or significant other debt already on their balance sheets, known as 'leveraged' finance scenarios. A major focus of corporate finance is helping clients – whether they are borrowers or financial institutions acting as arrangers, lenders or underwriters – design and negotiate creative leveraged financing structures and terms.

Flexibility is important. Companies looking for financing solutions have a broad array of products to choose from, any of which may be more or less desirable at a given moment due to market forces, current political events, strength of the company's own projected business profile, the company's corporate structure, and other pre-existing indebtedness. While historically there were two separate and distinct sources of funding in these scenarios – traditional bank lenders providing secured senior debt on the one hand, versus a broader market of investment funds, CLOs, hedge funds and others playing for high returns in the capital markets, often through unsecured or subordinated bonds – these two markets, while still distinct in terms of legal process and deal execution, now see many crossover investors.

Ever-changing lending regulations have opened up new opportunities for non-traditional sources of funds to enter the lending market, particularly following the recession. Innovative non-traditional products such as covenant-lite loans and second lien loans and bonds have become common as ideas and concepts from one product are adopted into another. With this confluence of funding sources and investor requirements, it is important to be agile enough to discuss all alternatives with clients and understand the considerations required in choosing a financing path (or creating a new one!).

Corporate finance is a collaborative practice, even with the parties 'across the table'. The interests of funding sources and those of issuers or borrowers will not be aligned completely, but all of the parties to each transaction are interested in generating a solution that brings each of the parties what they need. Financing sources and borrowers look to their legal advisers to help them structure increasingly creative options that work for all parties on a long-term basis in the face of challenging and potentially volatile financial environments.

'With multinational corporations and private equity investment becoming more global in nature, pressure grows to expand traditional lending structures to include new locations in creative cross-border financings.'

Keeping abreast of market trends and financing considerations is a must in this dynamic environment. Because both the capital markets and the leveraged lending worlds are subject to significant fluctuation based on a number of factors – including everything from recent case law involving financings, collateral security, and bankruptcies, to the global political and regulatory environment – the 'best' answer for a client in a given scenario can change at any time. Recent developments may require new investor risk protections on any given transaction, or may dictate that companies in a specific sector or geopolitical area will be viewed as more or less stable. Our depth of market knowledge allows us to help clients structure creative solutions to complex situations while understanding the parameters of what investors will require, whether during a peak or a trough moment in the financial markets.

In addition, the practice of corporate finance requires a global view. As markets of the world previously viewed as unstable or less legally mature begin to evolve and set up legal structures that allow them to be seen as viable jurisdictions for investment, the complexity of transaction structures and the volume of financing alternatives increases. With multinational corporations and private equity investment becoming more global in nature, pressure grows to expand traditional lending structures to include new locations in creative cross-border financings. Corporate finance lawyers are often called upon to find balance between allowing an issuer or borrower to capitalize on its assets on a more global basis, while maintaining the integrity of the investors' risk.

The life of a junior corporate finance associate

Corporate finance associates act as the "hub" of the transaction wheel. In order to be sure a financing is ex-

Practice Areas

ecuted efficiently and properly, he or she will coordinate with experts in other areas relevant to the transaction, including bankruptcy attorneys where there are questions of enforcement or protection in a "worst-case" scenario, tax attorneys involved in structuring the issuance or loan on a cost-efficient basis, real estate and environmental attorneys where real property will be taken as collateral, and litigators involved to evaluate various risks existing at an issuer or potentially created by a financing.

Corporate finance associates work directly with clients; junior members of the client team are similarly involved which affords the opportunity to develop long-term client relationships in the process.

Corporate finance associates at all levels are crucial to the drafting of disclosure documents for securities offerings, and junior associates often are the real "experts" on the issuer, having conducted much of the due diligence evaluating the company's operations and business, through review of corporate documents and material contracts, discussions with management, and on-site visits.

Corporate finance associates will be involved in drafting contracts from a very early stage in their careers, and will participate in the negotiation and documentation of final deal terms on an increasing basis as they become more familiar with market terms and client desires.

Junior corporate finance associates serve as "masters of ceremonies" as a financing transaction reaches conclusion. Particularly on a transaction involving secured debt, many documents will have to be executed, certifications delivered, and filings made — and the junior associates will be tasked with verifying all is done properly in order to ensure the business deal is reflected accurately and security has been granted properly.

Suggested coursework for a future corporate finance attorney

Junior corporate finance attorneys may find it helpful to complete a basic accounting or finance course, preferably at the business school affiliated with their law school. Learning the language and fundamental elements of these disciplines provides one with a foundation upon which to set the day-to-day experiences as a corporate finance lawyer.

'Courses in securities regulation, secured transactions, contract negotiation and drafting all prove helpful after law school graduation.'

For capital markets transactions, aspects of the US securities laws, including SEC rules and guidelines and general disclosure issues, are central to the work we do. On transactions involving leveraged lending, knowledge of the regulatory landscape, creditors' rights and Uniform Commercial Code matters all play a primary role. Courses in securities regulation, secured transactions, contract negotiation and drafting all prove helpful after law school graduation.

Because corporate finance associates bring together expertise from specialists in other relevant areas, a basic familiarity with related areas such as M&A, corporate tax, bankruptcy or real property law is beneficial in helping round out an associate's skill set and foster an appreciation of the 'bigger picture' surrounding a finance transaction.

About Cahill Gordon & Reindel LLP

Cahill has a prominent global corporate finance practice operating from New York and London. In 2015, it was ranked #1 by Bloomberg for representing investment banks in the over $250 billion (2015) US corporate high yield debt markets and #1 by Thomson Reuters for representing lenders and arrangers in the over $900 billion (2015) US corporate leveraged (i.e. non-investment grade) syndicated loan markets.

Author

Jennifer Ezring

Jennifer B. Ezring is a partner in Cahill's corporate practice. She advises commercial and investment banks in leveraged finance transactions, including acquisition financings, leveraged buyouts, going-private transactions, recapitalizations, project financings, bridge lending and loan commitments, out-of-court debt restructurings, exit facilities and other secured lending transactions. Jennifer has practiced in a variety of industries, including gaming, energy, manufacturing, media, and internet technology. She has a broad range of financing experience in both US and international transactions. Jennifer received her BA from Princeton University and her JD from NYU.

CAHILL

Practice Areas

Climate Change and Renewable Energy

In a nutshell

Climate change attorneys advise on four core aspects of law. Transactional advice is the most common aspect, and mainly involves negotiating carbon-related deals (such as carbon credits or projects to reduce carbon emissions, most of which have international dimensions). Next up is litigation; it involves challenging climate change rules, regulations and laws, as well as defining the boundaries of the law. Regulatory advice is a growing area, due to the increasing number of climate change regulations being issued. Companies are therefore relying on lawyers more than ever to ensure that their activities are compliant with the latest regulations. Failure to comply leads us to the final aspect, enforcement, which is also rising in prominence as the body of regulations expands.

> *"You have a role to play in solving some of the world's most important problems. A lot of the industry focuses on making sure developing parts of the country and the world provide people with reliable and affordable energy in as clean a way as possible."*
>
> – Partner, Sidley Austin

What lawyers do

- Climate change and renewable energy practices attract a broad client base, which can be split into three categories: environmental groups, government groups, and corporations.
- Companies seek advice on reducing their carbon footprint, as well as broader issues such as employment, IP and finance. As a result, it's also important to have a good working knowledge of other legal areas, such as general corporate law, M&A and tax.
- What lawyers focus on depends on their location. Washington, DC, for example, is at the heart of federal climate change regulation, so lawyers here are most likely to be involved in policy drafting. A practitioner in Texas, on the other hand, is more likely to spend their time advising fossil fuel companies on regulatory compliance. Renewable energy work, meanwhile, is mostly concentrated around large cities such as New York, DC, Chicago and San Francisco.
- Geographical connections also play a part in determining the scope of matters. For example, a lawyer based in California is more likely to be working with Asia on international deals than one in New York. Head to

a regional firm if the scope you're after is smaller and more localized: firms in cities like Oklahoma City attract energy work but aren't known as 'practice area hubs' in the same way San Francisco and DC are.
- Associates tend to do a lot of hands-on work to gain expertise in areas that are still developing. **Roger-Martella**, who was until recently environment practice head and climate change expert at Sidley Austin, explains: *"This is a rapidly growing practice and constantly evolving, so my associates are becoming experts in areas that will become more mainstream within a few years. We are preparing them for what we see as an inevitability on these issues."*

Realities of the job

- Climate change is a niche area, so it's unlikely that you'll be able to specialize full-time in it. Many lawyers specialize in a broader practice area – such as energy, environment, international law or litigation – and then work on climate change matters as part of their portfolio.
- Advising environmental organizations and government bodies may be your ultimate goal in this area, but the reality is that most of the work involves assisting corporations with climate change compliance.

> *"I think the work is very intellectually stimulating, as it touches on so many different aspects of the law: tax, policy, bankruptcy, finance and many more. The work is not monotonous and every day brings something different."*
>
> – Todd Alexander, Norton Rose Fulbright

- As the body of climate change law is comparatively small, knowledge can be built up quite quickly. However, it is also important to be have some technical knowledge, so science and engineering degrees can be particularly useful in this respect.
- In terms of approach, being able to adapt to a client's style is important, as Todd Alexander of Norton Rose Fulbright explains: *"Some clients like a harsh, direct and pushy person, while others prefer someone conciliatory and facilitating. It depends on the client and situation."*
- One of the most rewarding aspects of the work is that it affects a large number of people, says Martella: *"You have a role to play in solving some the world's most im-*

portant problems. A lot of the industry focuses on making sure developing parts of the country and the world provide people with reliable and affordable energy in as clean a way as possible. There is a social justice aspect to this."

- On the transactional side, no deal is like the last, as Alexander reveals: "*It is hard to create standardization because every deal is so unique. It is interesting and challenging, as you have no form to follow on a daily basis; each deal requires separate analysis and negotiation, so intellectually it is very rewarding as you are constantly challenged and learning.*"

- This strand of work often involves international deals and a lot of travel. Although that may sound glamorous, the reality is that extensive travel is exhausting, and you may need to get used to working while jet lagged. As is the nature of transactional work, schedules can be unpredictable and demanding, so Alexander tells us that it's important to have a passion for the area: "*If you try to force yourself to go into this and you are not happy to make the sacrifices needed it won't be worth it. You have to find what the right balance is for you.*"

- Climate change is also a highly contentious practice area, as new regulations are likely to be challenged both by those who think they go too far and by those who think they do not go far enough. Martella explains that as a litigator in the field it's important to detach oneself emotionally from the issues at hand: "*This is perhaps one of the most emotional and passionate areas of the law. On both sides people have very strong views which create clashes outside of the courtroom. The impact goes beyond just legal issues; there is a strong nexus between climate change law and controversies.*" A litigator must act in their client's interest, even if that goes against their personal views or ethics.

"This is perhaps one of the most emotional and passionate areas of the law."

Current issues

- Climate change is the subject of huge political debate at the moment, and the legislation that surrounds it has become increasingly complex. The recent focus has been on enacting measures within the energy sector, which has become increasingly intertwined with climate change from a regulatory perspective.
- The improvement in electric vehicles in recent years is likely to make them an increasingly prominent part of climate change discourse and action.

Rankings in *Chambers USA*

Top ranked

Hunton & Williams	Sidley Austin

Highly Recommended

Baker Botts	Hogan Lovells
Baker McKenzie	Kirkland & Ellis
Bracewell	Latham & Watkins
Crowell & Moring	Vinson & Elkins

For more detail on ranking tiers and locations, visit www.chambersandpartners.com

- The renewables market is experiencing record-breaking growth year-on-year. Solar energy is seen as the leader of the pack thanks to steadily decreasing solar installation costs, which have made it a highly competitive area of the market.
- Another major development in the renewable energy sector is the development of battery storage. This advance will go some way to tackle the difficulties posed by energy which has been produced from renewable sources.
- The current and future construction of transmission lines is important, as they will ensure that renewable energy plants are reliably connected to the grid and contribute to the power supply consistently.
- Global corporations such as Apple and Amazon are becoming increasingly interested in using and promoting renewable energy. They are now entering into purchasing contracts to buy energy directly from renewable energy producers, thereby helping these producers to operate more profitably.
- The Clean Power Plan shaped climate change legislation during the last few months of President Obama's administration. However, with Trump at the helm it's looking increasingly likely that the new administration will not follow this particular course of action. Expect a widespread re-evaluation of the previous administration's climate change and renewable energy policies.
- At an international level, the Paris Agreement demonstrates the shift in focus from carbon trading to policy making, although the extent to which this agreement will be implemented effectively by the signatories remains to be seen.
- Although it is yet to fully develop its presence on the market, China is seen as an emerging player, especially in connection with emissions trading.

Corporate/M&A

In a nutshell

Corporate is sometimes defined as a catchall practice area that includes everything that isn't litigation or tax. The higher you go in the BigLaw tree, however, the more corporate becomes synonymous with mergers and acquisitions (M&A) and corporate governance. Some big firms include capital markets and private equity under this umbrella, but these areas are so complex and distinct that *Chambers Associate* prefers to treat them separately.

This practice area can involve advising clients from cradle to grave: from starting up and going public, to raising capital, selling, acquiring and combining businesses, to looking at the overall framework for operations and advising the board of directors on special transactions. Typical M&A work involves advising on selling, combining and acquiring businesses. BigLaw firms often focus on **public M&A**, advising either the buyer or seller in a transaction involving a public company. This area of corporate law routinely provides the biggest deals, is often cross-border and can involve cash and/or stock considerations. **Private M&A** takes place between private companies and can also be multifaceted, particularly where partnerships are involved. M&A lawyers can act as transactional coordinators too, because for every takeover or disposal, there will be employment, antitrust or tax implications to consider.

Corporate governance involves advising companies on crucial board affairs (including director duties) and their relationships with shareholders, which are paramount during transactions or shareholder disputes.

What lawyers do
Public M&A for buyer
- Identify the client's business objectives.
- Identify the legal issues – these vary depending on factors like whether the deal is friendly or unfriendly.
- Build a 'road map' for the client from start to finish, and include a timeframe.
- Advise on deal and negotiating tactics.
- Conduct due diligence on other side.
- Determine – with the help of tax attorneys – the tax implications and if they require special structuring.
- Work with antitrust attorneys to assess regulatory obstacles, gain regulatory approval and analyze any other required regulatory approvals.
- If cross-border, work with local counsel. Review all the client's contracts: business, employment, outsourcing, debt instruments, preferred stock, etc.

- Obtain third-party consents from lenders or parties to other contracts.
- Negotiate agreement, sign, announce publicly, close the deal.
- Attorneys for the target decide whether to negotiate, refuse the buyer's overtures, sell, or do a deal with another company.

Realities of the job
- *"The most important thing for a corporate lawyer is to develop an understanding of what's most important to your client – what they are really trying to accomplish and what issues really matter to them and why,"* explains **Victor Lewkow** of **Cleary Gottlieb Steen & Hamilton**.
- **Robert Townsend** of **Cravath, Swaine & Moore** highlights some of the characteristics common of those working in corporate/M&A, which include being *"driven and motivated to maintain a high level of quality. You need to be intellectually curious in order to identify issues, but also practical so that you can figure out how to best solve those issues – that's where we add value."*
- An M&A transaction can have *"a whole laundry list of tactics to choose from and issues to consider, depending upon what side you're on,"* says **Alison Ressler** of **Sullivan & Cromwell**, meaning that no two deals are exactly the same. Similarly, each deal will have a unique life cycle and so some will naturally take longer to complete than others.
- A key part of M&A work is explaining issues in a way that makes sense to the client. *"Lawyers often use enormous amounts of jargon, with great expertise and complexity, which is not necessarily helpful for the business people involved,"* Lewkow tells us. He adds: *"Often there is no perfect answer, so some of the time you'll be helping the client figure out what the least 'bad' alternative is."*
- Townsend adds: *"You need to have the ability to articulate your position in a way that is clear and concise so that a business person can understand. It is also important to listen carefully to what your client and the other side are saying in negotiations in order to know how to modify your strategy accordingly."*
- Due diligence will largely fall to associates and, though it can be tedious, it's crucial for attorneys to understand what's in the documents. *"Law students tend to think of us as just reading and marking up documents, but a key characteristic of a top corporate lawyer is the ability to negotiate and construct arguments on your feet,"* states Ressler.

- Delaware, where many corporations are incorporated, has among the most pronounced and expansive laws on the duties of the board and rules concerning special committees, which have tremendous implications for M&A transactions and corporate governance work. Lewkow confirms: *"Many of the corporate law court decisions in Delaware influence how we address problems and generally go about structuring transactions."*
- Public companies, particularly those in the Fortune 500, are slick operations with considerable legal budgets and expertise, and usually need less hand-holding than smaller, less sophisticated clients.
- The high-pressure nature of the work is a result of *"not only having the chance to be involved in issues that are very important to your client, but also making a genuine difference to those issues,"* says **Adam Emmerich** of **Wachtell, Lipton, Rosen & Katz.**
- *"Many deals have a lot of moving pieces, whereby solving one problem could actually create another problem,"* according to Lewkow. *"What works well for IP purposes, for example, might not work well for tax purposes."*
- Clients often expect transactions to be completed in a matter of days, which can mean working 18-hour days and weekends. This expectation can create an atmosphere of cooperation and expediency among parties. *"You break down the walls between who's doing what, and just dive in and do it,"* **Josh Bonnie of Simpson Thacher & Bartlett** says.
- It also means that flexibility is key. *"Sometimes you may have a plan to go on holiday, then find out that you need to be on the spot and fully engaged,"* says Emmerich. However, this comes with the territory of it being *"a dynamic, interesting and exciting practice."*
- *"I don't think there is one style which makes you an excellent or effective M&A lawyer,"* explains **Louis Goldberg** of **Davis Polk & Wardwell.** He adds that at one end of the spectrum you have those who are *"thoughtful, determined and tactical,"* while at the other end there are the 'deal junkies': *"They have the charisma and love the ins and outs of the deal climate."*
- The broader category of corporate finance includes representing borrowers in lending transactions with banks, though most firms organize themselves so that the lawyers who advise the lenders and borrowers are part of the banking and finance team.

Rankings in *Chambers USA*

Top ranked

Alston & Bird	Kirkland & Ellis
Baker Botts	Latham & Watkins
Brownstein Hyatt Farber	Morgan, Lewis & Bockius
Cooley	MoFo
Cravath	Nixon Peabody
Davis Polk	Perkins Coie
Dechert	Reed Smith
DLA Piper	Ropes & Gray
Foley & Lardner	Sidley Austin
Gibson	Simpson Thacher
Goodwin	Skadden
Greenberg	Snell & Wilmer
Hogan Lovells	Squire Patton Boggs
Holland & Knight	Sullivan & Cromwell
Hunton & Williams	Venable LLP
Jones Day	Vinson & Elkins
K&L Gates	WilmerHale
King & Spalding	Wilson

Highly recommended

Akin Gump	Kramer Levin
Allen & Overy	Mayer Brown
Arnold & Porter	McDermott Will & Emery
Baker McKenzie	Milbank, Tweed
Bracewell	Mintz Levin
Cadwalader	Munger
Choate Hall	Norton Rose Fulbright
Cleary	Orrick
Clifford Chance	Paul Hastings
Cozen O'Connor	Paul, Weiss
Crowell & Moring	Pillsbury Winthrop Shaw
Debevoise & Plimpton	Pittman
Duane Morris	Proskauer Rose
Dykema Gossett	Schulte Roth & Zabel
Fox Rothschild	Seward & Kissel
Freshfields	Shearman & Sterling
Fried, Frank	Sheppard, Mullin
Gibbons	Thompson & Knight
Haynes and Boone	Vedder Price
Hughes Hubbard & Reed	Waller
Jackson Walker	Weil, Gotshal & Manges
Jenner & Block	White & Case
Katten Muchin Rosenman	Willkie Farr & Gallagher
Kilpatrick Townsend	Winston & Strawn

For more detail on ranking tiers and locations, visit
www.chambersandpartners.com

Top career tips

George Bason Jr, partner, **Davis Polk & Wardwell**:
"The key to it is that law is a service profession. I think all personality types are welcome, but having that availability and enthusiasm 24 hours a day, 365 days a year is very important – once you accept that as a base line it's a wonderful profession. And, with a few exceptions, clients treat their lawyers with respect and view them as a valued part of the team. It's such a human thing, but a lot of people lose sight of the fact that it's a service business."

Alison Ressler, partner, **Sullivan & Cromwell**:
"There are three primary courses that students who are interested in corporate law should take. Securities regulation is key – you need to understand securities law and what's involved in issuing securities. A general corporate law course explains the different forms of corporate entities and how federal and state regulations affect mergers. A business combinations or mergers class teaches the case law on mergers and the difference between hostile and friendly takeovers. Two key ancillary courses are corporate income tax and accounting for lawyers."

"The best thing law students can do in preparation is read the Financial Times *and* The Wall Street Journal *while in law school. Those papers will really give you a sense of what's happening in the business world."*

Adam Emmerich, partner, **Wachtell, Lipton, Rosen & Katz**:
"Like most things in life, if it's your passion and you find it engaging then it's relatively easy to do well. If you've gotten the idea that it sounds good on paper, or is remunerative or prestigious, that won't carry you through; you actually have to find it interesting."

Victor Lewkow, partner, **Cleary Gottlieb Steen & Hamilton**:
"I think what surprised me the most is how much I actually enjoy being a corporate lawyer. I had no background or experience in business, but quickly discovered that mergers and acquisitions was an interesting and challenging practice that I found fun – and still do."

Robert Townsend, partner, **Cravath, Swaine & Moore**:
"I think it's important not to be afraid to make mistakes. Think for yourself and don't rely on precedent. Be assertive in identifying issues and asking questions."

Practice Areas

"Despite all the thinking law firms do around hiring, most often it still depends on what school you went to, your GPA and whether you were on the journal. Those credentials are the given. Then, maybe the next most important thing is that you're a fully-formed adult. Law firms do want candidates with some maturity, and some experience."

- Jim Leipold, executive director of NALP

Skadden's lawyers lift the lid on life in M&A

Attorneys in our M&A practice advise clients on mergers, acquisitions, divestitures, spin-offs, proxy contests and joint ventures, as well as on strategic alternatives. Additionally, we advise clients on corporate governance, securities law and general corporate matters.

The practice represents a diverse array of US and international, public and private clients, including multinational corporations, emerging companies, private equity and hedge funds, individual investors, sovereign governments and other stakeholders. Clients often are undergoing fundamental changes in their strategy and business, and our M&A attorneys help them navigate this period of profound change.

Business Climate

While global M&A volume in 2016 declined from the record levels set in 2015, activity remained strong by historical standards. Global dollar value of deals was approximately $3.7 trillion, an annual total behind only 2015 and 2007. Dollar value of US transactions was approximately $1.7 trillion.

Market Drivers

Despite political and economic developments that caught many observers by surprise, M&A volume in 2016 was again dominated by two strategic forces: the need to grow revenues and earnings in a low-growth environment, and the need to be competitively positioned in the global marketplace. M&A has provided corporations a means to grow revenues faster than would be possible organically, and synergies resulting from transactions have yielded expanded margins and rapid earnings growth. Deal activity also allowed strategic players to enhance geographic or portfolio footprints and transformed some into industry disruptors through the acquisition of new technologies.

One noteworthy development was an increase in inbound US M&A activity to record levels. In 2016, inbound deal volume surpassed $500 billion, with significant activity coming from Canada, China and the UK. While there are numerous potential headwinds that may temper this this increased activity — robust asset prices, a strong dollar, the potential impact of changes in Chinese policies limiting foreign investment and concerns regarding the potential for growing economic nationalism — significant cross-border deal flows into the US appear likely to continue.

Hostile and Unsolicited Activity

Hostile and unsolicited M&A activity has continued to play a small but important role in the M&A market. In 2016, unsolicited transactions accounted for nearly $400 billion in global deal value. However, as in prior years, success by hostile offerors was far from universal. In 2016, several target companies successfully defended against unsolicited proposals without an alternative transaction being present. One notable example was the withdrawal by Canadian Pacific Railroad of its unsolicited offer for Norfolk Southern Company after Norfolk Southern determined that the value generated under its own strategic plan was higher than Canadian Pacific's proposal and that the proposed transaction was highly unlikely to receive regulatory approval.

Abandoned Transactions

2016 saw a number of large proposed transactions withdrawn after announcement, with more than $800 billion in deals withdrawn throughout the year, almost one-fifth of total transactions value announced over that period of time. Transactions were abandoned for a wide range of reasons and at various stages. Certain announced unsolicited offers never took flight due to the target's unwillingness to engage, while other signed deals ultimately were terminated as a result of shareholder dissatisfaction with the proposed terms, emergence of a topping bid or regulatory issues.

Several large pharmaceutical transactions were terminated following changes to tax regulations seeking to halt so-called "inversion" transactions, in which a US company would be acquired by a smaller foreign company effectively moving the home tax jurisdiction of the publicly traded parent out of the US. Several large transactions were abandoned in 2016 in the face of aggressive antitrust enforcement at the Department of Justice and the Federal Trade Commission, reflecting increased government willingness to litigate in order to enjoin, rather than accept proposed settlements in, transactions raising substantive antitrust issues.

Potential Impact of the Change in Administration on US M&A Activity

Equity markets to date have reacted favorably to the outcome of the presidential election and the expected changes to fiscal and regulatory policies. But speculation on the impact of the Trump administration on M&A activity remains precisely that — speculation. However, likely policy changes could result in a meaningful, and generally favorable, impact on the M&A environment, such as adopting a more business-friendly approach to regulation, increasing the competitiveness of the US corporate tax regime and adopting incentives to repatriate offshore cash. The impact of possible changes to fiscal policy, trade policy and national security review are more difficult to predict and could lead to positive or negative impacts on the deal environment.

Life as an M&A Associate

The M&A lawyer's role is truly unique within the range of corporate law disciplines. Each deal requires the M&A team to work closely with lawyers in other groups, such as corporate finance, banking, executive compensation and benefits, intellectual property, labor, real estate, tax, antitrust and litigation, as well as a host of others with regulatory subject-matter expertise. It's a bit of a hub-and-spoke model and feedback from other groups typically flows through the M&A team. Consequently, an M&A associate's knowledge of corporate law will grow broadly and exponentially. From the career development standpoint, gaining exposure to and an understanding of these varied areas of law is a major benefit of being an M&A associate. In comparison to the steadied pace of learning in law school, practicing M&A may feel a bit like drinking from the fire hose.

M&A assignments are rarely static and never straightforward. An overload of information, novel and complicated issues, and shifting objectives are the norm — flowing swiftly and steadily from both your client and the counterparty. Managing the M&A process is a master class in organized chaos. Although this can be stressful, it's also exhilarating. Distilling this varied information in order to best relay it to your client and appropriately address related issues in negotiated deal documentation is at the crux of the job. Some issues will be straightforward, while others will require innovative thinking and skillful creativity. M&A associates often have to be comfortable getting in the weeds of an issue while simultaneously viewing the entire situation from the "20,000 foot level."

How Best to Prepare

From the soft-skills perspective, multitasking, time management, attention to detail and the ability to think critically will prove immensely valuable to any new M&A associate. In terms of classes, there is no mandatory curriculum. Many law schools offer specific classes in M&A and contract drafting, which introduce law students to the different sections of M&A agreements, provide exposure to relevant legal vernacular and highlight many key transaction drivers. Classes in securities law, corporations, business taxation, finance and accounting are useful as well. However, given the diversity of deals and clients, there are always areas of law you will need to learn on the job. Perhaps the best preparation you can have is getting comfortable saying, "I don't know, but I'll find out."

M&A associates work in different industries and across varied geographies. They also learn to make sense of the unknown and leverage past experience to assist on future deals. No transaction takes place in a vacuum — clients and their businesses exist within the wider, global business, financial and regulatory markets. To that end, start reading **The Wall Street Journal**, **Financial Times** and other business news publications. Nobody will quiz you on the front page, but familiarity with the business world will pay dividends as you begin to provide clients with a range of strategic advice.

Authors

Jeremy Gaspar

Thomas Kennedy

Thomas H. Kennedy is a partner and **Jeremy R. Gaspar** is an associate in Skadden's New York M&A practice. In 2015, Skadden became the first law firm to handle more than $1 trillion in global announced M&A deals in a single year, ranking first by value globally and in the U.S. according to Bloomberg, Mergermarket and Thomson Reuters.

Practice Areas

Skadden

M&A in the middle market: Jenner & Block's perspective

A strong transactional practice group can assist clients in a wide variety of complex transactions. For example, Jenner & Block LLP assists clients in areas including mergers and acquisitions, corporate finance, securities, and private equity and investment management. A broad understanding of companies and the markets is key to helping clients decide how to structure transactions to attain the most desired outcome.

Business Climate

In 2015, improved economic conditions resulted in record-setting M&A activity, both in terms of deal volume and proceeds. Among the largest transactions was Pfizer's planned merger with Allergan for $160 billion. This transaction became a hot topic in April 2016, when the deal fell apart after the US Department of the Treasury announced a new regulation that some argue was designed specifically to block the Pfizer–Allergan merger. Also in 2015, Anheuser-Busch InBev proposed to acquire rival SABMiller for $107 billion.

'Middle-market transactions remained the dominant arena for private equity investors.'

Given the flurry of activity in 2015, it was not surprising to see activity slow in the first quarter of 2016. First-quarter deal volume declined by 16% from 2015, year to date. Sectors that have remained strong and growing include industrials, which saw a 3% increase in deal volume, and utilities, which saw a 213% increase in deal proceeds.

Private equity sponsors were able to quickly raise funds and saw strong distributions from exits in 2015. The year saw a continuing trend of distributions exceeding contributions, inspiring more limited partners to invest and reinvest in funds. Middle-market transactions remained the dominant arena for private equity investors.

Life of an Associate

This climate provides excellent opportunities to junior corporate associates. Specifically, associates can get exposure to a variety of businesses, industries, cultures and clients. Companies continue to look to do deals, and with more regulatory regimes, corporate lawyers are needed as much as they have ever been.

Deals are like puzzles, and associates must be prepared to understand how pieces fit together. Savvy junior associates take the initiative to figure out where their assignments fit in to the bigger picture and how they can develop their skill sets so as to take on additional responsibilities in future transactions.

While all transactions are different, junior corporate associates at Jenner & Block may find themselves doing any number of the following on a day-to-day basis:

- conducting due diligence and preparing due diligence reports;
- assisting senior associates and partners in drafting and revising transaction documents;
- preparing corporate resolutions and attending to general corporate housekeeping matters;
- drafting and reviewing ancillary documents related to a transaction (for instance, a junior associate may be asked to prepare an escrow agreement for use in an M&A transaction or to check a company's securities filing against the relevant securities rules);
- coordinating the drafting of transaction documents and review of due diligence materials by the firm's subject matter experts; and
- conducting research on a specific issue raised by a client or a general topic applicable to numerous clients or matters.

While all of the above may require practice-specific skills, they also require certain fundamental skills that apply to lawyers at all levels. Specifically, associates need to be organized and communicate well. A willingness to work hard and pitch in as a team player is also important.

As a junior associate, you should not wait for the work to come to you. Go out and find assignments, especially assignments that interest you. Consider not only the type of transaction (e.g., M&A versus securities), but also the industry involved and the size of the transaction. Larger transactions provide associates with the opportunity to observe and learn from the resolution of complex legal issues, while smaller transactions allow junior associates to draft, negotiate and handle other components of a transaction. You should continue to seek opportunities for training, learn from senior lawyers about the work you are doing, and ask for tips and feedback. Such interactions help your professional development.

Law school does not always prepare you for life as a junior corporate associate. For instance, law school doesn't teach you how to call a specialty partner – perhaps someone in tax, IP or labor – to request that he or she take on a task related to the transaction. While you should take appropriate courses, including contracts, business organizations and secured transactions, be aware that many of those courses are theoretical in nature. The best courses will be taught by practitioners, often adjunct professors, who are in the field and can give practical insight about the day-to-day nuances of the role. Look for opportunities to take classes in contract drafting, mergers and acquisitions and anything that has to do with accounting. These are skills that will serve you well.

> ‘You need to appreciate your client's business and be interested in what the client wants to accomplish.’

Life as a junior corporate associate varies with the peaks and valleys of deal flow. You may go a few weeks with very little work, then get slammed when a transaction gets underway. Being flexible, prepared and up to speed on all of your matters are key to successfully navigating your time as a junior associate. If you work hard, demonstrate a genuine interest in the area and produce high-quality work, the opportunities to work on more complex matters will present themselves.

More and more, clients expect their counsel to be true advisers who advise not just on the relevant legal issues, but also the full scope of the business. Clients do not want to always hear "that is a business issue" or "we should ask the business people what they think." They want your perspective on those points, too. To effectively counsel your client in these areas, you need to appreciate your client's business and be interested in what the client wants to accomplish. The concepts can sometimes be difficult, and the work will vary from industry to industry, but if you develop an understanding of the underlying aspects of the business, you will be more likely to succeed.

This is a time of technological and innovative change, and the new economy offers challenges and opportunities for innovation in the practice of corporate law. At Jenner & Block, we hope that by leveraging improvements in technology and thinking creatively, we can continue to provide excellent service to our clients and remain competitive in the changing legal market.

Authors

Michael Bolos

Michael Bolos focuses his practice primarily on mergers and acquisitions, domestic and cross-border complex business transactions and other general corporate matters for public and privately held companies.

Brendan Donahue

Brendan A. Donahue's practice includes corporate law, mergers and acquisitions and private equity. He represents public and private companies in a variety of domestic and cross-border transactions.

Hannah K. Costigan Cowles

Hannah K. Costigan Cowles focuses primarily on middle market mergers and acquisitions and private equity transactions and works with private equity and mezzanine funds on matters that arise throughout the lives of those funds.

Practice Areas

JENNER & BLOCK LLP

Environment

In a nutshell

Environment attorneys advise companies on federal, state and local laws and regulations relating to public health, welfare and the environment. The type of conduct that is regulated includes industrial activity, the development of natural resources, the use of land and everyday activities like driving a car. BigLaw attorneys primarily defend companies that are subject to these laws and regulations.

The laws attorneys work with will depend on the environmental medium: for example, air, water, waste and natural/cultural/historical resources (this touches on historical preservation, land use and endangered species) all have their own statutes and programs. The Clean Air Act – *"one of the most complex pieces of legislation on the books,"* according to **Hunton & Williams** partner **Bill Brownell** – is one example.

The types of proceedings handled by environmental lawyers are also varied. Administrative agency work involves dealing with agencies. In federal government, that includes the Environmental Protection Agency (EPA), the Department of the Interior (DOI), the Department of Agriculture (DOA), the Department of Energy (DOE) and the Nuclear Regulatory Commission (NRC). Legislative work involves working with Congress and advising companies on federal legislation and lobbying.

What lawyers do

- *"I tell students that the practice of environmental law touches on everything a lawyer can do. An environmental lawyer will practice before Congress, administrative agencies, federal and state courts, and international tribunals and organizations. The practice of environmental law also involves politically controversial subjects that one reads about in the papers every day,"* says Hunton's Brownell.
- He adds: *"When a statute or law is changed it initiates a process that can last for years, from lobbying legislators, to working with agencies that develop rules, to challenging or defending those rules in court, to seeking permits and licenses under those rules, to defending clients in enforcement proceedings."*

Realities of the job

- The laws and regulations have become increasingly complicated over the years. Thus, much of what environmental lawyers do on a daily basis is to *"make sure that clients understand all the rules to which they are subject and work with them to ensure they are complying with those rules,"* says **Hunton & Williams** partner Andrea Field.
- *"Often, the first time a client realizes that there's a problem is when the EPA starts an enforcement action, charging the client with breaking federal law."* Because the laws are often unclear, *"it is the attorney's job to determine if legitimate arguments can be made that, in fact, the client has not violated the law. And if there are violations, then it is the lawyer's job to negotiate a reasonable – and, if possible, nonpunitive – way for the client to come into compliance."*
- This field of law is *"constantly changing,"* according to Field. *"International tribunals, Congress and state legislatures enact complicated laws. That prompts regulators to adopt complicated rules and issue guidance to implement the laws."*
- According to **Patrick Dennis**, co-chair of **Gibson, Dunn & Crutcher**'s environmental litigation and mass tort practice group, young environmental lawyers will find that *"many of the issues are recent and have not been the subject of litigation."*
- He also remarks: *"It's a practice area that is very much subject to politics, legislation and developments in science. For example, now with mapping of the human genome, you can determine if in a birth defects case the causes are hereditary or might be external."*
- So, are science qualifications important in the environmental field? Dennis does not think so: *"Some of the best lawyers I've worked with have no scientific background at all."* He adds: *"Lawyers, particularly in this field, need to be really good advocates and good writers. They have got to be flexible and do not have to understand every nuance of science."*
- *"Day to day we might be involved in rulemaking, consulting with clients or defending an enforcement action, but in each of those contexts we are essentially engaging in the larger debate about how to use the world's resources in a responsible way,"* says **Robert Wyman**, partner and environment don at **Latham & Watkins**.
- Wyman adds: *"Almost everything one does touches on an important area of public policy. Most environmental law practitioners find the job personally rewarding because they have strong views about how environmental risk should be addressed. The practice of law can become routine, but if you're passionate then it never gets old."*
- Some lawyers reckon that large commercial practices are downsizing their environmental departments. However, **Sive, Paget** and **Riesel** principal **Kathy Robb** comments: *"I wouldn't say that big firm practices are*

Practice Areas

Rankings in *Chambers USA*

Top ranked

Arnold & Porter	Kilpatrick
Baker Botts	King & Spalding
Bracewell	Latham & Watkins
Cravath	Morgan, Lewis & Bockius
Davis Polk	Nixon Peabody
Gibbons	Perkins Coie
Gibson, Dunn	Schiff Hardin
Greenberg Traurig	Sidley Austin
Hunton	Simpson
Jenner	Snell & Wilmer
K&L Gates	Waller

Highly recommended

Allen & Overy	Mintz Levin
Alston & Bird	MoFo
Baker McKenzie	Norton Rose Fulbright
Brown Rudnick	Nutter McClennen & Fish
Brownstein Hyatt	O'Melveny & Myers
Cahill Gordon	Paul Hastings
Crowell	Pillsbury Winthrop Shaw
Debevoise	Pittman
Fox Rothschild	Shearman & Sterling
Goodwin	Sheppard, Mullin, Richter
Goulston & Storrs	Sullivan & Cromwell
Haynes and Boone	Thompson & Knight
Hogan Lovells	Venable
Holland & Knight	Vinson & Elkins
Jackson Walker	Weil, Gotshal & Manges
Katten Muchin Rosenman	White & Case
Kirkland & Ellis	
Mayer Brown	

For more detail on ranking tiers and locations, visit
www.chambersandpartners.com

de-emphasizing their environmental practices; rather they aren't growing as much as they were 15 years ago." She suggests that this is because clients favor specialist environmental firms with highly experienced practitioners who can deal with *"sophisticated environmental issues."* Market sources also explain that environmental work tends to attract lower fees than other commercial practice areas, making it less palatable for big, corporate firms.

- What advice does Kathy Robb have for upcoming lawyers? *"Do as much reading as possible and study the background on the policy that is driving some of the changes. You can deal better with the nuts and bolts of the day-to-day work if you understand what the theory is behind the regulatory program."*

Current issues

- Climate change is certainly an issue that has formed part of President Barack Obama's political agenda. It has also been championed by non profit organizations, such as the The Natural Resources Defense Council. Most government action to curb greenhouse gas emissions has been achieved not through congressional but executive powers. The 2010 cap-and-trade bill was famously blocked by Congress.

- In 2013, Obama announced a new national action plan to tackle climate change. It outlined measures to reduce pollution and the impact of climate change. It also focused on America's role in driving international environmental efforts. However, in February 2016, the Supreme Court stayed enforcement of the Clean Power Plan for existing power plants.

- There is ongoing speculation about how the Trump administration will affect the environmental legal market: *"In terms of climate change, there is currently a fair amount of civil litigation and I think that is going to continue regardless of the Trump admin,"* says Patrick Dennis.

- It is fair to say that Trump is unlikely to follow Obama's green footprints on the domestic or international stage. Trump has said that he intends to withdraw from the Paris Climate Change agreement, which was signed and ratified just last year (2016). Nonetheless, the agreement is binding for three years with an additional notice period of one year, which limits his influence – at least in the short-term. It remains to be seen how the Mexico-Canada-US environmental pact made in June 2016 will fare; the countries have agreed to generate 50% of their energy from clean sources by 2050.

- Market sources believe that the Trump administration is likely to relax state and federal environmental regulations, hampering national and global efforts to cut carbon emissions. It is likely that there will be a significant easing of regulation with regard to fracking and coal extraction.

- Moreover, it is expected that the US will see a radical reduction in the number of enforcement cases brought by the EPA. The resultant drop in work might however be balanced by an increase in compliance cases associated with a surge in traditional energy development.

- According to some legal practitioners, the Trump administration is likely to lead to a rise in litigation, chiefly in citizen suits. NGOs will also become more vocal.

- While Superfund cases are becoming less common, compliance cases, typically involving the Clean Air Act and Clean Water Act are becoming more widespread. There has been an increase in brownfield development recently as the economy has picked up, which is particularly beneficial for attorneys working in the transactional sphere of environmental law. This

Practice Areas

type of work will receive an even greater boost if the new administration slashes taxes.

- The Flint, Michigan toxic tort case continues to make headlines across the world. Between 6,000 and 12,000 children are believed to have been exposed to drinking water with high levels of lead. The crisis led to a federal state of emergency being declared by Obama in 2016. Criminal charges were brought against several officials.

- Patrick Dennis does not anticipate that traditional toxic tort class actions (for example, litigation pertaining to contaminated air or water) will increase under the Trump administration, as *"courts are not particularly favorable to class actions for that kind of tort. He notes that they tend to be more open to product liability cases, such as contaminated food and imported retail goods, but each case is different."*

- Environmental work has become increasingly international in scope: *"Much of the environmental law that is applicable to those operating any facility manufacturing goods has become regulated not just by US environmental law but by laws from other countries, and harmonizing legal requirements in different jurisdictions is increasingly part of our engagement,"* says Kathy Robb. Moreover, the compliance issues associated with international climate change treaties at a global and national level will continue to give rise to opportunities within the environmental legal sector.

To learn more about the growing practice of Climate Change law, head to p.117

Food & Beverages, Retail and Franchising

In a nutshell

Food and beverages, retail, and franchising law are three overlapping practice areas, which center on the trade of products and services. They encompass the sale of goods and services to consumers, as well as business-to-business (B2B) matters. Attorneys who specialize in these fields must take a holistic approach to their work, as they deal with a wide range of issues; matters can encompass real estate leases, franchise documentation, M&A deals, antitrust compliance and IP regulations. There is a contentious side to these practices, where the work is similarly varied: false advertising class actions, GMO (genetically modified organism) labeling claims and data breach investigations are covered alongside other issues. Practitioners act for an unsurprisingly broad list of clients, including multinational food distributors, international fashion houses, shopping centers and trade associations.

The global flow of products and services, facilitated by the rise of e-commerce, means that lawyers typically have expertise in both international and domestic regulations. The latter are issued by the likes of the Food and Drug Administration (FDA), the United States Department of Agriculture (USDA), the Drug Enforcement Administration (DEA), the Department of Justice (DOJ), and the Federal Trade Commission (FTC).

What lawyers do

Food & Beverages/Retail (contentious)

- Receive instructions from a client who has been accused of false advertising.
- File for a motion to dismiss.
- If it's a class action, conduct 'class' discovery. This involves working with experts to try to defeat class action certification. Attorneys will depose the experts before filing and defending their reports.
- If class certification is granted (or if the case was never a class action in the first place) attorneys carry out 'merits' discovery. They obtain all the relevant documents and conduct depositions about liability and damages.
- Apply for summary judgment. If summary judgment is denied, the case goes to trial. Attorneys determine the evidence and depositions to use, produce the exhibit list, and decide on what sort of discovery or motions to advocate.
- Go to trial. Handle post-trial steps.
- Attorneys for the plaintiff conduct due diligence before filing a complaint, oppose motions to dismiss, defend class action certification and oppose summary judgment.

Franchising (transactional)

- Receive instructions from a franchisor who would like to establish a franchise agreement with a franchisee.
- Draft a franchise disclosure document (FDD) and send it to the franchisee to review.
- Negotiate any revisions to the disclosure document in consultation with the client.
- Apply to have the FDD filed by a state agency if required under state law.
- Draft the franchise contract and ensure that it is signed by both parties.

Realities of the job

- **Miriam Guggenheim**, co-chair of **Covington & Burling**'s food, drug & device practice group says: *"The issues in the food and beverages industry are quite broad. There is nutrition and public health policy; engaging with congress and the FDA; considering what consumer advocacy groups and NGOs think about a particular issue; helping companies think through acquisitions and about the value of the brand; giving labeling advice; and preventing consumer fraud litigation."*

> *"There will be enforcement actions and recalls where you need to drop everything and help a client make a decision and interact with regulatory agencies."*

- **Martin Hahn**, a food and beverages partner at **Hogan Lovells**, asserts: *"The typical day is unpredictable. There will be countless calls and people that will stop by your office. There will be enforcement actions and recalls where you need to drop everything and help a client make a decision and interact with regulatory agencies."* He jokes: *"I never accomplish what I intend to do when I come into the office!"*
- Food and beverages cases are often filed in California with the US District Court for the Northern District of California, which is fondly referred to as the 'Food Court.'
- Lawyers in this field must maintain a thorough understanding of various acts, especially the Nutrition Labeling and Education Act (1990) and the FDA Food Safety Modernization Act (2011).
- An interest in science is essential within the food and beverages domain: *"You have to be willing to engage*

Practice Areas

with scientific studies and grapple with them," Guggenheim points out.

- Guggenheim also emphasizes the importance of time management, especially as a regulatory attorney: *"We tend to work on several different matters at a time, compared to litigators or corporate attorneys who might work on one deal for an extended period. I have 14 to 16 client matters on any given day, which is fun but can also be challenging."* However, she also notes that *"the hours are still lower compared to typical litigation or corporate practices."*

"You have to be willing to engage with scientific studies and grapple with them."

- **Deborah Coldwell**, a franchising litigator at **Haynes and Boone**, flags the difference between a litigator's and a corporate attorney's schedule: *"50% or more of my colleagues are transactional lawyers. They are very busy at year end, whereas we are not so busy. However, we work really hard when we are going to trial— 24/7 in some instances."*

- Working with foreign jurisdictions is common for a transactional franchising lawyer. *"We do a significant amount of work for US-based clients expanding internationally,"* states **Stuart Hershman**, a franchising partner at **DLA Piper**. He explains that most overseas jurisdictions do not have governmental franchising agencies: *"You have to comply with laws internationally, including franchise-specific laws in an increasing number of countries, but overall (there of course are exceptions) there isn't government interaction and oversight like there is in the US."* In contrast, franchising litigators find that most brawls tend to be domestic in nature. *"I have not seen that many cross-border court cases,"* Coldwell tells us. *"Typically if they are cross-border they end up in arbitration."*

- Many firms actively seek out candidates with professional work experience. **Warren Karp**, chair of **Greenberg Traurig**'s global retail practice, notes: *"We look for people who have taken a year or two after college to go out into the real world, to do volunteer work or gain business experience. We find that when they come into the firm as a young associate they have a different, beneficial perspective."*

Current issues
Food & Beverages

- There has been much debate in recent years over what constitutes 'natural' food, with some courts staying lawsuits until the FDA clarifies its definition of the term. One case that hasn't been granted a stay is Claudia Morales et al v. Kraft Foods Group: questions over Kraft's use of artificial colors in its shredded, fat-free

cheddar mean that the case will hit the courts soon.

"We're seeing a continued interest by consumers to learn more about their food."

- Consumer concern over misleading food labeling and health and safety issues continues. PepsiCo recently found itself the subject of a lawsuit filed on behalf of consumers after traces of the pesticide glyphosate were found in Quaker Oats (a brand owned by PepsiCo, labeled '100% Natural Whole Grain).

- As a result, transparency is on the rise, as Miriam Guggenheim explains: *"We're seeing a continued interest by consumers to learn more about their food. Companies are intending to be more transparent about their products, by stating what the ingredients are and where they come from."* This can, however, create new problems: *"They are using more plain English and can come up against regulatory bodies if they aren't consistent with defined terms."*

- The FDA has announced that food manufacturers will have to introduce a new 'Nutrition Facts' label for their packaged foods by July 2018. Martin Hahn tells us that this has resulted in *"a tremendous economic burden on the industry."* He hopes that the new administration will be *"more sensitive to industry concerns."*

- According to Hahn, *"litigation continues to be one of the biggest threats to the food industry. People are looking for new and creative ways to bring actions against the industry. It is a tremendous drag on resources and companies' ability to produce high-quality food products."*

- Like many practice areas, the food and beverages market is becoming increasingly international in its focus. Guggenheim reports: *"Foreign companies are interested in entering the US and domestic companies are looking to acquire foreign companies and bring new food products to the country."*

- There is much uncertainty over how the Trump administration will affect the market. Guggenheim tells us: *"I don't think food safety rules will change, as they are tied to legislation issued from Congress. Whether there will be less enforcement and fewer inspections remains to be seen."* She adds: *"I don't think private litigation will go away; it will continue to grow."* Hahn comments: *"I'm optimistic we will continue to see fair trade between the US and its trading partners."*

Retail

- The popularity of online shopping has inevitably affected the commerce of bricks-and-mortar retailers; retail space in shopping malls has consequently become cheaper.

- Furthermore, the sector has suffered from the lackluster economy, leading to an increased number of com

Rankings in *Chambers USA*

Top ranked

DLA Piper	Jones Day
Gibson Dunn	McDermott Will & Emery
Greenberg Traurig	Perkins Coie
Hogan Lovells	

Highly recommended

Baker McKenzie	King & Spalding
Foley & Lardner	Latham & Watkins
Goodwin	Morgan, Lewis & Bockius
Goulston & Storrs	Nixon Peabody
Haynes and Boone	Paul, Weiss
Holland & Knight	Pillsbury Winthrop
Hunton & Williams	Venable
Kilpatrick Townsend	Wiley

For more detail on ranking tiers and locations, visit www.chambersandpartners.com

panies filing for bankruptcy.

> *"There is a move to consumer-centric, omnichannel retailing where the consumer has multiple choices."*

- The digitalization of the retail market (via increased use of mobile devices and the spread of social media) has given rise to many opportunities for lawyers – particularly in the area of advertising and its associated privacy issues. Attorneys must assess the merits of false advertising claims in relation to the The Federal Trade Commission Act (1914) and consider state statutes, such as the California Consumer Legal Remedies Act. Warren Karp identifies an important trend in this digitalized retail market: *"There is a move from multichannel retailing to consumer-centric, omnichannel retailing where the consumer has multiple choices. They can get products from anywhere, delivered directly from a fulfilment center or store."*
- Intellectual property is an important strand of retail

work. Companies often look to protect their designs under trade dress – a constituent of the Lanham Act. In 2012, for example, the fashion designer Christian Louboutin succeeded in protecting his red shoe sole under trade dress in the US.

- Products are also becoming 'smarter' in line with technological developments. E-textiles are of great interest to apparel manufacturers, who are looking to patent their new technologies.
- How will Trump affect the retail market? As with other practice areas, our sources predict a decline in enforcement from regulatory bodies. Karp asserts: *"For me, from the supply chain side, I see tariffs being imposed and free trade being tightened."*

Franchising

- The main issue in the franchising market concerns the 'joint employer' model. It has thrown up the following question: which party is responsible for employees? The franchisor (the owner of the franchise) or the franchisee (the company or individual licensed to operate under the franchise)?
- *"Over the last two-plus years there has been an increasing effort by certain administrative agencies in the US to hold franchisors liable for things that happen at the franchisee level,"* Stuart Hershman tells us. Consequently, a lot of franchising lawyers are advising on employment dispute resolution matters.
- In October 2016, the world's biggest franchise, McDonald's, agreed to pay $3.75 million to workers, finally settling a dispute over pay. A District Court in San Francisco had previously ruled that McDonald's could be sued for franchisee level violations as it was a joint employer.
- Elsewhere, Deborah Coldwell notes that technology poses a challenge to the franchising market. She explains that there are laws for everything *"from drone delivery, to online ordering, to website franchise sales,"* adding: *"Keeping up is going to be a challenge for lawyers and companies because technology moves so quickly."*

Practice Areas

Government and Government Contracts

In a nutshell

Government contracts lawyers *"don't just sit at their desks reviewing contracts,"* says **Richard Rector**, chair of **DLA Piper**'s government contracts practice. *"Actually, what we do involves a broad range of legal skills, as over half of what we do is litigation."* Bid protests form the bulk of contentious work, along with disputes involving costs recovery or performance problems; lawyers also defend contractors accused of fraud or other misconduct. In addition, attorneys here help contractors to navigate the regulations and special rules tied to providing goods and services to federal government. Advising on subcontracts, scheduling and organizational conflicts are all common activities too.

> *"Law firms that lobby are not selling access, they are selling skills."*

"Law firms that lobby are not selling access, they are selling skills," says **Nick Allard**, current dean of Brooklyn Law School and former chair of **Squire Patton Boggs**' lobbying, political and election law practice. *"They are litigators serving as advocates in a broader array of arenas."* More specifically, government relations lawyers directly lobby the federal and state government on behalf of a variety of businesses – including healthcare, education and defense entities – on specific legislation or ongoing issues. They promote or oppose new initiatives to Congress or the administration; attempt to persuade government to amend legislation; and try to convince courts to reinterpret laws. *"You get exposed to a wide range of industries,"* says **Richard Rector**, *"and so it never gets boring."*

Political law specialists advise on the organization and financing of election campaigns, which includes assisting corporations and other groups with election-related activities. On the litigation side, they help to challenge decisions made by electoral authorities, such as the Federal Election Commission.

What lawyers do
Government contracts

- Virtually every government agency procures external services, but the Department of Defense is far and away the largest consumer. Other major areas are aerospace, construction, healthcare, homeland security, education and IT.
- When external services or goods are required, the government will issue a procurement solicitation (or 'Request for Proposal'). The process of procurement and

contracting is run by a government official called the contracting officer.

- Lawyers help guide potential contractors through the solicitation procedures: pointing out the key risk issues; how the evaluation factors will influence the selection decision; and how this contract differs from previous ones. However, they do not advise clients on how to obtain a contract or how to market themselves.
- **Rand Allen** of **Wiley Rein** says: *"We advise a lot of companies on how to get into the government contracts arena without creating undue compliance risk, for instance by qualifying for a status which will minimize the intrusiveness of government in their business."*
- Government contracts tend to use 'boilerplates' or standardized terms and conditions. In contrast to a commercial setting, there isn't as much room to negotiate the requirements that form part of the contract. Lawyers also negotiate subcontracts and teaming agreements between contractors.

> *"Where good, but not great, credentials may once have been sufficient for being hired, popular areas of the law now have their pick of the most elite students on the market."*
>
> — The Big Interview with... Marc Elias, Hillary Clinton's general counsel and partner at Perkins Coie. Visit www.chambers-associate.com for the full interview.

After the formation of the contract, lawyers act for both plaintiffs (the disappointed bidders) and defendants (the awardees) during bid protests. A typical bid protest challenges the award of a contract at an administrative forum: the US Government Accountability Office (GAO) or the US Court of Federal Claims (CFC). These cases are usually resolved over three months, which means associates don't get bogged down by document review for prolonged periods. The GAO is required by statute to issue a ruling within 100 days. Plaintiffs have ten days to put together protest documents, and government agencies have 30 days to respond. CFC proceedings take about the same time, sometimes slightly longer. Associates prepare drafts of protest filings and identify applicable legal precedent. This involves close scrutiny of the original Request for Proposal; the government agency's award decision;

and the proposals and negotiation responses submitted by both the awardee and the protester.

- Disputes also arise over the performance of existing contracts. Lawyers represent contractors in alternative dispute resolution or litigation in front of the Armed Services Board of Contract Appeals, the Civilian Board of Contract Appeals or the Court of Federal Claims.
- Lawyers defend contractors against allegations of fraud, as well as waste and misconduct under various federal criminal and civil statutes, including the False Claims Act.
- Lawyers also act in disputes between prime contractors and subcontractors in federal and state courts.

"Lobbying involves so much more than this image people have of the glad-handing door-opener."

Government relations

- Government relations lawyers are approached by clients from all industries; they call upon lawyers when they believe a certain piece of legislation will either benefit or harm their business, and therefore seek to either promote or change that legislation.
- The service that government relations lawyers provide involves *"analyzing laws, writing memoranda to clients advising on legal provisions (telling them what their responsibilities are under new legislation) and preparing advocacy pieces for hearings,"* Nick Allard tells us.
- Besides advocacy there's legal research into current statutes, drafting of proposed rules and legislation, and drafting of clients' comments on legislation.
- Government relations lawyers form a link between their clients and politicians and administrators. But Allard is eager to clear up a misunderstanding: *"Lobbying involves so much more than this image people have of the glad-handing door-opener. That is not interesting or high-end work. What we do is analyze, advise and advocate. We seek to understand our clients' business, their mission and what they want to accomplish."*

Realities of the job

- *"Government contracts is a very litigation-oriented area,"* explains **John Chierichella** of **Sheppard Mullin**. *"You don't just have the opportunity to litigate though; you get to do so in relation to things that are incredibly interesting, whether it be a bid protest, debarment proceeding, False Claims Act case or a subcontract dispute."*

"If your eyes glaze over when reading a detailed technical or cost proposal, this is not the area for you."

- Bid protests are typically intense affairs, packed with information that must be absorbed in a short space of time. *"If your eyes glaze over when reading a detailed technical or cost proposal, this is not the area for you,"* says **Tom McGovern**, **Hogan Lovells'** government contracts practice area leader. Richard Rector confirms that *"you have to have a very good analytical ability when reviewing a contract to understand how it applies to a particular industry. When we are interviewing, we look out for people who are detail-oriented and don't shy away from digging into the documents and enjoying the analysis and the investigation."*
- Associates working on a smaller bid protest may have the opportunity to actually lead the case. During a larger bid protest it's more likely that they'll work on a particular aspect of it.
- Cost issues can be daunting to analyze due to the vast body of regulations and complex wording to grapple with. However, Chierichella tells us that *"if you can understand that logic chain and overcome those concerns, there's a lot of benefit you can give to clients by working through cost issues to maximize the amount to be paid and the amount they will retain."*
- While most traditional law practices deal with questions pertaining to what the law is, political law mainly involves the question of what the law should be.
- Lobbyists' main clients include corporations, trade associations, universities, healthcare institutions, states and municipalities. Lawyers also do pro bono lobbying work on behalf of charities and other nonprofit organizations.

"It's vital to understand how decisions will play out if they get picked up by the media."

- *"One of the most important things to understand is that every company in the US is affected by the government's policies,"* **Tom Boyd** of **DLA Piper** tells us. *"Whether it's in the form of legislation, regulation or the exercise of executive power, it's going to impact the marketplace and every one of our clients."*
- Nick Allard describes the public policy process as *"never-ending,"* adding that *"anything that is done can be undone."*
- It is usually easier to shoot down a planned bill than to get one passed.
- *"Whenever you're representing a corporation, part of the picture will involve a high-profile public official,"* says **Ken Gross** of **Skadden**. *"So it's vital to understand how decisions will play out if they get picked up by the media."*
- The famous 'revolving door' relationship between the administration and lobbying shops provides lawyers at all levels with the opportunity to work in-house for the

Practice Areas

government.

- *"I think having some exposure to government service is very helpful in this practice,"* explains Gross. **David Nadler** of **Blank Rome** confirms this: *"I would advise working for the government before a law firm, as it's rewarding in its own right, but it also paints a picture of what it's like to work on both sides of the table."*
- Government lawyers are also active at the state level. Smaller state-based firms – grouped together into the State Capital Global Law Firm Group – advise on business regulation, ethics codes, campaign finance and state government procurement.
- *"Clients come from all over the globe,"* Tom Boyd says. *"So we're not only interested in the political issues concerning Washington, DC, but also those that relate to client interests in London, Paris, Berlin and Brussels."*
- *"There is a relatively small Bar and you deal with the same people regularly on the other side,"* states Allen. *"That generates more comity and less hostile behavior than some lawyers are used to."*

Current issues

- Contractors and the government are always at odds as they attempt to achieve the best prices from their respective positions. McGovern explains that *"contractors are consulting us for advice on how to protect themselves from government budget cuts and austerity measures."*
- Potential budget cuts in light of the 'fiscal cliff' has been a significant issue, requiring lawyers to assess what their clients' rights would be if the government decided to cease financing certain services or projects. While a deal was reached to avoid substantial spending cuts – albeit narrowly – a lot of work still needs to be done and it remains a primary concern for contractors.

"Contractors are concerned about mounting cybersecurity threats."

- The budget cuts and reductions in overall government spending have made the competition for any government work all the more competitive. *"With tighter budgets come fewer contract awards, so contractors are more likely to seek redress through the bid protest process if they lose contracts they previously held,"* McGovern reports.
- Technology is having a major impact on the relationship between government, the public and corporations. The amount of information provided online is driving up the quality of counseling and advice demanded from lawyers.
- Data security has become a significant area of activity, especially in light of Edward Snowden's revelations

Rankings in *Chambers USA*

Top ranked

Akin Gump	Perkins Coie
Arnold & Porter	Skadden
Crowell & Moring	Wiley Rein

Highly recommended

Allen & Overy	King & Spalding
Alston & Bird	Mayer Brown
Cozen O'Connor	MoFo
DLA Piper	Pillsbury Winthrop
Fried, Frank	Sheppard, Mullin, Richter
Gibson Dunn	Squire Patton Boggs
Hogan Lovells	Venable
Holland & Knight	Vinson
Jones Day	WilmerHale
K&L Gates	

For more detail on ranking tiers and locations, visit www.chambersandpartners.com

about the activities of the security services. This affects all contractors who have access to government information, whether they store it on their own systems or are tasked with securing the government's own storage facilities.

- *"Contractors are concerned about mounting cybersecurity threats,"* emphasizes McGovern, *"both in relation to their own networks and those they maintain for government customers. The government is greatly concerned about the security of its own data entrusted to contractors and expects contractors to adhere to strict information assurance guidelines and to cooperate and share data about cyber attacks in order to counter such threats. At the same time, there have been news reports of government intelligence agencies attempting to access data in commercial networks, including those operated by their own contractors, which is somewhat ironic."*
- When asked about the effect of the incoming Trump administration, David Nadler is reluctant to make any predictions: *"He's such a wild card. With a more conventional politician you can make predictions, but not here."* At the same time, Richard Rector emphasizes a development that could boost work in the area: *"Trump talked about spending more on infrastructure development including highways, public work and IT. A surge in government spending on infrastructure is good for government contractors and there seems to be bipartisan support for it."*

Practice Areas

Healthcare

In a nutshell

Healthcare is an industry-specific practice area that encompasses a number of traditional law practices such as corporate and litigation. Because the industry is highly regulated, specialist healthcare lawyers are often needed to monitor and react to new regulations.

Typically, the matters that healthcare lawyers deal with encompass three different categories. First is the transactional element – essentially the buying or selling of healthcare businesses. Second is any litigation among healthcare companies, and third is advising on the regulatory sphere and in relation to any governmental legislative issues.

Healthcare is a massive part of the US economy. In 2015 healthcare spending was almost 18% of GDP, and by 2021 it is predicted to account for just under one-fifth of the country's economy. Many major firms have healthcare practices and there are many niche or boutique health firms, with many of them tied to specific states.

It is also a practice that continually evolves because of ever-changing laws. The passing of the Patient Protection and Affordable Care Act in March 2010 (aka Obamacare), for example, remains a landmark moment. One thing is for certain: the nationwide demand for healthcare advice and representation has never been greater.

Clients include investment funds who are interested in investing in healthcare, and established providers, like hospitals.

What lawyers do

Healthcare: transactional

- Healthcare lawyers are sometimes brought in as troubleshooters at the same stage of a deal that tax and antitrust attorneys are brought in. This is often the case for smaller BigLaw health practices and local healthcare boutiques.
- At other times healthcare lawyers will run a deal from soup to nuts. This happens when there are numerous health industry clients or statutes involved, so lawyers who understand the regulatory context of a deal need to be involved from the outset. This happens more often in larger BigLaw healthcare practices and boutiques, but is increasingly common given the complexity of new healthcare reforms.
- Healthcare transactional work involves putting a deal together and doing the due diligence as normal. According to **Jeffrey Schneider** of **Hogan Lovells**, however, *"these are usually very complicated deals because of the regulatory constraints that exist, so you have to structure them in ways that you might not in other industries."*

Healthcare: litigation

- Litigation work – especially in relation to government investigations – is *"the high end of regulatory healthcare work for people who have been at it for a long time and are really good,"* **Doug Hastings** of **Epstein Becker & Green** says.
- Government-funded Medicare and Medicaid payments are a major source of litigation and government investigations. *"There is a whole set of rules on how you can get paid as a healthcare provider for Medicare and Medicaid services,"* explains Hastings. *"Anyone that provides healthcare – hospitals, physicians, hospices, home care providers – will have some Medicare patients. Not only are there questions surrounding the eligibility and amount of payment, but providers might face anything from a routine government audit to an investigation into healthcare fraud."*
- Healthcare and life sciences practices see a lot of qui tam litigation – cases in which someone who assists with a government prosecution can receive all or part of the financial penalty imposed.

Healthcare: advice

- Outside the times when healthcare lawyers are called in for litigation and transactions, they are constantly providing regulatory advice. Schneider says: *"It's about making sure clients comply with the vast array of regulations out there that limit a company's conduct, as well as helping clients think through problems and do things in the correct manner."*
- The advice covers more than just the regulatory side. *"There are nonregulatory issues to deal with as well, such as contractual issues with physicians and medical staff relationships,"* **Dennis Barry** of **King & Spalding** states.
- Among the key pieces of legislation governing Medicare fraud and abuse are the antikickback law and the Stark Law. The latter governs physicians' referral of patients to medical facilities in which that physician has a financial interest.
- Federal antitrust laws and Food & Drug Administration regulations also form an important component of health lawyers' work.

Practice Areas

Realities of the Job

- *"Like every lawyer you have to be able to listen and to communicate but I think particularly for health care law you have to be able to read the law and fully understand its nuances. It is a highly regulatory practice area so you cannot be afraid of diving into statutory text and regulatory text,"* says **Edward S. Kornreich** of **Proskauer**.

- Kornreich continues: *"The joy I get from solving a problem for a client is what drives the practice. In healthcare, clients tend to be people who are interested in serving the public and by solving any issues you advance the public interest."*

- Kornreich adds that the type of person who would thrive in this area would be *"somebody who is a good communicator, thoughtful and has the ability to and enjoys reading, understanding and explaining the law, as well as applying it in various contexts. It is also useful to have someone who is orientated toward social welfare."*

- On working hours, Kornreich states: *"I think they are reasonable on average. This is generally because of the nature of people as they tend to be more willing to tolerate personal lives on the part of their employees."*

- *"I think what I like the most is I'm representing clients who are dedicated to making people better. It is a very human-orientated practice. It's not just about numbers or strategy or markets. The consumers really matter,"* says **Greg Luce** of **Skadden**.

- To succeed in this practice area, Luce goes on to say: *"You have to have a thorough understanding of how this business and its sectors work. Every industry has its qualities but you need to understand how a healthcare provider or manufacturer operates to understand the implications of the legal regime. You really need to know your client."*

- Luce continues in offering general career advice for this practice area: *"I think you need to match your expectations to your interests. If you want to be a litigator and test yourself and you want to be in the cauldron of a court room then do. If you want to be in healthcare and get into the policy and regulations and interested in how industry is evolving, it is a great field. It is an area that offers a lot of opportunities for entrepreneurial thinkers."*

- *"You need to be solution-orientated and practical. There is a lot of gray area in the law because it is always developing so you have to review the facts and law carefully and provide a practical solution. It is a very complex practice area so you need to be able to take something complicated and explain it in a straight forward way for your clients,"* says **Jim Owens** of **McDermott Will & Emery**.

- Owens tell us his favorite aspect of working in healthcare: *"I love representing providers. Doctors and nurses and other healthcare professionals want to help people. They have good intentions and are very selfless – it makes me happy to work with those people. Everyone has healthcare in their life, its a personal thing. To be able to work in an industry that is doing good is rewarding."*

- However Owens warns against the trickier aspects of the practice area: *"The amount of change is difficult so you have to keep on top of it. You always have to check what the current law is as you deliver advice. There are so many aspects to what we do which makes it very complicated."*

- *"I would say that if you have an interest in healthcare or background in healthcare you should consider this field. In the US the population is aging and the demand is rising. Because of this demand it will be a specialism in demand,"* Owens tell us.

Current issues

- Under the new Republican administration, a huge issue is the repeal of Obamacare.

- The future of regulatory enforcement is also uncertain. The assumption is that there will be less regulation but this is not known for sure.

- There is an increasing consolidation amongst care providers and integration of hospitals with other facilities. There is an increasing focus on the social determinants of healthcare, where the discourse concentrates on how services are provided and finding preventative means to keep people out of hospital.

- Edward Kornreich says the Trump administration could mean *"ACA repeal, and its unknown replacement, if any. Uncertainty is enhanced by possible Medicare and Medicaid program changes. While there is the possibility of substantial regulatory reform, this is less certain in healthcare."*

- Greg Luce offers his opinion on the Trump administration: *"I think it will be very significant. It's hard to imagine a single sector that will be more affected than healthcare, with combined House and Senate interest in repealing and replacing Obamacare. It will make a sea of change in the way healthcare will be delivered. The main difference I think will be less of a role for federalist healthcare policy and increased private enterprise and state-directed healthcare."*

- Jim Owens says: *"I think right now the general view is that it will be positive for most businesses and sort of the same with healthcare. Trump said he wants to repeal Obamacare, but Congress cannot do so successfully without coming up with a replacement law. If a replacement law is passed, it will provide a large amount of legal work for healthcare lawyers."*

- Monitoring legislative changes is a major task for all healthcare and life sciences lawyers. Junior associates especially can be involved in writing up summaries of the implications of new legislation for various client sectors.

- The ACA has also placed an emphasis on providing quality, value-for-money care; consequently hospitals are trying to maintain financial competitiveness while

Practice Areas

Rankings in *Chambers USA*

Top ranked

Akin Gump	King & Spalding
Alston & Bird	McDermott Will
Duane Morris	Mintz Levin
Epstein Becker	Norton Rose Fulbright
Hogan Lovells	Proskauer Rose
Jones Day	Ropes & Gray
K&L Gates	Waller

Highly recommended

Arnold & Porter	Jackson Walker
Cadwalader	Katten Muchin Rosenman
Choate	Latham & Watkins
Cozen O'Connor	Morgan, Lewis & Bockius
Crowell	Nixon Peabody
DLA Piper	Reed Smith
Foley & Lardner	Sheppard, Mullin, Richter
Fox Rothschild	Sidley Austin
Gibbons	Skadden, Arps
Greenberg Traurig	Thompson & Knight
Haynes and Boone	Venable
Holland & Knight	

For more detail on ranking tiers and locations, visit
www.chambersandpartners.com

still providing excellent services. Mergers have become an increasingly popular method to try and boost savings but hospitals need to ensure they don't fall foul of antitrust laws or regulators in the process. Law firms will continue to see a range of healthcare clients seeking advice on mergers, and regulatory and antitrust matters.

- Pharmaceutical, biotech and medical companies have also seen a rise in mergers as they aim to continue producing high-quality products without excessive spending.
- Pharmaceutical company mergers will be further driven by the expiration of several pharmaceutical patents. It's expected that those losing patents will seek to protect themselves from profit losses by acquiring companies with lucrative products.

Practice Areas

Life as a Healthcare lawyer: insights from Waller

Home to nearly 20 publicly traded healthcare companies, many of the nation's largest privately owned healthcare entities, and several of the most successful healthcare start-ups, Nashville is the healthcare capital of the nation. Based in Nashville, Waller has several decades of experience providing pragmatic, trusted advice to leading healthcare organizations, and the firm's expertise spans virtually every segment of the healthcare industry.

Over the last 50 years, Waller has played a key role in shaping the healthcare industry and contributing to the success of our clients. We have developed a cross-disciplinary, collaborative environment to meet different strategic goals and respond to significant and complex challenges, while constantly adapting to the shifting regulatory environment. Waller's healthcare practice has evolved to meet clients' changing needs, from helping HCA, Inc. grow into the world's largest investor-owned operator of healthcare facilities to navigating high-stakes compliance issues for clients across myriad segments of the industry, including outpatient healthcare, post-acute care, behavioral health, home health, and dentistry.

For more than a decade, Modern Healthcare has ranked Waller among the nation's largest healthcare law firms, and we have been recognized by the American Bar Association's (ABA) Health Law Section as the largest health law firm in the South. Waller also is recognized annually on the American Health Lawyers Association's (AHLA) industry-esteemed "Top 10 Firms" list.

Waller attorneys are widely known for their industry insight and are regularly quoted on cutting-edge healthcare topics in Modern Healthcare, The Wall Street Journal, The New York Times, and other industry publications. Our attorneys also serve key leadership roles in the AHLA and ABA Health Law Section, and regularly speak at leading healthcare conferences throughout the nation. Additionally, Waller alumni fill C-suite, general counsel, compliance, and other senior roles at many leading healthcare companies and organizations, a reflection of the firm's deep relationships with the companies and organizations driving the healthcare industry in the 21st Century.

Waller's multidisciplinary healthcare department includes more than 125 experienced attorneys across the firm's four offices in Austin, Birmingham, Memphis, and Nashville. Waller has built a national reputation for handling sophisticated, high-profile corporate transactions in the healthcare space, and our corporate transactional capabilities are complemented by attorneys with specialized expertise in nearly all areas of the law affecting our healthcare clients.

Healthcare Operations and Compliance

Healthcare organizations must navigate a minefield of state and federal regulatory issues in both their day-to-day operations and their long-term objectives. Waller's healthcare operations and compliance attorneys work closely with clients to understand the clients' business objectives and assist in implementing creative approaches to achieve those goals in a compliant manner. Due to the complexity of the regulatory landscape, healthcare attorneys are often brought in by attorneys in other practice groups to advise and assist in a variety of matters for healthcare clients (e.g. commercial finance, government investigations, and private equity transactions).

To be successful, healthcare attorneys need to be both highly technical and detail-oriented in order to align client objectives with the constantly changing regulatory environment. Matters can involve both state and federal laws, so it is important for healthcare associates to develop strong research and issue-spotting skills. Additionally, healthcare associates need to be effective communicators in order to distill complex issues and laws into clear, concise summaries for clients and provide the strategic solutions.

Typical areas in which healthcare compliance associates will be involved include:

- analyzing or drafting arrangements involving referral sources (e.g. physicians) to ensure compliance with state and federal anti-kickback and self-referral laws;
- structuring mergers, acquisitions, and joint ventures to ensure compliance with federal and state regulations;
- assisting in the development of innovative models for hospitals and physicians to work together (e.g. through clinical co-management agreements and foundation models, within accountable care organizations, and through joint venture arrangements);
- assisting with Certificate of Need and licensure applications; and
- drafting policies and procedures relating to HIPAA patient privacy/security regulations.

Practice Areas

Government Investigations and Enforcement Defense

Companies and individuals operating in today's healthcare regulatory climate increasingly find themselves the subject of criminal, civil, or administrative investigations and enforcement actions. The Department of Justice (DOJ), Office of Inspector General (OIG), and other key agencies continue to step up their enforcement activities, and 702 new qui tam lawsuits – an average of 13.5 cases every week – were filed last year by whistleblowers under the False Claims Act. In addition to the enhanced level of government scrutiny, recent hikes in the civil monetary penalties associated with violations of the healthcare fraud and abuse laws have made the stakes higher than ever.

From publicly traded companies to individual health care providers, clients turn to Waller's high-profile team of government investigations and white collar defense attorneys. The investigations team comprises seasoned litigation and healthcare industry professionals, as well as several former federal prosecutors, and is bolstered by our nationally recognized healthcare regulatory and compliance team to help clients carefully navigate everything from non-routine audits and qui tam lawsuits to criminal enforcement actions. We help clients respond to such actions with strategies aimed at minimizing – or completely avoiding – penalties, negative publicity, and disruptions to their business operations. While we strive to proactively resolve matters short of litigation, our attorneys have the experience necessary to litigate a case through trial in order to obtain favorable results for the client.

As part of our government investigations and enforcement defense practice, associates may be called upon to assist with conducting sensitive internal investigations, including participating in witness interviews, reviewing documents, and preparing correspondence to relevant government agencies. When deemed appropriate for the client's situation, associates may also be asked to help draft voluntary disclosure submissions to DOJ, OIG, the Centers for Medicare and Medicaid Services, and other regulators. Finally, in the event litigation becomes necessary, associates play a critical role in reviewing and compiling evidence to support the client's position, drafting pleadings and other court filings, and assisting with other trial preparation activities.

Healthcare Transactions

Public and private healthcare companies and their investors rely on Waller's transactional attorneys for advice and counsel on mergers and acquisitions, joint ventures, recapitalizations, commercial finance transactions, and securities offerings. Waller handles a significant number of complex transactions in the middle market, and our associates frequently work opposite peers in national law firms located in most major cities. In addition, Waller is committed to identifying and developing expertise in emerging areas, as evidenced by the firm's growing healthcare information technology practice, our reputation as a trusted advisor to dental support organizations and related multi-site specialty practices, and our ability to guide private equity and venture capital clients through cutting-edge transactions.

Associates working in Waller's corporate practice play a key role in virtually every transactional matter the firm handles. Typically, senior associates are directly responsible to the lead partner for managing all aspects of a transaction, including drafting purchase agreements and other material documents and coordinating with the firm's healthcare regulatory, tax, and other specialized practitioners. Junior associates also play critical roles in transactions, assisting with the drafting of transaction documents, monitoring and managing deal deadlines, and providing support to the lead senior associate or partner working on the deal.

Waller's corporate transactional attorneys have earned a lofty reputation in the healthcare industry due to their keen understanding of the sector and willingness to always "go the extra mile" to help clients achieve their business objectives. To maintain that reputation, associates must be attentive to detail, driven, skilled at multitasking, and capable of effectively communicating and working collaboratively with other members of the deal team. Waller does not rest on its laurels, and firm leadership has historically stayed a few steps ahead of the competition in analyzing the market and determining what impact changes in the economy, the regulatory environment, and our clients' needs will have on the development of niche practices and other specialized legal offerings... so stay tuned.

Practice Areas

waller.

Intellectual Property

In a nutshell

There are four different types of intellectual property: patents, trademarks, copyright and trade secrets. Patents are issued by the US Patent & Trademark Office (USPTO) to the creators of new inventions or processes. They're practically a monopoly on the manufacture and sale of the patented invention, but they only last for 15 years. Trademarks can potentially last forever, but only protect the words, symbols or phrases used to distinguish the brand or identity of a good or service.

Somewhere in between is copyright, which protects works of authorship such as books, movies, music and plays. Copyright is a complicated system of restrictions on copying, performing and otherwise profiting from protected works, and lasts for the life of the author plus 70 years. Finally, trade secret law protects the holders of proprietary information from having their information stolen or disclosed to the public in certain circumstances. Think Coke's secret formula.

Companies big and small rely on IP to give them an edge over their competitors, and IP-intensive industries directly or indirectly account for over 45 million US jobs, or a third of the workforce. Clients can include a tech startup looking to patent the latest gizmo to a film distributor trying to stop its content from being pirated. As well as being financially rewarding, IP law also offers some fascinating ethical questions, including:

- Do pharmaceutical patents give life-sciences companies an incentive to invest in creating life-saving drugs, or do they just keep their prices high?
- Should people named 'McDonald' be able to name their restaurants after themselves?
- And is your Happy Potter fanfiction copyright infringement, fair use, or just weird?

What IP lawyers do

- Engage in written correspondence to see if the alleged infringement can be resolved through a license and royalty agreement or other amicable resolution.
- If not resolved, attorneys representing the rights-holder file an infringement claim. Defense attorneys then respond with a counterclaim stating that either their client has not infringed or that the IP is invalid and unenforceable.
- Engage in discovery. Examine public records held in the USPTO that document the correspondence between the patent holder and the USPTO. Prepare interrogatories, requests for admission, and document requests seeking more information about the other side's positions. On average, discovery will take three years.
- Engage in the summary judgment motion phase. Engage in a Markman hearing, during which the judge interprets the language of the claims, ruling on any disagreements between parties on their interpretation. Markman hearings can take place any time before the case goes to the jury, but usually occur before trial.
- Go to trial, normally in front of a jury. This usually takes between four and ten days.
- Perform IP due diligence – review a third party's IP portfolio prior to your client entering into a transaction with them. Assess the strengths and weaknesses of the portfolio so that the client can understand the risks of doing business with the rights-holder.
- Draft commercial agreements between owners of IP rights and those who want to use the protected invention, design or artistic work. The most common agreements will either transfer ownership or grant a license.

Realities of the job

- In order to become a member of the patent Bar, you must pass an exam administered by the USPTO, which requires you to have completed a minimum number of technical or scientific courses in college or university. You don't actually need to be a member of the patent Bar to appear in federal district court on a patent case. Membership of the patent Bar is only necessary for attorneys who want to do patent prosecution work. **Paul Parker**, firmwide co-chair of **Perkins Coie**'s intellectual property practice, affirms that science qualifications are not a prerequisite for trademark and trade secrets work.
- Patent owners can file claims in any district court they want; some districts are considered more patent-friendly and are therefore more popular than others. The most notable of these is the Eastern District of Texas, based in Marshall, TX (population 24,000). Critics say its unorthodox rules and conservative jury pool favor patent-owners, while its supporters cite the court's efficiency.
- An IP portfolio can be the most valuable of a business's assets, particularly in the pharmaceutical sector. This means that IP lawyers need to form part of the deal team from an early stage.
- Overseas companies and inventors view the USA as a prime venue for patent litigation.
- As a result of globalization, the current manufactur-

Practice Areas

Rankings in *Chambers USA*

Top ranked

Alston & Bird	Kilpatrick Townsend
Baker Botts	Kirkland & Ellis
Debevoise & Plimpton	Latham & Watkins
Finnegan, Henderson	Morrison & Foerster
Fish & Richardson	Perkins Coie
Foley & Lardner	Pillsbury Winthrop Shaw
Goodwin	Pittman
Hunton & Williams	Sidley Austin
Irell & Manella	Sterne, Kessler, Goldstein
Jones Day	WilmerHale

Highly recommended

Akin Gump	King & Spalding
Arnold & Porter	Mayer Brown
Baker McKenzie	McDermott Will & Emery
Bracewell	Morgan, Lewis & Bockius
Brownstein Hyatt	Norton Rose Fulbright
Choate Hall & Stewart	O'Melveny & Myers
Cooley	Orrick
Cravath	Patterson Belknap
Crowell & Moring	Paul Hastings
Dechert	Paul, Weiss
DLA Piper	Proskauer Rose
Duane Morris	Reed Smith
Fitzpatrick, Cella, Harper	Ropes & Gray
Gibbons	Skadden
Gibson Dunn & Crutcher	Thompson & Knight
Greenberg Traurig	Venable
Haynes and Boone	Vinson & Elkins
Hogan Lovells	Weil
Jenner & Block	White & Case
K&L Gates	Wilson
Katten Muchin Rosenman	Winston

For more detail on ranking tiers and locations, visit www.chambersandpartners.com

ing and importation process has become enormously complicated and creates considerable challenges for patent owners seeking royalties or compensation at all levels of the manufacturing and distribution chain.

- Every patent infringement appeal is filed with the US Court of Appeals for the Federal Circuit. If parties don't like the result there, the only option is to file a petition for certiorari with the Supreme Court, which has taken more patent cases in the last decade.
- Patent cases bring great risk to Fortune 500 companies, which can incur enormous damages dating back up to six years from the filing of the complaint. This explains the rise of non-practicing entities or patent trolls, which buy up portfolios of patents and make their money threatening to sue other businesses for patent infringement. Faced with such stiff penalties,

and without the resources to fight the case in court, smaller companies and inventors pay the patent trolls hefty license fees.

- Different types of IP work means differing workloads, explains Professor **Tim Holbrook** of **Emory University**. *"Patent prosecutors tend to work more independently, as it's often just you and the PTO,"* he explains. *"Patent litigation often goes on for years, and requires long term thinking,"* he adds, *"while trademark litigation is all about speed. Cases are decided off a preliminary injunction, so if something's happening, it's happening now."*
- IP candidates who can demonstrate that they have business expertise will fare well: *"I think it's very helpful to hire people who have been in industry for a couple of years or more"* says Paul Parker. He also notes: *"Unlike in a lot of areas where law is a cost center, in patent prosecution, as opposed to litigation, you are an asset creator – you create value for companies."* **Dale Cendali**, a partner of **Kirkland & Ellis**, remarks that lawyers *"must stay nimble because what we think the world is today is likely to not be the case in ten years."*
- Good communication skills are a must, particularly in transactional IP and IP litigation. Lawyers need to be able to simplify and explain complex technical matters to lay judges, juries and clients.
- What do our expert lawyers enjoy most about their profession? Dale Cendali says *"I like the theater of trials and depositions and court hearings,"* adding: *"I really like working with my team."* Paul Parker enthuses: *"Being in IP law is a continual learning process about science and the world around us."*
- **Trent Webb** of **Shook, Hardy & Bacon** tells us: *"Being competitive and having a drive to win is very important, because every case involves trying to beat the other side. Creativity is also essential; we strive to find unique approaches to solving problems. You also need to be able to simplify and explain very complicated technical issues to lay juries. Communicating effectively to your audience is extremely important."*
- What challenges might an associate face? Paul Parker affirms: *"For mid-level associates there is a period of time when there seems to be a lot of basic preparation and prosecution. It's a threshold you have to get through before operating at a much more strategic level with clients."*
- Dale Cendali advises budding IP lawyers *"to dig a little deeper to figure out the nature of the IP practice at different firms. What is it they do? How many associates are working in that group? What are the potential opportunities to make partner?"*

Current issues

- In 2011, the America Invents Act was passed, which replaced the first-to-invent patent system with a first-to-file patent system. The act enables anyone to challenge the validity of patents through inter-partes review proceedings. The aim of the act is to impede non-practicing entities or patent trolls from initiating costly litigation: *"Non-practicing entities have been restricted by the changes in the law and are in the process of adapting to the new limitations,"* reports Paul Parker, noting: *"There are fewer cases being filed in the technology area."* However, inter-partes review has itself been abused by so-called reverse patent trolls: hedge funds which challenge strategic patents, causing the patent holder's share price to drop. They then make a profit shorting the rights-holder's stock.

- The House Judiciary Committee announced its first policy proposal in December 2016, following a lengthy assessment of US copyright law. The Committee aims to establish advisory committees to facilitate communication with federal agencies about marketplace developments and new policies.

- The Apple-Samsung patent wars have yet to reach their final conclusion, as the matter of how much Samsung owes Apple in damages is still being debated in the Supreme Court; a decision is expected in June 2017.

- There is an ongoing debate about 'patent-eligible subject matter'. The 1980s days of patents for 'anything under the sun that is made by man' are long gone, with patents becoming increasingly difficult to obtain. The Alice Corp. v. CLS Bank was a landmark case in the software industry (not withstanding the fact that software was not explicitly discussed in the case), as the Supreme Court ruled in 2014 that Alice Corp.'s patents were based on an abstract idea and were, therefore, invalid. Software giants including Microsoft and Google announced their respective stances in the legal wrangle, filing amicus curiae briefs.

- The Lanham Act has been the subject of fierce debate in the past few years. The Washington Redskins case went from court to court with the Supreme Court finally refusing, in October 2016, to validate the club's trademarks.

- However, in 2016, the Federal Circuit ruled that the provision of the Lanham Act that allows the refusal of scandalous or immoral trademarks is unconstitutional, as it breaches the Free Speech Clause of the First Amendment. The Supreme Court is now set to review this ruling; it has accepted the US Patent and Trademark Office's petition for writ of certiorari in Lee v. Tam. The contentious Tam case involves the band, The Slants, which considers that it has culturally re-appropriated its name. A ruling in The Slants, favor could reopen the Redskins case.

- In May 2016, The Defend Trade Secrets Act became law. According to Dale Cendali, *"it's certainly true that trade secrets theft is becoming a growing issue relating to intellectual property."* This act means that trade secrets are now governed by federal rather than state law. Some have questioned whether the act is even necessary: *"Almost all the states have their own type of trade secret law,"* says Dale Cendali. She does, however, add: *"At least now there is a federal overlay that is intended to be uniform."* The act notably allows employers to claim damages in trade secret cases. It also stops whistleblowers from falling victim to retaliatory accusations of trade secret misappropriation.

International Arbitration

In a nutshell

International arbitration addresses any case or potential dispute between parties – usually located in two different countries – and is the most common form of alternative dispute resolution (ADR). *"At the most basic level, international arbitration attorneys are international litigators in a transnational justice system,"* says **Donald Donovan** of **Debevoise & Plimpton**. *"It's a system that's validated by both national and international law, but not run directly by any given state."* Arbitrations often arise from clauses included by companies in their commercial contracts with one another. This means that, if a dispute arises between them, they are obliged to arbitrate their dispute rather than pursue traditional litigation.

Arbitration provides a binding solution to the dispute by way of an arbitral 'award'. The award can be enforced internationally through the provisions of the 1958 New York Convention on the Recognition and Enforcement of Arbitral Awards, which more than 140 states have ratified. *"Private parties often prefer international arbitration because it provides a neutral and relatively confidential forum, specialist arbitrators and greater ease of enforcement of the award in multiple jurisdictions. The New York Convention is unique in that there is no equivalent international treaty in force around the globe to ensure the international currency and enforcement of domestic court judgments,"* explains **David Lindsey**, partner and cofounder of international arbitration boutique **Chaffetz Lindsey** in New York.

The types of cases heard in international arbitration are typically cross-border commercial disputes that occur in situations like joint ventures or corporate transactions (including M&A). *"The types of disputes run the gamut, but they are all really linked to investment and transactions outside the home jurisdiction of the claimant,"* **Nigel Blackaby** of **Freshfields Bruckhaus Deringer** says. Disputes commonly originate in the oil and gas, telecom, privatized public utilities and construction industries.

One specific type of international arbitration is 'investment arbitration', where a claim is brought by a foreign investor directly against the host state of its investment. This arises from the likes of multinational ventures, such as energy projects, and can be instigated in two ways: investors and host states either consent in contracts to use international arbitration to resolve disputes, or investors make claims under bilateral (or multilateral) investment treaties (BITs). BigLaw firms – as well as specialist boutique firms in some instances – represent both claimants

and defendants in such cases, though they must be careful about conflicts.

The disputes are often considered under a foreign applicable law and resolved under the arbitration rules of the International Chamber of Commerce (**ICC**), the International Centre for Dispute Resolution of the American Arbitration Association (**ICDR**), the London Court of International Arbitration (**LCIA**), The World Bank's International Centre for Settlement of Investment Disputes (**ICSID**), or the United Nations Commission on International Trade Law (**UNCITRAL**). The nature of the dispute largely determines the relevance of each set of rules. Investor-state disputes, for example, are usually arbitrated under UNCITRAL or ICSID, while the LCIA and ICC rules are suitable for virtually all types of arbitration – though the latter is more appropriate for commercial disputes.

What lawyers do

- Receive instructions from the client, who thinks, for example, that their contract has been breached or that their rights under an applicable investment treaty have been infringed.
- Review the contract or treaty, solicit and review relevant documentation and speak to potential witnesses.
- Provide the client with a memo on the merits of the case. This may involve working with local counsel in the relevant jurisdiction.
- If a client wants to proceed, draft the necessary initiation papers – usually a 'Request for Arbitration' in accordance with the applicable arbitration rules, such as ICDR, ICC or ICSID – and submit to the relevant arbitral institution.
- The case is then registered and the request is communicated to the respondent, usually by the arbitral institution. The respondent answers, possibly with an objection to the jurisdiction and with a response to the case's merits. They name an arbitrator.
- In order to establish the tribunal, each party proposes an impartial and independent 'party-nominated' arbitrator. The party-nominated arbitrators then usually seek to agree on a 'president' or 'chair' of the tribunal, failing which, the president/chair will be nominated by the institution. Once constituted, the tribunal will invite parties to the first procedural hearing at the (usually neutral) seat of hearing (often jurisdictions with favorable arbitration laws and culture such as New York, London, Paris, Geneva and Singapore), where the calendar and procedural order for the next steps

Practice Areas

will be established.

- In commercial arbitration, there is a period for exchanging documentary evidence, during which each side will produce the documents upon which it intends to rely. This does not typically include 'US-style' discovery, but a far more limited disclosure process.
- The next steps usually include a very detailed presentation of the facts and evidence by the claimant (including written witness/expert statements and all relevant documentation). This is called a 'Memorial' – it may also be included in a pre-hearing brief shortly before the hearing on the merits.
- Defense attorneys submit a 'Defense Memorial' or response brief with a similar presentation.
- There will often be a further round of 'Reply' and 'Rejoinder' memorials or briefs.
- Final hearing takes place, where witnesses are questioned and cross-examined before the tribunal, and oral argument is made. The written witness statements filed with the Memorials often take the place of direct testimony at the hearing.
- Submit final, post-hearing briefs. In complex cases, these can be lengthy.
- Tribunal determines award, which must be 'reasoned' (ie, the tribunal's reasoning for the award must be set out), in writing, and signed by the members of the tribunal. With a three-person tribunal, a majority determines the award.

Realities of the job

- *"The international context is fascinating because, regardless of whether it's a commercial or investor-state arbitration, you're always experiencing different cultures, countries, languages and personalities. It really is such a wonderful dynamic and mix,"* says **Carolyn Lamm** of **White & Case**.
- *"You can assist yourself greatly by having a real command of more than one language,"* Donovan explains. *"English is of course important, but having a command of other languages as well really helps."* Spanish, Mandarin and Russian are three languages in demand. Portuguese is also increasingly valuable for international arbitrators, in conjunction with the growth of the Brazilian market in particular.
- *"International arbitration isn't entirely different from courtroom advocacy,"* according to Lamm. Compared to US litigation, however, international arbitration typically relies more on written, instead of oral, advocacy and on contemporaneous documents, rather than on witness testimony from parties. In final hearings, for example, written witness statements often take the place of oral direct testimony.
- *"In many ways the skills that make you successful in international arbitration are no different from the skills that make you successful in litigation,"* **Joe Profaizer** of

Paul Hastings tells us. Elliot Polebaum of Polebaum Arbitration concurs, elaborating:"It's a good idea to have a grounding in disputes more generally. Working in the litigation department of a law firm is a good place to start, before getting specialized. There are opportunities to become enmeshed in the factual development of a case, learning and handling the disclosure process, including the deposition process in US litigations, and managing the documentation."

- The job involves a lot of travel to identify relevant documents and interview witnesses. Depending on the circumstances, associates may also travel.
- It's important for international arbitration lawyers to build up their knowledge of economic and financial issues, as these form an important component of the work. *"Those language skills can't be at the expense of deep analytical and substantive skills. A comprehensive understanding of international economics, politics, business, finance, and how companies operate across borders is a necessary foundation,"* according to Joe Profaizer.
- *"Currently there is no overarching set of rules to account for all the various national backgrounds that lawyers in an international proceeding come from, so if you have lawyers from different legal systems they may not be conducting themselves in the same way,"* Lamm tells us. Despite this, the differences between European, US and Asian practices, and between civil law and common law, are not as great as they once were. Some say a more universal practice is developing; the International Bar Association's now widely used evidence rules are an example of this.
- In commercial arbitration, demands for documents from the other side are allowed, but not as much as in the discovery phases of US litigation. Depositions are rarely allowed, unless US parties are involved and the arbitration clause itself calls for them. [See the aforementioned IBA evidence rules for a good summary.] *"American litigations use oral depositions as part of the discovery process. Taking part in that process can be a useful vehicle for young lawyers to develop their skills in questioning witnesses. In international arbitration by contrast, witnesses are not subject to depositions (unless the parties agree). That means that the only witnesses who are questioned in international arbitration cases are those who testify in the arbitration hearing. In that setting, the witness testimony is typically handled by partners, and occasionally by talented senior associates,"* according to Polebaum.
- International arbitration has provided an effective platform for female practitioners to excel, which is demonstrated by organizations such as ArbitralWomen.
- David Lindsey says: *"Participants in the international arbitration bar share a mutual respect and camaraderie that I have not witnessed in other areas of legal practice."*
- International arbitration is generally a difficult profes-

Practice Areas

Rankings in *Chambers USA*

Top ranked

Debevoise & Plimpton	White & Case
King & Spalding	

Highly recommended

Arnold & Porter	Jenner & Block
Baker Botts	Norton Rose Fulbright
Baker McKenzie	Reed Smith
Cleary Gottlieb	Shearman & Sterling
Curtis, Mallet-Prevost	Sidley Austin
Freshfields	Simpson Thacher
Hogan Lovells	Skadden
Hughes Hubbard	WilmerHale

For more detail on ranking tiers and locations, visit www.chambersandpartners.com

sion to enter, and so it's typical for juniors to develop their skills as trial lawyers first. *"The bottom line is you must learn advocacy– how to present on your feet with care, thoroughness and confidence. You also need to know whether you love to do that, because some people just don't excel in that kind of situation,"* Lamm informs us.

Current issues

- New York, London, Paris and Geneva have traditionally been favored as the arbitrators' venues of choice, but Hong Kong and Singapore are quickly becoming popular alternatives. Don't expect newcomers to displace old favorites: commentators reckon the growth of Asian venues is thanks to a wider increase in international arbitration and a desire to emulate successful models found in the Europe and the USA. The Middle East has also seen an increase in venues for international dispute resolution, with the UAE and Dubai offering viable options for arbitration processes.

- Arbitral decisions have been increasingly challenged over the last ten years; while most of these failed to overturn initial rulings, the last five years have seen a few succeed. Recently the world's largest arbitral settlement between the shareholders of Yukos Oil and Russia was challenged and defeated in a court in the Netherlands. This decision has been appealed and it will be interesting to see the effects the ruling will have on the enforcement of international arbitration awards. ConocoPhillips has sued the Venezuelan government concerning asset dumps before the Delaware Uniform Fraudulent Transfer Act. So far the Venezuelan government has succeeded in the delaying of proceedings, the result of this case may have a key impact on the enforcement of arbitral rulings against states.

- **Jenner & Block**'s **Anton Valukas** tells us: *"Arbitra-*

tion has become as complex as civil litigation. It's not unusual for arbitrations to involve extensive discovery, motion practice and protracted resolutions. As a result, arbitration may not continue to be the alternative choice for resolving matters."

- Reacting to complaints that arbitration has become increasingly costly and slow, at the start of 2016 the International Chamber of Commerce (ICC) announced new time scale expectations for the submission of awards to try and combat the problem.

- Class arbitrations have been around in the USA for some time but thanks to some companies prohibiting customers from pursuing class arbitrations these actions are on the decline. Outside the USA it's a different story; although still infrequent, class arbitrations are increasingly springing up and commentators expect this to continue in the coming years.

- The number of investor-state disputes has increased considerably in recent years, with energy, oil, gas and mining companies leading the charge. As governments begin imposing limitations and conditions on investors' abilities to take on foreign governments, this incline in cases could soon start leveling off.

- *"A longer term trend is that ordinary disputes are becoming larger and more complicated, involving more money, more parties, more parallel proceedings, and more complex substantive issues,"* according to Joe Profaizer.

- According to Elliot Polebaum of Fried Frank, *"international arbitration has become the dispute resolution mechanism of choice for international business. Big transactions involving important contracts can lead to significant and high-stakes disputes, and there has been an increasing number of such disputes in recent years."*

- Keep an eye on the dispute between ConocoPhillips and Venezuela over the illegal expropriation of oil investments to watch how another sovereign state attempts to push back against arbitral decision: Venezuela is currently trying to get the ruling overturned.

- The status of a series of international trade deals which have been in the process of being negotiated over the last year has been placed under threat in a volatile political climate. The new president has announced his intention to withdraw from TPP, a deal to which the US was a signatory but which had not yet been ratified. It remains to be seen if this position will continue to be the case upon Trump's inauguration. The Comprehensive Economic and Trade Agreement between Canada and the EU has been signed.

Practice Areas

International Trade

In a nutshell

The work of international trade lawyers is split between two main areas: the application of domestic law to international trade, and treaty-based international law governing trade flows. On the domestic side, work covers export controls, embargoes and economic sanctions, import relief actions such as antidumping, countervailing duties and safeguards, and customs classifications, valuation and rules of origin matters. In relation to international treaties, attorneys advise on World Trade Organization (WTO) rules, preferential trade regimes such as the North American Free Trade Agreement (NAFTA) and bilateral investment treaties (BITs).

Lawyers advise on the implementation of these domestic and international rules, and counsel clients in disputes related to their violation. Clients include US organizations doing business in foreign jurisdictions and foreign businesses operating in the USA; they include major corporations, trade associations and national and regional governments.

What lawyers do

Domestic

- Lawyers represent clients before the International Trade Commission (ITC) and the Department of Commerce (DOC), the two main bodies that review petitions related to import laws. They are the first port of call for disputes and protests related to issues such as dumping, countervailing duties and safeguards.
- The first port of call for protests over customs classifications, valuation and rules of origin matters is US Customs and Border Protection (CBP).
- Lawyers assist US companies to secure a license from the DOC for the export of 'dual use' goods (with both military and commercial applications), or from the Department of State for the shipment of military goods.
- They also assist clients before the Treasury Department's Office of Foreign Assets Control (OFAC), which administers and enforces economic and trade sanctions against targeted foreign countries, terrorism-sponsoring organizations and international narcotics traffickers.
- Parties can protest determinations made by the ITC, DOC and CBP at the Court of International Trade. This court also hears protests against trade-related worker assistance decisions made by the Departments of Labor and Agriculture.
- Antidumping duties are imposed on imports to com-

bat 'dumping' – selling a product in an export market at a price less than its home market value, which injures a domestic industry.
- Countervailing duties are similar to antidumping duties, but are imposed by a country to counter the effects of subsidies in foreign markets.
- Safeguards are 'emergency' measures in response to an unforeseen increase in imports which damages or threatens to damage a specific domestic industry. Unlike 'unfair' activities like subsidies and dumping, increased shipments by themselves are not deemed to be unfair, so safeguards must be applied in a nondiscriminatory fashion.
- Section 337 of the Tariff Act of 1930 provides an alternative to US court actions to challenge imports that infringe patents or other intellectual property rights. These cases are dealt with by administrative law judges in the ITC.
- Lawyers also assist companies involved in an acquisition of a US target under review by the Committee on Foreign Investment in the United States (CFIUS). Established in 1975, CFIUS (pronounced 'sifius') is tasked with reviewing the national security implications of investment in US assets.

International

- On the treaty side, trade lawyers practice *"global regulatory law,"* according to **Andy Shoyer**, partner and chair of **Sidley Austin's** international trade and dispute resolution practice.
- Disputes are the largest source of work. The WTO is the main international arbitrator of trade disputes. Its Dispute Settlement Body makes rulings on agreements made between member states under WTO negotiations. Only sovereign states can bring disputes to the WTO so lawyers for private stakeholders will be involved in lobbying governments to bring cases or in assisting to defend them.
- Neither the US government nor the EU hires outside counsel to represent them in front of the WTO, so US attorneys often find themselves representing other nations, such as Brazil.
- Disputes relating to BITs are heard in arbitral tribunals administered by the International Centre for Settlement of Investment Disputes (ICSID), an arm of The World Bank, or similar arbitration centers.
- Treaty-focused attorneys will also engage in lobbying to influence the development of new international rules. *"We listen to what companies tell us about the regulatory barriers they face and translate that into po-*

Practice Areas

tential treaty language. Then we will help businesses affect the negotiations within the US and internationally," Andy Shoyer explains.

Realities of the job

- **F Joseph Warin**, partner and chair of the Washington, DC litigation department at **Gibson Dunn**, advises: *"Adventurousness and a willingness to take risks are necessary in this practice. If you're dealing with, for instance, stock options in Norway, you need a sense of intellectual curiosity to understand and process all this and then give advice that's nuanced to the environment. Cultural sensitivity is a must. Being a good listener is imperative. I urge young associates to be keen listeners and not to leapfrog that step because it's absolutely essential in order to give good solid advice."*
- International trade work is often closely tied to headline-making current events, and associates grapple with key policy as well as legal issues.
- One associate who works in an international trade department told us: *"I had focused on international studies throughout college and demonstrated an interest in international trade."*
- *"Unlike domestic litigation, we don't have substantial document production and discovery work in WTO or other treaty disputes,"* Shoyer informs us. *"That saves junior associates from some of the drudge work. But that doesn't mean that lawyers don't have to get on top of the facts! Arbitrations can involve hundreds of pages of documents and younger associates will get involved in that."*
- *"International trade practices with a significant policy focus tend to be partner-heavy because clients demand high-profile advice,"* Shoyer explains. *"It's hard to generate the knowledge base required just by reading the case law: you need to have the experience. You build up your knowledge base slower."*
- Trade lawyers need to be politically aware and keep track of negotiations at the WTO and other multilateral, regional and bilateral regimes. **Joe Dorn**, former partner at **King & Spalding**, says: *" Many WTO cases are very intellectually challenging. You're often covering new ground, so that's very stimulating."*
- Andy Shoyer tells us: *"The greatest challenge and joy in this area is that you are really practicing the law of globalization. You're at the forefront of those business and policy forces that drive the world. Anyone in this practice needs to appreciate that the nexus of law and policy is very important."*
- Shoyer adds: *"While the ability to work comfortably in several languages is so helpful, a fluency with culture is vital. You need to be comfortable putting yourself in the shoes of someone from another culture. Creativity and openness is a must, perhaps more so than in any other area of the law because it's still emerging."*
- F Joseph Warin says: *"I'm constantly globe-trotting. I'll*

go to London, then Abu Dhabi, then two weeks later I'll be in New Delhi. It's fascinating but it also keeps me away from my family, so this big plus is also the biggest negative."

Current issues

- The nature of international trade means that it is important for lawyers to be aware of ongoing diplomatic and political developments across the globe.
- International trade laws increasingly intersect other regulatory frameworks and cut across multiple borders, which makes compliance challenging. **Beth Peters** of **Hogan Lovells** informs us that *"typically regulations within the US, EU, UK and other regions may be triggered simultaneously when trade issues arise, whether that's in international trade litigation or in international trade compliance matters. Some examples are export controls, sanctions, anti-money laundering, cybersecurity and securities reporting regulations."*
- Lawyers in this practice have to be acutely aware of the sanctions imposed on foreign nations. *"In the last year governments have continued the use of 'smart sanctions' – those that are targeted to particular industries and transactions,"* Peters reports. *"They have been implemented in particular with respect to Russia and Ukraine, as well as in Latin America, where they relate to narcotics traffickers and other designated nationals."*
- In addition, US sanctions on North Korea have been strengthened and expanded recently. In February 2016, President Obama signed into law the North Korea Sanctions and Policy Enhancement Act in response to Pyongyang's recent ballistic missile activities.
- The nature of international trade means that it is important for lawyers to be aware of ongoing diplomatic and political developments across the globe.
- From an export perspective, **Matthew Nicely**, a partner in **Hughes Hubbard** & Reed's international trade and customs practice group, explains that *"the opening up of Myanmar and its re-entry into the world economy will be important. Many companies are interested in changing the way they go about doing business in the country now that US and other countries' trade and investment restrictions are being lifted."*
- In February 2016, the Trans-Pacific Partnership (TPP) trade deal was signed by the United States and 11 other Asia-Pacific countries: Australia, Brunei Darussalam, Canada, Chile, Japan, Malaysia, Mexico, New Zealand, Peru, Singapore and Vietnam. TPP writes the rules for global trade among members, seeking to promote trade and strengthen relationships between the nations.
- The upcoming election has seen *"some interesting dialog"* with respect to TPP and a range of other multilateral and regional agreements, according to Beth Peters.

Practice Areas

- President Obama's trip to Cuba in March 2016 marks the most recent development in US-Cuba diplomatic relations; commercial air travel was also restored in February 2016. Peters notes that *"dialog with respect to Cuba will continue to come up in this election."*
- Britain's exit from the EU – Brexit – will completely change the legal basis of Britain's trade links with the world. *"This is an area that requires complex study,"* Peters tells us, as *"the USA and Britain have a very close trade and national security relationship."*
- Matthew Nicely stressed that *"there's always a lot of focus on the origin of goods imported into the United States. This is true with all products, but particularly those that have been subjected to antidumping or countervailing duty cases, which inevitably lead to allegations of transhipment."* In the recent past the most frequent target of antidumping and countervailing duty cases was China, but recent cases include *"multiple other countries, including Korea, Japan and Turkey, and others, particularly as the US steel industry has resumed its heavy use of this kind of import relief."*
- Increasingly, both US and foreign clients are becoming more aware that nations outside the USA also have complicated and important trade laws. Beth Peters highlights that *"we've certainly experienced clients addressing trade issues in Singapore, Brazil and India,"* in particular.
- Export control and trade compliance are becoming an increasingly busy area due trade control being seen as a means to exert geopolitical influence. **David J.Levine** of **McDermott Will** and **Emery** explains: *"In a broader sense, there is a tendency, as our election made clear, for countries to become more insular and retract from global trade deals. No one really knows what exactly will happen with the incoming Trump administration, but people are watching carefully as trade was highlighted during the campaign, and Trump is still talking about how to implement some of the issues he campaigned for."*

Rankings in *Chambers USA*

Top ranked

Baker McKenzie	Sidley Austin
Fish & Richardson	Skadden
Hogan Lovells	White & Case

Highly recommended

Akin Gump	Latham & Watkins
Alston & Bird	Mayer Brown
Arnold & Porter	MoFo
Crowell & Moring	O'Melveny & Myers
Curtis, Mallet-Prevost	Pillsbury Winthrop
Davis Polk & Wardwell	Stroock
DLA Piper	Vinson
Finnegan, Henderson	Wiley Rein
Gibson, Dunn & Crutcher	WilmerHale
Hughes Hubbard & Reed	Wilson
King & Spalding	Winston & Strawn
Kirkland & Ellis	

For more detail on ranking tiers and locations, visit www.chambersandpartners.com

Practice Areas

Labor & Employment

In a nutshell

Labor & employment law governs the workplace and the relationships between employers and employees; managers and unions; and employers and the government. BigLaw firms tend to represent employers.

Employment work involves both litigation and counseling. The former tackles claims of discrimination, including age, disability, national origin, race, religion, whistle-blower/retaliation, sex and sexual harassment. Such claims are brought by individuals or administrative agencies like the US Equal Employment Opportunity Commission (EEOC). Other common disputes concern unpaid overtime ('wage and hour' claims) under the Fair Labor Standards Act (FLSA), and claims relating to the Family and Medical Leave Act (FMLA), both of which may be filed with the US Department of Labor (DOL).

Lawyers who offer employment counseling advise on compliance with various employment laws. This involves advising on clients' wholesale employment policies and practices, as well as on 'difficult situations', be they sexual harassment complaints or reductions in force. They will often advise on the employment aspects of business transactions like M&A or restructurings. Attorneys will either provide both litigation and counseling advice, or specialize in one discipline.

BigLaw labor lawyers commonly advise management on union matters governed by the National Labor Relations Act (NLRA), which is administered by the National Labor Relations Board (NLRB). They have expertise in collective bargaining, union and strike avoidance, and strike breaking. They will also advise on Occupational Safety and Health Act (OSHA) matters, which the DOL (via the Occupational Safety and Health Administration) enforces. Labor attorneys may also engage in litigation of NLRA and OSHA disputes.

Employee Benefits, Executive Compensation & ERISA

Many firms have a distinct practice focused on executive compensation, employee benefits and ERISA work. For the uninitiated, ERISA is the Employee Retirement Income Security Act of 1974 – the federal statutory framework that governs the administration of employee benefit plans and the rights of the beneficiaries. **Kyoko Takahashi Lin**, partner at **Davis Polk**, tells us: "*The work we do is really about people: how do you motivate them? How do you get them to be incentivized and work hard and do the right thing and treat employees well? That*

is what we are trying to advise companies on." There is much, much more to this specialization, however.

What lawyers do

Employment litigation

- Receive notice of a charge or complaint filed with the EEOC or DOL, respectively.
- Advise client on how to respond to the EEOC, DOL or other government investigations.
- Negotiate with the agencies, work with them in investigations, and try to come to settlement in appropriate cases.
- If a class action, oppose class certification.
- If no settlement can be reached, begin discovery – paper and electronic. Settlement can occur at any stage of a case.
- Provided the case is not settled, standard litigation will commence.

Employment counseling

- Review and draft employment contracts and policy documents.
- Advise client on the steps to take when problems arise.
- Keep client abreast of new changes to laws and regulations, often by way of newsletters or seminars.
- Advise on the employment implications of business transactions.
- Focus on minimizing risk for the client, by instilling a proactive and preventive approach.

Labor relations

- Act as a liaison between management and unions.
- Lead negotiations between the different sides.
- Litigate cases before the NLRB and in federal courts.

Realities of the job

- Only a small percentage of cases filed in the courts are putative class actions. Most are wage and hour or discrimination cases.
- Cases are heard in state and federal courts, as well as before administrative and regulatory boards.
- Many labor and employment laws will sound familiar: Americans with Disabilities Act, Civil Rights Act of 1964, Equal Pay Act, Age Discrimination in Employment Act and National Labor Relations Act.
- Most charges are found to have 'no reasonable cause' and many others will be settled before litigation.

Practice Areas

- The EEOC and NLRB are separate administrative agencies and are not part of the DOL. The best labor lawyers will have good people skills, because they will be interacting with both management and unions. The most successful ones will be able to convince both management and unions that they have common goals.
- According to **Thomas Linthorst**, a partner in **Morgan Lewis & Bockius**' labor & employment practice: *"Those that really can get close to their clients, understand what the client needs, and can think creatively about meeting the client's needs will find that to be a successful approach."*
- When the economy is down, clients are concerned about surviving, which often involves downsizing. Advising on reductions in force is never pleasant.
- **Alison Marshall** of **Jones Day** says: *"I do think that we move more quickly in comparison to some of the big commercial litigation cases. Also, our cases are not always as big, so associates often get more responsibility. That is a plus, but juniors need to be prepared to take on that responsibility."*
- Sometimes the intensity of the workload is high, especially when lawyers are gearing up for a big trial. Being responsive is critical.
- Often lawyers will be dealing with a non-lawyer – a HR professional for example – so they need to be able to translate complex legal principles into clear concepts for them. It's critical to be able to write well, with a view toward addressing practical problems, and not overwhelming the client. This is also true when it comes to explaining elements of a case or situation to the judiciary.
- **Bettina Plevan**, partner at **Proskauer Rose**, says: *"Sometimes clients have pressing emergencies, and you have to be responsive immediately."*
- **Joseph Costello**, partner at **Morgan Lewis**, warns: *"This is an area of law that requires flexibility and adaptability. Every day there's a new challenge, and the issues are not always predictable: an employee may have a disability that needs to be accommodated; there might be a union-organizing drive; or maybe an employee has complained about a posting on a social media website, which another employee has published. Any of these situations could trigger a call to us."*
- **Stephen Poor**, chairman of **Seyfarth Shaw** informs us that in this field, *"there is still that focus on the real world, which can be messier and stickier than the relatively sterile laboratory of the justice system. In other words, success in this field requires a practical bent and a propensity to solve problems rather than win arguments."*

Current issues

- A very significant development is the death of Justice Scalia in February 2016. He was part of a Supreme Court majority that issued a number of significant decisions in labor and employment, *"including in the areas of class actions, arbitration agreements, and on the merits of wage and hour issues,"* Thomas Linthorst informed us. *"I'm looking with great interest at who his replacement will be for their impact on those areas."*
- *"Whistle-blowing is an area that is clearly on the rise, by virtue of additional legislation under Dodd-Frank, and some high-profile announcements from the SEC,"* Linthorst reported. Recently, the SEC announced that a $30 million bounty was given to someone who provided original information to them, which led to a successful enforcement action.
- The extent of the protection afforded by the Sarbanes-Oxley (SOX) whistle-blower anti-retaliation provision was expanded by a 2014 decision of the Supreme Court. The Annual Report on the Dodd-Frank Whistleblower Program, released by Office of the Whistleblower (OWB), reported an increase of 8% of tips from whistle-blowers in 2015 compared to 2014.
- An increase in SOX retaliation claims has resulted from *"a series of decisions by the Department of Labor extending SOX protections for conduct not previously considered protected,"* according to Linthorst. In February 2016, the Whistleblower Augmented Reward and Nonretaliation Act of 2016 (or WARN Act) was introduced, and aims to strengthen the protections and incentives available to financial crimes whistle-blowers.
- One area that has also been very active is the SEC's stance on policies and agreements that it contends may chill reporting to regulators, such as overbroad confidentiality agreements and non-disparagement provisions. *"The SEC has brought several enforcement actions against companies where it claimed the policies or agreements were overbroad,"* Linthorst informed us. *"This means companies are generally reviewing their policies and agreements to make sure they don't preclude or chill employees from reporting potential violations of law to regulators."*
- Another hot area is that of wage and hour claims. According to Linthorst: *"There has been lots of class and collective action litigation as everyone seems to be suing for overtime."* Some of the claims are being brought by those covered by the 'white-collar exemptions' to the overtime requirements, while others have been brought by employees claiming that they have not been properly compensated for 'off-the-clock' work. *"One of the reasons for this spike,"* explains Linthorst, *"is that under the federal overtime law, the Fair Labor Standards Act, a claim can be filed on behalf of all those who are 'similarly situated' to the plaintiff and, upon a determination by the court that the case is appropriate for notice, notice can be sent to all others 'similarly situ-*

Practice Areas

Rankings in *Chambers USA*

Top ranked

Alston & Bird	Morgan, Lewis & Bockius
Gibson, Dunn & Crutcher	Nixon Peabody
Greenberg Traurig	Paul Hastings
Hunton & Williams	Perkins Coie
Jones Day	Proskauer Rose
McDermott Will & Emery	Waller

Highly recommended

Akin Gump	Mintz Levin
Baker McKenzie	MoFo
Bracewell	Munger
Brownstein Hyatt	Norton Rose Fulbright
Cozen O'Connor	Nutter McClennen & Fish
Dechert	O'Melveny & Myers
Duane Morris	Orrick
Dykema Gossett	Reed Smith
Epstein Becker	Ropes & Gray
Foley & Lardner	Sheppard, Mullin, Richter
Fox Rothschild	Sidley Austin
Gibbons	Snell & Wilmer
Goodwin	Squire Patton Boggs
Haynes and Boone	Thompson & Knight
Holland & Knight	Vedder Price
Jackson Walker	Venable
K&L Gates	Vinson & Elkins
Kilpatrick Townsend	Weil
King & Slding	Winston & Strawn
Mayer Brown	

For more detail on ranking tiers and locations, visit
www.chambersandpartners.com

ated'. When that happens, there can suddenly be hundreds of claims."

- More generally, Linthorst pointed to *"the rise of labor and employment laws, regulations and ordinances at the state and local level."* He continued that *"a lot of state and local governments are passing laws; some of them are around wage theft, some relating to paid sick leave, and some are just new posting requirements for existing laws, but it creates a real challenge for those employers that operate nationally."*

"If you're in a courtroom you need to listen to what the judge and opposing counsel are saying. So many lawyers at the beginning and end of their careers are tied to their scripts for their outline or witness examinations and are not listening to what the judge, opposing counsel or witnesses are saying."

- Brad D Brian, co-managing partner of
Munger, Tolles and Olson

Practice Areas

Life Sciences

In a nutshell

Life sciences is an umbrella term that denotes all of the medical and scientific products and services that fall under the following areas: biotechnology, pharmaceuticals, medical devices, dietary supplements, foods, cosmetics and environmental agents.

For lawyers, the practice area is particularly diverse as it encompasses several areas of traditional practice including regulatory, criminal investigation, enforcement, compliance, competition, intellectual property and many more. Clients range from governments to major global pharmaceutical manufacturers to start-up companies that are inventing new medical drugs.

All of this variety is broken down into three core areas for lawyers: regulatory, intellectual property and corporate. Regulatory work encompasses the likes of market authorization of products, government affairs, competition matters and compliance work. Life on the intellectual property side is focused on protecting clients' patents, while corporate lawyers assist companies with both their everyday and transformative matters, from basic employment needs and governance issues to business-altering M&A deals.

What life science lawyers do

Regulatory

- Assist clients with getting their products to market in various jurisdictions.
- Liaise with the government when there are objections to clinical trials.
- Help companies to improve their manufacturing techniques.
- Advise clients on how to distribute their products in line with healthcare laws.

IP

- Represent clients during patent infringement proceedings.

Corporate

- Advise on complex contractual relationships like collaborations and alliances.
- Facilitate commercial transactions involving a life sciences element.
- Assist with M&A and venture capital work containing a life sciences element.

- Take the role of lead negotiator in business transactions.

Realities of the job

- Working hours vary across the three core areas. Regulatory work offers the most flexibility, while the hours experienced by patent trial lawyers – especially as a case heats up – can be intense. Corporate hours, as you might expect, are dictated by the peaks and troughs of the deal cycle, so periods of late nights are followed by lulls of more standard hours.
- *"It is important to be a specialist but also to learn about other fields and how they impact on each other, e.g. how the area of product liability might influence regulatory advice,"* says **Scott Bass** of **Sidley Austin**. *"One of the main challenges is keeping up with fast-changing developments and staying informed."*
- This fast pace is at the same time one of the most exciting elements of the practice, Bass feels: *"The sector is constantly changing, so there's the opportunity to break new ground often. You get to help industry but also assist governments and consumers in a lot of what you do."*
- **Latham & Watkins'** **Judith Hasko** agrees: *"I think you have got to have a comfort level with an ever-changing legal and regulatory environment, and you have to be interested and comfortable with change. It is an exciting industry, but people who do well like change."*
- *"You also have to be commercially sophisticated and have an interest in the commercial drivers as to why a company wants to do something,"* Hasko continues. *"In my experience you need to work well with your client. They have critical information you need. You need the full input of your client and it's your job to do that. It is also challenging to tailor advice so that it makes sense to them. You just need to fully understand their goals. What is also tricky is the ability to keep a lot of different elements in your head about the law and the client's business at the same time when you are negotiating."*
- *"There is a lot of opportunity in life sciences as the legal frameworks and government's policies are constantly changing,"* Hasko explains. *"This creates opportunities for lawyers. It is very exciting and rewarding to help to move products forward that will help people. It's not a practice for everyone as it can be very technical, but for those who have a connection with the industry I would say go for it."*
- On the corporate side, **Covington & Burling's** **John Hurvitz** tells us: *"You have an opportunity to be involved in all phases of the deal cycle from structuring to negotiating to implementation. Also, there is a lot of*

Practice Areas

Rankings in *Chambers USA*

Top ranked

Cooley	WilmerHale
Latham & Watkins	

Highly Recommended

Arnold & Porter	McDermott Will & Emery
Dechert	Mintz Levin
DLA Piper	Morgan, Lewis
Finnegan, Henderson	MoFo
Gibson, Dunn	Perkins Coie
Goodwin	Reed Smith
Hogan Lovells	Ropes & Gray
Irell & Manella	Sidley Austin
Jones Day	Wilson Sonsini
Kirkland & Ellis	

For more detail on ranking tiers and locations, visit
www.chambersandpartners.com

deal activity in the industry so you have an opportunity to work with clients over many years and multiple transactions. These deep and longstanding relationships are very rewarding, both professionally and personally."

- Hurvitz adds: *"A scientific background is useful but not necessary. It is more important to have an interest in the underlying science and technology, as there is ample opportunity to learn about the latest innovations and breakthroughs. The practice is multidisciplinary so to be successful you need to be comfortable working across a range of legal disciplines, such as IP, competition, corporate, and also to have a business mindset. The business issues and legal issues are inextricably intertwined in this practice."*

- Life sciences collaborations are, Hurvitz tells us, *"very complex. In addition to working across legal disciplines, there are often multiple facets of the deal that have to be managed in parallel. It is like four or five dimensional chess at times. People who are smart, curious, have good memories and attention to detail will do well. You also need to be comfortable in making judgment calls. There are often so many business and legal issues at play in any given deal, that the clients typically look to the lawyers to offer practical guidance."*

- When it comes to regulatory work, *"the most challenging thing we face in our practice is the challenge faced by industry as a whole: it is an extremely difficult and long*

process from invention to product," says **Daniel Becker** of **Fenwick & West**. *"In a 25-year career only two or three inventions that I've worked on have become a marketed pharmaceutical product. We don't get instant or even near-term gratification."* However, *"every time I come to work it's nice knowing that the work I am doing makes a difference. Very few products I work on make it to market, but when they do and you see the positive benefits it is so thrilling."*

Current issues

- *"A key issue at the moment is how governments will regulate emerging technology such as diagnostics, wearables, and home testing kits,"* Sidley Austin's Scott Bass explains. *"There is also an issue when it comes to the regulation of breakthrough drugs like biologics and genetically based drugs."*

- While the full effect of the Trump administration remains unclear, our interviewees made some predictions. Scott Bass takes a glass half-full approach: *"The prevailing view is that it will provide more incentives for companies to explore new areas with less government regulation."*

- In contrast, **Fenwick & West**'s **Daniel Becker** adopts a somewhat bleaker view: *"It's going to be a disaster. There will be many fewer individuals who have medical insurance; there will be an uninformed and unnuanced assault on drug pricing; and there will also be a chill on bringing in talent from other countries, as collaboration will become more difficult."*

- **Latham & Watkins**' **Judith Hasko** raises another Trump-related issue: *"What Trump is going to do is really unclear. He has made comments recently that he would impose some types of limits on drug prices or reimbursement for drugs, which would have a ripple effect across the industry. There are also some concerns that conservative government leaders may implement policies that could hinder certain types of scientific research."*

- On a positive note, the 21st Century Cures Act was enacted in 2016. $6.3 billion has been set aside for funding medical research, including former vice president Joe Biden's 'Cancer Moonshot' program. The law could speed up the approval process for prescriptions and medical devices, increasing activity in the sector.

- Elsewhere, IP-related laws continue to keep lawyers busy. A recent law stipulated that genetic sequences were not patentable, which had large ramifications across the industry.

Practice Areas

Litigation

In a nutshell

Litigation attorneys help their clients resolve disputes. If disputes are not settled by negotiation, they will be concluded either by court litigation or by an alternative form of dispute resolution, such as arbitration or mediation, both of which are potentially more expeditious, less costly and out of public view.

Disputes may concern anything from unpaid bills or unfulfilled contract terms to problems between landlords and tenants, infringement of IP rights, construction-related claims, the liabilities of insurers, shipping cases, defective products, entertainment industry wrangles… the list is endless. Since the recession, many general litigators have become increasingly involved in conflicts arising out of securities, white-collar crime and bankruptcy scenarios.

Some litigators will concentrate on specific types of claims, making use of particular industry knowledge; others will remain generalists, applying their legal experiences – especially trial experience – to all manner of cases and clients. The onus is often on young litigators to specialize early: *"You were almost discouraged from being a specialist 30 years ago. It is more important now to think about a speciality. A good litigator is a generalist: they can try any case, but also having a speciality is key to marketability now,"* according to **David Lender** of **Weil Gotshal.** Some litigators will focus on appellate matters – see our Appellate chapter for more info.

What litigators do

- Pre-litigation counseling and advisory work. Part of the job involves mitigating the risk of future wrangles by counseling clients on the ramifications of business decisions and ensuring compliance with laws and regulators. *"We focus on risk analysis,"* **Anton Valukas** of **Jenner & Block** stresses. *"All good litigators understand that an appropriate evaluation of a matter in the first instance can significantly reduce exposure to litigation."*
- Advise clients on whether they have a valid claim, or whether to settle or fight a claim made against them. *"One of the biggest mistakes lawyers can make is to oversell the chances of winning,"* **Robert Giuffra** of **Sullivan & Cromwell** tells us. *"The client needs the best possible assessment of the chances of victory and what it will entail to get them there."*
- Draft pleadings; for example, if acting for a defendant a litigator will prepare a motion to dismiss or an answer.
- Assuming that the case goes beyond the pleading stage, litigators will ordinarily proceed to the discovery phase, where each side serves discovery requests on the other in order to gain access to evidence that is relevant to the case.
- In modern litigation cases *"virtually all of discovery now is e-discovery; in large major commercial litigation it is rare now to have paper discovery,"* according to David Lender. In part this is due to a growth in cross-border litigation, as well as technological development. For smaller and mid-sized firms, e-discovery work is often outsourced. **Eugene Stearns** of **Stearns Weaver Miller** notes: *"Lawyers now have to be IT specialists as well as traditional litigators. It is critical for young lawyers to develop these techniques."*
- There is a vast amount of document review, during which litigators attempt to find the 'smoking gun' that will win the case – for example, an email that indicates strong evidence of a conspiracy. *"There is a perception that a stunning moment in a trial will turn it all around,"* Valukas tells us. *"The reality is if you have two really talented lawyers who work exceedingly hard, the facts will determine the case. For every hour in the courtroom there have been dozens of hours spent outside it, getting ready for that moment. All that preparatory work for trial is so important."*
- Draft evidentiary objections. This involves constructing arguments on the admissibility of evidence that may be prejudicial, or beneficial, to either side. Represent clients at pretrial hearings.
- Prepare and conduct depositions.
- Senior litigators, normally at partner level, are responsible for the way the case is presented and conduct the trial itself, deciding which arguments will resonate with jurors and undertaking witness cross-examination and closing arguments. *"You always want to litigate a case through the rubric of your main themes. One mistake lawyers make is to overcomplicate a case,"* says Giuffra. *"It's very important to figure out and focus on the four or so issues that matter most."*

Realities of the job

- *"The great thing about litigation is the variety; everything is new almost all of the time,"* says **Carey Dunne**, formerly of Davis Polk and currently general counsel of the Manhattan District Attorney's Office. *"The legal issues can be similar, of course, but the industries are frequently different and so are the facts, which means the strategy and analysis are always challenging and evolving."*
- Everything is driven by procedural rules and the time-

Rankings in *Chambers USA*

Top ranked

Alston & Bird	Latham & Watkins
Cleary Gottlieb	Morgan, Lewis & Bockius
Cravath	Munger, Tolles & Olson
Davis Polk & Wardwell	Nixon Peabody
Debevoise & Plimpton	Paul, Weiss, Rifkind
Dechert	Perkins Coie
DLA Piper	Proskauer Rose
Foley & Lardner	Reed Smith
Fried, Frank	Ropes & Gray
Gibbons	Sidley Austin
Gibson, Dunn & Crutcher	Simpson Thacher
Goodwin	Skadden, Arps
Hogan Lovells	Snell & Wilmer
Hunton & Williams	Sullivan & Cromwell
Jenner & Block	Waller
Jones Day	Willkie Farr & Gallagher
K&L Gates	WilmerHale
King & Spalding	Wilson Sonsini
Kirkland & Ellis	

Highly Recommended

Akin Gump	Kasowitz Benson Torres
Allen & Overy	Katten Muchin Rosenman
Arnold & Porter	Kilpatrick Townsend
Axinn, Veltrop & Harkrider	Kramer Levin Naftalis
Baker Botts	Mayer Brown
Baker McKenzie	McDermott Will & Emery
Bracewell	Milbank, Tweed, Hadley
Brownstein Hyatt Farber	Mintz Levin
Cadwalader	MoFo
Cahill Gordon	Norton Rose Fulbright
Choate Hall & Stewart	Nutter McClennen & Fish
Clifford Chance US	O'Melveny & Myers
Cooley	Orrick, Herrington
Cozen O'Connor	Patterson Belknap Webb
Crowell & Moring	Paul Hastings
Duane Morris	Shearman & Sterling
Dykema Gossett	Sheppard, Mullin, Richter
Fox Rothschild	Squire Patton Boggs
Freshfields Bruckhaus	Thompson & Knight
Goulston & Storrs	Vedder Price
Greenberg Traurig	Venable
Hangley Aronchick	Vinson & Elkins
Haynes and Boone	Weil
Holland & Knight	White & Case
Irell & Manella	Winston & Strawn
Jackson Walker	

For more detail on ranking tiers and locations, visit
www.chambersandpartners.com

table of the courts. Good litigators understand how best to maneuver within the system, while also developing case-winning strategies.

- As litigators need to abide by tight deadlines, the nature of the work is often cyclical. *"There may be periods when you just have a tremendous volume of work that needs to be accomplished in a short amount of time, but there's also a level of rush and excitement about that,"* says **David Zinn** of **Williams & Connolly**.

- *"You have to be someone who is willing to deal with uncertainty; litigation is inherently uncertain,"* Giuffra tells us. *"Planning goes out the window; I've had to learn how not to plan,"* confirmed one Fried Frank associate. *"It's an adjustment and some people aren't ready for that. You need to be adaptable."*

- *"Searching through documents is often like looking for a needle in a haystack; it can be a taxing and tiring process,"* explains **F Joseph Warin** of **Gibson Dunn**. However, for junior attorneys this is not as prominent a task as it once was. While initial document review is often outsourced to contract attorneys, litigators at all levels of seniority need to have excellent knowledge of the key documents in a case.

- Juniors do also perform written work, like first drafts of pleadings, and the preparation of questions to be asked, and sometimes conduct depositions.

- Technology is changing the face of the litigation process: *"The ethics bars of each state are even passing ethics rules that you are obligated to have technological skills in the modern era, to provide your client with effective counsel,"* says David Lender. Young lawyers developing a practice in the area should consider developing these skills.

- Litigators need to express themselves succinctly and precisely in all their communications.

- *"Taking apart a set of arguments is like a labyrinth of pros and cons,"* Warin says. *"You need to figure out which are likely to be the most persuasive for a judge or jury, as well as discarding arguments that you eventually find out are flawed."*

- Deciding upon which arguments will be the most effective is made easier by jury simulations. *"You don't go to trial in a big case without having some testing of which key points resonate with potential jurors,"* according to **Jonathan Lerner** of **Skadden**.

- Front-line participation in full-blown trial advocacy generally isn't something that litigators experience until later in their careers. *"Sometimes young lawyers don't get the opportunity to be in the courtroom,"* says **Randy Mastro** of **Gibson Dunn**. *"I always encourage them to take on additional pro bono assignments where they can get that experience."*

- Litigators may be known for having the gift of the gab but it's just as important to put your ears to good use. **Brad D Brian**, co-MP of **Munger, Tolles & Olson,** tells us: *"If you're in a courtroom you need to listen to what* *the judge and opposing counsel are saying. So many lawyers at the beginning and end of their careers are tied to their scripts for their outline or witness examinations and are not listening to what the judge, opposing counsel or witnesses are saying."*

- The overwhelming majority of cases will settle before reaching trial; however, in the current environment, cases often settle later in the process. Eugene Stearns of Stearns Weaver Miller notes that *"litigation is becoming very expensive for those looking to solve disputes. Clients are trying to figure out how to avoid court proceedings."*

Current issues

- As clients tighten their budgets for full-blown trials, law firms are having to compete far more for the fewer matters that are going around. Cash-conscious companies are turning instead to mediation or arbitration to settle disputes or directing their lawyers to keep costs down. While the amount of litigation may have fallen, cases that do make it to trial are increasingly complex or high value.
- Recent high-profile data breaches have catapulted cyber security and privacy into the spotlight. It's now one of the fastest-growing practices out there. Data breaches; a growing push for consumer protection; and regulatory shifts concerning privacy and data sharing have highlighted the need for businesses to have a strong understanding of the law in this area. For example, the Federal Communication Commission's (FCC) 2015 ruling on the Telephone Consumer Protection Act increased the scope of liability businesses face, while in Europe the European Court of Justice ruled that national regulators have the power to stop companies transferring EU citizens' data to the US.
- Class action lawsuits are another booming area. Privacy class actions are increasingly hitting the courts as consumers take on companies whose data breaches exposed personal data. Other busy areas right now include class actions against inaccurate food and beverage labeling, and securities fraud. 2016 was also a high water mark for class actions concerning minimum-wage increases across several states, and independent-contractor classification in the 'gig economy'.
- The SEC announced it has filed the most enforcement cases in its history for the third year in a row. While mortgage-related matters stemming from the financial crisis have tailed off, litigators are more active in relation to financial services activity such as price fixing, municipal bond disclosures, and other securities litigation.

- Contentious IP matters in the healthcare and pharmaceutical space are tipped for an uptick. *"There's a growing need for litigation services in the biosimilar area,"* **Evan Chesler** of **Cravath** highlights. 'What on earth are biosimilars?' we hear you cry: they're basically generic copies of branded bio-pharmaceutical drugs. *"The legal issues with biosimilars are similar to those which surround the development of generic drugs in the traditional chemical pharma space,"* Chesler continues. *"I think that will be a very big litigation focus in the coming years."* 2016 saw a significant uptick in patent litigation filings, a trend which shows little sign of abating.
- Whereas previous years saw a large amount of antitrust litigation due to the tough enforcement stance of the Obama administration, President Trump's rhetoric implies a more pro-business stance, so it is likely that there may be a decrease in litigation stemming from this source, but a possible increase in M&A activity.
- The last year has seen a large amount of healthcare trials taking place before the Supreme Court concerning the Affordable Care Act. It remains to be seen what, if anything, will replace it. The Court's decision over Texas's onerous abortion law will likely deter other states from pursuing the same line.
- The Trump administration's dismissive view of global warming is being met with legal challenges. Environmental nongovernmental organizations (ENGOs) are increasingly fighting new energy developments with regulatory and legal weapons. Using social media to mobilize support, ENGOs are drumming up considerable funding to enable them to pursue these challenges.
- In late 2015, the Department of Justice revealed its new white-collar crime policy which places an increased focus on the naming of individuals involved in corporate wrongdoing. Previously, companies could cooperate with investigators and hand over information about improper practices without having to identify those involved but, in part thanks to criticism that Wall Street execs have remained largely unscathed in the fall out from the financial crisis, the DOJ has toughened its stance. Credit will be given to companies who hand over such details, but commentators are concerned that in the interest of protecting employees, organizations may refuse to cooperate with the DOJ.
- The question of immigration reform is more pressing than ever under Trump. His travel bans continue to be met with fierce legal challenges all over the country.

White Collar Litigation: Cahill's experts reveal how it works

White collar tops the chart for the happiest practice area for associates, according to our recent survey. We caught up with a few white collar litigators at Cahill to find out more about their intriguing practice.

What is white collar law?

Helena Franceschi, associate: "White collar" law refers to the broad range of finance-related offenses that can be subject to regulatory investigations and enforcement actions. It covers a broad range of conduct and can implicate antitrust, the Foreign Corrupt Practices Act, antimanipulation, and fraud statutes. Because white collar laws often concern the practices of global institutions, these investigations may involve cross-border proceedings before multiple regulators.

Ivan Torres, associate: I view white collar law as the practice of investigating and defending financially motivated misconduct that typically occurs in connection with commercial activity.

What are the highs and lows?

HF: The work is sophisticated and above-the-fold *Wall Street Journal* consequential. That is certainly one of the highs. Discovering the facts of any given case and piecing together the advocacy to support those facts – just as you would with any litigation – is also one of the highs. The lows include a significant amount of document review that is to be expected in today's modern society given the significance of email and electronic forms of communication.

IT: The highs and lows typically come together. Whenever an investigation really gets moving the work typically gets very intense, but this is also when you start to see all your hard work pay off. This pay-off can either be realizing patterns in the documents and financial records that you didn't appreciate at the beginning of an investigation, taking an interview where the interviewee's body language and reactions make it clear that they are surprised to see certain documents that you have shown them or surprised to hear certain questions, or being able to piece together the facts of a situation to explain what might look like misconduct on first glance was actually legitimate.

What do associates do?

Cydney Swofford Freeman, associate: White collar matters can be an excellent way to gain substantive experience as a very junior associate, as the teams are frequently quite small. As the junior associate (and occasionally the only associate!), I typically handle document analysis, am involved with various client and third-party interviews, and will often write the first draft of reports and client memoranda.

HF: Associates review documents and develop the facts and timeline of the case. Associates also participate in subsequent witness interviews as well as draft pieces of advocacy, involving presentations to regulators and white papers.

IT: I have been on investigation teams that were 20+ people where my primary role was to do second or third line review of documents and to build out chronologies based on those documents, but I have also worked on teams of less than five where I was visiting clients to take interviews, preparing and attending presentations to government regulators, and was involved in building out and executing our overall investigation plan. But as a general matter, the work on a white collar investigation usually includes a mix of document review with an eye towards building out the story of what happened, preparing for and taking interviews of key personnel, working with accountants to follow the money trail, preparing presentations detailing your findings for the client (which typically include the general counsel, the board of directors, or independent board members), and either cooperating with the relevant government regulators or working with them to best protect the rights and interests of your client.

How does your work interact with general litigation?

HF: Regulatory investigation and enforcement work often comes hand-in-hand with civil litigations concerning the same conduct. Thus, associates have the opportunity to experience a white collar matter from both the investigatory and litigation perspectives.

Practice Areas

157

CSF: Our firm divides its associates into two categories: corporate and litigation. Our white collar matters are generally run through the litigation department. There is no third set of associates who only do white collar, though because Cahill uses a free market system, people who would like to exclusively work on white collar cases may choose to accept only white collar work. I personally work on a variety of both litigation and white collar matters simultaneously.

IT: I personally have maintained a balance of at least one white collar investigation and one more general litigation matter since I started at Cahill because the two offer you different experiences and challenges.

How soon should a litigator specialize?

HF: A litigator should make her own decision when to specialize, and in part the natural trajectory of a litigator's career will determine it. Some experience many matters as a "generalist" for some time before affirmatively choosing to develop a competency. On the other hand, others may inadvertently develop a competency through working with the same team over a period of time.

CSF: Unless a person comes to a firm absolutely certain that they want to specialize in a particular area, I do not think a litigator needs to specialize early. I am a second-year associate, and have by no means worked only on white collar cases. I think my varied experience benefits my practice as a whole.

IT: At least at Cahill, there is no push to specialize early on. If anything, litigation associates are encouraged to maintain a diverse practice that includes both general litigation and investigations work. This diversity gives you a different perspective and helps you see the big picture on matters better. For example, the typically less formal path investigations take lets associates get earlier experience with interviews that becomes helpful down the line when taking depositions. Likewise, having experience with the more adversarial environment of litigation is helpful as it makes you more critical in the way you approach an internal investigation.

Where can new associates expect to be in five years?

HF: The hope is to leverage one's training at the junior level to become a highly effective manager/midlevel associate.

IT: By your fifth year, associates working on white collar investigations and cases have usually worked on a number of different matters that often relate to different industries, and in doing so have taken a number of interviews, have been involved in presentations to both the client and government regulators, and have also had the chance to see a number of their investigations to a close, which will typically include settlement negotiations with the government and assisting companies with remedial efforts.

What personal qualities make good white collar lawyers?

HF: Attention to detail and a good attitude, always, and a willingness to learn and adapt – being part of an investigation team requires learning the client's business.

CSF: Some of the best white collar lawyers I know are thorough, measured, and detail-oriented.

IT: Curiosity and a willingness to learn and think on your feet. Often when you start an investigation you will have little background knowledge on the workings of a particular industry. To understand the motivations of the people who work at the company you have to really understand the work they do.

What are the trends and big stories in the white collar market?

HF: Coming out of the financial crisis, we have seen regulators focus on benchmark rigging (e.g., LIBOR, foreign exchange, and others) as well as fraud more generally with respect to certain complex assets (e.g., RMBS). As algorithms and automated processes begin to play a bigger role in banks and other large institutions, I predict that regulatory enforcement/white collar will eventually shift its focus to policing predatory behavior in this area.

IT: Over the past few years there has been more of a push for companies to assist the government in investigating which individual directors or executives were involved in misconduct. In terms of big stories, over the last five years or so you have the interest rates-related investigations and prosecutions both here and in the UK, a number of anti-corruption investigations that focus on Latin America, including, for example, the ever growing Petrobras scandal and the fallout from the Mossack Fonseca leaks.

How should students brush-up on their white collar knowledge?

IT: Following the news, including legal news and blogs related to white collar work is helpful because these resources give you pretty good insight into the trends going on. Law schools also often have great guest speakers who have either worked on these cases on the defense side or have prosecuted these cases.

HF: Apart from taking Securities Regulation in law school, they should read the *Financial Times*, the *Wall Street Journal*, and check out popular books and films that concern white collar crime.

What are your tips for passing the interview process?

CSF: As cheesy as it sounds, I think that being yourself is most important in an interview. Sure, firms will evaluate your resume and transcript, but as an interviewer, what I want to know is whether I would enjoy working with you on a daily basis for the foreseeable future. The reverse is equally as important. Of course, it is also important to understand the contours of the firm before the interview – for example, Cahill prides itself on its free market system.

IT: Be well prepared to discuss your own background and interests and also why you are interested in working at the firm you are interviewing at. Also, be yourself, remember that interviews are not only about finding the smartest candidate but also about finding people that will be good members of a team.

HF: Demonstrate how you are self-motivated and able to multi-task with different projects and meet deadlines.

Describe the opportunities unique to Cahill

HF: With excellence comes opportunity: Cahill staffs cases leanly and thus associates may be able to assume more responsibility early, at a more junior level. Associates also benefit from the collegial environment and mentorship by more senior attorneys, including partners.

CSF: Cahill's free market system may not be entirely unique, but was one of its strongest selling points when I made the decision to join. I relish the ability to craft my caseload based on my interests, rather than immediately pigeonholing myself into a specific practice area as a very young associate. As only a second year, I already

have been able to explore white collar, First Amendment, trademark, and financial litigation matters, just to name a few.

IT: I have been able to work on a range of different projects including FCPA work, securities litigation, complex financial litigation, and first amendment work. By allowing associates to develop their own practice rather than having more rigid departments, Cahill allows associates more flexibility with the experiences they get and with partners and clients they get to work with. I have also found Cahill to be very willing to let associates take on work that typically would be reserved for more senior associates when they show an interest and an ability to take on greater responsibility.

Learn more about associate life at Cahill on p.237

Authors

Helena Franceschi
Associate

Ivan Torres
Associate

Cydney Swofford
Freeman, Associate

CAHILL

Practice Areas

The Big Interview: **Elkan Abramowitz**, star white collar litigator

Elkan Abramowitz (JD NYU School of Law 1964) was awarded a *Chambers USA* 'Lifetime Achievement Award' in 2016. He is a name partner at white-collar boutique Morvillo Abramowitz Grand Iason & Anello in New York and is ranked as a senior statesmen in New York for Litigation: White-Collar Crime & Government Investigations by Chambers USA.

Abramowitz built his name defending high-profile, often political or commercial, clients. One of this most famous cases saw him represent Woody Allen in the filmmaker's custody battle with ex-wife Mia Farrow in 1993. More recently, he successfully undermined the prosecution in the marathon case against former Dewey & LeBoeuf chairman Steven Davis, resulting in a deadlocked jury and a mistrial. Abramowitz has also served as Assistant Deputy Mayor for the City of New York and as a Special Counsel to the Select Committee on Crime for the US House of Representatives.

Why did you decide to become a lawyer?
In my Brooklyn neighborhood there were really only three career options: the law, medicine, and going into business with your father. My father was an accountant and I couldn't add two and two, so I really thought I couldn't be an accountant. Also, I couldn't stand the sight of blood. So by default, I just kept saying I was going to be a lawyer. Despite briefly fancying the idea of becoming a high school teacher, I have been dedicated to law.

Starting out, what did you expect from a career in law?
Early on, I viewed myself as being very shy. I did not know that I had the chops to be a trial lawyer. However, after my summer job in the US Attorney's office, followed by a District Court clerkship right out of NYU Law, everything changed (including my expectations). Watching the trial work of the great trial lawyers of the day reassured me that I was cut out to follow in their footsteps.

> *"Trying white collar cases has evolved into an exercise as to which side has the more significant electronic evidence."*

How did you get into white collar defense? By design? By chance?
I went to law school before trial-practice courses were offered, so I had to learn from other ways. During my clerkship in the S.D.N.Y., I watched and learned from really good trial lawyers on both sides, and I realized this is something I really could be competent doing. I learned by watching, as opposed to doing. I also noted what came naturally to me as well as what skills of mine might need sharpening. With the skills I learned in the US Attorney's Office, it was natural for me to specialize in white collar defense.

You took a lot of cases to trial very early on in your career. What do you consider to have been your big break?
Yes, I tried 30 cases to verdict before I was 30, which certainly kick-started my career. In 1976 when US Attorney Bob Fiske asked me to return to the government as Chief of the Criminal Division I accepted his offer, solidifying another pivotal milestone. He wanted someone with defense experience, which is a perspective that I wish more career prosecutors understood.

What's been the most eye-opening experience of your career and what has it taught you?
Trying white collar cases has evolved into an exercise as to which side has the more significant electronic evidence. Instead of cases involving just oral testimony, too many cases now rely on ill-conceived emails which are expensive to retrieve and sometimes difficult to explain.

What single achievement are you most proud of?
I am extremely proud of my recent representation of Steven Davis, the former Chairman of Dewey & LeBoeuf, and the related marathon trial. Indeed, the trial was referred to as the legal industry's trial of the year. It centered around allegations that Davis and two other executives engaged in a long-running scheme to defraud investors. But prosecutors failed to tell a coherent story, which allowed me and my team to prove that there was no crime. Once you really believe that – and I did believe it before the trial – all your cross-examinations and all your openings and summations fall into place.

What do you consider your greatest failure or regret?
Not trying more cases. Because of the sentencing guidelines and the expense and complexity of modern white collar prosecutions, fewer and fewer cases are going to trial. This ends up giving the government too much pow-

er in defining what is criminal conduct. In my view, we need more juries to intervene in reviewing the government's judgment.

"How best to deal with business activity that damages the public good? I stand by my conviction that prosecuting CEOs is generally not the answer."

What have you enjoyed most during your career in the legal profession?

Reflecting on my career, I am particularly proud of my defense work involving prosecutions that, I believe, have represented misguided efforts to address an important national policy question: how best to deal with business activity that damages the public good? I stand by my conviction that prosecuting CEOs is generally not the answer.

And the least?

The drudgery of discovery in civil cases.

What do you want your legacy to be?

A dedicated family man who had the courage and support to navigate and conquer a challenging area of the law.

What law would you change, abolish or create?

The question of guilt or innocence is something that is not so stark in white collar cases because often the problem is not whether somebody did something, but whether what they did was knowingly wrong. There's no question that what went on in the financial crisis was a disaster on every level, but the answer is not to stretch traditional notions of criminality to try to put people in

jail. The answer is to create a regulatory environment where these things can't happen again. I firmly believe that the clamor to prosecute the bankers of the 2008 stock market collapse is unwarranted. The public's focus on senior executives deflects attention from the core issue – poorly regulated financial instruments.

Who is your legal hero?

I've had three bosses in my career: Inzer B. Wyatt, Robert M. Morgenthau, and Robert B. Fiske, all of whom are my legal heroes. I learned the importance of scholarship, precision, compassion, thoroughness, craftsmanship, and integrity – things that I hope are reflected in my work to this day.

What differences do you see in today's legal market compared to when you started?

When I started out, white collar law was less ubiquitous. Today, white collar law has become a standard practice area in BigLaw. The other significant change is the globalization of law firms, which have increased exponentially in size. Unfortunately, our profession is still struggling with diversity and inclusion.

What advice would you give to students trying to enter the legal profession today?

Work hard, evaluate your strengths and weaknesses, and pursue opportunities of interest.

And to those looking to become a trial lawyer?

Trial practice is not for everyone, but if you find your way to the first chair remember my most important trial motto: KISS (keep it simple stupid), followed by one of my favorite courtroom rules: when you're winning the argument with the Court, stop speaking. Sometimes the more you argue, the more you might convince the Court that it was wrong in initially agreeing with you.

Practice Areas

"The problem is not whether somebody did something, but whether what they did was knowingly wrong."

Securities litigation: an overview by Cleary Gottlieb

Our team of litigators in this area has had a significant impact in obtaining precedential rulings that shape securities law in the nation's preeminent courts. Our work is challenging and often presents new factual scenarios which push each of us to work through complex issues. The opportunity to develop creative and novel legal strategies for our clients, with whom we have deep and long-standing relationships, makes each week that much more interesting and meaningful.

What type of work you can expect to do in this practice?

A week can vary widely. It can include a deposition or representing clients in investigatory interviews, drafting briefs, preparing and presenting arguments in court, or meeting with clients to discuss strategic direction. I am fortunate to work at a firm that is comprised of so many intelligent and creative lawyers. I work with many of our associates on a daily basis and I enjoy educating and mentoring them.

What preparations can you make to succeed in this practice?

Read the New York Times, the Wall Street Journal, the New York Law Journal, and newsletters describing cases and other legal developments. There is no better training and preparation than being knowledgeable about both the law and the facts. Take advantage of opportunities to ask questions from other practitioners and to write. Be courageous and confident in your views. And, as it relates to law school coursework, classes on civil procedure, evidence, and securities litigation would be beneficial. I would also encourage everyone to develop a practice of reading cases beginning to end in order to understand the stories they tell and the legal principles involved in the case.

Some recent securities litigation cases from Cleary's standpoint.

- We are representing **Petrobras**, **PGF**, and **certain current and former Petrobras executives**, in securities fraud litigation in the U.S. District Courts for the Southern District of New York and the Eastern District of Pennsylvania.
- We represented financial institutions – including **Bank of America, BBVA, BNY Mellon, Caja Madrid, Citi-**

group, and **HSBC** – that underwrote securities issued by Lehman Brothers in the 18 months prior to its collapse in the settlement of a class action arising out of the Lehman offerings; and in securing the dismissal or settlement of actions brought before the class settlement was achieved.

- We represented global financial institutions, including **HSBC, BNP Paribas, Credit Agricole, Citigroup** and **BNY Mellon**, in defending matters arising from the Madoff fraud and the bankruptcy of Bernard L. Madoff Investment Securities. The case spanned the US, Italy, the UK, Ireland, Luxembourg and Bermuda.
- We acted for **The Dow Chemical Company** in winning the dismissal of a federal proxy case brought against the company's directors and principal officers in the U.S. District Court for the District of Delaware.
- We represented **Warburg Pincus** and one of its managing directors in securing dismissal of a complaint alleging federal securities fraud claims in the U.S. District Court for the Central District of California.
- We are representing the current and former board of directors of **Kindred Healthcare** in shareholder derivative litigation brought in state court in Kentucky.
- We represented **Goldman, Sachs & Co.**, as financial advisor to the board of directors of **Volcano Corporation** in its acquisition by Philips in securing the dismissal of post-closing damages claims in the Delaware Court of Chancery.
- We represented **Google** in securing the dismissal of a shareholder class action filed in Illinois state court, arising out of Google's 2011 acquisition of Motorola Mobility; our firm also represented Google in the underlying transaction.
- We represented **Nationstar Mortgage Holdings, Inc.** in winning a motion to dismiss a putative securities class action filed on behalf of shareholders in the U.S. District Court for the Southern District of Florida.
- We are representing lender **OneMain Holdings** and

several of its officers in a putative securities class action under the Exchange Act, challenging public statements about the company's financial condition, results of operation, and anticipated benefits from the $4.25 billion acquisition that created OneMain Holdings.

About the author

Lewis Liman's practice focuses on commercial and securities class action litigation, government enforcement, and appeals. He has been retained to represent leading financial institutions and Fortune 100 companies in securities litigation, and companies and senior executives in governmental enforcement actions. Mr. Liman joined Cleary in 2003 as a partner. Prior to joining Cleary, he worked for over five years as an Assistant U.S. Attorney for the Southern District of New York, during which time he was appointed Deputy Chief Appellate Attorney. He has also served as a law clerk to the Honorable Pierre N. Leval of the U.S. District Court for the Southern District of New York, and to Justice John Paul Stevens of the U.S. Supreme Court. He received a J.D. from Yale Law School, an M.Sc. in Economics, with distinction, from the London School of Economics, and an undergraduate degree, magna cum laude, from Harvard.

To learn about associate life at Cleary turn to p.243

Practice Areas

CLEARY GOTTLIEB

Privacy & Data Security

In a nutshell

The issue of privacy and data security is one of the most pressing and controversial in our digital age – so naturally it's a growth area for lawyers. The law in this area is still relatively new, but nonetheless it struggles to keep up with rapid technological advances. Lawyers advise clients on the collection, use and transfer of personal information. Multinational companies, developers of products and public bodies are all under pressure to comply to ever-changing regulation that protects the consumer.

"Cybersecurity is going to be a hot button issue."

– Mary Ellen Callahan, Jenner & Block

Attorneys might focus on compliance and take a proactive approach, ensuring clients adhere to their obligations to protect personal information either from outside attack or from misuse by employees. Alternatively, lawyers might assume a more reactive role and deal with data breaches, as well as contentious matters and investigations conducted by data protection authorities. This part of the practice is also known as the enforcement side.

The rise of social media companies, smart technology and data transmission means that lawyers in this field are increasingly relevant. A growing awareness of what is being shared between organizations has prompted the need to protect not only personal data but intellectual property too. *"Cybersecurity is going to be a hot button issue,"* **Mary Ellen Callahan** of **Jenner & Block** says. *"There is more interest than ever in keeping information protected."*

What privacy and data security lawyers do

- Advise companies on data transfer and storage.
- Advise companies on risk factors that make them vulnerable to cyber attacks.
- Negotiate settlements for clients accused of neglecting their legal obligations.
- Litigate on behalf of clients whose data has been breached.
- Are sometimes employed on a 'just in case' basis to take action in tricky situations.
- Work with engineers and developers to ensure that software adheres to regulatory obligations.

Realities of the job

- Given that this area affects all types of businesses, you'll *"work with a whole range of clients,"* Mary Ellen Callahan tells us. Her practice covers everything from *"the entertainment industry to government contracts. I like the variety. I like the fact that I deal with six to 12 clients a day."*

"The matters that arise are a really big deal for the client; it's like heart surgery."

– Doug Meal, Ropes & Gray

- On the reactive side of the practice, the pressure can be high. *"The matters that arise are a really big deal for the client; it's like heart surgery,"* says **Doug Meal** of **Ropes & Gray**. *"Dealing with a major security breach feels truly life threatening for the client so it's really rewarding when, first of all, you get engaged by a client who needs help in this scary and stressful situation."* However, this can also *"put significant stress on you; the clients are really counting on you and you feel tremendous responsibility for them."*

- This burgeoning area of law provides plenty of hands-on experience for young lawyers. Callahan tells us: *"I have a woman working on international data transfers and another on mobile data protections. They will work somewhere between one and four hours and then meet to talk about the issues. They might participate once a week in client calls to follow up on aspects and do a status check. When we are in reactive mode we need a more rapid pace, perhaps with hourly calls. On a breach, for example, we need to be all hands on deck."*

- With new territory comes the need for creativity. *"This body of law barely existed 10 years ago,"* says Meal. *"On every matter you're dealing with legal issues that have never been dealt with before. There are not enough prior decisions out there to really decide for you what the answer will be to an issue that arises. As a lawyer you have an opportunity as you're not bound by a whole body of established law. You have the ability to argue and have a role in making the law."*

- Although a technical background *"can be useful and give you some credibility,"* it is not necessarily required, says Callahan. Meal agrees: *"Prior experience in computer technology is valuable but certainly not essential."*

- Variety is key in the beginning, says Meal: *"I would want the opportunity to do both compliance and enforcement for some period of time. I would be looking*

Rankings in *Chambers USA*

Top ranked

Hogan Lovells	MoFo

Highly recommended

Alston & Bird	Perkins Coie
Arnold & Porter Kaye	Ropes & Gray
Baker McKenzie	Sidley Austin
Cooley	Venable
DLA Piper	Wiley Rein
Hunton & Williams	Wilson Sonsini
McDermott Will & Emery	

For more detail on ranking tiers and locations, visit
www.chambersandpartners.com

*hard for a law firm that would give you a chance to do
this in the area – it's quite important."*

Current Issues

- The Trump administration could affect the Federal Communications Commission's (FCC) scope. *"The FCC has been under Democratic control for the last eight years, and during that time it has dramatically expanded its regulatory reach in privacy and data security,"* explains Meal. *"The FCC will now be moving under Republican control, so you could see a significant rollback of what has been occurring under Democratic control."*

- Privacy and data security legislation could also take a new turn following the appointment of Neil Gorsuch as the ninth member of the Supreme Court. *"In issues where the Supreme Court is going to be asked to speak about how to interpret various statutes and what the scope of the FCC's authority is, you could see those situations coming out more pro business than pro consumer,"* says Meal.

- The alleged Russian hacking of the Democratic National Committee highlighted priorities for lawyers in the field. *"Good data governance and hygiene"* will become increasingly important factors, says Callahan. *"It's very sobering,"* she adds, pointing to the rising stakes of cyber attacks: *"CEOs have been fired over breaches that occurred due a lack of data security."*

- *"On the privacy front, the focus on the EU will increase as we receive more data from Europe,"* says Callahan. New regulations on the movement of personal data have been adopted in the EU in the form of The General Data Protection Regulation: the regulations aim to simply the transfer of personal data for businesses while offering EU citizens control over how their data is processed. While data transfer between the USA and EU may become easier, business with the UK could be affected by the *"complexities created by Brexit,"* according to Meal.

- Businesses are also keen to keep their information under wraps. *"They need to protect their intellectual property,"* Callahan points out. Recent high-profile hackings and leaks – such as the Panama Papers – mean that risk mitigation will be especially relevant in the months ahead.

- The Federal Trade Secrets Act may produce some interesting cases brought by companies whose trade secrets have been stolen. On a related note, lawyers will see an uptick in *"drafting employment contracts to comply"* to ensure employees don't pass information on to competitors, according to **Lori Lesser** of **Simpson Thacher & Bartlett**.

- Government surveillance of companies and individuals will continue to be discussed. Recent news stories accuse governments of collecting personal data to analyze security threats, while whistleblower Edward Snowden is still making headlines for exposing the US government's tracking of personal emails and phone calls. In addition, Apple recently got into a courtroom brawl with the FBI, which demanded that it help them access an iPhone formerly belonging to San Bernardino shooter Syed Rizwan Farook. Going forward, the law will need to adapt to balance the individual's right to privacy with the perceived safety of the population at large.

- The advance of technology – especially 'smart' devices – has already caused a number of privacy concerns. For example: the potential to track the movement of an electric car; to monitor the activity of smart technology; to reach private spaces with drones; and to watch a user through their own webcam are all possibilities which the law will need to keep up with.

- The popularity of mobile apps means that personal information is more accessible than ever. Many apps ask the user to input details about themselves; most people neglect to read the small print and remain unaware of the extent to which their information could be shared.

- The ethics of using personal data for targeted advertising is being called into question. Facebook was recently criticized for drawing on messages sent via WhatsApp – which it acquired – to provide advertisements that it believes will appeal to its users. The question of whether it is acceptable or not to build a profile of app users in such a way will no doubt shape future legislation.

Practice Areas

Private Equity

In a nutshell

Private equity and investment companies operate funds that pool the investments of anybody prepared to part with their money for a sustained period of time. The private equity firm takes this cash – often alongside a large portion of bank debt (making it a 'leveraged buyout', or 'LBO') – to buy companies or other assets with the goal of selling them on at a massive profit. Investment management lawyers, therefore, have two primary functions: they form the funds (which are typically structured as limited partnerships) and help the private equity firm negotiate the terms on which investors contribute their money, and they act for the private equity fund when it buys and sells its investments.

Venture capital is a subset of private equity that sees investors put money into startup companies or small businesses in the hope they will be sold to a private equity firm or taken public. Although this typically entails high risk for the investor, it has the potential for above-average returns. The higher risk compared to private equity proper is offset by investing smaller amounts over a shorter timespan, typically.

Investment management is the professional management of various securities (shares, bonds, etc) and assets in order to meet the specified investment goals of investors. Investment management lawyers may work in any of the specialist areas described below, but ultimately advise on the structuring, formation, taxation and regulation of all types of investment funds.

A **hedge fund** is a private, actively managed investment fund. It aims to provide returns to investors by investing in a diverse range of markets, investment instruments and strategies. Hedge funds' investment strategies aim to make a positive return on investment regardless of whether markets are rising or falling. Expertise on the derivative markets helps hedge funds achieve this.

A **mutual fund** is a collective investment vehicle that pools money from many investors to purchase securities. The term is most commonly applied to collective investments that are regulated and sold to the general public.

A **real estate investment fund/trust** is a publicly traded investment vehicle that uses investors' money to invest in properties and mortgages.

Both hedge funds and mutual funds generally operate as **open funds**. This means that investors may periodically make additions to, or withdrawals from, their stakes in the fund. An investor will generally purchase shares in the fund directly from the fund itself rather than from the existing shareholders. It contrasts with a closed fund, which typically issues all the shares it will issue at the outset, with such shares usually being tradable between investors thereafter.

What lawyers do

- Advise clients on how to structure new funds.
- Help private equity firms negotiate the terms on which investors contribute their money.
- Act for the private fund when it buys and sells its investments.
- Assist clients throughout the fund-raising process. This includes the preparation of offering materials, the preparation of partnership agreements, advising on and documenting management and compensation arrangements, and closing fund formation transactions.
- Draft the numerous organizational documents necessary to form an investment fund, including a private placement memorandum, a limited partnership agreement (if the fund is a limited partnership) or an operating agreement (if the fund is a limited liability company), and investor subscription agreements.
- Conduct diligence and negotiate contracts.
- Inform and advise clients on the constantly changing regulatory and compliance issues arising under US and international securities, tax and ERISA laws.
- Provide day-to-day advice with respect to issues such as performance and advertising, and brokerage and portfolio trading practices.

Realities of the job

Funds lawyers often work for clients in very small teams, meaning there is the chance for even the most junior associates to gain great experience. *"When you start out, you will work on private placement memos, draft key documents and review the transfer agreements,"* says **Bruce Ettelson** of **Kirkland & Ellis**. *"In funds, you may negotiate with hundreds of parties at the same time so typically you get the chance to work in negotiations as a young associate."*

Structuring funds requires an intimate familiarity with relevant securities and investment company rules. Understanding and being able to apply knowledge of key legislature, such as the Securities and Exchange Com-

Rankings in *Chambers USA*

Top ranked

Goodwin	Simpson Thacher
Proskauer Rose	WilmerHale
Ropes & Gray	

Highly recommended

Choate Hall & Stewart	Kirkland & Ellis
Cleary Gottlieb	Latham & Watkins
Cooley	Paul, Weiss, Rifkind
Davis Polk & Wardwell	Skadden, Arps
Debevoise & Plimpton	Weil, Gotshal
Dechert	White & Case
Fried, Frank, Harris, Shriver	Willkie Farr & Gallagher
Gibson, Dunn & Crutcher	

For more detail on ranking tiers and locations, visit
www.chambersandpartners.com

mission (SEC) guidelines as well as federal and state laws, is a vital skill.

Setting up funds also requires a significant amount of tax, ERISA and industry knowledge. Funds lawyers often work in close collaboration with their tax and finance colleagues to realize the best value for clients.

Private placement memoranda must contain risk factors and material disclosures about the investment manager and the strategy to be employed by the fund.

Form ADV is the uniform form used by investment advisers to register with both the SEC and state securities authorities. It consists of two parts: part one requires information about the investment adviser's business, ownership, clients, employees, business practices, affiliations, and any disciplinary events of the adviser or its employees; part two requires investment advisers to prepare narrative brochures written in plain English that contain information such as the types of advisory services offered, the adviser's fee schedule, disciplinary information, conflicts of interest, and the educational and business background of management and key advisory personnel of the adviser.

Being responsive to client needs and understanding the time-sensitive nature of fund organization is essential. *"A lot of work involves helping clients to understand what the market is and how they can best use such information. As private funds attorneys, we often play a strategic counseling role,"* says **Bruce Ettelson**.

"I would recommend taking a securities regulations course," says **Lisa Schneider** of **Fried Frank**. *"Having a*

basic understanding of securities law is an important foundation for the practice of asset management and other areas of corporate law."

"A key personality trait often overlooked that you need in this practice area is emotional intelligence – people skills. One of the things I love about this practice is that in fundraisings I don't really do one-on-one negotiations, and in terms of large private securities offerings you will be dealing with numerous different law firms. Finding a common denominator and getting everyone to agree to pretty much the same terms means that being able to read, understand and gently move people helps tremendously," explains **Jordan Murray** of **Debevoise & Plimpton**.

"Attention to detail and the ability to take a step back and understand the big picture" are key attributes for success, according to **Lisa Schneider**.

Current issues

- Global private equity assets under management (AUM) are around $2.5 trillion, the highest ever (source: Prequin).
- 2016 was another strong year, the fourth consecutive year when fundraising surpassed $300 billion ($347 billion was raised by 830 funds in 2016).
- There is a trend of fewer funds managing more money. The average size of private equity funds closed in 2016 was $471 million, a record high.
- Private equity accounted for 57% of all private capital raised in 2016, up from 52% the previous year.
- According to Prequin, 95% of investors are happy with their private equity portfolios' performance, up from 81% in 2011.
- Healthcare IT company MultiPlan was both one of the largest private equity buyouts and exits in 2016 when GIC, Hellman & Friedman, and Leonard Green & Partners bought it for $7.5 billion from Ardian, Partners Group, and Starr Investment Holdings.
- 2016 saw 9,719 venture capital deals valued at $134 billion, representing a 13% drop in the number of financings from 2015 – reversing the upward trend of the previous six years.
- Private equity-backed IPOs in 2016 yielded proceeds of only $8.8 billion, down from $11.3 billion in 2015 and $25 billion in 2014. The 2016 figure was the lowest since 2009 (source: Renaissance Capital US IPO Market).
- VC-backed IPOs in 2016 were worth only $3.5 billion, less than half of 2015's $8.9 billion and a fraction of 2014's $35.3 billion. Again, it was the worst result since 2009.
- The slowdown in IPOs began in August 2015 over China growth fears; political uncertainty in the US, conflicts in the Middle East, Brexit, and interest rate

Practice Areas

rise fears are some of the other reasons why IPOs were fewer in 2016.

- 'Trumponomics' could have a significant effect on the private equity market. Details right now are scant, but the potential repeal of the Dodd-Frank Act would mean less regulation in financial services, including PE and VC.

Advice from the gurus of private equity and investment management

Bruce Ettelson, head of the private funds group, **Kirkland & Ellis**:

"A real benefit of funds work is that you meet very senior people at the clients early on in your career and become a general corporate counsel to those clients. You're able to represent clients from cradle to grave. You're not only doing the transfers, but also helping them with reports, regulatory compliance, structuring transactions within a fund's permitted transaction parameters and other issues. A wealth of challenges will come up over ten years of working with a client. It's a very dynamic and challenging practice. The work doesn't end with structuring and closing a fund."

Lisa Schneider, corporate partner, focused primarily on the structuring and representation of hedge funds and other alternative investment products, at **Fried Frank**:

"One of the great things about this area of law is that the role of a junior associate is not that different from that of a senior associate or partner. In many fields, junior associates are often relegated to lower-level tasks, such as diligence, and are not exposed to high-level deal negotiations. Juniors in this practice really get exposure to the whole picture. Transactions are leanly staffed, so that junior associates are able to be involved in all aspects of a transaction, including drafting and negotiations."

"The private fund space is dynamic and is continuously evolving. As the client businesses and products adapt to changes in the market, our practice must change and evolve as well. This is what keeps the private funds practice both challenging and rewarding. It's great to be at the cutting edge of the industry."

Jordan Murray, deputy chair of the firm's corporate department and member of the private equity funds and investment management groups, **Debevoise & Plimpton**:

"I really view myself as a commercial business lawyer who does everything for these private investment firms other than their acquisitions and dispositions. We handle their private securities offerings – which could be viewed as the sexy part of the job – and deal with a whole range of projects, including opening non-US offices, high-level personnel changes, firm restructurings and liquidity events, securities filings, investor reports and communications, incentive arrangements and regulatory and compliance issues, which have become ever more burdensome. My job often involves marshaling the right teams within Debevoise for our clients. It's like being the quarterback who directs everything."

"For me the real reward is that our clients are so easy to work with. So many of the folks I work with are so entrepreneurial and smart and grasp onto issues and concepts so quickly that it really is quite fun. They are also the type of people who recognize the good work and loyalty we bring to the table – they let you know they appreciate that. For most of my clients I feel like I'm an extension of their organizations. When I speak of my clients it's about 'we'. We enjoy our clients' successes and, thankfully with less frequency, suffer and fight through their challenges as well."

Product Liability

In a nutshell

Product liability involves personal injury or property damage litigation arising from alleged design and manufacturing defects, or information/warning deficiencies, in products. Litigation can consist of individual cases arising from one-off injuries, but in recent years much of it has been conducted through mass torts. These comprise class actions and/or multiple related individual cases brought by plaintiffs. Most cases within a mass tort do not go to trial as they tend to be resolved early through mediation or settlement.

Product liability lawyers also advise on how to avoid litigation, since clients are increasingly interested in prevention and mitigation of the costs and risks of significant product liability litigation. Attorneys are also often required to advise on related, nontraditional product claims, such as government investigations, which frequently arise alongside private claims. This quasi-criminal aspect involves defending the client against suits filed by state attorneys general and investigations conducted by the Department of Justice, often simultaneously.

The major industries that see the lion's share of product liability suits are tobacco, pharmaceutical, consumer products, chemicals and medical devices. BigLaw firms normally defend the manufacturers of the products.

What lawyers do

- Meet with company witnesses to put together the company's defense.
- Fact investigation and discovery – find out what actually happened.
- Product investigation – get to know the product.
- Choose and prepare experts; arrange for experiments if necessary.
- File motions under the Frye or Daubert doctrines to dismiss inadequate plaintiffs' experts.
- Write briefs on evidentiary, class action and dispositive motion issues, as well as legal analysis.
- Take and defend fact and expert depositions.
- Argue cases before juries.
- Manage post-trial steps.

Realities of the job

- Mass torts will typically include some form of consolidation or aggregation of the claims, ranging from a class action – in which plaintiffs have significant issues in common – to a federal multidistrict proceeding coordinating all the cases for pretrial purposes.
- Cases are heard all across the country, though plaintiffs may favor certain jurisdictions for tactical reasons. These include East Texas, Atlantic County in New Jersey, and Philadelphia. The 'bank district' in Los Angeles is popular for its history of awarding multimillion and billion-dollar verdicts. It has been described by advocates of tort law reform as *"judicial hell on earth."*
- Not all cases are tried the same way. There are a variety of different trial models that judges are experimenting with, including the bifurcated, reverse-bifurcated and bellwether models. Depending on the model, different strategies will be needed, and will sometimes require a mock jury exercise to see what will work best. Attorneys can suggest alternate trial plans, though the judge has the final say. Once the trial has begun, it is difficult to change how it is tried, though with mass torts involving many cases it is possible to try iterative cases differently.
- The main drivers of complex product liability litigation are the business and strategic decisions made by the plaintiffs' Bar, which do not necessarily involve pure scientific analysis of a product.
- Plaintiff lawyers jump from product to product and industry to industry, and try to apply the same model to different cases. The tobacco industry has often seen plaintiffs' innovations before any other, whereafter plaintiffs will experiment with those approaches in different industries.
- Many clients work extensively with the FDA, so current FDA employees cannot be used by the defense as expert witnesses, due to the conflict of interest. Instead, attorneys will work with retired FDA employees to learn about the regulatory and approval processes.
- Much of the work done preparing for trial will turn out to be for cases that never make it to trial, since most mass torts are resolved before then. But attorneys do not know which of the 20,000-30,000 claims filed will actually be tried. There is, however, a winnowing process whereby judges eventually select a smaller pool of cases to be tried.
- There is a large amount of routine paper and electronic discovery required, though many firms use staff and contract attorneys to do this job.
- You don't have to have a background in science to be a product liability lawyer, though to be a successful one you will have to learn about areas outside the law like engineering, medicine and science. You will also have to be able to communicate complicated scientific ideas to a judge or jury in a clear and simple fashion.
- You may work with some of the leading scientists and

doctors in the country and the world. The job often involves extensive travel for trials and meeting with experts., but most product liability work is domestic.

Current issues

- Consumer fraud class actions continue to be on the rise across the United States, particularly in California. These actions tend to be filed when plaintiffs' counsel allege that *"defendants mislead consumers as to the benefits of their products,"* explains **Michael Davis**, former head of **Sidley Austin**'s product liability and mass torts practice. These actions often arise when a product *"claims to be 'natural' or have a specific health benefit, or when there are technical issues with labeling."*
- Some frequently named defendants, in addition to the traditional consumer, food and pharmaceutical companies, are *"energy drink manufacturers who allegedly fail to adequately label their products, helmet manufacturers, and NFL franchises for concussion injuries players allegedly suffered over time,"* according to Michael Davis.
- Another interesting development has been the advent of 'innovator liability'. According to **Paul Boehm**, partner at **Williams & Connolly**, this has been driven *"by plaintiffs lawyers' desire to circumvent the Supreme Court's decision in Mensing. Since plaintiffs, under Mensing, cannot sue a generic drug manufacturer for failure to warn, plaintiffs' attorneys have advanced the theory that the 'original innovator' of the product, rather than the manufacturer of the product plaintiff actually used, can be liable under state-based 'failure to warn' claims. This theory would represent a fundamental change in some basic principles of tort law. Three state courts have allowed 'failure to warn' cases founded on the theory of 'innovator liability', but most courts continue to reject it."*
- Plaintiffs' attorneys continue to bring cases on purely speculative bases. These actions are often based on supposed economic loss or the mere risk of a loss in future. *"Such cases are often brought when the actual product works as it should, but it is claimed that negative press coverage about possible damage has reduced the product's value,"* according to Davis.
- The development of driverless cars has generated new queries for the practice area – does an accident involving one constitute a product liability case, or is a crash the fault of the, for want of a better term, 'driver'? Current consensus suggests this will indeed be a product liability issue, but the conundrum demonstrates how technology can evolve faster than the law surrounding it.

Rankings in *Chambers USA*

Top ranked

Sidley Austin

Highly recommended

Arnold & Porter	Kirkland & Ellis
Baker Botts	Mayer Brown
Dechert	Morgan, Lewis & Bockius
DLA Piper	MoFo
Goodwin	O'Melveny & Myers
Greenberg Traurig	Orrick
Holland & Knight	Perkins Coie
Hughes Hubbard & Reed	Reed Smith
Jones Day	Skadden
King & Spalding	Venable

For more detail on ranking tiers and locations, visit www.chambersandpartners.com

What top product liability lawyers advise

Harvey Kaplan, partner and chair emeritus of the pharmaceutical and medical device litigation division, **Shook, Hardy & Bacon**:

"Thorough preparation is the key. You have to dedicate yourself. Turn over every stone and develop the drive to nail down the facts, which sometimes means – lo and behold! – you'll have to get out of your office and interact with people. The facts are all-important."

"An understanding of the science involved is paramount when you're dealing with pharmaceutical and medical device litigation. You have to educate yourself."

"As a junior associate you'll be working with busy partners who may be very experienced but don't know all the details about a particular case. It's a great opportunity to make yourself indispensable by being the person with the in-depth knowledge of the documents."

Will Goodman, member, **Watkins & Eager**:

"Defending big companies at trial is an exceptional challenge – I've been able to work with some top national and international firms along the way and to try cases outside my home state. If you want a more regular lifestyle, you might consider a practice area other than trial work, where you have some control over your schedule. In product liability we just do what we have to do. My record is 47 consecutive days away from home. There are a lot of long hours, and a lot of time and effort goes into preparing and trying complex cases."

Projects & Energy

In a nutshell

Energy and projects are two distinct but overlapping areas of law. When combined, they focus on the development, construction and financing of major natural resource (oil/gas, mining), power and infrastructure projects. The construction of pipelines, refineries, mines, power plants and petrochemical plants is a massive business, with high stakes and massive dollar values. Emerging economies are frequently the most hungry for infrastructural improvements, meaning a lawyer's work increasingly takes on an international flavor.

In addition, the projects component of an energy practice consists of both transactional and regulatory work (with regulatory work more prevalent in US domestic projects). There is a clear demarcation between transactional and regulatory work, and lawyers usually specialize in one of the two.

Non-energy projects are all about infrastructure. Typical examples might be road, airports, rail, shipping, telecoms and, most glamorously, sewage and water systems. The work would also include the construction of major multi-investor public buildings such as jails and stadiums.

What lawyers do

Energy – transactional & regulatory

- Transactional work can cover anything across M&A, joint ventures, capital markets, private equity, venture capital and project development and finance work.
- Energy lawyers deal with three types of clients: upstream, midstream and downstream. Upstream businesses deal with getting energy out of the ground – oil, gas, coal, sometimes geothermal. This includes mining and minerals companies. Midstream clients are in the refining, treating and transportation of resources industry and its offshoots. Downstream clients are energy distributors: gas stations, electricity providers, gas companies.
- Lawyers advise clients on negotiating and drafting agreements related to things like energy projects, the sale of power companies, investment in and development of upstream resources and the financing of various energy investments.
- Certain states, such as Texas, have a very particular regulatory structure, so lawyers are often called upon to provide clients that are new to the state with regulatory advice on purchases and sales, contracts between companies and users, public authority requirements and licensing.

- Many firms' energy work focuses either on infrastructure and construction projects or on representations in front of the Federal Energy Regulatory Commission (FERC). FERC is a US government regulatory agency. It regulates electricity sales, electric rates, hydropower projects, natural gas pricing and oil pipeline rates. Its decisions can be reviewed by federal courts.
- *"I like that it involves public policy. I find that very interesting. I like that what I do will have an effect on a wide variety of people and also that there is a lot of variety in what I do from one day to the next. I can do individual client counseling, I can contest cases and I can be involved in rule-making where policy issues are heavily debated all in one day. I find it interesting to have variety,"* says **Catherine Webking**, partner at **Scott Douglas** & McConnico.

Projects

- Projects lawyers have three or four types of clients: sponsors/developers who put together the project; financiers (banks, international development agencies, foreign export credit agencies); the provider or contractor (who supplies raw materials or undertakes construction); and sometimes the 'offtaker' who purchases the products produced by the project. The most significant roles for lawyers are representing either the sponsors/developers or the financiers.
- **Keith Martin**, partner and co-head of the project finance group at **Norton Rose Fulbright**, says: *"Project finance transactions are complicated exercises in risk allocation that take a lot of time and generate lots of paper. The complexity is increased by the involvement of different countries and the number of people in different roles – sponsors, senior and subordinated lenders, tax and true equity investors, landowners, offtakers. These are interesting puzzles to put together – they take an ability to listen carefully, spot common ground and solve problems."*
- The overwhelming majority of international work for projects lawyers is handled in New York – which remains the 'money center' for transactions in Latin America. The Energy Policy Act of 2005 created a host of new regulations by which companies in the industry are required to abide. These include loan guarantees for technologies that avoid greenhouse gases, subsidies for alternative energy producers and incentives to drill for oil in the Gulf of Mexico.

Practice Areas

Realities of the job

- This area of law is not widely publicized on legal courses. However, it can be a highly rewarding area of law to work in, as Catherine Webking of Scott Douglas & McConnico explains: *"It is certainly not an intuitive area to go into from law school. But what is interesting is that the utility business is ultimately affecting everyone in the States so it is an area that really has a broad impact but is not well-known from law school."*

- Texas is *"the land of opportunity"* for energy lawyers focused on US-based projects. Its law schools – most notably the University of Texas – are some of the only ones in the country to provide energy classes. In Texas the energy industry is regulated by the Railroad Commission of Texas. Alaska is the country's second oil state. With the recent explosion of natural gas (and oil) shale development, many other states have seen increases in energy activity.

- Work is often international or related to projects overseas, as there is hyperactive development of infrastructure and the energy sector in many economies. *"Just look at where development is roaring to find out where we work: China, India, Brazil, Mexico, Indonesia, Peru, the Gulf states. There are giant infrastructure developments there – things are moving much faster than in the developed world."*

- The international nature of work means lawyers often have to deal with *"shaky jurisdictions. Structuring a deal to take into account political risk is very much a part of being an international projects lawyer. And that's not just in less developed countries – there could be similar issues surrounding a mining deal in California."*

- Working hours can vary greatly across the spectrum of work. While regulatory lawyers often work long hours, their schedule is often more predictable and manageable than that of transactional lawyers.

- In regulatory and advisory work, new recruits are often placed on contentious cases, as the hands-on approach is considered by many firms to be the best introduction to gaining expertise within the practice area.

- Energy transactional schedules are far less stable and this area of work may not be ideal for those with responsibilities or hobbies outside the work environment. Litigation work, on the other hand, is more predictable even when working long hours.

- Transactions can typically last anywhere between six months and three years. In a typical transaction, the partner's role is to manage the workflow and relationship with clients while other team members do the necessary groundwork and work in parallel to ensure the various elements of a deal fall into place.

- An excellent sense of organization is a must across all areas of energy and projects. It is also important to be comfortable with general administration law, and have good litigation and transactional skills. Eventually, an attorney can specialize in the types of cases they find

Rankings in *Chambers USA*

Top ranked

Baker Botts	Perkins Coie
Bracewell	Shearman & Sterling
Foley & Lardner	Skadden
King & Spalding	Squire Patton Boggs
Latham & Watkins	Sullivan & Cromwell
Mayer Brown	Thompson & Knight
Milbank,	Vinson & Elkins
Morgan, Lewis & Bockius	White & Case
Nixon Peabody	Winston & Strawn
Orrick	

Highly recommended

Akin Gump	Kirkland & Ellis
Alston & Bird	MoFo
Brownstein Hyatt Farber	Munger
Cadwalader	O'Melveny & Myers
Cleary Gottlieb	Pillsbury Winthrop Shaw
Crowell & Moring	Pittman
Debevoise & Plimpton	Schiff Hardin
Gibson, Dunn & Crutcher	Sidley Austin
Greenberg Traurig	Simpson Thacher & Bartlett
Haynes and Boone	Venable
Hogan Lovells	Wilson Sonsini
Hunton & Williams	
Jackson Walker	
K&L Gates	

For more detail on ranking tiers and locations, visit www.chambersandpartners.com

the most rewarding.

- **Thomas Eastment**, head of the energy regulatory group at **Baker Botts**, tells us: *"A nice broad understanding of the key areas of law is crucial. This would include classic energy law but also environmental, finance and general commercial law. The issues we grapple with span all these, so you need to be nimble. The answer is not simply taking an energy course."*

- Another important skill is being able to handle numbers and technical issues. Catherine Webking says: *"I have an engineering undergraduate degree, which was very useful. There is a lot of number crunching to be done and our clients are engineers or accountants so being comfortable with numbers is important."*

- Webking also tells us that the variety of work on offer can be simultaneously stimulating and challenging. There is little repetition and the day will not be monotonous, but gaining an in-depth knowledge in a specific area will take longer: *"It is an ever-changing landscape in terms of corporate structures, there is a lot of activity related to companies acquiring other companies or merging with other companies so the clients themselves change quite often."*

Practice Areas

- As it is a relatively small practice area, an attorney in this area will often be co-operating with the same small groups of people. Consequently, your opponent on one deal may become your ally on the next, and so it is important to maintain a professional attitude at all times.
- Particularly on the transactional side, it is important to be able to gauge what level of detail is sufficient. As **Todd Alexander**, partner at **Norton Rose Fulbright** explains: *"Unlike being in school where there is no cost to seeking perfection and you can research for as long as you like to write the best article you can, in a firm time is money. You may stop at 90% of the way there, thinking this is efficient, because the extra time doubles the price of the services provided. For half the price you get 90% certainty and sometime juniors struggle with that because they are used to being measured by having gotten the right answer. Perfection is not always what you're looking for."*

Current issues
- There has been a strong surge of activity in renewable energy as corporations increasingly diversify their energy sources and turn to renewables: *"One of the most high profile issues right now is the incorporation of renewable technologies in our market. Customers are able to install their own facilities which then can assist the centralized grid,"* says Catherine Webking.
- Solar energy has seen a particular boost. Todd Alexander of Norton Rose Fulbright tells us he sees this as a major area of growth in the future: *"Solar installation costs continue to decline and are now competitive in many markets. Looking forward, solar energy is going to be leading the charge."*
- Alexander also explains that battery storage is likely to become a significant subject: *"The problem with renewable energy is that it is intermittent in nature and not*

dispatchable. You can't ask for it on demand. There have been continuous improvements in battery storage which would allow all renewable energy to be generated when available and dispatched as needed."
- Shale oil exploitation has been a big thing since the 2000s, with a nearly 80% increase from the 2006 levels being reported by the US Energy Information Administration. Although the price of oil and gas is slowing the level of activity in this area, and some smaller companies who got rich quick from the earlier shale boom are now going out of business, this is still seen as a strong area of economic production.
- Internationally, Brazil, East Africa, Australia and the North Sea are attracting increasing attention. Chinese and Indian companies especially are investing heavily in infrastructure and exploration in these new areas, as well as existing markets. South Africa looks ripe to become a key player in shale gas exploration.
- On the projects side, there is a lot of current investment in the transmission grid and new projects are being constantly proposed in connection with it.
- As ever, a change in administration often brings about some level of shift in policy. The Trump administration is expected to place more focus on energy sourced from fossil fuels than the Obama administration, and in that respect bring a level of regulatory predictability in that area.
- At the same time, renewable energy sectors are currently very strong in terms of economic production and as such it is likely that support for this industry will also be maintained. This is an industry where growth is driven by the decreasing cost of production, and as the cost of renewable energy is constantly significantly declining this will likely remain a very competitive area of the market.

Practice Areas

173

Life as a Project Finance lawyer, by Milbank, Tweed, Hadley & McCloy LLP

What is project finance?

Project finance involves the development and financing of infrastructure, and spans various industries and locations around the world. It focuses on the financing of a specific asset (it could be a solar power plant, a petrochemical facility, a pipeline, or any number of different assets) in which lenders or investors look principally to the revenues generated by the asset for the repayment of the loans for the asset's development (such as revenue from the sale of power from a solar power plant or sale of copper oxide from a copper mine). As collateral for the loans, the lenders or investors take a lien over all the assets of the project, including the cash flow the project generates and the contracts that assure the stability of its costs and its revenues. This type of structured finance is deployed most commonly in the development of large infrastructure projects and the exploitation of energy/natural resources.

Our industries

We are a very diverse practice group and in order to stay nimble and flexible regardless of what the economy is doing, we practice in a wide variety of industries. These range from power projects powered by conventional means, like natural gas, to a cutting-edge renewables practice where we regularly work on a wide range of wind, solar and biomass power plants. We have a strong oil and gas practice involving gas pipelines, liquefied natural gas projects, petrochemicals and other processing facilities. Our mining practice is also one of the most prominent in the world. We are also involved in all kinds of pure infrastructure projects, such as ports, airports, toll roads, bridges and other similar assets. Occasionally, we also are asked to apply project finance principles to other industries such as the construction of new satellite constellations. We once were even involved in the construction and financing of the world's largest cheese factory!

The international element

The international part of project finance is one of the reasons why it is such an interesting discipline. We regularly work on infrastructure projects around the world, and often in less developed economies, as those are often the places where additional infrastructure is most needed. As we follow international investment flows, many different nationalities are often involved in our deals. For example, we have worked on the financing of liquefied natural gas import terminals in Mexico where the primary investors are Japanese and Korean trading companies, the banks are international government banks from Japan and Korea as well as commercial banks from the United States, and the party purchasing all of the natural gas produced by the project is Mexican government institutions. One of the most fascinating parts of our job is getting together with all of these different actors into a conference room (in New York or somewhere else in the world) to negotiate a commercial transaction. As a result of our international projects, there is often also travel involved in our jobs – associates never know when they may need to travel to Brazil, Chile, Colombia or somewhere else for last-minute meetings!

Key issues and trends, and what shapes our practice

There are many different factors that affect the kinds of projects we are working on. The first factor is the price of commodities. For example, when prices for natural resources such as gold, copper, silver or other commodities are high, we usually see an influx of mining projects around the world. Conversely, when the price of natural gas is low, we see larger numbers of projects that need cheap natural gas, such as gas-fired power plants, petrochemical facilities (that use natural gas as a "feedstock") and liquefied natural gas export terminals, where natural gas is super-cooled to allow it to be loaded onto massive ships and sent around the world.

Legislation also shapes our practice. Due to government incentives over the past ten years, there has been an explosion of renewable energy projects, and we have developed one of the most prominent renewable energy practices in the world, from massive utility-scale solar projects in the desert that are so large that they can be seen from space, to domestic roof-top solar projects.

Of course, the general state of the world economy also shapes our practice. Luckily for us, we are diversified in industries as well as in global regions, so we are always well positioned to take advantage of positive trends and to ride out negative ones. For example, we were extraordinarily busy in Brazil a few years ago when that economy was booming, but that work has subsided as a general economic slowdown (as well as some large scandals) have hit that country. At the same time though, other countries – such as Colombia and Mexico – have emerged as economic engines, and we have been well positioned to take advantage of work opportunities there.

Life of an associate

A project finance associate can expect to represent major financial institutions, sponsors and developers in complex domestic and cross-border project financings. Associates are responsible for structuring, negotiating and drafting the financing documentation that accompanies transactions of this type, including loan agreements and various types of security agreements. Given the cross-border nature of our practice, associates will be involved in not only the negotiation and drafting of the New York law governed documentation, but will also be expected to review and comment upon the documentation being drafted by attorneys located in each other jurisdiction applicable to the transaction. As a result, associates are often required to take the lead in discussing key documentation issues with all attorneys representing the client, who may be located in other parts of the US or the world.

A project finance associate also spends a great deal of time reviewing the project agreements, including the construction contracts, the revenue contracts and the supply and service contracts applicable to a project, in order to prepare detailed due diligence reports for our clients. The purpose of such due diligence reports is to advise our clients on contingent liabilities and legal risks associated with a project that would be material to an investment or a lending decision. Such contingent liabilities and risks are ultimately allocated among the transaction participants in the financing or investment documentation. Given the technical nature of the project agreements, associates will be expected to take the lead in coordinating input from the various technical, financial, insurance and market consultants hired by our clients to assist in the due diligence and documentation process.

Here are some typical examples of work that a junior project finance associate would be involved in:

- Due diligence review and preparing issues memos about the risks in project documents (such as construction contracts, equipment supply agreements, operation and maintenance agreements, fuel supply and transportation contracts and offtake agreements)
- Coordinating the due diligence review with local counsel and specialists (regulatory, environmental, real estate)
- First cut of drafting the financing documents (such as credit agreement, security documents and note purchase agreements)
- Conforming exhibits, schedules and ancillary documents from previous transactions and conforming them to the new transaction
- Listening in on conference calls with clients and lawyers as the deal is being negotiated
- Making a checklist of the conditions in the credit agreement that need to be met prior to the deal closing. Reviewing items delivered to satisfy these conditions and tracking their delivery in the checklist
- After a deal closes, preparing a closing set of all the project and finance documents

What you need to succeed

A balance of skill sets is necessary for success as a junior associate in project finance. Attention to detail and organization are highly prized. Junior associates need to pay attention to things like defined terms changing or being added as drafts are passed back and forth between lawyers, to make sure that changes are reflected throughout the deal (potentially across seven or eight documents). When a deal is closing, numerous emails will fly back and forth between lawyers and clients, and junior associates need to be able to take initiative to track down those conditions that are required before the deal will close. Intellectual curiosity is also important, especially when conducting due diligence. Senior associates and partners look to the juniors to have a good handle on the project documents and to note potential red flags that they raise, because these in turn affect how the financing documents will be drafted.

Most lawyers don't come into project finance with a background in the area, and few law schools teach courses in the subject matter. Learning happens on the job, first, with the development of the general skill sets needed to succeed as a junior associate. As associates become exposed to different types of projects and types of financing structures, they begin to learn about the market, what is more or less risky for a client and how to manage those risks, along with the various industries, from solar, to infrastructure, to natural gas pipelines.

Author

Dan Michalchuk

Daniel J. Michalchuk is a partner in the New York office of Milbank and a member of the firm's Global Project, Energy & Infrastructure Finance Group. Mr. Michalchuk has represented project sponsors and financial institutions in numerous domestic and international project financings. Mr. Michalchuk's experience spans various industries and sectors, including: oil and gas, power and transmission, renewable energy, mining and metals and infrastructure.

Real Estate

In a nutshell

Real estate has multiple branches. Certainly, the practice no longer simply involves the sale of property by A to B; it now encompasses acquisitions and disposals, financing, leasing, development, joint ventures and funds.

Financing is a significant component of most transactions, and can involve sophisticated structuring, capital markets transactions, mortgage and mezzanine loans, debt restructurings, private placements, sale and lease-back financings, governmental incentives and tax aspects.

Another branch of real estate is land use, which requires attorneys to advise on state and local laws, such as zoning regulations, which affect the behavior and development of the real estate market. There are also aspects of real estate work that sometimes require advice on tax, litigation, restructuring and bankruptcy, and environmental law.

What lawyers do

- Draft a letter of intent, which sets forth the basic parameters of a transaction.
- Conduct due diligence. Make sure what the client is purchasing or underwriting holds no unwelcome surprises.
- Obtain municipal and/or state approval, where needed. Negotiate the contract, which allocates responsibilities among the parties.
- Negotiate financing documentation.
- Close the contract, joint venture and/or financing.

Realities of the job

- According to **Joseph Shenker** of **Sullivan & Cromwell**, there are three aspects to every deal: *"Of course you have the legal element, but on top of that there are the business and psychological elements to take into account."*
- These are also integral to the practice as a whole. *"The practice of real estate law involves the confluence of legal and business strategy,"* he adds. *"It's ideal for someone who is interested in both business and law, as well as in meeting entrepreneurial people and understanding their mindset."*
- Typical clients include developers, owners, institutional investors, lenders, tenants, underwriters, pension funds, insurance companies, private equity and hedge funds.

- Working in real estate requires sensitivity to each client's needs and expectations. While private clients are motivated by profit margins, the public ones are driven by policy and politics. Lenders tend to be cautious in their approach, while developers are bold and visionary. Harmonizing parties' competing goals can be tricky.
- Real estate is cyclical by nature. When the economy is bad, the real estate sector is often adversely affected. This means that *"if you have skills to put a deal together, you should also have the skills to take it apart – if and when it gets into trouble,"* says **Laura Ciabarra**, partner at **Dechert**. *"Prior to the financial crisis you didn't need to know both sides, but now there's a wonderful opportunity for young attorneys to acquire both sets of skills and they should definitely take advantage of that."*
- A transaction is truly a team-oriented affair; there will always be more than one attorney working on the deal. Therefore, having the ability to collaborate well with others is a must, in addition to coping with the stressful nature of deadlines.
- *"In the week or so leading up to the completion of a deal, you'll probably find yourself in the office every day working until midnight,"* explains Ciabarra. *"I don't think I've ever worked on a transaction without there being that final week or two of craziness."* However, she describes real estate lawyers as *"deal junkies"* who thrive on the hectic nature of the closing stages, with everyone pulling together to reach a successful conclusion.
- Real estate lawyers tend to have a variety of projects in hand at any one time, which requires exceptional organizational skills.
- The work is often highly tax-driven. When it comes to the more complex transactions, understanding the tax goals and limitations that exist is particularly useful.
- Unlike corporate lawyers, who may have no more than a CD-ROM to mark the end of a deal, real estate lawyers have a physical result that can be seen, touched, visited, lived in and worked in.

Current issues

- *"We're seeing a volatile market at the moment,"* says Shenker. *"The debt markets have not fully recovered from the global financial crisis and we are still dealing with over-leveraged properties which need to be refinanced."*
- Despite this, there has arguably been more of a recovery than many expected – especially in the commercial real estate market. In 2012, for example, the number of home sales rose to 4.65 million, which is a 9.2% in-

Rankings in *Chambers USA*

Top ranked

Arnold & Porter	Hunton & Williams
Baker Botts	Jackson Walker
Brownstein Hyatt Farber	Jones Day
Cadwalader	Katten Muchin Rosenman
Cleary Gottlieb	King & Spalding
Cooley	Kirkland & Ellis
DLA Piper	Latham & Watkins
Foley & Lardner	Paul Hastings
Fried, Frank	Perkins Coie
Gibson, Dunn & Crutcher	Simpson Thacher & Bartlett
Goodwin	Skadden
Goulston & Storrs	Snell & Wilmer
Greenberg Traurig	Sullivan & Cromwell
Haynes and Boone	Thompson & Knight
Holland & Knight	Waller

Highly recommended

Alston & Bird	Morrison & Foerster
Bracewell	Munger, Tolles & Olson
Brown Rudnick	Nixon Peabody
Cozen O'Connor	Nutter McClennen & Fish
Debevoise & Plimpton	Orrick, Herrington
Dechert	Patterson Belknap
Duane Morris	Paul, Weiss
Dykema Gossett	Pillsbury Winthrop
Fox Rothschild	Proskauer Rose
Gibbons	Reed Smith
Hangley Aronchick	Ropes & Gray
Hogan Lovells	Schulte Roth & Zabel
Jenner & Block	Shearman & Sterling
K&L Gates	Sidley Austin
Kasowitz Benson Torres	Stroock & Stroock & Lavan
Kilpatrick Townsend	Venable
Kramer Levin Naftalis	Vinson & Elkins
Mayer Brown	Weil, Gotshal & Manges
Milbank, Tweed, Hadley	White & Case
Mintz Levin	Willkie Farr & Gallagher
Morgan, Lewis & Bockius	WilmerHale

For more detail on ranking tiers and locations, visit www.chambersandpartners.com

crease from the previous year and the highest figure since 2007. Experts say this improvement is likely to carry on.

- *"There is an unusually large inflow of non-US capital into US real estate – particularly from Asia – so we're beginning to witness again the investment thesis that the US is a sanctuary for foreign capital,"* Shenker tells us. This is particularly true in Manhattan, where in 2015, foreign buyers were snapping up iconic buildings at an above-market value: in the past such transactions would have commonly taken on the form of joint ven-

tures, but these buyers have been stumping up the cash to own these buildings outright.

- Besides the more iconic buildings, foreign buyers purchased $102.6 billion of residential property in the US between April 2015 and March 2016.
- Disasters like Hurricane Sandy have made people focus a lot more on their leases. *"There are a number of clauses, such as casualty and interruption of services provisions, that some may not have paid sufficient attention to before – both in terms of the language used and what the insurance provides,"* explains **Jon Mechanic** of **Fried Frank**.
- Large institutional investors have taken advantage of the dip in real estate prices and the demand for rentals by moving into the 'single occupancy family homes' segment of the market: Simpson Thacher recently represented the world's largest alternative asset manager, Blackstone, during its creation of Invitation Homes, a national platform that has purchased over 39,000 distressed single family homes – it's now the largest owner of homes in the country.
- According to PwC and the Urban Land Institute (ULI), changing demographics in the US are likely to impact all real estate sectors. The growth of 'generation Y' (those born between 1979 and 1995) will continue to dictate how space is developed and used. Generation Yers don't use their cars so much, prefer urban spaces and at the same time very much treasure their mobility. Expect an uptick in collaborative office spaces and intown rental housing. Developers are also looking at where this generation is literally moving to, and popular cities include Austin, Seattle, Portland and the Twin Cities in Minneapolis.
- Retiring baby-boomers will also play their part: it is predicted that many will leave their suburban homes behind, in favor of urban locations which can offer better amenities and convenient healthcare. This trend, paired with generation Y's habits, means that interest in developing suburban areas has dropped.
- These changing demographics will also affect the labor pool – with more millennials seeking higher education, they remain out of the workforce for longer. Retiring baby-boomers as well as the clampdown on Mexican immigration will also reduce the labor pool significantly. Labor availability and shortage will therefore mean longer development times for projects, which cuts into returns.
- DC is no longer so hot for real estate. The federal government sector made the market more resilient during the economic downturn, but in light of government shutdowns and hesitancy over the future of government spending, confidence in the market has waned. According to the ULI report, in 2011 only New York and DC had decent prospects for investors and developers – this year DC didn't even make the ULI's list.
- Second-tier cities are hot, and are fueling recovery.

Practice Areas

Investors and developers are beginning to turn away from major cities like NYC and San Francisco, as there are more housing deals to be snapped up in places like Dallas and Portland. Interest is growing in areas like downtown Detroit, which has seen a series of successes and struggles in recent history. Emerging from its 2013 bankruptcy, Detroit has seen significant progress, with about 5,000 new housing units either planned for construction or being built.

- The multifamily sector is flagging. In short, too many multifamily apartment blocks were built to cater for the demand which sprung from the recession. However, in 2014, that demand has dipped, so development in this sector will cool off.
- Our online shopping habits and impatient desire for speedy deliveries will influence how industrial spaces are both designed and situated: ideally as close to densely populated urban areas as possible, to guarantee that promise of a swift same-day delivery.

- Many are hopeful that President Trump, being a long-time real estate mogul, will be a friend to the real estate market. Recently the Federal Reserve raised interest rates – the average interest rate on a 30-year fixed mortgage jumped from 3.5% to 4.25% in the week following Trump's election. The Federal Reserve expects this to rise again in 2017.
- Experts expect advantageous tax structure changes and fewer business regulations with the new administration. Trump's 'Buy American, Hire American' policy will theoretically lead to more jobs, and therefore a steady increase in real estate values as a result.

"You need to be intellectually curious in order to identify issues, but also practical so that you can figure out how to best solve those issues – that's where we add value."

- Robert Townsend, head of North American M&A practice at Cravath, Swaine & Moore

Sports, Media, Entertainment & Advertising

In a nutshell

Media and entertainment, advertising and sports are distinct yet overlapping areas of the law. Some aspects of their practice are common to them all – contracts law, for example – but ensuring a '100% beef burger' abides by the rules stated by the Federal Trade Commission (FTC) is clearly a matter for an advertising specialist.

Whichever strand you practice, one thing is for certain: the work is incredibly varied. None of these specialisms has its own distinct branch of law. Rather, they involve piecing together elements of a broad range of legal disciplines and applying them to one particular industry sector. It is also an incredibly challenging and fast-paced area, where one needs to stay abreast of the latest developments and innovations to catch up with the dramatically changing legal landscape at the cutting edge of new media technology.

Media and entertainment

Media and entertainment lawyers provide legal advice and representation to those working in the entertainment industries, including the fields of theater, television, music, publishing, gambling, film and digital media. The practice has a major fault-line down the middle, with most lawyers falling on either the transactional or the contentious side. Many entertainment lawyers hone one particular specialism – the music industry, for example – while others remain generalists.

Advertising

Advertising lawyers advise on every aspect of brand promotion, from drawing up contracts and deploying 'viral' campaigns to settling false advertising disputes. Again, the role of 'advertising lawyer' is somewhat of a misnomer as its attorneys tend to fall into subspecialisms – generally using their expertise to advise on regulatory, transactional or false advertising matters.

Sports

Split between transactional and litigation work, sports lawyers help out individuals and companies involved in the sports industry. That involves anything from drawing up player signing contracts, purchasing and selling stadia and negotiating branding agreements to litigating licensing issues.

What lawyers do

Media and entertainment

- Draft and negotiate record, publishing, producer, management, distribution, touring, merchandising, corporate sponsorship, licensing and internet agreements.
- Consult with artists, record companies and publishers regarding their financing, entertainment and internet strategies, plus the protection of their IP rights.
- Advise media and entertainment companies on their M&A activities and joint ventures.
- Assist various companies with investments and financings of media entities.
- Provide pre-publication content advice to broadcasters and publishers.
- Litigate matters including contractual, copyright and trademark, employment, and payment disputes.
- First Amendment law is a substantial specialism in itself – advising on issues of free speech, censorship and defamation, among other contentious issues.

Advertising

- Advise advertisers on playing by the rules according to advertising watchdogs including the FTC, and legislation such as the Children's Online Privacy Protection Act.
- Counsel manufacturers on all facets of food and drug labeling, marketing and advertising requirements.
- Advise on sweepstakes and other commercial promotions.
- Litigate false advertising claims, from single party to consumer class actions – particularly those falling under the Lanham Act, the federal false advertising statute.
- Provide copyright advice on advertising issues.
- Negotiate advertising-based content licensing agreements, for a whole range of different media.
- Assist companies with issues related to new technologies and digital media, such as adoption of innovative advertising and promotion strategies, social media initiatives and regulation, and other technology-related services, as well as advising on digital distribution models, e-commerce and related data security concerns.

Sports

- Advise broadcasters and other sports bodies on audio-visual media piracy issues.
- Sports-related litigation – anything from athlete con-

Practice Areas

179

tractual disputes to stadium construction and copyright issues.

- Advise professional sports leagues, club owners, investors and other financial institutions on sports-related licensing agreements, project finance, securitizations, and security offerings.
- Act on M&A transactions involving sports-related bodies, and in the purchase and sale of sports teams.
- Advise sports administrators, commercial bodies and municipal authorities on hosting major sporting events.
- Manage IP portfolios for sports brands.

Realities of the job

- You need to be prepared that an actual job of an entertainment lawyer is not going to be all that different from that of any other lawyer. *"The day would be the same as that of a junior associate working on a matter in any industry: reading, drafting, spending a long time on the phone with clients. It's no different than work for any similar transactional or litigation practice group,"* confesses **Ruth Fisher**, a co-chair of **Gibson Dunn**'s media, entertainment and technology practice group. You will be expected, however, to understand very industry specific requirements, such as *"where the rights are owned and how they are owned."*
- *"If you could visualize it, you have to think about it as a wheel, where there's IP, advertising, data content, and technology – all of those are interrelated,"* illustrates **James D. Taylor** at **Loeb & Loeb**. You will need to master many different disciplines whether you are sports or media lawyer, and excel at those. Although it means more work, he stresses that *"the value and benefit of this is that you develop a holistic approach."*
- Work in the fun sector is far from being just fun! There is an awful lot to learn as you go: *"It takes a great deal of hard work to stay current. Projects move very quickly,"* warns **Kenneth Florin**, co-chair of advanced media and technology and chair of digital and social media groups at **Loeb & Loeb**. *"It's not a nine to five job, but if you want to dig deep, there's plenty of opportunity."*
- The fast pace and an ever-changing nature of the job is what actually makes it so exciting and special: *"I think what's of particular interest to younger attorneys is that the legal landscape is changing fairly dramatically because of technology,"* says James D. Taylor." What's unique is that what we are doing hasn't existed before: we are at the very beginning of digital revolution with things continuing to accelerate." On the other hand, some elements of work do not change, so you can expect some continuity: *"Whether it is a talented director creating a new movie, or an artist creating a new recording, you have issues around that. Disputes arise between actors and studios. Those existed 30 years ago and stay the same,"* reveals **Glenn D. Pomerantz**, liti-

Rankings in *Chambers USA*

Top ranked

Akin Gump	Munger
Cahill Gordon & Reindel	Patterson Belknap Webb
Cravath, Swaine & Moore	Paul, Weiss
Debevoise & Plimpton	Proskauer Rose
Gibson, Dunn & Crutcher	Skadden
Jenner & Block	Weil, Gotshal & Manges
Kramer Levin Naftalis	Wiley
Latham & Watkins	Winston & Strawn

Highly recommended

Arnold & Porter	Kirkland & Ellis
Cooley	Morgan, Lewis & Bockius
Davis Polk & Wardwell	O'Melveny & Myers
DLA Piper	Reed Smith
Foley & Lardner	Sheppard, Mullin, Richter
Greenberg Traurig	Stroock & Stroock & Lavan
Hogan Lovells	Venable
Holland & Knight	Waller
Hughes Hubbard & Reed	Weil
Irell & Manella	WilmerHale
Katten Muchin Rosenman	

For more detail on ranking tiers and locations, visit www.chambersandpartners.com

gation partner in the Los Angeles office of **Munger, Tolles & Olson**.

- *"I have wonderful clients,"* enthuses Pomerantz, *"but the entertainment industry tends to attract more volatile, eccentric people than other industries, not only as business people but as lawyers too."* If the idea of working with eccentric people scares you away, you may find some consolation in the fact that you do not need to change yourself or your style to fit the industry: *"I think so many types of lawyers that other industries need, this industry needs too, so there is wide room for lawyers with different styles."*
- *"In some ways it's high profile. When you go to a dinner party most people have understanding of issues you work on,"* says Pomerantz. However, he goes on to add: *"Much of what you do is what you'd do in other industries, it's just that it tends to be of more interest to wider community."* Ruth Fisher has a strong view on this: *"The point I'm trying to make is that it's a wonderful practice intellectually but it's not all about the glamor. We don't meet the stars!"* You should be prepared instead to meet studios, people dealing with large studios and distributors, remembering that *"clients are all the same: they expect you to do excellent work instantly."*
- With tough competition and few jobs, the path to becoming a lawyer in this discipline may be a long and arduous one, so it is for the patient. It's important not to overestimate one's chances just because of some ex-

perience at an entertainment company: *"No one should think they have an in because they have worked for an entertainment company. Half of students have experience in media companies."* Glenn suggests you pick a firm that does some entertainment work so you have a chance to practice it, but *"if not, do general work and that will give you experience relevant for industry."* It may sound a little obvious, but all sources agree that the rule number one is simply to be a first-rate lawyer.

Current issues

- Probably the most significant trend affecting the media industry today is the massive displacements across the sector caused by technological disruption. Lawyers must be aware of the potential new opportunities and challenges to their practice as a result of technological innovations. Ruth Fisher at Gibson Dunn sees *"a lot of opportunities now in helping clients navigate new distribution methods and finding ways for the ever-increasing number of channels to get to audiences."* Glenn Pomerantz says that dramatic changes in the music business from rampant piracy in the early 2000s led to legitimate businesses launching their own music services, like Apple's itunes, Spotify, and Amazon Prime: *"A lot of companies turned towards streaming services, and lawyers are affected by that… deals, issues, disputes."*
- New technology presents new threats to media industry in terms of IP infringement. To take new-real time piracy as an example, we can expect to see more copyright holders litigating for copyright infringement. However, the owners of live-streaming platforms may find an easy escape considering that current US law is still not firm on this point. Another option for copyright holders is to harness new technology to their own advantage to protect themselves from piracy. *"Every company is thinking of how to take advantage of this great opportunity whilst at the same time trying to combat illegal distribution of their crown jewels,"* explains Glenn Pomerantz.
- Digital forms of advertising are clearly overtaking the traditional channels. America's TV ad-revenues are expected to slow down, whereas Internet advertising is forecast to expand considerably. Amazon and Hulu will present a further challenge to traditional TV players by showing live TV from 2017. Facebook shall continue to own the biggest share of the total online ad spending. Notwithstanding these trends, TV and print advertising is not going away, as James D. Taylor clarifies: *"There is not a movement away from one form of advertising to another,"* but rather *"advertisers look across different channels and leverage what their capabilities are."*
- The latest update on the controversy in sports law surrounding the rights of college athletes for compensation is the Supreme Court's decision October 2016 not

to hear the O'Bannon versus NCAA case. The previous ruling in the case overturned NCAA restrictions on the athletes' ability to receive compensation for the commercial use of their images, and guaranteed athletes up to $5,000 a year. The latest denial of certiorari was a rather inconclusive end to the six-year trial, but the amount of publicity it received brings hopes of larger reform to the college sports establishment.
- As a consequence of the continuing debate over the legality of online fantasy sports games, more and more states are enacting laws legalizing and regulating the industry. New York passed the bill in June 2016, allowing players to play the games for cash under gambling laws, apart from English Premier League. At least 20 other states have failed or not taken the action to pass the laws in 2017.
- The recent trend of new money coming into the industry from China, following big acquisitions of Hollywood studios by Chinese film groups, may be undercut amongst uncertainty with US politics and the possibility of changes under the new administration. Although the impact of the current administration remains *"a 64 thousand dollar question, less regulation could certainly mean more deals and acquisitions,"* according to Kenneth Florin.
- Ruth Fisher adds: *"Putting aside regulated deals, like TV broadcasting – it's very hard to see why a creator or a distributor would fear new foreign investments in the industry. There are so many distribution channels."*

Advice from the gurus

Kenneth R Florin, deputy chairman at **Loeb & Loeb** with expertise in advertising law:

"Be committed to the pursuit and learning of disciplines. In your free time learn about advertising and IP. But if you don't get in as a graduate right out of law school, it doesn't mean you can't learn strong legal skills as a corporate litigator and then present yourself with these skills."

"It's important to try to understand as many interrelated disciplines, whether advertising or IP, and have general understanding on how different platforms work, as well as technology and business."

James D. Taylor, co-chair of **Loeb & Loeb**'s advanced media and technology department and chair of the firm's advertising and promotions practice:

"Understand the business, and most important, develop good solid legal and communication skills. Keep in mind that in media and entertainment, your work as a lawyer is usually much less glamorous than the business itself. It's more about getting the best results for your client and developing strong negotiating and drafting skills."

Practice Areas

"We look for people with outstanding legal and communication skills. Those people with solid litigation and corporate background tend to succeed. Don't think too narrow. Don't think you just need to understand social media and IP."

Ruth Fisher, a transactional partner and co-chair of **Gibson Dunn**'s media, entertainment and technology practice group based in Century City:

"Here is the problem for most of people who try to enter this field: there are more people than those who can get in. I think it's not ideal. The way that most people get to this job is that: first, they are very good at an area like litigation, corporate, employee executive compensation, etc. So first, they are a lawyer who is good at a specific area, and only then in the special industry. What a client needs is, for example, a good corporate lawyer who can do a complicated venture or M&A. But going to a law firm and saying: 'I want to be an entertainment lawyer,' for sure you won't get that job.

Glenn Pomerantz, litigation partner specialized in media and entertainment industries in the Los Angeles office of **Munger, Tolles & Olson**:

"Read everything you can and get a hand on what's happening in these industries. It's important to stay in touch with current developments: what are major independent studios doing? Any court decision that may affect that? Policy statements? What's Netflix doing? The more sophisticated you are on issues and how industry works the better the lawyer you are going to be."

"The most import thing you have to do is to deliver A+ legal work – do it! The idea of going out for dinner or sports event is secondary. The single most important thing is to do a great job. It makes it more likely they will call you again and you'll gain greater reputation. It's not just about networking. Clients are very smart and they know that no matter how much they like somebody, if they don't give them great product result, they won't be on their list. It takes a while to wait for next opportunity. Work hard and be patient."

Life in Media and Entertainment law, by Sidley associates

With two offices in Southern California, and lawyers across the globe who provide services to numerous clients on media and entertainment-related projects, Sidley has a dynamic and growing media and entertainment practice and is involved in virtually all phases of content creation, protection, production, financing and distribution.

Sidley represents various media businesses including commercial banks, financiers and investors, film and television studios, production companies, and producers of entertainment and new media content. Sidley assists our clients in a range of entertainment-related transactional work, including with M&A and finance deals, general corporate governance and corporate organizational work. As a transactional media attorney, day-to-day life is dictated by the transactions, which tend to build in intensity until a scheduled closing date. Transactional lawyers serve as deal team leaders, and oversee the negotiations, diligence and drafting efforts of a team of specialist lawyers.

"Working in Sidley's media and entertainment transactional group, I regularly engage with media power players in Hollywood and around the world. My practice in Sidley's Century City office is focused on entertainment M&A, although I also work on entertainment-focused finance deals. My experience working at Sidley has been challenging and filled with long hours and late nights, but extremely professionally rewarding. As a film and television fan, it has been quite rewarding to the see the fruits of our clients' labor on billboards, television, streaming online, and on the big screen."

– Aerin Snow

Sidley's litigation lawyers handle a variety of entertainment matters, including breach of contract, copyright infringement, trademark infringement, and appeals, and provide general legal guidance to entertainment and media clients. The clients that Sidley serves include television and film studios, television networks, production companies, music companies, recording labels, fashion companies, and online and print publishing companies. A litigation attorney will handle all facets of the litigation process, from drafting the initial complaint or answer, through motion practice and discovery, all the way until the case is resolved. Litigation associates in particular can expect a hands-on experience, as these types of cases are typically staffed with a single partner and a single associate. This lean staffing enables litigation associates to take leadership roles in drafting pleadings, interfacing with the client and opposing counsel, attending hearings, and conducting discovery.

"Already in my short time at Sidley, I have had the opportunity to work on several intellectual property matters for media and entertainment clients. I think what makes these matters fun and exciting is the challenging areas of law, the sometimes unbelievable facts, and the popular, well-known clients."

– Lauren M. De Lilly

Becoming a Media and Entertainment Lawyer

Sidley assigns its associates to a single practice group such as litigation, bankruptcy or real estate when they begin practicing. However, associates have a few years to experiment with different practice areas within a group to determine their best fit. In Sidley's Los Angeles and Century City offices transactional associates are assigned to the corporate and finance group and have the opportunity to work in areas such as structured finance, restructuring, M&A, technology transactions and investment funds. Associates interested specifically in transactional media deals have the opportunity to try their hands at media-related deals to gauge whether they enjoy the work. Sidley places a strong emphasis on formal and informal mentoring, and associate and partner mentors frequently assist with navigating the tricky decision of selecting a practice area.

"Sidley's transactional media partners are some of the best in the business, and they take an unparalleled interest in mentoring their associates. I feel lucky to be working with them, and grateful for the interest they have taken in my professional development, and the professional development of every other member of our team of media deal lawyers." – Aerin Snow

Practice Areas

Sidley's litigation attorneys are placed into the general litigation group where they have the opportunity to be staffed on all types of litigation matters, including those for media and entertainment clients. In the Los Angeles office, a distinct group of partners form the backbone of the entertainment and media practice. Associates interested in working on entertainment-related cases will likely find themselves working for this core group. Litigation associates have several options as to how to become involved in media and entertainment matters. For example, an associate can express interest to the litigation group staffing partners, who then work to pair the associate with an entertainment-related matter. Alternatively, a partner in the entertainment practice may reach out directly to an associate to assist on projects for a media client. Associates working on entertainment matters frequently also work on cases in other litigation areas including product liability, class actions, copyright, trademark, appeals, complex commercial litigation, and investigations.

"One of my more memorable cases was defending multiple television networks and a former television executive against claims of copyright infringement related to a popular reality television show. This case was leanly staffed, allowing me to work one-on-one with one of the co-heads of the Los Angeles litigation group and to take on key responsibilities in the case including an ownership role over drafting our motion to dismiss, reply brief, discovery responses and requests, as well as communicating with opposing counsel. This case gave me hands-on experience during my first year as an associate and proved a stepping stone in terms of building my media and entertainment litigation practice, as now I find myself recommended by partners to assist on media and entertainment-related intellectual property cases." — Lauren M. De Lilly

Current Issues for Media and Entertainment Lawyers

Transactional

Technological change continues to disrupt the media industry resulting in massive disaggregation. Deal making across the industry is requiring practitioners to be aware of the latest innovations while anticipating future changes and their impact on deal making.

Significant consolidation of the media industry is occurring in response to continuing disaggregation. Horizontal and vertical consolidation strategies are being pursued, as well as sponsor-driven roll-up strategies and branded content strategies. Demand for M&A practitioners with media deal-making expertise will remain strong for the foreseeable future.

Deals require capital. There are significant financial resources looking for alternative investment strategies, and media investments remain an attractive option for everyone from wealthy individuals to banks, hedge funds, private equity, family offices, sovereign funds and others. Practitioners adept in representing those deploying or obtaining capital will remain in high demand.

Litigation

Technology has disrupted the traditional business models of content delivery. There is considerable friction between content owners and those developing new means to deliver content outside of traditional channels, resulting in a fair amount of litigation.

We should see continued publicity rights litigation in light of the Supreme Court's refusal to hear the Electronic Arts v Davis case, where former NFL players objected to the use of their images in the Madden NFL games. The lines between regarding "fair use" and what uses are protected under the First Amendment are quite murky now, and that breeds litigation.

Litigation respecting the scope of copyright fair use should play out in interesting and unexpected ways.

Authors

Aerin Snow

Aerin Snow is a fifth-year associate in the Century City office, Corporate and Finance group

Lauren De Lilly

Lauren M. De Lilly is a third-year associate in the Los Angeles office, Complex Commercial Litigation

Practice Areas

Tax

"Do you do the cross-word puzzle? You have to have that knack for seeing how things fit together."

In a nutshell

"Tax touches virtually every aspect of the economy," says **Les Samuels**, tax counsel at **Cleary Gottlieb**. Accordingly, tax law encompasses a variety of activities, from transactional support and structuring to tax planning and tax controversy.

Working alongside corporate lawyers, tax attorneys ensure that transactions are as tax-efficient as possible, be they centered on public or private M&A, capital markets, investment funds (private equity, REITs and mutual funds), joint ventures or partnerships. Tax planning advice requires familiarity with all relevant domestic and international laws, and it is essential to have an understanding of clients' overall objectives and the structuring of their businesses.

Tax controversy is more of an independent category, covering a range of contentious tax issues. These include tax-based litigation, IRS examinations and tax shelter investigations. Disputes are usually resolved at the administrative level. Transfer pricing is also grouped with tax controversy.

See page **190** for the new section on Wealth Management.

What lawyers do

- Advise clients on the tax elements of transactions.
- Analyze cases and regulations to develop a real understanding of the tax implications of transaction structures. Findings are summarized as memoranda or given through direct counseling.
- Negotiate terms dealing with the tax aspects of transactions.
- Draft agreements, especially for M&A and joint ventures, which are particularly tax-intensive. An important element is the drafting of tax disclosures.
- Liaise with other non-tax lawyers and clients to ensure the smooth running of transactions.
- If working in tax controversy, negotiate with the IRS, respond to IRS questions, and draft memoranda and briefs.

Realities of the job

- It's vital to have an affinity for reading case law and regulations, as this is how juniors will spend a lot of their time. **Christopher Rizek** of **Caplin & Drysdale** says: *"Do you do the cross-word puzzle? You have to have that knack for seeing how things fit together. For young associates the legal research is very heavy and to be a tax controversy lawyer you also have to enjoy the give and take of the adversarial process."*
- **Maria Jones** of **Kramer Levin** explains *"there is so much to learn and it's not easy, other parts of law aren't as bookish as tax. People think tax is boring, it's not; it's very intellectually challenging, but you have to like the challenge."*
- By keeping up to date with changing regulations, tax lawyers can become real experts and even innovators within the legal landscape. With experience, they may be able to offer a solution to a tax issue that has previously been unsolvable. For example, the tax lawyer will produce a new financial instrument that becomes accepted by the market. This will sometimes prompt the government to review its regulations. Jones says: *"You may spend your entire career on one area of tax law and become an expert, so you need to figure out if you want to seek opportunities to specialize."* One of the advantages of being an expert in a particular area is not only that you have the possibility of innovation in the application of the law in that area, but to influence the drafting of regulations and legislative proposals due to your expertise.
- Tax lawyers need to express themselves clearly and concisely. Solid technical knowledge is essential, as is the ability to explain technical information to non-experts.
- In order to ensure that commercial transactions are as tax-efficient as possible, tax practices work closely with corporate departments and understand the non-tax issues that drive transactions. *"It's quite common for their to be a tax person involved in a transaction from the beginning so they can keep an eye on things, so you need to be able to explain difficult tax issues to people who aren't tax lawyers,"* says Jones.
- Tax controversy cases can be very long and drawn out disputes, so patience and a keen eye for detail is important. Rizek explains, *"When you're a tax planner you need to know a lot about the law in a lot of different areas, but when you're a controversy lawyer you go an inch wide but a mile deep on an issue already highlighted by*

the IRS."

- **Michael Desmond** of **The Law Offices of Michael J. Desmond** also stresses the importance of attention to detail in tax disputes. *"A complex-seeming case might come down to a couple of key issues, so you need to be able look through boxes of paper and focus on the key issues and not be intimidated or lost by the apparent complexities of a case."*
- Excellent interpersonal skills are a must. Tax controversy can sometimes involve liaising with the IRS, and it is important that lawyers be upfront and straight-talking. They may also work with international clients, so cultural awareness is important. Tax lawyers also work closely with other departments, advising on transactions in real estate, corporate law and banking.
- Lawyers have the chance to work on a variety of matters, including charity and pro bono. They are expected to comment on proposed regulations and may also give tutorials to colleagues and clients.
- Tax lawyers sometimes break up their career by spending time working for the government, notably the IRS.

Current issues

- Tax reform is something that the new administration has made a key policy. Both Donald Trump and Paul Ryan have proposed substantial tax reforms, cutting corporate tax by either 15% or 20%, massively reducing corporate tax loopholes and creating various tax incentives to encourage US companies to support the domestic economy.
- Globally, there has been more cooperation regarding tax havens and information exchange to address the role of businesses in eroding countries' tax bases. As of December 2016, 113 jurisdictions have Foreign Account Tax Compliance Act agreements with the IRS, which has helped create greater lines of communication between the IRS and foreign financial firms. Also the IRS's offshore voluntary disclosure program allows overseas account holders to rectify any tax shortcomings, thus warding off the threat of penalty action.
- As recent, high-profile cases involving Amazon, Apple, Facebook and McDonald's have shown throughout 2016, international transfer pricing cases are becoming increasingly prominent for controversy lawyers. Rizek explained: *"The largest tax controversy cases tend to be international transfer pricing related."* Desmond also explained: *"McDonald's and Apple are happening in Europe; they're out of the US headlines but they're important so you can understand cross-border tax issues."*
- Following the Supreme Court's approval of same-sex marriage in June 2015, gay and lesbian married couples may now file joint tax returns at state and federal levels.

Rankings in *Chambers USA*

Top ranked

Alston & Bird	King & Spalding
Baker Botts	Kirkland & Ellis
Baker McKenzie	Latham & Watkins
Cleary Gottlieb	Mayer Brown
Cravath	McDermott Will & Emery
Davis Polk & Wardwell	Morgan, Lewis & Bockius
Dechert	Ropes & Gray
Gibson, Dunn & Crutcher	Simpson Thacher & Bartlett
Goodwin	Skadden
Greenberg Traurig	Sullivan & Cromwell
Holland & Knight	Vinson & Elkins

Highly recommended

Akin Gump	Munger
Arnold & Porter	Norton Rose Fulbright
Bracewell	O'Melveny & Myers
Cadwalader	Paul Hastings
Choate Hall & Stewart	Paul, Weiss
Clifford Chance	Pillsbury Winthrop
Debevoise & Plimpton	Proskauer Rose
DLA Piper	Reed Smith
Duane Morris	Schulte Roth & Zabel
Fried, Frank	Shearman & Sterling
Haynes and Boone	Sidley Austin
Irell & Manella	Thompson & Knight
Jenner & Block	Weil, Gotshal & Manges
Jones Day	White & Case
Katten Muchin Rosenman	Willkie Farr & Gallagher
Kilpatrick Townsend	WilmerHale
Kramer Levin Naftalis	Wilson Sonsini
Milbank, Tweed	Winston & Strawn
MoFo	

For more detail on ranking tiers and locations, visit www.chambersandpartners.com

What top tax lawyers advise

Leslie Samuels, senior counsel, Cleary Gottlieb:

"It's important to keep your eyes and ears open to make sure you understand everything about the transaction so your advice is the most effective it can be."

"You don't have to be a math genius to be a very successful tax lawyer. You're dealing more with concepts. We don't prepare tax returns, and we certainly don't get busy before the tax filing dates."

Technology & Outsourcing

In a nutshell

Technology lawyers are experts on the rapidly changing laws and regulations surrounding complex communication technologies. Their classification as an attorney can vary – some fall under the IP umbrella, while others work within corporate or trial departments – but tech lawyers are united in their specialized industry expertise. Many narrow their focus to the telecommunications field, which deals with media such as telephones, cable, radio and the internet; others focus on information technology – which involves software, e-commerce and data privacy issues – or outsourcing, which oversees the provision of third-party services.

Whatever their specialty, a tech lawyer's primary role is to help clients abide by the complicated policies that pertain to certain technologies. In the US, such policies are by and large enforced by the Federal Communications Commission (FCC). Typical matters range from working on behalf of the government to promote fair market competition, to overseeing disputes between telecoms corporations, to advising merging companies on contract negotiations. They may also advise on protection of intellectual property.

Rapid advances in technology mean each generation of tech lawyers faces a shifting workload – attorneys today regularly contend with smartphone and internet-related matters, while their 20th Century counterparts mainly dealt with telephone line technology, and attorneys in the 19th Century grappled with the telegraph and other disruptive innovations.

What lawyers do

- Advise companies on commercial transactions, including mergers, acquisitions, investments and the purchase of services, particularly those with antitrust issues.
- Negotiate contract terms for companies acquiring new technologies or enhancing existing ones.
- Handle diligence and draft transaction documents, including provisions for any future developments between providers.
- Assist with dispute resolution, often between telecoms companies. Many disputes are cross-border and often fall under the IP bracket – for example, patent infringement cases.
- Represent clients at trial, usually in the state court.
- Counsel communications companies, such as cable or internet providers, on their regulatory obligations.
- Help companies learn how to protect their IT and web-based assets and defend themselves against cybersquatting and other data protection issues. For more information about data protection, see our Privacy & Data Security chapter.
- Represent clients seeking the provision of IT services through a third party.
- Assist the government to promote competition between telecom and other technology companies, and ensure services don't interfere with national security.
- Advise start-up companies on compliance, potential pitfalls and protection of their intellectual property.
- Assist with software deals such as licensing or buying subscriptions to cloud services.

Realities of the job

- Technology transactions often require attorneys to work as part of a multidisciplinary team that incorporates lawyers from multiple fields, including IP, tax and corporate. *"My role is like that of a quarterback,"* **Baker Botts**' technology sector chair **John Martin** tells us. *"I coordinate lawyers from other practice areas and disciplines to develop and implement an integrated solution and to address the client's many issues. It's a multifaceted approach."*
- Technology is a perfect field for those wanting to experience ingenuity. *"It is energizing and exciting to be around creative and inventive people,"* says **Lori Lesser** of **Simpson Thatcher & Bartlett**. *"These people are changing the world, saving the world and affecting how we work, how we get to work and run our lives online. It's a real privilege to work with these people."*
- The field is constantly changing thanks to developments in technology, which means *"every deal is different and every transaction has its own challenges,"* Martin says. *"There's no cookie-cutter matter out there; each deal is unique, which makes this a challenging and intellectually stimulating field. Nothing is rote or routine, and the learning curve never plateaus."* This shifting workload also means *"practitioners should be comfortable with ambiguity,"* **Chérie Kiser** of **Cahill Gordon & Reindel** advises. *"The law surrounding communications issues is constantly changing because the technology is dynamic. Developments are happening in real time in this sector, and lawyers are called upon by their clients to help shape and influence those laws. One should be comfortable with that lack of stability."*
- Because technology lawyers are specialists, they typically *"handle the majority of matters themselves rather than delegating projects or issues completely,"* Kiser

Practice Areas

187

says. This means even top-level partners are obliged to contend with grunt work like diligence at times. *"Fortunately, matters are interesting!"* she adds. Technology and telecoms matters have *"a language of their own that's highly technical and full of acronyms,"* Kiser warns. As such, attaining a good grasp of the relevant jargon – accessible through industry trade journals and magazines – is a crucial aspect of the job. It's not unusual for a tech lawyer to have an undergraduate degree in engineering, business or computer science, and many have held previous careers in those industries before making the change to law.

- Although a strong interest in technology is essential, a related degree is not necessarily a prerequisite. *"You don't need to have a technology background from university,"* says Lori Lesser. *"You have to enjoy technology and working with people who are technology experts. You need to have the self confidence to know that you can be educated."*

- The area is a very good place for a lawyer who wants to hit the ground running. *"It is an emerging field; it's very easy to make a name for yourself early,"* says Lesser. *"It's not a field with people with decades of expertise. The law is brand new and every time there is a law on trade secrets, patent law enforcement or EU law, everyone starts on day one. If you're eager to learn, inhale as much knowledge as you can you will quickly be as experienced as someone older."* **Michael Steinig** of **Eversheds Sutherland** backs this up: *"Associates get more client interaction. They are negotiating what needs to go into documents very early in their career. One pro is the learning curve the associate goes on to advance."*

- When working on the transactional side, building good client relations is at least as important as the outcomes of certain cases. *"You can do a good job for your client and they say thank you but you don't win,"* says Michael Steinig. *"You don't have that high and low that you have in some other areas of law."*

- A job as a tech lawyer isn't limited to a BigLaw firm, though an increasing number of matters are now handled by teams at private firms, thanks to the manpower and other resources such establishments have at their disposal. Options outside of BigLaw include serving as legal counsel for the FCC and going in-house with a tech firm.

Current issues

- The rapid rise of cloud computing has made it a *"very hot topic"* in the sector in the last few years, Baker Botts' John Martin tells us. *"It's at an active and evolving stage, which lends itself to many interesting issues in terms of stability of service and allocation of risk. Think about your mobile device and all the data it contains – that's now being stored in the cloud rather than the device itself, which means you as a consumer will require

Rankings in *Chambers USA*

Top ranked

Baker McKenzie	Morrison & Foerster
DLA Piper	Pillsbury Winthrop Shaw
Gibson, Dunn & Crutcher	Pittman
Harris, Wiltshire & Grannis	Weil, Gotshal & Manges
Hogan Lovells	Wiley Rein
Latham & Watkins	Willkie Farr & Gallagher
Mayer Brown	Wilson Sonsini
McDermott Will & Emery	

Highly recommended

Akin Gump	K&L Gates
Arnold & Porter	Kirkland & Ellis
Baker Botts	Morgan, Lewis & Bockius
Bracewell	Orrick, Herrington
Choate Hall & Stewart	Proskauer Rose
Cooley	Sidley Austin
Foley & Lardner	Skadden, Arps
Goodwin	Venable
Greenberg Traurig	Vinson & Elkins
Haynes and Boone	WilmerHale
Hunton & Williams	
Jenner & Block	

For more detail on ranking tiers and locations, visit www.chambersandpartners.com

on-demand services and updated info from the technology provider."*

- The sector used to center around the US regulatory landscape exclusively; however, thanks to an increasingly global market, most technology and telecoms companies have expanded their business internationally, *"which in turn requires us to broaden our capability as legal advisers by collaborating with foreign counsel to apply our US-based knowledge transnationally."*

- As content-sharing technology becomes increasingly dominant, companies need to be as inventive as possible to protect their intellectual property and remain profitable: *"As we have more and more devices we change how people view content and make money off content and there are winners and losers,"* says Lori Lesser.

- Content on social media has also had seismic affects on the real world. Recent political decisions have arguably been affected and badly predicted by the patterns in which people share content, as well as the perceived rise in 'fake news'. The use of these platforms by the media as well as the provider's responsibility to keep their service 'clean' will undoubtedly be hot topics as they continue to expand.

- From delivering pizza, to filming, to helping to find lost mountaineers, the potential civilian and commercial uses of unmanned aerial vehicles (more commonly known as drones) have proliferated. Clients are increasingly keen to discover how best to utilize these flying machines, and that means navigating a host of legal and regulatory issues. With all these unmanned aircraft whizzing about the sky, safety is a prime concern, but considering that drones were developed for intelligence purposes, so is privacy. Law firms have been setting up practice groups to help their clients navigate this spaghetti-esque tangle of regulations.

- 3D printers have also created quite a stir, particularly in the IP and product liability worlds. All that is needed to 3D-print something is an electronic schematic and a 3D printer, and the technology is already capable of producing prosthetics, aircraft parts and even rudimentary firearms. 3D printers are becoming more affordable and accessible, which raises the specter of their being used to produce unauthorized copies of patented inventions.

- The continuing development of self-driving cars will bring with it numerous ethical issues concerning with whom the culpability would lie in the case of an accident and whether the technology will protect the itself, the operator or other road users.

- With a main focus on making our lives easier, technology has the power to simplify outsourcing deals. *"Large outsourcing deals usually take nine months with several people working on it. Cloud deals are a lot less work and a lot quicker; they are more of a commodity. The power of that technology is able to replace the larger service agreements,"* says Michael Steinig. *"You don't need a 20-page establishment document, just click a button. The volume of the deal increases, but not so much the complexity."*

- The result of the recent US election will have an impact on policy, but the general consensus is that work in technology law is a fairly safe bet. *"Some of this stuff might be done differently, but it's not going away,"* says Steinig. *"The quality of what's done and the benefit of it are a powerful combination."* Indeed, as Martin points out, *"the landscape in the technology sector is constantly evolving, so there's a high demand for smart, hard-working lawyers to get involved. Technology is an attractive sector for new lawyers because there's always something over the horizon. This will be the case for the foreseeable future."*

Practice Areas

"The worst answer I have ever had to a question was the person who told me about working on a group project at college where no-one pulled their weight, so they did all the work. They were really proud of it, but it tells me they might not work well in a team."

- a BigLaw hiring partner discussing OCIs

Wealth Management

In a nutshell

Private client lawyers advise wealthy families, individuals, trustees and fiduciaries on all aspects of estate planning, including asset management, tax planning, wills and trusts, charitable contributions and various types of estate litigation. Matters can be purely domestic or have an international element if, for example, a family has non-US resident members, is seeking asylum in the country, or has invested wealth overseas.

A great deal of private client work is tax-based, especially with regards to income and estate tax. However, specialists in this area also need to ensure their corporate tax knowledge is up to date, as it's not unusual for their family clients to have multimillion-dollar businesses to their names. As **Carol Harrington** of **McDermott Will & Emery** highlights: *"In addition to the original family business, one client owns casinos, two major league sports teams and a charitable foundation – that's a similar situation for a lot of clients."*

"The ability to deal with numbers is important. You don't have to be a maths wizard, but you can't be afraid of spreadsheets."

– Carlyn McCaffrey, McDermott, Will & Emery

Compliance is another important aspect of wealth management. Lawyers need to cultivate a lot of regulatory knowledge in order to advise their clients, who may have multiple requirements as shareholders of corporate entities, trustees of charitable foundations, charitable donors and recipients of trusts.

What wealth management lawyers do

- Structure assets to create tax-efficient structures for private individuals seeking to transfer assets to family members or executives of estates.
- Draft wills, trusts and estate documents.
- Regularly meet with clients.
- Aid families and wealthy individuals with their personal tax liabilities and solutions.
- Establish and structure charitable organizations, as well as charitable endowments and funds.
- Provide families with multi-jurisdictional advice pertaining to their international estates.
- Liaise with private client lawyers around the world.
- Represent trustees in litigation regarding their conduct when handling of an estate.
- Communicate and discuss strategy within a team.

Realities of the job

- **Basil Zirinis,** a leading wealth management partner at **Sullivan & Cromwell**, says: *"Our practice is a mix of drafting, meeting, advising and researching."*
- Wealth management tends to offer young lawyers more direct client contact than they'd typically get in a larger corporate or litigation department. *"If you're a strong associate and you show drive, there is always the opportunity to be very involved with families face-to-face,"* says Zirinis.
- Building relationships with clients is an important part of the job, as **Carlyn McCaffrey** of **McDermott Will & Emery** explains: *"Many private client attorneys end up with hundreds of clients over their careers. They don't work for them all at the same time, but they don't finish with a client either. Estate planning is a lifetime enterprise. If you had a client 20 years ago that you did good work for, chances are you're still working with them today."*

"Any one of my clients could call me with something crucial to them; their dad's had a heart attack, so what do they do?"

– Carol Harrington, McDermott, Will & Emery

- Harrington also drives home the importance of empathy and client-care skills. *"These are real-life people-problems; sometimes kids aren't financially responsible, for instance, and sometimes families don't get on."* She adds: *"There's a crisis every minute and each client wants to be the only client you have. Any one of my clients could call me with something crucial to them; their dad's had a heart attack, so what do they do?"*
- Research forms a large part of the role. *"We're fortunate enough to have a practice where the questions are unusual and complex, and there are often no clear answers,"* Zirinis notes. *"We add value where the answer is unsettled, so the associates are doing research, but it's creative research. This makes it more challenging and more interesting."*
- Attention to detail is vital, especially when structuring assets for high net worth individuals (HNWIs). *"It's important that you understand the law; it's technical, complex and it can get pretty complicated,"* Harrington points out.
- Private client lawyers tend to juggle several matters at once. *"This element is a challenge, but at the same time it's a high point. There's so much variety and you never*

Rankings in *Chambers USA*

Top ranked

Alston & Bird	McDermott Will & Emery
Baker Botts	Pillsbury Winthrop Shaw
Choate	Ropes & Gray
Cooley	Snell & Wilmer

Highly recommended

Arnold & Porter	Nutter, McClennan & Fish
Baker McKenzie	Paul, Weiss
Cadwalader	Perkins Coie
Goulston & Storrs	Proskauer Rose
Greenberg Traurig	Schiff Hardin
Holland & Knight	Schulte Roth & Zabel
K&L Gates	Sheppard Mullin
Katten Muchin Rosenman	Sidley Austin
Kirkland & Ellis	Sullivan & Cromwell
Milbank, Tweed	Thompson & Knight
Norton Rose Fulbright	Willkie Farr & Gallagher

For more detail on ranking tiers and locations, visit www.chambersandpartners.com

charitable donations from the current 39.6% rate to 33%. Whether congress accepts the plan in full is yet to be seen.

- According to a 2012 report complied by Emmanuel Saez and Gabriel Zucman, the top 0.1% of families in the US own almost the same share of wealth as the bottom 90% combined – signaling levels of wealth inequality not witnessed since the Great Depression. On a global level, a 2015 Oxfam report found that just 62 people own as much as 50% of the worlds' population combined. All of this, Carol Harrington believes, means that *"there is a lot of work here to do. In the next ten to 20 years there is going to be the greatest transfer of wealth in the history of the world."*

> *"When families are fighting they want you to help them settle it, but given the emotions and family history it can very difficult... there is often no clear or perfectly right answer."*
>
> – Basil Zirinis, Sullivan & Cromwell

see the same thing over and over again. It's thrilling, exciting and fresh," Zirinis enthuses.

- An interest in tax and a good feel for numbers is a must. McCaffrey says: *"The ability to deal with numbers is important. You don't have to be a math wizard, but you can't be afraid of spreadsheets."* Often clients will have business interests that need to be factored in, but the more complex sums are usually sent to the firm's corporate tax teams to figure out.

Current issues

- *"The global nature of wealth certainly has an impact on the practice,"* says **Amy Heller** of **Skadden**. *"It's increasingly common for wealthy families to have family members and assets in multiple jurisdictions, so it's important to have – at the very least – an awareness of other countries' laws and a sensitivity to other cultures."*
- The changing nature of the law means that lawyers must remain flexible in their drafting of wills, trusts and other documents; they require many additional clauses to ensure their smooth adaptation to shifting regulations.
- The new US administration's proposed tax plan aims to abolish the estate tax, which is currently set at 40% of estates larger than $5.45 million, or $10.9 million for those filing jointly. However, it is still unclear whether this proposed plan will go ahead in full, or whether amendments will be made.
- Another significant proposed tax change by the new administration involves reducing the deductibility of

Basil Zirinis' advice for aspiring wealth management lawyers:

- Hone your diplomacy skills. *"Because it's such a human area of the law, it can be extremely emotional. Do you leave assets outright? Do you trust your family? There is no right answer. When families are fighting they want you to help them settle it, but given the emotions and family history it can very difficult. It's not about 'right' or 'wrong' family members, it's just that there is often no clear or perfectly right answer."*
- Tax it up at law school. *"Students should definitely take as many tax courses as they can in law school – including corporate tax. The more of a background they have in tax, the more helpful it will be."*
- But still keep it broad. *"We do everything from corporate law to litigation in our practice – so the broadest possible academic experience is also important."*
- Expand your language skills. *"An international perspective on the world is helpful, especially because the explosion of wealth is global. It's not just the US and Europe anymore; it's China, Latin America and many other jurisdictions. That's where the most interesting work will ultimately be for young lawyers, so languages are extremely important."*

Practice Areas

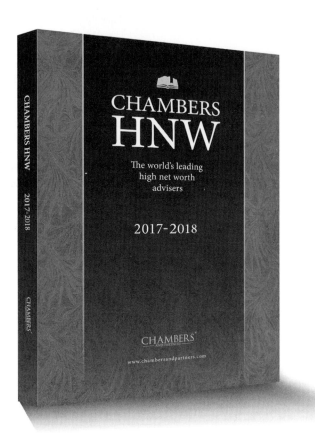

Chambers HNW 2017-2018

The world's leading high net worth advisers

Chambers' global reputation provides unique access to this notably difficult to reach audience. The guide is used by family offices and professional advisers to wealthy individuals, providing objective guidance on an international scale.

The 2018 edition of *Chambers High Net Worth* offers an even more in-depth view into high net worth markets all over the world. It features 14 new jurisdictions as well as all 50 US States. We also take a closer look at three key US markets for Family/Matrimony; New York, California and Florida.

The Inside View

The Inside View

As you will read in The Inside View, law firms can vary massively – all have their own quirks – but most share common features as businesses. Here's what JD grads should expect...

What firms have in common

- At most BigLaw firms juniors join a **single department** on their first day. Some firms allow rotations either within a broad practice area (like corporate) or across the whole firm.
- Usually entry-level associates begin life at a firm with low-level **'junior' tasks** – the grunt work like due diligence, document review, document production, collecting closing signatures and so on. You have to start somewhere, but things do get better: drafting, advising clients, negotiating with opposing counsel. How steep the learning curve is depends on the firm, but there are usually certain responsibilities that fall to individuals at each level. For instance, a BigLaw junior is unlikely to be taking depositions, but they may second-chair one. The higher the dollar value of a matter, the lower a junior's level of responsibility tends to be.
- If a firm is known for a certain area of practice, don't assume this is all it does (for example, there's a lot more to Weil Gotshal & Manges than just bankruptcy). Boutiques aside, at most BigLaw firms corporate and litigation are the two biggest departments. Either a **specialist department** – like IP or labor & employment – will exist alongside these, or specialities will be discernible in a firm's corporate or litigation work (for example, a focus on product liability or energy).
- Junior associates usually **have their own office**, although at the largest firms – especially in New York – juniors will share with another lawyer for their first one or two years.

- The most common cliché about BigLaw is true: lawyers do work some long hours. Client and partner demands can mean long days and all-nighters when the going gets tough. Where firms differ is in how often such 'firedrills' occur, how regularly you're expected to work weekends and late at night, and how frequently you end up canceling events in your private life for work.
- Many firms have a formal **billable target**. Others don't. But that doesn't mean lawyers work any less. All firms expect attorneys to work an amount which reflects how active their department is. If you're significantly below the average, that's bad news. Billing is the be all and end all of lawyer life.
- Law firms are increasingly relaxed about where lawyers do their work. Most juniors try to be in the office during **business hours**, but few partners expect juniors to be at their desks every day from 9am to 9pm. At the same time, many firms allow and expect flexibility from their juniors. This means that working from home in the evenings and on weekends is common. Associates are expected to check emails on their smartphones and be communicative outside office hours.
- Devoting a proportion of your time to **pro bono** is encouraged at most firms. Some allow a certain number to be counted as billable; at others this number is essentially unlimited. In practice, juniors are usually free to pursue pro bono projects provided they do not interfere with paid work. Only rarely do juniors devote more than 5–10% of their time to pro bono.

The Inside View

Adam Leitman Bailey, P.C.

Lawyers per state

Largest US office: New York
US offices: 1
International offices: 0
First-year salary: no lower than $150,000
Billable hours: requirement varies by associate
Summers 2017: 3 (all 2Ls)
Revenue 2016: undisclosed
Partners made in 2017: 1
Famous for: real estate work, especially condos and foreclosures

Adam Leitman Bailey is a small, gutsy firm operating in the buzzing world of New York real estate law.

INVOLVED in a mortgage foreclosure dispute? Are you a residential landlord with problem tenants? Or a tenant with a shark landlord? Got a noisy or disruptive neighbor? Then call Adam Leitman Bailey: the man; the firm. New York real estate lawyer Adam Leitman Bailey founded the firm that bears his name in 2000 when he was just 29 years old. *"Adam is a very passionate and strong person and he is definitely inspiring,"* one of his associates told us. His clients and peers agree, as *Chambers USA* awards Bailey an individual ranking for his work in the New York real estate market.

This firm's USP is clear: *"We only practice real estate law. We practice one type of law in one state,"* its website states. Attorneys here are primarily litigators, working on matters related to condos, landlord-tenant disputes and mortgage foreclosures, although there's some transactional work too (mainly the buying and selling of residential property). *"What I like about real estate law is that what you are working on is actually tangible – you can see it in real life,"* one associate said. Another told us why they enjoy the litigious aspects of the work, proudly reporting that they had *"found a lie in a deposition which the opposition had taken – it was the key to winning our case."*

Some of our associate interviewees had a background in the real estate world before joining the firm, but some did not. All were attracted to the firm's entrepreneurial culture and the promise of being able to work independently early in their career.

Work & Offices

Juniors work within small specialized teams, usually consisting of a partner and one or two associates. The firm's litigators – including juniors – are variously specialized in foreclosure, landlord-tenant, condominium/cooperative, title insurance, commercial real estate, and appellate matters. Clients include some well-known names like Verizon, Wells Fargo and Citibank, plus title insurance companies Stewart and Fidelity National. The firm also acts for many individual property owners, residents and apartment cooperatives.

"New York has a lot of foreclosure-related statutes," a junior litigator in this field told us, *"so we assist foreclosure clients from the beginning to make sure they are sending out 90-day pre-foreclosure notices and 30-day notices of demand. When a loan is ready to be referred for foreclosure we draft all the necessary documentation. If the borrower does not contest the action you move toward default judgment which is straightforward. When actions are contested it requires a lot of time and more litigation – a lot can go wrong so we need to pay a lot of attention to detail."* An associate who works on more general real estate disputes told us: *"I have gravitated toward clients that have*

On chambers-associate.com...

• The Ground Zero Mosque case

See firm profile on p.569

The Inside View

particular problems: property owners who want to stop construction taking place next door; or individuals who want to build something and their neighbor opposes it; or people who feel the cooperative board of their building is displaying favoritism."

"I will review the case, come up with my own arguments and write the initial draft of a motion."

All our interviewees noted the "hands-on experience" the firm gives them – "clients know me and I am their point of contact," one junior told us. The structure of the firm means all associates technically work under a partner who supervises them. In practice, juniors are given a lot of independence. "I draft motions, replies, complaints, discovery demands..." one told us. "I also draft creative arguments: I will review the case, come up with my own arguments and write the initial draft of a motion." Juniors also undertake oral arguments during hearings and may second-chair trials. "Some weeks I will be in court twice a week to argue a motion," one reported.

Court visits are so frequent, in fact, that proximity to the Lower Manhattan courthouses is key to the firm's location. It was previously located in the Equitable Building, one block from Wall Street, but moved to One Battery Park Plaza in March 2017, which is still within walking distance of the courts.

Hours & Pro Bono

Juniors said they usually arrive in the office at 9am (sometimes heading straight to court) and "normally leave at 7pm, sometimes at 8pm or 9pm." Weekend and evening working does happen – the firm has a policy of responding to all client queries within 24 hours – although one source described staying till midnight as something which "happens once in a blue moon." Another source said: "I don't work to the exclusion of all else. The firm understands if I have things I need to do in my personal life." That said, during office hours "you are constantly working and it's fast paced the whole time."

"It's fast paced the whole time."

There is also a significant incentive to work more hours: associates receive a third of what they bill and collect over and above their base salary as a profit-sharing bonus (and that amount is then also their raise the following year). We heard from some that the firm has a 1,600-hour billing requirement, but most aimed to work significantly more than that: one source said they aim to bill around 1,900 hours annually, while another had billed well over 2,000 hours in a year.

Recent work highlights

- Back in 2011 the firm successfully won a $5 million settlement from Donald Trump on behalf of the buyers of condos at Trump SoHo who alleged that the inflated claims made by Trump about the property amounted to fraud
- Won a $20 million case on behalf of tenants of an apartment building on the Upper East Side against their landlord who had demanded a rent increase after claiming to have made $2 million in improvements to the building
- Won a case in the lower courts and on appeal for US Bank, defending it against a motion brought by the high bidder in a foreclosure sale of a property in Queens, which was seeking to make changes to the mortgage
- Won a boundary dispute case for a couple living on the Upper East Side whose millionaire neighbor objected to them putting up a fence on the property boundary on land which was theirs, but over which the millionaire claimed 'squatters' rights' as he had occupied it for over 20 years

Pro bono hours cannot be counted as billable, but one associate told us they had helped Adam Leitman Bailey with a pro bono matter. "We only take on pro bono cases presenting significant real estate issues that have serious public implications," says Bailey. He himself worked pro bono on the so-called Ground Zero Mosque case, defending the Islamic center's developer against a lawsuit aimed at preventing the center and mosque's construction near the site of the former World Trade Center towers. Bailey was even grilled on Fox News' The O'Reilly Factor over the case.

Pro bono hours
- For all attorneys: undisclosed
- Average per attorney: undisclosed

Training & Development

There is some formal in-house and external training, but associates agreed that most training happens on the job. "You need to learn and pick things up as you go, and if you don't understand something you are expected to go ask for help," one source reported. Happily, "the relationship with the partners is very interactive: you draft a document, get comments back on it, then work on it again, add to it and send it back. If you make a mistake you are called out on it and you rectify it."

The quality of associates' work and billing is monitored by Adam Leitman Bailey himself, but there are no formal annual reviews or appraisals.

See firm profile on p.569

Diversity	Partners (%)	Associates (%)
Women	25	30
White	Undisclosed	Undisclosed
Black/African American	-	-
Hispanic/Latin American	-	-
Asian	-	-
Mixed/Other	-	-
LGBT	-	-

Culture & Diversity

Besides being an *"eye in the sky"* when it comes to hours and performance, Bailey is also the point around which the firm's culture pivots. *"He is the central figure of the firm,"* an associate said. *"It is his baby. He operates at 100% all day, every day. He is excited and passionate about his work and that translates to his employees."* The associates we spoke to were all chatty, ambitious, entrepreneurial and enthusiastic. One associate said of Bailey: *"His philosophy is simple: work as hard as you can and earn as much money as you can for yourself and for your team."*

"Adam Leitman Bailey is the central figure of the firm. It is his baby."

Bailey enthusiastically shares his gains with his attorneys and staff – and not just by means of the profit-sharing bonus mentioned above. There are a bunch of perks on offer: summer and winter parties, cakes to celebrate birthdays, massages and manicures every other Friday, sponsored gym memberships, and regular bagged lunches in the office (or a nearby park in summer). Bailey even buys employees any theater and sports tickets they request and pays for a tailored business suit for every new associate – the office dress code is business formal except on dress-down Fridays.

Get Hired

"I would rather have someone from a second, third or fourth-tier school who is ambitious, than someone from a top school who just got there because they are from a wealthy background. I need to see that people can do well in competition with others..." Find out the full story on www.chambers-associate.com.

A third of the firm's associates are women, and a couple are from ethnic minority backgrounds. *"We have people from different walks of life and different backgrounds,"* one source told us. *"And people are in different stages of their life. For example, some people already have big families, while some are just starting families."*

Strategy & Future

We asked Adam Leitman Bailey what made him start his own law firm 17 years ago. *"I learned a lot from my Grandma Betty who grew up during the Great Depression – we balance out our practice areas to allow us to succeed when the market falls and we do types of real estate law that every one needs – everyone needs a place to live and an attorney to handle the purchase or sale or to litigate when a home or office ownership or tenancy is being challenged."* A key way Bailey decided to provide good customer service was by specialization – *"one type of law in one state"* – not just at the firm level, but by having every attorney specialized in a sub-field of real estate law.

"50 to 60% of our clients have been with us for over a decade."

Bailey also believes the strength of the firm lies in the countercyclical nature of real estate law practice. *"We actually do better when the real estate market is doing worse,"* says Bailey. *"During the financial crisis in 2007/08 we were hiring and growing. We also keep significant reserves for a rainy day."* It helps that he has many loyal clients who turn to the firm regularly. *"We have many clients – including Fortune 500 companies – who have been with us for many years. 50 to 60% of our clients have been with us for over a decade."*

These relationships bode well for the future. *"We turn away a lot of transactional business because we are so busy,"* says Bailey. It is this area of the firm which he expects to grow most in the near future. *"We are hoping to hire more new transactional attorneys in the future."*

See firm profile on p.569

The Inside View

Akin Gump Strauss Hauer & Feld

Lawyers per state

233
215
19
101
182

Largest US office: DC
US offices: 11
International offices: 9
First-year salary: $180,000
Billable hours: 1,950 soft bonus target
Summers 2017: 76 (55 2Ls, 18 1Ls, 3 SEO)
Revenue 2016: $980 million (+5.4%)
Partners made in 2017: 18 (8 US)
Famous for: Transatlantic restructuring power-house; helping Native Americans; DC lobbying

High-ranking Texan with global outlook seeks energetic associates for congenial career courtship.

BLEND an achin', entrepreneurial desire to serve clients with a whole lotta legal gumption and you've got yourself an Akin Gump. In the decades since its founding in post-WW2 Dallas, this outfit's amassed 20 offices spread across the Middle East, Asia, Europe and the USA. Although Texas is where it all began, DC is the biggest base, in keeping with the firm's predilection for lobbying work. In addition to its government expertise, the firm's bankruptcy, investment funds, international trade and energy practices all earn recognition on a nationwide level from *Chambers USA*. *Chambers Global* also recognizes the firm as among the world leaders in international trade, hedge funds and restructuring.

The Work

The litigation department receives the largest amount of new associates, followed by corporate. Several join the oil and gas/natural resources group – which is a Texan specialty – while there are other practices like investment funds and cross-border transactions that take on a sprinkling of juniors. The larger departments have an assigning partner who *"keeps track of what's on everyone's plate,"* but as associates find their feet they can receive work directly from partners or take a *"walk down the hall"* to seek out assignments *"if I have extra hours to fill."*

On chambers-associate.com...

- Get hired at Akin Gump

A corporate junior let slip that *"earlier this year we had an issue when associates were billing 300 hours for multiple months in a row. It came to a head and partners set up a meeting. Now they're spreading out work from Dallas to New York and Houston so it doesn't happen again. It was good, I feel like communication was opened up amongst partners to associates."*

A litigator described their practice as one *"combining three broad areas: one is white-collar, then there's some bankruptcy litigation, which is huge in New York and brings in a lot of work, and besides that there's general commercial litigation."* Another source told us that *"on the white-collar side of things, I have insider trader investigations that I'm doing most of the legwork on. I coordinate with the client and contract attorneys. Since I'm junior, there's a certain amount of doc review but partners want you to present the case to them and analyze the facts. They're eager to have you sit in on preparation for interviews or depositions. It's not just isolated doc review."*

For commercial litigation, *"most of our clients tend to be investment funds"* while *"there are big energy clients in other states, Texas in particular, that affect the work we get in New York."* A junior's daily grind might consist of *"some doc review, but also research and motion practice over discovery disputes. I've taken a first draft of a brief and that writing experience is really helpful."* Over in bankruptcy, *"there's lot of research and seniors encourage me to get involved in depositions and drafting outlines."*

See firm profile on p.570

Rankings in *Chambers USA*

Appellate Law	Investment Funds
Bankruptcy/Restructuring	Labor & Employment
Capital Markets	Litigation
Corporate/M&A	Media & Entertainment
Energy & Natural Resources	Native American Law
	Projects
Government	Tax
Healthcare	Technology
Intellectual Property	Telecommunications
International Trade	

For detail on ranking tiers and ranking locations, visit
www.chambersandpartners.com

"It's not just isolated doc review."

Meanwhile, over in the corporate department, juniors get stuck into M&A, plus securities offerings and debt work. *"For M&A, we mainly represent private equity companies and their portfolio companies although there's a little bit of work for public companies. Early on I did a lot of diligence, but in the last six to eight months I've gotten more client contact. It's actually very demanding – when the partner's gone out of town I interface directly via email and calls. I've been very surprised at the level of responsibility – it's above and beyond."* Other tasks include *"drafting portions of purchase agreements, creating issues lists and dealing with comments from the other side."* Over in Houston, an associate in the oil and gas business revealed that *"we do a large number of asset deals and I assist with the drafting and negotiating of the deal documents."*

Training & Development

Novices have a week of initial training covering basics like *"here's how HR works and these are the computer systems, etcetera,"* and some practice-specific sessions on *"advocacy and the life cycle of litigation, plus a writing workshop run by an external coach."* Several sources agreed that *"there's not a whole lot of formal training targeted for first-years apart from CLEs offered throughout the year, and I was a bit concerned, like 'what am I missing?' I have friends at other firms who were training for a whole month!"*

Experience of informal feedback and practical *"on the job training"* varied from source to source. *"It wasn't something I was expecting and it happened, which is wonderful,"* reported one gratefully. *"In my first case I had to draft a discovery request. It wasn't difficult but I'd never done it before, and after I turned it in the partner took me out for coffee and went over the reasons for changes. He has any number of other cases but he took 30 minutes out to sit down, for my education. It doesn't always happen but it was really nice, and you improve faster than shooting in*

Recent work highlights

- Advised 7-Eleven in $3.3 billion purchase of 1,108 convenience stores in 18 states from Sunoco LP
- Advised EP Energy in asset sale of Texas and Louisiana shale plays to Covey Park Gas for $420 million in cash
- Acting for Pechanga Band of Luiseño Indians regarding access to an increased water supply to tribally-owned land
- Representing an endowment fund, pension plan and investors in a $27 million dispute with the former general partner of certain real estate private equity funds

the dark and inputting edits." On the other hand, another junior told us: *"I don't want to say that I don't feel supported, but I don't want to say that partners are taking time out to teach me things. It's not like people don't care that there isn't that type of extra support, but nobody's saying 'oh, you're a first-year, what opportunities do you need?'"* Juniors are assigned partner and associate mentors.

Offices

A Dallas junior complained that *"the office is in the southern part of the downtown area, which is not quite as new and vibrant as uptown. Our office has a lot of dark colors and dark paneling, and people want newer, more modern space."* Well, their wishes were granted – shortly before we went to press it was announced that Akin Gump's Dallas base will move uptown to a gleaming new building. DC juniors also reported that an office move was in the pipeline.

"...everything seems to match."

Over in the Big Apple, attorneys proudly declared that their digs are *"very nice. We're in the Bank of America Tower where they film the HBO show The Newsroom."* First-years share an office but then graduate to their own space. *"I'm on the 31st floor with a good view of Manhattan through big windows,"* murmured one, but demurred when asked about the décor. *"I'm the wrong person to critique the interior design. I mean, everything seems to match."*

Over in Houston, a chatty associate told us: *"There's a wellness room where you can take a nap. They provide bottled water and soda. The carpets are regularly washed and there's nice art and stuff on the walls."*

Hours & Compensation

Associates need to rack up 1,950 hours to qualify for a bonus but there's no official billing target. The lack of a set figure *"is probably one of my favorite things about this place,"* said one junior. *"The work can ebb and flow, so right now it's really, really busy and I'm working a lot, but*

See firm profile on p.570

Diversity	Partners (%)	Associates (%)
Women	20.2	44
White	86.9	72.7
Black/African American	2.2	3.3
Hispanic/Latin American	3.7	2.8
Asian	6.72	8.9
Mixed/Other	0.4	1.9
LGBT	0.7	1.5

then there are the slower months, in fall and summer. As a first-year I got super-worried when I didn't have much work, but people reassured me, 'hey enjoy this time you have when you're not swamped.' Even when it's super-busy it's manageable: you know what the project requires of you and can prepare your life."

"It's not like I'm here until 3am for weeks at a time."

Another junior admitted that "some matters are more unpredictable, like a fast-paced restructuring case, whereas with white-collar, it's easier to plan your life around deadlines. If I want to do something on a Saturday like go to a concert, then I'm happy to stay later on Thursday. Overall the work/life balance is pretty good but it's definitely not perfect. But I didn't expect to work nine to five." Indeed, some interviewees reported staying into the wee hours, but "those are discrete times to do with a deadline. It's not like I'm here until 3am for weeks at a time." An 11-hour work day is common, but "there's not a huge face time requirement. In your first year you want to be in the office as much as can to give the impression you're a hard worker, but once you establish that and people know you they won't be looking for you if you're not busy." Taking a vacation isn't off the cards: "After a busy period I took an international vacation for two weeks. I didn't get work emails, only emails asking how my trip was going."

Culture

In Big D, "people buckle down and get it done, but they're also very open and friendly. We talk about fantasy football and then go back and do our work. It's a congenial place." Associates have a happy hour every couple of months, plus "there's always a lot of informal stuff, like a bowling night which is a lot of fun, and associates go to dinner with each other's families."

A New Yorker mused that "some firms are very private, where people do their own thing, while there are others where the expectation is that you're going to go out on Friday night. Here, it's in between. It's common to grab a drink or two after work with a few closer friends but it's not like this is going to be your social life." Apparently, "the diver-

sity committee puts on pretty fun events, like wine tasting, a meal at an Indian restaurant, or showing a movie like Selma."

"We talk about fantasy football and then go back and do our work."

In the capital, "there's a very collegial atmosphere. I feel extraordinarily lucky, folk here have great personalities and a sense of humor, we don't have scary people screaming at associates. We're fun-loving and don't take ourselves super-seriously."

Pro Bono

"Pro bono is the norm around here," stated a source, a declaration that every interviewee lived up to – all of them were working on pro bono matters at the time of our calls. Associates appreciated that "there's no cap on hours – you can count it all toward the billable total. There are so many avenues so it's easy to find the type of project you're interested in. I got five emails in the past two days about projects. It's like going into a candy store: you pick out what you enjoy."

"There are so many avenues."

Unsurprisingly, some of these matters are tough. We heard of sad cases including "a mother accused of abusing her child in the Bronx family court," a murder-suicide, and "trying to get a juvenile lifer re-sentenced." Others had taken on landlord-tenant cases, civil litigations against municipalities, breach of contract cases for local businesses, and human trafficking research.

Pro bono hours
- For all US attorneys: 83,761
- Average per US attorney: 100

Diversity

A diverse associate told us that "at the partnership level there's not a lot of diversity. I know that the firm's aware of diversity issues and is actively working on them, or planning to. I don't know how widespread that is. There are specific people who care a lot about it, but I personally think it's a little behind other firms." There's a women's group that puts on events like happy hours, plus a range of intiatives to help recruit diverse lawyers. As well as an overarching national diversity committee, there are local groups in each office representing LGBT and ethnic minority attorneys. There's an LGBT retreat and a working parents' forum in New York and DC.

See firm profile on p.570

Get Hired

We all know that law firms everywhere are looking for good grades and good experience. But managing partner Kim Koopersmith lets us in on a few insider secrets that will help hopefuls through the interview process and beyond. First up, she advocates making the most of law school. *"Use law school as much as you possibly can to explore your own interests and get a foundation in what you think you'll focus your future on."* Pretty standard stuff. In our discussions with her however, she tells us that things like moot courts, law clinics and *"involving yourself in groups where you have a speaking role, are great experiences that will give you more confidence later on."* On a more general note, Akin favors candidates that *"are on the offensive to get a seat at the table. We want spunky associates who are willing to think for themselves and express their thoughts to better serve clients."*

So how do you show that? *"Don't be shy about talking about yourself or about asking questions."* Questions are a good way to engage interviewers to let them know that firstly you've thought about the firm in a bit more depth, but also *"in the course of your questions it can show how you articulate your thoughts and whether you're comfortable having a back and forth with the interviewer. This way we get more of a sense of who you are and whether you'll be a good cultural fit."*

Strategy & Future

2016 was a busy time for firms across the country. The new administration is taking some getting used to in the legal sector. Akin Gump lawyers were among those who pitched up at airports to help out people affected by Trump's immigration ban *"and we will continue to do so as part of our commitment to pro bono,"* says Koopersmith. In an attempt to balance things out however, the firm also hired a prominent Republican lobbyist *"to better serve all our clients' interests by taking a bipartisan approach."* Other firm additions include new offices in Dallas and DC, which are currently under construction and scheduled for completion in 2019. *"We live in a different environment to how we did 20 years ago when we first moved into these offices. Now it's all about collaboration and innovation, so we wanted to shape the new spaces to facilitate those goals. We've even included associates in helping with the design plans."*

"A total home run."

Other than that, things seem to be chugging along quite nicely at Akin. Three years on from the Bingham acquisition, Koopersmith says that *"it's been a total home run. They're so completely connected with our firm."* When we asked if there were any plans to repeat the success of the Bingham deal, the powers that be kept it broad saying: *"We will focus on finding geographical opportunities or overlapping circles of expertise that will fit well with us."* While there weren't any specifics offered up as to what areas of expertise they wanted to find opportunities in, we were told that at the moment *"our financial restructuring practice continues to be a dominant player in the distressed space and we are becoming more dominate in white-collar crime and global trade. We've been very successful in the things we care most about, which we will continue to do in the future."*

"We live in a different environment to how we did 20 years ago when we first moved into these offices. Now it's all about collaboration and innovation, so we wanted to shape the new spaces to facilitate those goals.

See firm profile on p.570

Allen & Overy LLP

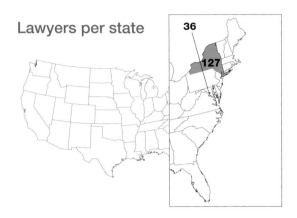

Lawyers per state

36

127

Largest US office: New York
US offices: 2
International offices: 42
First-year salary: $180,000
Billable hours: 2,000 target
Summers 2017: 20 (all 2Ls)
Revenue 2016: $1.97 billion (-4.4%)
Partners made in 2017: 24 globally (0 in US)
Famous for: British magic circle credentials; cross-border work; project finance

Equipped with *"the resources of a global behemoth, but the culture of a much smaller firm,"* A&O's got the 'magic' formula.

BUDAPEST, Bangkok, Barcelona, Beijing... We can name eight exotic A&O locations beginning with the letter 'B' alone. And while you're entertaining your dinner guests with this fun fact, you might also point out that flag-planting alone doesn't make a law firm great. Numerous firms can claim international credentials, but for this British-born giant, *"international work is not just a recruiting gimmick,"* insisted the associates we spoke to. *"It's a way of life at A&O – it's 80% or 90% of our work."* Consider this: a staggering ten practices at A&O are ranked top-tier in the *Chambers* global-wide rankings, and the firm is awarded the third spot in the *Chambers Global Top 30*.

Allen & Overy is one of London's mega-prestigious 'magic circle' law firms, but its Stateside offices in New York and Washington, DC are cozier than many USA-headquartered peers. Though *"A&O does not have the same name recognition in New York that big local firms have, it's really investing in US associates for that reason,"* one junior felt. The US drive in recent years has yielded strong *Chambers USA* rankings in areas including project finance, commercial litigation, antitrust, real estate and environment work.

On chambers-associate.com...

- Get hired: all the essential info
- Allen & Overy's connection to the British monarchy

The firm is awarded the third spot in the Chambers Global Top 30.

The Work

In New York, incoming associates submit a list of preferences to the firm, which rotates them through two practice areas for a six month stint in each, though *"there is the option to stay where you are if there's room and everything went well."* The main options are project finance, banking, real estate, corporate and litigation. Rotation is popular as *"people think they're interested in one area, then end up going down a completely different path. You get to work with as many people as possible and naturally find what you're most interested in."* Contrastingly, in the smaller DC office *"you're technically assigned to an area, but float around and keep working with lots of different groups. Day to day work can greatly vary."* Insiders revealed that *"the class coming in this year will be put into a pool system, and not assigned to a group at all."* DC newbies will, however, still rank practice areas to give an indication of their interests.

The project finance team *"works for a lot of big banks, private equity and hedge funds."* Associates saw *"a lot of due diligence – I don't mind, it's really great exercise in drafting. After about six months you get more involved in negotiating substantive documents: operative credit agreements, process agent letters, legal opinions."* Less popular were *"lots of closing and post-closing tasks – somebody has to do it, that's just life. It's very important, but very tedious."* Though associates *"would love more renewable*

The Inside View

See firm profile on p.571

Rankings in *Chambers USA*

Antitrust	Government
Capital Markets	Latin American Investment
Corporate/M&A	Litigation
Environment	Projects
Financial Services Regulation	

For detail on ranking tiers and ranking locations, visit
www.chambersandpartners.com

Recent work highlights

- Represented the Bank of China in a case to determine whether US courts had the ability to force disclosure of information on Chinese accounts
- Worked on $148.8 million purchase of Manhattan Holiday Inn, advising lender Deutsche Bank
- Advised Thomson Reuters on its $3.55 billion sale to Onex and Baring Asia
- Represented Macquarie and Skanska in the $875 million design and build of the Maryland Purple Line rail project

energy and power work," they enjoyed *"directly answering client queries, with plenty of oversight. Direct client contact is culturally very normal."*

"Direct client contact is culturally very normal."

A&O litigators reported *"a fair amount of document review, drafting advocacy work and research assignments for senior associates and partners. Days can be incredibly varied and unpredictable."* The work is *"primarily investigation,"* and because both offices are *"leanly staffed, you do a lot more sub-drafting and procedural work."* Juniors thrived in the high-responsibility environment. *"On one conference call, other firms only had partners talking; here they allowed me to do the call myself."* Workload was seen as *"manageable. I don't want to work 70-hour weeks, and I don't, but it's enough to keep you busy."*

Most practice areas feature *"a big international dimension, constantly working with people in other offices."* Interviewees worked with *"a lot of overseas clients, and on most projects you need to coordinate with people in multiple different timezones. International harmonization is very important."* In addition to liaising with colleagues in other offices, there are ample opportunities to spend a bit of time abroad. *"The international secondment program is pretty regular. They're typically from third year on, earlier than that you need more experience,"* so don't book your flight just yet.

Get Hired

One associate made it clear that A&O is *"looking for people interested in doing cross-border work, not looking to be a tourist."* Head to chambers-associate.com for more tips.

Training & Development

Converging on New York, all incoming attorneys attend a week of orientation followed by department-specific training. Beyond that there's *"lots of learning by doing, and really good workshops for things like depositions. We're*

certainly not struggling to meet CLE credit hours."* An annual performance review *"provides junior and mid-level criteria, showing what you should be striving for,"* though in the rotational first year this is less rigid. Interviewees reported inconsistent levels of on-the-job assessment. *"Feedback isn't part of your job description,"* quipped one associate, but most felt *"people are very willing to share feedback that facilitates our ability to grow."*

Culture & Diversity

Upon arriving at A&O, newbies were relieved to find *"everybody speaks to each other as a human being, and it makes a huge difference liking the people you work with. It turns it from a job into a profession."* Though culture *"differs from group to group, there is a British influence in that everybody's extremely polite."* New Yorkers reported *"going across groups for drinks all the time,"* as well as socializing within teams. One *"had a cooking party – all the partners came along,"* while *"people could bring their kids and significant others to a Hallowe'en event"* in DC. *"Everybody in the office can still fit into the break room"* for *"weekly happy hours,"* after which people tended to head home for some family or relaxation time.

"If there's anything you want to know you can ask."

"There isn't a weird super-intense hierarchy" between partners and associates, regardless of *"enormous respect for people up the chain."* Juniors felt they were *"at the forefront of senior attorney's minds, entrusted with important work and made to feel like I'm playing an important role."* Washington sources praised their managing partner for being *"very transparent, if there's anything you want to know you can ask."* Not to be outdone, Big Apple associates enjoyed *"a good sense of transparency from what the firm shares internally about our goals, and growing a presence in New York."*

Interviewees acknowledged typical BigLaw diversity issues, particularly concerning ethnic minorities, but *"secondments from different offices bring not just ethnic, but national diversity."* The firm's 'A&Out' forum signifies *"a*

See firm profile on p.571

The Inside View

Diversity	Partners (%)	Associates (%)
Women	18.4	44.7
White	89.8	70.7
Black/African American	0	2.3
Hispanic/Latin American	0	4.1
Asian	10.2	13.4
Mixed/Other	0	2.3
LGBT	10.2	4.9

good presence of LGBT attorneys," and there's a '20:20' drive to increase the female membership of Allen & Overy's global partnership by 20% by 2020. US managing partner David Krischer tells us *"in the US we're already at 20% women partners, the US offices are at the forefront of the diversity program."* Associates admitted that *"there's recognition across the firm that more has to be done. Multiple female attorneys have recently made partner, and you witness a lot of people emphasizing the importance of diversity."*

Hours & Compensation

Sources reported *"very deal specific-working hours,"* ranging from standard 9.30am to 6.30pm days to *"nights working until 2am or 3am, though that's not regular."* They agreed that *"you do have time for a private life. It's tricky during the weekdays, by nature of being a junior, but weekends are pretty free."* Officially the billing target is 2,000 hours, but *"it's not a hard minimum and it's never been mentioned"* – one associate only found out *"reading about it in* Chambers Associate!" Washingtonians were particularly optimistic about hitting the 2,000, as *"not being locked down to one practice means you're never worried about work slowing down."*

"If they know you're doing a good job you'll get your bonus."

"It was important" to associates that A&O matched the new Cravath pay scale, as *"you want the firm to be attractive to new hires. I think it would have said something about the health of the firm if they hadn't."* Bonuses match market level but aren't directly correlated to the hours target – associates weren't certain how the system works, but were confident that *"if partners know you're doing a good job, you'll get your bonus."* Juniors also get 20 days, vacation a year, five of which can roll over, though *"taking it is a bit of a learning curve. It's your responsibility to bring it up, but everybody encourages it."*

Pro Bono

Weekly lists of opportunities advertize *"everything from child custody and tenancy disputes to global immigration cases."* Associates can count 50 pro bono hours toward their billables target, and sources *"would be surprised if anybody wasn't hitting that."* Those we spoke to felt A&O was *"very welcoming of pro bono, I've never seen any indication the firm wouldn't want you to do it. I emailed a partner about it and she said 'yes, we all need to do pro bono'. Nobody struggles to meet the bar."* Though some were *"slammed with billables, and would love to do more,"* others took on a broad range of cases. These include *"a massive pro bono undertaking in international sex trafficking, looking at global regulations to find loopholes"* and, on a smaller scale, *"working on establishing a local nonprofit."* The firm elects a global charity partner in London to oversee pro bono worldwide.

Pro bono hours
- For all US attorneys: 5,611
- Average per US attorney: 31

Offices & Strategy

Associates described the New York office as *"really cool, right in Midtown. Because it's connected to the Rockefeller concourse, you can literally take the subway into the work building."* From years one to three, attorneys typically share offices, *"which is great – you can use your senior roommate as a mini mentor and informal resource for questions,"* before getting their own room around their third or fourth year. DC's office was *"planned with growth in mind, so there's lots of space."* Though *"people are constantly going between US offices,"* some practice areas including restructuring saw less of this. Twice a year the firm sends an email around all its offices listing secondment opportunities across the globe – for example, *"there have definitely been some Dubai placements."* Some groups take their newbies to London for two weeks of training, *"a crash course in financial law. Lots of time is spent not just on training, but talking about firm strategy."*

"There have definitely been some Dubai placements."

Speaking of strategy, A&O is pushing forward a plan to boost its IP practice internationally, and a US IP litigation offering is in the works. Recent successes have left attorneys optimistic: *"We're in a sustained period of profitability here in the States. We're showing that we're a good investment, and being as busy as we are is a good thing for justifying expansion."*

The Inside View

See firm profile on p.571

Alston & Bird LLP

Lawyers per state

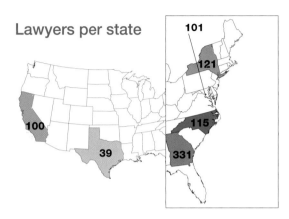

Largest US office: Atlanta
US offices: 8
International offices: 2
First-year salary: $155,000 - $180,000
Billable hours: 1,950 target
Summers 2017: 53 (45 2Ls, 8 1Ls)
Revenue 2016: $730.5 million (+6.2%)
Partners made in 2017: 20 (all US)
Famous for: friendly Southern culture; big dogs in Atlanta

"The firm has the Southern culture that Georgians like, but you still get to work with huge international companies."

"WHEN you say the firm's name to people in this state, they know what you're talking about," associates told us proudly. Such is Alston & Bird's reputation in the Peach State that it's rated top by *Chambers USA* in no fewer than eight different practice areas here. Among Alston's seven other offices, Charlotte's IP group is one of three top-ranked in the North Carolina region, while DC houses a robust healthcare practice. Standout practices in California are construction, environment and securities litigation.

Many of our sources hailed from Georgia themselves, and even those based in other states also appreciated the firm's unique Southern vibe – *"a combination of local personality and big sophisticated work."* They were also hopeful of one day grabbing a slice of the equity peach pie – *"in my interview the hiring partner said that Alston & Bird has one of the highest proportions of homegrown partners in BigLaw,"* one explained. The firm's 1:1 ratio of partners to associates is uncommon at firms of this scale.

On chambers-associate.com...

- Get hired: insider tips and tricks
- Interviews with managing partner Richard Hays and professional personnel partner Liz Price
- Human trafficking pro bono at Alston & Bird, and interview with pro bono and community service director Cheryl Naja

The Work

Many of the firm's entry-level associates swoop into the litigation & trial practice or IP litigation departments; one or two a year join securities litigation. The rest spread across transactional practices including finance, financial services & products, corporate transactions and real estate. Once they're in a nest, Alston's baby birds are fed work from *"a combination of systems, it varies a lot by group."* Most have some degree of formal allocation, but in many cases *"folks don't rely on that. It's very entrepreneurial, which I think is a huge benefit because there is opportunity to seek things out."*

The litigation & trial group links juniors to partners or senior associates through work pairings, so *"theoretically work can come down from the pipeline,"* though it's easy to seek it out from others. White-collar, antitrust, insurance, class actions and commercial disputes all fall into the broad team. Interviewees were *"working all the aspects of a case – discovery, developing strategy, some research memos. It's really fun as a junior to feel like you're managing the project."* There was an element of jumping in at the deep end, as newbies are *"really expected to hit the ground running – it's hard to know when to say no to something."* Smaller litigious groups such as product liability also provide *"surprising responsibility. Partners forget what year we're in when they give us work."* Client contact *"varies depending on the case,"* those in smaller groups seeing more more quickly.

"I think I won the lottery!"

See firm profile on p.572

Rankings in *Chambers USA*

Antitrust	Government
Banking & Finance	Healthcare
Bankruptcy/Restructuring	Immigration
Construction	Intellectual Property
Corporate/M&A	International Trade
ERISA Litigation	Labor & Employment
Employee Benefits &	Litigation
Executive Compensation	Privacy & Data Security
Energy & Natural	REITs
Resources	Real Estate
Environment	Tax

For detail on ranking tiers and ranking locations, visit
www.chambersandpartners.com

IP litigation covers *"everything from patent trolls to competitor vs competitor, there's nothing in the practice area Alston doesn't take on."* Newcomers *"have obviously done document review, which can be fine because it's mindless,"* but were also trusted with *"motions to transfer, writing portions for big briefs and summary judgments. Decisions are made by partners; associates get them down on paper."* Snowed in by an avalanche of patent infringements, the group was *"struggling to find associates to fill the work that's coming in. We're definitely not sat here twiddling our thumbs!"* Our sources considered the workload *"sustainable at least for a few years, but if it doesn't slow down we won't get a very balanced life."* They were far more pleased by the hefty responsibility levels, and after a *"feeling out period"* were off and away with *"a lot of autonomy that builds over time."* Several highlighted depositions as the next entry on their legal bucket list.

Public M&A makes up the bulk of Alston's corporate practice, with an additional dose of securities and some office specialities (startups in Silicon Valley, private equity in Charlotte.) Early onjuniors tackle *"mostly diligence, reviewing contracts and typing up summaries of important provisions,"* as well ancillary documents. Several interviewees found *"the workload the hardest adjustment – it's a little bit feast and famine. Overall it's fine, I'm not overwhelmed."* As in litigation, the rush provides challenging work quickly, and smaller transactional groups like construction lack *"a typical big firm hierarchy, where work passes up the chain so the bottom only does a tiny part of the project."* One corporate source exclaimed: *"I think I won the lottery! I'm very happy here. There's a good amount of being challenged but I'm not out here on my own."*

Get Hired

"I could tell they didn't really want to be in Atlanta. Something like that will make the firm not want you," told an interviewer.
Find out more at chambers-associate.com.

Recent work highlights

- Represented Dell in $24.9 billion appraisal dispute over management-led buyout
- Lead defense counsel for Coca-Cola against accusations it had infringed patents held by equipment distributor Beverage Dispensing Solutions
- Acted for Home Depot in three public offerings totaling $7 billion
- Served as counsel to New Jersey governor Chris Christie in Fort Lee lane closure case

Training & Development

In yearly reviews, associates write self-evaluative memos and submit them to partners on the associates' committee, who then review their charges in categories including leadership, initiative and critical thinking. Pleasantly *"surprised how in-depth the comments are,"* sources told us *"generally people are pretty good about constructive criticism and praise,"* though noted *"it is partner-dependent. I work for some people that just don't give feedback, which can be tough."* But more helpful mentors *"want to sit down and explain changes they make. It's not like a partner will take a motion, put it in a black hole then submit something else."*

> *"...surprised how in-depth the comments are."*

Before they get into the nitty-gritty training, all new starters attend a week long orientation on the usual nuts and bolts. They then head back to school for litigation academy (*"a two-year program of talking through different topics with a well-respected retired litigator"*), M&A college or IP training. Star pupils thought their education was *"super-helpful, though a lot of it is learning as you go."* A mock trial *"pulls it all together"* for litigators. Transactional sources felt management had made *"real attempts to come up with a good practical program"* in recent years.

Culture & Diversity

Alston *"has a reputation of being the happy law firm,"* reinforced by its placement on the *Fortune* '100 Best Companies to Work For' 18 years in a row. Looking beyond the accolades, juniors suggested: *"it's not entirely without problems, but overall I do think it's a good place to work. Everyone's highly motivated and wants to do a really good job."* In smaller offices, *"the majority of people know each other,"* and across the A&B flock *"partners are really invested in wanting associates to succeed."* Several had got chummier with partners than you might expect – *"we obviously get work from them and they are our bosses, but they'll also grab us to go to lunch. It's not like they're in an ivory tower ordering us around."* Noting that *"one of Alston's principles is financial transparency,"* associates

See firm profile on p.572

Diversity	Partners (%)	Associates (%)
Women	22.8	45.6
White	92.2	71.1
Black/African American	2.5	8.0
Hispanic/Latin American	1.1	6.0
Asian	3.1	9.5
Mixed/Other	1.1	5.4
LGBT	3.1	3.4

were pleased to be kept in the know about the state of the firm's coffers.

"It's not like they're in an ivory tower ordering us around."

A *"surprising"* social scene includes an end-of-week bar in several of the firm's bases, where *"buddies always go and enjoy a drink or two."* Come the holiday season there are both office and practice group Christmas parties; some sources also attended *"lots of social events with the women's and diversity committees, informal stuff like going to coffee or drinks."* On top of that, there's *"a lot of pro bono and community service events – trivia games, talent shows. They make for a nice break in the work day."* Whatever they were getting up to, associates maintained *"relationships that aren't exclusively work-based."*

As with most firms, the higher up the tree you look the less diverse things appear. Associates singled out the *"fantastic"* parental leave program for praise – *"it's difficult to keep a tiny human alive then come back to work, but the firm is really supportive of working moms."* Alston & Bird is also *"known for its good work with the LGBT community."* The Women's Initiative operates its own mentoring system; other minorities (LGBT, ethnically diverse) are also assigned a mentor. *"A lot of the younger partners are very focused on diversity, and the leadership is very aware of it,"* though interviewees noted Alston *"still has a lot to do, but so does every firm. When you make diversity a big issue, you might not realize there's a way to go."*

Offices

Alston's Atlanta attorneys *"in the heart of the legal community"* have seen some big improvements to their office recently. *"They've spent God knows what renovating the place, it's now all marble and glass. It looks like a magazine or PR firm office."* The firm is based in what was the IBM Building, a midtown landmark recognizable to Atlanta clients. Associates there felt *"this is the hub, everyone knows it,"* and that their base rules the roost over the firm as a whole – though colleagues in other locations protested that they do have distinct autonomy.

"It looks like a magazine or PR firm office."

New York tackles cases with more of a financial bent, while government work is a greater focus in Washington, DC; the office is *"at the heart of everything, a few blocks from the White House."* Because *"all associates have a window,"* they get a chance to enjoy the view – *"certainly not the case everywhere."* A&B LA is also favorably located, next to Bunker Hill. Closest to the HQ is the Charlotte office – *"the location is top notch. Charlotte in general is very affordable."* Good news for juniors, as starting salaries there and in Atlanta are $25,000 lower than the New York BigLaw standard. Overseas, Alston has offices in Brussels and Beijing.

Hours & Compensation

It's easy to disagree over money, and Alston & Bird associates had conflicting opinions about how their firm dealt with the 2016 market leap to the new Cravath salary scale. *"They did terribly, to be honest,"* one aggrieved party felt. *"The firm was behind the ball. Atlantans felt slighted by the differences between offices."* Contrastingly, others argued A&B *"realized change was coming and adjusted quickly,"* and that *"the firm took care of us, so associate morale is high."* Similarly divisive was a change in vacation policy. The shift from four weeks to *"officially unlimited"* leave *"has pros and cons – it sounds nice in theory but can have the effect of making people take less."*

"They're aware we have lives and don't ruin our weekends."

Alston & Bird has no formal billable hours requirement but associates are bonus eligible at 1,950 hours (up from 1,900 before 2017). How easy it is to reach that *"varies a lot by group,"* but the busy people in IP and litigation felt *"you'd have to be trying very hard not to hit your hours!"* Juniors were glad not to be chained to their desks, as *"there's no real face time requirement. Partners let you know what you need to get done and in what time."* Another plus was that higher-ups were *"aware we have lives and don't ruin our weekends. I never get assignments at 5pm on a Friday to be done by Monday morning."* Weekend work *"is on a when-needed basis,"* and interviewees were often out of the office by 6.30pm.

Pro Bono

Up to 150 hours of pro bono count toward the firm's bonus eligible target (before 2017, only 100 counted). Many took full advantage, and applauded *"the firm's activeness in getting pro bono work to associates."* One junior had gone as far as to bill 250 hours one year, and 200 the next. Most matters are sourced through the firm's internal pro

See firm profile on p.572

The Inside View

bono portal. Options have included *"a project drafting wills for those who can't afford them,"* and custody matters which provided *"great opportunities for direct client contact."* The annual ABBY awards, a *"big party and spectacle,"* include prizes for those demonstrating outstanding commitment to pro bono. Interviewees who hadn't got involved chalked it down to time constraints: *"I wish I'd had more time for it. I'm hoping to do more next year."*

"Great opportunities for direct client contact."

Pro bono hours
- For all US attorneys: 49,514
- Average per US attorney: 64

Strategy & Future

"They're pretty transparent," said one associate we quizzed about how open the firm was to sharing its strategy and future plans, *"but maybe I'm just duped!"* Colleagues agreed *"Alston isn't one to over-promise,"* and were certain of *"no fears of having one pulled over on us, and suddenly being in deficit."* Associates had no knowledge of Alston spreading its wings to new territories any time soon, but were confident that they'd be the first to know, as *"they're very careful before opening a new office, and get people's opinions on it."* Managing partner Richard Hays confirms: *"We communicate consistently that growth is driven by investing in the people we already have, identifying our strengths and playing to them. To do so, we've expanded business development to all levels of associates as well as our summer associates."* For more from Hays, head to www.chambers-associate.com.

To learn about becoming a lawyer in the Southeast, visit chambers-associate.com

See firm profile on p.572

Arnold & Porter Kaye Scholer LLP

Lawyers per state

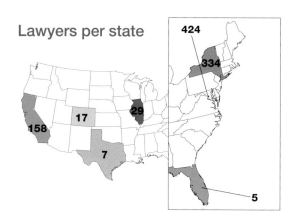

424
334
29
17
158
7
5

Largest US office: Washington, DC
US offices: 9
International offices: 4
First-year salary: $180,000
Billable hours: 2,000 target
Summers 2017: 64 (59 2Ls, 5 1Ls)
Revenue 2016: $945 million
Partners made in 2017: 8
Famous for: the headline merger of 2016; pro bono; public policy and IP

This merger between a DC and a New York firm wasn't just about complementary practices; a common *"humanity"* binds the two together.

"WE'RE all very excited about the combination," revealed Richard Alexander, chairman of the newly merged Arnold & Porter Kaye Scholer. "I said to our colleagues that change is hard," continued Alexander, but "I think the change will represent really wonderful opportunities and will enhance our competitive position as a law firm." The theme of the merger has been consolidation rather than expansion, beefing up bases in DC and New York, and combining complementary practices in litigation, regulatory areas, public policy, corporate work and IP. Bucking recent merger trends, the growth will be largely on American soil: AP brings just Brussels to Kaye Scholer's international network of Frankfurt and Shanghai, but their combined strength in London should now pack more punch.

But if this marriage is going to work, they need to click on a personal level. "When I interviewed here everyone I met seemed down to earth and enjoyable to be around, and I didn't get that impression from every firm I went to," confided a source from the Kaye Scholer side, but this could equally have come from our AP interviewees who told us: "They spare a few moments to joke around with you and ask after your partner or dog. Folks have an interest in you beyond the work you're doing." The humanity of both firms stands out,

and both share a passion for pro bono too: "There's such an emphasis on pro bono here that it attracts people who care." The firm formerly known at Kaye Scholer once had the artist formerly known as Prince on its books, but both firms' client lists read like a who's who, particularly in the IP and government contracts spheres, including such names as AT&T, Samsung, Google, Disney and Airbus.

The Work

When we interviewed litigators from both legacy firms, it became even clearer why these two firms merged. In New York, DC and elsewhere, litigation is by far the largest department for juniors, where they begin as generalists before specializing. "The workload is very diverse – you find yourself on securities cases, white collar investigations or product liability cases," said one New Yorker. While "most people aren't big on a hierarchical structure," juniors will do a fair amount of doc review and research. However, associates across the network "felt very involved and that's what's most exciting about working on these matters." Those from A&P thought that "partners are interested in your view of the case, especially when you've been immersed in the documents. Most of my research assignments into specific legal questions haven't been one-off tasks with no context of the wider case. I don't feel like a horse with blinkers on; I'm looking at the fuller picture." And a KS junior in New York echoed this: "After a call a senior team member will ask me, 'does that person seem credible?' They value my opinion and that feels really good."

On chambers-associate.com...

- Training and development
- Interview tips

See firm profile on p.573

Rankings in *Chambers USA*

Antitrust	Intellectual Property
Appellate Law	International Arbitration
Bankruptcy/Restructuring	International Trade
Capital Markets	Leisure & Hospitality
Corporate Crime &	Life Sciences
Investigations	Litigation
Corporate/M&A	Media & Entertainment
Environment	Privacy & Data Security
Financial Services	Products Liability
Regulation	Real Estate
Government	Securities
Healthcare	Tax
IT & Outsourcing	Telecommunications

For detail on ranking tiers and ranking locations, visit
www.chambersandpartners.com

"I don't feel like a horse with blinkers on."

Opportunities are there for the taking: *"If you're proactive they let you do pretty much anything within reason. I've drafted motions, attended and defended depositions as a first and second-year, assisted at client site interviews, drafted disclosure reports, drafted letters to the other side, undertaken all facets of discovery – some great, some not so great – you name it, I've done it,"* one interviewee listed. *"We tend to staff matters leanly. It works to an associate's benefit, but it can also be a bit hair-raising in the process."*

Alongside litigation, other departments available to first years in the new firm include government contracts & national security; life sciences & healthcare regulatory; intellectual property; corporate & finance; real estate; tax; antitrust; telecommunications, internet & media; and environmental.

"I always feel very involved and that's what's most exciting."

Over in real estate, most of the clients (often "institutional clients like big banks") are on the lender side of transactions, and "maybe 25% of my work is representing borrowers. I've been fortunate in being able to do both – if you express an interest, you can get that sort of work." Junior associates are expected to "keep tabs on the life of a deal – we're relied upon to maintain checklists, do the due diligence, run public searches on entities, draft loan documents and review opinions – it's everything coming in the door with the exception of drafting the main meat of the loan agreement."

Rookies in the corporate department are called upon to *"draft parts of merger agreements, limited partnership agreements, investor manager agreements and memos"* as

Recent work highlights

- Defended American cruise company Carnival Corporation against claims brought by hundreds of passengers who had been on board the Costa Concordia cruise ship when it sank off the coast of Italy
- Acted for Ernst & Young to challenge the government's award of a $58 million health contract to PwC
- Advising AT&T on the antitrust aspects of its proposed acquisition of Time Warner
- Represented Trump Hotels in a $91 million valuation dispute over the development on the historic site of the Old Post Office on Pennsylvania Avenue, Washington, DC
- Acted for retinal surgeon Dr Salomon Melgen who is accused of healthcare fraud and bribing his friend Senator Robert Menendez to secure business connections
- Acting as counsel for Swiss pharma company Novartis in product liability litigation relating to claims that blood pressure medications cause kidney damage.

well as handling the diligence on deals. *"Other folk in my year have spent more time doing securities work, but I've done a lot of work with pharma companies and the buying and selling of biotech companies. I've also worked on fund formations and helped institutional clients to invest in funds."*

"You really have the opportunity to carve out the areas you want to work in," we were told. At both A&P and KS, associates started out largely relying on a flow of work from assigning partners in each department, but *"they really encourage you to be entrepreneurial"* and build your own practice. Associates advised *"talking to people you worked with on your summer placement or have spoken with once or twice,"* one litigator told us. And it's not uncommon to *"cold call and see if people are free to chat about the work they do,"* with an eye to working with them in the future. Once they'd established connections in their department, many of our sources had ceased to rely on the assigning partners.

Training

From trial workshops to the firm's own take on TED talks, *"the firm's made an effort to increase"* training opportunities for juniors. Visit chambers-associate.com for more about the training opportunities.

Culture & Development

In any merger there will always be some cultural differences, but, reassuringly we found a lot of common themes: *"Everyone feels human. You're not expected to be a robot and just churn out work,"* one interviewee told us.

See firm profile on p.573

Diversity	Partners (%)	Associates (%)
Women	20	49.8
White	89.1	76.8
Black/African American	2.2	5.2
Hispanic/Latin American	1.9	4.2
Asian	5.3	11
Mixed/Other	1.6	2.9
LGBT	3.1	5

"We work hard and you need to pull out all the stops, but they respect important personal stuff," clarified another. *"People stop to talk with you in the hallways. It's not like everyone is always rushing around or too busy to develop relationships,"* one source stressed.

"This is the most supportive atmosphere I could have found with BigLaw."

"This is the most supportive atmosphere I could have found with BigLaw," asserted a KS associate. Asked if they found the job fulfilling, one replied that *"it's not like I'm helping orphans or working for charity, this is a for-profit company, but with that said I'm generally happy."* This culture hasn't come about by accident: *"It's weird if I don't see my mentor every week. It's nice to have that built-in support network,"* one source told us. *"To encourage open dialogue the firm provides an allowance for weekly lunch or coffee. I frequently go out with my mentee to give them time to get comfortable with me and say anything they don't want overheard within the firm,"* confided one mentor.

"People here are willing to get to know each other on a personal level, have fun and spend time with each other." Again, this is encouraged by the firm, which hands out a lunch fund to new starters to encourage them to get to know one another. New York associates also appreciated that *"the firm does a good job at transparency on financial side."*

At both firms, our associate sources welcomed the weekly *"free booze, light snacks"* and things like *"corn hole games."* At both legacy firms, the socialising gets competitive. In DC there are the summer and winter Olympics. *"It's really fun, they divide us into teams and then we compete"* in events such as desk chair volleyball, ping pong and *"a gymnastic dance thing."* How gymnastic, exactly? *"I didn't attend,"* our source admitted. *"I just saw the aftermath…"* The winter Olympics were apparently inspired by the real thing in Sochi with a Russian-themed event with ice sculptures and medal ceremonies. In New York, KS first years were welcomed into the firm with a Halloween costume competition, and we heard of a costume competition in San Francisco too. A recent winner was a mid-

level associate whose pirate costume included a treasure chest with a mermaid attached.

KS associates told how their firm doesn't mess around when it comes to summer events. *"We had a 007-themed casino night for all associates, no partners invited,"* chuckled an interviewee. What else? *"We went to a Beyoncé concert, picked out a pair of sunglasses at Warby Parker, and had a rooftop party at the Hotel Hugo, overlooking the Hudson."* Not too shabby. There's also the annual holiday party and department-wide events. Whatever the social scene in the new firm morphs into, we expect it to be lively and definitely competitive.

Offices

In 2017 the following offices are welcoming first year associates: DC, NY, San Fran, Silicon Valley, LA, Denver and Houston. New York office will have the largest intake, closely followed by DC.

"Oh it's gorgeous."

The DC HQ of A&P relocated to the Mount Vernon Triangle in 2015. The *"brand new building is squeaky clean and awesome. It feels a bit like a cruise ship with long walkways and glass sliding doors, and the building comes to a point. It's very streamlined"* and littered with art work, keeping it *"vibrant and colorful."* Outside of DC, we're told the artwork is just as impressive. *"On every wall, there's a photo or painting. It's very creative,"* approved one Los Angeles source.

"Oh it's gorgeous," purred a junior when asked what they thought of the Big Apple base, which the firm also moved into in 2015. After the merger, the KS office welcomed in their new A&P colleagues. *"I love it! Everything is immaculate, we have a cafeteria with coffee bar and an outdoor terrace – it brightens everyone's day to sit out there in the few months when the New York weather is nice. We have happy hours out there and play corn hole."*

Pro Bono

"Once again we've had extraordinary results in 2016 in terms of our pro bono work," beamed chairman Richard Alexander. This was a huge pull factor for a lot of our sources: *"The fact it was so supportive of pro bono really stood out."* The range of matters available apparently feels like *"pretty much everything under the sun and then some other stuff I didn't know existed. Immigrant and asylum work are very prominent. We also handle death row cases and can work on a criminal defense program,"* which sees associates rock up to court and pick up a case on the day. Others have worked on matters concerning disability or voting rights, gun control work, clemency petitions,

See firm profile on p.573

domestic violence, prevention against gun violence and incorporation of non-profits.

"Everything under the sun."

Pre-merger, A&P was one of the top pro bono billers in the USA, posting more than double the hours at KS. But it's clear there's no clash of attitudes towards pro bono and this culture will prevail. "We get emails all the time," a KS associate assured us and pointed out that the firm works with a non-profit organization to facilitate transgender name changes. Interviewees had also taken on landlord-tenant issues, death penalty appeals, drugs cases ("I got to listen to wire-tap conversations between 23 gang members") and an international project helping refugees from Syria and Iraq to come to the USA. "It's been very rewarding."

Pro bono hours
- For all US attorneys: 92,873
- Average per US attorney: 93 (combined figures from the two legacy firms)

Diversity

All new employees attend diversity training upon arrival. The workshop "walks you through different approaches, backgrounds and ways of handling situations and sensitivities as they pertain to diversity." Both legacy firms bring with them a good range of affinity groups – African American, Asian, Latino, LGBT, women, veterans and working parents are all represented – and they "have their own retreats, meetings, mentoring and networking events so people can feel comfortable working here."

"I think that there's a strong emphasis on diversity in recruitment," both sets of associates agreed, it's still "not diverse enough, which is a little disappointing as I know we try hard." When you look at the numbers, A&P matches KS on gender, but shows a little more success in retaining ethnic minorities. But the figures are in keeping with the BigLaw norms.

Hours & Compensation

To be bonus eligible, associates must bill 2,000 hours, which can include up to 200 hours of pro bono or business development hours in things like firm service, shadowing and training. "Overall it's a realistic target," asserted sources. "I don't feel swamped or destroyed but it is difficult at the beginning, because it takes a while to get ramped up on the billable work, so the 200 non-billable hours go by very quickly!"

Attorneys are granted an unlimited supply of holiday. "What you get is incredible but it is hard to fit in," one source cautioned, though at least the firm's making the right nois-es: "In my first week here, a partner told us we should take vacations. He acknowledged there's never going to be a perfect time to go and you're always going to be busy so you just have to make time for it," one New Yorker reported. Once sizzling on a beach or hurtling down black diamond ski trails, our interviewees appeared to have been left alone. "I've never been bothered when away, which was fantastic," one source told us, while another admitted: "I responded to an email while on vacation and was told to stop looking at them. That's a good remark to hear."

Most of those we spoke to "try to get in at around 9.30am – some days I'll leave at 6.30pm, some days 11pm. It really does vary. They don't expect you to be burning midnight oil all the time." One appreciative source noted that "flexibility increases with seniority – now I'm entering my third year, people know they can trust me and I can work from home." There's no strict policy on flexible working and generally it depends on the partner you're with and the proximity of a deadline. It's normal to do "a little something on the weekends. For the most part, I'm left alone unless there's something pressing, but generally I do a few hours on a Saturday or Sunday, to catch up on a few things or get a head-start for Monday."

Strategy & Future

"We had a shared vision of what we wanted to accomplish," said chairman Richard Alexander in an interview with us. A&P was hankering after a "strong presence in New York," while KS "clients were, with increasing frequency, really needing more regulatory expertise," and A&P's answer to that "was something very appealing," Alexander explained. This merger was much more about consolidation. "There are some new practices to each legacy firm but this merger was not about expansion," Alexander adds. Both legacy firms' strong practice and sector-based identities look to continue: "We see ourselves in a couple of key industry areas like science, financial services and bankruptcy. Both firms have heavily invested in those areas." Alexander's upbeat mood on the new venture was palpable – "We're going to work hard to make it very successful." And, echoing the story we heard from the associates, Alexander stressed that "we are very focused on talent and making sure we continue to be a place where our associates and staff want to work and make a career with us."

See firm profile on p.573

The Inside View

Axinn, Veltrop & Harkrider LLP

Lawyers per state

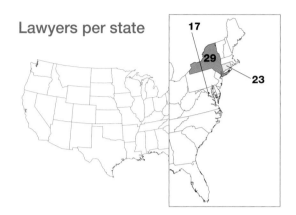

Largest US office: New York

US offices: 3

International offices: 0

First-year salary: $170,000 (CT) - $180,000 (NY/DC)

Billable hours: 2,000 target

Summers 2017: 9 (all 2Ls)

Revenue 2016: undisclosed

Partners made in 2017: 1

Famous for: antitrust and IP work; being a young, growing firm

Youthful Axinn punches well above its weight.

NEW York boutique firm Axinn celebrated 20 years of existence on April Fool's Day 2017, but its enviable reputation for patent, antitrust and litigation work is no joke. *"The firm is doing very well,"* managing partner Jim Veltrop tells us. *"Our antitrust deal work continues to be exceptionally strong, and our litigation practice has been especially vibrant."* A recent uptick in tech sector work has been an added bonus for the firm's three core practices.

Axinn's expertise is further demonstrated by its rankings in *Chambers USA,* where it is among the front runners both for general commercial litigation in Connecticut, and antitrust in New York. With just 29 lawyers in New York, 23 in Hartford and 17 in DC, such recognition is a big accolade for a firm this small.

"Axinn is unique in that it might be the smallest firm in the world that handles matters as large as it does," Jim Veltrop expands. *"There are unique challenges to taking on $60 billion dollar deals at a firm this size, and juniors are asked to take on a lot of responsibility – a lot more than they might in a larger firm. That exposure from such an early stage breeds excellent lawyers, which is why entry-level hiring is so important for us."* If this all sounds like your kind of thing, then you're in luck. Axinn's 2016 summer program welcomed nine summer associates, which is its highest

number ever. 2017 also welcomes nine. *"It's a great time to get involved,"* said juniors already here.

The Work

All of Axinn's lawyers are litigators, and newbies are evenly divided between antitrust and IP, plus one in the general litigation group. The latter does a lot of corporate-level insurance and commercial contract litigation, as well as some high-level labor & employment cases. The past year has also brought *"a substantial increase in litigation relating to financial services,"* MP Jim Veltrop adds. Wherever they end up, juniors' work is allocated formally via an assigning partner. Workload reports are submitted every week and *"the assigning partner will try and staff you on matters that fit your interests."* Take note: *"There's a culture here of being assertive and independent, so it's on you to communicate with people to make sure your priorities are accounted for."* In the past year the firm has been busy working on a number of major antitrust cases, including *"a major price fixing case and a class action that could be the largest in US history,"* Jim Veltrop enthuses. The team *"definitely leans toward tech, life sciences and healthcare work,"* associates pointed out, *"but also works with more down-to-earth industries, like manufacturers of auto parts and forestry products."*

With deal work, counseling, criminal cases and litigation all on the cards, juniors rated the department's variety of cases on offer. *"I had the chance to work as part of a very large team on a cross-border merger transaction,"* recounted one. *"With so many people, I figured I'd be doing the grunt work, but I ended up on a substantial filing for*

On chambers-associate.com...

- Get hired
- How to succeed at the boutique end of BigLaw

See firm profile on p.574

Rankings in *Chambers USA*

Antitrust

Litigation

For detail on ranking tiers and ranking locations, visit
www.chambersandpartners.com

Recent work highlights

- Won over $16 million in damages for DePuy Synthes, following Globus Medical's infringement of three spinal implant patents
- Served as lead antitrust counsel to Dell across 20 jurisdictions in connection with Dell's $67 billion acquisition of EMC Corporation. The transaction is the largest technology merger in history
- Achieved significant appellate victories for Natco, allowing the pharmaceuticals company to offer the first generic version of popular flu treatment Tamiflu

a foreign jurisdiction." On smaller transactions, *"there's usually just one associate working on the planning stages. When things heat up, guess who's best placed to lead the team? Having that responsibility for the product and the direction of the team was not something I expected a couple of years into my career."*

"I'm now the leading associate on a case for an important product, and I'm barely out of second year!"

Axinn's IP practice continues to carve a name for itself as one of the leading practices in the country. The team works a lot with medical devices and generic pharmaceutical companies (generic drugs being those whose patents have expired). Technology has also been a growing industry for the firm in recent years, with cases related to developments in the biotech field – like spinal implants – common fare. When it comes to the work itself, *"patent litigation is a big part of what we do,"* one junior outlined, *"but we're not just a straight lit shop. There are plenty of counsel and Freedom to Operate opportunities on offer too."*

On litigious matters, our sources have been busy preparing depositions and tackling first drafts of motions and briefs. Those staffed on counseling matters focused more on legal research and preparing memos for clients. *"It's very much a meritocracy,"* so *"there are a lot of opportunities for advancement,"* we heard. *"I'm now the leading associate on a case for an important product, and I'm barely out of second year!"*

Training & Development

Rookies' speedy progression begins during the summer program, where they're *"given meaningful and substantive tasks, like writing memos to be presented to clients. You're expected to take initiative, work independently and submit your work on time. It's a real assessment of how you'd function as a first-year at the firm."*

"You're treated like an adult."

This on-the-job style continues once juniors begin at the firm. *"There are a few days of admin training when you start and a handful of periodic meet-ups over the next few years, covering things like case management and effective use of resources. Still, the best training comes through working one-to-one with partners,"* we heard. Juniors

liked this up-front approach, adding: *"You're a member of the team and you're treated like an adult. People trust you, they motivate you, they guide you. Ultimately they get the best out of you because they see the best in you."* Formal feedback comes in the form of two annual appraisals, held with juniors' head of department.

Offices & Culture

In the capital, rookies told us their office *"has the benefit of being close to the DOJ and the SEC, so we tend to work on a broader mix of litigation and antitrust matters."* Attorneys here all have their own office and there's also an in-house gym. *"That's particularly useful,"* one junior joked. *"We're near Chinatown so there's a lot of good food nearby!"* Over in Hartford meanwhile, *"the lifestyle is more suburban, but we work on the same high-level cases as New York and DC. The work here isn't necessarily Connecticut-focused."* The office predominantly deals in IP matters.

The New York HQ is mainly focused on the merger control side of antitrust work as well as litigation, and associates agreed the office *"definitely feels like our main base. It's got a larger associate-to-partner ratio and a lot of the associate-centric training happens here."* Perhaps the biggest coup for Big Apple attorneys is the quality of snacks on offer. *"We get much healthier stuff than Connecticut or DC,"* one New Yorker reckoned. *"It's a perpetual in-joke when the offices get together for Skype training sessions: we'll be chowing down on fruit and nuts, whilst they're stuck with chips!"*

"Everyone is on first name terms."

Associates revealed that attitudes to work differ between offices, and that DC and Connecticut offer *"less erratic hours and a more laid back atmosphere"* than New York. Still, it's important to remember that *"when it comes to numbers, Axinn is a relatively small firm, even in New York. Everyone is on first name terms, and people take a considerate interest in each other's professional and personal lives."*

See firm profile on p.574

The Inside View

Diversity	Partners (%)	Associates (%)
Women	12.5	33
White	100	61
Black/African American	0	3
Hispanic/Latin American	0	0
Asian	0	30
Mixed/Other	0	6
LGBT	4	6

It's an attitude that stretches from the top down. Founding partner John Harkrider *"is always stressing the importance of being comfortable being yourself here,"* one junior mentioned. *"He's a keen movie-maker. Another attorney publishes sci-fi novels. It's not a place where you have to fit a certain mold to succeed."*

Hours & Compensation

"We're a firm that asks a lot of our associates, and that means we have to work extra hard to make sure those associates are also able to maintain a good work-life balance," Jim Veltrop acknowledges. *"We are committed to creating and improving policies that allow associates to strike that balance – things like enhanced caregiver leave and support and sabbatical leave options."*

"People are mostly reasonable with their demands."

Associates corroborated this view, and were particularly impressed with the firm's acceptance of family commitments. *"There's the option to do some of your work from home if you need it,"* we heard. *"If you have to go collect your kid no one will begrudge you."* Associates need to bill 1,800 hours to be eligible for a portion of their bonus, and 2,000 for the full amount. *"There aren't too many crazy 14-hour days,"* but we did hear of the odd early hours finish around trial time. Thankfully *"no one will set you meaningless deadlines. People are mostly reasonable with their demands."*

Pro Bono

100 pro bono hours can count toward billables at Axinn, though *"there's no hours requirement. Pro bono is definitely encouraged, but often people are so busy it can be hard to see where to slot projects in."*

Regular emails are sent out listing opportunities, which range from veterans' rights affairs to refugee cases through the International Rescue Committee. Attorneys in New York have worked for Volunteer Lawyers for the Arts, which provides legal representation for low-income artists and non-profit arts organizations.

Diversity

"The firm isn't as diverse as I would like," grumbled one antitrust junior. *"There's a definite deficit of female partners in my department."* It was the same story in IP and litigation, where associates have found *"the firm has trouble retaining female lawyers, particularly after they've had children."* Ethnic diversity *"could be better too,"* with figures showing that 100% of Axinn's partners are white, while just 12.5% are women. Juniors couldn't list any specific initiatives in place to counter this imbalance, but did praise the women's affinity group, which organizes monthly conferences, as well as social events such as dinners and lunches.

Strategy & Future

"An exciting combination of stability and exceptional performance" has fueled another successful financial year at the firm, according to MP Jim Veltrop. In the years ahead, he envisions *"major growth in our biotechnology practice, including both patent litigation and regulatory matters."* Furthermore, *"we also see strong client growth in our criminal antitrust practice."*

See firm profile on p.574

The Inside View

Baker McKenzie

Lawyers per state

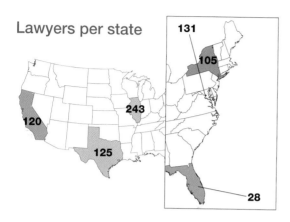

131
105
243
120
125
28

Largest US office: Chicago
US offices: 7
International offices: 70
First-year salary: $180,000 ($145,000 in Miami)
Billable hours: 2,000 required
Summers 2017: 51 (41 2Ls, 10 1Ls)
Revenue 2016: $2.64 billion (+8.6%)
Partners made in 2017: 15 (US only)
Famous for: humongous headcount; tax prowess

Baker may have dropped the ampersand from its name, but nothing else has been edited out from this global firm's offering.

"YOU have to think anyway, so why not think big?" So quipped a certain new political figure. The president's motivational saying might equally sum up Baker McKenzie. In the lists of the world's biggest firms, it always features near the top by both headcount and revenue. It houses over 13,000 employees in 77 offices dotted across the planet. Several associates we interviewed had *"wanted to join a firm that emphasized their global operations,"* and felt *"Baker did that more than any other."*

Recently, this big firm has seen some big changes, dropping the '&' from its name as part of a worldwide rebranding exercise and appointing a new global chair, Paul Rawlinson. *"The new management is doing a very good job dealing with issues as they come,"* according to our associate interviewees. Top *Chambers USA* accolades for the firm's signature tax practice are the tip of an iceberg of rankings for numerous practice areas including corporate/M&A, litigation, employment, international trade, immigration and outsourcing.

On chambers-associate.com...

- Get Hired: insider tips and tricks
- Interviews with North American managing partner Rick Hammett and hiring partner Scott Brandman
- Baker McKenzie's overseas offices

The Work

A sizable portion of juniors joins the tax or corporate & securities team, the rest heading into IP, international commercial, compensation & employment, banking & finance, or litigation & government enforcement. Projects are usually staffed by practice area rather than office, so juniors *"can get work from the entire North American group"* – many took advantage of this, but the majority focused on work from within their own base. The free market system can mean *"there's not a lot of structure to allocation. It tends to be fairly informal,"* with associates naturally slotting into work relationships with partners. *"On the whole it's a good system,"* according to our sources.

"I can get work from the entire North American group."

Baker's tax practice covers both transactional and litigation matters. The latter focuses on clients' relationship with the IRS, and the firm regularly defends corporations' stated positions in disputed tax returns and filings. There is some domestic work on offer, but lawyers typically *"deal with clients with large global footprints: the firm's value is it's a one-stop shop for international issues."* Newcomers dive headfirst into brief and memo writing, background research and planning. Those we spoke to were frustrated that *"some weeks I'll be twiddling my thumbs, others I'll bill 50 hours,"* but felt *"happy with the client contact side of things. Straight away it was more than I expected and my first thought when corresponding with them was 'oh, wow!'"*

The Inside View

See firm profile on p.575

Rankings in *Chambers USA*

Climate Change	International Arbitration
Corporate/M&A	International Trade
Employee Benefits &	Labor & Employment
Executive Compensation	Litigation
Environment	Outsourcing
FCPA	Privacy & Data Security
Franchising	Tax
Immigration	Technology
Intellectual Property	

For detail on ranking tiers and ranking locations, visit
www.chambersandpartners.com

Recent work highlights

- Advised oil and gas company Lonestar Resources on relocation from Australia to the US and subsequent NASDAQ listing
- Counseled FedEx on its $4.8 billion acquisition of courier service TNT Express
- Acted for medical device firm Medtronic in potential $1.36 billion tax dispute; reparations were reduced to $14 million
- Represented Facebook in dispute with IRS over asset value transfer

Corporate encompasses M&A (frequently with a cross-border element), securities, capital markets and funds, as well as the firm's specialty of *"global reorganization: not bankruptcy, but tax-oriented movement of money. Different offices do different things but by and large there's a big emphasis on reorganization."* International cases inevitably evolved as juniors slept, so each day they *"woke to wade through a ton of emails!"* Following this info-rich breakfast, an average day consists of *"drafting base agreements, attending to ancillary documents and running the diligence."* Varying responsibility levels mean some days were *"happier"* than others but sources acknowledged *"it's necessary to learn the basics, you can't skip that experience."*

Newbies in compensation & employment revealed *"on the global side we're doing much the same as juniors in corporate, helping with cross-border work and putting resources together."* The group has a hand in corporate transactions, as *"if a union is involved in the acquisition we'll advise on that aspect."* Varied day-to-day tasks were *"one reason why I've enjoyed what I've done so far,"* said one junior, even if that included less desirable tasks like *"a lot of not terribly complex document review."* Interviewees were disappointed to have had fairly little client contact, but noticed it increasing as they became more senior.

"I got to travel to Japan a couple of times."

Litigation at Baker McKenzie is *"mostly driven by big investigations"*– the firm handles commercial cases too but *"compliance and criminal work are the bread and butter."* Associates tackled *"a lot of document review and analysis, or preparing for interviews, depending on where the project was."* Though *"some partners micromanage more than others,"* juniors got *"a surprising amount of responsibility straight away; even when the stakes are higher and I have less I'm never shut out."* The international nature

of the work sometimes necessitated a spell abroad; one interviewee *"got to travel to Japan a couple of times"* for one case alone.

Offices & Culture

The firm's Chicago hub featured in *Transformers: Age of Extinction*, but don't let that put you off. It's just far enough to the edge of the city's main 'Loop' that attorneys *"feel nicely separated from the hustle and bustle, but it's a bummer to commute."* Glass doors proved *"divisive – they provide natural light but no privacy,"* but overall it's *"a good, modern space."* Baker McKenzie DC sits in a *"trophy location looking over the White House, it's an awesome place to work,"* while New Yorkers are right next to Bryant Park. Down in Texas, the Houston office is in the *"iconic"* Bank of America Center. Dallas is in the process of relocating to new digs. Summer associates have the option to spend a few weeks abroad in one of the firm's sister offices, and fully fledged associates can also jet off overseas thanks to Baker's Associate Training Program.

"The firm seems smaller than it actually is."

Undaunted by the scale of the Baker McKenzie network, juniors told us they *"talk with everyone all the time – the firm seems smaller than it actually is."* Most felt *"there is an overarching culture, they've done a good job pushing for a one-firm mentality,"* but noted *"each office does have its own flavor."* For instance, *"Chicago is a bit stuffier than other places, perhaps as it's the HQ."* On the other hand, there's *"a distinctive California vibe"* in Palo Alto and San Francisco. *"It's good they're trying to maintain that."* Wherever they were, juniors got the impression *"management make an effort to be transparent"* about future growth and strategy, *"but it's a big firm, and that will always be a hurdle."*

Though it's *"not firm policy that you have to hang out with your colleagues, everyone's amicable if not good friends,"* associates told us. *"Outside of work-related functions*

See firm profile on p.575

Diversity	Partners (%)	Associates (%)
Women	28	50
White	88.4	73
Black/African American	0.6	5
Hispanic/Latin American	4	4
Asian	5	14
Mixed/Other	2	4
LGBT	0.8	4

there's not always a ton of people socializing together." They were happy to get opportunities to let their hair down, even if Baker Mac lacks a "huge party culture." Appropriately for a Chicago-born firm, pizza plays a role in many social stories, from "associate pizza nights and happy hours" in Houston to a DC "goodbye party for a colleague when we went bowling and for a pizza." Sources told us that certain partners display "no sense of hierarchy at all – some still show up to associate pizza night!" "I wouldn't interact with a partner in the same way I would a fellow junior," one interviewee explained: "it's not like 'Mr' this and 'Ma'am' that: interaction with partners is usually much more low key and I feel comfortable cracking jokes with some of them."

Get Hired

"What's different about Baker is that we're practice-group driven, we have certain specialties and are looking for people with interests that fall there." Get clued in with more recruitment tips at www.chambers-associate.com.

Training & Development

Newcomers immediately noticed "one thing Baker does best is putting on a lot of conferences," which play a big role in associate training: "It's really nice in a place as big as Baker to see the faces of the people we're emailing." Each office hosts "fairly regular" internal CLEs which "tend to be on practice group-specific topics." Some interviewees felt "you need to get your hands wet to really learn to do something," and thus appreciated on-the-go training that acts "more as constructive criticism than patting you on the back."

"Feedback goes both ways."

Asked if they got regular work feedback, one diplomatic junior suggested "that's not the strongest of our strengths," but felt "very comfortable with my superiors, and if there were a problem, I'd know." Monthly cross-office webinars and annual reviews help to fill in any gaps, while the firm also runs a mentoring system wherein juniors have quarterly check-ins with an assigned partner. Most sources

were "happy overall, it seems people let you know if you've done something incorrectly or there's something to work on," and were pleased to note "feedback goes both ways" so they could let partners know how helpful they'd been.

Diversity

Associates felt Baker McKenzie is "fairly diverse for a large firm," with the caveat "it is mostly white lawyers at the very top." Juniors suggested "the international nature of the firm helps diversity," as lawyers globe trot across different offices. Nonetheless, like at many peer firms, some felt there has been "a struggle for ethnic diversity." Fortunately, there are corrective initiatives in place including a global diversity and inclusion committee; one source predicted "we'll see the fruits of their labors within the next few years." Associates were much more positive about gender balance; a female interviewee "constantly saw people like me that I could identify with in leadership positions." The firm recently appointed Anna Brown as its new North American director of diversity and inclusion, and in 2017 close to 40% of its US partner promotions were women.

"I constantly saw people like me that I could identify with in leadership positions."

Hours & Pro Bono

Associates who clock up 2,000 hours are eligible for a bonus. "For most, that's pretty achievable," though multiple interviewees reported that "it varies by practice group. One bad month where you're significantly under-target can derail you." Corporate associates in particular saw "no trouble hitting the 2,000. I've had bad months but no real problems and overall the hours have been good." There was some grumbling about lack of information on bonus payouts, but associates commended the firm for "realizing how important it is we match market" and swiftly meeting the nationwide BigLaw rise to a $180,000 and up starting salary. "Everyone's pleased they didn't give us the run around." The firm's 'unlimited' vacation policy also drew mixed feedback; several juniors saw it as "a way to discourage vacation" while others argued "it's totally fine, we don't get judged for taking breaks."

"Though it can be emotionally difficult, the work is extremely rewarding."

There's "never a shortage of opportunities" to do pro bono at Baker McKenzie, though sources' overall impression was that "people are happy for you to do it, but there's no huge expectation or requirement." Many of those who'd got stuck in had handled immigration cases (some prompted by President Trump's executive orders), while other op-

See firm profile on p.575

The Inside View

portunities included work for disability organizations, youth homelessness charities and corporate pro bono.

Matters are coordinated by two pro bono partners *"who are very committed and do a ton of great work,"* juniors told us. *"Though it can be emotionally difficult, the work is extremely rewarding. It's a very different challenge."* Associates can count 100 hours of pro bono toward their billable target. A few interviewees opined that *"it would be nice for more to count toward the target, as it's the easiest way to make up hours when billable work is slow,"* but realized *"there needs to be a limit or people would start to avoid paying work!"* Some dedicated their time to volunteering work with local organizations instead of legal pro bono.

Pro bono hours
- For all US attorneys: undisclosed
- Average per US attorney: undisclosed

Strategy & Future

So why did Baker McKenzie drop its '&'? Rick Hammett, the firm's North America managing partner, explains *"we were known to many simply as Baker McKenzie already, so it made sense. We've continued to have the strongest global law brand in the world while strengthening our brand recognition in the USA."* Alongside the branding shift, Paul Rawlinson became the firm's first British global chair in 2016. With the re-branding complete, Hammett tells us to expect further growth from Baker McKenzie going forward – *"there are no specific new offices in the pipeline at this point, but I definitely see us continuing to grow into new markets both in North America and globally. In particular, I see us growing in New York."* The full interview is available in the Bonus Features for the firm on www. chambers-associate.com.

"In particular, I see us growing in New York."

See firm profile on p.575

Baker Botts LLP

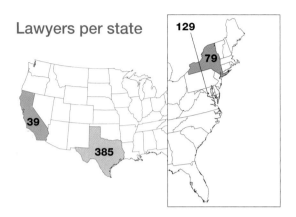

Lawyers per state

129
79
39
385

Largest US office: Houston
US offices: 7
International offices: 7
First-year salary: $180,000
Billable hours: 2,000 requirement
Summers 2017: 96 (64 2Ls, 32 1Ls)
Revenue 2016: $846.5 million (+20.2%)
Partners made in 2017: 8 globally (all US)
Famous for: being the oldest firm in Texas; a slick energy practice

There's a lot more than oil and gas at Texas' oldest law firm.

OIL prices may have hit rock bottom over the past couple of years, but Baker Botts has blossomed. *"Although to our core we're an energy firm, we're very focused on continuing to grow in other areas,"* hiring partner Van Beckwith explains. Associates were likewise keen to stress that *"we do more than just energy."* These days, the 177 year-old Texan practices many different types of law in 14 offices across the globe, conducted by 725 lawyers who between them speak 50 languages and handle matters in over 145 countries. *"I wanted to join a general practice firm with prestige and a great reputation – and that's what you get here,"* one junior associate told us, and others said similar. Big-name clients include ExxonMobil, Shell, Petrobras and Dell.

Unsurprisingly, Baker Botts' energy practices radiate through *Chambers USA's* hottest national rankings. In Texas, the best marks also go to corporate/M&A, environment, tax, real estate and IP. This breadth of expertise once again yielded glowing financials – in 2016 revenue soared by over 20% to $846.5 million. *"We've held as strong as the year before, which was a relief during the challenging times of uncertain commodity prices,"* says Van Beckwith. High tech work of all description is one particular growth area: He adds: *"In the next ten years we want*

to have an even deeper tech bench. We currently have 180 lawyers with tech degrees and I can see us taking more."*

The Work

Candidates should know which location specializes in what practice area. Most beginners join one of the three Texan offices and they gave us the run-down of who practices what and where: *"New York is primarily corporate and IP work,"* which are the two practices *Chambers USA* ranks here, although other practices are active too. *"There's a lot of IP and emerging companies work in Palo Alto. San Francisco does real estate,"* plus IP and litigation. *"DC does a lot of antitrust, white-collar, environmental work, and international arbitration."* Energy regulatory and general litigation also feature prominently in DC. *Houston and the other Texas offices are generally treated as one unit and are mostly full service. There's a lot more energy work, specifically energy litigation, in Houston because the chair of that practice is there."* A large number of rookies join litigation, corporate and IP, with projects, environmental and tax following not far behind.

> *"You get to pick partners whose practices you want to emulate."*

"There's no structure to getting work," insisted insiders. Initially, starters are given their first work by formally assigned mentors to ease their transition into the firm. *"But as more people hear about your work you get it from other people."* Sources liked the freedom *"to go get work from people you actually want to work with and you get to pick partners whose practices you want to emulate."*

On chambers-associate.com...

- Interview with hiring partner Van Beckwith
- Energy law under the Trump administration: the views from top energy lawyers
- More on getting hired

See firm profile on p.576

The Inside View

Rankings in *Chambers USA*

Antitrust	Intellectual Property
Banking & Finance	International Arbitration
Bankruptcy/Restructuring	Latin American Investment
Capital Markets	Litigation
Climate Change	Products Liability
Corporate/M&A	Projects
Energy & Natural Resources	Real Estate
	Tax
Environment	Technology

For detail on ranking tiers and ranking locations, visit
www.chambersandpartners.com

However, others reasoned that *"for first-years it can be a double-edged sword, because it can be difficult to get your bearings."*

Litigators commonly *"do a lot of research in the beginning and help other people write briefs."* Pretty standard fare, but *"what was surprising was that it wasn't as much doc review as I had thought, and what you do review is like the meat and potatoes of the case."* More substantive tasks include *"drafting discovery motions and motions to dismiss in the federal court."* Some have also *"been there for jury testing and voir dire for a trial."* Traditionally, newbies start off as generalists and can take on work from different sub-groups that can include bankruptcy, securities litigation, ERISA and energy litigation.

Texan transactional associates get energy work as well. Permeating both general corporate and global projects, insiders told us that *"despite the crappy market last year, we are still going to make our hours."* Corporate sources felt that there was *"a fair amount of drafting things like contribution agreements and lots of sitting in on client calls."* Different offices have different focuses: for example, DC is mostly energy regulation and trade sanctions, while Houston is the epicenter of transactional energy work. Interviewees said that *"from day one partners are very open with you and tell you to speak up if you think something is legally incorrect."* Purchase and sale agreement drafting was usual, as was the opportunity to be seconded to a client for *"around three to five months. It's great for client contact."*

IP juniors detailed that *"we do everything here like litigation, patent prosecution and also trademarks."* Litigation tasks were a good mix of *"taking the first crack at drafting discovery motions, second chairing a deposition"* and *"working directly with clients. I was on a two hour conference call with a client. I didn't expect that as a first-year."* Prosecution assignments involve *"interviewing inventors to write and file patent applications, responding to patent office actions and writing appeal briefs."*

Recent work highlights

- Represented Schlumberger in its $14.8 billion acquisition of Cameron International, creating the world's largest oilfield services company
- Defended AT&T in a location privacy technology patent trial against Enovsys LLC
- Represented the conflicts committee for Antero Midstream Partners in the $1.05 billion acquisition of Antero Resources Corporation's integrated water business

Training & Development

"The first few weeks are 'drinking out of a fire-hose'-type training, like how to use the computer, send emails and other soft skills," as well as initial legal training on how to be a good associate. After this, practice groups tend to run fundamentals training that cover the basics for each group. For example, new litigators got *"training in depositions and discovery, plus bi-weekly email updates on changes in the law."* Newbies in global projects went through *"everything oil and gas-related. We do general contract drafting and then more specific things like international contracts for oil companies. There are also lessons on the lingo like what does 'upstream' mean?"* As associates progress through the years there's evidence of partnership-track training, and *"how to bring business into the firm through networking and stuff like that."*

> *"You're going to get lost in the weeds if you're not a self-starter."*

There's a formal annual review. Usually two partners take each associate through the conglomerated feedback from all supervisors they've worked with for more than 20 billable hours. *"Partners aren't going to remember all the small things you did. It's a bit lackluster – you hear things you've heard before."* Informal feedback is a mixed bag. *"The most helpful feedback I get is after each assignment in real time. Mid-levels are really good at giving it. Seniors struggle a bit more because they're so busy, but the partners are fantastic and really take the time to make sure you understand."* However, others qualified that it depends who you work with: *"You have to ask for it and it's tough. You're going to get lost in the weeds if you're not a self-starter."* The overall consensus was that while the quality of feedback was generally good, insiders wished that *"there was more communication as a whole."*

Offices & Culture

Baker Botts has developed seven domestic and seven overseas offices, and boasts a strategic alliance in Kuwait with the International Legal Group. Closer to home, the Houston HQ contains the *"top brass."* Renovated around three years ago, the Houston office is *"beautiful. We're at 1 Shell Plaza and there's glass everywhere. It's awesome,*

See firm profile on p.576

Diversity	Partners (%)	Associates (%)
Women	17.2	42.4
White	76.9	91.1
Black/African American	2.1	2.4
Hispanic/Latin American	4.6	2.4
Asian	11.8	3.1
Mixed/Other	4.6	1
LGBT	3	4

but sometimes I wonder how useful doors are when everyone can just see in anyway!" All associates get their own offices regardless of location. Austinians told us that "sometimes we can feel like a bit of a support office, but that's probably because we're smaller. We still originate our own work here though." New Yorkers were more than happy being "in a landmark location in 30 Rockefeller Center. I'm looking straight at the Empire State Building right now. Tourists pay for the view I've got."

> "Tourists pay for the view I've got."

"Wherever we are, the culture translates as still being a bit Texan." That boils down to "being really friendly and you're not taken for granted. I get a lot of 'thank you' emails. It means a lot." Most felt that while the atmosphere is "chummy," it's normally "a little more 'business first' compared to some other firms." This did affect BB's social side. "The social life might be one of the firm's weaknesses. Most people do their own thing: there's not a firmwide culture of frequent events." But the events on offer weren't disappointing. Along with the usual sprinkling of monthly happy hours, more unique events have included a lip-sync battle for charity and "a Thanksgiving pot luck lunch, for all the lawyers and staff. People bring stuff in and there's always really good pie."

Hours & Compensation

Most juniors work around ten hours per day on average, with some logging back onto the system from home. Most people get in around 8.30am and normally stay till 7pm. In global projects "it's been a slower year, so sometimes it's more like 9-6pm. But when a deal is on, you're billing around the clock." Some told tales of working until "3.30am and then coming in for 7am the next day."

Attorneys have a 2,000-hour billable target to be bonus eligible. Some didn't "really understand the bonus system." Others explained that it's "unique. Instead of locktstep, we have this strange level system." Rather than bonuses being determined by class year, BB operates under four levels that house two or three associate year-groups. Insiders liked this approach: "If you're doing amazing work, you get more money based on your attributes within your

level and it doesn't matter what year you are." However others were more reasoned. "Just because you hit 2,000 hours, you're not guaranteed the maximum rate. It's more like 2,200 and then it's more about how your group leaders view bonus allocation."

Pro Bono

"They can give you credit for every pro bono hour you do and it goes toward your bonus." While some had been clocking up to 400 hours, others warned that "while they say it's unlimited, I don't think they mean for you to spend all your time doing it." However, "it gives you the confidence to start acting and thinking like a proper lawyer." Litigators were the most enthusiastic: "It's the best training because you get to go in front of judges as the lead attorney." Corporate newbies also get in on the action, partnering up with their counterparts in lit. "We do a lot of domestic violence work and divorces. So corporate associates do the run-down of the assets and the litigators handle the actual court part." Most people recounted how they'd interviewed clients, drafted the case documents and spent a good amount of time in court and mediations. "It makes you pay closer attention to what you're doing because there's no partner fail-safe to lean on."

Pro bono hours
- For all US attorneys: 33,932
- Average per US attorney: 80

Diversity

While some urged that "it's not all WASPS," others disagreed: "We're not very diverse. It seems like an issue that the firm cares about, but doesn't really know how to address." Others continued that "we talk the talk and know it's important, but we're not fully there in terms of inclusivity." There's a diversity committee that orchestrates the running of different affinity groups representing women, LGBTQ, Black and Hispanic attorneys. But "there used to be monthly meetings and break-out sessions and that's gone away now. It's understandable because everyone is so busy." However, the firm is still trying to remedy the situation. Working with pipeline initiatives like the National Black Pre-Law Conference and CLEO [Council on Legal Education Opportunity] has helped to ensure that incoming classes are more diverse.

> "The commitment to diversity and the attempts at diversity are disconnected."

"I'm very comfortable here. In terms of gender, it's pretty even. In fact, in the class that just started, there are three women and one male." Others were more blunt about ethnic diversity. "It's something we are always going to strug-

See firm profile on p.576

The Inside View

gle with in Texas. We do have diversity outreaches. But given the political climate, I don't blame diverse people for not choosing to live and work in this state." It was clear that associates appreciated the firm's attempts, but thought BB fell short in terms of results. "It just feels like the commitment to diversity and the attempts at diversity are disconnected." Initiatives to remedy this include programs for LGBT, minority, and female summer associates, plus celebrating events like Asian Pacific heritage month.

Get Hired & Strategy

Van Beckwith lets us in on what's in store for the future. "I'm very excited about what the future holds for us. Even during this challenging time for oil commodity pricing, we're on track to have a record year. In 177 years as a firm, management has never taken for granted who we are. We've continued to reinvest in people and as students arrive here we hope that they feel that energy too. It's definitely made people excited to come and work at Baker Botts." But what do you have to do to get through the door? Sources suggested "trying to gear activities in law school to future practice. If you know you want to be a litigator, get on the mock trial team." For more advice on the inside track, go online.

"We've continued to reinvest in people and as students arrive here we hope that they feel that energy"

The Inside View

See firm profile on p.576

Bracewell LLP

Lawyers per state

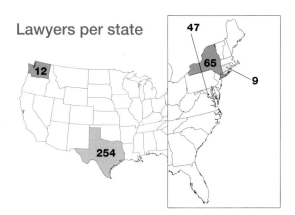

47
65
9
12
254

Largest US office: Houston
US offices: 8
International offices: 2
First-year salary: $180,000
Billable hours: 2,000 target (or 1,800 reduced compensation track)
Summers 2017: 30 (20 2Ls, 10 1Ls)
Revenue 2016: $277 million (-6.6%)
Partners made in 2017: 7
Famous for: energy work; being a "destination firm"

It's less 'Houston, we have a problem' and more 'Houston, we have lift off' at this energy-fueled firm.

BRACEWELL'S Texas background means it knows what's watt in the energy sector. The firm generates legal expertise from its four bases in the Lone Star State, three on the East Coast, and also a small office in Seattle, plus across the seas in London and Dubai. As an energy-focused (though not energy-reliant) firm, the drop in global oil prices may cause concern, but newish managing partner Greg Bopp explains that *"you have to be adaptive to the environment you're in. Our focus is to continue to be universally recognized in the 'Big 3' sectors of energy, finance, and technology, as well as strategic areas like M&A, capital markets, complex commercial litigation, white collar defense, and government regulatory and policy."* He also reiterates that *"fortunately the market continued and has improved in 2016."*

Next to energy, *Chambers USA* ranks the firm highly in areas including banking & finance, bankruptcy/restructuring, environment, tech, labor & employment and corporate/M&A. However, associates told us: *"Our motto is 'we know energy',"* so as a result *"people in finance, environment, or even litigation are connected to energy on some level."*

On chambers-associate.com...

- More on getting hired and culture at Bracewell
- Interview with managing partner Greg Bopp
- Energy law under the Trump administration: the views from top energy lawyers

The Work

Whichever practice groups associates are in, the work often has an energy slant. Most juniors are in litigation, closely followed by corporate, and finance. Others go into areas including real estate, environment, IP, restructuring and tax. Work allocation is generally through a pooling system. *"People end up with working relationships quickly; you tend to develop and get on partners' radars."* In smaller offices, things tend to be more informal: *"I work for a partner or group of partners,"* a Dallas source revealed, *"but it's definitely encouraged to branch out from your main partner for work."*

Corporate sources in the Houston HQ reported doing a fair amount of doc review and due diligence, with one describing themselves as *"a repository of information about the deals."* Another spoke of drafting clauses: *"They're usually completely wrong at first! But it's great that partners take the time to let me try, then explain their feedback."* The department deals with a mix of public companies, private equity clients, and energy clients, primarily in the Texas area. Deals worked on have included *"one of $120 million, and one of $12 billion."* But regardless of size, there's a hefty amount of client contact: *"I help coordinate with the company and agent banks, and that's cool for me because I was the one making sure everything was moving forward. I was talking to these people, and if the clients needed something they would contact me directly."* Another experienced *"ending the day feeling like you helped the clients, and that definitely helps with maintaining morale."*

The Inside View

See firm profile on p.577

Rankings in *Chambers USA*

Banking & Finance	Intellectual Property
Bankruptcy/Restructuring	Labor & Employment
Capital Markets	Litigation
Climate Change	Projects
Corporate/M&A	Real Estate
Energy & Natural Resources	Tax
Environment	Technology

For detail on ranking tiers and ranking locations, visit www.chambersandpartners.com

Recent work highlights

- Succeeded in reversing the verdict against former Countrywide executive Rebecca Mairone, as well as Bank of America and Countrywide Bank, for allegedly selling fraudulent mortgages to Fannie Mae and Freddie Mac in the years leading up to the 2008 financial crisis
- Advised food service giant Sysco on a $1.7 billion loan facility with Deutsche Bank AG Cayman Islands Branch
- Represented Facebook in a patent infringement case involving an Australian company
- Represented energy infrastructure company Kinder Morgan when it purchased from Shell the 49% of the joint venture, Elba Liquefaction Project (ELC), that it did not already own

"It's great that partners take the time to let me try, then explain their feedback."

Litigators are abundant in New York as well as Houston. White-collar crime is split between civil and criminal work. Criminal defense clients tend to be individuals. Occasionally larger companies appear, for example in relation to alleged FCPA [Foreign Corrupt Practices Act] violations. Sources mentioned that regulators are currently hot on the tail of public corruption and bribery. *"80% of the time it's just me and a partner on a case,"* a New Yorker noted. *"I'm doing tasks that would usually be given to mid-level associates, which is great! If you show you're able to do the work, no one has any reservation about giving it to you."* Tasks include meeting with potential clients and evaluating their case, preparing memos, preparing interviews with clients, and then helping interview them. In a cross-over with the cyber-security department, a litigator described *"drafting incident response plans, and cyber-security policies for companies."*

Finance associates, largely based in Texas and New York, deal with *"the lending side of oil and gas"* through credit agreements, representing agent banks, and helping negotiate current agreements. Houston associates have also worked with borrowers – *"really interesting, seeing things from both sides."* Public finance associates mostly work for governmental and non-profit entities. Regular duties include changes to contracts, due diligence, and even attending client dinners: *"You wouldn't typically see a first or second-year invited to those!"* Such a level of responsibility *"could be overwhelming if you're afraid to ask for help. You just have to know when to ask questions and when it's time to rely on the people around you."*

Training & Development

"You can't beat the quality of training you get here. Sometimes you don't know what you don't know, but we have the resources to help you figure it out." Training kicks off with two days of new associate orientation in Houston, cover-

ing everything from IT to confidentiality. Meetings with partners take place, as well as dinners where associates can get know their peers from other offices. Orientation used to take place two months after first-years started, but in response to feedback that *"some things would have been better to learn straight away,"* the firm moved it earlier. Finance and corporate associates talked about a boot camp which takes place every Friday for the first few months. The training process in litigation is more informal.

Reviews start with a self-evaluation and used to occur annually, but in response to associate feedback they now happen every six months. *"A year is a long time that you could be doing things consistently wrong,"* one junior reflected. The AEC [Attorney Evaluation Committee] speaks to partners you've worked for and compiles a review.

Culture & Offices

The firm's HQ is located in Houston's snazzy Pennzoil building – *"architecturally very beautiful, and cool to be in a piece of Houston culture."* Renovation of the office is helping to *"promote a more uniform culture."* A tradition of Monday morning video conferences involving all offices and led by the managing partner helps *"show you your place in the big machine,"* according to associates. *"It's clear we're all playing for the same team."*

While different cities have different cultures, a New Yorker felt the Big Apple office has certain aspects of Texas culture: *"Everyone knows people's spouses and kids' names, which isn't really a New York thing."* Juniors also praised the ability to work remotely: *"It's rare that you need to be in the office all the time,"* a corporate associate explained. *"Even partners sometimes work from home – the remote connections are very good."* They also agreed that *"the firm doesn't like to do things on weekends – they know people*

The Inside View

See firm profile on p.577

Diversity	Partners (%)	Associates (%)
Women	21	45
White	92	83
Black/African American	3	3
Hispanic/Latin American	3	5
Asian	1	3
Mixed/Other	0	3
LGBT	0.5	2

work hard enough, and don't try to take any more time than that."

Hours & Compensation

The 2,000-hour annual billable goal is *"definitely a target. Not a requirement disguised as a target."* Some associates in smaller offices thought there might not always be enough work to reach the target, but assured us that *"the firm is really reasonable. A couple of years ago we had two massive trials and everyone was exhausted but billed crazy amounts of hours. The next year's hours were lower because everyone wanted vacations after the hectic year. The firm understood – everyone got full bonuses and the firm was fine with it."* Unlike the coffee-fueled law firm stereotype, all-nighters at Bracewell are rare: *"I can count on one hand the number of times I've been here past 10pm. Unless it's an emergency, it's really not the norm."*

"It will make you a better lawyer if you really care about the issue."

Pro Bono

Bracewell allows attorneys to bill 100 hours of pro bono and diversity-related work toward their billing target. Former managing partner Mark Evans was said to be working on a pro bono case – indicative of the *"spirit of the firm."* Cases have included working on divorces, housing and tenancy matters, immigration and asylum cases (for example, for Kids in Need of Defense (KIND)). Bracewell also helps Legal Lines, a hotline people can call for legal advice. The firm *"allows you to say 'I'm really passionate about this organization or cause, and want to do legal work for them.' They also know it will make you a better lawyer if you really care about the issue."*

Pro bono hours:
- For US attorneys: 9,258
- Average per US attorney: undisclosed

Diversity

Interviewees agreed that *"the legal profession as a whole has a problem with diversity,"* but differed about which area they thought the firm is better at. Some highlighted women's diversity as the firm's biggest strength, with initiatives like 'Minute Mentoring' – *"like speed dating, but for mentoring."* However, associates in Dallas found that *"there are not many women in our office, but there's good racial diversity. Even higher up – there's significant diversity in partnership levels in our group."* A New Yorker was more critical of BigLaw as a whole: *"Maternity policies don't really facilitate the retention of women. BigLaw isn't kind to people who want to step out for a while and come back, but I don't think it's through lack of caring."* In Bracewell's case, we did hear of multiple attorneys coming back after their parental leave.

Juniors emphasized that Bracewell *"genuinely wants to improve diversity, and is actively trying. There's just a lot of competition between law firms when it comes to recruiting diverse candidates."*

Strategy & Future

With multiple changes in the last year – the departure of Rudy Giuliani and a few partners, and a new managing partner – some associates were curious about the future direction of the firm. *"It was a bit worrying coming from law school to an office that's in flux,"* a New Yorker remembered, *"but things are starting to settle down now, which is comforting."* MP Greg Bopp tells us: *"For those currently in law school, they'll continue to see us focus on our strengths – energy, finance and technology, as well as our strategic practice areas like complex commercial litigation and M&A."*

"Effort on entry-level hiring."

He concludes: *"We will continue to have a strong focus on entry-level hiring... and the organic growth that results from that. We consider ourselves to be a destination firm for talent – a firm you can join straight out of law school with the hope and expectation that you will have a long-term career here, if that's what you are interested in. I'm an example of that, having been here for my entire legal career."*

Get Hired

"We want to know if you're someone we can bring in front of clients, and someone that will represent the firm well." Read tips on how to get hired in our online Bonus Features on Bracewell.

See firm profile on p.577

Brown Rudnick LLP

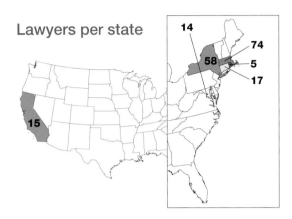

Lawyers per state

14
74
58
5
17
15

Largest US office: Boston
US offices: 6
International offices: 2
First-year salary: $180,000
Billable hours: 1,900 target
Summers 2017: 10 (8 2Ls, 2 1Ls)
Revenue 2016: $191 million (-0.7%)
Partners made in 2017: 4 globally (1 in US)
Famous for: bankruptcy expertise

Boston's own Brown Rudnick knows bankruptcy is no tea party...

IN a memorable moment from *The Office*, Steve Carrell's dim-witted character Michael Scott acts on a colleague's advice to declare bankruptcy. Taking this ever-so literally, he proceeds with misguided confidence to shout: *"I declare bankruptcy!"* If only it were that simple – bankruptcy of big companies is a sticky issue – and that's where Brown Rudnick steps in. Though far from being the largest law firm out there, it excels when companies hit the rocks financially, regularly diving head-first into Chapter 11 litigation to pull distressed investors from the wreckage. Such are this plucky Bostonian's talents in restructuring that it secures top tier recognition from *Chambers USA*, beating plenty of legal heavyweights that do this kind of law.

"We're staffed pretty leanly, and there are some definite benefits," associate sources explained. *"Even as a second-year I'm the most senior associate on cases or have the most time to devote to them. So you're the master of facts, you know what's going on and partners very much need you. It feels good to be a working part."* In this environment associates have to be *"entrepreneurial – that's the firm's term for it, but I would call it scrappy. You need to be able to adjust."*

On chambers-associate.com...

- Our interview with chairman and CEO Joe Ryan
- We talk recruitment with co-hiring partner Jeff Jonas
- More on recruitment from associates

The Work

Most new associates join the Boston or New York office, and at the time of our calls around two-thirds of juniors were in litigation & restructuring. Elsewhere, the corporate & capital markets department covers sub-groups like tax, finance, and IP. Both departments have an associate development manager who is supposed to assign juniors work based on their availability. But *"in practice it's only true that you get your work from the allocation system to begin with. Since then it's been different."* Another associate continued: *"In practice you go through partners – they come to you and ask 'can you do this?' Then they shoot it up to the assignment coordinator."* Circumventing the system allows associates more flexibility to gain and keep good work, but it can also cause hiccups. Some associates said they felt obliged to say yes when partners came knocking, causing *"inefficiency in how work is distributed. Some people are slammed and others are twiddling their thumbs."*

"Cases are leanly staffed."

For restructuring associates, *"the things you do over and over are research and first drafts of pleadings. There's also some letter drafting and client management. That you'll do consistently. The things which are a bit more unique come when you are working on smaller cases. You may go to court, second-chair a hearing or work with counsel to strategize. That stuff means you're not just sat at your desk, insulated. You're more out there and feeling involved."* And *"cases are leanly staffed. It's nice to step into the shoes which are normally filled by someone more senior,"* even if

See firm profile on p.578

The Inside View

Rankings in *Chambers USA*

Bankruptcy/Restructuring
Environment
Real Estate

For detail on ranking tiers and ranking locations, visit
www.chambersandpartners.com

Recent work highlights

- Represented the Official Committee of Unsecured Creditors in the Chapter 11 case of New England Compounding Pharmacy. The pharmacy was at fault over a well publicized deadly fungal meningitis outbreak which began in 2012. $200 million was secured to compensate creditors and victims
- Represented the law firm Lippes Mathias against a malicious prosecution claim made by Facebook and Mark Zuckerburg against several law firms who had fought Zuckerburg over Facebook's ownership
- Lawyers in the UK and US advised commodity trading group ED&F Man on its acquisition of Maviga, a specialist crops trading firm. The firm provided cross-border legal advice and due diligence covering 11 jurisdictions worldwide

it left juniors *"juggling a handful of cases"* and was *"sometimes stressful."* This lean staffing extended across teams.

Commercial litigators noted that *"because we have such a robust restructuring practice you will see a lot of related work, even though it's not our focus."* But this was just one part of a varied mix which also included *"contract disputes and IP."* Interviewees recalled drafting motions and briefs, tackling management tasks like overseeing doc review and some even prepared for and attended depositions. Meanwhile, in corporate, associates get to grips with mid-market M&A, contributing *"pretty standard junior work"* like due diligence. More positively, *"once you get your foot in the door,"* it's very common *"to have the first crack at drafting some fairly significant documents,"* such as operating agreements.

Training & Development

Incoming juniors head to Boston for a week of orientation before starting in earnest. From then on *"there's a great deal of training."* As *"first-years we had two or three trainings a week"* which *"run the gamut,"* coming from every department. *"It's usually mandatory to go to your practice group's and optional to go to the others."* Associates went on to tell us about specific deposition training where *"the firm brings in an outside group"* and *"a lot of lunch sessions."*

Associates receive formal feedback through a yearly review which *"identifies the people you have worked with a lot. Each of them writes a review of you and you are given a summary."* But some associates found that *"other than that I don't get a lot of feedback."* Interviewees gave the impression that informal feedback was variable. *"It's really person to person. Overall I'd say you usually do get feedback, but it's generic and difficult to ascertain what specifically you did do well: 'great job' for example."*

Culture

Last year's research uncovered some issues with partner-associate interaction, so naturally we asked this year's interviewees about it. *"At the beginning of my experience there were some partners who could be very direct, not quite shouting, but certainly making sure they were get-*

ting their point across, maybe if you needed to be more attentive over typos. But there has been a conscious effort to make sure that is not the first approach partners take in providing feedback." Specifically, associates placed the problem in the Big Apple: *"There's a big difference as far as atmosphere goes. New York is a lot tenser, a little less friendly and casual and a little more high-stress, high-tension."* Still, some reveled in this. *"We are the New York office and there is an intensity, a busyness and an hours expectation that comes along with that. As a first-year it is stressful, but not more than other places. It only comes from the higher responsibility and tasks that people elsewhere often wait until their fourth or fifth year to do."*

> ### "There's a big difference as far as atmosphere goes."

"In the last few months there's been a real push to try and make sure that associates are happy here, to try and boost associate morale. They rolled out a survey asking what could be improved and one of the responses to that survey was an increase in quarterly functions outside of the office." That chimed with associates telling us that *"we will organize drinks ourselves and go out, but there's not a lot of firm social events."* It's important to make clear that associates were still positive on the whole, describing partners who are *"very invested in mentoring you and developing your skills,"* and *"real bonds and friendships"* between colleagues. Boston associates declared their office *"friendly and laid back. You can take a break and talk to people for example. People just get their work done and there's no real face-time needed."*

Hours & Compensation

While the billable hours target of 1,900 a year was seen as *"reasonable"* and *"certainly doable"* by most, we heard a few associates, across a couple of departments, complain

See firm profile on p.578

Diversity	Partners (%)	Associates (%)
Women	16	42
White	-	-
Black/African American	-	-
Hispanic/Latin American	-	-
Asian	-	-
Mixed/Other	-	-
LGBT	-	-

Pro bono hours
- For all US attorneys: 9,159 (including summer associates)
- Average per US attorney: 59 (including summer associates)

about a lack of available work. Whether the affected associates met the target and got their bonus was *"going to be a close call – it's certainly a concern,"* they said. Most juniors described a steady working day lasting from around 9am until 7pm, though *"when you're busy you will probably leave between 10pm and 11pm."* Associates from all departments could recall occasional early morning finishes and weekend work, but *"normally I'm not looking around asking 'can I leave yet?'"*

Offices

A swift tour of the Boston office would reveal that *"the interior décor is pretty modern – there's a lot of white furniture around. There's a café downstairs that has seating and we're right across from a bunch of food trucks. There's grilled cheese, pizza, and a cookie truck – it gets pretty busy."* New Yorkers were very satisfied with their own glass monolith, a stone's throw from Times Square, but some thought the glass was best kept on the outside. *"It's pretty weird that someone can watch you eating lunch."* By a few months in, associates in both Boston and New York had their own workspace. Across offices, the firm *"encourages you to establish personal relationships"* – Boston and New York's restructuring teams work particularly closely, for example. The firm also has US offices in Hartford, Orange County, Providence and DC.

"We're right across from a bunch of food trucks."

Pro Bono

"I think they take a lot of pride in pro bono," associates told us. *"They recently changed the policy on credit: the limit used to be 50 hours but now it's unlimited and you get full credit, which is great."* However, many associates struggled to fit pro bono around their *"demanding billable work. It's a lot of work and it kind of creeps up on you."* But the larger workload means more responsibility. *"In my case I've taken depositions and argued a summary judgment motion. It's given me a unique opportunity."* Associates have tackled *"Chapter 7 individual bankruptcies to help people without financial means get representation"* as well as working with Kids In Need of Defense on immigration cases.

Diversity

Associates came up with a common assessment of the firm's diversity. *"At associate level I think it's fairly even on men and women. The bigger problem is at partner level. There are fewer female partners and that's something the firm is trying to address. I also think it's accurate to say that the firm is white dominated."* Brown Rudnick achieves an almost 50-50 split on gender at associate level. Our interviewees used a set of new hires as evidence of the firm's commitment to diversity. There's a new diversity partner, Sunni Beville, and a director of equity, inclusion and diversity, Ari Joseph, in New York. *"They're making a concerted effort to make sure it is a central part of how we operate."*

"At associate level I think it's fairly even."

Get Hired

"We are looking for people who like to be pushed," says co-hiring partner Jeff Jonas. *"You want a third-year associate with five years experience."* For more tips on recruitment, head to chambers-associate.com.

Strategy & Future

Despite the firm's aptitude for restructuring, *"as a firm I know it's trying to expand the type of work it does, especially in the European offices,"* according to one associate. London is best known for white-collar litigation, and recently hired a new partner in emerging markets. Paris, meanwhile, does a lot of international arbitration, and has a relatively new restructuring team. Until recently, the firm also had a small office in Dublin, Ireland. Another US associate let us know that the firm is *"growing its IP department,"* plus *"they're still growing white collar."* CEO Joe Ryan tells us that *"we're alert to opportunities and one thing we pride ourselves on is being nimble and being able to react to changes in industry or in the legal environment. We are able to make quick decisions. But it's not a fly-by-night approach that we take."* The firm's own website confirms: *"Throw out the old paradigm. In fact throw out the word paradigm – and anything else tired, trite, sluggish or slow."*

See firm profile on p.578

The Inside View

Brownstein Hyatt Farber Schreck

Lawyers per state

11

2

31

34

142

4

Largest US office: Denver
US offices: 11
International offices: 0
First-year salary: $135,000
Billable hours: 1,900 required
Summers 2017: 7 (5 2Ls, 2 1Ls)
Revenue 2016: $173 million (+0.6%)
Partners made in 2017: 6
Famous for: being a key player in Denver; lobbying shop

This firm's small intake means mile-high opportunities for rookies, so Denver's Brownstein Hyatt is hunting for associates who are *"all in."*

COLORADO-founded Brownstein Hyatt is relatively young by BigLaw standards. Established by three law school friends in 1968, the firm has since ventured out from its Denver base and established a string of offices across the western states. *"We're right in the sweet spot between a large and regional firm,"* associates told us. *"It feels small but you have all the resources of a big firm with a national reach and different practice areas."*

Managing partner Adam Agron tells us the firm considers itself *"a national boutique with a handful of practices that are complementary with one another. We're not trying to be a full-service firm that is all things to all people."* Brownstein's corporate and real estate practices muster top-tier *Chambers USA* rankings in Colorado; Denver's IP, labor & employment, litigation, and energy & natural resources teams here are also worth a mention. It's also a dab hand at gaming and licensing law, scooping up *Chambers USA* rankings in this area in Nevada and nationwide. Over in the east, the firm's Washington, DC office has an established – and rapidly expanding – lobbying focus. Visit chambers-associate.com for more from Agron on the firm's connection to Capitol Hill.

On chambers-associate.com...

- We speak with managing partner Adam Agron
- We talk hiring with director of attorney recruiting Jamie Olberding

The Work

Brownstein's Denver office absorbs most of its junior associates but a handful are also scattered between Las Vegas and Santa Barbara. Of the juniors on our list, four were in litigation, three apiece in IP, energy & natural resources and real estate, two in corporate and one in government relations.

The Denver summer program is split into two halves. During the first half *"work is free flowing from each of our four major groups: corporate, real estate, litigation and natural resources."* Other areas to dabble in include IP and government relations. A mid-summer check-in allows summers to identify the areas most interesting to them and after that *"they funnel you work from that practice."*

"They do a good job at making sure you're not sat in your office, holding your knees and crying."

Once they're through the door as full-time associates, work is allocated in a free market system. *"You work primarily for specific attorneys in your department,"* sources told us. *"They do a good job at making sure you're not sat in your office, holding your knees and crying"* over a mountain of work.

Transactional associates were pleased to get a fair amount of client contact. *"I've had a lot of client interface, directly emailing back and forth with them, especially with regards*

The Inside View

See firm profile on p.579

Rankings in *Chambers USA*

Corporate/Commercial	Labor & Employment
Corporate/M&A	Litigation
Environment	Natural Resources
Gaming & Licensing	Real Estate
Intellectual Property	

For detail on ranking tiers and ranking locations, visit www.chambersandpartners.com

Recent work highlights

- Advised Blackstone in its $500 million purchase of three Denver high-rise buildings
- Represented gaming company Penn National on licensing and regulatory matters concerning the development and management of a casino for the Jamul Indian Tribe near San Diego
- Acted for Denver-based IT and consulting company NexusTek in its purchase of assets from IT services providers Illumen and iPremise
- Represented communication company MDF Holdings in two class actions concerning the Telephone Consumer Protection Act

to compliance work," one energy & natural resources junior told us. *"The headcount and lean staffing in our group gives great opportunities for responsibility."* This sentiment was echoed by counterparts in real estate: *"I'm often corresponding with clients over email or phone. I also have plenty of access to partners,"* one told us. *"For big institutional clients I get the more menial due diligence work, drafting and scanning documents, while on the smaller deals I'm responsible for drafting purchase and sale agreements and taking a transaction to closing,"* another real estate attorney outlined.

How do litigators fill their days? *"My top task is research,"* one told us. *"There's a lot of research and writing memoranda to explain the legal implications of the issue at hand, a lot of doc review and condensing the findings from that into a usable work product. I might help someone prepare for a deposition too."*

Training & Development

Brownstein's first-years are *"considered apprentices. As part of the apprenticeship program the billable hours requirement is lower."* Newbies shoot for 1,400 billable hours, 200 pro bono and 300 shadow hours. Shadow hours can be used for *"a variety of things. In litigation you could attend a hearing or trial that would be above your level. Transactional associates could sit in on client calls."* Following a one-day orientation, the *"pretty solid training program acclimatizes attorneys to the firm"* by connecting them with a peer mentor. They then enter *"a formal mentor program which pairs you up with an older attorney in your department."* CLEs and departmental training occur regularly throughout the year; in real estate, for example, a series of luncheon sessions during the first half of the year *"covers all the basic real estate issues."*

The firm operates *"a step program as opposed to counting us as first, second or third-years. You're considered a level one to four instead."* Each level typically counts as two years so, for example, a third-year associate attorney is a level two attorney. Everyone gets an annual review. First-years and those approaching a level change also have a mid-year review.

Hours & Compensation

Attorneys aim for 1,900 billable hours a year, 100 of which can be made up of pro bono. First-years are also aiming for a *"modified 1,900 hour target"* – 1,400 hours can be client billable, 200 pro bono and 300 shadowing.

> *"Does an extra $30,000 a year justify you being in the office 'til midnight and then going in again at five? I don't think it does."*

Juniors slated the 1,900 target – modified and standard – as very achievable. *"Oh yeah, there's definitely enough work,"* one busy interviewee chuckled. Our sources reported putting in roughly ten hours a day at the office, with some taking work home a couple of nights a week: *"The office is pretty dead after 6pm as people go home to their families."*

Bonuses kick in once the 1,900 hour threshold is breached and is based on a combination of hours and merit. Denver associates told us, on their $135k salary: *"We don't get paid on the Cravath scale as we don't work on that scale. I have friends at bigger firms with sleeping bags in their office. Does an extra $30,000 a year justify you being in the office 'til midnight and then going in again at five? I don't think it does."*

Pro Bono

Brownstein's 200 pro bono hour requirement for newbies *"is a really positive part of being a first-year,"* one interviewee reckoned, while another added: *"I did a ton of it, you can get really involved in the community."* A pro bono partner matches up attorneys with projects and everyone's encouraged to bill at least 50 hours a year. Juniors have got stuck in helping non profits draft foundation documents or assisting them with transactions, or advising clients on employment issues. We even heard of one

See firm profile on p.579

Diversity	Partners (%)	Associates (%)
Women	29	42
White	94	85
Black/African American	2	4
Hispanic/Latin American	0	1
Asian	2	4
Mixed/Other	2	6
LGBT	Undisclosed	Undisclosed

first-year who'd worked with the coordinator to build a monthly legal aid drop-in clinic from scratch.

Pro bono hours
- For all US attorneys: 12,749
- Average per US attorney: 49

Culture

"We take what we do seriously but we don't take ourselves too seriously," juniors told us. *"It's definitely more laid back than a bigger firm. Part of that is just that Colorado is a casual kind of place."* You won't find the *"the stuffy old law firm dynamic here. We have a mindset that feels more collaborative, social and fun. I genuinely enjoy the people I work with,"* another interviewee reported. *"At Brownstein, people have known each other for years and their families take weekends or vacations together."*

"Colorado is a casual kind of place."

Back in the office, *"no-one closes their door; the partners never kick us out or have full power plays. It feels very friendly."* We were also told there's *"definitely a lot of energy. They do a good job of engaging people with the firm and ensuring we all come together for social events."* In Denver everyone gets together on the third Thursday of the month for drinks. Once a quarter the firm hosts an ice-cream social where *"they put up a picture of everyone hired in the last quarter so everyone can come and meet them."*

An annual all-associates retreat is supplemented by an all-attorney retreat every other year. The latter tends to be *"more CLE and strategy-focused like 'this is what's happening at the firm, and this is your role.'"* The former, dubbed *"associate spring break"* by one excited attorney, is aimed at *"community-building."* Associates are whisked away to a client's property for activities such as golfing, pool-time, horse-riding and drinks.

Offices

Aside from the retreats, associates haven't had much interaction with colleagues in other locations. Eleven offices make up Brownstein's US offering: five in California, two in Nevada and one each in Colorado, New Jersey, New Mexico, and Washington, DC.

HQ Denver is the firm's largest base. Interviewees described the recently renovated office as *"nice but not like the flashiest office."* One reckoned the décor *"fits the model and mindset of the firm; the service we provide to clients is not premised on the white shoe law firms of old but more the millennial mindset."* Modern artwork dots the walls and everyone gets their own office *"with good views of the city on all sides."*

Diversity

Interviewees reckoned location was the firm's biggest barrier to improving diversity at the firm. *"Denver is just less diverse than New York or DC,"* sighed one, while a colleague elaborated: *"The pool of talent we're attracting our attorneys from has a lack of diversity and I think the firm suffers from that. I think it takes recruiting diverse attorneys very seriously but it's fighting an uphill battle and has to take really proactive steps."* Consequently, *"minorities are a minority here,"* but juniors did think the firm was *"pretty diverse gender-wise."*

The Women's Leadership Initiative is undergoing *"a strong push right now. We've set up small mentoring circles for women in the firm"* and the group meets once a month to discuss *"an article which talks about the unique challenges of being a woman."* Brownstein also participates in the Colorado Pledge to Diversity Program, offering a place on its summer program for a diverse 1L student.

Get Hired

Local connections can be a selling point for those interested in getting a foot in the door. Visit chambers-associate.com for more on the recruitment process from the firm's director of attorney recruiting, Jamie Olberding.

Strategy & Future

Brownstein sticks to its focus on specialty groups when it comes to building the firm: *"We're not keen on adding practice groups just to add revenue and we're not keen on adding groups that don't synergistically benefit the firm or our people,"* managing partner Adam Agron tells us. *"We've added depth in the hot area of cyber and data security."* Read more from Agron in our Bonus Features on Brownstein on our website.

See firm profile on p.579

Cadwalader, Wickersham & Taft LLP

Lawyers per state

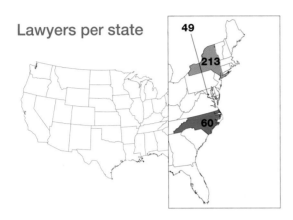

49
213
60

Largest US office: New York

US offices: 3

International offices: 2

First-year salary: $180,000

Billable hours: 2,000 (incl. 200 non-billables) target

Summers 2017: 26 (23 2Ls, 1 1L, 2 SEOs)

Revenue 2016: $452 million (-2.5%)

Partners made in 2017: 8

Famous for: being New York's oldest law firm and a panache for all things finance

Wall Street supremo Cadwalader is New York's oldest law firm.

ONCE upon a time, Cadwalader had a reputation for being a scary place to work. All that's changed, and associates here told us that *"if you're working 16-hour days, you know you're around people who are friendly, willing to invest in you and help you grow."* Cadwalader's website has a useful timeline charting its incredibly long history from its founding in 1792 – when George Washington was president – to today. Given its longevity, associates weren't fazed by reports of partner departures or the closure of two offices in China in 2016 (Beijing and Hong Kong) plus a tiny office in Houston: Most *"aren't worried at all. Some of us started our careers in 2008 when things were shaky, and this feels nothing like that."* In DC, *"four antitrust partners left and took a few associates with them"*– resulting in the cancellation of the DC office's summer program in 2017. The firm said it would instead hire 3Ls to start in DC in fall 2018. In New York and Charlotte, things are normal.

Managing partner Pat Quinn tells us that *"we have a very clear strategy for growth that is underpinned by understanding what Cadwalader is as a firm and where we are going in the future. We're the oldest firm in New York – 225 years in 2017! – and so we naturally have thrived in the finance, funds and securities space, serving financial institutions, big corporations and private funds. We like to say that we are a quintessential Wall Street firm. We want to continue to be leaders in all areas of need for our clients."* Top and highly ranked practices in *Chambers USA* (especially capital markets, corporate/M&A, and litigation) were big draws for associates we spoke to in New York, while DC sources were attracted by Cadwalader's strong energy, capital markets, and white-collar groups, among others here.

The Work

Each team has its own assignment system: some use a professional development manager who dishes out work, while others have a more *"informal approach. As you become known, you get more work through relationships."* New York is the firm's largest office, with a rep for capital markets, corporate and M&A expertise. At the time of our calls, 44 of 64 juniors were based in Manhattan. While most occupied the aforementioned bigger groups, there were also associates in global litigation, private client, financial services, restructuring, and tax. DC claimed ten associates, spread between the office's main areas of practice: antitrust, energy, white-collar defense & investigations, and capital markets. Charlotte had ten, mostly in capital markets.

It came as no surprise that New Yorkers in capital markets were comfortably busy: *"It's Cadwalader's bread and butter work."* Sources were mainly doing commercial backed securities. *"Basically we deal with three parties: underwriters, the issuer and the loan sellers. It's a lot of review and amendments of all the separate documents for each deal."* Others were quick to stress that *"our group*

On chambers-associate.com...

- Interview with managing partner, Pat Quinn
- Cadwalader's pro bono work: Malala Yousafzai
- More on getting hired

See firm profile on p.580

The Inside View

Rankings in *Chambers USA*

Capital Markets	Financial Services
Corporate/M&A	Regulation
Employee Benefits &	Healthcare
Executive Compensation	Litigation
Energy & Natural	Real Estate
Resources	Tax

For detail on ranking tiers and ranking locations, visit
www.chambersandpartners.com

Recent work highlights

- Worked on 25 corporate spin-offs and acquisitions in the last 12 months worth over $20 billion
- Advised multiple major banks in the issuing of over 8,000 structured products worth over $18 billion
- Represented the International Swaps and Derivatives Association, developing an industry-wide solution to the Dodd-Frank Act documentation requirements for security-based swaps

deals with other asset classes too. You can securitize most things: credit cards, student loans and tax. They can all be turned into investment vehicles."

"You get more work through relationships."

DC sources were keen to mention that *"the antitrust group is still chugging along, but it's a lot more focused toward litigation."* White-collar is now the largest team there. *"There are a lot of investigations going on that cover both international components and governmental aspects."* Recent work has included assisting *"several individuals from a European bank are being investigated by the US authorities."* Responsibility might take the form of *"doing client interviews, taking notes and traveling to Europe to inspect documents that can't leave that jurisdiction. You travel a lot in this group."*

The old commercial, corporate and securities group was re-branded as 'corporate' recently. Corporate works closely with global ligation, *"because most of our work comes from corporate clients."* Securities work comes more under the capital markets umbrella. The team still does *"securities litigation, M&A shareholder actions and derivative law suits."* While those in DC found that *"it's 50% doc review,"* New Yorkers reported that *"I've second-chaired a deposition after only 30 minutes' sleep. It's a lot of research and drafting parts of briefs. I've even attended a hearing."* Other transactional work found newbies in the finance group. *"It used to be under corporate but now we've split away and are divided between real estate finance and banking finance."* Charlotte insiders spoke of their time in *"syndicated leveraged finance transactions representing international banks and hedge funds."* Typical tasks included the first drafts of credit and securities agreements. *"It's the most edifying experience so far."*

Training & Development

First Year Fundamentals *"used to be a week-long training where everyone goes to New York. But now it's three days of programs, stretching out more training over the coming months."* Instruction covers everything from *"how to conduct research, to the firm's databases."* After this, there are

monthly departmental updates and CLEs. Each group does things a little differently. Capital markets, for example, covers the basics on mortgage-backed securities. *"This is all about how deals are structured and the documents we should be familiar with."* This is also aided by a mentorship program, which sees starters paired with both a partner and junior mentor. Each coupling is given *"a quarterly budget of around $225 to get coffees and ask literally the dumbest questions ever."* Others pooled their resources and organized *"to go see Beyoncé."* Lucky for some.

First-years have bi-annual reviews, and everyone else gets an annual review. *"You list all the attorneys you've worked with and they evaluate you. You go through what they've said with the partner you've worked most with."* Interviewees were happy with this set-up and enjoyed the opportunity *"to upward review, so we get to comment on the partners."*

Diversity

Most interviewees could reel off the firm's various diversity initiatives, and acknowledged an effort is being made to improve. One capital markets New Yorker commented that *"we're fairly diverse, at least in my department."* Those in DC and Charlotte had a slightly different experience: *"While the firm definitely tries to promote diversity, my office is small so I don't think it's that diverse."* MP Pat Quinn explains that *"we are committed to creating a firm with diversity from top to bottom, which is why we focus on developing diverse associates into future leaders."* Charlotte newbies told us that *"when I first started there were about five women in my group. Now, it's closer to 19, so they're hiring in the right way."*

"You have to give the firm credit for trying."

Cadwalader's many affinity groups put on different events throughout the year. The accolade for most original event goes to collaborative trial re-enactments. *"The last one was hosted by three separate groups and we re-enacted famous cases that have specifically impacted our group's history."* Another impressive get-together was a

See firm profile on p.580

Diversity	Partners (%)	Associates (%)
Women	22.5	39.7
White	90.1	71.9
Black/African American	1.4	4.1
Hispanic/Latin American	2.8	4.1
Asian	4.2	15.2
Mixed/Other	1.4	4.6
LGBT	4.2	2.3

luncheon hosted by the Cadwalader Black and Latino Association, with special guest Cornell William Brooks, president and CEO of the NAACP. *"It brought the issues surrounding racial tensions in our country right to the table. You have to give the firm credit for trying. The issue is now about retaining diverse associates."*

Pro Bono

A dedicated pro bono manager helps associates engage in different projects, as do affinity groups. *"I've worked with the women's group and The Legal Aid Society on New York housing projects, helping a woman get her house back. It was lot of back and forth getting to a settlement offer and then coordinating the signing."* Sources felt that the firm was good at incentivizing participation. *"We can bill up to 200 hours which goes toward our bonus."* There's also an internal awards ceremony that recognizes pro bono pioneers.

Pro bono hours
- For all US attorneys: 8,186
- Average per US attorney: 24

Hours & Compensation

Some prefer to get into the office early (around 8am) during the week to try to keep weekends (mostly) free. Some have even *"worked two back-to-backs until 4am, but it's rare."* After 8pm *"they send you home in a car and they pay for dinner."* Cadwalader's hours requirement was scrapped in January 2014, but it's back. *"It's a bit of a bummer, but it's pretty easy to reach."* If associates bill 1,800 hours plus 200 'quality non-billables' they will get the full bonus, and 2,200 hours will bag them 120% of the base amount. *"It's to stop people working 2,600 hours and getting paid the same as someone who isn't working as much."*

Culture

What of Cadwalader's 'shark tank' reputation in days of yore? *"They've made a lot of effort to fix that,"* a representative junior told us. *"I mean some partners can be intimidating still, but that's because they've had copious years of experience."* Regardless of location, *"I genuinely enjoy the people I work with and we all socialize with each other outside of work – which I think is unique compared to other firms."* Washingtonians felt that *"it's probably a bit more relaxed here than in New York, because partners don't care what hours you're in or what you're wearing."* However, New York and Charlotte sources said the same, with many citing this as one of the key reasons they chose Cadwalader in the first place. *"Out of all the interviews I did, the people were more interested in me as a person."*

"We all socialize with each other outside of work."

Offices

The Big Apple *"is where all the big decisions are made."* However, Charlotte and DC *"don't feel removed: there's a lot going on here. We're just a little further away – that's all!"* All associates in all locations get their own offices, with summers and first-years getting in on the action in DC and Charlotte right from the off. New Yorkers have to wait until their second-year.

In DC, the office is based in Chinatown, *"with really great restaurants just a short walk away and a free gym in our building."* In Manhattan, associates joked that *"we call the décor 50 shades of beige,"* but it's the views that made sources gaga. *"They're fantastic, I can see the Statue of Liberty and we have a huge high-powered telescope in the reception so that people can look out."* Taking a closer look inside, you'll discover a quirky gem. Rumor has it that there's a partner who also owns a toy company and has decked a corner of the office in *"Disney statues and Game of Thrones figurines. The weird thing is, I've seen the nik-naks, but never the partner!"*

Get Hired & Strategy

Our sources told us that *"we're looking for a good personality fit more than anything."* But how does this play into the firm going forward? For the complete break-down on how to get hired and what's in store for the future, go online.

See firm profile on p.580

Cahill Gordon & Reindel LLP

Lawyers per state

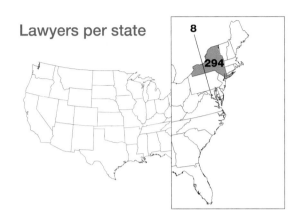

Largest US office: New York
US offices: 2
International offices: 1
First-year salary: $180,000
Billable hours: no requirement
Summers 2017: 33 (all 2Ls)
Revenue 2016: $382.6 million (+5%)
Partners made in 2017: 4
Famous for: the legendary Floyd Abrams; sky-high remuneration; corporate prowess

Few firms offer more freedom to shape your practice. Even fewer pay associates such big bonuses.

"WHAT attracted me to Cahill? That's easy: the partners who interviewed me, their personalities. They were old school New York lawyers – outspoken and brutally honest, not über formal or deferential." In New York BigLaw it certainly pays to have a bit of moxie, but at Cahill a get-up-and-go attitude will really reap dividends. At the center of the firm's culture is its much-vaunted free market assignment that *"offers the average associate the chance to cultivate their own practice"* – but more about that later.

> *"Free market means you can realize what you're good at, even though for the first few years you are a complete generalist."*

Another big draw is Cahill's First Amendment practice headed up by the *"legendary Floyd Abrams."* One source was quick to urge caution – *"the name you always hear is Floyd's but associates said, 'you know you probably won't get to work with him'. But I actually have, and it was great!"* His practice is under the umbrella of the bigger litigation department, which takes roughly half of all incoming associates. The other half enter through the corporate corridor. These are, however, general terms: *"We don't have specific departments that you specialize in. Free market means you can realize what you're good at, even though for the first few years you are a complete generalist."*

Chambers USA recognizes Cahill's versatility, awarding top-tier nationwide rosettes for its banking & finance and capital markets work while also recognizing its first-rate New York insurance and media litigation practices. Other ranked practices are telecoms in DC and environment in NY.

The Work

Now, about that free market assignment system. Purely and simply: *"It's as free market as they come."* From your first day partners approach associates and vice versa. *"It's something that makes the experience completely distinctive from other firms. You don't get an email or phone call saying 'you're working on this.' You get a call saying the firm is getting involved in this matter, do you want in?"*

That said, all markets need oversight, and our interviewees felt the system could be improved even further to avoid uneven workloads or senior associates forming the same teams. Management listened and responded. Jonathan Schaffzin, a member of the firm's executive committee, tells us: *"There won't be any differences in the free market system but there will be more focus and attention*

The Inside View

See firm profile on p.581

Rankings in *Chambers USA*

Banking & Finance	Insurance
Capital Markets	Litigation
Environment	Media & Entertainment

For detail on ranking tiers and ranking locations, visit
www.chambersandpartners.com

Recent work highlights

- Represented the lead arrangers in credit facilities that backed the $4 billion acquisition of UFC [Ultimate Fighting Championship] by WME [William Morris Endeavor]
- Represented Coca-Cola Enterprises in connection with its agreement to combine its Spanish and German arms to form Coca-Cola European Partners Plc, a new UK company that created the world's largest independent Coca-Cola bottler
- Represented the debt financing sources in the largest leveraged buyout in history – the $67 billion acquisition of EMC by Dell, which created the US's largest privately-controlled, integrated technology company
- Secured a victory for Deutsche Bank in a long standing multibillion-dollar litigation brought by Sebastian Holdings, an offshore investment fund, in the New York Supreme Court

on the younger associates to make sure they are getting the right mixture of experience. It'll still be free market but with more attentive monitoring."

Litigation juniors mostly work on matters *"involving large financial clients, usually banks."* But within that *"there's a range – some antitrust and a lot of general commercial litigation."* As they gain experience, tasks vary to include *"a lot of motion practice, a lot of brief writing and sometimes you can even be involved in strategy."* Some litigators can choose to take a year out to do a judicial clerkship. The firm supports you and writes a recommendation when needed. When you get back *"your responsibility levels increase and you're treated as a more senior associate."*

> To learn more about white-collar and corporate finance at Cahill, head to the practice areas chapter.

Over in corporate *"the bread and butter is credit agreements and leveraged finance,"* though they also *"do a little bit of M&A and equity work."* Teams feel smaller than litigation, where *"they'll often have several first-years on one case,"* while in corporate *"if you have two first-years on a deal, that's an anomaly."* As a result, responsibility increases incrementally. *"When you start you're doing due diligence, then it evolves to drafting ancillary documents, and eventually you're the first one to hold the pen to credit agreements and major transactional documents. As a third-year you get to do almost everything, including communicating directly with clients."*

Culture

Part of the reason that the free market system is able to flourish at Cahill is because of its size. It's effectively a one-shop firm, give or take a few lawyers in DC and London. As a result, sources said it felt smaller than its closest city rivals and *"it's definitely a place where you make your reputation, it's small enough that people know what you're about pretty quickly."* Once they do *"you see the difference in the type of work you are given."*

> "One of the biggest reasons that I love my job is the people who work here."

Outside of that work, sources agreed that they were more likely to hang out with their peers informally than at organized dos. This interviewee's response was pretty typical: *"One of the biggest reasons that I love my job is the people who work here. I hang out with people from work separately from work because the people they bring in are of such high quality."* For those looking for a bit of function to their functions, *"a lot of the social life is centered around the summer – that's when they'll often put a card down at a huge bar and say go have fun."* Cahill summers can also enjoy *"going to the Mets as a guest of the firm or catching dinner and a show on Broadway."* That's not to say the firm doesn't let its collective hair down in the winter months. Recently, there were separate litigation and corporate parties at Cipriani's with dinner and dancing and a raffle where they gave away stuff like *"Beyoncé tickets and gift certificates to really fancy restaurants."*

Hours & Compensation

Another thing Cahill is known for is its unflinching attitude to hours – *"obviously New York BigLaw means New York big hours but there's a bit more expected of associates here."* A quiet day could see an associate arriving for 9.30 or 10am, and strolling out at 5.30pm, *"though you'll probably go home and log into the system later that evening."* But a busy one can take home-time right up to midnight: *"You just know there are some days that you can't make evening plans."*

Cahill's juniors are some of the best remunerated in the city.

In return for that extra mile, Cahill's juniors are some of the best remunerated in the city. On top of their market-rate salaries (which in June 2016 rose to $180,000 for first-year associates) in the past the firm has doled

See firm profile on p.581

Diversity	Partners (%)	Associates (%)
Women	18	45
White	91	79
Black/African American	3	3
Hispanic/Latin American	0	6
Asian	4.5	12
Mixed/Other	1.5	0
LGBT	6	3

out bonuses twice a year. However, sources we spoke to hadn't seen their mid-year bonuses in 2016. When quizzed on this, Jonathan Schaffzin replies: *"This year we decided to look at the work for the whole year and decide from that."*

But don't be despondent, those bonuses still don't hinge on any kind of hours target – *"we don't have an official billables number. What was thrown around among associates is that people were trying to hit 2,100, but if you get 1,800, or 1,900 you'll be fine."* Technically junior associates get four working weeks of vacation a year. *"Partners do make sure you take it all"* but *"because of the way we do things, we can't really take short vacations."* Taking time off can be tricky: *"That's the negative side of the free market: getting work on your plate is easy but when you need to get it off it can be really hard."*

Pro Bono
Another way to get those hours up is by taking advantage of the firm's very active pro bono commitments, which the powers-that-be count the same as billable work. It's also a good way to get on your feet as *"you'll often be the one in court arguing on a case."* If you are interested in pro bono then it's good to make it clear during the summer when a lot of the opportunities become available. The firm works a lot with The Door – a youth charity based in New York. They run things like an emancipation clinic and SIJS [Special Immigrant Juvenile Status], a family law clinic working to secure young immigrants green cards. Cahill lawyers are also heavily involved with Sanctuary for Families, a non-profit dedicated to aiding victims of domestic violence and their children.

Pro bono hours
- For all US attorneys: 11,989
- Average per US attorney: 37

Training & Development
To prepare juniors for the hard work that will come their way, first-years start their time at Cahill with a week-long training program aptly referred to as *"boot camp."* Sources described it as *"pretty standard stuff, but helpful.*

Because it's so early on you're still trying to get your head around everything else. I would say the informal on-the-job training we receive frequently is definitely more useful."

"At 3pm every day they set out some trail mix, fruit and granola bars..."

There are supposed to be formal reviews every January delivered by specially assigned *"liaison partners."* However, this system of mentorship has been found wanting – the liaison partners are each assigned around four associates, who may not all work with them. As mentioned previously, management is in the process of reforming the mentoring program to make it more comprehensive. As a result, reviews are more informal procedures: *"If you ask any of the partners you work with, they will give you substantive feedback on a regular basis."*

Offices
Cahill occupies floors 14-21 and 26 of a fairly standard downtown office block. But there is widespread belief that people are a bit harsh about Cahill HQ – *"lawyers generally complain about the office space. But it's not that bad: all the desks and stuff are new. I mean some of the lower floors look kind of beat up but there are little kitchens on each floor with vending machines and at 3pm every day they set out some trail mix, fruit and granola bars, which is nice,"* a source explained. *"Though they used to give out cookies..."* Aside from cookie grumbles, the biggest complaint was that *"it's either freezing or 100 degrees,"* which we hope is an exaggeration.

Diversity
When it came to diversity at the firm is a belief that *"Cahill could do a lot better"* but most agreed, *"I would never for one minute think that candidates are not hired purely on credentials and merit."* That said, there is definitely an understanding on the partners' part that they need to improve. As Jonathan Schaffzin put it, *"we are proud of the strides we are taking. It's a priority of management to have the lawyers of the firm be reflective of what we see in the world at large, and that's not just lip-service."* Cahill has various affinity groups, including for African Americans, LGBTQ, and parents.

See firm profile on p.581

Choate Hall & Stewart LLP

Lawyers per state

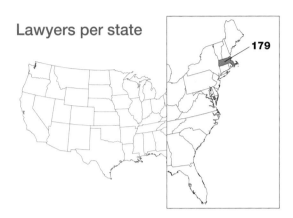

179

Largest US office: Boston
US offices: 1
International offices: 0
First-year salary: $180,000
Billable hours: 2,000 to be bonus eligible
Summers 2017: 19 (18 2Ls, 1 1Ls)
Revenue 2016: $218.5 million (+7.8%)
Partners made in 2017: 2
Famous for: Bostonian brand; one-office model

With its one-office model and Bostonian gentility, Choate is a good bet for self-starting associates.

"I'M very pleased and proud to report that 2016 has been the best year in the firm's history," Choate's chairman Jon Nadas declares. These Bostonians have always managed to punch above their weight, but Nadas explains: "In terms of work, we've never received more interesting matters. In terms of talent – which is the key – I don't think we've ever had more success recruiting at all levels. And financially, our revenue is up 2.9% per partner and 10% overall." So far, so good; and to what does Nadas attribute the firm's continued upward trajectory? "One of the most significant keys to our success is our 'under-one-roof' business model."

Indeed, that very same thing was a big draw for many of the associates we spoke to. One particularly effusive source responded: "Choate is really great... it's like the dream. It's a big firm with sophisticated clients that does proper work. But it feels like a small firm where people really do take care of each other." But that wasn't just the company line being toed with incredible diligence, it was a sentiment corroborated by most – "the model works really well. There's one office, with all the attorneys together in the same place and really a lot of interaction between the groups." Once again, this is not mere hyperbole, as

On chambers-associate.com...

- More on training
- Choate gets a makeover
- Interview with Choate chairman Jon Nadas

evidenced by wreaths of top-tier *Chambers* rankings for a plethora of practices, including antitrust, banking & finance, restructuring, and corporate/M&A.

The Work

Having a relatively small operation doesn't necessitate pigeonholing juniors. In fact, most Choate freshmen and women only have to choose between one of three broad umbrella departments when they join – litigation, business (as the corporate practice is known), or wealth management. There's also real estate, and patent. "You have two to three to four years to specialize... though I know several at those levels who still dip and dabble." So, basically, it's up to you to find the work you want. And, though each team has an assignment partner for juniors (and one for seniors), "who pools assignments from all the other partners and sends them your way," really "you have to be proactive if you want to meld your own practice – which shows the faith they have in juniors here."

"When choosing a firm I looked on a macro level ..."

For those who pick the shade of the litigation umbrella, the main sub-groups are IP, complex trial & appellate, white-collar, labor & employment, government enforcement, and insurance & reinsurance. Depending "on the size and complexity of a case," juniors will be doing "doc review, briefing partners, drafting motions and practicing preparing exhibits for trial." But really, as with other

See firm profile on p.582

Rankings in *Chambers USA*

Antitrust	Intellectual Property
Banking & Finance	Litigation
Bankruptcy/Restructuring	Private Equity
Corporate/M&A	Tax
Healthcare	Technology
Insurance	

For detail on ranking tiers and ranking locations, visit www.chambersandpartners.com

Recent work highlights

- Acted for Momenta Pharmaceuticals defending the company against a rival that filed an antitrust suit
- Represented Achievers Corp on its $111 million sale to Blackhawk Networks
- Represented Liberty Mutual in an environmental coverage dispute involving a pollution site in Woburn, MA
- Advised Wells Fargo regarding a $100 million term loan to Sports Authority, involving complex intercreditor issues

teams, in litigation it's all about *"the smaller case teams which allow you to quickly ramp up the value added based on how well you've done on earlier assignments; because the groups are so lean there's not this whole raft of mid-level associates in the way of getting seriously substantive work."*

The business department is a similar story – *"when choosing a firm I looked on a macro level and Choate has smaller, leaner deal teams where associates seem to have more client interaction than peers at other firms."* Over here, finance & restructuring, private equity, tax, and business tech are the main players, with the latter enjoying special success due to the richness of Boston's start-up scene. It's a mixed bag and *"very collaborative. Everyone works on a lot of different things. They want you to be very well-rounded because the practice is so varied."* This means that juniors *"do just about everything,"* which includes *"all the diligence inquiries, looking over all existing documentation, reviewing all the documents for the clients, and sitting in on all the partner's calls."*

Culture

As mentioned above, Choate's one-office model has a major impact on the firm's culture. One source described it as *"like a specialized boutique firm that deals with big matters – sort of like an East Coast Irell."* Another opined that *"its size means leaner staffing and more opportunity to do substantive work, with a workload that more accurately reflects my ability."* Interviewees felt the good vibes emanating as soon as they set foot in the office – *"I got the feeling walking down the halls for the first time that everyone knew each other."* Yet another explained that Choate's culture was *"all about team work, supporting others and working together to provide the best service for clients."*

"The first-years do a skit usually poking fun at the partners and then we have a big cocktail reception and dinner."

After hearing so much about the tight-knit work culture, it was quite surprising that many felt that the firm wasn't the most social of places. Sources spoke fondly of the pizza and beer nights that take place every three weeks

in the office, but apart from that it was down to the summer social flurry to sate the gregarious. A relative lack of formalized functions was attributed more to the fact that *"we have a leadership that is not particularly 'fratty'"* and *"they try and keep socializing at a level that everybody, including those with young families, is comfortable with."* That said, those summer events should not be scoffed at. There's *"usually a party at one of the big Boston museums,"* and that's before mentioning the firm's annual day-long country club retreat – *"the first-years do a skit usually poking fun at the partners and then we have a big cocktail reception and dinner."*

Training & Development

In recent years management has put professional development at the top of its list of priorities and this has meant lawyers *"have more contemporaneous feedback from partners on a case, who have been told to provide feedback as often as possible."* This increased focus also manifests itself in Choate's mentorship scheme. All newbies are assigned two mentors – one mid-level associate and one partner – who are encouraged to spend a certain number of hours with them a month. However, *"rather than this be burdensome, it's great to have allotted down time with people you don't directly work with, and I don't know anyone who doesn't really get on with at least one of their mentors."*

Hours & Compensation

It used to be that juniors were required to bill 1,900 hours to *"be in good standing"* but now there's only one target – the 2,000 needed to be bonus eligible. After that, *"the managing partner [with input from partners] decides how big your bonus will be, and when you get your annual review [in March] a month later the reviewing partner will explain the reasoning behind it."* Despite the ultimate decision being taken behind closed doors, interviewees insisted *"it's as transparent as it could conceivably be without them telling everyone what everyone else is getting paid."* The firm also sweetens the deal by allowing first and second-years to count up to 100 hours of on-the-job training and an unlimited number of pro bono hours (within reason) toward the target.

The Inside View

See firm profile on p.582

Diversity	Partners (%)	Associates (%)
Women	19	55
White	97	84
Black/African American	1.5	1
Hispanic/Latin American	1.5	8
Asian	0	7
Mixed/Other	0	0
LGBT	4	4

"The system allows for great flexibility."

Sources didn't sugar-coat the fact that Choate expects its lawyers to work hard, this being a fairly typical response: *"On average I'm spending between 50 and 55 hours at the office every week."* That said, the firm does make sure rumbling bellies don't resound through the wee hours by buying attorneys dinner if they're in the office after 7.30pm. Moreover, for those who prefer homecooking, *"the system allows for great flexibility. There's no face-time whatsoever and people with young families can go home and log onto the system very easily."*

Office

Choate HQ has recently undergone major renovation and there was unanimous praise among sources for their fresh new digs. The firm has six floors of a skyscraper in downtown Boston and the renovation has seen the space turned into an open-plan, light-filled office. In other words, *"it's all glass,"* which initially meant *"everyone was concerned about privacy."* However, most attorneys *"stopped caring after a while,"* and appreciated that *"it's all soundproof and really is conducive to having person-to-person communications."* In fact, one source gave us cause for considerable jealousy when they described *"sitting down right now and looking out of floor-to-ceiling windows at Boston Harbor and the Atlantic Ocean."*

"Sitting down right now and looking out of floor-to-ceiling windows at Boston Harbor and the Atlantic Ocean."

Pro Bono

As mentioned previously, there is no cap on the number of pro bono hours associates can count toward their billable target – something interviewees put down to the fact the firm *"wants you to be a great attorney but also recognizes that you are part of the community."* Choate is a Boston institution and has a number of affiliations with charitable organizations in the city. One is the Citizens Schools program – *"where we go in and teach middle school students about constitutional law and in the end go through a mock trial."* Choate lawyers are also heavily involved with a local legal clinic called Lawyer's Clearing House that provides pro bono work to those on lower incomes.

Pro bono hours
- For all attorneys: 4,115
- Average per attorney: 35

Diversity

In some respects Choate is ahead of the curve, diversity-wise: *"We've got more female associates than male."* However, there is a recognition that when it comes to racial diversity, the firm has to improve. As Nadas puts it, *"it's a priority for us that to be a better organization, we need to be more diverse."* The firm has a diversity committee that includes senior people from various departments, and a diversity fellowship is on offer to 1L law students from diverse backgrounds. At the beginning of 2017, the committee invited Professor Jerry Kang from UCLA – a world expert on implicit bias – to come and talk to the firm.

Strategy & Future

Partners are very open about whether or not associates are on the partnership track – *"I've got a friend at quite a small firm in the city where, once you get hired, it's sort of understood that you'll stick around forever. That's not the vibe here – people leave laterally a lot, but at the same time, if they think you're doing a good job they will tell you. Also, people who are struggling are alerted to the fact politely."* For those that do leave, *"Choate is excellent at keeping the door open: they have regular alumni events and the people who've left never say a bad word. They're back here the whole time."*

Get Hired

"I think we are looking for people who are grateful – this is a wonderful opportunity." On chambers-associate.com we interview chairman John Nadas about the ideal candidate and the view of the firm from management.

See firm profile on p.582

The Inside View

Cleary Gottlieb Steen & Hamilton LLP

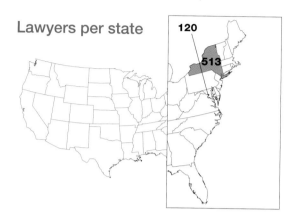

Lawyers per state

120

513

Largest US office: New York
US offices: 2
International offices: 14
First-year salary: $180,000
Billable hours: no requirement
Summers 2017: 160 (155 2Ls, 1 1L, 4 others)
Revenue 2016: $1.272 billion (+4.9%)
Partners made in 2017: 8 (7 in US)
Famous for: international reach and informal work practice

It's all change at the top of this elite New Yorker, but *"consolidating our gains"* is more likely than any radical overhaul.

CLEARY Gottlieb rang in New Year 2017 by handing over the reins to a brand new managing partner. Mark Leddy – who'd held the position for six years – made way for investment funds partner Michael Gerstenzang. Hiring partner Lisa Schweitzer reassures us that dramatic change under new managing partners doesn't happen at this firm: *"Cleary's unique lockstep partnership creates a culture of collaboration and respect allowing our partnership to decide all important firm matters under the guidance of the managing partner."* She added: *"We're very excited to have Michael Gerstenzang as our new managing partner. He's deeply devoted to our firm's culture, the work we do for clients and the strategic growth of our business."*

One thing we're sure of is that Gerstenzang will be racking up plenty of air miles zigzagging across the firm's prestigious global network. As well as a huge New York and smaller DC office, Cleary has 14 international offices covering Europe, Asia, the Middle East and Latin America. Its pedigree is highlighted by a host of *Chambers Global* rankings, including top global-wide recognition for its antitrust and capital markets prowess.

While Cleary's international expertise was *"a given"* among the associates we spoke too, back home the firm racks up first-class *Chambers USA* rankings in New York for its employee benefits, Latin American investment, white-collar crime, real estate, and tax work. Washington, DC's star group is the antitrust practice, while on a nationwide level the firm is noted for several stellar practices including antitrust (yet again), capital markets, banking, regulation, and tax.

Strategy & Future

Don't expect big changes to accompany the recent managerial transition: *"We're focused on consolidating our gains at the moment,"* associates understood. *"We weathered the financial crisis and did well in the aftermath. We opened new offices in recent years"* in China, South Korea, São Paulo and Abu Dhabi, *"but at the moment we're focusing on integrating those in the lifeblood of the firm."* We heard that, closer to home, the antitrust practice is in line to increase its depth, particularly in DC where David Gelfand – former deputy assistant attorney general for DOJ's antitrust litigation division – recently rejoined the firm as partner.

The Work & Offices

Cleary encourages both summer and junior associates to dip their toes in a variety of practice areas. Departments that take a lot of junior associates in New York include capital markets, M&A, litigation/arbitration, private eq-

On chambers-associate.com...

- Hiring at Cleary
- Diversity at Cleary
- We chat with hiring partner Lisa Schweitzer

The Inside View

See firm profile on p.583

Rankings in *Chambers USA*

Antitrust
Banking & Finance
Bankruptcy/Restructuring
Capital Markets
Corporate Crime &
  Investigations
Corporate/M&A
Employee Benefits &
  Executive Compensation
Energy & Natural
  Resources

Financial Services
  Regulation
International Arbitration
Investment Funds
Latin American Investment
Litigation
Private Equity
Real Estate
Securities
Tax

For detail on ranking tiers and ranking locations, visit
www.chambersandpartners.com

Recent work highlights

- Advised Dow on antitrust clearance matters in China, Brazil, the EU and the US following the announcement of the chemical giant's merger with DuPont
- Assisted Barclays, JP Morgan and Morgan Stanley who represented the underwriters of a $5 billion debt offering by Chevron
- Instructed by mining companies BHP Billiton, Vale and Samarco Mineração to lead an investigation into the collapse of the iron ore tailings Fundão dam in Brazil in 2015
- Advised brewers SABMiller on tax aspects of its $100 billion-plus merger with fellow drinks company AB InBev

uity/fund formation, and real estate. In DC most associates operate within corporate, litigation and antitrust, though they can also sample structured finance and regulatory work.

"*The flexibility is why I love working for them,*" one source gushed, while another told us: "*It keeps things really interesting and gives you the chance to learn a lot. I imagine at some point I will start specializing, but as a young attorney it's very good to have the opportunity to put my toes in the water and learn new skills doing different things.*"

"There is no pre-defined set of tasks."

Assignment coordinators are responsible for distributing assignments and checking that associates are doing a spread of work they're interested in. Most of our sources had gotten their first assignments through the coordinators but had since branched out to seeking work directly from partners.

Generalist litigators could latch onto anything from securities or bankruptcy disputes to white-collar crime, employment and general commercial disputes. The vast majority of litigation work in DC is antitrust related. "*We have a strong e-discovery group so associates aren't doing first-level doc review, which is pretty great. Instead we take a second-level review or review relevant flagged files,*" one interviewee told us. That said "*as the matters we're handling are often huge the teams can be large, so you may be on a number of less significant but still important tasks; that's everything from taking notes during calls to preparing summaries, reviewing drafts others have written or taking first drafts of documents.*" There's still room for juniors to get stuck in on leaner staffed or exceptionally busy cases: "*We were taking depositions as first-years. It was incredible but there were hundreds to be done so everyone had a chit.*" Others had drafted motions or briefs and assisted with depositions.

Capital markets, finance, restructuring, M&A and private equity can all be sampled by transactional folks. "*This place is not good with definition,*" one source told us as they mused how best to explain their daily docket: "*There is no pre-defined set of tasks*" correlating to seniority. "*On a small team you handle everything from the start whereas on a big team you could be doing due diligence for a few months. I don't think anyone has said 'this person isn't senior enough for that' – often the question revolves around whether they should give it to you outright or pair you with a sixth or seventh-year in case you have any questions.*" Interviewees had dug down into or coordinated diligence, drafted or revised disclosure materials or agreements and directly liaised with clients to answer queries.

"Connectivity to the global arena."

Both litigators and deal-doers regularly get the chance to work with their colleagues around the globe. "*Many deals tend to deal with cross-border issues or are international in nature. I like that connectivity to the global arena.*" Summer associates may even get the chance to spend some of the summer in one of the firm's overseas offices.

Washington, DC and New York make up the firm's US offering. The latter houses most rookies. DC juniors get their own office from the get-go while Big Apple newbies begin firm life sharing with another junior. "*It's a God-given when you start as someone is suffering with you,*" but most sources were glad to transition into their own digs after a year.

Training & Development

All new associates are eased into the firm with a "*two-week mini MBA program*" in New York. After this initial flurry of classroom activity, there are fairly regular CLEs. Corporate College is open to first-years and above. The weekly classes "*cover a different topic each week giving an in-depth run-down on things like corporate reporting requirements or valuations in an M&A deal. During the*

See firm profile on p.583

Diversity	Partners (%)	Associates (%)
Women	17.4	49.7
White	89	64.1
Black/African American	2.8	9
Hispanic/Latin American	3.7	8.8
Asian	3.7	13.3
Mixed/Other	0.9	4.7
LGBT	4.6	5.6

second-year we have a lot of soft skills trainings on things like how to make a client presentation.”

Litigation Academy runs over a shorter space of time but is more intensive. *“We all fly to New York for a two-day training session,”* one DC associate told us. *“The first day was basically presentations on good deposition methods and some examples of tactics and then the next day we held a simulation. We all prepared to defend a witness and to depose a witness twice. Partners stand in as judges and gave feedback after the first set of sessions and then we had the opportunity to try and improve it in the second session.”* Annual global practice area retreats also host hands-on practical training sessions for associates: antitrust folks, for example, were swept off to Salzburg, Austria where they analyzed a mock potential merger and pitched a presentation to partners who pretended to be clients.

“She's an oracle.”

The appraisal system veers off a bit from the more straightforward curriculum. In New York, for their first two years, associates' annual reviews are given by Mary Watson, a senior attorney and director of professional development. *“She's an oracle,”* one associate found. *“She helps you interpret the reviews and can say ‘don't worry, this partner says this to everyone’ or on the other hand note ‘this is a weird comment for this partner, let's talk to him some more about it.’”*

Hours & Compensation

Cleary doesn't specify an annual billable hours target but we pressed our sources to discover if there was an unofficial figure floating about. *“If there is, I've never heard of it,”* one source responded, while another told us: *“I really don't think so. People work hard enough that they don't have to think about it.”* Those we spoke to told us that ten to 12-hour stints in the office were fairly typical, with those leaving earlier putting in a couple of hours from home.

Exit times can fluctuate wildly: *“I've been leaving at 5pm recently but when it's busy there are months where I get four to five hours’ sleep a night, and the rest of the time I'm*

in the office, weekends, holidays, whatever,” one deal-doer told us. *“We're certainly compensated for working hard,”* another source conceded. The *“hazard pay”* falls in line with the BigLaw market ($180,000 for first-years). Lockstep bonuses also match the market rate.

Culture

Juniors credited the lockstep bonus and lack of billable hours target for *“driving the cooperative environment. The compensation and culture go hand in hand as everyone is on the same level regardless of hours and cases.”* Others agreed: *“It doesn't feel like we're competing with other associates for hours – your team is supportive. But while on the one hand it is cooperative and collaborative, there are very high expectations. We get a lot of really great opportunities very early on but they can be stressful.”*

“Busy and intense.”

Despite the pressure *“those moments are smoothed by working with people you have ongoing positive relationships with. This role requires the type of personality that is open to and thrives on collaboration, which is important for building relationships when times are stressful.”* Another told us *“it's busy and intense – it's not all fun and games but we have a cheese and wine event every week. They do a good job of keeping morale up despite how much work we're doing all the time.”*

Cheese and wine may keep attorneys going week to week, but the big event of the year is the skit-tastic ‘Wranglers’: *“Everybody goes and it's a fun way for first-years to introduce themselves to the firm.”* Newbies are split into groups and tasked with producing a themed video skit *“making fun of firm life. It's shown to the rest of us before we have a huge party.”* Past themes ranged from 80's movies to sit-coms and tacky infomercials.

Diversity

An all-white, mostly male partner and counsel promotion round in November 2016 left diversity *“a touchy subject”* when we spoke to our sources. Many felt that although *“Cleary does a good job at being committed, they're not always successful in the result. I do think they haven't quite figured out how to get the diverse associates all the way through to partnership.”* Another agreed, noting *“I don't think anyone is talking about issues in recruiting.”* Since the partnership promotions, *“we've had a lot of discussions about the situation and the firm recognizes it's a huge priority.”*

Visit chambers-associate.com for a full run-down of associates' thoughts on diversity levels at the firm.

See firm profile on p.583

Pro Bono

No billable hours target means no limit to the amount of pro bono associates can do. *"When things were quiet I had a month where half my work was pro bono,"* one source told us. Many interviewees have worked on immigration and trafficking rights cases, including working toward removing prostitution convictions for sex trafficking victims. The firm also had a hand in overturning the conviction of Clifford Jones, who in 1981 was convicted of rape and murder based upon unreliable testimony. The firm also helped create a *"social venture obligation"* for the Osborne Association to help finance a furniture business which employs ex-offenders. Cleary also put lawyers on the ground at JFK and Dulles airport following Trump's executive order to halt immigration from largely Muslim countries – over 100 Cleary attorneys were on hand to assist with immigration and asylum issues.

Pro bono hours
- For all US attorneys: 56,647
- Average per US attorney: 80

Get Hired

"People are very independent – they're able to advocate for themselves and come up with ideas," one associate told us when we asked what kind of person the firm hires. To find out more and receive hiring tips from current associates, read our Cleary feature on chambers-associate.com

For a snapshot of life as a securities litigator, read Cleary's expert view on chambers-associate.com

See firm profile on p.583

Clifford Chance US LLP

Lawyers per state

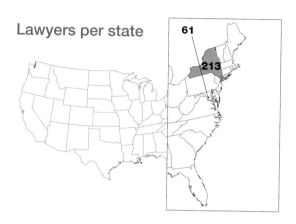

Largest US office: New York
US offices: 2
International offices: 31
First-year salary: $180,000
Billable hours: no requirement
Summers 2017: 29 (28 2Ls, 1 other)
Revenue 2016: $2.06 billion
Partners made in 2017: 3 (in US)
Famous for: being one of London's magic circle firms; reigning champion of *Chambers Global*

With a British pedigree and global command behind them, Clifford Chance's US offices are looking to boost their domestic clout.

IF Clifford Chance were an actor it could be Tom Hiddleston: an elite British export with broad appeal and a track record of quality performances (let's forget that acceptance speech for a moment). But put him in a room with one of Manhattan's greats, say, Robert De Niro, and would he still steal the scene? And so it is with the actual Clifford Chance Stateside. *"To be credible in the market you have to have domestic strength in a number of key areas, and we have that,"* says Evan Cohen, regional managing partner for the Americas. Indeed, CC has robust corporate, finance and litigation practices in the US; credibility isn't lacking, but – for now – size is: *"So we're looking to grow in corporate M&A and litigation,"* Cohen tells us. *"We've hired some laterals and promoted some talented associates, but we're still under-sized in comparison to the M&A powerhouses and big litigation teams at other New York firms."*

> **"We're looking to grow in corporate M&A and litigation."**

What could be better to support these plans than a prestigious reputation and vast global network? CC is one of London's exclusive 'magic circle' firms, a merry quintet of top-notch players traditionally known for their corporate and finance panache. But some are a tad more magical than the others, and CC has cast its spell on *Chambers Global*, which bestows more top rankings on the firm than any other. Incoming associates could see the advantages of signing up for junior life at CC, with a global grasp tightened on 23 countries across five continents. *"You have CC and you have a traditionally US-centered firm. They both have a Brussels office, for example, but antitrust work here versus antitrust work there is on another scale: they're not equals."* And who says being smaller than the New York hotshots is necessarily a bad thing? *"The deals are staffed leanly in comparison to other big firms in the city, so juniors get substantive work."*

Offices

Like its fellow 'magic circle' expats, CC has kept its US presence focused in New York and DC. At the time of our calls, 39 second and third-year associates were based in New York, while 13 called DC their home. The Big Apple base is *"centrally located and right by the Rockefeller Center."* Juniors inhabit internal offices for two years – and share for the first – before graduating to their own window-adorned room. *"But all of the windows are tinted so it's still too dark!"* Let's hope the *"wonderful and subsidized"* cafeteria serves vitamin D-rich meals... Sources pointed to the office's REITs, derivatives, M&A and as-

On chambers-associate.com...

- Interview with regional managing partner of the Americas, Evan Cohen
- Interview with New York hiring partner Nick Williams
- Additional get hired tips

The Inside View

See firm profile on p.584

247

Rankings in *Chambers USA*

Capital Markets	Projects
Corporate/M&A	REITs
Insurance	Tax
Latin American Investment	Transportation
Litigation	

For detail on ranking tiers and ranking locations, visit
www.chambersandpartners.com

Recent work highlights

- Advised Mondelēz International (formerly Kraft Foods) on its $13.9 billion acquisition of coffee maestro Keurig Green Mountain
- Represented Goldman Sachs as arranger of the $965 million financing of three toll road projects in Colombia
- Acting for Dubai Islamic Bank (DIB) during eight civil cases that will determine whether it should be held liable for allegedly providing retail banking services to al Qaeda affiliates

set finance practices as particular areas of strength, and boasted: *"We have one of the best Latin America practices in New York for sure."*

Likewise in DC: *"Lat Am project finance work is a massive part of our practice, although our sanctions and export control expertise is also represented strongly."* Juniors here bragged of having their own offices from the get-go, but did admit that *"it's a bit of a nightmare at the moment"* due to a hefty renovation project that will connect CC with the building behind it. Still, the prospect of a new *"state of the art lobby, gym and other facilities"* kept interviewees happy, as did the bustling K Street location.

Strategy & Future

Leveraged finance has also been earmarked for growth alongside corporate M&A and litigation. In addition, the Trump administration will influence future domestic work, says Cohen: *"First, in infrastructure. There's an opportunity for us to leverage our PPP expertise out of Europe, and to use our project finance expertise too."* Regulatory advice will also be in demand. *"Regulations will change. Dodd-Frank will be revisited. There will be a lot of questions, and we have the only US/Europe regulatory practice on the ground in New York."*

"There's an opportunity to leverage our PPP expertise."

Further afield, work pertaining to Latin America is booming: *"We represented Goldman on Colombia's 4G toll roads* [see work highlights, below] *and now Goldman is looking into Paraguay and Argentina. The latter is on the up and is a focus for us in the Americas. We're seeing some infrastructure, finance and corporate M&A work there."*

The Work

In the Big Apple, the vast majority of second and third-year associates – almost 80% – could be found in CC's transactional group; only three juniors were litigators, while the rest were split between separate tax, real estate and ERISA groups.

The transactional group is divided into three arms: corporate, banking & finance, and capital markets. Those who join it are assigned to the 'transactional pool' and sample all three areas. *"The idea is that you organically fall into the group you want to be in. We have around three years to decide, but have the option of formally joining a group before then too."* An assignment coordinator is on hand to help: *"She monitors our schedules and makes sure the work is evenly distributed. But it's a two-way relationship; we express our interests and she tries to get us the assignments we want."*

"You organically fall into the group you want to be in."

Banking work includes regulatory matters, *"where you draft lots of disclosures,"* as well as project finance deals: *"We're establishing power plants in Guatemala, building airports in Peru and we've completed the first ever project bond in Colombia."* Over in capital markets, both debt and equity offerings are on the table. *"The deals are big and doc-heavy, with many moving parts, so there's a lot of project management alongside drafting filings and registration statements."* Corporate covers the likes of fund formation, M&A and insurance deals. Juniors become masters of due diligence and *"get to know each company very well – you're constantly liaising with them to research any issues."*

In DC, a handful of juniors could be found in the projects and capital markets groups, but most were litigators. Across the office *"assignment is more organic,"* especially for junior litigators, who are *"given a great deal of latitude"* to sample and no *"ultimatums"* about specializing. There's a mix of civil litigation; international arbitration; and regulatory & investigatory work. The latter spans white collar crime, FCPA sanctions, securities law and cyber security matters. *"With sanctions work, you might be drafting OFAC license applications and analyzing transactions to report on issues – these are fourth-year tasks, but because of the size of our office, you get to do them earlier."* Juniors in civil lit and international arbitration must hone their drafting skills while on the move: *"Our associates travel early and travel often."* We heard of one

See firm profile on p.584

The Inside View

Diversity	Partners (%)	Associates (%)
Women	11	47
White	82	64
Black/African American	0	2
Hispanic/Latin American	4	9
Asian	3	17
Mixed/Other	11	8
LGBT	1	3.5

associate visiting *"Peru, Uruguay, Argentina, Chile, Spain and Paris – all in the past two and a half months!"* Other duties include preparing for hearings, drafting memorials and assisting with client pitches.

Training & Development

CC is *"huge on formal training,"* enthused sources in the transactional pool. *"During the first four months there are bi-weekly trainings that cover all the groups. They give you booklets to keep, which are very helpful!"* Litigators don't get the same introductory blast of training, as *"they expect you to learn a lot through experience."* However, litigators and deal-doers alike participate in the Clifford Chance Academy, which runs class-tailored sessions throughout the year.

Juniors meet with their assigned career development partner and the head of their practice group to discuss their annual reviews, which consist of feedback provided by colleagues. *"We discuss the class-based goals that we set at the start of the year and whether we think we met them. To get the most out of the process you have to be open and make sure you ask all the questions you want to ask."*

Culture

"We're not trying to be a typical New York firm," juniors insisted. *"We're intentionally operating a different model: here the partners are not directly competing against one another and all of the groups share profits."* As a result, *"there's a strong sense of community. We share the work and we get along – no one gets jealous."*

"We're not trying to be a typical New York firm."

With all this collegiality flying around, the social life is pretty good. In New York, the associates' network hosts a monthly happy hour in the office, usually with a theme to abide by: *"For Hallowe'en we dressed up as Where's Waldo!"* These are accompanied by more formal dos, like an office-wide holiday party. *"These events are held to keep us connected and promote interaction. The partners, the* seniors and the juniors all enjoy the drinks and laugh a lot." The DC office is, however, quieter in comparison.

The atmosphere may be warm and fuzzy at times, but the approach to the work itself is much more hard-nosed. *"We're very practical people and it's not a very esoteric firm: we don't like to spend hours pontificating. Clients come to us for very real-world solutions delivered at a very real-world deadline."*

Hours & Compensation

There's no formal billing requirement, but sources were conscious of an unofficial 2,000-hour target. *"For the first two years you still get a bonus even if you don't hit it, as they acknowledge you have less control over your workload."* After that, the policy isn't *"super obvious."* Officially, CC takes *"a holistic approach, and considers your pro bono work, firm activities – like BD – and your reviews."* However, many felt that hours were still the most important factor in determining bonus eligibility.

"It's like that Rihanna song: work, work, work, work, work!"

Luckily, most deemed the target *"very achievable,"* as life at CC *"is like that Rihanna song: work, work, work, work, work!"* If a deal is closing *"you can be working 12 hours a day, every day, for several weeks."* When things quieten down 10am starts and 8pm exits are pretty standard. Litigators can also work some *"crazy hours"* thanks to the amount of travel in their schedules, as well as the need to accommodate other time zones: *"When we're working with China we stagger our working days to cover the full 24-hour period."* Ouch. To reward their hard graft, CC gives its lawyers a $400 certificate if they bill 250 hours in a month: *"It's meant to go toward an evening of entertainment with your family or whoever – the people you don't see enough!"*

Pro Bono

There's no cap on pro bono hours and all CC lawyers are encouraged to devote at least 50 hours to this noble pursuit each year. *"It's actually more of an expectation,"* juniors clarified, *"and our managing partner likes to see it on everyone's time sheet."*

It's easy to rack up those hours: an intranet page and two designated pro bono partners disseminate projects *"constantly,"* while *"individual associates and partners will have their own projects that they'll ask for help with."* New Yorkers had been devoting their time to domestic violence charity My Sisters' Place, while their DC counterparts had poured their efforts into the Children's Law Center. In addition, *"the cool thing about CC is that you*

See firm profile on p.584

The Inside View

can do pro bono worldwide; there might be an organization in the UK you're interested in, or an NGO in India,
for example."

Pro bono Hours
- For all US attorneys: undisclosed
- Average per US attorney: undisclosed

Diversity

"As a global firm we do attract and need a more diverse
group of people," sources declared, pointing to a promising representation of ethnic minority and LGBT associates. CC's global-wide LGBT network, Arcus, is especially active: the group recently organized Pride art
exhibitions in both DC and New York, as well as several
international offices.

*"We've just instituted more flexible
maternity leave policies."*

However, "we don't have enough female partners," moaned
juniors. "This has been acknowledged, but we need to put
in place more measures to support women, like childcare
facilities." Regional managing partner for the Americas,
Evan Cohen, says: "I am personally committed to including more women in the partnership and supporting female
associates; I have four daughters and I want them to have
the same opportunities. We've just instituted more flexible
maternity leave policies, and we're looking at other ways
we can support female lawyers so they stay at the firm and
become partners."

Get Hired

To get a foot in the door, you'll need "cream of the crop
academics, plus a genuine interest in international work at
a truly global firm." Foreign language skills go down well,
as does a passion for travel, especially if you're a future
litigator en route to DC: "There's so much travel involved,
so people have to enjoy it." For more associate tips, plus
words of wisdom from CC's New York hiring partner,
Nick Williams, go online.

*"There's so much travel involved,
so people have to enjoy it."*

See firm profile on p.584

250

Cooley LLP

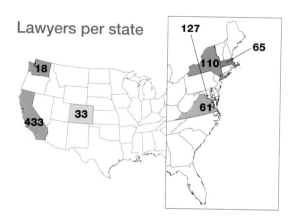

Lawyers per state

127
65
18
110
433
33
61

Largest US office: Palo Alto
US offices: 10
International offices: 2
First-year salary: $180,000
Billable hours: 1,950 target
Summers 2017: 56 (48 2Ls, 7 1Ls, 1 other)
Revenue 2016: $974.3 million (+6.8%)
Partners made in 2017: 13 (all in US)
Famous for: emerging companies; cool California vibes

Cooley's increasingly global legal experts are often the go-to lawyers for high growth companies of all descriptions.

COOLEY and Silicon Valley's histories are intertwined: in the 1950s, for example, the firm's lawyers helped set up one of the West Coast's first ever venture capital firms. VC work remains one of Cooley's best-known strengths. It also advised a profusion of tech companies in Northern California whose computer chips and mind-bending gadgetry put the 'Silicon' in the 'Valley'. These days, life sciences, pharma and media industry companies feature as prominently in the client roster as pure tech. The common link is high growth.

"A firm made for the present."

Juniors we spoke to were attracted to the firm because of the type of work it deals with, but also because culturally *"it's a firm that is looking forward – a firm made for the present."* Cooley's own rapid growth in recent years also created a buzz among associates: *"We're growing, but not for the sake of growth. Rather, we're growing strategically – expanding in both expertise and practice groups, but also offices."* Unsurprisingly, the firm achieves several top *Chambers USA* rankings for VC and startup-related expertise, and other ranked practices cover life sciences, corporate, capital markets, IP, litigation, and tech.

On chambers-associate.com...

- More about getting hired at Cooley
- Interview with CEO Joe Conroy
- A few Silicon Valley facts

The Work & Offices

The 'business' (corporate) practice takes about two-thirds of juniors, with the remaining third in litigation. Traditionally starting as generalists within their designated group, newbies are free to explore different areas. For litigators this means a mix of antitrust, commercial disputes, IP and white-collar crime cases, whereas transactional hopefuls keep busy in subgroups like corporate/M&A, emerging or public companies, technology, and venture capital. While work assignment partners are usually on hand to dish out work, this varies from office to office. Many reported: *"No one describes it as free market, but you can get the work you want or seek out individuals you like working for."*

"I could be running deals that are hundreds of millions of dollars."

Newbies in the business group start out broad, doing a mix of things which could range from startups to M&A and IPOs. Emerging companies work sees juniors deal with companies through their whole life cycle: *"The beginning can be incorporation and formation of the entity, hiring employees, and venture capital financing, which is a big part of what we do. We help companies manage those transactions."* Responsibility-wise, juniors reported receiving *"more oversight from partners with bigger VCs, although generally you get a lot of autonomy. I could be running deals worth hundreds of millions of dollars."* The final stretch of the cycle sometimes sees the group taking companies public. Tasks include *"a certain amount*

See firm profile on p.585

Rankings in *Chambers USA*

Antitrust	Media & Entertainment
Capital Markets	Privacy & Data Security
Corporate/Commercial	Private Equity
Corporate/M&A	Real Estate
IT & Outsourcing	Startups & Emerging
Intellectual Property	Companies
Investment Funds	Technology
Life Sciences	Telecommunications
Litigation	

For detail on ranking tiers and ranking locations, visit
www.chambersandpartners.com

Recent work highlights

- Advised biopharmaceutical company Medivation in its sale to Pfizer for $14 billion
- Defended Mark Zuckerberg in contract dispute with a real estate developer, concerning the developer's $1.7 million sale of an estate property in Palo Alto
- Defending Pokémon Go-developer Niantic against class actions filed by property owners who complained that nearby PokéStops are creating a public nuisance
- Advised online fund-raising platform CrowdRise on its sale to GoFundMe, the world's largest social fund-raising platform

of procedural work" like doc review and due diligence, but also *"thoughtful analysis of documents"* including investment reviews, and drafting various agreements. A Palo Alto source reflected: *"I talk to friends at other firms who are still stuck doing data entry, which is frustrating for them. There's some level of that to any job, but at least here, you're given not only the room to grow, but the tools to grow."*

"The companies tend to be small, so I get a lot of interaction with the owner or CEO."

Given Cooley's high volume of work with startups, corporate juniors here weren't short of client contact: *"The companies tend to be small, so I get a lot of interaction with the owner or CEO."* Many reported being *"the main point of contact"* for these clients, as well as negotiator with opposing counsel. *"It's daunting at first, but people were willing to review emails I was sending out. It was good to just jump right in."* The unpredictable workload meant *"sometimes it's like trying to drink water from a fire hydrant"* – but *"that's going to be the case anywhere."*

Litigators *"get to work on all different kinds of cases, depending on the partner you work for and what's available at the time."* Junior litigators often see repeat clients because *"once familiar with one, if anything else comes up with that client you're expected to work on it too because you know the business."* The work includes legal research, discovery, advising clients on particular laws, and drafting documents. A San Diego junior highlighted *"it's definitely not all doc review – it's actually a surprisingly small amount of what we do. I almost would have liked more!"* Sources also appreciated *"getting great experience in different areas, not just writing, but being able to manage a case and have ownership of it."* A downside juniors highlighted was that *"it's harder to get client contact on the litigation side,"* though most noted they'd *"had it here and there."* Client contact was more common with smaller clients, usually in employment cases, where *"the businesses can't really afford to take up lots of time with partners."*

Generally, though, *"partners are happy to give you more responsibility if they feel you're capable of handling it. If you do good work, you'll get given plenty of substantive work."*

"California firms are already laid back, but San Diego is especially laid back – that's why I love it."

Most juniors are based in the Palo Alto HQ, followed by San Diego and San Francisco. The PA branch is *"shaped like a horseshoe – you always get lost at first, ending up at one end of the horseshoe then walking back."* Those in San Diego felt *"California firms are already laid back, but San Diego is especially laid back – that's why I love it."* Juniors on the East Coast can be found mostly in DC, Boston, and New York. A New Yorker described their office as like *"the Wild West – it's slightly disorganized just because it's growing so fast!"* Another noted that *"Cooley's other offices were built more recently and they're much more hip and modern, which is Cooley's brand. We look more like a traditional New York office."* Smaller offices like Reston, Seattle, and Broomfield were said to be *"very close knit."*

Training & Development

Training gets under way with a week of Cooley College in Palo Alto. It covers *"everything you're meant to know in a condensed period."* This includes educating juniors on the firm's identity, initial practice-specific training, and meeting fellow juniors from across all offices. *"They kind of give you too much information, where you can't really retain all of it,"* one source had found. Luckily, juniors receive *"a handy dandy binder to refer to for everything you need."* Formal training is then practice-specific and usually occurs monthly. One source enthused *"they're always talking internally about how to make it better, but I actually already think it's very good."*

See firm profile on p.585

Diversity	Partners (%)	Associates (%)
Women	22	56.5
White	87.4	75.6
Black/African American	1.4	3.1
Hispanic/Latin American	2.9	2.7
Asian	6.9	12.9
Mixed/Other	1.1	4.5
LGBT	1.8	2.7

Pro Bono

For the Cooley gang, the sky's the limit when it comes to pro bono. The firm is *"very, very committed"* to this type of work and doesn't cap the hours associates can spend on it. Sources had been involved in a range of cases including immigration and asylum, work for KIND [Kids In Need of Defense], and clemency projects that address sentencing disparities. Juniors also said *"the firm is happy to encourage other projects we want to look into, within our practice area or something different."* As well as getting experience in different fields, juniors valued the *"experience with clients, and in courtrooms"* that pro bono work can bring.

Pro bono hours
- For all US attorneys: 43,858
- Average per US attorney: 57

Culture

"Cooley is a firm that values individuals," sources described. *"It's still BigLaw – there's still the expectation that you can jump on something at a moment's notice, but they want everybody to be themselves."* Many highlighted the *"Silicon Valley-cool"* vibe that permeates each of the offices, whether East or West Coast. Even with dress code, the firm sheds that stereotypical *Law & Order* look: *"People are okay with you dressing casually, and that matches our client base."* Juniors emphasized that *"an important aspect of our culture is having smart lawyers, but also good people."* Collaboration is also key: one source noted *"people that tend to do well here are people who are capable of saying "hey, I don't know everything," and that's fine, but be confident to work with other people to find solutions."*

"Silicon Valley-cool."

The firm hosts monthly happy hours, and while *"it's a little different to places where everyone wanders down to the pub, we do a good job of having a good time as a group."* The social scene varies by office, with San Diego sources, for example, feeling their city was *"sleepier than New York or San Francisco,"* and *"more family-focused."* Palo Alto, meanwhile, boasts its own softball team (*"we won the championship which was a big deal!"*).

Hours & Compensation

"Over time you're able to achieve more balance, but the most negative part of this job is that it demands so much time," one associate mused. *"The realistic approach for law students starting a career with a big firm is to understand that you're going to put in a big time commitment earlier in your career. It's just what it takes to become competent at your job."* The yearly target for Cooley's associates is 1,950 hours, which *"people think is a fair number. Not everyone achieves it, but that's the point of a bonus."* On average, juniors put in ten to 12 hours in the office a day, and some said they could log back on at home *"after putting the kids to sleep."* Others stressed that it's *"flexible enough to get what I want to do done, and still meet work expectations."*

Associates also gave the thumbs up to the speed with which Cooley matched Cravath in the recent salaries hike. *"Given our size, I think it's great we're matching it. I don't think it's a given considering we're not a New York firm."* As for bonuses, *"this year they're emphasizing that it's completely discretionary."* Many felt it was *"a little bit of a black box. Cooley send out a letter talking about the decision-making and bonus process, but it's not 100% transparent."*

Diversity

"The Bay area is generally very diverse, very liberal, and very accepting," a Palo Alto junior reminded us. However, the general consensus on Cooley's diversity was that *"they're making an effort but it's tough. The recruiting pool isn't particularly large and that's a big problem. It's certainly a high priority for the firm."* The firm promotes several affinity groups, and has a diversity fellowship program for law students. Recipients can spend their 1L and 2L summers with the firm and receive a total of $30,000 toward law school tuition (the third and final $10,000 installment is paid when they join as an associate). Offices vary when it comes to gender diversity – for instance, New Yorkers said *"partnership is slightly less diverse than the group as a whole"* while San Diego sources claimed *"we have several very established women partners who are very supportive, and that's been great."*

"We have several very established women partners who are very supportive."

Strategy & Future

"I think the firm is looking closely at where the economy is going and where law practice is going, and intends to be on the forefront of 21st-century law firms going forward," juniors reckoned. The plan is *"to continue to grow and expand strategically."* CEO Joe Conroy confirms this: *"Our*

See firm profile on p.585

strategy involves continued investment in our power cent-ers," namely "California/Silicon Valley" and "the Boston to DC corridor, including New York." Globally, Conroy ex-plains, "we will also be expanding to other markets where it makes sense." He highlights Germany as "a likely target as it's a nexus to what we do really well."

Get Hired

"It's important that both sides find the right fit, and that can only happen when both the student and the firm is being candid about what they are seeking." Visit chambers-associate.com to learn some tips from Carrie Wagner, director of legal talent at Cooley.

Tech-savvy Cooley is one of the few firms leading AI development in the law. Read our feature on chambers-associate.com

See firm profile on p.585

Cozen O'Connor

Lawyers per state

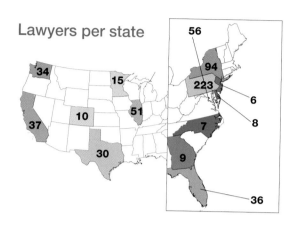

Largest US office: Philadelphia
US offices: 22
International offices: 2
First-year salary: $125,000 – $160,000
Billable hours: vary by practice area, between 1,600 and 2,000
Summers 2017: 23 (17 2Ls, 6 1Ls)
Revenue 2016: $376 million (+10.1%)
Partners made in 2017: undisclosed
Famous for: a healthy work/life balance; devising subrogation

Young and energetic Cozen O'Connor is still expanding, but will it retain its much-cherished culture?

AFTER a jam-packed 2015, 2016 was a quieter, calmer period at Cozen O'Connor. The preceding year saw the saw the launch of a State Attorneys General Practice in DC, the relocation of six of the firm's 24 offices and the acquisition of Chicago firm Meckler Bulger Tilson, making Cozen one of the fastest-growing *Am Law* firms of 2015. While things may have slowed over 2016, growth's hardly come to a standstill: Cozen swiped 15 intellectual property lawyers from IP boutique Feldman Gale and continued to bulk out its New York, Miami, Minneapolis and Washington, DC offices with hires into a string of departments.

The Philadelphia-headquartered firm was launched barely 50 years ago as an insurance and commercial litigation boutique but today it covers a wide array of practice areas, earning *Chambers USA* rankings in everything from corporate/M&A to labor & employment, construction, insurance and litigation. And though the firm's now moved beyond its original focus on the last two, founding fathers Stephen Cozen and Patrick O'Connor still roam the halls to this day.

On chambers-associate.com...

- Interview with managing partner Vince McGuinness
- Recruitment tips and advice
- Subrogation: Cozen's insurance specialty

The Work

Upon arrival, first-years are assigned to one of Cozen's transactional practices – such as corporate, real estate, energy or IP – or the so-called litigation pool. Litigators enter the pool for up to 18 months, taking a dip in different sub-groups like commercial litigation, global insurance or subrogation. All practice areas have an assignment coordinator who *"keeps track of how we're doing and divvies out work, but you're more than welcome to walk around the office to find something."*

"I can't overstate the value."

The litigation pool garnered almost universal praise from our sources. *"One of Cozen's best assets is that it has a strong plaintiff and defense side and the pool allows you to practice in both. I now primarily do defence work but I can't overstate the value of doing plaintiff work when I was first learning, as I'm able to understand the pressures on and thought processes of the plaintiff side,"* reported one litigator. Another revealed: *"It was great for internal marketing. I was able to make connections not only in my office but in offices and departments across the country."* For their first six months litigators receive an evaluation email after each assignment: *"You can get a ton of feedback in your first six months, more than I ever got in law school."*

"Involved in the nitty gritty."

See firm profile on p.586

Rankings in *Chambers USA*

Construction	Labor & Employment
Corporate/M&A	Litigation
Government	Real Estate
Healthcare	Transportation
Insurance	

For detail on ranking tiers and ranking locations, visit www.chambersandpartners.com

Recent work highlights

- Continued to represent the Executive Committee for Commercial Claims in a post-9/11 dispute over the alleged involvement of Saudi Arabia in funding Al Qaeda. The firm is currently appealing Saudi Arabia's successful motion to dismiss the suit
- Represented National Fire & Marine Insurance in an $80 million subrogation claim following a fire at the Empress Casino Joliet in 2009
- Acted for the estate of musical theater composer Mitch Leigh in a licensing dispute between the copyright holders of the music, lyrics and book of the musical Man of La Mancha

While immersed in the pool *"I've gotten to work on every stage of litigation,"* one source outlined. *"The majority of what I do is either research, drafting motions or responding to discovery requests, but I also attend conferences and conduct doc review."* Another spoke of *"spending a good amount of time in depositions – they were not afraid to send me out there, which was great as I could come back and talk to them about my experience. They're more than amenable to go over it with me. If I'm writing a brief and propose some ideas, the partners are willing to put my contribution out there."* Those working within smaller groups *"manage the cases from start to finish. I do most of the work by myself. If I have any questions or it's strategy-related I can go to my supervisor and ask what they think."* We even heard of juniors becoming *"really involved in the nitty-gritty communications with the client and opposing counsel."*

Training & Development

Orientation takes places in Philadelphia, with first-years flown in from across the country. Over a three-day period newbies *"familiarize themselves with the firm and its resources. We also received a session on how to use our support staff."* Juniors congregate at various offices in the network every couple of years to attend the all-firm retreat or associate symposium. When we spoke to our sources, plans were underway for the 2017 symposium; the itinerary included *"sessions on managing staff, how to bring in business and how to network."*

Monthly departmental training sessions drill juniors on the need to know skills within their practice area. Litigators can attend COTA [Cozen O'Connor's Trial Academy] and CODEP [Cozen O'Connor Deposition Program] where *"people watch you taking a practice deposition and give you feedback on how to improve. More of the CODEP style training would be useful."*

Hours & Compensation

Billable targets differ by practice area: corporate aims for 1,600, real estate 1,650 and litigation 1,800. Although these are relatively low for BigLaw and *"don't sound too bad, there are months or weeks when it can be crazy."* When times are good juniors can expect to put in around ten-hour days at the office. *"It's a ghost town here by 7pm,"* one Philly junior told us. But while the office inhabitants may have migrated to their couches and dinner tables, many are *"plugging back into"* work during the evening.

Cozen associate salaries are below market rate and have proved something of a contentious topic in the past. Before Cravath instituted the new New York scale ($180,000 for first-years) and caused a mass scramble in the market to match, Cozen had already increased its associate salaries, but since then Cozen raised its salaries further – this time to $150,000 for first-years in Philadelphia and $160,000 New York and DC. Associates felt the firm's decisions on salaries have been prudent: *"It's only going to hurt us if Cozen foolishly overspends on salaries and then we find ourselves without a bonus."* Another reasoned: *"If we were offered a $10k raise but had to bill 100 hours more, I'd say 'don't raise my salary'."*

Culture

Growth in the DC base over the past few years has created a *"culture in flux,"* after this office *"brought in some great attorneys from higher-intensity law firms."* These additions came with ups – *"high-profile clients"* – and downs – *"I'm working as hard as friends at bigger firms who are earning much more. Before I arrived I was told that although I wouldn't make market, I would leave at a decent hour. I don't think the new partners were made aware of this. The culture in DC used to be great, and it might still be, but people are wondering what's the deal?"* Despite the uncertainty, our DC sources agreed *"there are very few assholes here. I genuinely enjoy the company of most people – they're approachable and informal."*

See firm profile on p.586

Diversity	Partners (%)	Associates (%)
Women	24	47
White	93	84
Black/African American	2.5	3
Hispanic/Latin American	2.5	4
Asian	1	5
Mixed/Other	1	4
LGBT	1	3.5

"We like practicing law but we also like doing other things too."

Cozen's reputation for striking a healthy work/life balance still holds strong in its other offices. *"People know you have a life outside the firm. We like practicing law but we also like doing other things too."* All this results in *"more of a laid-back culture."* Sources were quick to emphasize that *"we're competitive in the market but not internally with each other."*

"I appreciate the level of respect I'm afforded," said one source. *"People understand I'm young and have a lot of learning to do but noone is condescending. They acknowledge my intelligence and have faith in my ability, which makes it a comfortable place to work."* Interviewees told us this respectful attitude is driven into them from day one: *"They communicated the need to be polite to everyone, from Brooke in the cafeteria to the guys in the mailroom. We're nothing without them – that's how it is here and why associates are also treated with respect. Cozen is the sum of its parts."*

Pro Bono
Melinda deLisle joined the firm in May 2016 as the new director of pro bono engagement. Described as *"fabulous"* by interviewees, deLisle has facilitated *"an absolute increase"* in the amount of pro bono opportunities associates come across. *"She's met with lots of us to ask what areas we're interested in helping out with, like immigration or LGBT rights,"* sources told us. *"Whatever you're interested in she'll find something for you,"* whether it's battling for prisoners' civil rights that gets your heart racing, aiding immigrants in securing asylum status, advising non-profits or working on the Innocence Project. Up to 75 hours count as billable, and you can ask for approval to go above that.

Pro bono hours
- For all US attorneys: 16,442
- Average per US attorney: 30

Diversity
Although many sources reckoned the firm wasn't *"super-diverse,"* it fares relatively well compared to others in BigLaw. Over half of Cozen's associates are female, as are a quarter of its partners. It falls short on racial diversity however; four-fifths of associates are white, while at the partner level it's over 90%. That said, *"when considering-inclusiveness I think Cozen's second to none,"* one associate stressed. Another source added: *"It's very supportive. That doesn't mean there isn't any work to do but I think diversity is a priority."* Diverse attorneys are invited a day early to the biennial firmwide retreat for networking events and panel discussions. A mentoring program pairs up diverse attorneys with members of the diversity committee.

Offices & Strategy
At the time of our calls junior associates were based in Chicago, LA, Houston, LA, New York, Philadelphia (where most juniors end up), Seattle and Washington, DC. The firm has a further 14 offices in the US. Although *"Philly is the largest office I don't feel it's overbearing,"* one West Coast source told us. *"Vince [McGuinness – managing partner] and others come out here pretty often."* McGuinness and CEO Michael Heller travel to each office to meet with associates for a state of the firm address. Juniors can submit anonymous questions in advance to discuss anything from diversity issues to compensation concerns.

Managing partner Vince McGuinness tells us: *"We stayed on course with our strategic objectives in terms of growing certain target areas; those are South Florida, California, New York and Washington, DC."* Go online to read the full interview with McGuinness and see how firm's meeting other core strategic objectives.

Get Hired
"Generally affable, down-to-earth people who have respect for others" help maintain the Cozen way. Sources were adamant there is such a thing as *"a distinct Cozen personality"* so visit chambers-associate.com to find out what this entails and check out hiring tips from our sources.

The Inside View

See firm profile on p.586

Cravath, Swaine & Moore LLP

Lawyers per state

492

Largest US office: New York

US offices: 1

International offices: 1

First-year salary: $180,000

Billable hours: no requirement

Summers 2017: 121 (119 2Ls, 2 1Ls)

Revenue 2016: $737.8 million (+10.7%)

Partners made in 2017: 3

Famous for: legendary business model (including Cravath pay scale); world-class M&A

This legendary New York firm has a business model for the long term.

ON a purely statistical basis, with just two offices – one in New York and one in London – and a headcount of less than 500, it would be easy to place Cravath into the category of 'smaller firm'. But to do so, you'd probably have to be living on another planet, or at least under a rock. For when it comes to names in BigLaw, there's Cravath, and then there's everybody else. Much of the firm's prestige derives from its famous business model. The Cravath System – a set of principles and procedures that govern everything from hiring, to training, to bonuses and compensation – is often imitated, but never equaled. And in 2016, Cravath once more set the tone when it announced that it would now pay a whopping first-year salary of $180,000 – a move which most other elite firms soon matched.

But the reason Cravath sets the tone when it comes to business practice is not because of its pay scale, but the results its unique model achieves. For example, its crème de la crème corporate outfit has been involved in three of the ten largest M&A deals of all time. The most recent of these was AT&T's $85.4 billion merger with Time Warner. *Chambers USA* recognizes these achievements, awarding the firm cool and refreshing top-tier nationwide rankings for its M&A, banking, capital markets,

securities, and tax work. In its Big Apple home it also gets the juiciest of accolades for its environmental, commercial litigation and media & entertainment practices.

The Work

Chances are that if you are seriously considering Cravath you have heard of the firm's renowned rotation system. Corporate lawyers switch practice group every 12 to 15 months, while their litigious comrades do the same every 15 to 18 months. While this might seem like a convoluted way of allowing lawyers the opportunity to find their niche, the system is in fact ingrained into Cravath's DNA and involves attorneys rotating around the houses until they settle down and make partner, *"though some even go beyond that point."* Ergo, *"if you are a partner at Cravath, you will have deep knowledge and experience of so many different types of law."*

From a class that *"fluctuates in size between 100-150, depending on the economy,"* the corporate department takes about 50 newbies, or just over half of all incoming associates. Around 40% of the intake enters the litigation practice, while the remaining attorneys are split between tax and trusts & estates. As mentioned previously, Cravath's corporate lawyers are best known for their M&A craft and the teams that deal with those transactions are the biggest in the department. Juniors are expected to get involved in every aspect of a deal, including plenty of the dreaded due diligence: *"Though some people complain, they get on with it because it gives you invaluable insight into the companies that we work with."* That said, due to the small sizes of the teams, high-level tasks also enter

On chambers-associate.com...

- Cravath's rotation system
- We chat with hiring partners Karin DeMasi and Eric Schiele
- The Cravath System

See firm profile on p.587

Rankings in *Chambers USA*

Antitrust	Environment
Banking & Finance	Intellectual Property
Capital Markets	Litigation
Corporate Crime &	Media & Entertainment
Investigations	Securities
Corporate/M&A	Tax
Employee Benefits &	
Executive Compensation	

For detail on ranking tiers and ranking locations, visit www.chambersandpartners.com

Recent work highlights

- Represented Time Warner in its $85.4 billion merger with AT&T
- Represented British American Tobacco in its $93 billion merger with Reynolds
- Acted as new counsel for the Republic of Argentina in overturning extraordinary injunctions in New York district court and in an expedited appeal. The victory cleared the way for Argentina to resolve the vast majority of its litigation with holdout creditors and return to the international capital markets for the first time in 15 years
- Won a favorable judgment for American Express after a seven-week trial and appeal in a civil lawsuit brought by the DOJ and 17 state attorneys general against AmEx

attorneys' repertoires early on – *"we have these foreign associate attorneys who come to us on exchanges from friendly firms. I worked with one on a recent deal and he was amazed at the level of responsibility that we get. From day one I was talking to clients on the phone."* Another source commented: *"You see first-years driving transactions, which would be highly unusual at other firms."*

"Amazed at the level of responsibility."

Over in litigation things aren't hugely different, except for the fact that juniors work with specific clients instead of in specific practice areas. This means that associates rotate between partners instead: *"You'll be working with a specific partner and their clients doing different things for each one. For example, if their client is American Express, you'll be doing a lot of antitrust, but you'll also be doing securities or investigations work as well."* Again, responsibility levels are high – *"as a first-year you are doing a lot of work that fifth-years would be doing. Of course, there are deposition outlines and doc review, but as soon as we finished that I was in full trial preparation mode, writing briefs, and doing research."*

Culture

Sky-high responsibility levels, a much-lauded rotation system, unapologetically long hours, and an almost unparalleled prestige – all of these things contribute to one of the most unique work cultures in all of BigLaw. Added to this is the fact that *"you can't really lateral to Cravath, so if you don't make it first time, you aren't likely to get a second chance."* Promoting only from within and possessing an incredibly selective recruitment process engenders a system *"built to have the best and brightest come here and try it out."* Many interviewees admitted that gaining a place in this hallowed institution was a *"source of pride"* and perhaps explained why Cravath lawyers are willing to work so hard for the firm – *"absolutely no one here shies away from working extremely hard."* At the same time, and despite their mega status, *"the firm only has two offices and our main competitors all tend to be much larg-*

er than us, so there's a definite focus on maintaining this small firm culture."*

"You can't really lateral to Cravath, so if you don't make it first time, you aren't likely to get a second chance."

Work hard-play hard has become a huge cliché in the world of business, but at Cravath it is a BigLaw trope that is alive and well. *"The pastoral care at the firm is second to none, and though we're not partying all night, the events teams are ever-present in our lives from an early stage. And personally they are some of my favorite people in the building."* Those events teams are very active, putting together a busy social calendar. There's a monthly happy hour at a local bar with an unlimited tab, while more family-friendly fun is afforded by the annual Central Park Zoo party, during which the firm *"rents out the entire zoo for the night and everyone brings along their families."* And it'd be remiss of us not to mention the Cravath Prom, a biennial black-tie bash that takes place at a swanky location somewhere in the city – last year it was Ellis Island's turn for a glitzy takeover.

Hours & Compensation

As mentioned above, long hours are part and parcel of a Cravath lawyer's life – *"I do think it's important to go into the firm with your eyes wide open and it's something they are very candid about in the interviews. They know it's in everyone's interest that you are fully aware of the hours here."* That said, assignments stem from the few partners that juniors work with, meaning *"if you're not busy, they strongly encourage you to go and live your life. Because when the work is there, it will find you."* Sources also felt the lack of an official billing target was *"very helpful, it means I'm not thinking just about a figure but about the work I am doing. It allows people to relax without worrying about hitting some arbitrary requirement."*

See firm profile on p.587

Diversity	Partners (%)	Associates (%)
Women	21	39
White	93	75
Black/African American	1	4
Hispanic/Latin American	1	4
Asian	5	13
Mixed/Other	0	4
LGBT	4	4

"If you're not busy they strongly encourage you to go and live your life."

Despite having no target, interviewees were certain that *"if there was a quota, we would easily fill it. It's not unusual to have 120-hour weeks quite regularly."* Nonetheless, *"you could be working late into the night one week and then billing five hours the next: it just really fluctuates."* What probably won't come as a surprise is the fact that Cravath associates had no qualms about their market-leading salaries. But they particularly liked that *"your bonus isn't dependent on hours and there's never any resentment between those who are busy and those who are not."*

Offices

All Cravath attorneys share an office until their third year, and tradition dictates that whoever is the more senior occupant has the window desk. And this isn't the only historic convention the firm indulges in: *"When I brought my girlfriend here for the first time she said the décor was exactly what she imagined an old school New York law firm to look like. There are a lot of oak bookcases and marble busts of old men."* The firm also has exclusive use of the Cravath cafeteria, which is subsidized by the firm and serves three hot meals a day. One discerning foodie has this to say about the fare on offer: *"It's above average for a cafeteria but not great if you want to eat healthy!"*

"There are a lot of oak bookcases and marble busts of old men."

For those latterly inclined, the office is in an excellent location. At 50th and 8th it sits on the doorstep of trendy Hell's Kitchen, which boasts great transport connections and *"a ton of wonderful restaurants and bars."* Cravath furnishes its lawyers with *"excellent secretarial support – it's about five associates to each assistant. We also have an admin assistant team on every floor who give us 24-hour support, proofing and reviewing lists to make sure they sync up."*

Training & Development

The rotation system means that Cravath attorneys are well-rounded renaissance individuals after a couple of years at the firm. Moreover, the smaller working groups make on-the-job training more viable. Most sources agreed that *"it's largely an ad hoc system of professional development. You learn the most by getting immersed in different types of work. Although there are formalized programs for those who prefer to learn that way."* The firm's mentorship scheme also came in for universal praise: *"When you start you get an associate mentor and they are given a budget to take you out for lunch a couple of times a month. Then, starting your second year you get a partner mentor who is in the same department as you but on a different team. Mine has been great, we talk at least once a week."*

Pro Bono

Further educational opportunities are afforded by Cravath's pro bono network which for many juniors represents *"the chance to go to court and argue on your feet for the first time."* However, owing to their hectic work schedules, participation is *"largely driven by professional interest, and whether or not you can be spared at the time."* The firm works with organizations like the Innocence Project, the Montefiore Children's Hospital, and Her Justice – *"a charity for low-income women who have suffered from domestic violence."*

Pro bono hours
- For all US attorneys: 25,874
- Average per attorney: 52

Diversity

Diversity was another area in which sources felt the firm could make more of an effort. There are several racial affinity groups, but *"they're not very active."* Cravath's women's initiatives make more headway, though – *"there are women's lunches once a month and departmental partners will host all their female lawyers at their apartments regularly as well."*

"You have an interview with the main partners."

Get Hired

There's no getting away from the fact that the Cravath recruitment process is a rigorous affair. After an initial OCI, the callback is a day-long interview with numerous partners and associates. Instead of the usual two or three-hour affair, *"you have an interview with the main partners but there's no time limit, it just goes on until the partners get what they want out of it. It reminded me more of how a family business is run."*

See firm profile on p.587

Interviewees were in no doubt as to where most new recruits come from – *"it's really the top 14 schools, there's a lot from NYU, and Harvard has a big contingent."* However, they were also keen to stress that personality plays a big part as well: *"If you're coming from Columbia and have certain grades, some firms will take you without even thinking. But Cravath's not like that – they are looking for people with great personalities as well as grades."*

Strategy & Future

Unsurprisingly, working at Cravath opens many prestigious doors: *"You can check out our Wikipedia page, there's a long list of famous people who used to be Cravath lawyers. It's rare that people lateral to other firms; if they leave it'll be to go into business or government."* Those who choose to stay are kept up to date about strategy at regular townhall meetings, which are mandatory to attend. In July 2016 it was announced – *"to much fanfare"* – that Faiza Saeed was taking over as presiding partner of the firm from C. Allen Parker in January 2017. *"Everyone's really excited, she has amazing clients and is the first Asian-American female head of a white-shoe firm."*

> *"You can check out our Wikipedia page, there's a long list of famous people who used to be Cravath lawyers. It's rare that people lateral to other firms; if they leave it'll be to go into business or government."*

The Inside View

See firm profile on p.587

Crowell & Moring LLP

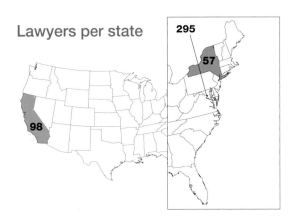

Lawyers per state

295
57
98

Largest US office: Washington, DC
US offices: 5
International offices: 2
First-year salary: $180,000
Billable hours: 2,000 required
Summers 2017: 21 (20 2Ls, 1 1L)
Revenue 2016: $434.3 million (+19.6%)
Partners made in 2017: 6 (all US)
Famous for: DC powerhouse; rubber ducks; amenable culture

Government expertise is just one of many draws for associates at this relatively young, multi-office DC institution.

"I WANT us to be different," Crowell's chair since 2015, Angela Styles, emphasizes to us. *"A lot of law firms seem to consider younger lawyers as commodities, not focusing on their careers. I want young associates to understand the business of law from day one."* She helps interview on campus herself and makes an effort to spend time with junior lawyers – *"I want to build careers with them."* One outcome of a nurturing culture is lower attrition, as one associate observed: *"Several partners, counsel and associates have been here a long time, and that's rare."*

Crowell has tried to do things a little differently ever since a group of lawyers broke away from the now-ginormous Jones Day in 1979 to set up this firm. As it continues to grow, some juniors highlighted tension between the better lifestyle associated with a newer, smaller firm and traditional BigLaw expectations. On the one hand, the billing target rose from 1,900 to 2,000 hours in 2016, following a Cravath-matching salary hike to $180,000 for first-years. On the other, associates tell us every year how much they appreciate a degree of *"flexible working"* which *"promotes diversity. The traditional law firm model of working ridiculously long hours is outdated and not sustainable."* One felt that Crowell *"is not a lifestyle firm,*

and I don't think it ever was, but there was a time when it wasn't as much of a big dog. Are we one of the big firms and do we want to play on that level? It's a good problem to have!"*

In 2016, Crowell closed two of its domestic offices (Anchorage and Cheyenne). Nevertheless, the firm enjoyed a super-successful year financially, with revenue shooting up almost 20% and partner profits jumping $412,000 to $1.45 million.

The Work & Offices

Well known for government contracts work, Crowell also secures excellent *Chambers USA* rankings in areas including litigation, white-collar crime, environment, healthcare, insurance, and transportation. Cyber security is a growing department, and crosses over into several of the firm's older practices. Most new associates head to the DC HQ, with the rest spread around four other offices: New York, LA, San Fran, and Orange County (although the smallest branches take juniors infrequently). Overseas, Crowell is in London and Brussels.

On arrival, associates are assigned to two departments from their list of preferences: *"As a young associate who doesn't know what they want to do yet, this really attracted me,"* a DC source enthused. Groups most populated by juniors are antitrust, commercial litigation, government contracts, and white-collar defense & regulatory enforcement. Juniors also go to practices including energy, envi-

On chambers-associate.com...

- More tips on getting hired
- Interview with chair Angela Styles
- A brief history of the Crowell & Moring ducks

See firm profile on p.588

Rankings in *Chambers USA*

Antitrust
Climate Change
Corporate/M&A
Energy & Natural
   Resources
Environment
Government

Healthcare
Insurance
Intellectual Property
International Trade
Litigation
Transportation

For detail on ranking tiers and ranking locations, visit
www.chambersandpartners.com

Recent work highlights

- Defending Blue Cross and Blue Shield in multi-district antitrust proceedings
- NRG Yield (Crowell client) acquired a 75% interest in a portfolio of 12 wind facilities from NRG Energy for $210 million
- Representing Bob Daisley in suit against Ozzy Osbourne, seeking $2 million in unpaid royalties
- Government contracts matters in relation to the split of Hewlett-Packard Co. into Hewlett Packard Enterprise and Hewlett Packard Inc.

ronment & natural resources, IP, healthcare, corporate, international trade, cyber security, tax, and advertising & product risk management. Each department has a staffing partner who assigns work based on associates' self-penned availability reports. *"That's the formal system,"* an associate explained, *"but a lot of work comes from people you know and have worked with before."* Another added: *"I feel I have control over what type of work I do, and that's important to me."*

"I feel I have control over what type of work I do."

The firm's government contracts group and those with a regulatory focus like advertising are centered on DC. The department primarily focuses on bid protests, where aggrieved contractors challenge the outcome of federal procurement process before the Government Accountability Office or Court of Federal Claims. It offers a fascinating peek into the murky world intersection of the public and private sectors. Juniors liked that *"Crowell does a good job of getting associates involved early,"* and *"from my first year I was interacting with clients."*

In antitrust and litigation, associates said they worked with larger companies, including *Fortune* 50 clients, so had less client contact – but *"that's just the nature of the work."* They got more client exposure on smaller cases where they *"slide up in responsibility"* and develop *"at a pace that isn't overwhelming."* Legal research, drafting and *"writing substantial portions for a case"* are par for the course in litigation teams. Juniors highlighted that regular cross-office staffing helps remove any sense of being in a *"satellite office"* for those outside DC. *"I've worked with attorneys from Orange County, San Francisco, and DC, and have been to these offices myself,"* one pointed out. Across the board, associates felt the responsibility they were given was appropriate to their level: *"A little bit more responsibility than you can handle is the perfect level because it forces you to be sharp. Sometimes it can be stressful, but what job isn't?"*

IP sources in DC found themselves doing tasks like *"writing briefs and memos"* but also *"liaising between our firm and the particular client. It was awesome for a junior associate to do that – it's unheard of in most firms!"* There's also a rising popularity to do IPRs – a condensed form of litigation in which *"everything moves quickly."* Corporate associates spoke of doing the usual due diligence, preparing reports, and *"drafting and editing provisions of agreements."* One felt that *"the person who brings in the deal is the heart of the deal – I just help out where I can, but I'm definitely an integral part of the process."* Excitingly for white-collar crime associates, there are often meetings with the Department of Justice and FBI: *"It's fun to get out from behind the desk!"*

Training and Development

Training for summer associates includes the opportunity to do a mock deposition, with feedback from a partner. For incoming first-years, formal training involves an orientation followed by practice area-specific bootcamps. *"It involves some legal training, but also some business training on how the firm actually works,"* a DC associate described. From then on it's about learning on the job, though *"you're never thrown in to cope by yourself. They allow you to learn things thoroughly from the ground up."*

"Learn things thoroughly from the ground up."

Associates were eager to mention a 'trial academy' that the firm organizes for third-years and up. It's a one-week intensive trial advocacy training program that you have to be nominated to do. *"You do a whole trial in one week, with the partners as the judges. It's the craziest work week, with people coming to DC from all offices."*

Pro Bono

Associates are required to bill at least 50 pro bono hours each year, but with the recent rise in billing hours, the firm has put a new policy in place and now has no cap on pro bono hours. *"In theory you could bill 500 hours to*

Diversity	Partners (%)	Associates (%)
Women	24	55
White	90	67
Black/African American	4	9
Hispanic/Latin American	2	5
Asian	4	17
Mixed/Other	2	1
LGBT	2	2

pro bono!" one associate exclaimed. Cases have included criminal defense, landlord and tenancy matters, and immigration cases, such as *"procuring a visa for an undocumented Polish immigrant who needed a specific visa for women who have been victims of crime."* There's also a full-time pro bono partner, Susan Hoffman, who helps coordinate this.

Pro bono hours
- For US attorneys: 35,855
- Average per US attorney: 78

Hours & Compensation

Associates are paid in lockstep, which helps to eliminate any competition between attorneys. But it's the salary rise that's been the talk of the town at Crowell recently. The firm's starting salary has gone up to $180,000. Associates were all happy with this, but expressed some concern about the increased billable hour target (2,000 up from 1,900): *"If you're in one of the big groups like government contracts or antitrust then there's no real worry, but if you're in one of the slower groups it might be tougher. Some people worry that it will make things more cutthroat with people trying to make sure they have enough work to do,"* one associate thought. But for many, the rise won't make much difference: *"People who consistently hit 1,900 will have no problem hitting the new target. It will be a good indicator of where people are. For me, there's a new found motivation to do even better."*

Culture

"The founders wanted to break away from 'big firm culture' and that's still prevalent. Old partners have left, but that doesn't mean the culture has changed," explained a DC associate. *"We're a big firm, but we don't act like it."* A shining example of this is Crowell's famous rubber ducks. Legend has it that someone placed a rubber duck in DC office's fountain soon after it was installed. Many more have appeared since then. *"They're like the calling card of the firm,"* an associate laughed, *"and a nice segue into the history of the firm."* The firm looks for people with a sense of humor, according to associates: *"Down to earth,*

not too formal, but hard working. After all, you want to sit with people who you enjoy working with."

"We're a big firm, but we don't act like it."

Juniors have noticed a slight difference in culture between offices and departments, but a lot of it comes down to size: *"In the LA offices there are about 30 attorneys, so everyone is pretty tight. DC feels much bigger, simply because it is!"* DC associates similarly observed that *"some bigger groups have some pride in their group, so there's a little separation there, but I wouldn't overstress that. I know a lot of people around the office and we socialize to an extent."* All staff are invited to happy hours, not just attorneys. The Christmas parties are a highlight for many – an associate told us how *"the leader of our practice group traditionally calls bingo every year."*

Diversity

"Crowell is better than most of its peers," one associate said of diversity, *"but the industry as a whole has a lot of work to do in that area."* Others praised gender diversity, pointing to the female firm chair, Angela Styles. A Women's Attorney Network regularly meets up and put on events like *"'Making Partner 101', where a panel of women – including one on the managing board, two that had recently been promoted to partner, and two on the promotions committee – discussed the unique challenges that women face in the industry. It was really well attended. Women want to answer these questions, but you have to ask."* For other diversity matters there's a diversity council, which *"really has an invested interest in someone's career."* One lawyer told us: *"I'm a minority here, and diversity is kind of there. I'm not worried about it."*

"Really beefing up our national brand."

Strategy & Future

Firm chair Angela Styles tells us the plan going forward is *"really beefing up our national brand, while making sure we have international capacity."* The firm's HQ goes toe-to-toe with other big DC firms, so *"now we're focused on expanding that to New York and California."* The real aim, Styles tells us, *"is to make sure companies know who we are, know what we're good at, and come to us."* Find our full interview with Angela Styles online.

Get Hired

DC associates tell us that *"beyond credentials, they have to have the 'Crowell personality'."* Find out what that is, and more about getting hired at chambers-associate.com

See firm profile on p.588

Curtis, Mallet-Prevost, Colt & Mosle

Lawyers per state

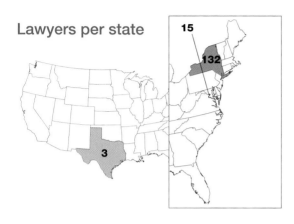

Largest US office: New York
US offices: 3
International offices: 14
First-year salary: $180,000
Billable hours: 2,000 target
Summers 2017: 9 (7 2Ls, 2 1Ls)
Revenue 2016: $177 million (+16.8%)
Partners made in 2017: 4
Famous for: expertise in international arbitration work

Fascinating international work is on offer here to the small intake of associates.

BEFORE you speak to anyone here, you should know it's not pronounced 'mallet' (as in hammer) but the more sophisticated 'malay'. But this is where comparisons with a clumsy tool end: when sovereign nations, governments or international corporations clash across borders, a delicate hand is needed to negotiate tense international arbitrations when so much is at stake. This is the firm's forte. Founded way back in 1830, the firm quickly expanded abroad and its 14 international offices today make this moderately sized New Yorker disproportionately global. Less conventional locations – like Astana and Ashgabat – join global financial centers like London and Dubai in the current office roster, and 2016 saw the addition of Geneva. The work in NY is usually international, though less so in litigation and tax. Some form of worldly knowledge is almost ubiquitous among associates, whether through travel experience or speaking a second language.

Curtis takes a refined approach to hiring, bringing in a select group of around ten associates each year. They gleefully told us they *"didn't want to join a giant and didn't want to get lost in the shuffle."* Hiring partner Carl Ruggiero explains that *"we're able to invest a lot more in*

the people who come here because of that." A strong dose of early responsibility for associates proves his point.

The Work

Although opportunities do occasionally crop up in groups like trusts & estates and restructuring & insolvency, the vast majority of Curtis' fresh faces splits between the 'corporate international' and litigation teams. In corporate there is an assigning partner, but newbies we spoke to felt it was more *"self directed – you go out and find the work you want to do."* This system means associates can experience everything on offer, including M&A, IP, investment management, securities, funds, and international arbitration, or commit to a more focused approach. *"If you wanted to do only funds and they like you there, then you could do just that."* But in changing it up, associates found partners *"very accommodating."* Corporate are big on client contact from day one. One associate recalled a *"positive"* experience *"being the only person on the call as a first-year. It was only a minor agreement and the partner was sitting in on it, but I was the only one talking – it did feel a bit sink or swim."*

> *"I was the only one talking – it did feel a bit sink or swim."*

Significantly, Curtis' esteemed international arbitration practice falls into the corporate bracket. Cases here are *"pretty leanly staffed,"* so associates happily reported having *"daily communications with partners."* As you might

On chambers-associate.com...

- More on Curtis' international arbitration work for nation states
- We talk to hiring partner Carl Ruggiero and get more insight from associates on hiring

The Inside View

See firm profile on p.589

Rankings in *Chambers USA*

International Arbitration	Tax
International Trade	

For detail on ranking tiers and ranking locations, visit www.chambersandpartners.com

expect, *"most of the matters are staffed across either the DC office or offices around the world."* Associates could look back on a strong variety of work: *"Drafting submissions, incidental correspondence or provisional measures. You also coordinate document production and assist in the preparation for hearings. And I've drafted the opening statement for the cross-examination of a witness."*

By contrast, the litigation group's clients and concerns are largely homegrown. Work assignment is also a *"more formal"* affair, where the assigning partner holds the cards. This drew the complaint that some partners *"reserve certain associates to have them on call,"* limiting which matters can be accessed. It's a broad group, though, with securities, commercial litigation and some arbitration on offer – *"a generalist department, to be honest."* Some *"fairly tedious"* doc review features, but associates assured us that *"you can do whatever you are capable of. Nobody gives you your tasks based on your class year."* They progressed to *"drafting motions and briefs"* and *"preparing witness statements,"* though *"the training wheels were definitely on to start with – the firm keeps a vigilant eye on your work."*

Training & Development

Associates were pleased with their level of client contact and regular partner interaction. *"It's a case of just diving in and hoping for the best, but everyone is cognizant that's what you're doing."* For support, juniors looked to their peers, *"going into each other's offices if you have a question. They'll share whatever experience they have with you."* They also lauded their partner mentors as *"a great tool to get close with one partner and to build a strong relationship."*

"I don't crave the formal experience."

Regarding organized training, *"it's impossible to exhaustively cover everything, but they do a good job."* First, basic subjects are covered like *"legal research and writing"* or *"how to use online research tools."* Then practice groups take up the mantle. *"Every month litigation has a breakfast meeting. They vary: some update the team on cases we're working on, and others are just training."* Interviewees generally preferred *"learning on the job. I don't feel I'm hanging out to dry, I don't crave the formal experience."* They did, however, lament a lackadaisical approach to formal reviews. There is one per year, but *"if feedback comes it's normally more informal and ad hoc."*

Recent work highlights

- Represented Venezuela in an arbitration worth $31.7 billion, which was initiated by subsidiaries of Conoco Phillips. The firm eliminated one-third of a claim of damages over the alleged expropriation of petroleum projects
- Defends India in an arbitration brought by Deutsche Telecom regarding the annulment of a contract in order to reserve S-band frequencies for national security
- Defends the Vietnam Association of Shrimp Exporters in the annual reviews carried out by the Commerce Department regarding an anti-dumping duty on frozen shrimp
- Represented salad-maker CHOPT over its sale and the issuance of new equity to investors including Catterton, a private equity firm

Pro Bono

Associates who'd done pro bono spoke enthusiastically about it – including the opportunity of *"getting experience in front of a judge."* The fact that pro bono counts hour-for-hour toward associates' billable hours target serves as further incentive. Nevertheless, some sources hadn't done any at all: *"I would like to do pro bono, but I don't feel I have had time to do it,"* was one typical response. While the firm sends out opportunities to get involved, associates stressed that *"nobody tells you to do it, but it's there if you want it."* Some felt certain partners simply prioritized billable work, or that working on larger billable cases made it impossible to find the time for pro bono. Ultimately, it is *"up to you to seize the initiative. It's up to the associate to get all of the work done. You make it fit because you want to do it."*

Pro bono hours

- For all US attorneys: 3,456
- Average per US attorney: 26

"You make it fit because you want to do it."

Diversity

"I do think it's diverse, but more because of our international practice than because of an active desire to recruit diverse associates," one representative interviewee believed. *"From my end, seeing who comes in, everyone seems pretty similar."* Well informed associates acknowledged the firm's good showing in diversity awards and rankings, but maintained that *"it's one of our biggest faults. We have very few African-American attorneys, a lot of female associates but very few female partners."* Besides *"a women's initiative, where we meet every month to talk about women in law,"* interviewees couldn't think of any other diversity initiatives.

See firm profile on p.589

Diversity	Partners (%)	Associates (%)
Women	10.5	38.5
White	81	71
Black/African American	3.5	3
Hispanic/Latin American	12	14.5
Asian	1.75	10
Mixed/Other	1.75	1.5
LGBT	5	1.5

Offices

Junior associates reside in New York. *"The location is great. It's a giant building in front of Grand Central so it's really easy to get to. The actual offices are pretty classic, they're not modern, they're formally decorated."* Others described the space as *"comfortable and warm."* A renovation is nearly finished, but it's nothing revolutionary: *"They're doing it in the exact same color!"* If the surrounds weren't reassuring and unchanging enough, most associates also share an office for around three years.

Culture

Despite its long list of foreign offices, we were reminded by associates that *"it's a fairly small firm in terms of New York BigLaw."* This fosters *"a tight camaraderie"* and ensures *"you don't get lost amongst hundreds of people."* Within practice groups, *"you say hi, you talk about politics and sports,"* but some felt that an air of formality ruled proceedings. Interviewees put this down to the *"offices not being modern or open plan,"* and *"people approaching work fairly seriously."* Undoubtedly *"it's pretty far from a Google or Facebook environment,"* but that's fairly symptomatic of NY law firms.

"If you push to get questions answered they won't hide anything."

The firm's long history is unavoidable – the firm wrote a book on the subject – but most antiquated ideas left long ago. It's still a little tight-lipped on business developments for some associates, but *"the partnership is responsive if you ask what's going on. If you push to get questions answered they won't hide anything."* A formal dress code was the most evident archaic rite. It's *"suits and ties every day* [for male associates] *except for Fridays, when you don't have to wear a tie – but you should still have one with you!"*

Chances to dress down aren't *"super-regular."* Instead, *"probably once a month there is some sort of firm spon-*sored meet-up or activity."* The firm also gets together when people join or leave the firm, for the Christmas period, or for summer events where people might *"play some pool or go bowling."* Be in no doubt, this is *"a tight-knit group,"* but *"many people come to work, are friendly to one another, then go home and have their friends outside of work."*

Hours & Compensation

"In law, there are gonna be times when your hours suck, that's just the reality of life," said one straight-talking associate. *"But here they suck the way you want them to suck. If you prefer coming in late and working late at night you can do it, as long as the work gets done."* Though weekends weren't quite sacred, with *"six or seven-day weeks"* cropping up occasionally, associates for the most part found these periods to be predictable. As recompense for going through the mill, we heard talk of the odd afternoon off work. Otherwise 6.30pm was a typical home time when the going was good.

The 2,000 billable hours target is *"easily achievable,"* most told us. Those 2,000 hours can include things like pro bono work and business development. The salary received no complaints as *"Curtis just moved to the market rate for the first four years. So I'm happy for the foreseeable future!"* But the bonuses received some complaints having been below market in 2015.

Get Hired

Interviewees told us the firm is *"particularly interested in people with international experience and foreign language skills,"* but equally high on the list was *"someone who's a hard worker, is diligent, but is also pleasant to be around, and not super-arrogant."* For the full interview with partner Carl Ruggiero, and more on recruitment, go to our write-up on Curtis on chambers-associate.com.

Strategy & Future

Associates adeptly assessed the firm as *"not static, but it is conservative. It opens its offices based on a clear need for them, not just for the sake of growing."* Another remarked that *"we're not suddenly going to have a new practice."* Those aboard this steady ship were reassured that *"most partners are people who started here and came up through the ranks."* Keeping that up, the firm promoted eight partners in the US this year, and HP Carl Ruggiero tells us *"we are looking for people making a career."*

"We are looking for people making a career."

See firm profile on p.589

Davis Polk & Wardwell LLP

Lawyers per state

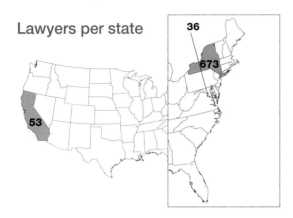

Largest US office: New York

US offices: 3

International offices: 7

First-year salary: $180, 000

Billable hours: no requirement

Summers 2017: 132 (126 2Ls, 6 1Ls)

Revenue 2016: $1.18 billion (+7.3%)

Partners made in 2017: 11 globally (10 in US)

Famous for: over 150 years of New York heritage; polite culture; capital markets and M&A prowess

Big egos don't make the cut at this New York corporate law titan.

ONE of the oldest New York firms, Davis Polk has acquired a formidable reputation for market-leading M&A, credit and capital markets work. Operating out of ten offices across the US, Europe, Latin America and Asia, this *Chambers USA* top-ranked firm advises on vast corporate and financial transactions for some of the world's highest-paying clients. Recently the firm helped mastermind the largest foreign acquisition by a Chinese firm ever recorded, advising Swiss seed giant Syngenta on its $43 billion acquisition by ChemChina. But there's more to DP than just mega deal-making. The litigation team makes up some 30% of the firm's workload, and is particularly big on antitrust and enforcement matters.

> *"The training opportunities and resume fodder here are unprecedented!"*

This prestige is a big draw for rookies. *"Every day you're exposed to market-leading work, brought in by market-leading professionals,"* marveled one junior associate. *"The training opportunities and résumé fodder here are unprecedented!"* The negative connotations of 'white-shoe' have long gone, associates told us: *"Davis Polk remains a cordial and respectful environment to work in,"* they pointed out. *"I'd heard it was a stuffy white-shoe firm, but that's just not the case. Sure, people take their work very seriously, expectations are high and the hours are long. But*

On chambers-associate.com...

- Tips on getting hired by Davis Polk
- Interview with managing partner Tom Reid

everyone here is willing to pull their weight for the good of the team. You'll not find many big egos here."

The Work

During the summer program, new starters have the option to sample work from across Davis Polk's corporate, litigation and tax departments. *"It's helpful to have that flexibility,"* one interviewee reflected. *"It limits the chance of any 'grass is greener' type situations arising."* Around two-thirds join the corporate department, which is split into sub-groups including capital markets, financial institutions, M&A, credit transactions, insolvency & restructuring, and executive compensation. Corporate juniors get the opportunity to have a shot at one, two, or occasionally three different areas before settling down, thanks to a six-month rotation system. *"Our intake is huge, so if there's a group you really want to try out then you have to be willing to fight for it,"* said one deal-doer. *"Talk to partners, ask questions. Don't be afraid to be the squeaky wheel!"*

Serving clients in the private, public, blue-chip and private equity sphere, rookies in the M&A team begin by taking on more *"menial"* bureaucratic tasks. *"The point of this is to get you familiar with deal structures and protocol,"* we heard. *"After nailing the basics you'll get to work on due diligence reports, and draft documentation under supervision."* Over in the financial institutions group (FIG), juniors help both foreign and domestic banks to meet US regulatory requirements. *"We regularly advise financial institutions on how best to navigate the Dodd-Frank Act,"* juniors explained, *"so there's plenty of research*

See firm profile on p.590

The Inside View

Rankings in *Chambers USA*

Antitrust	Financial Services
Banking & Finance	Regulation
Bankruptcy/Restructuring	International Trade
Capital Markets	Investment Funds
Corporate Crime &	Latin American Investment
Investigations	Litigation
Corporate/M&A	Media & Entertainment
Employee Benefits &	Private Equity
Executive Compensation	Securities
Environment	Tax
FCPA	

For detail on ranking tiers and ranking locations, visit
www.chambersandpartners.com

Recent work highlights

- Advised Syngenta on its $43 billion acquisition by ChemChina
- Helped GE sell most of its financing arm, GE Capital, in a spate of transactions valued at over $50 billion
- Defeated an investor lawsuit alleging that Facebook's underwriters improperly earned $100 million in short-swing profits following the social network's 2012 IPO

The Menlo Park office takes on a handful of entry-level associates each year. The Western spur *"is a little more independent in that it takes on work that reflects the Bay Area's client base,"* Tom Reid continues. *"It mainly helps high-tech clients with IP litigation, capital markets work, IPOs and M&A, things like that."*

"New York and DC are joined at the hip."

Elsewhere, the firm has attorneys in Beijing, Hong Kong, London, Madrid, Paris, São Paulo and Tokyo. Both summer associates and associates have the opportunity to spend time abroad.

about regulations, rules and laws to get stuck into." FIG used to be one of our smaller corporate groups, but *"in the wake of the financial crisis its profile exploded."* Juniors here seemed excited to be a part of it all: *"The only other firms that represent Wall Street at this level are perhaps Cleary and Sullivan & Cromwell,"* thought one.

"Don't be afraid to be the squeaky wheel!"

M&A, credit and capital markets may be where the firm made its name, but with around 25% of beginners entering the litigation department, it's a bigger taker than any of the corporate sub-groups. As you might expect, corporate and financial litigation crops up regularly, though associates also have the opportunity to get involved in areas such as antitrust, white-collar crime, securities, bankruptcy, and international arbitration. Juniors here were delighted with the opportunities they'd been extended: *"I operate more as a fourth-year,"* one beamed. *"They throw you in at the deep end but seniors are there with the rope if you need it!"* Our sources had been busy preparing briefs, working on pre-merger filings, and even counseling clients directly.

Offices

At home, Davis Polk has offices in New York, DC and Menlo Park, California. Occupying 25 stories in midtown Manhattan, the Big Apple HQ is a full-service shop welcoming some 160-ish juniors each year. According to managing partner Tom Reid, *"New York and DC are joined at the hip, as the practices there link closely with our practices here in New York. DC mainly focuses on three regulatory areas – financial regulation, antitrust and enforcement. For our clients in New York to know that we have a presence in those areas in DC is a big selling point."* DC takes on one or two first-years each year.

Training & Development

With such a large New York intake, juniors got the impression that *"as much as we're all employed to work at Davis Polk, the reality is that most of us won't make partner here."* Davis Polk hires well over 100 junior associates each year, and only a handful of people make partner. Still, juniors were far from disheartened. *"Lots of people come here because it provides you with a brilliant launchpad for your career,"* said one. *"It's a strong brand that gets junior associates involved in sophisticated work. Once you are four or five years into your career, plenty of attractive opportunities start cropping up."*

"A brilliant launchpad for your career."

In DC, *"many people have long-term plans to work for the government at some stage in their career. I think the firm understands the attraction of making policy rather than enforcing or complying with it, and there have been several cases of people heading into public service for an extended period before returning to the firm later in their careers."*

Regardless of where they end up, all starters begin their Davis Polk careers by congregating in the Big Apple for Lawyering 101: an initial week of orientation where new starters cover the office essentials such as computer training, document management training and billing. Skills sessions also feature, honing fundamentals of good lawyering like time management, formatting and compliance matters. Lawyering 101 is followed every second

See firm profile on p.590

Diversity	Partners (%)	Associates (%)
Women	19	43
White	88	67
Black/African American	1	5
Hispanic/Latin American	4	5
Asian	7	21
Mixed/Other	0	2
LGBT	2	8

year by Lawyering 301 and Lawyering 501. Corporate juniors on rotation receive six-monthly partner reviews, and those more firmly rooted attend annual check-ups.

Most sources were happy with the opportunities they'd had to find their feet in the meantime: *"Obviously partners and senior associates are incredibly busy people, so if you ask them for feedback on something you've drafted they may not have the time to sit down and talk it all through in extensive detail,"* one junior reasoned. *"Still, most will at the very least mark it up so you can see what you could improve upon next time round."* Juniors had also found that *"it's worth reaching out to other members of the department with questions and queries, if your supervisor is busy or out of the office. I've sent out mass emails when I've been stuck and I've immediately received four or five responses with solutions and examples to help me out."*

Pro Bono

Pro bono is also a good way to notch up some valuable experience. The firm doesn't set a minimum requirement, but most of our sources had a few stories to tell. *"You can bill as many pro bono hours as you want,"* one junior told us. *"Once you're on a matter you can list the amount of hours you've put in on your weekly workload report. Staffing partners will then factor it into next week's schedule in the same way as they'd do for any billed work. If you're busy on a pro bono case, that's really respected."*

In NYC, juniors had helped push clemency petitions for federal prisoners, taken on criminal defence cases, assisted non-profits in sorting their foundational documents, and lent their skills to immigration petitions. The latter also crops up regularly in the Menlo Park office, where alongside eviction hearings, associates had knuckled down on plenty of U visa cases for juveniles and victims of domestic abuse.

Pro bono hours
- For all US attorneys: 40,676
- Average per US attorney: 45

Culture

In our last few *Chambers Associate* features, DP has always been praised for its collaborative and supportive internal environment. This continues to be the case, with one insider confirming: *"Professionally there is a hierarchy, but socially it is very casual. I feel comfortable talking to partners, and don't feel that I need to act differently with them than I do with those who I summered with. The firm stages a lot of social and professional events – formal dinners, happy hours, auctions etc – which give you a good opportunity to get to know people at the firm, but really there's very little pressure to take part if you don't want to."*

As one of the world's top law firms, it's quality of work that can really help put your name on people's radar. *"Davis Polk is a place where you are objectively assessed based on the product you are delivering,"* another junior added. *"We're all here to do a job, and you don't have to conform to any arbitrary social conventions to meet those professional expectations."*

Hours & Compensation

With no billing target, bonuses are lockstep based on seniority. Sources commended this system for creating a working environment where *"there's an appreciation from the top that there's a lot more to this job than just billing hours. A lot of non-billable work – presenting to clients, analyzing rules and regulations for a newsletter, things like that – could open the door for future billed business. By not setting a formal billing target, the firm acknowledges that our value isn't just in making numbers."*

"A lot more to this job than just billing hours."

Eleven hour days in New York compare to Menlo Park's ten hour norm, though respondents from both offices conceded that *"on busy stretches you could easily be here for most of the night."* Consequently *"you need to be pretty motivated to work here, and it's important to like what you're doing."* Still, *"seniors aren't afraid to show their appreciation when you've billed long hours,"* rewarding associates with lunches, dinners and thankful emails. *"I remember one partner bringing in masseuses when things were really crazy,"* one FIG associate laughed. *"There were dozens of us working as hard as was humanly possible, and that gesture really made a big difference in getting us through the home stretch."*

Strategy & Future

"It's really been a terrific year," managing partner Tom Reid tells us. The firm's *"diversified"* business model has been key to this continued success: *"Obviously we have a strong US presence, but it's worth noting that around 10%*

See firm profile on p.590

of our work comes out of Asia, and another 10% comes from Europe. In terms of our practices, I'd say that about 30% of our work is litigious, whereas the corporate and tax department – which encompasses the likes of M&A, capital markets, financial regulation and leveraged finance – makes up the other 70%. Over the last 12 months all of those practices have been at the top of their game, often working hand-in-hand to secure incredible results for our clients."

Happy with the state of affairs, Reid doesn't expect Davis Polk to steer from its current course too dramatically in the near future. "I don't envisage there being any large-scale strategic growth projects. We're happy with the firm's current size, and we see ourselves growing gradually from here onwards. There are growth opportunities across the board that we intend to capitalize on, but in terms of the business model I don't anticipate there being many proportional shifts."

Diversity

"The idea of someone being treated differently because of their race, gender or sexuality is unthinkable," attorneys agreed. Like most BigLaw firms, "there's plenty of work to do to get our numbers to where they need to be," but sources were confident that "management recognizes this is an issue, and is making resources available to improve the balance going forward." A "wide spectrum" of diversity groups regularly stages events, "which helps ensure that minority issues are an ongoing discussion." Our interviewees had attended diversity dinners, seminars, and even theater visits, and were pleased to report that "the events are open to all."

Entry-level recruitment was stressed as a key focus in balancing the books in the coming years. "We may be a white-shoe firm, but our summer program doesn't just fast-track Yale and Harvard graduates," one junior explained. "The firm is making a big effort to reach out to other schools. We need brilliant people with cutting-edge skills, and there's a real appreciation that by interviewing at a wide range of law schools we'll be able to hire an associate class with a diverse range of skills and personalities."

> "The idea of someone being treated differently because of their race, gender or sexuality is unthinkable."

The Inside View

See firm profile on p.590

Debevoise & Plimpton LLP

Lawyers per state

Largest US office: New York
US offices: 2
International offices: 7
First-year salary: $180,000
Billable hours: no requirement
Summers 2017: 78 (72 2Ls, 6 others)
Revenue 2016: $735 million (-3%)
Partners made in 2017: 7
Famous for: polite culture ("the nice firm"); West Wing mentions

Polite people praised distinguished Debevoise's considerate culture.

IN a profession where firms live and die by their standing, *"Debevoise has the reputation of being the gentleman of BigLaw firms,"* associates here reminded us. *"It's all about a culture of lawyers treating each other with respect and politeness."* Combine that image with top-tier work, and it's easy to see why the firm sits at the top table of the New York legal scene. Founded at the height of the art deco period in the 1930s, this sleek outfit is perhaps still thought of as 'white-shoe', although that label has fallen out of fashion in recent years. In 2016, the modern Debevoise opened a Tokyo office, cementing Japanese client relationships going back decades. London is the firm's second largest office after New York, and there are six other overseas bases within this prestigious network.

A legacy initially built on private equity funds work led associates to reassure us that *"we're still a PE shop,"* but that's far from the full story. While Debevoise certainly excels in private equity fund formation (achieving a top ranking from *Chambers USA*), other highly regarded practices include litigation, M&A, white collar crime, insurance, media & entertainment, IP, real estate, and sports law. The deal-clincher for associates deciding which firm to join, however, was Debevoise's *"culture of*

co-operation and openness, where everyone is helping each other. It resonated with me during recruitment and it has proved true."

The Work

The New York office takes nearly all the firm's first-years, though several start out in Debevoise's Washington, DC base. Most associates tend to head into corporate or litigation with a handful slotting into tax (which includes employee benefits). There's also a cyber security group which utilizes both litigators and corporate juniors when needed. Both the larger groups offer two ways of acquiring work: either staffing partners will assign you work or you can solicit work directly from partners.

Corporate rookies head straight into one sub-group, which they switch for another at the end of their first year. Crunch time arrives at the start of the third year when they must choose their permanent area from the two they've experienced, or head into a third they haven't tried. (They spend longer in their first rotation to allow for a period of acclimatization.) On offer are: M&A, real estate, capital markets, finance, bankruptcy, investment management, and insurance. Sources appreciated the *"chance to try out a different group and compare, as well as just getting to know the wider team which I'm a part of."*

Juniors cut their teeth on plenty of first drafts in corporate. In investment management *"tasks for a junior like me will include doing the first draft of a letter or of a subscription agreement, perhaps even a small section of the partnership agreement."* Other associates reported re-

On chambers-associate.com...

- Interview with Michael Blair – presiding partner of Debevoise & Plimpton
- Interview with director of legal recruiting Sandra Herbst and Nicole Mesard, chair of the firm's hiring committee

See firm profile on p.591

The Inside View

Rankings in *Chambers USA*

Advertising	Intellectual Property
Banking & Finance	International Arbitration
Bankruptcy/Restructuring	Investment Funds
Capital Markets	Latin American Investment
Corporate Crime &	Litigation
Investigations	Media & Entertainment
Corporate/M&A	Private Equity
Employee Benefits &	Projects
Executive Compensation	Real Estate
Environment	Securities
FCPA	Sports Law
Financial Services	Tax
Regulation	Transportation
Insurance	

For detail on ranking tiers and ranking locations, visit
www.chambersandpartners.com

viewing purchase agreements, but drafting was kept to ancillary documents: closing certificates, resolutions and the like. Associates found due diligence is particularly heavy in M&A – *"something most juniors will have to do"* – but it cropped up in most groups. Others described administrative work, putting together opinions, certificates and closing checklists.

"If you write a summary it doesn't just disappear into the ether."

Litigators start out as generalists for the first two years before specializing in one of the four following areas: general commercial, international dispute resolution, IP, or white-collar crime. Associates described white-collar as being *"mostly doc review"* – a standard junior task. They complimented the department's efforts *"to make sure that your knowledge built up through the doc review has an impact. If you write a summary it doesn't just disappear into the ether; partners will ask you about it and make changes to documents accordingly."* The size of the department means it is *"hierarchical – but they do a great job of keeping you included."*

Training and Development

Newbies from offices around the world begin their time at the firm by flying into New York and attending a mini-MBA course: *"A business education. It's great, they sit you down to learn about financial institutions and the global economy."* This is *"not only incredibly useful for learning certain concepts, but also for getting a sense of who your co-associates are, and building a sense of community."* From then on there's plenty of formal training, and despite it *"feeling very organized,"* some felt *"you will sit down every week or two for some training but it's not as effective as a classroom environment."*

Recent work highlights

- Represented Oaktree Capital Managment in its formation of two private equity funds worth $11 billion in total
- Represented Toyota after an investigation by the Consumer Financial Protection Bureau and Department of Justice over fair lending. It resulted in a payment of $22 million in damages
- Advised the Canada Pension Plan Investment Board as it acquired underwriter Ascot, the Lloyd's platform of American International Group, for $1.1 billion

Litigators appreciated the chance to *"sign up for a mock trial program."*

Like last year, the occasional associate linked the firm's *"nice or genteel"* culture to a *"passive aggressive"* atmosphere surrounding feedback, which one described as *"cold air in the room."* But once again this was not the majority view. *"You read between the lines,"* one explained. *"It's not hard to understand if you need to do something over – you will know exactly why."* Another believed that *"rather than avoiding the truth in any way, I've found we are very honest,"* so *"when something is wrong they are quick to tell you and help you correct it."*

"It's an amazing reason to join."

Overall, associates felt the firm tries *"to make you a great lawyer: They don't just use you up and toss you aside, they want to develop you."* To that end, associates recalled *"coffee meetings with your partner adviser to talk over your career."* Not everyone can be a partner though, and we heard that *"the typical path is to stay for a few years and then go in-house."* Hiring committee chair Nicole Mesard acknowledges *"they maybe don't want to spend their entire career with us"* and feels time spent at the firm sees *"doors open in a different way for them. It's an amazing reason to join."*

Culture

"Respect" was the watchword when it came to culture. *"They have your back, nobody's getting screamed at,"* said one, while another claimed: *"I'm still to find a mean person in the building! Everyone's voice matters. You can speak up and participate by providing your thoughts – it's collaborative."* Interviewees *"didn't feel judged for taking vacation,"* nor were *"partners breathing down your neck."* Ultimately *"saying that you can't handle the amount of work you have isn't frowned upon, it isn't a sign of defeat. People will step in to help and maybe you'll cover them next time in return."*

See firm profile on p.591

The Inside View

Diversity	Partners (%)	Associates (%)
Women	20.8	53
White	89.6	65.8
Black/African American	0.9	7.5
Hispanic/Latin American	3.8	8.8
Asian	4.7	15.7
Mixed/Other	0.9	2.2
LGBT	4.7	6.3

What motivates lawyers here? *"It's very driven and people are intellectually curious. As opposed to being poked and prodded, people want to do their work."* Some might call them *"nerdy"* – *"I personally see it as a badge of honor! We really enjoy our work and we'll dive into difficult, intellectual problems. Our goal is not to speak first, but to get things right."* In summary *"people here aren't just in it for the money or for prestige, they are genuinely interested in the legal issues at play."*

This culture's no product of indoctrination, in fact *"there's very little coaching on it."* Instead *"the ethos we have ema-nates from the leadership. They lead from example: You will see partners working at 1am."* Politeness too *"trick-les down"* from the top. *"I have never hesitated to talk to a partner, despite being awestruck about how much they know sometimes! They aren't mythical creatures locked away somewhere; I have plenty of interactions and every partner has been friendly and down to earth. They share war stories and talk about their personal lives, and we see them with their families at the summer event at Central Park Zoo – they're always willing to talk."* Zoo trips aside, the firm isn't rife with party animals. *"You can find the social stuff if you're looking for it, but it's not a crucial el-ement of getting to know people and being a part of the culture. You don't have to party."*

Get Hired

Since *"the people here aren't really eat-what-you-kill or aggressive,"* associates felt the firm *"really wants team players who will fit in."* Being *"business-savvy"* helps too. Hiring committee chair Nicole Mesard tells us: *"Doors open in many different ways for associates, and it's another compelling reason to join us."* For the full inter-view and more information on recruitment go to chambers-associate.com.

Hours & Compensation

"When you come into BigLaw you expect to work hard, and I've done the late nights and worked at weekends," confessed one associate. *"There are days when I finish at midnight or later and depending on closings, a few all*

nighters too, where you just go home to shower." Hours tend to fluctuate: *"Some circumstances are out of your control, like last-minute requests – there's only so much you can do to protect your nights and weekends."*

"There aren't people breathing down your neck to do X amount of hours."

An associate pointed out that *"I have dialed down my hours when necessary – there aren't people breathing down your neck to do X amount of hours."* Debevoise doesn't apply pressure with any billable hours requirements, and operates a lockstep compensation scheme. *"If you are looking for something to give you direction the unofficial target they set is 2,000 hours, but in the first year nobody is counting hours."* Besides, *"most partners are aware of how much work is going around – as long as you are finding work, how could they be upset?"*

Pro Bono

Pro bono is treated the same as billable hours, ensur-ing the firm bills more pro bono than almost any other US firm. *"Around a quarter of my hours have been pro bono,"* one junior reported. *"A commitment to pro bono was something I looked for, and Debevoise certainly walks the walk."* Indeed, associates felt no pressure to shirk pro bono as *"the firm knows I will get a lot of experience draft-ing briefs through pro bono."*

"Debevoise certainly walks the walk."

A New York-based pro bono coordinator emails out op-portunities, but juniors can *"express an interest in some-thing you've found, and they'll be very receptive."* Matters include asylum cases, death penalty appeals, various things through Volunteer Lawyers for the Arts, securing the lease of a community garden in NY, student debt re-negotiations and helping startups to form LLPs.

Pro bono hours
- For all US attorneys: 66,268
- Average per US attorney: 133

Diversity

Debevoise was shortlisted in the *Chambers Diversity* awards for the 'most pioneering firm for female lawyers'. Associates struck an upbeat note when discussing diver-sity, though our 2017 survey shows fairly average figures for their market: 10.4% of partners are of an ethnic mi-nority and 20.8% are women. *"At the junior and mid levels you can see that there's a lot of progress, but any higher and I think it's unbalanced,"* one junior assessed.

The Inside View

Associates' positivity focused on it being *"tremendously open on diversity."* At a yearly firm dinner *"everyone gets together and the firm talks about where it currently stands on diversity and where our emphasis is going to be placed in the future."* Other initiatives include *"a monthly lunch with the Asian affinity group, which is great for meeting people from other departments. Our lunch for Chinese New Year was one of the best attended events I've seen!"* Affinity groups for other minorities also meet on a monthly basis.

Offices

Associates in New York told us *"the office feels clean and crisp,"* and were fans of the *"fantastic cafeteria."* They set the scene: *"It's in Midtown East and has a view of Central Park. Typically, as a first or second-year, you either get a window room which is shared with another associate or you have an interior room to yourself."* Window or no window, *"it's good to be able to ask dumb questions to your office-mate, or just shoot the breeze."* Also, *"every day from 4pm to 5pm we have a coffee break where they set out coffee and cookies in the cafeteria. Quite often they'll have sports on the TV or there's a Foosball table which people take advantage of."*

With international offices only a phone call or email away, associates felt *"the firm could be better about offering more international opportunities, to go abroad on secondment, or for international conferences."* While it isn't out of the question to go on a working sojourn, *"it wouldn't just be a case of expressing my interest, I would have to jump through hoops. If I wanted to leave NY it could take several years,"* one junior reckoned.

Strategy & Future

Associates were relieved to announce the firm is addressing *"everyone's old complaint"* by *"joining the rest of the world!"* They're *"changing all the technology, swapping out desktops and monitors for new computers."* Despite this, and the expansion into Tokyo, associates perceived Debevoise as a firm holding its course. *"It has a commitment to do what it does excellently, and then looks for opportunities to spread that excellency to new areas."*

> *"We know it's a solid and consistent firm."*

Some grumbles over transparency were evident, but even though associates *"aren't privy to strategic conversations, we know it's a solid and consistent firm which values long-term, steady growth."* And so *"associates are seen as an investment and as an important asset."*

> ## *"Our goal is not to speak first, but to get things right."*

See firm profile on p.591

Dechert LLP

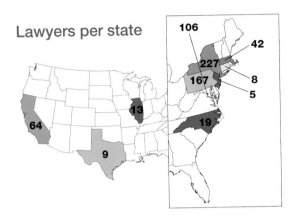

Lawyers per state

106
42
227
167
8
5
13
64
19
9

Largest US office: New York
US offices: 13
International offices: 14
First-year salary: $180,000
Billable hours: 1,950 target
Summers 2017: 46 (42 2Ls, 4 1Ls)
Revenue 2016: $911.6 million (+2.4%)
Partners made in 2017: 5
Famous for: focus on a handful of practice areas; Philly origins

Philadelphia-born and raised, the fresh prince of *"global specialist"* law spends most of its days with massive clients.

BIG firms love to shout from the rooftops about their international prowess, but Dechert's juniors are happy to back up the boasts: *"I feel like we've got a lot of clients who engage the firm because of its expertise across the entire world,"* said one. Another commended Dechert as *"one of the few firms with both a fully fledged Philadelphia office and an international footprint."* This Philly-born go-getter clearly has a taste for global expansion: it's opened 13 new offices since the turn of the millennium, including five in 2012 alone.

CEO Henry Nassau characterizes Dechert with its broad footprint as *"having domain expertise in four or five areas, and we try to stay focused on those. We don't try to be all things to all people."* Our interviewees highlighted *"stellar white-collar and exciting securities litigation practices,"* while *Chambers USA* ranks these and many corporate-related practices, regionally and nationally. Visit chambersandpartners.com and search 'Dechert' for the firm's detailed listings and achievements across the various global *Chambers* guides.

On chambers-associate.com...

- Get hired: Interview tips and tricks
- Interviews with CEO Henry Nassau and hiring partner Jim Lebovitz
- More on Dechert's overseas offices

The Work

Almost all new associates join the litigation, corporate & securities, finance & real estate, or financial services teams. A few go into antitrust, international arbitration or tax, and Silicon Valley gets a cohort of IP juniors. Associates tend to get work initially through a formal assignment method, sending weekly availability reports to practice group coordinators, as *"early on you have less ability to find your own work, because you've got no track record."* After that, it's much more informal: *"If I want to branch out into a new area, I'd just look for that work."*

"We might lead a conference call and directly implement their feedback."

There are, however, variations by practice area: in financial services, associates are *"split into four or five different client teams. It's a pretty good system. The teams are large so if somebody's overworked it's easy to recommend they assign work to somebody else."* Work covers *"every corner of the market,"* split generally into *"mutual and private funds. We represent the funds themselves and independent trustees generally."* The daily grind is to the tune of *"a regular hum of filings and various board memos. We're reviewing client documents, making sure they're compliant with requirements and providing comments."* After a settling-in period, interviewees found climbing the totem pole easy. *"What I like about Dechert is once you gain the trust of someone you move on quickly."* Some third-years even got given *"supervisory work, reviewing more junior*

See firm profile on p.592

Rankings in *Chambers USA*

Antitrust	Labor & Employment
Bankruptcy/Restructuring	Life Sciences
Capital Markets	Litigation
Corporate/M&A	Private Equity
Financial Services	Products Liability
Regulation	Real Estate
Intellectual Property	Securities
Investment Funds	Tax

For detail on ranking tiers and ranking locations, visit
www.chambersandpartners.com

Recent work highlights

- Advised the government of the Republic of Georgia on $2.5 billion Black Sea Deep Water Port Project
- Counseled auctioneers Ritchie Bros on $758 million acquisition of online equipment marketplace IronPlanet
- Represented chemicals giant Dow in $1 billion price-fixing litigation
- Acted for employment website Monster Worldwide in its $429 million sale to recruitment agency Randstad

attorneys," relishing the chance to be the boss at such an early stage.

In corporate, practice group coordinators allocate work initially, though in offices with fewer corporate partners *"it comes more directly from them."* Associates thought *"the good thing about Dechert is we do a little bit of everything,"* including life sciences, capital markets and private equity work. Newcomers inevitably come up against due diligence, but also *"take the first cut at drafting a lot of documents. On the M&A side, ancillary documents outside the merger agreement are the ball in our court."* Associates felt the firm *"wants you to gain more responsibility early on, and gives you tasks so you can get that."* As such, *"there's a lot of direct client contact quickly. We might lead a conference call and directly implement their feedback."* Interviewees took varying work volumes in their stride: *"We always joke about being preconditioned to be nervous wrecks when things aren't busy!"*

Those who fall under the 'general litigation' banner can take on anything for two years, before choosing between either the complex commercial or white-collar and securities group. Initially taking work from both, juniors *"do a lot of legal research and writing memos. There's a lot of document review in the first few years, and as litigation goes forward we do deposition prep and prepare witness kits."* Clients tend to be *"pretty variable, mainly* Fortune 500 *companies."* The firm deals with *"a lot of breach of contract cases and other contractual issues."* As in other areas, juniors found *"the workload ebbs and flows; it's nothing I wouldn't have anticipated. Averaged out, the firm does a pretty good job of giving associates enough interesting work."* Client contact tends to be minimal at first, then

increases with experience, with a big jump around the third year.

"It's nothing I wouldn't have anticipated."

Training & Development

"Very practice group-specific training" includes *"bi-weekly lunch sessions"* for litigators, *"covering the whole litigation process over a year."* Corporate hosts *"annual programs that ping-pong between private transactions one year, public the next,"* while in financial services *"training covers general topics in investment management law."* For the firm as a whole, the monthly Critical Skills Institute program is designed to develop communication, leadership, client relations and management skills, but many felt *"the most valuable thing is Dechert places a large emphasis on individualized instruction and mentoring."* The firm incentivizes exceptional mentors with $10,000 cash rewards.

"Individualized instruction and mentoring."

Formal reviews take place twice a year, for which associates fill out forms that highlight what they've worked on for more than 15 hours, and who with. Partners and seniors then send written evaluations – *"you end up having dozens of reviewers."* When quizzed about the everyday, most juniors felt higher-ups *"take the extra two minutes to give some feedback, so when I go into the reviews I'm not surprised by what I hear."* Some desired more consistency between partners in this regard, but commended senior associates for being *"more likely to provide lengthy feedback"* on a day-to-day basis.

Culture

"What I think is really great is that we are all proud to be at Dechert, but our lives are not just Dechert," was the neat summary provided by one associate we interviewed. Suggesting that *"we don't socialize with co-workers as much as some other big firms, but we're very respectful of each other's time,"* most agreed that *"it's more relaxed when we*

Get Hired

"When I went through OCIs, I over-analyzed my answers and tried to memorize them. The process is getting to know you as a person, not a play-by-play analysis." chambers-associate. com has more tips, and an interview with hiring partner Jim Lebovitz.

See firm profile on p.592

Diversity	Partners (%)	Associates (%)
Women	14.1	42.7
White	92	75.4
Black/African American	2.4	3.3
Hispanic/Latin American	2.8	3.8
Asian	2.4	15.5
Mixed/Other	0.5	2
LGBT	2.8	1.6

At the Chambers Diversity Awards 2016, Dechert was nominated for the pro bono program of the year.

"A big reason why some people end up coming here."

Pro bono hours
- For all US attorneys: 77,671
- Average per US attorney: 103

do have social events because we're not forced to go." These *"relaxed"* events range from Monday breakfasts in Washington, DC (*"it's popular, but a bit grab and go!"*) to a firmwide Hallowe'en costume contest (*"the winning office got an extra happy hour."*) Cultural perceptions varied geographically: a Boston junior thought their smaller team was *"more tight-knit, so things are more relaxed,"* whereas in Chicago *"the culture is different because people here are young and hours-driven."*

"Across the board here, partners are close to associates and try to include them rather than being totally above them." Several interviewees happily trashed the scary BigLaw partner stereotype: *"The Dechert way is to encourage, not scare associates. A great thing here is constant reinforcement that you're fully capable of doing anything – there will be setbacks, but you'll improve."* Though many *"haven't really heard about management decisions until they come down from above,"* others were *"very confident"* in the firm being transparent – opinions differed by office. Several felt *"it's not something I'm concerned about, but my impression is things are going well."*

"We don't socialize as much as some other big firms, but we're very respectful of each other's time."

Pro Bono & Diversity

Juniors gushed about the firm's commitment to pro bono: *"It's a major way that Dechert distinguishes itself, and a big reason why some people end up coming here."* All attorneys are required to devote at least 25 hours to pro bono, and juniors can count up to 200 hours toward their billing target, after which permission is required to count more. But everybody we interviewed reported *"it's really easy to ask for an extension, especially in litigation where everybody goes over 200."* Firm-run pro bono clinics supplement longer-term projects including landlord/tenant work, education hearings and prisoner rights cases. Awards ceremonies celebrate those who go above and beyond, but interviewees didn't need a trophy to feel rewarded. *"You learn a lot about other work from non-profit cases. It has a direct impact on your skills going forward."*

Less overjoyed on the diversity front, associates explained *"it's diverse at junior level, but there's not good representation at the top. That's as good as it gets in BigLaw!"* That said, the two largest offices have female partners running them, while those in smaller offices including Chicago, Los Angeles and Orange County celebrated having an *"incredibly diverse"* workplace, with the caveat that *"the firm as a whole is not so much from what I've seen."* One noted *"a lot of turnover of diverse attorneys, I don't know why,"* but to counteract this Dechert has an array of affinity groups that include Asian, Black, Latino and LGBT groups, and most visibly the Global Women's Initiative. Associates were happy that *"the firm doesn't overemphasize diversity initiatives, it's not in your face. I think it's a good balance of making sure you know where to go, but it's not over the top."*

Hours & Compensation

Reaching the yearly billing target of 1,950 hours makes you bonus-eligible. *"If you hit the total you get a market bonus. There's a chance you can get more for going beyond that but there's no real clarity about how that works."* Juniors thought *"the target's fairly easily achievable when you include the generous pro bono set-up,"* though some went on to say *"you need to take the initiative if your practice area isn't busy all the time."* Most felt that left time for a decent private life: *"If you're in professional services and you make plans before 8pm you might be late, but 1,950 hours at least leaves room to make plans."* Associates get 20 days of vacation a year, and when some didn't take it *"the firm sent out an email saying people weren't using their vacation, encouraging those who hadn't to do so."*

"There was doubt they'd stay committed, but they did."

Dechert matched the new market associate salary scale (starting at $180,000) in all of its offices, which some considered *"a nice surprise."* A minority felt that *"based on the firm's aspirations and who they consider their peers, I thought they'd have matched more quickly,"* but most were simply happy to get paid more. Philadelphia and Princeton associates were particularly chuffed, as they'd only been boosted to the $160,000 scale in spring 2015.

See firm profile on p.592

"Management had then agreed to pay everybody in the US the same. There was doubt they'd stay committed, but they did and carried through on that promise."

Offices & Strategy

Dechert's story began in Philly, but New York juniors implied their base had become the mothership. They enjoyed *"glass walls in very modern, nicely sized offices. There are pretty amazing views of the Empire State Building."* Not to be outdone, Philadelphians declared *"the building is great. It's convenient because we're right next to the station. The only negative is we're not in the center of the city."* First-years normally get their own office, except New Yorkers who share for the first few months. Boston juniors loved being on the *"40th and 41st floors, overlooking Boston harbor,"* while in Los Angeles *"the actual building is okay but the downtown location is perfect."*

> *"You don't need to be rooted in an office to work on something."*

From coast to coast, interviewees felt *"Dechert has done a good job of establishing continuity across offices. Everything is integrated, and communication is one of the great strengths of the firm."* This extended to international col-laboration (for a closer look at Dechert's overseas offices, head to the firm's online profile Bonus Features). One junior characterized it as a *"very nimble approach. You don't need to be rooted in an office to work on something – they find who the best person is."* Financial services, for instance, is practiced by attorneys across the country but mostly coordinated in DC.

CEO Henry Nassau explains: *"With the use of new technologies, we as a firm have evolved to be less focused on where a lawyer is seated, and instead consider where the best lawyer is available. On the East Coast, we frequently staff projects as a collaboration between New York, Philadelphia and DC."* He points to the Big Apple office in particular as a future growth opportunity, and reveals the firm has *"no current plans to open any new offices. We're very focused on where we're going to build out – the next location would likely be Shanghai, but we have a lot of building out to do in Asia."* Find the full interview on chambers-associate.com.

> *"You don't need to be rooted in an office to work on something."*

See firm profile on p.592

DLA Piper LLP (US)

Lawyers per state

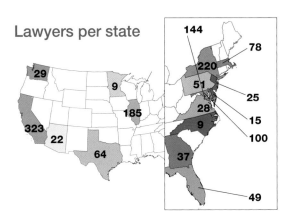

144
78
29
220
9
51
25
185
28
323
15
22
9
100
64
37
49

Largest US office: New York
US offices: 28
International offices: 67 (plus 20 affiliates)
First-year salary: $180,000 in major markets; $160,000 elsewhere
Billable hours: 2,000 target
Summers 2017: 49 (37 2Ls, 12 1Ls)
Revenue 2016: $2.47 billion (-2.9%)
Partners made in 2017: 17
Famous for: global expansion; massive mergers

When a law firm morphs into a global giant, local know-how and a respect for work-life balance can go out of the window – unless you're DLA Piper.

IF you're bored of researching law firms, why not play the game: 'name a movie with a DLA office in the title'? We'll start you off with Casablanca. You get the picture – the firm's big. Of the world's continents, only Antarctica has yet to be conquered by DLA's 100-something offices. The associates we spoke to were drawn almost unanimously to the firm's *"global reach"* and whopping revenue, which fixes DLA in second place on the *Am Law 100*. The reality is that associates get to work with colleagues across the country and the world, with the potential for international travel as well. Juniors were excited about *"handling complex international deals."* But the culture also appealed: *"From speaking to people at DLA who had been here for 20 years or so, it seems this is the kind of place where once you're here they want you to stay. Attorneys here still love their jobs, and love the firm."*

DLA Piper unsurprisingly covers a plethora of practice areas. *Chambers USA* ranks the firm in 16 US states alone, cementing the firm's reputation for local business expertise. But on a nationwide level, the firm also receives plaudits in a broad array of practices, from corporate M&A to international trade to sports law, life sci-

ences, tax, and start-ups. A glance at the rankings – in areas like franchising, privacy or retail – shows a firm with a pronounced sector focus. Juniors themselves can be found most abundantly in litigation, closely followed by corporate, then real estate. After those junior-heavy practices, associates are principally spread among tax, finance, restructuring, IP, and employment.

The Work & Offices

Although the firm spreads its legal wings across several states, the bulk of juniors appear in the New York, Chicago, and Palo Alto offices. DC, Boston, and Baltimore are next in line. At the time of our research, the New York office was preparing for a major renovation, and the Chicago office was in the process of moving to a brand-spanking new office on the Chicago riverside. Other smaller offices have a more relaxing vibe: *"It's in the middle of nowhere,"* a Baltimore junior laughed, *"but there's walking paths, trees, and deer – if you need a break you can take a walk around. I think that contributes to the culture too. Here, we're more chilled than New York or DC."* And this may sound trifling, but all juniors have their own offices with windows – a rarity in BigLaw. The glass doors in the Boston office were met with mixed views: *"it definitely helps create a transparent community. The downside is it's not great if you want to take a nap under your desk!"*

"It's not great if you want to take a nap under your desk!"

See firm profile on p.593

The Inside View

Rankings in *Chambers USA*

Bankruptcy/Restructuring	Life Sciences
Chancery	Litigation
Construction	Outsourcing
Corporate/Commercial	Privacy & Data Security
Corporate/M&A	Products Liability
Franchising	REITs
Government	Real Estate
Healthcare	Retail
IT & Outsourcing	Sports Law
Insurance	Startups & Emerging
Intellectual Property	Companies
International Trade	Tax
Leisure & Hospitality	Technology

For detail on ranking tiers and ranking locations, visit
www.chambersandpartners.com

Recent work highlights

- Provides Dr. Seuss Enterprises with ongoing trademark, copyright, and media advice
- Victory for pharmaceutical giants Pfizer in a product liability litigation about alleged cardiovascular injuries associated with testosterone replacement therapies
- Represented the City of Oakland in a lawsuit filed against the federal government to prevent it from foreclosing the property where the country's largest medical cannabis dispensary conducts its business in compliance with California law
- Defended the Home Depot in a trademark and false endorsement litigation filed by Ernest Evans (aka Chubby Checker) related to the alleged use of the Chubby Checker mark and stage name

The sizable litigation group covers areas from contractual disputes to government investigations, FCPA matters, and professional malpractice in what juniors term *"a large bucket for all things litigation."* Juniors tried their hand at *"accounting malpractice, ponzi schemes, and direct lawsuits"* among other issues. White-collar crime involved more investigatory work, often involving the DOJ and FPC. Juniors reported the classic tasks like legal research, fact development work, as well as prepping witnesses and deposition prep. Other regular tasks included *"producing memos for clients and interviewing various government entities."* Some experienced ample responsibility even on bigger cases when *"there's more managing to be done."* For example, a San Francisco junior *"managed a contract review team that was split between Chicago and San Francisco."* As for support, *"it depends on the personality of the partner I'm working with,"* a litigator explained. *"Some are eager to be mentors. Others are more closed off – but not to the point where I'd feel uncomfortable asking them questions."*

Corporate juniors are spread across most of the country, handling a mix of M&A, private equity and corporate governance issues. Then there are emerging growth specialists who advise startups, investors, and venture capital firms. The average day will no doubt involve some due diligence, doc review, and memo writing, but *"a good thing here is that juniors get a lot of early experience with drafting transactional documents."* Our sources reported *"coordinating with specialists"* and *"direct emails and calls with clients."* A Chicago associate reflected, *"they keep deals pretty leanly staffed which means you have the opportunity to do true substantive work early on."*

The real estate practice takes up around half of the firm's Boston office, but juniors can also be found in New York, North Carolina, and dotted along the West Coast. The transactional side deals with acquisitions, depositions, financing, and leasing, while the development side navigates *"permitting hoops to get permits for clients to build a building from the ground up."* Juniors most commonly work on purchases and sales of real estate usually in their respective cities. Tasks include due diligence, summaries of leases, and drafting purchase agreements. One junior described *"trying to sublet space in a New York office building. I was negotiating with the current tenants and regularly talking to the counsel of the client."* Juniors were happy with the firm's support: *"Everyone here is good about teaching and supervising, but your hand isn't held the whole time."* And when it came to workload and responsibility, a Boston junior enthused that *"it keeps me on my toes. I always feel like I'm being pushed to what I can handle – in a good way!"*

> *"I always feel like I'm being pushed to what I can handle – in a good way."*

Most practice areas adopt a more free-market system of work allocation and *"the global reach of the firm means we could be working with someone in another state, Spain, the UK… anywhere! And thanks to technology it's almost as if you're in the same office!"* Across all the practice areas, juniors agree that *"as you move up they set clear benchmarks that we try to meet each year. With that comes more responsibility or more senior roles on a case, or supervising others."*

Training & Development

"They're open to giving you feedback because they're invested in you and your success." Learn more on chambers-associate.com

Culture

"It's been a good balance between the expectations they have for you as an attorney, and understanding that you're a human and have other things going on," a Baltimore jun-

See firm profile on p.593

Diversity	Partners (%)	Associates (%)
Women	20.6	43.2
White	86.5	73.4
Black/African American	2.2	4.1
Hispanic/Latin American	2.7	1.8
Asian	4.8	14.6
Mixed/Other	1.7	5.8
LGBT	1.3	1.8

ior reflected. At a firm of this breadth and born out of recent mergers, some viewed the culture as *"slightly disjointed."* Glass-half-full types might interpret this as the regional offices retaining their own character, which is typical of a Swiss Verein structure, especially where the firm has strong ties to regional businesses. Then it's perhaps no surprise to hear *"stories about New York and DC being more intense – that's just the nature of those markets."* Nevertheless, everyone agreed that *"there's definitely a firm consensus on striking a work-life balance."* The firm achieves this through allowing a more flexible working system: *"There are people who leave consistently at five to get back to their families, and people understand that. They might sign on later in the evening, but they allow you to have that balance to be a productive individual."*

"They allow you to have that balance to be a productive individual."

A junior in North Carolina declared *"my favorite part about this office is working with such smart people who you can learn from, but are all very approachable."* Associates we spoke to wrongly expected a firm of this scale to be less collaborative and collegial, and many noted the premium the firm places on personality at recruitment. So it's no surprise to hear from a Chicagoan that *"people here are friends, not just co-workers."* Lunches and *"pretty frequent happy hours and get-togethers,"* fill the social calendar, *"but since we all have busy schedules there's a fair amount of stopping in the halls and chatting,"* juniors acknowledge. Many prefer this as *"we're not pressured or required to hang out all the time. Many of us have young families we want to get home to, or a social life outside of the firm."*

Diversity

"Leadership cares a lot about it, and makes people feel welcome and want to stay" a Bay Area associate expressed. The firm holds a diversity conference where every self-recorded diverse person is invited to meet each other and strengthen relationships across offices. *"I think diversity is at the forefront of what the firm is thinking about as they move forward,"* a Bostonian articulated, *"although diversity at partner level is definitely a work in progress."* At as-

sociate level however, it's reported to be pretty diverse, especially concerning gender: *"As a woman they've told me about groups and organisations I can get involved in. My mentor is female – it's great having her to bounce off all sorts of questions."* Indeed, this culture is an expectation when you're working with *"people from different countries, speaking different languages. It makes for a really interesting workplace."*

Hours & Compensation

The 2,000-hour billing target was *"definitely achievable,"* most associates found. One admitted, *"some years it might be hard to meet, and others not so, but it never feels overbearing – I never feel like I'll have to pull an all-nighter."* Those who rack up the 2,000 hours are then eligible for a bonus. Juniors reported an average day from 9am to around 6.30pm, then often logging on at home after dinner. *"They're flexible when it comes to letting you spend time with your family, as long as you're getting the work done,"* one commented. Some late nights and weekend work was considered unavoidable because on some matters *"it's more important to be with the team and discussing it together,"* but when we asked our sources if they still had time for a private life, the consensus answer was *"yes. Absolutely."* Would associates at many other global mega-firms respond like this? We think not.

Pro Bono

Juniors keenly emphasized that pro bono was *"not just lip service"* and felt that *"there are very few firms as committed as DLA."* Up to 100 hours can go toward the billing target, but up to 400 hours can be billed if it's for one of the firm's 'signature projects'. These address domestic violence, education, and juvenile justice issues among others. One junior spoke about *"a civil rights matter defending an inmate that was abused by a police officer."* A corporate junior tried their hand at an asylum case, which was *"interesting because I'm not a litigator, so I got to stretch my legs in a space I don't usually work in."* Some associates mentioned that *"despite the robust program, some practice group leaders may not be as enthusiastic about having associates doing pro bono because of billable hour targets."* But on balance reports were very positive, such as the Seattle associates who got pro bono credit for volunteering at food banks, *"which is fantastic!"*

Pro bono hours
- For all US attorneys: 117,108
- Average per US attorney: 85

See firm profile on p.593

Strategy & Future

In the past twelve months, DLA have opened another four offices internationally. Co-managing partner Stasia Kelly explains that *"the market is continuing to evolve and we want to be on the forefront of meeting those challenges and shaping them in our position as one of the largest law firms in the world."* Kelly also notes that DLA wants to *"focus on the markets where our clients are."* With that in mind, co-managing partner Mike Poulos explains that *"Latin America is clearly a focus for us, so we can expect additional expansion there. And like other firms, we're also interested in Asia."* Aside from new offices, Poulos tells us: *"We have realized our clients are very focused on having a sector-based approach, so as we expand this is something we will be conscious of."*

Get Hired

"We're looking for people who not only respond to challenging situations well, but are creative problem solvers." Find out more about getting hired at chambers-associate.com

"Diversity is at the forefront of what the firm is thinking about as they move forward"

See firm profile on p.593

Duane Morris LLP

Lawyers per state

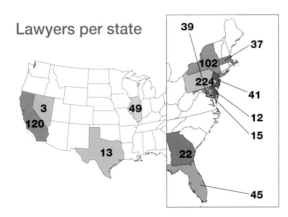

39
37
102
224
41
3
120
49
12
15
13
22
45

Largest US office: Philadelphia

US offices: 20

International offices: 8

First-year salary: $165,000 (Baltimore, New York, Philadelphia, DC and Chicago); $150,000 (San Diego); $140,000 (Miami/Cherry Hill, New Jersey)

Billable hours: 1,950 required

Summers 2017: 16 (15 2Ls, 1 1Ls)

Revenue 2016: $454.3 million (+4.6%)

Partners made in 2017: 10

Famous for: uniform décor; huge national coverage; Harvard Business School case studies

With 20 US offices, Duane Morris is more tight-knit than you might expect.

WHEN asked how such a big business maintains a unified culture, Duane Morris's chairman, John Soroko, quickly replies: *"We put a huge emphasis on people interacting and getting to know each other personally as well as professionally. This is the explicit aim of our annual firm-wide get togethers. We've got every Duane Morris employee in the same place, having fun but also learning."* DM, as it's affectionately known, also has another trick up its sleeve when it comes to creating that aforementioned unity, it models every one of its 20 US offices on its Philadelphia HQ – *"right down to the paintings on the wall,"* as one associate put it.

A focus on smaller, compact offices with identical furnishings, and an emphasis on tight-knit working relationships is complemented by a healthy respect for associates' abilities. Add attentive pastoral care to the mix, as evidenced by the firm's annual retreats – that alternate between funky Philadelphia and sunny Boca – and you're on to a winner. It's a happy mix, and revenues in 2016 rose again: to $454.3 million, up 4.6%. *Chambers USA* also recognizes its success, awarding the firm top-notch rankings for its bankruptcy, construction, corporate and IP practices.

The Work

In the firm's bigger offices (New York, Philly and Chicago), summer associates are given a form on which they rank their three preferred practices. After you've received a job offer there's *"a bit of a waiting game while they decide where you'll be placed."* Then, *"about two or three weeks before you join,"* you are told your practice. Most incomers will find themselves in litigation (or 'trial' as it's known at DM), the firm's largest department. Other groups newbies go to are corporate, IP, bankruptcy, real estate, wealth planning, labor & employment. Assignment across the board is fairly free market and associates are given a few years to find their niche.

Litigators need not worry about being pigeonholed, because Duane Morris's gargantuan operation deals with *"almost every dispute under the sun."* Sources spoke of being involved with everything from construction, to product liability, to insurance disputes. Other areas include CSAL (commercial securities & antitrust litigation), appellate, construction, insurance, IP, product liability, tax, white-collar corporate investigations & regulatory. Since cases range from *"two guys arguing over a home extension"* to *"two banks arguing over the mis-selling of debt,"* juniors' tasks encompass *"top-to-bottom stuff."* One pretty typical interviewee had *"drafted preparation documents, prepared for trial, gone to trial and argued on my feet on my own."* Another lauded the faith that senior lawyers have in raw recruits: *"I know that most of our motions for summary judgment have been drafted by associates. They have a lot of faith that we can get the job done."*

On chambers-associate.com...

- Interview with firm chairman John Soroko
- Doing business with Cuba
- More on culture

See firm profile on p.594

The Inside View

Rankings in *Chambers USA*

Banking & Finance	Insurance
Bankruptcy/Restructuring	Intellectual Property
Construction	Labor & Employment
Corporate/M&A	Litigation
Healthcare	Real Estate
Immigration	Tax

For detail on ranking tiers and ranking locations, visit www.chambersandpartners.com

"They have a lot of faith that we can get the job done."

Over in corporate, juniors have similar freedom to find their niche. Though the practice is pretty evenly split, *"when you come here there is no point at which you need to decide whether you are an M&A or finance lawyer."* With the former, associates will *"do all the diligence, draft the purchase agreements, usually take initial calls with the client – really as much as you feel you can handle."* Other areas on offer include private equity, venture capital, securities, and emerging growth. Healthcare finance is a big source of the corporate team's work and one attorney described a typical deal: *"I'll draft all the ancillary documents, draft the credit agreements, track them once they've been sent off and generally keep the partner organized and up-to-date."*

Culture

A combination of small class sizes and fluid practice groups means associates *"work with and get to know a lot of people quite quickly."* Because of this tight-knit environment, senior lawyers are more invested in their juniors – *"they have a personal interest in my life and will always ask me about my weekend."* And this cordiality even extends to clients: *"Partners here have a great relationship with their clients. We don't regularly have midnight emergencies because the clients aren't going to ask that from their friends."*

"We don't regularly have midnight emergencies because the clients aren't going to ask that of their friends."

This friendly approach makes DM a sociable place to work across the board. In Baltimore there are *"events with cake and balloons and singing for whoever's had a birthday that month."* In LA things are a bit more formal, with *"bi-monthly all-office lunches at a nice restaurant round the corner."* Over in the Big Apple, some attorneys like to get their families involved – *"we'll all go to a local bar and, rather than make our excuses, we'll get our spouses to join us and just hang out all night."* The Chi-

Recent work highlights

- Represented the President of India in privatization program of public sector units in deals totaling more than $600 million
- Obtained defense verdict on all counts for a global medical device manufacturer facing claim that metal-on-metal hip implant products were unreasonably dangerous
- Advising developer and investor with plans to build and operate solar power plants in Myanmar
- Advised on the sale of NCell (the market-leading Nepalese telecommunication operator) by TeliaSonera to Axiata, at an enterprise value of US$1.37 billion

cago office takes socializing seriously with *"a get-together every month, whatever the weather"* and a *"seriously fun summer party."*

Training & Development

Associates mentioned the words 'fun' and 'sun' maybe a dozen or so times when describing Duane Morris's annual conference, whose location alternates between Philadelphia and Boca Raton. It brings together every lawyer from all of the firm's 27 international offices for *"breakout events, dinners, dances and group meetings."* The Boca location perhaps unsurprisingly came in for the most amount of praise: *"We're all put up in this luxury resort and after attending the meetings, everyone heads to the beach."*

"Everyone heads to the beach."

After that, other formal training might sound decidedly dull, but following some *"pretty uninspiring IT instruction"* at the start of their careers, associates have a *"comprehensive offering of CLEs, online videos and courses"* to aid their development. There was also praise for the firm's very own direct messaging system that allows lawyers across the firm to communicate with one another at lightning speed.

Hours & Compensation

When it comes to salaries, the firm is *"below Cravath"* ($165,000 in major markets), but *"the fact that we have lower billables makes up for that."* As for those billables, there's an official target of 1,950 firmwide, but that includes up to 100 hours of pro bono, which sources agreed *"seriously sweetens the deal."* Overall, this sweetened deal was viewed much more favorably than the higher pay/increased pressure at other firms. *"Duane Morris lawyers obviously still work extremely hard but there's an appreciation that we've got a much better work/life balance than other BigLaw firms, and I think this makes everyone that bit happier."*

See firm profile on p.594

The Inside View

Diversity	Partners (%)	Associates (%)
Women	23.4	39.4
White	90.5	80.6
Black/African American	2.5	3.1
Hispanic/Latin American	2.5	3.7
Asian	4.5	6.2
Mixed/Other	1.7	3.7
LGBT	1.5	1.5

"A much better work/life balance."

Respect for people's family lives permeates the firm from the top down. "*There are absolutely no face-time requirements here. I've not once been asked 'where were you?' if I've left early for something. Anyway, some partners are gone around 4.30pm – they're off coaching their kids' sports teams and going to recitals. You can basically have the kind of family life you want.*" This attitude extends to vacation: "*We get four weeks a year and unless something major is going down, you won't be required to be constantly taking phone calls and replying to emails.*"

Offices

With 20 US offices – stretching from San Diego to Boston to Miami – you'd think it'd be hard to develop a sense of home for visiting attorneys. But the powers that be came up with a foolhardy solution: make all of their offices look exactly the same. This might seem like hyperbole but it's true, and every single source that we spoke to attested to their identical nature: "*Even the paintings on the wall are the same! It makes it feel like one huge worldwide office – when you video call anywhere in the world you feel like you're in the same building, just in different rooms.*"

Pro Bono

Further uniformity is offered by pro bono work, which is "*a big deal across the firm.*" Though associates aren't forced to take part, all of the resources are there and the 100-hour allowance acts as a big incentive. New York associates had worked a lot with Girls Education Monitoring (GEM), "*an organization that helps victims of trafficking.*" And, besides the obvious benefits of helping a good cause, this had allowed some of them "*experience in court, on our feet.*" Over in Philly, the firm has relationships with a heap of local organizations including "*the Inner-City Law Center, Advancing Justice and the Children's Rights Alliance.*"

Pro bono hours
- For all US attorneys: 31,725
- Average per US attorney: 49

Diversity

Uniformity might be good for wallpaper but when it comes to a workforce, diversity is the key to success. To this end, Duane Morris is definitely making moves in the right direction. In fact, the firm's efforts were so well regarded that in 2015 Philadelphia's newly elected mayor Jim Kenney picked head of diversity and inclusion Nolan Atkinson to head the city's diversity drive. Interviewees were proud of DM's achievements. "*We were one of the first firms to have a special retreat for diverse lawyers. Every May they meet with the executive committee in Philly and discuss how to improve the prospects of diverse attorneys.*" Gender diversity is also heavily promoted – "*We have women's book clubs in the bigger offices where female lawyers get together and read books related to women in business. They're also good for offering tips to junior associates who are just embarking on their careers.*"

Get Hired

One way the firm recruits to its smaller offices that lack a summer program is by offering 'externships' to students from local colleges. These are basically work experience placements that offer participants extra school credit as well as "*invaluable insight into what life is like for junior lawyers at Duane Morris – what kind of work you will be involved in, and really what day-to-day life is like at the firm.*" For those entering by more conventional avenues, recruiters make sure you interview with a wide array of attorneys, so that "*when you start you recognize a lot of friendly faces.*" When asked what kind of attributes recruiters looked for, many agreed that "*you have to have a desire to develop business and take a more entrepreneurial approach. From the beginning they really encourage business development. They force you to attend events.*"

"You have to have a desire to develop business and take a more entrepreneurial approach."

Strategy & Future

Sources opined that most partners at the firm had been summer associates there too – "*That's another thing I noticed. They must be doing something right if they are retaining people that long.*" And when it comes to looking to the future, John Soroko, has his eyes fixed on reinforcing the home front. "*We've added a new group from Carlton Fields to our Miami Office and added a new corporate and banking team in LA.*" That said, DM isn't ignoring emerging international markets, in 2016 the firm opened a new office in Taiwan and continues to build on its existing presence in places like Singapore and Sri Lanka.

See firm profile on p.594

The Inside View

Dykema Gossett PLLC

Lawyers per state

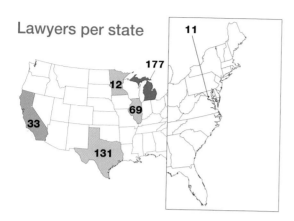

Largest US office: San Antonio
US offices: 15
International offices: 0
First-year salary: $120,000-$150,000
Billable hours: 1,950 target
Summers 2017: 18 (13 2Ls, 5 1Ls)
Revenue 2016: $218.9 million (-2.7%)
Partners made in 2017: 6 (all US)
Famous for: being big in San Antonio; long-term relationships in the automotive industry

Dykema has enviable vintage in Motor City but is also revving up its reputation a long drive away in all directions.

MUCH like fellow Michigan native Madonna, Dykema just gets better with age. While the largest office is now San Antonio, the double Michigan offering in Detroit and Bloomfield Hills reminds attorneys of their roots. Against the backdrop of a ravaged auto industry, 2008 to 2014 was also particularly hard on the city, which famously filed for bankruptcy. But Motown is getting its mojo back, and Dykema associates were especially keen to be part of the rejuvenation, citing it as one of the reasons they were drawn to the firm in the first place. *"There's a lot going on and there's a lot of regeneration in property. This was specifically why I wanted to work in real estate at Dykema,"* one told us. But it's not just real estate that earns the firm recognition. *Chambers USA* also awards high rankings for its Michigan-based litigation, M&A and labor & employment, and employee benefits practices. Elsewhere the firm receives accolades in Texas and Illinois. Clients include the likes of Ford, Fiat Chrysler and Bank of America.

Approximately 430 lawyers are dotted around each of Dykema's 15 domestic hubs, with a significant influx of fresh faces in Texas in the wake of the merger with San Antonio-based Cox Smith. A year on chairman and CEO Peter Kellett tells us that *"we've been given new vigor since the merger and we've successfully integrated. Legacy partners from Cox Smith permeate all of our management committees and we've seen real growth in cross-office and cross-client sharing work, which has been a continued focus of ours."*

The Work

When new summer associates begin their work experience, they're *"encouraged to try whatever they want to try."* At the end, future associates select their three top choices and most participants were pleased to be assigned to their preferred group. No department runs a formal assignment system, instead operating a free market: *"You get work organically through relationships."* Most of our sources were transactional associates. *"Corporate has different sub-groups like public company, M&A, securities, finance, IP transactions and compliance, but everyone starts off as generalists,"* sources explained. Many had dabbled in corporate finance. Around *"40% is due diligence,"* which was balanced with *"drafting board resolutions, ancillary and collateral access agreements and filing the UCCs [Uniform Commercial Codes]."* It's a research -heavy group: *"I've had to work out what happens when the borrower is in default and if we can collect on their assets."* While most were happy with what they'd experienced, others sometimes felt the heat: *"Sometimes clients refuse to have other associates work on their matters apart from you, so you're working 15-hour days."* However, *"at the same time I get to work at a higher level of sophistication, so overall it's worth it."*

On chambers-associate.com...

- Interview with chairman and CEO Peter Kellett
- More on getting hired

See firm profile on p.595

The Inside View

Rankings in *Chambers USA*

Bankruptcy/Restructuring	Immigration
Corporate/M&A	Labor & Employment
Employee Benefits &	Litigation
Executive Compensation	Real Estate

For detail on ranking tiers and ranking locations, visit
www.chambersandpartners.com

"I get to work at a higher level of sophistication, so overall it's worth it."

Real estaters were happy with the spread of work and responsibility levels. *"We do a load of land use and landlord/tenant work. There's a ton of leasing, especially with one client who works in the cell phone tower industry."* Tasks include *"setting up easements, doing lease amendments, and the client interaction is great. You're literally talking directly to clients and responding to their emails daily."* Chicago insiders explained that the preponderance of their work comes from the commercial lease sphere with a sprinkling of real estate finance in the mix too. *"Because of the market at the moment we don't do as much financing, but when we do we represent a lot of banks and lenders. Younger associates are in charge of reviewing the documents involved in the logistics of closings. This is anything from finalizing loan documents or settling statements of title when a deal is co-financed."*

Litigation houses sub-groups such as class actions and product liability, commercial, business, or financial services. Associates have free reign to work across practice groups. While there are obvious benefits, some suggested *"the downside is that there's no one group you can be certain of getting work from. It can be frustrating at times."* A lot of litigation comes from automotive product liability, despite the industry decline in recent years. Typical tasks in this area include *"doing the grunt work creating cases summaries. But it's great because you see the case from beginning to end."* Responsibility is generally good: *"Eight months in I was working closely with the director of the department and I could run my own cases. I've managed discovery, drafted discovery responses, motions and mediation statements."*

Training & Development

Training kicks off with a new associates retreat *"in Detroit for several days, learning about all the firm's systems. Then we have practice group-specific trainings to learn the basics."* Chicago-based corporate newbies get treated to a *"transactional bootcamp, where you have to draft deal documents and close a pretend deal with live negotiations, and you're rated on how you did."* However, most other

Recent work highlights

- Recently helped Ford to close a significant investment in Velodyne LiDAR, a company that provides a key component for autonomous vehicles. Baidu (which is akin to Google in China) was the co-lead investor with Ford
- Advised a large national hamburger chain in the launch of its mobile customer app dealing with in-app payment functions, mobile rewards/loyalty, mobile app-related patent research and regulatory advice on FDA requirements
- General counsel for the private nonprofit corporation that is building the M-1 Rail project in Detroit, which has capital costs of over $140 million

associates had experienced the *"learn as you go"* approach to development. They *"wished it was more formal throughout. But to be honest, I don't know how helpful that will be as you only take it on board when you physically do it."* Assigned mentors *"help you think strategically about your own career. I've been given 100% of my mentor's attention, and I know how busy they are."*

Reviews occur once a year, where associates have to detail the substantive work they've done. Usually, practice group leaders and a member of the professional personnel committee take you through the conglomerated feedback from supervising attorneys. Some felt that *"it's not possible to get a true reading, because there's just too many deals to mention and I know the partner won't really remember what I did."*

Hours & Compensation

Hitting the hours target of 1,950 means eligibility for a merit-based bonus, *"except for first-years,"* who don't get any bonus. Which was just as well, as a few of our sources revealed that *"some people, especially first-years, are not even close to hitting that."* However, lawyers weren't stressed. *"The expectation is that you do everything you can and if you don't meet it, don't worry. It's not unfair and they appreciate that sometimes the work isn't there."*

"We get paid fairly for the work we do." Starting the day at around 8.30am and leaving at *"7pm ish"* was standard. However, it varies between departments and as usual we heard that those in corporate should prep for the occasional all-nighter. In 2016, Dykema announced pay rises. *"From what I understand, first, second and third-years got more,"* thought one junior. *"Where I think the problem lies is that the straight increase didn't affect mid-level associates. If I was a fourth-year, I'd be upset."* Fourth-years and above still got merit-based rises in 2016, as usual.

See firm profile on p.595

The Inside View

Diversity	Partners (%)	Associates (%)
Women	23	54
White	90	80
Black/African American	3	7
Hispanic/Latin American	5	5
Asian	1	4
Mixed/Other	1	3
LGBT	0	1

Pro Bono

Up to 100 hours can count toward bonus eligibility with prior approval. However, 30 a year are compulsory. Those who fail to reach this mark have to pay $500 to a charity of their choosing. Associates were happy with this set-up: *"It opens so many great opportunities. If people don't want to do it, they just have to suck it up!"* Associates had been involved in a plethora of good causes, all managed by a *"full-time pro bono coordinator who emails us with all the latest matters."* These include *"helping to release a person from jail who had served seven years after being wrongly convicted."* Others had *"drafted Amicus briefs for a not-for-profit in Detroit. There was a big, bad, cement-crushing company building a facility next-door to a children's charity day care center. So we had to defend the not-for-profit in front of the Board of Zoning Appeals."*

Pro bono hours
- For all attorneys: 15,776
- Average per attorney: 42

"It opens so many great opportunities."

Diversity

"It's something that the firm struggles with," juniors felt. *"They're conscious of it and they really try to hire diverse candidates, but right now it's not as diverse as it was when I was a summer."* However, they were quick to defend Dykema's efforts to promote diversity. Initiatives like the Wolverine Bar Association's summer clerkship program for diverse 1Ls, and diversity scholarships in partnership with the University of Michigan and University of Illinois, have done their bit to make things better. *"When I look around I'm very happy compared to other places I've been to. In my class of 16, six of us are people of color, there's some LGBT attorneys and we are about 50:50 men to women."* Overall, Chicago attorneys felt the results of the diversity efforts more strongly than those in other offices. While leadership is still *"pretty much Caucasian, last summer class we had no Caucasians, so it shows there's an aim to diversify the pool we hire from."*

Offices

"Even though we have all these offices now, Detroit is still officially the HQ," insiders asserted. *"Most of our committees are made up heavily with Michigan-based lawyers, so Michigan is the power center."* Some chuckled that *"people call Bloomfield Hills the country club because it's just outside of Detroit, which makes it a little bit calmer and bit easier to work in."* That said, associates further afield didn't feel left out. Chicagoans stated that *"we never feel like we're the step-child; we generate our own work so it's an important office."* This independence was probably helped by the fact that Illinois-based attorneys were *"made up of a composition of smaller firm mergers and we've adopted some of their rules. For example, anyone can go into anyone's offices at any time to get help. That was a rule from a previous firm."* The latest merger saw Dykema join forces with Texas firm Cox Smith in 2015. However, at associate level *"we haven't really felt the effects of it across the board. But we now do a lot more cross-staffing with Texas."*

Associates all have their own offices straight away regardless of location. Michigan newbies are treated to a more traditional law firm feel with *"dark wood furniture, but you can make it your own by personalizing your office and hanging up anything you want."* Those in Texas felt that *"our buildings are a lot nicer, they're brighter and more modern feeling with a lot more glass."* Yet Bloomfield Hills pips them to the post with a rooftop terrace, which is the sometime setting of monthly socials.

Culture

Across all offices and practice groups, juniors agreed that *"we sort of go for people that we think are going to work hard but then can go out for a beer later. It's not always the person with cream-of-the-crop grades, because you can be number one in the class and have a sucky personality."* Michigan sources acknowledged that *"it's such a cliché to say people care and that it's collegial, but it's true here."* Don't be surprised if you get an invite to a colleague's wedding, in other words.

"... because you can be number one in the class and have a sucky personality."

In the wake of the merger, associates were glad of the opportunity to get to know their new comrades. *"We had our first retreat in Detroit with the Cox Smith associates. It really helped us to start working together so that it's no longer 'them' and us.'"*

Chicago-based sources had a few qualms. *"It is collegial, but we're all on separate floors. Sometimes you feel insulated from the rest of the office. Partners work across departments all the time, but we don't as much."* However,

See firm profile on p.595

"everyone has their door open all the time so you can just walk in. Like right now I've got my door closed because I'm talking to you, and everyone is wondering why."

Strategy & Get Hired

Chairman and CEO Peter Kellett lets us in on Dykema's future strategy: *"We want to have a greater full-service offering on the national platform. That's why we've grown purposefully in Texas after the merger, as well as in the Twin Cities in Minneapolis. We're not growing just for the sake of it, and we didn't just throw darts at a map to choose where we grow."* What about recruitment? Hiring partner Lisa Brown advises to *"not sit back. Take advantage of every work opportunity you're given. Take ownership of them, express your ideas and prove that you're going to be a valuable member of any team. A big part of this job is going out and taking the ownership to get clients. So people with those types of skills are very attractive to us."* For more on strategy and how to get hired, go online.

> **"A big part of this job is going out and taking the ownership to get clients. So people with those types of skills are very attractive to us."**

See firm profile on p.595

Epstein Becker & Green PC

Lawyers per state

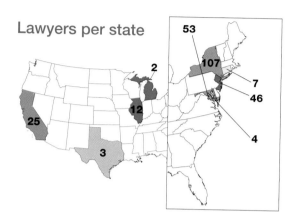

53
2
107
7
46
12
25
4
3

Largest US office: New York
US offices: 12
International offices: 0
First-year salary: varies by practice and location ($130,000 - $140,000 in DC and NYC)
Billable hours: 1,950 requirement
Summers 2017: 12 (10 2Ls, 2 1Ls)
Revenue 2016: undisclosed
Partners made in 2017: 5
Famous for: labor & employment law; healthcare law

We'd prescribe a healthy dose of Epstein Becker & Green if healthcare or labor law gets your pulse racing.

EPSTEIN knows what it wants: healthcare and labor law are front of mind at this specialist, mostly East Coast-based firm. *"Focused excellence"* is its tagline, and keeping an eye on the dual prize has paid off: *Chambers USA* consistently awards a flurry of rankings to Epstein's two core practice areas in New York, New Jersey, DC, and nationwide.

Being focused is an attitude the firm also seeks out when choosing its incoming associates: *"I only went to law school to do healthcare law!"* one successful applicant told us. Industry experience of some kind is pretty much guaranteed among Epstein's attorneys, and even the few who come straight through from law school will have taken healthcare or labor modules while studying. *"We really look for people who can prove they're absolutely interested in one of those two areas,"* a junior with hiring experience stressed to us. *"This isn't a firm where you rotate through departments during the summer."*

Strategy & Future

Epstein's not veering from its successful tried and tested dedication to healthcare and employment/labor law. *"In healthcare, we continue to have very strong demand from private equity clients that are making investments in healthcare entities,"* chairman Mark Lutes tells us, also citing government investigations and information security as other current key drivers. Data protection is also prevalent on the employment/labor side. *"Employee data and security risk management is at the top of the agenda for many employers,"* Lutes explains, also noting that an increase in *"class action litigation is keeping the employment and labor group pretty busy."*

The Work

Most first-year associates join the Washington, DC or New York office while a handful are absorbed into Newark. At the time of our calls around three-quarters of Epstein's Big Apple juniors were in the employment practice, with the remainder divided between healthcare and litigation. DC predominantly recruits into healthcare.

"You have a lot more control over your experience."

Departments may line up a couple of matters to get newbies out of the starting blocks but ultimately it's up to juniors to hunt down work. Sources reckoned the procedure's not too painful once you're over the initial discomfort: *"It does require effort to go out and drum up work and*

The Inside View

See firm profile on p.596

Rankings in *Chambers USA*

Employee Benefits & Executive Compensation	Healthcare Labor & Employment

For detail on ranking tiers and ranking locations, visit www.chambersandpartners.com

that can be stressful," one associate admitted. *"But once you're accustomed to it you have a lot more control over your experience and that's a big plus."*

Healthcare rookies operate on anything from M&A to government investigations, regulatory advice or data protection issues. Epstein often partners with other law firms to provide advice on healthcare specific issues of large M&A transactions but it also handles plenty of takeover deals on its own, often for private equity clients investing in *"pharmacies, hospitals, physicians' practice, drug or medical device manufacturers,"* one deal-doer listed. Associates take the lead on due diligence, reviewing existing contracts and facilitating the transfer of licenses.Overseeing diligence also falls to associates tackling large regulatory matters. This area tends to be research-heavy, though we heard of sources on smaller projects *"taking charge of cases from beginning to end; I draft memos as I see fit but a partner may suggest revisions to ensure it fits the client's bill."*

"A significant amount of client interaction."

Epstein's DC office specializes in advising clients on government investigations into fraud and abuse, such as false billing or issues arising under anti-kickback legislation (which bans the offer of rewards for healthcare referrals). Rookies frequently respond to government subpoenas for the production of information, but matters also afford *"a significant amount of client interaction; I often conduct onsite visits to interview clients for additional information."*

Healthcare frequently bleeds into the firm's employment and labor practice; the industry, along with financial services, hospitality, retail and technology, makes up the bulk of the firm's sector focus in this area. Newbies begin life as generalists, sampling both labor and employment work. Associates have seen an uptick in traditional labor relations matters in recent years thanks to the Obama administration's encouragement of unionization. Associates could find themselves gainfully employed on union election, unfair labor practices or labor relations advice matters. On the employment side our sources had toiled away on single and class action discrimination suits, wage and hour cases, trade secret violations, and whistleblowing claims. Matters tend to be staffed by one partner and one associate, so juniors are often in the thick of it:

Recent work highlights

- Advised non profit California hospital chain MemorialCare Health System on a five-year arrangement to provide medical care to employees of aircraft titan Boeing. This is the first direct-to-employer healthcare network in the Golden State
- DC and NY healthcare and labor/employment attorneys clubbed together to advise wound care company RestorixHealth in a False Claims Act and employment discrimination case after a former employee alleged Restorix submitted false medical bills
- Represented Fox News chief Roger Ailes to settle a headline-grabbing discrimination case after former News host Gretchen Carlson filed a sexual harassment and retaliation suit against Ailes and Fox News
- Acted for insurers AXA after a former broker, who was fired for selling unapproved investments, sued AXA for breach of contract

"I've had the opportunity to interact with opposing counsel, attend hearings and second-chair depositions. Partners review my first drafts of complaints and pleadings, but in several cases I've almost entirely produced the documents we've filed."

Culture & Training

"Success at the firm is dependent on associates charting their own path," one source stressed. *"There's not much hand-holding so you have to be ambitious and entrepreneurial."* Take training for example: rookies cover the basics like the email system and billing in their first few days. The *"biggest chunk of training"* comes in the form of the summer program's EBG Academy but juniors are invited along all the same. The firm also subscribes to various webinars and fledgling healthcare lawyers are sent off to the annual American Health Lawyers Association conference. Beyond that, *"healthcare changes so much that formal training sessions can be outdated. We pride ourselves on being at the cutting edge of the area, so a lot of the time you're discussing issues with a partner and learning as you go,"* one interviewee explained. *"You're expected to do a lot of self-learning and associates who are ambitious in that way get better and more challenging work assignments."* Another added: *"Most senior attorneys are invested in teaching you and providing feedback on your work, but it's up to you to speak out and ask for it."* Juniors didn't feel there was too much of a hurdle to overcome in doing this, telling us *"interactions between partners and associates are not pompous. I'm never concerned about knocking on an unfamiliar partner's door and saying 'hey, I know you're an expert on this, can you teach me the background?'"*

"A lot of self-learning."

See firm profile on p.596

Diversity	Partners (%)	Associates (%)
Women	28	53
White	88	82
Black/African American	1	4
Hispanic/Latin American	2	1
Asian	6	10
Mixed/Other	3	3
LGBT	2	3

Epstein recently advised iExhale on the launch of a happiness and mental health app, but how well does it help the well-being of its own attorneys? One source conceded: *"There are times when everyone is busy, and when deadlines are approaching the tension can get high, but generally it's very calm."* Others credited a lack of suit-wearing with creating a *"non-stuffy"* and *"low-key atmosphere."* Although Newark associates believed their office is *"a little more laid back than New York,"* the general consensus – whatever the location – was that *"people are friendly with one another. Associates rely on everyone else to give us work so there's no reason to be burning bridges."* Another highlighted that *"although there's a lot of work to be done, no one looks in at my door to see when I'm coming or going. It's very production-based; the real stuff matters, not nonsense"* like face time.

Hours & Compensation

Epstein's salary falls below the market rate and varies by practice and location. Although all our sources admitted to craving a pay rise, they had mixed feelings about their take-home pay. *"We're targeting a cost-sensitive market which determines our billing rate,"* one rationalized. Others were less pleased: *"It's the one area that has room for improvement. I'm willing to take a pay cut for the quality of life, but within reason."*

> *"We're targeting a cost-sensitive market."*

We also heard a few gripes about the bonus, which juniors become eligible for once they've billed 1,950 hours. *"It's difficult to comprehend how it works,"* one grumbled. *"It's a very murky issue but it's so below market it's not even worth fighting about."* Others took a more sanguine view: *"It reflects the lower rates for the markets we work in but I don't think I've been treated unfairly."* Nearly everyone felt the 1,950 bonus target was achievable; to reach it, interviewees reported pulling ten-hour days at the office plus a few additional hours from home each week.

Offices

Associates in the Big Apple might prefer home comforts as their office looks *"1980s frumpy!"* But on the plus side *"it has nice large offices and almost every attorney gets their own. It's not very modern or chic but neither am I."* Excited juniors in the capital are about to see their office undergo *"a full-tear down"* refurb, which will introduce lots of glass and a new cafeteria, among other things. The DC, New York and Newark offices take on juniors, but Epstein has plenty more places in its national network: Baltimore, Boston, Chicago, Houston, LA, Princeton, San Diego, San Francisco and Stamford

Pro Bono

Associates can bill up to 100 hours of pro bono once they've met the 1,950 billable requirement. Several told us the policy meant they'd personally put pro bono on the back-burner but others hadn't let it stop them. A pro bono committee keeps juniors informed of any opportunities, though one source recommended *"being a self-starter to find what you want."* New Yorkers had seen plenty of work advising non-profits and start-ups, while the DC office *"tends to handle a lot of social security disability cases"* as the hearing office is in the same building.

Pro bono hours
- For all attorneys: 5,500
- Average per attorney: 21

Diversity

Associates repeatedly highlighted the high proportion of female partners at Epstein; at 28% it's higher than the typical BigLaw average of around 20%. *"I applied here because it stood out as a good place for women,"* shared one junior. *"I've found it's very supportive."* A women's initiative regularly hosts cross-industry events which provide *"a great networking opportunity; anyone can invite clients or female big players along."* Associates told us Epstein's *"not particularly ethnically diverse but it is an inclusive environment"* and there's a pipeline scheme for minority 1Ls.

Get Hired

Whether you've interned at a labor union, spent a decade in HR or loved healthcare classes at law school, a demonstrated interested in healthcare or employment/labor law is vital for aspiring Epsteiners. For more tips and advice on the firm's hiring process visit chambers-associate.com

The Inside View

See firm profile on p.596

293

Finnegan, Henderson, Farabow, Garrett & Dunner LLP

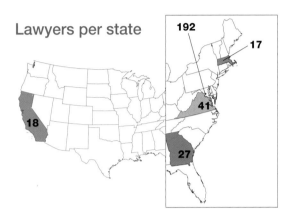

Lawyers per state

Largest US office: Washington, DC

US offices: 5

International offices: 5

First-year salary: $180,000

Billable hours: 2,000 target (or 1,900 plus 100 pro bono hours)

Summers 2017: 30 (23 2Ls, 7 1Ls)

Revenue 2016: $309.9 million (+0.6%)

Partners made in 2017: 11 globally (10 in US)

Famous for: IP, patents are really their thing

"The go-to IP firm in the US," according to associates here, has five offices around the country and five more globally.

FINNEGAN's lengthy full name crams a lot in, and the firm too *"prides itself on being able to do any patent law under the sun."* The DC-founded 52-year-old has amassed ten offices worldwide – not bad for a firm that specializes in just one area of the law, intellectual property. Its focus, however, is broad: consumer products, medical devices, biotech, pharma, electricals, and alternative energy are just some of the categories. Finnegan has over 300 professionals with science degrees, around 75 of which have PhDs, and over 40 have been former US Patent Office examiners. 2015 saw the firm celebrate its 50th anniversary, which coincided with the launch of a fourth Asian office, in South Korea.

"Its reputation made me want to come here."

Managing partner Mark Sweet explains that *"our strategy over the next few years is to expand our market share as a premier global, full-service IP law firm in the increasingly complex field of intellectual property."* Finnegan scores top marks in *Chambers USA* in DC for IP litigation, patent prosecution, and trademark, copyright & trade secrets.

National nods also go to life sciences and Section 337 [mostly patent infringement disputes] cases as well, and the firm's also ranked in California, Georgia, Massachusetts, and Northern Virginia. This clearly struck a chord with associates: *"Its reputation made me want to come here. Year after year it's ranked as one of the top IP firms in the world."*

The Work

Most juniors are in DC, and the rest are sprinkled around Atlanta, Boston, Palo Alto and Reston. Based on their academic and technical backgrounds, new starters fall into one of the following practice groups: electrical, chemical, mechanical, biotechnology & pharmaceuticals, or trademark & copyright. Assignment *"is mostly informal. There are pros and cons to that. In my first month, I was left to find work on my own. I wish someone had pre-assigned me something. But it made me go and get the work I actually wanted."* While most told similar stories, there's also a catch-all availability report, which *"is where you can formally request work if you're light."*

Depending on which groups they get involved with, Finnegan's associates can expect to work on matters relating to the following: electronics, computers, industrial manufacturing, consumer products, medical devices, biotechnology, pharmaceuticals, chemicals, or alternative energy. Within each practice, newbies take on a mix of both patent prosecution and IP litigation work. *"You're not just a litigator or a prosecutor."*

On chambers-associate.com...

- Interview with managing partner Mark Sweet
- Schools bout for summers: alternative routes into Finnegan
- More on getting hired

See firm profile on p.597

Rankings in *Chambers USA*

Intellectual Property	Life Sciences
International Trade	

For detail on ranking tiers and ranking locations, visit
www.chambersandpartners.com

"It made me go and get the work I actually wanted."

"I get the sense that our bread is definitely buttered on the litigation side." Around two-thirds of the firm's juniors in DC spend at least half of their time doing litigation. They'd been involved in a healthy array of matters. *"I've worked on two district court cases, ITC cases* [disputes in front of the International Trade Commission – quicker than traditional trials], *an IPR* [Inter Partes Review] *and an appeal, all in less than a year at the firm."* Alongside the usual doc review, other tasks include first drafts of discovery letters, opinions and motions to compel. Sources had even *"second-chaired and defended a deposition."* Insiders advised: *"Just ask, no one hogs work."*

Patent prosecution work sees juniors guide clients through the patent application process. As well as preparing drafts of claims for the initial filing, interviewees had *"worked on a mechanical client patent portfolio trying to assess the strengths and weaknesses, because they're about to go against their main competitor. There are so many patents involved, so it's been great to look at the big picture, which you normally don't get to do."* Newbies said that patent prosecution gives you ample opportunity to get more experience because *"the cases are quicker than litigation and leanly staffed, so you're forced to get involved."*

Training & Development

Training begins with a week's orientation in DC, attended by all starters and focusing *"on everything from the more boring IT instructions to around eight hours of prosecution and litigation training."* After this initial intense program, training happens informally throughout the year. Some remembered *"the most helpful lunchtime session we had was how to take and defend depositions."* Others described that *"over the first six months we've had around eight lectures on PTAB* [Patent Trial and Appeal Board] *cases. It's a new area and they have completely different rules."* One of the greatest tools at associates' disposal is Ed Good, a resident legal writing coach: *"He's a legend. He runs seminars on the active voice and the power of persuasion. He encourages you to submit writing samples and we workshop them."* Read our feature on good legal writing, including tips from Ed Good, on our website.

"He's a legend."

Recent work highlights

- Persuaded the US Court of Appeals for the Federal Circuit to vacate and remand the Patent Trial and Appeal Board's decisions that adversely affected three patents related to coaxial cable connectors owned by client PPC Broadband
- Provides strategic worldwide intellectual property counseling to pharma company Vertex with a focus on Vertex's FDA cystic fibrosis products
- Direct worldwide protection of Under Armour's trademark portfolio and representation in numerous US trademark enforcement matters
- Defended ABBYY Software and Lexmark in district court against infringement accusations directed to two patents related to optical character recognition (OCR) software and a third patent directed to distributed document processing over a computer network

A mentorship program teams starters with a partner and senior associate, allotting them a budget to socialize and get advice. Come review time, first-years have biannual appraisals, which drop to yearly meetings in the second-year. For both, *"you fill out online reports and you say who you've worked with most. They review you and then your practice group leader and a reviewing partner sit down and talk it through with you."*

Diversity

At associate level, ethnic minorities are well represented. Standing tall at 24%, Finnegan's Asian American showing is particularly noteworthy among newbies. The playing field is pretty level when it comes to gender diversity too, with 44% female associates. *"All IP firms suffer handicaps from a female standpoint. It self-selects because not many women do engineering or science and then go to law school."* But that said, *"this is the best firm I've seen for women advancing to leadership. The head of the electrical group is a woman."* This is partly to do with the efforts of the Women's Forum. Recent events included a panel discussion *"made up of three female judges, two district, one federal and a partner from our firm, discussing the underrepresentation of women in first-chair roles in trials and appeals. It was so insightful."*

"This is the best firm I've seen for women advancing to leadership."

Strategy & Get Hired

"Our IPR practice is really exploding, I think it's our most up and coming area," insisted insiders. *"Take IP-specific classes, intern at the Patent Office in the summer, don't just sit around. If you want to show enthusiasm for our work, get experience."* Managing partner Mark Sweet says that *"the most successful candidates that we see are those who demonstrate a sincere interest in Finnegan – a commitment to IP, a collaborative spirit, and a geographic tie*

The Inside View

See firm profile on p.597

Diversity	Partners (%)	Associates (%)
Women	26	44
White	88	66
Black/African American	3	6
Hispanic/Latin American	0	3
Asian	9	24
Mixed/Other	0	1
LGBT	2	2

to one of our global offices." For more insight from both associates and the powers that be, go online.

Culture

"In general practice, everyone is the Type A gunner," reflected one associate. "What I love about Finnegan is that deep down we're all nerdy scientists or engineers. We've all had similar experience suffering through engineering college and then coming to the law." Others boasted that "I feel really comfortable here. We have a team mentality and everyone wants each other to succeed." While a lot of attorneys here have PhDs and masters degrees, sources stressed that "you're not looked down upon if you don't have that. It's not a prerequisite." In fact, Finnegan focuses more on what associates achieve during their time at the firm, rather than what they've done before: "You're not allowed to hang your diplomas in your office. It's pretty cool. It's about what you can add to the firm and how you can help your clients now."

"We have monthly happy hours on our roof terrace. But most of our socials are in the summer and we do a lot of kayaking, hiking or rock climbing." However those in Atlanta had the most fun playing "Whirlyball" (a cross between lacrosse and bumper cars.) Firmwide shindigs include the reintroduced "all-attorney retreat. We spend two days in a hotel outside of DC and do activities in the morning, panel discussions about the firm strategy in the afternoon and then a casino night in the evening. I think we're going to do this every other year."

Offices

"DC is the main office and it's in a phenomenal location right in the city center. Location is key." Washingtonians get more than just easy transport links, though: "We have a free gym in our building and a good cafeteria." Nevertheless, the best place to catch a tan remains the HQ's roof garden. "It's great to go to lunch there," with some departments hosting happy hours here too.

Novices had the impression that satellite offices were perhaps a little more laid back than Finnegan central, because as one associate remembered: "Each office has its own thing going on. Palo Alto has a different vibe. It's a little bit more relaxed. I don't know why, maybe it's the nice weather." Those in Atlanta were equally as chilled and were very taken with their new office building. "It's very modern. We're in this really hip area in Atlantic Station." What generated most buzz though "is the excitement over our new standing desks. We deal with the cutting edge of technology so now the office has developed specific Skype stations and huddle rooms so that different teams can cross-conference." Regardless of location, associates had their own windowed offices. In DC, sources said that summers typically share and this set-up is called "barns. I'm not sure why."

Hours & Compensation

"It's remarkably humane. I try to bill around eight hours a day. I get in around 8.30am and leave around 7pm," which was common among associates. Finnegan's billing target is 2,000 hours to be eligible for a bonus (or 1,900 plus 100 pro bono hours). Insiders broke it down further: "Once you hit the hours component, there's a qualitative component. For each chunk of time you go over, you get a certain percentage of the base rate. But even if you haven't gone over by the full 'chunk' and you've done killer work, then you'll get a higher bonus too."

Pro Bono

"They're extremely committed" explained one source. "We have a dedicated pro bono coordinator. Any case you want, she can get." Criminal defense representation, asylum cases and veterans appeals tend to flood the docket, with the latter particularly common. "We do more veteran pro bono than any firm I know," revealed one insider. "Also if we win a case we donate all of our court awarded attorney fees to charity. We donated upward of $300,000 last year from just our veteran work." Besides helping out some of the country's bravest, associates found pro bono involvement to be a great way to earn new responsibilities. "There's a 20-hour seminar that teaches you how to do criminal defense work." The firm works with the Clemency Project to "help people appeal against unfairly long sentences. I drafted everything, and did all the client interviews. It gives associates the chance to stand up in court, because in IP you won't get to do that for a least a few years."

Pro bono hours
- For all US attorneys: 11,732
- Average per US attorney: 93

The Inside View

See firm profile on p.597

Fish & Richardson PC

Lawyers per state

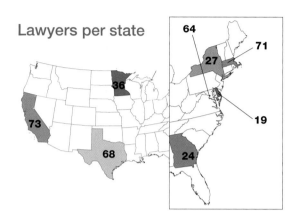

Largest US office: Boston
US offices: 11
International offices: 1
First-year salary: $180,000
Billable hours: 1,900 required
Summers 2017: 36 (28 2Ls, 8 1Ls)
Revenue 2016: $407.68 million (+3.2%)
Partners made in 2017: 10
Famous for: top-notch IP work; "loveable nerds"

Fish is so famous for IP it even made it onto the nation's TV screens...

ARE you a fan of the TV show *Jeopardy*? If so, you may remember an episode last year featuring a law firm trivia round: *"Tops for patent litigation per* US News & World Report, *Fish & Richardson specializes in IP. Short for this."* After one contestant, Bill, answered incorrectly (*"what is an 'initial'?"*), fellow player Jill came up trumps with *"what is 'intellectual property'?"* Absolutely right, as Fish is one of the most famous IP specialists out there (others in this guide are Finnegan, Fitzpatrick, and Sterne Kessler). In 2016 alone, for example, it filed well over 5,500 US and 4,500 foreign patent applications. Needless to say, Fish's *"prestige in the patent and IP field"* is the main reason associates come to this firm.

Fish's president Peter Devlin highlights that *"what makes us unique is the sheer number and caliber of our technically trained lawyers, for instance, we have a large number of attorneys with PhDs."* Its specialist knowledge gains it top rankings in *Chambers USA* for all aspects of IP. The firm has also recently been growing its commercial litigation practice, but Fish is sticking to its roots as most cases here tend to have a tech slant of some kind.

The Work
New starters join either patent litigation or prosecution, then later divide into small subgroups based on their in-

terests. Subgroups include expertise in trademark, copyright, regulatory & government affairs, and post-grant reviews. The vast majority of this year's associate pool were in patent litigation, and although juniors are spread across the country, most were in DC, Boston, Silicon Valley, Atlanta, and New York. Fish's clients include tech giants like Google and Microsoft, but it also deals with its fair share of start-ups and individual inventors.

A litigator defined their practice area as *"complex litigation directed toward issues of patent infringement and invalidity."* Clients include drug companies, software designers, individuals, and some *"big recurring clients"* – often in the *Fortune* 500. *"A case I've worked on was one individual who wanted to start his own website. On the other hand, there are really big pharmaceutical clients, and everything in between."* Juniors also see *"a lot of defense work."* Tasks range from *"pre-due diligence, through to trial and appeal."* This includes the typical doc review and discovery, as well as supporting deposition prep and drafting opinion letters and motions: *"I'm sometimes the main person to draft the motion,"* a New Yorker enthused. Others reported attending trials and playing a *"supporting role in getting witnesses ready, and some involvement on appeal briefs to federal courts."* A DC junior described that there's *"a lot of grunt work, but at the same time, a lot of substantive experience."* When it comes to international opportunities, one junior highlighted that *"within four months I was on a plane to Europe to interview an inventor. It was a ton of work, but awesome."* Other juniors we spoke to had not had experience abroad, but many had heard from colleagues who had gone overseas.

On chambers-associate.com...
- More on getting hired at Fish & Richardson
- Interview with firm president Peter Devlin

The Inside View

See firm profile on p.598

Rankings in *Chambers USA*

Intellectual Property	International Trade

For detail on ranking tiers and ranking locations, visit
www.chambersandpartners.com

"You can become pretty independent."

Over in patent prosecution, it's *"generally more low budg-et, short projects."* Work involves coordinating with in-ventors, learning about their new tech, and then drafting patent applications. *"You can become pretty independent where the partners are only taking quick reviews. It's always a good feeling when you get the first couple of drafts back with minimal changes,"* one reported. Before this stage, juniors conduct searches to see if anything might prevent a client obtaining a patent, or *"look for ways to differenti-ate the idea from tech or patents already out there. As you go up and gain more experience, you get more involved in patent portfolio management and help clients make more strategic decisions – whether to file items as patents or trade secrets."* The group works for big companies and start-ups alike: *"It's fun to work with start-ups because you're effectively their in-house counsel, talking directly with CEOs."* Technical backgrounds play a more pivotal role here compared to litigation: *"Occasionally an email will come across where a partner isn't so familiar with par-ticular tech for a client, asking if anyone has experience in say, robotics, or maybe computer learning. You can raise your hand and get the chance to work for someone differ-ent, or someone in a different office."*

All juniors described the assignment process as fairly free market, but there are also group leaders: *"If you're looking for more work, they're happy to help."* A litigator explained the pros and cons: *"Sometimes it's hard to prove you're going to be helpful to a case and bring something to the table. This can be frustrating, but the free market system also gives you control over your workload and the cases you want to work on."* The system also lends itself to flexibility: *"At Fish, when there's need for someone to do something, they don't care about boundaries – we can all help each other out."*

Training & Development

Formal Fish bootcamps take place for new starters, tai-lored to either patent prosecution or ligation. In litiga-tion this involves *"training for taking expert depositions, for fact witness depositions, and for being more articulate,"* followed by additional sessions on software programs and admin. Then there's *"hands-on training maybe four or five times year,"* according to a New Yorker. *"Space is limited though. I've only been able to join two of those."* A Texan junior also thought that *"it would be good to have senior bootcamps a little more often."*

Recent work highlights

- Represented eBay in defense of four patent infringements brought against them by Paid Inc in regard to online ship-ping calculators
- Defended LG Chem against Celgard over infringement of a patent involving lithium batteries
- Representing Microsoft in suit filed against Corel for alleg-edly infringing nine Microsoft patents on various aspects of the user interfaces in Corel's products
- Obtained reversal of $200 million verdict against Gilead, filed by Merck regarding its Hepatitis C drug patent

Biannual reviews take in place in which *"people you work for submit reviews of your work to the group leader who will then go over the feedback. You discuss where you are at in terms of average milestones for a person in your year. I have heard of people getting ambushed but generally they're pretty transparent about it."*

Culture & Offices

"If you want to socialize, the opportunities are there, but if you want to go home, nobody will fault you for it either," an Atlanta junior explained. There are regular attrorney breakfasts and lunches, but when it comes to after-hours, many prefer to head back to their families. It's reported that there are more social opportunities in the summer, like *"dinners and pool parties at partners' houses,"* or *"a trip to Napa for wine tasting."* However, *"if someone is looking for a vibrant social life generally, they might not find it here."* The offices themselves have their own unique culture, although sadly we must report that the Dallas of-fice's famous 'Bat Cave' – *"a conference room filled entirely with Batman memorabilia"* – is no more as the attorney responsible has left the firm. In Austin, meanwhile, the office managing partner occasionally buys 'fish art' – *"monster fish that we hang on the walls and get to name!"* Maybe it's a Texas thing...

"Kind of geeky, but in a good way!"

Many juniors liked the *"hard-working yet laid back cul-ture"* at Fish, and praised it for having a family-like envi-ronment: *"Even partners look out for you and make sure you're not getting burnt out."* Due to the extensive range of technical backgrounds, one junior described the culture as *"kind of geeky, but in a good way!"* However, *"you can't have people that are really smart, but can't communicate"* a Bostonian pointed out. *"I don't want to say 'be a de-cent human being', but that's mostly true."* There are also programs in place for flexible working or reduced hours. *"People are very understanding of your other responsibili-ties, and are willing to help you manage your workload. The firm has such a focus on quality that if you don't have the*

See firm profile on p.598

Diversity	Partners (%)	Associates (%)
Women	17	33
White	87	69
Black/African American	1	5
Hispanic/Latin American	2	2
Asian	8	21
Mixed/Other	2	2
LGBT	2	4

bandwidth to do a good job, they don't want you to take on so much that the quality suffers."

"The way our firm is structured is that we don't really have a headquarters – every office is at the same level as others," a New Yorker explained. "The Boston office is older, but the DC office is actually bigger. There's a lot of cross-staffing, so it doesn't matter where you are, you can still get the same level of work." Sources told us that the DC office will be moving location in two years to a building "two blocks away from the federal circuit, where you can see the White House from the top." The Silicon Valley office was noted to be more airy and spacious, and the Boston office was praised for its "modern feel, great tech resources" and "really cool lighting fixture that has a hologram."

Hours & Compensation

The firm's 1,900 billable hour target is a breeze for most litigators because "on average, people go significantly above that." For patent prosecutors it can be "more of a challenge, because prosecution is a lower budget practice. But it's definitely reasonable." The new tiered bonus system is tied to hours. "We're told if we hit 2,100 hours then we'll get bonuses comparable to big firms." However, a few associates would push for more transparency on this front because "when it comes to bonuses, it's like a black box. It's hard to know what to expect before you get it."

"Most people have nice home offices to work from."

The working day varied slightly from associate to associate, but the average was 9am to 7.30pm. The option of remote working means they can log back in at home if they have to leave for any reason. "I leave to walk my dog, but then log back in and work from home," one reported. Fish also gives associates a tech budget of $500 a year which can be "used for any purpose related to tech, so most people have nice home offices to work from." In terms of vacation, "it depends on the status of your cases. Vacations aren't discouraged. You just have to fit them where it makes sense."

Pro Bono

Juniors can bill up to 200 hours of pro bono work toward their billable target, and many said "the firm really wants you to use those hours. Most of the time, you get to do a bit more and experience things that might not come up as easily in billable cases, but still get the hours." Juniors have been involved in everything from "helping people apply for citizenship to cases ongoing in district courts." In an unfair dismissal case, "the client was representing himself when we stepped in and did some briefing. I got to read statements in court, but it ended up going to mediation where the client got a favorable settlement. I kind of wanted it to go to oral argument just because I was so ready! But it was still a good experience."

Pro bono hours

- For all US attorneys: 19,253
- Average per US attorney: 56

Diversity

"I'd say it might not be where it needs to be, but everyone tries to do more in terms of recruitment and retention," an associate assessed. Many juniors admitted that diversity in IP "is hard because the profession is self-selecting – you can only draw from the candidates who present themselves." Only a third of Fish's associates are female. But in spite of this, the DC office has seen a growing female presence, and hiring partner Betty Chen tells us of the firm's participation in a program called the OnRamp Fellowship. "This program helps women who have taken time off from their careers get integrated back into the legal industry," she explains. "We are among the first law firms to participate in this program." There's also a women-only retreat, where female attorneys discuss new ways to recruit and retain women. Consequently, juniors think: "Fish is really trying to acknowledge its weaknesses and areas that need improvement, and build a community." In terms of ethnic diversity, Fish fares better than most BigLaw firms: almost 40% of associates are racially diverse.

Strategy & Future

"We're very pleased with where the firm's gone and we're looking forward to a strong fourth quarter," firm president Peter Devlin tells us. "We spend a lot of time in Asia in particular, so we're growing our client base in South Korea and China." On top of that, "our pharmaceutical litigation practice is growing, as well as our commercial litigation practice."

Diversity is also high on his agenda, he says: "In 2016 we hired a new chief professional development and diversity officer for the firm. We're also growing our pro bono program, which provides new lawyers with great opportunities for professional growth."

See firm profile on p.598

The Inside View

Fitzpatrick, Cella, Harper & Scinto

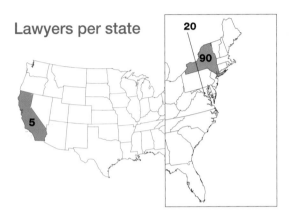

Lawyers per state

Largest US office: New York
US offices: 3
International offices: 0
First-year salary: $180,000
Billable hours: 2,160 target
Summers 2017: 10 (8 2Ls, 2 1Ls)
Revenue 2016: not disclosed
Partners made in 2017: 3
Famous for: top patent work for pharma and electronics clients

The *"nerdy"* lawyers of this sizable boutique put the 'intellectual' in intellectual property.

"ALMOST everybody here has at least an undergraduate degree in hard science or engineering. That makes for a unique atmosphere at a law firm." Associates proudly dubbed Fitzpatrick *"one of the premier firms for name brand patent litigation,"* and not just because it's the source of their paychecks. The firm scores highly in *Chambers USA* for its IP work both in New York and nationally.

Historically, its forte has been pharmaceuticals – Fitzpatrick was involved in the first ever 'Hatch-Waxman' drug patenting lawsuit – but electronics work is on the increase for clients including IBM and Canon. Though the firm has bases in Washington, DC and Orange County, its New York HQ is the center of the action. Size matters: *"The firm is fairly large"* for an IP boutique, but *"almost all the attorneys are in the same office, so you get to know everybody better and develop relationships quite quickly."*

The Work

Newcomers almost exclusively begin in the Big Apple, DC traditionally taking one a year. The firm's main practice is divided between patent litigation and prosecution. Most New Yorkers focus on litigation, while DC attorneys normally take the prosecution route. The latter have a docket for work distribution and are supervised by one partner, whereas litigators operate in *"teams that come and go as cases do."* There is a weekly survey to identify who needs work, and assignment partners who *"try to match you with cases fitting your technical expertise."* Associates used this system to steer their practice where they chose. *"I wanted to do some transactional work, so I put in a request and was almost immediately put on a transactional assignment."*

"There's no real routine."

On the litigation side, tasks include *"a lot of legal research, document review, drafting discovery requests and letters to opposing counsel,"* alongside the inevitable due diligence. A handful of lucky juniors got to go to trial within a year of starting, *"prepping witnesses and taking research assignments directly from the client. It was cool to get that exposure as a first-year, and hugely helpful as you can then apply the experience to the early stages of a case."* As a lawyer progresses, so does the nature of the work, though *"it changes a lot and it's nice that there's no real routine"* day to day. *"Senior colleagues never want to test you, they legitimately try to find answers to questions through you."*

On chambers-associate.com...

- Get hired: tricks and tips for getting into Fitzpatrick
- Interviews with recruiting committee chair Ha Kung Wong and management committee member Mike Sandonato
- The Hatch-Waxman Act of 1984

Rankings in *Chambers USA*

Intellectual Property

For detail on ranking tiers and ranking locations, visit
www.chambersandpartners.com

Patent prosecutors in DC commonly saw more mechanical and electronics clients than their pharma-focused New York counterparts. *"We're typically responding to office actions, involving the US Patent and Trademark Office and international obligations. There's a lot of filing information and disclosing statements to patent offices, as well as miscellaneous letters to clients."* DC associates also got to tackle inter partes review (IPR), which operates under a low burden of proof and faster time-frames than traditional litigation. One was *"personally in charge of compiling IPR statistics for pitches, checking new files and collecting information on them,"* and relished the chance to do it all again.

"I'm not overwhelmed but still get a good number of hours."

Interviewees praised the *"merit-based system. If you show you're responsible doing something, they give you greater responsibility. There are not a lot of arbitrary roadblocks based on what year you graduated."* Even from the start, juniors were *"sometimes surprised with how much you get trusted. You'd think as a first-year you'd be on training wheels, but you're trusted with a lot."* Some felt that *"work was lighter at times than I'd like,"* partly down to the natural litigation ebb and flow. Most associates saw *"a good amount of work. I'm not overwhelmed but still get a good number of hours."*

Training & Development

Newbies are initially enrolled in a two-week bootcamp in New York. This is built upon by monthly presentations by senior lawyers, covering different topics depending on your class year. *"They're very practical, and tell you where to look for answers to problems."* Juniors are also given bi-annual coaching with the National Institute for Trial Advocacy (NITA), with actors playing witnesses in a mock trial situation. Juniors were *"happy with the level of training – it's just enough that it's not annoying."* Those in DC had the downside of *"not being there in person for a lot of it, but it would be impractical to come to New York for everything."* Some *"would like more"* day-to-day assessment of their work, but others *"worked with very receptive feedback, there haven't been any issues,"* suggesting that *"you have to be proactive."* A formal annual review around November helps clarify any *"macro-level"* problems.

Recent work highlights

- Won dismissal of complaints against Japanese pharma company Daiichi Sankyo over blood pressure medication, establishing Supreme Court precedent for personal jurisdiction law
- Represented Amgen in a challenge brought against the company's patent on a $1 billion drug used in the treating of hyperparathyroidism (which can cause weak bones)
- Acted successfully on behalf of banking association subsidiary Askeladden to invalidate patents related to loyalty reward programs
- Obtained dismissal of lawsuit levied against clothing giant PVH regarding laser-faded jeans

Get Hired

"For IP in general you need to be able to think scientifically, but the legal aspect requires a different kind of thought." For top tips from Fitzpatrick associates, and chair of the recruiting committee Ha Kung Wong, head to chambers-associate.com.

Culture & Diversity

Sharing science backgrounds, *"everybody's a little nerdy, but still very friendly and social – not stereotypical awkward engineers! Recruitment brings in a good mix of people who you want to talk to and work with."* There are differences between offices: *"DC is very laid back and more personable, New York a bit more intense – but it's not stressful, nobody's yelling at secretaries!"* The firm encourages a familial atmosphere with happy hours and summer events like the highly popular Fitzpatrick Olympics. *"You're in teams with people you don't generally work with for events like rock climbing, dodgeball and giant Jenga."* Though Washingtonians saw less fun outside of the summer period, they *"make it up very well for ourselves,"* running teams in local sports leagues. Across the board *"there is a lot of camaraderie, the mood is always good, but this year there's been a downside because people are unclear as to where the firm is going."*

"Not stereotypical awkward engineers!"

A general lack of transparency was seen by many as a problem. One junior described it as their *"biggest criticism. The firm is very opaque in terms of management decisions. There was an instance where some administrative staff were let go and people here only found out about it online."* Town hall meetings are held at least once a year, and are *"usually informative."* This opportunity to ask *"literally any question"* was credited as one way the firm provides some transparency, but in general *"they could be more detailed in what they tell us."*

The Inside View

Diversity	Partners (%)	Associates (%)
Women	16	45
White	92	74
Black/African American	0	1.5
Hispanic/Latin American	0	1.5
Asian	6	18
Mixed/Other	2	5
LGBT	0	1

Many reasoned that *"given that engineering and science is male-dominated, there will inevitably be more men here,"* but sources were pleased to report that *"diversity is on the rise. The latest class is 50/50 male and female, and we have colleagues representing almost every ethnic background and sexual orientation from all over the world."* New York was seen as holding the diversity edge over DC, partly a result of the latter's smaller overall headcount. Projects including a Woman's Initiative Program prompted associates to conclude that *"the firm is doing well and going in the right direction."*

Hours & Compensation

"180 hours a month is the official target," but sources *"don't think that's a hard goal. You definitely want to get around that many but it's not something I've had to worry about. They're flexible."* A typical day was *"9am to 6pm, creeping toward 7pm,"* with some reporting longer hours around trial time. Juniors are encouraged to take their vacation, and while enjoying time off *"you don't have to look at your email. I responded to an email while I was on vacation just before trial, and was told to not respond to any more!"*

"It's something we'd like them to be more transparent about."

At the time of interviews, associates were *"pretty happy with the salary, but it's a little frustrating that other firms went up and Fitzpatrick hasn't made a decision or told us what they're doing."* Compensation is lockstep, and bonuses are awarded based on hours plus other important factors including quality of work, marketing activity, pro bono and recruiting support. Many were frustrated to be left in the dark about the chances of a raise to match the market. *"That's something we'd like them to be more transparent about."* The firm did go on to confirm it was matching the $180,000 market starting salary.

Pro Bono

Every pro bono hour counts toward billables, making it *"a lot more inviting, and a lot of first-years use pro bono to fill out their time, which is definitely encouraged."* Juniors took on cases including housing projects, asylum cases,

veterans' claims and contracts work, relishing the chance to step out of their comfort zone – though pro bono IP was also available. *"I got a ton of motion-writing experience, and a lot more autonomy getting to see the running of a case."* Although there is no definitive pro bono target, a conscious effort is made by the pro bono partner to alert associates to opportunities.

Pro bono hours
- For all US attorneys: 3,710
- Average per US attorney: 28

Offices

"Everybody gets their own office," unlike many other firms in Manhattan, *"with one or two windows – as you work up you get two!"* There was friendly competition over which base is best: one source liked DC *"a lot more than New York – there's a lot more room and you get tons of privacy,"* whereas those in the firm's headquarters championed their location. *"You're in the center of everything, it's easy to commute to. The lobby is beautiful and there's really nice décor."* The only disadvantage was congestion over the holidays as *"we're right by the Radio City Christmas tree!"*

New York's mothership sets the tone for all offices and *"most decisions are made by the management committee there."* Associates reported reasonably frequent communication between bases, and *"some teams are cross-staffed,"* particularly for litigation. *"We do manage some clients autonomously in DC, and definitely make client decisions here,"* suggesting some degree of devolution.

Strategy & Future

If business stays healthy, associates fancy their chances at partnership down the line. *"People reckon the chances are pretty decent because of the relatively small class sizes, better than at a larger firm."* Last year the chair of the firm's recruiting committee, Ha Kung Wong, told us about a boom in electronics work at Fitzpatrick, and this year's interviewees suggested this was set to continue. *"We're getting a pretty decent influx of work in the tech space, including software and electrical engineering, it's still on the increase."* Management committee member Mike Sandonato tells us the firm will *"be maintaining our emphasis on pharmaceuticals and electronics, and at the same time expanding to other sectors that are interesting to us."* For the full interview, go to chambers-associate.com.

"We're getting a pretty decent influx of work in the tech space, including software and electrical engineering, it's still on the increase."

Foley & Lardner LLP

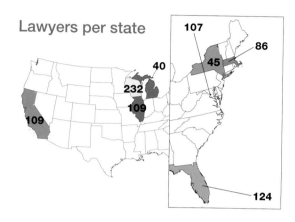

Lawyers per state

107
86
40
45
232
109
109
124

Largest US office: Milwaukee
US offices: 17
International offices: 3
First-year salary: $140,000 - $180,000
Billable hours: 1,900 required
Summers 2017: 60 (49 2Ls, 11 1Ls)
Revenue 2016: $671 million (-1.76%)
Partners made in 2017: 14 (all US)
Famous for: friendly, down-to-earth atmosphere and being Wisconsin's oldest and largest firm

Wisconsiner Foley & Lardner – 175 years old in 2017 – exports its Midwestern atmosphere and *"small town vibe"* across the States.

FOLEY may have branched out from its Wisconsin origins long ago, but the Badger State is where it remains peerless. Here, the firm tops the *Chambers USA* rankings tables for meaty practice areas like banking, corporate/M&A, general litigation, real estate, and intellectual property. In these areas in Wisconsin there is no better law firm than Foley.

It wasn't just *"the prestige and reputation"* of Wisconsin's largest and oldest firm that motivated our associate interviewees to get a foot in the door: *"Even though we're in Wisconsin, we've also got a national reach."* Beyond America's Dairyland the firm has offices in no fewer than 17 different locations spread all over the country. *Chambers USA* ranks its work in California, Florida, Illinois, Massachusetts, Michigan, and Washington, DC. Foley's sports law, franchising and healthcare teams gain nationwide recognition. In 2017, Foley is celebrating its 175th birthday. Merger rumors involving Foley have swirled around the legal blogosphere for some time, and as we went to press the latest contender for a possible tie-up was New York boutique Friedman Kaplan.

The Work

Juniors are assigned to the IP, litigation or business law (transactional) departments upon arrival at Foley. Work is predominantly assigned through relationships with partners though some groups also make use of a coordinator to help delegate projects.

IP juniors are split between IP litigators, IP transactional and patent prosecutors. The latter are slotted into further subgroups of chemical, biotech & pharma, mechanical & electromechanical technology, or electronics. IP litigators *"prepare trial and oral argument outlines but there's also a substantial amount of doc review and coordination. Cases are all fact-intensive so you spend a lot of time in the documents, but I also undertake loads of research and writing."* Patent prosecutors are *"assigned to a case that's on your docket until the patent is granted. Most of my work involves drafting applications, reviewing filings associated with the patent, and recommending strategy."* Another told of off-site visits *"to meet engineers to come up with a strategy for patent approval."*

Business law is an umbrella practice housing subgroups such as tax, transactional & securities, finance & financial institutions, healthcare, real estate and private equity. Juniors are assigned to a subgroup though can reach out to other teams to take on work. Our sources had tackled everything from investment management funds to M&A, securitization, regulatory compliance and general commercial matters. *"For the first year and a half I didn't get to draft any major project or transaction documents. More*

The Inside View

See firm profile on p.599

Rankings in *Chambers USA*

Banking & Finance	Intellectual Property
Bankruptcy/Restructuring	Labor & Employment
Corporate/M&A	Litigation
Franchising	Natural Resources
Healthcare	Projects
IT & Outsourcing	Real Estate
Insurance	Sports Law

For detail on ranking tiers and ranking locations, visit
www.chambersandpartners.com

Recent work highlights

- Assisted Harley-Davidson to secure a $1.44 billion credit agreement
- Represented Major League Baseball Advanced Media after Baseball Quick accused MLB of copying its method to create shortened highlights of baseball games
- Acted for CVS Health in several class action suits brought by independent pharmacies which allege CVS misused patient data to secure new patient business

and more now I'm the only associate staffed on a matter, running weekly calls, reviewing documents and answering client questions directly instead of running them through a senior or partner," one third-year told us. *"For the larger M&A deals, I'm still doing the diligence and drafting of ancillary documents and escrow agreements but on other deals I'm drafting some of the primary deal documents."*

Unlike the other two departments, litigation is a generalist group where associates try out different types of work before they specialize. Labor & employment, business litigation, government enforcement & white-collar crime, antitrust, appellate and privacy are all areas juniors can get stuck into. They had gained a wide range of experience, with one telling us: *"On a couple of matters I just did the standard first-year doc review and research but I also got some pretty good opportunities to draft full motions."* Another outlined: *"I was on a huge matter which really relied on the first-years for tasks above what's usually expected. We were writing expert and interrogatory reports, drafting complaints and were typically the second attorney in interviews. I also worked on the client management side, answering their questions."*

Training & Development

New starters are given a brief overview on the firm when they first start, before all being flown to one office. Once here they're broken into department groups to *"dig a little deeper"* into practice area processes, deal or case mechanics and any issues they're likely to run into. Beyond this, juniors can attend practice area or subgroup-specific training sessions fairly regularly, ranging from *"something we could run into such as environmental or ethical issues"* to *"a drafting program where we drafted up financial documents and made a library that all associates could access as a starting point."* Litigators also have access to *"professional trainers"* to assist with mock depositions and other litigation skills.

Culture

Associates in offices around the US lauded Foley's Wisconsin roots as the reason behind its amicable environment and lack of aggressive colleagues. Milwaukee

juniors told us: *"It's pretty much Midwestern. It's not cut-throat and I don't feel my colleagues are trying to take work off me. People keep an eye out for each other."* A fellow Wisconsinite noted: *"It feels like a team environment. You don't see a lot of politicking."* Although Foley's *"a big law firm it's got a small-town vibe. We're humble; we don't think we're the greatest lawyers in the world but everyone wants everyone else to succeed."*

Despite being over 600 miles away, *"we have a typical Midwest atmosphere in the DC office,"* one rookie here told us. *"It's got a laid back attitude, we don't kill ourselves over our billables and people respect your family time."* One was quick to stress that *"it doesn't mean that people are expecting less of you as the standards are high but the atmosphere feels laid back."*

"A good job of easing unnecessary pressures."

Boston juniors agreed with their fellow East Coasters: *"The people we work with are grounded and appreciate we have lives outside of work. People are realistic; as the long as the work is getting done it doesn't matter where you do it. It creates a calmer environment; stress is unavoidable in this job but they do a good job of easing unnecessary pressures."* Colleagues are *"willing to help out. I had a weird question on a pro bono matter and called someone I'd never spoken to before. She spent ages helping me out despite it being the end of the day."*

Offices

"Holy cow, this is nice!" visitors to one of Foley's offices are said to exclaim. Visit chambers-associate.com to find out which office they're talking about.

See firm profile on p.599

The Inside View

Diversity	Partners (%)	Associates (%)
Women	19.4	43.7
White	91.9	74.4
Black/African American	0.7	4.4
Hispanic/Latin American	4	6.6
Asian	2.9	13.3
Mixed/Other	0	0
LGBT	1.4	5.5

Diversity

The location of many of Foley's offices doesn't necessarily lend itself to shining diversity statistics, our sources explained. *"Our offices in places like Milwaukee – which isn't the most racially diverse place – or Jacksonville, Orlando and Madison aren't that diverse but it is in places like Boston and DC."*

"I think we're a little behind across the board but Foley makes strides to improve it," one Bostonian told us. *"Our women's committee is really active. We have tons of events for clients and a very strong internal support network; our office managing partner invited all the women over to her house for a Christmas party."* The firm has a diversity 'action council' and supports affinity groups for women, LGBTQ, African-American, Asian Pacific-American and Hispanic-American attorneys. Offices also hold an annual diversity week: *"They put on lunchtime presentations on topics like bullying or LGBT issues in the workplace,"* one Milwaukee interviewee told us. Foley's summer associate class in 2017 is its most ethnically diverse ever at 37%.

Pro Bono

Several sources had used their pro bono practice to further the skills and type of matters they handle on a day-to-day basis. We spoke to associates who'd helped clients draft patent applications, assisted non profits in applying for tax exemption status, or drafted corporate governance documents. Many were just as keen to get stuck into matters totally different to the day job, undertaking landlord/tenant, family and immigration matters or helping domestic violence victims obtain orders of protection and secure housing, for example.

The first 100 hours of pro bono work can count toward billables, which can be extended with prior approval. *"I'll call it a soft cap as they almost always grant it,"* one source told us and we heard of several attorneys racking up over 200 pro bono hours. *"You just need to give them a justification explaining how it helps your career."*

Pro bono hours
- For all US attorneys: 46,656
- Average per US attorney: 56

Hours & Compensation

In July 2016 it was announced the firm would raise is billable requirement from 1,850 to 1,900 hours; its bonus eligibility threshold remains at 1,950 hours. Alongside this announcement came news that the first-year salary for associates in Boston, Chicago, New York, California and DC would be matching the $180,000 Cravath-scale. First-years in other offices received a $20,000 raise. Great news for newbies, but not so much for the other years *"as they didn't tell the rest of us what our salary would be."* The firm eventually announced they would be raising salaries for second-years and up but the *"drawn out process"* had left our interviewees a little peeved. One source reasoned: *"Management can at times move slowly with the decision-making process; I think they're a bit risk-adverse which does have its benefits in the legal market."*

As for the increase in billable targets, *"I think at first a lot of us baulked at it but we've realized it's not a big deal. It's still completely doable."* An 8.30am to 6.30pm stint in the office was fairly common among interviewees, with many putting in an additional hour or so at home if needed.

Get Hired

The range of associates at Foley *"runs the gamut from introverted to extroverted"* but *"we tend to attract grounded, down-to-earth people."* Visit chambers-associate.com for more on hiring at Foley.

Strategy & Future

Rumors of a merger with global firm Eversheds were quickly put to bed in 2016 when chairman Jay Rothman announced preliminary exploratory talks had come to nothing. Is the firm still on the merger hunt to expand its international presence? *"We are still looking but we have not found the right combination partner for us at this point,"* he tells us.

On the domestic front, Foley aims to continue to grow its presence across the US in the upper mid-market. Rothman tells us: *"We've added a number of new lateral partners in some specific, strategic focus areas including private equity, energy, privacy & security, securities enforcement and wage and class action defense."* Visit chambers-associate.com for more insight from Rothman.

See firm profile on p.599

Fox Rothschild LLP

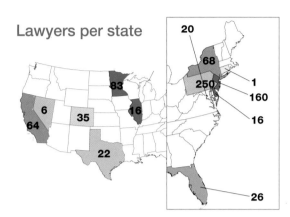

Lawyers per state

20
68
83
250
6
35
16
64
22
1
160
16
26

Largest US office: Philadelphia
US offices: 22
International offices: 0
First-year salary: $115,000 - $160,000
Billable hours: 1,850 required (1,900 litigation)
Summers 2017: 25 (20 2Ls, 5 1Ls)
Revenue 2016: $416.3 million (+14%
Partners made in 2017: 15
Famous for: being entrepreneurial; lots of US offices

A mid-sized, "*non-hierarchical*" firm with great national reach, this Fox is a lot more approachable than its four-legged namesake.

FANTASTIC Mr Fox and the equally excellent Mr Rothschild founded their Philly law firm exactly a century ago. These days, Fox Rothschild's stalking ground comprises no fewer than 22 different offices spread all around the country (as the map above illustrates). For some associates, joining full-service Fox was a fairytale come true as "*some other firms aren't as collegial, it's not adversarial or intimidating here and I immediately felt comfortable during the callback. Fox is a large firm with 750 lawyers around the country but my office is relatively small, giving me substantive work faster.*" Most of Fox's offices are small to medium in size, and even the largest – Philadelphia – houses a comfortable 250 attorneys.

Interviewees also liked Fox's steadily improving financial performance, helped from time to time by strategic mergers, like 2016's acquisition of Minneapolis's Wolff & Donnelly. "*Apparently we've never laid anyone off. Not ever – even during '08,*" one junior reflected. Recent lateral attorney hires include six entertainment lawyers from Lommen Abdo to the Minneapolis, New York and DC offices. "*We are a multi-practice firm with entertainment practices in several offices, so we had the leverage to attract other laterals,*" managing partner Mark Silow tells us. "*It's been a very smooth transition.*" The entertainment

On chambers-associate.com...

- Interview with managing partner Mark Silow
- More on getting hired

team boasts clients including husband and wife duo Angela Bassett and Courtney B Vance, the latter of whom recently played defense lawyer Johnnie Cochran in TV's *The People v. OJ Simpson. Chambers USA* awards Fox top prize nationwide for its gaming & licensing expertise, and ranks various other transactional and litigation-related practices in Pennsylvania, New Jersey, Minnesota, DC and Colorado.

The Work

At the time of our calls, the largest cohorts of juniors were in Princeton, Philly, New York and Atlantic City, with others spread across Minneapolis, Dallas, Miami, Wilmington, Denver, Montgomery County, Roseland, Pittsburgh, Exton, Warrington, Blue Bell, West Palm Beach and LA. Corporate and litigation take on the most juniors, followed by real estate, labor, and IP. The entertainment, and financial restructuring & bankruptcy departments also had a resident junior associate at the time of our calls. It's worth asking which office specializes in what. Insiders told us that "*in LA it's pretty much just litigation and bankruptcy, Atlantic City does a lot of gaming and casino law. New York does a lot of local counsel work for generic patents in IP and anything from commercial disputes to contested estates and super funds. There's also a pretty big entertainment practice.*"

In most teams, assignment is fairly informal: "*It's mainly relationship-based and you get work from partners who trust you.*" Over in litigation, however, there's a caveat for

See firm profile on p.600

Rankings in *Chambers USA*

Bankruptcy/Restructuring	Healthcare
Corporate/M&A	Labor & Employment
Environment	Litigation
Gaming & Licensing	Real Estate

For detail on ranking tiers and ranking locations, visit www.chambersandpartners.com

Recent work highlights

- Secured a $390 million verdict in favor of the Chapter 7 trustee of the Downey Financial Corp
- Negotiated $150 million worth of leases during the 'de-malling' of a shopping center and the reconstruction of an open-air mall
- Defended film producer and former Disney exec Todd Garner against claims his company 'stole' ideas from the actress Elizabeth Banks

first-years who *"are supposed to have all their assignments cleared through the head of the department to make sure they are not under water."* Speaking of litigation, *"if you're not afraid to do it, they'll throw you straight in at the deep end."* Sources had *"drafted every level of litigation document that there is, everything from motions to appellate briefs."* Some had also gone to court: *"I've gone to federal and state court and second-chaired a trial – it wasn't a big case though."*

"I've gone to federal and state court and second-chaired a trial."

Juniors in the corporate department told us that *"it's very much a general corporate practice but each partner varies in terms of what they specialize in."* In Princeton, newbies explained that *"we have three partners who are well respected in securities law and three in healthcare. We have several in M&A, but in this office we really stick out for health law."* Insiders shed some light on what tasks they'd tackled: *"Corporate work is cyclical so at points it can be quiet, but normally it's a lot of drafting things like purchase and acquisition agreements and basic contract formation drafting."* On mergers, some had *"drafted resolution documents for subsidiary companies to approve the merger of the parent company and the sale of stocks and shares."*

Over in real estate, *"we've been working on local zoning ordinance to determine what we can do for a particular housing development."* Others told us that despite the overriding transactional nature of the work, there's the odd overlap with litigation. *"It's like a mini court trial when you have to appear in front of the zoning board. You have to put up witnesses, so I spend a lot of time prepping experts. In court appeals, I've drafted all the pleadings and argued general summary judgment motions."*

Training & Development
Training kicks off with an initial orientation in Philly that lasts for around three days and covers basic skills like billing, IT and general admin. Following this, transactional associates and litigators have their own practice-specific training program, with the hours clocked up counting toward the overall billable total. There's mandatory writing training: *"The most useful session was when an expert came in and told us how to write emails without annoying people."* There's also a mock trial program and plenty of lunchtime seminars and CLEs available in-house. Litigators described their *"deposition weekend where we all go and take mock depositions while the partners critique you. I still use what I learned then to this day."*

"It's a pretty steep learning curve and I'm still on it."

Corporate attorneys get sessions on *"how to conduct due diligence and all of the important provisions of purchase agreements."* However, transactional newbies wished there was more on offer because *"corporate lawyers don't really get taught in law school because it's so geared towards litigators. It's a pretty steep learning curve and I'm still on it."*

Offices
Although Philly is officially the homebase, insiders were keen to stress that *"it doesn't seem Philly-centric, at least not in terms of work. Each office has its own identity."* How so? *"In New York it's a bit more casual. I know, I was surprised by that, but compared to Philadelphia the people here just feel more personable,"* a Big Appler reckoned. Usually newbies get their own office straight away. Philly locals told us that *"I have my own windows. Obviously that's the only thing you look for in a law firm!"* Princeton sources revealed that *"it's nothing flashy but I have a huge window and I don't feel like I'm in a prison."* New Yorkers were effusive about their impending move to a new purpose-built space: *"Everything is going to be brand new. We thought this building was fine but then we saw the new one and we were like 'oh wait!' Plus it's across the street from Grand Central station."*

"I don't feel like I'm in a prison."

Hours & Compensation
Litigators have a billing target of 1,900 hours, while it's 1,850 for everyone else. *"It's pretty achievable. You don't see people running around the corridors with their hair on fire trying to get more hours."* The average day starts at around 9am and finishes at 6.30pm-ish: *"By 8pm no one is in the office."* Most weren't fussed about hitting the target and they didn't mind the different goals between groups. *"I think litigators have a higher target because*

See firm profile on p.600

The Inside View

Diversity	Partners (%)	Associates (%)
Women	23.4	41.9
White	93.7	81.4
Black/African American	1.1	3.3
Hispanic/Latin American	1.3	3.7
Asian	2.3	7.9
Mixed/Other	3.7	1.7
LGBT	0.6	2.8

there's always plenty of work to go round. In corporate it's more hit and miss."

The base salary was upped in 2016 to $160,000 in major markets, and starting at $115,000 (depending on location). "We're always a bit behind the market and even though we raised recently, it's not as high as other firms." However, sources appreciated the reward for associates who bring in substantial new business. "It's great. If we bring in matters worth over $10,000, then we get a 10% bonus." General bonuses increase for every 25 hours associates clock up in excess of the billing target.

Culture

"The most unique thing about our culture? It's not hierarchical, it's me and the partner in the trenches." This was a common theme, and some associates described regularly "being taken out for drinks or dinner by the partners." Sources also wanted to stress that there was a strong sense of collaboration: "You don't get that walled-off feeling that you can get in other firms. We like to work together." Location also played a role in the Fox vibe. For example, "Atlantic City is a lot more laid back because we're right near the beach. It's a lot less formal and everyone lives more or less in the same area, so you regularly bump into partners doing their grocery shopping." Most had no qualms about the partner-associate dynamic at the firm, although some mentioned that "the legal work is the easiest part of life here. Managing your day-to-day interactions and partner expectations can be challenging."

Socially, there are usually happy hours every fortnight in Philadelphia, although these sorts of get-togethers happen less frequently in suburban offices, as you might expect. Insiders told us that "trying to get regular events sorted is a real difficulty." But there's a national associates' weekend, which happens every other year and comprises "different skill-based training in the day and then dinners and drinks in the evenings."

Pro Bono

Associates can count 50 hours of pro bono work toward the bonus program; "if we need more we can just ask." Most interviewees had got involved with a few matters that included "a guardian ad litem case [a guardian appointed by the court to represent the interests of children or incompetent people]." Others had "helped out a lot with legal name changes. In Pennsylvania we have a different process for changing the name on official documents, so it can be difficult to navigate." Tasks had seen newbies "first-chairing hearings, leading client meetings, and drafting all the relevant documents."

Pro bono hours
- For all attorneys: 1,793
- Average per attorney: 10

Diversity

"It's definitely emphasized, but it's not anything amazing," explained associates of diversity. "It's not tremendously racially diverse." Newbies in a regional office rationalized that "it's not management's fault, we just don't have the same scale of recruitment pool that a major city would have. Here we tend to recruit people who have a local connection and they tend to be white and middle class." Sources felt that New York was the most diverse even compared to the firm's main hub in Philly. In terms of gender, "we have a Women's Initiative that's really active. Every office has a partner and an associate head and there are lots of events to go to." Most common were drinks or networking with speakers who tackled topics like the track to partnership. Others spoke of "virtual conferences which are streamed into every office and there are panel discussions on topics that affect female attorneys. Last year's conference was all about how we can make men more aware of our issues and how to discuss them freely."

Strategy & Get Hired

"One of the key things about our firm is that they put a premium on a 'good fit'," an associate reported. "We're not super-obsessed about getting a 4.0 student who can sit in a room and bill 14 hours a day." Others continued that "it sounds pie in the sky, but we're more about building a firm where we can collaborate and work in a nice environment. So in the interview be honest and be yourself." Other than building a platform for collaboration, what else is the firm looking to build on? Managing partner Mark Silow tells us, "we will try to expand into other major metropolitan areas around the country. The cities that are very interesting to us are places like Boston, Seattle, Houston and Kansas City. Our second goal is to grow our newer existing offices that we want to make more vital in our current offering." For more from the experts, go online.

See firm profile on p.600

The Inside View

Freshfields Bruckhaus Deringer LLP

Lawyers per state

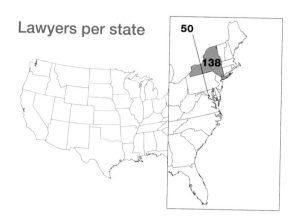

Largest US office: New York
US offices: 2
International offices: 24
First-year salary: $180,000
Billable hours: no requirement
Summers 2017: 19 (17 2Ls, 2 1Ls)
Revenue 2016: £1.327 billion (+6.6%)
Partners made in 2017: 18 globally (1 in US)
Famous for: magic circle prestige; international prowess

An incredibly global firm with a relatively small US base, Freshfields may not be fresh-faced but it's certainly outward-looking...

DON'T be fooled by a name that evokes new shoots of grass: Freshfields is actually the oldest of the five elite firms that make up Britain's historic magic circle. That said, its presence in the US is still relatively fresh – it only opened its inaugural New York office in 1977, and it remains small. But as has often been the case in the city's history, if you turn up in the Big Apple with a couple of bucks and some good ideas, you can reach for the stars. Not just literally – Freshfields occupies four floors of *"one of the tallest buildings in Midtown"* – but also figuratively: *Chambers USA* recognizes its chutzpah and ranks the firm for its capital markets, international arbitration, projects and tax work.

"Many of us get to visit Europe three times in our first year."

"We are incredibly well-integrated globally," juniors told us. *"I speak with colleagues in London and Brussels on a daily basis."* This kind of emphasis on the international is obviously a big draw and sources described as *"tremendous"* the fact that *"many of us get to visit Europe three times in our first year."* Then there's the close relationship between New York and DC – the latter of which opened

in 1998 – described by one associate as *"pretty much one entity."* All of which proves that the firm's claim on its website to be 'one partnership' across borders is far from hyperbolic.

The Work

Freshfields' New York juniors are stationed in capital markets, finance, corporate and dispute resolution; while in the smaller DC office they can also find themselves in the firm's antitrust team. The popular dispute resolution group is split into three subgroups: international arbitration, investigations and civil litigation. First and second-year associates will *"move between all three"* and then *"usually around the beginning of your third year you will start to specialize as you begin to find your niche."*

As you might expect, *"all of the stuff you work on as a junior has an international aspect"* with investigations involving *"regulators from multiple jurisdictions."* From these multiple jurisdictions come clients of an international caliber and interviewees had handled cases for big name financial institutions, pharmaceutical companies, universities, airlines and publishers. Those fearing hours and hours of *"dreaded doc review"* need not fear: *"If you come and work at Freshfields there is no way you'll be doing doc review for two years. When there's a lot of it to be done, senior associates will always chip in."*

The Inside View

See firm profile on p.601

Rankings in *Chambers USA*

Antitrust	International Arbitration
Capital Markets	Litigation
Corporate/M&A	

For detail on ranking tiers and ranking locations, visit www.chambersandpartners.com

Recent work highlights

- Advised Formula One and CVC Capital Partners in connection with the $8 billion sale of Formula One Group to Liberty Media
- Advised Henderson Group on its $6 billion all stock merger of equals with Janus Capital to form Janus Henderson Global Investors, a leading global active asset manager with AUM of more than $320 billion
- Advised InterContinental Hotels Group as a third party respondent in the DOJ merger investigation of the Marriott International and Starwood Hotels & Resorts merger
- Advising Volkswagen on the settlement reached with the US government to resolve criminal and federal environmental and other civil claims against the company

The corporate tree too contains multiple branches, with the department split between capital markets, finance, IP and corporate/M&A. These subgroups work closely together and, with the exception of IP – *"which is tiny"* – fresh-faced corporate associates may find themselves getting work from different teams, at least initially. Cross-selling is rife across all departments but none more so than in corporate where *"different subgroups will most often be working on particular aspects of one huge deal."* One such mammoth deal has been the acquisition of the world's second-largest brewer by the first-largest. Freshfields took the lead on Anheuser-Busch's $100 billion purchase of SABMiller and pulled in every corporate hand in the firm.

"Begin to find your niche."

Work on this most frothy of deals saw corporate sources *"running due diligence, reviewing contracts and drafting ancillary documents."* Over in antitrust – or *"antitrust, competition and trade, to give it its proper name"* – *"we've been working for a year doing merger control on the deal."* Outside of that, the team deals mostly with *Fortune 500* companies, though there's a *"growing niche working with private equity firms."*

Assignment used to be *"informal across the board,"* and in most smaller teams it still usually just involves *"a conversation or email."* However, in New York, after some minor grumblings, the system has been reformed – *"we now have an email distribution list and when a new assignment comes in it will go to people on the list. We also have an Excel spreadsheet into which we put our weekly hours; assigning partners will look at this when deciding who to approach about work."* This system ensures associates don't become over-burdened.

Culture

Sources believed that Freshfields's culture was more than a little bit influenced by the firm's European heritage – *"I think people are more open-minded here about interacting with other cultures. And, especially in New York, I think it makes it a little bit less aggressive."* That said, the office's cosmopolitan feel is no secret – indeed it's what attracted many to the firm in the first place. *"There are always lawyers here on secondment from all over the world and they aren't just sitting in a corner: they are fully integrated into the work."*

On top of this, juniors are trusted with high-level tasks from early on: *"The partners trust us to work stuff out for ourselves. Also, because a lot of the US groups are quite small, you're give a lot of responsibility. At times it can feel like too much!"*

What there could be more of are firm-organized social events. *"Obviously during the summer there are loads of events: we go to dinner at a swanky restaurant and then out to a Broadway show [Hamilton]; we even go on a fishing trip to Brooklyn. No one catches much fish but it's great fun."* But other than that, there's only really *"the Christmas party and the occasional happy hour."* Nonetheless, the relative paucity of organized fun belies a place where *"everyone gets on really well, office doors are kept open and you'll often have seniors stroll into your office for a chat."*

Training & Development

It may be that management keep its powder dry for the firm's regular global gatherings – *"when it comes to international conferences and training opportunities, Freshfields really put its money where its mouth is."* Juniors attend annual practice area conferences, *"always in pretty plush locations,"* with the worldwide dispute resolution team having recently enjoyed a three-day get together in Prague with *"loads of workshops, lectures and teambuilding exercises."*

Given the size of the US offices, practical on-the-job training also works well. That said, there's still *"plenty of formalized in-house stuff."* Sources described a typical first-year exercise: *"A partner will typically pair up with a newbie for a mock presentation. The junior will do all the work and preparation and then they'll both present to their group."* This practical development runs parallel to a firmwide 'career milestones' training and assessment program, which garnered more of a lukewarm response from interviewees. *"It's more like a set of skills that are listed and you're supposed to work toward but it's hard to*

See firm profile on p.601

Diversity	Partners (%)	Associates (%)
Women	27	48
White	92	77
Black/African American	3	4
Hispanic/Latin American	5	8
Asian	0	11
Mixed/Other	0	0
LGBT	Unknown	Unknown

articulate all of these different milestones." Nonetheless, there was near unanimous relief that *"unlike London, the milestones don't affect our compensation."*

Appraisals take place annually, *"though I think first-years get one after six months."* Juniors approach senior associates and partners they've worked with and ask them to submit a short appraisal on a sheet. Then meeting with a partner, *"they more or less explain what you're doing well and what needs improvement."* Freshfields also encourages partners to give regular informal feedback.

Offices

"It is absolutely gorgeous," effused one source about the firm's NYC digs. *"I'm talking to you right now from the 56th floor and looking out over Central Park and upper Manhattan, the sun is shining and it's pretty sweet."* As well as this awestruck individual's 56th floor, Freshfields has the one below and two above, meaning they take up floors 55–58 of *"one of the taller buildings in Midtown."* Besides the panoramic views, the building's location directly above the East 51st subway station was also lauded – *"especially when it's minus 20 on a February morning."*

> ### "The décor has kind of a Scandinavian vibe – simple, wooden and clean."

DC is more of a modest affair. Again it's conveniently located for commuters *"right by the Metro Center stop in the middle of town,"* and *"we're right next to a church whose bells toll every hour, on the hour."* Inside *"the décor has kind of a Scandinavian vibe – simple, wooden and clean."*

Hours & Compensation

The lockstep salary and bonus system was universally praised by sources. However, there's no billings target at Freshfields, which was a relief to some but others found it quite stressful because expectations and transparency vary, partner-to-partner. When it comes to those bonuses, the firm *"isn't at Wachtell's level but we did do a salary match when Cravath went up."* In terms of hours, juniors felt Freshfields was pretty standard for the Big Apple – with most days ending around 8 or 9pm – while DC is

"a little less crazy." That said, *"there are plenty of lawyers who have young families and so will leave the office at six, go home and have dinner, and then start working remotely again later – that's definitely encouraged by management."*

Vacation is a pretty standard *"20 days, with six that you can carry over."* Though *"unlike our European colleagues, who disappear for a week or two in August, we're still expected to be contactable."*

Pro Bono

Pro bono fits into Freshfields's ethos of juniors being expected to dive into things head first. Their willingness to do so is rewarded – every February there is a reception where *"the highest pro bono billers are commended in front of the whole office."* All of the work is coordinated out of New York so most of it is centered in the Big Apple, although DC does a lot too. Interviewees had worked with New York's Legal Aid Society, mostly on work with asylum seekers, while others had been involved with the Bronx Defenders and the UN.

Pro bono hours
- For all US attorneys: 11,743
- Average per US attorney: 70

Diversity

Associates recognized that Freshfields is taking the requisite steps in the right direction, especially with regards to gender. The firm has a formal female mentorship program that couples junior partners with mid-level associates with the aim of *"counseling them to show what it takes to move up the chain to the top."* There's also an active LGBT group that does a lot of pro bono work on transgender and same-sex rights and – like the practice areas – convenes globally every 14 months for a two-day conference in London.

Get Hired

While being bilingual and attending a prestigious university are by no means essential to success in the Freshfields recruitment process, they certainly aren't a hindrance. *"Languages and top schools"* kept popping up when we asked about the ideal Freshfields candidate: *"Looking at the biographies of my colleagues, they all listed fluency in at least one other language."* But never fear, recruiters are also looking for a sharp intellectual curiosity – *"I did a lot of interviews and I felt Freshfields went into more detail about school. They asked a lot about the academic work I'd done. I think they are maybe looking at people who have done more humanities-focused subjects."* After surviving the interviews, potential recruits are treated to a cocktail reception, though one nervous source quipped: *"I kind of wish it had been before."*

The Inside View

See firm profile on p.601

Fried, Frank, Harris, Shriver & Jacobson

Lawyers per state

90

351

Largest US office: New York
US offices: 2
International offices: 3
First-year salary: $180,000
Billable hours: 2,000 target
Summers 2017: 70 (63 2Ls, 2 1Ls, 3 3Ls, 2 SEOs)
Revenue 2016: $556.4 million (+10.3%)
Partners made in 2017: 5 globally (all US)
Famous for: all things corporate, with a strong sprinkling of real estate and litigation too

This Wall Street firm's delicious array of practice areas has a distinctly transactional flavor.

FRIED Frank is Manhattan-born and bred. Not to be confused with a meal at a diner, the 'Fried' is pronounced 'freed'. But the firm offers its own mouthwatering menu of opportunities to associates. Some of the world's largest financial institutions are on the client roster. One repeat customer is Goldman Sachs, which it advised on a whopping 167 M&A deals in 2016 alone.

While most of Fried Frank's 450 strong US team is housed in New York, just under 100 attorneys are in DC. There's also a sprinkling of offices in global financial centers Frankfurt, London and Paris. The firm was also in Asia but closed its offices in Hong Kong and Shanghai in 2015. While chairman David Greenwald assures us that Asia is not permanently off the menu, *"our focus is on building our core practices – asset management, M&A, private equity, real estate, capital markets, finance, tax and litigation. We are also focused on aligning our European practices with our practices in the US."* Associates were drawn here in part by *"the firm's great reputation for M&A, but it covers all areas of corporate law which is why it's very popular."*

Other specialist areas include litigation and finance, which along with corporate/ M&A receive rankings from our sister publication *Chambers USA*. But the highest accolade goes to the New York-centered real estate practice, which acts on some of the city's biggest developments. *"The real estate group is super-competitive to get into, but that's because we're known for it,"* insiders emphasized.

The Work

At the time of our calls, 37 of 71 junior associates were part of the corporate group in New York. Real estate in the Big Apple claimed eight junior lawyers, while litigation housed seven. The rest were in executive compensation, tax and bankruptcy. Twelve of the 71 were in DC: most in corporate, a handful in litigation, and one in each of tax, antitrust, real estate and executive compensation & employee benefits. Each department assigns work slightly differently. Staffing in corporate is controlled by an assigning partner, who mediates between partners and newbies. For the first eight months or so, new associates used to rotate around the department, but now they are placed in a specific group for three to six months. If they want to move then, they can. *"It's pretty flexible and most end up where they want to be."*

Corporate houses seven subgroups: asset management; capital markets & corporate governance; corporate real estate; finance; M&A & private equity; environmental; and IP transactional. The majority of our sources had sampled asset management. *"Generally it's a lot of fund*

See firm profile on p.602

The Inside View

Rankings in *Chambers USA*

Banking & Finance	Investment Funds
Capital Markets	Litigation
Corporate/M&A	Private Equity
Employee Benefits &	Real Estate
Executive Compensation	Tax
Government	

For detail on ranking tiers and ranking locations, visit
www.chambersandpartners.com

Recent work highlights

- Representing Goldman Sachs, UBS, Deutsche Bank, and Citigroup in a securities class action concerning the issuance of around $26 billion of residential mortgage-backed securities
- Acting as counsel to Medicare company Humana in its proposed $37 billion sale to Aetna
- Advising Citigroup in its $2 billion purchase of its HQ at 388-390 Greenwich Street in Tribeca from SL Green Realty
- Advised on Anbang Insurance's $1.95 billion purchase of the Waldorf Astoria from Hilton

Pro bono hours

- For all US attorneys: 32,984
- Average per US attorney: 74

formation and maintenance. It involves negotiating with investors, drafting purchase agreements, due diligence memos, SEC filings and opinion letters." All enthused that "they expose you to substantive work very early on, and you can see deals from start to finish." Corporate real estaters described a focus in "four major types of transactions: acquisitions, leasing, refinancing and development. There is also a sub-sub-group which does land use work." Insiders had been "prepping and reviewing ancillary documents, researching title issues and distilling leases." Others described their role as "the keeper of the documents." As Tolkienesque as that sounds, they explained that "it means that you have to keep everything organized. It's not the most glamorous role, but it gives you ground-up experience."

A practice group manager in New York and various partners firmwide handle the staffing of litigation associates – DC included. "There's a big white-collar practice, there's also real estate litigation, commercial litigation, and bankruptcy." Tasks include drafting parts of briefs, the usual doc review and some client interaction. However, a few insiders who had either come from previous careers or clerked found it took a while to adjust to the department dynamic. "It's good that we have a hierarchy to look over work, but sometimes it feels like the firm underestimates our ability."

Pro Bono

A pro bono counsel circulates opportunities to associates, who must do at least 20 hours a year to be bonus eligible. However in reality "you can count anything up to 300 hours, which is extremely generous." Associates were keen to relay the various partnership programs with organizations like HerJustice and Sanctuary for Families. "There's tons of opportunities to get involved with things like domestic violence." But the most common cases were immigration matters. New attorneys generally had "conducted client interviews for U visa applications [visas that give victims of crimes temporary legal status] for abused women." Others had "written appellate briefs, led the discovery process and drafted affidavits."

Training & Development

There's a Fried Frank Academy for summers and Fried Frank University for first-years, who all schlep over to the Big Apple for tutelage. Speaking of the latter, associates described it as "a one week program where they dump all this info on you. It's a little overwhelming – it caused a lot of knowledge leakage and I'm not too sure what went in." Insiders were grateful for monthly refreshers that included CLEs on topics like "document drafting and depositions."

Newbies prepare for formal reviews by listing supervisors they've worked with for more than 30 hours and then "write a blurb about what you did." This is a fairly comprehensive personal statement. Two partners then go over the conglomerated feedback. "They add a bit more color to what's been said about you." You can upward review partners: "They say it's anonymous, but that being said, people are hesitant to say too much."

Hours & Compensation

The 2,000 hours billing target is very achievable, partly because 125 hours can be from "qualified non-billables, which are things like recruiting for the firm." Additionally, up to 300 hours of pro bono can count toward the total. Associates generally worked from 9.30am to 7.30pm, but we heard of different schedules depending on what group people were in. "M&A is cyclical, so some days I can leave at 6pm and others I'm working until 12am and on weekends too." Yet insiders stressed that "if you've stayed here until 3am, then they tell you to go home the next day. Plus we're paid well."

"If you've stayed here until 3am, then they tell you to go home the next day."

See firm profile on p.602

The Inside View

Diversity	Partners (%)	Associates (%)
Women	15	43
White	97	76
Black/African American	0	6
Hispanic/Latin American	1	4
Asian	2	10
Mixed/Other	0	4
LGBT	1	6

How well? Interviewees gave us the elevator pitch: *"We were worried that they weren't going to raise the salary lockstep with other BigLaw firms, but they did. It went up to $190,000 for second-years."* Bonuses are tiered. *"Over 2,200 hours is 15% above the base rate. You get a 'super bonus' over the 2,450 mark, but at that point it's not really worth it for the hours you have to work to reach that."*

Culture & Diversity

Surprisingly, *"it's not what I had in mind for Manhattan BigLaw,"* insisted insiders. *"I thought it'd be cut-throat because all lawyers are competitive, but not here and not with each other at least. No one's crazy."* There's a healthy mix of monthly cocktail and happy hours and associate pizza lunches to keep things ticking along. But it's the summer that sees most gatherings, like open-air Shakespeare in Central Park. Both offices also have a sporty side: *"There's a yoga instructor once a week and we have 'Fit Club' where the firm pays for groups of four of us to have a personal trainer."* A few felt that *"some partners are very much still in the old guard and don't really account for change. Some expect your work to be perfect first time when they haven't explained how to do it right."*

"No one's crazy."

But what does that say about diversity? *"Is the partnership diverse? No. But that's a problem throughout the industry. It's also harder to recruit diverse lateral partners because if they've made partner at a firm, they're less likely to leave."* This year insiders were happier with the increased numbers of females in leadership: *"There's a lot of women here so they're trying to make it better. One woman has just made partner working part time, which is encouraging as it says you can raise a family as well."* There is the usual range of affinity groups, though the most visible was said to be the women's forum. *"They run sessions with partners where we talk about work/life balance and things like that."* However, *"there are very few African American or Hispanic partners. While we have a culture of inclusivity, this area is lacking."* The stats bear this out at partner level (0% African American, 1% Hispanic and 2% Asian partners), although at associate level the figures are bet-

ter than average: 6% African American, 4% Hispanic and 10% Asian associates.

Offices

The waterfront New York office was a hit with associates. The dark wood interiors give it a *"traditional law firm feel, but it's really beautiful. The views are gorgeous."* First-years usually have to share an office and liked the company. New Yorkers raved about their new associate lounge, *"which has free snacks and drinks only for associates. There's also a ping-pong table, foosball, a TV and extra coffee machines that make amazing cappuccinos."*

"It's easy to take for granted how great the office is."

A stone's throw away from the White House, DC associates said that *"sometimes it's easy to take for granted how great the office is."* They were adamant that *"no one shares an office – ever!"* Not even first-years. Unlike the NY mothership, the DC hub is drenched in *"natural light with glass everywhere. If you're working in a law firm, it's nice to be in beautiful surroundings."* DC pips Manhattan to the post on the artwork front as sources gushed that *"there's Lichtensteins everywhere."* Even though New York is the main hub, DCers were sure that *"there's a lot of workflow between offices – we never feel like a dinky satellite."*

Strategy & Get Hired

With a history at Fried Frank and a 20-year career at Goldman Sachs, David Greenwald returned as chairman in late 2014, and his presence is most definitely felt by juniors. The firm runs regular *"town-hall meetings,"* where Greenwald has an open forum to go over the firm's strategy. *"It's about an hour and a half and he goes over the firm's financials and what each department is doing."* Insiders said that he encourages questions and *"does a really good job of listening to suggestions."* Recent discussions have included *"a clearer explanation of the bonus structure, plus where the firm as a whole is going."*

David Greenwald tells us that *"in September 2017, we have 54 new associates joining us, which is the largest incoming class we have had since 2008."* Considering the big focus both now and in the future in transactional work, associates advised that people should come with *"corporate experience, because all law school prepares you for is litigation."* Greenwald adds: *"We continue to invest in associates as the future of the firm, and we are committed to creating opportunities for them to work on cutting-edge matters and build strong relationships with clients."* For more tips, go online.

See firm profile on p.602

The Inside View

Gibbons P.C.

Lawyers per state

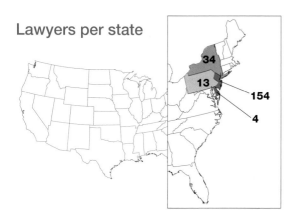

Largest US office: Newark
US offices: 5
International offices: 0
Second-year salary: $135,000
Billable hours: 1,980 required
Summers 2017: no summer program
Revenue 2016: $102.35 million (-5.3%)
Partners made in 2017: 4
Famous for: hiring judicial clerks; Newark stronghold; branding

Gibbons is a huge legal brand in New Jersey that welcomes judicial clerks.

FOUNDED in Newark in 1926, Gibbons has spent the best part of a century on its feet honing its advocacy prowess for clients across a multitude of different sectors. Almost all juniors at this litigation hothouse are based in the Newark HQ, though at the time of our calls there was a lone junior associate in Trenton too. Further afield, the Jersey stalwart's network extends out of state to offices in New York, Wilmington and Philadelphia. Across its network, Gibbons' big earner remains its top-ranked litigation team, but *Chambers USA* also recognizes other practices including corporate/M&A, IP, healthcare, real estate, and bankruptcy.

As a PC [professional corporation] rather than an LLP, Gibbons' partners are referred to as 'directors', though all the associates we spoke to called them partners anyway. The firm's litigious *"pedigree"* has helped it to develop and attract a garrison of directors that includes some of the Garden State's finest litigators. Take James Zazzali, who formerly served as chief justice of the Supreme Court of New Jersey. Or Edwin Stern, who is acting justice on the New Jersey Supreme Court. All in all *"if you're studying law in New Jersey – hell, even if you're not – you can't miss Gibbons!"*

On chambers-associate.com...

- Tips on getting hired by Gibbons
- Gibbons' Top Bananas

The Work

At the time of our calls most juniors were in the large business & commercial litigation (BCL) group; a couple were in product liability; and there was one apiece in criminal defense, employment & labor law, and government affairs. Other options in past years have included corporate, financial restructuring & creditors' rights, IP, and real property & environmental law. All incoming associates are assigned a staffing partner to help them manage their workload. *"Each department has a dedicated attorney,"* but *"after a few months they act as more of a safety net. Once you've established a few relationships with partners, you're set."* Associates are also welcome to try out work from other departments: *"It's not uncommon for people to explore another interest area based on informal conversations they've had with partners,"* we heard.

"Business and commercial litigation (BCL) is the firm's largest group," mentioned one litigator. Work here varies from class action defense in consumer protection work, to general business disputes, like breaches of contract. For first-years, *"the likelihood is that you'll initially try out a bit of everything."* Gibbons' clerkship-honed juniors are rarely swamped with paperwork: *"Most people land here with polished legal research and writing skills already, so it's not long until you're really getting into the nitty-gritty practical tasks. By the end of my first year I'd already taken depositions, written briefs and had lots of regular client contact."*

Over in product liability, clients include pharmaceuticals companies – of which there's a high concentration around Trenton and Newark – oil & gas, and telecom-

The Inside View

Rankings in *Chambers USA*

Bankruptcy/Restructuring	Intellectual Property
Corporate/M&A	Labor & Employment
Environment	Litigation
Healthcare	Real Estate

For detail on ranking tiers and ranking locations, visit www.chambersandpartners.com

Recent work highlights

- Successfully defended an appeal against the New Jersey Sports & Exposition Authority's decision to issue $1.15 billion in bonds to help finish the construction of 'American Dream Meadowlands', a mall and entertainment complex
- Helped Canam, North America's largest fabricator of steel components, in its majority stake purchase of New Jersey steel erector Stonebridge
- Helped a prominent New Jersey hospital avoid paying millions of dollars in damages, in a government investigation concerning fraudulent federal healthcare claims

munications corporations. On big litigations, juniors had been entrusted with *"research and investigation tasks,"* but had also *"participated in internal strategy conversations, and drafted motions."* On smaller cases, *"it's very often just you and a partner, so you get first crack at everything that comes in the door! I've held several one-to-one calls with clients and general counsel, without my partner supervising."* Still, juniors did stress that *"while there are lots of opportunities to pick up and run cases, partners make it known that they're there as a safety net if you need it."*

Client meetings and court trips are common in the criminal defense team, which mainly covers federal, white-collar and government investigations cases. Over in employment & labor meanwhile, rookies are straight in at the deep end. *"From the very start I was attending witness interviews, discussing strategy with the supervising director, and helping devise cost-effective solutions to settle claims,"* we heard.

Offices

Gibbons has around 210 attorneys firmwide, with the vast majority of associates based in Newark. *"Newark gets a bad rep, but it's come a long way even since I was at law school,"* we were told. *"There's a tremendous amount of opportunity appearing, and tons of companies are getting in on it. There are a lot of start-up accelerators, and we've even got a Whole Foods now!"*

As for the office itself, *"we're well positioned to take advantage of this uptick, as our office is attached to Penn Station – a major transportation artery."* The firm's proximity to Seton Hall and Rutgers *"makes us feel like we're part of a network of excellence,"* particularly as *"we do a lot of events with them."*

Gibbons' other offices are much smaller than Newark's: New York, with just over 30 attorneys, and Philly (with around 15) have a similar spread of departments; Trenton handles a lot of lobbying and other government-related work; and the Delaware office focuses on bankruptcy.

Training & Development

Fresh starters are automatically enrolled into The Gibbons Academy, which delivers monthly presentations to help juniors flesh out their on-the-job learning, while

also bagging their CLE requirements. *"It's great that we can do that on-site,"* said one. *"It saves a lot of trekking about!"* Past talks have included 'Corporate governance 101' and 'Protecting your license from litigation landmines.'

There's also an annual review process. *"The feedback you receive isn't tied into whether or not you've made hours; it's more about the quality of your work."* In most departments juniors submit a self-evaluation, and further feedback is provided by any partners they've spent over 50 hours working with. *"A neutral partner then puts together a comprehensive evaluation measured against certain key competencies, such as writing or interpersonal skills. It helps you to target in on certain areas in the year ahead."*

Culture

St. Patrick's Day is a big deal at Gibbons. *"Last year the firm put on a big spread, and there were games too. We're mostly litigators here so the limerick contest was pretty competitive!"* The firm also marked its 90th anniversary in 2016. *"A big birthday party was thrown and all of the other offices turned up,"* said one Newark local. *"But on a day-to-day basis I wouldn't wouldn't say Gibbons is a super social place. There certainly isn't a regimented party plan you have to adhere to."*

Informal socializing is far more common, and *"it's really easy to making friends and connections here. I've done that with a few partners, and they all seem really keen to pull me along in their endeavors. That could mean the opportunity to write an article with them, or to accompany them to trade events and interact with lawyers at other firms. I've had so many opportunities come from informal streams that have helped deepen and broaden my industry knowledge."*

There are also a number of social events put on at an early stage to facilitate these interactions. *"The welcome reception for the new associate class was the one I found most beneficial,"* another junior recounted. *"It lay the founda-*

See firm profile on p.603

Diversity	Partners (%)	Associates (%)
Women	20	43
White	92	94
Black/African American	3	1
Hispanic/Latin American	3	5
Asian	2	0
Mixed/Other	0	0
LGBT	2	5

tions for future relationships with colleagues more senior to me, and from different practice groups."

Diversity

"Gibbons has made real efforts to invest in pipeline diversity schemes," associates agreed. Since 2008 the firm has worked alongside the New Jersey Law and Education Empowerment Project, running week-long work placements for young urban students. It also offers internships to upcoming minority scholars, as part of the United States Higher Achievement and Advancement Foundation Fellowship.

Attorneys can also attend *"regular"* presentations on diversity issues, provided by Gibbons' Diversity Initiative Program. Consequently *"there's a lot of positive sentiment about diversity and equality at the firm, particularly for female attorneys."* Family life seems particularly well-supported: after parental leave, attorneys have the option to return on a 60% basis, and after a year they can remain on an 80% schedule for as long as they need.

Get Hired

Gibbons abandoned its traditional OCI and summer program well over a decade ago in favor of hiring worldly-wise judicial clerks. This makes sense as almost all junior associates work in Gibbons' top-ranked litigation team where they can put their experience with judges to good use. For further application tips, check out chambers-associate.com.

Pro Bono

Associates can count 50 hours of pro bono toward their billable target. *"It's not necessarily a requirement,"* pointed out one caller, *"but it's certainly highly encouraged. It's a litigation-heavy firm so pretty much everyone surpasses that mark. As a young associate it's a great way to get onto a deposition, own a case, or stand on your feet."*

The firm provides pro bono support to a catalog of different organizations. Associates in the Newark office had drafted wills for first responders through the Wills for Heroes program, offered advice on child custody at a domestic violence clinic, and helped push asylum applications for undocumented children from South and Central America.

Pro bono hours
- For all attorneys: 13,109
- Average per attorney: 70

Hours & Compensation

Though associates' billable target is set at 1,980 hours, *"it's not necessarily a strict requirement. I won't hit my target this year, but the firm has explained that as long as I fill my time with other activities – writing, doing research for partners, participating in business events or pro bono – this shouldn't be an issue."*

Few interviewees regularly worked later than 7pm, with most clocking off at 6.30pm at the latest. *"The nature of litigation means that this can fluctuate,"* but the latest night we heard of ended at around 10.30 pm. During these periods *"you're welcome to tailor your schedule to fit with your life outside of work. If you've got kids you can get home for dinner, and then put in a few hours remotely in the evening if you need to. That balance is encouraged."*

Strategy & Future

Associates tipped the lobbying-focused Trenton office as one to watch over the coming years. *"The firm is really looking to grow in the political sphere, particularly when it comes to working with lobbyists. Our goal is to expand that offering beyond New Jersey to become a national presence in the field."*

Managing partner Patrick Dunican confirms that *"for the past nine years Gibbons has been named the top lawyer-lobbying firm in New Jersey. We have long-established relationships with elected politicians and policy makers and are known for producing the state's best work in the political field. We believe the next step will be to expand our reach to Washington, DC. This isn't a new aspiration – we have many long-standing relationships with members of the US House of Representatives and Senate – but now we're actually putting the wheels in motion and setting up in DC. We've been actively exploring opportunities for about six months, and expect to have an office open within another six."*

> *"We've been actively exploring opportunities for about six months, and expect to have an office open within another six."*

See firm profile on p.603

The Inside View

Gibson, Dunn & Crutcher LLP

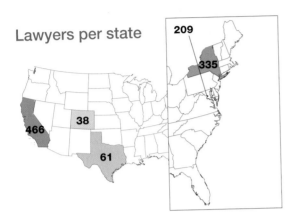

Lawyers per state

209
335
466
38
61

Largest US office: New York
US offices: 10
International offices: 10
First-year salary: $180,000
Billable hours: no requirement
Summers 2017: 123 (116 2Ls, 6 1Ls, 1 other)
Revenue 2016: $1.61 billion (+4.4%)
Partners made in 2017: 13
Famous for: helping to overturn Proposition 8; huge presence on East and West Coast

Content juniors relish *"taking control of their careers"* in the free market system at this mighty LA-founded institution.

GIBSON Dunn is a powerful presence with extensive territory. The firm's 1,200 lawyers are spread across ten US offices, with a further ten overseas – the latest additions being a domestic base in Houston and a new offering in Frankfurt. Kudos abounds around Gibson – it tops the *Chambers USA* charts for heaps of litigious and transactional practices, including antitrust, appellate, regulation, FCPA [Foreign Corrupt Practices Act], M&A, IT and outsourcing. Roam the hallways and you might spot big shot lawyers like Ted Olson (who helped overturn Proposition 8), Orin Snyder (attorney to Bob Dylan and Jerry Seinfeld) and Debra Wong Yang (the first Asian American woman to serve as a federal prosecutor). With such prestige in abundance, it's no wonder that the firm is a magnet to ambitious law students looking for a place to start private practice.

The Work

First-year associates join Gibson's offices across the country, but the largest cohorts are based in New York, LA and DC. During their first two years, juniors have the opportunity to formally rotate between practice areas at six-month intervals. However, *"most people usually come in knowing that they want to be litigators, for example, and stick with that."*

On chambers-associate.com...

- Interview with Chairman Ken Doran

Thanks to the firm's free market system, *"you have the freedom to develop your own practice and build relationships with the people you want to build relationships with. You're not forced onto projects or at the mercy of an assigning partner."* As such, *"you need to take charge of your own destiny, figure out what you wanna do and go get it!"*

Associates acknowledged that *"there are a couple of downsides"* to this system: *"Time management can be an issue, especially as a first year when you don't know how many things you should take on and nobody but you knows what's on your plate. Things come up at the same time, so you're doing a ton of hours in one day and then not much at all. There's no great way to control that."* Despite negotiating this *"learning curve"* associates concurred that *"the positives outweigh the negatives for personalities who are drawn to the free market system."* It was also reassuring to hear from a former summer associate: *"It was clear that interviewers had put a lot of effort into matching me with people working in my areas of interest. I appreciated that."*

"Every matter is different and so exciting!"

We heard from juniors who'd tried their hand at employment cases, data privacy, patent, legal malpractice defense, government investigations, appellate, antitrust work, healthcare, and securities cases. *"I've been doing everything from researching and writing memos, to making calls to clients and doing witness interviews, to a bit of doc review."* A happy associate commented that *"every*

See firm profile on p.604

The Inside View

Rankings in *Chambers USA*

Antitrust

Appellate Law

Banking & Finance

Bankruptcy/Restructuring

Capital Markets

Corporate Crime &
  Investigations

Corporate/M&A

ERISA Litigation

Employee Benefits &
  Executive Compensation

Energy & Natural
  Resources

Environment

FCPA

Government

IT & Outsourcing

Insurance

Intellectual Property

International Trade

Investment Funds

Labor & Employment

Leisure & Hospitality

Life Sciences

Litigation

Media & Entertainment

Outsourcing

Private Equity

Projects

Real Estate

Retail

Securities

Tax

Technology

Transportation

For detail on ranking tiers and ranking locations, visit
www.chambersandpartners.com

Recent work highlights

- Acted for Nike and Converse in a $1 billion case against Chinese counterfeiters
- Represented Seattle-based Group Health Cooperative in its $1.8 billion sale to healthcare consortium Kaiser Permanente
- Advised 2015 NBA champs Golden State Warriors on its $1 billion acquisition of land from Salesforce, which will be turned into an arena and entertainment complex

Training & Development

The firm offers weekly practice-specific training sessions for new associates that are beamed out via videolink across the offices. *"Each one covers a different topic like filing a complaint, or filing a motion to dismiss,"* explained a source. *"They're pretty helpful – it's good to cover the basics."* Of course, *"you learn the most from actually trying to do the job!"*

There's also the annual New Lawyer Academy – a retreat in Tucson, Arizona, attended by all new starters, including laterals, from offices across the world. In addition to litigation and transactional classes, there's ample opportunity to *"drink, dance and have fun!"* Activities include skeet shooting, horse riding, spa treatments and karaoke contests.

"I've been impressed with the partners here; they're concerned with how I'm developing."

Interviewees tended to be pleased with the level of feedback received from seniors during the daily grind. *"I've been impressed with the partners here; they're concerned with how I'm developing and are good about taking the time to walk me through things."* Naturally, it's all *"personality-dependent."* While some folk have *"strong mentoring skills"* and readily offer advice, others are *"less proactive, but will give you red lines on your draft."*

Culture and Offices

All our sources appreciated that Gibson is *"not unnecessarily aggressive, like other BigLaw firms might be."* According to associates, *"everyone here is so smart and has something to teach you all the time. The people and the work keep me on my toes, but at the same time it's a warm place – ego is checked at the door!"* One emphasized that *"in the law there's a lot of competition, and often a dog eat dog attitude, but I've never felt it within the firm. There are some competitive, intense people here but their energies are directed toward the other side!"* The free market system is integral to the culture, thought interviewees. *"It's a huge positive – regardless of rank, it forces people to be kind, respectful and nice. If they're not, partners won't get good associates to work with them. If you don't adopt*

---

matter is different and so exciting! What I love about the free market system is that you can dive into a new subject matter every couple of months. I've immersed myself in pharmacy regulation and done diligence with respect to FDA regulated entities. Then I parachuted into something different – I'm currently involved in a very large diesel emissions case along the lines of the VW matter."

Over in corporate associates are able to try out a range of areas, including capital markets, M&A, finance, private equity and funds. An insider who'd got stuck into IP transactions explained that *"as a junior on deals, I've had a lot of responsibility, way more than I expected. I communicate with clients and the other side face to face and on calls, which is a really amazing experience. I'm often keeping track of around 50 or 60 documents and I've drafted trademark and patent licenses."*

Meanwhile, associates in the real estate department pointed out that *"in terms of clients, we work for the majority of large institutional names that everyone knows, in this country and internationally, but we also have the ability to work with more local players, because of the firm's connections to LA and California. As well as a global reputation we have intricate knowledge of locales and the smaller clients who are doing sometimes faster paced work require on-the-ground knowledge."* Typical tasks for juniors include attending meetings with clients and government regulators, research, reviewing and drafting documents like development agreements, easements, and purchase and sale agreements. *"I also review a lot of documents that make sure we comply with California's environmental quality laws."*

The Inside View

See firm profile on p.604

Diversity	Partners (%)	Associates (%)
Women	16.6	45.2
White	89.9	76.6
Black/African American	1.6	2.3
Hispanic/Latin American	1.3	4.2
Asian	6	13.5
Mixed/Other	1.3	3.4
LGBT	2.2	6.2

a positive attitude and way of interacting then you won't survive here."

"It's definitely a place where you can make really good friends."

As for regional culture, those in DC "are known for dressing a little more conservatively, but it's just a superficial stuffiness. People here are very down to earth and willing to take the input of juniors. Everyone is very supportive. If I'm trying to get away on vacation and something comes up, I know that a colleague is eager to take on work to make sure that I get my vacation, and I'm happy to return the favor. The mindset is that we're in this together."

Do Gibson's West Coast roots result in laid back vibes? "Laid back is a relative term," laughed a source. A West-coaster noted that "I've worked in the DC office and on the East Coast, and even within the firm itself there's definitely a slight divide in terms of seriousness." An LA interviewee thought that "we have a pretty West Coast culture here, people are pretty relaxed and want to have a life outside work."

When it comes to socializing, there's plenty going on across offices, like happy hours and informal drinks gatherings, but sources made it clear that there's no pressure to mingle after-hours if family comes first or you're just not in the mood. In 2016 the firm celebrated its 125th anniversary with a big bash that featured Lenny Kravitz and "cool speakers like Madeleine Albright and Malcolm Gladwell." Many of our interviewees emphasized that "I'm very close with my people from my class year – we work out together, we go to dinners, go to each other's weddings. It's definitely a place where you can make really good friends."

Hours & Compensation

The firm has a "soft target" of 1,950 hours for the year. All of our interviewees were relaxed about meeting this. "I've never been concerned about it – there's more than enough work to go around." Many mentioned that they'd "surpassed the suggested target without any trouble." However, it's understood that "for first-years the hours might be difficult to meet when you're ramping up at the beginning."

Everyone we spoke to was pleased to confirm that pro bono hours "count one-for-one toward the target, so there are a plenty of ways to make up the 1,950 hours." As usual, attorneys emphasized that "things really ebb and flow – sometimes I can come in at 10am and leave at 5pm with an hour for lunch, but if a case is going crazy then I'll be up late." Juniors weren't too clear about the specifics of the bonus system, although everyone is eligible for a merit-based bonus, even if they don't hit the 1,950.

Pro bono

As mentioned previously, the firm credits all pro bono hours and there isn't a formal cap. Every insider we talked to had at least one pro bono matter on the go. A source spoke of being involved in an "exceptional" Innocence Project case, "working to exonerate two men in Maryland wrongfully convicted of murder. It's been an ongoing commitment for the firm over the past three or four years, and the firm has thrown a remarkable amount of resources into it in terms of man hours and money! It's really impressive." Other interviewees mentioned that they'd worked on clemency petitions, immigration and adoption cases, helped to form a non profit dog shelter and undertaken employment work for a local ballet institution.

Pro bono Hours
- For all US attorneys: 152, 912
- Average per US attorney: 131

Diversity

Juniors admitted that, as with most big firms, diversity levels definitely need to improve. However, all of them agreed that Gibson "makes diversity a priority" Many mentioned that "the firm is very attentive to women's issues. They have regular lunches and events that encourage women to stay on track for partnership. There aren't as many women in senior leadership roles as men, so everyone agrees that this needs to be addressed." There's also an all-women retreat "to talk about retention and celebrate female lawyers."

"A priority."

Get Hired

Associates weren't short of things to say when asked about the sort of person who thrives here. "They certainly look for people who are going to take advantage of the free market system. You need to be the type of person who wants to knock on doors or network in order to develop your career. Fit is very important because the firm is proud and protective of the culture." Various lunches and dinners form part of the selection process ("They put a lot of emphasis on seeing how you perform in a more casual setting").

See firm profile on p.604

Leslie Ripley, chief recruiting officer, confirms that *"it's not just about law school academics; part of the equation is the personalities of the people we're hiring, and whether they fit into our culture. That's why we have an extensive OCI program and generally include meals during the callback process – we want to spend more time with our potential recruits."* This emphasis on personality was certainly echoed by our interviewees. *"I came for interviews as a summer and really hit it off with everyone I met with, people seemed generally happy, doors were open in hallways,"* said a DCer. Then a Manhattanite told us: *"I guess when I was interviewing for firms to work for as law student, I was somewhat overwhelmed by the number, and how similar they all are, but here I felt at ease with people I met."*

In an interview with the firm chairman and managing partner Ken Doan, he told us: *"Our practice is very dynamic, so we're looking for lawyers who appreciate a challenge, relish cutting-edge work, and thrive in an ever-changing market environment."* To read the full interview with Doran, go online.

"I came for interviews as a summer and really hit it off with everyone I met with."

See firm profile on p.604

Goodwin

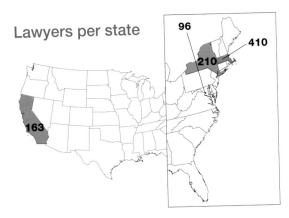

Lawyers per state

96
410
210
163

Largest US office: Boston
US offices: 6
International offices: 4
First-year salary: $180,000
Billable hours: 1,950 target
Summers 2017: 60 (59 2Ls, 1 1L)
Revenue 2016: $912 million (+5.4%)
Partners made in 2017: 15 (14 in US)
Famous for: top tech work; good work/life balance

"You get a ton of responsibility early on if you demonstrate you can handle it" – the Goodwinner takes it all.

LAW firm re-branding is becoming a bit of a trend right now. Mighty Baker & McKenzie dropped its ampersand; Nutter is another recently 'refreshed' firm in this guide that springs to mind. In 2016, Goodwin Procter LLP became known simply as Goodwin, as you can see for yourself on the firm's snazzy new website. Around the same time, Goodwin's huge Boston office relocated to brand new premises; comparing old to new, associates raved: *"it's literally night and day. The new space is really impressive."* Hiring partner Ken Gordon reveals *"it's designed to be more open and collaborative. Everyone sees the design as state of the art so people are happier to be in the office."*

"Goodwin has a really low tolerance for assholes."

Goodwin may be going through changes but it remains one of Boston's most prominent law firms. *Chambers USA* ranks it top in Massachusetts for an array of litigious and transactional practice areas. Happily, success hasn't gone to attorneys' heads: *"Goodwin has a really low tolerance for assholes,"* one junior observed. *"People are willing to go out of their way to work you through the finer points*

of being a lawyer." All six of the firm's US offices accommodate newcomers each year, with the majority heading to Boston or the Big Apple.

The Work

Incoming juniors join one of two *"buckets,"* litigation or business law, and spend their first two years as general resources before specializing. Goodwin *"encourages getting experience across a broad range of areas"* while you're housed in the bucket. Work is coordinated by staffing managers but associates *"can 100% pick and choose what we want to do."* One provided an example: *"I wanted to write a motion to dismiss, sent an email and a week or two later got a case where I could do that."* On the flip side, *"there's a broad latitude to say no to stuff"* if the workload has piled too high.

Business law juniors can sample a range of areas including M&A, real estate, tax and life sciences. Drawing from one or many, *"the beauty of it was every day is different. Some days you get an email from a client and everything changes!"* Typical tasks include *"standard diligence stuff; more menial tasks come with the territory. By your second year you're pretty involved in the mechanics of a deal and not just burying your head in documents."* Most felt the process was more of a manageable learning curve than a rollercoaster: *"Goodwin does a good job of striking the balance between providing education and responsibility. As soon as I know how to do something I've started doing something else, so you're always a little bit outside of your*

See firm profile on p.605

The Inside View

Rankings in *Chambers USA*

Banking & Finance	Investment Funds
Bankruptcy/Restructuring	Labor & Employment
Capital Markets	Leisure & Hospitality
Corporate Crime & Investigations	Life Sciences
	Litigation
Corporate/M&A	Private Equity
ERISA Litigation	Products Liability
Employee Benefits & Executive Compensation	REITs
	Real Estate
Environment	Securities
Financial Services Regulation	Startups & Emerging Companies
Food & Beverages	Tax
Intellectual Property	Technology

For detail on ranking tiers and ranking locations, visit www.chambersandpartners.com

Recent work highlights

- Represented real estate investment trust Mid-America Apartment Communities in $4 billion acquisition of Post Properties
- Defended former president of pharmaceutical company Warner Chilcott against a federal conspiracy charge
- Advised Medical Properties Trust on $1.25 billion acquisition of nine acute care hospitals
- Represented American Farmland Company in merger with Farmland Partners, to form the largest public farmland real estate investment trust in the United States

comfort zone," and associates *"wouldn't prefer it any other way."* Responsibility was dropped in juniors' laps from the get-go, leading to some unusual situations. *"Before I was sworn in with the bar, on my third day here I got a call directly from a client. When I'd given my advice they said 'okay, you're the lawyer' – inside I was like 'well technically I'm not!'"*

"You're always a little bit outside of your comfort zone."

"A good chunk of the work" in litigation deals with consumer finance, but there's also antitrust, white collar, securities and other areas on offer. *"As a first-year there's a lot of document review, as is normal for all firms,"* but higher up the ladder comes *"a lot more research and drafting motions, subpoena responses and requests for production. There's a good mix of stuff that's comfortable and scary to start with."* Client contact comes quickly more often than not, and work was broad enough that juniors *"couldn't name something I'm dying to do that I haven't,"* and sufficiently plentiful. *"If I wanted to bill a million hours a week I could,"* according to one. *"If not it's pretty easy to push back and say my plate is full."* A restless colleague agreed *"I'm the kind of person who hates being bored, so I like that we're busy."*

Toward the end of their second year, associates typically pick a 'business unit' to officially specialize in – we say officially because associates remain free to seek work from outside their chosen unit. Associates felt the bucket system worked well for *"seeing different work styles. You can shape your career along the path you want,"* and several took up the option to delay specializing. Others identified their niche and narrowed their scope more quickly,

while laterals found it easy to build on what they'd done previously.

Get Hired

"You don't need to know what all of an M&A deal looks like, but having a handle on why you're going for BigLaw is important." To find out what else is important, head to chambers-associate.com.

Training & Development

A week-long orientation at the firm's Boston office includes *"talks from business folks to boost your financial literacy,"* and newbies take additional *"quote unquote mandatory"* training sessions twice a week (*"attendance peters out around four or five months in..."*) The staggered approach was popular among associates, who theorized that *"if you did all your training up front, it would be like reading all the rules of Monopoly in one go before playing – you need to learn by doing."*

"It would be like reading all the rules of Monopoly in one go."

Formal feedback comes through an initial six month review then yearly evaluations, in which *"the firm collects reviews from all senior attorneys who work with you, and distill a general narrative,"* a system that *"works well. Informal feedback is encouraged, but some of the onus is on juniors to get it."* Those who did *"always had a sense of how I'm performing"* and saw no surprises come review time.

Culture and Diversity

"In law school you don't meet many normal people. Goodwin's filled its halls with people who are funny and pleasant to work with." Whether they agreed with this one colleague's view of law students or not, associates concurred: *"We're not viewed as tools for work. There's a much better work/life balance than other firms."* Californians trumpeted their offices as the most *"laid back. People elsewhere*

See firm profile on p605

Diversity	Partners (%)	Associates (%)
Women	23	49
White	93	76
Black/African American	1	4
Hispanic/Latin American	2	3
Asian	3	14
Mixed/Other	1	3
LGBT	2	4

are pretty envious of the West Coast culture." They also asserted: *"We don't feel like satellite offices. We're continuing to grow, who knows where the expansion will end!"* Even away from the Cali coastline, juniors described partners as *"pretty relaxed – I'm not going to barge into their office whenever I want but doors are usually open."* While there was *"a certain level of deference,"* that didn't prevent *"constant interaction with higher-ups. There's no palpable divide."*

"There's a much better work/life balance."

When not talking business, partners and associates were hanging out at the bar. *"There are senior attorneys I feel I can work with 60 hours a week then go for a beer with them on Friday night,"* said one, while another described *"themed Thursday get-togethers – we've done pie for Thanksgiving, a soup and salad event in winter, and a beer and pizza night."* Not all social events were alcohol-fueled: sportier juniors took to the basketball court for *"games every Tuesday. We'll play for two hours and invite clients to join us."*

Associates appreciated that *"events aren't just old white dudes telling us how great law is."* The firm's affinity groups include a women's initiative, an LGBT group, and the Committee on Racial and Ethnic Diversity (CRED). Attempts to emphasize diversity through hiring are *"starting to show in the partnership."* Clear openness to increase LGBT diversity also impressed interviewees. One credited this to Massachusetts' history as the first state to legalize gay marriage: *"Diversity has been a focus here longer than at other firms because they're based here, and having that reputation has drawn diverse people to the firm."* Though *"every firm could do better,"* Goodwin juniors *"can't knock them for trying."* Lately the firm has partnered with the Leadership Council on Legal Diversity on its 'pathfinder program,' and it also works with headhunters to bring in diverse candidates.

Offices

The glass walls and modern design of the firm's new Boston digs have encouraged *"more ad hoc interaction than the old office,"* but associates noted a trade-off. *"It's definitely not as good a location as previously, but it's less bad than everyone expected."* Bostonians agreed: *"It is a much better office overall."* San Fran lawyers also moved to a new space recently. Big Apple-based juniors reported theirs is in *"a fine building. We're expanding and picking up more space."* The team is situated in the New York Times Building, where lawyers share a cafeteria with the paper's staff.

"More ad hoc interaction than the old office."

Washington, DC is on the small side, so its attorneys regularly collaborate with Boston and New York. They described the building as *"nice enough, though I've seen nicer,"* but the downtown location was popular. LA lawyers likewise appreciated their *"very central location: we're directly across the street from the tallest building in California,"* unlike those in the *"restaurant wasteland"* of Silicon Valley. Associates tended to see more inter-office communication with their coastal neighbors than the US as a whole.

Pro Bono

There's no cap on pro bono counting toward hours targets, so the firm *"incentivizes you to do it and get more of a leadership role. It makes life so much easier that pro bono is weighted the same as billables."* Goodwin offers the usual panoply of pro bono projects, including immigration and asylum cases, landlord and tenant work, First Amendment matters and advising nonprofits on their corporate governance – *"the firm is flexible about what people take on."* Every year it dedicates some training to how to get involved in pro bono, and *"they bring in a panel to explain how it enriches your practice."*

"Nobody bats an eyelid about billing a lot."

Congratulatory paperweights landed on the desks of those who went above and beyond; these top-billers found *"pro bono clients are treated no differently to paying clients. You shouldn't bill 500 hours every year, but nobody bats an eyelid about billing a lot."* The ensuing conclusion was that *"there is a real transparent commitment on the part of the firm. It's not something they encourage then push you back on."*

Pro bono hours
- For all US attorneys: 59,877
- Average per US attorney: 67

See firm profile on p.605

Hours & Compensation

The firm has a billable hours target of 1,950 hours, and *"unlike at other firms, where you can get a pro-rated bonus if you don't hit hours, here you either hit it and get the bonus or don't and you don't,"* although contrastingly *"if you bill more you usually get above market."* Juniors we spoke to were all confident that Goodwin will consistently match the New York market for compensation, and looked back on the Cravath-led salary jumps with the view that *"as long as we got bumped up it didn't matter how long Goodwin took."* Starting salaries increased to $180,000 for associates in all the firm's US offices.

"Everybody's done all-nighters, but that's definitely rare."

Most agreed that *"in first year you may have trouble getting up to speed, but we've been really busy as a firm so it's hard not to hit 1,950."* Busy interviewees described an average ten hour working day with some catching up on the weekend, and while *"everybody's done all-nighters, that's definitely rare."* Particularly in the business law bucket, *"the workload is cyclical so if you're slammed one month you're not busy the next."* Associates get four weeks of vacation a year, and as partners *"know you're grinding throughout the year"* they mostly let their charges enjoy the time off. One interviewee who'd had a filing to do while vacationing *"talked to other associates, and they were astonished I had to do anything."*

Strategy & Future

Layoffs a couple of years back left some juniors feeling wary. *"It was a weird year, and it made me feel uncomfortable at the time."* However, interviewees believed *"since then the firm has tried to be more open and honest, so we aren't freaking out."* Most agreed *"formally or informally you get the sense of direction in which the firm is going,"* though some felt *"more transparency would always be a good thing. But things seem to be running smoothly, and people tend to be happy."* They felt *"it's hard to tell the chances of making partner, but there are multiple upward career trajectories."* New York business law leader Jennifer Bralower confirms: *"This is a great place for people who want to actively manage their career. We give our lawyers a lot of flexibility."*

"There are multiple upward career trajectories."

See firm profile on p.605

Goulston & Storrs

Lawyers per state

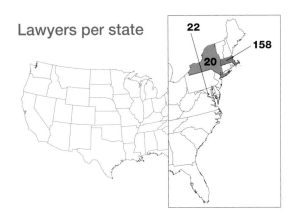

Largest US office: Boston
US offices: 3
International offices: 1
First-year salary: $180,000
Billable hours: no requirement
Summers 2017: 7 (6 2Ls, 1 1L)
Revenue 2016: undisclosed
Partners made in 2017: 2
Famous for: Boston-based; real estate prowess

"The best place to do real estate in Boston, bar none – other firms advised me I should go to Goulston!"

BUSINESS in Boston is booming thanks to a thriving life sciences industry and healthy M&A environment, but the city remains *"a small community which breeds professional courtesy,"* according to Goulston's associates. Almost all of the firm's small intake takes up residence in Beantown, where they enjoy a waterfront location. One junior explained that Goulston *"doesn't hire 50 people then aim to make five partners. Folks really believe you only get hired here if you have a realistic shot at partnership."*

Real estate is the firm's bread and butter: the practice here has baked up impressive *Chambers USA* rankings in DC as well as Massachusetts (our online Bonus Features on Goulston have more info on the local market). Associates suggested that real estate *"drives the firm in a lot of ways,"* but areas including finance, bankruptcy and commercial litigation also pick up plaudits. As well as Boston, Goulston's own properties are found in New York, DC and Beijing.

Offices

Practically all Goulston's first-years are hired into Boston, but because work allocators staff matters across offices, attorneys may sometimes find themselves working with colleagues in the Big Apple and DC. The HQ spreads over two buildings, occupying one floor of a waterside hotel (*"a more traditional space than next door, but I still like it"*) alongside the *"stunning"* main office. Dubbed *"traditional brick-and-beam Boston"* by associates, it's in *"a pretty awesome waterside location right near the heart of the city."*

The smaller New York base sits in midtown east; a more compact space means *"there's really not a hierarchical feel."* Goulston DC's location also comes up trumps – it's just a short walk from the White House. Eager for associates to get to know the firm's own real estate, management is *"very encouraging of inter-office visits. There's a big emphasis on making everyone feel part of one firm,"* juniors reported.

The Work

Incoming associates list three practice groups they're interested in, and *"you normally get your first or second choice."* Real estate absorbs nearly all of Goulston's six or so annual new first-years, though the odd junior may sign up with another area like litigation, corporate or private client & trusts. Every group has two formal work allocators who *"check in pretty regularly to ask about our workloads."* Associates described the structured system

See firm profile on p.606

The Inside View

Rankings in *Chambers USA*

Banking & Finance	Litigation
Bankruptcy/Restructuring	Real Estate
Environment	Retail
Leisure & Hospitality	

For detail on ranking tiers and ranking locations, visit
www.chambersandpartners.com

Recent work highlights

- Represented real estate investors Beacon Capital Partners in $304 million sale of Canal Park real estate
- Assisted in securing affordable housing status for 59 homes in the Dorchester and Mattapan areas of Boston
- Administrative agent for financial giant JPMorgan in $78 million construction financing
- Advised investor consortium on $305 million acquisition of healthcare multinational Novo Nordisk's North American HQ

as *"wonderful – it's not an eat-what-you-kill firm so you're not rushing to cut the next person off from work."* Partners can approach juniors directly, but still run assignments past the allocators to keep everyone in the loop.

Transactions, financing, and permit & development matters make up the lion's share of Goulston's real estate work. *"The bulk of our attorneys represents developers: we cover each piece of a real estate life cycle, and you won't just be pulled into a tiny piece of it."* Newbies got a stab at *"some drafting, and you might take the first crack at certain agreements and leases"* while also *"handling due diligence. You're generally responsible for moving the deal along."* Heading into the third year *"there's a transition into new aspects, like helping with loan documents."* Client contact *"takes every form, it's very deal specific,"* and the firm has a 2:1 ratio of partners to associates so teams are leanly staffed more often than not. *"They give you the chance to take the ball and run with it,"* so there's *"a lot of responsibility"* off the bat. Interviewees found it *"a little intimidating sometimes, but you have a support network to rely on if you have any questions."*

The corporate team tackles *"finance, M&A, corporate governance... as a junior you get staffed on everything: there's no strict focus."* Juniors got stuck into *"drafting deal documents, taking comments from opposing counsel and vetting them with the partner. I'm not drafting the hundred-million dollar deals, but on smaller ones there are good opportunities to get my feet wet."* Part of a small team with few associates, corporate sources noted: *"You can't avoid client contact: by virtue of the way we're staffed, you have to be ready at all times."* They summarized the opportunities on offer as *"challenging, but really amazing."* Peers in litigation kept themselves busy with *"research, drafting discovery responses and submissions for mediation – it varies a lot."* The *"diverse"* group spans employment, legal malpractice and general commercial litigation.

Training & Development

Newbies are assigned a mid-level associate sibling and a partner mentor:*"The expectation is they'll train you to be the best you can be."* Goulston & Storrs University provides a general program for juniors who *"can ask for certain things, or to not do things we already know. There's a pretty good input process."* Practice-specific training includes a once-a-month course in real estate (*"an inch-deep, mile-long experience"*), and quarterly meetings in corporate *"to go through things we'd like to work on."* Boston associates are often joined by their counterparts from New York or Washington, DC during training sessions.

"An inch-deep, mile-long experience."

Juniors get an official review every six months in which they sit down with two partners from outside their group, who provide feedback from partners they've worked with. *"Apart from the first one,"* sources noted, *"the reviews are pretty substantive."* This culminates at the five-year mark in a higher-level review. Away from the formal system, *"there's good feedback from partners generally. It's not like you're at school, but people are more than happy to answer questions."*

Culture

"This firm has a reputation as the good guys – they're ethical, uphold a high standard and treat people fairly." Taking a break from a massive group hug (probably), Goulston juniors told us they were *"amazed how cohesive a group our class were"* and boasted: *"We're a firm that's never merged. We take community very seriously when hiring."* Though some remarked: *"Most young associates don't find families too challenging,"* others detected a cultural shift – *"from what I've heard it was strongly family-friendly, and now there's a lot of young, single associates who want to be social."* Chances to do so include *"holiday and summer parties, and cocktails and hors d'oeuvres at partners' houses. It's always nice to hang out and get to know each other."* New York and DC attorneys are encouraged to head up the coast for firmwide events but *"there's no pressure"* to be at every party.

The day after each monthly partner meeting, associates are kept in the loop through a lunch with the firm's managing partners at which *"there's a run down almost to the bullet point of what the partners discussed."* The frequency of open forums lead juniors to conclude: *"We have a more transparent management than I'd expect there to be at other places,"* and they were happy to note: *"It doesn't*

See firm profile on p.606

Diversity	Partners (%)	Associates (%)
Women	21	56
White	99	75
Black/African American	0	9
Hispanic/Latin American	0	7
Asian	1	9
Mixed/Other	0	0
LGBT	3	4

feel like there's a class structure where associates are lesser than partners." One credited this to the low ratio of associates to partners; another simply declared themselves "very pleased with the lack of hierarchy."

Pro Bono & Diversity

Good feeling at Goulston extends to pro bono, "a very robust part of what the firm is all about" according to interviewees – "they're extremely committed, there's an expectation everyone will do it." As all pro bono hours count the same as billables, there is little need to keep track of which is which, and as cases often come through the allocation system "you might not know it's pro bono until you're doing it!" The firm's diversity committee also invites associates to take on pro bono cases which deal with minority issues and communities in Boston. Other opportunities include immigration and asylum cases, and "if there's a cause you feel strongly about you can raise it with the committee."

Pro bono hours
- For all US attorneys: 11,843
- Average per US attorney: undisclosed

"You might not know it's pro bono until you're doing it!"

There's more to the diversity committee than organizing pro bono matters; a speakers' program, social events and community outreach projects are all on the cards. Associates noted "a desire to continue to diversify and be a true representation of society" on Goulston's part, one source telling us: "It's one of the main reasons I chose this firm. They were really intentional about making that a priority." The firm put its money where its mouth is with an entirely female summer class in 2015, four of the six coming from a diverse ethnic background. Confident "that was simply because they were the best candidates," associates concluded that "gender-wise

it feels very balanced, though racial diversity does need some work," especially at partner level.

Hours & Compensation

Some associates seemed surprised when asked about the hours they work, having "never been in a conversation where the numbers were brought up." Goulston doesn't stipulate a billable hours requirement, though associates get anonymous reports "to see where we fall compared to other people." Some admitted that "even without a requirement, I don't want to be the person with the lowest!"

So why isn't there a target? "Not having one allows for a lot of flexibility," juniors explained. "If you get stuff done on time there's no expectation for you to just be here." The flip side is Goulston's bonuses are nonexistent – "it goes hand in hand with the lack of hours target." Associates were generally pleased with the system, one reasoning that "I much prefer the flexibility of being able to have a personal life without stressing about hours." Compensation is lockstep through the third year; thereafter salaries are more merit-based

Get Hired

"One thing the firm finds very important is whether a person can be put in front of a client." Head to chambers-associate.com for insider tips on recruitment at Goulston.

Strategy & Future

The Boston real estate market is healthier than ever, and Goulston's heritage in the city makes it well placed to capitalize. Co-managing partner Barry Green explains: "Boston has a remarkably dynamic economy with a highly educated workforce. Pretty much everything you look at in the city will have the Goulston stamp; we take a lot of pride in that and our position in the market." Like its home city, the firm is in the driver seat for steady expansion in the future. According to Green the priority is "growing our footprint in New York and DC. The associate ranks in both offices are continuing to grow, which we're delighted about – it's not expansion at the pace you might see at a larger firm, that's not our style, and we've been very pleased with the progress." Our interview with Green and his comanaging partner Marty Fantozzi is available in full on our website.

"Pretty much everything you look at in the city will have the Goulston stamp: we take a lot of pride in that and our position in the market."

See firm profile on p.606

The Inside View

Greenberg Traurig, PA

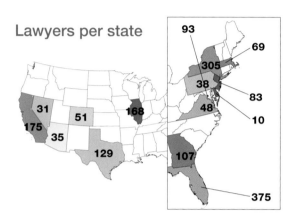

Lawyers per state

93
69
305
38
83
31 51 168 48 10
175 35
129 107
375

Largest US office: New York
US offices: 29
International offices: 9
First-year salary: $110,000-$180,000
Billable hours: no official target
Summers 2017: 44 (43 2Ls, 1 1L)
Revenue 2016: $1.38 billion (+4.4%)
Partners made in 2017: 36 in US
Famous for: megafirm with a flair for real estate

No greenhorn, Greenberg Traurig famously produces associates with a knack for business.

NATIONAL and international coverage like GT's doesn't appear out of thin air. It is, however, only a spritely 50 years of age. Founded in Miami in 1967, the firm quickly developed its excellent reputation for real estate work. Plenty of expansion later and New York is now its largest office, but you'll find sites in a total of 19 states offering expertise way beyond just real estate. This giant's not built on mega-mergers, but in 2016 it considered changing course, engaging in merger talks with British suitor Berwin Leighton Paisner. It wasn't to be: instead Greenberg backed itself to keep getting bigger and stronger while staying solo for now.

"Nobody is micro-managing at all."

The firm values independence among its associates too, who told us that *"nobody is micro-managing at all. Work is left to my discretion and I'm given significant input on cases. They definitely let you stand on your own two feet and get you involved in client contact so that clients know who you are."* The firm places a premium on associates developing new and existing business themselves.

The Work

Greenberg's real estate achievements need little introduction, and associates in Miami believed it's *"still the main office for real estate."* However, not only has the real estate team expanded across the US, now comprising over 250 lawyers, but litigation actually surpasses it in size. Of the 115 associates who made up the 2014 and 2015 year classes at the time of our calls, 36 were stationed in litigation or IP litigation. Compare that with the 22 real estate associates and 27 corporate associates and it's clear to see that the firm's focus is diverse. It's also worth noting that New York had the most associates, and Miami the second most.

Assignment is generally based on informal relationships where partners (formally known as shareholders) reach out to juniors, and associates also occasionally seek out partners for work. Corporate, however, tends to be slightly more formal, as do the larger offices. More formal arrangements have *"a master spreadsheet of who is assigned to which cases."* The overarching approach is to give juniors a broad range of work within their departments, while encouraging associates to be forthright. *"They tell us and remind us that if there is a client or a case you want to pursue, or if there are other types of work which you have an idea about, the firm will make it happen – they're all ears."*

On chambers-associate.com...

- We talk recruitment with global chairman of professional development and integration Brad Kaufman
- Associates give us their insight on getting hired
- Our interview with CEO Brian Duffy

See firm profile on p.607

Rankings in *Chambers USA*

Banking & Finance	Labor & Employment
Bankruptcy/Restructuring	Latin American Investment
Construction	Leisure & Hospitality
Corporate/Commercial	Litigation
Corporate/M&A	Media & Entertainment
Energy & Natural	Native American Law
Resources	Natural Resources
Environment	Products Liability
Franchising	REITs
Gaming & Licensing	Real Estate
Healthcare	Retail
Immigration	Tax
Intellectual Property	Technology

For detail on ranking tiers and ranking locations, visit
www.chambersandpartners.com

"Basically the deal is that I have the flexibility to handle my own deals. Partners trust me to come to them with hiccups."

Real estate newbies reported tackling *"negotiations, leases, and handling clients directly"* – a lot of responsibility. *"Basically the deal is that I have the flexibility to handle my own deals. Partners trust me to come to them with hiccups or situations which might need their level of expertise – they lean on me to identify those."* With it being such a developed real estate practice, Greenberg takes on all elements of real estate: *"You either buy, sell or lease something, or you use the real estate as collateral for a loan, so that means there's lending and borrowing work."*

Litigators told us that on *"pretty much any really tangible aspect of the things to be done we are brought in to do the leg work: research on legal issues, analyzing pleadings, strategy, drafting responses. Then in discovery we're drafting discovery requests or responses, and before the summary judgment we're preparing research, writing briefs, and preparing for the hearings."* Juniors also handled project management tasks – *"making sure the day-to-day is running."* For the most part, *"shareholders give you a long leash and let you take things as far as you can."*

Pro Bono

Associates informed us that the firm's *"pretty good about circulating opportunities"* and that it's *"very supportive with pro bono. We get credit up to something like 100 hours,"* and associates can apply for more credit if they look like they will exceed this. However, they commonly told us: *"I haven't done a ton."* One associate told us that *"in real estate it is very tough; litigation lends itself more to getting matters."* Sources had similar difficulties in the other transactional practices.

Recent work highlights

- Represented JMP apartments in its purchase of Jefferson Marketplace in DC, which consists of 281 apartment units, an acquisition of $141 million
- Represented Miami Worldcenter Associates in multiple stages of the development of a 24-acre plot of land as part of the Miami Worldcenter project. The development is valued at $4-5 billion
- Represented JPMorgan Chase in a number of mortgage backed securities litigations brought by Ambac Assurance, Syncora and other plaintiffs
- Represented Jarden Corporation during its $15.4 billion acquisition by Newell Rubbermaid, forming Newell Brands

"Spend a day with a middle school class while they're learning to run a business."

Associates told us that the majority of work comes in from *"large organizations"* dedicated to pro bono. The firm maintains relationships with a whole host of these, including KIND [Kids in Need of Defense] and Her Justice. One associate told us about *"a relationship with Junior Achievement which does outreach to middle schools doing programs on business and finance."* This allowed associates to *"spend a day with a middle school class while they're learning to run a business."* The firm is also a sponsor of the Holly Skolnick Fellowship in partnership with Equal Justice Works, which allows recent law school grads to work in various nonprofit organizations.

Pro bono hours
- For all US attorneys: 25,603
- Average per US attorney: 16

Training & Development

After an initial orientation, training is department led. Litigators, for example, are enrolled into the GT Skills Academy, which offers around six two-to-three day seminars on different topics, bringing associates together from different offices. *"They range from deposition training and motion practice all the way to trial training,"* via mock trials. Transactional newbies have a corporate boot camp. In addition, Greenberg provides regular lunches, CLE sessions and webinars. *"I think GT has a great training program. Every week there are different CLEs or seminars which you can tune into. Sometimes it's in-house to watch a program or hear someone speak or there are broadcasts you can tune into – those are really helpful."* Beyond formal training, associates remained positive. *"Most shareholders are very willing to help you out; they all realize that everyone is new at some point and that nobody coming out of law school really knows anything."*

See firm profile on p.607

The Inside View

Diversity	Partners (%)	Associates (%)
Women	22.4	47.2
White	87.8	77.1
Black/African American	Undisclosed	Undisclosed
Hispanic/Latin American	-	-
Asian	-	-
Mixed/Other	-	-
LGBT	1.7	1.1

Associates have one formal review each year. They sit down with the heads of their department and *"go over the feedback from shareholders based on the work you have done. You see exactly what they've said, the good things and the not-so-good things. Sometimes it's eye-opening as some aren't as good at giving feedback as it happens."* Associates agreed it was *"a good way of checking in."*

Offices

GT's global network consists of 38 offices. Nine overseas outposts include Shanghai, Tel Aviv and London, with an additional strategic alliance in Italy. Back home, GT doesn't designate any office as the official headquarters. Miami's steeped in history, New York wins on size, but the firm prefers to place emphasis on the sum of its parts. *"That's one of our selling points for getting work. Say if you have a deal in California, we'd have the people to do it."* Encouragingly, despite it's scale, associates in the smaller offices didn't *"feel on the outskirts of where everything is going on. It's not a satellite."* Even so, associates weren't in constant contact with other offices, and cross-staffing was only occasional.

The Miami base takes up five floors in the Wells Fargo building: *"We have a kitchen on every floor with coffee, tea and a soda machine. On the 44th floor where all the conference rooms are we have a cafe where you can buy lunch and dinner. We're also a block a way from Whole Foods which is basically an extension of the cafeteria!"* Associates usually start with an office to themselves, though in New York sharing is more common initially.

Culture

Law is a business just like any other, and GT doesn't hang about in informing associates of that fact. *"It's very entrepreneurial,"* one said of the culture. *"They want you thinking from day one about your practice down the road, whether that relates to your specialty or your clients."* Another confirmed that rather than having associates *"on track each year doing certain tasks, limiting you, telling you 'put your head down and work, don't worry about BD [business development] yet',"* the firm is *"always happy for you to try new things, to sponsor it and to get you train-*

ing. They never say you're not ready for that, and I think it's something they very much instill in you." GT's slogan, 'built for change', is the crystallization of this approach.

"They want you thinking from day one about your practice down the road."

This entrepreneurial spirit doesn't necessarily come with any survival-of-the-fittest ruthlessness, however: *"It's not overly competitive. Everyone is willing to work together to help each other out. That's one thing I like; it's collaborative, open-door and not political at all."* One associate called the office *"quiet,"* another *"corporate. People come in serious about performing their duties and practicing, but everyone's quick with a joke."*

Any thirst associates have for socializing is met with a healthy trickle of events, rather than a downpour. *"People aren't planning a happy hour every week, but every few weeks we have one."* There are also monthly lunches and the typical holiday parties, but elsewhere New York associates told us about an Oscars themed party as well as a St. Patrick's Day parade which brings bagpipe players honking their way through the office.

Hours & Compensation

Greenberg doesn't have an official billable target, but most associates we spoke to thought they should aim for 2,000 hours – *"not a crazy number at all. It's a bit of a fuzzy target."* Miami was piloting a concrete 1,900 hour target, so change may be on its way firmwide. *"As you would expect, it's ebb and flow"* when it comes to associates' workloads and the hours they have to clock to keep up. However juniors could regularly *"leave at 7 to 7.30pm and definitely take a lunch every day."* In part this is because associates could work from home in the evenings to meet the often taxing demands of clients. When they did have to stay late at the office, *"yours isn't the only light on at the end of the hallway; you're never alone in the trenches."*

"You're never alone in the trenches."

Bonuses are merit-based, which split our associates. Some were thankful, as *"it gives you an incentive,"* but others felt that if work stopped being provided by partners, they'd be powerless to bill high enough. Also, beyond hours, *"it's completely black box here for bonuses."*

Diversity

Greenberg's diversity figures are comfortably average. *"They do as well as they can – it's not for a lack of trying."* The even gender split among associates is certainly a promising indicator, and associates were positive that

The Inside View

See firm profile on p.607

the firm endeavors to improve the figures which aren't as promising – female and ethnic minority partners, for example. *"They definitely have a lot of women's events,"* falling under the umbrella of a women's initiative. *"There are meetings every two months or so. They'll plan different events or meetings for women to get together and talk about issues women face in the workplace, like what resources there are for maternity leave."* It sometimes involves bringing speakers in, and some associates mentioned a cooking class. We also heard about a recent increase to maternity leave. One associate took solace in the not-so WASP-ish roots of the firm. *"GT was started by a group of Jewish men because at the time it was hard getting jobs at very traditional firms. They've instilled the idea of having a much more diverse group."*

Get Hired

"Many interviewing 2Ls will want any job at a large law firm. If you're looking for a law firm that you'll stay at for a few years you want a place where you can branch out a bit, where they will retain you and train you – you have to be honest about what you want." For more recruitment insight form associates go to chambers-associate.com.

Strategy & Future

GT's strategy of targeted growth means its sights are firmly set on its core practices. *"I think they're definitely trying to grow the corporate group,"* said one New York associate. *"Just in terms of hiring partners who do slightly different things, and also having more associates in the corporate department."* New York associates particularly noticed the firm *"bringing in more laterals, both shareholders and lateral associates."* Texas too, is on the up – they've hired roughly 40 attorneys since June 2015, including a former Supreme Court Justice who'll head up the appellate practice. Associates also expressed confidence that they'd be a part of this growth. *"If you're committed to being a partner in Miami you can do it,"* said one Floridian.

This suggests that in spite of the merger-which-never-was with UK firm BLP, the firm's immediate concern isn't finding a willing substitute. Besides the failed merger, GT's appeared in the legal press a lot because of Rudy Giuliani. The addition of the ex-Mayor of New York as a shareholder is impressive, but his outspokenness is more bothersome. Did this concern associates? *"Personally no, because Richard Rosenbaum sent an email clarifying that whatever he thinks doesn't reflect the firm; he doesn't speak for the firm and I don't personally think it is a reflection of the firm's views."*

"They've instilled the idea of having a much more diverse group."

See firm profile on p.607

Hangley Aronchick Segal Pudlin & Schiller

Lawyers per state

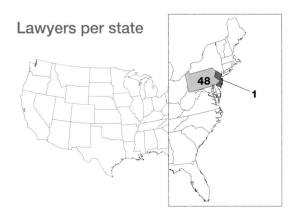

Largest US office: Philadelphia
US offices: 4
International offices: 0
First-year salary: $135,000
Billable hours: no requirement
Summers 2017: no summer program
Revenue 2016: undisclosed
Partners made in 2017: 0
Famous for: life-sized model cow in the HQ; its sense of humor

Jovial young firm Hangley isn't joking around when it comes to litigation...

HOLY cow, it's Hangley – the Philly firm with a funny bone and a fondness for serious business. While a lot of places pay lip service to office-based lightheartedness, it's built into the constitution at Hangley. This firm, the website boasts, prizes its *"wicked sense of humor."* Need proof? There's an entire page devoted to amusing attorney vignettes, including a mention of the giant decorative fiberglass cow (bought at auction) that resides in the office conference area. That said, there's more to Hangley than heifers and pure whimsy. Despite its petite size, this 22-year-old has accumulated an impressive clutch of *Chambers USA* rankings for its litigation, insurance, real estate and bankruptcy work in Pennsylvania.

The Work

Sources were keen to point out that they were drawn to *"the size of the firm, given the quality of the work that's done here. It's a firm of about 50 lawyers which does the same sorts of work that much larger firms do. Cases are very leanly staffed so you get good experience right away. On most cases I'm the only associate, which is phenomenal."* Interviewees praised the firm's lack of hierarchy: *"You have close contact with the partners – or shareholders as we call them – and they respect your views. It's not the kind of firm where juniors are given orders and expected to carry them out without thinking or questioning issues. Partners expect you'll have own ideas, not just defer."*

Hangley's particular culture and reputation for *"extensive"* pro bono work also attracted associates, who cited the firm's efforts to legalize same sex marriage in Philadelphia as a major draw. One revealed that *"I was very wary of going to a firm at all – I was trying to avoid it in fact – but Hangley has a better approach and philosophy than most. It doesn't emphasize the same things, like compensation; it's able to attract people who care about achievement and working hard but are not necessarily interested in the rat race."*

Hangley doesn't have OCIs or a summer program (for more on hiring see below) and so *"there are no real first-years who are right out of law school. A lot of people have been clerks, so it's typical get a lot more experience like editing, drafting, taking first stabs at documents and speaking directly to representatives of the client."* The overwhelming majority of new associates begin Hangley life as litigators, and there's a very broad range of work on offer, including antitrust, bankruptcy, business/corporate, environmental law, insurance coverage and real estate. *"In terms of cases, it really runs the gamut. There's a lot of work on behalf of governments. For example we've represented the city of Philly in trying to uphold the legality of a recently passed tax on sugary drinks. I'm working on an international contract dispute between an Israeli and an American company, a tort case and a domestic breach of contract. There's insurance work on behalf of insurers, labor and employment stuff, a bit of white collar... really just about every kind of litigation!"*

On chambers-associate.com...

- The lighter side of Hangley

The Inside View

See firm profile on p.608

Rankings in *Chambers USA*

Bankruptcy/Restructuring	Litigation
Insurance	Real Estate

For detail on ranking tiers and ranking locations, visit
www.chambersandpartners.com

"It's able to attract people who care about achievement and working hard but are not necessarily interested in the rat race."

As such, the daily grind *"varies tremendously. There's a lot of writing, like drafting memos, briefs or motions."* What about the dread doc review? *"There's a fair amount of discovery work but not like reviewing tons and tons of docs all the time. A lot gets outsourced. We tend not to have as many huge doc heavy cases, and generally speaking I get to handle the more interesting aspects of discovery."* In addition, there's *"certainly legal research. I've not got to take a deposition yet but I've been involved in prepping witnesses and partners for depositions. I'm optimistic that I'll be able to take or defend a deposition soon."* Sources also highlighted that juniors cover *"a lot of case management work because of the firm's size. I keep the schedules, make sure everything's on track, reach out to co-counsel and coordinate with them, and ensure partners are on track and reviewing what they need to. It's a lot of responsibility over the cases."*

Training & Development

Aside from a few days of computer training, *"there's no real formal training program"* at Hangley. Insiders explained that *"it's part of the environment. Because it's a smaller firm that tends to hire people who have clerked or have some experience, you're expected to hit the ground running. There's a lot of learning on the job, and fortunately the size of the place means there are lots of opportunities to see partners in action, participate in strategy calls with the client, and talk things through. Partners and associates are always willing and able to help when you're unfamiliar with things. There's a lot of support if you seek it out and if you need it."* Juniors are assigned a shareholder (partner) and an associate mentor.

"You're expected to hit the ground running."

Get Hired

Only a few junior-level associates are hired each year, so Hangley can afford to be scrupulous in its selection process. High academic achievement is a must, of course. Many juniors have clerked for at least a year, although it's not a formal requirement. *"Pretty much everybody has come off a clerkship – the firm actively seeks clerks,"*

Recent work highlights

- Obtained the complete dismissal of a high-profile challenge to the Philadelphia Beverage Tax. Hangley continues to defend the City of Philadelphia on appeal
- Acted for Comcast in a patent infringement dispute with telecoms company Sprint
- Represented 2,400 juveniles and their parents in a class action concerning two Pennsylvania judges who received payoffs of $2.6 million to maximize the number of children committed to two private detention units
- Represented a class of mushroom purchasers in a price fixing case against the Eastern Mushroom Marketing Co-operative

emphasized juniors. However, *"a lot of it is about fit and having the right personality for the firm – they want smart people who can get along with others and make it a pleasant place to work."*

"Pretty much everybody has come off a clerkship."

Managing partner David Pudlin tells us that *"we hire laterally for specialty areas like corporate, real estate or family – we prefer that people get their training in these specialties elsewhere. With litigation, we like to train them internally. We look for a strong academic background, a strong federal clerkship or even two, and for self-starters, because our firm is very hands on. One cannot hide in the library! Early on they will be going before judges. We want them to progress rapidly, whereas at bigger firms associates are given such opportunities much more slowly."*

Offices

All the newish associates on our list were in the Philadelphia HQ, which houses 42 of the firm's attorneys. The other offices are in Harrisburg, Norristown and Cherry Hill. The Philly office was recently renovated. *"They did a good job – it's not luxurious by any stretch, but you get a stipend to decorate your office. I have some art work and finally had my diploma framed and my bar certificates. Some people get a rug. It's very homey."* Juniors mentioned eagerly that *"our offices are huge and they're not hierarchical about it, so I have a bigger office than some of the partners. They just give you a space!"*

"It's very homey."

Culture

Hangley's website says it provides *"down-to-earth legal counsel"* with *"a healthy sense of humor."* But what's the reality like? Juniors told us that Hangley *"tries to live up to its humorous image, but it's still a law firm where serious work happens and people are serious about stuff."* That

See firm profile on p.608

The Inside View

Diversity	Partners (%)	Associates (%)
Women	29	40
White	Undisclosed	Undisclosed
Black/African American	-	-
Hispanic/Latin American	-	-
Asian	-	-
Mixed/Other	-	-
LGBT	-	-

said, it's as *"informal as a law firm can be! We have a lunch every Friday. People are approachable. You can talk to partners whose names are on the door about anything, be it career issues or your experience at the firm. They're open and willing. The size of the firm and the fact that people have been here a long time helps. There's camaraderie. Everybody knows everyone. There isn't space here for people who are going to be disrespectful or yelling at others. That's not something that's accepted here. There's an ethos that people are treated with respect and that includes associates, staff and paralegals. A real effort is made to make this a nice place to work. It's not like people are cracking jokes all day, but we'll get a funny email circulating every once in a while and we all get along, and so far it's been fantastic."*

"It's not like everybody is getting together and doing shots at the bar."

Juniors added that *"it's not a place where you're chained to your desk 24/7. A lot of us have families, and partners understand when, for example, you have to take a morning to go to something at your child's school, so long as it's not interfering with work it's no problem. The partners are the kind of people who went to events at their kids' schools."*

On the social calendar, there's a holiday party and occasional happy hours planned by the associate development committee (*"people attend but it's not like everybody is getting together and doing shots at the bar – a lot have families"*). Plus there are *"periodic family events and informal get-togethers. We have a rule of four where the firm will cover a lunch bill if four people organize a lunch together."*

Hours & Compensation

There's no official billing requirement at Hangley, although billables are connected to the budget: associates are budgeted for 1,800 billable hours a year. *"Nobody has any complaints about billables – it's not all about the hours like at many firms. If you're not turning things down, nobody's going to say how come you didn't find enough work to meet your target? We need to work hard and be responsive to clients, and some times are busier than others, the idea here is that we don't want people being here every*

night until midnight and weekends and not getting to see family and friends."

A source emphasized that Hangley is *"pretty much a nine to six kind of place – the office is pretty quiet after 6pm. If there's more to be done I'll have dinner and put my kids to bed and then do another hour or two of work."* A very busy time might mean *"getting in at 8am and leaving more like 7pm or 7.30pm and working one day of the weekend."* A junior summarized: *"It's as good as it can be in this line of work."*

"It's as good as it can be in this line of work."

Pro Bono

Associates reckoned that pro bono at Hangley is *"definitely encouraged"* but pointed out that *"unlike bigger firms, they don't give you credit to count toward the 1,800 target."* That said, *"the billable target means less, because the bonus isn't based on it."* According to sources, who'd worked on family and immigration cases, *"Hangley also differs from a big firm in that there's no structured pipeline for pro bono, so you have to be more proactive about getting it and finding your own projects. The firm takes a broad view, so community involvement is also encouraged even if it's not a legal project per se. Attorneys here sit on various boards of community and social welfare organizations."*

"You have to be more proactive about getting it."

Pro bono hours
- For all attorneys: Undisclosed
- Average per attorney: Undisclosed

Diversity

On the subject of diversity, associates pointed out that firm's small size skews the figures somewhat. *"They only generally hire one or two people every year, so it's tougher to get the diversity we want to have. There's an effort made to reach out to diverse candidates and encourage them to apply. The diversity here is more aspirational than anything. We don't have as much diversity as a lot of us would like."* One thought that *"diversity should be something people address more than they do."*

However, in terms of gender diversity, *"we have a large number of female partners compared to a lot of other firms."* In fact, there are 29% female partners, and 40% female associates. Sources partly credited the firm's approach to work/life balance: *"A lot of people here are able to raise kids and have a successful career."* Interviewees commented that *"there are not very many people of color here at all."*

See firm profile on p.608

"We don't have as much diversity as a lot of us would like."

Unlike bigger outfits, Hangley doesn't have a range of diversity groups or committees. *"There are so few of us, the relationships are personal, not mediated through an affinity group."*

Strategy & Future

Looking back at the previous 12 months, CEO David Pudlin tells us that the firm's *"had another terrific year – our fifth really terrific year in a row. We have continued to hire wonderful young attorneys including Harvard and Yale Law graduates. The strategy for the future involves a 'more of the same' approach. Our commercial litigation department, which is the majority of the firm, continues to do very well, and real estate work has picked up quite a bit so we have had growth there. Our family law group continues to grow and do well, and environmental work also is increasing."*

Hangley's pulling power is demonstrable. *"We have been approached by several partners at large firms who are interested in joining us. The fact that we are attractive to partners in other firms who have portable business is flattering also."*

"There's camaraderie. Everybody knows everyone. There isn't space here for people who are going to be disrespectful or yelling at others. That's not something that's accepted here."

See firm profile on p.608

The Inside View

Harris, Wiltshire & Grannis LLP

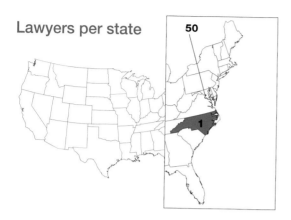

Lawyers per state

Largest US office: Washington, DC
US offices: 2
International offices: 0
First-year salary: $178,500
Billable hours: no requirement
Summers 2017: 2 (2 2Ls)
Revenue 2016: undisclosed
Partners made in 2017: 3
Famous for: boutique BigLaw telecoms masters; firm gong

HWG triumphs at telecoms with an approach that's petite and elite, rather than large and in-charge.

SOMEWHERE in a parallel universe the very best law firms, serving the most well known clients, are rather different. Associates do stimulating work from the start and get treated with unflinching respect, even having a stake in the business' success themselves; everyone gets along too – of course, people still work exceedingly hard, but there's fun, frivolity and bacchanalia without the dark cloud of an hours target looming over them. And you can forget bureaucracy – people speak face to face and actually listen, whatever their rank. One other thing: these firms are tiny. That's no fault, however; in fact it's their defining feature. This is SmallLaw. Or rather SmallBigLaw.

We don't know if the founders of HWG took a trip to that universe nearly 20 years ago, but their firm, a DC-based telecoms boutique, is the spitting image. Telecoms work is king, and the firm earns itself a top ranking from *Chambers USA* in recognition. With this success, HWG is gradually increasing in size and diversifying its work – does this mean it's becoming more... BigLaw? *"God I hope not! I really hope not,"* exclaims cofounder and managing partner Bill Wiltshire. *"I feel we've really captured something here that a lot of firms don't have."*

On chambers-associate.com...

- We talk to managing partner Bill Wiltshire
- Chair of the hiring committee Jonathan Mirsky gives us the lowdown
- More insight on recruitment from associates

The Work

The firm's boutique size is evident in the way the business is run. Interpersonal relations, discussion, and common sense are all valued, not the formulaic over-management you sometimes get at bigger firms. A prime example is work assignment, where *"people have a general sense of how busy you are, and will knock on your door and ask."* Associates also took control, chasing the work they wanted, with the people they wanted: *"Associates don't really have to specialize and you can drive the direction you want to go in,"* said one associate who typified the frequent movement between practice areas, of which the main two are telecoms and litigation. Outside of matters which associates are fully involved in – *"working with a set team"* – they also picked up *"one-off"* assignments which partners need doing. *"There's an email to associates and they coordinate among themselves to decide who is in the best position to take it on, deciding on both interest and availability."* This process of self-assignment is fairly unique.

"You can drive what direction you want to go in."

Clients are typically high profile and international. Telecoms provides the largest share of work, but there's an increasing diversity on offer, of which associates get a fair mix. A glance at the firm's client list reveals big names like Google, Microsoft and Facebook, and the work can be niche, technical and specialized. Much of the work concerns *"fairly high stakes proceedings involving the FCC, sometimes trying to change policy."*

The Inside View

Rankings in *Chambers USA*

Telecommunications

For detail on ranking tiers and ranking locations, visit
www.chambersandpartners.com

Taking this complexity into account, it's perhaps more remarkable that associates get the responsibility that they do. *"It's not the sort of place where you wind up getting into discussions about hierarchies."* Since *"the teams are small everyone, whether a partner or an associate, has to do essential work,"* and *"you're always pretty close to the end product."* Associates get substantive work from the start and *"partners are invested in giving increasing responsibility,"* so the opportunity for depositions and court appearances comes relatively soon in comparison with most of BigLaw. One litigator gave an idea of what they'd handled: *"I've been the primary drafter on court documents, on court filings, I've helped draft memos to clients – so there's been plenty of outward facing things but there's also the essential groundwork for cases. I've done doc review and research and all of those things which need to be done, but there's a focus at this firm about why you do everything. I wouldn't be complaining about doing doc review as I understand why it is so important."* The egalitarian approach *"goes both ways."* While fairly junior associates had *"led meetings at the FCC"* and interacted with clients regularly, *"maybe you'd do the normal tasks of a first-year when you're in your fourth year."*

> *"Partners are invested in giving increasing responsibility."*

Training & Development

The firm's approach to training *"is pretty informal"* and *"learning by doing."* Associates were fully aware of *"the expectation that the firm throws people in and they have to figure it out – the firm will be there to help and support."* This support is the crucial part: associates stressed that, while there wasn't much hand holding or spoon-feeding, *"partners help you figure it out. If you're confused you can go to their office and ask them about it."* Nevertheless, associates can still *"seek out CLEs that would be useful,"* though that's *"self-driven."*

> *"Learning by doing."*

But HWG does add something a little different to the mix: its famous 'Anything But Law' and 'Nothing But Law' talks. There's one of each per month, alternating between the two extremes. The former features a presentation by someone from the firm on *"a topic which is totally unrelated"* to the profession, instead focusing on a personal interest. *"We had someone talk about Quidditch and someone talked about fencing."* Associates appreciated *"the value in things like this; it builds a sense of community."* The 'Nothing But' talks have *"associates or

Recent work highlights

- Represented Facebook, Microsoft and Telxius as they tried to obtain the necessary FCC license and national security clearance to invest in the MAREA fiber optic cable system linking the US and Spain
- Successfully represented Sprint in its challenge, through an FCC rulemaking proceeding, to the prices set by AT&T and Verizon for business data services
- Aided Comcast and the National Cable & Telecommunications Association in securing a new band of WiFi in the US 'Spectrum Frontiers' proceedings

partners talk about an area they are familiar with or a case they have worked on."* A recent example was *"Telecommunications 101."*

Offices

HWG's carrying a little more weight these days, and the addition of new personnel looks set to continue. *"We're already maxing out where we are now,"* says Bill Wiltshire, *"but we have an option on the floor below us so we will be expanding! The location couldn't be better."* The current office building used to belong to the FCC itself and is located in downtown DC. Its most prominent feature is a large central room, whose *"primary purpose is that every day we are all in there eating lunch: partners, associates and legal assistants. It's not compulsory but a lot of us choose to and that is emblematic of the lack of hierarchy. Everyone knows each other and hangs out and eats together. It's also used for happy hours, 'Anything Buts' and 'Nothing Buts.'"*

Culture

Associates put this fellowship down to *"the tone set by the people who founded it. They make clear that they started it to be a place with a friendly culture where people like to work."* This is perpetuated because *"it's kind of infectious; and if you hire people who value this culture it makes sense to keep it going."* It's tight knit, we certainly got that impression, and associates were appreciative of what partners did for them. *"Partners are really treating you like a colleague rather than an employee. Part of that is your development; they're helping you learn as you go, part of that is giving you responsibility, but part of it is also just being friendly and, I want to say... treating you like a human."* Statements like this forgive the lack of formal mentoring or training opportunities. *"It is still a pretty small place and it has a small place mentality – most stuff is pretty casual."*

> *"If you hire people who value this culture it makes sense to keep it going."*

See firm profile on p.609

The Inside View

Diversity	Partners (%)	Associates (%)
Women	24	46
White	83	61
Black/African American	3	8
Hispanic/Latin American	0	0
Asian	7	31
Mixed/Other	7	0
LGBT	10	0

Conversely, monthly pizza lunches, an annual picnic, annual karaoke, frequent bowling nights and weekly Friday happy hours mean that associates' social calendars can be altogether more serious. Happy hours take place in the office and are signaled with the ringing of an office gong, which also gets a sounding *"when someone has had a success, big or small, maybe if they've won a case."* The bowling is *"especially ingrained in the culture, there's always a big turnout for that."* As part of an old tradition *"all people starting that year get a bowling shirt"* emblazoned with their starting year. *"It's really cool to see how long people have been here."*

Hours & Compensation

"People really appreciate their co-workers. That puts a lot of emphasis on living normal lives. People care about birthdays and vacations – you can take them and people treat them with respect, and if you have to leave the office it's something people take seriously." Underpinning this is the fact that *"there is no billing target at all. Every year management will give a presentation on how the firm is doing financially. Part of that presentation includes an average of what people worked, so people know the number, but they don't target it, nobody is looking at your hours."* Associates could regularly *"be home for dinner. Stuff comes up, and I've certainly had days, weeks, months that have been much busier than that. Finishing your work to a high quality comes first, that sometimes means late nights but the firm is designed so that when work settles down, if someone has been crushed they should get to take it easy."*

"There is no billing target at all."

The firm's bonus system bucks convention, allocating tracking points and paying attorneys quarterly. What they are paid *"depends only on seniority and the firm's profitability that quarter, not on hours. It's a way of spreading the wealth."*

Pro Bono and Diversity

The pursuit of pro bono work at HWG is tacitly encouraged because *"pro bono hours are treated the same"* as any other billable hour, but our sources also told us *"there's no pressure"* around getting involved – some hadn't

done any. Associates reported seeing both opportunities *"which associates seek out themselves and find a partner to oversee it"* and occasions where associates were *"helping a partner with something they were already involved in."* In 2016 the firm did significant work advising Bread for the City, a charity aiding DC's vulnerable residents.

"It's a priority in hiring."

As we checked in on the state of diversity at HWG, we were greeted with a common response: *"They're working on it."* Associates with a few years under their belts could see progress, telling us *"it's a priority in hiring to include that as a consideration."* One source informed us that *"recent hires have helped ethnic diversity."* As well as telling us about flexible working options for parents and a new approach to interviewing utilizing objective criteria, chair of the hiring committee Jonathan Mirsky believes the firm's innovative tech clients gives diversity added importance: *"They are looking for us to be diverse."*

Pro bono hours
- For all attorneys: 2,236
- Average per attorney: 43

Get Hired

"Associates should initially think of themselves as Washington lawyers rather than telecom lawyers," says Jonathan Mirsky, hiring chair. To read him elaborating on this, and for more insight on hiring from associates, go to chambers-associate.com.

Strategy and Future

Bill Wiltshire says of the firm's expansion: *"We're not aiming to increase our personnel just for the sake of getting bigger, but we'll continue to grow as we need people to service our clients' demands."* Those demands come in a number of new areas, appellate being one, energy being the other. *"Although the firm began with a focus on telecoms, there has been more diversity in the type of work that has been coming in."* But he stresses his openness to change: *"We don't put our thumb on the scale, we take our business wherever the clients are coming from."* If this sounds a little vague, one must remember how young the firm is. *"Our executive committee decided last year that it was time to develop an overall vision of what we want to be when we grow up and we're still in the early stages of deciding that."*

"Although the firm began with a focus on telecoms, there has been more diversity in the type of work that has been coming in."

See firm profile on p.609

The Inside View

Haynes and Boone, LLP

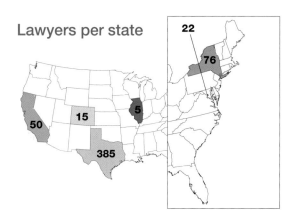

Lawyers per state

22
76
5
15
50
385

Largest US office: Dallas
US offices: 12
International offices: 3
First-year salary: $180,000
Billable hours: 2,000 in Texas, 1,800 in New York
Summers 2017: 33+ (33 2Ls, 1Ls still interviewing when we went to press)
Revenue 2016: $375 million (+3.6%)
Partners made in 2017: 13 (all US)
Famous for: its *"no-jerk"* culture; being able to have a life outside of work

You can take Haynes and Boone out of Texas, but you can't take the Texas out of Haynes and Boone.

DENVER and Chicago joined the Haynes and Boone party in 2015, followed by London in 2016, thanks to a merger with shipbuilding and energy specialist Curtis Davis Garrard. *"London has been on the firm's drawing board since 2005, so we're absolutely delighted about being there,"* managing partner Tim Powers tells us. *"Our focus in energy and tech will align very well with the market there."* Haynes and Boone's strong appetite for expansion means *"we're constantly looking at opportunities in New York and DC, and focusing on growth on both the East and West Coast while also keeping and extending our place in the Texas market."*

Founded 47 years ago, the firm may not quite be the biggest T-bone on the Texan grill, but it picks up juicy rankings from *Chambers USA,* most notably in antitrust, energy, environment, bankruptcy, banking, insurance, IP and real estate. Tim Powers says: *"the biggest growing practice area is definitely private equity and funds. Surprisingly, the healthcare practice is also growing substantially. IP and tech are growing, and real estate continues to be strong."* Rankings outside of Texas and overseas reflect Haynes and Boone's broader development in recent years.

The Work and Offices

Outside of the Lone Star State, Haynes and Boone has offices in New York, Chicago, Palo Alto, Orange County, Denver, and DC. Mexico City, Shanghai and London feature on its global map, though few junior associates we spoke to had dealt with international matters themselves. One noted that *"understandably, Dallas itself doesn't have all that many cross-border deals."* Communication is encouraged between US offices, and for example we heard of a lawyer who *"just took a trip to New York – she simply asked if she could work from the New York office for a few days and they made the arrangements."*

"If you ever need something to do, it's comfortable to ask."

During the summer program, people experience a range of practice areas during a formal rotation. At the end, they state a preference from options including business litigation, corporate/M&A, real estate, IP, and restructuring. The firm *"really tries to get you your preference. If it needs an associate in a particular area, you've got a high chance of getting your first choice."*

Most associates are generally assigned work from a supervisor, but *"if you ever need something to do it's comfortable to ask."* In smaller offices, it's more common to walk around and ask for work. Some preferred this informal system as *"it models the way partners get clients in the real world. It helps make you more extroverted."* A *"good variety"* of typical junior tasks for litigators includes research,

On chambers-associate.com...

- More on getting hired at Haynes and Boone
- Interview with managing partner Tim Powers

See firm profile on p.610

Rankings in *Chambers USA*

Antitrust	Insurance
Banking & Finance	Intellectual Property
Bankruptcy/Restructuring	Labor & Employment
Corporate/M&A	Latin American Investment
Energy & Natural	Litigation
Resources	Real Estate
Environment	Tax
Franchising	Technology
Healthcare	

For detail on ranking tiers and ranking locations, visit
www.chambersandpartners.com

Recent work highlights

- Defended the NFL in a lawsuit brought against it by organizers of a fantasy football convention
- Defended Ericsson against a patent suit by Sycamore IP Holdings
- Antitrust counsel and advice to American Electric Power on its sale to American Commercial Lines
- Revised and negotiated a software license agreement, maintenance and support plan, and statement of work for new workforce management at American Airlines
- Advised HRSmart on transfer of IP, IT, and software in its sale to Deltek

"*drafting motions, preparing depositions and hearing outlines, conferring with counsel, attending and arguing at hearings, as well as doc reviews. There's a lot of responsibility compared to friends at other firms, especially on smaller cases.*" Corporate sources found themselves "*drafting stuff in the first year, then getting more responsibility and being involved in client meetings.*" Others concurred: "*In the first year you prove you can do good work; they can trust you to know what you're doing, so in the second year you get more responsibility.*"

In real estate, we heard the "*amount of responsibility is both uncomfortable and beneficial – you definitely learn a lot when uncomfortable! When you come to the firm, nobody knows your skills so you have to gain trust from the partners. When they have confidence in your ability, you'll get assigned more work.*" Jobs include drafting loan documents and lease amendments. Several in various practices reported feeling loved: "*They really valued my opinion, making me more invested in the work I was doing – they really cared about my input.*"

Training and Development

Training kicks off with a three day program in Dallas known as 'HayBoo U', followed by department-specific training by attorneys in different specialized areas. From here on, it's all systems go – one associate revealed that "*the training wheels come off right away which helps you learn on the job. You're not thrown to the sharks by any means, but you do learn rather quickly!*" Another associate mentioned the firm's subscription to PLI [Practising Law Institute], which allows free access to online webinars and some in-person training for all Haynes and Boone attorneys.

"The training wheel come off right away which helps you learn on the job."

Juniors generally found there are no nasty surprises in their mid and end of year reviews: "*If they're having a problem with you, they're not going to spring it on you.*"

Anybody will generally be happy to give you informal feedback throughout the year."

Culture

A big reason associates were attracted to HayBoo was the friendly culture that exists alongside high-level and challenging work. One summed it up as: "*Easy going people that still take their work very seriously.*" Despite the firm's ever-growing size, many championed its one-firm culture, with offices outside Texas maintaining the same friendly Texas vibe. A New York associate noted a slight difference, with the culture here closer to that of other high-caliber New York firms. But across the board, there's a "*no-jerk policy.*"

"It was very special to see he had such concern about us having a good time."

The busiest time in the social calendar is of course the summer. One interviewee recalled a story of how "*several students came to Dallas and felt let down that it didn't live up to its Western 'cowboy' image. One of the older associates then took it on his own initiative to organize an outing in Fort Worth to country music concerts, dances, and all things Texan! It was very special to see he had such concern about us having a good time.*"

Associates felt kept in the loop, communication-wise. There's a monthly newsletter from MP Tim Powers, who occasionally appears at each of the offices in person. He apparently updates employees on what's happening and lets associates ask questions. One source explained that "*it's hard to be completely transparent from a business standpoint, but the firm still tries nonetheless.*"

Hours and Compensation

Several interviewees were vague about the exact annual billing target, which is 1,800 hours in New York and 2,000 in Texas. Usually, those that make it are put on a 'high-base' bonus system, while those that don't quite reach it go on a 'low-base', though things like pro bono

The Inside View

See firm profile on p.610

Diversity	Partners (%)	Associates (%)
Women	22	40
White	88	69
Black/African American	1	4
Hispanic/Latin American	6	7
Asian	4	17
Mixed/Other	1	3
LGBT	2	2

Pro bono hours
- For all US attorneys: 12,915
- Average per US attorney: 45

will also be taken into consideration. *"The firm will review your performance for bonuses as well – it isn't just about the hours."*

Most sources reported an average day of roughly 9.30am to about 7pm, but this depends hugely on workload. Litigators tend to get in earlier than their transactional colleagues. One described a nice tradition in their corporate team if they have to stay late: *"Someone will order dinner, and everyone staying late will eat together. It really builds a team environment – there's an undeniable sense of solidarity and camaraderie."*

Pro Bono
In all offices, associates can to bill up to 100 hours of pro bono work. There was mixed feedback on the topic from those in the New York office, but elsewhere, every first-year gets assigned a pro bono case after a few months and *"even if they're not assigned it, people do it just because they want to!"* The firm regularly emails out pro bono opportunities, but you can bring your own case to the table if you have one. Associates reported being involved in drafting wills for low-income clients and working on a number of immigration cases. One example involved an associate obtaining asylum for a client who had been subject to inhumane treatment in their home country. The client was subsequently allowed to stay in the US.

"It's great to invite them to the office and do everything you can to help."

Junior associates also jumped at the opportunity to experience an area they wouldn't usually work in. One corporate associate worked a pro bono litigation case and said *"I knew nothing about litigation, but I went to the lit floor and asked for advice. Everyone was more than willing to help!"* Associates describe a *"special feeling when clients are grateful that you've taken the time to help. In most cases they don't have the means, so it's great to invite them to the office and do everything you can to help."*

Diversity
Associates generally praised the firm's approach to diversity, with many highlighting a real push to improve. Some believed the firm isn't yet diverse enough and want to see further improvements, but admitted that *"the firm recognizes it's an issue, and partners are very supportive of diversity measures."* Haynes and Boone holds a diversity retreat every other year, which some of our interviewees had participated in. One considered diversity *"very real and raw. They're not just doing the retreat to say they do it – it's informative and supportive."* Diverse associates are also paired with a diverse partner mentor they can go to for help.

Strategy and Future
In our last edition, managing partner Tim Powers speculated about expanding to London, and within a year the merger with London-based Curtis Davis Garrard was finalized. So what's next for Haynes and Boone? *"Currently there are not necessarily any new offices on the drawing board. We want to focus on domestic growth. We're not a firm that wants to be Baker McKenzie or Akin Gump – we only want to go into markets where we think we can make a difference and differentiate ourselves."* Find our full interview with Tim Powers online.

Get Hired
"Spend the little time you have making a connection with the interviewer. They already know your grades; they have your resumé." Find out more about getting hired at Haynes and Boone on chambers-associate.com

Hogan Lovells

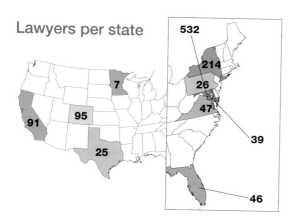

Lawyers per state

532	
214	
7	26
	47
91	95
25	39
	46

Largest US office: Washington, DC
US offices: 13
International offices: 36
First-year salary: $180,000 in most cities
Billable hours: 2,000 target
Summers 2017: 129 (111 2Ls, 16 1Ls, 2 others)
Revenue 2016: $1.93 billion (+6%)
Partners made in 2017: 29 (18 in US)
Famous for: transatlantic merger; diverse practices and geographies

Industry focus is now the name of the game at this *"supportive"* international maestro.

"2016 WAS a strong year. We had a particular focus on developing our industry sector capabilities," the managing partner of Hogan Lovells' largest region in the States (DC), Eve Howard, tells us. Why the industry focus? It's *"a powerful mechanism for bringing the whole of the firm to the whole of our clients. This approach also acts as a significant force in bringing together our different practices to align behind significant market issues, allowing us to be thought leaders in the industry."* In other words, a healthcare client (for example) can come to the firm's healthcare team for advice on a raft of legal specialisms, like regulatory, corporate/M&A and litigation, to name a few. *"Demonstrating a deep understanding of their industry really resonates with clients,"* Eve Howard adds.

Other differentiators of Hogan Lovells are its diverse geographies – 13 domestic and 36 international offices – and numerous practice areas. Unsurprisingly, these are a big draw for new recruits, but so too is the unique *"personality of the firm – it's a very warm place,"* according to one junior. Helping this side of things further, in early 2016 HL rolled out a firmwide 'agile working' policy, giving lawyers and staff more flexibility over their own schedules compared to the the old reduced hours system. Associates also mentioned the firm's great rep for *"com-*

On chambers-associate.com...

- Get Hired
- Interview with hiring partner Tim Lloyd

mitment to pro bono" – demonstrated in early 2017, for example, when a huge pro bono team (20-plus lawyers) sprang into action against President Trump's travel ban, helping detainees at various international airports, and setting up an internal task force to coordinate efforts.

The Work

Incoming juniors join one of five main groups: litigation, arbitration & employment (LAE); corporate; government regulatory; finance; or IP. Only a sprinkling of newcomers join the latter two areas, while LAE, corporate, and government regulatory take on a fairly even load of juniors.

In DC – the flagship office – new recruits have the chance to do four-month rotations in different practice areas to get a feel for where they might best fit. There's even a popular pro bono rotation (for more on that, see below). However, rotating is by no means compulsory but sources appreciated the chance to dabble. *"I did a few rotations and settled in my group after a year. All of those rotations happened because I wanted them to, but I could have settled at any time."* Of course, *"people tend to have strong preferences coming in about litigation or transactional work."* In offices outside of DC, there's no rotation system. In most practices, work assignment comprises *"a mix of a formal system, with a weekly email reporting what we have on and our capacity, and an informal free market system,"* whereby associates *"connect with partners or pick up things here and there when people are looking*

See firm profile on p.611

The Inside View

Rankings in *Chambers USA*

Antitrust

Appellate Law

Climate Change

Corporate Crime & Investigations

Corporate/M&A

Employee Benefits & Executive Compensation

Energy & Natural Resources

Environment

Financial Services Regulation

Food & Beverages

Government

Healthcare

Immigration

Insurance

Intellectual Property

International Arbitration

International Trade

Latin American Investment

Leisure & Hospitality

Life Sciences

Litigation

Media & Entertainment

Natural Resources

Privacy & Data Security

REITs

Real Estate

Securities

Telecommunications

Transportation

For detail on ranking tiers and ranking locations, visit
www.chambersandpartners.com

Recent work highlights

- Tokyo, New York, DC and Singapore lawyers advised leading US nuclear operator Exelon on the formation of a 50:50 joint venture with The Japan Atomic Power Company
- Advised the State of Hawaii in its challenge of Trump's travel ban
- Secured a major copyright victory for TV broadcasters in the Ninth Circuit in *Fox Television Stations, Inc. v. Aereokiller, LLC*. The case was about third parties re-transmitting content online, a major issue affecting clients including Fox Television Stations, CBS Studios, NBCUniversal Media, American Broadcasting Companies, and Disney Enterprises
- Represented Petróleos Mexicanos (Pemex), a Mexico-owned exploration and production company, in an agreement with Australian multinational BHP Billiton to develop the deep-water Trion Block, a $14 billion project

for bodies on a project." A government regulatory junior told us "*the head of our group does an incredible job of making sure everyone's getting the experience they want, but I also pester certain partners with specific practices to get staffed on their work.*"

Over in litigation in DC, "*when you first start, you are assigned a partner mentor and they physically give you you first assignment and organize others. Another partner sends out emails asking you about staffing. I think it's pretty effective.*" Sources had tackled areas including white collar investigations, healthcare, general corporate litigation, construction, insurance, accounting disputes and entertainment issues. "*I've done a lot of motions to dismiss, drafted briefs, coordinated all the depositions of 100-plus named plaintiffs and taken ten of the depositions myself,*" said one junior. Transactional attorneys take charge of "*a lot of paper that gets pushed and things like ancillaries. Then there's the more exciting and fun stuff like taking an initial draft of a credit agreement and helping with the negotiation process.*" A transactional source in a smaller department said there's a formal "*weekly reporting system*" but "*I get all my work informally!*"

> "*I've handled discrete client questions, policy analysis and government investigations.*"

In government regulatory, some sources focus their practice on FDA work. "*I'd be the one to review FDA guidance, I'd chat with the partner about what I've found and how we should present the information. Then I draft an email with guidance as to what the client should do going forward. If a client is doing a product recall, I file a report with the*

Commission, interface with the client and take first draft of a report." Other associates in government regulatory might home in on trade or cybersecurity work. "*We tend to represent foreign companies being investigated and there's more of a disputes flavor,*" a trade source reported. "*I've been to the Court of International Trade, worked on a couple of briefs and a lot of exhibit preparation.*" In cybersecurity, "*the clients are top in their field – cutting edge* Fortune 100 *companies and start-ups looking to do innovative things with data and information. My role varies a lot. I've handled discrete client questions, policy analysis and government investigations.*"

Training & Development

Newcomers have an initial administrative orientation in their respective offices, which gets them up to speed with "*an introduction to the firm covering things like how to bill your time.*" Then, in late September or early October, everyone comes to DC for a week of more substantive legal orientation, with tips on the transition from student or judicial clerk to lawyer, and practice-specific training, which continues thereafter. A training highlight for litigators is NITA training in Colorado over three days, with actors assisting in witness interviews and deposition sessions. There are also legal writing classes and "*really wonderful*" public speaking training. "*In my group there's a ton of institutional knowledge passed on, through Power Points and client alerts,*" a government regulatory junior told us. Another source remarked that "*one of the great things about being at a big firm is the massive amount of resources, but it requires initiative from associates. People are busy and so it's incumbent on associates to seek out feedback, but I certainly feel very supported by senior associates and partners. If I have questions I don't feel shy about asking them.*"

See firm profile on p.611

The Inside View

Diversity	Partners (%)	Associates (%)
Women	25	50
White	90	73
Black/African American	1	6
Hispanic/Latin American	4	7
Asian	3	11
Mixed/Other	0.5	4
LGBT	1.7	4

First-years are assigned both an associate and a partner mentor, although *"people also develop their own informal relationships."* As one commented: *"I'm lucky to have some close mentors who will take the time to give me some substantive feedback if they think I'm missing a key point."*

Hours & Compensation

Sources had different feelings about the 2,000 hour billing target. For some, hitting the figure is *"entirely realistic and not a concern."* Others, especially those in smaller groups, found that *"sometimes the work doesn't trickle down so it's not realistic for a lot of associates. Historically I have not made my hours."* However, *"talking to mid-levels it's never been an issue, it's understood that the work ebbs and flows. I've never really gotten pushback against my hours. I do a ton of pro bono and business development. They look at you holistically, so as long as you're not a slacker it's okay."* The first-year starting salary is $180,000 in all US offices except Miami, Minneapolis and Colorado Springs.

> *"They look at you holistically, so as long as you're not a slacker it's okay."*

On a typical day it's normal for juniors to spend around ten hours in the office, although they appreciated that *"there's a lot of flexibility. I like to leave earlier and work from home in the evenings. Partners don't really care where you are as long as they can reach you."* However, this being BigLaw, *"it's a demanding environment"* and *"working from dawn until dusk"* is sometimes par for the course. Asked for an example of a late finish, one interviewee told us *"5am the next day... but that was a unique circumstance."* Associates were pleased to note that time off is respected. *"I just came back from a ten day vacation where I checked my emails twice and nobody called me."*

Pro Bono

All our sources spoke enthusiastically about Hogan's approach to pro bono. *"It really sets the firm apart from others – it's definitely a very significant priority. We have a dedicated pro bono department with a full time partner [T. Weymouth, known as "T"] assisted by a senior fellow who's a mid to senior level."* First-years can do a four month rotation where they work exclusively on pro bono work. However, *"even if you're not a rotator, most people do pro bono work."* Indeed, all of our sources had taken on projects, including immigration issues – most recently, the travel ban – and death penalty cases, including through the Innocence Project. One noted cheerily that *"you can devote as much time as you want to it because the firm policy is if you hit 1,850 billable hours you can count an unlimited number of pro bono hours after that toward your total."*

Pro bono hours
- For all US attorneys: 87,864
- Average per US attorney: 85

Culture

The buzzword at Hogan Lovells is *"collaborative,"* but what does this actually mean? A *"supportive, non-competitive, challenging environment,"* was one junior's assessment, a sentiment echoed by others. *"It feels like everyone is available to help and make sure you're succeeding. People are very affable and candid. Unlike a lot of workplaces, you can show your true personality and build real friendships."* Another associate commented that *"people genuinely enjoy each other's company. I went on a hike with a couple of co-workers recently."* What else is going on socially? *"The easiest answer is I went to a see a local Nineties cover band, who are popular in DC, with a bunch of Hogan folks. We then bumped into four other groups of Hogan people, from mid levels to juniors. Folk here are very social and fun to hang out with."*

> *"You can show your true personality and build real friendships."*

There are practice-specific gatherings, like lunches, happy hours and dinners, plus a monthly a firmwide happy hour, known as 'pub night' in true British style. *"We are known in the market to be a very collaborative and friendly firm,"* regional managing partner Eve Howard points out. *"Lateral associates and partners from other firms also say that's true."* Her personal testimony bears this out: *"I came to Hogan & Hartson nearly 30 years ago not only because of the great corporate practice, but also because it was known for its collegiality and warm culture. I'm proud to say that Hogan Lovells has retained that culture 30 years later."*

Offices

Renovation is taking place across the entire DC office: *"It's currently a work in progress but the new developments are fabulous – open, light and with collaborative spaces."* There's even a rooftop solarium, as well as a new cafeteria and conference rooms. The LA and Denver offices

See firm profile on p.611

The Inside View

have also been transformed. *"There's a ton of glass, lots of big windows, and funky furniture, all staff and attorneys have standing desks. It looks like a law firm merged with a Silicon Valley tech start up."* New Yorkers told us that *"in 2018 we're moving to a very modern space that has a better flow. The issue in our office is that corporate and litigation are on separate floors with another company in between, so to help with that situation the managing partners created a lounge space that's light and comfortable, with free apples and nice coffee and tea, and beer and wine after 5pm on Fridays."* New Yorkers won't be moving far: only a few blocks away on Madison Avenue. DC sources applauded their subsidized cafeteria: *"It's a great social space and everyone uses it, including partners."* Most offices have their own pet name for their common areas: in DC it's called 'The Hive', while in Denver it's 'The Junction', and in Baltimore 'The Nest'.

> *"like a law firm merged with a Silicon Valley tech start up."*

Diversity

A notable hire in 2016 was the appointment of Leslie Richards-Yellen as director of inclusion for the Americas region. *"Diversity is something that the firm is very aware of and focused on promoting,"* associates told us. Diversity initiatives include affinity groups for African-Americans, Latin-Americans, LGBT people, and women. Every year or two the firm hosts its 'Pathways to Success' conference: the firm's African-American associates are invited to the capital, where they meet with diverse law students and offer advice on their career paths.

"We have a diversity committee and every month there's an event, like a documentary showing or a speaker. The partners are involved, which is really nice. They did a film showing the other day about disabilities, and people were encouraged to take time off from their day. A movie and food: who's going to say no?" Other associates mentioned that *"there are still efforts to be made, in terms of diversity in the upper echelons of the firm, which many firms suffer*

from." On the topic of the new firmwide agile working policies, regional MP Eve Howard says: *"Personally, it's an issue that's very important to me. We have always been open to working flexibly and I spent 15 years here on a reduced schedule to help balance the needs of my family. We encourage our people to work in the way that is smartest for them within the demands of the job. It's a powerful tool for retaining and attracting the best talent."* In March, the firm won an award from The Diversity & Flexibility Alliance for its new initiative.

Get Hired

Hogan Lovells recruits from around 35 law schools each year. Find out more in our Bonus Features online.

Strategy & Future

Hogan Lovells was formed by the 2010 mega-merger of the then 800-plus-lawyer US firm Hogan & Hartson and the UK's Lovells. The strategy since then of integration, organic growth (but no more mergers thus far), and occasional lateral partner hires has continued into 2017. In April, for example, the firm added four high profile attorneys in North California from Weil Gotshal, with collective expertise in M&A and IP in various industries, including tech and life sciences. M&A, incidentally, has been *"strong around the globe"* for the firm and *"we worked on some very large transactions, particularly with complex regulatory aspects."* according to regional MP Eve Howard.

Government-related practices, meanwhile, have taken advantage of the *"revolving door"* of talent freed up by the change in administration from Obama to Trump: recent hires include a former solicitor of the US Department of the Interior to the environment practice, and a senior Department of Justice official to Hogan's antitrust, competition and economic regulation (ACER) team.

> *"A powerful mechanism for bringing the whole of the firm to the whole of our clients."*

See firm profile on p.611

Holland & Knight LLP

Lawyers per state

Holland & Knight LLP also has an office in Alaska with ten attorneys

Largest US office: Washington, DC

US offices: 24

International offices: 3

First-year salary: $180,000 in major markets

Billable hours: 1,900 target

Summers 2017: 26 (21 2Ls, 5 1Ls)

Revenue 2016: $802.9 million (+7.9%)

Partners made in 2017: 23 globally (all in US)

Famous for: big presence in Florida with a big national network

This Florida-founded firm's many offices around the country offer *"interesting and demanding work"* with *"a very civilized culture."*

ALLURING as Florida's Key lime pie may be, two-thirds of Holland & Knight's 1,100 attorneys these days work outside the sunny state, where the firm can trace its roots back to the 1880s. The first non-FL office, in Washington, opened almost a century later, and is by a smidgen the largest of H&K's 27 offices by headcount. London is the most recent addition (2016) – the firm's third international base after Bogotá and Mexico City – and was set up to boost market-leading aviation and maritime finance practices.

These business areas are just two of many at Holland & Knight that *Chambers USA* singles out as high-fliers in the legal industry. Others include real estate, corporate/M&A, private equity, media & entertainment, litigation (general and white-collar), environment, retail, and all things government-related. Check out chambersandpartners.com for the full list with commentaries. Speaking of government, in early 2017 the firm caught the news media's attention when it hired one of Trump's transition team, lobbyist Scott Mason, as a policy advisor in DC.

On chambers-associate.com...

- Interview with managing partner Steve Sonberg
- Energy law under the Trump administration: the views from top energy lawyers
- More on getting hired

The Work

Work at H&K is split into four sections – business, litigation, real estate and government – which are then divided into different groups. The business section, which comprises about 60% of new starters, is made up of the following groups: corporate finance, corporate/M&A, financial services, international & cross border transactions, private wealth services, public companies & securities, structured finance, and syndication. Most groups tackle assignment in the same way, with sources describing *"a mostly informal process where partners approach you, and visa versa."* While most had no qualms, others suggested *"that it might be nice for at least first-years to have a formal system because it can be daunting approaching partners."*

> *"If they think you're able to argue in court in your first or second year, they'll let you do it."*

Structured finance newbies told us they did *"a lot of asset-backed finance mostly in the aviation, maritime and transportation sectors. We mostly represent lenders and companies that want to acquire vessels."* On smaller matters, insiders had *"run conference and client calls, drafted ancillary documents – we're never micromanaged."* Litigators also felt trusted with responsibility: *"If they think you're able to argue in court in your first or second year, they'll let you do it."* Obviously we're not talking first-chair, but *"motion arguments and doing the first draft of appellate briefs"* were a common occurrence.

The Inside View

See firm profile on p.612

Rankings in *Chambers USA*

Banking & Finance	Leisure & Hospitality
Bankruptcy/Restructuring	Litigation
Construction	Media & Entertainment
Corporate/M&A	Native American Law
Environment	Products Liability
Food & Beverages	Real Estate
Government	Retail
Healthcare	Tax
Labor & Employment	Transportation
Latin American Investment	

For detail on ranking tiers and ranking locations, visit
www.chambersandpartners.com

Within real estate, most juniors do commercial real estate work within their region, although a few were specialized in areas such as transactions or land use & government. Most revealed that *"it's a lot of drafting leases, consignments, third party approvals and speaking with local counsel."* Those in the land use subgroup said that *"we land use lawyers straddle the line between transactional work and administrative board presentations. So we do a lot of drafting pleadings and applications."* Over in government, the smallest of the four sections, associates can get involved with either public policy & regulation or West Coast land use and environmental work. Regarding the latter, newbies engaged in *"cases that try to clean up contaminated soil, researching local codes, doc review, and doing the first drafts of documents."*

Training & Development

"We have a training program called 'a day in the life of' and it goes through all the things you'll need to know on a daily basis here." Education then becomes practice-specific, with lectures, a CLE series, legal updates and interactive workshops that are all put online for newbies to peruse at their leisure. For example, some sources in relevant practices had been encouraged to attend the environment-focused Yosemite Law Conference, *"which counts as CLE credits too."* Insiders told us that *"you're a little on your own and it's up to you to make sure you're watching these presentations."*

Juniors are assigned a peer and partner mentor, and while most had found theirs helpful, others were less convinced: *"Some people use theirs more than others, and some don't know who their mentors are!"* One enthusiast said: *"I'm close to my associate mentor and they've been really successful so I know it's good advice."* Additionally, third-year female attorneys get assigned a female mentor through the women's initiative. *"This mentor will be from another office so you get to network more with people you might not have met before."* Reviews are bi-annual for the first two years and subsequently once a year. Feedback is *"all kept anonymous and goes as far as any review system*

Recent work highlights

- Representing CNN in two defamation lawsuits concerning reports on infant death rates at a Florida hospital
- Acted as special maritime counsel to Citibank concerning its $1 billion revolving credit facility for the construction of two drillships
- Represented Irish fruit company Fyffes in its $113 million acquisition of Canadian mushroom producer Highline Produce

can, really. There's an inherent limitation in systems like this because it asks people to remember what you've done in the past. I learn best from real-time feedback."

Offices

Among Holland & Knight's 24 domestic offices and three international outfits, there's no official HQ. Insiders told us that *"since the firm was founded in Florida there are a certain amount of centralized decisions that come out of there. But everything is handled by each office's management committee, so it never feels factioned."* Boston and Miami had the largest number of second and third-years (13) on this year's interviewee list, closely followed by New York, Chicago and Washington, DC. The rest were found in: Tampa, Dallas, LA, Jacksonville, San Francisco, Orlando, Atlanta, Denver, Fort Lauderdale, Portland, Tysons, Anchorage, and Tallahassee.

While New Yorkers *"have to share offices for several years,"* most associates we spoke to had their own space to call their home from home. *"It's understandable,"* reasoned one San Franciscan. *"New York real estate prices are crazy!"* Bostonians were proud of their *"miniature golf green on the Tudor patio outside. There's also shuffle-board."* However, DC-ers took it one step further: *"There's a really nice gym in the basement, we have a roof terrace, and the 10th floor has an indoor putting green and a smart room with a Wii and Foosball."* On top of that, *"we're pretty much round the corner from the White House, so whenever there's a bomb threat we're put on lock-down."*

Culture

"I'm never made to feel guilty about something stupid like not being at my desk at 9pm," one associate told us. *"I'm not going to get crap from an old person who thinks good work is purely down to a well-tied tie."* Insiders explained further: *"It's very busy and demanding and everyone will be all hands on deck if a deal is going down. But associates are respected and you're treated like an adult."*

H&K has a few tricks up its sleeves to keep things ticking over in *"collegial"* fashion. New Yorkers told us that *"there's quite a few young associates here and you can get*

See firm profile on p.612

Diversity	Partners (%)	Associates (%)
Women	22	49
White	88	74
Black/African American	2	6
Hispanic/Latin American	7	11
Asian	2	7
Mixed/Other	1	2
LGBT	2	1

close to people organically. We're always going out for dinners and drinks after work." In DC, there's an active push to "make happy hours more of a thing so that we get to see each other, because you can be in a bit of a bubble and you have to watch out for that." Some offices have their own softball teams that compete in local leagues against other firms. However, those in Miami have had a bit of a football setback: "There were quite a few injuries, so word on the street is that it's been shut down." While most felt that there was enough social stuff on offer, some felt that "we don't have as many events – or as elaborate – as some other firms. So if you're looking for loads of socials then that's probably not us here."

Hours & Compensation

Attorneys are encouraged to hit a 1,900 billing target. Most thought it was doable, "but it depends on how busy your group is. Some years you can cruise past 2,000 by August, but when it's slow there's not a lot you can do." Insiders were thankful that 100 pro bono hours could count toward billables as well. There was a little confusion about exactly how associates are compensated. Salaries matched the market "in March 2016 and then when New York went up again a few months later, the firm followed suit." While this should be a cause for celebration, not everyone was in the party spirit: "Younger associates benefit most from it because we didn't adopt the full-scale increase for the top years. For first and second-years it's $180,000 and $190,000 respectively. After that you have a range and the top of that range is the market rate." As in the past, compensation is discretionary for third-years and above, with a separate bonus for things like commitment to the community and diversity.

Pro Bono

We heard of various activities, including working for "a non profit that makes documentaries and we had to draft all the finance agreements and coordinated all the production agreements too." Others had "worked for the Bronx Zoo on a few matters," "researched into exoneration for

people on death row," and some had "helped low income households who were in rented apartments find paths to ownership and negotiate leases." Sources also explained that "here there's an expectation to do at least 50 hours, and we get reminders listing people who haven't participated."

Pro bono hours
- For all US attorneys: 65,908
- Average per US attorney: 65

Diversity

At H&K "there's a diversity committee, so there is an active pursuit of diversity. But whether or not it's that effective I don't know." The firm fares better with female employment, at least at associate level. The most prominent of H&K's affinity groups is the Woman's Initiative: "We have monthly meetings, discuss career advancement, and there's mentorship, but it depends on which office you're in as to how involved people are. To be honest we're not super-involved because we're just trying to make our billables." However, insiders felt that "the firm is very encouraging in helping interest groups and events get set up. For example, we had a whole lot of people involved in the Women's March the day after the inauguration."

In terms of ethnic diversity, "racially I don't think we're that great compared to the rest of the world, but compared to other law firms I think we're good." Yet, activity varied depending on location. "There's an Asian Pacific interest group but I don't think it's as active here in New York because there isn't as large an Asian population here. This group tends to be more visible in California."

Strategy & Get Hired

"The most important thing for you to do," one associate advised, "is make sure you talk to practicing lawyers to see what their lives are like, because there's a lot of difference between a firm's published billable hours requirement and what it actually works out as." Continuing in this vein, sources extolled the importance of "getting as much real work experience that you can while you're still at law school. Get involved with a clinic." Looking toward the future, managing partner Steve Sonberg lets us in on the firm's strategy. " We've identified a number of industry groups in which we are particularly strong and want to continue to distinguish ourselves. They are healthcare, real estate, tech, transportation, financial services and energy. We are investing in those areas to showcase to clients the industry expertise and understanding we have of their business needs." **For more insider info, go online.**

See firm profile on p.612

The Inside View

Hughes Hubbard & Reed LLP

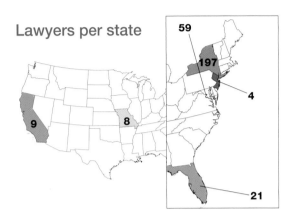

Lawyers per state

59
197
4
9
8
21

Largest US office: New York
US offices: 6
International offices: 2
First-year salary: $180,000
Billable hours: 1,950 target (1,750 billable)
Summers 2017: 23 (22 2Ls, 1 LLM)
Revenue 2016: not disclosed
Partners made in 2017: 2
Famous for: founding father Charles Evans Hughes; historic diversity achievements

With an historic past, newly-renovated offices and international reach, this mid-sized law firm has a lot to recommend it.

WHEN asked to define the typical Hughes Hubbard attorney, one source took a moment to search for the perfect analogy, before replying: *"We're really just a bunch of golden retrievers – very goofy, but nice, helpful people... I would feel comfortable talking to absolutely anyone at the firm."* But don't worry, no one's going to ask you to play fetch: HH (as it's affectionately known) places great emphasis on associates finding their own way. The firm – founded in 1888 – is a New York institution whose founding father – Charles Evans Hughes – served as the 36th Governor of New York, Chief Justice of the Supreme Court, United States Secretary of State, and was once a Republican presidential candidate.

But it is perhaps the firm that bears his name that remains his most lasting legacy. That's not to say that HH is an institution stuck in the past. Its recently-renovated HQ can be found among the shiny towers of downtown Manhattan, and its lawyers – spread between six US offices as well as outposts in Tokyo and Paris – constitute a modern, mostly litigation-focused international practice. *Chambers USA* recognizes its prowess, giving the firm a couple of nationwide rankings for its international arbitration and international trade work.

On chambers-associate.com...

- Interview with George Tsougarakis, hiring partner

The Work

New York takes the vast majority of incoming associates, while a handful go to DC, with Miami taking at least one a year. Litigation is the main destination for newly-minted attorneys, with that department representing *"about 75% of the headcount in New York and even more than that in DC."* A scattering of juniors can also be found in corporate, tax and IP. Summer associates *"are able to give their departmental preference,"* but really *"they want you to get as rounded an experience as possible and encourage you to take work from everyone."*

"They want you to get as rounded an experience as possible and encourage you to take work from everyone."

After accepting their offers to come back, incomers are earmarked for a practice. However, it is one of HH's core principles that most lawyers don't specialize until they are mid-level, an approach lauded by many but criticized by some sources who opined: *"There are a lot of associates who have left the firm because they found the process of not specializing made it difficult for them to develop expertise."*

A large proportion of the firm's contentious work concerns product liability, most often for large pharmaceutical companies. Elsewhere, the white-collar investigations and international arbitration teams are *"big and growing."* Lean staffing is a fact of life and it means *"juniors get a lot of responsibility"* purely because *"there are so few attorneys."* These 'few' still *"do things like doc review,"* but also

See firm profile on p.613

Rankings in *Chambers USA*

Bankruptcy/Restructuring	Latin American Investment
Corporate/M&A	Media & Entertainment
International Arbitration	Products Liability
International Trade	Transportation

For detail on ranking tiers and ranking locations, visit
www.chambersandpartners.com

Recent work highlights

- Represented Epic Pharma in its sale to China's Humanwell Healthcare Group and PuraCap Pharmaceutical
- Won historic 'champerty' victory for Portigon in New York's highest court
- Advised underwriters in $1.3 billion Viacom bond offering
- Counseled United Airlines in nearly $2 billion of EETC offerings [a type of debt financing]

"get the opportunity to do a lot of really substantive stuff like write briefs, and do depositions and expert reports." One litigious interlocutor even reported how *"one partner let me do an oral argument all on my own."*

The much smaller corporate department is more relaxed than its contentious counterpart: *"I think the hierarchy is less pronounced, the entire department is about 30 attorneys, so it's fairly informal – a lot of my projects in the first year were just me and a partner!"* In New York – where there are M&A, structured finance, securities and funds teams – juniors are expected to spend their first three years as generalists. But in DC *"it's mostly just aviation finance and compliance,"* so if you make up part of the small corporate contingent, you'll be specializing early on. Again, thanks to low numbers, associates are given a lot of autonomy: *"By the middle of the first year I was pretty much running a lot of the smaller deals,"* one reported.

Culture

Associates agreed that HH *"has a reputation for being more traditional,"* in large part because *"it's been around for more than 100 years and has that prestige."* On top of that, *"almost all of our partners are homegrown and we have this institutional longevity with clients – there's a sense of continuity in that regard too."*

Again the word that came up most when talking about the firm's social scene was 'traditional'. But it's a fair comment – the New York office's holiday party has been held at the same Downtown steakhouse for over 50 years. Other than the requisite quarterly happy hours and Christmas events, sources admitted that HH wasn't the most social of places. But this was put down to the fact that *"a lot of people have families and would prefer to go home."* And it'd be remiss of us not to mention the informal lunches that take place every second Thursday of the month in both offices – *"they're always well attended and there's a 'no work talk' rule that is strictly enforced."*

Training & Development

All incoming associates attend a formal week-long training in New York called The Hughes Institute. You won't be required to don lab coat and fire up the bunsen burner; the program is purely dedicated to your role as an HH attorney: *"How things work in the office, who the*

librarians are, everything you need to know about the firm, really." There is legal stuff but it's mostly litigation-based. As a result, corporate associates attend their own trainings spread out over their first few months. And the Institute isn't the end of substantive legal training for juniors – there is a *"grueling but gratifying"* three-day mock trial for litigation first-years. Their corporate counterparts are offered a comprehensive range of lunchtime trainings to whet their appetite.

Despite the excellent formalized training, interviewees believed that the most valuable learning happened on the job. To this end, the firm's *"world class"* mentorship scheme comes to the fore. When someone joins, *"they get a junior associate mentor, a senior associate mentor and sometimes a partner mentor as well."* Mentors are incentivized to take their mentees out to catch up over coffee or some food – *"it's great to have a network of people with a bit more experience to draw on for advice."* Recently the firm also launched its 'business development program': *"They pair up a partner with three or four associates. You'll have meeting every few weeks to talk about contacts and marketing yourself within the firm."*

Hours & Compensation

Eschewing New York convention, HH deploys a tiered system for bonuses. Associates must hit 1,950 hours to be eligible for a first-year bonus, which is half of market – *"you can bill 1,750 and if you have 400 substantive nonbillable hours it can bump you up to eligible."* After that 2,100 billable hours gets you market, 2,300 gets you market and a half and 2,500 gets you double market. Most agreed with one source who declared: *"I'm in no way resentful of the tiered system. If I was really killing myself and I knew I was getting the same bonus as someone who'd billed 2,000, I'd be pissed."* Bonuses are paid out at the end of February after attorneys' annual reviews, then *"they'll retroactively increase your pay for January."*

Due to a general ebb and flow of work, sources reported great fluctuation in the number of hours they usually worked. Nonetheless, most agreed that hours at HH weren't as tough as they'd anticipated, and that, unlike other firms, there really is no culture of face time – *"I'll be home by seven most nights. A lot of people here have*

See firm profile on p.613

Diversity	Partners (%)	Associates (%)
Women	23	49
White	91	69
Black/African American	1	11
Hispanic/Latin American	3	8
Asian	4	9
Mixed/Other	1	3
LGBT	2	5

Diversity

HH has always been a BigLaw leader in diversity: it was the first Wall Street firm to hire a female associate and the first to appoint a black female partner. Its current chair is Candace Beinecke – the first woman to head a major law firm in New York City. That said, sources felt that *"though we're not doing worse than any other big NYC firm... the eye has been taken off the prize somewhat."* The stats are pretty good for BigLaw, though: almost half of associates are female and over 30% are ethnically diverse.

come from more intense firms where they expect associates to stay at their desks until everyone's gone home – it's not like that here." Others spoke of busy weeks but expressed relief that weekends were still sacred: *"A very light week is 40 hours but partners understand that weekends are still by and large our own."*

There are a number of affinity groups *"but they could be more active, there's lunch or dinner once in a while but down in DC I hear they regularly organize events."* We asked a DC source to corroborate: *"The diversity committee meets up once a quarter to talk about goings-on. We've hosted a few panel discussions with legal professionals and academics about how to make the legal field more diverse."*

Offices

The firm's Big Apple HQ has recently undergone extensive renovation and sources happily reported that *"everything's nice and glass and new."* On the second point, a new found lack of privacy came in for some criticism: *"The offices all have glass walls – but I don't know anyone who's been happy about that."* Though the fact that every attorney now had their own space was widely praised. In greener news, the office's cafeteria has been *"vastly upgraded"* according to interviewees who were effusive about its new salad bar – *"it's really great!"*

DC is a lot smaller, meaning *"after a few weeks you've pretty much met everyone"* and *"it feels pretty tight-knit and homely."* Compared to its flashy open-plan older sibling, as one discerning source put it, *"the décor is pretty outdated – the offices are all painted eggshell/cream and the desks are all dark brown, cherry wood."*

Get Hired

Juniors agreed that *"HH doesn't look for any particular type – there's all kinds of people here. What's important is that a person is likeable or coachable."* Potential recruits are interviewed initially by two partners – one from corporate and one from litigation. Then those who are chosen for a callback are invited to something called 'Super Saturday' – *"you have breakfast and/or lunch with the other candidates and some partners and associates. I think it's to see if certain relationships and chemistry works out."* So it's worth brushing up on those table manners if you want to impress...

Strategy/Future

Partners and management are candid about how the business is performing. There is an annual state-of-the-firm address in the spring – *"the executive committee does a presentation, they go through the top clients and future projects and discuss projected revenue."* After a recent slowdown on the litigation front, *"they were very open and have ended up moving some associates to the Paris office,"* which was less affected.

Pro Bono

Pro bono work is not just encouraged, it's required: *"Every associate has to do at least 20 hours a year."* After they've racked up 50, attorneys can count up to 200 pro bono hours toward their bonus target, a sign that *"HH really takes its commitments seriously."* The firm has long-standing relationships with a number of worthwhile organizations including Volunteer Lawyers for the Arts, *"that helps artists or groups out with everything from becoming a non-profit to actual litigation;"* Her Justice, *"who we help with immigration cases;"* and New York Legal Assistance Group (NYLAG), *"who provide free legal service for low-income New Yorkers."*

Pro bono hours
- For all US attorneys: over 50,000
- Average per US attorney: 140

See firm profile on p.613

Hunton & Williams LLP

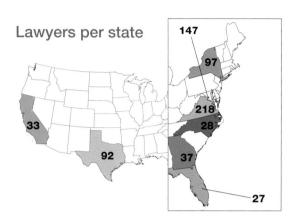

Lawyers per state

147
97
218
28
33
92
37
27

Largest US office: Richmond
US offices: 14
International offices: 5
First-year salary: $160,000 - $180,000
Billable hours: 2,000 target
Summers 2017: 31 (26 2Ls, 5 1Ls)
Revenue 2016: $568 million (+7.6%)
Partners made in 2017: 9 (all US)
Famous for: Southern charm; data security and climate change practices

With its forward-looking practices, we have a feeling the world is going to need Hunton's lawyers…

A PIONEER attitude has embodied Hunton & Williams since it set up in Virginia 1901. From its eagle's perch on the banks of the James River, this Richmond firm has defined itself by its avant garde practices – environment law and tech, notably – which have always ensured demand for the firm's expertise and that looks set to continue. Managing partner Wally Martinez reassures us: the firm aims *"to be known as a leader in adopting, using, and deploying technology for the benefit of our clients,"* and like a few other tech-savvy firms in this guide, Hunton is looking to its newer recruits to help shape the firm.

In the 1960s Hunton took its brand out to DC and then established a larger network across the US, principally along the East Coast, and then onto Texas and California. Overseas the firm has set up five strategic bases that play to its strengths in areas like energy, infrastructure, tech and environmental law.

"The real experience has been very different from the expectation."

On chambers-associate.com…

- More on getting hired at Hunton & Williams
- Interview with global managing partner Wally Martinez
- Training and development

"We haven't experienced any of the horror stories of BigLaw here," associates told us when we interviewed them. *"The real experience has been very different from the expectation."* Some were attracted by its *"excellent energy and infrastructure practices"* – in *Chambers USA* Hunton gets top marks nationwide for its climate change, environment, and privacy & data security practices. Regionally, it also ranks top for bankruptcy/restructuring, general litigation, and labor & employment in Virginia, and corporate/M&A, real estate, and IP in Southern Virginia, and the firm picks up various rankings across seven other US states. MP Wally Martinez highlights *"financial services, retail & consumer products, energy, and real estate investment & finance"* as the firm's leading industries.

The Work & Offices

We found large numbers of juniors to interview in the corporate and capital finance & real estate groups, closely followed by litigation. Others were split between administration law, tax & ERISA, labor & employment, energy & infrastructure, and competition. Each practice group is then divided into more specific sub-groups. The Richmond HQ has the largest intake of juniors across a range of practices. The Big Apple's office on Park Avenue follows in junior numbers, and emphasizes energy and transactional practices, and DC's labor, energy, environment and antitrust-heavy office is a close third. *"Someone here has a great eye for art,"* a DC junior noted about the particular office's style. Among the smaller branches, the firm's fairly long-standing McLean office is soon to close

See firm profile on p.614

The Inside View

Rankings in *Chambers USA*

Antitrust	Latin American Investment
Banking & Finance	Litigation
Bankruptcy/Restructuring	Outsourcing
Capital Markets	Privacy & Data Security
Climate Change	Projects
Corporate/M&A	Real Estate
Environment	REITs
Intellectual Property	Retail
Labor & Employment	

For detail on ranking tiers and ranking locations, visit
www.chambersandpartners.com

Recent work highlights

- Advised Nigeria Bulk Electricity Trading in its $1.76 billion purchase agreements to buy 1,125MW of solar power
- Ongoing advice to Google on numerous aspects of US and EU privacy law, notably advice on compliance with new and existing EU rulings, monitoring and mobile issues
- Lawyers in Miami, Atlanta and Dallas advised Promerica Financial Corporation in its acquisition of Banco Citibank de Guatemala and affiliate Cititarjetas de Guatemala Limitada
- Advised Bank of America and Allianz in its tax equity investments on a portfolio of wind projects being developed by EDF Renewables in New Mexico

its doors, with current attorneys there moving to the DC office down the road.

The capital finance & real estate group represents both the banks and the developers. Deals are *"all kinds of sizes, from people buying one building, to those buying a portfolio of properties. Values can be anywhere between $30 million to $300 million."* The group also represents landowners, and meets with local officials and citizen groups as *"they're the ones to make decisions on what's allowed."* Tasks include the usual due diligence and research, as according to one source, *"it's a junior's job to handle the underlying, non-loan type things."* But juniors have also reported regular writing tasks in the form of lease summaries and drafting deeds. One source summed it up in saying *"it can sometimes feel like some things are above you, but sometimes you're thinking that a paralegal could do this..."* The group sees a range of sizes of clients, so client contact is a regular thing for juniors. *"They call me instead of my boss sometimes, and it's nice to be able to answer their questions"* one enthused. Even with bigger clients, a New Yorker explained that *"there are all levels of staff with big clients, so I interact with people equivalent to my level all the time."* Juniors also highlighted that *"the firm does a good job of having a lot of client events. People will introduce you to principals at banks – it's pretty cool to meet those people."*

> *"The expectation to pick up new things and learn on your own."*

Meanwhile, corporate juniors experienced a range of work, from *"M&A to finance, to corporate governance."* This included public and private securities offerings, and M&A for private equity clients, among other work.

New on chambers-associate.com...

- Privacy & data security: a career guide
- Artificial intelligence and the law

Clients include businesses in the auto industry, industrial manufacturing clients, and financial institutions. Corporate juniors reflected that *"as a junior there's always going to be some level of diligence, but I think I'm fortunate that I get to handle a lot of high level documents."* Beyond due diligence and ancillary documents, juniors reported revising drafts of purchase and contribution agreements as well as being *"on calls with clients on a daily basis."*

The energy branch of the corporate practice deals with energy M&A, oil & gas work, project finance, renewable energy, and tax. On top of the previously mentioned tasks, juniors reported advising stakeholders in aspects of financing, and reviewing and interpreting contracts to determine the risks. One corporate junior reckoned that *"there's a high degree of independence, and the expectation to pick up new things and learn on your own. You can chat with partners for high level issues, but generally there's not much hand holding."* Another explained that *"if you develop a reputation for good work, you get sought out more and more."* A Dallas junior advised that *"with that responsibility comes a steep learning curve, and you have to be able to handle that."* The deals were described as *"middle market,"* often dealing with foreign companies coming in to the US market, or vice versa. The energy side reported a couple of major projects, upward of $4 billion.

Litigators had *"the chance to dive into a lot of different things"* as a result of the firm's range of litigation subgroups. A DC junior noted doing *"some privacy cases, some retail cases, and financial credit report cases."* One laughed saying *"I enjoy working for clients whose stuff I personally own."* Other juniors veered toward energy and environmental lawsuits. One source explained *"we'll usually represent clients when they get approval from the federal agency to do something, and environmental groups then challenge that decision in court."* Tasks across the group include writing motions to dismiss, drafting legal holds, drafting mediation statements, and the inevitable research assignments. *"When I started I expected to be a drone doing doc review all day. I've done a little of that, but*

See firm profile on p.614

Diversity	Partners (%)	Associates (%)
Women	18	49.5
White	90.8	82.8
Black/African American	2.8	3
Hispanic/Latin American	3.2	5
Asian	2.8	6.9
Mixed/Other	0.4	2.3
LGBT	0.7	1.7

I've also had the opportunity to do more substantive work." When it came to work assignment, one junior noted *"of course you need to do work that needs to be done, but everyone seems to be a kind person, so if you're working for someone that has your best interests at heart, they're going to look to give you work that you enjoy."*

Culture

"My thoughts when I had my callback were that these people are people I'd want to go for a drink with, and wouldn't mind spending time with. And that has held true," a DC source recounted. A New Yorker described a positive *"Southern-type vibe"* spreading firmwide, in the form of barbecue cook-offs in the summer and *"nice, friendly people."* A Richmond junior confirmed this: *"Richmond is technically the main office, but I think they try to make sure the culture runs through the entire firm."* Although some sources *"wouldn't say the social life is the strongest aspect,"* there are still Friday happy hours and many events for summer associates. One source explained *"it's kind of a mix. If you're looking to socialize after work there are opportunities there, but also, people are trying to raise families. It's supportive of whichever way you want to go."*

"At no point do you feel like a minion slogging away..."

Juniors described their fellow associates as *"motivated and driven, ready to take on responsibility."* All agreed on the respectful and service-oriented culture, and highlighted that the firm's attorneys are *"great communicators."* Juniors also felt *"the firm is invested in the success of its associates."* A Richmond junior expressed that *"when there's work to be done, people are very serious about the final product being very good and getting it right, but at no point do you feel like a minion slogging away in your office."*

Hours & Compensation

Most juniors felt the firm's 2,000 hour billing target to be achievable, but *"it depends a lot on what sort of year it's been and what work is coming in."* Either way, sources told us they're not penalized if they don't make it and they're

"told not to stress too much about it." On average, associates spend about ten hours a day in the office, *"subject to ebbs and flows in the work."* Almost all of our sources agreed that it was very rare for them to work on weekends, but again, it *"depends on the clients' needs and what stage any transaction is at."*

"We get paid extremely well for Richmond."

"I'm happy with the salary, but unhappy with the uncertainty," sources reported. By this, juniors referred to the rise in junior salaries to match the Cravath scale, which is good news but left *"concern about not necessarily moving to lockstep"* thereafter. One source described the new system as *"black-boxed"* and was resigned to *"waiting to see how it pans out."* However, Richmond juniors had fewer concerns, saying *"we get paid extremely well for Richmond – it doesn't cost much to live here, and we're highly paid."*

Pro Bono

Associates can bill up to 50 hours of pro bono work. Beyond that, there is an award, named after co-founder E. Randolph Williams, for those who provide over 100 hours of pro bono service. Juniors also mentioned that *"if you're not participating, you're going to be asked why."* Cases include asylum, domestic violence, and landlord/low income tenants disputes. Some juniors had worked at a clinic for *"people who wouldn't normally be able to afford a lawyer to write out their will."* Sources loved the degree of responsibility they got on pro bono cases: *"I got to litigate a case on my own in front of a judge!"* Global MP Wally Martinez reinforces the firm's duty to society: *"For the eighth year running 100% of our US lawyers have participated in pro bono projects."* A recent highlight was winning clemency from then-President Obama for William Ortiz, commuting Ortiz's 50-year prison sentence for nonviolent, low-level drug offenses. He had already served 26 years.

"I got to litigate a case on my own in front of a judge!"

Pro bono hours
- For all US attorneys: 37,285
- Average per US attorney: 55

Diversity

Sources felt the firm *"does well for women"* compared to the rest of BigLaw. *"They could definitely improve racial diversity and LGBT diversity, but they are working on it and moving forward."* Many juniors agreed the firm's efforts in recruiting women were very good, noting that women partners were well represented across the offices. The firm holds a diversity retreat – *"I wasn't expecting to*

See firm profile on p.614

see over 100 attorneys there, but that's what happened!"
There's also a diversity program for 1L summers where
the firm *"brings in diverse students and hopes to jump start
their efforts to retain them."* Overall, juniors feel there are
"plans in place," but with *"definite work to do there."*

Get Hired

*"Sometimes people come to interview with an
ego. That's not a good route to take – we can spot
it a mile away. We want to maintain our jovial culture."* Find out more about getting hired at www.
chambers-associate.com

Strategy & Future

On the strategic front, managing partner Wally Martinez
tells us that *"last year on the strategic front, we strengthened our focus on our four leading industries: financial
services, retail & consumer products, energy, and real estate development & finance."* Going forward, Martinez
explains: *"Our plan is to build internationally and develop
greater depth in two US markets where we're already invested – Texas and California."* When asked about particular plans for new offices, Martinez says there's nothing
in particular at present, but says *"we continue to explore
opportunities where they align with best serving our clients."*

Another area of focus is *"utilizing technology to its
fullest extent in all aspects of our practice."* On this front,
Martinez is *"looking to the next generation to move the
rest of the firm forward, helping us to adapt and create
new ways of working so that we can better deliver the
excellent quality of work that clients have come to expect."*

**" ...looking to the next generation to
move the rest of the firm."**

See firm profile on p.614

Irell & Manella LLP

Lawyers per state

130

Largest US office: Century City
US offices: 2
International offices: 0
First-year salary: $180,000
Billable hours: 2,000 target
Summers 2017: 12 (10 2Ls, 2 1Ls)
Revenue 2016: not disclosed
Partners made in 2017: 1
Famous for: bow-tie clad IP supremo Morgan Chu; high associate autonomy; California casual

La La Land's very own IP virtuoso...

THIS Californian star began to shine just before the Roaring Twenties and the Golden Age of Cinema propelled American culture worldwide. Indeed, Irell's first clients were the Garbos and Bogarts of that world, as well as their studio employers. And, though the latter still fill the firm's rolodexes – with the likes of Warner Bros. and MGM on the books – in recent years the tech companies and start-ups of Silicon Valley have become its bread and butter.

A big reason for this is the firm's IP practice, the *"single biggest"* at Irell, and *"probably the best in the West,"* headed up by the *"legendary, bow tie-clad supremo"* Morgan Chu. Moreover, though it might not factor into prospective clients' decision making, the firm shares key attributes with those tech pioneers. There is an entrepreneurial and academic culture that sees clever recruits given a lot of autonomy early on. On top of this is a healthy respect for attorneys' work/life balance: *"What struck me about Irell is that I could have my life and I could have my work,"* one junior told us. And as for that work, *Chambers USA* fully recognizes Irell's caliber, awarding it top rankings for its IP practice, while giving similarly high nods to its litigation and media & entertainment teams. Bankruptcy, tax, and life sciences also come in for praise.

On chambers-associate.com...

- Interview with managing partner Andrei Iancu
- Interview with hiring partner Ellisen Turner

The Work

Most newcomers are drafted into litigation, which *"accounts for probably about 75% of what we do here."* That includes the firm's world-beating IP lawyers who, as across the practices, *"mostly work with large technology firms."* That said, aside from working within the broad categories of 'litigation' and 'corporate', attorneys are given the freedom to cultivate their own niche – *"you don't actually ever have to define or decide clearly which specific field you want to work in, and the assignment system really enables that."*

"Hey, I'd love to join your team."

Some sources labeled that assignment system 'holistic', which is a very Californian way of saying 'informal'. *"You can walk up to a partner and say, 'hey, I'd love to join your team'. Or you can speak with the work coordinators and let them know that not only do you need work, or want work, but what kind of work you want to do."* Really what it comes down to is the fact that *"if you are a member of a team, regardless of seniority, you will be handed work. And if you get it done, you will get more of it."*

Junior lawyers in all departments said they had daily tasks that ranged from the menial to the high-level. In IP, lawyers had done *"standard research, drafted opening briefings, drafted motions and responded to them."* One had even *"worked on a brief for the Supreme Court."* Over in corporate – where the team's work is split *"about two-thirds M&A to one-third finance"* – it's a question of *"the more you ask for, the more you get. I'm still doing some due diligence but I'm also taking a hand in running the main*

The Inside View

See firm profile on p.615

Rankings in *Chambers USA*

Bankruptcy/Restructuring	Litigation
Intellectual Property	Media & Entertainment
Life Sciences	Tax

For detail on ranking tiers and ranking locations, visit
www.chambersandpartners.com

Recent work highlights

- Represented Miramax in its acquisition by Qatari-based media and entertainment company beIN Media Group
- Represented Dalian Wanda Group on its acquisition of Legendary Entertainment for $3.5 billion. The transaction has been heralded as China's largest cross-border cultural acquisition to date
- A federal jury in Wisconsin found that Apple owes Irell client the Wisconsin Alumni Research Foundation (WARF) $234.2 million for patent infringement related to a WARF-owned computer processing patent

transactional documents." One litigation source had *"provided research, drafted outlines and done witness preparation support."*

Culture

Interviewees were quick to point out the defining feature of Irell's culture – *"to put it simply, it's 'autonomy'. That's the prevailing work culture. I haven't yet experienced a situation where a superior ever suggested that they are in charge of or have control of my time and space."* Perhaps this trust in attorneys' ability – *"if you can handle it and do a good job, you're going to get the work"* – stems from the *"intellectual vibe"* that permeates the firm. Recruiters tend to target the top schools and the top students at those schools: *"The idea is that people want to be around people who are smart."* However, less conventional candidates needn't be deterred: *"There are people here from a mélange of backgrounds, there's some from academics, some from business, some from government, there's even a few from the military."*

"If you can handle it and do a good job, you're going to get the work."

As for socializing among this mixed bunch, sources spoke of *"holiday parties, weekly happy hours and annual summer retreats"* to local resorts that involved activities like yoga, golf and horse riding. There was also talk of weekly firm breakfasts that *"do a good job of bringing everyone together regularly."* But mostly, interviewees agreed that *"the vibe is more live and let live"* and to that end, *"people tend to have lives outside of work, that's not because people don't get along or are friendly – the vast majority are. Just that, especially in a place as big as LA, people have a lot of other stuff going on."*

Training & Development

New recruits are given a week-long orientation in how to use the basic systems at the firm, which many found helpful due to the myriad of support staff in each department. Other than that, there's pretty frequent formal practice-specific training, plus occasional sessions like *"deposition and legal writing workshops."* It would be remiss of us not to mention the three-day retreat at a Palm Springs hotel for Irell newbies. But this retreat isn't all pool parties and palm trees – back in the office, lawyers have to prepare a

deposition in front of partners, using hired actors to play the part of witnesses.

When they join, juniors are assigned to a mentoring pod with three to five junior people, a mid-level associate, and a partner or counsel. In theory they are supposed to meet monthly, but sources admitted that this was an area the firm could do more in – *"I think mentorship and monitoring could use some improvement. It wasn't really an issue in the past because there were only two or three associates in a group. But now that we're quite a bit bigger, you can see occasions when juniors get a bit lost."*

Offices

One place associates won't get lost is on the firm's switchboard. With only two offices – HQ in Century City and a smaller outpost in Newport Beach – Irell might seem like a small operation, especially since *"given modern technology, it's really just one office with two zip codes."* However, as previously stated, it's a Golden State supremo, and its Avenue of the Stars home reflects that status. Everyone has access to the firm's gym and personal trainer and new starters are given *"big bright offices"* replete with *"massive desks"* on their first day. There is no cafeteria but, as one helpful source reminded us, *"this is Century City, every building has a cafe, there's a mall across the street with some pretty good restaurants, and once a week there's a local farmer's market."*

"Given modern technology, it's really just one office with two zip codes."

Newport Beach, despite containing a third of the firm's lawyers, has very few juniors. It's mostly made up of *"partners who want to live the more casual life that the OC affords."* Because of their absence *"you have to be a bit more strategic about getting work from them. If there's a partner there that you want to work with, make sure you regularly check in via email or over the phone."*

See firm profile on p.615

The Inside View

Diversity	Partners (%)	Associates (%)
Women	9	40
White	82	82
Black/African American	2	0
Hispanic/Latin American	2	0
Asian	14	13
Mixed/Other	0	5
LGBT	2	4

Hours & Compensation

Most associates agreed that *"I almost never stay really late. Obviously we're still working for BigLaw and once a month I will probably stay in the office until midnight, but generally I come home around dinner time."* This was attributed to the fact that *"you can tell that partner's work is important to them but you can tell that their families are more important."*

A 2,000 hours billings target was described as *"eminently achievable"* by associates, especially since they can count *"an unlimited amount of pro bono toward the total."* However, the intensity of those billables varied between practices, with one corporate source opining: *"It's different here to litigation, they're more calendar-driven. I've had two or three months in a row when I'm really slammed. Then I'm only in the office four days a week and leave at five for a month."* When it comes to vacation, *"we get an unlimited number of days and, as long as you're billing enough, I've never had a problem taking time off."*

Pro Bono

As mentioned above, *"the firm treats pro bono and billable work as the same for juniors."* This is in part because *"it gives us an excellent opportunity to get up on our feet in court."* Interviewees had worked with a number of worthy organizations in the LA area including Public Counsel, the Inner City Law Center and Bet Tzedek, all of which offer free legal advice to people from low-income communities.

Pro bono hours
- For all attorneys : 18,086
- Average per attorney: 147

Diversity

Diversity isn't a huge issue here, associates told us, which they attributed more to the fact that *"you're not viewed as a diverse or female candidate – you're a person and that's why you're on the team."* A women's network curates events such as talks by inspirational women. Sources were also quick to point to the work of Irell's diversity committee and the firm's new diversity scholarship as evidence of Irell's credentials.

"You're a person and that's why you're on the team."

Get Hired

We have nodded to Irell's proclivity for academically-gifted candidates before – the firm only really considers those with top grades. That said, recruiters are also looking for people with a passion: *"Whether it be polo or paleontology, partners here like when you have worldly or intellectual interests."* As if to prove this exact point, another source recalled that *"during the interview I had a conversation with one of the partners. But it wasn't anything to do with recruitment or law, just topics of general interest. You know, abstracts of philosophy, that kind of thing."*

Strategy & Future

At the beginning of 2015, Irell was rocked when partners John Hueston and Brian Hennigan took over 30 of Irell's lawyers to form their own firm. For many associates this was a shock – *"you feel like you're one big team and then that happens."* However, most agreed that *"despite a reduced headcount, in terms of incoming work there's been no difference."* And many were positive about the defection's impact: *"If anything I feel like the firm's more cohesive now. Before Hueston-Hennigan, the groups were more insulated."* In an interview with managing partner Andrei Iancu, he told us: *"from the very beginning we are thinking – can these individuals be our future partners?"* See the full interview online.

See firm profile on p.615

Jackson Walker LLP

Lawyers per state

375

Largest US office: Dallas
US offices: 7
International offices: 0
First-year salary: $180,000
Billable hours: 1,950 required (2,000 bonus target)
Summers 2017: 28 (17 2Ls, 11 1Ls)
Revenue 2016: $246.65 million (+11.3%)
Partners made in 2017: 10
Famous for: Texan heritage, conservative culture

This *"traditional Texas firm"* celebrating its 130th birthday gives young associates a *"lot of responsibility,"* they told us.

OPENING its doors long before the invention of the pocket calculator, liquid paper, Fritos and Dr Pepper (all Texas inventions), Jackson Walker has a long history in the Lone Star State. With age comes experience, and the firm earns plaudits from *Chambers USA* for practices in Texas including real estate, energy, construction, environment, and healthcare. Unlike many Texan rivals, JW has stayed firmly within the boundaries of its home state – all seven offices are based here.

Several of the associates we interviewed felt the firm *"reached out to me more than the other way around,"* and welcomed the personal touch. This reinforced their belief that Jackson Walker isn't *"an associate mill that will burn you out – they care about your advancement."* As you might expect at a firm with a strong Texan character, almost everybody we spoke to had personal ties to the Lone Star State.

The Work

Most juniors join the litigation, corporate & securities, and real estate groups, while a handful head to smaller groups including wealth planning, finance, and labor & employment. The majority get work through *"a mix of*

both allocation and seeking it out ourselves. That comes with challenges, as when partners don't always communicate,"* although ordinarily *"they do ask me how busy I am and don't want to overload me."* Experience makes things easier to manage as *"you've established relationships with certain partners. But there's not a ton of control in the first and second years."*

"There's not nearly as much document review as we were led to expect!"

Litigators *"represent all kinds of clients, mostly mid-sized companies. We're a traditional Texas firm so there's a lot of oil and gas work."* Associates found it hard to identify mainstay tasks because *"it varies a lot week to week,"* but narrowed it down to *"writing briefs and memos, pretty informal research. There's not nearly as much document review as we were led to expect!"* Many got plenty of opportunities to get to know the clientele. *"I'm on two or three phone calls with clients or opposing counsel everyday. There's not a ton of courtroom time, that's the nature of the beast, but I think there's more than at other firms."* The overall workload was *"about right on balance,"* litigation's fluctuating nature taken into account.

"In corporate, our bread and butter is mid-sized clients," and a booming mid-market in Texas left associates with full bellies. Starting out with *"closing checklists, drafting ancillary documents and due diligence, you get more stuff on your plate as you move up."* One interviewee had *"helped negotiate main agreements. The lean structure of*

On chambers-associate.com...

- Get hired: All the essential info
- JW, Oprah Winfrey and mad cow disease

See firm profile on p.616

The Inside View

Rankings in *Chambers USA*

Bankruptcy/Restructuring	Healthcare
Corporate/M&A	Immigration
Energy & Natural	Labor & Employment
Resources	Litigation
Environment	Real Estate

For detail on ranking tiers and ranking locations, visit
www.chambersandpartners.com

Recent work highlights

- Acted in $725 million sale of the W.T. Waggoner Ranch to a billionaire NFL team owner
- Represented midstream energy partnership Blueknight in $135.9 million acquisition of nine asphalt terminals
- Handled contract negotiations for $100 million Southport Logistics Park
- Counseled debtors on the $9 billion Linn Energy bankruptcy case

Get Hired

"A big thing we're looking for is any kind of past experience that would lend itself to a particular practice area," according to one associate who'd helped conduct interviews. Head to chambers-associate.com for tips on getting hired by JW.

the firm means you take on major roles in deals a lot faster. You need to become a Swiss army knife of business law." A sweet-toothed corporate junior described the variety of work as *"like Baskin Robbins – there's loads of flavors to try!"*

"Swiss army knife of business law."

Lean staffing models provided similar opportunities elsewhere. Real estate associates *"do a lot of drafting – that comes with the territory. What I didn't expect was a good amount of time on the phone with clients."* Acknowledging that *"you'll never have a perfect amount of work, you'll always be fast or slow, it does balance out,"* most interviewees were happy to lean toward the busier end. The finance team tackles things like *"amendments to different loan agreements. For loans under $5 million I'll just handle the whole thing on my own."* Fortunately for high-flying newbies, there's a safety net: *"We're given a lot of responsibility but there are always people there to answer questions."* Most were *"absolutely happy"* with their responsibilities.

Training & Development

All new starters in the fall congregate in the Dallas HQ for a two-day bootcamp which kicks off two weeks of training before they start practicing. They also return throughout their junior years, and get regular opportunities for CLEs and NITA programs. Corporate associates felt they got less training than litigators, although since our calls the firm has appointed a coordinator here to focus on corporate training. For both litigators and transactional associates, *"it's mostly trial by fire. You get the best training just by doing."* Annual and mid-year reviews are *"not a big formal ordeal. You chat to the practice leader and get a rating from 0-5 for how good you're doing."* Though all interviewees were happy with their feedback, some reported that the amount is *"very practice group-dependent: some are a lot more structured than others."*

Culture

Dubbing Jackson Walker *"laid back for a law firm"* – though of course, it's all relative – juniors were relieved to find *"there's no demonic slave-driver partner like in* Suits! *We really pride ourselves on being kind to each other. I'm yet to find anybody who's really unreasonable."* The firm's conservative culture came in for praise (*"you don't have the same worries as at other firms"*), but some interviewees were less glowing and thought *"it's a bit of a Texas boys' club."* They reasoned *"everyone's good natured and nice, but for better or worse they only know one way to run the firm, so you see an attitude that 'this is the Jackson Walker way'."*

"You definitely meet people you wouldn't at other jobs!"

Happy hours are a weekly occurrence, the core of *"a pretty good workplace social life"* that is admittedly less well-engrained in offices with fewer attorneys. A firmwide retreat every 18 months helps balance this, and *"summer is a good time, with bigger events where people from different sections meet and mingle."* The firm Christmas party brings festive cheer, and other events may even provide unique experiences: *"At one I sat next to the general manager of the Dallas Mavericks and got to chat to him. You definitely meet people you wouldn't in other jobs!"*

Different offices exhibit different cultures: Fort Worth is *"old-fashioned, but the city's like that in general,"* compared to the *"really laid-back and familial"* Houston and *"quieter, very open"* San Antonio. Similarly divided when asked about transparency, certain juniors implied *"because there are so many partners and offices run semi-autonomously, it takes a while for decisions to be made and explained."* Others felt they could *"talk to the managing partner any time I want. Nobody's hiding the ball."*

See firm profile on p.616

The Inside View

Diversity	Partners (%)	Associates (%)
Women	21.8	48
White	86	73
Black/African American	3.5	7
Hispanic/Latin American	7	9
Asian	2.5	7
Mixed/Other	1	4
LGBT	1	2

Interestingly, contrasting views came from within offices rather than between them.

Offices

Upping sticks to the Dallas's Arts District, the brand new HQ was taken over by the firm in 2015 and provides an *"absolutely stunning space in a better location. Everybody has their own room, and the technology is really advanced."* Similarly popular, the Houston base is in a *"good downtown location, right by a mall with lots of food options,"* while Austin interviewees loved the social side of their city: *"There's a ton of stuff to do, a lot of bands come through here."* The smaller Fort Worth and San Antonio offices only take in one or two newbies a year. Collaboration was prevalent *"to an extent: some offices talk to each other more than others."* Videophones provide the chance to *"feel like you're meeting the people there even if you don't in person,"* and are used in monthly meetings between some practice groups and to link smaller outposts to the mothership.

"Some talk to each other more than others."

Hours & Compensation

The associate salary hike of summer 2016 sent waves of excitement through BigLaw; delays at Jackson Walker in matching Texas rivals stirred some consternation at the time, though everything's fine now. Many interviewees felt *"when all the firms raised they pretended it didn't happen. It created a lot of angst about why they took so long – they could have handled it better."* In hindsight, some associates *"liked that they took the time to consider if they could afford it, and it's good they can give people a boost."* Despite *"some vagueness about how compensation will now work, it's great that they did raise salaries with the market."*

"You have to be self-motivated and lucky."

However, alongside the increases, the associate bonus eligibility target has climbed from 1,950 to 2,000, including 100 citizenship hours that can include pro bono. The

number to remain in good standing and get a salary rise remains at 1,950. Juniors thought their chances of hitting the goals were *"hit or miss depending on business. You have to be self-motivated and lucky depending on what cases you're on."* Some were *"resigned to never getting raises or bonuses"* as a result, criticizing *"rewarding quantity of work over quality,"* but more optimistic associates felt the push will *"make us better attorneys"* in the long run.

Pro Bono & Diversity

The increase in the citizenship hours requirement from 50 to 100 is partly *"how they encourage people"* to do pro bono. Associates felt that otherwise *"there hasn't been a huge push. Those opportunities exist if you want but you have to make the effort."* Cases tend to be close to home, such as *"a friend of a friend having divorce or insurance problems, who the firm would like us to help out."* Transactional juniors found it relatively more difficult to find time for pro bono.

Pro bono hours
- For all attorneys: 6,253
- Average per attorney: 16

"The firm tries hard to attract minorities."

"I notice every year that summer attorneys are heavily women, and they try to include minorities." Initiatives including the JW² women's network are in place to address diversity issues, but Texas-based juniors usually comment on the region's overall struggle, and this year was no exception. *"It's a sea of white. They have initiatives, but in our office I see less of that in action,"* according to one associate, while another acknowledged that *"the firm tries hard to attract minorities, but it can be difficult to keep them."* More positive sources pointed out *"we're really good with women in our office,"* suggesting varying success at achieving diversity overall.

Strategy & Future

Assured associates *"have a lot of faith in the firm because it's pretty stable, there's not going to be a big global merger. Over 200 years the dedication to staying in Texas hasn't changed."* They echoed managing partner Wade Cooper, who suggests *"the economic advantage of staying in Texas is we don't have the higher overheads of New York or elsewhere. That gives us rate flexibility so we can straddle different markets; clients from out of state are often happy to hire us because of that. We want to continue to be the go-to firm for issues in Texas whether they be transactional, litigation or government-related."*

See firm profile on p.616

The Inside View

Jenner & Block LLP

Lawyers per state

92

80

313

52

Largest US office: Chicago
US offices: 4
International offices: 1
First-year salary: $180,000
Billable hours: 2,100 target
Summers 2017: 47 (44 2Ls, 3 3Ls)
Revenue 2016: $457.6 million (-1.5%)
Partners made in 2017: 18 (17 in US)
Famous for: pros at pro bono; Chicago litigation legends; LGBT-friendliness

Born in the Windy City, this litigation powerhouse's commitment to pro bono is more than just hot air.

IMAGINE if Jenner & Block were a Chicago deep-dish pizza. Built on a crust of tolerant values and *"a much friendlier culture than other firms,"* it's filled to the brim with the pleasingly pungent cheese of litigation excellence and a nutritious tomato sauce of pro bono fame. This latter juicy practice was a huge draw for associates, who described *"an unparalleled reputation"* for charitable work that *"tends to attract unpretentious people with an inclination for social justice. It's not a firm of robots!"* Then there are the toppings – pepperoni, peppers, mushrooms, or whatever you feel like – which correspond to other appealing staples on the menu at Jenner like its excellent diversity (not least LGBT), strong mid-market transactional practices, and technological innovation.

Our associate sources stressed that *"Jenner is one of the top litigation firms in Chicago,"* and *Chambers USA* agrees – the firm gets top rankings for general commercial and white collar litigation in Illinois, not to mention an array of accolades in other practice areas including environment, corporate/M&A, intellectual property, and bankruptcy/restructuring. Jenner also picks up rankings in New York, DC, California, and nationwide. Comple-

menting its quartet of US bases, the 113 year-old Chicagoan opened a London office in 2015.

The Work

The overwhelming majority of newcomers can be found in litigation, but a few head into smaller groups like corporate and IP, and the DC office takes a couple for government contracts work. Juniors get tasks through an open market system *"so you can seek out partners to work with,"* though there are assignment partners who *"allocate you based on need if you don't get enough work."* During the firm's summer program, newbies can try transactional work or focus purely on contentious, and it's not uncommon for associates in smaller groups to get work from the larger litigation practice.

Entry-level litigators are generalists for four years before choosing where to specialize. The group covers *"complex commercial cases, and quite a lot of white collar investigations – some are ginormous, others are smaller and take a couple of weeks."* Each office has unique specialties: media & entertainment is one of the larger sub-sections in New York; DC tackles *"a lot of appellate and Supreme Court stuff;"* and Los Angeles deals in soft IP (copyright and trademarks). Juniors typically take on *"a fair amount of document review"* as well as *"drafting outlines and preparations for witness interviews."* One explained that *"if there's work to be done, it almost doesn't matter what level you're at."* Client contact comes more quickly for juniors on smaller cases. *"They put me on a small matter where I*

On www.chambers-associate.com...

- Get hired: all the insider info
- Interview with chief talent officer Charlotte Wager
- *Lawrence v. Texas*

The Inside View

See firm profile on p.617

Rankings in *Chambers USA*

Appellate Law	International Arbitration
Bankruptcy/Restructuring	Leisure & Hospitality
Corporate Crime & Investigations	Litigation
Corporate/M&A	Media & Entertainment
Environment	Real Estate
Insurance	Tax
Intellectual Property	Telecommunications

For detail on ranking tiers and ranking locations, visit www.chambersandpartners.com

Recent work highlights

- Won dismissal of pensions class action levied against chemicals giant Dow
- Represented Motion Picture Association of America in copyright infringement suit against file-sharing site Megaupload
- Counseled snack giant Snyder's-Lance in $1.91 billion acquisition of Diamond Foods
- Filed an amicus brief challenging Mississippi's 'unnatural intercourse' laws

was the primary contact. The partner did it specifically so I could get client exposure." Some described the workload as *"more than I'm comfortable with, but they're pushing you to grow. It's not heaven, but it's not hell either!"*

"It's not heaven, but it's not hell either!"

Jenner's patent litigation and counseling group is *"pretty heavy on petrochemicals, life sciences and biotech, but we also have a robust computer sciences practice."* Assigned based on their technical expertise, newbies found themselves *"typically working through discovery and general document review."* Restructuring & bankruptcy *"represents a lot of creditors, and several partners are court-appointed trustees in Chapter 7 cases* [in which a company ceases all operations]. *They'll send me to court on routine matters two or three times a month."* When not in court, associates were deep in research or motion drafting.

Other smaller groups including private wealth and government contracts put *"a lot of responsibility on associates to step up and be an important part of the team."* Government contracts covers *"many internal investigations, so there's a lot of document review. I'm doing grunt work but also making major, substantive contributions – it's a good challenge."* Across the board, associates declared *"the expectation is to be proactive, and take control of your own destiny."*

Pro Bono

Coming in with the knowledge that pro bono is *"a major selling point for the firm,"* newcomers had high expectations, but were relieved to find *"Jenner is awesome about letting you do whatever you want."* All pro bono hours count toward bonus targets. One source felt they *"might have abused the system a bit,"* but their colleagues reassured us *"partners see pro bono as a time for associates to gain substantive experience."* Several juniors took on "Section 1983" work (enforcing the provisions of the Fourteenth Amendment) as well as social security and veterans' appeals. Acknowledging *"this is a business,"* interviewees concluded *"pro bono is very much part of the culture."* Jenner recently hit the headlines by taking on a

case challenging Mississippi's 'unnatural intercourse' law, which remains despite the Supreme Court striking down homophobic laws like it well over a decade ago.

Pro bono hours
- For all US attorneys: 75,419
- Average per US attorney: 141

Get Hired

"If you don't talk about pro bono, you haven't done your homework." Get started on that, and find out more about recruitment at Jenner, at chambers-associate.com.

Training & Development

Following an initial orientation there's *"a lot of training in place, especially for first-years. There are CLEs for everything under the sun, and quite a bit targeted at the nitty-gritty."* On top of that is deposition training and NITA programs, as well as a mentorship scheme. Most juniors, however, preferred to cut to the chase and *"a lot of people get training while practicing because of pro bono."*

Six-monthly reviews for first-years and 12-month reviews thereafter keep juniors clued in on their progress: *"Partners you've worked with fill out reviews, address any issues, discuss goals and provide tips for meeting them. It's fairly comprehensive and helpful for knowing where you stand."* Most felt that *"informal feedback is more important,"* even if it came at varied levels because *"while some partners are fantastic about offering feedback as you go, with others you have to initiate the conversation yourself."*

Culture & Diversity

Acknowledging *"the firm is pretty liberal,"* interviewees clarified *"it's not in the sense that we're socialists, but that everyone's very tolerant here."* One cheerful associate revealed they'd *"imagined BigLaw culture to be kill or be killed, but we don't have that at all."* That's partly because *"the firm is a bit smaller than some others, so we're more*

See firm profile on p.617

Diversity	Partners (%)	Associates (%)
Women	28.8	44.9
White	90.9	79
Black/African American	2.1	3.4
Hispanic/Latin American	2.5	4.9
Asian	3	9.8
Mixed/Other	1.7	2.9
LGBT	4.2	12.7

tight-knit," albeit with some differences between offices. Those outside of the HQ considered it *"a bit more intense"* than elsewhere, but Chicagoans countered *"the feeling here is 'nice nerds', there's no ruthless competition. Everyone takes work seriously but it's a pretty laid back environment."* Several credited the cheery mood to the firm's pro bono propensity.

It's unsurprising then that volunteer work is part of the social program for associates. As well as the typical summer events, the firm also hosts a weekly happy hour in every office; in Chicago it takes place in the *"beautiful top-floor conference room."* A ring of donut shops around the office kept those with a sweet tooth happy; more savory palettes relished the information-meaty *"monthly associate meetings, where they literally present all the financials."* Satiated juniors dubbed the firm *"shockingly transparent"* as a result.

"I joke that the only thing not tolerated is intolerance!"

Through *"workshops and training to educate partners and associates alike on issues,"* the recruiting committee *"has made great inroads"* promoting diversity in associates' eyes. Jenner is known for doing a sterling job with hiring and retaining LGBT attorneys, and is consistently at the top of our charts for its success in this area. *"The policies for LGBT lawyers and women are especially strong – they've elevated a lot of women to partner, including those on reduced schedule,"* and female associates appreciated *"that sends a really good message about the firm's values."* Two-thirds of Jenner's 2017 partner class were women, LGBT or ethnically diverse. Juniors identified the latter as an area for improvement: those in smaller offices reported less diversity among their colleagues by virtue of size. They were nonetheless confident in Jenner's inclusiveness – *"I joke that the only thing not tolerated is intolerance!"* – and ability to improve in the future.

Hours & Compensation

Jenner's official associate annual hours target is 2,100. However, insiders revealed that *"people see the 2,100 and think it's more than other firms, but that includes pro bono and firm-approved hours like CLEs and article writing."* Averaging ten hour work days with *"a couple of hours on weekends,"* juniors found *"2,100 is fairly easy. What's more difficult is the 2,000 billable hours goal."* Several identified this additional benchmark, but were quick to add *"I didn't hit the 2,000 billables target and still got the normal bonus and raise."*

Bonuses aren't strictly lockstep, which stirred mixed feelings among associates: some argued *"they're really upfront about the information ahead of time,"* but others *"wished it was lockstep and everyone got the same. It's supposedly merit-based, but it's difficult to know what quantifies that."* Associate salaries are more consistent, and rose in 2016 in all offices to match the Cravath scale.

Offices & Strategy

The Chicago mothership is *"fancy in the sense that we work in a gleaming skyscraper in a hip part of downtown."* Associates get cozy with their colleagues, noting *"they're trying to pack more people onto each floor,"* but few minded as *"things are livelier now."* Jenner New York sits in midtown east with *"convenient access to subways,"* while the DC base *"has a very modern vibe, right in the city center."* Angelenos are housed in the US Bank Tower, which has *"just gone through a massive overhaul. They're trying to make it a big tourist attraction."* Those who fancied a bit of work tourism found *"working fluidly across offices is completely normal. Each has its own strengths and culture."* Chicago may be the focal point, but nobody outside the hub complained: *"I never feel like we're a satellite, we're valued in our own right as we should be."*

"Working fluidly across offices is completely normal."

So where does Jenner go from here? *"There are no immediate plans for new offices or moves into new practice areas,"* according to chief talent officer Charlotte Wager, but the firm will be *"focused on London, Los Angeles, New York and DC for continued growth."* Firmwide revenue soared by nearly 15% in 2015, although it dropped a smidgen in 2016 to $457.6 million. Charlotte Wager notes that *"pro bono numbers were significantly up even during growth."* For the full interview, including more info on both strategy and recruitment at Jenner, visit our website.

See firm profile on p.617

The Inside View

Jones Day

Lawyers per state

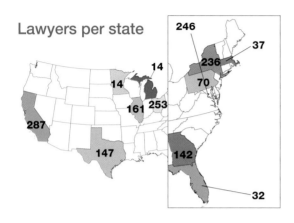

246
37
14
236
14
70
161 253
287
147
142
32

Largest US office: New York

US offices: 18

International offices: 26

First-year salary: $180,000 ($160,000 in Cleveland, Columbus, Detroit, Miami, Minneapolis, and Pittsburgh)

Billable hours: 2,000 target

Summers 2017: 213-214 (174 2Ls, 30 1Ls, 1 3L, others 8-9)

Revenue 2016: $1.98 billion (+1.9%)

Partners made in 2017: 47 globally (33 in US)

Famous for: Being one of the world's biggest, most prestigious firms.

Despite being one of the legal industry's big fish, Jones Day associates say the firm is *"not looking for sharks."*

AS one of BigLaw's most recognizable names, it's no surprise that associates were enchanted by Jones Day's *"great reputation"* and *"sheer number of offices."* But one thing sources didn't wholly foresee was *"how friendly everyone is."* Many highlighted that *"Jones Day is able to pick associates that are personable, genuine, down-to-earth, and fun to be around."* They found the firm to be *"truly international. Some firms call themselves international, but only hire those who have been through the US education system. Jones Day recognizes good schools abroad too."*

This global titan that originated in Cleveland a century and a quarter ago spans five continents in 19 countries, with a grand total of 44 locations. *Chambers USA* gives top notch kudos for the firm's antitrust, bankruptcy & restructuring, labor & employment, and retail practices nationwide, while countless practices score highly in lots of states (check out www.chambersandpartners.com for the full breakdown). Sources also commented on JD's financial robustness, and one remembered *"reading that Jones Day was one of the only firms that didn't let go of juniors during the 2008 financial crisis, which was comforting."*

On chambers-associate.com...

- More on getting hired at Jones Day
- Interview with hiring partner Sharyl Reisman
- Jones Day and Detroit

The Work

First-years join the New Lawyers Group (NLG) when they start: *"The idea behind it is to give associates the chance to try different areas before committing to one."* Sources felt this was *"very appealing – some people come in with a strong idea of what they want to do, then go after that work. Other people have less of an idea, so can try out a few things."* The work assignment was generally free market, though fresh recruits had the safety net of a *"weekly system where you record what you're working on, and how much availability you have. You can easily be forgotten if you don't show your face."* However, *"you can go out and expand that pool of people you work for"* and there are *"a lot of opportunities,"* but *"you have to be a go-getter at all times."*

"You have to be a go-getter."

Business & tort litigation had the largest chunk of juniors by a hefty margin. The practice covers a wide range of litigation matters including commercial, securities, product liability, and regulatory enforcement matters. Clients are often *"huge Fortune 500 companies and banks."* Juniors noted doing *"the ground work that's important, but non-intellectual – that's just the nature of being a junior associate."* They also experienced some pretty substantive tasks too. *"There are three large silos of litigation for juniors: discovery and document management; legal briefing, writing, and research; and trial work."* Especially with smaller cases, these *"usually require contact with opposing counsel, and negotiating the settlement."* A DC junior recalled

See firm profile on p.618

The Inside View

Rankings in *Chambers USA*

Antitrust	Government
Appellate Law	Healthcare
Banking & Finance	Insurance
Bankruptcy/Restructuring	Intellectual Property
Capital Markets	Labor & Employment
Construction	Latin American Investment
Corporate Crime &	Life Sciences
Investigations	Litigation
Corporate/M&A	Products Liability
ERISA Litigation	Real Estate
Employee Benefits &	Retail
Executive Compensation	Tax
FCPA	

For detail on ranking tiers and ranking locations, visit
www.chambersandpartners.com

Recent work highlights

- Represented STERUS in its $1.9 billion acquisition of Synergy Health
- Advising retail pharmacy chain Rite Aid as antitrust counsel in connection with the proposed $17.2 billion acquisition of Walgreens Boots Alliance
- Defending SharkNinja Operation against allegations that its Shark Rocket vacuum cleaner infringes three Dyson design patents
- Defending McDonald's in a large National Labor Relations Board litigation matter, regarding nearly 300 unfair labor practice charges

that *"one thing we all fear going into BigLaw and big cities is getting sent to the warehouse for months to sift through documents. I have pretty much avoided that and feel like I've been able to work on the more interesting, substantive stuff you imagine in law school as more lawyerly."*

Transactional practices like M&A and restructuring also take on many juniors. The M&A group deals with public and private transactions and corporate governance matters. Juniors reported being *"in charge of a lot of diligence matters on a deal, which entails reviewing documents and providing summaries and analysis of documents."* Interviewees also mentioned *"there's a lot of drafting with M&A."* This includes *"not only deal documents, but also commercial contracts."* Juniors felt like they were *"getting opportunities to grow as the firm gives us increasing responsibility as time goes on."* Restructuring folk also reported much writing and research, as well as communicating with various parties involved – *"a lot of creditors and vendors"* – and regular contact with bankruptcy courts. Older juniors felt they had *"gotten a lot more experience than most third-years elsewhere. I think I'd be lying if I said it wasn't overwhelming at times, but people here have made it a lot easier than it could have been. If I have questions, they take the time to help. I don't feel like my questions are a burden to anyone."*

Labor & employment and IP were also popular with Jones Day juniors. The IP department is split into three sections: patent prosecution, patent litigation, and transactional. Associates usually *"pick one, maybe two of those. In patent prosecution, you get in front of the client more quickly than with the other two."* Tasks across the board include drafting discovery responses, research, and diligence for M&A matters. Responsibility reportedly *"varies wildly depending on the partner and how the case is staffed."* In labor & employment, juniors praised getting *"great experience already"* in the form of *"appear-*

ing in court and drafting pleadings. In the first year I did some doc review, but I haven't done any since." Juniors felt they were *"definitely challenged, but also given a good amount of guidance."*

Training & Development

Newbies from across the world are flown into DC to take part in the New Lawyer Academy. There is a series of presentations and workshops, with training on everything from writing to *"how to work with a partner."* After this, there are CLE events as well as semi-regular lectures and meetings on new developments that may be relevant to each practice. For litigators, the firm partners with the National Institute for Trial Advocacy (NITA) for multi-day trainings. The group also hosts mock trials where associates are assigned litigation teams and argue a case in front of partners. Transactional recruits take part in an M&A bootcamp, which *"takes you through an M&A deal from start to finish."* Some sources believed the firm is *"trying to formalize some trainings, as previously you could only learn by doing it yourself."* Others admitted that learning by *"just getting more work"* was most effective, although the firm also used pro bono as a way to get live training.

Offices

The highest intake of juniors is in the New York, DC, and Cleveland offices, followed by Atlanta and Chicago. Other domestic offices that host juniors are Boston, Columbus, Dallas, Detroit, Houston, Irvine, LA, Miami, Minneapolis, New York, Pittsburgh, San Diego, San Francisco, and Silicon Valley.

The New York office recently moved downtown. Now settled, juniors in the new office considered it *"spectacular"* and described the change as *"a very positive move."* It has floor-to-ceiling windows and a view of the Statue of Liberty. The DC office is a unique combination of two very different buildings: one *"older federal building that's very stately and faces the Capitol,"* and a new building de-

The Inside View

See firm profile on p.618

Diversity	Partners (%)	Associates (%)
Women	36.4	48
White	90.9	92
Black/African American	0	0
Hispanic/Latin American	3	0
Asian	0	0
Mixed/Other	6.1	8
LGBT	Unknown	Unknown

signed by Richard Rogers *"made of glass and steel, with a very modern atrium."* The location was also praised – *"most big law firms are over on the west side nearer to the White House. It's much more crowded there, with packed, narrow streets. Down here it's a lot quieter, with trees lining the street. It's generally a more pleasant place to be."*

Culture

If you've even just glanced at Jones Day's website, you won't be able to miss its 'One Firm Worldwide' slogan. Juniors themselves vouched for this: *"Already in my first year and a half, I've worked with different partners and associates across several offices, including those abroad."* Others keenly highlighted the *"team-oriented atmosphere – it's not about doing everything possible to make sure you personally impress the partner; it's important that the team does well, and then that positive energy reflects on everyone."* One source emphasized they had *"never felt like I had to watch my back in case someone was trying to take credit for my idea or anything."* Another reiterated this: *"I really would say it's non-sharky."* Juniors also noticed that the firm *"cares about its people – it's clear they're not just trying to burn you out or use you just to bill hours."* As for fellow associates, *"they want to know you personally, not just as a colleague."*

> *"It's clear they're not just trying to burn you out or use you just to bill hours."*

Despite BigLaw's reputation, many felt that Jones Day was *"less aggressive than I would have imagined. It's definitely less of a fancy Ivy League, stuffy firm compared to typical New York and DC top law firms."* Things are pretty active on the social side, and most of the offices have weekly happy hours, with the occasional firm-sponsored event. As at most firms, the social scene lights up most during the summer with *"a lot of events during that period."*

Hours & Compensation

Most sources found Jones Day's 2,000 hours target to be achievable, and if associates don't reach it it's *"not because they are lazy, but because there hasn't been enough work that year or in that group."* Interviewees' working hours

varied considerably, and they felt the firm offers a degree of *"flexibility, so long as you do the work you need to do."* For example, *"if I need to go to the doctor, I will go, then connect after."* Another admitted: *"I'd say that I have worked more weekends than I expected, but it's not always forced; it's just sometimes that has to happen in order to have a slightly less stressful week ahead."* Most agreed that for the majority of the time, working on the weekend was *"a matter of choice."* The firm stresses that there is absolutely no facetime requirement.

Potential for *"higher than lockstep."*

As for compensation, things are done slightly differently at Jones Day. There's no typical bonus structure, but it's explained to associates that *"it's folded into the salary"* and works as an *"annual raise."* This *"black box compensation"* system met few complaints, although some wondered *"how do you know if you're being undervalued if you don't know the baseline?"* That said, others reckoned *"our system allows for really strong outstanding associates to earn higher than lockstep would allow,"* and overall most sources felt *"very privileged for what we get paid."*

Pro Bono

"When I work with partners, they take pro bono matters just as seriously as billable matters." Juniors across all offices emphasized the firm's commitment to pro bono, and highlighted that there's *"no hard cut off"* for pro bono hours, although it is understood that they shouldn't be the primary source of hours. Everyone was also *"very excited about the firm's initiatives;"* the firm has had significant involvement with the Unaccompanied Minors Project. The project aims to help mothers and young children who have crossed the border into the US gain refugee status and apply for citizenship. This year, juniors reported *"a big push for veterans' rights"* with VetLex. Other cases have included working on clemency cases, and various family law matters.

Pro bono hours
- For all US attorneys: 108,334
- Average per US attorney: not disclosed

Diversity

Sources reckoned *"diversity at the firm is increasing every year."* Gender diversity is a *"bright spot,"* most evident from females in leadership positions. *"The firm does a very good job of recruiting and promoting women, and having women in all levels of leadership."* This is bolstered through the firm's participation in Women's International Networking (WIN), an organization active in women's leadership and diversity. Opinions were more divided when it came to racial diversity. Many believed *"the firm is doing better with minority groups, but it can definitely*

See firm profile on p.618

continue to improve." However, *"those groups are relatively under-represented. It could be that it is a self-selecting profession."* Despite this, the firm is *"definitely aware of diversity and committed to improving things."*

Strategy & Future

Many juniors thought that *"Jones Day is one of the best firms to make partner. They give opportunities to people here from day one. If you do good work and you're here for a long time, then it's likely you'll be able to make partner."* That's not to say associates don't leave for one reason or another, but *"it seems like a lot of partners here came up through the ranks."* As for Jones Day's future, Sharyl Reisman maintains that Jones Day will *"continue to provide innovative and seamless client service."*

"If you do good work and you're here for a long time, then it's likely you'll be able to make partner."

See firm profile on p.618

K&L Gates

Lawyers per state

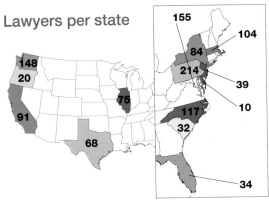

155
104
84
148
214
20
39
75
10
91
117
32
68
34

K&L Gatesalso has an office in Alaska with four attorneys

Largest US office: Pittsburgh
US offices: 24
International offices: 22
First-year salary: $140,000 - $180,000 (varies by office)
Billable hours: 1,950 target
Summers 2017: 65 (56 2Ls, 9 1Ls)
Revenue 2016: $1.179 billion (+10.7%)
Partners made in 2017: 13 (8 US)
Famous for: rapid mergers; huge number of offices

It's the end of an era and the start of a promising new one at one of the fastest-expanding firms in recent history.

AFTER two decades at the top, K&L's chairman and global managing partner Peter Kalis stood down in 2017, and the keys to the Gates (sorry) passed to new management. Interviewed just as Mike Caccese and Jim Segerdahl took the reins, associates told us *"it seems like there will be a lot of positive changes"* going forward. Executive committee member Craig Budner says the firm is *"very excited about the transition. We've been investing in our platform and we're poised to take real advantage of it."*

That platform merits a plethora of *Chambers USA* rankings spanning dozens of practices, from commercial litigation and corporate/M&A to more specialist areas like maritime regulation and technology outsourcing. Interviewees described K&L as *"the best of both worlds"* in that it boasts *"the resources of a larger firm"* as well as *"the local connections and culture"* of the smaller firms that came together in a series of mergers ever since the K&L (for Kilpatrick & Lockhart) combined with the Gates (Seattle's Preston Gates) to form K&L Gates in 2007. Today's firm can trace its history back to the 1850s.

On chambers-associate.com...

- Get Hired: how to get inside the K&L Gates
- Interview with global integration and strategic growth partner Craig Budner
- K&L Gates takes on revenge porn

The Work

Juniors join an umbrella practice group upon arrival: most head into corporate and transactional, IP, litigation and dispute resolution, or policy and regulatory. Each operates a free market system that encourages newbies to approach partners for tasks and gives them *"more control"* over their workload – it's *"a little challenging in the first six months, but I grew to like that you can pick and choose who to work with."* Some reported frustration that *"you might be busy working long weeks and see people who are doing less,"* but Seattle has a workflow coordinator to help the overburdened.

"I wasn't expecting such a great opportunity that quickly."

Corporate & transactional at K&L Gates covers *"a very wide range"* of sub-practices including M&A, securities, debt and equity financing, venture capital and healthcare. *"The whole menu is available"* to hungry juniors, whose plates were full with *"anything from drafting documents to preparing all the required ancillaries."* As they got more senior our sources noticed *"I don't do as much due diligence as I used to; I appreciate the opportunities I get to grow and progress,"* and one suggested *"all the partners are aware that the only way an associate can grow is to give them greater responsibility."* The workload can be *"very up and down, that's the nature of it, particularly in M&A."* Long days become the norm toward the ends of deals but *"overall the work/life balance seems better than at some peer firms,"* interviewees indicated.

See firm profile on p.619

The Inside View

Rankings in *Chambers USA*

Bankruptcy/Restructuring	Insurance
Corporate/Commercial	Intellectual Property
Corporate/M&A	Investment Funds
Energy & Natural Resources	Labor & Employment
Environment	Litigation
Government	Real Estate
Healthcare	Technology
	Transportation

For detail on ranking tiers and ranking locations, visit
www.chambersandpartners.com

Recent work highlights

- Represented Yum! Brands in Delaware on $2.3 billion securitization of Taco Bell's royalties in the US
- Defended World Wrestling Entertainment in various class action cases alleging brain injuries in former WWE talent
- Counseled recycled packaging producer Cascades on acquisition of packaging plant in Newtown, CT
- Advised technology group Hexagon AB on $834 million acquisition of MSC Software

Junior litigators filled their days with *"research, writing portions of motions and a little bit of document review, though that's slowed down as I've got more senior."* The *"all stripes group"* handles *"bread and butter commercial contract disputes"* as well as securities, insurance and tort litigation. Client contact can be limited by deal size, but interviewees looked *"to build toward it, I see it coming in the future and it doesn't bother me now."* They brushed off hefty workloads and reasoned *"that's the nature of the beast, sometimes it will be overwhelming and stressful."* Some patent litigation filters through into their team, but the dedicated IP group handles the majority as well as patent prosecution and post-grant review. A general day there consists of *"working on a draft application or response to office action. Things were slow to begin with but it's pretty consistent now."*

In policy and regulatory, work focuses on representing financial institutions in cases of *"government enforcement, white collar crime, a lot of internal investigations... any matter where the government could be the adverse party."* For newcomers that means *"a lot of document review, internal preparation and research,"* but there's also the chance to *"travel across the US and internationally with a partner."* One interviewee recalled *"quite soon after I started we had to travel to prep the client for testimony. I wasn't expecting such a great opportunity that quickly."* Policy and regulatory work is also a fixture in financial services, where juniors get *"a lot of drafting, but also frequent phone calls with clients, answering regulatory concerns."* Days in that group tended to be *"more consistent than in most practices, and it's always been manageable."*

Offices

K&L's Pittsburgh epicenter has outgrown DC, which was until recently the largest office. *"The building and location are great,"* according to interviewees. *"The offices have giant windows looking out over the city that provide loads of natural light."* Other larger bases include Seattle (*"we've got a pretty big presence here"*), Boston (*"the combo of having your own office but maintaining an open door policy is nice, you can ask for help when you need*

it"*) and Chicago, in which *"the décor is a little outdated, but we're trying to update within the next year."* They're lagging behind most other places, as *"a few years ago the firm decided to brand every office the same,"* the identikit surroundings designed to help *"associates feel at home no matter where they go."*

> *"It feels the same calling someone across the country as it does co-workers on a lower floor."*

Internationally-minded associates felt *"very encouraged to reach out to other offices and visit if we're nearby; they really promote the global platform. I definitely get international exposure."* Those prone to travel sickness can stick to K&L's sister office program: every year, each office pairs with another of comparable size and keeps in touch via quarterly video-conferences. Sister locations mix business and pleasure – last year Pittsburghers enjoyed *"a tour of London in pictures!"* The network's connectivity prompted one source to declare *"it feels the same calling someone across the country as it does co-workers on a lower floor."*

Culture & Diversity

Juniors in various offices suggested *"there's a lingering culture from the firm that was here before we became K&L Gates,"* so local character tends to bleed into the personality of each office. Pittsburgh has *"a blue collar work ethic that fits the city, it's a very close-knit community,"* while in Seattle there's *"a lower expectation to be billing New York-style hours"* and Raleigh's *"pretty family-friendly: everyone knows we're not a major city and acts accordingly."* Others, however, argued *"there is a culture that permeates all the offices, and associates tend to have a more global outlook than partners."* Quizzed about relationships with their superiors, insiders agreed *"it's pretty collegial overall, but different partners are different people. Some prefer a more traditional hierarchical set up but I've never met anyone I'm afraid to talk to."*

> *"Associates tend to have a more global outlook than partners."*

See firm profile on p.619

The Inside View

Diversity	Partners (%)	Associates (%)
Women	24	46
White	89	83
Black/African American	2	3
Hispanic/Latin American	2	3
Asian	5	7
Mixed/Other	2	4
LGBT	2	3

Chicago is *"very social – we have monthly cocktail hours where staff and attorneys get together."* Not to be outdone, Pittsburghers hosted *"a pot luck dinner program run by the associate committee – it's a good way to meet associates across the firm."* Contrastingly, in Boston there's *"not as robust a social life as in other places, due to both the firm and people's attitudes."* Perhaps they could take notes from DC, who host *"a nice holiday get-together every year, it's a good opportunity to boost morale and get people excited."* Juniors were similarly pleased with the situation in Seattle: *"The social aspect is one my favorite things about the firm. I'm grabbing lunch or coffee with the people I'm working with multiple times a week."* Annual retreats bring lawyers from different offices together to help them put names to faces.

Gender diversity has come a long way in the law, and K&L juniors applauded the firm for *"moving in the right direction with younger associates, there's a strong emphasis on female leadership."* The Women In the Profession (WIP) group hosts networking events as well as happy hours. On the flip side, several sources felt *"we're not great on ethnic diversity, but they're actively trying to remedy that at recruitment level."* Since 2013, K&L Gates has granted 140 diverse students summer associate positions in California, Chicago and North Carolina through its Kickstarter Program, while the Pittsburgh and Seattle bases have distinct diversity fellowships. Some interviewees worried that *"it's hard to see positive results"* from these initiatives, but others thought they *"will do wonders"* in due time.

Get Hired

The firm tells us it *"wants to know about a student's successes in all parts of their life, and how that translates into them being an excellent lawyer."* Get more insider info at chambers-associate.com.

Training & Development
"The first year has an incredible amount of training packed in," which helped *"to make the free market system more comfortable."* If anything, the deluge of information was too much – *"sometimes I feel we get too much training, it seems like we have CLEs available everyday!"* Transactional associates can sit in on merger workshops, negotiation training or sessions on compiling documents like audit response letters. Larger offices like Pittsburgh and DC host training sessions which are broadcast firm-wide: *"Because of that capability we're exposed to more things than a smaller firm would have resources for,"* something juniors *"really appreciated."* Annual reviews evaluate associates' progress each year spanning September 1st to August 31st, though many felt *"there's only so much the formal process can do."* Thankfully, partners are *"generally good about giving direct feedback; some you need to ask but others give it unprompted."*

"It makes the free market system more comfortable."

Hours & Compensation
Associate salaries at K&L Gates vary depending on where you're working, but start at $180,000 in Boston, Chicago, Dallas, Houston, Los Angeles, New York, Orange County, Palo Alto, San Francisco and Washington, DC. Other offices work to different scales, and the firm got mixed feedback on its response to the 2016 market salary rise; some aggrieved sources grumbled that *"they handled it quite poorly. I wish there'd been more communication."* However, others gave more positive impressions – *"they did a good job explaining what they did and why. It was important to keeping us competitive, and it was done fairly."*

"Remote working is definitely encouraged."

Most juniors tended to work ten-hour days with *"some weekend work depending on how busy the practice is."* They were pleased to find *"remote working is definitely encouraged"* if they needed to leave the office a bit earlier: *"I've never had any issues."* Associates become bonus-eligible once they hit 1,950 hours. How achievable is that it? *"It depends a lot on your practice area and the partners you work with,"* one junior summarized. *"I think it's achievable most years for most people, but there don't seem to be repercussions for not hitting 1,950."* All those we spoke to *"definitely had time for a life outside the firm, that's a necessity,"* and had no problems taking vacation in quieter periods.

Pro Bono
Every hour of pro bono counts toward the bonus threshold. *"I've never felt a push back, it's always encouraged,"* according to juniors, with the caveat *"they probably wouldn't like it to be 50% of our hours! But they definitely respect and think highly of pro bono, we have a strong

See firm profile on p.619

initiative." Matters up for grabs included asylum cases, prisoner rights litigation and various contract disputes, delivered via *"weekly emails listing contacts who can help you engage with cases. At the same time, the partners in charge of pro bono are receptive to juniors' ideas if it's something K&L isn't already engaged with."* In one example *"a group of associates conceptualized an idea where the firm would harness its network in a global volunteer effort to help those affected by hunger,"* the firm explains *"they pitched the idea to management, who immediately approved it."* Several interviewees got involved with the firm's 'revenge porn' cyber civil rights program; you can find more information in our online Bonus Features on K&L Gates.

Pro bono hours
- For all US attorneys: 53,620
- Average per US attorney: 44

Strategy & Future
We've covered reports of partner defections and other behind the scenes happenings in previous years, and interviewees voiced concerns about being *"often kept in the dark. There were a lot of staff layoffs recently; it could have been managed a little differently."* Optimism pervaded that *"it seems like they're moving in the right direction to keep us informed."* Executive committee partner Craig Budner confirms K&L Gates is *"free of debt despite our investments in building a globally integrated platform. Young lawyers coming in know that when they make it to partnership it's been paid for, and there's no ongoing obligation to pay off the debts of past generations."* Looking back at the firm's rapid rise, he reveals *"we've done the expansion, the next phase is to take advantage of the resources that we now have."* The full interview with Budner can be found on our website.

"We've done the expansion, the next phase is to take advantage of the resources that we now have."

See firm profile on p.619

Kasowitz Benson Torres LLP

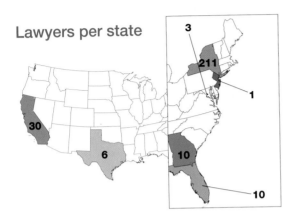

Lawyers per state

Largest US office: New York

US offices: 9

International offices: 0

First-year salary: $180,000

Billable hours: no requirement (2,150 for top bonus level)

Summers 2017: 11 (9 2Ls, 2 1Ls)

Revenue 2016: undisclosed

Partners made in 2017: 7

Famous for: representing Trump; aggressive litigation stance; founder Marc Kasowitz

Lean, mean courtroom wolverine Kasowitz should appeal to bold, dynamic and proactive types.

TOUGH as nails Kasowitz's aggressive litigation stance has put it firmly on the map. Its formidable courtroom approach attracts go-getting, self-assured associates; there's no room for the timid among this bunch. The eponymous Marc Kasowitz heads up the New York-centered firm, which recently grabbed a lot of headlines in the run up to the US presidential election thanks to its longtime representation of Donald Trump. The litigation shop could often be found fighting Trump's corner in thorny legal battles or defamation suits; Marc Kasowitz wrote *that* letter to the *New York Times* demanding the retraction of an article about an alleged groping incident. Name partner David Friedman was also recently appointed by Trump as the US Ambassador to Israel, described by associates as *"very exciting."* As a result of Friedman's departure, in late March 2017 the firm was renamed Kasowitz Benson Torres LLP.

Chambers USA counts Kasowitz among 'The Elite' for its general commercial litigation offering in New York. The firm also has corporate and real estate practices. Nearly all of Kasowitz's juniors are swallowed up by the firm's commercial litigation practice where they tackle anything from business disputes, antitrust, IP, securities to product liability. A handful of juniors join transactional practice areas – like IP, real estate, bankruptcy, and employment – but are usually put there because of prior work experience or educational background.

The Work

Every Monday rookies fill out a drop-down box, indicating their active matters, what they're working on and future availability. Two assignment partners oversee this process: *"They often funnel work to you if they know you have an interest in a certain area."* Many of our sources were comfortable reaching out to other partners directly for work.

"It's been hectic the entire time but I've loved it."

A few years back the firm laid off a number of associates, and consequently when the current crop of rookies arrived *"everything was scarcely staffed, so in three to four months we were drafting papers to court and doing pretty substantial legal stuff,"* one source told us. Another added: *"It's been hectic the entire time but I've loved it."*

Interviewees attached to smaller cases dove into legal research and writing motions, briefs and complaints. *"On some of the bigger staffed cases I'm still doing research and writing, but there are more layers of attorneys to go through,"* one source reported. Numerous sources had second chaired depositions or trotted down to court *"a bunch of times; I don't speak but I get to sit in on oral argu-*

On chambers-associate.com...

- Interview with hiring partner Aaron Marks
- Get hired at Kasowitz

See firm profile on p.620

The Inside View

Rankings in *Chambers USA*

Bankruptcy/Restructuring	Litigation
Insurance	Real Estate

For detail on ranking tiers and ranking locations, visit
www.chambersandpartners.com

ments." We even heard a few sources had the chance *"to prep Marc Kasowitz on an oral argument. I had to understand the facts, get into the weeds better than anyone else and answer his questions. He was relying on me to have the answer – that was a highlight!"*

While juniors do have the chance to get their teeth into meatier matters, we'd be remiss not to point out they do *"experience more mundane tasks."* Interviewees had come across *"a lot of discovery and doc review, or responding to and drafting discovery requests."* As a result of *"handling everything top to bottom,"* juniors find themselves switching gears pretty often: *"One minute you're fielding client phone calls and the next, photocopying."*

Training & Development

As a result of the firm *"being on the lean side, they need to get associates out the gate and running"* from the get-go. New starters enroll at 'Kasowitz University' where they're *"brought up to speed on everything that goes into litigating a case."* Everyone's assigned to a fictional case where they're tasked with things like carrying out the discovery process, writing complaints and responses, exchanging interrogatories and conducting mock depositions and arguments. *"You sit down with partners and you get line by line, point by point feedback for each assignment."* Beyond Kasowitz University, juniors can attend CLEs.

A couple of years back the firm revamped its review process after juniors claimed confusion over bonus calculations. The review now takes place in March so there's *"more of a connection in an associate's mind between their review and their bonus."* Juniors fill out a self assessment which is submitted to partners they've worked with. These partners then weigh in on rookies' performances and once everything's been collated, reviews are delivered by a partner associates haven't worked with.

Outside the formal process juniors were quick to reach out to partners for advice on their progress, telling us *"the firm attracts litigators and big personalities; the people who come here are the type who seek out feedback anyway."* Not that they always need to seek it out: *"People aren't afraid to tell you how they feel about the work. They don't try hard to hide it if they feel you should have done something different or need to hone your skills."*

Recent work highlights

- Representing the Schaghticoke Tribal Nation in a $600 million property suit with Connecticut. The state seized land from the American Indian tribe over 100 years ago
- Acting for Resolute Forest Products in a defamation suit launched against Greenpeace. The firm is using anti-mafia legislation to seek redress from Greenpeace, after the forestry giant claims the organization slandered it to garner donations
- Taking on the role of both plaintiff and counsel in a whistleblowing case against the Dow Chemical, Bayer Material Science, BASF and Huntsman International. The firm alleges the four chemical companies neglected to inform the EPA of the negative health effects of a common chemical

Offices & Culture

Self-confidence is a fairly common trait among Kasowitz juniors: *"They won't babysit you. If you're not outgoing it's not a problem but it's a bit more difficult to succeed. You've got to take the bull by the horns and manage your own career trajectory; I think that plays into the free market system. You've got to look out for yourself and take charge of what you do."* Consequently the firm *"attracts people who are go-getters and aggressive."* That's less toward their colleagues, interviewees were keen to add, and more to do with the firm's *"litigation style. We've got to be aggressive in creating solutions."* Sources also painted the firm as *"pretty tight knit"* and somewhere *"people ask you about your life. We focus on more than work."*

"Sit in client meetings with Marc Kasowitz himself."

Having the name partners on site creates *"a bit of a unique culture. All four founders are practicing here and are really invested in the firm. It's pretty cool to see them and be able to sit in client meetings with Marc Kasowitz himself. People really buy into what the founding partners' vision of the firm is and understand that Marc runs the show,"* one interviewee reckoned.

Most of the firm's junior associates are based in the firm's New York mothership, though a handful are scattered across other bases. Kasowitz has built up a national network of offices over the years, spanning California, Texas, Florida, Georgia, New Jersey and Washington, DC.

New York newbies start out sharing an internal office, before getting their own (still internal) digs in second-year. After that they graduate to a window office. *"It's my biggest gripe,"* said one source. *"I loved sharing but it's no fun having no windows."*

See firm profile on p.620

Diversity	Partners (%)	Associates (%)
Women	20	40.8
White	87.8	80.8
Black/African American	1.1	7.2
Hispanic/Latin American	6.7	4.8
Asian	1.1	3.2
Mixed/Other	3.3	4
LGBT	1.1	4.8

Hours & Pro Bono

Unofficially attorneys are tasked with getting 2,150 billable hours under their belt. This can include pro bono, business development and recruiting hours. Bonuses are calculated by a combination of hours and reviews; doing well in both affords attorneys a full bonus. Reviews are conducted close to bonus payouts, to give juniors a better understanding of the amount they receive.

"You have to learn to take advantage of the quiet times and not feel guilty."

One source told us: *"We've been so incredibly busy that you don't even have to think about hours as they happen on their own. There are times when you actively need to take time off to spend with your friends and family and take a breather."* That said, juniors did note that as the firm has brought on a few more associates, recently *"it's become more manageable"* and *"face time is really not pivotal,"* so they don't need to be stuck in the office at all hours.

Our sources tended to rack up about ten hours a day in the office, plus some evening and weekend work but *"as we're a litigation shop, every month just varies so wildly. You have to learn to take advantage of the quiet times and not feel guilty."*

Perhaps as a result of all this work, we were hard pushed to come across rookies who completed much, or any, pro bono. *"It's widely available,"* one such source explained, *"but it can take quite a bit to balance pro bono work with normal cases."* While there might not be much take up, there is *"something for everyone. You can work on anything you can think of, like asylum matters or advocating on behalf of students and educational resources. If you reach out to the pro bono partner, he'll make contact with organizations."*

Pro bono hours
- For all attorneys: 9,903
- Average per attorney: 38

Diversity

Juniors reckoned that diversity at the firm leaves *"room for improvement."* One interviewee described their class as *"mostly white men,"* though others felt there was *"a nice representation"* of female associates. Women make up less than half the associate ranks while minority attorneys count for 16% of the associates. All that said, we should note that of the seven attorneys promoted to partner in 2016, four of them were women. And *"in the last few years it seems like there's been more of a push in our summer and incoming classes for diversity,"* one source reckoned. *"It's moving in the right direction but we could do better."* The firm points out that of the eight current first-years, three are diverse.

The firm supports minority organizations (such as the Cuban American Bar Association and the Long Island Hispanic Bar Association) and sponsors a variety of networking events. It also recently introduced a women's committee.

Get Hired

"If working for a high powered partner puts you out of your comfort zone, this isn't the place for you." Find out what you'll need to make the grade by visiting chambers-associate.com for more hiring and interview tips.

Strategy & Future

Kasowitz sees no reason to deviate from its litigation focus; the firm reckons it will continue to expand its work in privacy, IP, banking, antitrust, and white collar.

In the past we've heard from associates that the firm keeps its cards pretty close to the vest when it comes to the game plan. Some reckoned this was still the case: *"When big decisions are made they email us but I'm not in the inner circle where things are going on – it's tight knit at the top."* Others felt they were kept relatively well informed: *"We have a committee that liaises with partners and passes along information. We were in the news a bit with the Presidential election and Marc Kasowitz was good at getting out in front and talking to associates and partners about what was going on."*

Katten Muchin Rosenman LLP

Lawyers per state

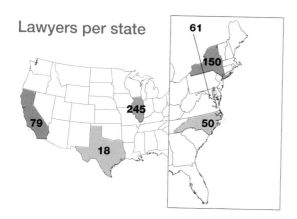

Largest US office: Chicago	
US offices: 11	
International offices: 2	
First-year salary: $180,000	
Billable hours: 2,000 (1,950 in Charlotte)	
Summers 2017: 35 (25 2Ls, 10 1Ls)	
Revenue 2016: $553.8 million (-1.4%)	
Partners made in 2017: 13	
Famous for: innovation and entrepreneurship	

Curiosity certainly didn't kill this fearless young Kat.

"WE'RE one of the newest firms in the Am Law 100," Katten's new chairman Roger Furey points out to us. *"We were created on the foundation of being innovative and unafraid to do things differently."* Since its foundation in Chicago in 1974, Katten has prided itself on having an inquisitive, go-getting culture, which is reflected in the type of hires it makes. *"We want those with a desire to be innovative and entrepreneurial,"* Furey explains, *"but we're doing it as teams. Collaboration is the mantra right now."* You can read our full interview with the chairman in Katten's Bonus Features on our website, where he talks about some of the ways lawyers are currently innovating. *"We recognize the legal world is changing, and we want to be on the front wave of being that entrepreneurial law firm that reflects our beginnings"* he adds.

"We recognize the legal world is changing."

The firm has 11 domestic offices spanning the East and West Coasts, Texas, and the Midwest, plus two overseas (London and Shanghai). *Chambers USA* ranks lots of practice areas including including capital markets, climate change, real estate, sports law, and wealth management – all on a nationwide level. Regionally, the firm weighs in with good rankings in healthcare, banking &

finance, corporate/M&A, and different types of litigation, among others.

The Work

Over a third of juniors on our interviewee list were in litigation, which has various sub-groups. Corporate and real estate had the next most associates, followed by the finance, IP, tax, and trusts & estates groups. Work assignment varies across offices: larger groups in Chicago have *"an assigned partner that's sparingly used, only right at the beginning when you start,"* while DC juniors experienced a *"hybrid of assignment methods."* In LA *"partners know your workflow better, so assignment is more ad hoc."*

Litigation sub-groups include white collar defense, financial services, construction, and commercial litigation. A Chicago litigator noted that *"white collar defense is probably the most popular, and it can be hard to get staffed on those cases – but I've been lucky and got to do a lot of that work."* The group tends to represent individuals whose companies are under investigation, and financial services firms. There's *"a lot of writing – drafting briefs and motions, working on discovery, witness prep, and meeting with clients to help get them ready for depositions."* On the commercial side, the group represents larger commercial developers, and in DC *"some relatively big names in the real estate game."* As a junior there's *"so much discovery to do because I'm the cheapest,"* but also general research and drafting. *"I'd like more challenging and involved tasks,"* one noted, *"but a lot of it is a learning process. Sometimes higher level work gets pushed down depending on workload, but much comes with time."*

On chambers-associate.com...

- More on getting hired at Katten
- Interview with firm chair Roger Furey

See firm profile on p.621

The Inside View

Rankings in *Chambers USA*

Banking & Finance	Litigation
Bankruptcy/Restructuring	Media & Entertainment
Capital Markets	Real Estate
Corporate/M&A	Sports Law
Environment	Tax
Healthcare	Transportation
Intellectual Property	

For detail on ranking tiers and ranking locations, visit
www.chambersandpartners.com

Recent work highlights

- US counsel to Royal Bank of Canada on compliance with US securities laws and other US regulatory matters
- Advised the Barack Obama Foundation regarding environmental issues related to candidate sites for the Obama Presidential Center
- Represented URL Pharma an antitrust and contract breach suit against Reckitt Benckiser over the right to sell generic Mucines – an anti-congestion drug
- Represented Ardent Health Services in the sale of Ardent to Ventas for $1.75 billion

"It's sink or swim, which is kind of intimidating, but a great way to get skills."

On the transactional side, corporate M&A juniors often *"help private equity firms acquire companies for their portfolios, to then sell off in a few years."* Tasks include due diligence, preparing memos, reviewing files on companies, and *"pulling people together."* Other offices are also on hand if specialist knowledge is needed. Deals are generally leanly staffed: one source said *"it's sink or swim, which is kind of intimidating, but a great way to get skills."* Another explained *"it's a fast learning curve. They give you as much responsibility as you want, but at any point if it gets too much, the partners are mindful of pulling back a bit."* Although leanly staffed, some sources were *"eager to get more drafting experience. They let me draft a license agreement, so I'm getting pieces slowly. I think they're ramping me up toward more."* On the commercial finance side, there's a lot of acquisition work, with some financing. Juniors enjoyed *"being able to do both sides. It's cool to get to see the full cycle."* Work volume is *"manageable if it's one deal at a time, but if it's multiple with two trying to close at the same time, it might be a bit insane! But even when it's insane, there's an end in sight."*

"I'll be the first or second person the client calls, which is pretty unique."

Real estate juniors do *"all things – a mix of acquisitions, financing, and a fair bit of joint venture work."* A Chicago source noted *"a good mix of deals. Some smaller deals have less oversight, especially once the purchase agreement is negotiated. I can run with it on my own."* Other tasks include due diligence, organizing the time lines for closings, and *"becoming an expert on the properties in question."* Juniors in this group should also be ready for direct client contact from the get-go: *"I'll be the first or second person the client calls, which is pretty unique."*

Offices

The firm's modern HQ is in Windy City, although chairman Roger Furey works out of the DC office. DC's smaller size means juniors felt *"you have the benefit of being a big firm, but it feels medium-sized."* The Chicago office is *"well located for social activities."* The only grumble was parking, which *"can be kind of a disaster."* Juniors in LA move interchangeably between downtown and Century City, although *"downtown feels like more of a satellite office."* Some of the smaller offices have more specific focuses: Austin serves clients in the energy and chemical sectors, while fellow Texas base Houston tackles environmental compliance and workplace safety matters. Environmental clients can also be found in San Francisco, while Charlotte focuses heavily on real estate and litigation.

Training & Development

Each department has its own formal training sessions, which some juniors *"haven't found to be the most beneficial experience, but that's something I think they're trying to work on."* This included some lunch programs, as well as web cast training via video conferences. Many found learning on the job to be the most effective training. Litigators participated in trial advocacy training in Chicago, as well as *"incredibly useful"* deposition training. *"The firm hired actors and set up depositions like it was actually happening. It was really useful, especially getting the feedback from the partners."*

The review process currently occurs twice a year, although word on the street is that juniors expect one to become more focused on career development and career goals. The biannual reviews held no surprises for juniors, who felt that *"generally partners are good at giving feedback as you go and telling you if you're doing something wrong."*

See firm profile on p.621

The Inside View

Diversity	Partners (%)	Associates (%)
Women	22.5	47.1
White	93.2	80.2
Black/African American	1.4	4.0
Hispanic/Latin American	1.1	4.0
Asian	3.9	11
Mixed/Other	0.4	0.9
LGBT	2.1	4.4

Pro Bono

"The opportunities are definitely there: it's on the associate whether they'll take advantage of them" a DC junior explained. Attorneys can bill up to 100 hours of pro bono, but can request more. Katten has a full-time pro bono partner who regularly emails out opportunities, which have included asylum cases, work with non-profit organizations, transfers of property, and a rising number of adoptions. The latter *"are obviously non-adversarial, so everyone is happy, which is nice."*

"I billed 170 hours of pro bono last year."

Pro bono hours
- For all US attorneys: 25,919
- Average per US attorney: 40

Culture

"In the grand scheme of BigLaw, it's pretty casual and informal," juniors felt. Katten makes it a habit to *"look for people we want to be around all day. It's a personality fit thing."* As a result, the partners are approachable, and *"my best friends are the people I work with. There's a real affection toward my co-workers."* The *"social aspect is alive and well"* despite not necessarily being firm-initiated. But juniors emphasized that *"it goes back to the quality of the people here – everyone is nice and people feel included."*

"Katten is thoughtful about expansion."

Culture can differ across groups and offices, and many felt *"siloed"* within their departments. But *"within the group, we feel close to everyone."* On the younger end, juniors *"socialize frequently after work"* but there's also *"a big contingent of people who have kids, so it's a good mix."* Juniors considered the firm conservative in terms of its growth: *"Katten is thoughtful about expansion – they're not rushing into mergers left and right which is good to see."* With the arrival of President Trump, some juniors believed that *"everyone in BigLaw is generally curious to see where things are going. The outlook feels very unsure right now."*

Hours & Compensation

"I don't feel the need to be in the office for like 12 hours – I can work from home if need be." The average working day for juniors was around 9am and 7pm, but *"depending on what's going on with a case, the hours are flexible enough to make billable time and work your personal life around that."* Happily, if work isn't pressing, *"they really try not to infringe on your weekend."*

Katten has a 2,000 hour billable target to get a bonus of some sort, but 2,100 hours for the market rate. A finance source noted that *"generally people bill over this, as a byproduct of the workflow."* Another explained *"the bonus at 2,000 doesn't match the Cravath scale, and that annoys people. But at the same time, it jumps up for every 100 hours more. If you bill 2,400 hours you might make more than an associate in New York."* Juniors praised the firm's quick reaction the market rise in salaries and the *"transparent discussions"* around it, but felt *"the firm isn't transparent about the hours bonus, and it can vary from year to year. If you do the extra hours it could be big, or it could be negligible."*

Diversity

"Leaders are asking 'what can we do better?' They're definitely listening." Opinions on diversity varied, but the general feeling was that *"the firm might not have the answers yet, but it's making concerted efforts to address these issues."* Katten has a 1L diversity program aimed at recruiting more diverse candidates, and offers a diversity scholarship of $15,000. The firm also held a diversity summit in Chicago, in which diverse partners spoke, addressing *"career development, mentoring, and things like that."* There's an active women's leadership forum to address retaining women, which has *"a new partner in charge who is fantastic!"* A DC junior noted: *"As far as female attorneys are concerned, there's a refreshing number of female partners and practice group leaders. Although when you get to partner level, you start to feel like there's not as many ethnically diverse people. That would be nice to see improved."* Juniors acknowledged the problem in recruiting and retaining diverse attorneys, but noted *"it's not uniquely problematic at Katten."*

Strategy & Future

Chairman Roger Furey explains that Katten's entrepreneurial history guides its future. *"We want to be on the front wave of being an entrepreneurial law firm that reflects our beginnings."* So what will tomorrow bring? *"We intend to invest time and resources in data intelligence and AI, and find out where it makes sense to roll those into serving our clients,"* he says.

See firm profile on p.621

"We have a strategic plan with a number of objectives. One is to focus and grow stronger in our core strengths... in private equity, in finance – commercial finance and structured finance are two of the most successful areas – and in the area of environment and workplace safety. High stakes litigation is also a focus. We have a great practice in financial services litigation as well as white collar, and we're getting stronger in IP too." For the full interview, go online.

What makes people stand out at interview? *"People who have done their research,"* juniors said, *"people who have given the sense that Katten isn't just another firm they're interviewing with."* Find out more about getting hired at chambers-associate.com

See firm profile on p.621

Kilpatrick Townsend & Stockton LLP

Lawyers per state

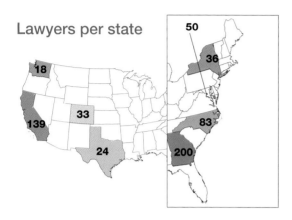

50	
36	
18	
33	
139	
83	
24	
200	

Largest US office: Atlanta
US offices: 15
International offices: 3
First-year salary: $120,000 - $180,000
Billable hours: 1,400/1,900 targets
Summers 2017: 27 (17 2Ls, 10 1Ls)
Revenue 2016: $416.4 million (+1.2%)
Partners made in 2017: 8
Famous for: strong IP practice; Atlanta HQ

"Entrepreneurial" Kilpatrick is a lot more than just an IP firm.

BACK in 1893, when the inventors of a sickly-sweet morphine substitute felt they were probably onto something, they turned to an IP firm to register their new brand. And thus the Coca-Cola trademark was born, registered by a firm that was to become Kilpatrick Townsend. Since then, the firm has been busy growing through mergers, and 2015 saw the launch of the firm's first Texas office after it merged with Dallas-based litigation boutique Crouch & Ramey. This new addition brings the firm's US office roster to 15 (it also has attorneys in Shanghai, Stockholm and Tokyo).

The firm's broad geographic spread – spanning both coasts and several states in between – is largely thanks to the 2011 merger between California-based Townsend and Crew and Atlanta fixture Kilpatrick Stockton. Both legacy firms were themselves products of historic mergers. Both had long been known for their stellar IP capabilities and the IP practice remains highly respected today. But, as one junior rightly pointed out, *"we're a full-service firm with an incredibly strong IP base."* Other robust practices where juniors can get involved include corporate, construction, labor, litigation and real estate, to name a few.

On chambers-associate.com...

- We check in with managing partner Susan Spaeth
- More on diversity
- Kilpatrick's unusual recruitment process

The Work

After rotating through three practice groups during the summer program, rookies rank them in order of preference. Around three-quarters of juniors tend to head into the various subgroups within IP. The remainder are split between Kilpatrick's litigation and CFRE (corporate, finance & real estate) departments. Although each group has access to a formal workload system where juniors can indicate their availability, some teams *"don't seem to use it too much."* Most assignments come from senior attorneys *"reaching out to those they're interested in working with."* But juniors needn't just wait to see what comes through the door as *"we're an entrepreneurial firm. If you want to reach out to partners they appreciate the initiative and find something for you."*

IP associates join one of five subgroups: patent litigation; trademark & copyright; medical & mechanical devices; chemistry & life sciences; and electronics & software. Attorneys in the last three groups tend to predominantly work on patent prosecution (applying for patent status), though they're not restricted from working on patent litigation matters. Trademark & copyright juniors are required to work on both sides. *"Depending on the complexity of the case, I could run the litigation or just be one of the hands,"* one patent litigator outlined. Regardless of complexity, technical and legal research is almost a given. Interviewees had also drafted discovery requests, reviewed deposition transcripts and prepared senior attorneys for depositions. Over on the patent prosecution side, juniors *"meet with inventors or in-house attorneys to learn about the invention and draft patent applications complete with technical drawings. We file it and then work*

The Inside View

See firm profile on p.622

Rankings in *Chambers USA*

Bankruptcy/Restructuring	Franchising
Construction	Intellectual Property
Corporate/M&A	Labor & Employment
Employee Benefits &	Litigation
Executive Compensation	Native American Law
Environment	Real Estate
Financial Services	Tax
Regulation	

For detail on ranking tiers and ranking locations, visit
www.chambersandpartners.com

Recent work highlights

- Acted for Expedia as intellectual property counsel on the travel company's $3.9 billion acquisition of HomeAway
- Acted for Adidas in trademark infringement litigation against Skechers, including protecting the company's distinctive three stripes
- Handled a dispute over the construction of a US Embassy compound in Wellington, New Zealand

back and forth with the patent office to make revisions to the claims."

"It's a bit of a chess game."

Sources acknowledged that even though tasks on offer *"can appear repetitive, we're always looking at different technologies. Someone may make one claim about the science involved; our job is to say 'we view it another way' and prove our point is valid. It's a bit of a chess game and I really like that aspect."* Others pointed out that the firm *"gives you responsibility so that you can become an expert. The partners are interested in developing a specialist area for each associate but it does pigeonhole you. Only one or two people here know more about my niche than I do, which is great but it can't be the only thing I do. It's a double-edged sword."*

Culture

In Atlanta *"the atmosphere depends on the level you're on."* The IP floor, for instance, has *"a very laid-back atmosphere. It's just very collaborative,"* with chairs being dragged into partners' offices for team meetings. *"If someone new walks by, people pop their heads out of their office to ask who they are."* The greetings don't stop once you become a familiar face: *"I always get a good morning when people walk past my office."*

"They have a magnetic aura."

One interviewee felt this attitude might surprise some people, as *"I don't know if you'd describe most lawyers as fun, and patent law is the most nerdy and esoteric area of law, but everyone is extremely friendly. People crack jokes that are not just nerdy, they're actual jokes."* Another IP junior put this ambience down to the team *"attracting people who others want to be around; they're charismatic. They don't have to be chatty or funny but they have a magnetic aura about them."* Beyond the IP pale, *"if you go up a couple of levels it doesn't have the same feel. The litigation floor is a bit more intense."*

Compared to the IP boutiques in town, Kilpatrick's Seattle base is *"probably more buttoned up."* But associates here felt *"people are really friendly and easy to talk to. I've known a lot of attorneys and there is not a lot of ego here."* Although lawyers *"get intensely into their work, it doesn't get super intense."* If someone becomes overloaded colleagues are generally up for *"transferring off matters. People are willing to help out."* Down in San Francisco, *"people ring each other with questions. It's not competitive at all."* Just like in Atlanta, the patent prosecutors are *"a little quieter than those on the litigation floor where four people are working on one document."*

Offices

Atlanta welcomes the largest concentration of Kilpatrick rookies, followed by Seattle and San Francisco. The rest are spread sparsely around most of the firm's 15 offices. At the time of our calls we also found juniors in Charlotte, Denver, Los Angeles, Raleigh, San Diego, Silicon Valley, Walnut Creek and Winston-Salem.

"We have two nerve centers."

Atlanta is also considered Kilpatrick's de facto headquarters although management is split between here and San Francisco. *"We have two nerve centers due to the merger. Currently our chairman is in Atlanta and our managing partner in Silicon Valley; it used to be the other way round."* Our sources tended to work most closely with offices in their region: *"Typically I'll be working with the East Coast,"* articulated one Atlantan. *"Lots of people spend time in another office to interact more with other teams."* Cross-office interaction appears visible early on but opportunities *"grow as your career progresses."*

Training & Development

New starters are all flown to one location for practice group boot camps. The *"three-day intensive training session"* covers things like *"what's needed to respond to an office action or conduct an interview."* This is topped up around the fourth year for *"more advanced topics."* Litigators additionally attend a two-day mock trial where they *"prepare and present to partners"* and can also take advantage of a three-day deposition training. A profes-

See firm profile on p.622

Diversity	Partners (%)	Associates (%)
Women	25.2	40.5
White	92	73.2
Black/African American	2.5	5.5
Hispanic/Latin American	0.8	3.2
Asian	4.6	13.6
Mixed/Other	0	4.6
LGBT	-	-

sional development series brings in speakers to *"chat about improving and tightening legal writing or client development."* It also, handily, covers *"dealing with difficult clients."*

"Dealing with difficult clients."

First-years are assigned a senior associate as mentor (mid or senior-level attorneys are paired with counsel or partners). But there are plenty of informal mentors around as *"lawyers are funny; they love to talk and feel important. If you ask someone to mentor you they get really excited about it."*

Pro Bono
In the Bay Area *"there's quite a lot of immigration"* matters helping children gain visas and asylum. *"Some are fleeing drug cartels and violence; their family members may have been killed. All kinds of horrible things happen to them. It's rewarding to do something for someone with a very tangible result."*

"Fleeing drug cartels and violence."

Kilpatrick's Atlanta office has *"a whole program devoted to grandparent adoptions."* Come Saturday, some juniors here can be found hanging around the Atlanta Volunteer Lawyers Foundation, *"interviewing people who need help. It's a pretty good way to pick up pro bono."*

Domestic abuse and landlord/tenant matters or advising indigent inventors on IP rights were popular assignments across the firm. Attorneys are required to complete 30 hours of pro bono a year and can credit up to 50 hours toward their annual billable target.

Pro bono hours
- For all US attorneys: 38,100
- Average per US attorney: 56

Hours & Compensation
Entry-level associates are required to bill at least 1,400 hours a year. Second-years and up shoot for an annual target of 1,900. *"It's achievable but easier for attorneys in*

certain practices." Patent prosecutors, for example, may struggle more than litigators. That being said, one interviewee felt: *"This isn't the kind of place that looks at an associate and blames them if they're not hitting the hours. It's a team effort and partners take personal responsibility if not enough work is going around."*

"Achieving just the minimum is not going to get you an A+ review."

For those able to meet the target, it's worth bearing in mind that *"achieving just the minimum is not going to get you an A+ review. There's an understanding you should strive to go above it,"* especially if you want to be seeing dollar signs in front of your eyes: *"If you don't exceed the target by a good amount, don't expect a bonus."*

Although *"lots of people are early birds"* and in by 8.30am, how associates notch up their hours is generally up to them. *"They don't insist we stay here for 60 hours a week. I may have to do 60 hours' worth of work but if I'm only in the office 40 hours a week, I can go home and be a decent parent."*

Diversity
Sources praised the firm's supportive attitude toward parent attorneys: *"It's one of the biggest things I love about this firm."* Juniors in Atlanta judged that *"compared to most firms, especially in the IP area, we have a much higher percentage of female partners and associates."*

"It compares favorably."

Females are *"still underrepresented"* in Seattle. It's also *"pretty homogeneous in terms of race. The Atlanta office is more racially diverse, but it's in a city with a large African-American population."* The Bay Area *"seems fairly diverse. I think it compares favorably to others."*

Get Hired
Kilpatrick scrapped the traditional callback interview format a couple of years ago. *"We felt we weren't getting a full picture of how the candidates would perform in real-world circumstances at a law firm,"* hiring committee chairman Charlie Henn explains. *"We weren't getting good information on teamwork, collaboration and creativity in trying to solve client problems in a group."*

Instead, the firm devised 'Super Call-Back Weekend'. Dinner and drinks with the firm's attorneys on a Friday are followed by a task-filled Saturday. Aspiring attorneys are put through their paces in a one-on-one interview, a writing exercise and group tasks including a client chal-

See firm profile on p.622

lenge. Read our online interview with Charlie Henn to find out more.

"See if people are fake or genuine."

Current juniors were on board with the changes: *"I think it's better. Some people don't interview well, or they interview well but can't work in groups. The assessments get at things which wouldn't come out in interviews."* And dinner the night before allows attorneys to *"see if people are fake or genuine. So much of this job is not academic as much as tolerating the people around you."*

Strategy & Future

2015 saw the opening of Kilpatrick's Dallas office to *"better support our Texas client base,"* managing partner Susan Spaeth tells us. *"We are looking to have our office footprint better match our national and international client base."* Spaeth is keeping tight-lipped about the possibility of additional offices to service this commitment but explains: *"Our firm is team-centric. When we look at strategic growth it's more around what growth we need to have in different practice offerings and where that affects a particular geographic region. We are very interested in further growing our corporate offering in California, for example."*

While IP will continue to be the firm's front runner, Kilpatrick will *"further expand and support our corporate and commercial litigation depth and breadth"* across the USA.

To learn about the life of an intellectual property lawyer, check out our practice area reviews on chambers-associate.com

See firm profile on p.622

The Inside View

King & Spalding LLP

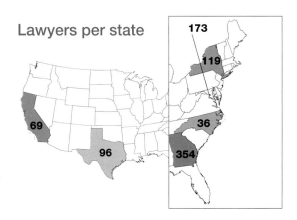

Lawyers per state

173
119
69
96
36
354

Largest US office: Atlanta
US offices: 9
International offices: 10
First-year salary: $155,000 - $180,000
Billable hours: no requirement
Summers 2017: 51 (46 2Ls, 3 1Ls, 2 3Ls)
Revenue 2016: $1.058 billion (+3.9%)
Partners made in 2017: 14 globally (12 in US)
Famous for: one of Atlanta's go-to firms; market-beating growth

Ten years ago, Georgia's most gorgeous law firm ranked about half way down *Am Law's* rankings – these days it's top 20.

MANY law firms took a nose dive following the Great Recession, but this one did the opposite: *"We have grown our revenue every year for the last 30 years,"* Atlanta-based chairman Robert Hays proudly points out. This Southern-tinged international firm hit the $1 billion landmark for the first time in 2015, and boosted revenue by another 3.9% in 2016. Profit also hiked (+8.2%), *"which is hard to do."* Troops-wise, King & Spalding has now surpassed the psychologically significant 1,000-lawyer mark – this is officially a Big Firm, as its turbo-charged ascent of *Am Law's* annual size rankings in recent years testifies. All these accolades are the culmination of an unusually busy decade that has seen K&S almost quadruple its office count to 19. The most recent are Tokyo and Los Angeles. *"We opened more offices than our peers,"* Robert Hays reflects. *"However, we didn't grow for growth's sake. There is a strategic rationale for every geography we are in. We would likely not open as many in future because we have opened a lot in cities that are either financial centers or have other strategic importance."*

Examining strategic opportunities in Asia, for example, led to Tokyo's opening in 2016, while the new LA office – built by a mix of lateral hires and existing Spaldingites switching offices – largely focuses on two of King & Spalding's six cash cow practice areas: global disputes

and healthcare/life sciences. The other core practices are: energy; technology/IP; financial institutions; and government investigations/regulatory. These six expert areas help define the firm's unique identity: *"We are not trying to be all things to all people,"* the chairman adds, *"and we are also not hyperspecialized in terms of practices like some firms. We seek a balance."*

The Work

Chambers USA showers top or high rankings upon numerous practices in these six categories, both nationally and at state level: Georgia, California, DC, New York, North Carolina, and Texas. Atlanta summer associates can rotate between different practices before expressing a preference. In New York and DC, summers generally don't rotate but are recruited into single groups, although the level of flexibility varies between practice groups and offices. Most K&S associates work in business litigation, but a significant number can be found in corporate, as well as 'special matters', which covers white collar crime. Other options include finance, healthcare, tort & environmental litigation, and international arbitration.

"The really neat thing about our group is that people do lots of different things."

A business litigator told us that *"the really neat thing about our group is that people do lots of different things."* Examples we heard about include antitrust, work for *"the*

On chambers-associate.com...

- Tips on getting hired
- From the K&S hall of fame: Griffin Bell

See firm profile on p.623

Rankings in *Chambers USA*

Antitrust	Healthcare
Appellate Law	Intellectual Property
Banking & Finance	International Arbitration
Bankruptcy/Restructuring	International Trade
Construction	Labor & Employment
Corporate Crime &	Latin American Investment
Investigations	Litigation
Corporate/M&A	Products Liability
Energy & Natural	Projects
Resources	REITs
Environment	Real Estate
Food & Beverages	Securities
Government	Tax

For detail on ranking tiers and ranking locations, visit
www.chambersandpartners.com

Recent work highlights

- Advised fast food chain Popeyes Louisiana Kitchen on its $1.8 billion sale to Restaurants Brands International (RBI), owners of brands including Burger King and Tim Horton's
- Acting for LNG export project developer NextDecade on its proposed combination with Harmony, a publicly listed special purpose acquisition company whose objective is to take a company public via reverse merger
- A K&S pro bono team working with Lambda Legal won a civil rights victory on behalf of a Georgia transgender client whose name-change petition had been denied by a lower court
- Represented Morgan Stanley and Raymond James as bookrunning managers and representatives of the underwriters in a public offering of shares by Rayonier, a timberland real estate investment trust (REIT)

big four accountancy firms," liability cases, trademark disputes, class actions, government regulation... the list is almost endless. One had worked on behalf of *"a large healthcare provider"* and another the American Automobile Association. In fact, clients can be small, huge, or *"some companies in the middle I'd never heard of. It's important to the assigning partner to make sure new associates get a variety of work."* This assigner is on hand for *"the first couple of years, to make sure I have work when I want it but am not overwhelmed. But once I've worked with a partner they come straight to me."* Assignment becomes more organic. Responsibility-wise, a healthcare source told us: *"I do anything from drafting motions and discovery requests, requests for production, writing memos and angry attorney letters, and on the regulatory side keeping up with regulations and advising clients. As a junior in this practice, you do get substantive experience pretty early. There's not so much doc review because we have a discovery center in Atlanta."*

In the corporate department, a junior's fare depends on the heftiness of the transaction: *"A deal for GE or Coca Cola will tend to have a lot of people staffed on it so there's a bit more hierarchy and I'd typically be assigned diligence. I'll be on calls with clients, help to draft disclosure schedules and ancillary agreements. I have less to do with drafting the actual purchase agreements, but with a smaller client there'll be me and one other partner or associate, so I get to do a lot. They put a lot of trust in you."* The capital transactions & real estate department is quite a broad group that includes private equity-related work like *"capital raising and fund formation. There's a lot of drafting: private placement memos, limited partnership agreements, operating agreements, negotiations and side letters between sponsors, managers and investors."*

Training & Development

An initial orientation called 'Starting Strong' incorporates various events and video trainings which cover, among other things, *"the ins and outs of the firm's systems, like billing, the availability of resources and who to contact if there's an issue,"* according to one interviewee. More broadly at the firm thereafter, *"we do have a lot of support staff who're always available for questions and issues, and that's hugely helpful."* 'King & Spalding University' (KSU) is the name given to a range of training programs for junior and midlevel associates, plus a diversity retreat and senior women's forum. There are KSU Skills Academies for transactional associates and litigators, which for the latter include *"programs on trial advocacy and how to improve your writing."* Another *"really great program is a two-day hands-on NITA training. People really prioritize going to it."* Each summer, transactional juniors congregate in Atlanta for their own skills academy. KSU programs also provide networking opportunities, for example at welcome dinners in partners' homes.

"Every new starter or lateral is assigned a partner 'link'."

There are also business development classes, and a mentoring scheme called 'LINK.' *"Every new starter is assigned a partner and an associate 'link' to help them with questions that they maybe don't want to go to their assigning partner with, like vacation and what's appropriate."* Interviewees felt well-supported on the whole. Unsurprisingly, the level of feedback *"depends on the person. Some people volunteer feedback, but I haven't been in a situation where I've felt I couldn't ask for any comments. Generally people keep their door open, so even if they didn't offer it you can ask for clarification."* Separately, partner Sam Matchett offers individual career counseling to first, second and third-year associates and all diverse associates.

See firm profile on p.623

The Inside View

Diversity	Partners (%)	Associates (%)
Women	23.5	46.5
White	91	82.3
Black/African American	2.4	4.8
Hispanic/Latin American	3	4.2
Asian	3.3	6.3
Mixed/Other	0.3	2.5
LGBT	1	3.2

Hours & Compensation

Although there isn't a formal billing target, we heard that it's necessary to rack up 2,050 hours in order to rake in a bonus. Associates agreed that *"it's pretty realistic. I haven't had trouble hitting it."* Hours billed above this goal gives associates more cash, and given how busy this growing firm has been in recent years, many interviewees found themselves in this category. Asked about work/life balance, they were phlegmatic: *"I mean, it's BigLaw, and like any other BigLaw firm there are demands placed on you beyond the normal 8am to 5pm. Having said that, the firm really makes an effort to encourage balance. I've gone on a number of vacations."* Another told us that *"everyone here encourages personal time when you have the opportunity, because they acknowledge that there will be times when it's so busy that won't be able to. The week between Christmas and New Year, I had one brief due on the Tuesday but the rest of week I enjoyed the time off – although I did a bit of work from home."*

"I mean, it's BigLaw…"

Pro Bono

Associates can count up to 100 hours of pro bono toward their billable total and sources concurred that King & Spalding *"definitely encourages us to get involved – and a lot of folks do."* There's a pro bono partner, Josh Toll in DC, who *"devotes a very large percentage of time to managing the program and sending out emails with opportunities which makes it easy to get into."* Sources had taken on a range of work, including clemency projects, special educational needs issues relating to DC public schools, and election protection work. We also heard about domestic violence restraining orders and residency cases in conjunction with non-profit abused women charity HerJustice.

Pro bono hours:
- For all US attorneys: 26,094
- Average per US attorney: 33

Culture

"There's definitely a Southern feel," chuckled an Atlanta associate when asked about the office's culture, *"but it's* not nearly as stuffy as I imagined it would be. It actually used to be all formal suits and ties but now it's business casual, modernized. People are very friendly."* Another emphasized that *"the Atlanta culture is defined differently between practice groups. If I'm in the elevator with people who aren't on my floor, often I don't know who they are, but within the smaller groups it's very comfortable. Everyone I work with is professional but they do want to get to know you on personal level as well."*

"It actually used to be all formal suits and ties but now it's business casual."

Big Apple juniors described their enclave as *"relatively laid back for a New York BigLaw firm, although we don't have a business casual dress code – it's not that laid back! I never hear yelling, and people generally like to work with one another. It's very collegial, not competitive or mean."* A source who'd lateraled in from another, larger firm confirmed that *"it's more formal here. People are very cordial and very professional, but at the end of the day they want to go home and be with their families, so it's less social than my previous firm. It doesn't feel stuffy, just a little bit distant in a certain way. People are here definitely to work."* The social calendar includes *"a couple of parties for summers, a holiday party and occasional happy hours,"* while departments get together for retreats and *"dinner or drinks every few months or so."*

Diversity

With 91% of K&S partners and 82% of associates being white, it's no surprise that respondents reckoned that the firm *"probably isn't one of the most diverse out there."* Nevertheless, K&S *"definitely does make an effort to ensure it is diverse, and does a good job, although there is always room for improvement."* Meanwhile, *"my biggest gripe with the New York office is that it's not nearly as diverse as it should be for New York."* Looking across all departments and offices, however, *"there is no glass ceiling: there are significant partners of color, and women. There are also the respective affinity groups and mentoring for associates."* Diversity partner Sam Matchett (see Training above) and associate director of HR & diversity Caroline Abney also visit offices to offer support.

"Tons of panels and talks by partners and clients. Diversity isn't a strength of the firm but it's valued."

Affinity groups include those for LGBTQ lawyers, women, and attorneys of color. In Atlanta the women's group *"has a lunch every couple of months, happy hours, and we try to do events every now and then."* Every other year there's a two-day diversity retreat in Atlanta, featuring *"tons of panels and talks by partners and clients. Diversity*

See firm profile on p.623

The Inside View

isn't a strength of the firm but it's valued." Chairman Robert Hays points out that large clients are nowadays *"extremely interested"* in diversity, and in fact monitor and grade law firms' success in providing diverse attorneys on their caseloads. This had led to collaboration with clients, including affinity programs, social events, and also *"seconding minority or other diverse associates to clients."*

Offices

Most junior associates are based in the Atlanta HQ, followed by DC and New York. The rest are spread around Houston, Austin, Charlotte, San Francisco, Sacramento, Silicon Valley, and the firm's newest domestic office, Los Angeles. *"We are in a high rise in midtown,"* an Atlanta source described, *"and they're in the middle of renovating the offices. We've been shuffled around and changed floors. They're trying to make it more modern, with glass."*

"They're in the middle of renovating."

New York recently underwent its own renovation, and associates were in two minds about the *"nice glass"* of internal offices used by staff and first-years, which can create a *"fishbowl"* effect – some *"people put up posters for privacy"* on the glass doors of their shared offices. Most attorneys still have solid wooden doors though, we should point out. Juniors elsewhere usually get their own offices, and DC-ers enjoyed having more office space generally (compared to New York). *"It's great we are next door to the White House: the perfect location."* One part of the building is *"a bit older, one part is brand new."*

Get Hired

King & Spalding is visiting 27 law schools for OCIs in 2017 as part of its junior-level recruitment drive, and participates in various job fairs and resumé collects as well, meaning you've got a good chance to find them. What sort of person does the firm look for? Find out in our Bonus Features on chambers-associate.com.

Strategy & Future

"There are six core practice areas identified, and we're focused on growing those," one clued-up associate believed. *"There's no imperative to grow out – it's more developing our reputation for what we are good at. Auditor liability will certainly continue to be a focus; also media, antitrust, regulatory, and others."* Perhaps chairman Robert Hays has associates like this one in mind when he comments that nowadays *"we are seeing associates with sophisticated knowledge of law firms as businesses. Associates are very attuned now to the footprint of law firms: where the resources are, their national and international reach."*

King & Spalding's remarkable growth over the last decade means there's never been a better time to impress recruiters here with your business-savvy legal world view. Lawyers need to have one eye on the future, as this associate demonstrates: *"Every other week our practice group has a meeting where we talk about client development, marketing, and what the plan is for our group moving forward. I can see that the firm's expanding in a strategic and smart way. It's on an upward trajectory."*

"We are seeing associates with sophisticated knowledge of law firms as businesses."

See firm profile on p.623

Kirkland & Ellis LLP

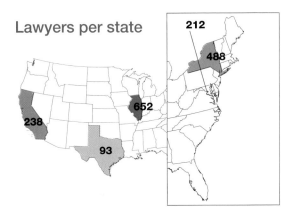

Lawyers per state

212
488
652
238
93

Largest US office: Chicago
US offices: 7
International offices: 5
First-year salary: $180,000
Billable hours: no requirement
Summers 2017: 247 (230 2Ls, 17 1Ls)
Revenue 2016: $2.65 billion (+15%)
Partners made in 2017: 81 globally
Famous for: eye-popping deals and tricky litigation

Beneath their 'Type-A' reputation, Kirkland associates are just *"normal people who like to work hard."*

KIRKLAND'S prestige is well-known throughout the legal industry. Its reputation precedes it: attorneys are driven self-starters who, in the words of one here, are *"committed to the work, but also enjoy it."* The conclusion? *"Kirkland is an unbelievable firm no matter who you talk to."* The firm's confident associates also pointed out that if there's a high profile lawsuit in the headlines, Kirkland's name may well crop up. But there's also a huge transactional practice that sources said is growing, and a glance at the firm's *Chambers USA* rankings shows the breadth of work on offer.

Kirkland rakes in numerous top national rankings in the *Chambers* directory for practices including bankruptcy/restructuring, IP, corporate/M&A, private equity, and general commercial litigation. It also garners ace rankings in its home state of Illinois for areas such as antitrust, insurance litigation, white collar litigation, banking & finance, real estate, and tax. Other regions with various ranked practices are California, DC, and New York. In 2016, Kirkland's revenue soared 15% to $2.65 billion, lifting the firm to second place in the *Am Law 100* for the first time.

The Work

Kirkland's growing transactional group had the majority of this year's junior cohort, with almost two-thirds of associates on our almost 330-strong interviewee list getting their teeth into various transactional practices. Lots of individuals were in litigation teams, with the remainder split between IP and restructuring. Across all groups, the firm implements an *"open assignment system,"* a rename of the free market system because *"incoming law students were afraid of it."* In spite of this system, many found they'd *"never had to ask for something – the phone is always ringing."* Juniors felt *"a formal system is more necessary when there isn't much work – we don't have that problem here; there's more than enough to go around."* The learning curve was more a matter of *"knowing when to say no."* The *"seamless"* cross-staffing element of the firm was also praised, with one DC source admitting *"I probably speak to other offices more than my own mother!"*

> *"The firm looks to associates to do the first draft of most documents."*

The transactional group covers both general corporate work as well as specialist groups such as investment funds, debt financing, international trade, and employee benefits. Investment funds folks focus on *"private funds and investment vehicles meant for sophisticated investors – usually private equity firms."* Deals tend to range from around $200 million to over $1 billion in size. Debt financing specialists described *"facilitating loan processes by working with the client to secure the syndicated loan*

On chambers-associate.com...

- More on getting hired at Kirkland
- Interview with firm-wide recruiting committee vice chairs Beth Deeley and Jason Kanner

The Inside View

See firm profile on p.624

Rankings in *Chambers USA*

Advertising	Insurance
Antitrust	Intellectual Property
Appellate Law	International Trade
Banking & Finance	Investment Funds
Bankruptcy/Restructuring	Life Sciences
Capital Markets	Litigation
Climate Change	Media & Entertainment
Corporate Crime &	Outsourcing
Investigations	Private Equity
Corporate/M&A	Products Liability
Energy & Natural	Real Estate
Resources	Securities
Environment	Tax
FCPA	Technology

For detail on ranking tiers and ranking locations, visit
www.chambersandpartners.com

Recent work highlights

- Defended Abbott Laboratories in a False Claims Act suit seeking more than $1 billion
- Advised Baxalta, a biopharmaceutical company, in connection with Shire's $32 billion takeover bid
- Victory for Converse (owned by Nike) against more than 30 companies seeking an order excluding knockoff shoes that infringe Converse's trademark from entering the US
- Victory for Samsung in patent suit brought by Nvidia

IP litigators deal mostly with patent work, with occasional bits of trademark and trade secrets work thrown in. As well as tech clients, the group also works for consumer appliance clients, among others. Juniors reported doing much legal research, writing memos, and *"doc review – though not as much as I expected. It can't be avoided as a junior altogether."* Initial drafting of documents and consulting experts is also part of a junior's work in this group. *"I'm generally not the point person for clients, but I do interact with them, especially for depositions and when we've gone to trial."*

they get." All groups involved some level of due diligence, but many also noted that the firm *"looks to associates to do the first draft of most documents. At first I was surprised as it's so much responsibility so early on, but it's the best way to learn."* Responsibility varies depending on the deal – on 'mega-funds' the *"junior's role is a bit more limited."* Smaller deals involves *"more responsibility, maybe negotiating terms a bit more with lawyers and investors."* On deals with a shorter lifespan, *"you really learn a lot in a short amount of time."* In terms of clients, *"we work with the best of the best."* These include portfolio companies for private equity firms, and larger companies on compliance issues. Juniors had been *"exposed to several different types of companies,"* and considered that to be *"a really valuable experience."* They also experienced being *"the point person for a client on smaller deals."*

"A great thing about this firm is getting real experiences."

Litigators, by contrast, were more likely to work on a more general basis. Cases *"run the whole gamut"* and include securities litigation, mass torts, antitrust, white collar crime, as well as commercial disputes. *"When I started, like any young litigator, I did a lot of doc review, but lately it's been more meeting witnesses and deposition preparation. A great thing about this firm is getting real experiences."* Juniors also assisted at hearings and with matters behind the scene. A DC source highlighted working on SEC investigations. Due to Kirkland's high-flying status, *"we're obviously not a cheap firm, so clients are usually big. Most of our work is done for institutional clients that we've had for years."* With that in mind, juniors admitted that *"in litigation, there's not as much direct client contact on the junior level. It's just the nature of litigation in BigLaw."*

Restructuring sources described their group as a *"hybrid of corporate and litigation. Restructuring is almost never 100% consensual from top to bottom, so we do a lot of motion practice, a lot of writing – which corporate attorneys don't always get to do, especially on the persuasive writing side."* Juniors also *"work closely with the litigation team to support the goals we're trying to achieve in a case."* A New Yorker believed that *"if you show aptitude, people are more than happy to give you responsibility,"* and backed that up by noting that *"within months of starting, I was the point person on a work stream, helping run it."* Interviewees felt it was *"nice to have ownership of something and develop your expertise."*

Hours & Compensation

The lack of an official billing target meant that most sources billed anywhere between 2,000 and 2,500 hours. *"We're so busy that I don't even have to focus on an actual number – it always hits or exceeds expectations."* Others believed that the lack of target meant *"more focus on quality of work than hours."* Despite the naturally high-billing culture, *"it's not a face-time firm – if you're given responsibility, they just trust you to get it done."* As a result, many reported going home for dinner, then logging back on for a bit afterward. This flexibility was popular: *"It's infinitely better than firms where the partner is walking in around at 9am, seeing who's in. The quality of my work isn't necessarily great at 9am, but it's fine to come in later here."*

See firm profile on p.624

The Inside View

Diversity	Partners (%)	Associates (%)
Women	22.8	36
White	88.6	76.8
Black/African American	1.5	2.4
Hispanic/Latin American	3	5.5
Asian	5.7	13.2
Mixed/Other	1.3	2.1
LGBT	2.6	4.8

"You feel like you're really being compensated for the work you've done, and you feel recognized."

Experiences differed when it came to striking a work-life balance. One junior laughed: *"I'm a junior associate at a big law firm. There's no such thing."* Others said *"it's a matter of setting boundaries – you've got to plan ahead if you want to maintain your personal life."* But one thing people agreed on was that the compensation is *"definitely the best part."* Bonuses are famous for usually being above market. *"If you're talented and doing good work, you'll walk away with a very nice bonus. You feel like you're really being compensated for the work you've done, and you feel recognized."*

Culture & Offices

"We have pride of work here. We want to do the most interesting work and want to do it better than anyone else." Juniors have an entrepreneurial flair, with *"people who are looking to take on responsibility early in their career."* Fellow attorneys are *"normal people who work hard and like to win cases."* Many felt the people were also very *"warm and welcoming,"* and although *"partners will be demanding in terms of quality of work and getting stuff done, everyone is nice even when setting the bar high."* Despite the firm's 'Type A' reputation, it's not as internally competitive as one might think: *"I thought people here would throw me under the bus, but everyone's got each other's backs."*

Kirkland's seven domestic offices stretch from coast to coast, and there are five international offices. A Cali source felt: *"The East and West Coasts operate differently – we're more chilled on the West Coast."* LA is generally considered a *"litigator's town,"* though sources reckoned the office was split 50/50 between litigation and corporate. On the other hand, San Fran hosts mostly transactional attorneys, and the Big Apple is reportedly becoming more corporate-focused. DC, based near the Supreme Court, has a large number of litigators. They will be moving to new digs in 2019, but for now, a popular aspect of the *"70s-style office"* is the free breakfast: *"It gives a pep to your step in the morning."* New York is currently mid-way through renovations, and one visible change is the *"360-degree view of midtown."* The firm's HQ is in Chicago, and every junior that has seen it agreed: *"The Chicago office is beautiful."* It also has a gym that's free to use for attorneys.

Training & Development

"One reason I really like it here is because they're very serious about training." New starters jet off to one office for general training, followed by practice-specific training. Ongoing practice area training sessions are delivered through the firm's Kirkland Institute program – the Kirkland Institute for Trial Advocacy for litigators, and the Kirkland Institute of Corporate Practice for transactional associates. Trial advocacy is made up of *"on-your-feet training and experience,"* *"deposition training,"* and *"mock trials."* Corporate juniors reported video conferences about *"general corporate matters"* as well as lunch trainings. *"I wish I could do more, but it can be hard to make time for it, especially when you have 50 other billable things to do."* Either way, at Kirkland there's *"lots of training, for good or bad."*

Pro Bono

Pro bono is *"such a part of the culture here,"* according to juniors. There's no cap on hours: *"I billed 300 hours of pro bono last year and it all counted toward my bonus."* The aim is for all associates to hit at least 20 pro bono hours. Matters have included immigration cases (on the rise right now), veterans' work, identity theft, and cases being considered for clemency. *"It can be difficult when our client matters are so busy – it can be harder to find the extra hours to do pro bono."* That said, *"everyone is happy to do it."*

Pro bono hours
- For all US attorneys: 109,481
- Average per US attorney: 66.6

Diversity

Kirkland associates have seen a *"huge push"* on the diversity front. However, many noted that *"while there's commitment, there's still progress to be made."* Many thought the firm *"very strong for women,"* with the Women's Leadership Initiative being particularly active, getting together *"almost weekly."* One female source explained that *"the partners leading the program are really inspiring, and it's good to know they're here."* As for ethnic diversity, *"we need more minorities – there's no other way to say it. But my understanding is that it's a priority."* The firm was also described as *"extremely LGBT-friendly,"* putting on various discussions and seminars.

See firm profile on p.624

The Inside View

Strategy & Future

Interviewees reckoned that when it came to making partner, *"if it's something you want and make clear that you want it, people will be honest with you about your chances."* Many juniors noticed the growth specifically in the corporate department. *"Some in litigation feel that's not a good thing,"* but *"corporate seems to be more of a revenue driver."* Others highlighted *"expanding the firm's international presence, with a lot of global work in Asia especially."*

Recruiting committee vice chairs Beth Deeley and Jason Kanner confirm the firm's continued growth. *"With such a huge restructuring practice, we're a little less sensitive to economic downturn. There will probably be a recession, but we're a little less concerned because our practice is so diversified. Litigation will be steady regardless, and corporate is currently booming, but if there's a downturn, restructuring will be booming."*

Several sources felt that *"spark and initiative go a long way"* at Kirkland. See more about getting hired at Kirkland at chambers-associate.com

See firm profile on p.624

Kramer Levin Naftalis & Frankel LLP

Lawyers per state

Largest US office: New York
US offices: 2
International offices: 1
First-year salary: $180,000
Billable hours: 1,950 target
Summers 2017: 18 (16 2Ls, 1 1L, 1 SEO)
Revenue 2016: $352 million (+6%)
Partners made in 2017: 3
Famous for: friendly work environment; advertising litigation; LGBT and pro bono initiatives

It's BigLaw but not too big; a New York litigation hot-shot but *"not so uptight"* – there's a nice balance to life at Kramer Levin.

IF you're going to sell a razor that claims to 'shave as well or better than a Mach 3', you'd better make sure it does, or you'll have Kramer Levin all over you like, er, a shaving rash. This was one recent case Kramer Levin fought on behalf of Gillette. A stream of fascinating cases – from defamation to misinterpreted pregnancy tests – flows through the firm's advertising litigation department, making it one of the very top in the country.

The firm's litigation department ventures way beyond advertising, of course, and wins commendation from *Chambers USA*, as do its teams in bankruptcy, capital markets, immigration and several others.

"A nice compromise on the big firm idea."

The firm has come a long way since 1968, when it had just 14 lawyers and full-service ambitions. It now numbers nearly 300 attorneys, with bases in the Silicon Valley and Paris as well as its Big Apple HQ. Associates appreciated that this isn't a whale of a law firm, nor a Manhattan shark tank – more of a canny koi carp with a genial personality. *"It's a nice compromise on the big firm idea – while we're a large firm, it has a better feel than a 1000-person firm. I feel a connection to the whole firm."* A

junior noted that *"when I interviewed here I got a really good vibe, I felt it wasn't so uptight."*

The Work

On the summer program, students can sample work from across departments. At the end of the summer, the firm doesn't give department-specific offers, but students' preferences are taken into account. Shortly before they arrive to begin full-time work, newcomers find out what department they'll join. While some sources didn't like the general offers system, others weren't concerned about it: *"I personally had nice experiences with a number of groups during my summer, so I thought I'd be happy wherever they placed me."*

Kramer's litigation and corporate groups take the most juniors overall, while most of the rest go to intellectual property, real estate and creditors' rights (bankruptcy) teams. The remainder are spread around tax, immigration, environment, financial services and the individual client group.

Each department has an assigning partner and associates fill out a weekly email detailing their availability. *"In the beginning a lot of work comes through the assigning partner but as you start to work with people they'll come back to you for other projects."* Reassuringly, the assigning partner is always there as *"a good resource if you're slow."* A junior in the corporate department remarked that *"I get an appropriate amount of work, although the work*

On chambers-associate.com...

- Training & Development at Kramer Levin

The Inside View

See firm profile on p.625

Rankings in *Chambers USA*

Advertising	Immigration
Bankruptcy/Restructuring	Litigation
Capital Markets	Real Estate
Corporate/M&A	Tax

For detail on ranking tiers and ranking locations, visit www.chambersandpartners.com

Recent work highlights

- Acted for the congregation of the nation's oldest synagogue, Touro Synagogue in Rhode Island, in a four-year dispute with a New York congregation over the ownership of the synagogue and silver bells valued at $7.4 million
- Defended boxing manager Al Haymon against a $100 million antitrust lawsuit filed by boxing promotion company Top Rank
- Represented BlackRock in its acquisition of digital wealth management company Future Advisor

flow is maybe a little inconsistent. It's the industry that's a problem – you can't control when things come up and I've definitely had weeks where I wish I was busier or slower."

> "Sometimes it's just a partner and me, which means I'm doing basically everything."

There's a good variety of work open to litigators and most of our sources had worked on general commercial cases, white collar and government investigations. *"One of my first cases was a large business divorce for a private company involving a lot of contract disputes between commercial parties. Recently I've been doing bankruptcy litigation too."* Typical tasks include *"a lot of research, drafting motions, writing memos or outlines detailing what the state of law is, what cases say and my opinion of whether something can or can't be supported."* Another source mentioned that *"I've had a good range of case sizes. Sometimes it's just a partner and me, which means I'm doing basically everything. Other cases have 20 lawyers on them, so then I'm doing more of the more junior things."* Inevitably doc review is on the agenda.

Meanwhile, over in the corporate department *"we don't have separate groups for M&A and securities, which big firms typically do."* Instead, *"we get exposure to both, so we develop an expertise in general corporate work, which is great."* Most of the clientèle is made up of middle market private companies. *"I've been coordinating with counsel about due diligence, doing legal research and keeping track of documents like the signature pages and the warranties. A lot of it is legal research, and there's some drafting of documents like registration statements for the SEC or resolutions."*

Training & Development

"Everyone is very willing to offer help." Go to chambers-associate.com to read about the training opportunities at Kramer Levin.

Offices

Sources uniformly praised the firm's New York location in midtown Manhattan – *"we're in the center of where law firms should be"* – and felt pleased enough with the office interiors. *"It's very nice although it would never be an exhibit in an architecture museum. In terms of décor it's not the nicest law firm I've ever been to, but it's very pleasant and there's lots of natural light and interesting art prints and lithographs on the walls."* Associates get their own office in the second or third year, but had no complaints about sharing. *"It was really kind of fun and I was sad when my officemate and I had to split up!"*

> "It was really kind of fun and I was sad when my officemate and I had to split up!"

The firm's only other domestic office, in Silicon Valley, has around 15 lawyers and specializes in IP litigation, particularly involving tech and life sciences. Kramer's single international outpost, in Paris, was acquired in 1999 as the unexpected result of Clifford Chance's merger with Roger & Wells. The Paris office of the latter firm decided not to participate in the transaction, so Kramer saw their chance, et tout le monde connaît la suite.

Culture

Nearly all interviewees echoed this: *"The reason I picked the firm was the informal feeling I got when I visited. It's very pleasant and humane: not a harsh, cut-throat place at all."* Another piped up that *"I love it here! The firm wants to foster this cordial environment. Even if I hated the work I'd still love where I worked."* And coming back down to earth for a second: *"Of course, it's not all rainbows and butterflies – there are definitely stressful moments, but that's not because people are driving me crazy or putting me down!"*

> "It's not fratty here."

"There's enough socializing but no huge expectation to spend tons more time away from your personal life," associates agreed. *"I have a few very good friends from my*

See firm profile on p.625

The Inside View

Diversity	Partners (%)	Associates (%)
Women	13.3	40.1
White	91.9	77.9
Black/African American	2	1.2
Hispanic/Latin American	0	4.7
Asian	6.1	13.4
Mixed/Other	0	2.9
LGBT	3.1	3.5

transgender youth. Kramer has longstanding links to domestic abuse charity Her Justice. *"The firm is very pro bono focused,"* insisted juniors. *"Although I doubt they'd be happy if you just did 2,000 hours of it."* That said, associates can undertake a full time pro bono secondment for four months.

Pro bono hours
- For all US attorneys: 19,633
- Average per US attorney: 66

summer class but it's not fratty here. People like working with each other, but don't feel they need to go out drinking all the time. Although maybe they do and I'm not invited!" chuckled an associate. As you'd expect, *"over the summer the social stuff heats up"* and Kramer attorneys hit the town with more regularity. Year-round, there are department-wide social gatherings *"with wine, beer and snacks"* every so often and an associate breakfast.

Hours & Compensation

Associates need to rack up 1,950 hours to get a bonus. This target was introduced in January 2017 in response to associate feedback – the previous target for a full bonus was a hefty 2,150 hours, a figure which associates agreed was too high when we interviewed them in fall 2016. The previous target was described as a *"common gripe"* and we weren't surprised to hear from a recruitment source that there was general jubilation among associates when the new target was introduced.

"I mean, it's a good amount of money but..."

It's typical for associates to arrive in the office around 9.30am or 9.45am and leave at around 7pm or 7.30pm, *"but if I do leave then it's not like I leave and then I'll be totally off; I'm still connected in case anyone needs something."* Of an evening, putting in some time from home is common, as is doing some work at the weekend. On the whole sources were at ease with the work/life balance. *"I would say coming into the firm it was a concern, because I have kids, but outside of a few months where I was overwhelmed with work, nobody has any problems if I leave at 6pm. I've found people to be very respectful of holidays and vacations and they're happy not to bother you. Other attorneys are willing to step in and take over work if necessary."*

Pro Bono

All pro bono hours count toward the bonus target and the *"fact that there's no cap on hours shows that they take it seriously,"* sources felt. All of our interviewees had taken on projects, including divorces, asylum cases, copyright matters and the creation of a non-profit organization for

Diversity

"It's an ongoing process," mused a junior on the subject of diversity at Kramer. *"When I was a summer, there were only four women in my class and one person who counted as diverse. I definitely see a change now – there's a more diverse presence. The firm has a way to go in terms of a female presence at the top, but we're moving in that direction – of the four people who became partners or counsel most recently, two were women. There are discussions about it – they're cognizant of the disparity."* The diversity committee *"puts on lots of interesting lunches. I recently went to one about living with mental illness as part of national disability awareness month."* The firm also has an extensive history of working for LGBT rights: in 1981 it helped to set up the Gay Men's Health Crisis.

"I definitely see a change now."

Get Hired

Juniors reckoned that the firm contains *"a big mix of folk, but what people have in common is that they're grounded, not flashy and out to impress other people. People are confident and self-motivated."* Managing partner Paul Pearlman adds that *"our culture is very important, and we look for those who'll fit in well – enthusiastic, approachable and well-rounded people."*

Strategy & Future

"Our strategy remains the same – we want to remain an independent firm. We're not seeking to grow for growth's sake, because big is not necessarily better – we'll grow organically and through selective lateral hires," Pearlman tells us, noting that the firm brought in three lateral partners in 2016. He adds that it's been a *"pretty active"* year for Kramer across a number of practice areas, including antitrust, white collar (*"we have a number of large ongoing investigations"*), restructuring, corporate, IP and real estate. *"We've also had some big pro bono wins such as protecting the custody and visitation rights of non-biological parents."*

The Inside View

See firm profile on p.625

Latham & Watkins LLP

Lawyers per state

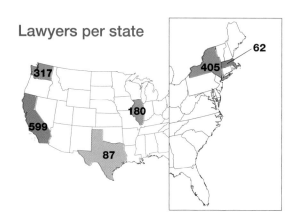

62
405
317
180
599
87

Largest US office: New York
US offices: 11
International offices: 20
First-year salary: $180,000
Billable hours: 1,900 target
Summers 2017: 197 (183 2Ls, 14 1Ls)
Revenue 2016: $2.823 billion (+6.5%)
Partners made in 2017: 36
Famous for: Am Law #1; unassigned junior associates; global reach

Latham & Watkins is a legal kingpin that will appeal to high-fliers keen to discover their own path to practice.

NABBING the top spot in the *Am Law 100* for a second consecutive year, Latham & Watkins bags *"some of the finest and most ground-breaking cases to hit the market,"* according to associates here. Latham is actually one of only four firms to have achieved the distinction of topping *Am Law* over the years, along with Skadden, Baker McKenzie and DLA Piper.

Latham employs over 2,000 attorneys in offices across the US, Europe, the Middle East, and Asia, and has built its name as a world leader in corporate transactions, environmental law, finance matters, litigation and tax services. Almost a third of the California-founded firm's 32 global offices are found in the States, where it earns a wealth of top-tier *Chambers USA* rankings in areas ranging from corporate, life sciences, and real estate matters to white-collar crime.

"If you're up to the task, you're up to the task."

Over the firm's 80 year history, New York has overtaken SoCal as Latham's most populous US hub. Still, associates were keen to reinforce that *"we haven't got an official headquarters, and we don't have satellite offices. There's no pecking order here where there's one money maker and a*

bunch of assistants." It's a model that is reflected in the firm's approach to associate development: *"If you're up to the task, you're up to the task. There's no sense that juniors are here to push paper for three years."*

But for associates, the most celebrated aspect of Latham's training program was undoubtedly the flexibility they'd had to fine-tune their legal interests. Thanks to the firm's 'unassigned' program, juniors *"can take as long as you need to grasp what you want to do."*

The Work

Associates begin life at the firm as 'unassigned' so they can experience different areas, whether that's a variety of corporate assignments or figuring out whether you want to be a deal-doer or litigator. Rookies needn't worry about being forced to sample the whole menu if you arrive with more definite ideas of what you want to do. One source stressed: *"It has to be one of the hallmarks of our training program. Over your first two years here you're welcome to try out work from whichever areas take your interest. If you want to focus on one particular practice, that's fine too. It's a great opportunity to help you realize what you're getting yourself into."* After two years, associates are encouraged to formally align with one of the firm's five core practices: corporate; finance; litigation & trial; tax; and environment, land & resources.

On chambers-associate.com...

- Tips on getting hired by Latham
- Interview with hiring partner Manu Gayatrinath

See firm profile on p.626

The Inside View

Rankings in *Chambers USA*

Antitrust	International Trade
Appellate Law	Investment Funds
Banking & Finance	Latin American Investment
Bankruptcy/Restructuring	Leisure & Hospitality
Capital Markets	Life Sciences
Climate Change	Litigation
Corporate Crime &	Media & Entertainment
Investigations	Outsourcing
Corporate/M&A	Private Equity
Employee Benefits &	Projects
Executive Compensation	Real Estate
Energy & Natural	REITs
Resources	Retail
Environment	Securities
FCPA	Sports Law
Financial Services	Startups & Emerging
Regulation	Companies
Healthcare	Tax
IT & Outsourcing	Technology
Insurance	Telecommunications
Intellectual Property	

For detail on ranking tiers and ranking locations, visit www.chambersandpartners.com

"By your second year you'll have built up a pretty strong bank of contacts at the firm."

Newbies can make use of Latham's formal assigning system, 'The Book', to pick up work. Juniors are staffed on projects based on their availability, but *"by your second year you'll have built up a pretty strong bank of contacts at the firm. They'll reach out to you personally with opportunities they think you'll dig."* Subgroups within the wider practice areas vary in their allocation process; some employ a staffing partner while others require associates to find matters themselves.

Deal-doers told us that *"departments have different approaches to staffing on matters, so the rate of progression can vary between practice groups."* In M&A, for example, *"we work on a lot of incredibly complex deals, so it takes at least a year to get your head round it all. When you start you're more likely to take administrative roles on larger cases, which helps you to understand how different deal structures work."* Once the nuts and bolts are suitably digested, new opportunities arise. *"Your level of responsibility is dictated by your ability,"* added another transactional rookie. Lull periods also offer a window of opportunity. *"When people have a bit of spare time on their hands you'll tend to get more drafting opportunities, as well as follow-up sessions to give you feedback on the work you've produced."*

Recent work highlights

- Helped Emirates Bank quash a $550 million claim raised by US tech company Infospan, which alleged that Emirates Bank misappropriated trade secrets with the intention of engaging in fraudulent activity
- Orchestrated Siemens' $970 million acquisition of CD-adapco, a developer of computer-aided engineering applications
- Represented Southern California Gas in the wake of the Aliso Canyon natural gas leak, that lasted from October 2015 to February 2016. The costs of the leak have been publicly estimated at $665 million

Litigators were similarly pleased with their ascent. *"From the very start my experience here has been fantastic,"* purred one second year. *"Even at an early stage I was doing far more discovery than I was doc review. It wasn't long before I was attending depositions, client meetings in advance of depositions, and witness interviews, and most of my second year classmates have taken a deposition themselves."* Where drafting is concerned, *"clearly there are more opportunities to draft on pro bono cases,"* but another sophomore added: *"I've had plenty of opportunities to draft subpoenas, or assist on drafting motions. We're a big firm that gets great work all round, locally, nationally and internationally. The varying levels of opportunity that scope presents means you can really check all the boxes."*

Pro Bono

Pro bono hours all count toward the billable target, and everyone's expected to do at least 20 hours. *"It's great for when you've got gaps in your schedule,"* one junior asserted. *"Though after a few years that's a relative rarity!"* Rookies were grateful that there's no limit to billing pro bono hours. *"It never feels like pro bono is a waste of time or detrimental,"* said one. Quite the opposite in fact: *"It's a really good way to run your own files,"* with rookies spearheading anything from asylum applications to veterans' benefits appeals.

Pro bono hours
- For all US attorneys: 144,334
- Average per US attorney: 94

Diversity

"You couldn't really describe the firm as diverse, particularly at partner level," admitted several of our sources. When it comes to gender diversity, *"there are lots of women in the junior ranks, but there's a problem when it comes to promotion of female lawyers to partner,"* like there is in all of BigLaw. Still, most agreed that *"the firm is sincerely working to improve the issue,"* and the stats at associate level are decent, with around 20% non-white associates,

See firm profile on p.626

Diversity	Partners (%)	Associates (%)
Women	21	41
White	92	81
Black/African American	1	4
Hispanic/Latin American	3	6
Asian	6	15
Mixed/Other	1	1
LGBT	3	5

for example. There's a *"comprehensive"* range of affinity groups on offer – six in total, covering women, different ethnicities, LGBT and parents – which *"help bring diverse attorneys' struggles into focus."* Latham has also created an impressive number of initiatives to help buck the trend, including a three-day Diversity Leadership Academy for law students and mid-level associates, the Women's Leadership Academy and the associate-led Multicultural Promotion & Attainment Coalition (MPAC).

"The firm isn't where it needs to be, but the arrow is pointing in the right direction."

As such, *"the firm isn't where it needs to be, but the arrow is pointing in the right direction."* In 2016 the firm was shortlisted for the *Chambers USA* diversity awards and in terms of recruiting, there are various diversity scholarships and internships available to students like the 1L Fellowship Program and 2L Diversity Scholars program.

Offices & Training

Interaction between the firm's 11 domestic and 20 international offices is fairly well oiled, and *"though New York is the biggest office, there's no sense that it's the control center bossing everyone else around."* A New Yorker added: *"I regularly work with associates and partners in DC and California. Nothing they say ever betrays a power imbalance between offices, and they're always proud to talk about the work they're taking on and the clients they've won."*

Latham's associate development program *"plays a big part in facilitating cross-office interactions."* A formal academy program sees first, third and fifth-year associates flown out to one location for a series of condensed training sessions and conferences. Summers and partners also attend. First-year academies *"tend to be out in Reston,"* with the third-year top-up typically out in San Francisco.

The academies help bring associates up to speed with what's expected of them over the next couple of years, and introduce new skills to help them develop into the role. First-year attendees *"are introduced to the basics of*

practice, but it's just as much an opportunity to meet people from other offices that you're likely to work with down the line."* Third-years focus more on leadership skills, and are invited to attend the Diversity Leadership Academy with first-year law students and future summer associates. *"The focus of the Diversity Leadership Academy is to build our community and empower future leaders at the firm,"* says immediate past recruiting committee chair Manu Gayatrinath. *"Whether they're already associates here, or first-year law students committed to diversity and inclusion that we hope will bring value to the legal profession."*

"It's very easy to grab a coffee with a partner in your department and talk it over."

Associates overwhelmingly approved the academy program. *"Latham is willing to mobilize large sections of its associate force, and a number of significant partners, to ensure that we receive the best guidance possible,"* raved one. *"For every second of those few days we're not billing a thing, so it must be a big hit. It's a huge commitment to our training, networking and professional development."*

Back in their home offices, first-years' legal education continues through 'core curriculum' sessions. Held every few weeks by partners and associates, these sessions feature presentations on different practice areas and key skills such as drafting and negotiation. Lunchtime seminars are also staged by individual practice groups, covering anything from recent court cases to legal updates in specific areas like leveraged finance. On a more one-to-one basis, associates benefit from a 'buddy mentor' – usually a second or third year associate – who *"serves as a great port of call for any 'teething problem' style questions."* Juniors are also assigned a partner mentor, but our sources were keen to point out that *"Latham has a strong culture of informal mentorship"* too, so *"if you're looking to try out a certain type of work it's very easy to grab a coffee with a partner in your department and talk it over."* More formally scheduled catch-ups arise during mid and end of year reviews.

Culture & Hours

Bar a few 'work in progress' comments concerning diversity, associates across the board admitted to being *"surprised at joining such a progressive working environment. White shoe firms carry a reputation as being overly fratty, but that's rarely true of Latham."* Associates are under little pressure to socialize outside of office hours. *"Latham is pretty big, so you're always able to find people who share similar ideas about socializing. Some people love to go out for a drink after a long day, but others will want to spend time with their families. You're under no pressure here."*

See firm profile on p.626

The Inside View

With long hours *"unavoidable,"* this discretionary approach is probably for the best. Nationwide, associates were averaging around twelve hours a day, and we heard plenty of stories of 4am finishes during busy spells. New Yorkers had found that *"Latham is doing its best to improve retention of associates, so instead of beating us to the ground with work, management prioritizes balance. Senior colleagues check in to see how your workload is going, or whether you need any help, and when you're out of the office people respect your privacy."* The office also boasts *"a strong team dynamic,"* so *"even if you're slaving away at 2am to help push through a deal, you won't be left to do it alone."*

"People are feeling more optimistic about retention in the years ahead."

This impression was fairly consistent among associates in Latham's larger offices, but in lesser populated outlets sources offered a few words of caution. *"As work allocation tends to be more informal here, it's important that you keep a keen eye on your workload,"* revealed one Orange County insider. *"Learn to say no when necessary, because there have definitely been cases of superstar juniors overloading themselves and burning out."*

To be bonus eligible associates must reach a target of 1,900 hours, but most of our sources had hit at least the 2,000 mark, with some billing several hundred hours above that. Not meeting the 1,900 means you won't get a bonus, but *"as long as you've worked hard to keep busy when there have been shortfalls, you're at no risk of losing your job."* All in all, *"Latham's efforts to let us balance our work with our personal lives means people are feeling more optimistic about retention in the years ahead. The workload here is heavy, but associates rarely leave to join another firm."*

Strategy & Future

Over the next few years Latham's entry-level hiring should remain fairly stable. Manu Gayatrinath tells us: *"Our summer program usually takes on about 200 new hires. With the firm continuing to top the tables and perform well financially I don't anticipate there being any vast changes to that number in the near future."*

This stability is a product of the firm's multi-disciplinary performance strategy. *"Latham has a broad base of practice groups, and is well-positioned in various markets across the globe,"* Gayatrinath continues. *"A lot of our practice groups perform counter-cyclically, which helps us to weather market ups and downs pretty fluidly. We haven't seen any change in what we are doing from a junior hiring perspective; we offer so many practices that the demand always seems to float at around the same level. There's no intention to shake things up when it comes to hiring."*

"Working here requires drive and self-motivation, but you can never let that come at the expense of mutual respect." Learn more about what the firm looks for on www.chambers-associate.com

See firm profile on p.626

Linklaters

Lawyers per state

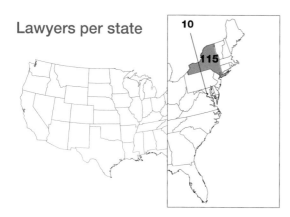

Largest US office: New York
US offices: 2
International offices: 27
First-year salary: $180,000
Billable hours: no requirement
Summers 2017: 26 (25 2Ls, 1 1L)
Revenue 2016: £1.31 billion (+3.1%)
Partners made in 2017: 2 US, 26 globally
Famous for: internationalist outlook and magic circle prestige

This magic circle firm's US operation is a shiny gold Link in its worldwide chain...

"I QUICKLY got the impression that this was one of the few international firms that truly uses all of its resources – there really is the 'one Linklaters' deal across the world." Sources were near unanimous in agreement about what first attracted them to this prestigious magic circle firm (nicknamed 'Links' by its employees): *"I came here for the same reason most people do: I mean I wanted to be a transactional lawyer and I wanted to do top-notch M&A. But mostly I wanted to work on high-level international stuff and that's what you get here. We have very few domestic clients."*

Linklaters has 29 offices and 2,600 lawyers worldwide. However, since its US operation only comprises around 125 lawyers spread between two locations, it can still feel quite cozy: *"We are this big global firm but the New York office is only a hundred or so people. You do recognize basically everyone's face. A big part of the culture is based on that, and the fact that they don't really hire jerks."* They're no jerks when it comes to business either – counting a horde of mega names among their clientèle such as AT&T, Credit Suisse, investment multinational BlackRock and pharma giant Novartis.

The Work
The majority of New York newcomers will end up in investment management, tax, banking, dispute resolution and corporate, with a few lone rangers scattered across antitrust, financial regulation and capital markets (LatAm). The firm recently phased out its system of assigning new recruits to a specific practice group and instead implemented a pool system. As a result, work allocation is becoming *"more informal across the board,"* one corporate associate observed. *"Now we get a list of deals quite regularly and we can then volunteer for the ones we're interested in. Either that or the assigning partners or senior associates just approach certain juniors and request their help."*

Links's investment management team *"is a little bit different from those you'd see in other firms."* They don't work with any mutual funds and mostly work on private ones for large private equity houses. Over in banking *"the most frequent work is arranging US guarantors for British companies that want to borrow money."* On 'network deals' – those not run out of New York – *"once you've done a few as a junior you're sort of allowed to run them yourself."* In litigation, work is likely to involve more variety, as one interviewee reported: *"I started with a breach of contract case for a bank. Now I've done a couple of antitrust cases and several internal investigations. Foreign clients also come to us with concerns about US sanctions."*

On chambers-associate.com...
• Interview with hiring partner Justin Storm

"Substantive work during the day."

See firm profile on p.627

Rankings in *Chambers USA*

Antitrust

Investment Funds

Latin American Investment

For detail on ranking tiers and ranking locations, visit
www.chambersandpartners.com

Perhaps due to the group's small size – *"there are only five partners in litigation, three in New York and two in DC"* – juniors can expect top-notch assignments: *"I've never been overrun just with doc review. Investigations usually have tight timelines so I haven't had to do months and months of it. In most cases, I prefer to get doc review done from my couch after work, and take on substantive work during the day."* In 2013, the firm added a new team to the wider dispute resolution department. The 'International Governance and Development' practice works with clients in developing countries, as well as NGOs focused on international development – further proof, if any was needed, of Linklaters' steadfast commitment to global growth.

Culture

Complementing its internationalism is Linklaters USA's pride in its ties to the old country. As one source opined, the 'British thing' *"affects the culture in a number of ways."* A few associates reported that *"people tend to dress more formally here – I'm not talking top-hat-and-tails but I compare it to other New York firms and both male and female lawyers here usually wear a suit."* On top of that there's *"a drinks cart every Friday, the closing book is called a 'bible', if you don't get stuff in on time they put you on a 'sinners list', and meetings are called 'prayers' – which is funny because no one knows what they are at first and nobody shows up!"* Here at *Chambers Associate* we like to think we do our bit in fostering Anglo-American relations but we can safely say we've never heard of this kind of lingo being used at another UK firm. *"We know playing up the British thing is just a bit of fun, and it's nice to have something that sets the office apart from your average New York BigLaw joint."*

"Though it's a social place, most get-togethers are informal and take place outside the office," juniors told us. In-house, there's the drinks carts, as well as *"popcorn socials and afternoon cakes"* on Wednesday afternoons. The firm also throws *"a pretty good holiday party toward the end of the year."* In 2015, *"it was at Chelsea Piers; there was a lavish dinner and then we all danced till 2am."* In 2016, it was held at the Estrela Penthouse at Le Parker Meridien.

Hours & Compensation

When it comes to working hours, Links dances to a different tune to most of its city rivals. Days rarely extend past 10pm with most sources echoing this associate: *"I*

Recent work highlights

- Advised Steinhoff – a South African retailer of household goods – on the acquisition of Mattress Firm, the largest speciality bedding retailer in the US, for $3.8 billion
- Advised Visa Europe on the sale of 100% of its share capital to Visa in a deal worth approximately €21.2 billion
- New York bankruptcy team currently advising Wells Fargo on a number of important mandates including Project Sabine – a roadmap for practitioners looking to value oil and gas assets in today's highly volatile market
- LatAm team has recently acted on a number of the first transactions in the re-opening of the Argentine capital markets, advising banks on provincial debt issuances and corporate issuances

don't really have late nights, like past ten or 11pm, but I do quite often work on the weekend." Sources attributed the less punishing hours to the British influence and *"a culture that's averse to ruining people's evenings and weekends for no reason."* That said, if you do end up staying past eight during the winter, the firm gets you dinner and a cab home, a perk that you earn after nine during the balmy summer months.

> *"A culture that's averse to ruining people's evenings and weekends for no reason."*

Interviewees appreciated that the firm doesn't impose a billable target – *"literally no one's ever told me you should be hitting this many hours."* And most agreed that *"as long as you're doing the same amount as those around you, you don't feel under pressure to take on extra assignments."* This casual approach extends to remuneration: *"Salaries are completely lockstep as are bonuses, which are tied to the Cravath scale."*

Pro Bono

Partners see pro bono as *"a good way for associates to get their feet wet"* and so encourage it from your summer onwards. The following response was not uncommon: *"I worked on 50 hours of pro bono last year and that's pretty typical for junior associates. We constantly get emails with opportunities and if someone's working on a pro bono deal he or she will often ask for help."* As for those opportunities, a lot of work comes through New York Lawyers in the Public Interest (NYLPI) and the Urban Justice Center. Juniors have also started giving legal assistance to the MinKwon Center for Community Action – a nonprofit that helps out in New York's Korean community.

Pro bono hours
- For all US attorneys: 4,236
- Average per US attorney: 34

The Inside View

See firm profile on p.627

Diversity	Partners (%)	Associates (%)
Women	14	43
White	86	59
Black/African American	2	2
Hispanic/Latin American	5	6
Asian	2	5
Mixed/Other	2	7
LGBT	7	6

Training & Development

Links's summer is the first opportunity for feet-wetting as associates dip their toes on both sides of the pond. Rookies can request to split their time, with five weeks spent in any two of the following locations: New York, London or Hong Kong, and occasionally other locations (e.g. Frankfurt). In between the split, newbies worldwide descend on the London HQ for a long weekend of socializing and training. Sources agreed that the former was more useful than the latter, *"because there are lawyers from so many different jurisdictions a lot of the stuff which is UK-specific doesn't relate."*

"Lawyers from so many different jurisdictions."

Once they get back to home base, there are regular practice-specific training sessions. If these don't suffice *"there's also a pretty comprehensive list of courses online and if you sign up to any of those they'll fly you to London to take part."* There used to be just one formal appraisal for associates but *"now we have quarterly informal reviews – the idea is to be able to catch things that could potentially be issues early on."* But never fear, *"it's all still fairly informal – at the end of the year you write a self-review and nominate people to deliver it."*

Offices

Juniors were slightly critical of Links's Big Apple home, which is right in the middle of a cluster of BigLaw names in Midtown. *"It's not not nice, just a bit shabby. I mean we've got views of the park, which is great, but I think the lease is up in a couple of years and right now it'd be nice to move into the next space."* Another associate clarified those remarks: *"The building isn't run down or anything but the administrative staff aren't great – it takes a while to get something fixed."*

The firm's DC office, which at time of writing has one first-year associate, occupies half of a small building on the city's South Side. This base is a bit more mod – *"a client the other day said it looks like the Apple Store."* For the moment the DC office isn't large enough to stage a comprehensive summer program.

Diversity

Linklaters actively promotes its internationalism and it's for this reason that many sources thought it *"does better at diversity than many other NYC firms."* There is an ever increasing contingent of Mandarin-speaking lawyers, but really *"people here are from all over the place."* On top of this there's an *"incredibly active"* women's committee that organizes regular networking events, a monthly breakfast and a book club where women come together and talk about their work and experience of the firm. There are also affinity groups for LGBT and ethnic minority lawyers – Linklaters offers a number of placement opportunities to 1Ls from these two groups.

Get Hired

As we alluded to above, speaking a second, third, or even fourth language is a mega plus during the Linklaters recruitment process. Justin Storms – the firm's hiring partner – explains the current strategy: *"Part of what we've done this year, at the request of our Hong Kong office, is to focus on recruiting fluent Mandarin speakers who can support our China-facing work."*

That said, monoglots need not be too disheartened: *"It's by no means necessary to be proficient in another language, and what we're looking for first and foremost is whether someone has an affinity with Linklaters and will work well in this environment."*

Strategy

Due to the fact that *"London is very much the headquarters"* of Linklaters, recent uncertainty due to the Brexit vote has obviously affected the whole firm. However, rather than be caught off guard, the powers that be had been planning for all eventualities – *"we were briefed on the potential consequences before the result and afterwards we set up a war room to help advise American clients with British interests."* As Justin Storms puts it: *"We know there'll be long-term uncertainty but for a law firm such as ours this can actually present a lot of opportunities."*

See firm profile on p.627

Mayer Brown LLP

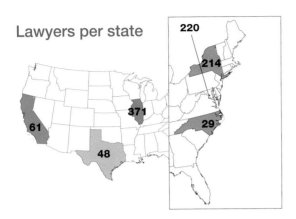

Lawyers per state

220
214
371
61
29
48

Largest US office: Chicago
US offices: 7
International offices: 13
First-year salary: $180,000
Billable hours: 2,000 required (2,100 to be bonus eligible)
Summers 2017: 60 (53 2Ls, 3 1Ls, 4 3Ls)
Revenue 2016: $1.26 billion (+0.2%)
Partners made in 2017: 21 globally (17 in US)
Famous for: Chicago institution; intellectual culture

As Chicagoan Mayer Brown keeps spreading across the map, its associates get to plot their own path.

"I THINK the firm is in a very impressive stage of growth right now," one of our junior sources told us. We'd have to agree. Look beyond the historic Chicago HQ and muscular US network which spans from East to West, and you'll still see Mayer Brown's influence stretching over the horizon. *Chambers USA* ranks no fewer than 25 practice areas nationwide, plus many more state-by-state. The latest addition is a new Dubai office, opened in 2016 to become its first Middle East base, only a year after the lights were switched on in Mexico City. Mayer Brown also has numerous well-established offices in Asia and Europe. Back on US soil, the DC office not long ago hired an entire consumer financial services team – over 30 lawyers – from K&L Gates.

"People are appreciative, and intelligent."

However, neither the recent growth spurt nor the go-getting free market system of work allocation alter the fact that *"people here are genuinely nice,"* associates told us. *"People here work hard, but I've appreciated the recognition I've got for working long hours. After a late night,*

or a weekend of work, partners will reach out. People are appreciative, and intelligent."

The Work

The two most populated groups are finance and litigation, each taking roughly a quarter of the cohort on our interviewee list. Not far behind was the corporate & securities group, while the remainder were scattered sparsely through real estate, IP, tax transactions & consulting, government & global trade, tax controversy, bankruptcy & insolvency, financial services regulation, and employment & benefits. During their summer program, newbies can try work from any of these practice groups, after which they make a decision on which practice area to join full time.

Most of our interviewees accessed work through a free market system. *"You have to be willing to ask for what you want. But you also don't get stuck with assignments you're not interested in."* Our sources were quick to note that *"there's zero negative energy"* around the search for work: *"There's no competitiveness."* The system provides associates freedom to choose who they work with, though *"you can get trapped quite quickly. When you're good at something, people want to keep staffing you on it."* Furthermore, associates tend to *"find who they like working with in the first year and stick with that."* Being less regimented, the system also had associates telling us that often the *"work is not evenly distributed."* An exception is the finance group in New York, where *"the firm implemented*

On chambers-associate.com...

- Interview with managing partner Ken Geller
- We talk to national hiring partner Brad Keck
- More on recruitment from associates

See firm profile on p.628

Rankings in *Chambers USA*

Antitrust	Insurance
Appellate Law	Intellectual Property
Banking & Finance	International Trade
Bankruptcy/Restructuring	Labor & Employment
Capital Markets	Latin American Investment
Communications	Litigation
Corporate/M&A	Outsourcing
Employee Benefits &	Products Liability
Executive Compensation	Projects
Environment	Real Estate
Financial Services	Tax
Regulation	Technology
Government	Transportation
Immigration	

For detail on ranking tiers and ranking locations, visit
www.chambersandpartners.com

Recent work highlights

- Represented HSBC in an antitrust matter against claims that competition was infringed in the trading of interest swaps
- Advised the California High Speed Rail Authority on the proposed state-wide high speed rail network
- Represented Tyco International, a security systems company, over $3 billion in potentially deductible interest paid to a Swiss finance company
- Successfully represented multinational Cargill to dismiss a price-fixing class action regarding the sale of road salt in Ohio

a system with an assigning partner who will manage your workload so that one person isn't overloaded and the work is spread more evenly."

"You have to be willing to ask for what you want."

Finance associates described *"primarily representing large financial institutions: banks, private equity funds etc. It's very broad: acquisition finance, securitizations – that's one of the shining stars of our practice – also project finance. As a first-year you start with closing checklists, edits and stuff like that. Once you show you can do that you can start drafting primary transaction documents or investor memos."* Associates had also taken part in client calls and deal negotiations.

Over in litigation, the work can be anything from mortgage-backed securities cases and fraud to breach of contract, antitrust and environmental matters. The work also threw up international travel opportunities for quite a few associates, regularly flying to Paris or taking a working sojourn to Singapore. *"There's absolutely no jealousy about people going to France or Spain!"* one associate joked. When on US soil, associates are certainly familiar with doc review, though one believed that *"every time I've had to do it there are mid-levels and seniors doing it too."* More interestingly there are tasks *"going from research and brief writing to trial and witness preparation."*

Training & Development

Training is tailored to junior, mid-level and senior associates. To start with, there's an initial 'Fast Track' training series offering weekly sessions for six months, *"usually at lunch on a Monday."* These cover *"skills which are applicable to anyone at the firm, like timekeeping and how*

to deal with partners." Each practice offers more specific training too: *"I get invited to litigation's sessions. They will have one on how to write a motion or a research memo. Some partners will also give talks on very specific issues,"* often covering recent legal developments.

"You need to be proactive."

At the six month mark, associates reach a *"check in point"* to talk over progress with a partner. Normally the formal reviews take place only once a year – a little too infrequent for some associates who felt *"they should check in more than once a year to see that we are getting enough opportunities."* More informally, associates told us they *"get a good amount of feedback on a day to day basis from senior associates and partners,"* though some felt *"you need to be proactive. If I reach out for feedback everyone has been good."* Juniors get assigned an associate and partner mentor, but we heard that *"because of the free market system everyone starts to look to the people they work for instead."* The firm also provides an internal career coach.

Offices & Strategy

Our list of junior associates showed that nearly half of them had joined the firm's original – and largest – office in Chicago, while around a quarter were in New York. DC takes the next largest number, and the remaining few associates are spread between posts in Charlotte, Palo Alto, LA and Houston. Chicagoans told us the office is *"in the process of renovation,"* including *"replacing the internal walls with glass."* One told us their *"favorite feature is the fact we have desks which you can automatically raise or lower. In terms of renovated space, they are trying to encourage more areas for people to hang out, so the lounge area is much more open. It's almost done!"* They've also got a cafeteria and a gym in the building, though lawyers' fitness fanaticism isn't subsidized.

"New and very modern."

See firm profile on p.628

The Inside View

Diversity	Partners (%)	Associates (%)
Women	19.7	41.8
White	90.8	75.0
Black/African American	1.2	3.0
Hispanic/Latin American	3.7	4.0
Asian	2.7	13.0
Mixed/Other	1.7	5.0
LGBT	2.4	3.3

New York's lawyers have only recently settled into their home, having switched to a spot on Avenue of the Americas in 2015. The office is *"connected to the Rockefeller Center, and we have a tunnel underneath with plenty of food options. It's nice not to have to leave the building when it's snowing or raining."* Inside, *"it's new and very modern,"* said one source. *"We have four floors and each floor is the size of an avenue block so it is quite big. One floor is just dedicated to client space, so we have a lot more events here."* Like Chicago, *"everything inside is glass – so you know who's in."* Unlike Chicago, however, where associates get their own office from day one, New Yorkers are in the sharing game for a year or two. Elsewhere, DC is notable for being *"very architecturally interesting."* We hear that *"everyone in DC knows it as the building with the night-club lobby as it's always changing color."*

"The night-club lobby."

Mayer Brown's timeline has of late been dotted with office opening after office opening – Mexico City and Dubai being the most recent. Another trend has been the *"steady stream of laterals,"* including the K&L Gates hires. Managing partner Ken Geller comments: *"From our standpoint it was opportunistic. We had lawyers who knew people over there, and we heard that they were thinking about a move. We got on their radar, they talked to us and we're really happy they came here."* The firm also recently added the ex-GC of Fiat Chrysler to its Chicago office.

Culture

"I'd say people are quite relaxed here," said one associate. *"They're not snobby or very uppity. You can talk to anyone at a social event. People are understanding about your personal situations, but at the same time people take work quite seriously and people are pretty hardworking."* Another called it *"friendly but professional."* However, many associates fell short of anything concrete, telling us *"it's just a bit of a grab bag: there's not a unified culture here. It's a collection of smart individuals who are maybe a little more introverted – but they're all traits common among lawyers. We're a little more introverted, a little more of the smart, intellectual type, but other than that I'm not sure."* Others put it this way: *"The firm embraces its nerdy persona.*

People here are smart and love what they're doing. There's a sense of camaraderie around the work itself."

"Friendly but professional."

Amid *"plenty of different types of people"* and the cornucopia of lawyerly styles, associates *"hit it off with certain partners."* While *"some are a lot more old school and want to sit down and talk things through; others are much younger – so we text a lot."* In fact, *"it can be as simple as whether a partner likes to get their work done in the morning."* Ultimately, *"you end up gravitating to who you vibe with."* How better to sense someone's vibe than in a videocall? *"Our office phones have a camera in them,"* associates informed us. *"It's nice to be able to see the person you're talking to, especially people in other offices."* Aside from regular happy hours in each office, a social highlight in Chicago is *"the annual attorney outing in the summer. It used to be at a country club years ago, but it was at a rooftop bar this year with a casino, a raffle and games."* Most associates agreed, however, that *"by and large most people's social life exists outside the firm."*

Hours & Compensation

Compensation is calculated using a rather complex system. In order to remain in good standing at the firm and advance to the next level in the pay scale, associates need to bill 2,000 working hours. That also includes pro bono, business development and recruiting work, and training sessions. However, there is a subset of the working hours – which the firm refers to as 'creditable hours' – which almost exclusively consists of billables and up to 200 pro bono hours. Associates have to rack up 2,100 creditable hours for a bonus in all offices apart from New York, where the hours threshold is not set in stone. It's *"a different system with no written policy – that can be worrisome."* In general though, associates found their targets achievable – *"it's not something that haunts me."*

"It's not something that haunts me."

In all offices, days lasting from 9am to 7pm were the norm, while the longer stretches synonymous with BigLaw also feature. *"The firm is not big on facetime,"* but exceptionally busy periods had required all-nighters from some associates. *"Here's the thing: everyone was still here at three in the morning,"* recalled one associate. *"It was a team atmosphere, all hands on deck. If you're up, I'm up."* Thankfully, most associates told us they felt entirely comfortable taking a couple of weeks' vacation: *"You just have to make sure it's not inconvenient."*

See firm profile on p.628

The Inside View

Pro Bono

Mayer Brown is signed up to the 'Law Firm Pro Bono Challenge,' which means it dedicates at least 3% of its billable hours to pro bono. Junior associates are expected to bill at least 60 hours, while *"the cap is at 200 hours – but I know people who do more than that."* A fair few of our interviewees had reached that cap, but most hovered around the 60 hour mark. *"I think it's huge, especially in litigation,"* said one associate. *"It is a way for the firm to get me involved and get me good experience early on."*

"We have a pro bono coordinator and she sends out opportunities from time to time," explained associates. Juniors had worked on a variety of matters, including *"working at an organization to help pensioners be able to access Medicare,"* working for Lawyers for the Creative Arts, tackling immigration cases, writing appellate briefs and helping people learn election laws.

Pro bono hours
- For all US attorneys: 52,608
- Average per US attorney: 60

Get Hired

"Obviously it's hard, and in no way a science, but even on campus one thought in our heads is: 'is this a partner to be some day?'" For the full interview with national hiring partner Brad Keck and more insight into recruitment go to chambers-associate.com.

Diversity

"I think it's becoming diverse," said one associate tellingly. *"Everything starts from the beginning."* While they struck a tone of optimism, juniors stressed that the firm *"needs to do more on retention and promotion,"* telling us *"the partnership skews pretty heavily male."* Across the board, the firm's figures are fairly average compared to the rest of BigLaw – but a diversity committee, headed up by Jerry DeBerry is in charge of amending that. Associates mentioned several *"affinity groups"* for minorities including a *"women's forum that has been around for a very long time. They have monthly meetings as well as splitting up into smaller mentoring groups."* There's also *"a diversity retreat every two years,"* held most recently *"in a Chicago hotel: people from all the offices flew in for three days. There was a program of events and lots of speakers, plus workshops on leadership issues."* The firm also offers four $15,000 scholarships to diverse members of its summer class.

See firm profile on p.628

The Inside View

McDermott Will & Emery LLP

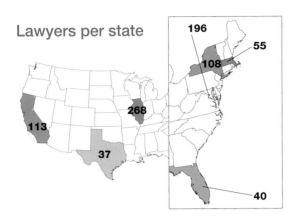

Lawyers per state

196
55
108
268
113
37
40

Largest US office: Chicago

US offices: 10

International offices: 8 (plus strategic alliance in Shanghai)

First-year salary: $180,000

Billable hours: 2,000 hours (target)

Summers 2017: 41 (37 2Ls, 4 1Ls)

Revenue 2016: $908.7 million

Partners made in 2017: 34

Famous for: being a healthcare whiz; Chicago roots; penchant for all things tax-related

The winds of change are circling around Chicago-born McDermott, which has a new chairman focused on growth and is hiring those in touch with their inner-Bruce Springsteen (we'll explain...)

McDERMOTT may have started as a humble Chicagoan tax practice, but banish notions of hushed offices and intense folk poring over dry statutes; this is a bustling global outfit where, as new chairman Ira Coleman – elected in September 2016 – explains, *"people can have fun at work – we say 'bring all your weirdness' and don't be a different person here to who you are at home."*

Associates agreed, adding that *"there's not a one-size-fits-all"* approach at the firm, which spreads its kooky know-how across ten domestic and eight international offices – seven in Europe and one in South Korea. In the US, McDermott's top-ranked healthcare practice is one of its star performers, but *Chambers USA* also bestows cream of the crop status on the firm's wealth management and food & beverages expertise. Other areas of strength include McDermott's perennial tax practice, as well as its corporate M&A, privacy, IP, commercial litigation and labor and employment work.

" We say 'bring all your weirdness.'"

Sources did point to McDermott's traditional rep as *"a conservative Chicago firm,"* but with Coleman at the helm it looks like any trace of that tag will be snuffed out once

On chambers-associate.com...

- Interview with new chairman Ira Coleman

and for all: *"We want to embrace and drive change, to be adventurous, creative and open-minded,"* vows Coleman. And while many of our interviewees came to McDermott with a specific practice in mind, Coleman will be pushing a more collaborative model of specialization: *"If you want to be good you've got to be a specialist, but you also need to learn to work in teams as our clients' problems are becoming increasingly complex and cross all kinds of practice groups."*

Strategy & Future

What else is on the agenda? *"We're going to focus on the areas where we are indispensable to our clients, and make ourselves even more indispensable,"* says Coleman. These areas, he adds, are known as the firm's *"power alleys,"* and cover *"trial and big ticket litigation; private equity and M&A; and health."* Further focus comes in the form of McDermott's key growth markets in New York and London, but the firm will also be *"continuing to grow out"* its west coast practice – especially in Silicon Valley.

"We're going to focus on areas where we are indispensable."

The Work

Every incoming associate joins a particular practice group. McDermott's corporate advisory group housed the largest percentage of second and third-year juniors (23%), followed closely by the firm's trial and health

See firm profile on p.629

The Inside View

Rankings in *Chambers USA*

Antitrust	Intellectual Property
Banking & Finance	Labor & Employment
Corporate/M&A	Life Sciences
ERISA Litigation	Litigation
Employee Benefits & Executive Compensation	Outsourcing
	Privacy & Data Security
Food & Beverages	Tax
Healthcare	Technology
Insurance	

For detail on ranking tiers and ranking locations, visit www.chambersandpartners.com

Recent work highlights

- Acted for healthcare system operator Steward during a $1.25 billion transaction with Alabama-based REIT Medical Properties Trust
- Advised German chemical company Evonik on its $3.8 billion acquisition of Air Products & Chemicals performance materials unit
- Secured a $13.5 million patent infringement award from South Korean company SBM on behalf of client Cummins-Allison, a manufacturer of high speed currency processing equipment

---

industry advisory groups. The remaining juniors were spread sparsely between a variety of groups, including private client, tax, regulatory and government strategies.

An informal approach to work assignment reigns across the practices. There is a safety net in the form of each practice's office head, who looks out for juniors in case they are under or over-burdened. The balance seems to be just right though, according to the majority of our sources: *"There is plenty of work to go around, and to be honest I haven't had to ask anyone for work; people approach me with assignments."* Some groups also have a *"busyness tracer,"* so *"if you're swamped you can indicate that you don't need any work, but if you're light you can give people the go ahead."*

"There is plenty of work to go around."

There are *"two primary arms"* in the corporate advisory group: *"M&A/private equity and finance."* Real estate and bankruptcy also fall under this group – although fresh-faced juniors don't tend to have exposure to these areas. *"Usually you're staffed on deals with two to four people. When you start out you draft more ancillary documents, like security certificates and escrow agreements, but as you progress on smaller deals it gets more hands-on and you start to produce first drafts of key documents like the purchase agreement."*

Over in the health industry advisory practice there are several 'affinity groups' to explore: *"We have an antitrust group, a fraud and abuse group, a hospitals and health systems group, a digital health group – it really runs the gamut!"* Juniors are encouraged to sample various areas before narrowing their field as they approach mid-level status. With lots to delve into, the work is unsurprisingly varied: *"You might conduct diligence on transactions, or contribute to a compliance project by analyzing HIPAA policies, or work on getting an entity Medicaid certification."*

Trial juniors also start out with a broad remit. *"You do a lot of commercial cases like contract disputes, as well*

as class actions, but you can also branch out into white collar work and collaborate with our private client group on fiduciary litigation."* Our eager-eyed sources found themselves *"doing a lot of research and writing up memos for partners, but also drafting court filings like discovery responses and pleadings, combined with some interaction with clients."*

Training & Development

It's all goal, goal, goal at McDermott: each year associates compile a career development plan using a set of key competencies tailored to their class year and practice. *"It's a really helpful exercise. Everyone picks five goals from the list of competencies, which is incredibly detailed: it has every law you should be learning and every document you should be drafting."*

"Everyone picks five goals."

"There's a lot of great training," to help juniors tick off those goals. McDermott University hosts sessions *"at least once a week: you can pick and choose what you want to attend, whether it's a general training on public speaking or a webinar on a legal update of interest."* These are supplemented by quarterly practice group trainings, which are class-tailored and mandatory. *"For example, all the trial associates went to DC for a two-day deposition training, while the corporate juniors gathered in New York for a two-day negotiation exercise."*

Offices

Together Chicago and DC housed 60% of the juniors on our list. Sources still considered the former to be the symbolic heart of the firm: *"When people think about McDermott they think of Chicago; the firm leadership is by and large here, and we're still the largest office in the network,"* confirmed one Windy City resident. Juniors here were looking forward to their imminent move to the brand new River Point skyscraper, a *"sleek, curved building with glass interior walls!"* The atmosphere was deemed *"more chillax"* than the *"serious"* DC office – the

See firm profile on p.629

The Inside View

Diversity	Partners (%)	Associates (%)
Women	29.7	52.7
White	82.9	61.4
Black/African American	1.7	4
Hispanic/Latin American	2.5	4.5
Asian	6.8	9.5
Mixed/Other	0.01	1.8
LGBT	2.3	2.7

next largest. *"That's more a reflection of the DC vibe as a whole though,"* clarified an associate here.

New chairman and former head of the Miami office Ira Coleman clearly has an eye for a good layout: *"Ira designed the entire office – it's modern and beautiful and overlooks the ocean!"* one Miamian raved. The office is set to become a template for the rest of McDermott: *"Ira wants to replicate the Miami culture throughout the firm. It's warm and friendly; we go on boat trips together and Ira takes us all out for happy hours after work!"* Elsewhere, associates were spread quite evenly between the New York, Boston, Houston, LA and Silicon Valley offices.

Culture

Ira Coleman may well wish to replicate the Miami culture throughout the firm, but he might not have to do much as the pervasive atmosphere sounds pretty warm already. *"People here are smart and nice,"* commented one Chicagoan: *"We work quickly and diligently but partners will make it clear when something is urgent and when it's not."* A colleague in New York agreed: *"At my last firm the firm-scheduled happy hours felt like work, but here they're always nice. Plus, people get together of their own accord too; this past Friday all the corporate associates got together for an informal lunch."*

"This isn't a firm that chews you up and spits you out."

It all reflects a culture where people stay for the long haul, as this LA-based junior suggested: *"A lot of the partners started as summers and have gone on to found new offices. This isn't a firm that chews you up and spits you out; they want to see you learn and grow."* Others pointed to the firm's mentorship program as evidence of this. *"When you start you're assigned a mid or senior-level mentor, and you have an ongoing dialogue with them about your day-to-day work and where you want your career to go."* McDermott's cohort group system also scored praise for breaking down barriers: *"Once a quarter you meet up with people from different practice groups – usually two partners and five associates – and the associates get to dis-* cuss their likes and dislikes, the steps they can take to move forward."*

Hours & Compensation

All associates work to meet a 2,000 hour billing target each year. Most deemed this *"pretty reasonable"* across the locations and practices. To help them get there, juniors can count 100 hours in pro bono and 75 in professional development toward the target.

"Frankly, it's a lot of money."

On average, associates aimed to bill seven to eight hours a day, equating to around ten hours spent in the office or working from home. Of course, *"it all depends on how busy it is"*; as matters heat up in groups like corporate, healthcare and trial, working 12 to 15 hours for a short spell is typical. Other groups, like tax and private client, tend to be *"more stable – so you can expect to work from 9.30am to 7.30pm most days."*

In 2016, McDermott implemented lockstep compensation and matched Cravath's latest salary hike. *"Frankly, it's a lot of money,"* chirped juniors, who also liked the shift to lockstep: *"It's much easier, as everyone knows how it works."* Hitting 2,000 hours grants associates a market-rate bonus, but a discretionary element means there's more up for grabs: *"It's not clear how much more you'll get, but extra hours and good reviews are taken into account."* It also means that those who don't hit the 2,000 hour target can still bag a bonus if they've consistently produced quality work.

Pro Bono

Those extra bonus-bumping hours can come in the form of pro bono: *"Once you hit your 2,000 hour target, you can count all pro bono as billable – a huge incentive, plus you get to help people!"*

"People here do quite the range."

There are pro bono coordinators in each office, and in some cases within practice groups too. *"In Chicago,"* for instance, *"the healthcare pro bono rep makes sure everyone steps up to meet their 20 hour target each year – he'll say we have this percentage of people who've met it and this percentage who haven't, which gets people moving!"*

"People here do quite the range," juniors stated. Indeed, in Boston we heard of associates running a domestic violence clinic; in New York sources had given their time to Volunteer Lawyers for the Arts; and in Chicago the American Health Lawyers Association received a lot of help from the firm.

The Inside View

See firm profile on p.629

Pro bono hours
- For all US attorneys: 46,993
- Average per US attorney: 46

Diversity

Sources flagged the *"excellent LGBT committee and affinity group,"* and also had good things to say when it came to the representation of women at the firm. During the latest partnership promotion round, 47% (16 of 34) of new appointments were women. The larger offices have formal women's initiatives, like the one in New York, where *"we do charity fundraisers, holiday parties, talks, poker nights – it's great to develop relationships with the partners."* In the smaller offices, like Miami, *"there's not a formal initiative, but all of the women know and support each other."* Sources did feel, however, that there's *"still a lot of work to be done"* when it comes to racial and ethnic diversity: *"I'm one of only a handful of lawyers of color in my office,"* one associate commented.

Get Hired

When it comes to catching McDermott's attention, the more Bruce you are the better. After observing Springsteen vigorously preparing for a concert in Philadelphia, chairman Ira Coleman thought: *"'Here's Bruce, 67 years old, worth hundreds of millions – why does he need to practice?' And the only reason is because he's passionate: every night he wants himself and the band to perform better than the night before. I want to hire people like that – people who want to constantly get better."*

"Why does he need to practice?'"

Aside from emulating New Jersey's finest, you better come down to earth too, as humility is a key virtue at McDermott: *"You can't ask someone straight out in an interview whether they're humble or not as they'll say 'of course I am!'"* quips Coleman. *"So what I do – even if someone's come through all of the interview rounds with the highest ratings – is ask our receptionists and staff if the candidate was nice to them. Nobody gets through if our receptionists and staff don't think they're nice."*

To learn more about becoming a lawyer in Chicago, visit chambers-associate.com

Milbank, Tweed, Hadley & McCloy

Lawyers per state

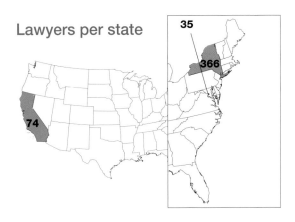

35
366
74

Largest US office: New York
US offices: 3
International offices: 9
First-year salary: $180,000
Billable hours: no requirement
Summers 2017: 86 (84 2Ls, 2 others)
Revenue 2016: $855.6 million (+11%)
Partners made in 2017: 5 (4 in US)
Famous for: early clients were the Rockefellers and Vanderbilts; projects and financial services expertise

This venerable old New Yorker offers excellent training and pro bono opportunities alongside high responsibility... meet thoroughly modern Milbank.

VERY soon Milbank – founded in 1866 and once counting the Rockefellers and Vanderbilts as clients – is moving. Its new home? The massive Hudson Yards development on Manhattan's West Side – marketed as *"a new neighborhood for the next generation."* The firm's ultra-modern new zip code should be the final nail in the coffin for what associates called *"the ball and chain of being known as old school."* That creaky image has long jarred with Milbank's very 21st Century work style and culture: *"Nobody's eyeing when you come in,"* juniors told us of Milbank's *unstuffiness.* *"They're not hounding you on the language you use or how you present yourself. You don't have to meet any formal expectations."*

Milbank traditionally helped clients build wealth, establishing hedge funds by the dozen, but nowadays it's also well known for work stemming from an opposite trajectory. The stellar bankruptcy and restructuring practice handles Chapter 11 cases, and gets plenty of plaudits from *Chambers USA.* The project finance practice is similarly esteemed, and more *Chambers* recognition comes for M&A, wealth management, aviation finance, and Latin American investment, among other areas. International work crops up in most corporate and finance

practices, and the firm's global reach is solidified by nine international offices, from London to São Paulo.

The Work

Litigation takes the lion's share of the firm's first-years, with the next largest chunk of newbies being scattered among the various finance-themed sub-groups. In a recent change, the firm now allows budding transactional lawyers to rotate through three six-month rotations before calling their chosen practice area home. This does not include the much lauded bankruptcy and restructuring group which, specializing in Chapter 11 cases and corporate restructuring, provides elements of both litigious and transactional work. Associates in financial teams told us the firm *"really expects you to do a lot; it is somewhat sink or swim."* Some even found themselves *"doing the full spectrum of managing a deal after the first year."*

"I was doing substantive writing."

Associates stepping into Milbank's litigation group will find that it serves private equity funds, global investment banks, individual investors, as well as big corporations, in a mix of general corporate litigation, securities, and white collar work. Associates happily reported that *"every case has been different, going from FX trading to more traditional contract law. I haven't stuck with securities."* Despite telling us that *"at times you are definitely doing the simpler tasks,"* with *"some weeks of doc review,"* sources felt

On chambers-associate.com...

- Our interview with chairman Scott Edelman
- Get Hired
- Milbank and the Rockefellers

See firm profile on p.630

The Inside View

Rankings in *Chambers USA*

Banking & Finance	Litigation
Bankruptcy/Restructuring	Projects
Capital Markets	Real Estate
Corporate/M&A	Tax
Latin American Investment	Transportation

For detail on ranking tiers and ranking locations, visit
www.chambersandpartners.com

Recent work highlights

- Acted as counsel to settle upon the re-organization of Alpha Natural Resources, previously one of the largest US coal mining companies before it filed for bankruptcy in 2015
- Represented beauty giant Revlon in its $870 million acquisition of cosmetics and fragrance company Elizabeth Arden
- Advised a group of lenders including Santander and BNP Paribas on their financing of a new natural gas pipeline in Mexico
- Represented Goldman Sachs and JP Morgan Securities (among others) as initial purchasers when Intelsat Jackson, a satellite services business, made a $1.25 billion offering

they had been *"really lucky"* with the *"75% substantive"* work they received. This included *"writing a full report which was sent out to a client,"* preparation of experts' reports, and trial preparation. *"I was doing substantive writing, of motions, drafting letters to the judge, and all of the responses and objections."* They even experienced responsibility when simply *"sitting in on calls and interviews as a note taker. You have to remember everything they said because your seniors will come and ask you about it afterward!"*

The global projects and infrastructure group is particularly known for working with lenders, often on renewable energy projects. *"What I like about this group is that you're building something tangible: it's not just corporate ladders moving money from one place to another."* A significant amount of the stuff getting built has something to do with Latin America. Associates were often focused on the closing checklist: *"Once the deal has some structure we develop a list of closing documents we need for the deal. The junior will draft that and then keep track of it as documents go back and forth."* This had associates *"reviewing and editing documents,"* which provided *"a good sense of managing and organizing our process."*

Pro Bono

Milbank has a pretty hot reputation when it comes to pro bono. *"It's our big thing!"* exclaimed one associate. For years the jewel in its crown was the Milbank fellowship, which gave the opportunity of three months uninterrupted pro bono work away from the firm. In a recent change however, it's instead plumped for pushing pro bono through a higher hours target and an emphasis on providing pro bono opportunities as soon as first years are through the door. *"While the fellowship was very successful, it effectively pulled our first-years away from their peer group for three months, at a time when training and developing bonds is critical,"* says hiring partner Rod Miller. *"We decided that having the entire class start at the same time is a better way to offer training and strengthen connections."* Miller points out that associates will now be *"benefiting from working side-by-side with more seasoned lawyers"* on their early pro bono. *"Our Advocacy@Milbank program for new litigators includes a program where*

new associates will work with senior associates and partners on pro bono appellate matters,"* adds Miller.

"A lot of work with Holocaust survivors."

Regarding the loss of the fellowship, one associate told us: *"it was such an absurdly generous program anyway, it would be hard to be angry."* But, despite Miller's assurances, current associates were worried about how the new system will match up when *"you are already managing your workflow. It's hard to turn down work for pro bono."* The proof will be in the pudding, as the system hadn't kicked in at the time of our research. Meanwhile associates recalled many interesting pro bono projects, including *"an immigration case to help someone get a green card,"* and *"a lot of work with Holocaust survivors, applying for reparations."*

Pro bono hours
- For all US attorneys: 49,855
- Average per US attorney: 101

Culture & Offices

Interviewees felt that Milbank *"has a sociable culture for the most part, and people are respectful."* However, inevitably *"it's very hard to talk about culture because the various groups are very different."* Litigation, projects and the rest all have *"different personalities."* Some *"hang out and drink a lot,"* while others *"appreciate not being forced to do a lot of social activities."* Litigation in particular was said to be less personable. Being such a large firm, this fragmentation is somewhat understandable. One litigator told us *"it's so big that I couldn't tell you who works in corporate – we even have separate elevators!"* Meanwhile, others sliced up the firm by class-year, telling us they wouldn't *"hang out with senior or mid level associates. If I'm not on a deal with a third-year, I wouldn't know who they were."* Those in LA weren't in the mood for surren-

See firm profile on p.630

Diversity	Partners (%)	Associates (%)
Women	15.2	40.5
White	88.4	70.4
Black/African American	1.8	5
Hispanic/Latin American	5.4	7.6
Asian	3.6	12.9
Mixed/Other	0.9	4.1
LGBT	2.7	3.8

dering their special identity either, declaring themselves *"different from New York"* because although *"we work a lot of hours, when we are done we go home. We won't do a happy hour – it's a very work-centric office."*

"The various groups are so different."

"When I first came to Milbank I thought it was pretty breathtaking, it being in a skyscraper with Wall Street nearby," recalled an associate. It's long been an image of the legal establishment, and though associates disagreed, they knew *"that some people liken Milbank to a country club. It's hard to shake the reputation of it being old school."* The soon-to-be-vacated New York office is *"dated"* (especially in its technology), and *"everyone hates the elevators, because normally three are down."* Happily, only a year after the LA office switched premises, NY is getting ready to follow suit, transferring to the über-modern Hudson Yard development as soon as it's finished, where the firm has the ability to custom-design its interior.

Training & Development

The centerpiece of Milbank's training comes in the third year, as it bundles associates off to Cambridge, MA for a week of learning at the Milbank@Harvard program. Taught by law and business professors at Harvard, it's an intense week spent learning business, law and soft skills topics. *"I've heard it's amazing – you don't have to do any work for a week!"* But there's more. For starters, *"the summer program is mostly training. That's where I got the theoretical basis for a lot of my work."* Then there's a week of orientation at New York, which is attended by all newbies, including overseas. There are also *"multiple CLEs and we have one on presentation skills. People also come in to help you with your writing."* Plus, *"there are half hour bi-monthly lunches. We have a bit of a gab and then there's a 20-30 minute presentation on new developments or law which people are unaware of."* To cap it all off, for litigation associates, there's Advocacy@Milbank which provides workshops on depositions, arguing motions, trial skills, leadership skills and much more from their first to their sixth year. One associate believed: *"I don't think there is much more structured training which they could do."*

"We have a joke here about how many mentors does a Milbank-er have?"

"We have a joke here about how many mentors does a Milbank-er have? They certainly aren't lacking." But *"it's variable how engaged they will be in your life."* The review system could also be improved, said some: *"In theory we have annual reviews, but I haven't had mine yet."* Another told us: *"I went in for my review and none of the people I had worked with on my busiest matters had filled out the review form."* Informal feedback and supervision are, however, common. *"There is a steep learning curve but everyone is open to questions if you're struggling."* One went as far as to say that *"everyone is in love with their group's mid-levels. They're helpful, patient and very good teachers."*

Diversity

Associates observed a split when it came to diversity, with the firm delivering *"a pretty good gender spread at associate level."* Feedback that *"diversity in the partner ranks isn't so good"* aligns with previous years' research, and currently only 15.2% of partners are women. Encouragingly, associates could easily point to improvements and initiatives, and were safe in the knowledge that *"this is definitely a meritocracy: They judge you on your work and don't worry about anything else."*

"This is definitely a meritocracy."

There are various different affinity groups, including ones for African-American, Asian, Latino and female lawyers, which attend recruitment events and bring in speakers. The women's group is more active than some, hosting a regular book club, for example. We also heard about *"a super-fancy cocktail party where you can invite any professional female friends."* Those in Los Angeles get a little less direct help, as *"it's all based in New York, they don't touch us here."* The firm's LGBT group is called Pride. There's also a new 1L diversity fellowship, with those hired joining the New York summer program.

Hours & Compensation

With a market rate salary and no billing requirement, the sun shines on Milbank associates. Nevertheless, the lack of an hours goal unsettled some, but most felt that as *"there's no requirement I don't feel any pressure to get a certain amount of hours."* Less satisfactorily, *"if you buy tickets for a concert it's in God's hands."* Transactional groups come off worse as *"the challenge relative to litigators is that you have to coincide your work with how the deal is progressing. We can't control the timing, and so we have to be very responsive."*

See firm profile on p.630

The Inside View

Critical points in deals or cases resulted in very occasional weekends and all nighters. *"Everyone has their own concept of work life balance but for me, I feel like the hours are humane. There are some horrible weeks and nights but overall it's not horrendous. It really does ebb and flow."* In DC associates get a slightly better deal on hours, but everyone else described average days of 9.30am until 7pm, and then a few hours' work from home. *"If you stay past 8pm you'll get a free dinner and a free ride home."*

"It really does ebb and flow."

Get Hired

"Personality is a big deal. People don't have to be overly extroverted or gregarious." That said, hiring partner Rod Miller still wants people *"to have the ability to instil confidence and trust in the client that their problems are being handled, so that they can sleep easy at night."* For more on hiring and the full interview with Rod Miller, read our Milbank feature on chambers-associate.com.

Strategy & Future

Associates saw the move to 55 Hudson Yards as a shift toward a different image, also telling us that *"we are trying now to bring in clients who aren't just old banks, particularly in the corporate groups."* The 16-year lease is a significant development and a statement of confidence. It is not however, a signal of expansion – the new office is 250,000 square feet compared to the 300,000 of the old office. Associates were realistic about their future too: *"They invest in us wherever possible, but people are sometimes here for years and don't make partner."* MP Scott Edelman tells us: *"Our move to one of the most vibrant new spaces in New York City is a reflection of the firm's young, vibrant and energetic culture. The firm has grown beyond its Wall Street banking roots and being in a new space in Hudson Yards, a new contemporary and energetic part of New York City, is consistent with who we are today and the high-energy, entrepreneurial spirit of the firm throughout our global offices."*

See firm profile on p.630

The Inside View

Mintz Levin Cohn Ferris Glovsky and Popeo PC

Lawyers per state

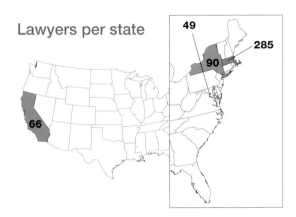

49

285

90

66

Largest US office: Boston
US offices: 6
International offices: 1
First-year salary: $180,000
Billable hours: 2,000 target (incl. 1,850 billables)
Summers 2017: 15 (11 2Ls, 4 1Ls)
Revenue 2016: $372.5 million (+2.5%)
Partners made in 2017: 5 (all US)
Famous for: life sciences, healthcare and tech specialisms

Cutting-edge life sciences help this Boston bastion keep its practice mint-fresh.

THE Bay State is recognized globally as a hub for life sciences and biotechnology, and the investment agency Massachusetts' Life Sciences Center is currently driving a $1 billion state investment in the sector. Luckily, Boston legal stronghold Mintz Levin loves all things life-sciencey: *"The market is very strong right now and we have a very strong practice,"* managing member Bob Bodian tells us. *"Our corporate department in particular has seen a lot of life sciences activity recently."* 2015 saw a massive 17.7% revenue jump, followed by 2.5% growth the following year.

In its home state, the firm picks up strong *Chambers USA* rankings for areas including corporate, healthcare, public finance and commercial litigation, complemented by healthcare accolades in New York and DC. Associates we spoke to recognized *"it is among the top firms in Boston, but the important thing is that people seem to commit to one another,"* agreeing that *"the culture is the biggest draw."*

Culture

Sources characterized Mintz as *"pretty collaborative – people hang out in the lobby and check in on each other. There's an open door policy and people can swing by and run questions by each other. I haven't seen any divas!"* An evident lack of face time culture was popular, with *"the opportunity to work remotely if we need to, providing time to spend with our families we might not get otherwise."* Despite the generally relaxed mood, some detected a change in the winds. *"When I was interviewing it felt very laid back compared to other firms. Now it has a bigger financial footprint, people are more worried about their billing and there's a bit more pressure."*

"I haven't seen any divas!"

This also had an effect on socializing, something *"we could be stronger in. Admittedly, lots of people have families and we are trying to do more."* Friday happy hours are *"a very good opportunity to meet people,"* though some reported sparse attendance. Red Sox fandom brings attorneys in the Boston office together, for both firm-run football TV nights on Mondays and weekend trips to games. Little things like *"an email letting everybody know somebody had a healthy baby"* go a long way for associate morale.

Managing member Bob Bodian was dubbed *"a straight shooter"* by associates: *"If you ask questions he really does try to be transparent. I think management understands the value of transparency."* In the main, partners came in for

On chambers-associate.com...

- Get hired: all the essential info
- Interviews with managing member Bob Bodian and director of legal recruiting Shannon Davis
- More on Mintz Levin's offices

The Inside View

See firm profile on p.631

415

Rankings in *Chambers USA*

Bankruptcy/Restructuring	Insurance
Corporate/M&A	Labor & Employment
Employee Benefits &	Life Sciences
Executive Compensation	Litigation
Environment	Real Estate
Healthcare	

For detail on ranking tiers and ranking locations, visit
www.chambersandpartners.com

Recent work highlights

- Acted for Synta Pharmaceuticals in its $253.9 million reverse merger with Madrigal
- Lead counsel for bakery chain Panera in suit against Papa John's over violation of a former executive's non-competition agreement
- Achieved first-of-its-kind dismissal of a class action against gym company Work Out World, accused of violating the Telephone Consumer Protection Act
- Represented borrower Spitzer Enterprises in $235 million loan for Brooklyn residential development project

praise for *"treating everybody on the same level. It's more of a horizontal landscape than a strict hierarchy when it comes to work. It feels like a team, and I like that."*

The Work

Splitting pretty evenly between the litigation and corporate departments (plus a few in IP, public finance, and employment law), almost every newcomer heads to Boston. Departments are overseen by a practice manager who *"gets you assignments when you first start, divvying out work based on reports you give."* That's how it works *"in a perfect world – when you start you're dependent on the practice manager, but in the end you have to do things yourself."* Interviewees happily shifted to receiving work directly from partners once they'd got settled, bypassing the formal system. *"It's tricky to balance, but getting tasks through informal channels represents a vote of confidence."*

Litigators worked with clients *"ranging from big businesses to insurance companies and high net worth individuals,"* often with a leaning toward life sciences and biotech. Associates were *"generally doing research to plug in to a brief. I often have to research a discrete issue, and have gotten to write briefs and motions."* Less glamorously, there is *"a fair amount of doc review, but less than I had anticipated after friends told me it's all you do in first year. There's a healthy balance between drudgery and substantive work."* Litigation tends to be high stakes rather than commoditized, commanding higher rates. Six months from starting, one junior *"got staffed as a semi-lead associate on a case, dealing with document production and management."* White collar litigation was in notably high demand, several associates hoping to get a slice of that (Boston cream) pie.

"I haven't been thrown to the dogs too often."

Mintz's corporate and securities group predominantly works with clients in the tech, biotech, health and life sciences industries. Interviewees' responsibilities had included *"a lot of drafting ancillary documents, engagement letters, everything required for approval. On smaller cases*

there's more drafting of major documents like purchasing agreements." Bigger M&A deals required more basic due diligence. Although some suggested *"the first couple of years you're completely under water all the time with the workload,"* they recognized *"the experience is designed to make you a thorough attorney, and however great you think you are, you have to go through that."*

Other practice areas saw work ebb and flow. One junior diagnosed *"a problem with Mintz that it's a big firm with BigLaw expectations but there are times when things are not very busy."* Most were nonetheless pleased with the responsibility afforded them. *"Mintz tries to staff cases leanly, which provides lots of client contact opportunities, especially once you get comfortable and more competent."* Another associate reasoned that they *"haven't been thrown to the dogs too often, but it's not super-easy-boring things all the time either."*

Get Hired

"As a person, will you fit in at Mintz? They know what's on your résumé – they want to see if you're sociable and a team player." For top tips from associates and an interview with director of legal recruiting Shannon Davis, read our Bonus Features on Mintz on our website.

Offices & Diversity

Situated *"conveniently right next to South Station in Boston,"* Mintz's HQ offers a room with a view for everybody. *"Some people complain the décor is dated, which is probably true,"* according to associates, but most *"really don't mind."* The firm's Big Apple base is set out in a helpful circle, while in San Diego *"we have one of the best offices in the city with an ocean view. The only downside is we're not downtown."*

"You can't fault the firm for not trying" to correct typical BigLaw diversity imbalances, including that *"the East Coast is more diverse than the West."* A yearly diversity retreat in New York (*"people from all the offices gather*

See firm profile on p.631

The Inside View

Diversity	Partners (%)	Associates (%)
Women	25	48
White	91	79
Black/African American	2	5
Hispanic/Latin American	3	3
Asian	4	11
Mixed/Other	0	2
LGBT	3	3

for it") was appreciated, as was the firm's annual Richard Mintz diversity scholarship. Policies allowing attorneys with children to work more from home while still being on the partner track were also highlighted as a strong positive.

Training & Development

An initial Base Camp program gets juniors acquainted, schooling them on firm logistics and practicalities of work outlined in *"binders of information you can refer back to."* This is followed by *"various trainings throughout the year; they bring in really good people to do lectures, and if you find a useful CLE they make it very clear you can go for it."*

"You know when you're doing a good job."

Newcomers get a check-in meeting soon after starting, and everybody receives two formal annual evaluations. Some suggested the system *"needs improvement: anybody who's worked with you more than 20 hours evaluates you, but you don't get to see your full review before meeting the practice manager and section head, you only get a summary. It's very silly."* Contrastingly, others felt *"they do a great job of compiling comments into a short narrative."* There were similarly mixed reports on everyday feedback, the consensus being that *"you typically know when you're doing a good job,"* one way or another.

Pro Bono

Part of the training for newcomers is a schooling in pro bono and how it is delegated. Interviewees were united in a strong commitment to community work, though *"it is hard to do things outside of client billables. Balancing the work is on you."* The firm's Domestic Violence Project is a pro bono staple, as are things like social security, immigration and asylum cases. A source of disappointment for some was that *"when we interviewed, pro bono counts toward billables, but now it doesn't [until 1,850 billables are attained]. It's a culture change as Mintz is known for its pro bono, and that's something which is slowly being chipped away, which is sad."* Others were less discouraged

by the change. *"They really encourage younger associates to do pro bono, and it gives you the opportunity to draft motions and go before a judge. I wouldn't have had those chances in my billables."*

Pro bono hours
- For all US attorneys: 14,715.8
- Average per US attorney: 30.66

Hours & Compensation

Associates aim for a client billable target of 1,850 hours, affording them an automatic bonus. Once they've hit this any training, pro bono and special projects count toward the hours-based bonus. Newcomers had some worries about hitting targets, but suggested *"everybody's aware of the slower times, and people are really understanding."* Most saw 1,850 as *"very achievable, I'm not concerned about it. There's a ton of work depending on the section you're in."* Corporate juniors were particularly confident, and all thought *"if you hit your hours nobody will bug you"* for taking vacation.

"It was a big relief when we found out."

There were *"a lot of mixed feelings"* about the slowness in confirming associate salary rises to match the Cravath scale, but most associates we spoke to *"had no problem with it. Some were definitely criticizing the firm for not confirming it earlier."* The firm put this down to its fiscal year starting in October rather than June. One source summarized: *"It was frustrating at first that the decision took a long time and updates would have been helpful, but it was a big relief when we found out and I appreciated why the firm took so long."* Managing member Bob Bodian clarifies that management *"took our time to evaluate everything, so when the increase was announced there was no mystery or doubt."*

Strategy & Future

After a record-busting 2015, Mintz did even better in 2016. Managing member Bob Bodian chalks this success up to lucrative lateral hires, as well as *"the firm becoming more collaborative. Three years ago, 20% of our clients used three or more of our practice areas – last year it was 35%."* There's no rush to push the envelope, though. *"We're not looking to create new offices, but we're definitely looking to grow on both coasts, and are recruiting to that effect."* For more from Bodian, check out www.chambers-associate.com.

"We're definitely looking to grow on both coasts."

See firm profile on p.631

Morgan, Lewis & Bockius LLP

Lawyers per state

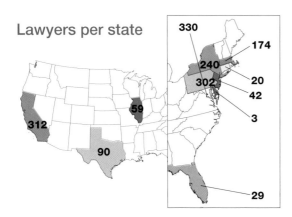

Largest US office: Philadelphia
US offices: 17
International offices: 13
First-year salary: $165,000 - $180,000
Billable hours: no requirement
Summers 2017: 75 (65 2Ls, 10 1Ls)
Revenue 2016: $1.86 billion (+1.1%)
Partners made in 2017: 33 globally (32 in US)
Famous for: biggest firm in the US; excellent associate training

America's largest firm continues to focus on associate development while advising clients at the highest levels.

WHEN asked what Morgan Lewis offers young lawyers that is unique from its rivals, hiring partner Christina Melendi replies in a heartbeat: *"We offer an exceptionally strong training environment, giving them an ability to not only develop their legal skills but also personal skills."* Both legal and personal development are the raison d'être for 'ML Experiences', whereby all summer associates can pick three different routes for their first ten weeks at the firm. They can stay in the office for the full ten, or stay for six weeks and go on a client secondment for four weeks, or spend those latter four weeks with a pro bono organization instead. All of which, as Melendi puts it, *"gives young lawyers invaluable insight early on into what a client, or general counsel, or a legal department expects of them and our firm."*

And having such a thorough focus on the individual is no mean feat considering the firm is America's biggest by headcount, with over 2,000 attorneys nationwide. Hundreds of these were previously Bingham McCutchen lawyers who came over in 2014 when their firm imploded, and associates agreed that the two were coming together nicely. *"The areas in which Bingham was strong and where Morgan Lewis is strong are completely different, and something that has been great about the combination has been*

a strengthening of both sides." *Chambers USA* recognizes many ML strengths, bestowing top tier nationwide rankings for practices including capital markets, corporate/M&A, ERISA litigation, and labor & employment. The firm made global news when partner Sheri Dillon represented Trump at his first press conference shortly before his inauguration.

The Work

Incoming ML attorneys join one of three groups that broadly represent *"corporate, litigation, and labor & employment."* When you start *"you get a specific offer from one of those groups and then it's just a matter of asking for particular work."* Juniors in corporate or finance find themselves in a pool system and *"the work you get depends on who's busy, so for the first two years you do a little bit of both, then you gradually find your way into one group."*

Assignment is organic and stems from the relationships you form in your first two years – *"as you get put on cases, if you do a good job, generally the partners come back to you with more of the same work."* That said, there are mechanisms in place to make sure juniors aren't overburdened: *"Each practice group has a workflow coordinator and twice a week they send out an email with a color system to gauge how busy you are."* This focus on preventing burnout stems from the fact that *"partners are very vigilant, they make sure that everyone is getting the experience that they want and they ask up front if there's anyone you'd*

See firm profile on p.632

The Inside View

Rankings in *Chambers USA*

Antitrust
Banking & Finance
Bankruptcy/Restructuring
Capital Markets
Corporate/M&A
ERISA Litigation
Employee Benefits &
   Executive Compensation
Energy & Natural
   Resources
Environment
Financial Services
   Regulation
Healthcare
Immigration
Insurance
Intellectual Property

Investment Funds
Labor & Employment
Latin American Investment
Life Sciences
Litigation
Media & Entertainment
Outsourcing
Products Liability
Projects
Real Estate
Retail
Securities
Startups & Emerging
   Companies
Tax
Telecommunications

For detail on ranking tiers and ranking locations, visit
www.chambersandpartners.com

Recent work highlights

- Represented Dr Pepper Snapple Group in its $1.7 billion acquisition of Bai Brands
- Represented social discovery public market leader Meet-Me in its acquisition of If(we), a social and mobile technology company that operates Tagged and hi5, for $60 million in cash. ML also represented MeetMe in its related $30 million credit facility
- Helped grocery distributor McLane Co. obtain a grant of certiorari and represented the company before the US Supreme Court in a case addressing the subpoena power of the Equal Employment Opportunity Commission
- Won summary judgment on all claims for American Society for Testing and Materials in a copyright infringement action that raised cutting-edge issues relating to the intersection of copyright law and the digital era

Interviewees who had initially thought they'd be joining Bingham were effusive about the lengths Morgan Lewis went to in order to make them feel at home: *"There was a big effort, especially in New York, to make sure that the unique things about Bingham's culture would live on. For example, today's Friday and I'm wearing jeans. 'Casual Fridays' were a big thing at Bingham and Morgan Lewis has made sure that hasn't changed with the merger."* And jeans aren't the only things that are standing strong in the Big Apple. The firm's all-attorney family event held at Dave & Buster's in Times Square toward the end of the summer remains a fixture.

especially like to work with, or anything you'd especially like to work on."

"Each practice group has a workflow coordinator."

Sources spoke of lean staffing across the board, meaning meaty tasks from an early stage. Litigious juniors reported a department that is *"not segregated into various practices"* meaning *"every first-year is expected to do some white collar, commercial litigation and securities work."* They also opined cheerfully that *"doc review is rare here. As a first-year you're more likely to be involved in preparing depositions, drafting motions for summary judgment, responding to discovery and even helping to decide client strategy."* Transactional associates told of similar goings on – *"we usually handle the transaction checklist. I don't really do much drafting, I mostly review the agreements and make sure they are all in order."*

"After two years all of the kinks have been worked out."

Over in Philly, the firm's HQ and the office that *"probably exerts the most influence culturally nationwide,"* attorneys can expect a packed social calendar with *"weekly happy hours and monthly associate lunches"* as well as a *"big soirée at the University of Pennsylvania Museum of Archaeology."* However, the jewel in the crown of the year comes every spring, when Morgan Lewis rents out the entire Philadelphia Zoo and invites the whole office and their families to join in the fun.

Culture
The powers that be had a job on their hands trying to meld the culture of 700 Bingham McCutchen lawyers and staff with the already big Morgan Lewis. In locations where both firms had a presence – such as Boston and New York – whoever's office was larger subsumed the other's. Sources felt that *"while it was initially tense when a lot of the Bingham partners left or didn't get offers,"* but because *"most of the associates stayed"* the *"initial 'us v. them' atmosphere quickly faded, and after two years all of the kinks have been worked out."*

Hours & Compensation
Sources reported differing adherence to face time depending on location. In offices with more young families, such as LA and Dallas, *"there's less pressure for you to be at your desk every single hour of the day. People who have kids work for part of the day here then pop back up online later."* While in the bigger offices, like New York and Philly, *"even if you have nothing on you'd still kind of be expected to be around just in case."* That said, work isn't hard to come by – *"in the past two years, there's never been more than a couple of hours when I've been looking for something to do."*

See firm profile on p.632

Diversity	Partners (%)	Associates (%)
Women	22.1	51.3
White	91.9	75.6
Black/African American	1.7	4.2
Hispanic/Latin American	1.1	4.2
Asian	4.8	13.5
Mixed/Other	0.5	2.4
LGBT	2.5	4.4

"About half of my hours right now are pro bono and I've never had anyone criticize me for that."

All of which makes the 2,000 billable hours requirement eminently achievable, especially since *"it's not really a requirement at all"* but *"more of a target."* Added to this is the fact that, at least in the first year, pro bono hours can count toward your target – *"about half of my hours right now are pro bono and I've never had anyone criticize me for that."* The one area that came in for slight criticism was bonuses. All bonuses are discretionary and 'individualized', meaning *"even if you don't hit 2,000 you are eligible"* but also that *"it's hard to build in accountability for the firm."* Nonetheless, those who had experienced the old lockstep system said that the reform – which had included a salary increase for first and second-years – was mostly intended to match market. First-year salaries are: $180,000 (Boston, Hartford, New York, DC, California, Chicago, Texas, Princeton and Philadelphia), and $165,000 (Pittsburgh, Wilmington and Miami).

Training & Development

Morgan Lewis has a rigorous training program for new hires. There's 'ML Experiences', but also three days of induction in Philly called 'New Lawyer Academy', *"where you're going through all kinds of things like the IT systems, and also where to go if you need more staples."* After that, associates receive practice-specific education. In corporate and finance there's formal training every other week at lunchtime. Litigation juniors can expect regular two-day deposition workshops with actors playing the roles of fake witnesses. Over time, deposition training becomes 'trial academy', a forum for associates to test their courtroom skills.

Complementing this comprehensive training is constructive and ongoing feedback. This reaches its zenith during associates' annual reviews, which are an incredibly thorough process: *"Each associate provides a self-assessment – you are rating what you think your performance was but you're also providing a written description of your matters. And then that's reviewed by any partner that has worked with you for more than 20 hours. That's*

then discussed in a meeting among partners and you end up getting a consolidated written review."

Offices

With 17 US offices, it'd be a long task to describe every one, so we'll stick to the largest. The Philadelphia HQ is located downtown, right above the train station, *"which is particularly handy in the middle of winter as you don't need to go outside at all."* On the top floor there's a cafeteria that serves hot breakfast and lunch and, once a week, something called an 'enhanced snack' – which, our sources reported, is *"not as exciting as it sounds."* In other snack-related news, the New York office is also building a new cafeteria. It's also right next to a big terminus, in this case Grand Central.

The firm's LA digs were described as *"exactly like the office in* Suits*"* by one interviewee, who went on to lament that fact that the West Coast was sometimes overlooked by those calling the shots in the East – *"on a couple of occasions I've got the impression that they think of us a bit as those cowboys out West,"* one joked. Bostonians stayed in the Bingham office after the merger – *"it's a great space, very modern; less oak-paneling and dark wood, more frosted glass and natural light."*

Pro Bono

As mentioned previously, *"100% of pro bono hours count toward billables."* And, if that weren't enough to incentivize it, there is also a 'pro bono challenge' – *"they ask all attorneys to book at least 20 pro bono hours a year and we get updates every quarter telling us how each practice and office is doing."* In Philly, the firm works closely with Philadelphia VIP, a legal non-profit that does some great local work. In Boston, interviewees had volunteered with Project Citizenship, a charity that helps immigrants fill out citizenship papers.

Pro bono hours
- For all US attorneys: 99,404
- Average per US attorney: 57

Diversity

A focus on diversity is one thing former Bingham sources felt might have been lost with their firm's name – *"during the Bingham recruitment process diversity was talked about a lot but since I've been here I haven't heard it mentioned once."* Associates all agreed though that if ML was succeeding anywhere it was in gender diversity: *"We have various affinity groups and committees but I think the best evidence is that, at least since I've been here, every class has been exactly 50-50 men and women."*

See firm profile on p.632

The Inside View

In March 2017, the firm made headlines when it announced that qualifying associates would be allowed to work from home for up to two days a week. Time will tell what the take-up will be and how it will work exactly – we will report back next year.

Get Hired

One source who had been involved in recruitment leaked a bit of info about the interview questions: *"They ask us to evaluate five key characteristics: intellectual and cognitive ability, planning and organizational skills, communication skills, working with others, and character."* This is all part of the firm's much-vaunted 'behavioral interviewing' which assesses how candidates have reacted in the past and how that might indicate their future behavior. Other interviewees stressed ML's appreciation of things like involvement with sport or the military – *"it's proof that you have worked well in a team atmosphere before and that you don't just have an individual mentality."*

Strategy & Future

Morgan Lewis focuses on hiring the right personalities for partnership one day and *"there are a large number of lawyers who stay here for their whole careers,"* according to associates. It's something that's talked about early on too: *"They bring it up during performance evaluations and if you were not on track, they'd let you know."* That said, in the bigger offices, the firm has become wary about being too top-heavy: *"What they've started doing is establishing a formal procedure to place mid-level associates at clients. We'll periodically get listings of jobs from our own HR department for positions at our clients."*

> ## *"They ask us to evaluate five key characteristics: intellectual and cognitive ability; planning and organizational skills; communication skills; working with others, and character."*

The Inside View

See firm profile on p.632

Morrison & Foerster LLP

Lawyers per state

112
192
16
41
420

Largest US office: San Francisco

US offices: 8

International offices: 8

First-year salary: $180,000

Billable hours: undisclosed (associates spoke of 1,950 target)

Summers 2017: 104 (77 2Ls, 24 1Ls, 3 others)

Revenue 2016: $945 million (-3.5%)

Partners made in 2017: 15 globally (9 in US)

Famous for: California-casual dress; unlimited pro bono hours; mega tech clients

For tech excellence in a "more livable" environment, it's MoFo, fo sho.

IN your arduous research of law firms – as you scroll through endless text on your screen or flick through the pages of weighty career books – you could be forgiven for falling asleep as the constant stream of law firm names wearies your eyes. MoFo, having the rudest name in the market, is at a distinct advantage. The firm's work and "laid back" Cali culture are pretty exciting too in the grand scheme of things. "This is the firm other associates lateral to," one reasonably relaxed associate here told us. Managing partner Craig Martin confirms all this when he says his goal is to have "the most respected and sought after culture in the industry."

MoFo is best known for its tech clients, many of whom download the firm's expertise in intellectual property law (especially litigation). MoFo famously represented Apple in the 'smartphone wars' against Samsung, and other big-name clients include Toshiba, DreamWorks and Netflix. As well as IP, MoFo's *Chambers USA* ranking highlights include corporate/M&A, various types of litigation, IT & outsourcing, financial services regulation, and government. These are serious, serious practice areas, so when associates use the phrase "laid back" we need to add the phrase 'for BigLaw'.

On chambers-associate.com...

- We interview managing partner Craig Martin
- We talk to chief legal talent officer Diane Cardona Downs about recruitment
- More on getting hired from associates

The Work

Many new junior associates join litigation and a sizable chunk ends up in corporate, and finance. A few join tax. Outside litigation, where juniors are generalists, associates are allocated to a specific practice group: for example general corporate, patent, capital markets, or technology transactions.

The assignment of work is a casual affair. Assigning partners do exist, but depending on which practice area and office you're in, they are relied upon to varying degrees. Generally, litigation associates take advantage of the assigning partners, said to be helpful in "making your preferences known." Litigators "are able to roam around," exploring the sub-groups on offer, which include securities, litigation, enforcement and white-collar (SLEW), commercial litigation, and financial services. Associates told us "people vary to the extent that they try to specialize early. Some people like to get a sense of different practices; others come in with set ideas." Describing their work, litigation associates told us "the typical thing would be drafting discovery responses, briefs and legal research and preparing deposition outlines and materials." That's no mean feat, and "there are definitely opportunities to step up and take on significant briefs if you're interested." Since "a lot of cases only have a couple of juniors and partners working on them, whatever you take on is appreciated."

"It's more fluid than it is formalized."

In other departments, such as corporate, "you tend to have partners or associates who either like working with you or need someone to work on a job. They reach out in-

See firm profile on p.633

Rankings in *Chambers USA*

Antitrust	Labor & Employment
Appellate Law	Life Sciences
Banking & Finance	Litigation
Bankruptcy/Restructuring	Outsourcing
Capital Markets	Privacy & Data Security
Corporate/M&A	Products Liability
Environment	Projects
FCPA	Real Estate
Financial Services	REITs
Regulation	Startups & Emerging
Government	Companies
IT & Outsourcing	Tax
Intellectual Property	Technology
International Trade	

For detail on ranking tiers and ranking locations, visit
www.chambersandpartners.com

dependently or drop by your office." This is possible because MoFo's corporate lawyers operate in much more niche teams – often with only one or two associates per practice area: *"It's more fluid than it is formalized."* Although work allocation varies, we heard from some sources about a *"weekly status report where we submit everything we're working on,"* so that partners can assess associates' workload. As in litigation, these small teams mean lean staffing. Though the tasks often vary, associates told us about being *"really exposed to helping cover roles that might feel beyond your years."* Many had experienced direct client contact too – *"it's great for people who want to jump in and learn on the job,"* said one. *"Honestly, I came in thinking I would have horror stories of due diligence for the first year or two: just mind-numbing work. But ultimately, at this point, I get to have a hand in most documents. It's more a reflection of the grace of the people I work for – even now I produce documents that are complete garbage! But they are giving me the chance to grow organically."*

Training & Development

San Francisco plays host to new attorneys' induction into the firm. *"It's a huge event; they rent out an entire hotel. People are flown in from every single office,"* and they mean every office... worldwide. *"A lot of it is meet and greet, there's lots of alcohol and mingling after the events are over."* There's training too, though *"it tends to go in one ear and out the other. But they spend a lot of money on having people teaching seminars from all over the country and making sure people feel welcome – it's much appreciated."*

Once they've dispersed, training covers general skills *"like public speaking, and then more tailored stuff for litigators or corporate."* Practice group training is called

Recent work highlights

- Represented Autodesk to stop the Chinese company ZW-CAD Software from selling a cloned version of the Auto-CAD design software under a new name
- Represented the medical robotics company Auris Surgical Robotics in its $150 million Series C financing
- Represented Unilever in its acquisition of Dollar Shave Club, a start-up based in California
- Negotiated the partnership between Visa and Google, on behalf of Visa, contributing to Google's Android pay scheme

"MoFo U," and a corporate source described *"mandatory seminars where they discuss the foundational skill sets for corporate. When training comes up someone prints out the materials for it and people call in from all over the country to join in."* Nevertheless, some associates wanted *"a little more formalized training and mentoring."* The formal mentoring scheme, going under the name *"Odyssey,"* did not last long enough in most associates' eyes, nor did it follow *"a very obvious structure."* Carving out time for informal feedback and mentoring could be difficult: *"We'd be back to work a minute later,"* one told us. *"That's not the type of mentoring I would want."* A source felt it vital to *"be able to learn as you go forward."*

Hours & Compensation

MoFo's billing target is set at 1,950 hours regardless of office: *"A very doable target,"* especially as *"MoFo does a good job of trying to count all of your hours."* Associates praised the flexibility they were afforded: *"I'm working a lot of late nights and weekends, so it's not relaxed in that sense. But if you get the job done nobody will be coming round to see if you're here."* One New Yorker felt they worked *"fewer hours than other law firms in New York,"* and though their hours might be slightly longer than their West Coast counterparts, they still liked that *"if you want to leave at 6.30pm for yoga and come back to finish, there's no problem. MoFo has shown me that it is possible to work in BigLaw but also enjoy respect for your time."*

To secure vacation, associates had to get organized. *"It does require a bit of coordinating, so people usually plan their vacations in advance, letting people know and getting coverage for their responsibilities."* MoFo follows a system whereby lawyers accrue holiday entitlement: 15 days maximum for first, second and third-years everywhere but New York, where they can earn 20.

Pro Bono

Pro bono is a big deal at MoFo. Managing partner Craig Martin tells us that *"client service, commitment to pro bono, volunteerism, charitable giving – they all run*

The Inside View

See firm profile on p.633

Diversity	Partners (%)	Associates (%)
Women	23.5	46.2
White	83.7	68.2
Black/African American	2.4	3.2
Hispanic/Latin American	4	5.3
Asian	10	19.1
Mixed/Other	0	4.2
LGBT	2	4.5

through the firm. They're important regardless of the geography one finds oneself in." Associates too described "a real, honest commitment to pro bono and social justice issues." That means that "right away you're staffed on pro bono matters and it's taken very seriously." To enable this, there's no cap on the number of pro bono hours attorneys can bill, and they all count towards their billable target. "When I started I had many more pro bono hours than billable, but I was never talked to about it."

"I had many more pro bono hours than billable."

Associates brought up a plethora of matters they'd been involved in, including immigration issues, "voting rights litigation," housing and environmental work. The firm has previously won significant victories championing gay marriage rights, tackling 'Don't Ask, Don't Tell' and fighting for the rights of those with disabilities in the Supreme Court. There are partners to coordinate the pro bono effort, frequently suggesting matters to associates, but juniors also reported suggesting and bringing in their own matters. A recent pro bono highlight was filing a civil rights lawsuit on behalf of two San Diego men jailed for posting rap lyrics on their social media pages, which the government claimed linked them to gangs. Charges were dismissed or not ultimately brought, so the duo are seeking compensation and other redress for their seven months inside.

Pro bono hours
- For all attorneys across all US offices: 86,000 approx.
- Average per US attorney: 123

Culture
You can take the firm out of California, but can you take the Californian out of the firm? We'd say not – though each office is its own blend, the culture always bears the distinctive marks of its San Francisco origins. "I think ultimately, as much as we might complain in Los Angeles, the strenuous requirements of BigLaw aren't as apparent." Nor is the uniform of BigLaw: "It's definitely business casual. It's not a suit and tie place" – casual Fridays and charity events even allow associates to saunter in Zuckerberg-

style (jeans and a T-shirt). One associate pointed out: "We do call ourselves MoFo! People are playful and it's a fun place to be. We don't take ourselves too seriously. We're serious when we need to be, but the firm in general tends to be laid back and feels very human."

"People are playful and it's a fun place to be."

The other side of the coin of course sees associates "working long hours – it's not all hunky dory. You're expected to work at a high level, but people have lives and they understand that." Inevitably, "demanding work and clients" could boil up a little stress, but "an attitude of mutual respect among everybody" was a helpful remedy. The absence of a strict hierarchy also delighted associates, who took full advantage. "If I have a question, I can just ask a partner – there's no need to politic, I just ask." One told us that "one of our global heads and I talk every day – the access to people high up in the firm is phenomenal!" Bringing the working week to an end, attorneys can attend cocktail hour in the office at 5pm on a Friday. Otherwise there's a mix of social events, usually team-specific. One associate told us about "practice group monthly lunches and a bake-off event. People tend to have families, and a lot are married with children."

Diversity
MoFo achieves good diversity figures (relative to the profession) in terms of ethnicity, gender and LGBT both at associate and partner level. "Quite a few powerful partners on my office floor are women, and there are a lot of female associates. It's maybe half and half women to men at this point. And there are people of all races and religions. It's quite a diverse place, I find." Significantly, MoFo was the first BigLaw firm to have an openly gay chairman, Keith Wetmore. The firm has active affinity groups too, organizing "a lot of events – they make it easy to participate and affirm the values of diversity." A member of the Asian affinity group told us they met up for "Korean barbecue or escape rooms." In addition, every two years the firm invites its diverse attorneys to its 'Diversity Summit,' replete with lectures and schmoozing opportunities.

Offices
MoFo's presence stretches well beyond California. Joining the West Coast sites in San Francisco, Los Angeles, San Diego, and Palo Alto are a small office in Denver and a huddle of East Coast sites which include DC, Northern Virginia and New York. San Francisco takes the largest number of associates, with Los Angeles and New York not far behind. Associates told us "there are always people emailing around offices asking for advice, and you can be working in teams across offices," but travel between them

"A huge loungebrary."

was rare for juniors. New Yorkers revealed that *"there are no facilities in the building: no cafeteria or gym – which I think is a shame. But it's very accessible, being near Columbus Circle, and on a lot of subway lines, and if you're lucky you get a view of the Hudson."* Meanwhile LA associates reside on the top floor of their towering building, and caught our attention by describing *"a huge loungebrary,"* which hosts their office cocktail parties.

Get Hired

Director of attorney recruiting Diane Cardona Downs tells us the *"summer program is about giving real work and training opportunities, so that summers can see what life is like here and we see how they fare."* For more insight on recruitment, read MoFo's Bonus Features on chambers-associate.com.

Strategy & Future

"Our strategy has been to play to our strengths, to leverage our market share," says managing partner Craig Martin. The future of the firm looks broadly similar, but recent years have seen *"a big push into the emerging companies and venture capital practice."* Though this is taking place on the East Coast too, he points out that *"it is a nice fit for us given our strength in the Bay Area. So much activity has occurred in Silicon Valley and San Francisco, so given our size and reputation, we're well placed to identify and assist clients in that area."* This work will embrace not only the tech industry, but also media and financial services.

"They spend a lot of money on having people teaching seminars from all over the country."

Munger, Tolles & Olson LLP

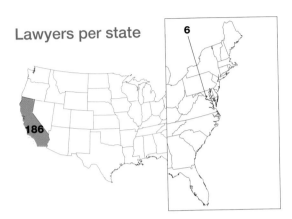

Lawyers per state

6

186

Largest US office: Los Angeles
US offices: 3
International offices: 0
First-year salary: $180,000
Billable hours: no requirement
Summers 2017: 19 (14 2Ls, 4 1Ls, 1 3L)
Revenue 2016: undisclosed
Partners made in 2017: 3
Famous for: unique committee-based democratic structure; some superstar clients

Munger recently broke out of California to open a DC office with a headline-grabbing hire...

MUNGER's long been a West Coast legend, generating dazzling work out of two relatively small bases, in LA and San Francisco, while eschewing the BigLaw preference for national expansion. But 2016 brought a new DC office out of the blue. Even co-managing partner Sandra Seville-Jones admits *"we had no plans to open an office."* However, the golden opportunity of bringing in former Solicitor General Don Verrilli to head the DC operation changed all that. *"His being available was really the driving force,"* says Seville-Jones. In fact, Munger's got form when it comes to big names. There's an ongoing relationship with superstar investor Warren Buffett for one, and plenty more household names line up as clients, including Walt Disney, Bank of America, and Warner Bros.

Chambers USA top ranks the firm's commercial, securities, and media litigation prowess, and its white-collar crime practice is also second to none. High rankings go to Munger's antitrust, energy, labor & employment, tax, real estate, corporate/M&A, and appellate work. Culturally, Munger sets itself apart with a uniquely egalitarian committee-based system: *"A show of hands"* among all

lawyers settles most firm decisions. And with an almost 1:1 partner-associate ratio, genuine power lies in associates' hands. *"We talked a lot before we opened the DC office, and we were involved in that decision,"* one junior source revealed. As a result, *"I feel integrated and invested in the firm."*

The Work

Munger doesn't allocate its fee-earners to specific, named practice areas. *"At Munger there's an emphasis on being a generalist. I wanted to practice in a number of areas and not be siloed off into one group doing the same thing over and over again."* That said, attorneys here do tend to develop areas of expertise over time. The vast majority of new associates stride into litigation territory, though you'll find one or two working on the corporate side.

"At Munger there's an emphasis on being a generalist."

Munger's work assignment is informal. A work coordinator presents possible cases to associates in their first six months, but from then on associates take over, communicating directly with partners. Associates felt this suited *"self starters,"* telling us that *"if you're the kind of person who will be sat there waiting for a partner to knock on your door and offer you the work you want – that won't happen."* Most liked *"the open system,"* though they believed *"learning to navigate it takes time,"* especially *"balancing and predicting your workload."*

On chambers-associate.com...

- Interview with co-managing partner Sandra Seville-Jones
- We talk to recruiting co-chair Carolyn Luedtke
- Who is Charlie Munger?
- More on recruitment from associates

See firm profile on p.634

Rankings in *Chambers USA*

Antitrust	Litigation
Corporate/M&A	Media & Entertainment
Energy & Natural Resources	Real Estate
	Securities
Labor & Employment	Tax

For detail on ranking tiers and ranking locations, visit
www.chambersandpartners.com

Recent work highlights

- Defending LG E lectronics against claims of alleged price fixing of cathode ray tubes the company uses in its monitors and TVs. Costco is one of the plaintiffs
- Represented Berkshire Hathaway in its $37.2 billion acquisition of Precision Castparts
- New DC office head Don Verrilli represents Airbnb in its federal lawsuit against the city of San Francisco over their provision of booking services for unlicensed property owners

Associates had been involved in all sorts of litigation, creating some unique experiences – but their tasks remained similar. They could all recall drafting multiple motions and briefs and praised the fact that *"doc review has been very limited. I don't feel I have many tasks which are those easy, fairly mindless jobs."* Some had to wait though, as in their experience *"after eight to ten months there was a big jump in my level of substantive work. That came after I drafted my first motion to dismiss."* A lucky few had taken depositions and prepared witnesses, while others reported regularly being *"the face of MTO to our client."* Lean staffing also left associates wholly *"responsible for the discovery side of things: managing paralegals and overseeing document production."*

Culture

Two elements lie at the core of Munger's *"distinctive culture."* Firstly, the firm's low leverage. A ratio of roughly 1:1 between partners and associates meant our sources were *"dealing almost exclusively with partners."* The effects are best seen in the responsibility they're showered with, but associates also felt *"in demand."* Having fewer associates up for grabs *"instills a culture where partners have to be a little more respectful."* A second leveler is the firm's system of committees, which help put almost all major firm decisions to a vote. On hiring, office moves and plenty more besides an associate has as much power as a senior partner: *"Open, democratic and transparent,"* one called it. Within this egalitarian framework, associates described *"a quiet place, with a lot of people in their offices working hard."* There's *"an emphasis on really high quality work"* – it's *"definitely a work focused culture."*

"Open, democratic and transparent."

Since the firm has a preference for recruiting those with clerkships under their belt, *"there are less 'straight-through kids.' People are a little older. Almost all of the people I know here are married or in a serious relationship so it's not a crazy going-out-type culture. People shouldn't be expecting that."* There's even an onsite daycare facility at the LA office. Despite the stress of diaper changes and temper-tantrums, associates still described *"a good amount of joviality."* There are weekly 'sherry-sips' (drinking-based get togethers), a firmwide retreat for lawyers and their

families, plus we're told the firm has *"four seats at the Staples Center,"* where associates can take clients.

Pro Bono

"One way the firm walks the walk is that people have no problems with me doing ridiculous amounts of pro bono. Others have spent 50% of their time on it and there hasn't been a peep from anyone about it." In fact there's no cap: *"It's treated the same as billable hours, it's given the same credit, it's displayed on time reports,"* and associates felt free to take advantage. *"The firm doesn't badger or force – some by choice or by circumstance haven't done any – but it's embedded in the culture of the firm to give back."*

"It's embedded in the culture of the firm to give back."

Associates praised MTO's *"longstanding relationship with Kids in Need of Defense* [KIND]. *It's good because we get to run with cases, we get client contact and we can argue in court or the immigration office."* The firm is also open to associates sourcing work themselves. One associate sorted their sports club's organizational documents and the firm famously aided unlawfully-arrested Ferguson protesters in 2014 after an associate rallied the partnership to their cause.

Pro bono hours
- For all attorneys: 28,273
- Average per attorney: 146

Training & Development

Unlike most rival firms with their comprehensive training programs, *"the focus is not on formal training."* Instead, Munger favors learning on the job. *"You get an assignment and then talk to associates and partners to figure out how to do it."* Associates found this **"pretty effective,"** more so than *"putting us in front of a projector for a week."* They explained that *"because you're working so closely with partners you need to get to know how they work. There's no exact way of doing anything."* That said, there's still an initial retreat for new attorneys and op-

See firm profile on p.634

The Inside View

Diversity	Partners (%)	Associates (%)
Women	22.4	40.6
White	82.4	74.0
Black/African American	0	4.2
Hispanic/Latin American	3.5	5.2
Asian	11.8	11.5
Mixed/Other	0	6.3
LGBT	2.4	8.3

tional *"workshops every so often."* Firm lunches two times a week also beam presentations and discussion to all offices via videolink.

"There's no exact way of doing anything."

Keeping associates on the straight and narrow are twice yearly formal reviews. *"The feedback is pretty detailed. They do a good job of talking to the people you've worked with and letting you know where you stand."* Associates also get an associate and partner mentor to *"help you navigate the environment."*

Hours & Compensation

Munger's bonus system is holistic, with *"no formal rubric, no 'work this many hours and get this many positive reviews,' but pretty much everyone gets paid bonuses."* There's no official billing goal, but associates felt that the 1,800-hour mark was regularly cleared. *"Some people here are workaholics, but it's not a crazy-hour firm."* As we often hear from West Coasters, the work-life balance at Munger is *"probably as good as you could expect."* It is *"still Big Law, so there are last minute things which mean late nights and weekend work sometimes, but I can't complain too much."* Associates were used to leaving around 6pm having rocked up to work around 9.30am – not too shabby – but most also logged on once they were home. *"They're flexible about the when and where,"* enabling associates with families to get home for a bedtime story or three.

Offices

The brand new DC office is based a short trundle from both the White House and Supreme Court, an apt home for its new head. When we went to press, three associates had been hired so far, but we're told *"the DC office already connects by videolink during lunches."* The original West Coast duo can *"work pretty seamlessly,"* with some San Franciscans finding that *"most cases involve working with people in the LA office."* However, some LA associates claimed little to no significant contact with San Francisco.

"There were a lot of meetings about design choices."

Change is also afoot in LA. Employees need only cross the street to their new premises, again on South Grand Avenue. *"Over the past year there were a lot of meetings about design choices,"* with the committee system giving associates a say on the details. *"One big decision was about the glass doors of the offices and how opaque they would be."* The dramatic conclusion? *"You can only make out someone's outline."* Unlike most big firm attorneys, Munger associates are given their own office as soon as they start work, moving to a larger office after two years. In a continuation of the democratic theme, this upgrade leaves juniors with the same sized offices as partners.

Diversity

Diversity was the one area in which all associates agreed the firm didn't live up to its high standards. *"I think like all firms we could be better at diversity. Part of it is a pipeline issue, finding law school students who meet the standard and want to be in LA. But we've also had some retention issues."* Associates were sure, however, that a *"desire for change"* exists. Some associates suggested that *"because it's so democratic and bureaucratic it can be hard to get things done. People spend time looking at the issue but I don't know how close that gets us to a solution."* Recruiting co-chair Carolyn Hoecker Luedtke explains *"we're trying a variety of things,"* and points us to a number of initiatives. The MTO Fellows Program aids a group of students to succeed at their law schools and there's also a new summer program for 1Ls.

Get Hired

Carolyn Hoecker Luedtke tells us: *"We don't just want people to passively sit in their office and execute their work. We want people to be leaders: with their clients, within the firm and in their communities."* For more insight on recruitment, go to our MTO feature on chambers-associate.com.

Strategy & Future

Co-managing partner Sandra Seville-Jones is adamant the firm's *"not trying to achieve anything different from what we are usually: bringing bright lawyers into a low-leverage environment and trying to solve distinctive problems."* She does however let slip that *"I'd like to see us spend some time working in privacy and data security."* As for the DC branch, that'll be *"just another MTO office, solving our clients' toughest legal problems."* Seville-Jones explains that *"of course, we anticipate the appellate practice being strong, but with somebody like Don who has handled many complicated cases, it's about more than just appellate."*

See firm profile on p.634

Nixon Peabody LLP

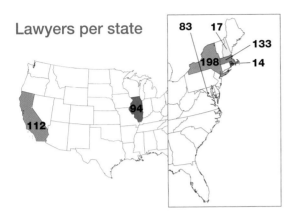

Lawyers per state

83	17
	133
198	14
94	
112	

Largest US office: New York
US offices: 12
International offices: 4
First-year salary: $160,000
Billable hours: 1,900 target
Summers 2017: 18 (14 2Ls, 4 1Ls)
Revenue 2016: $458 million (-0.7%)
Partners made in 2017: 14 (all US)
Famous for: entrepreneurial spirit and an urge to merge

"Embrace change," Nixon's MP exhorts. Like its new website, Nixon Peabody's future looks bright.

ALTHOUGH Nixon Peabody can trace its history back over a century, it is actually less than 20 years old. Confused? Well, back in 1999 a firm in New York state with the word 'Nixon' in its name merged with a Boston firm called Peabody & Brown. Further mergers since then have seen Nixon Peabody grow to today's 650 lawyers in 16 offices worldwide. The most recent combination was in 2015 with Chicago's Ungaretti & Harris. Nixon's CEO and managing partner Andrew Glincher tells us *"we have a solid platform of offices with a strong, cohesive culture. We continue our tradition of building office space that reflects our view of the future workplace."* He emphasizes that *"above all, we need to embrace change."*

There's a definite buzz around the firm right now, which not long ago underwent a snazzy re-brand complete with dazzling new website (you might need to wear sunglasses when you look at it). Around the same time, some offices moved to shiny new digs (see the Offices section below for more info). Glincher highlights some of Nixon's global activities. *"As part of our global strategy, we expanded our presence in Asia in 2016 by opening a representative*

On chambers-associate.com...

- Interview with CEO and managing partner Andrew Glincher
- Interview with hiring bigwigs Stacie Collier and John Snellings
- More on getting hired

office in Singapore. Singapore is an important gateway for our Asian clients investing and doing business in the US." Back home, Glincher continues that the firm is *"pursuing growth of our major metro offices and deepening our talent in major practice groups. We are currently focused on expanding our offerings in New York, California, Chicago, Washington, DC, and Boston based on client demand."* Furthermore, *"we have also made diversity a top priority,"* and to that end Nixon recently hired a full time diversity and inclusion manager and instituted new training.

The Work

Summer associates are taken at seven offices (Boston, Rochester, Chicago, Long Island, NYC, Rochester and San Fran). They rank three practices by preference, *"I've never heard of anyone not getting their first choice."* Most juniors end up in one of the firm's corporate or litigation teams, while others go to groups including healthcare, labor & employment, and real estate. However, some go into the *"business department pool,"* which is a generalist group that usually houses associates who have preferenced oversubscribed groups. While they waited for a specific spot to open up, juniors took on broad transactional work. *"In the beginning I didn't like it as I felt I was just doing work for the sake of it. It doesn't let you create relationships from day one which is what you need to do."*

Work assignment was simpler. *"It's heavily based on relationships, but there's a coordinator to help if you're slow."* While most were happy, others warned that *"you have*

The Inside View

Rankings in *Chambers USA*

Corporate/Commercial	Franchising
Corporate/M&A	Healthcare
Energy & Natural	Labor & Employment
Resources	Litigation
Environment	Real Estate

For detail on ranking tiers and ranking locations, visit
www.chambersandpartners.com

Recent work highlights

- Represented the daughter of Pablo Picasso in negotiations concerning the ownership of his 1931 work 'Bust of Woman'
- Advised Constellation Brands in the $1 billion acquisition of Ballast Point Brewing and Spirits
- Represented Exeter Health Resources after a member of staff allegedly infected patients with hepatitis C
- Advised NYC-based affordable housing developer Hudson Valley Property Group on its joint venture to acquire a 1,000+ unit housing portfolio in New Jersey

to be proactive. If you're unmotivated it's easy not to make your hours." On the flipside, others discouraged taking on too much. "It's tough in the first year to say no to work. The biggest lie you tell as a junior is: "Yes, I'd love to help with that!""

"If you can't handle responsibility, this might not be the place for you."

Transactional newbies had "mostly done M&A work, private equity securitization for public and private companies, done all the client calls, drafted ancillary documents and contracts, plus there's some due diligence." Rookies interact with clients by themselves. "I was told at law school that I wouldn't speak to clients until the third year – that's not the case here." In healthcare, insiders told us that they'd "worked a lot on the regulatory side, researching into abuse concerns, payment and HIPAA issues." Litigators had "conducted witness interviews and depositions." Others described "class actions with over 300 parties and I'm managing the deposition schedules and working on discovery disputes." One interviewee joked that "up until last month, I'd made it through two years without having to do doc review. But I suppose it's good I've done it now because it would be embarrassing as a fourth-year if I didn't know how to do it." Regardless of practice area, all associates stated that "if you can't handle responsibility, this might not be the place for you."

Training & Development

Orientation for new attorneys in Boston "is fantastic. The first two days are specifically firm orientation and then they break us up into either transactional or litigation groups. There's a transactional crash course and I still look at that material to help my work today." However, most early training comes through non-compulsory programs and conferences. "There's lots of different training on witness interviews and depositions." Mentors also play a role in development. Newbies get assigned an associate mentor straight away and then "after a year you choose a partner mentor who you think you can jive with. There's room for improvement because some are more hands on than others."

Associates have two six-monthly reviews in their first year, then an annual review after that. "You do a self evaluation and then ask the partners and seniors you've worked with most to review you." Two partners take the reviewee through the comments. "It's never a surprise: you know where you stand before you have the sit-down."

Pro Bono

Up to 60 pro bono hours can count toward the 1,850 billable requirement. Insiders felt that "it's an excellent opportunity to work on assignments that you wouldn't be responsible for in your billables for a number of years." Newbies get to cut their teeth on whatever takes their fancy. Matters had included "helping female immigrants who had been the victims of domestic violence find pathways to citizenship." The general consensus was that "it's a great chance, especially if you're a litigator, to get into a court room."

"It's a great chance, especially if you're a litigator, to get into a court room."

Pro bono hours
- For all US attorneys: 33,754
- Average per US attorney: 47

Hours & Compensation

As well as the 1,850 requirement (and 1,900 target to be bonus-eligible), there's an additional 400-hour requirement for personal development, which covers everything from keeping up with legal news to getting involved with the local community. The 400 hours are officially mandatory. "It's more important for fourth or fifth-years to help them develop client skills. It's more of an aspirational goal for the rest of us and there are no repercussions if we don't hit it."

"I don't hate my life here!"

Speaking of bonuses, the firm not only has a discretionary model, but an hourly one too. "Every 50 hours you go

See firm profile on p.635

The Inside View

Diversity	Partners (%)	Associates (%)
Women	25	48.2
White	90.4	74.6
Black/African American	1.5	5.4
Hispanic/Latin American	2.5	5.4
Asian	4	10.7
Mixed/Other	1.5	4
LGBT	3.4	5.4

above 1,900 you get a certain percentage above the base rate, until you get to 2,400 hours which gives you 15%." Unlike its peers, Nixon P. didn't increase the salary with the market. "It's because we raised in 2014 to $160,000." But there weren't complaints. "I think we're paid really well for what we do and I don't hate my life here!" To meet these targets, most insiders clock in around 9am and out by 6.30ish.

Culture

"We joke that NP stands for 'Nice People', but I really agree with it. It's not as cutthroat as other places and people don't dread coming in," juniors told us. A few felt that "because there have been so many mergers, each office has its own flavor. But the firm's atmosphere overall is one where everyone is interested in helping you out." Others explained further: "You never look at the person next to you and think they're my competition. They tell us that we can all succeed and make partner if we want to, we just have to work hard."

"We joke that NP stands for 'Nice People', but I really agree with it."

Like at most firms, summer brings the most social events. Everything from "wine tasting in Napa" to "casino nights" and "outings at the Boston aquarium" are on offer. While most offices have quarterly happy hours, social events aren't hugely frequent. However, sources weren't complaining: "It's not the type of firm where everyone is single and works hard and goes out every night. Most people have families, so they go home."

Offices

"Boston and New York are really like the two headquarters." However, Bostonians were quick to stress that "it's not like we're the Boston lot and everyone comes to us. Each office has its own identity and they're not satellites." In DC, "we recently moved to an up-and-coming area and there's glass everywhere. It's really cool because it's pushed all the other offices to change." Following suit, LA moved in April 2016. "Our office was essentially built from scratch, so we don't have a typical law office look. There's

lots of color and a roof terrace where we can eat lunch and have happy hours. Plus everyone has their own office."

"Bigger than some apartments, with views over the Bay."

New Yorkers are the next to get the upgrade: "We're transitioning to new offices in 2017." San Franciscans joked that their individual offices "are bigger than some apartments, with views over the Bay." They added for good measure that "yes, Boston is the home base, but we've never been left out. We're definitely not the awkward stepchild." Ironically, the only one out of the loop in terms of upgrades is Boston, but insiders revealed that "we're working toward a renovation, so hopefully we might be next!"

Diversity

"Every firm has a problem with this and we're no different. Ethnicity and female to male ratios in the partnership is a problem, but at least the firm recognizes it," said juniors. In an effort to address this, professional personnel partner Stacie Collier tells us about the firm's recruiting drive: "We work with a number of law schools in our efforts to recruit diverse candidates. We participate in a number of law school programs, organize our own programs, and participate in well-known diversity career fairs such as Lavender Law, which targets LGBT law students. We recently created an internship with Howard University Law School in which we invite diverse students to work in one of our practice groups for a semester to give them insight into the firm."

"It's not going to change overnight, but that doesn't mean we're not welcoming."

Associates could reel off a list of the usual affinity groups, but the most visible was the women's initiative. Across different offices, the group hosts "quarterly lunches where female rainmakers come in and talk about their experiences." On top of this, there are "mentoring circles made up of partners and juniors in different practice groups, so that you can get advice and interact with women that you might not have met before." However, when it came to racial diversity, insiders commented that "in my office I can name the attorneys of color on one hand." Yet sources were quick to add that "it's not going to change overnight, but that doesn't mean we're not welcoming."

Strategy & Get Hired

Stacie Collier's predecessor, John Snellings (now serving as of counsel) tells us what NP wants in new recruits: "In addition to academic excellence, we are also looking for candidates with practical experience." He goes on to

See firm profile on p.635

The Inside View

describe the importance of cultural fit too: *"We're also looking for law students who are a good fit with our firm culture. We are team-oriented and want to work with people who are entrepreneurial and creative."*

Looking to the future, Andrew Glincher tells us about the firm's growth. *"Our future growth is tied directly to our client focus and prioritizing their needs for services. We have expanded globally through opening a representative office in Singapore and creating associations with other international law firms. In doing so, we have cultivated good working relationships with these firms and many mutual clients."* For more info, go online.

"In addition to academic excellence, we are also looking for candidates with practical experience."

See firm profile on p.635

Norton Rose Fulbright

Lawyers per state

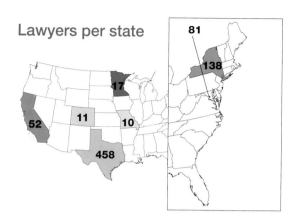

Largest US office: Houston
US offices: 11
International offices: 46
First-year salary: $180,000
Billable hours: 2,000 target
Summers 2017: 45 (31 2Ls, 14 1Ls)
Revenue 2016: $1.686 billion (-3%; $2 billion approx. post-merger)
Partners made in 2017: 12
Famous for: Texas vibe; giant international scope

"An air of humanity" defines this giant firm as much as its appetite for merger-led global expansion.

[Please note: headcount and revenue figures reflect the data available as we went to press and prior to the merger with Chadbourne & Parke .]

NORTON Rose Fulbright has catapulted into BigLaw stardom over the past few years, thanks to a series of smart combinations with firms across the globe. In 2017 the firm welcomes in Chadbourne, bringing extra wattage to Norton Rose Fulbright's already buzzing energy practice, and a shared enthusiasm for projects in emerging markets. It also helps this once Texas-focused firm gain a much stronger foothold in New York. The merger boosts headcount to approximately 4,000 lawyers spread across more than 50 cities worldwide, and is likely to nudge the firm up to sixth place in the *Am Law 100*.

The firm's long history of mergers is characterized by marrying-up complementary practice areas and amassing strategic locations for its globetrotting clients. But the merger that changed it all was in June 2013, when UK banking and projects heavyweight Norton Rose merged with Texas-based litigation powerhouse Fulbright & Jaworski. The firm's global headquarters are in London,

On chambers-associate.com...

- Justice for Jara: Chadbourne's pro bono work for the murdered folk singer
- Recruitment tips
- More on the training

but Texas remains an important command center for the firm. San Antonio-based partner Daryl Lansdale recently succeeded Houston's Linda Addison as the firm's US managing partner, and the Houston office stands strong as NRF's biggest US office.

'Expertise in the driving forces of globalization has propelled the firm's very own global expansion.'

In Texas, *Chambers USA* ranks Norton Rose Fulbright in areas including antitrust, bankruptcy & restructuring, healthcare, intellectual property, and labor & employment. Elsewhere, the firm wins plaudits nationwide for (among others) energy projects of all description, corporate/M&A, general litigation, product liability, retail, tax and aviation finance.

The *Chambers Global Top 30* places Norton Rose Fulbright as the world's seventh most capable global firm. Few firms can rival Norton Rose Fulbright's experience across the world's emerging markets – and with this comes a network spanning the Americas, Asia, Europe, Australia and Africa. Project finance has underpinned the firm's success in helping developing economies establish infrastructure: expertise in the driving forces of globalization has propelled the firm's very own global expansion. The newest additions to the network are in Monaco and San Francisco, and a merger with Vancouver's Bull Housser & Tupper. In spring 2016 the Houston office established a Latin America team to help support

The Inside View

See firm profile on p.636

Rankings in *Chambers USA*

Antitrust	International Arbitration
Banking & Finance	Labor & Employment
Bankruptcy/Restructuring	Litigation
Corporate/M&A	Products Liability
Energy & Natural	Projects
Resources	Retail
Environment	Tax
Healthcare	Technology
Insurance	Transportation
Intellectual Property	

For detail on ranking tiers and ranking locations, visit
www.chambersandpartners.com

Recent work highlights

- Defending Shell in a $40 million lawsuit concerning the alleged underpayment of federal oil royalites.
- Guided CeloNova BioSciences through the $70 million sale of its interventional radiology business to Boston Scientific Corporation
- Helped Qualcomm successfully rebuff over 130 patent infringement claims raised by consumer electronics giant NVIDIA.
- Assisted General Electric on the acquisition, development and franchising of the $2.7 billion Desert Sunlight Solar Farm in California
- Represented Argentinian oil and gas producer YPF relating to allegations brought by the State of New Jersey and Occidental Chemical concerning the pollution of the Garden State's Passaic River

the booming projects and energy trade emerging from the firm's Rio de Janeiro, Bogota and Caracas offices.

"All of our recent hires seem to have a very global perspective."

Juniors here were attracted to the firm's reach and ambition, and had found that *"all of our recent hires seem to have a very global perspective. The firm is actively trying to recruit people who are keen to work with offices around the world, and driven to further strengthen those ties,"* an associate told. The work *"is consistently challenging,"* but reassuringly, *"people here are far from a bunch of automatons."* In fact, our sources found their colleagues *"fun, interesting people who aren't afraid to go out for a drink every now and again."*

The Work

The 90 junior associates on our list of interviewees were spread across as many as 17 practice areas. The corporate, M&A and securities group was the most populated with 15 juniors, but now with the inclusion of Chadbourne, we expect more junior opportunities in New York for litigation and project finance. Before the summer program begins, participants are asked which types of work they'd like to experience. *"We give them a true idea of what it's like to be an associate,"* says hiring partner Doug Wabner. Summers *"very often have client contact and their work would be shown to clients."* The hands-on experience helps new joiners make an informed decision on the practice group they join.

NRF's assignment system functions as a managed market economy. *"You get work by reaching out to partners and chasing up matters yourself,"* explained one insider, *"but partners will keep an eye on everyone's workload."*

For sources in Houston's corporate team *"there's a steep but well managed increase in responsibility."* When first starting, juniors take on *"a lot of research and due diligence, which helps you to flesh out an understanding of*

entire project and deal structures." Once they've shown they can handle that, rookies begin to communicate with clients. In their first six months, juniors here had reviewed confidentiality agreements, drafted contracts, and even run their own deals. *"It was a straightforward asset purchase, but I was understandably pretty nervous,"* recalled one deal-doer. *"Thankfully, whenever I was stuck my supervising partner would mark up my work and talk me through what needed changing. That helped a lot going forward."*

"A lot more collaboration with offices across the US, and across the world too."

Aside from corporate, associates could also be found in areas including IP transactions and patent prosecution; other strands of IP; straight finance as well as financial institutions and insurance; and regulations, investigations, securities and compliance. There are various groups dedicated to the energy sector, such as energy and infrastructure, energy transactions, and power and alternative energy. Certain offices are best known for specific expertise, like Dallas with its litigation know-how. Since the big merger in 2013, associates had noticed *"a lot more collaboration with offices across the US, and across the world too."*

The legacy Chadbourne practice in project finance was popular with our interviewees. *"We do wind, solar, geothermal, a little non-renewable and a lot of gas deals. They could be domestic or international and if they're international they tend to be in Latin America or Africa."* First-years are channeled toward *"process-driven tasks"* such as maintaining closing checklists and getting people in the right place to sign documents. Lean staffing on this team means *"you get to build up broad expertise early on."*

See firm profile on p.636

Diversity	Partners (%)	Associates (%)
Women	20.9	47.8
White	91.8	73.1
Black/African American	1	4.8
Hispanic/Latin American	3.4	4.9
Asian	3.4	12.9
Mixed/Other	0.3	4.3
LGBT	Undisclosed	Undisclosed

New York litigation is split into subgroups such as IP, securities regulation, international arbitration and white-collar crime. Associates are *"hired as generalists and it takes time to specialize. I didn't realize how much dedication I would have to show to an area."* But several interviewees had made the most of sampling the department's delights: *"One of my favorite things about the group is being able to steer myself toward great work."* People had spent time doing *"a lot of research and a ton of drafting."* One recalled: *"A year and a half in, I was able to draft motions by myself, albeit with a senior's input."*

Get Hired

¿Hablas español? Você fala português? *"We have a big presence in Latin America"* plus a slew of other international matters, *"so it's pretty common for people to be multilingual."* Both multi and mono-linguists alike should check out www.chambers-associate.com for recruitment tips and advice from associates.

Offices

Before this merger happened, each firm looked at the other's US market and decided they could do with a better presence there. So energy-focused Chadbourne finally got a base in Texas, and global finance giant Norton Rose Fulbright got a significant boost in Manhattan. Conveniently, the two firms are based one on top of the other in the same tower in Midtown New York – the firm assures us this merger was more than just a chat in the lift taken too far. Integration in New York will be almost effortless, but in the other cities where there are now two offices – DC and LA – the firm expects a slower integration.

"A lot of the legendary partners are based here."

Houston was the firm's biggest US office before the combination (now it's New York), and houses far more junior associates than any other base. *"It's where Fulbright really made its name. A lot of the legendary partners are based here and the sheer amount of people in the office lends it*

that feeling too. We have three floors dedicated solely to litigation!" The firm occupies the top dozen floors of Fulbright Tower, and all partners and associates have their own window and offices. But despite Fulbright's long history in Space City, *"there's no feeling that we're the command center and our other offices function as satellites. Our workforce is so global and the remote access technology is so advanced that big US meetings can be held anywhere really."*

Dallas, Austin, and DC are the next most junior-heavy offices, followed by LA, San Antonio, Minneapolis and St. Louis, which claim between one and three each. *"It feels like all of our US offices are growing in importance as one,"* another insider affirmed. *"It used to be the case that the Texas offices functioned independently of one another, but now we work together a lot more regularly. There's a lot of interaction with DC and New York too."*

Diversity

"There's been a huge emphasis on bringing the firm into the 21st century," juniors highlighted when questioned on diversity. *"NRF is making ground in a way that you don't see among other Texan firms."* Spearheading this effort is the firm's 2020 vision, a legacy project first conceived by outgoing US managing partner Linda Addison. *"The idea is that by 2020 we want 30% of our board and management committees across the globe to be female,"* explained one source, *"as well as 30% of our partners globally."*

"NRF is making ground in a way that you don't see among other Texas firms."

Plans seem to be moving along well. Summer classes are *"extremely diverse,"* and *"the firm also funds and supports a whole range of affinity groups and awareness events,"* catering to demographics such as ethnic minorities, LGBTQ and female attorneys. Associates were proud to tell us: *"If you come in my hallway you'll hear a lot of Spanish!"* And this progressive culture looks in safe hands: *"We've always believed in diversity, and we will continue to believe in it under my watch,"* declares Wabner.

Pro Bono

"As a young associate you're encouraged to do a lot of pro bono work," interviewees agreed. Litigators we spoke to had tackled divorce cases, death penalty appeals and asylum cases, while transactional lawyers had helped veterans draft wills and formed entities for not-for-profits. Chadbourne had thrown a lot of its pro bono muscle behind immigrant cases in recent years and enjoyed some *"long fought battles."* Sources felt *"there are usually more litigious opportunities available, but the pro bono commit-*

See firm profile on p.636

The Inside View

tee does its best to find opportunities that will interest you." One rookie remembered their first case, where *"I was too nervous to take it all on by myself. The pro bono team put me in touch with a partner who helped co-pilot the case, and that gave me the confidence to do my next one alone."* 100 hours of pro bono can be counted toward associates' 2,000 hour target.

Culture & Hours

Charitable work also forms the basis of one of Norton Rose Fulbright's most exciting social opportunities. Every year a selection of attorneys from across the world make their way to Houston to compete in the MS 150. This two-day fundraising bike ride is organized by the National MS Society, and sources told us that *"over seventy members of the firm turned up last year to make the big cycle from Houston to Austin. It was a great way to meet colleagues you may not otherwise get the chance to meet, and made me feel a part of a fully-integrated global organization."*

"Fulbright's hallmark is its kindness."

"Fulbright's hallmark is its kindness," reflected one Houstonite. *"Southern hospitality is alive and well here!"* Interviewees across the board praised their colleagues for their *"air of humanity,"* with one adding: *"We all work really hard but if a family emergency crops up you'll have loads of people willing to cover for you."* This isn't always the case at the biggest global firms: *"There's an understanding here that facilitating an outside life makes for better lawyers."* Insiders felt that office culture and working styles vary depending on which branch you're in. *"Austin is a bit more relaxed than Houston,"* claimed one Austin source. *"It's a more casual working environment, and people don't wear suits every day. More people in Austin are on flexible schedules, or work remotely, and Dallas it's the same. People are busy in waves here, but there's no expectation you'll be in the office if you're not needed."*

Over in Houston, *"things are a little closer to the New York-style BigLaw culture."* Still, Houstonites didn't seem too aggrieved. *"Things are a little busier here, and we all work hard to ensure the firm continues to compete at a global level,"* one junior voiced. *"But I really don't feel like I'm part of an all-consuming rat race. I have children, and feel I'm able to leave at five to spend time with them, before putting in a few hours' work later on."*

"We all work hard to ensure the firm continues to compete at a global level."

The New York office of Chadbourne stood out for fostering independence in its junior attorneys: *"There's an emphasis on people going out and bringing in new clients. We have a lot of networking events geared toward it, including one where we invited peers graduating from business school."* We expect this culture to continue.

Irrespective of where associates are based, there's no billable hours requirement during their first year. When first-years bloom into second-years, a target of 2,000 hours kicks in, on which hangs standard bonus eligibility. *"There's an expectation you'll make 2,000, but it's not a hard expectation,"* associates reckoned. *"If you don't hit it it's unlikely you'll be fired!"*

Strategy & Future

Norton Rose Fulbright's track record is set to continue in the coming years. *"As Monaco proved, it's clear that the firm will continue to look for expansive growth opportunities,"* associates maintained. The firm's key industries – financial institutions; energy; infrastructure, mining and commodities; transport; technology and innovation; and life sciences and healthcare – are set to maintain their importance, though with Fulbright historically a Texas-based litigation shop, *"we'll be looking to grow our New York and DC offices, and add more US-based transactional work within our key industries."*

"We've definitely retained our prestige in the local community..." For more on how things have changed post-merger, head to the Bonus Features online.

See firm profile on p.636

Nutter McClennen & Fish LLP

Lawyers per state

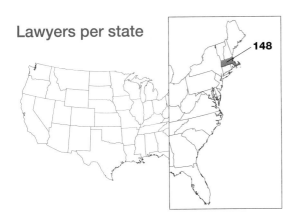

148

Largest US office: Boston
US offices: 2
International offices: 0
First-year salary: $160,000
Billable hours: 1,900 required
Summers 2017: 8 (7 2Ls, 1 1L)
Revenue 2016: $89.4 million (+2.8%)
Partners made in 2017: 3
Famous for: a top firm in Boston; link with legendary SCOTUS Justice Louis Brandeis

In a nutshell, this Bostonian is uncommonly good.

FOLLOWING a rebrand in 2016, Nutter now has a slogan: *Uncommon Law.* Several of the firm's select group of associates explained to us that they were attracted by Nutter's 'uncommon' reputation compared to larger firms: *"The buzz was that it's a different place, really collegial, it fosters associates, and staffs leanly so you get substantive work early on. It was incredibly nice and welcoming. Firms can seem the same, and it came down to atmosphere."* Others spoke of *"feeling valued"* and how *"they hire people with the expectation they will become partners at some point."* Managing partner Deb Manus was equally enthusiastic: *"People are truly energized by the new Uncommon Law brand. The 'discovery phase' of the project involved all of the members of the Nutter community: clients, attorneys, staff and industry experts with whom we work. We unveiled the brand in May with a major internal brand launch event."*

Nutter also has unique history – it was co-founded by Supreme Court Justice Louis Brandeis, no less, in 1879. Deb Manus adds that *"the other thing about a good brand is that is a way of reminding people that we have to constantly aspire to delivering on the brand promise. A good brand inspires people to do that."* Today's 150 or so lawyers still operate from Boston, plus a small Hyannis office. *Chambers USA* ranks the firm highly for banking & finance, litigation, real estate, environment, and labor & employment work.

The Work

Juniors begin at Nutter in one of the following practices: real estate & finance, trusts & estates, tax, IP, litigation, or

On chambers-associate.com...

- Interviews with managing partner Deb Manus and hiring chair Matthew Bresette

business (Nutter's word for corporate). Associates must fill out weekly reports to their department chair so that their workload can be assessed, and new work assigned. *"That's the formal system,"* associates revealed, *"but it's not uncommon that partners you've worked with will talk to you or the chair and give you work themselves. There's the formal process and then some of it happens more organically."* The system's loosest in the smaller departments, but everyone reported that *"the firm has been very receptive to the types of work I've enjoyed doing."*

Litigation is Nutter's largest department and handles *"anything and everything,"* making forays into business and commercial, product liability, environmental, IP, white collar and employment and labor law as part of its wide roaming practice. Associates handle doc reviews, discovery requests, brief writing and research, but they were positive about how *"we leanly staff deals so you do get more opportunities."* These include *"progressing to manage the people doing doc review,"* witness interviews and drafting memos. *"I think it's a nice balance of some core junior tasks, which you know come at a law firm, but also of more interesting, substantive work."*

"I've worked with every lawyer here already."

The Inside View

See firm profile on p.637

437

Rankings in *Chambers USA*

Banking & Finance	Litigation
Environment	Real Estate
Labor & Employment	

For detail on ranking tiers and ranking locations, visit www.chambersandpartners.com

Nutter's real estate department throws commercial finance matters into the mix too, involving financing, acquisition and lending on the one hand, and development, leasing, land use and zoning on the other. They do this for a mixture of banks, developers, investors, property owners and public sector clients. For associates it's a case of being *"exposed to every part of the department – in a kind of utility role. I've worked with every lawyer here already, but you specialize after a few years."* They'd met with clients – *"absolutely key to an associate at my level"* – and saw their fair share of drafting ancillary documents and leases.

In the petite business department, associates can find work which is *"wide ranging."* As well as providing corporate and regulatory services to banks and other well-established clients, the department also picks up work from emerging companies: *"It's nice to get experience with both the investors and the start-ups – it's good, pure corporate work, and you're seeing it work on the ground."* Juniors can get up to their necks in drafting: *"Things like the financing documents and the term sheet: I'm usually in charge of drafting them in the first instance."*

Culture

One associate spoke of Nutter's more relaxed *"liberal arts"* vibe, and most explained the culture in terms of the firm's smallish size: *"Everyone knows you, nobody is a stranger – I like that. I didn't want to be an anonymous person, I wanted a community."* Associates also felt *"partners and associates are treated as equals – partners will ask you questions and really value your opinion, maybe on research or on strategy. They actually want to hear from you."* Hiring the right sort of people is key: *"Everyone gets along with each other, partly because the firm is mindful of hiring people who get behind the Nutter vision of being client-focused and respectful of each other. You can end up making good friends."* Moreover, *"because people want you to stay here and become a partner down the road, you feel like you're given a high level of responsibility – that trust goes a long way."* Fewer associates also means less competition: *"All these partners are invested in you and so you work to make sure you give bang for your buck."* To help with their development, juniors get two formal reviews a year plus an associate and partner mentor.

"We have what the firm calls 'wine down Thursdays'."

Recent work highlights

- Represents Fidelity bank concerning an international pyramid scheme. The Telexfree alleged Ponzi scheme has yielded government and internal investigations plus a class action across districts, and was worth around $3 billion
- Represented the financial adviser Sandler O'Neill Partners as it helped Provident Bancorp with its $42 million IPO
- Aided Houghton Mifflin Harcourt, an educational publisher, on the relocation of its headquarters, the largest lease transaction in Boston in 2015
- Represented the City of Haverhill Massachusetts over allegations by the United States that its water treatment plants were not meeting requirements

As for socializing, *"we have what the firm calls 'wine down Thursdays': they put out wine and cheese for us and we hang out for a bit, then it might spill over into something more..."* A holiday party at the end of the year and a summer attorney outing give further cause for mirth. *"Nutter does a good job of hiring people who are funny, kind and personable so you tend to be able to get a drink with other attorneys in the department."* However, even the best of friends need a little separation: *"The reality is that while everyone has a strong relationship here, they maintain lives outside of work. It's very family-friendly, the younger associates might go out around Boston, but others use the free time to spend it with their families."*

Offices & Training

Nutter goes as far as bricks and mortar to enshrine its culture, giving associates and partners alike the same sized offices: *"It's just a small example of how they treat you but I think it's a good demonstration of their commitment."* Several juniors told us they were *"in and out all the time. Rarely am I just in my office. We're encouraged to work on our assignments but at appropriate junctures go and ask a partner some questions for a minute – I'm very comfortable doing that."*

"They are devoted to developing us."

More structured training begins with the aptly titled Nuts and Bolts program, consisting of *"maybe six or seven training sessions over a few months to give an overview of the big things you'll work on as a junior associate – it's pretty comprehensive."* Some praised a 'critical skills curriculum' the firm is putting in place: *"The fact they're willing to develop an entire series shows they are devoted to developing associates."*

Pro Bono

Nutter has an historic connection to pro bono – co-founder Louis Brandeis was a big fan. Flash forward 140-

See firm profile on p.637

The Inside View

Diversity	Partners (%)	Associates (%)
Women	28	55
White	97	81
Black/African American	0	7.5
Hispanic/Latin American	3	4
Asian	0	7.5
Mixed/Other	0	0
LGBT	1	4

Hours & Compensation

Interviewees were content with their salary, which went up from $145,000 to $160,000 following the Cravath scale raise to $180,000. *"Although it's very important that we responded to the recent hikes, we aren't trying to be a '180' firm – nobody wants associates working that hard!"*

"Nobody wants associates working that hard!"

Associates' billing requirement is 1,900 hours with an extra 100 of *"additional firm accountable time"* too: a number both first-years and those in quieter departments found this tough. *"You're given some flexibility in first year about hitting that,"* as training sometimes intervenes, but it didn't have associates too concerned either way. *"Not getting a bonus is a small sacrifice for having a life through the year."* People tend to leave the office around 7pm on average, though they spoke of working occasional weekends.

odd years and you'll still find *"the overall attitude toward it is very positive. You can just pop up to talk to the people from KIND* [Kids In Need of Defense]*"* – the charity is based in the same building. Associates had also worked on things like immigration, helping people gain tax exempt status, and residential landlord-tenant disputes: *"It's a great chance to get some autonomy."* The firm lets associates loose by allowing unlimited pro bono in their billable hours.

Pro bono hours
- For all attorneys: 6,106
- Average per attorney: 46

Diversity & Get Hired

Good female representation aside, associate opinion was unanimous: *"There is a lot of work to be done."* But *"the firm is making the investment it has to to make any strides."* Deb Manus explains exactly how: *"Another thing I am very proud of is the progress we have made in making diversity and inclusion a priority at Nutter. We spent a full year developing a Diversity and Inclusion strategic plan."* The proof is in the pudding, and against a backdrop of 97% white partners, she highlights that *"of the lateral attorney hires we made in the past year, 83% were diverse candidates. That represents real progress for us. We're making it a priority."*

For anyone applying to Nutter *"the biggest question that they ask is why Nutter? And moreso, why Boston?"* Candidates should should prove their Beantown commitment and *"be a good fit."* And Nutter's policy of minimal hiring, maximum development? MP Deb Manus says *"Nutter will continue to make very significant investment in the professional development of our people. We have no plans to change that model. Hiring the right people, and then watching them succeed is one of the most satisfying aspects of my job."* For more detail on hiring, read outgoing recruitment partner Matt Bresette's interview online.

Strategy & Future

"I'd like to know a little more about the fundamental aspects of the firm," some juniors told us. *"I'm glad you mentioned that,"* MP Deb Manus tells us. *"After we spoke last year, I decided to start giving the associates periodic State of the Firm presentations. I did one in the fall and am doing another later this month. Organizationally, we continue to make an effort to involve associates in our formal client teams and internal committees, such as Hiring and Diversity and Inclusion. From a professional development standpoint, it's important that our up and coming talent understand how the firm works. After all, some day it will be up to them to run it."*

One junior had this to say on the firm's strategy: *"Nutter does a great job at doing what it does best, recognizing that, and being profitable. It's not going to be making humongous decisions like acquiring firms: it's more of a conservative approach."* Deb Manus notes that *"we don't rule out increasing the number of lawyers or opening offices in other jurisdictions, but the fit would just have to be right for us and for our clients. Given how vibrant the Boston economy is, it's a little hard to make an urgent case for diversifying out of this market."*

"Given how vibrant the Boston economy is, it's a little hard to make an urgent case for diversifying out of this market."

See firm profile on p.637

O'Melveny & Myers LLP

Lawyers per state

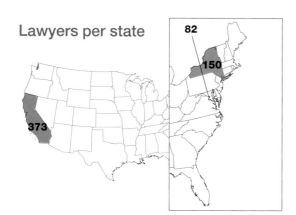

82

150

373

Largest US office: Los Angeles
US offices: 7
International offices: 8
First-year salary: $180,000
Billable hours: no requirement
Summers 2017: 70 (56 2Ls, 8 1Ls, 6 other)
Revenue 2016: $725 million (+5.1%)
Partners made in 2017: 8
Famous for: California heritage; strong on pro bono

Long before Ryan Gosling and Emma Stone hit the scene, O'Melveny & Myers was already lighting up La-La Land.

CAN you imagine Los Angeles as a small 19th Century frontier town? None of the glitz and glamor of Hollywood? Little more than 5,000 occupants? Well, this was the LA where the firm that is now O'Melveny & Myers first made its mark in 1885. O'Melveny today has over 700 lawyers in 15 offices worldwide, but still plays a pivotal role in the bustling LA scene. The BigLaw firm has a reputation for *"laid back California vibes,"* which interviewees found to be *"100% true."* Some found their OCI here *"the only interview where I really felt I could be myself."* Others said *"it didn't feel like they were trying to interview me to be an attorney; rather, to be a part of their organization."*

> **"The only interview where I really felt I could be myself."**

The firm gains Oscar-worthy rankings in *Chambers USA* for numerous practices in its California stronghold, plus New York and DC, including antitrust, bankruptcy, general commercial and white collar litigation, media & entertainment, and tax. Nationwide, the firm also gains recognition in areas including ERISA and insurance litigation, securities regulation, and projects, including renewables. While sources characterized O'Melveny as *"definitely a litigation firm,"* they pointed out that *"we're trying to bolster our transactional groups to even it out a bit."*

The Work

Just under three-quarters of juniors on our interviewee list were in litigation. The remaining quarter dealt with transactional matters. In both areas the work stays pretty general; it isn't until the third year that rookies can specialize. During this time, *"the people are really good at getting you exposed to a variety of areas, and working on things you're interested in."* Both litigators and transactional folks have a work advisers who *"ensures you are being fed assignments from the expressed interests you've talked about."* However, work assignment can also be more free market if you want it to be: *"As you get more senior it's a little less rigid. You develop relationships with certain partners and end up working for them."* The work coordinator meant they *"felt protected if I accidentally take on too much."*

Litigation's ample umbrella covers many areas including securities litigation, white collar and investigations, insurance litigation, antitrust, and general commercial disputes. This allows juniors the option to *"explore many different areas"* before specializing. Juniors were often in charge of *"a broad overview of the entire case"* and *"keeping tabs on everything."* They also spent much time speaking with experts: *"I'm in a position where there are some*

On chambers-associate.com...

- More on getting hired at O'Melveny & Myers
- Interview with firm chair Brad Butwin
- Becoming a lawyer in California

See firm profile on p.638

Rankings in *Chambers USA*

Antitrust	Intellectual Property
Appellate Law	International Trade
Bankruptcy/Restructuring	Labor & Employment
Capital Markets	Litigation
ERISA Litigation	Media & Entertainment
Employee Benefits &	Products Liability
Executive Compensation	Projects
Environment	Securities
Insurance	Tax

For detail on ranking tiers and ranking locations, visit
www.chambersandpartners.com

Recent work highlights

- Represented Donald Trump and Trump University in two class actions over false marketing allegations
- Representing Kesha in her ongoing dispute with long-time producer Dr Luke
- M&A and antitrust counsel to Alaska Airlines in its $4 billion acquisition of Virgin America
- Successfully invalidated all claims of three patents asserted by Visual Real Estate against Google involving Google's mapping products and GPS

subject matters that nobody else understand as well as I do. The partnership trusts us to understand what's going on because there's so much going on. They can't take the time to learn everything."

"I'd say less than 5% of my time is spent on doc review."

Juniors said they didn't do much doc review: "I've had one doc review assignment all year. I'd say less that 5% of my time is spent on it." Others relished substantive tasks like writing briefs and motions, calls with opposing counsel, witness prep, and witness interviews over the phone. One even said "I had the opportunities as a first-year to do witness interviews on my own." Many interviewees felt they had "enough oversight that it's not totally overwhelming, but enough responsibility that I'm growing as an attorney and not stuck in one place." Others reckoned "it's definitely a priority of the firm to try to give juniors as much responsibility as is appropriate on the case." Even with client contact, sources felt they had "significant opportunities to have my voice heard." This came especially with smaller matters where juniors were "the first point of contact to the client."

Transactional groups cover areas such as M&A, public companies, venture financing, and general banking and financing. Areas like bankruptcy felt more like "a good mix of litigation-side bankruptcy work and transactional bankruptcy work," despite being a "technically transactional" group. A third-year banking associate felt that "in the last year or so, the work has been transitioning to more substantive tasks." Initial work included classic junior tasks: legal research, keeping track of checklists, having documents printed and ready for the team, and setting up the logistics of calls. This increased to drafting ancillary documents, reviewing and summarizing contracts, "low-level" negotiating, and assisting on closings. "In terms of how they progress us, I think it's great," a junior explained. "Because it's a smaller practice, you don't really have a choice – you've got to take on more responsibility just because there aren't that many people." Some felt "the

unique benefit of being at a big, top 50 law firm in terms of resources, but because the corporate team is smaller and everyone seems to know each other, you develop a rapport with people faster and are entrusted with more substantive stuff quicker." However, "client contact is a bit limited at my level, but on smaller deals there's a bit more."

Pro Bono

At O'Melveny, attorneys are "100% committed to pro bono work." There's no cap on the number of hours you can bill, and there's "an expectation that everyone will do at least 20 hours a year." Sources explained "you're basically running a case by yourself, which is invaluable experience as a junior." Pro bono cases included asylum and visa cases, disability cases, environmental litigation, and family law matters. The firm is also involved in a program that helps provide Special Immigrant Juvenile Status to children that have been abandoned, neglected, or are escaping violence. Juniors also felt that pro bono provided "great opportunities to speak in court and do things you're not going to get to do on multimillion dollar cases as a first year."

Pro bono hours

- For all US attorneys: 60,914
- Average per US attorney: 104

Training & Development

"When you first come to the firm, there's a good amount of training to refresh you on everything you learned as a summer." After that, there's regular lunch trainings, and although these aren't compulsory, a lot of it goes toward CLE credit "making it more in enticing to go." There's also an associate and counsel off-site retreat every year where "they send out the kind of trainings we want, from networking to drafting to research. We asked, and they listened." Other juniors felt that "most training is on the job." One source tackled training by "going to one of the more senior associates I trust and asking them to send me what they've done on a particular task, then trying to emulate that."

See firm profile on p.638

Diversity	Partners (%)	Associates (%)
Women	19.1	45.1
White	89.4	75.8
Black/African American	2.1	1.9
Hispanic/Latin American	0.5	5.3
Asian	8.0	14.4
Mixed/Other	0	2.6
LGBT	2.7	5.8

Offices

The New York office of this Californian firm is located in Times Square. As of 2017, first-years share their office with another first-year, then everyone gets their own after that. In LA, where there's a lot of high profile entertainment work (litigation and transactional), many juniors highlighted the *"great associate lounge"* where you often find people taking it easy on a Friday evening. Apparently partners' key cards don't work for the lounge – *"but we do let them in!"*

Culture

"To compare us to high school," one associate joked, *"we're not the most popular kids, but we're not the unpopular ones – just the ones hanging out and having fun."* Attorneys here are *"people who like to laugh,"* although perhaps *"a bit goofy."* Juniors emphasized that their senior colleagues are not *"all high-strung, and don't yell or throw things."* Overall, they thought O'Melveny has a *"professional but family-type culture. The people here are both bright and capable, but 'normal'."* Sources also noticed that *"people can transfer between offices all over,"* and cited the firm's culture as one of the reasons why, if people have to relocate for personal reasons, *"they don't look to exit the firm, but look to stay within the firm wherever they move."*

"Bright and capable, but 'normal'."

Because the firm *"gives people the opportunity to interact with clients from a pretty early stage, they want people who are comfortable doing that as opposed to having their noses stuck in books constantly."* Sources also felt that the firm *"doesn't want a hierarchical barrier between partners and associates."* To help achieve this, a mentor-mentee budget pays for juniors to take a partner to lunch. The social life differs from office to office, but all have regular happy hours. In some there are *"a lot of attorneys with kids, so after-hours socializing isn't as big."* But juniors were keen to highlight the *"real close friendships"* between attorneys, and the overall *"friendly and social work environment."*

Hours & Compensation

The unofficial expectation is for associates to bill at least 1,900 hours. *"Nobody has a problem meeting that given the amount of work we have."* One source explained that *"when I look at my daily average, I feel like the firm respects my time and that I have other things in my life I want to do. I never feel like they are demanding so much that I'm questioning any aspect of my job."* But unsurprisingly *"there are definitely times when you don't have any free time. For example, if I'm filing something on Friday, I wouldn't make dinner plans on Thursday."* Broadly speaking, *"it's more about doing the work by the deadline – it's not necessarily vital that you're here working between 9am and 6pm."*

Juniors had no qualms about the compensation system – the firm matched the market rate in all offices when it was raised. As for bonuses, they are also at market *"plus sometimes a bump for doing a lot more hours, or a merit bump."*

Diversity

Many highlighted diversity as a *"high priority in recruiting"* and felt the firm to be *"extremely inclusive."* However, associates recognized that *"an expressed value doesn't necessarily always translate,"* although *"it does at associate level, at least."* There is *"a big push to make sure there are programs in place for women to not feel like they need to leave the firm at any point."* A women's leadership retreat also takes place where *"women partners encourage and prime associates to make partner."* Some felt that *"the make-up of people isn't that diverse, not for lack of trying,"* but observed that *"it's not like I'm always staring across the table at six old white guys."* Overall, juniors believed *"there's still work to be done everywhere in BigLaw, but I would say we're ahead of the curve."*

Strategy & Future

Juniors were under the impression that the firm is becoming *"focused on industry groups instead of just practices – practices centered around say, life sciences or transportation, for example."* They also felt that O'Melveny will *"continue to play to its strengths, rather than expand into things it doesn't really understand. The firm isn't going to try and unseat the king of some other practice area to become the best – we're going to stick to what we're already good at and maintain our position there."*

Firm chair Brad Butwin says the firm's strategy is *"about being client-centric."* He explains that *"the onus is on us to stay top of mind and work hard to deliver outstanding results and exceptional service every single time."* This means becoming much more efficient: the firm has now *"invested heavily in our software and have our own AI*

See firm profile on p.638

build into our database which houses 132 years worth of documents." Butwin emphasizes that these investments will lead to "*increased efficiency and decreased cost to the client*." He also admits that "*none of us can predict the full range of client needs in the future*," so expresses that associates themselves should be "*multidimensional*." In terms of new offices, Butwin asserts that "*we don't subscribe to the whole 'build it and they will come' strategy. We will continue to talk to clients about which locations and practices are important to them, and continue to play to our strengths. Whether that's opening offices or developing new practices, we'll only do it if it is in our clients' best interests*."

Get Hired

Hiring partner Allen Burton says the candidates that stand out are those who have "*a combination of enthusiasm for practicing law, and enthusiasm for our firm in particular*." Find out more about getting hired at O'Melveny at chambers-associate. com

Learn more about becoming a lawyer in California on chambers-associate.com

The Inside View

See firm profile on p.638

Orrick, Herrington & Sutcliffe LLP

Lawyers per state

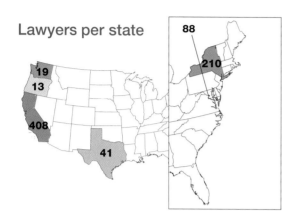

Largest US office: New York

US offices: 12

International offices: 14

First-year salary: $180,000 ($165,000 in Portland, Sacramento and Seattle)

Billable hours: no requirement (2,000 encouraged)

Summers 2017: 66 (63 2Ls, 3 1Ls)

Revenue 2016: $929.1 million (+1.7%)

Partners made in 2017: 18 (15 US)

Famous for: Bay Area origins; energy, finance and tech work; start up clients

"The work is cutting edge, but everyone retains their humanity" at the Californian colossus cultivating the tech giants of the future.

LAW students (probably) don't need to worry about artificial intelligence getting clever enough to replace human lawyers any time soon, but technology like AI is undoubtedly revolutionizing the legal profession. Orrick associates who noted their firm is renowned for a *"strong reputation in tech and with start ups"* were quick to assure us they're not treated like machines: *"The first thing that struck me was how concerned people were about my ideas. They go out of their way to make you feel you're not just a cog in the wheel."*

Coming in, juniors *"wanted to be part of important cases with decisions that set the landscape,"* and *"knew that would happen at Orrick."* Their hopes were no doubt encouraged by a broad smattering of *Chambers USA* rankings – including top marks for project finance nationwide and energy in California – as well as the landmark opening of a shiny new Houston office in 2016. In early 2017, the firm opened another new base, in Santa Monica.

The Work

Energy & infrastructure, technology and financial services are the firm's core strengths. Within these broad areas, Orrick offers incoming associates a range of corporate, litigious and specialist practice areas to get stuck into. Projects are often staffed across offices, *"depending on the practice area and case,"* and some juniors got exotic work with an international flavor. One was even *"geared up to go overseas for three months. The case ultimately settled, but I was surprised they trusted me with that as a first-year!"*

The large litigation group has a formal allocation system involving a central assigning partner. Interviewees also had partners reach out to them directly, *"so you get work from a mix of both. It's a pretty good system: the coordinator makes sure you're not drowning in work, and have time for sleep!"* New associates spend three years in a general pool where they can get work spanning tort, white collar, securities, and complex commercial litigation among other things. Keen to make it clear they play an integral role in cases, juniors told us they *"do a lot of research and drafting, and there is some document review, but it's all for a specific purpose and not for the sake of it."* The majority picked up *"a good amount of work – it's up to the individual to push back if needed so you're not completely overwhelmed."*

On chambers-associate.com...

- AI and the law: what does the future hold?
- Get Hired: interview tips and tricks
- Interview with chairman and CEO Mitch Zuklie
- What is a unicorn?

"I was geared up to go overseas for three months!"

See firm profile on p.639

The Inside View

Rankings in *Chambers USA*

Antitrust	Insurance
Appellate Law	Intellectual Property
Banking & Finance	Labor & Employment
Bankruptcy/Restructuring	Latin American Investment
Capital Markets	Litigation
Corporate/M&A	Native American Law
Employee Benefits &	Products Liability
Executive Compensation	Projects
Energy & Natural	Real Estate
Resources	Startups & Emerging
IT & Outsourcing	Companies

For detail on ranking tiers and ranking locations, visit
www.chambersandpartners.com

In corporate, most associates tend to be immediately placed into specific subgroups, which include capital markets and general corporate (covering M&A and private equity). On the West Coast, most go into the technology companies team, *"handling all stages of the corporate life cycle"* of fast-growing start ups (to find out more about Orrick's work with 'unicorn' companies, head to www.chambers-associate.com). Newcomers took the chance to *"dive right in. It's a bit nerve-racking but a great way to learn."* Many were impressed how quickly they progressed – *"the first financing I worked on I just collected pages and organized checklists; now I've essentially done the entire thing myself with a paralegal."* Suggesting they saw *"almost too much client contact,"* corporate associates were also *"generally happy with the workload,"* finding *"there are rarely unmanageable periods"* within the ebb and flow.

Overlapping with corporate (*"we do straight corporate formations and project financing"*), associates in the energy & infrastructure area saw a mix of renewables and traditional oil and gas work, noting *"different niches across different offices"* – for instance, the new Houston base is an oil hotspot. *"A lot of the work is standard junior tasks in a corporate role,"* but juniors saw *"significant responsibility growth over the years; even across the first year there's been the chance to take a first stab at drafting a major agreement."*

Public finance (to which the Portland office is almost wholly dedicated), real estate and restructuring teams fall under the broader 'finance' umbrella. Here, work can include *"a mix of litigation and transactional – I've never done the same thing twice."* Because these sub-groups are smaller than others, associates typically get work directly from partners, and those we spoke to agreed that *"if I want to be a part of something, I get the chance. Depending on how ambitious you are, you can take on as much as you want."*

Recent work highlights

- Advised Tokyo-based technology manufacturer Lintec Global on $375 million acquisition of MACtac Americas
- Represented cloud computing company Apigee in $625 million acquisition by Google
- Employed national strategy to successfully lobby for legislation legalizing daily fantasy sports on behalf of contest providers FanDuel and DraftKings
- Achieved favorable verdict for LG Electronics and AT&T in $30 million patent dispute

Culture & Diversity

West Coast-founded firms are renowned for being relatively more laid back than New York giants, a stereotype Orrick is happy to keep alive even in its East Coast offices. An NYC junior described *"a cocktail reception we had in summer for law school kids. To reinforce the Cali cool thing, they were blasting Bob Marley! We thought it was pretty funny, even if it seemed a bit forced."* Over in San Francisco, a corporate associate noted *"people dress casually at the start ups we work with, which lends to a laid back atmosphere. It's always weird seeing litigators in full suits!"* Juniors were glad to not worry and be happy, as *"the expectation here is that people are normal here and not just machines. Everybody has a real life and does interesting things outside of work."* As such, the common knowledge that *"in BigLaw there will always be stress and egos"* didn't dampen spirits.

"They were blasting Bob Marley!"

Each office has its own social traditions, from *"a closing event at the end of summer in a swanky hotel with a view of the White House"* in DC to Los Angeles' monthly *"martinis and mentorship events."* Meanwhile, practice group retreats brought together all associates from America and beyond. Energy & restructuring *"held it in Dublin, and brought the whole group from around the world there for a long weekend. It showed a good commitment to being one firm globally."* Small things like *"coordinating what we're eating if we work late"* helped associates foster group camaraderie. For women in the firm's affinity group, this involved *"going out to get lunch, or get our nails done. The men were a bit jealous!"*

As well as affinity groups, the firm runs an annual 'Dive In' diversity and inclusion event, with *"a changing theme each year talking about various issues. This year everyone got an ancestry subscription and could research their own background."* Are Orrick's efforts paying off? Juniors generally thought *"it's diverse within the context of the law, and they make sure people are exposed to different topics and issues"* including a Black Lives Matter panel in Los Angeles. But some argued *"the partnership stats could be better. They want to address it, and last year the partner*

The Inside View

See firm profile on p.639

Diversity	Partners (%)	Associates (%)
Women	21.9	46.1
White	78.5	59.6
Black/African American	2.8	2.5
Hispanic/Latin American	1.7	4.8
Asian	8	14.4
Mixed/Other	9	18.7
LGBT	2.4	6.2

class was majority women – but the fact that 2016 was the first time it happened was frustrating." In addition to recruiting from diversity careers events, Orrick was involved in hosting the first ever veterans' legal careers fair. It proved successful enough to become a regular fixture, and the third was held in 2017.

Training & Development
The Talent Model career development program is designed to help associates with business development, and fast-track high-fliers more quickly than traditional lockstep. Currently, attorneys opt to join either the partner track or the career associate track, the former of which is more popular by far. It includes three levels to work through: associate, managing associate and senior associate. Interviewees thought *"it's good to reward associates who work hard with an increase in compensation. It doesn't seem like the Talent Model could hold you up. I haven't met anyone frustrated. It only seems to help."*

"It's not like all of a sudden you make partner or don't."

Progress is discussed in annual evaluations, and first-years get an additional review. They appreciated *"all the work put into the formal system, and when reviews come around they're really helpful."* The level of day-to-day feedback *"is more dependent on the person you're working with. It could be better. The firm is aware of this and figuring out how to improve."* In the long term, the Talent Model provides *"a lot of metrics so you know where you stand. It's not like all of a sudden you make partner or don't"* – something associates welcomed.

Strategy & Future
Chairman and CEO Mitch Zuklie tells us Orrick has some exciting plans for the future of career development, including *"a new approach to flexible working called Agile Workplace. Our plan is to eliminate the concept of being on partner track or not, as we recognize the best opportunities can take a variety of routes."* Not only does the firm want to be *"the best place to work,"* but also to make room for more newcomers to enjoy what they're offering. *"We ex-*

pect to grow our summer class – 58 came out of it this year. It'll be closer to 70 next year which parallels our growth as a firm."* The full interview with Zuklie is on our website.

Hours & Compensation
"When gossip started that firms in New York were making moves" to a new salary scale starting at $180,000, associates *"got an email saying management was considering it. We then later got another email about matching the new scale."* Associate pay is less generous in Seattle, Sacramento and Portland, but juniors pointed out *"we're in a different market. The cost of living is very different."* Some in the larger bases *"thought we could have announced increases sooner,"* but chalked the delay down to the recent Houston opening and the need to invest there. The cherry on top came when the firm announced it would offer associates an additional $100 a month directly towards repayment of student loans – the happy recipients were *"encouraged to see Orrick go above and beyond."*

"Encouraged to see Orrick go above and beyond."

While Orrick doesn't have a formal billing target, partner-track attorneys are encouraged to bill at least 2,000 hours, compared to the lower 1,600 to 1,800 hours for associates on the other tracks. Most thought *"that seems achievable considering pro bono and shadowing count toward the target,"* and one unlucky junior who'd *"had a couple of slow months"* assured us *"they're not going to fire me. We talked about it in my evaluation and discussed ways to increase my numbers next year."* Even the higher target left room for some personal time, associates explaining that *"partners consider their own private lives important to them. That mentality trickles down."* Many took the chance to complete work from home after leaving at a reasonable 6 or 7pm.

Pro Bono
"It's something the firm really prides itself on" according to associates, who were pleased that there's no limit to the number of pro bono hours you can treat as billable. Having *"leapt at the opportunity,"* some felt they'd *"probably done more pro bono than I should have! There's a practical restraint, but it's highly encouraged."* Many took the chance to pursue personal passion projects. *"I told the pro bono partner I was interested in women's rights, so he gave me cases I'd be interested in."*

"I've probably done more than I should have!"

Opportunities on offer vary from local community clients to international issues. All attorneys are urged do at

See firm profile on p.639

The Inside View

least 20 hours, but *"every year they honor the people who crush that,"* and the office that clocks up the most hours wins a pizza party. *"They wouldn't reward us like that if they thought it mattered less than billables,"* our sources concluded.

Pro bono hours
- For all US attorneys: 82,420
- Average per US attorney: 137

Get Hired

"It's really surprising how often people don't take the time to prepare, and don't know what practices there are in the office." Get prepped with insider info at chambers-associate.com.

Offices

The firm's San Francisco HQ sits in *"one of the prettiest buildings downtown."* Associates were, however, disgruntled by *"a move to switch juniors to internal offices without windows,"* and saw *"some doubling up of first-years"* for the first time. Buddying up is the long-established norm for newcomers in New York, where *"each office has glass walls. It's nice because it feels like more of a community."* Washington sources described the DC base as *"like the Starship Enterprise – it's a very good modern building, though some complain there's too much empty space."*

"It's like the Starship Enterprise."

Orrick's Los Angeles base occupies the 31st through 33rd floors of a centrally located office block. Associates dubbed it a *"very professional space. It's a good place to bring clients because it's so impressive."* The Silicon Valley office is set in a cluster of four low-rise buildings set in a park in the suburbs, a stone's throw from Stanford University. Newest to the party is Houston – interviewees described the initial building as *"kind of terrible,"* but the firm is currently relocating to a new space. Collaboration between offices *"depends on the practice group and level you're at,"* often involving cross-ocean communication with London, Tokyo and elsewhere.

The Inside View

See firm profile on p.639

Patterson Belknap Webb & Tyler LLP

Lawyers per state

200

Largest US office: New York
US offices: 1
International offices: 0
First-year salary: $180,000
Billable hours: 2,100 target (incl. 250 non-billable)
Summers 2017: no summer program
Revenue 2016: $185.5 million (-1.3%)
Partners made in 2017: 3
Famous for: being fans of judicial clerks; litigation expertise; strong focus on mentoring

These days, litigation hotshot Patterson Belknap mostly fills its new associate classes with judicial clerks.

FOR the last few years, this pint-sized New York litigation ace has been hiring most of its associates from the ranks of judicial clerks (although it also takes on a handful of 3Ls each year). *"Everyone told me to look at Patterson Belknap,"* said one former clerk, now a Patterson associate. Another chimed: *"I just seemed to know loads of people who all spoke very highly of the firm. They take mentoring very seriously and its size means you're not in danger of falling through the cracks."*

Two-hundred-lawyer Patterson is best known for its litigation work. *Chambers USA* gives it a top tier ranking for advertising litigation, while the media & entertainment, securities and IP litigation groups also come in for praise. There's also a noncontentious side – home to practices like corporate, real estate, IP and tax – although usually all new junior associates are litigators.

The Work

Most juniors head into Patterson's litigation department. The firm's generalist approach to dishing out contentious matters proved attractive to many of our associate sources: *"After clerking I was used to the wide variety of cases and being able to do all sorts of things. I really wanted*

to go somewhere I wouldn't be slotted into one specialty straight off the bat.*"* Juniors can take up anything from false advertising to antitrust matters, white collar investigations, products liability or patent disputes, or just plain old contract bust-ups.

"Gives you a buffer."

Two assigning partners are on hand to allocate matters to juniors. Rookies check in with them every six weeks to talk about availability, *"what we're working on and what we want to work on. It's a great system which also gives you a buffer. It would feel hard to say no directly to a partner but here you won't find someone banging down your door saying they need you at the weekend. You have an advocate in the assigning partners."*

Judicial clerking experience stands associates in good stead to jump right into matters. *"For the most part I've gotten a lot of substantive legal writing, research and drafting"* – such as motions to dismiss – *"and I'm increasingly participating in client or co-counsel meetings,"* one third-year told us. Many of our sources had second-chaired depositions and we even heard of a few juniors being tasked with leading them: *"The first time a partner asked me to go and take a deposition I was like, 'I appreciate the compliment but I am scared shitless',"* one source laughed. *"I've been take aback – in a good way – about the responsibility I've been given."*

On chambers-associate.com...

- Diversity at Patterson
- Interview with hiring partner Bob Lehrburger

See firm profile on p.640

The Inside View

Rankings in *Chambers USA*

Advertising	Media & Entertainment
Intellectual Property	Real Estate
Litigation	

For detail on ranking tiers and ranking locations, visit www.chambersandpartners.com

In the run up to trial sources had *"drafted witness outlines and pulled together evidence. I've also read depositions and come up with ways to cross-examine witnesses. I'm not reviewing thousands of documents – my role is much more helping with strategies for pre-trial hearings and the trial."*

"Talking about strategy with partners."

Doc review is still on the cards, especially for some of the larger cases, though juniors were relatively upbeat about it: *"I know a lot of people loathe discovery and doc review but I think it's good to learn about e-discovery. You have to think of it as your vegetables and dessert: the doc review is my vegetables and the legal writing is my dessert."*

Get Hired

Although it hires a few candidates straight out of law school, Patterson focuses most of its efforts on wooing judicial clerks. Visit chambers-associate.com for more on the firm's hiring process from hiring partner Bob Lehrburger.

Training & Development

There's plenty of work for associates to chow down on, but how easy is it to swallow feedback on progress? Reviews occur every six months and *"give everyone a chance to comment on a wide range of skills. They put names to comments so there are no anonymous pot shots. People are honest too,"* one source appreciated. For entry-level associates (but not laterals), *"our first ever review is off the record, which is cool,"* another told us. *"It's not circulated to the partners, so you have an opportunity to make corrections."*

A whole buffet of easy digestible training is available from the get-go. A week of orientation covers things like using the IT systems and how to work with paralegals. Then there's a series of one to two hour long CLEs called 'nuts and bolts', which teaches lawyers how to manage a case from beginning to end. Writing and public speaking coaches are on hand to deliver *"really helpful individual sessions."* Attorneys also undertake a two-week externship with the City of New York's law department *"taking depositions for cases against the City of New York."*

Juniors are each assigned to an 'Associate Learning Group' consisting of a partner and five or six associates.

Recent work highlights

- Represented Coca-Cola in a false advertising dispute with pomegranate beverage manufacturers Pom Wonderful. Two consumer class action disputes were also brought over the same advertising
- Acted for Johnson & Johnson and Ethicon Endo-Surgery in a $176 million surgical device patent infringement dispute brought by Tyco Healthcare
- Represented law firm Garvey Schubert Barer in a malpractice suit filed by rapper 50 Cent

Each ALG comes together around three times a year for team building events like *"going to oral arguments or debriefings"* or *"doing something fun like attending a concert or going to a pizza-making class. It's fun but it can feel like enforced fun when you're really busy,"* one source admitted, before conceding *"it's a fairly new program and they're still figuring it out."* Actually, the ALG is driven by associates and optional rather than *"enforced."*

Managing partner Lisa Cleary also meets with each associate every couple of months to make sure they're happy with their experiences at the firm: *"She's fantastic and a big reason why Patterson's culture is the way it is. She gives everyone an outlet to have a conversation with her and I feel very comfortable doing so,"* one source exclaimed.

Culture & Offices

Patterson's juniors characterized the firm as *"a quiet, nerdy place. They only hire clerks and people who are attracted to clerkships are on the nerdier side,"* one ex-clerk believed. Other sources described Patterson as a *"fairly reserved place"* where people *"can be quite buttoned up."* That said, many were keen to stress *"it's very easy to have a conversation with someone and build a relationship. People are incredibly friendly."* There's not much in the way of a social scene: *"We don't have weekly happy hours and there isn't a sense of work hard/play hard. It's work hard and go chill with family and friends. I think that takes off a lot of stress."* Another added: *"I think it's a little bit more businesslike than some firms. People work hard during the day and go home at night."* This probably explains why none of our sources had seen people make use of the TV or video games in the firm's associate lounge. More in demand, however, were the lounge's *"free snacks and drinks – they tend to run out pretty quickly."* Everyone's given their own office at the firm *"except for a handful of first-years who haven't clerked – they share but get their own in the second year."*

"A pretty positive place."

One interviewee characterized the firm as *"a throwback"* clarifying: *"We take a lot of pride in lawyering. We are

See firm profile on p.640

Diversity	Partners (%)	Associates (%)
Women	17.6	51
White	90	75
Black/African American	2	2
Hispanic/Latin American	2	3
Asian	4	12.5
Mixed/Other	0	8
LGBT	9.8	6.7

very cordial in the office, people take being kind and respectful seriously. Partners don't have the stereotypical New York law firm partner 'holier than thou' attitude." Instead, *"everyone is very level-headed. There's an emphasis on being nice to people and respecting your work and time. We consider ourselves humane when it comes to hours. It's a pretty positive place."*

Hours & Compensation

Juniors shoot for a billable hours target of 1,850, and a target of 250 hours' worth of relevant nonbillable work, including pro bono. We heard the latter is *"very attainable as a lot of things count toward it; CLEs, Bar Association matters, client development, writing blogs for the firm."* A colleague joked: *"Almost everything except for vacation counts as non-billable."* As for hitting the billable target, *"you don't have to kill yourself to meet it."* Most of our sources reported spending time in the office between 9-9.30am and 7pm. *"It's not the kind of place where calls for a 10pm meeting would fly."*

Associates become eligible for a full bonus upon hitting both targets, but anyone falling short on one or other of those goals but who still hits 2,100 overall will be assessed on a case-by-case basis. Junior attorneys had heard rumors that the salary for senior associates was *"below market"* but were pleased to find their own pay was raised to stay in line with the recent market uplift.

Pro Bono

Who says 13 is an unlucky number? Probably not Patterson; the firm's just achieved a 100% pro bono participation rate for 13 years running. Everyone's handed a pro bono case among their first batch of work assignments and if you happen to *"go a month or two without one, you're often asked to take on a project."* Landlord/tenant negligence cases, challenges to housing benefit assessments and *"a veterans' law initiative to improve the discharge status of those who are dishonorably discharged from the military"* are just some of the opportunities on offer. The firm recently successfully represented a group of New Jersey Muslims who challenged their town's decision to ban them building a local mosque.

Pro bono hours
- For all attorneys: 23,749
- Average per attorney: 135

Diversity

"I'd like to see more diverse faces in leadership but the tone of support is there," one associate told us. Check out chambers-associate.com for an in-depth look at the firm's diversity initiatives and plenty of thoughts from our interviewees.

Strategy & Future

"We're happy with our size and our practices and do not anticipate many changes," hiring partner Bob Lehrburger tells us. *"Over the past several years one of the predominant forms of litigation we've handled has been residential mortgage-backed securities litigation. That cycle is slowing."* Lehrburger goes on to tell us that *"false advertising, one of the areas we are particularly known for, has seen a tremendous uptick"* in recent years. He also highlights patent litigation, antitrust, white collar investigations and cybersecurity as areas undergoing growth.

Managing partner Lisa Cleary is *"fantastic and a big reason why Patterson's culture is the way it is. She gives everyone an outlet to have a conversation with her and I feel very comfortable doing so."*

See firm profile on p.640

Paul Hastings LLP

Lawyers per state

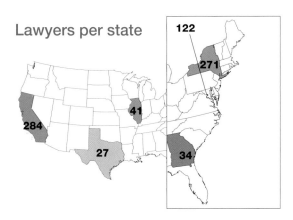

122
271
41
284
27
34

Largest US office: New York
US offices: 10
International offices: 11
First-year salary: $180,000
Billable hours: 2,000 target
Summers 2017: 84 (74 2Ls, 9 1Ls, 1 3L)
Revenue 2016: $1.075 billion (+1.7%)
Partners made in 2017: 5 (4 US)
Famous for: its LA office skyscraper which keeps getting destroyed in movies/on TV

Can it be possible for Paul Hastings to offer *"the best quality of life for its associates"* while keeping up with the best of BigLaw?

SINCE opening its doors in LA in 1951, Paul Hastings has grown across the US and opened a string of overseas offices, most recently launching a base in São Paulo. The 21-office firm is prominent in the US legal scene and highly regarded by *Chambers USA* for its work in numerous disciplines and locales. Its New York office (now the firm's largest) performs well in areas such as litigation, corporate/M&A, leisure & hospitality, real estate, and labor & employment. The New York office, incidentally, made the news in March 2017 when it hired most of Boies Schiller's corporate department. The California bases also earn a nod for the latter two practices, alongside the likes of tax, finance, environment, and employee benefits. Check out chambersandpartners.com for the full run down of the firm's US and global rankings.

It was recognition of a different kind, however, that attracted several of our interviewees to the firm: *"It's revered for having the best quality of life for its associates,"* one claimed. *"It's like the worst kept secret that everyone here is happy!"*

On chambers-associate.com...

- Managing partner Greg Nitzkowski on strategy and innovation
- How to get hired at Paul Hastings

The Work & Pro Bono

The biggest groups for junior associates to join are litigation and corporate, then real estate. Smaller groups include employment and tax. Corporate and litigation are divided into subgroups and although newbies begin life as generalists, once they have a foot in the door they're able to pursue assignments in specific areas.

Work allocation is office and group-specific: associates in larger groups tend to fill in weekly status reports which are submitted to an assigning partner, although juniors are also able to reach out directly to partners. Smaller groups usually rely on the latter method. Sources were generally content with the systems on offer, with one junior stating: *"As cumbersome and annoying as the forms are to fill in, they do ensure everyone has enough work and no one falls through the cracks."*

The many available corporate subgroups include M&A, private equity, investment management, project finance, and private investment funds. Most of the work rookie deal-doers take a stab at covers the usual junior associate tasks of due diligence, producing memos and schedules, running diligence calls and drafting ancillaries like a Secretary's Certificate delivered when a deal closes. Sources were keen to stress that *"they give you as much rope as you want. I said during my review that I wanted more substantive tasks. The response was that they trusted me and I was then given the reins to take on more."*

See firm profile on p.641

The Inside View

Rankings in *Chambers USA*

Antitrust	FCPA
Banking & Finance	Intellectual Property
Bankruptcy/Restructuring	Investment Funds
Capital Markets	Labor & Employment
Corporate/M&A	Latin American Investment
ERISA Litigation	Leisure & Hospitality
Employee Benefits &	Litigation
Executive Compensation	Real Estate
Environment	Tax

For detail on ranking tiers and ranking locations, visit
www.chambersandpartners.com

Recent work highlights

- Advised Merck & Co on its acquisition Afferent Pharmaceuticals for $1.25 billion
- Represented former Deutsche Bank employee Matthew Connolly after the DOJ accused Connolly and another employee of manipulating Libor rates. Connolly was the first American to be accused as part of the DOJ's high profile investigation into Libor manipulation
- Acted for DreamWorks Animation in selling 25% of its AwesomenessTV business to Verizon
- Assisted LinkedIn on an exchange of multiple properties in Mountain View, CA with Google

"A vital part of the team."

Litigation encompasses numerous subgroups such as white collar investigations, complex litigation and arbitration, securities, and patent litigation. *"We're sheltered from a lot of doc review as that's done by contract attorneys, so instead of being sat in front of a computer for hours we get to review documents tagged as important. Doc review gets a bad reputation, but when you're looking at relevant documents you become a master of the facts and therefore a vital part of the team tasked with writing documents for the clients,"* or attending witness interviews.

Due to *"the nature of real estate being leanly staffed, there is always a need for associates to show they're competent and capable for more"* in this group. *"Even in my first year I was trusted to either handle conference calls with clients or engage in email correspondence with them. I'm not thrown into the deep end and there's a lot of oversight, but the people I work under do recognize I can handle some things on my own,"* one junior told us. Another noted that thanks to paralegals taking on lower level tasks, juniors can undertake *"initial drafts of documents and get involved in negotiations."*

Pro bono was still considered by juniors to be *"the best way to get even more substantive work."* Aiding asylum seekers fleeing persecution, assisting tenants with housing claims and advising non-profit corporations are just some of the matters juniors can take a pop at. Everyone's given the target of meeting 20 hours of pro bono per year. Most tend to go beyond this.

Pro bono hours
- For all US attorneys: 84,672
- Average per US attorney: 109

Hours & Compensation

Despite the firm's policy of unlimited vacation, associates were aware that trying to reach the 2,000 hours annual billable target *"restrains what you can take."* Those busy enough to hit it early enough in the year *"could take off all of December,"* theoretically. While that situation might be a bit of an outlier, our sources had little qualms about failing to meet the 2,000 mark. They become bonus eligible once they've reached this threshold, with bonuses decided by a combination of performance reviews and number of hours past the target – 'productivity and merit', in the firm's official parlance.

"A few of us weren't going to torture this person by just leaving them to it, so we stayed and all worked together."

We came across few associates who'd pulled many all-nighters – where possible most tried to head home after 7pm to finish up anything which couldn't wait. Of course, there's always the unavoidable deadline which might keep you chained to your desk, but others usually try to pitch in: *"I once stayed until the early morning to help out a colleague. A few of us weren't going to torture this person by just leaving them to it, so we stayed and all worked together. Everyone has their down moments so we said 'let's do this in the most efficient way possible'."*

Training & Development

First-years can get a boost toward reaching the firm's billable target thanks to the inclusion of 150 billable client readiness hours. *"It's an opportunity to get credit for doing development activities like shadowing partners or sitting in on calls or an interview; it allows you to participate in meetings where you're new on the case and the client doesn't want to pay for you. I took advantage to sit in on a few things I'd otherwise never have had the chance to do in my first few months,"* one fan of the scheme enthused.

Paul Hastings uses the catchy acronym PH DNA [it stands for Paul Hastings Developing New Associates] to describe its training program. It kicks off with the associates assembling at one location for a few days to discuss the firm's culture, offer practice group-specific training

The Inside View

See firm profile on p.641

Diversity	Partners (%)	Associates (%)
Women	22	42.6
White	88.7	65.7
Black/African American	2.9	3.7
Hispanic/Latin American	3.3	3.7
Asian	4.9	23.3
Mixed/Other	0.4	3.7
LGBT	2	2.4

and *"get you up to speed on the basics you don't get in law school. It teaches us about the structures of client businesses and how that affects deals, due diligence or an investigations. There's also a section on accounting for lawyers."*

Culture and Offices

"We don't think of ourselves as an old, established firm," interviewees reported. *"We're innovative in terms of answering questions for clients which have not been answered before, and we're encouraged to think outside the box."*

On a more tangible level, the firm decided to shake up its New York office layout after moving to the Met Life Building above Grand Central Terminal in April 2016. First and second-years now sit in an open plan layout while the firm's introduced 'collaboration spaces' so associates have an informal area to gather for group projects. *"It's about the culture we're trying to shape,"* managing partner Greg Nitzkowski explains, highlighting the desire to *"emphasize flexibility and mobility."* Although the initial announcement on the layout was greeted with some grumbles, the juniors we spoke to believed the change had created *"a more collaborative environment. In the old office we never used to have our doors closed and we worked through noise and chatter. We're just trying to develop that atmosphere"* in the new digs.

"It feels like a coffee shop."

The Big Apple base is Paul Hastings' largest office by far, followed by LA and Washington, DC. All the firm's other offices also take juniors in varying numbers: Atlanta, Chicago, Orange County, Palo Alto, San Francisco, San Diego, and Houston. There are a further 11 bases overseas.

Although DC hasn't shifted to an open plan layout it has recently introduced a 'collaboration space'. *"It feels like a coffee shop with booths and couches. If you need a change of scenery you could take your laptop and put your feet up."* Another reckoned the new addition *"helps people touch base. DC doesn't have a stuffy environment and you won't find everyone in suits. It might have more of a Californian vibe in that respect."* New Yorkers likewise credited the

firm's LA origins with creating a kinder, collaborative atmosphere in their own office: *"The attitude is not so much 'we're paying you money so suck it up' but more 'we're in all this together so let's reach our goal',"* said one New Yorker.

"People aren't unnecessarily trying to up the stress level."

Sources across the US referenced the firm's attempts to ensure that Paul Hastings is *"not a daunting place to work. People aren't unnecessarily trying to up the stress level."* Among associates there's little *"sense of competition,"* felt one source. Others appreciated an environment which *"treats you like an adult – that's earned depending on who you work with – but generally there's not a structure imposed to ensure you're in the office between certain hours. It's expected you're doing what needs to be done."*

Strategy & Future

Over the past couple of years the firm's M&A, private equity, finance, IP and white collar litigation practices have undergone a healthy amount of growth. Managing partner Greg Nitzkowski tells us the firm will continue to focus its efforts on developing these practices.

The firm's also pinpointed a few offices where it expects a bump in headcount – London, New York, Washington, DC and the Bay Area – but Nitzkowski's keen to highlight the growth of a different kind: *"If you look at growth in terms of revenue you would have to note Asia and Latin America as big contributors to the success of the firm in both 2015 and 2016."* Visit chambersassociate.com to read more from Nitzkowski about plans for growth.

Diversity

Paul Hastings' gender split falls roughly in line with the national average (22% of the firm's partners are women and 42.6% of its associates are female) but when it comes to attitudes it gets a pat on the back from associates: *"As a woman in this industry you're terrified that before you have a kid people will look down upon you or be annoyed, but no one treats me any differently here,"* one mother told us. Another female associate believed *"they're very good at making sure women can come back to work in whatever capacity they prefer. It's nice to see women with families in the partnership ranks."*

Sources were less loquacious when it came to discussing racial diversity but did express a general consensus that although *"it could be better"* the current make up was *"reasonable"* and *"they try pretty hard"* to recruit and retain diverse associates. There are several Paul Hastings Affinity Networks (PHANS) for women, Asians, Afri-

See firm profile on p.641

can-Americans, Hispanics, and LGBT attorneys. These all provide mentoring advice and networking events.

"It's nice to see women with families in the partnership ranks."

The Inside View

See firm profile on p.641

Paul, Weiss, Rifkind, Wharton & Garrison LLP

Lawyers per state

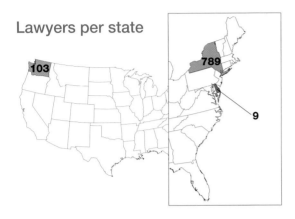

Largest US office: New York

US offices: 3

International offices: 5

First-year salary: $180,000

Billable hours: no requirement

Summers 2017: 134 (110 2Ls, 18 1Ls, 2 3Ls, 4 others)

Revenue 2016: $1.22 billion (+9.9%)

Partners made in 2017: 3 (all in US)

Famous for: star litigators; being one of New York's largest law firms; pro bono

---

Juniors at this Big Apple leader are an upbeat bunch, and a high percentage of partners began their careers here.

"IF you want to do litigation or white collar defense work in New York, there's no place better than Paul, Weiss!" boasted an associate. Growing revenues and profits for the twentieth consecutive year, Paul, Weiss offers much more than its headline litigation practice, with the firm earning multiple *Chambers USA* rankings in areas including corporate/M&A, capital markets, bankruptcy/restructuring, media & entertainment, IP, and financial services regulation.

Chair Brad Karp informs us that the firm is focusing on *"five key practice areas"* – public M&A, private equity, litigation, white collar defense, and restructuring. It's also added some serious weight in the past year thanks to a spate of top-dollar lateral hires: *"Scott Barshay joined us this April from Cravath. His world-leading expertise has enhanced our public M&A practice. David Bernick is as skilled a trial lawyer and strategic counselor as you'll find in the US. He joined us in May. We also hired Rick Rule in August,"* who Karp proudly describes as *"America's leading antitrust and merger clearance lawyer."*

As impressive as these hires are, some 80% of Paul, Weiss' partners came up through the ranks. Entry-level hiring remains a priority, and this is reflected in *"a supportive*

learning environment where you're given every opportunity to prove and push yourself."

The Work

Although litigation is the firm's largest practice, many juniors join the corporate group and rotate through subgroups before specializing in their third year. A handful of juniors join the smaller practices of tax, real estate, personal representation, employee benefits, and bankruptcy.

"Assignment is a three-pronged system," we were told. *"When you start, an assigning partner allocates you work based on your availability and your interests. After you've worked on a few cases people start to reach out to you, and if you want to get involved you just need to let your assigning partner know. You can also reach out to partners and ask them to get involved with cases too."* Rookies appreciated this flexibility, commenting *"it's great to be able to pursue matters you're specifically interested in, but it often surprises me how interesting some of the cases assigning partners have put me onto have been. It's nice to have someone point you in certain directions from time to time."*

Paul, Weiss' litigators are generalists, so *"it's completely up to you where you take that. If you want to do exclusively securities work you can do that. Some people do choose to specialize, but many stay as generalists because they like going into court. There's no pressure either way."* As such, juniors had worked on a wide range of matters, touch-

---

On chambers-associate.com...

- Interview with chairman Brad Karp
- Pro bono at Paul, Weiss

See firm profile on p.642

The Inside View

Rankings in *Chambers USA*

Antitrust	Financial Services
Banking & Finance	Regulation
Bankruptcy/Restructuring	Intellectual Property
Capital Markets	Investment Funds
Corporate Crime &	Litigation
Investigations	Media & Entertainment
Corporate/M&A	Private Equity
ERISA Litigation	Real Estate
Employee Benefits &	Retail
Executive Compensation	Securities
FCPA	Tax

For detail on ranking tiers and ranking locations, visit
www.chambersandpartners.com

ing on areas such as IP, antitrust, securities, mass tort, white-collar, and FCPA [Foreign Corrupt Practices Act] compliance. *"The variety of different cases on offer meant that you really get a comprehensive legal education,"* and rookies here had analyzed financial documents, drafted interview outlines, prepped partners for witness interviews, presented to the government and assisted companies with compliance programs.

> ### "It often surprises me how interesting some of the cases have been."

Over in corporate, juniors are unassigned until their third year when they specialize in one of the subgroups, which include securities, M&A, finance, funds and IP. *"For the first three months you're really just trying to get your head round various sorts of matters coming in, so there's lots of basic stuff to get you started: due diligence, drafting ancillary documents, stuff like that."* Nevertheless, transactional juniors were *"surprised"* to be given opportunities for client interaction from an early stage. *"You won't begin with anything too complex, perhaps the odd email or memo, but it helps you to get familiar with the client and means you feel comfortable to take on more complex stuff later on."* Supervisors are *"willing to give give you more responsibilities quickly, as long as you're ready,"* which some saw as a double-edged sword: *"It is easy to get swamped as you rise through the department and become more of a go-to for clients,"* we heard. *"You need to feel comfortable delegating to more junior associates when that happens."*

Training & Development
When they first start, juniors can expect an *"intensive first week of training,"* as well as *"more periodically-spaced sessions over the next few months."* Generally, though, training is offered on-the-job. *"Paul, Weiss correctly recognizes that juniors learn more by working on briefs than sitting in seminars,"* one source observed.

Recent work highlights
- Represented Time Warner Cable in its $78.7 billion merger with Charter. At the time this was the sixth largest global transaction of all time
- Defending the Arizona Cardinals against a class action lawsuit, which claims the NFL club deliberately concealed the harmful effects of concussions
- Organized an $840 million senior secured credit facility for Oak Hill Capital Partners, which was used to fund its $1.34 billion buyout of Berlin Packaging

Associates are kept up-to-date with a formal annual evaluation, as well as regular feedback. *"It usually lasts about half an hour,"* one litigator told us. *"You sit down with your assigning partner and they'll read out reviews of your performance submitted by all of the senior associates, partners and counsel you've worked with. Then you get the chance to tell them what you'd like to work on going forward. It's a good opportunity to voice your interests, as your assigning partner can then work toward staffing you on matters that will help you achieve your goals."*

For more ad hoc queries, juniors felt comfortable seeking out advice themselves: *"I don't think anyone wants new starters feeling like certain partners are unapproachable or untouchable,"* said one. *"People realize that our work product will always be better if we're in the know and comfortable with who we're working with, so there never tends to be a problem with knocking on doors for advice."*

Culture
With that approach in mind, it's no surprise juniors were pleased with the working environment at Paul, Weiss. *"I couldn't ask for more,"* said one. *"There's a reason that a lot of people who paralegal here come back to work as associates. People here tend to have a good sense of humor, and though the work can be tough no one is out to make your life crazier than it has to be."*

> ### "I wouldn't worry if I cursed in front of a colleague."

The firm's *"friendly, relaxed"* atmosphere allows for a little breathing room: *"It's not a super buttoned-up place,"* one rookie reflected. *"OK, its not Quinn Emanuel – we wear trousers not jeans, and if you're meeting a client you're expected to be in a suit – but I wouldn't worry if I cursed in front of a colleague."*

Good working relationships lead to active social lives and *"most would be happy to go for drinks after a hard day's slog."* More scheduled social opportunities include a weekly cocktail party on Fridays in New York, as well as an annual summer event, held at MoMA. *"They rent*

See firm profile on p.642

The Inside View

Diversity	Partners (%)	Associates (%)
Women	22	40
White	87	78
Black/African American	3	5
Hispanic/Latin American	2	2
Asian	7	12
Mixed/Other	2	3
LGBT	6	6

out the whole museum!" juniors exclaimed. *"The food is great, there are plenty of drinks floating about, and you're welcome to go off and explore the museum at your leisure!"*

Hours & Compensation

There's no billing target at Paul, Weiss, but the consensus among associates was that *"superstars bill anything up to 2,600 hours a year, whereas 1,800 is probably seen as a bit slack. Most people average at around 2,000-2,100."* Juniors appreciated not having a target hanging over their head: *"People ask if it puts pressure on us to overcompensate, but that's not the case,"* reasoned one deal-doer. *"I just try to approach it deal-by-deal, and it's nice not to have to worry about a number while I'm doing that."*

"Our clients pay a lot of money and expect us to be ready to go..."

Juniors tend to start work at 9am and leave any time between 7.30pm and 10pm. That being said, we did hear of a few all-nighters *"in exceptional circumstances,"* so *"be ready to work hard when you get here. Our clients pay a lot of money and expect us to be ready to go when they need us."* As for vacations, *"you're expected to keep on top of your emails, but the traffic tends to slow down,"* said one caller. *"No one made any requests of me while I was away, so it wasn't like I had to pull out my laptop periodically to keep people happy."*

Offices

Paul, Weiss may have eight offices but the vast majority of the people are in the New York HQ. At the time of our calls, junior associates based in the Big Apple covered a range of different practices such as litigation, corporate, real estate, bankruptcy and tax. DC is much smaller in comparison and *"does more government-facing work, FCPA stuff, white collar investigations, and some IP too."* Still, plenty of New Yorkers had worked on teams with colleagues in both DC and Wilmington, Delaware: *"It's a New York-centric firm, and case teams often stretch across several offices, depending on which locations best suit our clients."* A base in Toronto makes up the firm's North

American contingent, while further afield Paul, Weiss has offices in Beijing, Hong Kong, London and Tokyo.

"Awestruck by what's hanging on the walls."

There have been ongoing renovations in the New York office for the last few years, and associates were happy to report that *"it's all feeling pretty homely."* There's a subsidized cafeteria, a physical therapy center offering massages to stressed attorneys, and an *"incredible"* art collection too. *"Often I'll just go to a floor I haven't been to before and end up awestruck by what's hanging on the walls,"* one marveled.

Diversity

"Looking back through its history, Paul, Weiss has a proud record for always being a liberal and accepting place to work," sources beamed. In 1927, the firm was one of the first to allow Jews to practice with Gentiles; in 1949, it hired an African American associate, Harvard grad and ex-SCOTUS clerk William T. Coleman, at a time when few if any did; and in the early 1950s Carolyn Agger joined to become the first female partner at a major law firm.

Nowadays, *"there's still work to be done at the partner level,"* which juniors described as *"not that well represented, particularly when it comes to ethnic minorities."* Still, many were encouraged by the fact that *"our network of affinity groups is really busy, and doing insightful research into the ways in which lawyers of different demographics tend to perform. This is helping us better understand how the focus and structure of our training can help facilitate professional advancement for all of our lawyers."*

"Paul, Weiss has a proud record for always being a liberal and accepting place to work."

Pro Bono

When it comes to pro bono, juniors felt *"you're free to join case teams that are interesting to you."* The firm attracts *"a good selection of higher profile work aimed at systemic change, and smaller cases where you're empowered to take strategic decisions."* In New York, a designated pro bono associate and counsel *"sit all the first-years down and present them with a list of available cases. Having the whole variety of cases readily available was really helpful, because it means you can get stuck in before you've even got a full network of contacts in place."* The pro bono committee also serves as *"a good sounding board for strategic decisions."*

The Inside View

See firm profile on p.642

"There are literally hundreds of organizations the firm couples with," so our associate sources had taken on all sorts. Litigators had worked on criminal tasks like robberies, drug conspiracy allegations, landlord disputes and unemployment benefit appeals, whereas corporate insiders had helped transgender people change their names, worked on Iraqi refugee programs and assisted at family law clinics.

There's no specific pro bono hours target, but most of our sources had plenty of stories to recount. *"The fact that pro bono hours are counted like any other hours helps,"* juniors commended. *"Partners appreciate it's an important tool for facilitating our development, and boosting the firm's profile."*

To find out more about Paul, Weiss' long history of ground-breaking pro bono work, head to our website.

Pro bono hours
- For all US attorneys: 74,167
- Average per US attorney: 74

Strategy & Future

With the firm performing well financially, Paul, Weiss' core practices – public M&A, private equity, litigation, white collar defense, and restructuring – are set to remain a priority in the years ahead. According to Brad Karp, *"we believe that, in view of prevailing market conditions and business opportunities, we're operating in the right practice areas and the right geographic locations, we have the right mix of clients and a rich talent base to help us best serve those clients."*

Moving forward, *"our principal goal is to represent the most important clients in the world on their most important matters, while delivering exemplary client service and results."* As for the path to achieving this, Karp is playing his cards close to his chest. *"In the next year at least, I don't see us opening up offices in any new locations. As for practice areas, we'll be looking to continue to make strategic investments in the five key areas I mentioned earlier."*

Get hired

"I interviewed people this summer who in addition to working in finance had taken culinary classes, worked in media, or done Teach for America. Strong personalities are common here." Visit chambers-associate.com to learn about getting hired at Paul, Weiss.

"though the work can be tough no one is out to make your life crazier than it has to be."

See firm profile on p.642

Perkins Coie LLP

Lawyers per state

Perkins Coie LLP also has an office in Alaska with eight attorneys

Largest US office: Seattle
US offices: 16
International offices: 3
First-year salary: $105,000 (Anchorage) - $180,000
Billable hours: 1,800 – 1,950 required
Summers 2017: 57 (42 2Ls, 15 1Ls)
Revenue 2016: $781 million (+4.3%)
Partners made in 2017: 25 (all in US)
Famous for: political law; tech clients; great culture

High-level work exposure and exceptional camaraderie greet associates at this ever-expanding Seattle-founded firm.

PERKINS Coie built its respected name on the West Coast but right now is seeing most expansion out East: *"Our growth in New York has been fairly substantial,"* DC-based managing partner John Devaney highlights. The almost 50-strong Big Apple office increased its headcount by a juicy 50% in 2016, and launched an emerging companies & venture capital group led by start-up guru Charles Torres, who joined from Lowenstein. A quartet of former Kramer Levin investment management pros gave a boost to that team, while the IP practice was bolstered by a duo of partners from Ropes & Gray and another pair of partners from WilmerHale. *"I'm very pleased with the progress we've made in New York,"* Devaney says. *"We intend to continue to grow this office in different areas."*

Financially, 2016 was also *a good strong year, with a healthy revenue increase* of 4.3%. Devaney credits the firm's political law practice as one of the key drivers of this growth. Perkins houses one of the foremost political law groups in the US and has a long association with the Democratic Party. You might have spotted Marc Elias's name around the time of the presidential election – the Perkins Coie partner was general counsel to 'Hillary for

America', and you can read our interview with him on our website. Alongside political law, product liability, privacy and cyber security, and regulatory compliance are other areas which contributed to the revenue rise of the Seattle-headquartered firm, according to the MP.

Perkins Coie hauls in a considerable number of top-tier *Chambers USA* rankings, among them aviation, political law, general commercial litigation, IP, real estate, and environment. Many clients hail from the tech industry – Facebook, Nintendo, Amazon and Microsoft are all on the roster.

The Work
Most Perkins rookies find themselves in the firm's business, commercial litigation or IP practice groups, though a handful slip into smaller teams like political law or product liability. The three largest groups are divided into subgroups, to which juniors are loosely assigned upon arrival. *"You work on whatever comes across your desk but you're encouraged to make relationships with those working on things you're interested in,"* one litigator told us. Juniors regularly fill out an email utilization survey so management can *"gauge who has availability,"* but rookies mainly tend to communicate directly with partners and associates to become staffed on cases.

"The primary point of contact for a client."

On chambers-associate.com...
- Interview with managing partner John Devaney
- Associate hiring tips
- More on hours and compensation

The Inside View

See firm profile on p.643

Rankings in *Chambers USA*

Bankruptcy/Restructuring	Litigation
Corporate/Commercial	Native American Law
Corporate/M&A	Natural Resources
Environment	Privacy & Data Security
Government	Products Liability
Insurance	Real Estate
Intellectual Property	Retail
Labor & Employment	Startups & Emerging
Leisure & Hospitality	Companies
Life Sciences	Technology
	Transportation

For detail on ranking tiers and ranking locations, visit
www.chambersandpartners.com

Recent work highlights

- Acts as general counsel to the Democratic National Committee
- Represented the League of Women Voters of Florida on a claim that the Florida Legislature voting map boundaries were biased in favor of one political party
- Acted for US movie and video game rental kiosk company Outerwall in its $1.6 billion acquisition by affiliates of private equity firm Apollo Global Management
- Represented real estate website Zillow after it was sued for $2 billion by competitor Move for trade secret misappropriation, following Zillow's hire of Move's former Chief Strategy Officer

Business has subgroups including corporate governance/transactions; emerging companies & venture capital; financial transactions/restructuring; private equity; and tech transactions & privacy. *"One of the things I love about Perkins is just how small the teams are staffed for each matter,"* one deal-doer told us. Combine this with juniors being handed the lead on smaller matters, and rookies *"could be asked to handle any aspect of the deal. Even as a first-year I was negotiating directly with partners on the other side."* Another told of being *"the primary point of contact for a client on day-to-day questions from the get go. I handled it to the point I felt comfortable and brought in supervisors or partners when I needed to."* Though rookies conceded this *"can be intimidating at first, the partners are extremely encouraging and get that we make small mistakes."* Juniors are still expected to dig in on lower level work too though: *"As a first through third-year you're generally expected to do due diligence, manage the workflow, close checklists, and draft ancillary documents."*

"The firm has an e-discovery group so juniors don't do a lot of doc review."

Within commercial litigation, juniors join one of: antitrust; business litigation; construction; environment; insurance recovery; securities; or white-collar/investigations. Perkins has *"an e-discovery group so juniors don't do a lot of doc review."* Instead, associates are more likely to be found *"working with a team of discovery attorneys to help oversee the document production and analysis process. I've done a lot of legal research and writing – when I first started it involved researching diverse issues and writing a summary or memo, but I've now written a lot of briefs on my own at this point,"* one third-year told us. Others told of taking depositions or putting together the first drafts of motions to dismiss or summary responses.

IP folks choose to specialize in patent prosecution, patent litigation, or trademark & copyright. Juniors believed

that *"if you're not getting quite as much responsibility as you maybe should or your professional development is low, there's an effort by group management to get you certain types of experience."* It appears to be working as one IP litigator quipped: *"I've only done about five hours of doc review this year – I was hoping there would be more of it so I can switch off my brain for a bit."*

Offices

Cross-office working is well embedded at the firm. Many associates – particularly those in smaller offices such as Phoenix – often work with colleagues across the US. *"We call each other all the time and interact on Outlook chat,"* one member of a well-connected group told us. *"It does depend on your team and what you're working on but the firm culture is such that people in other locations are open to working with you."* One associate reckoned *"the firm's conscious that it wants attorneys to work across offices and develop relationships."*

"It wants attorneys to work across offices and develop relationships."

Outside Seattle, Perkins Coie has 15 other offices spread around pretty much most of the country. While *"it's pretty apparent that Seattle's running the show, it does feel like we have discretion and a fair amount of autonomy,"* one California source told us.

Training & Development

Each January, the firm's newbies converge on Seattle for a new starter retreat. *"We start around late September so having the retreat in the New Year means you've gotten your feet wet and know the lie of the land. I appreciated the balance rather than having everything front-loaded."* The get together's largely aimed at *"meeting other first-years and acclimatizing to the firm and its resources. It's not as focused on work as some of the other retreats, but it's nice to meet your peers and keep in touch with them when you*

See firm profile on p.643

Diversity	Partners (%)	Associates (%)
Women	25	48
White	88	75
Black/African American	2	3
Hispanic/Latin American	3	5
Asian	4	13
Mixed/Other	3	4
LGBT	2	3

visit other offices." On a more substantive level, monthly departmental training sessions are broadcast by video conference across offices.

Annual reviews are delivered by the associate evaluation committee and the firm makes "a deliberate point of ensuring you speak with someone who isn't in your office" or practice group, as well as someone who is. This allows associates to get objective feedback on their experience. First-years also receive a mid-year review.

Culture and Diversity

"At the first-year retreat I could tell that our office and New York have a more buttoned up culture than Seattle, Portland and Palo Alto," one DC-based source informed us. "But on the whole the firm has a pretty laid back West Coast vibe." There are a few exceptions: the Phoenix office was established by a merger with Arizona firm Brown and Bain in 2004, "so they have their own culture." Meanwhile a Chicagoan felt their office was "definitely West Coast in terms of dress" but "has a more intense atmosphere."

"There aren't any petty tyrants."

By and large though, the Perkins Coie way seems to have flowed from the Seattle office: "Everyone is polite and respectful. I'm respected as a human being and not just an hours generator. If I have to work on weekends it is not because I feel it is expected of me, but because it is required. Whenever it's tough there's an appreciation for the work we do." And where does Seattle get its vibe from? "Being able to see the mountains from the office is a daily reminder of things outside the law that are important," one junior reckoned. "I get the sense that people care about the important things; we won't take a lazy attitude to completing a project or getting a result for a client – we're serious about that – but the people I interact with are fun and enjoy themselves and their lives. It's not really intense."

Another reassured us that "there aren't any petty tyrants. Everyone just wants to get the work done and we get along." Naturally you'll find "a pressure to perform but in a very supportive atmosphere. Even when I was interviewing here I noticed that people were walking in and out of each oth-

er's offices, feeling free to ask questions." Others were keen to point out the supportive nature of their colleagues: "I have a lot of people who have been looking out for me in an informal way since I started three years ago, and they don't have to do that."

"Put pressure on management to do more."

Juniors also believed the firm's atmosphere was driven by its strong political law practice and association with the Democrats: "We have a left leaning body of associates and I think that tends to put pressure" on elements such as "increasing diversity," one junior surmised. "We have a very open and accepting environment where people feel comfortable and make an effort to be inclusive. Junior and mid-level associates constantly put pressure on management to do more than they're doing."

Already in place are two firmwide diversity retreats every other year: one for women, and one for all other minorities. At the time of our calls our female sources were "really looking forward to the women's retreat. I've heard it's everyone's favorite as it focuses more on networking than training and has lots of interesting speakers." The firm also has several affinity groups and offers a 1L diversity fellowship scheme. There's also a chief diversity officer, Theresa Cropper.

Statistically speaking, "there's always work to be done," but many sources were keen to point out that "the numbers don't always reflect our attitude to diversity." In Phoenix, for example, although there are "not a lot of women, we all do a good job of looking out for each other. Our committee is the most active in the office. We get together for lunch every month, discuss work and life challenges and celebrate wins, which really fosters the strong bond between us." Across offices others talked of working with "a lot of strong women." All that said, several did point out the need to increase the firm's racial diversity.

Get Hired

Associates felt the firm suits "easy-going people who have interests outside of work and a drive to keep those hobbies going" while practicing law. Visit chambers-associate.com for more insight into what the firm looks for during the recruitment process.

Hours & Compensation

Billing targets and salaries are linked to local markets, with the former ranging from 1,800 to 1,950 hours. Visit chambers-associate.com for a full run down on billing targets and compensation, and what associates make

See firm profile on p.643

The Inside View

461

of these. Generally, our sources *"didn't feel pressured to physically be in the office for obscene amounts of time. It's not like there's a big crowd here late at night. We do put in the time and the work, but in terms of offices hours I think the firm is understanding and accommodating,"* reckoned one interviewee. *"One thing I like about Perkins is that people don't keep tabs on when I come and go. I take my laptop home every night; I don't always use it but I check my emails regularly."*

Pro Bono

Whether it's immigration assistance, clemency petitions, landlord/tenant disputes or helping people draft their wills, there's *"a strong sentiment toward"* pro bono at Perkins Coie. Sources reported being actively encouraged to take on cases – *"I've recently been told to make more time for it,"* one pro-bono lacking source said. *"It's true what they say about it being a good way to get more stand-up-in-court experience,"* an avid pro bono fan enthused. *"I'm working with a partner mentor on one of my cases who'll help me with my first oral advocacy experience."*

Pro bono hours
- For all US attorneys: 52,075
- Average per US attorney: 51

Strategy & Future

Managing partner John Devaney identifies the firm's future growth areas as *"regulatory and compliance, privacy and cyber security, private equity, M&A and fintech – financial technology transactions – where we are a market leader in the US. There's a lot of demand among financial institutions in this area."*

Devaney also informs us that the firm will be *"exploring our international strategy to decide whether to make investments."* Visit chambers-associate.com to read more from Devaney on what the future holds.

"One of the things I love about Perkins is just how small the teams are staffed for each matter."

See firm profile on p.643

The Inside View

Pillsbury Winthrop Shaw Pittman LLP

Lawyers per state

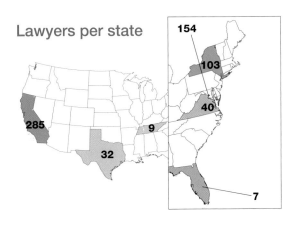

154
103
40
9
285
32
7

Largest US office: Washington, DC

US offices: 14

International offices: 7

First-year salary: $180,000

Billable hours: 1,950 target (bonus eligible at 1,900 and 2,000)

Summers 2017: 38 (all 2Ls)

Revenue 2016: $573.5 million (+3%)

Partners made in 2017: 8 globally (6 in US)

Famous for: California casual; historic diversity

Pillsbury won't be defined by its Cali roots, but it's hard to find a BigLaw firm with a pleasanter culture...

PILLSBURY is a name associated with dough, but in BigLaw circles it signifies a leading California-founded firm known for its tasty work/life balance and toothsome practices. *"There are a lot of laterals who move here from other big firms,"* associates pointed out. *"They come for the better hours, which are part of the more relaxed workplace culture here."* It's also known for kneading and shaping (as it were) excellent diversity, and was for example the first *Am Law 100* firm to be led by a woman, and one of the first to extend benefits to same-sex domestic partners.

The above must of course be mixed with a pinch of salt before baking – we're in no way saying that Pillsbury lawyers don't work hard. This firm is still a judicial juggernaut – with 13 US offices and five overseas – and also counts some mega clients in its roster, including Amazon, Visa and Disney. Many customers are served by various practice groups, *"which is kind of Pillsbury's motto: we try to be a one-stop shop for clients."* Chambers USA recognizes this versatility and awards the firm upper crust ratings in energy, environment, corporate/M&A, tax, and real estate, among others. The cherries on the icing (Band 1 rankings) are for construction, technology, outsourcing, IP, and transportation work.

The Work

When it comes to assignments for junior lawyers, *"generally it's a free market thing – you do something for someone and you just end up mostly working with them."* That said,

efforts have been made to formalize the process, especially for transactional newbies, who felt that *"sometimes senior lawyers were unaware of how much we had on our plates."* As a result, about a year ago the firm introduced a *"first-year firmwide assignment portal – you enter what you've billed and what you're going to bill next week and it gets sent around everywhere so people have an idea about your capacity."*

"You do something for someone and you just end up mostly working with them."

Perhaps the transactional confusion was down to the fact that newcomers are given the freedom to move between teams in order to get a flavor of the different practices. Indeed, in the firm's bigger offices – DC, New York and San Francisco – there is emphasis placed on allowing juniors a choice. As one Big Apple attorney explained: *"I was initially unsure about what I wanted to go into and they consulted me on my callback and when I started and asked if I'd be comfortable joining a certain department."*

Those departments include corporate & securities (where most first-years were based at the time of our calls), as well as: litigation; global sourcing; environmental; public practices; IP; communications; real estate; insolvency; finance; estates & trusts; and tax – though smaller offices only offer a handful of these. The corporate department is split pretty evenly between capital markets and M&A work. Associates' work encompasses *"all the things you'd*

See firm profile on p.644

Rankings in *Chambers USA*

Capital Markets	Insurance
Construction	Intellectual Property
Corporate/M&A	International Trade
Employee Benefits &	Outsourcing
Executive Compensation	Real Estate
Energy & Natural	Retail
Resources	Tax
Environment	Technology
Food & Beverages	Transportation
Government	

For detail on ranking tiers and ranking locations, visit
www.chambersandpartners.com

Recent work highlights

- Led on one of the largest single real estate transactions in New York City recently, advising FSP 787 Seventh in its acquisition of 787 Seventh Avenue in New York for just under $2 billion
- Advised NTT Data on its largest acquisition ever – the $3.06 billion purchase of Dell's IT services arm, Dell Systems
- Developed the legal infrastructure for the Delaware Blockchain Initiative, an effort to expand the use of distributed ledger and smart contract technologies by Delaware-incorporated businesses

expect from a first-year: making a checklist, drafting ancillary documents and officer certificates, and dealing with signature pages." However, while this might not seem like the stuff of fairy tales, sources were keen to stress that *"they make sure you get a good grounding so when you enter your second year you can start running smaller deals."*

Litigation encompasses white collar, insurance recovery and *"a lot of construction and real estate disputes."* As with most practices, responsibility levels vary greatly from office to office. In DC – where litigation is the biggest group – juniors can expect their first years to involve *"a substantial amount of doc review and researching."* However, most were pragmatic about this: *"I think everyone would say I wish I could be in trial more, but I'm still in the early stages of my career and it's important to build the skills."* In LA and the smaller offices things are a little more accelerated: *"From early on I was drafting several motions on construction defects cases and other big financial services-related litigation."*

Culture

Some associates attributed Pillsbury's more relaxed approach (compared to some BigLaw firms) to the firm's Californian heritage. Moreover, especially in practices like real estate, *"a lot of the firm's clients are based in and around San Francisco and it contributes to a much more contemporary business culture. I'm not in a suit and tie every day – if I'm meeting my direct partners I won't even put my jacket on."* That said, DC attorneys were keen to assert their office's influence within the network: *"I think the Cali thing can be a bit over-egged sometimes. It's an important part of our history but DC's our biggest office and it's very much a center of gravity."* The fact that it's bigger than the *"more work hard, play hard"* New York office means it *"sets the tone for the East Coast as a whole in terms of culture."*

"I'm not in a suit and tie every day."

"There are a lot of lawyers with young families at Pillsbury so there's more of a focus on work/life balance and perhaps less on the happy hours," sources told us. That's not to say that the firm's attorneys don't get together, but when they do it's more of a civilized affair. The following response was pretty typical: *"I've met everyone in my team's families and been to dinner at their houses. We work in small groups and I think that's pretty indicative of the firm as a whole."* In New York, *"there's a happy hour every other week in the break room, which has a pool table and music."* San Francisco's attorneys are probably the most sociable nationwide bunch, and the office's associate development committee puts on mixers and charity fundraising events like *"trivia and casino nights, where all the proceeds go to charity."*

Training & Development

First-years are all enrolled at Pillsbury University (PU) but don't worry, you won't be asked to re-don mortarboard and gown: this is simply the name of the firm's in-house CLE training department that caters for specific practice areas. While some sources found it *"incredibly useful for touching up on things you'd forgotten from law school,"* others questioned how practical lecture-based learning was: *"As with a lot of legal training, I don't think the format is the most helpful. It's usually someone just talking at you for 15 minutes. I think I've learned the most from being involved on deals and doing some high-level tasks, which is something that happens early on here."* Perhaps the most popular feature of the PU curriculum is that first-years are allowed to bill 150 hours of the training as billable work.

"I've learned the most from being involved on deals."

Pillsbury also has a much-lauded mentorship scheme – *"we all get a partner mentor when we join, someone you don't directly work with so you always feel comfortable reaching out to them, and vice versa. It's not like some firms that say they believe in mentorship: here they really care about personal and professional development."* Tales

See firm profile on p.644

Diversity	Partners (%)	Associates (%)
Women	22.4	47.9
White	87	67.8
Black/African American	1.2	3.4
Hispanic/Latin American	2.7	4.2
Asian	7.6	20.8
Mixed/Other	0.9	2.5
LGBT	4	5

of senior lawyers going the extra mile abounded and this one was pretty typical: *"Both partners I work with do an awesome job helping me with client interaction. One of them will always drop my name in emails and make sure I get credit for the work I've done."*

Hours & Compensation

Pillsbury lawyers have a firmwide billing target of 1,950 that affects bonus eligibility as well as class advancement – *"if you make 90% (1,900) of that you will advance in class year, if you don't, advancement is based on performance reviews. Making 2,000 means you're bonus eligible."* However, *"these figures are by no means set in stone."* The firm offers a standard bonus and a second discretionary bonus if you hit 110% of your hours.

Pro Bono

There is no cap on the number of pro bono hours associates can bill and it all counts toward their 1,950. Juniors *"get weekly updates with opportunities"* and *"you're given an award if you do more than 25 hours."* An unofficial target of 60 pro bono hours per associate has recently been introduced nationwide. Sources had worked on some really interesting stuff. Many in DC had worked with Kids in Need of Defense (KIND), an organization that provides unaccompanied immigrant and refugee children with representation in deportation proceedings, among other help.

Pro bono hours
- For all US attorneys: 36,696
- Average per US attorney: 65

Offices

With offices in San Francisco, Los Angeles, Silicon Valley, Sacramento and San Diego, it's not surprising that Pillsbury is well-known in California. However, offices in Texas, Nashville, Northern Virginia, DC, New York

and Florida ensure that the firm's presence is felt coast-to-coast. The Big Apple base is in a tall building right on Times Square. A lot of interviewees had mixed thoughts about this, with more than one *"getting off the subway a stop early,"* because *"it's not that nice having to walk through sharp elbows and naked ladies every morning!"*

The DC office – the firm's biggest – is housed in *"beautiful, open-plan"* purpose-built surroundings right next to Farragut North metro station, *"about two blocks from the White House."* LA lawyers are in a similarly A-list location occupying *"three floors of a big office building downtown."* There was praise aplenty for a recent renovation that saw *"new carpets laid and everyone get their own standing desk."* In the past, associates have been allowed to attend Lakers, Clippers and Dodgers games with clients thanks to Pillsbury's complimentary seats. Up north in San Francisco, attorneys will find themselves sitting on the dock of the Bay, with their office having uninhibited views of the Golden Gate and Bay Bridges.

Diversity

There is certainly recognition that Pillsbury has a way to go with improving racial diversity at the firm, though there are concerted efforts in the right direction. Every three years an 'attorneys of color' conference takes place in order to bring together, foster and develop diverse talent. In terms of gender, Pillsbury has been consistently praised for its diversity and has been named in the *Working Mother*'s '100 Best Companies List' for 11 consecutive years.

Get Hired

Pillsbury moves quick to secure its recruits. *"They tend to try and get all the candidates they want from OCIs and they extend offers pretty quickly. I interviewed on Friday and got an offer on Tuesday."* Associates are involved in the interview process early on in their Pillsbury careers and offered sage advice to potential greenhorns: *"We are looking for people with an interesting background, it's not just about academics – people who have experienced other careers, traveled the world or done a lot of volunteering are really valued here."*

"We are looking for people with an interesting background, it's not just about academics..."

See firm profile on p.644

Proskauer Rose LLP

Lawyers per state

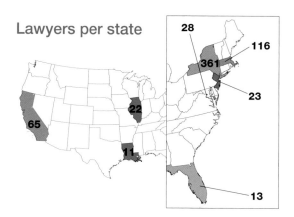

28
116
361
23
22
65
11
13

Largest US office: New York

US offices: 8

International offices: 5

First-year salary: $125,000 (New Orleans) - $180,000

Billable hours: no requirement

Summers 2017: 86 (82 2Ls, 2 1Ls, 2 others)

Revenue 2016: $852.4 million (+3.7%)

Partners made in 2017: 7 (all in US)

Famous for: labor & employment expertise; sports practice; keeping in touch with alumni

Proskauer regularly hits the headlines for representing celebs and sports teams, but this is only a small part of the work on offer.

WHAT unites Madonna, Lady Gaga, the New York City Ballet and impressively coiffed 80s pop duo Hall & Oates, apart from a certain familiarity with leotards? Proskauer Rose, of course. This 141-year-old New Yorker counsels them all, plus a whole host of other big-name clients from the arts and entertainment world. It's also known as a sports law champion, with major teams on the books and a rankings mantelpiece groaning under the weight of consecutive Band 1 trophies from *Chambers USA.*

Sports and showbiz work are a specialty within the firm's broader corporate and litigation practices. Actually, the firm was originally renowned for its labor & employment prowess and it retains a top-notch rep for this practice today, as a junior in the department was quick to point out: *"Coming to Proskauer is a no-brainer if you want to do labor and employment work in Manhattan."* Aside from its Big Apple HQ, the 725-plus attorney firm has seven other US bases and overseas outposts in London, Paris, Hong Kong, Beijing and São Paulo. The London office in particular has grown a lot recently.

The Work

Juniors can jump straight into the corporate, labor & employment, litigation, healthcare, real estate, tax, or private client services departments. Most newbies slot into the corporate group. Labor and litigation take in the next largest batches and a small handful are sprinkled among the remaining groups. Broadly speaking, those in litigation, labor and corporate begin life as generalists, and in each department a legal director coordinates work allocation. After a year or two, most juniors join a more focused practice area, although some like to keep things broad. Work assignment tends to be allocated on an informal basis, though you're still able to reach out to the director if things run quiet. A junior summarized: *"The firm rewards entrepreneurial behavior. If you're very proactive and like to network internally, or there's a partner whose style you'd like to emulate, then they encourage that. A lot of people here know what they want and will get out there and get it. That's not to say it's competitive, but Proskauer very much supports associates to steer their own careers."*

Corporate rookies could find themselves working on the usual milieu of M&A, private equity, capital markets and bankruptcy matters for clients like banks, private equity funds and companies in the healthcare, real estate, retail and leisure industries. *"There's definitely a lot of grunt work stuff like diligence,"* admitted an interviewee, *"but it's not as concentrated as I assumed it was going to be. The work is more substantive than I thought it would be. I've had drafting experience, of board resolutions and other an-*

On chambers-associate.com...

- More about the 'Proskauer Institute'
- Proskauer's "phenomenal" offices

See firm profile on p.645

Rankings in *Chambers USA*

Advertising	Investment Funds
Banking & Finance	Labor & Employment
Bankruptcy/Restructuring	Latin American Investment
Capital Markets	Leisure & Hospitality
Corporate/M&A	Litigation
ERISA Litigation	Media & Entertainment
Employee Benefits &	Private Equity
Executive Compensation	Real Estate
Healthcare	REITs
Immigration	Sports Law
Insurance	Tax
Intellectual Property	Technology

For detail on ranking tiers and ranking locations, visit
www.chambersandpartners.com

Recent work highlights

- Advised longstanding client AccorHotels (based in Paris) on its integration of 26 hotels from Brazil Hospitality Group (BHG), valued at R$200 million. In 2016, lawyers advised AccorHotels on its $2.9 billion acquisition of Fairmont Raffles Hotels International
- Represented private equity giant KKR in its $4 billion acquisition of mixed martial arts organization UFC
- Represented GRAMMY Museum and The Recording Academy in its international expansion to open a first-ever GRAMMY Museum in China
- Advised Discovery Communications on its agreement to invest $100 million and enter into a strategic partnership with digital content holding company Group Nine Media
- Defended Madonna and her manager in a trademark infringement suit over the use of the name 'Hard Candy'

cillary documents, and I coordinate the signature pages at the end of a deal." As well as praising the drafting opportunities, another rookie mentioned that they'd *"had good amount of client contact – I send docs directly to clients, get feedback and incorporate it."*

"The firm rewards entrepreneurial behavior."

A litigator proclaimed: *"I can't imagine having a broader range of work! I've worked on shareholder demands and derivative suits, some sports work relating to television contracts, trademark and copyright stuff, insurance cases, general contract disputes, arbitrations, false advertising and a couple of entertainment matters."* Another junior told us that *"since day one I've been on a dispute that's now going to summary judgment. Right now I'm helping experts to find materials – I'll be meeting with an accounting expert later today. Plus I'll be in client meetings later. I don't expect to say a ton, but I will be helping to prepare deposition outlines."* Research assignments, discovery requests and discovery responses are also typical tasks, along with drafting complaints and motions. *"I've actually been quite happily impressed with the amount of responsibility given to me so early on. As a junior I thought I'd be staffed on doc reviews and diligence, and during my first week or so that was the case, but once I volunteered myself and stepped up, the substantive work came almost immediately. I've written briefs, gone to client pitches, communicated directly with clients, done everything short of arguing in court."*

The labor element of labor & employment work involves managing the relationship between labor unions and companies, and dealing with issues and litigation which may arise. Employment tends to cover things like writing employee handbooks, employee benefits, and handling discrimination cases. *"I've drafted pleadings, briefs and motions, handled all of the discovery and led the discovery*

team. If you're somebody who can demonstrate ability and is prepared to hustle, then you'll get the more complicated assignments."*

Training & Development

Newcomers descend on the New York HQ for the 'Proskauer Institute', a week of initial training – *"getting to know the firm's resources and systems"*– and socials. Practice-specific sessions, including 'Training the Street' financial classes, continue in the first year. *"Almost every Friday for the first six months, they'd bring in pizza or lunch and attorneys from different practice groups give presentations on areas of practice, and we get CLE credit."*

Proskauer also recently introduced a 'Leadership Training' program to *"give you strategies for dealing with certain situations, like when you make mistakes or become overloaded,"* according to one interviewee. It's run by external consultants with input from partners about real life scenarios they have experienced which associates can learn from. After piloting this scheme, it's being rolled out to include summer associates too. *"I thought it was very insightful,"* mused another source. Rookies also get to do *"a mini MBA"* in the form of financial training sessions run in conjunction with Columbia Business School. A junior explained: *"It's important as a lawyer to see balance sheets or income statements and not to be overwhelmed. A lot of people become lawyers because they're afraid of numbers and not good at math! So we had three days involving textbooks and lectures to make us comfortable with financial information."*

"A mini MBA."

Sources were content with the support they received from seniors day-to-day. *"If I'm given an assignment I haven't done before, then someone will sit down and take me through the steps. People's phonelines are always open*

See firm profile on p.645

Diversity	Partners (%)	Associates (%)
Women	15.4	48.9
White	93.2	76.8
Black/African American	2.3	2.3
Hispanic/Latin American	2.7	4.8
Asian	2.3	13.6
Mixed/Other	0	2.5
LGBT	1.8	3

and they're happy to give me instruction." Many of the juniors we spoke to had positive things to say about the firm's mentoring scheme. Newcomers are assigned an associate mentor "who's your sounding board. A lot of things are foreign, so you can ask all your questions." In the second year, juniors get a more senior mentor who "helps you put together career development plan, and introduces you to clients. They're like your older brother or sister in the firm."

Hours & Compensation

There's no formal billing requirement at Proskauer, but do associates shoot for a certain number of hours? "I've heard the informal requirement is 2,000 hours," a litigator told us, while "in corporate number to hit is 1,800, because corporate is a bit more erratic in terms of workflow." These unofficial goals include things like pro bono, marketing, and other work for the firm. Bonuses are decided on a case-by-case basis, reflecting these things as well as the quality and quantity of billable work done. One associate revealed that "in some ways I'd prefer if there were a hard target, which would clear up some confusion about the hours target." However, others weren't ruffled by this at all: "The firm understands that workflow is not under your control and that as a first-year you're not going to get so many hours. I don't feel pressure at this stage. As long as you're not turning down work, it's ok."

"Everyone is given independence."

A pretty positive outlook on work/life balance was echoed among associates. "Partners and management embrace the idea of technology and remote access here. Everyone is given independence with regards to how they get their work done. You could leave at 6pm and log back on at home, or stay until 10pm in the office. If you have a dentist's appointment, you just go! You need to get the work done and keep the client happy – if those boxes are checked, then whatever!"

According to other associates, "they understand here that you're real human people. They don't want you to work weekends unless you absolutely have to. I'm always busy, I always have something to do, but there have not been many points at which I've felt overwhelmed. Some times I've been swamped, but they've never gone on for such a long time." Another junior concurred that "my February was extremely busy, and I was working until 2am for some time, but luckily those oppressive times are not prolonged." At Proskauer, "everyone is very respectful and mindful of your personal life, and I've never had an issue with taking time off. They care about your well-being, and your development, and want to make sure you're getting the most out of your experience."

Pro Bono

Proskauer places "a huge emphasis" on pro bono. Sources told us eagerly that the firm recently "welcomed a new pro bono partner and all newcomers are now assigned a pro bono matter. It's important to get started on one immediately, to set the trajectory for career involvement." The pro bono partner was a new role in 2015 (previously there was a pro bono counsel) when Bill Silverman filled it from Greenberg Traurig. In 2016, he was joined by a senior associate from Hogan Lovells, Erin Meyer, as pro bono counsel.

"They're focusing on getting more corporate pro bono work. People often think of it as more litigation-focused."

Whether litigator or deal-doer, "there's a lot of flexibility. They're focusing on getting more corporate pro bono work. People often think of it as more litigation-focused." Every interviewee had taken on at least one project, including immigration and Uvisa issues, non-profit mergers and company dissolutions. "I'm working on an asylum case with a partner and senior associate, but they've given it to me to run almost entirely. I file papers with the court and talk with immigration services directly. It's a great way to cut your teeth and manage a case." In one high profile case, Proskauer, New Jersey's ACLU and Disability Rights Advocates (DRA) are suing New Jersey's prison and education departments for failing to provide education to young prisoners with disabilities, including those in solitary confinement.

Pro bono hours
- For all US attorneys: 42,228
- Average per US attorney: 59

Culture

Nearly every one of the juniors we spoke to praised "the people" of Proskauer. "There's a lot of camaraderie," reported one. "What I find very appealing about the workplace is that no one thinks too highly of themselves. It's a

See firm profile on p.645

The Inside View

very egalitarian atmosphere." A junior explained that *"I'm easygoing generally and tend not to get stressed, so I wanted an environment that supports that. Here it's a laid back but serious environment. You have smart conversations about the law daily but can also talk about things that are completely not work-related."* Another source praised the firm's *"no BS approach"* to career paths. *"They don't pretend that partnership is right for everybody. We're all figuring it out year by year and they're very transparent about offering pathways to clients. One of the first panels I went to as a summer was 'Life after Proskauer.' I was thinking, 'I just got here, now you're telling me how I can leave?!' Of the alumni who spoke, one had opened a restaurant, one founded an app, one went in-house. They recognize that alumni are just as important as associates and that they're part of the family."*

"Alumni are just as important."

A frenetic social calendar *"is not a thing"* here, although there is a big holiday party and lots of summer events, plus occasional happy hours. *"Does the department go out for beers every week? No! Do I want that? No!"* exclaimed an associate. *"I want to live my life! You're not obligated to show up to mixers, there's no pressure, but if you've got buddies within the firm then you can go grab dinner or whatever."*

"Proskauer realizes that just because you've got a 4.0 or 4.2 GPA that doesn't mean you're the best candidate. I can tell you that every person I speak to here, I wouldn't mind sitting back and having a drink with," commented a junior. *"People are well-rounded, enthusiastic and optimistic, collaborative and not afraid to roll up their sleeves. We're not looking for people who are elitist. It's all about attitude."*

Offices

The New York office is definitely boast-worthy. *"It's a game changer! People that come and see our offices fall in love with them! It's like something you'd see on a TV show or a movie, and think 'oh offices don't really look that nice!' We're spoiled to have such nice premises."* Plenty of glass means that *"there's lots of sunlight coming in, and we're the only firm I can think of with its name on the building, which adds an extra sense of pride when you step into the office!"* The office artwork (cataloged in a *"coffee*

table book") and the subsidized cafeteria also drew high praise. *"Everyone eats lunch there. It's gorgeous, it looks like a restaurant that you'd go out to dinner at."* Among our sources, popular dishes include the sushi (there's a special Proskauer roll) and the grilled cheese.

Most juniors are in the New York office, and the next most are in Boston. LA takes on the next largest group and at the time of our calls there were also a few rookies spread across New Orleans, Chicago, Newark, DC, and Boca Raton. LA, New York, Washington, DC and Chicago offer a broad range of the firm's practices, while other offices have more specialized focuses.

Diversity

Proskauer has affinity groups for ethnic minority attorneys, religious observers, women, LGBT and flex-time lawyers. The Women's Alliance meets monthly. Proskauer's Silver Scholar Program offers summer associate places to diverse 1L or 2L students. Diverse associates are also matched up with someone from the Diverse Lawyer Mentoring Circle Program. *"I've been part of recruitment cycles now, and I'm seeing more women and candidates of color. It's refreshing that the firm is open about its commitment to diversity and the fact that it doesn't have the numbers we'd like."* Proskauer recently launched a program, CaRe 'Caregiver Return', that allows lawyers returning from primary caregiver leave to work a 75% schedule for up to six months to help them transition back to work.

"I can tell you that every person I speak to here, I wouldn't mind sitting back and having a drink with."

Strategy & Future

Chairman Joe Leccese confirms that *"we've had significant growth in the litigation practice over the past 12 months and we continue to develop our core competencies in M&A, finance and capital markets."* Looking overseas, he admits that *"growth in Hong Kong has been slowed by some of the economic disruptions in the Asian markets"* but *"the London office continues to grow dramatically – it's one of our strategic areas of expansion. Much of our growth is in the areas of M&A, private investment funds, finance and private equity real estate."*

"Everyone eats lunch there. It's gorgeous, it looks like a restaurant that you'd go out to dinner at."

See firm profile on p.645

Reed Smith LLP

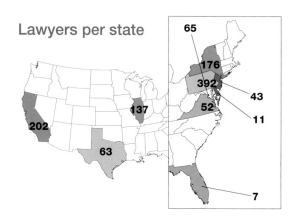

Lawyers per state

65
176
392
43
137
52
11
202
63
7

Largest US office: Pittsburgh

US offices: 16 (including a Global Customer Center)

International offices: 12

First-year salary: $130,000 - $180,000

Billable hours: 1,900 target (1,950 to be bonus eligible)

Summers 2017: 57 (52 2Ls, 5 1Ls)

Revenue 2016: $1.075 billion (-4.3%)

Partners made in 2017: 25 globally (16 in US)

Famous for: international reach, especially for shipping; Pittsburgh steel heritage.

Steel yourself for tons of opportunities at this huge firm, which even has its own university...

HEINZ tomato ketchup, the Big Mac, the Jeep, Reed Smith... The connection? All Pittsburgh-born, in 1877 in the law firm's case. Fast-forward 140 years: Reed Smith has a big presence across not only the US but the globe – 28 offices, including New York, DC, Chicago, San Fran, LA, and, as of April 2017, Miami. Associates liked the work opportunities size provides: *"It gives you the resources to do the work you want to do."* They also sang the praises of Reed Smith University, an ongoing formal training program: *"The firm really invests in you from day one."* See the Training section below for details.

Numerous ranked practice areas in *Chambers USA* include banking & finance, bankruptcy/restructuring, corporate/M&A, private equity, insurance, labor & employment, IP, and litigation. Founding partner James H. Reed was lawyer to one of the titans of 19th Century industrialism, Andrew Carnegie, whose steel company – US Steel – remains a Reed Smith client to this day.

The Work

Juniors are in either litigation or business & finance. Within each are subgroups: *"The fact they have a lot of*

practice groups was very attractive" sources noted. *"Initially it's hard to know what you want to do!"* Complex litigation is the biggest litigation subgroup, while others include IP, life sciences, labor & employment, and data security & privacy. Transactional associates split into corporate & transactional advisory, real estate, energy & natural resources, and financial services, among others.

"If you can show you're capable then people will let you take on things."

In complex litigation, *"the practice is so broad there are lots of opportunities for doing different things."* There is undeniably *"a lot of research and writing,"* but going to trial has seen juniors *"preparing witnesses for cross-examination, which involved setting up mock crosses and going over their responses."* A Pittsburgh associate highlighted they were *"lead drafter on a motion to dismiss. You can get hands-on experience in small matters, and on larger cases you get to observe a lot and see how senior attorneys deal with things."* Clients are often *Fortune 500* corporations, and juniors see things like product liability cases, contractual cases, class action cases, and shareholder disputes. A Chicago junior explained: *"If you can show you're capable then people will let you take on things. It's a lot of work – but the more you can do to take the pressure off the partners, the better."*

The global corporate group deals with matters including M&A, capital markets, and corporate governance work. *"It's not uncommon to work with clients in China, Europe,*

See firm profile on p.646

The Inside View

Rankings in *Chambers USA*

Advertising	Intellectual Property
Antitrust	International Arbitration
Banking & Finance	Labor & Employment
Bankruptcy/Restructuring	Life Sciences
Construction	Litigation
Corporate/M&A	Products Liability
Healthcare	Real Estate
Insurance	Tax

For detail on ranking tiers and ranking locations, visit
www.chambersandpartners.com

Recent work highlights

- Win for US Steel in antitrust suit brought by Stanislaus Food Products, a purchaser of tin mill products
- Assisted health distributor McKesson on its acquisition of Vantage Oncology for $1.2 billion
- Represented Volvo on its proposed auto manufacturing plant outside Charleston, SC
- Represented United Overseas Bank as the lender to Alchemy Properties in a $220 million deal that will finance the conversion of the upper floors of the Woolworth Building into condos

or elsewhere in Asia." Tasks include due diligence, drafting ancillary and transaction documents, as well as *"going on data sites and reviewing contract leases."* Juniors staffed on a deal *"do whatever is required."* Fluctuating workloads mean *"you can't see what's coming, which can then be hard to plan for."* A New Yorker found *"folks here trust you to do more than normal – it can be daunting at times, but overall I think it's a good thing."*

> ### "You know you're being allowed to exercise your judgment in decision-making."

IP folks deal with either privacy and data security or patent matters. Work on the former may involve *"drafting privacy policies for websites and apps,"* and on the trial side *"research, or preliminary drafts of motions to dismiss."* Juniors experienced *"independence but with supervision. You still have support, but you know you're being allowed to exercise your judgment in decision-making."* Clients on the privacy side include automotive companies and advertising companies, while the patent side sees more pharmaceutical companies. Patent juniors can be found *"reviewing office actions and prior art cited, coming up with strategies and drafting responses."* If a trial is involved, associates might get stuck into *"case review to see how certain judges behave."*

Energy & natural resources work varies by office. In Pittsburgh, for example, the main focus is construction litigation, with some environmental regulatory work thrown in too. Clients include pipeline companies and power generation plants. *"Research and drafting are a huge component of my day."* Other common tasks include discovery work, answering complaints, and doc review. *"To be honest, I expected less responsibility because whenever you hear about big firms there is this stereotype that you'll be doing grunt work and putting together binders. In a lot of cases here, the junior is responsible for managing the case, managing deadlines, and figuring out the response."*

Offices

Most juniors were in Pittsburgh, Philadelphia and New York. A strong force occupied offices across California, Chicago, and DC, with a smaller number across the firm's Virginia, Delaware, and New Jersey offices. Most do a little bit of everything, but the Pittsburgh office has a bigger focus on energy, insurance and corporate, while Chicago is best known for its insurance recovery group, and DC its life science group. Juniors have their own offices except in New York, where space is significantly more expensive. New Yorkers enjoyed the new cafeteria in their building, and the post-refurb open glass offices. *"I think everyone is getting used to the new-paint smell!"* one laughed.

> ### "Everyone is getting used to the new-paint smell!"

Training & Development

Reed Smith University is the firm's training resource and is linked to CareeRS, its firmwide career development program. There are a certain number of mandatory training sessions, then a calendar of sessions that you can choose to attend or not. *"There's a guiding system to help you look at what you're supposed to be dealing with, but I do think you have to really make what you want of it, and seek out what you really want,"* a New Yorker explained. Another enthused: *"I've liked the training because I've been able to learn from experiences of attorneys here and abroad."* Others mentioned practical *"on the ground training."*

The review process starts with a self-evaluation in which juniors list partners they've done work for, who in turn review them. The practice group leader then goes over both evaluations in person with associates, and these are used to determine compensation and bonuses. *"The system is fine, it's just sonorous when you have to write a ton in two weeks on top of the other work you have,"* one noted.

See firm profile on p.646

The Inside View

Diversity	Partners (%)	Associates (%)
Women	23.2	49.1
White	88.6	79.2
Black/African American	3.8	4.4
Hispanic/Latin American	1.7	5.4
Asian	4.6	9.1
Mixed/Other	1.3	1.9
LGBT	undisclosed	undisclosed

Culture

"The best way to describe the culture? People I work with are people I also hang out with on weekends," a Pittsburgher found. The friendly environment came as a surprise to some who *"didn't know what to expect coming into a large firm."* Many described the culture as entrepreneurial in the sense that *"you're encouraged to make your own career, even at junior level. The firm encourages you to do whatever you need to do to be successful."* Having said that, juniors were keen to clarify *"it's not overly competitive, but people work really hard."*

"You don't have to worry about letting your guard down."

"You don't have to worry about letting your guard down at inter-office events." The social scene ranges from *"charitable events that turn into social events"* to cooking competitions to an *"Oktoberfest-y event,"* plus occasional happy hours, *"a nice social gathering to let loose and talk about what's going on."*

At the beginning of 2016, the firm announced some layoffs that affected a handful of attorneys globally. One source said *"the leadership was upfront about it when it happened, and I didn't get a sense of panic,"* while a DC-er admitted *"when people have slow months they get really scared. The layoffs came with no notice."* But overall, many agreed *"it hasn't had a long-term impact on the atmosphere"* and the firm has *"come out stronger."* Some thought *"partners in a different generation maybe value different things. It seems they don't really value work/life balance."* But others pointed out that *"it's not uncommon to find senior attorneys at the local bar, hanging out and getting a beer."*

Hours & Compensation

"When everyone went to the New York scale [$180,000 for first-years], Reed Smith took about a week to chime in and follow suit." That said, salary still varies regionally, starting at $130,000 in Richmond. The billing goal is 1,900 hours, although to be eligible for a profit-sharing bonus, associates need to bill 1,950. Those in litigation and transactional groups had no trouble hitting the tar-

get, but some explained that *"it's not really achievable if you're in a specialized group. And it's harder to meet target when a lot of work is given to overseas."* Others elaborated: *"When you first start, it's hard to get workflow – you're still getting your legs and building a reputation. But from then on it's easier."*

Being in the office 9am to 7pm is fairly standard, with home work too. *"They expect you work when you need to, but also they're not oblivious to the fact that people want a work/life balance."* For most, this was achievable, but corporate associates noted that *"the unpredictable factor does affect it."* Some have to *"build a private life around work. It all depends where you are and what deal you're on."*

"You're often the lead attorney."

Pro Bono

Reed Smith encourages juniors to do pro bono, not least because *"you're often the lead attorney so it's good practice handling a matter on your own,"* a New Yorker explained. Associates can count 120 hours of pro bono work as billable, for individual cases or as part of the firm's formal program. Cases range from asylum, immigration, and domestic abuse to corporate governance matters and non-profit mergers. Several juniors mentioned their involvement in the Name Change Project – helping transgender people to change their names.

Pro bono hours
- For all US attorneys: 54,384
- Average per US attorney: 56

Diversity

The legal industry has plenty of work to do on the diversity front, but Reed Smith associates reckoned *"we're the cream of the crop in making sure women make partner."* The WINRS Women's Initiative Network of Reed Smith program focuses on developing women attorneys to their full potential and encouraging their advancement in the industry. *"For women, there's a bunch of seminars,"* a female junior noted, but they could have a wider impact: *"I feel like men need to get those trainings!"* That said, there is a firmwide implicit bias seminar. The firm also recently started an initiative for attorneys with disabilities. *"Reed Smith continues to support diversity efforts. There's a budget there if you have a diversity idea."*

Strategy & Future

Associates agreed that the firm *"offers a pathway to partnership that is much clearer than other firms"* and that they *"put in extra effort to cultivate relationships with you."* Managing partner Sandy Thomas emphasizes the effort the firm put into *"the investment we're making in people*

See firm profile on p.646

The Inside View

and capabilities." His general strategy is *"to be the leading global firm in five global industries"* – energy & natural resources, financial services, life sciences & health, entertainment & media, and shipping. To achieve this, *"we've added capabilities in each one of those and seen some really great recognitions in the market as a consequence."* Besides practice areas, Reed Smith is also focusing on its *"robust diversity and inclusion program"* which Thomas highlights *"has earned us the nickname 'Rainbow Smith'."*

Get Hired

"The questions we ask are designed to suss out what their interest is in being a practicing lawyer," global head of legal personnel Casey Ryan tells us. Find out more about getting hired at Reed Smith on chambers-associate.com

"Our strategy at Reed Smith is to be the leading global firm in five global industries."

The Inside View

See firm profile on p.646

Ropes & Gray LLP

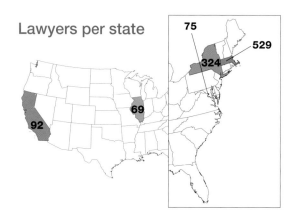

Lawyers per state

75
529
324
69
92

Largest US office: Boston
US offices: 6
International offices: 5
First-year salary: $180,000
Billable hours: no requirement
Summers 2017: 145 (144 2Ls, 1 1L)
Revenue 2016: $1.486 billion (+6.9%)
Partners made in 2017: 11 globally (8 in US)
Famous for: its Boston roots; second-to-none training

Associates learning the ropes get just enough slack at this Boston-HQ'd go-getter.

TWO years into Ropes & Gray's five-year growth plan – which culminates in 2020 – managing partner David Chapin is sensibly *"focused on executing plans"* right now. Chief among them is *"a real focus to beef up our New York presence and profile."* We should point out the NYC office is already pretty beefy, with over 300 lawyers. Ongoing lateral partner hires are an effort *"to build historically strong areas like private equity, bankruptcy, M&A, and investment funds, as they all complement the practices we have around the world."* The firm is investing in the financial centers of London, Hong Kong and New York in particular, *"the logical nexus for the financial institutions practice"* and where *"historic clients are clustered."* In March 2016, the firm announced the spin-off of its IP rights management practice, headed by several Ropes partners.

Unusually at Ropes & Gray, *"for the second year in a row, we didn't open any new offices,"* David Chapin explains. Instead, the goal is to *"make offices as integrated as we can."* Associates discerned a level-headed vibe at Ropes in general: *"There's none of that craziness you expect in BigLaw,"* they told us. *"The energy level is never low, but*

the stress level is also not huge. It's far from a frantic pace: it's more respectful."* All this is achieved while winning many *Chambers USA* rankings, not least for investment funds, M&A, banking & finance, healthcare, IP, tax, and litigation clients.

The Work

A strong work assignment system lies in wait for arriving associates. *"An ADM [associate development manager] is assigned to a practice group, and each week they assess everyone's availability thanks to an online system, and their knowledge of people's skill levels."* It's then down to the ADM to dish out the work; but as associates progress, ADMs play second fiddle to a more human approach. *"It's a good hybrid. Through networking and cultivating relationships you can build the work that you want to do. But there's still the built-in level of support with ADMs. When you're unsure of your next step or are a little slow in networking, that's a perfect time to go to the ADM."* Most junior associates are in the litigation, tax & benefits, and corporate groups. Within corporate, subgroups include private equity, investment management, and IP transactions, and people tend to specialize in one by their third year.

Corporate provides plenty of transactional work for associates, with private equity a particularly heavy presence. Juniors explained that *"you will do due diligence – that comes with the territory and it's necessary to have a solid understanding of the contracts before you take the lead on*

On chambers-associate.com...

- Interview with David Chapin, managing partner of Ropes & Gray
- We talk to Ropes' former hiring partner Richard Batchelder

See firm profile on p.647

Rankings in *Chambers USA*

Antitrust	Intellectual Property
Banking & Finance	Investment Funds
Bankruptcy/Restructuring	Labor & Employment
Capital Markets	Life Sciences
Corporate Crime & Investigations	Litigation
Corporate/M&A	Privacy & Data Security
Employee Benefits & Executive Compensation	Private Equity
FCPA	Real Estate
Healthcare	Securities
	Tax

For detail on ranking tiers and ranking locations, visit
www.chambersandpartners.com

Recent work highlights

- Represented Gawker Media as it filed for bankruptcy, and as it underwent restructuring following the $130 million litigation judgment against it regarding Hulk Hogan's sex tape
- Helped to form investment firm Atairos Group, founded by the former chief financial officer of Comcast and in possession of over $4 billion in committed capital
- Represented pharma giant Pfizer on $14 billion acquisition of biotech company Medivation

drafting anything. But our contract attorneys ensure you won't be staffed on 50 hours of DD in three days – the firm understands you won't develop that way." Opportunities to draft ancillary documents come associates' way, along with the possibility of a project manager-esque role. *"Someone explained it as being the quarter-back of the team, communicating to make sure everyone is on the same page and the process is flowing."*

"There's nothing rote about it."

Healthcare is a more niche practice within the corporate gamut, but it's also top ranked nationally by *Chambers USA*. Associates spoke of *"massive mergers between US healthcare companies and the regulatory red tape around doing that"*; hence a blend of transactional and regulatory work here. In contrast to the more conventional corporate experience, *"research is a big part. When questions come in from clients the answer often isn't clear – there's nothing rote about it. So you have to sift through a lot of information."*

Associates in litigation told us *"because you're put into general litigation you get all sorts,"* but *"it's mainly two buckets"* – business and securities, and government investigations. These two practices make up the largest chunk of the litigation department, but some people in most offices specialize in IP litigation instead. They work on *"district court cases, International Trade Commission litigation, and patents and trademarks,"* focusing on two markets: electronics and life sciences.

"The thing about being a junior is that you are cheap!" chuckled one litigation associate. *"It means you do everything you can possibly do. From things you would expect like doc review to what my role is now: drafting witness interviews, attending witness preparations, taking notes in interviews and meeting clients as a result."* And in between there's *"legal research, of course, and drafting motions."*

Offices

We found the firm's offices to be the cause of some playful inter-office rivalry: *"This office is awesome! Boston should be jealous of us,"* a San Franciscan joked. A NYC associate was sure *"they make an effort to have all the offices looking similar: the layout here is very like Boston."* The location, within spitting distance of the Rockefeller Center, is (as everyone knows) *"a popular tourist destination so it does get pretty busy around the building at times."* Associates share an office in their first year and sometimes in the second year too, a setup greeted with split responses. *"As nice as it is to learn with another person, I'd prefer my own office. It's great for the first three months, but if either of you are on a call it can be a distraction."* For fitness fanatics, *"the biggest disappointment is that there's no gym!"* We should point out, however, that the firm does offer reimbursement for fitness and weight loss programs, and corporate discounts at local health clubs.

Ropes HQ occupies nearly 20 floors of the *"coolest building in Boston,"* the Prudential Tower. Again, *"you share for the first year with another associate."* Those in the smaller San Fran office usually enjoy solitude from the start. An SF native described being *"right on the water with a view of the Bay and the bridge; it's basically all glass windows and we have standing desks for all on the fourth floor."* Ropes also has offices in DC, Chicago, and Silicon Valley.

"I know someone in every office."

"The firm is always talking about us being 'one firm,'" an associate remarked, *"but it does play out in the cross staffing – I know someone in every office."* Indeed, while geographically clustered offices tend to have the most frequent contact, one associate felt it was *"as easy as saying 'hey, I want to go somewhere else' for whatever reason and if it isn't problematic the firm's impetus is to say yes."*

Culture & Get Hired

One associate made this unusual observation to make a point about Ropes's decent culture: *"It's apparent to me that a lot of the people at the firm have stayed married. Normally big firms work you and work you until you burn*

See firm profile on p.647

The Inside View

Diversity	Partners (%)	Associates (%)
Women	25	47
White	84	70
Black/African American	2	4
Hispanic/Latin American	1	3
Asian	5	12
Mixed/Other	unknown	4
LGBT	2	5

out." Across offices, interviewees agreed that *"the part-ners I met interviewing were the kind of people that I felt I wanted to be."* We heard of *"an unspoken 'no asshole' rule – if you want to work here don't be an asshole!"* In essence, this means both a *"professional"* and *"human culture,"* in which *"people might send each other flowers when some-one has a baby or to thank them. I sit between two partners who are as willing to walk me through a complex question, without asking for a billing code, as they are chatting about wedding plans."* No surprise, then, that *"we are looking for people we want to work with, above the obvious academ-ics."*

"All you can ask for is the shot."

With juniors lining up alongside some *"very intellectu-ally rigorous people,"* a sense of responsibility cropped up in our interviews on more than one occasion: *"It is a little daunting to know that people really do listen to you and trust you – but it's no bad thing that you are actu-ally playing a role and not just shadowing. That gives me confidence."* As one put it: *"All you can ask for is the shot."*

"I would say that people don't feel any sort of pressure to go out after work. This is not a hard-partying firm." There are the usual *"firm sponsored happy hours,"* holiday parties, summer events, and *"a bowling event,"* the cause of *"some trash-talking between offices!"*

Hours & Compensation

Although there is no billable hours target, associates we spoke to believed they should aim for 1,900 hours: *"A sane and reasonable goal."* Most were confident they would meet it while acknowledging *"a built-in under-standing that you might not meet it in your first year."* There was much talk between offices of differing work-ing hours, primarily based on the belief that *"on the East Coast more hours are spent in the office."* If any difference exists, however, it is relatively slight. Most interviewees turned up around 9am and left between 6pm and 7pm, before logging on from home. Busier times bring una-voidable post-midnight finishes, something Eastern as-sociates seemed more used to. *"Even though it's obviously*

a stressful time, nobody is yelling; people are just getting stuff done; everyone is still working as a team."

"You can follow your own unique schedule."

"Generally people don't care where I'm working from. If I need to be at home because my fridge needs fixing, nobody minds having to email or call me." Offsite work is made easier still because *"at your request you can get a monitor and a docking station too, so that you're connected to the Ropes network via VPN."* This means *"you can follow your own unique schedule as long as you're there when all hands on deck are needed in the office."*

Diversity & Pro Bono

Ropes doesn't do badly on diversity figures – our sur-vey for 2017 shows that 47% of associates are women, 30% are from ethnic minority groups and **5%** identify as LGBT. Associates highlighted that appellate partner Douglas Hallward-Driemeier argued successfully before the Supreme Court in *Obergfell v. Hodges*, the historic gay marriage victory. MP David Chapin believes this and other noteworthy pro bono matters *"enhance the profile of the firm for taking on difficult matters, and attract a more diverse base of associates because of it."*

Diversity initiatives include *"a program where people are matched up with a mentor"* from their practice group, and meetings organized by both the Ropes Multicultural Group and the Women's Forum. The firm also offers a diversity scholarship, and a professional development advancement fund for diverse associates. Pro bono hours are treated the same as billable hours.

Pro bono hours
- For all US attorneys: 112,039
- Average per US attorney: 103

Training & Development

Right off the bat associates fly into an introductory training *"bootcamp"* in Boston. From there the training doesn't die away, as associates described a full calendar consisting of *"writing workshops, presentations about notable cases and professional responsibility training."* It's nothing if not regular, and one associate told us *"it's a lot to take in!"* Fortunately, *"there is an online database so that we can access any training materials we've missed if we're about to start work on something new."* One associ-ate surmised that *"your training is better as a result of the culture. My senior would pop into the office all the time and say 'for your own development I think you should per-haps address this point', and I knew he wasn't criticizing*

See firm profile on p.647

The Inside View

me." Or as another put it *"partners know you won't get everything right; they just steer you in a positive way."*

"Most people have a good run at the firm."

Associates receive formal annual reviews plus two quarterly informal reviews and an annual professional development discussion. They are also *"assigned an associate development partner. We don't get the sense that they are developing us like this just to have us leave."* Instead they felt *"most people have a good run at the firm, and they're in no rush to leave."* The GO program is an extra incentive to stay, as it offers chances to try working in a new, possibly international office either temporarily, or with the intention of a permanent move.

Strategy & Future

Interviewees were clued up on what they saw as *"a big push for more of an international presence and more international interaction."* It's a part of the day-to-day work for many, chatting away to the overseas offices when needed, and it's only going to increase. To ensure associates are mindful of strategy, there's an annual *"state of the firm meeting"* – they can pick up on faster-moving changes like the hires in NY via *"firmwide emails and a video about the new partner's practice. That's a good way of understanding the firm's general direction."* MP David Chapin believes *"we're already seeing how emphasis on the globalization of our client base is providing opportunities to work on matters cross-border and with clients in other geographies."*

"You can follow your own unique schedule as long as you're there when all hands on deck are needed in the office."

See firm profile on p.647

The Inside View

Schiff Hardin LLP

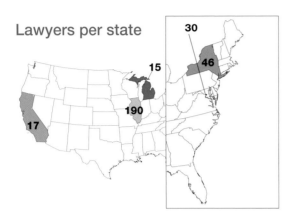

Lawyers per state

30
15
46
190
17

Largest US office: Chicago
US offices: 6
International offices: 0
First-year salary: $180,000
Billable hours: 2,000 required
Summers 2017: 14 (12 2Ls, 2 1Ls)
Revenue 2016: $222 million
Partners made in 2017: 9
Famous for: reputation in Chicago; lets associates roam free for a year before they have to pick a practice area; family-friendly

One of Chicago's oldest law firms has renewed vigor under its first female managing partner.

"CH-ch-ch-ch-changes," the late, great David Bowie sang. Around the time he left this world in early 2016, this leading 150 year-old Chicago firm experienced changes of its own when a group of 22 partners led by its former chairman and managing partner left Schiff to set up a new firm. The move came after a record year financially (thanks in part to a one-off $32 million contingency fee in 2015), when Schiff's revenue soared almost 15% to $277 million and partner profits jumped 21%. Since then, current managing partner Marci Eisenstein – appointed Schiff's first ever female MP in 2015 – has led a renewed push for growth, albeit with some refocusing (seven existing and four incoming associates were let go following the partner departures, and more recently the firm closed its small Dallas office). *"It was quite a shock but I don't know that there has been a major shift in focus,"* associates told us. *"We did lose a couple of elements of our litigation practice and we used to have a much larger products liability division, but a lot of groups were unaffected."* Marci Eisenstein confirms: *"The partner departures were certainly unexpected, and they were followed by a necessary but painful reduction-in-force. We went through some necessary re-*structuring, but we came through it more unified, cohesive, and focused than we've ever been."*

These things happen in BigLaw, and interviewees remained bullish about the firm, particularly its famously friendly culture which gives *"a real sense that we are human beings."* A high proportion of senior attorneys, including Marci Eisenstein, have spent their entire careers at Schiff, and juniors believed this goal remains true today: *"They are looking for people to be invested in the firm and to stay here for a long time."* There are openings for entry-level associates in several of Schiff's six offices spread around the country, and sources spoke highly of the decent responsibility and support they receive. The firm has also hired multiple lateral associates in the past year. *Chambers USA* singles out construction and environment as Schiff's strongest practices, and also highly rates its banking & finance, litigation, insurance, and wealth management teams.

The Work

Associates described the work assignment system as *"a completely free market system. It can be challenging, you have to be comfortable with finding work, with putting yourself out there. On the other hand, they really do allow you and encourage you to try things out."* For up to a year associates are at liberty to remain *"undesignated,"* with no need to declare allegiance to a group. *"To the heads of individual practice groups you can say 'hey, I'm looking for this type of experience' and they will direct you to part-*

On chambers-associate.com...

- Our interview with managing partner Marci Eisenstein
- We talk to hiring partners Dave Blickenstaff and Lisa Brown
- More on recruitment from associates

See firm profile on p.648

The Inside View

Rankings in *Chambers USA*

Construction	Environment
Energy & Natural Resources	Insurance

For detail on ranking tiers and ranking locations, visit
www.chambersandpartners.com

ners. Also, partners will call you out of the blue sometimes or talk to other partners to get referrals on associates. It goes in both directions." How long associates took to settle into one practice depended on their existing interests, but they felt *"no pressure"* to choose. *"I'm not sure how people could start fully knowing what they want to do,"* one associate mused.

"I'm not sure how people could start fully knowing what they want to do."

General litigation has the most junior associates. Quite a few go to the environmental practice, and you'll find one or two in general corporate & securities, finance, private client, real estate, IP, energy & public utilities, labor & employment, and product liability. Though litigation sources spoke about some large scale cases, on smaller cases *"it is typical to be staffed with just me and a partner. When something is in court, I will be in there addressing the court, or watching it, or doing a filing, or drafting for it. I'm drafting motions and discovery. It's harder to find these smaller cases but the opportunities are definitely out there."* Associates from many departments reported good client contact, like this finance source: *"Even as a first-year it was my responsibility to call the client and update them. As a second and third-year I'd be walking through the agreement with the client, doing it myself about a quarter of the time."* Across the board, associates gave rave reviews about the amount they were entrusted with: *"The thing I love about Schiff is that it is a place which will give as much responsibility as you are willing to take."*

Training & Development

Associates' ability to shoulder their high levels of responsibility rest in part on their legal writing. Schiff employs a full-time writing coach, Julie Schrager. *"Any time I write anything over two or three pages I would send it to her. She gives a lot of suggestions: she's so thorough you can get 50-60 comments,"* one associate reported. Stylistically, *"she knows the partners really well and even knows what certain judges are looking for."* Importantly, *"it's clear that it's outside the review process."* On that subject, there are annual formal reviews *"where you sit down with your practice group leader and they give a summary of the feedback given to you."* Informally, *"if you turn in work you get a lot of red ink – you see feedback that way. But you can also just walk into a partner's office or talk to associates after a deal and ask what you did well."*

Recent work highlights

- Worked on procurement, contract management, regulation and dispute resolution for Kansas City Power and Light regarding the La Cygne Generating station, comprising two coal-fired units, worth $1 billion
- Representing National Grid in the cleanup of the Gowanus Canal in New York
- Represented Michael Jordan in a five-year lawsuit against now-defunct supermarket chain Dominick's for advertising its 'Rancher's Reserve' steak with his name and number without permission. Jordan was awarded $8.9 million in damages

"If you turn in work you get a lot of red ink."

For litigation associates *"there's almost too much training, to the point where we were still being trained in April, and by that point I'd learned it on the job already!"* Over in finance, however, there's *"no specific finance group training. The training I get is more from actual work."* 50 of associates' billable hours are designated *"observational hours."* Many used them to *"attend a meeting or a hearing or something where the client wouldn't pay for you to go, or you have no direct role, but it would be a good learning experience."* Associates we interviewed felt the firm has *"made a lot of changes based on feedback from last year."*

Hours & Compensation

The 2,000 billable hour target caused no issues for associates. *"If you hit it you get a bonus and the amount is discretionary."* Some associates felt the movable element was *"not particularly well explained,"* nor was it *"particularly conducive to transparency."* At least one associate felt *"it should just be lockstep, then at least everyone knows."*

"There's the concept that you are a person with a family and a life."

"I've had some late nights but it's not a regular occurrence," said one associate. Most seemed content, suggesting their hours, though often long, weren't taking a severe toll on them. *"There's the concept that you are a person with a family and a life,"* so while weekend work wasn't unheard of, there's flexibility around face time. *"If I have a doctor's appointment at 10am nobody will ask where I am. If you need to leave to pick up your kid from daycare, nobody is shaming you."*

Pro Bono

Good news too on the pro bono front. Previously, *"you had to get approved for all of your pro bono hours above 75,"* but *"they've got rid of that now."* Instead, the pro bono hours counting toward associates' billing targets are un-

See firm profile on p.648

Diversity	Partners (%)	Associates (%)
Women	26.8	47.7
White	86.7	75
Black/African American	3.9	3.4
Hispanic/Latin American	2.2	2.3
Asian	4.4	11.4
Mixed/Other	1.7	2.3
LGBT	2.2	1.1

limited. Several reported doing over 200 hours, with one feeling *"encouraged to do that. There was no mention of me having billed too many hours."*

"The firm has continued to promote a whole bunch of opportunities. It got to the point where I was turning things down as so many partners were coming up with really cool stuff," gushed one associate. *"We have a clinic with Chicago Volunteer Legal Services where we go monthly to meet with lower income individuals who need legal assistance."* Associates had worked on and run *"a variety of civil matters, some family law, some benefits cases, and some landlord/tenant disputes."*

Pro bono hours
- For all attorneys: 16,943
- Average per attorney: 1,978

Culture

Beyond the writing coach, associates gave further evidence to suggest Schiff is an environment focused on long-term development. *"I can say 'can I take the first draft?' Even if the partner knows they'll have to revise it, I never get a 'no,' I get a 'sure!' Because that's how you learn. That's something I've felt the most, that they are invested in the learning."* As a result *"when you meet someone at Schiff, in a meeting or in the hallways, they will always tell you how long they've been at the firm – some partners have been here for 20 years and they are looking for that commitment."*

> *"It's friendly and easygoing without being particularly tight knit, rambunctious or energetic."*

"I would say it is a friendly place, but not an overly social place. I think everybody is friendly with each other in the hallway, everyone knows your name and a bit about each other. People's office doors are open, but at the end of the day most people go home to their families." Most associates felt the same way: *"I like the atmosphere here,"* said a Chicagoan. *"People aren't fussy about what you look like or whether I'm in the office all the time. It's friendly and easygoing without being particularly tight knit, rambunctious or energetic."* A big firmwide meeting is the highlight of the social calendar, traditionally combining a dinner, mixers, and business updates.

Offices

The Windy City headquarters are the most associate-heavy and their location within the landmark Willis (once Sears) Tower was a point of pride among its young occupiers. *"I love the tower!"* one declared. *"It's very conveniently located and super-easy to get to."* Associates get an office each too. Those in offices beyond Chicago reported frequent and fairly seamless work across offices, but we still heard comments that smaller offices had a sense of independence, and don't always subscribe to the Chicago model: *"They follow the beat of their own drum."* Beside the HQ in Chicago, there are offices in Ann Arbor, Lake Forest, New York, San Francisco, and DC.

Diversity

Diversity *"is a major concern of the firm,"* agreed associates. *"You can notice that among the summer associates there is a lot of diversity, and particularly in gender we do have diversity. There is a big focus on it. I think the challenge is to retain diversity: our diversity is much more among associates than in the partner ranks. But our managing partner is a woman and that is an important step for the firm to have made. It sends a strong signal about where we want to head."* Indeed, with managing partner Marci Eisenstein's help, the firm has done a lot to provide flexible parenting arrangements – there's even a specific New Moms Group. But as with so much of the legal profession, *"the fact is we don't have many non-white attorneys."*

Strategy & Future

The partner departures and subsequent lay-offs created uncertainty, but the opinion of most associates was that: *"It seems like the firm has figured out an equilibrium."* They felt Schiff was *"really listening to associates' concerns"* via meetings between partners and associates. Unlimited pro bono, the installation of WiFi and the matching of salaries have resulted: a process of *"shoring up morale."* Going forward *"everyone who is still here wants to be here, and that contributes to the atmosphere."*

Managing partner Marci Eisenstein tells us: *"We've had a really terrific year, which we were not necessarily expecting after the events of January 2016. Certain practices had breakout years: our IP group tried 11 cases in 12 months. That's remarkable for any IP group, and more remarkable for a firm of our size."* Read our full interview with Marci Eisenstein online to find out the rest of the story.

See firm profile on p.648

The Inside View

Schulte Roth & Zabel LLP

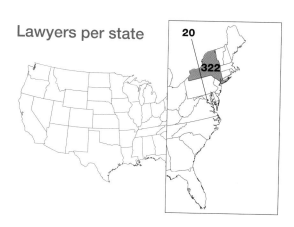

Lawyers per state

Largest US office: New York
US offices: 2
International offices: 1
First-year salary: $180,000
Billable hours: 2,000 target
Summers 2017: 38 (all 2Ls)
Revenue 2016: $409.5 million (+1%)
Partners made in 2017: 4 (all US)
Famous for: investment management and lots of hedge funds work

Schulte's hedge fund clients alone could stretch to the moon and back (probably).

THE year 1969 was noteworthy for all sorts of reasons: Richard Nixon swore the president's oath, The Beatles recorded their iconic Abbey Road album in London, and Neil Armstrong took a man's first step on the moon. Over in New York, meanwhile, seven young men (all under 35) were taking their own giant leap by leaving their law firms to set up a new one. Today, Schulte (pronounced *shultee*) is one of the top legal advisers for investment management work – representing nearly half of the 100 biggest hedge funds and over 3,000 investment funds worldwide. It has around 360 lawyers spread across offices in the Big Apple, DC and London.

Chambers USA confirms this reputation by awarding Schulte a top ranking nationwide for its investment funds prowess. It also gives decent marks to Schulte's capital markets, corporate/M&A, bankruptcy/restructuring, real estate, and tax practices, and recognizes its expertise too in white-collar litigation and government investigations. Executive committee chair Alan Waldenberg tells us that *"we're not trying to be all things to all people. Instead, we have a successful spot in the market representing clients we genuinely like."* Speaking of clients, notable cus-

tomers include Cerberus Capital Management, Veritas Capital and Credit Suisse.

The Work

Most juniors join the New York base, although at the time of our calls there was a sprinkling of associates in the DC branch. The latter comprises around 20 attorneys in total, most of whom are litigators working on either securities matters or white-collar defense. Associates usually submit status reports to indicate availability, and also get work via *"informal relationships that you've built up."* In investment management, *"we have two assignment partners, one for juniors and one for seniors, who look over our hours to make sure we're not lagging behind. But we're also usually assigned a client and we stay with them for our tenure at the firm. It's great because we get to build institutional knowledge and trust."*

"You have to keep on top of so many things."

Investment management *"is the place to be at Schulte,"* some here proudly felt. *"There's a small compliance subset in the group, but associates mostly get a good mix of private equity and hedge funds."* Expect to work *"on everything from handling fund-raising, launches, drafting fund documents, managing requests from investors, drafting partnership agreements, and interfacing with counsel over in the Caymans."* Other insiders told us that *"you feel like the quarterback because you have to keep on top of so*

The Inside View

See firm profile on p.649

Rankings in *Chambers USA*

Bankruptcy/Restructuring	Investment Funds
Capital Markets	Real Estate
Corporate/M&A	Tax

For detail on ranking tiers and ranking locations, visit
www.chambersandpartners.com

Recent work highlights

- Represented Marathon Asset Management, during Blackstone Strategic Capital Holdings Fund's acquisition of a minority interest. Marathon manages approximately $12.75 billion worth of assets
- Defending the former executive of SunTrust Mortgage, whose banks have total assets of $194 billion, against an indictment for wire fraud
- Represented Cerberus in the $38 million sale of Nova Technologies to casino slot machine maker Ainsworth Game Technology

many things." There's also a managerial element, *"because when there's a fund launch you have to make sure you've got all the proper documents drafted according to the correct terms. It's very intense."*

Litigators told us: *"In your first year, you spend a lot of your time doing doc review, which is kind of typical."* As associates progress, they get more responsibility, and DC sources told us they get high responsibility from the get-go. Regardless of location, meaty associate tasks included *"second chairing depositions, liaising with clients to prep for trial, and getting exhibits ready."* White-collar work sometimes requires international travel.

Associates in the M&A & securities group get stuck into *"a lot of contract review."* However a common theme across all departments was that because of the slight deficit of mid-level associates, younger lawyers get thrown in pretty early on. *"The firm has a great recruiting team and has taken on some good associates; the problem is retaining them. But because of this I've transitioned to higher level work."* This has seen corporate sources *"doing the initial drafts of sale and purchase agreements, corporate governance documents, and ancillary and contribution agreements."* Over on the shareholder activism side where shareholders of a publicly-traded company use their position to bring about change, insiders had *"drafted all notice and proxy statements and press releases. Activist work allows you to get client contact really early on."*

Training & Development

Incoming juniors gather in New York for a week of initial training that covers *"general orientation, IT, and how to research and email properly."* Training then becomes more specialized, with most groups running monthly sessions on case law updates. Recent topics included *"the 9th Circuit arguments on the immigration ban."* While corporate newbies were instructed *"in how to close deals and write opinion letters,"* litigators had a more interactive experience: *"In the summer we had a mock trial. It was my favorite bit of the program. The firm hired people to play witnesses and we had a jury which we could watch while they deliberated to see which bits of our advocacy were the most effective."*

General mentoring could be better, we heard: *"It's a struggle to know who to ask questions to. With seniors, sometimes I feel a bit like they're over the whole thing."* Formal feedback is given in the annual review, *"where you fill out a form evaluating what you've worked on and who you've worked with."* The reviewing partners then collect comments from the supervising attorneys and present the reviewee with conglomerated feedback.

Culture

"I never envisaged myself liking private practice," one associate confessed. *"I thought I'd do it for a few years and then look elsewhere. But now that I'm here I don't want to leave, purely because of the people. I like all of them and not just in a casual 'say hi' kinda way, but we're actually friends – both partners and associates alike."* Other echoed these sentiments, although a few mentioned the camaraderie *"can cool off"* among some seniors. Corporate sources said *"there's group lunch every other Friday and the occasional happy hour."* In DC, *"there's a drinks fridge and every couple of Fridays a partner has an open bar in his office. You can go over there and drink the type of whiskey that I can't justify buying on my salary!"*

In terms of career progression, juniors felt that *"the party line is that no one makes partner. The opportunities just aren't there. I think it's possibly because we're a smaller firm, but it does affect your plans for the future because you start looking at different options sooner than you would at other firms."* Chair Alan Waldenberg tells us that *"there are fewer opportunities for new associates today than there were when I started in 1978. Having said that, we've really focused on increasing opportunity. Last year we made a 5% increase in the partnership because we understand that unless we create the opportunities, people will leave, and we need new and young lawyers. They're the life-blood of this firm."*

Offices

Since early 2016, the NY HQ has been undergoing a huge revamp. *"We're about half-way done right now. It's*

See firm profile on p.649

Diversity	Partners (%)	Associates (%)
Women	13	42
White	87	74
Black/African American	2	1
Hispanic/Latin American	3	2
Asian	3	14
Mixed/Other	1	3
LGBT	2	4

completely different and very modern. It's all glass. Even though we still have wooden doors there's less privacy. At least it's very, very pretty." New Yorkers have to share digs in their first and second years, which they liked: "I really appreciated having someone to ask questions to and get a lot of info about the firm." DC was refurbished a few years ago and now everyone has their own office. "For a while it was really noisy because they were rebuilding the Washington Post building next to us. It's a lot quieter now and they're turning it into a shopping center with a beer garden, which I'm sure we'll go and use."

Hours & Compensation

In order to be eligible for a bonus, associates need to hit 2,000 hours. Up to 200 hours of pro bono, marketing or recruiting work can count toward the billing target. "I would like the target to be less, because you can be hurt by one slow month. Sometimes work can be cyclical so it's the luck of the draw." We heard that M&A has been a bit slower recently, and in August 2016 "the co-chair [John Pollack] left for Gibson Dunn." Others thought that "the uncertain political climate might be the reason why not as many deals are going through. Who knows!" However, in other departments it was full steam ahead. Some had worked "until 11pm every night for the past three weeks." Thankfully, "if you're burning the midnight oil they realize you need to catch up on sleep at some point. They're also pretty respectful about giving you two weeks uninterrupted vacation if you've been working hard."

The first-year salary was raised to $180,000 – "it's competitive, I mean we're at market." Bonuses are dependent on hours and increase by $10,000 increments for those who clock up 2,300 and 2,500 hours. "They're quite transparent, they send emails telling us what the bonus scales are. But my problem is that it shouldn't be based on hours. It should be more on quality and other factors that make good attorneys," some opined.

Diversity

Like much of BigLaw, "it's not particularly diverse. When you walk down the hall, it's mostly white people, although I know they're putting an effort into recruiting." One theory

why ethnic diversity wasn't better was that "our clients aren't Fortune 500 companies who sign pacts with each other to hire law firms with good diversity goals. Our clients are mid-market and aren't as diverse themselves, so it doesn't really play much of a role." Others suggested that "it feeds into why we don't have many mid-levels. When there's no one to mentor you who's also diverse, it's understandable why people leave. But we know that a lot of other firms care even less." The firm points out that a lot of attention and resources are focused on diversity right now, and the past two summer associate classes have been the most diverse ever at around 40%. Also, the most recent partner promotions included an Hispanic male and two Asian female attorneys, "which was a shock, because not only are they women and Asian, but one of them is also pregnant."

Female diversity is generally better, and while there are affinity groups for LGBT, black and Asian attorneys, the women's initiative is most visible. "We have women's happy hours and get-togethers to welcome new female associates."

Pro Bono

Schulte appointed Danny Greenberg – who spent nearly a decade as president and attorney-in-chief of the Legal Aid Society in New York – as special counsel overseeing the firm's pro bono program. 200 hours can count toward the billing target, although more litigators tend to get stuck in than transactional attorneys. Tasks have included "writing a brief for a case concerning an anarchist who was attempting to sue the UN for its role in a cholera outbreak in Haiti." In investment management, "at the moment we've got an associate doing a six-month fellowship at a non-profit. The firm still pays their salary." This is the program named in honor of former pro bono chair Brooks Burdette, which is open to all associates each year.

Pro bono hours
- For all US attorneys: 12,583
- Average per US attorney: 37

Strategy & Get Hired

"I've been on the executive committee for more than 30 years, and every year someone predicts the downfall of the mid-sized firm, and they're always wrong," explains exec committee chair Alan Waldenberg. "Other firms get bigger, but we like not having a whole lot of offices. It's so much easier with the advancement of technology to have a global practice right here in New York." Hiring partner Bill Gussman tells us that "we want bright students. Grades are a factor but not the complete package. We seek out personality and good communication skills." For more, read our Bonus Features on Schulte on chambers-associate.com.

See firm profile on p.649

Sedgwick LLP

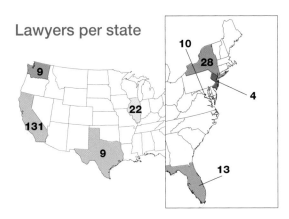

Lawyers per state

10
28
9
4
22
131
9
13

Largest US office: San Francisco
US offices: 12
International offices: 2
First-year salary: varies (case-by-case)
Billable hours: 1,950 requirement; 2,000 target
Summers 2017: no summer program
Revenue 2016: $170.6 million (-6.8%)
Famous for: litigation prowess; defenders of insurers

Sedgwick's prowess as a trial and litigation firm has been firmly bolstered since it opened its golden gate to a range of other practices...

FOUNDED in 1933, Sedgwick has grown considerably from its humble two-attorney beginnings in San Francisco. Nowadays laying claim to 14 offices across the USA and a further two abroad in London and Bermuda (an affiliated office), the firm most recently opened an office in Kansas City in 2014 to house its staff. And with growth has come variety: although it began life as a litigation firm, Sedgwick has since diversified to include areas such as business law, IP and real estate. In particular, this San Franciscan has an impressive insurance practice, ranking highly in *Chambers USA* within California for this area. It also ranks highly statewide for its construction work.

That said, Sedgwick's practice of origin still seemed to be the main draw for the associates we spoke to: "*I was very interested in litigation coming out of law school, and Sedgwick is one of the premier trial firms in San Francisco.*" And the work itself wasn't the only pull, as another explained: "*It sounds like such a cliché, but I didn't want to end up being another cog in a machine. I was very excited to be at a place where if I proved myself early, I would get more substantive work early, and that has really panned out for me.*" As well as California (San Fran, LA, Orange County), attorneys are to be found in Chicago, Dallas, Austin, Houston, Newark, New York, DC, Miami, Fort Lauderdale, and Seattle.

On chambers-associate.com...

- Pro bono at Sedgwick
- Diversity at Sedgwick

Get Hired & Strategy

We asked juniors what sort of person the firm looks to hire, and most agreed that social skills were a must. "*I found out that in my first interview,*" one newbie told us. "*They were pre-screening me to see if I would be cool enough to take for drinks with the client!*" Another noted that "*Sedgwick doesn't necessarily look for the applicants from the best schools with the highest grades. Obviously grades are important, but it's more important to make sure the person will fit into our culture.*" And be certain that the firm fits your interests; firm chair Michael Healy says that he looks for "*those that are interested in, and committed to, the type of practice we have.*"

In 2015, Sedgwick changed its formal summer program. Certain offices now take summer associates on a case-by-case basis – so candidates now have to apply directly to Sedgwick rather than through OCIs. This seems to be part of a broader strategy to focus on existing areas rather than expansion, as Michael Healy explains: "*Sedgwick is different than some of our peers in that we're committed to growing and bolstering our traditional areas of strength in our traditional cities.*" He adds: "*We're comfortable with our geographical footprint. We'd like to strengthen and broaden our expertise in the current offices.*"

And the removal of the summer program isn't the only change at Sedgwick. Michael Healy was appointed firm chair in 2015, and in addition, "*there is a new insurance division chair, a new commercial division chair, and a new at-large member*" on the five-person executive commit-

See firm profile on p.650

The Inside View

Rankings in *Chambers USA*

Construction

Insurance

For detail on ranking tiers and ranking locations, visit
www.chambersandpartners.com

Recent work highlights

- Representing the Judicial Council of the California Courts in a dispute with Jacobs Engineering regarding the construction of a court project. The client argues that Jacobs Engineering performed the work without a proper California Contractor's License and is subject to penalties
- Defended National Union Fire Insurance Company in a case where a manufacturer was unwittingly caught up in a Ponzi scheme and lost millions of dollars
- Representing engineering firm Leo A Daly over three class actions from residents of the city of Flint, Michigan alleging the firm knew or should have known that switching water sources without proper corrosion control treatment would result in lead contamination of water supplied to residents

tee. While hefty expansion isn't on the cards currently, Healy tells us that the firm has been bringing laterals into the cybersecurity & privacy group, an area which *"continues to grow in the US and in Europe,"* as well as *"five maritime partners to our San Francisco office earlier this year."*

The Work

The three main pillars of work are complex litigation, commercial, and insurance, and newbies join one of these three groups. Despite this, the work is not strictly segregated according to practice area: *"The divisional differences don't actually affect my day-to-day, it's just the way they lump us into groups for organizational purposes."* As such, overlap between groups is fairly commonplace; we heard of newcomers in insurance, for instance, who had handled contract disputes and commercial litigation matters. Work allocation is an informal process, meaning *"you've got to get out there. Thankfully I've never been in need of work here, and now there's a few partners I work for on a regular basis."*

"The firm encourages you to go out and build a book of business."

In the insurance group, some had focused mainly on insurance coverage: *"When insurance claims come in, the insurer comes to us to give them an opinion as to whether or not the claim is covered by the policy."* Others, meanwhile, had done more on the litigation side – always on behalf of the insurer. Over in complex litigation, we heard of newbies who had worked on cases involving the school district, as well as *"a lot of landlord-tenant work and environmental toxic torts."* In the commercial group meanwhile, we spoke to juniors who had done work in construction, business litigation and retail. The latter usually involves defending retailers, with false advertising and deceptive pricing cases being cited as particularly common.

Our interviewees were generally very pleased with the level of responsibility they'd been offered. *"I'm going to court regularly, I'm taking depositions, and appearing in front of arbitration panels,"* one insurance junior told us. Another in the commercial group added that while some paper shuffling can be expected, *"they also encourage you to branch out – we're not just stuck doing doc review every day. I've been able to take and defend depositions, take*

hearings, argue motions, and I'm about to second chair a deposition." Direct client contact is also fairly frequent; associates informed us that they are *"regularly on calls with clients,"* and one newbie appreciated that *"the firm encourages you to go out and build a book of business."*

Training & Development

Sedgwick organizes its training schedule through 'Sedgwick University', a program that offers classes and online resources on anything from *"how to manage complex litigation to the correct way to bill entries to clients."* The training sessions are officially split into seven schools: law, ethics, leadership, personal and professional development, finance, marketing and business development, and technology. Our interviewees also mentioned a weeklong 'Trial Academy' for midlevel associates. The course is conducted in Dallas *"with partners who act as judges, and you try two cases during the week. Everyone says it's one of the best experiences they've had at the firm."*

"Partners take time to go over things that I write."

Juniors *"have to attend a certain number of in-house training sessions to be in good standing,"* although many remarked that they had been given *"a ton"* of informal training and feedback too. One source noted that *"partners take time to go over things that I write and send them back to me, so I can see how to improve."* There is also a yearly formal review, at which point associates *"get a printout of feedback and constructive criticism, which is helpful."*

Offices

The majority of newbies are herded into Sedgwick's San Francisco HQ, *"right in the heart of the financial district."* Associates loved their *"floor-to-ceiling windows,"* and the great views were a definite plus: *"I can see*

See firm profile on p.650

Diversity	Partners (%)	Associates (%)
Women	32	44
White	82	74
Black/African American	4	3
Hispanic/Latin American	7	16
Asian	2	13
Mixed/Other	4	3
LGBT	4	1

the bay and various iconic places in San Francisco like the *Golden Gate Bridge.*" Chicago juniors meanwhile enjoyed their "*very spacious*" offices and "*nice big windows.*" The on-site gym and cafeteria were also appreciated – "*that's where I tend to eat breakfast and lunch.*"

"It's really got that wow effect when you walk in."

Over in LA, the office is allegedly "*like a spa! We recently had the entire place remodeled from top to bottom,*" chirped an eager newcomer. "*Everything was repainted, there's a new kitchen, new fixtures, new lights – it's really got that wow effect when you walk in.*" Another remarked that "*the main conference room has a view from Hollywood to Century City to Santa Monica, and on a clear day you can see the ocean – it's a pretty panoramic view.*"

Culture

We've mentioned Sedgwick's cordiality in past editions of *Chambers Associate*, and we were told that little has changed on that front: "*For the most part, everyone here is very friendly and approachable. I'm not working with condescending or arrogant people.*" One source highlighted that "*I never feel competitive with the other associates; there's no real cut-throat culture here.*" They went on to add that although "*working at a firm of this nature is going to be stressful and intense, it's good to know that you don't have to look over your shoulder as you're facing the challenges!*" And this friendliness isn't limited to associates – partners too are "*very accessible, and they do a good job of communicating with younger associates. I go to informal lunches with partners, or into their offices to chat – I was just now talking to a partner about our weekends.*"

"There's no real cut-throat culture here."

The phrase 'a good work/life balance' was frequently bandied about by the associates, but how does the firm promote this? "*I like the fact that it's very hands-off, and I very much make up my own hours,*" one source enthused. "*Most of my team have kids, so the firm is very diligent about keeping work off our plate for weekends as much*

as possible." Others pointed out that socializing among colleagues helped support a more balanced lifestyle. "*We have a group that goes out regularly, and partners come along too,*" one junior told us, adding that "*there's a wine bar and cellar down the street and we go there all the time.*" We heard that the firm itself is also good at arranging events: "*A couple of years ago Sedgwick instituted an associate retreat, which is in a different office each year,*" an interviewee informed us. The two-day event consists of a social gathering "*something like a baseball game,*" and "*an open forum to hear about what's going on at the firm and within your division, which is always interesting. It's a great way to meet other people across the firm.*"

Hours & Compensation

The 1,950 billable hours requirement at Sedgwick was generally considered "*very achievable.*" While the firm expects associates to hit this number, one junior commented: "*I know some people have not hit their hours before, but it hasn't resulted in anything besides the firm helping them to get more work.*" As far as base salary goes, "*we don't start at market, but it shows in the way we are afforded more flexibility with our hours, and I think it's a fair trade-off.*" The firm tells us that salaries are "*extremely competitive*" given its size. Incoming associates' salaries vary on an individual basis depending on where they're based.

"We are afforded more flexibility with our hours."

Juniors need to bill 2,000 hours to get the first tier of bonus, which increases with every 50 additional hours above this. Once you hit 2,150, the increments increase to 75 hours. There were gripes about the salary in previous years – more specifically due to a lack of transparency. Unfortunately, "*that is a recurring issue. It's not 100% clear to me how they choose the raises or what to pay you,*" one newbie grumbled. Another added: "*Basically you show up for your end-of-year review and they tell you what your salary is for next year – there's no negotiation.*"

This somewhat undiplomatic approach was criticized in a separate instance: "*They've just announced that they aren't going to give us a fee-sharing bonus if you bring in a new client.*" Despite the grouching, however, many were satisfied with the system. "*If I wanted to take it easy and only hit 1,950, I could,*" one conscientious junior informed us, "*and some people do that who are very content. I far exceeded that number this year, but I was also well rewarded for it – it's really what you make of it.*"

"It's really what you make of it."

See firm profile on p.650

Seward & Kissel LLP

Lawyers per state

14

168

Largest US office: New York
US offices: 2
International offices: 0
First-year salary: $180,000
Billable hours: 2,000 target
Summers 2017: 11 (all 2Ls)
Revenue 2016: undisclosed
Partners made in 2017: 2
Famous for: investment funds, maritime finance; topping the Associate Satisfaction Survey in 2017

If investment funds and shipping law put the wind in your sails then plot a course for the island of Manhattan, the home of Seward & Kissel.

FIRST things first, it's pronounced 'soo-wood' and not 'sea-ward'. Ironically, this mispronunciation would be more apt as S&K's prowess in all things maritime and shipping finance has been buoyed up by top marks from our sister publication *Chambers USA* in recent years. High marks also go to S&K's hedge funds work, which it's most famous for. In fact, the firm (founded in 1890) set up the world's first hedge fund, A.W. Jones & Co., in 1949. Expertise in these two areas were key reasons that associates picked the firm in the first place: *"Not only is its reputation in funds incomparable, but I'd heard horror stories of New York firms being cut-throat and there was none of that here."*

This is partly due to S&K's careful growth strategy. While some firms have expanded over seas, S&K has kept things anchored in the US, opting to run a two office operation out of New York and DC alone. Managing partner Jim Cofer tells us that *"we're happy being US-centric and from a strategic perspective we have a number of great relationships with non-US firms. This way, clients end up with folks who are at the top of their game from around the globe."* Associates liked this approach: keeping numbers down in the flagship gave Seward a *"boutique firm feel*

On chambers-associate.com...

- Interview with managing partner, Jim Cofer
- You're only 125 once! S&K's big birthday bash
- More on getting hired

that still does high-speed work. I think it's our biggest selling point. We're not a huge a firm so everything is leanly staffed and you get stuck in with work as soon as you start."

The Work

"You list three practices and most people get their first choice." Investment management takes the lion's share of new juniors, leaving a few to head to litigation, business transactions, corporate finance, global institutional finance, capital markets, ERISA, and maritime. *"In my class six went to investment, four to corporate, two to litigation and one went to global banking."* Different year-groups painted similar pictures. When it comes to work assignment, there's no formal system: *"Sometimes people just approach you and see if you're free."*

"It's a lot of hands-on experience very early on."

Seward & Kissel's market share is second to none in the investment management sphere, servicing some 40% of the top 100 hedge funds based on assets under management, and representing 13 of the top 100 private fund mangers. New starters are exposed to the full gamut of hedge funds work from day one, so expect to tackle *"everything from fund launches to researching questions on compliance."* New York insiders estimated that their *"department does about 80% hedge funds, 15% private equity and about 5% mutual funds."* Regardless of the type of fund greenhorns were staffed on, they had *"drafted of-*

See firm profile on p.651

The Inside View

Rankings in *Chambers USA*

Corporate/M&A	Transportation
Investment Funds	

For detail on ranking tiers and ranking locations, visit
www.chambersandpartners.com

fering documents, prospectuses, subscription agreements – and we're the go-to people for client calls."

Over in litigation, SEC civil investigations, contractual disputes and securities litigation are all common concerns. Budding litigators *"do pretty much everything, but there's a lot of employment, tax, IP and maritime lit."* White collar work has been on the up. Insiders explained that *"it's mostly securities stuff like company valuation issues or insider trading and embezzlement. The majority of cases are when the government investigates a big financial institution like a bank, we help them launch internal investigations and cooperate with governmental requirements."* Tasks might include a cornucopia of *"client interviews, note-taking and memo research."* While most found themselves lumped with discovery for a lot of their time, sources pointed out that *"it's expected."*

Business transactions is another popular destination for newbies. Juniors are assigned to one of a number of subgroups, such as M&A, capital markets and real estate. Maritime finance and other transactional shipping work also feature. Here lawyers are likely to assist clients worldwide on matters such as loan agreements, ship purchases and joint ventures. More generally, associates had done anything from *"drafting board consents to registration and rights agreements."* One rationalized: *"I'm not going to lie, it's a lot of due diligence. But even though it's grunt work, it's really important foundational work for these deals."*

Pro Bono

Sources were keen to describe their work with HerJustice, an organization that works in collaboration with New York law firms to provide legal services to indigent women. *"We tend to deal with contested divorces, domestic abuse and battered women cases."* Asylum matters also took up a healthy chunk of time. *"It was a pretty solid experience. I and two colleagues interviewed the client, wrote the brief, drafted expert affidavits and then went to a full hearing at the immigration court."* Not only is this a good cause, but insiders felt that *"taking the lead on these cases equips you with skills for your billables and I think partners are more willing to put you on things that would traditionally go to seniors."* All pro bono work can be counted toward associates' billable hours totals.

Pro bono hours
- For all attorneys: 8,820
- Average per attorney: 39

Recent work highlights

- Represented Saguenay Strathmore Capital in its sale to US-based Titan Advisors. The combined firm manages around $4 billion
- Represented Cypriot company Geveran Trading Co., relating to the US law involved its block sale of 37.8 million shares, worth $510 million
- Represented oil tanker shipping company Frontline in its merger with Frontline 2012, creating one of the world's leading tanker companies with a total market cap of $1.2 billion

Training & Development

Juniors undergo a week of orientation training, covering all the basics like how to bill, practice-specific seminars and a handful of CLEs. Corporate newbies have sessions explaining *"what a stock purchase agreement looks like and getting all the technical vocab down."* Litigators tended to have *"informal discussions on important legal developments every two months. We also had a jury trial CLE – that was great."* Most liked the informal approach, with a few even commenting that the *"week orientation was too long, I was ready to get out of there by day two."* S&K's more laid back approach was a definite hit when it came to mentorship: *"We don't have a mentorship program per se; we naturally work closely with the partners and everyone is willing to help."* Formal reviews are at year-end. Normally the partner you've worked with most will take you through the conglomerated feedback from other supervisors. Everyone was certain that *"if there are any real problems, they address it with you before your review."*

Offices

Most new Seward & Kisselers head to the New York HQ, located in Battery Park Plaza. Not all are lucky enough to have their own office – *"we normally transition first-years into the firm by making them share with second-years"* – but they liked the Lower Manhattan location for its waterfront calm. *"We're pretty much the last office on the edge of Manhattan, so we have this great view. We all have windows, which really makes a difference on a long day because you actually get to see outside."* Sources told us that the décor had just been updated, which most were happy with, but left a few querying the choice of art work. *"It just seems a bit weird. There's this painting of a pig surrounded by money – I don't quite get it!"* But if that's the only bone of contention, then newbies have nothing to worry about.

"You get to actually see outside."

See firm profile on p.651

The Inside View

Diversity	Partners (%)	Associates (%)
Women	8.8	46.6
White	93	83.5
Black/African American	0	2.9
Hispanic/Latin American	1.8	1.9
Asian	5.3	10.7
Mixed/Other	0	1
LGBT	0	0

DC is noticeably smaller with around 15 lawyers in total. Focusing predominantly on investment management, *"there's a strong mutual funds and capital markets practice there,"* MP Jim Cofer explains. *"Forty years ago the DC office was much more New York-centric and depended on New York for work. Now DC is the strongest it's ever been."*

Hours & Compensation

Most agreed that days in the office usually average around the ten-hour mark. However, interviewees felt that there's little pressure to stay in the evening if you're not busy. *"It's rare to work past 10pm. People are normally in until about 7.30ish."* Obviously, because the bulk of their practices have a transactional tenor, sources were quick to qualify that *"some months are busier than others, and it depends on the matter you're working on."* There's no formal billing requirement, though associates do qualify for a bonus by hitting 2,000 hours. *"It means you really don't have to kill yourself to reach it. I just do my work and if it happens it happens."*

Associates were keen to explain that at junior levels *"the bonus is in tiers depending on how many hours you're over. The first tier is $10,000, the second tier is $12,500 and the salary goes up to $190,000 for second-years. If I'm honest, they pay me so much money for something I find pretty enjoyable."* Despite being considerably smaller than many rival New York-based firms, Seward pays its associates the market rate.

Culture

"I know the word 'collegial' is brought up a lot when you describe law firms and I hate it, but it really is collegial here..." Most put this down to the smaller intake, allow-ing lawyers *"to get to know everyone."* Others were more pensive and explained that *"it's such a hard concept to define, but let me put it this way: No one is going to destroy your schedule for their own work or give you something and just leave."*

"We turned a conference room into a casino."

The occasional social helped things along too. Events are usually centered around the holidays and schmoozing the new summer intake. *"There was a really cool poker night. We turned a conference room into a casino, it was so much fun."* However, most people were keen to stress that S&K's social scene is more of an *"impromptu drinks type."* Some go the extra mile (literally): *"A bunch of us go hiking, and these people have really become my friends."*

Diversity

Interviewees judged the balance between male and female entry-level associates to be around 50:50, but they admitted that *"it doesn't feel particularly diverse. In fact it's almost exclusively white."* The figures match up too, with Caucasian attorneys making up 93% of partners and 83.5% of associates. However, sources reasoned: *"That might just be the nature of being a lawyer in New York. It's a problem for the whole profession."* To date, there are no affinity groups (for example, a women's forum), and associates considered that *"it's probably not one of the firm's strong suits, but they are trying. At least we've all come to the firm with different life experiences, which I think goes a way to helping."*

Strategy & Get Hired

"People who ask a lot of questions about the firm to demonstrate their enthusiasm are the ones that tend to do well in interviews," insiders advised. *"I hate it when I leave ten minutes for candidate questions and they're like 'nope I got nothing'."* So to prep a list of insightful queries and do your homework. You might start by researching what the firm has in store for the future. MP Jim Cofer tells us that *"we're not trying to be all things to all people, but focus more on our industry expertise and do more work for those clients."* For more insider tips, go online.

See firm profile on p.651

The Inside View

Shearman & Sterling LLP

Lawyers per state

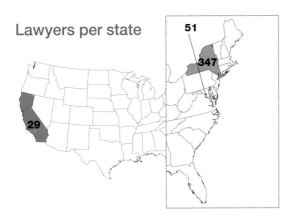

Largest US office: New York
US offices: 4
International offices: 16
First-year salary: $180,000
Billable hours: no requirement
Summers 2017: 64 (59 2Ls, 2 1Ls, 3 others)
Revenue 2016: $912 million (+6%)
Partners made in 2017: 6 (3 US)
Famous for: international work, white shoe heritage

What makes Shearman unique? Well, three-quarters of its offices are outside the US, so there's a clue...

SHEARMAN & Sterling has an international way of looking at things. Top law firms love explaining in as many different languages as possible why they're 'truly global', but Shearman has the facts to back up the chat – 80% of its offices are outside of the US, and its lawyers come from 80 different countries. The ones we spoke to declared *"it truly is a global firm. I feel like I know everyone even if we haven't met."*

International arbitration is a Shearman trademark, and during the time of our research it was fighting for the largest potential award in arbitral tribunal history, a whopping $50 billion from Russia on behalf of former controlling shareholders of bankrupt oil giant Yukos. Proud arbitration associates declared *"the practice here is second to none"* (read more about it in our feature on Shearman on our website). *Chambers USA* extends the praise to a range of areas including commercial litigation, capital markets and project finance. *Chambers Global* awards Shearman rankings for pretty much every region of the globe.

On chambers-associate.com...

- Get Hired: inside Shearman's interview process
- Interviews with global managing partner David Beveridge and the hiring partners
- Inside international arbitration

The Work

Nearly all new starters begin life in Shearman's NYC mothership, where most begin as generalists in either the corporate or litigation pools before specializing a few years in. Interviewees happily found this system provided *"a healthy mix"* of tasks early on, and come crunch time *"almost everyone ended up getting the group they wanted to specialize in."* The handful of juniors that begin in the Bay Area and DC are channeled more toward particular practices. In the smaller bases, work allocation is *"formal in theory, but in practice the partners just give you work and connect you with what interests you,"* contrasting with the more rigid *"formal process to keep track of business"* in New York.

"Right now litigation is incredibly busy," someone told us. *"You're catching us at an interesting time!"* Primarily representing *"financial institutions (that's what we're known for),"* Shearman associates jump into *"corporate governance-related investigations, antitrust class actions and regulatory work. There's a wide variety."* Though inevitably *"there is document review (that's the nature of litigation),"* tasks for juniors include *"discovery, drafting requests, legal research, taking depositions, preparing to defend, drafting briefs... it's pretty much litigation 101."* A busy firm can mean a tidal wave of work for those at the bottom, and one source reckoned *"a lot of people probably feel overworked, but on the whole it's been a fair amount, what one would expect."* The rush means high responsibility work comes quickly, leaving some *"a little terrified, but happy!*

See firm profile on p.652

Rankings in *Chambers USA*

Antitrust	Financial Services
Banking & Finance	Regulation
Capital Markets	International Arbitration
Corporate/M&A	Latin American Investment
Employee Benefits &	Litigation
Executive Compensation	Projects
Energy & Natural	Real Estate
Resources	Securities
Environment	Tax
FCPA	

For detail on ranking tiers and ranking locations, visit
www.chambersandpartners.com

I'd always love less work and more sleep, but it's great when you realize you're being a lawyer all by yourself."

"Pretty much every deal has an international element."

The corporate cohort is overseen by a practice coordinator for their first two years, who gives associates the chance to *"rank your top three practice areas each month. They make a deliberate effort to give you work from that top three."* Popular areas for interviewees included real estate (*"anything from acquisitions of property to working on the real estate portions of M&A deals"*) and asset management (*"investors can be a very wide ranging group"*). They inevitably grappled with *"some diligence, but not as much as I expected as a first-year,"* and also tried their hand at *"preparing closing documents, and taking the first stab at contracts and financing documents. If you put your hand up and say 'I can do X thing', people will be happy to help you through it."*

More niche groups cultivated *"very personal relationships – it's like working in a firm within a firm."* IP transactional involves *"a lot of joint ventures and joint development work that requires ancillary documents. I do first draft then get comments."* Lean staffing means associates are *"trusted to learn quickly."* In the dedicated antitrust team, work is *"primarily on the transactional side, advising on mergers. Pretty much every deal has an international element; we have to engage with colleagues around the world."* But they may be beaten in the global stakes by the international arbitration sub-group, *"dealing mostly with commercial arbitration between large companies. I get to do pretty meaningful tasks, and it's not like somebody else is then re-doing it."* Many said a big benefit of being in a smaller practice is the important role they played in deals.

Recent work highlights

- Advised B/E Aerospace on its $6.4 billion sale to aviation technology company Rockwell Collins
- Sought $50 billion of damages from the Russian Federation on behalf of former controlling shareholders of Yukos, the largest potential award in arbitral tribunal history
- Represented investment company Olayan America in a $570 million mortgage loan
- Acted for Citibank and Wells Fargo on a $200 million loan for real estate investment trust Hersha Hospitality

Get Hired

"Recently, we've moved more toward behavioral interviewing to produce more objective responses." Learn about these changes and more in our Bonus Features for Shearman on chambers-associate.com.

Training & Development

After an initial orientation week in their home offices, new starters flock to New York for a first-year conference. Later there's one for mid-level associates, then another called 'Associate Leadership Academy' for high-achieving sixth and seventh-years. Corporate newcomers get a *"bootcamp to get you up to speed,"* while litigators get schooled in the *"litigation academy, an ongoing program of lunches and presentations."* Interviewees received *"a mix of classroom and more hands-on workshop-style training – the formal programs aren't lacking at all."*

"The formal programs aren't lacking at all."

Associates get one formal review a year, plus an annual career development meeting: *"One is a performance evaluation, the other more a case of telling partners how we feel we're doing."* Outside of these, juniors felt *"the majority of partners are good at real-time feedback overall, though there are certainly people I wish gave more."* Annual career development meetings give associates the chance to tell higher-ups what they'd like to do more of in the future to build their practice.

Culture & Diversity

"Nobody screams or yells here," we heard. *"I was on a deal where a major deliverable was not there on the morning of closing. Nobody raised their voice, everybody just got to work to fix it."* Many pointed toward contrasts between offices: for example, *"DC is more relaxed and flexible and probably more family-oriented than others."* Though some dubbed *"New York more strait-laced"* because *"everyone's in suits, it's very different,"* others celebrated *"a very so-*

See firm profile on p.652

Diversity	Partners (%)	Associates (%)
Women	18	41
White	90	68
Black/African American	3	5
Hispanic/Latin American	2	5
Asian	6	19
Mixed/Other	0	2
LGBT	1	4

cial culture where you develop friendships quickly. It's very tight-knit for such a large office." Some sources mentioned that "although the older end of the partnership has a white shoe feel, it doesn't feel that way on the ground. The firm is more progressive than its image might project."

Does that translate on the diversity front? "It feels diverse, but not so much at the partnership level. That's something we have to work on." Though one source labeled recent partner promotions "a giant sausagefest" (all six in 2016 were men), another thought "the firm knows it needs to elevate more women partners" and address concerns. The presence of "so many international associates" was highlighted as a positive, and affinity groups are in place to help boost diversity – WISER (The Women's Initiative for Success, Excellence and Retention), BLAQUE (Black Lawyers Aligned in the Quest for Excellence) and AVALANCHE (The Association of Various Asia-interested Lawyers Aligned for Non-discrimination, Community, Honor and Excellence, of course!) are just some of those on offer.

"At the end of the day we're an office, not a summer camp!"

Associates hailed a strong social scene as "one of the firm's strong suits. We have sports teams for kickball and basketball, and most people get involved in something." Summer is the peak social period and associate committee members revealed they're "trying to increase the frequency of events" outside of the usual season, but there's no pressure for those with other interests to get involved. "I have a lot of friends at Shearman, and we'll grab drinks after work, but I'll also go out with friends from college and turn down events happening here, and that's totally fine." One pointed out that "at the end of the day we're an office, not a summer camp!"

Offices

The firm's DC and San Francisco bases have both relocated recently, and associates love their new nests. Washingtonians revealed the shift means "people talk to each

other a lot more – it's a much better laid-out space," while their Cali cousins were happy to swap "a good old boys' wooden office for a modern glass one." New York associates sounded like they could do with a similar upgrade: "Most people think it's dated; there's a very old school white shoe feel. The building won't win any prizes, but it's perfectly comfortable." Unlike elsewhere, New Yorkers share offices for their first two years.

"London and Asia feel like they're next door."

A sojourn overseas is a very real possibility, and every year a few entry-levels get the chance to work abroad permanently as US-track associates in one of Shearman's international offices. Even the majority left behind thought "London and Asia feel like they're next door." It's a good thing offices are strongly connected, as some felt the DC and West Coast bases "are definitely satellites," and one junior joked that "I'm surprised they didn't ask us to pray to New York three times a day!" Others were keen to assert theirs are "not just feeder offices" and reported more collaboration than delegation.

Pro Bono

Shearman does "a phenomenal job of making pro bono opportunities available," according to its philanthropic associates. Three full-time pro bono attorneys provide "constant resources for assistance," and "if you express interest in something specific the firm is good about hooking you up to a project you'll find interesting." Such projects range from veterans' benefits claims to work with the Animal Legal Defense Fund. Though "the firm is excited for juniors to gain experience," certain partners support these charitable ventures more enthusiastically than others, associates told us.

"Associates take weeks off to fly to Africa and teach pro bono courses."

As with many things at Shearman, associates found that the most distinctive element of pro bono is the capacity to take it all over the world. "The international side is a big point of differentiation from other firms. Associates take weeks off to fly to Africa and teach pro bono courses." All attorneys are required to do 25 hours of pro bono, a target which "everybody hits, and many go above and beyond." Some even argued "the requirement is very low," revealing "there have been discussions about increasing it."

Pro bono hours
- For all US attorneys: 37,416
- Average per US attorney: 85

Hours & Compensation

For billed work, Shearman doesn't enforce a particular target or requirement. Some associates tipped us off about an unofficial target of 2,050 hours, but *"never felt pressured"* to reach that benchmark. While litigators nonetheless found that *"easy to hit,"* in transactional groups *"it can be a little tougher because workflow is more and hit and miss. Because I'm given work directly, I would feel stressed if I had to hit a certain target to get a bonus."* In 2016 the firm announced a more solidified remote working policy so associates can work *"two days a month from home, no questions asked. They even bought everyone a laser printer and USB headset."* It makes sense then that *"there's very little face time requirement,"* particularly outside New York where sources *"saw the email and people looked at each other like, 'two days at home, is that it?'"*

> *"They bought everyone a laser printer and USB headset."*

When Cravath revealed its new associate salary scale, Shearmanites had *"no real fear we weren't going to match. We don't expect our firm to be a leader in bonuses and salaries, but we'll match the market."* Bonuses are lockstep, and any variation is based on individual merit, leaving associates *"not exactly thrilled, but there's some level of comfort to it."* The lack of hours target provides *"a lot of flexibility for associates"* to take all four weeks of vacation they're allotted. *"You definitely get the opportunity to take it, and as long as you make the transition in your work seamless it's fine."*

Strategy & Future

Proposed changes to the Shearman partnership track hit the headlines recently. *"The way it was handled internally was not great, it came out in the news before we were told."* The proposed introduction of non-equity partners would theoretically provide an easier leg-up to partnership for many, but several associates weren't convinced – they *"don't know anybody thrilled about it"* and felt there'd still been *"no real explanation."* Others were happy to give management the benefit of the doubt as *"there's a lot of willingness to talk about business decisions."* Managing partner David Beveridge explains *"we've introduced more flexibility into our operations. Each of the markets we operate in works differently, and our approach is no different to most global firms."* For more from Beveridge, head to chambers-associate.com.

> *"There's a lot of willingness to talk about business decisions."*

See firm profile on p.652

Sheppard, Mullin, Richter & Hampton LLP

Lawyers per state

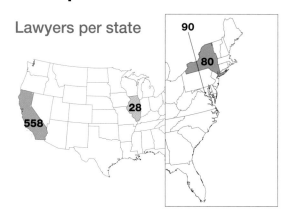

90
80
28
558

Largest US office: Los Angeles

US offices: 10

International offices: 5

First-year salary: $180,000

Billable hours: 1,950 required (1,800 client-charge-able)

Summers 2017: 34 (33 2Ls, 1 1L)

Revenue 2016: $607.17 million (+8.5%)

Partners made in 2017: 15 (all US)

Famous for: uninterrupted growth since 1992; Cali cool

Are you mulling over which Cali firms have a national presence and more relaxed vibe? Sheppard should be top of your list...

"WE'RE one of the very biggest law firms in California, which in and of itself is the sixth largest economy in the world," chairman Guy Halgren highlights to us. *"On top of that, we have vibrant offices nationally and internationally, and a very nice business plan in place."* Indeed, Sheppard's *"very nice"* business has achieved revenue growth every year since 1992. In 2015 it jumped 10% and another 8.5% in 2016, breaking the $600 million mark for the first time. It's no wonder associates here said they're *"more laid back"* than peers at other firms or why *"from the first day, everybody seems to be in a really good mood."*

> *"From the first day, everybody seems to be in a really good mood."*

A friendly atmosphere is one thing, but nothing motivates like success. *"A lot of people have been here since they were summer associates,"* junior interviewees pointed out. *"You can expect attrition at most large firms, but the churn and burn model is not in place at Sheppard."* Guy Halgren confirms that *"we want career people, and we make a lot of partners from associates every year. Fundamentally, we want people who will stay with us and finish their careers*

with us."* There are plenty of practices for aspiring attorneys to choose from, including litigation ('business trial'), corporate, labor & employment, IP, government contracts (mainly out of DC), finance & bankruptcy, and antitrust.

Offices

The bulk of newcomers shore up on the West Coast, primarily Los Angeles, Century City, Del Mar and San Francisco. A handful head to New York and Washington, and less frequently Chicago. The Big Apple base is *"very clean and modern, with an unlimited supply of caffeinated beverages."* DC boasts a *"spacious new building"* after the firm relocated in 2014. Housed *"on Bunker Hill like all the other law firms,"* LA sources admired *"lots of really interesting art"* brought in by *"a founding partner [Gordon Hampton] who was really into it."* Down the road in Century City, *"the outside doesn't look phenomenal, but inside is very nice and warm-feeling."* Collaboration between offices is frequent, particularly across the Cali coastline (*"in San Diego everyone has done something for LA"*), but it *"varies by practice group."*

> *"Everyone has done something for LA."*

The Work

Each office slots newbies into multiple different practice areas, some with less variation than others. DC is, unsurprisingly, Sheppard's government contracts hub while Century City is known for hosting the firm's me-

On chambers-associate.com...

- Get Hired: all the essential interview info
- Interviews with chairman Guy Halgren and chief human resources officer Bess Sully
- The Native American niche

See firm profile on p.653

Rankings in *Chambers USA*

Antitrust	Healthcare
Banking & Finance	Insurance
Bankruptcy/Restructuring	Labor & Employment
Construction	Litigation
Corporate/M&A	Media & Entertainment
Environment	Native American Law
Government	

For detail on ranking tiers and ranking locations, visit
www.chambersandpartners.com

Recent work highlights

- Defended Starbucks against claims of systematic failure to serve properly filled drinks
- Successfully defended Taco Bell in a $112 million dollar class action alleging the chain did not provide adequate rest breaks
- Campaigned on behalf of industrial supply company W. W. Grainger to successfully reopen bidding for US navy contract
- Represented American Fruits and Flavors in its $690 million acquisition by Monster Energy

dia & entertainment group and Del Mar is an IP hotspot. Firmwide, the business trial and corporate teams (both well-regarded in *Chambers USA*) take the most new associates, with finance & bankruptcy coming in third place. Labor & employment, real estate and antitrust also attract incoming attorneys.

Litigators in business trial typically worked on *"depositions, drafting motions and a range of pre-trial documents"* with *"lots of latitude to go out and get your hands dirty,"* and *"everybody gets the opportunity to work in every field."* Rookies tend to start out as generalists, but some offices have specialisms: *"San Francisco deals extensively in construction."* A free market system of work allocation split opinion: *"You can take more control over what assignments you want to be doing,"* but it left some feeling frustrated *"getting the same salary as someone doing less."*

"There are very few times when you're not doing anything."

The local economy tends to influence the type of work carried out in finance & bankruptcy: *"Real estate is specific to Orange County,"* for instance. *"The way the group operates means there's lots of communication,"* and associates found it *"pretty easy to form relationships."* They were kept busy with *"contract and lease reviews, due diligence, sub-lease negotiation, survey work and drafting,"* and *"if you have time available, someone will jump in to fill it."* Labor & employment associates were more *"up and down"* workload-wise, but *"if things ever get slow you know who to ask."* Their clients range *"from the biggest in their industry to those owning one restaurant,"* while Del Mar's IP team similarly *"works with both the country's biggest tech companies and individual ventures."* IP associates embraced *"the opportunity to work in both patent litigation and prosecution – nearly all other firms require you to choose one."*

Corporate juniors *"primarily deal with M&A, though it varies from office to office,"* encompassing a lot of *"healthcare, financing and public"* work. Everyday tasks include *"due diligence, but also reviewing agreements and draft-*

ing ancillary and formation documents." One corporate source enjoyed *"lots of substantive experience, which is my favorite part of the job. Every day is different."* Across the board there was *"a ramp up period for workload,"* but associates were happy to get full plates. *"There are very few times when you're not doing anything, and as you get experience you become better at managing your time."*

Newbies were commonly happy to take on cases great and small. *"Not only working huge cases but a wider array of values is a good thing for a young associate, as you get more varied opportunities than you would on just multi-billion dollar cases,"* they reasoned.

Training & Development

Following concerns in previous years about lack of formal training, the firm introduced *"Shep talks"* to cover *"general topics,"* providing a *"how to do well in the job guide,"* which was welcomed by associates. *"Generally happy"* with the new program, they acknowledged *"it's difficult to cater to individual interests, and they do ask what we'd find interesting."* Some felt that *"a lot of it is still train as you go,"* but appreciated mid-year and ongoing feedback from assigned partner mentors. This however varied *"depending on the partner, there's no consistent way they appraise work,"* leaving some more satisfied than others.

Culture & Diversity

"Transparency" is a buzzword Sheppard loves to throw around, according to interviewees who were subsequently *"pleased to be kept very in the loop. The firm prides itself on that."* Chairman Guy Halgren gives a yearly state of the firm address in January to all non-partners covering *"financial stats, associate attrition and which practice groups are under or over-performing. It gives you a nice sense of where you are. The best part is the chairman takes the time to come to every office to do the presentation."* Juniors *"went for lunch with partners"* and *"frequently dropped into their offices."* Despite *"clear demarcation between new and longstanding people,"* relationships *"feel like more of a*

The Inside View

See firm profile on p.653

495

Diversity	Partners (%)	Associates (%)
Women	17	48
White	89	61
Black/African American	2	4
Hispanic/Latin American	2	5
Asian	4	15
Mixed/Other	3	15
LGBT	3	2

team than a boss telling you what to do." Another source suggested partners do "a good job making us feel like we're not just minions!"

Associates considered Sheppard "fairly casual compared to stuffier firms" but acknowledged that "BigLaw will always be somewhat stressful." Summer socials have included musicals, baseball games and days at the races. More informally, practice groups host "associate morale events" – code for after-work drinks – though sources clarified "we're not a party firm!" Yearly retreats bring together practice teams from each office, as well as groups like the Diversity and Inclusion Network, for "a great weekend to help put names to faces."

"Sheppard is not just putting up figureheads."

Associates registered "good momentum" and a "huge push lately" on the diversity front. Those who attended the firm's diversity retreat "enjoyed and appreciated the opportunity to discuss such topics. It's an issue for every firm, it's good that Sheppard is not just putting up figureheads." The women's group "meets monthly to discuss business development and more casual themes. All the female partners attend, providing an opportunity for one to one talks where you're not afraid to ask questions." Though some saw theirs as a "relatively white office," juniors applauded the firm for "interviewing a lot of candidates from diverse backgrounds."

Get Hired

"The most important thing when choosing a firm is the culture – plenty of my classmates chose for prestige and are now unhappy." For more top tips, head to chambers associate.com.

Hours & Compensation

Matching the new Cravath scale of associate pay was unsurprisingly popular, "important to making associates feel equal" and "a nice little surprise." We've previously reported on confusion surrounding Sheppard's bonus sys-

tem, including grumblings from associates that bonuses didn't match market rates, but after "a few months of uncertainty," juniors praised the firm for "clarifying prior discrepancies, and it put people's minds at ease. Sheppard's response time was poor, but it's encouraging that they're going to match the market."

"You have time for a private life."

A billable target of 1,950 hours is "reasonable given the general flow of work, as pro bono and training hours are included." Daily hours vary by practice area, including "some work on weekends," but associates agreed "you have time for a private life." Vacation is "technically unlimited, and fairly flexible. In summer I took a bunch of three-day weekends."

Pro Bono

"A very large component of being a lawyer at Sheppard Mullin is pro bono," and associates can clock unlimited hours toward their billable target, once they've billed 1,800 hours to clients. While it's possible to take on "any project you want," asylum cases are common and "most people get involved with that." Some associates signed up for more than others, and certain eager beavers had done "over 100 hours of pro bono" without feeling pressured to take on more paid work. One Shep talk is dedicated wholly to pro bono, pushing the program from the outset. First-years with more free time appreciated using it to fill their hours, though "if you're doing more than 30% pro bono, other work will be found for you." Commitment to pro bono varied by practice area, but was fairly uniform between different offices.

"Most people get involved..."

Pro bono hours
- For all US attorneys: 29,630
- Average per US attorney: 39

Strategy & Future

Chairman Guy Halgren credits Sheppard's consistency to cautious expansion policies, and has "never believed in the idea of 'build it and they will come'. We are always in close contact with our clients, to know what they need from us." Associates were "excited about the organization and where it's going." In the immediate future, the East Coast looks likely to see the most growth. "New York and Washington, DC have certainly been our fastest growing offices over the last few years, and that looks set to continue – we're certainly not done in either city," according to Halgren.

See firm profile on p.653

The Inside View

Sidley Austin LLP

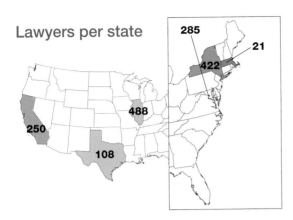

Lawyers per state

285
21
422
488
250
108

Largest US office: Chicago
US offices: 10
International offices: 9
First-year salary: $160,000
Billable hours: generally 2,000 target
Summers 2017: 127 (119 2Ls, 7 1Ls, 1 3L)
Revenue 2016: $1.93 billion (+3.4%)
Partners made in 2017: 16 globally (15 in US)
Famous for: Chicago-born, meeting place of the Obamas

This versatile Chicagoan behemoth offers juniors high-level tasks and the opportunity to dabble in lots of practices.

SAUL Bellow's picaresque masterpiece and Great American Novel *The Adventures of Augie March* begins with the line, *"I am an American, Chicago born – Chicago, that somber city – and go at things as I have taught myself."* You might say the same for Midwestener Sidley. Over the past decade it has cemented its reputation as the go-to shop for appellate law – in fact for most litigious practices. On top of this, the firm can also claim a starring role in the nation's recent narrative, for it was at its Windy City HQ that a young summer associate named Barack was assigned a mid-level mentor called Michelle. The rest, as they say folks, is history.

"Shocked at the breadth of our expertise."

But Sidley is much more than the place where the Obamas first met, and much more than just a litigation shop. Its ten US offices are distributed to gain maximum coverage across the country, and sources attested that *"whatever office you're in, Sidley has a top-tier practice there."* Indeed, one interviewee expressed themselves *"shocked at the breadth of our expertise in different areas of the law."* And *Chambers USA* also recognizes the firm's versatil-

ity, awarding the highest Band 1 ratings in a plethora of fields nationwide including: appellate; climate change and environmental law; financial services regulation; insurance; international trade; hedge funds; product liability; and rail transportation.

The Work

Sidley has a strong appellate reputation but really its uniqueness derives from the fact that *"it's one of the few BigLaw firms that has such strength across the board, especially in litigious practices,"* according to associates here. An informal assignment system reflects the fact that groups aren't *"hardened silos"* and it's *"usually in their fifth or sixth years that associates really find their niche,"* though *"even partners might occasionally dabble."* As a summer associate, *"you start cultivating relationships with partners"* and though *"the firm does give you an off-the-bat assignment or two"* almost all of a junior's work *"comes from people you've worked with in the past."*

"It's one of the few BigLaw firms that has such strength across the board."

While it's always been a fluid, free-market kind of place, Sidley has in recent years moved to make its famous litigation practice an even broader church – *"when I started there were four or five litigation groups and then about two years ago they changed the organization to just one general department, meaning attorneys have more freedom and the teams can do more cross-selling."* Under this

The Inside View

See firm profile on p.654

Rankings in *Chambers USA*

Antitrust	Insurance
Appellate Law	Intellectual Property
Banking & Finance	International Arbitration
Bankruptcy/Restructuring	International Trade
Capital Markets	Investment Funds
Climate Change	Labor & Employment
Corporate Crime &	Latin American Investment
Investigations	Leisure & Hospitality
Corporate/M&A	Life Sciences
ERISA Litigation	Litigation
Employee Benefits &	Privacy & Data Security
Executive Compensation	Products Liability
Energy & Natural	Real Estate
Resources	REITs
Environment	Securities
FCPA	Tax
Financial Services	Technology
Regulation	Telecommunications
Healthcare	Transportation

For detail on ranking tiers and ranking locations, visit
www.chambersandpartners.com

all-encompassing umbrella sits a plethora of sub-groups, including: complex litigation; regulatory & economic; international arbitration; white-collar; IP; and criminal & constitutional. Perhaps unsurprisingly, flitting between practices can mean responsibility levels are not easily accrued – *"if you avoid specializing in favor of trying lots of different stuff, you'll be doing a lot of doc review in order to build up your knowledge of every area."* However, litigious lawyers who find their feet earlier on can expect to be *"drafting motions to dismiss, writing research memos and managing discovery issues."*

Sidley's transactional teams, though smaller, are no less prestigious. Specialization usually takes place earlier than it does for their contentious counterparts, though this varies office-to-office. New York's corporate department is split between M&A, capital markets, private equity, and governance, with newbies encouraged to pursue one of these early on. Over in Chicago, however, with more practices to choose from – on top of the above three, there's also insurance, securities, regulatory, global finance, private equity, and real estate – comes an acceptance that juniors might take longer to find their niche. Again, the earlier you specialize, the meatier your tasks are: *"I chose to specialize in private equity after a few months and the level of experience has been phenomenal. After less than a year I was on a $2 billion deal where there was only one other associate and a partner on our side."*

Culture

One thing that kept cropping up among interviewees was Sidley's shrewd financial planning – *"they don't make*

Recent work highlights

- Represented insurance company Athene Holding in a $1.24 billion IPO, the second largest in the US and among the top ten largest worldwide in 2016
- Advised Yum China in connection with its $10.2 billion spin-off from Yum! Brands
- Represented Bayer in a high-profile case that pitted the life sciences company against the Federal Trade Commission in a three-week bench trial that returned a complete verdict in favor of Bayer
- Acts as primary US counsel for hedge fund Man Group and its affiliates, including over 20 new fund launches in 2016, and US offerings of over 20 existing offshore funds

plans they can't follow through on and they prepay expenses. This spreads confidence in the fact that the firm isn't going to fold or be bought up, and that extra job security is always a plus in BigLaw." The honesty with which numbers are discussed reflects a general culture of managerial openness that permeates the firm.

Sources also kept mentioning lean staffing at the firm, but insisted that while a lot of its competitors pay lip-service to the practice, Sidley's numbers mean it's a necessity. *"Every BigLaw firm says they staff leanly but we really have to since we don't have a lot of associates. We probably only have 1 ¼ per partner."* All this means *"there's enough oversight that you're not getting yourself in trouble and you end up learning quickly because you don't have the filter of three associates on a deal."*

> *"Every BigLaw firm says they staff leanly but we really have to."*

Perhaps as a result of the aforementioned fiscal conservatism, the social life at Sidley wasn't reported to set the world alight. A pretty standard event across the board is the quarterly Friday afternoon parties – *"we have some beers in the office then head to a local bar for food and drinks till pretty late."* There's also something called 'March Madness': a fun-filled week of spring shenanigans that includes activities like mini-golf and bar crawls.

Hours & Compensation

The most basic hours requirement at the firm is the 1,800 needed in order to progress to the next year. After that, sources were unsure what was a target and what was a requirement. To be bonus eligible it was generally agreed that *"you should be hitting 2,000, though 200 of those can be pro bono."* That said, one litigation sources reported: *"On my first day they got the whole group together for a meeting, and one of the things that was said was everyone should be hitting 2,000 billable hours. I think this is a new thing because I spoke to a senior associate who said they'd*

See firm profile on p.654

Diversity	Partners (%)	Associates (%)
Women	24.6	47.3
White	89.2	72.1
Black/African American	1.7	4.3
Hispanic/Latin American	1.7	6.4
Asian	6.5	14.9
Mixed/Other	0.9	2.3
LGBT	unknown	unknown

never heard that." And as for that bonus, *"it's discretionary, so it's easy to be cynical about them not paying market. But they do take you through whatever you've received."*

2,000 is by no means a horror target and most interviewees told of working late *"probably two to three nights a week,"* all of which adds up to a total of about *"50-55 hours a week."* All in all, many felt their expectations for the worst were largely unrealized: *"I went in with my eyes open and was expecting to be constantly working into the wee hours, but most days I leave between 7pm and 7.30pm."* When it comes to taking time off, the firm doesn't have an official vacation policy, which theoretically means attorneys can take as many days as they want. In reality, *"it probably works in the firm's favor because people usually end up taking less than they would."*

Training & Development
Sidley has a *"phenomenal training program – it almost annoyed me how much training I had in my first year!"* Newbies undergo a solid week of orientation in their respective offices – *"stuff like how to use the systems, office culture, and instructions like 'don't use emojis'"* – after which they are whisked away to Chicago for a three-day firmwide training-fest. Then it gets specific. Transactional tutees are enrolled in something called 'Corporate College', while their disputes colleagues attend 'Litigation Bootcamp'. The former involves *"flying to a Sidley office for three days of presentations and seminars on specific topics."* Litigation Bootcamp offers sessions on cross-examination, direct examination, deposition training and closing arguments, concluding in a mock trial.

"Really it's about the networks that you build."

Further guidance comes in the way of a retention committee – *"a group of associates who meet regularly and are able to pass on any grievances or suggestions to partners."* And then there's Sidley's mentorship scheme: *"Although you get a new mentor when you start, people build lasting relationships in the summer so partners you meet then still kind of guide you through. It seems like the firm's general approach is that there's a safety net that everyone has a*

connection to if they need but really it's about the networks that you build."

Offices
With ten offices spread from the East to the West Coast, Sidley truly enjoys nationwide coverage. Its Chicago HQ remains the firm's focal point though recently *"DC has risen in importance because of Carter Phillips – chair of the Executive Committee – who is based there."* Perhaps another reason for DC's ascendancy is the office's recent renovation that has transformed it into a *"bright, open space with standing desks and plenty of breakout space."*

Back in the Windy City, lawyers have got fantastic views of Lake Michigan as their home occupies floors 23-28 of a 38-floor skyscraper *"in the heart of Downtown."* Attorneys might also be distracted by the office's *"fetching mint-green interior"* or its *"excellent cafeteria."* Elsewhere, Dallas sources praised their office's *"free parking and shiny new gym,"* while occupants of Sidley's Century City digs had nice words to say about their own parking provisions as well as the *"really quite groovy modern art"* that adorns their walls.

Pro Bono
"A full-time pro bono counsel" based in Chicago sends out *"at least ten different emails a week"* with pro bono opportunities. Partners also allow associates to bring in work that they might be passionate about – *"the firm is very supportive, especially for young lawyers, to get whatever experience they can."* Sidley has strong relationships with many not-for-profit organizations including Her Justice, *"a group which helps victims of domestic violence,"* in New York. They also work closely with DC Legal Aid, and a number of Sidley attorneys have recently represented death row inmates in Alabama.

Pro bono hours
- For all US attorneys: 120,473
- Average per US attorney: 67

Diversity
A diversity committee and committee on the retention and promotion of women both *"put on loads of networking and client events focused on diversity."* The former hosts an annual reception at the Staples Center where clients and diverse attorneys come together to watch a Lakers game. There are also group-specific mentoring circles – such as the 'Mother's mentoring circle' – that host lunches and webinars on subjects like time management and recognizing unconscious bias.

See firm profile on p.654

Get Hired

Unsurprisingly, given its status, Sidley doesn't really look at candidates outside the top ten schools. But, after that filter is applied, *"the firm's focus is slightly more on personality."* As one associate who'd been involved in interviews put it: *"We can only tell so much from your résumé and transcripts. Really it's more about whether or not we want to spend 50 hours a week working with you. Can you make sound decisions and can I sit you down at a client lunch?"* Flexibility and time-management are also highly valued. *"You don't succeed at Sidley if you have to have a set schedule. The ability to get work done without having to constantly look to the client is a major plus for partners."*

Strategy & Future

As we've mentioned a few times, Sidley is a firm that prides itself on its conservative management. The firm is currently in the most recent *AmLaw 100* list. As a result of their reluctance to open in new locations, smaller existing offices – like Dallas and Century City – are seeing the most growth, with both purchasing new floor space as they rapidly expand. *"Zero debt has been our policy and our practice,"* exec committee member Anne Rea confirms. *"We have a culture of investing for the future."* For the full interview, read our Bonus Features on Sidley on chambers-associate.com.

Media & Entertainment associates at Sidley tell us all about their eventful practice on p.183

See firm profile on p.654

The Inside View

Simpson Thacher & Bartlett LLP

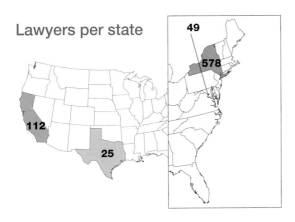

Lawyers per state

Largest US office: New York
US offices: 5
International offices: 6
First-year salary: $180,000
Billable hours: no requirement
Summers 2017: 127 (115 2Ls, 6 1Ls, 3 3Ls, 3 others)
Revenue 2016: $1.302 billion (+1.8%)
Partners made in 2017: 11 globally (8 in US)
Famous for: its elite status and polite culture

Not only does big fish Simpson offer work on some of the meatiest corporate deals around, it is, crucially, a *"pleasant place to work."*

FOR top dollar deals, one of the few law firms the denizens of Wall Street turn to is Simpson Thacher. Since its founding in 1884 by a couple of Columbia law school grads, the firm's cultivated a stellar pedigree. It's advised on the five biggest LBOs in business history, including the $44 billion acquisition of TXU by private equity kingpins KKR and the $39 billion buyout of Equity Office Properties by Blackstone. Simpson attorneys handled the four largest M&A deals of 2016, including ChemChina's $43 billion acquisition of Syngenta and Microsoft's $26.2 billion acquisition of LinkedIn. The beginning of 2017 saw the firm join forces with Microsoft again, advising it on a massive $17 billion bond offering.

To show for it all, Simpson's got a bulging collection of top-drawer *Chambers USA* rankings at national level for corporate, banking, private equity and real estate work. Simpson is strong at contentious work too, evidenced by premier rankings for securities litigation and insurance disputes.

The Work

The corporate department takes most junior associates, and litigators accounted for roughly a quarter of our interviewee list. The rest are sprinkled across real estate,

tax and executive compensation & employee benefits (ECEB). A lone junior was assigned to 'exempt organizations' – tax-exempt entities like charities.

Before settling on a specific group, corporate novices go through a rotation system that allows them to sample three (out of four) different areas within the overall department. The four main groups are banking & credit, securities & capital markets, M&A, and fund formation, although smaller practices like real estate, ECEB and public company advisory can be rotation destinations. *"It's an attractive system because it's tough at the outset to know what you want to do."* An associate who'd sampled private funds told us that *"I was involved in running several mega fund closings, which entailed coordinating with clients, drafting and getting back to investors with comments on subscription documents. Plus I negotiated side letters and took a first cut at a partnership agreement."*

Over in M&A, *"I've had a chance to work with strategic and private equity clients. Mostly I've been doing diligence work, but I've also drafted portions of documents like resolutions, parts of the SPA and a registration rights agreement,"* noted a junior, adding that *"I feel very much involved, and to the extent that there's time, people encourage me to take first draft at things. They don't shy away from giving you assignments."*

On chambers-associate.com...

- Interview with chairman Bill Dougherty

"The breadth and depth of experience is remarkable."

See firm profile on p.655

The Inside View

Rankings in *Chambers USA*

Antitrust	Insurance
Banking & Finance	International Arbitration
Bankruptcy/Restructuring	Investment Funds
Capital Markets	Latin American Investment
Corporate/M&A	Litigation
Employee Benefits &	Private Equity
Executive Compensation	Real Estate
Energy & Natural	Securities
Resources	Tax
Environment	Technology
Financial Services	
Regulation	

For detail on ranking tiers and ranking locations, visit
www.chambersandpartners.com

Recent work highlights

- Represented Barclays Capital, Citigroup Global Markets and Wells Fargo Securities as bookrunning managers in connection with a $750 million public offering by electronics manufacturer Amphenol
- Won appeals to the Second Circuit on behalf of two whistleblowers who exposed Medicare fraud
- Represented Platinum Equity in the formation and raising of Platinum Equity Capital Partners IV, which closed at $6.5 billion with over 200 limited partners from 28 countries
- Advised JPMorgan Chase Bank and Merrill Lynch, Pierce, Fenner & Smith as joint lead arrangers and bookrunners of a $40 billion bridge loan for AT&T to finance its acquisition of Time Warner

Meanwhile, litigators take a less structured approach to their Simpson salad days. *"The firm's known for its generalist style and I was really drawn to that – it's a perfect place for young lawyer to train,"* one reckoned. *"The breadth and depth of experience is remarkable. I do insurance, antitrust and general commercial litigation, diligence on large transactions and regulatory work."*

"Day to day, I often write research memos, draft legal analyses and memos for clients," told one litigator. *"On the regulatory side I speak directly to clients and am on calls with the government."* A source revealed that *"I'm working on one very large FCPA investigation that's been going for a few years now. I do a lot of document production and numerous witness interviews – I've been able to prepare outlines, meet the client and go over testimony. I've also been staffed to a compliance development case for an international client required lot of travel to South America for eight months, which was a little stressful at first but very rewarding."*

In most groups, *"the workflow comes through an assigning partner system who keeps track of your capacity. You receive work from staffing folks and partners directly but as you get more senior people reach out to you on an ad hoc basis."* Juniors thought that *"in theory the system works well. The centralized system means you don't have as much control over who you work with and there's not a lot of transparency in how and why things are assigned, but on the other hand it makes people less competitive, which is good."* One declared that *"I like that Simpson isn't an eat-what-you-kill firm. That appealed to me at the time I applied and it's definitely lived up to the importance placed on it – I knew that working at a firm would be nerve racking as it was and I was concerned about having to network while I knew nothing. This way, you're at ease, you have work and show your chops by doing assignments. It's egalitarian in that respect."*

Training & Development

All new associates congregate at the New York office for a few days of orientation. *"It's pretty comprehensive. There are some lecture-style sessions, some interactive ones like drafting practice, and presentations."* After this initial period, there are *"lunch time trainings within practices that partners in the group put together. I recently went to a government investigations practice lunch where partners discussed new cases and how they'll impact our practice. It was really interesting to hear what partners think especially as a lot come from government."*

> ## *"The learning curve is steep but that's not for a lack of people explaining things and teaching you."*

Rookies are assigned an associate and partner mentor. *"In my experience they're very receptive to questions, but generally speaking I've found that I can reach out to anyone and to the extent that they have capacity they will help you out with queries, although obviously seniors are sometimes really busy and it's hard to catch them."*

A junior noted that *"the learning curve is steep but that's not for a lack of people explaining things and teaching you."* First-year ECEB associates shadow a senior associate for a few weeks when they first start. *"If I couldn't see how a certain task fitted into the bigger picture, then they'd always stop and explain,"* said one.

Hours & Compensation

There isn't a set billing target at Simpson, something sources thought helps to foster *"a positive environment, where we work hard and support one another. I often speak to friends at other firms who seem hyper-focused at hitting a certain number."* That said, Simpsonites aren't exactly kicking back and relaxing. *"Obviously you wouldn't feel comfortable if your hours were low every single month,*

See firm profile on p.655

Diversity	Partners (%)	Associates (%)
Women	20	43
White	90	72
Black/African American	2	3
Hispanic/Latin American	3	3
Asian	5	17
Mixed/Other	0	5
LGBT	3	5

most people probably hit around 1,800 to 2,000. I don't feel stressed, I just get there organically."

"A combination of adrenaline and coffee."

Some juniors thought that, if anything, "the problem is there's too much work and you have no control and feel overburdened. I've billed an incredibly high number of hours. Things are leanly staffed which means you get more experience and that's a benefit, but the downside is that you are really really stretched. There's usually no solution other than to manage everything...people are very understanding of the fact that it's busy, but ultimately you'll be working a lot of late nights and weekends. It's very unpredictable, especially in M&A, and I work late or at weekends often without notice. Anyone who tells you they have a great work/life balance is lying!" Another insisted that "we certainly come in expecting to work a lot of hours, but also the people here are respectful of vacation time or when you have other obligations. It's do-able to manage your personal life and still be on top of work." Despite "hugely intense bursts" of work, during which sources are fueled by "a combination of adrenaline and coffee," there'll often be "a period where not much is happening for a few days."

Culture

"Polite" was the word on everybody's lips when we asked about the cordial Simpson culture. "It's a very pleasant place to work where people understand that the profession can be particularly demanding. It's certainly a reserved place, very polite," confirmed a junior, who concurred with others that there's occasionally a bit too much politeness: "People aren't very direct. A lot of communication is by email and phone rather than face to face and people tend not to give you constructive criticism until they get frustrated with you, which comes off like you're being scolded when actually they're totally in the right but didn't say anything to you beforehand." That said, each year we detect a distinctly supportive culture here.

The Simpson social calendar isn't exactly chock-full but most saw this as a positive. "One of the things I like is that there's never expectation go out for drink every Thursday

or Friday, or 'forced fun' that's tied to career advancement. People here work hard and then tend to go home but I've definitely made a lot of close friends here and we go out and grab coffee or get lunch, but I like that it's not expected." One summarized the situation: "You know how you have your settled-down friends and then your crazy party friends. Simpson is like the former."

Offices

The New York HQ is "not super fancy" but associates had "no complaints" about office esthetics. Recent renovations mean that attorneys now have glass offices. "Some people got scared at first because of privacy issues, but actually folk are mindful and don't stare weirdly into your office. I like it because there's more light." The cafeteria is a big hit. "It's fabulous – the food is delicious and highly subsidized so I eat here every day. There's a grill, a salad bar, lots of fresh fruit and baked goods."

Simpson's second largest office is in Palo Alto. The offices in DC, Los Angeles and Houston also hire entry-level junior associates.

Diversity

"The firm's tried hard in past few years to address the lack of diversity," mused an associate. "The summer class this year was more diverse than mine and we now have the first black partner in New York for very long time, which is appreciated by attorneys of color." There are active affinity groups for women, LGBT and ethnic minority attorneys, which "bring in speakers to educate partners on implicit bias and organize events" such as a theater trip to watch "a one woman play called Notes From The Field which was heavy stuff and far to the left on the matter of social justice."

Pro Bono

Juniors reckoned that pro bono "is taken very seriously and not sidelined. That's the culture here: a deep institutional commitment to serving others is part of the fabric." There's a pro bono co ordinator "who's wonderful and very engaging – the range of things on offer is extensive and if you find a project you're passionate about you can present it to the firm and they'll support you." Corporate associates had taken on projects "supporting small businesses or minority-owned businesses, helping with contract issues, entity formation for non-profits and regulatory compliance issues." Litigators mentioned that "there's always a ton of immigration work that can be done."

Pro bono hours
- For all US attorneys: 47,492
- Average per US attorney: 62

See firm profile on p.655

The Inside View

Get Hired

Academic excellence is obviously a priority, but the firm doesn't just let anyone with a raft of A-pluses through its doors. *"They try hard to get the fit right and listen to associates' opinions of candidates when we meet them during callbacks – they send juniors out to lunch with candidates, so we're thinking 'are you a weirdo?! Are you nice?!'"*

"The firm has a certain cut-off for academics – you have to meet a standard – but beyond that we recruit people who want to learn and work hard, for the most part, and people have other interests outside of work," an associate advised. *"They want to recruit impressive people who can interface well with clients and who have a genuine interest in the work we do."*

Strategy & Future

Chairman of the executive committee Bill Dougherty tells us that *"2016 was a very good year – we had solid activity across the board."* Although no other offices are in the pipeline, Simpson will *"continue to invest in our core strengths, including our funds and real estate groups which are doing extraordinarily well. We don't have plans to open any new offices, but expect to continue to expand our regulatory capabilities with a few strategic hires in our DC office, and we'll continue to expand our Houston office as we remain very optimistic about that market."*

"We recruit people who want to learn and work hard, for the most part, and people have other interests outside of work."

See firm profile on p.655

The Inside View

Skadden, Arps, Slate, Meagher & Flom LLP & Affiliates

Lawyers per state

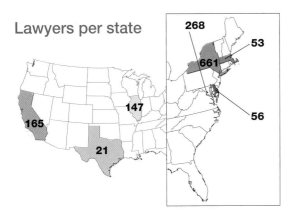

Largest US office: New York
US offices: 8
International offices: 14
First-year salary: $180,000
Billable hours: 1,800 target
Summers 2017: 236 (200 2Ls, 28 1Ls, 2 3Ls, 6 others)
Revenue 2016: $2.495 billion (+3.5%)
Partners made in 2017: 12 (11 in US)
Famous for: mega M&A, tough reputation, stand-out brand

A titan among law firms, Skadden rewards the determined and the ambitious.

FEW firms have as formidable a reputation as Skadden. It's a reputation so fierce that Skadden consistently features in industry surveys among the top four firms General Counsel dread facing. Aggression and an uncompromising attitude of throwing everything it's got at a matter make Skadden a firm clients want at their backs, whether they're negotiating tough terms of an M&A deal or batting off some seriously high stakes litigation. The firm's best known for its mega M&A deals – it made its name on these during the 80s – but it hauls in over 30 top-tier *Chambers USA* practice area rankings.

Skadden's success has made it one of the most recognizable BigLaw brands out there. *"Its prestige"* was repeatedly thrown out by our associate sources as the driver behind their desire to get a foot in the door. *"I thought if I'm going into BigLaw to do M&A, I should go big or go home,"* said one, with an attitude similar to that displayed by the firm. Punishing hours and high standards have given Skadden a reputation for being a tough place to work, but the rewards – *"cutting edge deals"* and *"a great jumping off point"* to positions elsewhere – still draw in associates in their hordes.

The Work

Skadden's corporate & transactional group soaks up around half of the annual intake of first-years. Outside of New York these deal-doers operate as generalists, while those in the Big Apple have the opportunity to pull two eight-month shifts in teams such as banking, corporate restructuring, finance, investment management, and M&A. *"You jump in, learn how to swim, get a little bit comfortable and feel like you're really picking up skills. Then you rotate and have to do it all again. It makes you a better lawyer, keeps you on your toes and I think it's nice not to have to make a final decision on your group before you walk in the door,"* one New Yorker told us. A handful of novices also slot into litigation & controversy or regulatory (which includes tax), though there's no rotation option in these groups. A centralized work allocation system exists in each department, though not every piece of work comes through it. Those in smaller groups were especially likely to rely on the old, informal, knock-on-the-door inquiry to recruit juniors onto matters.

"Keeps you on your toes."

Skadden's M&A team is the largest within the corporate group. Unlike in the smaller transactional subgroups – such as corporate restructuring or investment management – task allocation in M&A follows *"more of a structure and is based on seniority. That has pros and cons but I think at the end of the day having a more formal process prevents people from slipping through the cracks,"* one junior reasoned.

On chambers-associate.com...

- Interview with executive partner Eric Friedman
- Recruitment at Skadden

The Inside View

See firm profile on p.656

Rankings in *Chambers USA*

Antitrust	Intellectual Property
Banking & Finance	International Arbitration
Bankruptcy/Restructuring	International Trade
Capital Markets	Investment Funds
Chancery	Latin American Investment
Corporate Crime &	Litigation
Investigations	Media & Entertainment
Corporate/M&A	Private Equity
Employee Benefits &	Products Liability
Executive Compensation	Projects
Energy & Natural	Real Estate
Resources	REITs
FCPA	Securities
Financial Services	Sports Law
Regulation	Tax
Government	Technology
Healthcare	Telecommunications
Insurance	

For detail on ranking tiers and ranking locations, visit
www.chambersandpartners.com

Recent work on highlights

- Advised DuPont in its $130 billion merger with Dow
- Assisted transport company Norfolk Southern in its consideration and subsequent rejection of a $28.4 billion unsolicited takeover proposal by Canadian Pacific Railway
- Represented Wells Fargo in a suit brought by the Consumer Financial Protection Bureau concerning illegal service of student loan accounts
- Advised Oracle on its $9.3 billion acquisition of cloud software company NetSuite

which starts with a two-week mini-MBA. The first three days see associates converge on New York. Once back in their home office, the rest of the program gives juniors a grounding in things like *"calculating balance sheets and income flow statements,"* which proves *"valuable to understanding a client's business."* After this, associates spend two weeks on Skadden-specific training where *"different practices give presentations on everything you need about their area,"* alongside practice area focused general skills training.

First-years can typically be found reviewing and summarizing contracts, and preparing diligence reports. While the first few months can be diligence heavy, sources maintained a sanguine view of their experience: *"Diligence allowed me to familiarize myself with the nature of a corporate contract and summarizing them meant I got to know the market practices and what to expect. As I've grown more senior I've drafted ancillary documents and made revisions on the merger and purchase agreements, but I think without the diligence expertise I wouldn't have been able to understand the nuance and finesse of the deal details."* Other sources had negotiated ancillary and non-disclosure agreements and even started working on negotiations for the purchase agreement: *"I'm not negotiating the terms at this point but I'm doing some drafting and revising and reviewing those sections. I feel pretty good about my experience in M&A. There's a nice balance; people check in on me and help with the process but they know when to back off and let me handle things alone."*

Outside of the corporate sphere, associates were likewise pleased with their development: *"It's a meritocracy. I never feel like I'm waiting for fifth year to roll around so I could finally take a deposition,"* said one litigator with second-chair experience. *"Juniors are expected to have a lot of responsibility for discovery and managing document review, assisting with depositions, preparing for oral arguments and brief drafting."*

Training & Development

Associate life begins with a four-week training program called ACE [Associates' Comprehensive Education],

Further down the line, group-specific training sessions are staged, and rookies receive annual reviews (biannual in their first year). Several juniors felt feedback was *"an area the firm could work on. Informally, it's good person to person but there needs to be a better culture of providing feedback."* Another conceded: *"They have made more of a concrete effort to improve this. Since I joined they've made strides but it's still a work in progress."*

Hours & Compensation

Juniors up to and including their third year are granted up to 100 productive work hours such as shadowing on *"a client call where a partner doesn't want to bill your attendance,"* creating internal training presentations or writing articles. Juniors can put all 100 of these hours toward reaching the firm's 1,800 billable target, as well as billing an unlimited amount of pro bono hours. *"Given all that, 1,800 is more than achievable,"* sources told us.

The 1,800 target came into play in 2015; before that the unofficial goal was 1,600 hours. *"There was some consternation! 1,600 is ridiculously low for BigLaw but people were expecting a pay rise with the increase to 1,800 and were upset that didn't happen."* But since Cravath increased base salaries in June 2016 and Skadden followed suit, *"no-one's complaining any more."*

Twelve-hour days were common occurrences for our sources. *"I get in at 9.30am and then stay until anything from midnight to 4am,"* proffered one interviewee. *"One week I left at 3am, 4am, 8am, 2am. It wasn't fun but I did*

See firm profile on p.656

Diversity	Partners (%)	Associates (%)
Women	21.9	46.6
White	92.1	70.7
Black/African American	1.4	5.9
Hispanic/Latin American	3.1	5.4
Asian	3.4	13.5
Mixed/Other	0	4.5
LGBT	1.3	4.8

feel efficient – I didn't spend too much time sitting around not billing anything."

Culture & Offices

By far the largest concentration of Skadden lawyers reside in the New York office, followed by DC, Chicago and then LA. The firm also has domestic bases in Boston, Houston, Palo Alto and Wilmington.

"Walk through walls for our clients."

Skadden *"gets a reputation for being cutthroat and a sweatshop,"* acknowledged one California source who disagreed with this assessment. *"Maybe that's the case in New York?"* And what did New Yorkers think of that? *"I hate hearing it,"* one groaned. *"Frankly it's not true!"* In fact, across the board, most interviewee swere keen to dispel the idea of a *"ruthless"* environment. *"It's a firm with high standards and people understand and meet those. Work comes first and we will walk through walls for our clients but at the same time we all have lives and people are respectful of that,"* a Chicago source reflected. A Los-Angelite protested: *"Skadden LA doesn't deserve the sweatshop label at all."* That being said *"this is not the place for people to be afraid of taking care of themselves. You are not super-coddled,"* one New Yorker told us, while a colleague elaborated: *"The more you take on the more work you get. It's okay to have boundaries. I didn't know that in the beginning and I got a little burned out. You have to be responsible for yourself. It's fast paced and intense."*

While the drive for excellence permeates across offices, our sources did pick up on a few differences between their bases. Several Chicago associates felt their office *"reflected the Midwest culture. People are a bit more open and easy to talk to. We recognize everyone has families and other commitments and there has to be a balance."* Of course *"there are nights when you're working late but people are grateful for it."* In DC, *"people are more likely than those in New York to leave at 6pm and log on from home. In New York they tend to stay later."* The same goes for LA where *"people get in sooner and try to leave earlier; we don't have the New York mentality of being in the office late."* LA's smaller size also means *"people are more famil-*

iar with each other across practice areas" than in larger offices like DC or New York, *"and it's a bit more informal and laid back."*

"Excel without being competitive."

New Yorkers maintained that the vast scale of their office left the culture in the Big Apple *"kind of what you make it."* That said, one source told us: *"Generally I've been treated respectfully. Friends have worked under those who feel work is the most important thing above anything else happening in someone's life, but people have been supportive and accommodating toward me. I don't feel like my peers are my competitors. Overall we're focused on trying to do a good job and excel without being too competitive."* And on being tied to their desks longer than their counterparts elsewhere? *"Skadden's not known for its work-life balance, but to do anything on this level you can't really expect to have one. You have got to work hard to do the best work."*

Pro Bono

"Skadden definitely encourages pro bono; we have so many incentives to do it. There are no billable restrictions on it and they all count toward the target which is great if things are slow. As a junior there will inevitably be lulls in deals and whatever spare time you have can be filled with pro bono," such as clemency petitions, landlord/tenant and asylum matters, assisting non-profits with incorporation, or drafting operating agreements. *"It's allowed me to draft more motions than I can count and I've argued half a dozen times in court. I'm basically running the case,"* enthused one junior. A corporate associate told of the benefits of using it to widen their skill set. *"I tried the litigation side. It really helped maintain my writing and client interviewing skills."*

Pro bono hours
- For all US attorneys: 152,616
- Average per US attorney: 97

Diversity

"I feel like it's moderately diverse for a big firm, but it's not the most diverse place, especially among the senior attorneys; most of them are white men," one junior told us. *"But the firm is trying to change it."* Chicago, for example, recently brought on a diversity manager to help efforts in the Windy City.

Elsewhere there are numerous events for attorneys to attend. The New York women's group meets once a month *"to brainstorm initiatives and discuss what issues women face."* We also heard associates in New York launched a book club co-sponsored by the firm's affinity groups.

See firm profile on p.656

"For African American month we read Ta-Nehisi Coates' Between the World and Me *and did a close reading of a Beyoncé music video."* Cultural events also took place in LA, where the firm screened historical drama *Loving*, based on a 1960s Supreme Court case concerning an interracial couple. Skadden holds plenty of other diversity events across the firm; recent sessions included a talk by civil rights activist Connie Rice in DC and a conversation with journalist Soledad O'Brien in New York.

Get Hired

"You will not make it at Skadden if you are not driven, diligent and a self-starter," stressed one associate. Visit chambers-associate.com for more insider info on getting into the firm.

Strategy & Future

"We continue to aspire to be the go-to firm for our clients on their most important legal issues, and to be the go-to firm for top talent. In order to achieve those objectives we need to be in the right markets with the right mix of practices," executive partner Eric Friedman tells us. That's meant *"building out some of our international capabilities,"* including Hong Kong and London. The firm also brought on board *"Kenji Taneda to build out our Tokyo corporate team and we're continuing to round out some of the international practice depths."* Check out chambers-associate.com for Friedman's round up of what's been happening at Skadden.

> *"It's a firm with high standards and people understand and meet those. Work comes first and we will walk through walls for our clients but at the same time we all have lives and people are respectful of that."*

See firm profile on p.656

The Inside View

Snell & Wilmer LLP

Lawyers per state

Largest US office: Phoenix

US offices: 8

International offices: 1

First-year salary: $115,000 - $160,000

Billable hours: 1,800 - 1,950 target (varies by office)

Summers 2017: 24 (22 2Ls, 2 1Ls)

Revenue 2016: not disclosed

Partners made in 2017: 10 (all US)

Famous for: Southwestern strength, "no-jerk" culture

Phoenix-born Snell spreads its wings over the Southwest, and associates here feel they have a real shot at making partner one day.

WHAT sounds more exciting – the raffish party town of Vegas, the glitz of LA, or perhaps the endless sunshine of Arizona? All three plus Colorado and Utah (and Mexico) provide a home to Snell & Wilmer attorneys. Associates were quick to sing the praises of their home city, Phoenix: *"The location is terrific, we're downtown but on the outskirts so the traffic isn't crazy. The top floor of the building has amazing conference rooms with beautiful city views."*

Chairman Matt Feeney is clear that new recruits should slot comfortably into Snell's Southwest vibe. *"Our credo is a focus on clients, our communities and each other,"* he says. *"With new associates, the first topic of conversation is always culture."* It's the *"no-jerk"* culture that drew many of our sources here, and *"the sense that people really care about each other."* Also attractive were *"amazing opportunities to work on business development,"* and realistic partnership chances further down the line. *Chambers USA* hands out top rankings for the firm's corporate, real estate and environment work in Arizona, and commercial litigation both here and in Utah.

On chambers-associate.com...

- Get Hired: all the essential info
- Interview with chairman Matt Feeney
- The Valley of the Sun

The Work

Snell's Phoenix HQ runs an open market system within practice areas, where *"the emphasis is on the associate to manage their own schedule and seek out work."* Juniors agreed this *"usually works fairly well. It takes some adjusting to, but you can find people you work well with and keep going back to them. One of the nice things is if you end up working with partners you don't like, you don't have to go back."* Litigators reported some dips in work availability, but *"it's managed well, and there's normally more than enough."* In smaller offices, work came directly from the top down. *"It's great because we get to handle ground floor stuff that's really important for training purposes."*

Industry specific sub-groups within commercial litigation include financial services, securities, product liability, election & political law, and natural resources. Enjoying *"a good balance of smaller companies and* Fortune 500 *clients,"* associates saw *"everything from breach of contract and shareholder disputes to trusts litigation; it spans the spectrum."* First-years got stuck into *"a lot of research and memo writing. There's some document review, but not a lot. As you get more senior you turn to more discovery-related tasks and take a stab at drafting motions. If you can handle it, you're off to the races!"* Litigation's cyclical nature didn't faze gutsy juniors, who were typically *"busy enough to pick and choose work. Things have never been so crazy you can't handle it."* Some felt litigators *"need to be assertive"* to get invaluable client contact, which varied by case.

See firm profile on p.657

Rankings in *Chambers USA*

Corporate/M&A	Litigation
Environment	Real Estate
Labor & Employment	

For detail on ranking tiers and ranking locations, visit
www.chambersandpartners.com

Corporate attorneys *"do a lot of middle-market M&A work."* With *"a lot of substantive experience early on,"* tasks might include *"drafting ancillary documents and some lighter drafting on main purchase agreements,"* as well as inescapable due diligence: *"That's just what juniors do!"* Increasing responsibility comes sooner rather than later: *"They want you to interact with clients and manage deals as much as possible."* That doesn't mean being thrown to the wolves: one associate got *"the sense they're trying to train me up by not just giving me super junior stuff."*

"Things have never been so crazy that you can't handle it."

The labor & employment team typically sees *"clients with large employee bases. We get involved with ICE investigations [Homeland Security] and I-9 procedures [eligibility to work in US]."* Days may revolve around *"switching between drafting letters and memos, and doing legal research into federal guidance on an issue. Workload varies, but the trick in our practice area is to remain calm and realize things even out over time."* Over in real estate, juniors had tackled *"anything from drafting complaints and development agreements to, rarely, document review. I have as much responsibility as I want but they don't ever put me in a situation I'm not comfortable in."* Work often crosses between practice groups and offices.

Offices

All newcomers have an office to themselves in Phoenix, and enjoy *"a really nice location. The decorations are a little old and outdated, with an 80s Arizona desert feel, but the views are great,"* with associates facing either South or Camelback Mountain. They're also treated to *"funky, fun local art pieces,"* attributed to a former partner. Other offices were similarly happy – Orange County voiced *"no complaints"* after a recent renovation – and reported a fair amount of collaboration with close neighbors (like LA with OC, and Denver with Salt Lake City). *"Emails asking you to greet people who are visiting"* fostered community feeling, and though *"Phoenix is definitely the flagship,"* associates felt *"being elsewhere doesn't limit who you get to know at the firm."*

Recent work highlights

- Represented Wells Fargo in arbitration over multi-million dollar investment damage claims
- Served as US counsel for investment trust American Hotel Income Properties in the $57.6 million acquisition of two Hilton Hotels Embassy Suites
- Acted as counsel to payments company BillingTree in its recapitalization investment by Parthenon Capital Partners
- Defended Hooters against claims that the restaurant chain sent commercial texts without recipients' requests

Culture & Diversity

The *"notorious no jerk rule, a backbone of the firm,"* means *"everybody is happy to be here, and many partners and senior attorneys have come from ground level up. We're not all best friends but they do care professionally about younger associates."* Formality is a Snell tradition, from omnipresent suits and ties to *"a serious mood – it's professional but not cold."* Some interviewees felt *"the culture is changing a bit, and there's more pressure to be thinking about billing and business development,"* but there was fun to be had too, particularly during summer associate season. Phoenix juniors tried their luck at a popular annual Halloween casino night – *"everyone wears costumes"* – while other offices had traditions ranging from white water rafting in Colorado to harbor boat cruises for Californian attorneys.

"They're trying to help you grow as an attorney."

At associate roundtables, *"questions are submitted anonymously, and management answer in front of everybody."* Most subsequently had *"faith in them to be transparent; they generally keep us apprised."* A few associates felt transparency was *"a huge issue, and a lot of times we don't know what's going on at the top."* In a more general sense, though, partners were praised for *"really investing in young associates. They're trying to help you grow as an attorney and take on more responsibility."* Juniors also unanimously commended the firm for laying out *"a clear partner track: from day one they talk about it as a realistic possibility if you step up to the plate and develop your practice."*

Interviewees gave the thumbs up to the Women's Initiative for providing *"multiple options for flexible schedules, and ramp up/down periods where you can remain on the partnership track without typical hour goals."* Snell is no stranger to typical BigLaw diversity issues: *"The firm's going in the right direction, but it's not super-diverse with minorities."* Sources agreed: *"Female representation at the top is still lagging, but people are very concerned about recruitment and retention of diverse and female attorneys."* The firm tells us it has a program that addresses these

See firm profile on p.657

The Inside View

Diversity	Partners (%)	Associates (%)
Women	15.3	37.9
White	91	86
Black/African American	0	1
Hispanic/Latin American	4	3
Asian	1	6
Mixed/Other	3	2
LGBT	1	0

issues, as well as advancement. There's also a student diversity scholarship available (FAR program).

Get Hired

"A lot of people think business development is very favorable, others are very adamant on grades and percentages." For more tips and tricks, head to www.chambers-associate.com.

Training & Development

Initial associate orientation is followed by *"practice-group specific trainings, developing skills and getting exposure to new kinds of work."* Universally happy with the levels of training, sources particularly valued the firm's business development portal, which chairman Matt Feeney told us has been *"beefed up"* recently. Annual evaluations with *"everybody in the group evaluating your strengths and weaknesses"* helped associates determine where they stood, though everyday feedback was typically seen as more helpful. *"When I started there was a lot of one-to-one help, over time that's decreased but if I have questions everyone's willing to answer."* 150 hours of training and shadowing can be counted toward the billable target by first-years.

Hours & Compensation

With typical days running 8am to 6pm for most, *"you absolutely have time for a private life."* Longer hours cropped up around trial period, but associates stressed *"we don't have set hours. If you want to get out at 5pm, you may need to do weekend work; if you're more flexible, you might never have to."* Flexibility extended to vacation, for which there is no formal policy. *"It's a matter of managing your workload to find time,"* but some eager beavers needed encouragement – *"they were pushing me to take time off. I didn't listen!"*

"If you're working hard that's factored in."

While 2,000 billable hours represent the *"aspirational target"* for all associates, actual bonus-eligibility now varies by office, ranging from 1,800 (Reno, Vegas, SLC, Tucson) to 1,950 (California). Most thought *"you can hit it while maintaining a work/life balance, particularly when you gain more experience. But partners recognize they can't blame you for lack of work opportunities."* Snell's closed compensation system attracted mixed feedback – some *"would appreciate more transparency to know what's expected and how things are rewarded."* Others *"really like the idea, if you're working hard that's factored in."* One summarized: *"I wouldn't be opposed to open compensation, but I think the closed system is pretty fair. Levels seem comparable even if nobody publicizes it."*

Pro Bono

Associates were unanimous in registering *"a huge push for pro bono – they encourage you to do 50 hours, and it counts unlimited toward billables."* First-years were particularly happy to throw themselves in. One had *"billed a couple of hundred pro bono hours. When you're younger that's great, but they want to see older associates focusing on paid work."* Early opportunities for client contact through pro bono were invaluable, something *"the firm definitely encouraged."* Cases varied from immigrant and asylum cases to tenancy issues, and more specialist options including *"helping a local impoverished children's charity with its employee handbooks."* Given a plethora of choice, *"it's up to attorneys to find what they're interested in,"* and though some found little that they wanted to pursue, they put this more down to personal preferences than lack of options.

"It's up to attorneys to find what they're interested in."

Pro bono hours
- For all US attorneys: 14,085
- Average per US attorney: 34.28

Strategy & Future

"Our expansion plans right now continue to focus on our existing offices first and foremost," chairman Matt Feeney highlights. *"Two offices in particular with a lot of opportunities are Denver and Los Angeles."* Walking the walk to back up the talk, *"we increased the size of our summer associate program this year, a trend not embraced by all law firms."* Meanwhile, cross-pollinating work between practice areas represents a new-found strategy for the firm going forward. *"We're now focusing on work moving from group to group and getting pretty good at breaking down geographical boundaries as part of that. It's been very eye-opening."* For more from Feeney, visit our website.

The Inside View

See firm profile on p.657

Squire Patton Boggs

Lawyers per state

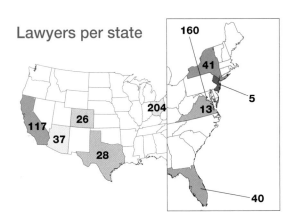

Largest US office: Washington, DC
US offices: 17
International offices: 29
First-year salary: $135,000 - $180,000
Billable hours: 1,950 required (1,900 for first-years)
Summers 2017: 31 (20 2Ls, 11 1Ls)
Revenue 2016: $983.1 million (+1.0%)
Partners made in 2017: 22
Famous for: numerous mergers and appetite for international growth

This firm's story over the past few years is one of mergers, both at home and abroad.

IN early 2017, Silicon Valley IP boutique Fernando & Partners joined Squire Patton Boggs in Palo Alto. The year before, a 50-attorney Californian litigation firm came under the SPB banner. The biggest recent merger, of course, was 2014's union of Cleveland-based global giant Squire Sanders with DC's smaller but still pretty big Patton Boggs, known in particular for its Capitol Hill connections. A few years earlier, in 2011, Squire Sanders had merged with top UK outfit Hammonds, adding around 500 lawyers in England, Europe and Asia.

All this begs the question: what might the firm's history of mergers and rapid growth do to its culture? *"That's a very fair question,"* global managing partner Fred Nance replies, *"and I will suggest that that's one reason I am in the job – I have been here for 38 years!"* A strong, unified culture is *"critical to expansion,"* he says. *"One of my responsibilities is to facilitate the basic firm culture remaining a part of our operations globally, to reinforce the glue that binds us. If you prioritize the right firm culture, good things including financial success will follow."*

At the time of writing, Squire Patton Boggs has 17 offices in the US and 29 overseas. Most lawyers are based in

Ohio and DC, followed by California, New York, Florida and Arizona. *"Our culture is that we are a one-firm firm,"* Fred Nance adds. *"Despite us being around the world, with 1,500-plus lawyers in 46 offices across 21 countries, every lawyer in every office has the same responsibility to the firm and to her or his colleagues throughout the world as though they were in an office down the hall."*

The Work

At the time of our calls, litigation had the greatest concentration of juniors, with the rest spread across practices including corporate, public policy, IP, and environment. As an associate in litigation *"you are a utility infielder who plays wherever you are needed."* That means dabbling in a range of matters including large commercial contract disputes, white collar investigations, and bankruptcy. *"The ethos is that you explore and find the type of law you enjoy working in."* Public policy juniors, who all reside in DC, are assigned to sub-groups including: international; transportation; healthcare; Florida & Latin America; and infrastructure & local government. Their role involves regularly climbing *"Capitol Hill, either presenting an issue on developments happening in the marketplace or for a policy summary meeting."*

> *"You are a utility infielder who plays wherever you are needed."*

Generally, the firm *"gives a lot of responsibility, and a lot of freedom to make your own way."* As one junior put it, *"for*

On chambers-associate.com...

- We chat with global managing partner Fred Nance
- We get recruitment insight from hiring partner Aneca Lasley and SPB associates

See firm profile on p.658

The Inside View

Rankings in *Chambers USA*

Banking & Finance	Government
Bankruptcy/Restructuring	Insurance
Corporate/M&A	Labor & Employment
Employee Benefits &	Litigation
Executive Compensation	Natural Resources

For detail on ranking tiers and ranking locations, visit
www.chambersandpartners.com

Recent work highlights

- A team from SPB was appointed by the Department of Justice and the City of Ferguson to monitor the federally mandated reforms of Ferguson's police department
- Represents Murray Energy, a coal mining company, in rule-making appeals to the Environmental Protection Agency, mostly concerning the EPA's attempts to regulate the emission of greenhouse gases
- Served as counsel to KeyBank in a $50 million revolving credit facility to United Fire Group

good and ill, I was surprised with the degree of autonomy I often get." Being given weighty tasks like *"a complicated motion to draft"* was *"good for morale; it made me feel like part of the team, and that I was contributing meaningfully."* Another told us: *"I like it a lot, but it's challenging and that does make it stressful. I don't like the stress but if you remove the challenge, it's not as fulfilling as a job."* Typical associate tasks across groups included drafting discovery requests, writing memos, plenty of legal research, doc review and, in corporate, some due diligence.

Work is allocated to juniors on an informal basis: *"Partners and associates will just ask me if I have time to help with something,"* or often *"you have to go partner-to-partner saying I'm in need of work – do you have something for me?"* Work often follows on organically from previous matters. *"Nothing is really formalized, there's not an assignment board or a faceless entity processing requests and sending them to me."* Some groups, however, like corporate and private investment funds, require associates to provide a weekly summary on their availability.

Offices

Interviewees were widely distributed: Columbus, DC and Cleveland had around five apiece; Cincinnati, Dallas, LA, and Phoenix each had a few, and the remainder populated San Francisco, Miami, West Palm Beach, Northern Virginia and Denver in ones and twos. Associates recalled many occasions where they'd taken advantage of the firm's huge office network, for example calling someone to ask for specialist advice. In public policy there are *"two-weekly calls with folks from all over the world, with partners from London, Brussels and all over the US. It's awesome to be part of such a global firm."* In big groups like litigation, *"there's a general pool of work if you are light on stuff: that can be from many other offices."*

Culture

In past years, associates have spoken to us about culture in relation to the 2014 merger of Squire Sanders and Patton Boggs. But for this year's bunch, *"as far as I'm concerned, the firm is fully integrated now."* It's *"a really relaxed environment,"* they agreed. *"It can be stressful, but I don't have to deal with rude people."* With all the

necessary integration, we were unsurprised to hear that *"it's very collaborative, it's very easy to talk to people."* That extended to *"both associates and partners among themselves, but also betwixt the two."*

"The firm is fully integrated now."

This communication encourages *"a lot of movement, a lot of cooperation and working across offices. People reach out in broad emails: 'who knows the language? Who has experience on this?' It goes back to the culture we have where we all work together. That's important in hiring – it's great if you're intelligent, but if you don't play well it's a non-starter."* Another junior speculated: *"I don't think we have the law school gunner type of person. People are very smart, but also kind of quirky. Everyone is allowed to be themselves."*

Lawyers are given similar wiggle room when it comes to socializing. One associate felt that at other firms *"there can be a pressure to socialize feverishly and it's seen as a mark of weakness not to go out partying on Wednesday. But here, there is a perfect mix of sociability, drinking and going out for lunch or dinner. It's a Midwestern firm and people have families or other responsibilities – they work together in an agreeable fashion."*

Training & Development

Most training at SPB tends to be *"on the job. Walk and talk about it as you're doing it. There's some sense of: 'you take a stab and we'll see how you come out, and if you have any questions now or going forward we'll address them.'"* This was viewed positively by most: *"The legal training is not properly characterized by sitting in an armchair and watching. Instead it's: go in, try it and they tell you how to do it better."* Still, the firm offers *"basic training, on how the phones work and how to save a file,"* and *"normal CLE training"* comes in *"monthly or bi-monthly sessions in the office."* It's up to associates to decide how much they need. One associate's final word on the issue was that *"given the cooperative atmosphere and willingness of partners and associates to see you learn and develop as a lawyer, I've*

See firm profile on p.658

Diversity	Partners (%)	Associates (%)
Women	21.2	50.6
White	85.6	79.4
Black/African American	4.4	2.3
Hispanic/Latin American	3.6	5.1
Asian	5.2	10.1
Mixed/Other	1.2	3.1
LGBT	unknown	unknown

never felt I didn't have the training to do what was asked of me."

Pro Bono

The extent to which pro bono figured in associates' experience varied wildly. We came across those who had knuckled down on plenty, those who were striving to get hold of something, and those who were blissfully removed from it. It is, associates told us, highly dependent upon the partners in their office. There are *"no standing opportunities. I found a matter I felt was important and so I do that every few weeks. It's nice to design your own opportunities, but there is not a strong emphasis on doing it."* That said, the firm does allow 100 hours of pro bono to count toward associates' billing target and there were many who had been heavily involved, even exceeding those 100 hours.

"You take a stab and we'll see how you come out."

One Columbus associate described *"a partner who is passionate about Legal Aid, so we have a great network. He gets cases and forwards them on to associates."* Another was *"grateful for the opportunity to be in court, to go to hearings, to file motions – you can strategize and I learned a ton about litigation in general. I was able to be the face of what I was doing."* In Cleveland, some had worked on Obama's prisoner clemency program.

Pro bono hours
- For all US attorneys: 18,825
- Average per US attorney: 27

Hours & Compensation

Newbies are eased into the firm with a billing target of 1,900 hours, increasing to 1,950 from the second year onward. This was no sweat for those who achieved it *"very easily. I surpassed that very quickly."* A picture emerged of a firm where *"you should be in the office from 9am to 6pm, but outside of those hours partners have said 'I don't care where you're doing your work as long as it is done.' I regularly work until 11 at night but I can work from home – I*

can leave at six and work at home all night. It doesn't feel that onerous." High pressure work and long hours mean life's not always a beach, but associates could take vacation providing they *"give enough of a heads up."*

"I regularly work until 11 at night but I can work from home."

Bonuses are dished out via a merit-based system, which takes into account billable hours, pro bono, firm citizenship and business development. *"It is unclear,"* said one associate. *"It's not lockstep and you're not given a structure in advance to help you. There's no way of knowing and it's a bit black box, so people don't rely on it as they don't know."* This was one example of a few associate complaints about *"clarity."* In addition to compensation-related career progression, some were unsure about how to best manage their workload.

Diversity

Associates' assessments of diversity varied by office. *"Certainly it is diverse in terms of gender, but in terms of race, at least in my smaller office it's not all that diverse. I do know that there are affinity groups and I know that we participated in a day of silence for the LGBT community."* The problem for this associate *"is that it is a large city but it's not New York, DC, LA, or San Fran."* We noticed those at Midwestern offices were more critical than those in DC, telling us *"they could do a lot better."* Taken as a whole, the firm's stats are fairly average, with 21.2% female partners and 20.6% diverse associates, but most believed *"they are trying, though something isn't working."* Associates could recall a number of diversity initiatives: in Phoenix, for example, *"a local law student comes and sits in the office and gets substantive writing projects to develop their skills."* Likewise there's *"a women's group that meets once a month"* where lawyers *"try to get together for lunch and just see where people are at, and that they are getting opportunities."*

Strategy & Future

With Squire Patton Boggs putting pen to paper on another merger this past year, albeit a small one, it's clear the firm remains on the look-out for growth opportunities. Meanwhile the acquisition of Fernando & Partners forms part of a recent attempt to strengthen the IP practice, which has also seen the hiring of partners in Germany. One associate gave us their thoughts on why a strategy of mergers works for the firm: *"They pick people that complement what we have, or help if we're lacking capabilities. They don't try and jam the puzzle pieces together: they look for a good fit on personality and capability. I don't know if every transition is seamless but I feel good about them and the people that matter do too."*

See firm profile on p.658

The Inside View

Sterne, Kessler, Goldstein & Fox P.L.L.C.

Lawyers per state

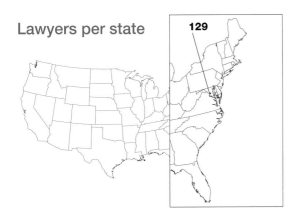

129

Largest US office: Washington, DC

US offices: 1

International offices: 0

First-year salary: $180,000 (2,000 hour track)/$165,000 (1,900 track)

Billable hours: 1,900 or 2,000 target

Summers 2017: 8 (4 2Ls, 4 1Ls)

Revenue 2016: undisclosed

Partners made in 2017: 5

Famous for: IP boutique with a strong emphasis on technical backgrounds

Why does E equal mc²? We've absolutely no idea, but Sterne Kessler's lawyers will know the answer...

ATTORNEYS walking the hallways of DC-based IP specialist Sterne Kessler lead a double life: skilled patent lawyers by day, and science and engineering savants by – well, by day too. Sterne Kessler has built its brand around that model, hiring attorneys with technical backgrounds, ensuring its IP advice comes from those thoroughly in-the-know. Advanced degrees and PhDs abound, plus plenty of relevant career experience: *"They bring to the team a depth of legal and technical analysis that very few firms have,"* says managing director Mike Ray.

The firm works in a wide range of industries, including computer software, engineering, and life sciences, servicing some very well known clients – Apple, Adidas and Google, to name a few. Not bad for a group of roughly 130 attorneys, but it's understandable, considering the firm's top *Chambers USA* ranking for patent prosecution in DC. This practice has existed since Sterne Kessler's founding in 1978, and today there are also busy patent litigation, patent office litigation, appellate, and trade commission teams, plus a trademark, advertising and anti-counterfeiting practice.

The Work

The emphasis on specialized know-how means that newbies are affiliated with a specific group from the beginning of the summer program. Litigation-designated associates solely handle contentious IP matters, while those in the electrical, mechanical, and biotech groups can experience both patent litigation and patent prosecution (applying for patent status). All have a hand in the firm's inter partes review (IPR) work, which it calls patent office litigation.

Biotech, electrical or mechanical newbies are allocated a point person whose *"responsibility is that you have enough work."* But *"after two years it's more about building relationships and opening yourself up to interesting projects."* Tasks are similar across all three teams and matters tend to fall into three categories: patent prosecution, opinion writing and patent office litigation. For prosecution, associates *"write the patent application, discuss it with the inventor, and then negotiate with the patent office."* As *"the responsible attorney"* on many of their cases, associates get client contact and plenty of writing, with some second-chairing depositions for IPRs. *"Clients give us more room to do research, analysis and strategy – it isn't a paperwork sweatshop."*

"It isn't a paperwork sweatshop."

A single coordinator oversees all workflow in the litigation department, but juniors are also free to reach out for assignments, provided they clear it with the coordina-

On chambers-associate.com...
- Interview with managing director Mike Ray
- We chat with hiring director Peter Jackman

The Inside View

See firm profile on p.659

Rankings in *Chambers USA*

Intellectual Property

For detail on ranking tiers and ranking locations, visit www.chambersandpartners.com

Recent work highlights

- Worked with Apple to protect the design of the Apple Watch worldwide
- Developed a patent for Biogen on the drugs Eloctate and Alprolix, which are used to treat hemophilia. Went on to successfully defend those patents at a USPTO re-examination
- Successfully represented Veeam Software against an attempt to invalidate four patents
- Represented Volkswagen against patent infringement claims made by Voxathon

tor first. *"The bulk of matters are district court litigation,"* but with *"a good amount of IPR litigation."* A wider brief means the team *"works hand in hand with the prosecution teams. Even if they didn't work on that patent they may be knowledgeable about the specific technical details."* Juniors had *"drafted pleadings, did discovery document review, and then started on expert reports, working to prepare them for deposition."* Being *"such a close knit team,"* associates didn't *"feel excluded from anything on the case."* Less positively, *"there is an ebb and flow of work, so if you're not staffed on a robust case it can be piecemeal work, taking what you can in the form of 'spot projects.' That can be pretty draining."* They pointed out that *"it's hard as a young associate to jump into a case that's been going on for years."*

"A close knit team."

Get Hired

Hiring director Peter Jackman tells us: *"Since we pride ourselves on being very tech savvy, we want candidates with advanced degrees, especially in the biotech and chemical areas."* For more on recruitment, go to our feature on Sterne Kessler on chambers-associate.com.

Culture

"On one side it's a group of highly intellectual scientists, but at the same time it's a very down to earth place." Similar evaluations were made by all sources, who jumped to inform us of the *"communal atmosphere."* The image of a law firm *"where the partner yells at you and you can't walk into someone's office to shoot the shit – that's not here. We are serious and good at what we do but the atmosphere is laid back."* Suits and ties are one casualty of that ethos; the dress code is *"not quite what you'd wear to the bar or the club, but it's casual."*

In *"working with partners daily,"* sources found their superiors to be *"very open and approachable. If I have an issue, I feel comfortable walking into their office and asking for five minutes – I've never been shunned."* In fact, *"you know all the partners and they all know you – there are no associates hidden away in a random office somewhere."*

"You know all the partners and they all know you."

In a concerted effort, the firm *"pushes partners to keep their doors open"* and *"tries to create an atmosphere that*

is not too stuffy, or critical, or competitive." In the same breath, associates mentioned their winter retreat at The Greenbrier in West Virginia. It provided *"speeches on the state of the market and sessions determining how to modify the firm for the better,"* but also *"plenty of team-building too. On top of all the meetings there are events and parties,"* plus *"paintballing, a tour of the whiskey distillery, caving and a bowling alley."* A summer trip to see the Nationals play baseball also comes at the firm's expense, plus there's a hike in the Blue Ridge Mountains every few years. That even includes a cook-out at retired name partner Sam Fox's farm. Beyond that, lawyers occasionally wet their whistles, but associates described *"a more family-centered approach,"* rather than *"a party scene."*

"An atmosphere that is not too stuffy, or critical, or competitive."

Offices

All attorneys reside in an office on New York Avenue – it's recently been renovated, and according to associates *"it's pretty awesome."* From the outside, it's the shell of an old bus station, complete with art-deco façade. Inside, visitors will find it to be *"really modern and very open. There are nice conference rooms with smart boards and integrated technology."* For unwinding, there's a *"cafeteria area with a football table and ping pong. There's a barista bar too – it's not just a coffee pot behind a bar, it's these crazy-expensive machines which can make any coffee you can think of."* As attorneys slurp their pumpkin-spiced-macha-frappa-skinny-vegan-lattes, one imagines conversation turning to the firm's best known piece of trivia. The 1990s film *True Lies* was filmed within the building, bringing the Austrian Oak himself, Arnold Schwarzenegger, swaggering through the hallways.

Training & Development

Associates' *"point person"* serves as their mentor, *"if and when I need them."* In addition, associates are paired up with a *"buddy"* of a similar level *"who you feel more comfortable talking with."* Sterne Kessler also launched a career coach program in 2014 to connect juniors with

See firm profile on p.659

Diversity	Partners (%)	Associates (%)
Women	21.4	24.3
White	77.8	72.9
Black/African American	3.7	2.9
Hispanic/Latin American	5.6	1.4
Asian	13	22.9
Mixed/Other	0	0
LGBT	1.9	2.9

partners outside of their practice group. *"When they hire associates they envision them being at the partner table with them. It's absolutely not guaranteed, but the ultimate goal is to allow people to work, grow and progress so that they could contribute as partner."*

Newbies kick off with two weeks' training on firm systems and the basics of patent prosecution. Thereafter, monthly practice group meetings offer discussion of legal issues and the opportunity for associates to present upon specific topics. In biotech, associates are *"taught by a senior partner throughout the first few years, which functions a lot like a college class."*

Pro Bono

Pro bono is pretty low key at Sterne Kessler. We weren't surprised when one associate told us: *"I don't know anyone who has done pro bono."* But it does exist, and for example lawyers in the past have helped Native American tribes with IP cases. Even participating associates admitted that *"as it's centered around IP, the work we can do is limited."* Associates felt that when it came to pro bono, *"the firm doesn't push us hard in that direction,"* while noting that *"our concerns have been heard, they're thinking about ways to work around it."* Since our calls, we heard that associates have taken on non-IP matters including immigration and family issues, among others.

"The work we can do is limited."

Pro bono hours
- For all attorneys: 1,000 approx.
- Average per attorney: 6.4

Hours & Compensation

Associates can choose their billable target to become bonus-eligible: 1,900 or 2,000 hours, though associates thought that *"most people go with 1,900 hours."* Some viewed it as *"risky to raise the bar for yourself and risk criticism,"* and associates did report that some colleagues fell shy of their target, particularly in litigation – but most found at least one of the two to be achievable.

"Most people go with 1,900 hours."

Interviewees tended to put in around ten hours a day at the office, with the majority leaving between 6pm and 7pm, but associates lauded the flexibility they were afforded. *"I have colleagues who aren't early people and they consistently come into the office between 10am and 11am and leave later – there's nobody waiting to see you punch your card in."* An associate described being *"able to go to the gym, eat dinner at home, hang out with friends and I don't work most weekends."* There was *"nobody expecting me to respond to my phone at 2am – it's healthy enough."*

Diversity

Women make up only 28% of the associates at Sterne Kessler – *"there aren't many female associates."* In the firm's defense, science and engineering already suffers a gender imbalance, and 27% of the firm's partners are female – a better proportion than at most firms. Sterne Kessler's ethnic minority representation is good, with minority attorneys making up a quarter of both associates and partners. Our sources noticed *"a good amount of Asian Americans compared to other groups."* Juniors could recall a number of initiatives: a *"women's litigation group,"* a mock trial organized by women's advancement non-profit Chiefs in Intellectual Property (ChIPs), and a *"diversity day, to share experiences with each other."* Hiring director Peter Jackman also tells us that *"one of the new initiatives for 2017 has us partnering with Howard University and doing a rotation with their College of Pharmacy."*

"There aren't many female associates."

Strategy & Future

The firm increasingly works on inter partes reviews: quasi-litigious cases overseen by the Patent Trial and Appeal Board. Since a shift in the law in 2012, it's been the hot area of patent law, and a dynamic one at that. *"The firm is always working to stay up to date with the changes to IPR and the concerning law. It feels like a new case comes out daily and you have to stay up on that."* Fortunately the firm's *"a market leader on this work"* – and has even written one of the first books on the subject. Managing director Mike Ray is keen not to get carried away, though: *"We think that it is important to maintain a balance between patent preparation and prosecution, court and ITC litigation, and patent office litigation. We are subject to the work that our clients want us to do – but we try to maintain that balance."*

See firm profile on p.659

Stroock & Stroock & Lavan LLP

Lawyers per state

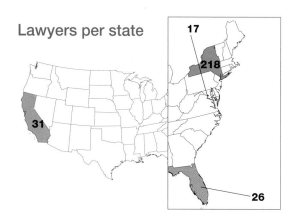

17

218

31

26

Largest US office: New York
US offices: 4
International offices: 0
First-year salary: $180,000
Billable hours: 2,000 target (incl. 200 non-billable)
Summers 2017: 14 (13 2Ls, 1 1L)
Revenue 2016: $270.7 million (+2.2%)
Partners made in 2017: 2
Famous for: big clients for a BigLaw firm that's on the smaller side

Lean staffing is the norm at this New York mid-sizer that punches well above its weight.

A FORMER hiring partner, Claude Szyfer, recalls being taught, as a young lawyer, the secret to success at Stroock: *"One of my mentors used to always say 'I want people to take ownership over a case and make it their own'. The type of people who succeed at Stroock are those who can work independently, because we staff so leanly."* The prospect of doing BigLaw in a more intimate environment had been an appealing draw for the current batch of juniors we interviewed: *"I'd heard this was a big firm in terms of the work you get,"* one told us, *"but not in the cut-throat attitude there is elsewhere."* Newly appointed co-managing partner Jeff Keitelman, the firm's first based in DC, suggests *"an opportunity to make a meaningful difference is one thing that sets Stroock apart."* A new hiring partner, Nicole Runyan, took over from Claude Szyfer in January 2017.

"Big" work comes from big clients including JP Morgan, Goldman Sachs, AIG and American Express. *Chambers USA* ranks Stroock for its work in New York, DC, California, Florida and nationwide, singling out for particular praise its insurance, international trade, and real es-

tate practices. New York, LA and now DC currently take new entry-level associates, and Claude Szyfer reveals that *"we're thinking more nationally as a firm, which involves the New York, DC, Los Angeles and Miami offices working more interactively in collaboration. That's something that's proven very exciting for our attorneys."*

The Work

Summer associates get to pick first-choice practice areas, so *"when making offers we can give them a sense of where they'll be,"* says HP Claude Szyfer. Litigation and corporate take in most new associates, who typically start as generalists within the team before finding a niche. Financial restructuring, IP, tax, real estate and other groups also accommodate newcomers. Associates reported that *"all the departments have an administrative partner. They're the central point for all assignments and as new matters come in they'll staff them."* Once they'd got to know partners and *"developed relationships, you get work informally, but it's a mix of both. Even in your second year you still get work from the formal system. Repeat work from certain partners is how people specialize."*

In litigation, juniors typically *"do legal research and drafting of papers. Many are put onto a large document review for a couple of months. There's also substantive drafting of briefs and motions."* For most, work wasn't hard to come by, and *"our group jokes that you have no problem hitting billable requirements."* The majority felt the rush wasn't constant, and breaks were welcomed as *"all of a sudden*

See firm profile on p.660

Rankings in *Chambers USA*

Bankruptcy/Restructuring	Media & Entertainment
Insurance	Real Estate
International Trade	

For detail on ranking tiers and ranking locations, visit www.chambersandpartners.com

Recent work highlights

- Represented JP Morgan Asset Management-advised fund in $1.65 billion sale of a Rockefeller Center building
- Acted for UK defense technology multinational QinetiQ in $100 million sale of Cyveillance subsidiary
- Advised the first ever peer-to-peer insurance company, Lemonade, during its launch as a licensed organization
- Represented director Oliver Stone on the $50 million financing and distribution of Snowden

a ton of work comes and you're harking back to the days it was quiet!" A broad mix of clients includes financial institutions and real estate agents. In many cases there's "a fair amount of client interaction, and juniors get significant responsibility. There's usually not several associates between junior and partner," thanks to lean staffing models.

"You have no problem hitting billable requirements!"

Corporate work spans "a whole plethora. There's a big private funds practice, mutual funds, derivatives, insurance, some energy work. We do smaller M&A." Specialization in a particular subsection over time was common, though not universal. Juniors initially got "familiar with checklists and closing documents. In the second year they're still part of the day-to-day, but there's a noticeable change from that to credit agreements, drafting ancillary and smaller documents. You get a lot more ability and autonomy." Happy to "generally do pretty substantive work," corporate associates felt "you're not buried, but given opportunities."

The financial restructuring team "typically does creditor-side representation in bankruptcies or out-of-court restructurings. It's pretty varied – as a first-year there's lots of research, but it's nice that once you've done a couple of things for someone they're willing to give you as much as you can handle." IP work primarily consists of patent litigation and prosecution, and trademark litigation. One junior enjoyed "immense responsibility. When things are busy I'll be writing motions and drafting briefs from start to finish. I even went to trial as a first-year!" The smaller teams provide more scope for specialization early on.

Training & Development

"There's a week's orientation at the start, which runs you through basic stuff. It's not entertaining but it has to be done!" Associates then attend CLE courses that run once a week for the first six months. "The cornerstone of training is the mock trial in summer: a lot goes into that." Otherwise, associates felt "the only real way to learn is in the trenches."

Associates get biannual, "informal" one-on-one reviews with the practice group's administrative partner. "They give you a snapshot of what people say about you." Daily

feedback comes through "informal conversations. There's not a lot of structured telling you how you did. Some partners are forthright with comments, others will give honest feedback if requested. The fact I have to ask sucks, but it is at least available."

Offices

Evoking Jay-Z, New Yorkers joked "we have 99 problems, and most of them are with the building! But it's going through renovations, and the improvements are nice." Associates' verdict was "it's not fantastic, but not terrible." Summers in New York share offices with first-years to integrate into the firm, and second-years get their own rooms when the new summer class arrives. Closer to Snoop Dogg's California cool, Los Angelenos lovedthe "building and Century City environment, with great views of downtown LA and the Hollywood sign." Communication between bases "depends on the deal and partners," but the firm is reportedly pushing for more.

Culture & Diversity

New York associates reported that "each department has a very different feel," as each is exclusive to one floor. Litigators felt "everyone's friendly, not particularly outgoing but generally nice," while the corporate team similarly has "a nice culture. The only thing I would say is some people think things are old-fashioned." Financial restructuring associates were happy to discover "it's pretty collegial, everybody keeps their door open." Partners firm-wide were considered "receptive to having associates involved with their discussions. Some are more old-school, but others will go out of their way to thank you."

"Each department has a very different feel."

Associates recognized that "Stroock is doing a big re-branding, and working on making things more unified." Transition was also underway in terms of transparency: "That's something that hasn't been quite as great in the past. They're aware people are unhappy and are trying to make it better." More social events were also on the reform agenda. Gregarious litigators felt they took more

See firm profile on p.660

The Inside View

Diversity	Partners (%)	Associates (%)
Women	17	35
White	93	77
Black/African American	0	5
Hispanic/Latin American	3.5	7
Asian	3.5	7
Mixed/Other	0	4
LGBT	1	3.5

opportunities to socialize with colleagues than those in other departments, but *"it's not like we're all dying to hang out. The work schedule is demanding enough that we want to go home after work. Last year's holiday party was really good and they're making an effort to encourage more"* along those lines.

Acknowledging that *"there are fewer females in senior positions, at associate level it's pretty diverse,"* though *"we are lacking in terms of ethnic minorities."* At associate level, only 35% are female, slightly lower than the BigLaw average. There are a variety of affinity groups including the Attorneys of Color, SSLGBT, and Working Parents, which all host regular meeting and events. While some associates suggested *"it doesn't feel very diverse,"* they acknowledged *"the firm is looking to address the issue – during recruiting it's something that's considered. We've seen they've hired more LGBT attorneys in particular."*

Get Hired

"Take advantage of mock interview programs. Try to get an idea of types of questions that come up and plan responses ahead of time." For help with that from associates, and our full interview with hiring partner Claude Szyfer, head to chambers-associate.com.

Pro Bono

The founding director of Stroock's Public Service Project, Kevin Curnin, coordinates pro bono work firmwide, and it's considered *"part of the firm's culture in a big way,"* according to associates. *"They're always encouraging people to take more and are very supportive of us dedicating time and effort to it. A lot of cases are personal passion projects of various partners, and they're a very different experience and nice complement to more typical work."*

Projects have varied from *"trust and estates pro bono work, and extremely rewarding cases for terminal illness sufferers,"* to a more time-consuming *"accusation of sexual assault."* One junior got involved in *"a lot of family*

law stuff, which was a really good experience." The firm has historically coordinated legal aid in the aftermath of the September 11 attacks, Hurricane Katrina and Superstorm Sandy. Our Bonus Features on chambers-associate.com have more information on Stroock's Public Service Project.

Pro bono hours
- For all attorneys: 17,970.5
- Average per attorney: 55.46

Hours & Compensation

An associate billing target of 2,000 hours, 200 of which can be non-billable legal work (pro bono, journal writing etc.) was considered *"attainable if you find the right work. Most people generally make it."* This translates to a ten hour working day: 9am to 7pm was the rough average, though corporate juniors tended to arrive and leave the office later. One source explained that *"on a good day you're out by 6pm, but plenty of times I've worked until 10pm or later."* Weekend work was exceptional, but expected, and interviewees felt *"Stroock is really good about a work/life balance"* for associates.

"Stroock is really good about a work/life balance."

"It took a while to hear anything" about the 2016 Cravath-led salary increases (to $180,000 for first-years), but the firm matched and associates thought *"they handled the increase well."* One reasoned: *"I think Stroock is careful financially, so change can be quite slow."* Los Angeles associates get the New York lockstep level for their first few years, then switch to merit-based compensation – *"they haven't given us a good explanation why."* In both offices, *"the firm encourages taking vacation. It's luck of the draw timing-wise, and it's sometimes hard to plan; but people are very understanding, rest is something they value."*

Strategy & Future

Former hiring partner Claude Szyfer tells us the firm *"wants to continue to grow, not so much opening more offices but strengthening those that we have. We've done some exciting five-year planning, in which we're considering the future of law firms. In particular we're looking at value propositions for clients."* Progress is underway in keeping associates more in the loop about firm strategy. *"They're making some serious effort"* according to interviewees, *"there's a new vision for the firm and it will be interesting to see how the transition goes."* Read our Bonus Features in Stroock's profile on chambers-associate.com for the full interview with Szyfer.

See firm profile on p.660

Sullivan & Cromwell LLP

Lawyers per state

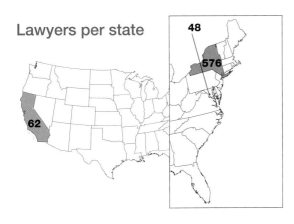

Largest US office: New York
US offices: 4
International offices: 8
First-year salary: $180,000
Billable hours: no requirement
Summers 2017: 133 (104 2Ls, 14 1Ls, 12 3Ls, 3 others)
Revenue 2016: $1.36 billion (+3.5%)
Partners made in 2017: 3
Famous for: perfectionism

Sullivan & Cromwell's perfectionist zeal rewards associates willing to give it their all.

CONFUCIUS once said: *"Better a diamond with a flaw than a pebble without."* Sullivan & Cromwell thinks differently. *"We have the saying here that perfection is not the enemy of good, and people take it seriously."* 200 years have seen S&C brew up a reputation for having the crème-de-la-crème of legal work and a painstaking approach to satisfying the client, where only the best will do. Its *Chambers USA* rankings are stacked high, with top marks for areas including white collar crime, securities litigation, capital markets, real estate, tax, plus of course the M&A practice, which recently advised on the gargantuan acquisition of Time Warner by AT&T, among other headline-grabbing deals. Chairman Joe Shenker is happy to report that *"we have been very busy with really trailblazing work,"* including work that will *"redefine the sports and media landscape."*

Associates found that *"the focus is on intellectual growth, on training – it's intellectual with a practical focus."* Add in exposure to stellar work, plus a generalist approach, and associates felt enabled to *"become the best lawyer you can be."* But the pursuit of perfection had juniors advising

that job candidates here carefully consider their *"work ethic."*

The Work

Litigation and the general practice group (which includes corporate and other transactional practices) take the bulk of new associates. Before settling down, GP associates *"can get work from any of the groups within general practice during the first 18 months."* A formal assignment system dishes out work, but associates also *"independently reach out to partners, or get recommended by them."* Of the two, *"developing work on your own"* seemed *"the way to get really interesting work."* And that, associates felt, gave the firm an edge: *"You wouldn't have that opportunity at other firms. I've appreciated having the flexibility to try different things and to figure out what I'm interested in."*

"I've appreciated having the flexibility to try different things."

Sources in the corporate department painted a pretty picture: typical splashes of low-level work, some due diligence here and there, but *"if anything it errs on the side of more responsibility rather than less."* Responsibility progressed quickly; one associate had *"worked with mid levels to draft documentation for a senior debt program. I took the first stab at drafting that from precedent. They weren't just giving me the busywork – it's very hands on."* Others drafted letters and transactional documents, took

On chambers-associate.com...

- Interview with chairman Joe Shenker
- Interview with global head of recruiting Sergio Galvis
- Sullivan & Cromwell's headline grabbing work

See firm profile on p.661

The Inside View

Rankings in *Chambers USA*

Antitrust	Financial Services
Capital Markets	Regulation
Corporate Crime &	Insurance
Investigations	Investment Funds
Corporate/M&A	Latin American Investment
Employee Benefits &	Litigation
Executive Compensation	Projects
Energy & Natural	Real Estate
Resources	REITs
Environment	Securities
FCPA	Tax

For detail on ranking tiers and ranking locations, visit
www.chambersandpartners.com

Recent work highlights

- Advised AT&T on its proposed $85.4 billion acquisition of Time Warner, fielding corporate, tax, IP, financing and litigation partners to support it
- Has served as counsel to Volkswagen in the multinational litigation emanating from the emissions scandal. Settlement has been reached on a number of fronts, including with the Department of Justice
- Advising German chemicals and pharma giant Bayer on its $65 billion acquisition of US company Monsanto
- Represented Columbia Pipeline Group in its $13 billion acquisition by TransCanada

part in negotiations and even ran the process for a securities offering. Close contact with partners was commonplace and responsibility soon came by the bucket-load. *"There have been times I've been out of my comfort zone, but it gives you the opportunity to expand your skills as an attorney."* One junior revealed that *"sometimes I have to remind them I've only been here for two years! It's nice that they trust me to do good work though."*

It's down to a staffer and associate development coordinator to sort associates' work in litigation. Associates stressed *"it's not free market. You can always speak to the staffer – they'll have a list of the available work and they can help you with it. Often your work follows on from what they give you."* Of the work, associates said: *"It's New York, so it's generally related to complex financial products and derivatives"* – but we should point out that many clients are in industries other than financial services. Securities litigation, white collar and regulation work feature heavily. Associates described *"getting doc review starting out. It's pretty hierarchical so you do a lot of administrative tasks. Once you show initiative and that you can manage your workload in a timely manner, and with precision, you will get leadership tasks."* Upon climbing the ladder associates worked on *"a lot of legal research"* and drafted witness depositions, motions and expert opinions.

Pro Bono

Most associates had done pro bono of some sort, but between those in general practice and litigation, there was a noticeable difference in the volume and variety. Some GP associates were even *"busy enough so that I haven't felt like taking any on would be a good idea."* The problem for those focused on corporate law is *"there's no real transferral of skills."* Since most pro bono on offer is litigation-based, it was *"hard to see any overlap."* But corporate associates could still work on things like transgender name changes: *"Quick, easy, and the firm is very invested in it."* In general, the pro bono picture is rosy: *"Not just good on*

paper, but really promoted and encouraged. There's no limit on hours, and plenty of opportunities."* Associates had worked on housing, child support and asylum matters, drafted appellate briefs, and told us about an opportunity to *"argue in court in the Bronx."*

> *"There's no limit on hours and plenty of opportunities."*

Pro bono hours
- For all US attorneys: 36,406
- Average per US attorney: 56

Hours & Compensation

While there's no specific pro bono requirement or official cap, and while there's no billable hours target either, associates advised that *"it's easy to take on too much with so many opportunities for responsibility. People need to keep themselves in check and learn to say no."* Associates work a hefty shift, with several telling us they regularly left the office at 8pm, often with more work at home. When needed, associates could work *"periods of 18-hour days,"* with one telling us that *"last month I worked every day until 11 at night."* Weekends weren't sacred, though associates were thankful for the advance notice they usually got. However, one associate went so far as to say that *"from Monday to Friday, they own you."*

> *"People need to keep themselves in check and learn to say no."*

Interviewees repeatedly highlighted the positive side of their deal, telling us: *"I do like that I don't have a billable minimum. People elsewhere are stressed and concerned about it, but I can use the quieter times to catch up on CLE credit or other matters. It gives you the flexibility to manage your life. I feel less stressed and not at all guilty about leaving around 5.30pm at quiet times."* The firm also *"offers equipment to work from home and, in my experience, as long as you communicate it's not a problem."* It seemed *"people are understanding about your hours and*

See firm profile on p.661

Diversity	Partners (%)	Associates (%)
Women	20	40
White	91	76
Black/African American	2	3
Hispanic/Latin American	4	4
Asian	3	14
Mixed/Other	1	2
LGBT	7	6

about when you take vacation. People told me to go ahead and take mine." Besides, "since salaries were increased" – in line with Cravath – "there's no stress about that."

Training & Development

Several associates told us good training was one of the things that drew them to Sullivan, which offers an impressive 400 formal programs a year. "Starting from the summer, associates get informal and formal training. There are practice group lunches once a month; we discuss technical issues and the legal market. They might talk about work volume and what clients have been up to – it's great both educationally and for career development." More formally there are seminars and occasional bootcamps: "Two days' intensive training on a mix of hard and soft skills." In line with the firm's generalist aims, associates can attend any practice group's training. However, litigation juniors told us it still could still come down to "learning by doing." They clarified that "when you get on a new case people explain to you and tell you what to do. Your senior always explains, so you're not doing things on the fly."

Once associates are assigned to a practice group, they can express a preference about who their formal mentor should be. Before that stage, though, "you technically have a formal mentor, but my go-to guy has been informal. People are friendly." Associates do also get the supernatural help of so-called "floor wizards." They're junior associates too, who "advise first years, and help them navigate the firm." S&C has also recently bolstered its support for departing associates. "They want to keep people as long as they can but they're also realistic that everyone won't be partner. So the firm launched a development plan for associates." It links associates with the firm's contacts, matching them to possible jobs. Go to chambers-associate.com to read more on this from the chairman, Joe Shenker.

Culture

Associates described their surroundings as "a culture of excellence," where they noticed "partners thinking a few steps ahead about every aspect of the matter" and an emphasis on immaculate work and client service. But what does this mean for associates? It applies "not to just to the

big things but the little." On the smallest scale, one associate found that subsequent reviews of their work would see "commas and words repeatedly switched around," finding their seniors to be "interventionists" and "very detail-oriented. This is not pejorative, but I'd call them control freaks. They like it done their way." Living up to this "higher scrutiny" meant there was an "adjustment curve," but associates found that "people are patient in pointing things out." Juniors leaned on helpful mid-levels who they found especially helpful in "explaining the background of a matter, so that you can see the bigger picture."

"This is not pejorative, but I'd call them control freaks."

The culture has "an intellectual tinge to it. People are very intellectually curious." They "like what they are doing, they enjoy law, they enjoy working hard and figuring out complex issues. I've met some of the smartest people I've ever met here!" The mask does slip every so often, though, as "you can have great conversations about the election or about a legal matter one day and then you can be talking about Justin Bieber the next." Amid the pursuit of perfection the atmosphere was still "personable" and associates assured us that "it's not mean or cold." But neither is the social life overly zealous; there's certainly "no pressure to go to events or to have a drink, people are mature about it."

Offices

S&C owns its NY office, "a really lovely building in the financial district, near to the Staten Island ferry." On the inside, a renovation is underway, with chairman Joe Shenker's critical eye "making sure we get a floor that tolerates wine stains." Actually owning the building allows for habitual improvement; "after Hurricane Sandy they re-did the basement and the gym." One gym-goer told us they'd "find it unbearable to be sitting here all day – it feels great to go downstairs for a class and a 30 minute workout." A 4pm snack time sounded like the gym's raison d'être – on offer are the standard "soda and chips" and occasionally posher fare like soft pretzels with a variety of dips, and cheese platters. "By 4.30 everything is gone!"

Diversity

As with many big firms, insiders acknowledge that "the firm makes a very real effort," but thought that "they could do more," particularly on racial diversity. "In terms of the resources it puts in, you can say that the affinity networks are well funded and do interesting programming. But like most firms, where the struggle comes in is recruitment and retention." The firm has an active women's network and various affinity groups. "The women's initiative is my favorite," said one female associate. "They now do office hours with partners and round table lunches for small

See firm profile on p.661

groups." The diversity figures are in line with the NYC norm, and hiring partner Sergio Galvis tells us that *"we regularly partner with law school groups to establish connections with their members on campus, deliver substantive programs, and provide information about the work we do."*

Get Hired

"A focus on what kind of work you want to do is key; being commercial, getting it right, being service-oriented, and all of that flows from your interest in the work – so you should start there." For the full interview with HP Sergio Galvis and recruitment insight from associates, go to chambers-associate.com.

Strategy & Future

In the past year, *"M&A – especially cross-border work – has been extraordinary,"* says chairman Joe Shenker. But he also draws our attention to *"the emerging area of financial technology, or FinTech, working with virtual currency exchanges, blockchain and distributed ledger developers, payment providers, and online lenders."* Shenker believes the firm's generalist approach breeds innovation like this, ushering in what he titles *"ground-breaking work."* That, he says, *"is what we strive for and recruit for."* And recruitment is at the heart of his strategy, believing the firm's *"most important task is to recruit the best and the brightest from around the world."*

"The most important task is to recruit the best and the brightest from around the world."

The Inside View

See firm profile on p.661

Thompson & Knight LLP

Lawyers per state

18	(New York)
2	(California)
288	(Texas)

Largest US office: Dallas
US offices: 6
International offices: 5
First-year salary: $180,000
Billable hours: 1,900 required (2,000 after first year)
Summers 2017: 12 (all 2Ls)
Revenue 2016: $213.4 million (+2.9%)
Partners made in 2017: 7
Famous for: Texas and oil

Associates pick Thompson & Knight for its strong reputation in Texas, its oil and gas work and *"the fact you get hands-on experience as it's a smaller firm."*

"ONE thing that really jumped out at me when I interviewed at Thompson & Knight was the shocking number of attorneys who had worked here all their lives!" exclaimed one associate. *"That attracted me as someone who values stability."* The firm is certainly stable: it was founded 130 years ago in Dallas by Bill Thompson and Bob Knight, two of the first law graduates of the University of Texas. In its history the firm was instrumental in the incorporation of Texas Instruments and the first so-called 'ABC Transaction' in the oil and gas sector.

Oil still runs through the firm's veins today and T&K is recognized by *Chambers USA* as one of the top firms in the nation for oil and gas work. In Texas too, *Chambers* rates T&K highly for its energy and environment work and grants it a top-tier ranking for real estate, plus recognition for its litigation, corporate, finance, tax and IP practices (among others).

The Work

At the time of research, 25 of the 40 junior associates on our interviewee list were based in Dallas, ten were in Houston, with one each in New York and Austin. Eight were based in the corporate & securities section ('section'

is the firm's name for practice group), seven in trial, six in real estate & banking and three or four in each of the tax, bankruptcy, IP and oil & gas sections. The trial section has a coordinator who oversees associate workload, but in all sections work assignment is mostly informal. *"I get assigned work when partners come by my office, email me or call to ask if I'm free. I don't really need to actively seek out work."*

The 60-lawyer corporate group does a lot of work for the oil and gas industry, although there is also a separate oil & gas section that focuses mainly on asset deals. Clients also come from the banking and finance, telecommunications, retail, transportation and healthcare sectors – they include energy explorer Warren Resources, investor EnCap, bedding manufacturer Tempur Sealy, and 7-Eleven. Private equity is also a significant focus. An associate told us: *"You can expect to be in charge of the wealth of documents related to a large transaction: making sure they are updated, that specialists are reviewing certain sections, and that documents are executed correctly. But there are also smaller transactions on which I work with just a partner. Then I undertake tasks like drafting and thinking through the documents strategically."*

The oil & gas section deals with oil and gas asset deals – the buying and selling of oil fields – and operational matters. Clients include energy giants BHP Billiton and Petrobras as well as banks. The low oil price means work's been a little slow recently in this section – *"when the price*

On chambers-associate.com...

- Get Hired

The Inside View

See firm profile on p.662

Rankings in *Chambers USA*

Antitrust	Healthcare
Banking & Finance	Intellectual Property
Bankruptcy/Restructuring	Labor & Employment
Corporate/M&A	Litigation
Energy & Natural	Real Estate
Resources	Tax
Environment	

For detail on ranking tiers and ranking locations, visit
www.chambersandpartners.com

Recent work highlights

- Represented the conflicts committee of oil and gas transportation and processing company American Midstream Partners in its $2 billion merger with JP Energy Partners
- Advised Alabama's Regions Bank on a $199 million loan to Texas financial services group USAA for the development of new offices for Amazon in Seattle
- Advised Houston-headquartered oil and gas company Ajax Resources on the $376 million acquisition of the Yellow Rose oil field in West Texas' Permian Basin from W&T Offshore
- Defended the owners of a shopping mall in the Rio Grande Valley against a court claim by the mall's operator that certain restrictive clauses in a contract prevented them from finding tenants for the mall

of oil was higher there was a lot more work." Still, we heard that in the last few months of 2016 activity levels started to pick up again and juniors remain active. One told us: "*I work on mortgage agreements and deal with the due diligence related to purchase and sales agreements.*"

> **"Despite the regional feel of the firm, we actually work on a lot of interesting cases across the country and around the world."**

The work of the trial group, with around 100 lawyers, covers oil and gas, healthcare, white collar crime, general commercial and antitrust. Clients include the Mark Cuban Companies, Indian steel manufacturer JSW, and oil and gas investor Double Eagle. The team deals with cases worth a couple of million dollars, and sometimes with bigger ones. "*Despite the regional feel of the firm, we actually work on a lot of interesting cases across the country and around the world,*" an interviewee reported. Juniors do research into black-letter law as well as "*drafting motions for summary judgment and documents in support of motions to dismiss.*" One source said they had "*managed a small breach of contract claim alone*" and we heard that some juniors even take depositions.

The firm's real estate clients are chiefly banks and other lenders and include Wells Fargo, Barclays Capital and Dunhill Partners. A real estate associate reported: "*I do a lot of title survey work and review operating agreements and commercial leases. I have direct contact with clients if they have a question about anything. I also draft loan documents and deal with post-closure tasks.*"

Training & Development

To help new associates understand the complexities of their work, T&K has an extensive program of CLEs and trainings: general ones on business development and legal writing and practice-specific ones on M&A, mezzanine finance and real estate. For litigators there's also the annual Trial Academy: "*We reenact a full jury trial at the George Allen Courts Building in Dallas and the as-*

sociates go up against each other with a partner acting as judge." Newcomers are also formally assigned associate and partner mentors – "*there's a big group of people I can reach out to for advice*" – and associates have yearly formal reviews and more relaxed midyear appraisals.

> **"Support from partners and other associates is always there."**

Day to day, "*support from partners and other associates is always there,*" said one source. "*If I'm given an assignment I haven't done before they tell me to come and ask if I have any questions.*" One source reported getting "*amazing feedback, especially during the editing process of documents I've drafted,*" while another said: "*There is not a lot of hand-holding, but there is follow-up to tell you why a certain decision was made about changes made to something you drafted.*"

Culture & Offices

Along with this supportive training, juniors told us that "*colleagues generally care about how your weekend was and how you are doing in life,*" with one source saying, "*I feel comfortable joking with the partners – I go for lunch and dinner with them.*" Further evidence of the attention paid to young lawyers is the new all-associate retreat organized for the first time in 2016; it included team bonding activities and a talk from managing partner Mark Sloan on firm strategy. There's also an annual client appreciation holiday party as well as section-by-section social events and occasional happy hours. Rather sweetly, the Houston office hosted a Hallowe'en party for the children of attorneys and staff.

Family is a focus for many at T&K – "*it's sociable here, but not in an over-the-top way. People come here to work and then go home to family.*" A Dallas source told us: "*We have TV screens around the office showing firm news and when*

See firm profile on p.662

Diversity	Partners (%)	Associates (%)
Women	26	48
White	94	83
Black/African American	1	6
Hispanic/Latin American	2	2
Asian	0	5
Mixed/Other	3	5
LGBT	unknown	3

someone has a baby or gets married a message goes up congratulating them." But not everything is family-oriented – "some people here are parents and some colleagues don't have children and I go for drinks and dinners with both." We heard that there's a good vibe during office hours too – "I joke that every hour someone will casually pop by my office just to see how I'm doing."

Dallas is the firm's headquarters and the largest office with around 150 attorneys. In Texas, a further 65 lawyers are in Houston, 20 in Austin and ten in Fort Worth. In mid-2017 the firm is moving from its current "dated" offices in Houston to an office nearer the center of downtown. "It looks very nice based on the sketches – we're basically designing it ourselves in a very modern way."

> "The partners stay in touch with the associates to make sure everyone has enough hours but is not overwhelmed."

Hours & Pro Bono
In order to be eligible for a discretionary bonus and advance to the next pay scale, first-years need to bill 1,900 hours (2,000 after the first year) including pro bono. They also need to rack up a further 200 hours of 'firm investment' time – "that seems like a lot at first, but it's a ludicrously easy target to hit and can include lunchtime CLEs, summer associate activities, lunch with clients, reading legal articles and so on." Overall, said one associate, "I have had zero trouble reaching the billing target."

"We work hard here," a junior told us, "but the partners stay in touch with the associates to make sure everyone has enough hours but is not overwhelmed." Juniors usually start work at 8.30/9am and leave anywhere from 6pm to 7.30pm on a regular day, though "if I'm busy I'll be here until 10pm," one said. Some like to work from home in the evenings, and "when we have a client emergency you have to work on the weekend – that's what we're paid for." And that pay just got better – T&K recently followed the market and increased associate salaries, with first-years now getting $180,000.

> "When we have a client emergency you have to work on the weekend – that's what we're paid for."

T&K awards up to 50 hours of pro bono toward the billable hours requirement, although associates can "send a request asking for additional hours to be counted, which is usually approved." Some juniors do as many as 150 to 200 hours; some do fewer. Associates work on probate, divorce, bankruptcy and corporate pro bono matters. The firm also works with the Dallas Volunteer Attorney Program and Habitat for Humanity, among other organizations.

Pro bono hours
- For all attorneys across all US offices: 3,254
- Average per US attorney: 27

Community Involvement & Diversity
Community involvement is something the firm seeks to promote beyond its pro bono commitments too. "We have identified various civic initiatives which partners and associates can get involved in. For example volunteering for various charitable organizations," says managing partner Mark Sloan.

The firm's Women's Initiative also "does events for charity. For instance, before the holidays we stuffed stockings to give to homeless children." Overall some associates said the firm "does what it can" when it comes to diversity, while others felt "more could be done." Sources agreed that "I think we're getting better – T&K used to be seen as a conservative old-school firm and unfairly still perhaps has that reputation." At the time of our research around half of juniors were women and a significant proportion were from ethnic minority backgrounds.

> "Our new managing partner is aiming for us to be a 'super-regional' firm."

Strategy & Future
T&K's strategy for the future is also focused on local links. One associate told us: "Our new managing partner is aiming for us to be a 'super-regional' firm – our roots are in Texas and that is our home, but we want to have a strong national presence too." Mark Sloan – who became managing partner in February 2016 – explains that the firm's focus remains squarely on Texas, as it seeks to maintain its market position in the face of competition from out-of-state firms entering the market. The out-of-state offices are specialized and focus on specific practice areas such as trial and real estate capital markets and the needs of specific clients within those areas.

The Inside View

See firm profile on p.662

Vedder Price

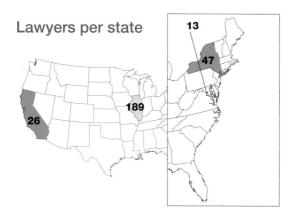

Lawyers per state

13
47
189
26

Largest US office: Chicago
US offices: 5
International offices: 2
First-year salary: $180,000
Billable hours: 2,000 required
Summers 2017: 13 (12 2Ls, 1 1L)
Revenue 2016: $239.8 million (+0.6%)
Partners made in 2017: 4 (all US)
Famous for: transport finance titan

A high-flier in asset finance, Vedder Price offers its junior associates great transport links to other practices too.

PLANES, trains and automobiles may call to mind the 1987 classic movie starring Steve Martin and John Candy, but they also (along with ships) make up Chicago-headquartered Vedder Price's rocket-fueled transportation finance practice. The aviation finance group especially speeds through the legal rankings stratosphere, and shipping finance isn't far behind. But a glance at Vedder's other *Chambers USA* rankings shows the firm offers a range of less niche practices too, including corporate/M&A, banking & finance, bankruptcy/restructuring, labor & employment, white collar litigation, and investment funds. While hiring partner Michael Waters acknowledges that his firm has *"one of the strongest transportation finance groups in the world,"* he also highlights that *"Vedder is very much a full-service firm."*

Junior associate interviewees considered the mid-sizer *"an excellent option if you're looking for a smaller place with the resources of a larger firm."* With close to 300 lawyers working from five US offices, Vedder is steadily growing. In 2016, it opened its second overseas office, in Singapore, to boost transport finance operations in the Far East. This followed a London launch five years before. Vedder's West Coast presence dates from 2013 and 2014 when it set up in San Fran and LA respectively.

The Work
The three groups on offer at Vedder are corporate, litigation, and labor & employment, and summers go straight into their department of choice. They will re-join their groups when they start as first-year associates (all being well). All three practices operate a free market system of work distribution, *"so it's up to you to fall into relationships and seek out work,"* we heard. Several interviewees had already forged links with partners during the summer so *"hit the ground running – since the first year I've never had to seek out work."* They were full of praise for the *"self-regulating system. It's really nice as it allows me to focus on what I want to do."*

Global transportation finance (GTF) is the highest-flying corporate subgroup, where at least some of the assets can fly. Newcomers quickly found lift-off themselves: *"They certainly challenge us. One of the ways we compete with larger firms is by asking a lot of associates."* Day-to-day this includes *"drafting credit and security agreements, managing closings, and directly contacting clients. The firm welcomes you reaching out to clients to move things forward."* The manner in which the wheels of asset finance turn means *"the workload is very cyclical, with no consistency month to month, but overall there's always enough"* to get airborne and hit hours targets.

"The incredible amount of responsibility is a double-edged sword."

On chambers-associate.com...
- More about aviation finance

See firm profile on p.663

Rankings in *Chambers USA*

Banking & Finance	Labor & Employment
Bankruptcy/Restructuring	Litigation
Corporate/M&A	Transportation
Investment Funds	

For detail on ranking tiers and ranking locations, visit
www.chambersandpartners.com

Elsewhere in corporate, the finance & transactions team tackles *"commercial finance work and M&A under the finance banner."* Associates had handled due diligence, document review and ancillary drafting, telling us they got *"an incredible amount of responsibility – a double-edged sword as it's high stress but great for learning."* Some who'd specialized in finance had been eager to see more M&A work, but recognized *"it's not a bad thing I haven't as I'd probably be overloaded."* Other corporate sub-teams include investment services (*"there's trustee, fund and adviser counsel as well as broker-dealer work; I'm pleasantly surprised to get a lot of autonomy"*) and financial institutions (*"banking, regulatory and M&A – under the Trump administration it looks like there'll be more of the latter."*)

There's some fluidity between the litigation and labor & employment groups, so interviewees here could swim in both pools. One had dealt with *"a lot of discrimination cases, securities work, accounting malpractice, and some IP,"* while another handled *"government-side litigation, as well as data privacy and some immigration stuff."* In these departments *"research is kind of standard; we also do a lot of writing of motions and memos."* People felt they got *"a lot of freedom. There were times I thought I was thrown in the deep end, but I always came out better for it."*

Training & Development

Associates are assessed twice a year in their first four years, and once a year after that. *"There's an interview process after the review committee meets,"* during which *"you get comments and recommendations from partners, then they assign you a grade."* While interviewees felt *"such a formal process doesn't always allow for day-to-day feedback,"* several were *"very proud to say I get constructive feedback every day."* Training on top of that comes from *"a pretty robust CLE program, especially practice-specific CLEs,"* though juniors again favored a more informal education. *"On the job is the only way lawyers learn; if you don't get your feet in the mud you're not learning,"* one declared. *"The busier you are the more likely you are to do well."* Others were satisfied by *"a good mix of formal and on-the-job training."*

"If you don't get your feet in the mud you're not learning."

Recent work highlights

- Represented a group of financial institutions to secure $1 billion funding for Alaska Airlines in its acquisition of Virgin America
- Advised investment firm (and aviation finance specialists) Castlelake on its second and third securitization issuances, with a combined value of $1.63 billion
- Acted for commercial bank PrivateBancorp during its $3.8 billion acquisition by Canadian 'Big Five' bank CIBC
- Defended Breaking Media – publishers of legal blog AboveTheLaw – in potential-seven figure defamation lawsuit

Get Hired

"I was asked what my favorite airplane was – I answered incorrectly, apparently!" chambers-associate.com has more interview insight and info on recruitment at Vedder.

Offices & Culture

Vedder has two offices on each of the East and West Coasts, complementing its 190-lawyer Chicago HQ: *"Location-wise it's great, right in the Chicago Loop."* One source described the décor as *"like out of* Beetlejuice*,"* but renovations are underway and *"the new layout looks really good."* The New York team has just moved to a different floor in Paramount Plaza *"right in midtown,"* and the new setup is *"a lot more modern – we have our own window offices."* Vedder also has smaller bases in Los Angeles, San Francisco and Washington, DC as well as London and now Singapore. Associates appreciated both the 'one firm' policy – *"my understanding is it's better than most firms because of our size and congeniality"* – and conservative thinking. *"Management won't spend money needlessly; we don't work in the biggest shiniest building because we don't need to."*

"We still have that Midwest mentality."

The *"more conservative setting"* also impacts culture *"in the sense that everyone comes here to work, but you don't make the firm your entire life."* That means *"when things are busy you work hard, but when they're not you take advantage of that and leave earlier."* Insiders reckoned *"the culture in LA is a bit different as people get in later and wear more casual clothing,"* but every office *"still has that Midwest mentality. Everyone works hard but I don't feel they're super-stressed out, and there's not one person I've met who's a total bummer."* Associates were also pleased with Vedder's conservative financial strategy, revealed via regular state of the firm addresses. These provide *"transparency,"* supplemented by emails providing daily

See firm profile on p.663

The Inside View

Diversity	Partners (%)	Associates (%)
Women	18	41
White	92	78
Black/African American	1	6
Hispanic/Latin American	3	3
Asian	4	10
Mixed/Other	0	3
LGBT	2	2

or weekly breakdowns of financials and anonymous lists of associates' billed hours.

"Opportunities are there" to get know colleagues outside of work, and like at many firms *"most of the social stuff happens during summer,"* from sports to wine tasting. Asked how many partake in events year-round, sources explained that *"some associates love going out, others would rather have more balance with their own lives. Relations between associates are very positive. The size of the firm means anyone brought in wants to rise to partner level; associates don't compete."* The firm's new women's initiative, WAVES Women At Vedder Empowering Success, *"does really well"* attracting associates to happy hours and book clubs.

Diversity

Acknowledging *"there's still a lot of white-haired white men at the top,"* Vedder juniors told us *"it's getting better across the board. Like at any firm, the higher up you get the more it's a relic of traditional ways."* The firm regularly visits various minority careers fairs and takes one diverse 1L summer associate each year. In 2015 it launched the WAVES initiative to complement Vedder Diverse (an affinity group for minority attorneys) and host *"great meetings"* to promote gender diversity. With these groups making waves, sources concluded *"the resources are certainly there. What the firm is up against is how to maintain good talent."* We heard that a female lawyer on maternity leave in 2016 was subsequently promoted to partner – strong evidence that the firm is tackling the issue in a supportive way.

"It's getting better across the board."

Hours & Compensation

"In true Vedder fashion, they took the time they needed" to match the increased Cravath salary scale. Some were concerned by *"radio silence – we had no idea whether to expect the raise and were kept out of the loop,"* suggesting *"a lot of advocacy by associates was needed"* to secure the

increases. Others argued *"they took the time to work it out properly"* and didn't *"fault them for taking the time to decide."*

"Some were more sensitive about the change."

To go with the salary hike, the firm also bumped its bonus eligibility target from 1,850 to 2,000 (though associates have been encouraged to aim for 2,000 for a while). So is the extra dough worth longer days? For many corporate associates *"2,000 is definitely achievable, and the extra money is a great added perk,"* but those in other practice areas were less thrilled. *"Some were more sensitive about the change as they found it hard to hit 1,850. There might be worries if you don't hit it, but what matters more is that you're billing as much as your peers."*

"There turned out to be additional expenses but the firm didn't bat an eye."

Pro Bono

Vedder has also doubled the pro bono hours associates can count as billable. While there was some complaint that the new 60 hour allotment *"is still a little low,"* the vast majority appreciated the increase. A pro bono coordinator sends out routine emails listing opportunities varying from prisoners' rights cases to divorce issues. One associate *"brought in my own pro bono matter, and ran it past the coordinator. There turned out to be additional expenses but the firm didn't bat an eye."* Some were too busy to get involved, but agreed *"Vedder is definitely committed to pro bono, and for some people it's definitely not underutilized."*

Pro bono hours
- For all US attorneys: undisclosed
- Average per US attorney: undisclosed

Strategy & Future

Vedder has slowly but surely grown its network over the last few years; Singapore is the latest addition. Operating shareholder Doug Hambleton explains *"the new location gives us ready access to Asian businesses in aviation and maritime finance. We're not looking to simply plant a flag in a new place."* Being relatively small and mighty suits the firm, according to Hambleton: *"Vedder doesn't seek to acquire other firms or merge, we're not a mega-firm and don't seek to be one. We try to build on the strengths we already have and maintain the edge we have in those areas."*

See firm profile on p.663

Venable LLP

Lawyers per state

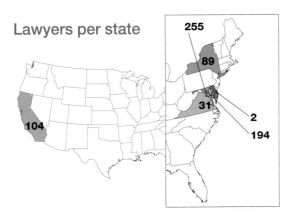

255
89
31
2
194
104

Largest US office: Washington, DC

US offices: 9

International offices: 0

First-year salary: $180,000

Billable hours: 1,950 to be bonus eligible

Summers 2017: 35 (all 2Ls)

Revenue 2016: $498.5 million (+4.4%)

Partners made in 2017: 11

Famous for: roof-top bocce court, all things regulatory

Rooftop bocce is just one of the things that distinguishes this DC and Baltimore-heavy national firm.

IT is often said of Baltimore that it's a southern city that just happens to be in the north. The reason for this is not because it has exquisite seafood – though it does – or because it gets mighty hot in the summertime, though that's true too; but because it has the kind of genteel and traditional culture that many people associate with Southern cities. A similar down-to-earth nature and warmth of personality was given time and again by sources asked what drew them to Baltimore-founded Venable. *"In my interview an associate told me he had to kick colleagues out of his office because they were having too much fun. That's a good cultural problem to have."*

The DC office eclipsed Baltimore's headcount a while back and is now officially the main office, but *"historically and spiritually Baltimore is home, even though Washington gets the most business and has the most variety of practices."* Further up the Eastern Seaboard, the firm has a growing presence in Delaware and New York. Over on the West Coast, its LA and San Francisco offices continue to expand. *Chambers USA* especially recognizes Venable's advertising, privacy & data, and REITs work nationwide. In its home state Venable gets top nods for real estate and corporate/M&A.

On chambers-associate.com...

- All you need to know about bocce
- Interview with hiring partner Larry Gesner

The Work

Regulatory is where the bulk of DC newbies will find themselves, but elsewhere commercial litigation, labor & employment and corporate are the firm's bread and butter. Under these umbrella practices sit specialist niches like product liability, real estate and IP. In the bigger offices (DC, Baltimore, LA and New York) placement is decided at the end of the summer – *"you rank all the practices available then about a week or two before you start you get a letter with your allocation. As far as I know they try hard to give you one of your top two."*

Assignment is fairly informal: *"You form relationships with partners early on, and then they usually just assign stuff one-on-one. It means you have to be quite open at first but everyone's really friendly so it's not hard."* This does mean that juniors have to be diligent about telling partners when they've got too much work on: *"There's no one controlling my workflow and quite early on I was a tad overwhelmed. So I talked to one of the partners I was working for and since then they've kept a track of what I'm doing."* Smaller groups have *"bi-weekly meetings with one partner during which assignments are given out."*

> *"You have to be quite open at first but everyone's really friendly so it's not hard."*

Sources reported high level tasks from the get-go: *"They staff very leanly here so on a deal it'll be just me and a partner or me and a mid-level associate. When it's the for-*

The Inside View

See firm profile on p.664

Rankings in *Chambers USA*

Advertising	Intellectual Property
Bankruptcy/Restructuring	Labor & Employment
Corporate/M&A	Leisure & Hospitality
Employee Benefits & Executive Compensation	Litigation
	Privacy & Data Security
Energy & Natural Resources	Products Liability
	Real Estate
Environment	REITs
Government	Retail
Healthcare	Technology

For detail on ranking tiers and ranking locations, visit www.chambersandpartners.com

Recent work highlights

- Advised Merkle Group as the marketing agency sold its majority stake in London-headquartered Dentsu Aegis Network
- Acted for Vibrant Media during a case that tested whether placing cookies on users' devices violated federal statutes
- Defending McDonald's in a nationwide class action that questions the purity of the fast food giant's mozzarella sticks
- Acted for BP as the energy giant filed a complaint against a Sunoco pipeline company for misconduct

mer, I'll be the one managing the calendar, which means you get to look at the master plan and speak up for the opportunities you want. They're looking for associates that want to take the reins on transactions." Over in litigation they're "doing the standard researching. But also a lot of the time first years will be doing the first draft of a brief." Real estate juniors cheerfully told of "starting out doing mainly due diligence and small lease drafting tasks," and then "after you've proved yourself you could be negotiating smaller leases."

Culture

Interviewees highlighted a discernible cultural difference between Venable's East and West Coast operations: "Obviously DC and Baltimore have had decades to define themselves and they both have hundreds of lawyers, whereas LA and San Francisco are new offices and need a bit of time to forge their own identities." As with most of Venable's newer outlets, the Californian duo were started by merging with local boutique firms and "bringing across lateral partners, who a lot of the time will come with their own associates." This often meant a "disparate collective made up of two or three tightly-knit groups."

On the East Coast, however, "the culture still very much stems from Baltimore." And, without paying too much heed to regional stereotypes, "there's a folksy down-to-earth atmosphere that I think you wouldn't necessarily get from a DC or New York-founded firm." This attitude prevails across all levels, associates said, and partners "aren't there to bring you down but really to guide you. They understand the stress of being an associate and they're very embracive when you make faults – there are no 'shouters' here."

"There's a folksy down-to-earth atmosphere that you wouldn't necessarily get from a DC or New York-founded firm."

In fact, the only time things seem to get competitive at Venable are during the annual summer bocce tournaments in DC. For all those unfamiliar with bocce, it's like the French game boules, played by throwing a ball and trying to get it nearest to a jack (smaller ball). This prosaic definition belies an intense competition – "you play with a partner and there are three rounds before the final. It gets pretty heated and there's a trophy that the winners parade around with." The firm is soon to move into new purpose-built DC digs, and "one of the first things that went on the blueprints was the roof-top bocce court."

Hours & Compensation

There is a reduced billable target for first-years of 1,800 hours, which increases to 1,900 for second-years and above. To be bonus eligible, juniors must hit 1,950 – of which 50 hours can be pro bono work. That bonus "increases in 50-hour increments over 1,900" and this, coupled with the fact that Venable matched the market salary in 2016, means "if you're thinking in the short-term, you can actually earn more here than at the traditional mega firms, even though our bonuses are way below market."

This is significant since "this is a firm that doesn't want you to be dying because of work," but it's also "a place where the work is there – there's not a day when you won't find eight hours to bill. As a junior you're never just sitting there and waiting for work."

Pro Bono

As mentioned above, pro bono is encouraged by the fact that associates can count 50 hours of it toward their billables. However, other than that "it isn't necessarily pushed to the front of the agenda, it's more about you putting yourself out there or expressing an interest in a particular area. If you do that, people will bring you opportunities." A lot of the firm's affiliates are in the DC/Maryland area and include the Historical Society of Washington, House of Ruth (a charity for sufferers of domestic vio-

See firm profile on p.664

The Inside View

Diversity	Partners (%)	Associates (%)
Women	undisclosed	undisclosed
White	-	-
Black/African American	-	-
Hispanic/Latin American	-	-
Asian	-	-
Mixed/Other	-	-
LGBT	-	-

lence), the Tahirih Justice Center, and Kids in Need of Defense. There's also a pro bono fellowship that sends an attorney full-time to a local non-profit, while the Venable Foundation, founded in 1983, donates to a wide variety of organizations.

Pro bono hours
- For all attorneys: 29,254
- Average per attorney: 43

Training & Development

Training is *"very much an informal process"* which sources preferred to *"time-consuming, sit-down sessions."* The firm understands that some might want an educational top-up once in a while and so is *"very receptive to you attending conferences and outside workshops and is very happy to pay for those."* With such a quick turnover of work and a more informal approach to training, associates felt that substantial feedback was sometimes hard to come by – *"there's an annual review and they're very fast. Mine was scheduled for 15 minutes but it lasted five."*

That said, there are ample forums in which junior attorneys can air their grievances: *"There's a junior panel which is a safe space to ask any questions to more senior associates and you are also assigned an associate mentor and a preceptor, the latter of whom takes you on client meetings and gives you training-type exercises to complete."*

Offices

Venable's DC contingent moved to new digs at the beginning of 2017. *"It's really pretty and all glass, so everyone at least has natural light. There's also a nice restaurant in the basement. Everyone's really excited because partners keep dropping by to say they've just been to Italy to choose new marble for the surfaces."* There's also a gym, bar and roof terrace. Over in San Francisco they're ahead of the curve of modernity – *"it's all glass interiors here and definitely not the standard law firm mahogany look. It fits with the culture of the city and our clients."*

All new starters at the firm get their own office from day one and Baltimore associates – whose home overlooks the city's historic Inner Harbor – praised the *"ample space, more than you'd get in other big cities. When you start they walk you into this big office with a great view over the harbor and you think, 'yes, I've arrived!'"*

"Yes, I've arrived!"

Diversity

Diversity, however, is an area in which Venables might still be waiting on the platform – *"I don't know how much they promote it,"* one associate reflected. *"I always felt like I wanted more, so I had to look outside the firm for networking events."* That said, *"there is a strong women's group, WAVE [Women at Venable], which meets quarterly and invites special guests to come and talk about female issues in the law."* There is also the Venable Success Group for diverse attorneys that holds biennial get togethers with speakers and workshops.

Get Hired

Many interviewees had been involved in the interview process soon after joining the firm. They advised: *"Venable generally looks for people who seem like they can hold their own. Like they can hold a conversation and that they have a life outside law school."* Another elaborated: *"Venable seems to place a lot of store on whether people have worked between law school or have some other passion or interest in the outside world."* Once they have passed through the OCIs, potential recruits can expect a callback where they'll meet with up to a dozen lawyers from the firm. *"It might sound intimidating but it's structured in a way where you meet one-on-one and everyone's really nice."*

Strategy & Future

Sources took succor from the fact that *"most of the partners in DC and Baltimore were first-years at the firm."* Across the board, there was belief that *"Venable is genuinely interested in people making partner. They tell you that from the start they will do their best to help you get to the top."* Going forward, associates believed the firm's strategy of acquiring smaller boutique firms in key locations and growing like that was going to continue – *"Venable occupies kind of a strange space in the legal market. It is Am Law 100 but almost right at the top of the mid-level. It means partners make a little bit less but they are invested in helping the firm grow so it can reach the top."*

"Venable is genuinely interested in people making partner."

See firm profile on p.664

Vinson & Elkins LLP

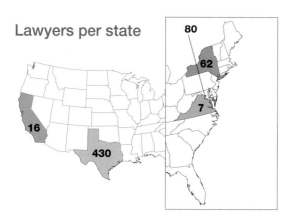

Lawyers per state

80
62
7
16
430

Largest US office: Houston
US offices: 8
International offices: 7
First-year salary: $180,000
Billable hours: 2,000 target
Summers 2017: 97 (75 2Ls, 20 1Ls, 2 others)
Revenue 2016: $653.9 million (+4.2%)
Partners made in 2017: 7
Famous for: Texan charm, energy supremos

As this Texan powerhouse celebrates its 100th birthday it continues to reap the rewards of a diverse practice...

INTERVIEWEES described Vinson & Elkins in impressive terms: *"It's THE name in Texas,"* proffered one. *"You don't really get much bigger in the energy sector,"* another said. *"In terms of prestige, it's the 'Cravath of the South',"* a third associate added. One thing's for sure, however you want to phrase it: this Texan powerhouse – which celebrates its 100th birthday in 2017 – has got the walk to match the talk.

> *"Those with an entrepreneurial disposition are best suited."*

Known primarily for its work in the oil and gas sectors, in the past ten years or so the firm has worked hard to diversify its practice. Despite nosediving oil prices, in 2016 Vinson posted the second-highest revenue in its 100-year history. And *Chambers USA* recognizes this versatility, awarding the firm top tier nationwide rankings for its energy practice, but also commending areas including general litigation, IP, capital markets, corporate/M&A, and tax in its home state. Diversification has also meant expansion out of Texas, with offices in New York, San Francisco, Palo Alto, DC, and most recently Richmond, complementing those in Austin, Dallas and firm HQ in Houston.

On chambers-associate.com...

- Vinson's vocations: more on the work
- Interview with hiring partner Doug Bland

The Work

At the end of their summer, associates are asked to rank their practice preferences as well as which office they'd like to join. Of the seven offices mentioned above, all except Palo Alto and San Francisco take first-years. And as for a practice, though you are officially designated a niche, *"if you want to experience it all you can. That means those with an entrepreneurial disposition are best suited, because you can pick up different work really easily in the beginning. Though, as you advance, there is pressure to specialize."*

As to where you can specialize, the corporate options are: capital markets/M&A (MACM), which accounts for around half of transactional associates; finance; tax; real estate; shareholder activism; and ETP energy transactions, only available in Houston. Those of a litigious bent can choose between: complex commercial litigation (CCL), which makes up about two thirds of the operation; appellate; environmental; international dispute resolution; securities; energy regulatory; and bankruptcy. And, there's also IP, *"which is sort of its own thing,"* but is still officially part of litigation.

Even though the powers-that-be recently moved to merge the capital markets and M&A teams, they are *"still pretty much distinct."* As a first-year associate you tend to be involved in at least some MACM work. Sources reported responsibility levels that were *"very deal and relationship-dependent"* and really *"based on how long you've been working for the company."* That said, they're still pretty high-level, *"anywhere from nearly running the*

See firm profile on p.665

The Inside View

Rankings in *Chambers USA*

Antitrust	Government
Appellate Law	Intellectual Property
Banking & Finance	International Trade
Bankruptcy/Restructuring	Labor & Employment
Capital Markets	Latin American Investment
Climate Change	Litigation
Corporate/M&A	Projects
Energy & Natural	Real Estate
Resources	Tax
Environment	Technology

For detail on ranking tiers and ranking locations, visit
www.chambersandpartners.com

Recent work highlights

- Advised Memorial Resource Development Corp. in a $4.4 billion all-stock merger with Range Resources Corporation.
- Represented Vantage Energy in a $2.7 billion purchase-and-sale agreement with Rice Energy Inc.
- Served as underwriters' counsel in Silver Run Acquisition Corp. II's $1 billion IPO
- Represented NorthStar Realty Finance Corp. in a $16 billion three-way merger with NorthStar Asset Management Group, Inc. and Colony Capital, Inc.
- Advised the sponsors, AES Corp. and the Motta Group, and their subsidiaries, Gas Natural Atlantico and Costa Norte LNG Terminal, in the $535 million project financing of the Colón LNG-to-Power Project.

deal" to *"a more quarterback role – consolidating all the work together and making sure the partners have all the necessary paperwork."* Things are pretty similar over in litigation, in the sense that *"you've got to be detail-oriented"* and *"do some grunt work"* on the bigger cases; but on smaller ones *"it'll just be you and a partner and in that case you're drafting motions, attending hearings and doing witness prep."*

Culture

While we are loath to indulge in regional stereotyping, almost every V&E associate we spoke to said that a certain Texas way of doing things permeates the firm. One NYC source expanded: *"I talk to my friends at the large white shoe firms and it's clear that the Texan culture shines through. It's open-door and you can talk to anybody. It's competitive but there's a lack of cutthroatedness."* Another interviewee spoke of a pervasive bonhomie – *"the word 'fratty' comes up on the* Vault *survey, which makes it sound quite negative. But I think it means that people tend to enjoy themselves in the office, to not be quite as dry. They like having people around at all times and everyone likes the people they work with."*

"The Texan culture shines through."

The social life at V&E reflects this – *"from junior associates up to partners, everyone's always up for getting together at least once a month."* These get-togethers usually take place during firm-sponsored happy hours at local bars. In DC the firm hosts an annual charity event where they make up a big space like a casino and bring in professional dealers to *"do it right and we all try to win money for a great cause."* Over in Houston spooky goings on were reported at the firm's annual Hallowe'en bash when *"everyone in the office brings in their kids to do trick or treat between floors,"* the other offices host similar gatherings. But the jewel in the crown of this year's social calendar must be V&E's 100th year anniversary party in April at Houston HQ. All-firm events usually take place every three years, but for the big 100 *"they're flying eve-*ryone plus a guest to Houston for three days of conferences and dancing."*

Training & Development

All attorneys will be familiar with the Houston base because everyone spends their first three days there doing team-building and general training. Then, when they return home, they'll have a week of *"meetings being taught how to use your computer, or who to contact if you need document processing, or the librarian will come in and show you how to get hold of certain materials."* After this initial flurry, there are weekly CLEs – *"one week it'll be a partner who does a lot of leasing and the next we might have one on real estate finance; next month we have tax lawyers coming in from a different office to impart their wisdom."*

The firm also has in place an extensive mentorship scheme designed to help juniors develop and grow. New starters are assigned both a partner and associate mentor to ease them into firm life. Then, after six months, you get to choose your own formal mentor. There is still further support offered by the firm's careers consultant, who travels around all of the offices imparting wisdom and offering an outlet for any associate concerns.

Hours & Compensation

Though there is no concrete billable target it's *"generally understood"* that associates need to hit 2,000 hours to be bonus-eligible. After this bonuses are tiered at 2,150 (x1.1) and 2,300 (x1.25) hours. There was universal praise for Vinson matching the increased Cravath scale in 2016. Sources didn't sugar-coat the fact that working at V&E means long hours. There's not exactly a face-time culture, but *"people would not be pleased if I just bolted before 5pm."* All-nighters aren't a given, but they do happen – *"in my two years here I've pulled four."* And interviewees agreed that the *"Friday afternoon document dump that ensures you're working the weekend"* was not unheard of.

The Inside View

See firm profile on p.665

Diversity	Partners (%)	Associates (%)
Women	15	38
White	90	79
Black/African American	1	4
Hispanic/Latin American	4	4
Asian	2	9
Mixed/Other	3	2
LGBT	3	2

Offices

Over half of the juniors on our interviewee list were based in Houston, which *"definitely feels like the home office,"* not least because *"it offers the fullest range of practices to incoming associates."* It also boasts the only private Starbucks in the country. The firm's second-largest office, Dallas, has plans to move to brand new digs in the near future – *"I can see it being built out my window... It's just a hole in the ground now but when it's finished it's going to be magnificent!"*

> *"It's just a hole in the ground now but when it's finished it's going to be magnificent!"*

New York associates appreciated the fact that their office has *"all the resources – librarians, subscriptions, CLEs and experts"* that *"a large firm can provide,"* but with *"the smaller office atmosphere of a more boutique establishment."* A discerning bunch, they did however have some qualms with the office's recent renovation – *"they seem to have changed the carpet though the new one is just as bad as the old one, which seems kind of pointless."* DC interviewees were pleased with their office's location both for its *"excellent transport links"* as well as the dozen or so nice bars and restaurants found in the retail space below.

Pro Bono

Pro bono is definitely on the agenda at V&E, though transactional lawyers – who of course make up the majority of the firm – thought it *"much easier to find litigation work."* That said, an unlimited number of pro bono hours count toward the bonus target which, coupled with twice monthly awards for those that bill the most, *"offers more than enough incentive to get involved."* In Texas, the firm is heavily involved with Houston Volunteer Lawyers who deal with things like immigration, helping veterans and the homeless, as well as landlord/tenant disputes for those who struggle with legal fees. Meanwhile, up in New York after President Trump's executive immigration ban, *"a bunch of V&E lawyers went down to JFK to help out those facing deportation."*

Pro bono hours
- For all US attorneys: 23,261
- Average per US attorney: 42

Diversity

Sources felt that when it came to diversity at the firm, more was being done to improve the gender rather than the racial ratio. The Women's Initiative is particularly active, holding a big all-firm lunch once a year as well as a new lunch series: *"You put in a request for a female partner. Then they set up lunches with you, another associate and two female partners."* There are also a number of diversity-related events taking place at the 100th anniversary weekender – *"the Women's Initiative is hosting a brunch for all the female attorneys and there is a big forum taking place for all the diverse attorneys."*

Get Hired

One source described V&E's OCI process as *"one of the more easy interviews."* But not *"easy in terms of the questions asked, just that it was more of a conversation instead of an interrogation – I felt like they were trying to get to know me as a person."* As far as the questions go, *"it's not weird behavioral stuff like at Google"* – they ask *"pretty standard stuff"* but *"I think potential recruits will find that we quickly try to get away from the résumé."* What it came down to, as one source succinctly put it, was *"when I'm sitting in a conference room at 3am eating my Seamless – do I want to talk to you about something other than work?"*

Strategy & Future

As mentioned previously, V&E has worked hard to diversify its practice away from its energy roots, a move that has proved incredibly shrewd in the long-run: *"We've actually got a really renowned restructuring group that have benefited from the oil downturn. Last year was our second most profitable ever. Showing that the firm's done a great job positioning itself."* Associates are offered an outlet for any grievances, and an insight into the firm's decision-making, at all-associate meetings – *"we can submit questions anonymously and discuss candidly the direction that the firm is headed."*

> **"I think potential recruits will find that we quickly try to get away from the résumé."**

See firm profile on p.665

The Inside View

Waller

Lawyers per state

Largest US office: Nashville
US offices: 4
International offices: 0
First-year salary: $115,000
Billable hours: 1,800 target
Summers 2017: 12 (9 2Ls, 3 1Ls)
Revenue 2016: undisclosed
Partners made in 2017: 7
Famous for: healthcare law; Tennessee heritage

Tennessee's top dogs have a healthy pedigree.

"NASHVILLE is the epicenter of healthcare in America, and the growth of Nashville has been great for the firm," several associates stressed. Indeed, Music City's biggest industry is actually healthcare – nearly 400 health companies are based here. Director of recruiting Bobby Weiss is quick to point out that *"Waller is unique in that we have the depth, experience and prowess of a healthcare boutique, while also providing full service offerings to the financial services, retail, hospitality, advanced manufacturing and technology industries."Chambers USA* backs this up, awarding Waller top rankings in Tennessee for these and other areas.

Most interviewees (but not all) had attended Southern law schools. All were attracted here by the 112-year-old's reputation: *"We've built that since our inception."* Bobby Weiss adds that *"you can do meaningful work on sophisticated matters. To an extent (it varies by office), Nashville and Austin in particular have become destination cities, and we've embraced that. This has helped to attract both solicited and unsolicited candidates without local backgrounds to the firm. We get a good mix of both locals and non-locals."*

On chambers-associate.com...

- We chat to chairman Matt Burnstein and recruiting director Bobby Weiss
- Get Hired: For those who want to holler at Waller for a job
- Music copyright and Waller

The Work

Most incoming juniors do either corporate or litigation work, some with a healthcare focus. A handful work in practices including labor & employment, IP, tax, immigration, and commercial finance. Even if they're not formally attached to the healthcare group, juniors should be ready to dish out some legal medicine as *"everyone at Waller does some healthcare work."* Interviewees generally had enjoyed *"a lot of client contact – not something that you need to push for. From day one you're involved in conference calls, and over time you get more direct client contact."*

"The firm as a whole has made its name in healthcare," associates emphasized. On the transactional side, they can expect to assist on M&A deals and/or securities offerings which *"can totally range in deal size from a small imaging center to a hundred million dollar hospital"* or *"from deals worth hundreds of thousands to a billion plus."* Over in litigation, juniors see *"a lot of medical malpractice, product liability, and government investigations for clients like hospitals and manufacturers."* The *"great thing about Waller is that unlike friends who practice in the big cities and spend 75% of their first year doing research, here we're in court straight away and take depositions."* Even newbies *"do everything from pre-suit background investigations and research to developing the complaint or answer, to preparing and answering discovery, and going to trial. If you're interested in something, you get to do it."*That said, there's still *"a lot of research and writing."* General commercial litigation includes *"lots of breach of contract work, fraud, and shareholder/partnerships disputes. The group also has a very strong white collar healthcare investigations and*

The Inside View

Rankings in *Chambers USA*

Banking & Finance	Labor & Employment
Corporate/M&A	Litigation
Environment	Media & Entertainment
Healthcare	Real Estate

For detail on ranking tiers and ranking locations, visit
www.chambersandpartners.com

Recent work highlights

- Provided special healthcare and real estate due diligence counsel in the acquisition of Ardent Health Services by Ventas, valued at $1.75 billion
- Worked as lead counsel to Spectrum Emery Development Company on the $350 million+ redevelopment of Nashville Convention Center
- Defended the songwriters and publishers behind Justin Bieber hit "Sorry" in a copyright infringement case alleging that the song's hook had been stolen
- Oversaw financing and branding of new $15 million Stanza Nashville boutique hotel

fraud practice, and some partners have developed more niche areas."

"If you're interested in something, you get to do it."

For corporate associates starting out there's a *"good variety of stuff too: a lot of due diligence, research, memos, drafting ancillary documents and smaller documents beyond purchase agreements. Larger scale deals are done by more senior associates. As you progress, partners allow you to take more responsibility in certain areas when you are ready."* The type of work juniors do *"runs the gamut depending on how the deal is staffed and how much rope the partners give you."* One summed up: *"At first, you do whatever needs to be done. In the second year you're given more freedom and responsibility to draft as you see fit and take more of a role in transactions."*

Associates usually fill in a weekly availability chart. This system works *"to an extent; it's not perfect but we know that would be impossible! I'm really happy as I never have to go looking for work."* Another source was also *"happy with the workload. I would rather have more work than less, and I've never felt overwhelmed. It feels like responsibility increases over time and you get opportunities to delegate to other people, including younger associates."*

Training & Development

A *"bit basic"* boot camp soon after starting orients new recruits. *"The best training is doing real work."* Practice-specific sessions include talks by partners, training lunches, and *"a lot of it is trial by fire, learning by doing."* Associates saw this as *"probably the best way to learn. It's a little nerve-racking, but provides good experience. You are kind of thrown into it, but there is oversight."* Appraisals involve an annual (February) and a mid-year review (August). The latter is *"especially helpful as it lets you know if anything's wrong before it's too late."* Interviewees also valued more informal advice, which *"varies from partner to partner."*

"A lot of it is trial by fire."

Culture & Diversity

"There's a close-knit culture within my practice group," a representative associate found. *"We're all on the same floor and all work together to some degree. It's a large firm so you don't necessarily know everybody, though events help with this. The firm does a great job of having things once a month – a retreat, reception, cocktail hour – so you can get to know people outside your bubble."* Southern hospitality appears to be alive and well in Nashville. *"The culture is laid back, welcoming, but the work needs to get done and done well."* Family-friendliness gets a boost from occasional events like *"Hallowe'en trick or treat where those with young children walk up and down the halls getting candy."* The firm's retreat is a *"fun weekend where everybody gets away to a resort, plays golf. It was interesting to see everybody on a more personal level."*

"Everybody wants to move and live here right now..."

Music City is a modern boomtown, and interviewees loved Nashville's social scene. You don't need to be a nine-to-five working Dolly Parton nut to enjoy life here: *"Everybody wants to move and live here right now. There's something for everyone. It's not just a music town: there are so many social opportunities you can barely keep up. Sports, arts, festivals – it's all definitely a draw."* Many understandably see working in Nashville as a big perk of the job.

Get Hired

Director of recruiting Bobby Weiss advises that prospective applicants for the summer program *"need to earn a job, which comes from good work and building relationships with others."* To find out more, including our full interview with Bobby Weiss, head to chambers-associate.com.

Regarding diversity, *"it's something they're working on."* Waller's chairman is heavily involved in the cause, and

See firm profile on p.666

The Inside View

Diversity	Partners (%)	Associates (%)
Women	16	34
White	97	86
Black/African American	1.2	6
Hispanic/Latin American	0	1.2
Asian	1.8	7
Mixed/Other	0	0
LGBT	0	0

the diversity committee works with organizations like the Leadership Council on Legal Diversity, as well as local schools. Associates believed regional factors are at play: *"Nashville and the South aren't as diverse as New York or California,"* though *"genderwise, things seem pretty diverse."* Overall then Waller does *"fairly well in terms of diversity, but there's always room for improvement."*

Pro Bono

Tennessee is known as the Volunteer State, so you'd expect Waller to be pros at pro bono. Opportunities come in *"weekly emails, and there are initiatives in place if you're interested. But it's not something that's driven home to the point that you feel you need to do it if you're not interested."* Some in areas like corporate felt their *"practice doesn't lend itself to pro bono"* so *"I haven't done much myself."* The amount done *"totally depends on the individual. Emails go out but it's not a requirement like at some firms."* Some people do pro bono *"all the time"* while others *"don't want to do legal work in their free time and prefer to do other community outreach. I don't know if there's an upper threshold – if you can juggle an ordinary caseload, the sky's the limit."* Examples include working with *"the legal aid group round the corner,"* domestic violence and protection order hearings.

Pro bono hours
- For all attorneys: 2,412
- Average per attorney: 12

Hours & Compensation

The 1,800 hour billing target is *"very achievable, coming out at about 150 a month. People in general are happy with it."* Litigators preparing for trial may find themselves working *"8am to 9/10/11pm, but other days or weeks aren't as busy – 9am to 5.30pm."* While hours in most practices *"ebb and flow,"* associates we spoke to tend to arrive between 8am and 10am and leave between 6pm and 9pm: *"It varies. Different partners have different schedules, and it depends on client locations."*

"It's nice to have a system that rewards you for working above and beyond."

Associates felt the salary ($115,000 for first-years) is competitive locally, as are bonuses, which are *"explained pretty clearly. It's nice to have a system that rewards you for working above and beyond,"* with a discretionary component. One source attested: *"When I was interviewing for the position, I was told that Waller was a meritocracy, and that's proven to be very true. Those who do a good job are taken care of."* Theoretically, those in their first couple of years at the firm get two weeks vacation, but that's not set in stone. *"It's pretty fluid. If you've been doing well they won't hold you to it. Some don't take it; some probably take more."*

Strategy & Future

2016 saw the acquisition of all 13 lawyers from Taube Summers: *"They're an Austin, Texas based bankruptcy and commercial litigation firm, and have really strengthened our capability in those departments,"* chairman Matt Burnstein tells us. Austin is nicknamed the 'Live Music Capital of the World' – so the firm's a neat fit for Music City's Waller in more ways than just business. He adds that Waller *"wants to continue to grow to meet the needs of clients without growing for growth's sake. We believe strongly in a future in Texas, and Austin specifically. One of the principal objectives of our strategic plan is continually enhancing our services to clients in financial services, which we're pushing in Austin in particular."* Read our full interview with the chairman online.

"We believe strongly in a future in Texas."

Offices

The firm's Nashville headquarters take in the vast majority of new associates. Everyone gets their own office, and juniors *"couldn't be more happy"* with the resultant freedom – nor with the window view. Nashvillians also found it easy to keep in contact with the firm's other offices. Associates suggested that the cross-country working relationship was *"fairly seamless – with technology you can coordinate pretty well."* Sources reported few face-to-face meetings between those in and outside of Tennessee, but some did arise from time to time. *"Nashville is definitely the hub"* where decisions are made.

To learn about becoming a healthcare lawyer, turn to Waller's review on p.138.

See firm profile on p.666

Weil, Gotshal & Manges LLP

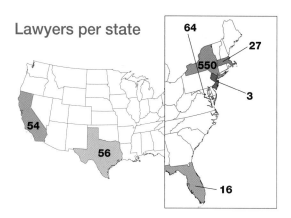

Lawyers per state

64
27
550
3
54
56
16

Largest US office: New York
US offices: 8
International offices: 11
First-year salary: $180,000
Billable hours: no target
Summers 2017: 139 (126 2Ls, 11 1Ls, 2 SEOs)
Revenue 2016: $1.26 billion (+8.6%)
Partners made in 2017: 13 (10 in US)
Famous for: high-profile bankruptcy cases and a booming M&A practice

Mammoth bankruptcy cases spring to mind whenever Weil's mentioned – but they're only one chapter in the firm's story.

THINK Weil, think bankruptcy? Sure, the octogenarian New York native has worked on some of the most colossal and high profile Chapter 11 bankruptcies around – Lehman Brothers, Enron, General Motors – but restructuring work is only a small part of Weil's offering. *"We have had our busiest and most profitable year ever in 2016 due to the true balance of our corporate, litigation and restructuring practices,"* executive partner Barry Wolf tells us. *"We've had three consecutive years of steady and significant growth in profitability leading up to this record year for us."*

"We've had three consecutive years of steady and significant growth."

The firm's corporate and litigation teams house most of its attorneys. Private equity and M&A have been major growth areas over the past 15 years, securing their status as key drivers for the firm. Both practices earn a nod from *Chambers USA*, along with other areas including bankruptcy (of course), litigation, IP, tax, banking, and media & entertainment. Weil also features as the 22nd most globally impressive firm on the *Chambers Global Top 30*.

On chambers-associate.com...

- Recruitment tips and advice
- Interview with executive partner Barry Wolf
- Weil's refreshed offices

The Work

Weil newbies are divided between four practice groups: most join sub-teams within the corporate or litigation department, while tax and business finance/restructuring each take a handful. It's worth noting that Boston only hires into private equity, that most first-years in Washington, DC slot into the regulatory, antitrust/competition, and white collar litigation groups, and that at the time of our calls all juniors in the Miami office were dedicated to complex, commercial litigation work, although real estate is on offer too.

Generally, associates in larger groups indicate their availability for work in weekly reports, while those in smaller teams often work with one or two partners who dole out work. Many associates get work through a mix of the formal and informal methods.

Corporate is divided into subgroups such private equity, M&A, banking & finance, capital markets, technology & IP transactions, structured finance, and real estate. Private equity and M&A absorb the largest number of associates; interviewees in these groups had typically started out tackling both private equity and M&A matters before gravitating toward one or the other with sources working on public mergers, private equity acquisitions, leveraged buyouts, oil and gas acquisitions, and bankruptcy asset sales.

"Negotiations fall to you."

See firm profile on p.667

Rankings in *Chambers USA*

Antitrust	Investment Funds
Banking & Finance	Labor & Employment
Bankruptcy/Restructuring	Litigation
Capital Markets	Media & Entertainment
Corporate/M&A	Private Equity
Employee Benefits &	Real Estate
Executive Compensation	Securities
Environment	Sports Law
IT & Outsourcing	Tax
Intellectual Property	Technology

For detail on ranking tiers and ranking locations, visit
www.chambersandpartners.com

Recent work highlights

- Advised Oracle on its $9.3 billion acquisition of cloud management software providers NetSuite
- Represented global helicopter company CHC and its subsidiaries in their Chapter 11 filing to enable the restructuring of $1.5 billion debt after plummeting oil prices pushed CHC into bankruptcy
- Acted for General Electric on the sale of GE Capital and its assets to Wells Fargo, Arval Service Lease and Marmon Holdings in deals totaling over $40 billion
- Succeeded in dismissing a $24 billion class action suit against Credit Suisse; the suit was lodged by resort property owners who claim they lost out after developers who'd been granted loans by the bank went into bankruptcy

Due diligence largely falls into the lap of first-years: *"Although it's not the most intellectually stimulating work, at least it's important to the deal."* In Dallas and Boston, first-years take on sole responsibility for non-disclosure agreements. *"You can ask questions of people but all the interaction with the client and negotiations fall to you. I liked having that responsibility early on as you can't always get involved in a deal right away,"* one junior told us. Firmwide, second-year sources had drafted operating or escrow agreements and commercial contracts, *"subject to someone more senior commenting on them"* they noted, with some even jumping at the chance to comment on provisions within purchase agreements.

Complex commercial litigation (CCL), securities litigation, antitrust/competition, and employment are just a few of Weil's litigation subgroups. The largest concentration of contentious-inclined juniors can be found in CCL; the catch-all group staffs associates on matters across the different subgroups so juniors can get stuck into the likes of bankruptcy, media, antitrust, and IP-related matters alongside traditional breach of contract claims. *"Starting out, I worked on a lot of doc review,"* one third-year told us. *"I've since been able to draft some motions, done some brief writing and helped create deposition and cross-examination outlines. If you've proved yourself and are willing to raise your hand to take on more substantive work, they're open to giving you something which would be reserved for someone more senior, as the firm is so busy."*

Training & Development

Just as it pays to raise your hand for more substantive work, so it goes for checking in on your progress. Outside of twice yearly formal reviews, associates told us *"it's up to you"* to request more than a returned red-line document. *"When you're in the middle of a deal and there's tons of work going on, feedback can be overlooked."* One proactive interviewee told us: *"I've never been turned away or feel shorted with an answer.*

Both partners and associates are more than willing to sit down and teach me."

First-year litigators attend regular classes on topics like *"how to do doc review, make privilege calls and draft summary judgment motions,"* which all gear up to a third-year trial skills workshop. Meanwhile, deal-doers get a crash-course in M&A and private equity over the first few days. After that they can attend *"periodic training"* on specific deals or topics, including practice group lunches. Training sessions are often beamed out across the firm's offices from New York.

Offices

While sources outside the Big Apple acknowledged that New York was the head honcho of offices, they didn't feel their own outfits were insignificant: those in Silicon Valley, Dallas and Boston emphasized the *"home grown"* nature of much of the work they handle, while a DC source added: *"We get the relaxed atmosphere of a satellite office with the clout of a wider group; we're not at all like the ugly step-sister who doesn't get any attention."* Visit chambers-associate.com to read about the firm's recent office overhauls.

"We're not at all like the ugly step-sister who doesn't get any attention."

Culture

Weil's lack of a billable hours requirement (more on that later) means *"we have a focus on collaboration,"* one junior thought. *"When people have an opportunity to work together, they ask questions. Practically I think people are quite laid back; that's not to say we're aren't formal or serious, but there's not so much of an emphasis on that. They want an environment where people feel comfortable collaborating and formality isn't always helpful in doing that."* Another illustrated: *"I feel comfortable offering up sugges-*

See firm profile on p.667

Diversity	Partners (%)	Associates (%)
Women	23	49
White	86	75
Black/African American	3	4
Hispanic/Latin American	3	5
Asian	4	14
Mixed/Other	0	2
LGBT	1	3

tions when drafting and people incorporate or comment on them – I'm never just dismissed outright."

"You can definitely take the initiative for different deals and responsibility and can make your career what you want," one interviewee told us. "You're not stuck in one place and people are open to offering you new experiences." Another added: "It's very entrepreneurial. You're motivated to go out, be proactive and shape you're experience. Multiple people have told me to make my Weil experience what I want it to be. Some people are here only for a short time or maybe they transition in-house; Weil has a program where you're able to meet alumni and ask about their career paths."

"There's not a lot of façade at Weil."

Of life in the Big Apple office, one New Yorker said: "It's a business and there are a lot of transactions but I think the partners try to put an effort into making it a nicer environment for associates. Each group has a liaison who mediates between the associates and partners. You can go to them with any issues; they're really willing to go to bat for you." A Dallas-based source found that "our small office promotes face-to-face interaction, so you find less passive aggressive emails and more genuine interaction with people. It's much easier to get a sense of who people are and what they need, which creates a good work environment. There's not a lot of façade at Weil." In Boston, "everyone is very available at every level, from staff to associates to partners; people care about those around them." DC has "a young vibe" and "sense of camaraderie" among its associates. Over on the West Coast, Silicon Valley juniors believed their office was "a bit different from the rest of Weil. We have a very relaxed culture- the vast majority of people are always wearing jeans and the environment doesn't require you to dedicate your life outside of work to be a reflection of your time in the office."

Hours & Compensation

Weil doesn't require its associates to hit a billable target, but everyone we spoke to had their own personal hours goal in mind. Some mentioned 1,800 hours, others 2,000, but we should point out that any unofficial goal can vary

between practice groups, and the firm emphasizes to us that there isn't a target at all. For litigators, the "work balance is either fairly busy or extremely busy," with many pulling between ten and 12 hour days. Corporate attorneys also pointed out the feast or famine nature of their practice: "No hard and fast routine: when we're slow I only work for six hours a day or I might consistently leave between 10pm and midnight for a month. When it's busy I can go weeks working every single day but at least I don't have to be in the office on weekends. I can get it done at home instead." Another reasoned: "We get paid a lot of money and they require a lot sacrifice from you. It's a constant struggle. I wish I had more free time but I understand the constraints."

Juniors felt encouraged to use all their annual leave. Longer stints away are your best bet for a clean break from work "as it's easier to haul you off something. If you're gone for two days you're probably still going to be on call and checking your emails."

Pro Bono

Weil associates are required to complete 50 hours of pro bono a year "but most people surpass that and go beyond 100." Over the past couple of years the firm's had a hand in everything from protecting an elderly cancer victim from abuse and ending indeterminate solitary confinement in California to aiding asylum seekers secure residency in the US and assisting small businesses and micro-entrepreneurs as part of Weil's partnership with a program called 'Start Small. Think Big.'

"It made me think a little bit."

Sources had tackled a similarly diverse array of matters, from reviewing inmate files as part of the Innocence Project to drafting tax advice and corporate charters for non profits. It may not be glamorous work, but interviewees liked the opportunities small pro bono cases bring. One junior found they'd taken the wrong track: "The matter I'm on is more like a large, typical billable case. The substance looked so cool I didn't think about how the opportunities would be limited."

Pro bono hours
- For all US attorneys: 36,800
- Average per US attorney: 52

Diversity

"It's an area we could improve," admitted most of our interviewees, though they did note that gender balance among the lower levels was pretty good. The firm "has placed a big emphasis on targeting diverse students at

See firm profile on p.667

law schools and hosting functions for law school diversity groups."

The firm's women's initiatives appeared the most visible to our sources: a Women@Weil task-force monitors issues such as *"flextime and the percentage of women pitching to clients. They're very transparent about what's going on in those areas."* Attorneys also attend diversity training sessions. *"They had actors come in to mimic situations and ask what we'd do. It's a good way to go about it; most people aren't going to be overtly disrespectful at a large firm but for minor things, like a man constantly talking over a woman – despite holding the same opinion – and then getting credit for her idea, that made me think a little bit,"* admitted one male interviewee.

Strategy & Future

A few years ago Weil instituted a major round of layoffs and lowered some partner compensation. Revenues rose slightly in 2014 and 2015. Executive partner Barry Wolf credits *"an uptick in restructuring activity"* and increased activity in the litigation and corporate practices for a further revenue rise in 2016 – up 8.6% to $1.264 billion.

Looking to the future Wolf expects *"continued growth in our public M&A practice – as we have become a destination firm for the C-suite and corporate boards – and more modest growth in private equity, which is already substantial in size. White collar investigations will also become a significant practice for the firm."*

Get Hired

"If you show initiative, are outgoing and have an entrepreneurial spirit you're going to do well," one associate told us. *"We put a huge premium on intellect and being articulate and personable."* Visit chambers-associate.com for a full rundown of tips and advice from Weil's current associates.

> ## "If you show initiative, are outgoing and have an entrepreneurial spirit you're going to do well."

The Inside View

See firm profile on p.667

White & Case LLP

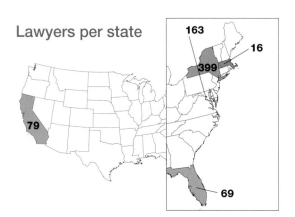

Lawyers per state

163
16
399
79
69

Largest US office: New York
US offices: 6
International offices: 34
First-year salary: $180,000 ($174,000 Miami)
Billable hours: 2,000 target
Summers 2017: 109 (101 2Ls, 6 1Ls, 2 SEOs)
Revenue 2016: $1.631 billion (+7.1%)
Partners made in 2017: 40 globally (17 in US)
Famous for: big international network; travel opportunities

Associates here should have *"a global mindset because pretty much everything we do is international."*

WHITE & Case never sits still, it seems. Office openings recently brought White & Case's global tally up to 40, a figure which has steadily risen over the past few years. *"We don't grow for growth's sake or just because of geography,"* exec committee member David Koschik stresses. November 2016 saw the launch of a base in Melbourne, Australia, which was quickly followed by one in Sydney in early 2017. *"Again, this was a focused move,"* Koschik reiterates. *"We were looking to expand throughout Asia and decided to move into Australia with a top notch group, particularly in project finance."* Around two-thirds of the firm's 2,000-plus lawyers are based outside the US.

That still leaves well over 700 attorneys in W&C's six home offices, the bulk of whom are in New York. *"We've opened the first new US office in 16 years in Boston [in 2016] because the US markets have been really busy across the board,"* says David Koschik. The Big Apple HQ houses most new associates, followed by DC, LA, Miami, and the tech-focused Palo Alto. As you'd expect for a firm with such a glittering global brand, White & Case is a star of the various *Chambers* directories – search for White &

On chambers-associate.com...

- Interview with executive committee member David Koschik
- Interview with global recruiting partner Brenda Dieck
- More on getting hired

Case on chambersandpartners.com to see all the rankings. In the US, particular strengths include corporate/M&A, litigation, banking, international arbitration and trade, antitrust, and projects. Beyond its reputation and the usual BigLaw benefits, W&C's relatively good-humored culture was a reason associates chose to come here, many told us. A glance at the *Chambers Global Top 30* shows White & Case ranked in 5th position among the firms with the most international clout: wherever the firm goes it rubs shoulders with the prestigious 'magic circle'.

The Work

Upon arrival, newbies in New York, DC and LA choose whether they'd like to go into litigation or corporate. Assignment is traditionally overseen by a coordinator. Associates submit time reports that detail their availability, *"but it's mostly relationship-based and anyone can poach me."* Normally people start out as generalists and are placed into work *"pools,"* before specializing later. *"In corporate it's normally for a year and in litigation it's normally about two years as a generalist. It makes you a better lawyer in the long run. If you don't understand what other groups do on a basic level then it will hold you back."* When it's time to choose, corporate associates can join sub-groups including banking, capital markets, energy, infrastructure, projects & asset finance (EIPAF), and M&A/corporate. Litigators join either the competition (where IP, trade and antitrust reside) or disputes sections, e.g. commercial litigation, arbitration and white-collar.

See firm profile on p.668

Rankings in *Chambers USA*

Antitrust	International Arbitration
Banking & Finance	International Trade
Bankruptcy/Restructuring	Latin American Investment
Capital Markets	Litigation
Corporate/M&A	Private Equity
Energy & Natural	Projects
Resources	Real Estate
Environment	Tax
Intellectual Property	Transportation

For detail on ranking tiers and ranking locations, visit
www.chambersandpartners.com

Recent work highlights

- Advised Blue Cross and Blue Shield insurer Anthem on its $54 billion acquisition of Cigna
- Represented Rolls-Royce in the disposal of its energy gas turbine and compressor business to Siemens in a $1.3 billion deal
- Defended global energy company Hess Corporation against a class action alleging consumer fraud
- Advised Saudi Arabian Oil Company on its joint venture with PT Pertamina, Indonesia's state-owned oil and gas company, for the $5 billion upgrade of a refinery in Indonesia

Litigators explained that *"most commercial lit is headed out of New York or LA. DC's a lot of international arbitration award enforcement, white collar crime and antitrust."* New York also does a lot of antitrust in collaboration with DC, and Boston does some too. Typical tasks include *"drafting briefs, motions, doing witness interviews, reviewing documents for production and drafting documents at federal, district and appeal levels too."* When it came to doc review, *"yeah it's grunt work but it was on a billion dollar trial."* LA residents can also get involved with the dedicated group serving Facebook, run out of that office. *"The group is its own thing. It's a really big client so there are a few people here who only work on litigation matters for them."*

"Some people like to micromanage and others let you run with something."

"There's a decent amount of responsibility," on the transactional side. While most newbies get involved with drafting, research and doc review, different locations see different work. In Miami, the projects team in the EIPAF group set sources to work on *"a lot of bank finance deals from Latin America. The firm generally has a focus in Latin America and typical junior work will be doing the initial draft of credit documents and closing checklists."* In LA, those in M&A explained that *"it's segmented into either public or private M&A, with a focus on private equity deals too."* Angelenos were happy to have *"drafted purchase agreements, tender documents, proxy statements and other public filings."* However, they gave more measured responses when asked if this was the norm. *"Responsibility depends on people's work styles. Some people like to micromanage and others let you run with something."* New Yorkers were the most vocal about their client exposure. *"I'm really satisfied with the responsibility because you have a lot of client contact early on. You do the ongoing advisory stuff, because you're expected to know about the whole deal."*

Training & Development

After office-specific IT training, newbies assemble in New York for *"the new associates' conference. Everyone in the US and Mexico offices goes there for two or three days"* of fundamentals tuition. *"After you start working, you then have group-specific training around three times a month on things like how to draft a motions or conduct discovery."* Transactional associates have a *"biannual M&A bootcamp. We get overviews of credit and purchase agreements that have been marked up and commented on."* Regardless of the practice area, all interviewees felt that *"most of the training is informal and on-the-job, which is the most valuable. The formal training could use improvement. The conference is fun and we learn some useful stuff, but it's a weird mix of the basics and then there's a lot on a much higher level which is not important to first-years."*

Annual formal reviews take associates through the conglomerated feedback from all the partners they've worked with. Some felt that *"it's fine, it was pretty bland and watered-down because the comments are all merged together so you don't know who says what, which can be a negative."* Others insisted that *"the best feedback is informal, but it depends who you work with. Sometimes people can forget."*

Offices

White & Case's offices are classed into three border-spanning designations: the Americas (which also ties in Mexico City and São Paulo), Asia-Pacific (which now includes Melbourne and Sydney), and EMEA (Europe, the Middle East and Africa). Practice groups across the Americas offices regularly work hand in hand, though plenty of juniors had worked with European and Asian teams too.

"It's an exciting time because we haven't moved in New York for over 32 years."

See firm profile on p.668

The Inside View

Diversity	Partners (%)	Associates (%)
Women	19	50
White	80	60
Black/African American	2	5
Hispanic/Latin American	6	12
Asian	10	17
Mixed/Other	1	6
LGBT	4	2

Insiders explained that *"New York and London are our co-motherships, but it's still pretty NY-centric."* However, they then qualified that *"all of our other offices are established in their own right. We're not comparable to other firms where they operate more like satellites."* Miami sources explained that *"NY is obviously the biggest place, but we hold our own here particularly in EIPAF."* Location dictates whether first-years get their own offices straight away. New Yorkers grumbled about their building: *"Thank God we're moving in 2017 because this is gross! It's just so old and cramped."* Juniors thought the new location is *"super swank."* David Koschik tells us more: *"It's an exciting time because we haven't moved in New York for over 32 years. We recently renovated DC and Miami and we moved offices in LA. In New York the new building has common spaces on each floor and client amenity floors."*

Culture

"It's hard to explain the culture," insiders pondered. *"For the most part hierarchy isn't important here. If you disagree with what the partners are saying they want to hear it."* Others went further: *"Everyone has a really good sense of humor, there are not a lot of egos and you can even make fun of the partners. Well…it depends who!"*

"We're lawyers so we like our happy hours."

On the social side, *"there are lots of married people so we don't go out partying that much."* However, *"the firm is trying to get attorneys to socialize a bit more."* Across all locations, the holidays saw the most action, with *"summer sailing"* in DC *"where we hired this boat and ate crab."* Corporate sources told us about *"pizza and beer every other Thursday – we're lawyers so we like our happy hours."* A standout event is the White & Case World Cup. *"It's in some European city each year and everyone in the firm is invited to go and either watch or play in this soccer and volleyball tournament between different teams in the firm. The firm even pays for you to fly over to the host city and stay."*

Diversity

A big factor of W&C's culture is the *"inherent diversity that comes being a global law firm. Because we pride ourselves in being international, the weight of our offices is outside the US so there are many different walks of life here, which naturally fosters diversity."* Insiders weren't saying that the firm is perfect: *"It could be 100 times better and we're definitely not representative of the broader population, but because we have so many foreign lawyers I would say we're more diverse than other firms."*

That's definitely true in terms of ethnic diversity, but *"beyond that I'm less confident in other forms. We hire a lot of women, but then it drops off dramatically like other firms."* To remedy this, *"the firm has brought in an external leadership coach to help women with business skills like 'being more assertive'."* Other topics include gravitas, political savvy, and networking. *"They're making an effort"* when it comes to diversity generally. *"It's just not that effective yet. But that isn't unique to this firm – it's everywhere."*

Pro Bono

"They're very committed: you have to do at least 20 hours and then you get a plaque. At least 50 people in my office got it this year." An NY based pro bono coordinator sends firmwide emails to get people involved with various matters. Associates had *"done a lot of Her Justice divorce and child custody cases and fact discovery for a big civil rights case."* Other tasks included *"researching the logistics of setting up a not-for-profit in different countries. Death row appeals in Florida and working out how to protect children who have been trafficked."* Insiders told us *"that you pretty much run these cases. You do everything from talking to clients to going to court."* Litigators found it easier to get involved and the skills they honed in pro bono were transferable to their billable work. In corporate, however, *"it doesn't translate as easily. Our work is very ebb and flow, so when we are really busy pro bono will get pushed aside."*

Pro bono hours
- For all US attorneys: 46,054
- Average per US attorney: 70

Hours & Compensation

2,000 hours makes you bonus eligible, 200 of which can be pro bono or firm mandated activities. *"It's stuff like recruitment or if you write an article,"* explained an associate. Operating in lockstep has meant that *"the firm has raised the bonus rates, following the market."* While this was generally a cause for celebration, the only bugbear that associates were left with was *"what the words 'bonus eligible' actually mean, because in some offices you can be eligible but not get the full bonus. So we've complained to*

See firm profile on p.668

the lawyers' committee to get more clarity and we're waiting to hear back."

Most worked ten hour days in the office, with a few *"leaving at 5am and then coming as usual the next day."* While this is rare, some sources observed that the international nature of their practice could make their diary unpredictable: *"It's the flipside to having international clients. There are so many different time zones to deal with. But people do recognize that if you have less sleep you're less productive. They're really good at letting you go early if you've been constantly working crazy hours."*

Get Hired & Strategy

"Global outlook is a big deal in everything we do because we work in so many different countries." While the obvious advice was to *"get good grades and law review experience,"* most interviewees extolled the benefits of *"having lived abroad or speaking a language. Don't come in here and just say 'oh yeah I really want to work with international clients' – show you have that perspective by doing something about it."*

David Koschik tells us that *"we want larger critical mass in practice areas rather than simply more geographic locations. To do that, much of our focus is on expanding our existing offices. We are very focused on becoming a much larger firm in the US by growing in targeted industries like tech, oil and gas, private equity and financial institutions."*

Chambers Global Top 30 shows White & Case ranked in 5th position among the firms with the most international clout. To view the firm's practice area rankings in the US and overseas, visit www.chambersandpartners.com

The Inside View

See firm profile on p.668

Wiley Rein LLP

Lawyers per state   **241**

Largest US office: Washington, DC

US offices: 1

International offices: 0

First-year salary: $180,000

Billable hours: 1,950 target

Summers 2017: 9 (8 2Ls, 1 1L)

Revenue 2016: undisclosed

Partners made in 2017: 5

Famous for: family friendly environment. government contracts, telecom and insurance work

Washington's Wiley Rein is the authority on government contracts.

"THREE is a magic number," once sang Bob Dorough. And who are we to disagree with the legendary singer-songwriter? While we're (almost) certain Dorough wasn't singing about Wiley Rein, the rule of three definitely applies to the Washington, DC native. The regulatory and policy pro is known for a trio of top practices: all things government-related, insurance, and telecom, media and technology (TMT), with each earning top tier rankings from *Chambers USA*. Other recognized practices include IP and international trade. The firm's grown to almost 250 attorneys since first setting up shop in 1983 with just under 40 lawyers.

Wiley's telecom practice has been a period of transition of the past year; two partners departed for DLA Piper, one for the FCC and one to Perkins Coie. The move follows the 2014 restructuring of Wiley's telecommunications practice into a TMT practice. Managing partner Peter Shields tells us: *"Our goal has been to continue to innovate and transform all of our practices, but TMT is particularly important because new technologies are being developed so quickly that it is a challenge for policy to catch up with progress. There is tremendous energy in some very exciting areas such as the Internet of Things, connected cars, and smart cities. That requires continued growth from the*

bottom up –so we are investing in our next-generation attorneys in this sector." Go online for more from Shields on the TMT group's development.

The Work

At the time of our calls, there were six juniors in the government contracts team, five in insurance, and three in TMT, with the odd attorney cropping up in the international trade, IP, election law, litigation and environmental departments.

"You need to be scrappy."

In the TMT and government contracts groups, there's a free market system for getting work: *"You need to be able to hustle,"* one source told us. *"A lot of the work at Wiley is regulatory based, not the kind of busy, larger litigation with a huge amount of doc review and discovery. Regulatory law lends itself to the need to develop an expertise and you see leaner staffed projects. On the one hand it benefits you to work on a project with just a partner or two, but it can be harder to find hours as they don't need as many associates. You need to be scrappy."* Despite the challenges this can pose in the first and second years, most juniors felt the benefits outweighed the downsides by the time they'd reached the third year: *"It's given me the chance to work with and develop close relationships with a lot of partners."* And if you're really struggling, we're told you can fall back on chief talent officer Kay Nash, who's *"very helpful in aiding you find work."* The insurance group, meanwhile, has an assigning partner. *"I think everyone else is very envious,"* one insurance junior confided.

On chambers-associate.com...

- Wiley's TMT practice
- Wiley Rein and Trump's new administration
- Hiring tips from recruiting committee chair Rachel Alexander

See firm profile on p.669

Rankings in *Chambers USA*

Franchising	Media & Entertainment
Government	Privacy & Data Security
Insurance	Telecommunications
International Trade	

For detail on ranking tiers and ranking locations, visit
www.chambersandpartners.com

Recent work highlights

- Lead counsel for insurance company CNA who are insuring Professor Alan Dershowitz in a defamation suit brought against him by two attorneys over statements alleging sexual misconduct
- Assisted aviation company M7 Aerospace in protesting the award of a $181 million US Navy contract for aircraft maintenance
- Represented electrical contractor M.C. Dean in FCC proceedings concerning allegations that M. C. Dean's management of the wireless network at the Baltimore Convention Center interfered with other wireless networks

Government contracts associates get a look in on *"everything from typical bid protest claims"* – challenging the award of government contracts – *"and contractor disputes to data rights issues, employment issues and compliance."* They may be helping clients to protest but juniors felt there was little to object to in this department: *"The partners are really good at pushing you and making sure you're never stagnant or just doing the bare minimum of research."* Sources had *"been in charge of coming up with a legal argument on my own and researching and drafting an entire pleading."* Another added: *"That's not to say you avoid doc review. It does come into it but it's often small and usually because you need to know the facts of the case when you're the only associate on it."*

"You're never stagnant."

It's a similar story in insurance where *"we don't have enormous cases which are doc review intensive. I think I've only done a grand total of maybe 30 hours of it this year."* Instead juniors spend their time *"writing a lot of coverage letters, push-back letters if someone thinks they should be covered and we disagree, and I've also written motions."* Others had tackled amicus briefs, complaints, answers and counter claims. *"It involves a lot of writing."* Matters here are split fairly evenly between *"monitoring underlying cases where our client, the insurer, could be on the hook for defense or settlement costs, and litigation involving a coverage dispute."*

Training & Development

Everyone receives an annual review, with first-years also benefiting from a handy mid-year check-in. Newbies are also assigned two associate mentors, who are usually in the same practice group. In addition to standard orientation sessions, new recruits have weekly practice-specific trainings. Each department offers a '101' series aimed at first-years. Insurance 101, for example *"talks you through the different areas of insurance and answers questions like 'what are pre-tender costs and why do people keep talking about them?' It's really helpful"* and also offers tips from older juniors on what they wish they'd known early on. In the second year juniors attend a 201 series on more advanced topics. Rookies can also make use of litigation skills workshops: *"The most recent covered writing and*

answering complaints, and crafting summary judgment motions."

Culture & Offices

Wiley associates have long noted the office décor is *"a little dated, but I think if it was too modern it wouldn't reflect us. We're not trying to be crazy fancy. We're very open with the fact we're not hoity toity."* We were told Wiley is populated by *"really nice, down-to-earth and relatable"* attorneys. *"People don't take themselves too seriously. They're funny and friendly."* Friendly yes, sociable? *"No, no no no,"* one source laughed. *"We're not a party firm, we're family friendly,"* explained another. *"During the work day people like to get their work done and leave at a reasonable hour if possible."* However, one source did note: *"I was a little anxious when I heard it was family-oriented as I'm young and single. It is family-friendly but it's not like there's no social interaction."* A bowling league, softball and flag football team exist for a *"small, core group"* who fancy more socializing with colleagues. *"I think the family-oriented spin comes from the fact people here treat you like family."*

"The partner replied that I put in the bulk of the work."

Juniors felt their daily efforts were valued: *"Partners do recognize your contribution and say thank you. There are times a client has responded very positively to a drafted product and the partner replied that I put in the bulk of the work and should be thanked too. Little things like announcing juniors on calls makes you feel like part of the team."* Another felt that *"partners are invested in your progress. They make sure you have client contact and that clients are comfortable speaking directly with the new generation who are coming up."* Others noted that colleagues keep an eye out for one another: *"You're expected to work hard, but if you're staying here until midnight people will not hesitate to tell you you're over-doing it and to go home. No-one wants you falling asleep at your desk."*

The Inside View

See firm profile on p.669

Diversity	Partners (%)	Associates (%)
Women	26	52
White	89	73
Black/African American	3	8
Hispanic/Latin American	3	5
Asian	5	13
Mixed/Other	0	1
LGBT	3	2

Pro bono hours
- For all attorneys: 11,576
- Average per attorney: 43

Hours & Compensation

Juniors shoot for an annual billable target of 1,950 hours. Sources felt reaching this figure was very practice group-specific but overall agreed it was a fair number to aim for. *"The firm is not unreasonable. High expectations are there and they are looking for you to meet them, but if the work isn't there and you've sought it out, they consider that."* Ten or 11 hour days in the office were common, with interviewees putting in a few hours from home when needed.

In summer 2016 the firm raised its first and second year salaries to $180,000 and $190,000 respectively. Beyond that, *"we matched the new industry standard until the fifth year and then the salary is decided on a case by case basis."* Bonuses are usually slightly below market *"but people don't come here expecting to get a large bonus,"* juniors reasoned.

Pro Bono

Fifty hours of pro bono count toward the billing target. A pro bono partner farms out opportunities to those who are interested. Juniors credited pro bono matters with promoting *"a little bit of internal networking"* and *"the opportunity to take on a large leadership role from the get go."* Landlord/tenant matters, family law issues and asylum cases are common. Attorneys can also attend a weekly pro bono clinic.

The firm recently took on a racial discrimination case which, at the time of our calls, was *"starting to generate a bit of press."* Along with the Department of Justice, over a half a dozen Wiley attorneys are representing three African-American Maryland police officers who allege they experienced racial discrimination from officials of Pocomoke City, the Worcester County State's Attorney's Office and the Maryland State Police.

Diversity

"I don't think it's a diverse firm," one newbie bluntly replied when we asked for their thoughts on racial diversity. Juniors did note, however, that *"there are a lot of visible efforts to change that and those efforts are appreciated."* A pipeline scheme is available for diverse 1Ls and the firm offers several affinity networks for various ethnic identities.

Other groups include parents-in-the-law and LGBT & Allies Lawyers. Events for the latter *"are always well attended."* A women's forum holds speaker events and quarterly lunches: *"Senator Amy Klobuchar came to one lunch – that was really cool,"* one impressed associate recalled. *"I agree for the most part that we're a good firm for women,"* another female source told us. *"The culture is pretty flexible, they do encourage a good work/life balance and there are a number of younger female partners."*

Get Hired

Associates noted *"a distinct lack of cockiness among people"* at Wiley, so check your ego at the door. Visit chambers-associate.com for hiring tips from associates and recruiting committee chair Rachel Alexander.

Strategy & Future

Wiley is poised to jump on opportunities brought about by the change in administration. *"Our International Trade Team has been extremely busy. It's an exciting time to be in that field and it will continue to be a key growth area for the firm,"* chief marketing officer Alina Gorokhovsky tell us. Managing partner Peter Shields adds: *"Our government contracts attorneys are getting a lot of calls from companies that already have contracts with the government or are interested in securing contracts. Our TMT team is handling inquiries on anything to do with the FCC. We are also seeing a large number of calls regarding health care and environment issues."* Visit chambers-associate.com for more from Shields and Gorokhovsky.

"Partners are invested in your progress. They make sure you have client contact and that clients are comfortable speaking directly with the new generation who are coming up."

See firm profile on p.669

The Inside View

Willkie Farr & Gallagher LLP

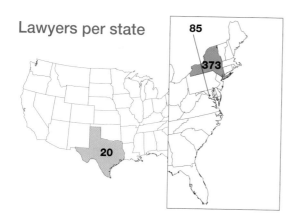

Lawyers per state

Largest US office: New York
US offices: 3
International offices: 6
First-year salary: $180,000
Billable hours: no requirement
Summers 2017: 62 (60 2Ls, 2 1Ls)
Revenue 2016: $691 million (+5%)
Partners made in 2017: 3
Famous for: insurance excellence; cross-practice group collegiality

Looking for a firm that's big on teamwork and busy all year round? You could go Farr at this New York institution.

IF we had a dime for every interviewee who described their firm as *"collegial,"* we'd be richer than the President. Juniors at Willkie were particularly quick to whip out this cliché, but had concrete evidence to back their claims: *"Even people I talked to at other firms all seemed to echo that Willkie is a collegial place. People get along across different practice groups, you really do meet and mingle."*

When not mingling, associates are living up to the firm's rich 130-year legacy (it has counted Thomas Edison, Ulysses S. Grant and National League Baseball on its client roster), and several saw *"a good reputation"* as a big draw. Fast forward to present day and Willkie has a healthy crop of *Chambers USA* rankings in bankruptcy/restructuring and insurance in particular, as well as nods for investment funds, commercial litigation and other areas.

The Work

Litigation and corporate are the two biggest intake groups, followed by asset management, real estate, executive compensation & employee benefits, restructuring and IP. You begin as a generalist and work is distributed

On chambers-associate.com...

- Get hired: the inside view on recruitment
- Interviews with chairman Tom Cerabino and personnel committee chair Tom Henry
- Major League Baseball and Willkie

through formal allocation systems, *"but if you want to get on a particular matter you can make a request to the assigning partner and they usually oblige."* Newcomers in several groups reported *"in your first few years you get a wide range of experiences,"* crediting the assignment coordinators with *"making sure you get exposure to different types of work. I liked that because I was trying to find out what I really wanted to do."*

> *"People are really reasonable, if you're drowning in work it's only temporary."*

In corporate *"the bread and butter is M&A, but insurance is also here and there's a fair amount of securities, private equity and capital markets work."* Handed the keys to the sweet shop, juniors got to pick and mix as *"the firm gives you a few years to figure out what you're good at before specializing de-facto."* First-years saw some due diligence, *"depending on deal size and how the team is set up,"* but also got their hands on meatier drafting and research. *"It's not that daunting to have lots of responsibility; everyone makes it clear the partners are there to answer questions."* The tight-knit asset management team (*"there's a lot of teamwork"*) deals with both private and registered funds. *"The workload's overwhelming at times, but that's the nature of the job,"* juniors reasoned.

White collar and FCPA Foreign Corrupt Practices Act cases make up a considerable chunk of litigation at Willkie, but there are also attorneys handling old-fashioned commercial litigation. DC in particular sees a lot

See firm profile on p.670

Rankings in *Chambers USA*

Antitrust	Litigation
Banking & Finance	Private Equity
Bankruptcy/Restructuring	Real Estate
Corporate/M&A	Securities
FCPA	Tax
Insurance	Telecommunications
Investment Funds	

For detail on ranking tiers and ranking locations, visit
www.chambersandpartners.com

Recent work highlights

- Represented Level 3 Communications in its $34 billion acquisition by telecommunications giant CenturyLink
- Resolved dispute to win $200 million insurance coverage for petroleum system and service provider Cameron International in Deepwater Horizon oil spill case
- Acted for a consortium of investors purchasing $5 billion of consumer loans from peer-to-peer lender Prosper
- Advised hedge fund managers Elliott on sponsorship of IoT start-up SIGFOX as part of the second-largest financing round for a startup in French history

of government investigations work, while New York handles more insurance and bankruptcy matters. Getting to grips with *"a lot of document review and summarizing,"* some juniors also had the chance to *"take and draft interviews from meetings with the client and government."* Even after leaping into the deep end of responsibility, *"people are really reasonable. If you're drowning in work it's only ever temporary."*

There was some frustration from sources in smaller practice areas who felt *"work isn't leveled out across juniors; the group's dynamic and politics can limit responsibility."* A lack of flexibility also rankled some, who lamented *"it's quite difficult to switch groups. It's frustrating having long periods with not much to do."* On the other hand, the restructuring group provided *"good exposure"* for associates, who got *"a combination of debtor and creditor work. I've been given assignments I don't understand 100% but next time I'll have a pool of knowledge to draw on."* Likewise, over in real estate *"people make a concerted effort to share the burden. On some deals I'm managing the transaction at a high level."*

Training & Development

Formal training programs *"go over general concepts, but the nitty-gritty depends on your mentor."* The firm assigns a 'Career Adviser' partner to each newcomer. An initial orientation *"isn't the most helpful thing, as getting it all at once isn't very practical,"* but there's enough training thereafter for one junior to have *"fulfilled all my New York bar credits within five months!"* Performance reviews take place annually, with a midyear review for first-years. Satisfied that *"it's difficult to know how you could do it better,"* interviewees felt *"you get a good idea of where you stand,"* but noted *"the firm would like to think it's a very open process. That depends on which partners you're working with."*

"It's difficult to know how you could do it better."

Offices

The New York HQ is *"currently remodeling, they've just opened up a brand new floor,"* but there's already *"a beautiful lobby, and most offices have really good views. The furniture isn't super-modern but it does the job."* Renovations have just finished in DC, introducing glass walls designed to *"bring more light in,"* which some felt was *"controversial"* now they'd lost their privacy. Less divisive was the introduction of office sharing for first-years, which *"helps you get into the groove of things."*

"Pretty seamless."

New York and DC frequently work in tandem, mostly within litigation as Willkie has only a few corporate attorneys in the capital. It's *"pretty seamless working between the two locations: we rely on the knowledge that people in the other office have and we can connect straight to them."* The Houston office opened in 2014 to serve Willkie's longstanding clients; many are in the energy sector.

Get Hired

"I don't think there's a magic bullet – whether you're a quieter or more gregarious person, they'll find value in you and give you a chance." For more insider info on recruitment at Willkie, check out chambers-associate.com.

Culture & Diversity

"Willkie does a lot to promote an 'all in this together' mentality even when it's super-busy," reflected by the fact that associates don't sit by group. Those we spoke to thought that *"adds a lot to the sense of camaraderie here,"* so though *"there are some nasty bits – we're lawyers after all! – the team atmosphere is unique and even at 2am when everything's miserable, you can joke with friends."* New Yorkers identified theirs as the *"more intense"* workplace, while firmwide *"there's definitely a hierarchy, but we do have partners who care about your career development."* Even less dewy-eyed interviewees conceded *"I don't know*

See firm profile on p.670

Diversity	Partners (%)	Associates (%)
Women	14.3	43.8
White	92.1	75.7
Black/African American	1.4	4.4
Hispanic/Latin American	2.9	5.9
Asian	2.1	10.4
Mixed/Other	1.4	3.6
LGBT	4.3	2.4

if any associates here are less happy than those at other places."

There's *"a fair amount of socializing – if you want to go out for a drink with peers there's always an opportunity."* Events range from holiday parties to March Madness pools and the usual plethora of summer activities. One interviewee recounted: *"Before the holiday season the senior associates spent the leftovers of their marketing budget on a group dinner for us juniors."* Not to be outdone, Willkie's management also stokes camaraderie with an annual state of the firm meeting covering financials, growth, practice areas for future focus and the general direction of the firm.

"Even at 2am when everything's miserable, you can joke with friends."

Befitting this transparency, *"the firm has admitted they have a way to go with diversity."* Associates felt *"New York is more diverse than DC."* The powers that be are aware of the situation, and the firm does have women's committees as well as cross-office mentoring programs aimed at DC associates. *"We really are trying,"* reported those involved in recruitment, and others felt *"impressed that diversity is something the firm wants us all to be aware of."* Speakers at 'diversity lunches' have included Dr Brigitte Vittrup, associate professor of child development at Texas Woman's University. Such events lead sources to conclude *"the firm takes inclusiveness seriously, and everyone's aware we need to do a better job."*

Pro Bono

There's no cap on the number of pro bono hours associates can treat as billable. As in previous years, corporate sources pointed out *"it's harder for us to use our skills pro bono,"* but *"there's plenty of people in the transactional group who do an incredible amount, and the firm does a good job circulating opportunities targeted at us."* The firm organizes a dedicated pro bono week in October, and regularly partners with the Lawyers' Committee in DC,

and Her Justice in New York which works with domestic violence victims – the two organizations regularly take a junior each for an externship. One associate told us while admiring the Willkie pro bono volunteer mug on their desk that they'd *"gotten to do child custody and protective order cases. Pro bono is taken as seriously as anything else here."*

Pro bono hours
- For all US attorneys: 30,663
- Average per US attorney: 67

Hours & Compensation

Willkie also has no hours targets for associates. That doesn't mean anybody's shirking work as *"people are competitive and want to say 'I billed X amount', and I think most people would hit a target if we had one."* Interviewees appreciated *"it makes a huge difference when we're not busy, we can enjoy the lighter weeks."* Some argued *"a requirement might force the assigning partners to make sure everyone has the same amount of work,"* but most *"generally have a sense of when we'll be busy or light"* and could adjust their schedule accordingly.

"Most people would hit a target if we had one."

Management had assured attorneys *"point blank in an open forum they'd match market for associate salaries,"* so when Cravath unveiled its new $180,000 and up scale there *"wasn't any question the firm would match."* Associates get 20 days a year vacation, and partners *"consider it part of your compensation, and vital to your work/life balance."* One source was even told *"don't be an idiot, make sure you take it"* in their annual review.

Strategy & Future

"The firm is conservatively managed," according to juniors confident that *"Willkie is run like a business. We're not going to suddenly go under. We weathered the last crisis, and something associates like about this place is the sense of job security."* That includes being clued in on future developments, for instance *"management talked to us about the Houston office before it was opened."* Chairman Tom Cerabino tells us the firm's *"blueprint for growth is built around six areas – M&A, private equity, commercial litigation, restructuring, asset management and antitrust. Houston has been very successful because we've managed to leverage expertise from other offices."* For the full interview, visit chambers-associate.com.

The Inside View

"Associates like the sense of job security."

See firm profile on p.670

WilmerHale

Lawyers per state

347
275
179
73
104
14

Largest US office: Washington, DC
US offices: 7 (including Dayton)
International offices: 5
First-year salary: $180,000
Billable hours: 2,000 target
Summers 2017: 77 (70 2Ls, 3 1Ls, 4 others)
Revenue 2016: $1.13 billion (-0.8%)
Partners made in 2017: 8 globally (7 in US)
Famous for: government-related work; antitrust; appellate

Associates at this prestigious firm praised a *"friendly"* culture where *"people are willing to give you opportunities for professional development."*

IN 2004, DC-based Wilmer, Cutler & Pickering merged with Boston old-timers Hale and Dorr to create the legal heavyweight that is WilmerHale. This international firm has a notable reputation for government-related work, with *"strong ties to people in the government."* In a recent headline-grabbing case, lawyers represented President Trump's son-in-law Jared Kushner in relation to nepotism and conflict-of-interest concerns. Other draws for new recruits include the firm's formidable antitrust practice, and *"the quality of its appellate group."* Both of these practices gain first-rate nationwide rankings in *Chambers USA*, as do financial services regulation, IP, life sciences, and securities regulation. Highly ranked areas include international arbitration, general commercial and white collar litigation, bankruptcy, corporate/M&A, and private equity.

Beyond the firm's prowess in multiple practice areas, several juniors we spoke to had been attracted here by *"Wilmer's commitment to pro bono work."* Sources also praised the people – *"really smart but not intimidating."* One explained that *"I very much enjoyed speaking to everybody who interviewed me – none had a vacant expression on their face, unlike some other firms."*

On chambers-associate.com...

- More on getting hired at WilmerHale
- Interview with co-managing partner Susan Murley

The Work

Each group has a work assignment coordinator, providing a *"formal path to take advantage of."* The general role involves *"matching people who have time with people who have need."* Juniors reported that this system *"works in tandem with a free market system,"* where partners that you have worked with over time start to come to you directly. A source praised the system, explaining it *"reduces anxiety as I've never had an issue of nothing for me to do. Not only do I always have something to do if I need it, but I also feel like I have some control over what it is."*

Most young litigators remain generalists until they are more senior. *"It's good because you can experience everything and get a taste for different litigation."* A few sources had veered toward more specific litigation in either antitrust, or securities and enforcement. These juniors dealt with *"securities class actions, enforcement of SEC and internal investigations,"* and clients were often involved in the financial industry in one way or another. Antitrust specialists saw a similar amount of government-facing work, as well as cartel defense and merger work.

"I've never had to pull an all-nighter or anything close to it."

Across the board, litigation juniors were responsible for doing the preliminary research, but *"pretty quickly I was drafting interview outlines and attending interviews."* Other work includes discovery and fact development, writing briefs, and taking depositions. One source ad-

See firm profile on p.671

The Inside View

Rankings in *Chambers USA*

Antitrust	International Arbitration
Appellate Law	International Trade
Banking & Finance	Life Sciences
Bankruptcy/Restructuring	Litigation
Corporate Crime &	Media & Entertainment
Investigations	Native American Law
Corporate/M&A	Private Equity
Employee Benefits &	Real Estate
Executive Compensation	Securities
FCPA	Startups & Emerging
Financial Services	Companies
Regulation	Tax
Government	Technology
Intellectual Property	

For detail on ranking tiers and ranking locations, visit
www.chambersandpartners.com

Recent work highlights

- Provided antitrust advice to Envision Healthcare regarding the company's merger with AmSurg Corporation. The combined company has annual revenue of over $8 billion
- Defending Twitter in a federal suit in California brought by estates of two terrorist attack victims alleging Twitter provided material support to ISIS
- Represented Google in a dispute with the Attorney General of Mississippi, who claimed Google was unlawfully disseminating harmful third-party content through its services
- Provides frequent advice to Bose on a wide range of privacy, data security, marketing and consumer protection issues that the company faces under federal, state, and international law

mitted *"it's unsurprising that some stuff that isn't intellectually taxing falls down the totem pole to junior associates."* However, a securities junior had experienced *"actually very little doc review – but certainly some. I almost wish I were doing more because it's less taxing and you can tune out a little more."* Sources reckoned that *"if you do your job well and express interest, then people you've worked with before are happy to let you take on as much as you can handle."* The volume of work was considered *"almost always manageable,"* with one noting: *"I've never had to pull and all-nighter or anything close to it."* Most had *"no complaints – as a junior you're trusted with quite a bit of responsibility right out of the gate, but there's also a lot of expertise to guide you."* As a result, juniors felt *"well supported."* When it came to client contact, *"the cases are big, so there are usually several lawyers working on them."* This meant that client contact was not as regular, and usually occurred more in the pro bono context. Juniors still felt that *"people are willing to give you opportunities for professional development."*

> ### "Legitimately, my first assignment on my first day, the partner told me to contact the client."

Corporate juniors also start out broad, dealing with everything from public companies and IPOs to M&A on both the buy and sell sides. There's also much work with start-ups: *"It's really cool because start-ups are usually talking to the most junior person on the team, so you get client contact right out the gate."* In contrast, *"M&A buy-side deals are often a lot bigger."* Interviewees reported classic diligence-related tasks and reviewing contracts, but also *"a lot of drafting."* This might include drafting small contracts, staff-related documents, and board resolutions for directors. Sources also felt encouraged to

branch out a little: *"I've been on deals with people who say "okay, why don't you try it." People have really been willing to let me try things, under their supervision."* As for client contact, *"legitimately, my first assignment on my first day of work, the partner told me to contact the client. I was like 'this is my first day!'"*

Training & Development

"The firm places a great deal of value on training – it's very comprehensive." Training starts as *"an overview of adjusting to firm culture"* and progresses to *"hands-on practice in specific areas."* Litigators receive deposition skills workshops, discovery drafting training, moot court practice and mock trials – *"all of which are very fun."* For corporate juniors, training covers diligence, filing proxies, how to read and understand documents used in financing, and Excel training, among other topics.

Associates felt training to be *"detailed and effective, which I appreciated because in law school you don't really learn the stuff you actually need to practice law."* They also found the extra practice *"gives a bit more confidence."* Other formal training is *"mostly clustered around when you move up to the next level – like if I were to become senior associate, there would be a big bunch of training centered around the responsibilities you take on at that time."*

Offices

As a result of the big 2004 merger, WilmerHale effectively has two headquarters – one in DC and one in Boston. The DC office is located just a couple of blocks from the White House, but really *"feels in the heart of DC."* The entrance to the main building has *"a ten-story atrium with a waterfall"* (see our Twitter feed for pictures) and the building has its own mock trial room with a jury box. The New York office is located in 7 World Trade Center and has *"an amazing panoramic view of midtown Manhattan,"* and the Boston office has a watery view of Bos-

The Inside View

Diversity	Partners (%)	Associates (%)
Women	24.7	49.5
White	89	76.8
Black/African American	2.7	5.2
Hispanic/Latin American	0.8	3
Asian	6.7	13.4
Mixed/Other	0.8	1.4
LGBT	0.8	5

ton Harbor. Other domestic offices are in Denver, Palo Alto and LA, plus a business services center in Dayton, Ohio. Overseas, the firm is in Beijing, Berlin, Brussels, Frankfurt, and London.

Culture

The general consensus was that the firm's personality is *"nice and nerdy."* A junior elaborated by explaining: *"We're a little bit nerdier than the stereotypes at other firms."* Attorneys at WilmerHale *"like law and like being lawyers"* but *"don't want work to be their entire lives."* The firm enables this as it *"strikes a good balance of pushing for top notch work without top notch stress."* Sources liked the way that *"everyone is interested in everyone else's well-being,"* and several said they were *"friends with people I think I would be friends with outside of the office."*

"I don't think I could find a BigLaw firm that has a better culture."

"I think for BigLaw there's a pretty good work-life balance, and people appreciate that. I don't think I could find a BigLaw firm that has a better culture." There are socials throughout the year and *"people tend to hang out, but it's a no-pressure situation."* Juniors described *"the crew that's going to go out, then the crew that has kids and goes home at five. Both of those exist here and no matter which you're looking for, I think you'll be fine."* The Boston, New York and Palo Alto offices each Friday host the 'Chowder and Marching Society' (CAMS) – an old Boston tradition but *"New York has taken out the chowder and the marching – we just have food and beer once a month. We simplified it."*

Pro Bono

WilmerHale's strong commitment to pro bono was a big draw for many juniors. Sources found the unlimited pro bono hours to be *"a tremendous policy."* Many considered it to be *"a part of the identity of the firm: I've spent a lot of time on pro bono matters and it's not something you get push-back on. There's no side-eye."* Cases have included clemency projects, immigration matters, appellate work, veterans' work, human trafficking cases, family law matters, and people seeking protection in the context of do-

mestic violence. Juniors found pro bono to be *"a great way of getting client exposure, but also do something good, something that is revolutionary to someone's life."*

Pro bono hours
- For all US attorneys: 99,198
- Average per US attorney: 99

Hours & Compensation

WilmerHale's 2,000 hours target (including pro bono) *"sounds like a big number, but we're never really short of work, so it's been manageable."* Many juniors admitted having to work a little most weekends, *"maybe an hour or two, but not filling the whole weekend. That's rare."* But when a weekend of work does happen, *"people are very very nice about it – they're actually upset that they're making you do it. They make it a point to thank you and say 'hey, this person works really hard'."* There's also the option to work from home as *"there's very little to no face time requirement if you're not needed to be at a specific place at a specific time."*

Associate salaries matched the Cravath scale when the market salary went up in 2016. The bonus system was a bit of a gray area for some juniors, but most recognized that *"it's pretty much based on market."* Some believed the bonus system to be based solely on hours, and how much over the target you go. One source explained: *"They'll give bonuses over market to people who put in a lot more hours than expected. They explained that the extra bonus isn't there to encourage people to go over target, it's just there to recognize the people willing to put in extra time if need be."* Others reckoned that the quality of work also affected the bonus rate.

Diversity

"WilmerHale is the kind of place where people feel welcomed." Although juniors agreed that there's *"a lot of straight, white dudes,"* many emphasized that that's *"industry-wide"* and the firm itself *"tries really hard. Certainly the incoming classes are diverse, and the firm is committed to making sure the partnership is diverse too."* The firm recently hired Nimesh Patel from the Department of Homeland Security to head diversity and inclusion. He *"has a history of successful diversity initiatives at other places,"* according to one associate, which will help with WH's efforts.

Strategy & Future

At the time of our research, the firm was preparing to have its annual state of the firm meeting. Juniors anticipated that the meeting would go through things like *"how the firm did last year, goals for the future, and what*

See firm profile on p.671

business they want to focus on," among other items. Regular emails go out as well updating attorneys on firm initiatives.

"We're only as good as our next generation of talent," co-managing partner Susan Murley tells us. *"Between now and when readers will be ready to join, we will continue to focus on building talent at the firm, to help us focus on areas such as litigation, intellectual property, crisis management, regulatory, all things transactional, and securi-* ties. *Those are strengths for us and will continue to be our focus."* In terms of geography, Murley explains: *"Some of our offices are more mature than others. For example, DC and Boston are both vibrant and key offices where we'll continue to recruit talent, but we probably will not look to see substantial growth in those offices in the next few years. On the other hand, we will see growth in California, New York, and in our newest office in Denver, Colorado, and we will continue to build our practice in all of those offices."*

"We're only as good as our next generation of talent."

See firm profile on p.671

Wilson Sonsini Goodrich & Rosati

Lawyers per state

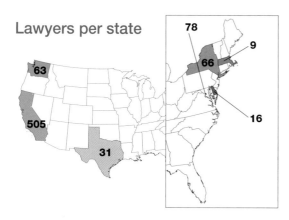

Largest US office: Palo Alto
US offices: 11
International offices: 4
First-year salary: $180,000
Billable hours: 1,950 target
Summers 2017: 56 (all 2Ls)
Revenue 2016: $755 million (+2.7%)
Partners made in 2017: 8
Famous for: start-up expertise; tech and life sciences focus

Long synonymous with Silicon Valley, Wilson Sonsini hires most new associates in California and Seattle, though there are openings elsewhere too.

TECH whizz Wilson Sonsini is Silicon Valley born and bred. The firm that handled Apple's IPO in 1980 cut its teeth in the booming emerging companies market of the 1970s, forging a USP for helping technology, life sciences and venture capital clients. Today it assists the likes of Google, Twitter, Netflix, Amazon and venture capitalists Sequoia, but big names are only half the package: Wilson Sonsini is still a major player on the start-up scene. *Chambers USA* considers it one of the best in the country for advising VC-backed newcos and it's this mix of little and large that sparked the interest of attorneys here when they were law students. *"We work with amazing tech companies,"* one new associate told us over the old-fashioned telephone, *"from early start-ups with two founders working out of an apartment to well-established public companies. We see a huge spectrum of clients."*

Chambers USA deems Wilson's capital markets, IT & outsourcing, securities litigation, corporate/M&A, and venture capital offerings among the best in California. Other ranked practices nationwide include capital markets, life sciences, antitrust, privacy & data security, and renewable energy. And much like the start-ups it's helped develop into international corporations, Wilson Sonsini

has expanded beyond Silicon Valley. The HQ remains in Palo Alto but other offices are to be found along the Western Seaboard and East Coast, in Texas, and overseas in China and Brussels.

The Work

Most of the firm's juniors can be found in the Palo Alto HQ. A handful reside in San Diego and Washington, DC, with the remainder scattered across the rest of the network, focusing on Los Angeles, Seattle, San Francisco and New York. The corporate department takes on the largest numbers of juniors – over half the rookies on our list were based here – with the rest split between litigation, technology transactions and IP. Work allocation tends to be largely organic in most groups, though teams have different ways of monitoring hours and activity.

Corporate newbies in Palo Alto spend their first two years at the firm in a 'launch' program. *"The corporate department is split into smaller practice groups which are very partner-centric,"* one source explained. *"People felt they were getting stuck working within these groups so the firm created 'launch',"* a corporate pool in which juniors can sample different areas. Interviewees appreciated the opportunity to launch themselves into a range of groups. *"I can't say enough good things about the staffing manager. You can request preferences and she ensures we get to experience working with different partners and practices."*

On chambers-associate.com...

- We speak with managing partner Douglas Clark
- Hiring partner Lisa Stimmell talks us through recruiting

See firm profile on p.673

The Inside View

Rankings in *Chambers USA*

Antitrust

Capital Markets

Corporate/Commercial

Corporate/M&A

Employee Benefits &
   Executive Compensation

IT & Outsourcing

Intellectual Property

International Trade

Life Sciences

Litigation

Privacy & Data Security

Projects

Securities

Startups & Emerging
   Companies

Tax

Technology

For detail on ranking tiers and ranking locations, visit
www.chambersandpartners.com

Recent work highlights

- Acted for data storage company Brocade in its $5.9 billion acquisition by semiconductor developer Broadcom
- Assisted Maxi Mobility, operators of Madrid-based ride-sharing app Cabify in a $120 million Series C financing round
- Represented cybersecurity service provider root9B in a securities fraud class action suit
- Advised electrophysiology development company Acutus Medical in a $75 million Series C financing round

Across the firm our associate sources had a hand in matters spanning *"the full life cycle"* of a company, from formation and incorporation all the way up to IPOs and M&A. *"We're working with start-ups at a very early stage who may have undergone a first few rounds of funding or venture capital financing. We might also help them with stock options and employee agreements. As they mature to mid-stage companies we handle more securities work and then as they mature they will be purchased or go public."* Others had worked with public companies *"on the day-to-day management of their corporate law needs like resolutions or stock option grants."*

"The sheer amount of deals and clients means that staffing is very light."

Day to day, tasks can be just as varied: *"The thing about working for different partner groups,"* one 'launch' interviewee told us, *"is that they all have different ways of using juniors. Some are very careful and you receive a lot of oversight; you do due diligence and maybe take the first crack of drafting basic forms or side letters. In other groups you're working with start-ups who don't want to spend a ton of money."* Juniors often find themselves *"able to kind of run the smaller deals"* which tend to be staffed by just a partner and associate. *"The sheer amount of deals and clients means that staffing is very light. You're given guidance but trusted to do everyday negotiating, making sure the deal is on track to close, communicating with the clients and managing their expectations"* as well as taking the first cut at drafting primary documents.

Many of Wilson's litigators find themselves in the securities and commercial litigation group, though other contentious departments include antitrust and patent litigation. One securities litigator told us: *"When I first started I was doing doc review and very simple drafting; the mid to senior associates would do the bulk of dispositive motions while I'd draft the requests for judicial notices. I had much more of a role on an investigation where I was preparing witnesses and a CEO to testify before a government agency."* Other junior sources had got stuck in on

legal research, kept clients updated on a case's progress, second chaired depositions and assisted senior attorneys in defending depositions.

Culture

"It's such a big firm and there's so much going on" – not to mention so many different offices – that juniors were cautious about ascribing a particular, overarching culture to the firm. That being said, we did come across a few commonalities. *"It's entrepreneurial; if you ask for a certain type of work you will get it but you have to be proactive. People appreciate it when you take the initiative to do things on your own, seek out answers and offer to take on more. The people who do well here are self-starters who are enthusiastic about getting their feet wet and not afraid to ask questions. They're self-motivated and don't need too much direction,"* one Palo Alto based-interviewee found.

"The exciting energy of start-ups."

"A lot of our clients are at a very early stage and that energy of emerging companies transfers into the office. At times it feels like we're part of a start-up; while I'm an IP lawyer I might be the only attorney my clients engage with for months at a time, so the legal advice I give is often beyond patent. The exciting energy transfers into all I do here," another source enthused. This dynamism is needed too: *"The pace at which the work comes in when you're working with early stage clients – it's like drinking water from a fire hose. It's become less overwhelming but for the first six months it was very intense."* Part of this is down to sometimes *"challenging clients."* A corporate junior noted: *"Some of these start-ups and entrepreneurs are living in a world of their own."* But interviewees were keen to point out that the flipside of working with emerging companies means *"you get a great degree of autonomy when dealing with them. It forces you to grow very early on."* Another elaborated: *"The needs and demands of clients mean things get pretty urgent quickly and then it's all hands on deck. They work you hard but we do try to be good at maintaining some kind of work/life balance."*

The Inside View

See firm profile on p.673

Diversity	Partners (%)	Associates (%)
Women	24	44
White	77.5	66.8
Black/African American	1.4	2.25
Hispanic/Latin American	6.6	2.3
Asian	14	24.2
Mixed/Other	0.5	4.5
LGBT	1.4	2.9

Despite the intense nature of work, juniors maintained *"we're still a West Coast firm. We work hard but people understand you have a life outside of the law."* A San Diegan quipped: *"It's BigLaw without the BigLaw part. We have the resources, the experts, the offices and all those kinds of perks but it's laid back and chilled."* Associates on the East Coast particularly appreciated the California mentality: *"It's midweek and I'm wearing jeans, a sweater and loafers. There are not too many other firms in DC where I could get away with that."*

Offices

Wilson Sonsini has 11 offices across the US. Boston's the most recent addition to the firm, opening in early 2016. Austin, Los Angeles, New York, Palo Alto (the firm's HQ), San Diego, Seattle, Washington, DC, Wilmington, and two San Francisco bases complete the US network. The firm also has hubs in Brussels, Beijing, Hong Kong and Shanghai.

Most of Wilson Sonsini's real estate is, reassuringly, decked out *"like a pretty generic law firm office"* and associates each have their own office. San Francisco's South of Market (SOMA) base, however, *"caters to start-ups, so it looks like a start-up. It's an open work space with exposed brick and beams. It looks very industrial. You often find clients working downstairs – I'm not sure if they like working here or just don't have an office yet."* Many of the associates we spoke to tended to predominantly work with colleagues in their own office, though we heard from litigators working cross-offices, and that teams reached out to specialists in other locations, like antitrust in DC.

Training & Development

'Launch' associates can also be sure of a monthly check-in on their progress; the staffing coordinator solicits feedback on a regular basis and juniors regularly meet with her for a fifteen-minute chat on their development. Outside of 'launch', everyone gets an annual review.

Newbies from across the firm are flown to Palo Alto for three days of intensive training as part of the 1st Year Academy. They later return for 3rd, 5th and 7th Year

Academies. The programs put associates through their paces in workshops covering things like due diligence, negotiation and management delegation. The first three months of first-year *"are slow on work; they do that on purpose and fill it with a lot of training."* Associates attend various training sessions giving them an insight into anything from specialty groups and how to tap into their resources, to practice classes on deal mechanics. Everyone's paired up with a 'First-Year Guide' to help integrate them into their new group. The firm also provides career guidance from coaches in the Career Management Center.

Hours & Compensation

Bonus eligibility starts once associates hit 1,950 hours. A hundred of these can be made up of non-billable work such as newsletter writing, interviews or client alerts, and juniors can also include an additional 50 shadowing hours. Unlimited pro bono also counts toward the target. Nearly all our sources, including those who hadn't tackled pro bono, had *"no trouble reaching"* the target. *"I think most people go over it,"* one source reckoned. *"We're consistently busy."*

On the *"biggest deals like IPOs and M&A you go full speed so you'll probably be here between 12 and 16 hours a day,"* one source told us. Otherwise ten or 11 hour stints in the office were common among our interviewees, with many also putting in an hour or two from home. The firm recently got rid of its *"black box"* merit-based bonus system and replaced it with a lockstep model. It matches market rate for both bonuses and salary.

"Expected to take the initiative."

Pro Bono

Unlimited pro bono hours count toward associates' billable targets. *"It's one of my favorite things about the firm,"* one interviewee declared. *"They're honestly not going to give you side-eye if you say 'sorry, I've got to do this for my pro bono case'."* Juniors are *"expected to take the initiative"* if they want to get involved and reach out to an unofficial coordinator. While several of our sources had sought out pro bono work, others were unaware of who to contact: *"I keep my eyes peeled but a lot of projects are hard to hear about."* The firm assures us there is an email, and the 'launch' program includes pro bono cases. Immigration cases are a dime a dozen but we also spoke to sources who had advised non-profit organizations on corporate issues, or assisted in guardianship cases, rent disputes, and unlawful detainment proceedings.

Pro bono hours
- For all US attorneys: 48,871
- Average per US attorney: 76

See firm profile on p.673

The Inside View

Diversity

"It doesn't feel un-diverse but it doesn't scream diverse," one junior mused. *"In some aspects it is very diverse, we have a lot of women partners and a lot of Asian American lawyers."* A quarter of associates are of Asian origin, and on this basis the firm performs better than market on ethnic diversity.

There is a Women's Task Force. *"It tries to bring women together to create a sense of camaraderie and highlights more senior people you can go to for advice about how to succeed in a law firm."* There's also an *"Asian associates' dinner every so often."* Interviewees were keen to point out that despite the lack of formal initiatives, the firm covers membership for external groups.

Strategy & Future

"Our strategy since the firm's inception more than 55 years ago has been to focus on tech, life sciences, renewable energy, and emerging growth companies," managing partner Douglas Clark tells us. The firm's in no rush to mess with a formula that works: *"We're going to retain our focus on industry sectors and continue to represent tech, life sciences, and renewable energy enterprises. One area of growth in the past several years has been our project and infrastructure practice; it has focused on renewable energy of late and will continue that focus as infrastructure and investment continues to expand in the US"*

Get Hired

"We're very enterprise-focused and we like to see people who understand that type of work," hiring partner Lisa Stimmell tells us. Visit chambers-associate.com for more from Stimmell on what the firm's looking for.

> ## "We're very enterprise-focused and we like to see people who understand that kind of work."
> ### Lisa Stimmell, hiring partner

The Inside View

See firm profile on p.673

Winston & Strawn LLP

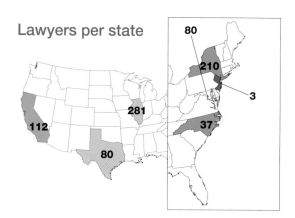

Lawyers per state

80

210

3

281

112

37

80

Largest US office: Chicago
US offices: 10
International offices: 7
First-year salary: $180,000
Billable hours: 2,000 required
Summers 2017: 68-71 (67-70 2Ls, 1 1L)
Revenue 2016: $822.8 million (+7.88%)
Partners made in 2017: 14
Famous for: Chicago's oldest firm; progressive parental leave policies; litigation heavyweights with a flourishing corporate group

This formidable litigator with a growing corporate side is dusting off its conservative image and investing heavily in its associates.

CHICAGO stalwart Winston & Strawn knows how to make an entrance. In early 2017 it strutted into Dallas with all the swagger of John Wayne to round up 23 partners from eight rival firms and open its very first Dallas base. *"We recognized that Dallas was a place where we could add to our national platform and expand in a city that has a lot of growth opportunities,"* managing partner Tom Fitzgerald tells us. The new addition will focus on adding to and strengthening the firm's litigation, real estate and corporate capabilities and gives Winston a grand total of 17 offices.

Winston's origins began much further north: it's the oldest firm in Chicago and, *"having been here forever, is extremely well respected and well known."* Age isn't the only thing earning Winston a good name; it's a beast in the courtroom, picking up a top tier *Chambers USA* ranking for its general commercial litigation practice. Intellectual property, transactional media & entertainment, energy, and shipping regulation also nab top spots. Meanwhile, the firm's corporate/M&A practice – which also earns a nod from *Chambers USA* – is in the midst of a flurry of growth.

Dallas isn't the only thing being shaken up by the firm. Winston's long enjoyed a reputation for being a conservative outfit but over the past few years associates had noticed *"a concerted effort to change that image from the top down."*

The Work

Around 60% of new associates go into litigation, while corporate accounts for roughly a quarter of juniors. The rest go into smaller groups including energy, employee benefits, labor & employment, real estate, and tax. Most practices dish out work through a free market system. *"As a young associate it can be difficult as the onus is on you to find work, but it's the best way to meet partners and get out there,"* sources told us. Should they run into difficulties an assigning partner is on hand to connect them with partners. The corporate group supplements its free market system by asking juniors to fill out a weekly form indicating their availability. New York deal-doers had been using this dual system *"for a while. It was working well to smooth out peaks and valleys,"* so it was recently adopted by other offices.

Litigation newbies spend their first few years as generalists, hopping between anything from securities and IP litigation to antitrust and general commercial disputes. Large scale doc review *"is farmed out to review companies,"* though our sources hadn't entirely escaped stints poring over the docs. One litigator outlined: *"My first year and a half was spent typically doing junior associate*

On chambers-associate.com

- Managing partner Tom Fitzgerald fills us in on a very busy year
- Getting hired at Winston & Strawn

See firm profile on p.674

The Inside View

Rankings in *Chambers USA*

Advertising	International Trade
Antitrust	Labor & Employment
Banking & Finance	Litigation
Bankruptcy/Restructuring	Media & Entertainment
Corporate/M&A	Projects
Energy & Natural	Sports Law
Resources	Tax
Intellectual Property	Transportation

For detail on ranking tiers and ranking locations, visit
www.chambersandpartners.com

Recent work highlights

- Represented AbbVie in a $93.8 million contract dispute with MedImmune arising out of the failed development of a new drug
- Acted for Illinois headquartered TreeHouse Foods in its $2.7 billion acquisition of the private brands operations of fellow Illinoisan ConAgra Foods
- Advised Goldman Sachs in an antitrust class action suit filed against the bank after US and European antitrust investigations into credit default swaps

tasks like case management, discovery related work and heavy research but in the last half a year I've taken on a substantial amount of drafting, taken control of briefs and second chaired depositions."

"A great way to get your name in front of people elsewhere."

Corporate rookies dip their toes into a bunch of transactional areas, like M&A, private equity and finance. *"In the first year you work on ancillary documents and diligence and figure out what a deal is and what all the different parts and aspects are,"* one third-year told us. *"As a second-year you tackle the drafting of ancillary documents and learn what they do and by the third year you're pushed into the more substantive documents. I've been working on a purchase agreement; I wasn't really sure if I was doing it correctly or not but the partner sat down with me afterward explaining why any changes needed to be made."*

Across practice areas, many juniors reported often working with colleagues in other offices – juniors in the smaller DC office were particularly likely to do this. *"You're not tied to what practices are physically in your office,"* sources told us. *"It's a great way to get your name in front of people elsewhere and build relationships among associates and partners."*

Offices

Most of the firm's associates are based in Chicago or New York. Washington, DC takes a handful and the rest are scattered between Charlotte, Houston, San Francisco and LA. New Yorkers share an office for their first two years: *"They try to pair us up with people we got along with on the summer program,"* so make sure any summer bromances are well publicized. Rookies in DC used to get lumbered with internal offices, *"but now everyone gets their own office with a window."* Chicago juniors also get their own digs complete with window from the get-go. In Chicago and DC, the firm has now moved to new premises.

Hours & Compensation

In June 2016, the firm announced salary rises for associates in all its US offices, not just New York. *"It was a great thing for morale and affirmed the firm's commitment to us. We were one of the first firms to match and the first in Chicago to do so,"* interviewees gushed.

> Winston's Dallas office brings the firm's number of US offices to ten. It also has seven international bases across Europe and China. Visit chambers associate.com for more on the new Dallas base.

Hitting 2,000 hours makes associates eligible for a base bonus. Provided they've got 1,900 in client billables under their belts, associates can count up to 100 pro bono or 40 firm citizenship hours toward the base bonus threshold. The latter encompasses time spent working on things like pitches or recruitment. After reaching 2,200 hours there's the likelihood of moving to a higher tier bonus which increases in 100-hour increments. Any additional pro bono hours can count toward these post 2,200 hour step-up bonuses.

There's no formal vacation policy at Winston and how much associates take off largely depends on the attitude within their group. We heard of some partners who insist people take at least two weeks, while some associates elsewhere felt taking that would be pushing it.

Juniors often put in at least nine hour days but warned it can get *"volatile. On a normal day when nothing's too crazy I could be out around 7pm. If things are hectic it's more 11pm but of course it can go all night,"* one source told us. Many of our interviewees worked with colleagues who were *"super flexible"* about where they expect juniors to get their work done, so heading home for dinner before plugging in for another hour's graft or working from home once a week or so was fairly common.

We also heard that Winston's Chicago office has recently become more *"open to reduced hours and alternative schedules. I think there's been a shift; management sat*

See firm profile on p.674

Diversity	Partners (%)	Associates (%)
Women	22	45
White	91	76
Black/African American	2	5
Hispanic/Latin American	3	5
Asian	3	9
Mixed/Other	1	5
LGBT	1	5

down and communicated what's available and how it can be used. It would be a great option for having kids and making this job work and hopefully eliminating the stigma around reduced hours will keep more women here," one source suggested.

Diversity

Winston recently rolled out a new gender neutral parental leave policy which affords new parents up to 20 weeks paid leave. "It's incredibly generous and has made a huge impact with women at the firm," one source told us. "It's a really good signal to us and was brought about by a push from the Women's Committee." While the gesture prompted very high praise from our interviewees, the question remains as to how much time parents will actually take. Sources informed us the firm has "held meetings about it and reiterated it's not just lip service – they want us to use it." We were told that since the move, "two associates took full paternity leave, which is unheard of." Others were more hesitant about taking the full allowance so time will tell how much use associates will make of the new policy. The firm also has a parental leave liaison to help with the transition period.

"A push from the Associates' Committee and Women's Committee."

Juniors noted the firm "could be more diverse," especially when it comes to racial diversity. Winston has a diversity committee and affinity groups for ethnic minorities and LGBT attorneys, and offers three scholarships to diverse summers every year.

Culture

Winston has long had a reputation for being a more formal and conservative kind of place. While some Chicago sources agreed they didn't think that description was "far off," many Windy City dwellers were keen to stress "it's changed over the last five years and a lot over the last year." One interviewee explained: "When I was a summer the door tags said 'Miss' or 'Mr', but now it's just your name." Another visible signs of change has been the introduction of jeans on Friday: "We used to just wear jeans once

a month and even that was a stretch but I think, thanks to a push back from the younger attorneys, the boundaries of business casual versus business professional tend to lean more toward the casual side," one source told us. Others pointed out that "the firm's more open to flexible and modern working arrangements," such as the increasing emphasis on reduced working hours and the new parental leave policy. One source posited: "I think the firm's realized that their employees, whether attorneys or staff, are their greater assets and they want to make working here as pleasant as possible."

"They want to make working here as pleasant as possible."

Over in New York, juniors didn't see much of the conservative reputation: "Maybe it's more among the senior partners?" one source suggested. "The interactions with people feel very casual," prompted by this office's commitment to weekly happy hours. "It's open to lawyers and staff and a great opportunity to unwind. Last week it was Super Bowl themed but it can range from Mardi Gras to tributes to Dolly Parton." In DC, "everybody is very friendly but only about half of us actually do the majority of our work with people in this location, so it's harder to have a homogeneous office culture."

Training & Development

Following grumbles in the past over the briefness of the review system, evaluations have undergone an overhaul. Juniors used to get oral feedback from a partner outside of their practice group. "The guy was very nice but it was weird as he wasn't in my practice area so it was harder to speak with him about my progress," one source recalled of the previous set-up. Juniors now receive a written copy of their feedback and the review is conducted by two partners, one of whom they've worked with, "to give you a better idea of how you're doing with your career and what you should be working on. It's a big change and a very positive one."

First-years at Winston are introduced to the firm with a week of orientation in Chicago, followed by weekly, hour-long sessions on various topics. For litigators, topics include how to prepare for trial, steps for discovery, and how to perform doc review, and every two years newbies gather in the Chicago office for firmwide deposition training.

Pro Bono

Attorneys are "given a lot of opportunities to do pro bono. We have a coordinator who sends out emails alerting us to matters and you can also reach out and ask for certain types of projects. A lot of people use it as a chance to de-

See firm profile on p.674

velop stand up skills like cross-examinations or oral arguments."

We're told there's "*a lot of immigration work to be had in Chicago,*" but sources had also gotten involved in adoption placement matters and helped clients appeal against the termination of housing vouchers. Assisting non-profits with corporate governance, drafting contracts and applying for tax exemption filled the dockets of corporate interviewees.

Pro bono hours
- For all US attorneys: 63,167
- Average per US attorney: 83

Get Hired

Associates kept flagging three key attributes when we asked them about what the firm looks for – "*grit*", "*confidence*" and "*pro-activity.*" Visit chambers-associate.com to find out what else you'll need.

Strategy & Future

Over the past few years the firm's been on a drive to be more transparent with associates about what's going down at Winston. "*They do it on a superficial level where they tell us they're adding these groups or focusing on these areas but they don't appraise us on big decisions until they've been made,*" one source told us. That said, juniors did note the situation "*has improved*" and if you do reach out and ask the partners "*they're typically very open about what is going on down the pipeline.*" Sources also praised the Associates' Committee: "*It has really developed over the last two years and the partners take it a lot more seriously.*"

Visit chambers-associate.com for a run down of what's in store for Winston from managing partner Tom Fitzgerald.

See firm profile on p.674

Leading Law Firms

Adam Leitman Bailey, P.C.

One Battery Park Plaza, Eighteenth Floor,
New York, NY 10004
Tel: 212 825 0365   Fax: 212 825 0999
Email: info@alblawfirm.com
www.alblawfirm.com

Main areas of work

Real estate

Firm profile

By uniting many of the best real estate attorneys of our generation, Adam Leitman Bailey, PC has become one of New York's most prominent real estate law firms. The firm excels by solely practicing real estate law and only taking on projects and cases where it is among the best in the field. Adam Leitman Bailey, PC has achieved groundbreaking results in the courtroom, in the board room, at the closing table, in the lobbies of legislative bodies and in every other venue where talented legal advocacy is key to its clients' interests.

Recruitment details

- Number of 1st year associates: 1   • Number of 2nd year associates: 1
- Associate salaries: 1st year: Base salary plus revenue sharing, plus bonus and depending on hours worked our pay is equal to larger firms
- Clerking policy: No

Summer details

Summer associate profile:

We choose the most talented applicants. When interviewing candidates for these positions, we look to see whether they have the potential to be great at our firm. Once we hire someone, the training, mentoring and teaching never stops. We strive for greatness in everything we do and expect our interns to do the same. We encourage you to express your opinions and share your ideas to improve our work.

Summer program components:

Our interns become lawyers in training and are part of the legal team and learn on the case or deal. Being assigned to active cases and made part of the team has given externs and interns the ability to produce amazing results. Only the very best law school students will make it at Adam Leitman Bailey, PC as we are considered among the best, if not the best, real estate law firm in New York City. Because Adam Leitman Bailey, PC practices only one type of law, all of our associates rapidly become experts. We have exciting cases that require hard work and sweat as well as the smartest most aggressive, passionate, loyal and committed students who are ready to change the world one real estate case at a time.

Interns will participate in a wide range of tasks that may include conducting case investigation, legal researc and discovery; meeting with clients and experts; and preparing memoranda, briefs and other legal documents for administrative, judicial and transactional proceedings.

Head Office: **New York, NY**
Number of domestic offices: **1**
Number of international offices: **0**
Partners (US): **8**
Associates (US): **17**

Main Recruitment Contact: **Brianna Loverich**
Hiring Partner: **Adam Leitman Bailey**
Recruitment website:
www.alblawfirm.com
Diversity officer: **Adam Leitman Bailey**

ADAM LEITMAN BAILEY, P.C.
NEW YORK REAL ESTATE ATTORNEYS

Firm Profiles

Akin Gump Strauss Hauer & Feld LLP

1333 New Hampshire Ave, NW, Washington, DC 20036
Tel: 202 887 4000 Fax: 202 887 4288
www.akingump.com

Main areas of work

Antitrust, communications and technology, cybersecurity, privacy and data protection, corporate, energy, entertainment and media, environment and natural resources, financial restructuring, global project finance, healthcare, intellectual property, international arbitration, international trade, investment funds, labor and employment, litigation, policy and regulation, Supreme Court and appellate and tax.

Firm profile

Akin Gump is a leading global law firm with more than 900 lawyers and advisors in the United States, Europe, Asia and the Middle East. Akin Gump is widely recognized for its strength in litigation and international arbitration, high stakes appellate work, financial restructuring, corporate transactions, investment funds, energy, global project finance and international trade and for its depth in regulatory and public policy, which allow the firm to provide a comprehensive suite of services for governments, companies and individuals worldwide. Collegiality, commitment, excellence, integrity and intensity form the bedrock of Akin Gump's core values. Akin Gump's dedication to the advancement of these values guides relationships within the firm and, most importantly, with its clients.

Recruitment details

- Number of 1st year associates: 43
- Associate salaries: 1st year: $180,000
- Clerking policy: Yes
- Number of 2nd year associates: 45
- 2nd Year: $190,000

Law Schools attending for OCIs in 2017:

American, Berkeley, Boston University, Cardozo, Catholic, Columbia, Cornell, Duke, Emory, Fordham, George Mason, George Washington, Georgetown, Harvard, Howard, Houston, Michigan, New York University, Penn, UC Irvine, UCLA, USC, SMU, Stanford, Texas, Tulane, Vanderbilt, Virginia, William & Mary

Summer details

Summer associate profile:

Akin Gump seeks motivated candidates with outstanding academic credentials, overall achievement, leadership and interpersonal skills, and work experience. In addition, the firm looks for candidates who demonstrate the firm's core competencies: ownership, professional excellence, service and teamwork and client focus.

Summer program components:

Akin Gump summer associates work on real matters for real clients. Summer associates gain in-depth exposure to the firm's practice and hands-on experience with clients and work that interests them. With training, mentorship, teamwork and social activities, summer associates get a realistic and meaningful picture of firm life. Summer associates participate in pro bono projects through organisations with which Akin Gump has a pro bono partnership. These projects are geared to summer associates' interests and maximize front-line responsibility while ensuring appropriate supervision from experienced attorneys. Summer associates receive feedback on a project-by-project basis and at mid-summer and end of summer reviews.

Number of domestic offices: 11
Number of international offices: 9
Worldwide revenue: $980,000,000
Partners (US): 268
Associates (US): 356

Main Recruitment Contact: David H Botter, Firmwide Hiring Partner.
For a complete listing of our recruiting contacts go to www.akingump.com/en/careers/lawyers/recruiting-process/contact-us.html
Recruitment website:
www.akingump.com/en/careers
Diversity officer: Karol Kepchar, Chair Firmwide Diversity Committee

Summer Salary 2017
1Ls: $3,500/week
2Ls: $3,500/week
1Ls hired? Select offices and through our Pro Bono Scholars Program
Split summers offered? Case by case
Can summers spend time in overseas office? No
Summers 2017: 73
Offers/Acceptances 2016:
52 offers, 45 acceptances

Akin Gump
STRAUSS HAUER & FELD LLP

Firm Profiles

Allen & Overy LLP

1221 Avenue of the Americas, New York, NY 10020
Tel: 212 610 6300   Fax: 212 610 6399
Email: legalcareers@allenovery.com
www.allenovery.com

Main areas of work

Banking, corporate, international capital markets, litigation, project finance, financial restructuring and insolvency, general lending, leveraged finance and tax.

Firm profile

We are one of a group of truly international and integrated law firms with approximately 5,000 people working in 44 cities in 30 countries. This network has allowed us to become one of the largest and most connected law firms in our peer group with a global reach and local depth that is simply unrivalled. As more than 65% of our work involves more than two countries, our US practice—which operates principally from offices in Hong Kong, London, New York and Washington DC—is fully integrated with our offices in Europe, Asia, South America, Australia and Africa. We believe we have a special culture at Allen & Overy, which is founded on quality work, excellent working partnerships and collegiality.

Recruitment details

• Number of 1st year associates: 18 (NY/DC)
• Number of 2nd year associates: 16 (NY/DC)
• Associate salaries: 1st year: $180,000   • 2nd year: $190,000
• Clerking policy: Yes

Law Schools attending for OCIs in 2017:

American, BC/BU, Brooklyn, Cardozo, Chicago, Columbia, Cornell, Duke, Emory, Fordham, Georgetown, George Washington, Harvard, Howard, Lavender Law, Michigan, NEBLSA, NLSC, Northwestern, NYU, University of Pennsylvania, Rutgers, Seton Hall, Stanford, St John's, Texas, UC Berkeley, UVA, Vanderbilt, Yale

Summer details

Summer associate profile:

At Allen & Overy, we operate in a dynamic, challenging environment which fosters creativity as well as professionalism. Our attorneys handle the most sophisticated and complex domestic and cross border transactions and cases for our clients. The ideal candidate should possess determination, vision, creativity, strength and breadth of character. He or she should be committed to working as part of an international team. One of the best features of the Allen & Overy team is the strength of the personal and professional relationships formed between colleagues. We maintain strong camaraderie around the world.

Summer program components:

We recruit on campus for all 3 summer programs (New York, London and Washington, DC). We typically host around 13-15 summer associates in New York, 3-4 in London and 4-5 in Washington DC. Summer associates are treated as full-time associates and we make a point of offering considerable responsibility, working on top-quality transactions in various areas. We place great value on feedback and go to great lengths to match individual preferences with the work we assign. Summer associates can expect to receive ample partner attention and to gain invaluable experience. We take mentoring and development seriously and both are fundamental aspects of our program. We also expect our summer associates to have fun and plan social events to integrate them into our firm culture.

Head Office: New York, NY
Number of domestic offices: 2
Number of international offices: 42
Partners (US): 48
Senior Counsel (US): 9
Associates (US): 115

Main Recruitment Contact:
Erin Manna, Senior Coordinator, Lateral & Staff Recruitment
Hiring Partners: Charles Borden (DC), Laura Hall (NY)
Recruitment website:
www.us.aograduate.com
Diversity officer: Elizabeth Leckie, Partner

Summer Salary 2017
1Ls: N/A
2Ls: $3,500/week
Post 3Ls: $3,500/week
1Ls hired? No
Split summers offered? Yes
Can summers spend time in overseas office? Yes, we run parallel summer associate programs in New York, London and Washington DC. Occasionally, summer associates have spent time in other offices with US capabilities on a case by case basis
Summers 2017: 20 (NY, LN, DC)
Offers/acceptances 2016:
23 offers, 21 acceptances (NY, LN, DC)

ALLEN & OVERY

Alston & Bird LLP

One Atlantic Center, 1201 West Peachtree Street, Atlanta, GA 30309-3424
Tel: 404 881 7000   Fax: 404 881 7777
Email: erin.springer@alston.com
www.alston.com

Main areas of work

Alston & Bird provides a full range of services to domestic and international clients. Our core practice areas are intellectual property, complex litigation, corporate and tax, with national industry focuses in healthcare, financial services and public policy.

Firm profile

Founded in 1893, Alston & Bird is a leading national AmLaw 50 firm. Counseling clients from what was initially a local context quickly expanded to regional, then national levels and now spans a global economic environment. Alston & Bird has overlaid its broad range of legal skills and business knowledge with a commitment to innovation and technology. Alston & Bird has been ranked on *Fortune* magazine's '100 Best Companies to Work For' list for 18 consecutive years, an unprecedented accomplishment among law firms in the United States. The recognition speaks to the culture of the firm and the environment in which we practice law and provide service to clients. Alston & Bird has been consistently recognized as a US law firm providing superior client service in the BTI Most Recommended Law Firms. This recognition results from interviews with approximately 300 corporate counsel at Fortune 1000 companies.

Recruitment details

- Number of 1st year associates: 39   • Number of 2nd year associates: 45
- Associate salaries: 1st year: $155,000-$180,000 (based on location)
- Clerking policy: Yes

Law Schools attending for OCIs in 2017:

American, Columbia, Cornell, Duke, Emory, Fordham, Georgetown, George Washington, Georgia, Georgia State, Harvard, Hofstra, Howard, Loyola, Mercer, Michigan, NYU, Northwestern, SMU, Stanford, Texas, UC Berkeley, UC Hastings, UC Irvine, UCLA, UNC, USC, Vanderbilt, Virginia, Wake Forest, Washington & Lee

Summer details

Summer associate profile:

Our lawyers have diverse backgrounds, varied social, cultural, civic, and educational interests and our summer associates are no exception. We value hard work, scholastic excellence and strong interpersonal skills.

Summer program components:

Our summer program provides students with substantive work for real clients, hands-on training opportunities, lawyer pairings to help foster relationships and a firm-wide retreat. Summer Associates work closely with their mentors to identify projects from our database that will allow for an authentic experience based on their legal interests. In addition to formal training programs, we offer out-of-office experiences to attend depositions, client meetings, hearings and other hands on learning experiences. Associate contacts ensure that summer associates have plenty of opportunities to interact with attorneys throughout the summer.

Head Office: Atlanta, GA
Number of domestic offices: 9
Number of international offices: 2
Worldwide revenue: $730,579,255
Partners (US): 345
Associates (US): 366

Main Recruitment Contact:
Erin L Springer
Hiring Partner: Elizabeth A Price
Recruitment website:
www.alston.com/alstoncareers
Diversity officers: Cari Dawson and John Latham

Summer Salary 2017
1Ls: $3,000/week (ATL, CLT, RTA) or $3,5000/week (DFW, LAX, NYC, SVA, WDC)
2Ls: $3,000/week (ATL, CLT, RTA) or $3,5000/week (DFW, LAX, NYC, SVA, WDC)
Post 3Ls: N/A
1Ls hired? Yes
Split summers offered? Yes, first half required
Can summers spend time in overseas office? No
Summers 2017: 55
Offers/acceptances 2016:
43 offers, 42 acceptances

ALSTON & BIRD

Arnold & Porter Kaye Scholer LLP

601 Massachusetts Avenue, NW. Washington, DC 20001-3743
Tel: 202 942 5000 Fax: 202 942 5999
Email: recruiting@apks.com
www.apks.com/en

Main areas of work

Our 1,000+ attorneys in 13 domestic and international offices practice across more than 30 areas, including corporate, finance, intellectual property, life sciences, litigation, real estate, and tax, provide clients a multi-disciplinary approach to their most complex legal issues.

Firm profile

Arnold & Porter Kaye Scholer LLP combines 100 years of business acumen and a common devotion to first-class legal work. With renowned regulatory experience, sophisticated litigation and transactional practitioners, and leading multidisciplinary practices, it is the firm of choice for 133 Fortune 250 companies. Recent commercial work includes representing AMC Entertainment in its $1.1 billion acquisition of Carmike Cinemas, creating the largest movie theater chain in the US, as well as a remarkable string of 26 international arbitration victories on behalf of various Latin American countries. Service is a core value of the firm, as demonstrated by our leading pro bono program. Firmwide, our attorneys performed more than 97,500 hours of pro bono work in 2016 on projects such as representing voting rights organizations and individual voters in federal and state courts, immigration and asylum work assisting detainees and victims of domestic violence, and partnering with commercial clients' in-house counsel on naturalization and consumer law projects. Our attorneys are also committed to government service, with many of the firm's lawyers previously holding senior positions in the White House and in US government agencies. Diversity and inclusion are core values, and the firm is committed to cultivating a positive and supportive work environment where all talent is accorded dignity and respect. Our firm values the contribution that each person makes as an individual, and all attorneys, regardless of experience level, are encouraged to participate fully in the work of the firm. For more about the firm, visit our website at apks.com.

Recruitment details

- Number of 1st year associates: 41
- Associate salaries: 1st year: $180,000
- Number of 2nd year associates: 38
- Clerking policy: yes

Law Schools attending for OCIs in 2017:

Brooklyn, Chicago, Columbia, Cornell, Duke, Fordham, George Mason, Georgetown, GW, Harvard, Howard, Loyola - Los Angeles, Michigan, NYU, Northwestern, St. John's, Stanford, Texas, Tulane, UC Berkeley, UC Davis, UC Hastings, UC Irvine, UCLA, U of Colorado, U of Denver, U of Houston, U Penn, USC, UVA, Yale

Summer details

Summer associate profile:

Our firm is a collection of independent, diverse personalities who share a common devotion to first class legal work and client service. We seek candidates with outstanding academic and extracurricular achievements, as well as relevant work experience.

Summer program components:

Our summer associates experience first-hand the firm's strong commitment to excellence, diversity, pro bono work, and professional development, working side-by-side with our attorneys on actual client matters. We seek to match assignments to the interests each summer associate has identified, including pro bono work. Our summer associates participate in the firm's extensive training programs, including attending a retreat in the Washington, DC office. All summer associates have mentors and receive feedback on each assignment. Our summer program features a mix of events designed to appeal to a broad range of interests.

Number of domestic offices: 9
Number of international offices: 4
Worldwide revenue: $944,732,000 (combined 2016 revenue for legacy Arnold & Porter and legacy Kaye Scholer)
Partners (US): 319
Associates (US): 479 (includes 49 staff attorneys)

Main Recruitment Contact:
Jennifer Gewertz, Firmwide Director of Attorney Recruiting
Hiring Partners: Ellen Fleishhacker, Catherine Schumacher and Darren Skinner
Recruitment website:
www.apks.com/en/careers

Summer Salary 2017
1Ls: $3,465 per week
2Ls: $3,465 per week
Post 3Ls: N/A
1Ls hired? Varies by office
Split summers offered? Yes
Can summers spend time in overseas office? No
Summers 2017: 64
Offers/acceptances 2016:
56 offers, 50 acceptances (2 offers outstanding) - combined numbers for legacy Arnold & Porter and legacy Kaye Scholer

ARNOLD & PORTER
KAYE SCHOLER

Axinn, Veltrop & Harkrider LLP

114 West 47th Street, New York, NY 10036
Tel: 212 728 2200   Fax: 212 728 2201
www.axinn.com

Main areas of work

Antitrust, intellectual property and complex litigation.

Firm profile

Axinn is a different kind of law firm. It combines the skills, experience and dedication of the world's largest firms with the focus, responsiveness, efficiency and attention to client needs of the best boutiques. Axinn was established in the late 1990s by lawyers from premier Wall Street firms with a common vision and has been joined by lawyers from the best firms and law schools who share that vision. Axinn is devoted to providing the highest conceivable quality of service in three practice areas: antitrust, intellectual property and high-stakes litigation. Axinn achieves that goal through world class skills and deep trial experience. Time and again, major companies have turned to Axinn for their biggest deals and cases, often on the eve of trial.

Recruitment details

- Number of 1st year associates: 4   • Number of 2nd year associates: 4
- Associate salaries: 1st year: $170,000 in CTO; $180,000 in NYO and DCO
- Clerking policy: Case by case

Law Schools attending for OCIs in 2017:

Berkeley, Chicago, Columbia, Connecticut, Duke, Fordham, George Washington, Georgetown, Harvard, Michigan, New York, Pennsylvania, Stanford, Virginia, Washington University in St Louis, Yale

Summer details

Summer associate profile:

Axinn is a top tier boutique practicing in antitrust, IP and high-stakes litigation. It seeks students who have achieved academic excellence and are entrepreneurial. Candidates must be among the top 25% of their law school class. Top 10% class ranking, law review and moot court experience is preferred. For the antitrust group, Axinn prefers that candidates have an economic or finance degree/ background. Science or engineering backgrounds are preferred for candidates who wish to work in IP. Patent bar admission is a plus for IP candidates.

Summer program components:

During their summer with Axinn, associates attend internal meetings and seminars to familiarize themselves with lawyers, clients and range of projects that comprise our practice. In addition, Axinn attorneys and outside professionals provide training in such topics as legal writing, litigation strategy and how to effectively utilize firm resources and support services. Each training experience emphasizes "learning by doing" and serves to enhance opportunities for summer associates to develop, exercise and build confidence in their skills. Each summer associate is assigned a partner and associate mentor, who are available to prioritize assignments and act as a sounding board. Axinn combines the prestige of a large firm with the collegiality of a boutique. Summer associates are invited to join events such as wine tastings, theater, sporting and museum outings and cooking classes.

Head Office: New York, NY
Number of domestic offices: 3
Number of international offices: 0
Partners (US): 24
Associates (US): 33

Main Recruitment Contact:
Rachel Rosado
Hiring Partners: Daniel Bitton, Jeremy Lowe and Thomas Rohback
Recruitment website:
www.axinn.com/careers
Diversity officer: Jeremy Lowe

Summer Salary 2017
1Ls: N/A
2Ls: $3,269/week (CT)
$3,461/week (NY/DC)
Post 3Ls: N/A
1Ls hired? No
Split summers offered? Case by case
Can summers spend time in overseas office? N/A
Summers 2017: 9
Offers/acceptances 2016:
5 offers, 5 acceptances

Firm Profiles

Baker Botts LLP

One Shell Plaza, 910 Louisiana, Houston, Texas 77002-4995
Tel: 713 229 1234   Fax: 713 229 1522
Email: info@bakerbotts.com
www.bakerbotts.com

Main areas of work

Based on our broad experience and our in-depth knowledge of our clients' industries, we are recognized as a leading firm in energy and technology. Core practice areas include project development and finance; corporate transactions; complex business litigation; international arbitration; antitrust; intellectual property; environmental; compliance and enforcement; tax; employee benefits; and real estate.

Firm profile

Baker Botts is a globally respected law firm with 725 lawyers and 14 international offices. We are driven by the highest ethical and professional standards. This professionalism, combined with industry knowledge and insights and our understanding of the law, helps us to deliver effective, innovative solutions for our clients.

For more than 175 years, Baker Botts has delivered results-oriented services, establishing us as a leading law firm. Our reputation is complemented by our leadership in government, the judiciary and our communities. Regardless of size, sector or jurisdiction of a client, our commitment is to help achieve their business objectives

Recruitment details

- Number of 1st year associates: 52
- Number of 2nd year associates: N/A – advancement based on levels system
- Associate salaries: 1st year: $180,000
- Clerking policy: Yes

Law Schools attending for OCIs in 2017:

Alabama, Baylor, Berkeley, Cardozo, Chicago, Columbia, Cornell, Duke, Fordham, Georgetown, George Washington, Harvard, Houston, Loyola Patent Program, LSU, Michigan, Northwestern, NYU, Pennsylvania, SMU, Stanford, Texas, UC Hastings, UCLA, UC Davis, USC, Vanderbilt, Virginia, Washington University, Yale, Bay Area Diversity Career Fair, Boston College/ Boston University Job Fair, Harvard BLSA Job Fair, Lavender Law Job Fair, San Francisco IP Job Fair, Southeastern Minority Job Fair, Southwest BLSA Job Fair, Texas in NY and DC Job Fairs.

Summer details

Summer associate profile:

Baker Botts lawyers are selected from the top graduates among the best law schools. We have formally established a set of core attributes we seek in candidates; some of which include leadership, collegiality, dedication, and commitment to excellence.

Summer program components:

Our philosophy is to allow summer associates to sample work in practice areas in which they are interested. Written and oral work evaluations are strongly encouraged and monitored. Each summer associate has both partner and associate advisors. All summer associates receive formal performance evaluations during the summer program. Baker Weekend, the cornerstone of our summer program, brings together summer associates and lawyers from all seven of our U.S. offices for a weekend of training and social events. Our summer associates learn about our firm through interactive panel discussions and informal break-out sessions with firm leadership and enjoy socializing with each other and our attorneys in a fun, casual setting.

Head Office: **Houston, TX**
Number of domestic offices: **7**
Number of international offices: **7**
Partners (US): **238**
Associates (US): **345**

Main Recruitment Contact: **Elizabeth Krichmar, Director of Recruiting**
Hiring Partner: **John Martin, Partner-in-Charge, Recruiting**
Recruitment website:
www.bakerbotts.com/lawstudents/
Diversity officer: **Sylvia James, Diversity Counsel**

Summer Salary 2017
1Ls: **$3,642/week**
2Ls: **$3,642/week**
Post 3Ls: **$3,642/week**
1Ls hired? **Yes**
Split summers offered? **Yes**
Can summers spend time in overseas office? **No**
Summers 2017: **96 (64 2Ls, 32 1Ls)**
Offers/acceptances 2016:
70 offers, 44 acceptances, 6 deferred acceptances, 4 undecided

BAKER BOTTS

Firm Profiles

Baker McKenzie

300 East Randolph Street, Chicago, IL 60601
Tel: 312 861 8000
www.bakermckenzie.com

Main areas of work

Antitrust and competition, banking and finance, dispute resolution, employment, environment and climate change, intellectual property, IT/communications, energy, mining and infrastructure, mergers and acquisitions, pharmaceuticals and health-care, private equity, real estate, securities, tax, trade and commerce.

Firm profile

For more than 60 years, Baker McKenzie has provided sophisticated advice and legal services to many of the world's most dynamic and successful organizations. Baker McKenzie serves more than half of the world's largest public companies as well as a broad spectrum of regional and local organizations. With more than 4,400 locally qualified, internationally experienced lawyers in 47 countries, the firm has the fluency to deliver a broad scope of quality legal services — consistently, with confidence and sensitivity for cultural, social and legal practice differences. Baker McKenzie professionals share common values of integrity, personal responsibility and tenacity in an enthusiastic client-service culture. The firm is still guided by the entrepreneurial spirit and demanding standards of its founders and works to forge close personal relationships among its professionals in order to foster the responsiveness and accountability clients rightfully expect. The firm has a diverse and welcoming culture. Its lawyers and other professionals are citizens of more than 60 countries and are admitted to practice in nearly 250 jurisdictions. They have offices in 77 locations worldwide, including in 26 of the world's 30 largest economies. Baker McKenzie also invests in communities where its people live and work and is a pioneer in teaming with its clients on corporate social responsibility efforts worldwide.

Recruitment details

- Number of 1st year associates: 34
- Associate salaries: 1st year: $180,000 in Dallas, Chicago, Houston, New York, Washington, DC, San Francisco/Palo Alto. $145,000 in Miami.
- Clerking policy: Case by case

Law Schools attending for OCIs in 2017:

Baker McKenzie is committed to recruiting the highest caliber of talent for their Summer Associate Program. Particularly, they take great strides in recruiting at more than 30 distinctive law schools.

Summer details

Summer program components:

The Summer Associate Program is designed to introduce law students to the practice of law at Baker McKenzie. Every effort is made to expose summer associates to all aspects of the firm's practice by receiving substantive legal work, professional training and networking opportunities. In addition, international clerkship opportunities are available for summer associates to gain meaningful work experience, aligned with their practice focus and intercultural experience, through a secondment in another office outside of North America.

Head Office: N/A
Number of domestic offices: 7
Number of international offices: 70
Worldwide revenue: $2.64 billion
Partners (US): 344
Associates (US): 342

Main Recruitment Contact:
Kristina Gajewicz, North America Recruiting Director
Hiring Partner: Scott Brandman, North America Hiring Partner
Recruitment website:
www.bakermckenzie.com/en/careers
Diversity officer: Anna Brown, North America Director of Diversity

Summer Salary 2017
1Ls: $3,462/week for all US offices, except $2,786/week in Miami
2Ls: $3,462/week for all US offices, except $2,786/week in Miami
1Ls hired? Case by case
Split summers offered? Case by case
Can summers spend time in overseas office? Yes, through our International Clerkship Program
Summers 2017: 51
Offers/acceptances 2016:
36 offers, 32 acceptances

Baker McKenzie.

Bracewell LLP

711 Louisiana St., Suite 2300, Houston, TX 77002
Tel: 713 223 2300   Fax: 1 800 404 3970
Email: client.services@bracewell.com
www.bracewell.com

Main areas of work

Bracewell's main areas of concentration are business and regulatory, technology, litigation and government. These areas breakdown into a number of core practices, including banks and financial institutions; energy; environmental strategies; financial restructuring; private investment funds; white-collar defense, internal investigations and regulatory enforcement; broker-dealer and market regulation; corporate and securities; finance; intellectual property; labor and employment; real estate and projects; strategic communications; tax; climate change; and public law.

Firm profile

Bracewell LLP is a global law firm with offices in Texas, New York, Washington, DC, Connecticut, Seattle, Dubai, and London. The firm serves Fortune 500 companies, major financial institutions, leading private investment funds, governmental entities and individuals concentrated in the energy, technology and financial services sectors worldwide.

Recruitment details

- Number of 1st year associates: 26
- Number of 2nd year associates: 20
- Associate Salaries: 1st Year: $180,000
- 2nd Year: $190,000
- Clerking policy: We encourage associates to pursue judicial clerkships if they are interested

Law Schools attending for OCIs in 2017:

Seventeen

Summer details

Summer associate profile:

Bracewell takes into account a number of factors when making its selection for summer associates. These include but are not limited to such academic-related areas as class rank, grade-point average and journal membership. In addition, the firm bases offers in part on the extracurricular endeavors of potential summer associates, such as professional/legal association involvement, internships and/or clerkships and law school fraternity memberships.

Summer program components:

The firm offers summer associate programs in all US offices, though demand in each office is determined from year to year. These programs vary by location, but range in length from 8-9 weeks. During this time, summer associates work in various practice areas – dictated by office locale – and attend hearings, depositions, trials, negotiations and client meetings. When not working at the firm, summer associates are encouraged to explore the city in which they live and are also invited to attorney dinners, all-clerk lunches and a summer associate retreat.

Head Office: Houston, TX
Number of domestic offices: 8
Number of international offices: 2
Worldwide revenue: $277,000,000
Partners (US): 169
Associates (US): 197

Main Recruitment Contact:
Jean Lenzner, Director Attorney Employment
Hiring Partners: Bryan Dumesnil and Ryan Holcomb
Recruitment website:
www.bracewell.com/careers
Diversity officer: Marredia Rogers

Summer Salary 2017
1Ls: $3,461.54/week
2Ls: $3,461.54/week
Post 3Ls: N/A
1Ls hired? Yes
Split summers offered? No
Can summers spend time in overseas office? No
Summers 2017: 33 (20 2Ls, 13 1Ls)

BRACEWELL

Brown Rudnick LLP

One Financial Center, Boston, MA 02111
Tel: 617 856 8200   Fax: 617 856 8201
www.brownrudnick.com

Main areas of work

Bankruptcy and corporate restructuring; complex litigation and arbitration; corporate, securities and M&A; distressed debt and claims trading; emerging companies; energy, utilities and environmental; finance; funds; government contracts; government law and strategies; healthcare; intellectual property; intellectual property litigation; international dispute resolution; life sciences; real estate; tax; white collar defense and government investigations.

Firm profile

Brown Rudnick, an international law firm with offices in the United States and Europe, represents clients from around the world in high stakes litigation, international arbitration and complex business transactions. Clients include public and private corporations, multinational Fortune 100 businesses and start-up enterprises. The firm also represents investors, as well as official and ad hoc creditors' committees in today's largest corporate restructurings, both domestically and abroad. Founded more than 60 years ago, Brown Rudnick has over 240 lawyers providing advice and services across key areas of the law. Beyond the United States, the firm regularly serves clients in Europe, the Middle East, North Africa, the Caribbean and Latin America. With its Brown Rudnick Center for the Public Interest, the firm has created an innovative model combining its pro bono, charitable giving and community volunteer efforts.

Recruitment details

- Number of 1st year associates: 17
- Number of 2nd year associates: 19
- Associate salaries: 1st year: $180,000
- 2nd year: $190,000
- Clerking policy: Yes

Law Schools attending for OCIs in 2017:

Boston College, Boston University, Columbia University, Fordham University School of Law, Georgetown University, Harvard University, Howard University School of Law, New York University, University of California – Irvine, Howard University School of Law, University of Connecticut, University of Texas

Summer details

Summer associate profile:

Brown Rudnick recruits summer associates who are highly intelligent and creative and also possess those personal qualities that define our firm: hard driving but value oriented and pragmatic, entrepreneurial, always honest and ethical and highly collaborative.

Summer program components:

Brown Rudnick allocates significant energy and resources to provide each summer associate with a first hand experience of life as a lawyer at our firm. We offer a wide range of assignments, provide a robust training curriculum, including core legal and writing skills, business development and networking skills, as well as a fun social calendar.

Head Office: **Boston, MA**
Number of domestic offices: **6**
Number of international offices: **2**
Worldwide revenue: **$191,000,000**
Partners (US): **85**
Associates (US): **74**

Main Recruitment Contacts:
Heather L. Cannady, Molly I. Childs
Hiring Partner: **Jeffrey L. Jonas**
Recruitment website:
www.brownrudnick/careers
Diversity officers: **Sunni Beville, Ari Joesph**

Summer Salary 2017
1Ls: **$3,461/week**
2Ls: **$3,461/week**
Post 3Ls: **$3,461/week**
1Ls hired? **Case by case**
Split summers offered? **Case by case**
Can summers spend time in overseas office? **Case by case**
Summers 2017: **10**
Offers/acceptances 2016:
9 offers, 7 acceptances, 2 outstanding (clerks)

Brownstein Hyatt Farber Schreck

410 Seventeenth Street, Suite 2200, Denver, CO 80202
Tel: 303 223 1100
Email: jolberding@bhfs.com
www.bhfs.com

Main areas of work

Practices: Corporate and business, gaming, intellectual property, energy and natural resources, government relations, litigation, real estate

Industries: Banking, investment, finance and money management; energy and mining; gaming; health care; life sciences; real estate; water; consumer products; entertainment; government, regulation and public policy; hospitality; professional service; and science and technology

Firm profile

Brownstein Hyatt Farber Schreck has developed a reputation as a high-powered law firm with unparalleled community and business connections. The firm has more than 250 attorneys and legislative consultants across 11 offices in Albuquerque, Atlantic City, Denver, Las Vegas, Los Angeles, Orange County, Reno, Sacramento, San Diego, Santa Barbara, and Washington, DC. The firm handles work for leaders in industries ranging from real estate, gaming, water, resorts and telecommunications to construction, energy, private equity and finance. The firm's broad resources allow it to assemble the right team of legal talent for any deal or case, no matter the size, complexity or location. Operating in partnership with their clients, Brownstein attorneys and policy advisors design integrated strategies that combine multidisciplinary teams to strive to become a seamless extension of in-house resources.

Recruitment details

- Number of 1st year associates: 7
- Associate salaries: 1st year: $135,000
- Clerking policy: yes
- Number of 2nd year associates: 7
- 2nd year: $140,000

Law Schools attending for OCIs in 2017:

University of Denver College of Law, University of Colorado School of Law, UCLA School of Law, UNLV School of Law

Summer details

Summer associate profile:

Brownstein's summer associate program offers an in-depth view of life at the firm, as well as the opportunity to develop the skills and relationships to establish a solid foundation for future success. For our structured, nine-week program, we look for current law students from law schools across the country dedicated to learning the life of the "real" legal world at a law firm. Associates must be open to mentoring and a comprehensive training schedule, including topics such as the billable hour, law firm survival skills and exploring major practice areas within the firm.

Summer program components:

Our summer associate program provides an in-depth view of life at the firm, as well as the opportunity to develop the skills and relationships necessary to establish a solid foundation for future success. The summer associates will have the opportunity to work with attorneys at all levels to learn about their individual practices and careers, and are also offered the opportunity to do pro bono work. In addition to a comprehensive training schedule, each summer associate is paired with a mentor who will help guide them through the program and facilitate their introduction to the firm. Brownstein offers education and training sessions each week during the program covering topics such as "The Billable Hour," "Law Firm Survival Skills," and exploring major practice areas within the firm. Additionally, the summer is filled with networking and social engagements to allow summer associates a chance to meet Brownstein attorneys and staff.

Head Office: Denver
Number of domestic offices: 11
Number of international offices: 0
Worldwide revenue: $173 million
Partners (US): 131
Associates (US): 79

Main Recruitment Contact: Jamie Olberding
Recruitment website: www.bhfs.com/careers

Summer Salary 2017
1Ls: $1,800
2Ls: $2,600
Post 3Ls: NA
1Ls hired? Yes
Split summers offered? Case-by-case
Can summers spend time in overseas office? NA
Summers 2017: 7
Offers/acceptances 2016: 4/4

Brownstein Hyatt
Farber Schreck

Cadwalader, Wickersham & Taft LLP

200 Liberty Street, New York, NY 10281
Tel: 212 504 6000   Fax: 212 504 6666
www.cadwalader.com

Main areas of work

The firm offers legal representation in antitrust, banking, business fraud, capital markets, corporate finance, corporate governance, energy, executive compensation, financial restructuring, healthcare, intellectual property, litigation, mergers and acquisitions, private equity, private wealth, real estate, regulation, securitization, structured finance and tax.

Firm profile

Cadwalader, Wickersham & Taft LLP, established in 1792, is a leading legal advisor to many of the world's top financial institutions and corporations, with offices in New York, London, Charlotte, Washington and Brussels. Our lawyers provide counsel on sophisticated and complex transactional, litigation, and regulatory matters to help our clients break new ground, achieve their business goals, and overcome challenges.

Recruitment details

- Number of 1st year associates: 44
- Associate salaries: 1st year: $180,000
- Clerking policy: Case by case
- Number of 2nd year associates: 27
- 2nd year: $190,000

Law Schools attending for OCIs in 2017:

American, Berkeley, Boston College, Boston University, Brooklyn, Cardozo, University of Chicago, Columbia, Cornell NYC Job Fair, Duke, Emory NYC Job Fair, Fordham, George Washington, Georgetown, Harvard, University of Michigan, Minnesota, Northwestern, NYU, Penn, Stanford, Vanderbilt, University of Virginia, Wash U and Yale

Summer details

Summer associate profile:

Cadwalader is a community of talented and driven individuals committed to innovation and premier client service. We seek candidates with a record of academic and personal achievement, who exhibit excellent communication skills and professionalism, and who are analytical and creative thinkers.

Summer program components:

Under the supervision of experienced attorneys, summer associates have an opportunity to make meaningful contributions to ongoing projects. You will work on diverse and challenging assignments in several of our areas, depending on your interests, participate in substantive and skills building sessions and take on pro bono work. Our goal is to expose you to the various aspects of the practice of law: meeting with clients; participating in strategy and negotiation sessions; conducting research; drafting memos, documents and pleadings; and attending closings, depositions and court appearances. Associate and partner mentors will work closely with you throughout the summer. In addition to getting feedback on individual projects by supervising lawyers, you will also participate in mid-summer and end-of-summer formal evaluations.

Head Office: New York, NY
Number of domestic offices: 3
Number of international offices: 2
Worldwide revenue: $452,000,000
Partners (US): 71
Associates (US): 172
Other attorneys: 79

Main Recruitment Contact:
Tara Conlon, Director of Legal Recruitment
Hiring Partners: Paul Mourning/Anne Tompkins
Recruitment website:
www.cadwalader.com/makehistory
Diversity officer: LaTonya Brooks, Manager of Diversity

Summer Salary 2017
1Ls: $3,462/week
2Ls: $3,462/week
Post 3Ls: $3,462/week
1Ls hired? Yes
Split summers offered? Case by case
Can summers spend time in overseas office? Case by case
Summers 2017: 24 (23 2Ls, 1 1Ls)
Offers/acceptances 2016:
43 offers, 32 acceptances

C A D W A L A D E R

Cahill Gordon & Reindel LLP

80 Pine Street, New York NY 10005
www.cahill.com/careers

Main areas of work

Antitrust, bankruptcy and restructuring, communications, corporate, corporate finance, corporate governance and investigations, crisis advisory, executive compensation and employee benefits, environmental, insurance, intellectual property, litigation, media, pro bono, real estate, tax and trust and estates.

Firm profile

Cahill has thrived for nearly a century by focusing on the most significant opportunities and the biggest legal challenges facing the top banking firms and global companies. Cahill is a firm where you can shape your own legal career. We believe that lawyers who practice in diverse areas are happier and more productive. We do not require immediate specialization and do not have formal departments or rotation policies. While among the most profitable New York-based law firms, our size is conducive to regular interaction between partners and associates. Opportunities abound for interesting work and unparalleled on-the-job training.

Recruitment details

- Number of 1st year associates: 34
- Associate salaries: 1st year: $180,000
- Clerking policy: Yes
- Number of 2nd year associates: 30
- 2nd year: $190,000

Law Schools attending for OCIs in 2017:

Albany, Boston College, Boston University, Brooklyn, Columbia, Cornell University, Duke University, Fordham University, Georgetown University, George Washington University, Harvard, Howard, New York University, Northwestern University, University of Michigan, University of Pennsylvania and University of Virginia (with job fairs and write-ins from a dozen more)

Summer details

Summer associate profile:

The firm seeks academically strong candidates who display good judgment, self-confidence and enthusiasm for the practice of law.

Summer program components:

Summer associates at Cahill gain first-hand experience of what it would be like to be an associate at Cahill. With substantive assignments and opportunities to gain valuable public interest work experience, attend client meetings, negotiations, court appearances and networking events, Cahill's summer associates develop a true understanding of the firm's practice. Formal and informal training, personal mentoring and comprehensive evaluations are components of the firm's summer program.

Head Office: **New York, NY**
Number of domestic offices: **2**
Number of international offices: **1**
Worldwide revenue: **$382,600,000**
Partners (US): **66**
Associates (US): **187**

Main Recruitment Contact:
Donna Manion
Hiring Partner: **Brian Markley**
Recruitment website:
www.cahill.com/careers
Diversity officers: **Susanna Suh and Luis Penalver**

Summer Salary 2017
1Ls: **N/A**
2Ls: **$3,500/week**
Post 3Ls: **N/A**
1Ls hired? **Case by case**
Split summers offered? **Yes, with government or public agencies**
Can summers spend time in overseas office? **No**
Summers 2017: **33**
Offers/acceptances 2016:
38 offers, 37 acceptances

Choate Hall & Stewart LLP

Two International Place, Boston, MA 02110
Tel: 617 248 5000
Email: legalrecruiting@choate.com
www.choate.com

Main areas of work

Private equity and M&A, life sciences and technology companies, intellectual property and related litigation, finance and restructuring, government enforcement and financial litigation, insurance and reinsurance, complex trial and appellate, and wealth management.

Firm profile

Choate is one of the nation's premier law firms. Choate conducts its national and international practice through a single office model, with all lawyers under one roof in Boston. The firm's associate-to-partner ratio is low, affording junior lawyers opportunities to play important roles on matters and facilitating rapid career development. Lawyers know each other well and work together in dedicated client teams. That familiarity, proximity and continuity allows them to share knowledge easily and respond to clients' needs efficiently, seamlessly and immediately.

Recruitment details

- Number of 1st year associates: 15
- Number of 2nd year associates: 12
- Associate salaries: 1st year: $180,000
- 2nd year: $190,000
- Clerking policy: Choate offers compensation and progression credit, as well as a one-time clerkship bonus, to candidates who join the firm immediately following the completion of a federal district or circuit court clerkship or a federal or state supreme court clerkship

Law Schools attending for OCIs in 2017:

Boston College, Boston University, Columbia, Cornell, Georgetown, Harvard, New York University, Northeastern, Suffolk, University of Virginia, Yale and UConn

Summer details

Summer associate profile:

Choate seeks candidates who have a record of academic excellence and professional achievement. In addition to academic success, we seek candidates who are committed and who offer perspectives and talents shaped by a broad range of socioeconomic, racial, ethnic and personal backgrounds. We value proven leadership, dedication to team success, a strong work ethic and the ability to approach challenges thoughtfully and creatively.

Summer program components:

Choate's summer associates are involved in real work with real clients from day one. In recent years, summers have performed legal and factual research, drafted memos and briefs, helped prepare transactional documents, conducted diligence and managed deal closings, assisted in fact gathering, drafted estate planning documents, observed depositions and trials and worked on pro bono matters. Each summer associate is matched with a junior associate, mid-level associate and partner mentor, who provide guidance and feedback. The summer training program provides the opportunity to develop professional skills, learn about working at the firm and work with writing and communications coaches.

Head Office: **Boston, MA**
Number of domestic offices: **1**
Number of international offices: **0**
Worldwide revenue: **$218,543,735**
Partners: **96**
Associates: **68**
Other Attorneys: **15**

Main Recruitment Contact:
Elaine Cohen Bortman, Chief of Legal Recruiting & Talent Development
Hiring Partners: **Diana Lloyd and John Nadas**
Recruitment website:
www.choate.com/careers

Summer Salary 2017
1Ls: **$3,462/week**
2Ls: **$3,462/week**
Post 3Ls: **$3,462/week**
1Ls hired? **Yes, through the firm's 1L Diversity Fellowship program, through which Fellows receive a position in Choate's summer program and are eligible for a stipend of up to $10,000**
Split summers offered? **No**
Can summers spend time in overseas office? **N/A**
Summers 2017: **19**
Offers/acceptances 2016:
12 2L offers, 12 acceptances

CHOATE HALL & STEWART LLP

Cleary Gottlieb Steen & Hamilton LLP

One Liberty Plaza, New York, NY 10006
Tel: 212 225 2000 Fax: 212 225 3999
www.clearygottlieb.com

Main areas of work

Antitrust and competition, banking and financial institutions, bankruptcy and re-structuring, capital markets, corporate governance, derivatives, energy, environmental law, executive compensation and ERISA, intellectual property, international trade and investment, leveraged and acquisition finance, litigation and arbitration, mergers, acquisitions and joint ventures, private clients and charitable organizations, private equity, privatizations, pro bono, project finance and infrastructure, public international-al law, real estate, sovereign governments and international institutions, structured finance, tax, white-collar defense, securities enforcement and internal investigations.

Firm profile

Cleary Gottlieb embodies the principles of collegiality, collaboration, individuality and legal excellence while cultivating the finest legal talent in the world. Operating as a single, integrated worldwide firm with 16 offices in 12 different countries, Cleary Gottlieb has helped shape the globalization of the legal profession for more than 70 years.

Recruitment details

- Number of 1st year associates: 92
- Associate salaries: 1st year: $180,000
- Clerking policy: Yes
- Number of 2nd year associates: 75
- 2nd year: $190,000

Law Schools attending for OCIs in 2017:

Boston College, Boston University, Brooklyn, Cardozo, Chicago, Columbia, Cornell, Duke, Fordham, George Washington, Georgetown, Harvard, Howard, Lavender Law Career Fair, Michigan, Midwest - California - Georgia Consortium, National Law School Consortium, NEBLSA Job Fair, New York Law School, NYU, Northwestern, Ohio State, University of Pennsylvania, Stanford, Texas, Tulane, Washington University - Washington and Lee, William and Mary, UC Berkeley, UCLA, USC Gould, Vanderbilt, Virginia, Yale

Summer details

Summer associate profile:

We seek candidates who are confident in their abilities and creative in their thinking. We look for academically strong men and women of all races and nationalities who are enthusiastic about practicing law. We place a premium on openness, diversity, individuality and collegiality and look for candidates who do so as well.

Summer program components:

Cleary offers summer associates the flexibility to enjoy assignments in many practice areas or to focus on a particular discipline. The summer program consists of formal and informal training, partner and associate mentoring, optional overseas office rota-tions, pro bono work, comprehensive evaluations and social/networking events.

Head Offices: New York, NY and Washington, DC
Number of domestic offices: 2
Number of international offices: 14
Partners (US): 109
Associates (US): 442

Main Recruitment Contacts:
Donna Harris (NY) and Georgia Emery Gray (DC)
Hiring Partners: Lisa Schweitzer (NY) and Michael A Mazzuchi (DC)
Recruitment website:
www.clearygottlieb.com
Diversity officers: Sandra Flow (NY), Larry Friedman (NY) and Derek Bush (DC)

Summer Salary 2017
1Ls: N/A
2Ls: $3,461/week
Post 3Ls: N/A
1Ls hired? Yes - Washington Diversity Summer Associate Program
Split summers offered? Yes
Can summers spend time in overseas office? Yes
Summers 2017: 149
Offers/acceptances 2016: 123 offers

CLEARY GOTTLIEB

Firm Profiles

Clifford Chance US LLP

31 West 52nd Street, New York, NY 10019-6131
Tel: 212 878 8000   Fax: 212 878 8375
www.cliffordchance.com

Main areas of work

Banking and finance, capital markets, corporate/M&A, litigation and dispute resolution, real estate and tax, pensions and employment.

Firm profile

Clifford Chance offers the opportunity to join a major US practice and the world's leading international law firm. We are the first fully-integrated worldwide firm to provide coordinated legal advice to the world's leading financial institutions, corporations and governments. The combination of a large US presence with unparalleled resources in Europe, Asia Pacific, Latin America, Africa and the Middle East makes us uniquely qualified to handle complex cross-border and domestic transactions, disputes and investigations.

Recruitment details

- Number of 1st year associates: 33
- Associate salaries: 1st year: $180,000
- Clerking policy: Yes
- Number of 2nd year associates: 31
- 2nd year: $190,000

Law Schools attending for OCIs in 2017:

American, Boston College, Boston University, Brooklyn, Columbia, Cornell, Duke, Fordham, Georgetown, George Washington, Harvard, Michigan, NYU, Penn, St. John's, Virginia

Summer details

Summer associate profile:

We believe in giving our lawyers a high level of exposure and responsibility from the very beginning. Over the ten week program, our clerks will work on a wide variety of assignments to not only gain exposure to our full range of practice areas, but to get to know the partners and associates in those departments as well. Through close attorney contact, formal training, time spent in one of our offices abroad, and social events that explore the city, our summer law clerks receive a realistic vision of what it means to be a Clifford Chance lawyer.

Summer program components:

We believe that the best learning is done on the job. In addition to the hands-on experience they'll receive working alongside our partners and associates on real assignments, our summer law clerks also participate in formal training programs focused on legal writing, negotiations training, as well as a seminar specifically geared toward working as an international lawyer. Feedback is consistent and given on a formal and informal basis, allowing our clerks to have a clear idea of their development.

Head Office: London
Number of domestic offices: 2
Number of international offices: 31
Worldwide revenue: $2,056,023,000
Partners (US): 74
Associates (US): 200

Main Recruitment Contact:
Sarah Posner
Hiring Partner: Nicholas R. Williams
Recruitment website:
www.cliffordchance.com/usrecruiting
Diversity officer: Zarrar Sehgal

Summer Salary 2017
1Ls: $3,461.54/week
2Ls: $3,461.54/week
Post 3Ls: $3,461.54/week
1Ls hired? No
Split summers offered? Case by case
Can summers spend time in
overseas office? Yes
Summers 2017: 28
Offers/acceptances 2016:
26 offers, 22 acceptances

C L I F F O R D
C H A N C E

Cooley LLP

3175 Hanover Street, Palo Alto, CA 94304-1130
Tel: 650 843 5000
www.cooley.com

Main areas of work

Advertising, antitrust and competition, capital markets, class actions, commercial litigation, communications, copyright, corporate, corporate restructuring and bankruptcy, debt finance, emerging companies, employment and labor, estate planning, financial services, fund formation, government contracts, healthcare, education, IP litigation, insurance/reinsurance, investment funds, life sciences, M&A, private equity, patent prosecution and counseling, privacy and data protection, public companies, regulatory, real estate, retail, securities, shareholder activism, tax, technology transactions, trademark, venture capital, white collar.

Firm profile

Cooley's lawyers solve legal issues for entrepreneurs, investors, financial institutions and established companies with a significant emphasis on technology, life sciences and other high growth industries. Clients partner with Cooley on transformative deals, complex IP and regulatory matters and bet-the-company litigation, where innovation meets the law. Cooley goes to great lengths to maintain the culture of teamwork, collaboration, respect and excellence upon which it was established in 1920. Cooley strives to maintain an environment of diversity and inclusiveness and to create opportunities for professional growth. It is proud to be one of *Fortune's* "100 Best Companies to Work For."

Cooley considers its commitment to the communities in which it operates to be one of its highest priorities and each year performs thousands of hours of pro bono legal services and other forms of community service.

Recruitment details

- Number of 1st year associates: 50
- Associate salaries: 1st year: $180,000
- Clerking policy: Yes
- Number of 2nd year associates: 53
- 2nd year: $190,000

Law Schools attending for OCIs in 2017:

Please refer to the Events portion of our website for a list of the job fairs and campuses we will visit during the 2017 OCI season

Summer details

Summer associate profile:

Successful summer associates are highly motivated, independent thinkers, with a collaborative spirit and an entrepreneurial mindset. They have excelled both in and beyond the classroom. They recognize that the greatest successes are those achieved by a team. They take ownership, inspire confidence and are motivated by a shared sense of purpose.

Summer program components:

Cooley's summer program is designed to give participants an unfiltered introduction to life and practice at the firm. It enables them to experience Cooley's commitment to providing extraordinary legal services in a professional and collaborative environment. Comprehensive training opportunities are provided through "Cooley College". Constructive feedback is provided at the conclusion of each assignment and in formal mid- and end-of-summer feedback sessions. Assigned mentors ensure that each summer associate is integrated into the firm over the course of the program.

Head Office: Palo Alto, CA
Number of domestic offices: 10
Number of international offices: 2
Worldwide revenue: $974 million
Partners (US): 300
Associates (US): 600

Main Recruitment Contact:
Carrie Wagner, Chief Legal Talent Officer
Recruitment website:
www.cooley.com/careers
Diversity officers: DeAnna Allen, Partner, Frank Pietrantonio, Partner and Amie Santos, Director of Diversity and Inclusion
Summer Salary 2017
1Ls: $3,462/week
2Ls: $3,462/week
1Ls hired? Yes, through Diversity Fellowship
Split summers offered? Yes
Can summers spend time in overseas office? No
Summers 2017: 56 (48 2L's, 7 1L's, 1 SEO)
Offers/acceptances 2016:
62 offers, 56 acceptances, 1 deferred

Cozen O'Connor

One Liberty, 1650 Market Street, Philadelphia, Suite 2800 PA 19103
Tel: 215 665 2000   Fax: 215 665 2013
www.cozen.com

Main areas of work

Business/corporate, commercial litigation, government and regulatory, insurance coverage, institutional response, intellectual property, labor and employment, real estate, private client services, subrogation and recovery, transporation and trade.

Firm profile

Established in 1970, Cozen O'Connor delivers legal services on an integrated and global basis. As a first-generation law firm, we have not forgotten our entrepreneurial roots and continue to provide top-notch client service at unparalleled value as we have grown to one of the top law firms in the country. Our business and litigation practice serves clients in the most effective and efficient manner, with professionals across disciplines working collaboratively to resolve any matter.

Recruitment details

- Number of 1st year associates: 12   • Number of 2nd year associates: 13
- Associate salaries: 1st year: $125,000-$160,000 (varies by office)
- 2nd year: Non lock step, merit-based compensation
- Clerking policy: Yes

Law Schools attending for OCIs in 2017:

Georgetown, Harvard, NYU, Penn, Penn State, Seattle University, Temple, UVA, University of Washington, Villanova, GW, Northwestern

Summer details

Summer associate profile:

Cozen O'Connor seeks summer associates who embody the best characteristics of our attorneys. We strive to find candidates who have distinguished themselves from their peers in academics, legal writing ability and oral advocacy skills. Our summer associates have diverse backgrounds including, but not limited to, prior work experience, military service and a demonstrated commitment to serving their communities through volunteerism.

Summer program components:

At Cozen O'Connor, we pride ourselves in providing our summer associates with a realistic experience of the responsibilities and high level of performance expected of the firm's associates. They take part in an extensive firm orientation and weekly training programs, such as a trial skills workshop where they have the opportunity to prepare and present a mock opening statement and take a mock deposition. Our writing mentors work closely with the summer associates to strengthen their legal writing skills and our associate mentors provide them with advice and guidance. Summer associates work on active cases and are relied upon to produce excellent work product. They are invited to practice group meetings and to attend hearings, depositions, or client meetings with their supervising attorneys. Summer associates receive assignments that allow them to become intimately familiar with the firm's various practice groups and their cases and clients and are encouraged to participate in pro bono matters.

Head Office: Philadelphia, PA
Number of domestic offices: 22
Number of international offices: 2
Worldwide revenue: $376,000,000
Partners (US): 403
Associates (US): 147

Main Recruitment Contacts:
Mindy J Herczfeld, Chief Legal Talent Officer and Jill M Caughie, Associate Director of Legal Recruiting
Hiring Partners: Dan Luccaro, Lezlie Madden
Recruitment website:
www.cozen.com/careers
Diversity officer: Kimya S P Johnson

Summer Salary 2017
1Ls: $2,200-$2800/week, varies by office
2Ls: $2,400-$3077/week, varies by office
1Ls hired? Yes
Split summers offered? Case by case
Can summers spend time in overseas office? No
Summers 2017: 17 (2Ls)
Offers/acceptances 2016:
13 offers,12 acceptances

Cravath, Swaine & Moore LLP

825 Eighth Avenue, New York, NY 10019
Tel: 212 474 1000   Fax: 212 474 3700
www.cravath.com

Main areas of work

Corporate, litigation, tax, executive compensation and benefits, trusts and estates.

Firm profile

Cravath is known as one of the preeminent law firms in the country. Each of our practice areas is highly regarded and our lawyers are widely recognized for their commitment to the representation of our clients' interests. We believe the development of our lawyers is our most important long term objective. Our partners come almost exclusively from the ranks of our own associates. We recruit the most talented law students and have our partners directly train the next generation of associates. Through our rotation system – a system in which corporate associates "rotate" from one practice group to another and litigation associates "rotate" from one partner to another – associates work directly with a small team of partners and associates. We have found that this system enables even our most recently hired associates to work directly with our clients and quickly to assume substantial responsibility for important matters, while at the same time preventing undue specialization.

Recruitment details

- Number of 1st year associates: 84
- Associate salaries: 1st year: $180,000
- Clerking policy: Yes
- Number of 2nd year associates: 70
- 2nd year: $190,000

Law Schools attending for OCIs in 2017:

Berkeley, Boston College/Boston University Job Fair, Brigham Young University New York Interview Program, Cardozo, Chicago, Columbia, Cornell Job Fair, Duke, Emory Job Fair, Fordham, George Washington New York Job Fair, Georgetown, Harvard, Harvard BLSA Job Fair, Howard, Lavender Law Career Fair, LeGaL LGBT Career Fair, Michigan, Midwest-California-Georgia Consortium, Northeast BLSA Job Fair, New York University, Northwestern, Notre Dame New York Job Fair, Stanford, Texas, Texas New York Job Fair, Tulane/Washington University Job Fair, Vanderbilt Job Fair, University of Pennsylvania, Virginia, Yale

Summer details

Summer associate profile:

Our summer program is designed to provide law students with an experience that mirrors the life of a first year associate. Summer associates experience the day-to-day working life of a Cravath lawyer and gain valuable hands-on experience working directly for, and with, our clients.

Summer program components:

Prior to the summer, we collect department and assignment preferences (type of matter or practice area, specific teams or partners). Upon arrival, summer associates are assigned to a partner from their selected department, along with an associate mentor. This partner is responsible for assigning work and providing feedback.

Head Office: **New York, NY**
Number of domestic offices: **1**
Number of international offices: **1**
Partners (US): **78**
Associates (US): **386**

Main Recruitment Contact: **Lisa A Kalen**
Hiring Partners: **Karin A DeMasi and Eric L Schiele**
Recruitment Website:
www.cravath.com
Diversity officer: **Kiisha J B Morrow**

Summer Salary 2017
1Ls: **$3,500/week**
2Ls: **$3,500/week**
Post 3Ls: **$3,500/week**
1Ls hired: **Yes**
Split summers offered: **Yes**
Can summers spend time in overseas office: **Yes**
Summers 2017: **2-1LS, 119-2Ls**

CRAVATH, SWAINE & MOORE LLP

Firm Profiles

Crowell & Moring LLP

1001 Pennsylvania Avenue, N.W. Washington DC, 20004-2595
Tel: 202 624 2500   Fax: 202 628 5116
www.crowell.com

Firm profile

Crowell & Moring LLP is an international law firm with approximately 500 lawyers representing clients in litigation and arbitration, regulatory, and transactional matters. The firm is internationally recognized for its representation of Fortune 500 companies in high-stakes litigation, as well as its ongoing commitment to pro bono service and diversity. The firm has offices in Washington, DC, New York, Los Angeles, San Francisco, Orange County, London, and Brussels.

Recruitment details

- Number of 1st year associates: 12
- Associate salaries: 1st year: $180,000
- Clerking policy: No
- Number of 2nd year associates: 17
- 2nd year: $190,000

Law Schools attending for OCIs in 2017:

We interview at the majority of the top 20 law schools and numerous diversity-related and IP-specific job fairs throughout the United States.

Summer details

Summer associate profile:

The firm looks for highly qualified, entrepreneurial candidates with diverse backgrounds. We prefer candidates with law review, journal or moot court experience and/or strong relevant legal employment experience, including judicial clerkships; as well as demonstrated leadership capabilities.

Summer program components:

The diversity in our summer program reflects the diversity of our firm at large. We want summer associates who take the practice of law and client service more seriously than they take themselves, who will contribute to the life of the firm, and who share our sense of responsibility to the community.

Most of our junior associates come from our Summer Associate Program. We want you to go back to law school knowing who we are, what we do, and how we do it. Work for summer associates includes mostly short-term projects that will allow you to experience as many practice areas and as many lawyers as possible.

Summer associates have the opportunity to participate in workshops and seminars on such topics as "The Law Firm as a Business and Negotiations Training" and "Negotiations Training." In addition, the firm offers summer associates the opportunities to participate in our Public Interest Fellowship program and sign up for Live Events, which are real-world activities such as court hearings, client meetings, depositions, presentations and negotiations that summer associates may attend in order to observe Crowell & Moring lawyers in action.

Head Office: Washington, DC
Number of domestic offices: 5
Number of international offices: 2
Partners (US): 167
Counsel/Sr Counsel (US): 132
Associates (US): 141

Main Recruitment Contact:
Torey Phillips, Director of Attorney Recruiting and Development
Hiring Partner: Ryan Tisch
Recruitment website:
www.crowell.com/Careers/Lawyers
Diversity officer: Melanie Priddy

Summer Salary 2017
1Ls: $3,462/week
2Ls: $3,462/week
Post 3Ls: $3,462/week
1Ls hired? Yes
Split summers offered? Case by case
Can summers spend time in overseas office? No
Summers 2017: 24 firmwide
Offers/acceptances 2016:
14 offers, 10 acceptances

Curtis, Mallet-Prevost, Colt & Mosle LLP

101 Park Avenue, New York, NY 10178-0061
Tel: 212 696 6000   Fax: 212 697 1559
www.curtis.com

Main areas of work

Curtis represents clients across industry sectors, including multinational corporations and financial institutions, governments and state-owned companies, money managers, sovereign wealth funds, family-owned businesses, individuals and entrepreneurs. Curtis' attorneys provide legal services in international arbitration, energy, renewable energy and climate change, project finance and infrastructure development, international tax, mergers and acquisitions, private equity, restructuring and insolvency, litigation, banking and finance, capital markets, investment management, international investment, corporate law and real estate.

Firm profile

Curtis, Mallet-Prevost, Colt & Mosle LLP is a leading international law firm that provides a broad range of legal services to clients around the world. The firm operates worldwide throughout its offices in Europe, the United States, Latin America, the Middle East and Central Asia. Curtis' international orientation has been a hallmark of its practice for nearly two centuries. Curtis attorneys are trained as internationalists with a deep understanding of the cultural as well as business sensitivities associated with conducting business across borders.

Recruitment details

- Number of 1st year associates: 14
- Associate salaries: 1st year: $180,000
- Clerking policy: Yes
- Number of 2nd year associates: 8
- 2nd year: $190,000

Law Schools attending for OCIs in 2017:

Boston College, Boalt, Cornell, Columbia, Duke, Fordham, Georgetown, Harvard, New York University, St. John's, Stanford, University of Chicago, University of Pennsylvania, University of Virginia, Vanderbilt, Yale

Summer details

Summer associate profile:

The Curtis Summer Program is small and highly selective. Curtis chooses approximately 10 to 15 second-year law students to participate in our program. The summer program, which lasts 10 weeks, starts in late May and ends in July. Grades and scores are not the only criteria for selection. Curtis looks for students who are confident, independent thinkers.

Summer program components:

The summer program is designed to give students a realistic view of the practice of law while at the same time teaching them real-world lawyering skills in a hands-on environment. Our summer associates quickly become assimilated as each summer associate is matched to a partner mentor and an associate advisor.

Summer associates receive assignments which are carefully selected to correspond with their interests and goals. Throughout the summer, summer associates join lawyers in meetings, closings, depositions and court proceedings. Formal training includes lectures, workshops, panel discussions and lunchtime programs on relevant topics.

Head Office: **New York, NY**
Number of domestic offices: **3**
Number of international offices: **14**
Worldwide revenue: **$151,500,000**
Partners (US): **58**
Associates (US): **71**

Main Recruitment Contact:
Raquel Lorenzo
Hiring Partner: **Carl Ruggiero**
Recruitment website:
www.curtis.com

Summer Salary 2017
1Ls: **$3,461.53/week**
2Ls: **$3,461.53/week**
Post 3Ls: **N/A**
1Ls hired? **Yes**
Split summers offered? **Case by case**
Can summers spend time in overseas office? **Case by case**
Summers 2017: **9**
Offers/acceptances 2016:
9 offers for 2Ls, 9 acceptances

Firm Profiles

Davis Polk & Wardwell LLP

450 Lexington Avenue, New York, NY 10017
Tel: 212 450 4000   Fax: 212 701 5800
www.davispolk.com

Main areas of work

Capital markets, mergers and acquisitions, credit, litigation (including antitrust, bankruptcy, general commercial, IP, securities litigation and enforcement, and white collar and government investigations), tax, private equity, investment management, insolvency and restructuring, corporate governance, intellectual property and technology, financial regulation, FinTech, environmental, executive compensation, real estate and trusts and estates.

Firm profile

Davis Polk & Wardwell LLP is a global law firm. For more than 165 years, its lawyers have advised industry-leading companies and major financial institutions on their most challenging legal and business matters. Davis Polk ranks among the world's preeminent law firms across the entire range of its practice. With more than 900 lawyers in New York, Menlo Park, CA, Washington DC, London, Paris, Madrid, Hong Kong, Beijing, Tokyo and São Paulo, the firm operates from key business centers around the world to provide clients with seamlessly integrated legal services of the highest caliber.

Recruitment details

- Associate salaries: 1st year: $180,000
- 2nd year: $190,000
- Clerking policy: Yes

Summer details

Summer associate profile:

We seek to hire applicants from a variety of backgrounds with outstanding academic and non-academic achievements, leadership skills and creativity and with a demonstrated willingness to take initiative. We strive to find exceptional lawyers who share our commitment to excellence.

Summer program components:

Our summer program is designed to allow students the opportunity to experience work as a junior associate. Summer associates are encouraged to work on matters in any practice area of interest. There are no required rotations. Work assignments are made through two associates who take leave from their regular practices to assist each summer associate in shaping their summer work experience. In addition to working with our attorneys on the firm's current billable and pro bono matters, summer associates have the opportunity to attend practice area overviews and participate in multi-day interactive training sessions and workshops. The program also includes a wide range of cultural, social and mentoring activities to assist summer associates in getting to know their peers and our attorneys.

Head Office: **New York, NY**
Number of domestic offices: **3**
Number of international offices: **7**
Lawyers (US): **762**

Main Recruitment Contact:
Cristobal V Modesto
Hiring Partners: **Maurice Blanco and Dana Seshens**
Recruitment website:
http://careers.davispolk.com

Summer Salary 2017
1Ls: **$3,500/week**
2Ls: **$3,500/week**
Split summers offered? **Yes**
Can summers spend time in overseas office? **Yes**
Summers 2017: **126 (NY)**

Debevoise & Plimpton LLP

919 Third Avenue, New York, NY 10022
Tel: 212 909 6000
www.debevoise.com

Main areas of work

Debevoise & Plimpton LLP has three main areas of practice: corporate (including mergers and acquisitions, private equity, investment funds, insurance, banking, leveraged finance, business restructuring and workouts, asset management, capital markets, corporate governance, structured and project finance, aviation finance, healthcare and life sciences, intellectual property, media and telecommunications, real estate, energy and environmental law), litigation (including white collar/regulatory, international dispute resolution, intellectual property, general commercial litigation, cybersecurity and data privacy, insurance, securities, antitrust, employment, bankruptcy and products liability) and tax and employee benefits.

Firm profile

Debevoise & Plimpton LLP is a premier law firm with market-leading practices, a global perspective and strong New York roots. The firm's clients look to it to bring a distinctively high degree of quality, intensity and creativity to resolve legal challenges selectively and cost efficiently. Deep partner commitment, industry expertise and a strategic approach enable the firm to bring clear commercial judgment to every matter. The firm draws on the strength of its culture and structure to deliver the best of the firm to every client through true collaboration.

Recruitment details

- Number of 1st year associates: 71
- Associate salaries: 1st year: $180,000
- Clerking policy: Yes
- Number of 2nd year associates: 75
- 2nd year: $190,000

Law Schools attending for OCIs in 2017:

Benjamin N Cardozo, Brooklyn, Columbia University, Cornell University, Duke University, Fordham University, Georgetown University, Harvard, Howard University, New York Law School, New York University School of Law, Northwestern, Rutgers University, St. John's University, Stanford, Tulane University, University of Chicago, University of Michigan, University of Pennsylvania, University of Texas Law School, University of Virginia, Washington University, Yale

Summer details

Summer associate profile:

Debevoise searches for dynamic, analytically strong and professionally curious individuals with an interest in and enthusiasm for the challenging deals and matters on which the firm works. In addition, the firm is interested in individuals from an array of different backgrounds as it prefers that its lawyer population is as diverse as its clients.

Summer program components:

Debevoise's summer program is structured to provide participants with the flexibility to explore as many practice areas as they wish. In order to accommodate the individual's evolving interests, the firm has chosen not to impose an assignment system that "rotates" participants through different areas of the firm. There are opportunities throughout the summer for formal evaluations, while informal feedback is given on a continuous basis. Social events are held for summer associates, which provide them with the chance to connect with other lawyers, of all levels, at the firm.

Head Office: New York, NY
Number of domestic offices: 2
Number of international offices: 7
Worldwide revenue: $735,000,000
Partners (US): 106
Associates (US): 319

Main Recruitment Contact:
Sandra Herbst
Hiring Partner: Nicole Mesard
Recruitment website:
www.debevoise.com
Diversity officers: Jonathan F Lewis (Diversity Committee Chair) and Rachel Simmonds-Watson (Diversity Manager)

Summer Salary 2017
1Ls: N/A
2Ls: $3,500/week
Post 3Ls: N/A
1Ls hired? No
Split summers offered? Yes
Can summers spend time in overseas office? Yes
Summers 2016: 72 (excluding SEOs and returnees; 70 in NY, 2 in DC)
Offers/acceptances 2016:
78 offers, 63 acceptances (NY and DC), some offers remain open.

Debevoise & Plimpton

Dechert LLP

Cira Centre, 2929 Arch Street, Philadelphia, PA 19104-2808
Tel: 215 994 4000   Fax: 215 994 2222

1095 Avenue of the Americas, New York, NY 10036-6797
Tel: 212 698 3500   Fax: 212 698 3599
www.dechert.com

Main areas of work

Dechert delivers legal expertise and commercial insight in our core practices: antitrust; banking and financial institutions; bankruptcy, business restructuring and reorganization; corporate; employee benefits and executive compensation; energy and natural resources; finance; financial services and investment management; intellectual property; international arbitration; international tax and private client services; international trade and government regulation; life sciences; litigation; pro bono; and real estate.

Firm profile

Dechert is a global law firm focused on sectors with the greatest complexities, legal intricacies and highest regulatory demands. With 28 offices in the United States, Europe, Asia and the Middle East, the firm offers attractive locations in which to live and work. Dechert is a leading global law firm for pro bono services. *The American Lawyer* consistently ranks us in the top 10 law firm pro bono programs.

Recruitment details

- Number of 1st year associates: 61
- Associate salaries: $180,000
- Clerking policy: Yes
- Number of 2nd year associates: 57
- 2nd year: $190,000

Law Schools attending for OCIs in 2017:

Boston College; Boston University; Catholic University; Columbia; Cornell; Duke; Fordham; George Washington University; Georgetown; Harvard; Hofstra University; Howard; New York University; Northwestern; Stanford; Temple; UCLA; UC Berkeley; UC Hastings; Chicago; Connecticut; Michigan; North Carolina; University of Pennsylvania; Pittsburgh; USC; Texas; Virginia; Vanderbilt; Villanova; Yale

Summer details

Summer associate profile:

Strong academic background and communication, leadership, management and client relations skills indicating a high likelihood of success as a lawyer at the firm.

Summer program components:

Summer associates will discover firsthand what it's like to work at one of the world's most respected and dynamic global law firms. Our summer associates do not formally rotate through practice groups or departments; rather, they work across all the practice groups. A variety of work assignments allows summer associates to gain a broad perspective and get a close-up view of the practice of law. Beyond client-based assignments, we encourage summer associates to attend closings, depositions, hearings, oral arguments, trials, negotiations, and board meetings. Summer associates are assigned at least one associate mentor and one partner mentor and attend practice group meetings and training. We offer summer associate-specific training sessions throughout the program. Through our program, we provide summer associates with a realistic view of what it's like to practice law at Dechert.

Main Offices: Philadelphia / New York
Number of domestic offices: 13
Number of international offices: 15
Worldwide revenue: $911,594,815
Partners (US): 216
Associates (US): 400

Main Recruitment Contacts:
Alison Bernard, Chief Talent Officer;
Paul Giangola, Global Director, Legal Recruiting
Hiring Partner: James A Lebovitz, Firmwide Hiring Chair
Recruitment website:
www.dechert.com/careers
Diversity officers: Hector Gonzalez, Deputy Chair for Diversity; Satra Sampson-Arokium, Director of Diversity and Inclusion
Summer Salary 2017
1Ls: $3,468/week
2Ls: $3,468/week
Post 3Ls: $3,468/week
1Ls hired? Yes
Split summers offered? Yes
Can summers spend time in overseas office? Yes, case by case
Summers 2017: 72 2Ls
Offers/acceptances 2016:
71 2L offers, 68 2L acceptances

DLA Piper LLP (US)

1251 Avenue of the Americas, 27th Floor, New York, NY 10020
Tel: 212 335 4500   Fax: 212 335 4501
www.dlapiper.com

Main areas of work

DLA Piper's core practices in the US are corporate, employment, finance, government affairs, intellectual property and technology, litigation, real estate, restructuring and tax.

Firm profile

DLA Piper is a global law firm with lawyers located in more than 40 countries throughout the Americas, Europe, the Middle East, Africa and Asia Pacific, positioning us to help clients with their legal needs around the world.

Recruitment details

- Number of 1st year associates: 32 (expected in 2017)
- Number of 2nd year associates: Not lock step
- Associate salaries: 1st year: $180,000 in most markets
- 2nd year: Varies by market
- Clerking policy: Yes; Article III Federal and Appellate clerkship bonus (market based)

Law Schools attending for OCIs in 2017:

TBD

Summer details

Summer associate profile:

We promote a culture that is inclusive of all, where everyone has the opportunity to grow their career and where pathways to success are transparent. We look for well-rounded, energetic and entrepreneurial people. We generally recruit from the top 1/4 to the top 1/3 of law school classes.

Summer program components:

During the summer, with guidance from lawyers in the roles of mentors, we provide summer associates with a stimulating, realistic and exciting taste of law firm life. Summer associates experience challenging days filled with client work, relationship-building opportunities and enriching activities. All summer associates attend a retreat hosted by one of our offices. During this three-day gathering, summer associates get to know one another and participate in team building and training activities. Our goal is for summer associates to experience what it is like to be on the DLA Piper team and, through the summer experience, envision their future as a knowledgeable, highly skilled, well-rounded DLA Piper lawyer.

More than 90 offices in 40 countries
Worldwide revenue: $2,470,207,395
Partners (US): 616
Associates (US): 522

Main Recruitment Contact:
Stacy Silverstone, Director of Legal Recruiting
Hiring Partner: Christina L. Martini, National Hiring Partner - Associate Recruiting
Recruitment website:
www.dlapiperlegalcareers.us
Diversity officer: Genhi Bailey

Summer Salary 2017
1Ls: $3,461/week in most markets
2Ls: $3,461/week in most markets
Post 3Ls: N/A
1Ls hired? Yes
Split summers offered? No
Can summers spend time in overseas office? No
Summers 2017: 37-40 2Ls,10-15 1Ls
Offers/acceptances 2016:
32 offers and 30 acceptances

Duane Morris LLP

30 S. 17th Street, United Plaza, Philadelphia, PA 19103
Tel: 215 979 1000   Fax: 215 979 1020

Main areas of work

Business reorganization and financial restructuring; corporate; employment, labor, benefits and immigration; energy, environment and resources; wealth planning, health law, intellectual property, litigation and real estate

Firm profile

Duane Morris LLP, a global law firm with more than 750 attorneys in offices across the United States and around the world, is asked by a broad array of clients to provide innovative solutions to today's legal and business challenges.

Recruitment details

- Number of 1st year associates: 13
- Number of 2nd year associates: 18
- Associate salaries: 1st year: $140,000-$165,000
- 2nd year: Non lock step compensation structure in place
- Clerking policy: Yes (federal only)

Law Schools attending for OCIs in 2017:

Boston College, Boston University, University of Chicago, Georgetown, Harvard, Howard, University of Maryland, Michigan, Northwestern, NYU, Penn, Temple, University of Virfinia, Villanova, among others

Summer details

Summer associate profile:

Duane Morris strives to attract the best law students and to offer the ideal environment for lawyers at the beginning of their professional lives. We endeavor to improve our Summer Associates Program each year to make Duane Morris a meaningful and valuable destination for summer associates. The firm's summer associates rated the firm's program #6 nationally in *The American Lawyer's* 2016 Summer Associates Survey and a #3 ranking in the Philadelphia City ranking for 2016.

Duane Morris offers interesting challenges to law students who participate in our summer program. We believe the program offers a realistic picture of our practice to aspiring attorneys who have an interest in sharing our goals and serving our clients. Our program balances challenging work assignments with constructive feedback, work-related activities outside the office and enjoyable social events.

Summer program components:

The growth and development of each Duane Morris attorney furthers the central goals of the firm to provide the best legal services possible, to develop and build client relationships, and to ensure the stature and reputation of the firm with its clients. Duane Morris's Attorney Professional Development Program provides its summer associates and associates with comprehensive training and mentoring to support development of individual knowledge, skills and abilities in three broad categories: legal skills and substantive law, best business practices for the firm and practice development. Aside from these specific responsibilities, the mentors help introduce the summer associates to other lawyers in the firm and provide general guidance on any matter, whether or not related to particular work assignments.

Head Office: **Philadelphia, PA**
Number of domestic offices: **20**
Number of international offices: **8**
Partners (US): **397**
Associates (US): **324**

Main Recruitment Contact:
Jennifer Davis, Manager of Legal Recruitment and Personnel
Hiring Partner: Kelly D Eckel, Esquire
Recruitment website:
www.duanemorris.com/site/careers.html
Diversity officer: Joseph K West, Esquire

Summer Salary 2017
1Ls: **$2,788/week (Phila)**
2Ls: **$3,173/week (Phila//NY/Chicago);**
$2,884 (San Diego);
$2,692 (Miami)
1Ls hired? **Yes, 1**
Split summers offered? **Case by case**
Can summers spend time in overseas office? **Case by case**
Summers 2017: **16 (15 2Ls, 1 1Ls)**
Offers/acceptances 2016:
16 offers (100%), 14 acceptances

Firm Profiles

Dykema Gossett PLLC

400 Renaissance Center, Detroit, MI 48243
Tel: 313 568 6800 Fax: 855 255 4354
www.dykema.com

Main areas of work

Dykema provides legal counsel to clients ranging from Fortune 500 corporations and middle-market businesses, to financial institutions, governmental entities and non-profits. Our practices include antitrust; appellate; automotive; banking; bankruptcy; class action; lending; litigation; construction; corporate; e-discovery; education; employee benefits and executive compensation; energy; environmental; estates and trusts; gaming; government policy; government investigations and compliance; healthcare; immigration; intellectual property and IP litigation; infrastructure; insurance; privacy, data security and e-commerce; private equity, venture capital and mezzanine finance; labor and employ-ment; life sciences; mergers and acquisitions; product liability; public finance; real estate; securities and taxation.

Firm profile

With more than a century of experience and nearly 500 attorneys and other professionals, Dykema is one of the top law firms for business in the United States. Serving clients from our 14 offices in California, Illinois, Michigan, Minnesota, Texas and Washington, DC, we help clients address their most complex and sophisticated issues. We provide the highest quality legal counsel and exceptional client service from a work environment that thrives on cooperation, diversity and inclusion. Many of our attorneys and staff have made Dyke-ma their home since the start of their careers. We consider this to be the highest compli-ment and one of the reasons for our ongoing success.

Recruitment details

- Number of 1st year associates: 8
- Number of 2nd year associates: 18
- Associate salaries: 1st year: $120,000-$150,000 (depending on office)
- 2nd year: Not lock step
- Clerking policy: Yes

Law Schools attending for OCIs in 2017:

Baylor, Detroit-Mercy, Illinois, Michigan, MSU, Northwestern, Notre Dame, OSU, St.Mary's, Texas Tech, Uof T - Austin, Southern Methodist (SMU), Wayne State

Summer details

Summer associate profile:

A successful summer associate candidate will show initiative, excellent analytical skills and strong writing ability. We look for associates who are willing to work hard, have dem-onstrated leadership potential and enjoy working in a team environment.

Summer program components:

Dykema's summer associate program offers challenging assignments and a real life law practice experience with opportunities to participate in client, court and other formal set-tings. We integrate our summer associates into the firm via practice area and professional development activities, including a writing workshop with a professional writing instruc-tor. We host social activities for summer associates to become better acquainted with us and our culture. We also provide summer associates with a senior and junior advisor. These advisors, together with our training, social activities and the substantive practice experience, have greatly contributed to the success of Dykema's summer program.

Head Office: Detroit, MI
Number of domestic offices: 14
Number of international offices: 0
Partners (US): 276
Associates (US): 141

Main Recruitment Contact:
Sarah K Staup
Hiring Partner: Lisa A Brown
Recruitment website:
www.dykema.com
Diversity officer: Sherrie L Farrell

Summer Salary 2017
2Ls: $1,900-$2,700/week
1Ls hired? Occasionally
Split summers offered? In Texas
Summers 2017: 32
Offers/acceptances 2016
14 offers, 8 acceptances

Firm Profiles

Epstein Becker & Green, PC

1227 25th Street, NW, Suite 700, Washington, DC 20037-1156
Tel: 202 861 0900   Fax: 202 296 2882

250 Park Avenue, New York, New York 10177-1211
Tel: 212 351 4500   Fax: 212 878 8600
www.ebglaw.com

Main areas of work

Healthcare and life sciences; employment, labor and workforce management; and litigation and business disputes.

Firm profile

Epstein Becker & Green, PC, is a national law firm with a primary focus on healthcare and life sciences; employment, labor and workforce management; and litigation and business disputes. Founded in 1973 as an industry-focused firm, Epstein Becker Green has decades of experience serving clients in healthcare, financial services, retail, hospitality and technology, among other industries, representing entities from startups to Fortune 100 companies. Operating in offices throughout the US and supporting clients in the US and abroad, the firm's attorneys are committed to uncompromising client service and legal excellence.

Recruitment details

- Number of 1st year associates: 9
- Number of 2nd year associates: 9
- Associate salaries: 1st year: Varies by practice and location
- 2nd year: Not lock step
- Clerking policy: Yes

Law Schools attending for OCIs in 2017:

American University, Boston University, Columbia, Cornell Law School, Fordham, George Washington University, Harvard Law School, Loyola University – Chicago, New York University, Seton Hall University, St Louis University, University of Houston, University of Maryland, University of Virginia

Summer details

Summer associate profile:

We look for law students who have a demonstrated interest in health law or labor and employment law through education and/or experience. EBG's summer associate positions are practice specific. Summer associate positions are either in the healthcare and life sciences practice or in the employment, labor and workforce management practice. We prefer top one-third, law journal experience and strong writing skills.

Summer program components:

Training and development is an important goal of the summer program. Each summer associate is assigned an associate and a partner mentor to help guide them through the summer program experience. Summer associates are provided feedback throughout the summer – formally and informally. They have a midsummer review and an end-of-summer review. In addition, there is a series of educational sessions offered throughout the summer – typically two per week. Summer associates are given real assignments to work on so they have the opportunity to understand what it would be like to be a junior associate at EBG.

Head office: **N/A**
Number of domestic offices: **13**
Number of partners (US): **127**
Number of associates (US): **118**

Main Recruiting Contact:
Amy Simmons
Hiring Partner: **William Milani**
Recruitment website:
www.ebglaw.com
Diversity officer: **Carrie Valiant**

Summer Salary for 2017
1Ls: **Varies by practice and location**
2Ls: **Varies by practice and location**
Post 3Ls: **N/A**
1Ls hired? **Yes, 2**
Split summers offered? **Case by case**
Summers 2017: **10**
Offers/acceptances 2016:
9 offers, 8 acceptances and one pursuing judicial clerkship

EPSTEIN
BECKER
GREEN

Finnegan, Henderson, Farabow, Garrett & Dunner LLP

901 New York Avenue, NW, Washington, DC 20001
Tel: 202 408 4000   Fax: 202 408 4400
www.finnegan.com

Main areas of work

Practice includes all aspects of patent, trademark, copyright, and trade secret law, including counseling, prosecution, licensing, patent office trials and litigation. Also represents clients on IP issues related to international trade, portfolio management, the Internet, e-commerce, government contracts, antitrust and unfair competition.

Firm profile

Finnegan is a full-service intellectual property law firm, with a diverse blend of legal talent and cutting-edge scientific experience. Finnegan represents clients in a variety of industries including: alternative energy, biotechnology, pharmaceuticals, chemicals, consumer products, industrial manufacturing, medical devices, electronics and computers. Finnegan is positioned at the forefront of evolving intellectual property law issues and is a proven leader in the field.

Recruitment details

- Number of 1st year associates: 19
- Associate salaries: 1st year: $180,000
- Clerking policy: Yes
- Number of 2nd year associates: 17
- 2nd year: $190,000

Law Schools attending for OCIs in 2017:

Alabama; American; Arizona State; Berkeley; Boston College; Boston University; Duke; Emory; Florida; George Mason; George Washington; Georgetown; Georgia; Georgia State; Harvard; Hastings; Howard; Maryland; New Hampshire; UNC at Chapel Hill; Pennsylvania; Santa Clara; Stanford; University of Texas, Austin; Vanderbilt; Virginia; Washington

Summer details

Summer associate profile:

Summer associates at Finnegan are committed to excelling in intellectual property law. They are expected to demonstrate the ability to analyze complex legal issues, write clearly and persuasively, show initiative and manage time effectively. Above all, they are expected to be team players who work and interact well with others.

Summer program components:

Finnegan's summer associates have an opportunity to work on a broad range of matters in all of our practice areas. They complete substantive work related to their interests, receive extensive training and often have the chance to observe oral argument at the CAFC, participate in client meetings and attend depositions. Finnegan's summer program aims to acclimate students to firm culture and to prepare them for life as an associate. All summer associates are assigned both a partner and an associate mentor. Feedback is given formally at midsummer and final reviews.

Head Office: **Washington, DC**
Number of domestic offices: **5**
Number of international offices: **5**
Worldwide revenue: **$309,849,000**
Partners (US): **120**
Associates (US): **144**
Main Recruitment Contact:
Laurie Taylor
Hiring Partner: **Scott Burwell**
Recruitment website:
www.finnegan.com
Diversity officer: **Raj Gupta**

Summer Salary 2017
1Ls: **$3,500/week**
2Ls: **$3,500/week**
Post 3Ls: **N/A**
1Ls hired? **Yes**
Split summers offered? **No**
Can summers spend time in overseas office? **No**
Summers 2017: **30**
Offers/acceptances 2016:
23 offers, 16 acceptances

FINNEGAN

Firm Profiles

Fish & Richardson PC

One Marina Park Drive, Boston, MA 02210
Tel: 617 542 5070 Fax: 617 542 8906
www.fr.com

Main areas of work

Fish & Richardson offers top-rated litigation, patent, regulatory, trademark, and copyright services to help clients maximize the value of their intellectual property.

Firm profile

Fish & Richardson is a global patent prosecution, intellectual property litigation, and commercial litigation law firm with more than 400 attorneys and technology specialists in the US and Europe. Fish is the #1 US patent litigation firm, handling nearly three times as many cases than its nearest competitor; a powerhouse patent prosecution firm; a top-tier trademark and copyright firm; and the #1 firm at the Patent Trial and Appeal Board, with more cases than any other firm. Since 1878, Fish attorneys have been winning cases worth billions in controversy – often by making new law – for the world's most innovative and influential technology leaders.

Recruitment details

- Number of 1st year associates: 26
- Number of 2nd year associates: 28
- Associate salaries: 1st year: $180,000
- Clerking policy: Yes

Law Schools attending for OCIs in 2017:

Boston College, Boston University, Cardozo, Columbia, Emory, Fordham, Georgetown, George Washington, Harvard, NYU, Santa Clara University, SMU, Stanford, Temple, Texas Tech, UC Berkeley, UC Davis, University of Georgia, UC Hastings, University of Houston Law Center, University of Iowa, UCLA, University of Michigan, University of Minnesota, University of Pennsylvania, University of San Diego, USC, University of Texas, University of Virginia, Vanderbilt Law School, Boston Lawyers Group Job Fair, Delaware Minority Job Fair, Patent Law Interview Program (Chicago), San Francisco IP Law Association Job Fair, Southeastern IP Job Fair

Summer details

Summer associate profile:

Fish seeks students with excellent academic credentials and superior writing ability. For many positions, a scientific or technical background is preferred (required for patent prosecution candidates). Summer associates at Fish are given meaningful work assignments and plenty of opportunities to interact with the attorneys. They may prepare patent and trademark applications; conduct research for litigation cases; and attend client meetings, depositions, and even trials. They also receive one-on-one training from attorneys and participate in the firm's nationwide video conferences. In addition to informal feedback from attorneys throughout the summer, summer associates are given feedback on their work during midsummer and end-of-summer reviews. To help integrate summer associates into the firm and the city in which the office is located, Fish plans social events and assigns a mentor to each summer associate based on common interests, educational background, and other criteria.

Head Office: Boston, MA
Number of domestic offices: 11
Number of international offices: 1
Worldwide revenue: $407,678,677
Partners (US): 181
Associates (US): 165

Main Recruitment Contact:
Kelly Mixon Morgan, National Director of Attorney Hiring
Hiring Principal:
Betty Chen
Recruitment website:
www.fr.com/careers/
Diversity officer: Ahmed Davis, National Diversity Chair

Summer Salary 2017
1Ls: $3,500/week
2Ls: $3,500/week
Post 3Ls: N/A
1Ls hired? Yes
Split summers offered? Yes, with minimum week requirement
Can summers spend time in overseas office? No
Summers 2017: 35, including 8 1Ls
Offers/acceptances 2016:
31 offers, 23 acceptances

FISH & RICHARDSON

Foley & Lardner LLP

777 E. Wisconsin Avenue, Milwaukee, WI 53202-5306
Tel: 414 271 2400 Fax: 414 297 4900
Email: rbradley@foley.com
www.foley.com

Main areas of work

With more than 850 attorneys spread across 17 domestic offices and 3 foreign offices, Foley's market-leading platform includes business law, government and public policy, international, intellectual property and litigation. Adding depth to our bench strength, we address and anticipate client needs across more than 60 core practice areas and 12 cross-disciplinary industry teams.

Firm profile

Foley provides award-winning business and legal insight to clients across the country and around the world. Creating legal strategies that help meet our clients' needs today – and anticipate their challenges tomorrow – Foley is continually recognized by our clients and the legal industry for our exceptional client service, thought-leadership, value, and innovative technology.

Recruitment details

- Number of 1st year associates: 46　　　● Number of 2nd year associates: 35
- Associate salaries: 1st year: $140,000-$180,000 (varies by geographic market)
- 2nd year: $150,000-$195,000 (varies by geographic market)
- Clerking policy: Yes

Law Schools attending for OCIs in 2017:

Boston College, Boston University, Columbia, Cornell, Duke, Florida State University, Fordham, George Washington, Georgetown, Harvard, Howard, Marquette University, New York University, Northwestern, Notre Dame, Stanford, UC-Berkeley, UC-Davis, UCLA, University of Chicago, University of Florida, University of Illinois, University of Iowa, University of Miami, University of Michigan, University of Minnesota, University of San Diego, University of Southern California, University of Virginia, University of Wisconsin, Vanderbilt, Yale

Summer details

Summer associate profile:

Foley is looking for summer associates with an entrepreneurial spirit who bring diverse life and work experiences. Key attributes also include intellect, academic achievement, judgment and leadership abilities and excellent communication and interpersonal skills.

Summer program components:

We aim to introduce our summer associates to life as a Foley associate. Making significant contributions from day one, our summer associates are immersed in real world, practical experiences. Work is assigned on a project basis, which allows summer associates to experience a variety of practice areas and choose projects that match their interests. Summer associates receive a dedicated mentor and our training programs highlight Foley's culture, practice areas and strategic goals while developing and strengthening professional skills. To round out the experience, our summer associates participate in entertaining social events, including a firmwide retreat, where summer associates hear directly from firm leadership, participate in interactive workshops and training programs and build and strengthen relationships with our attorneys and other members of their class.

Head Office: Milwaukee, WI
Number of domestic offices: 17
Number of international offices: 3
Worldwide revenue: $671,000,000
Partners (US): 411
Associates (US): 457

Main Recruitment Contact:
Rebecca S Bradley
Hiring Partner: Robert A Scher
Recruitment website:
www.foleyrecruiting.com
Diversity officer: Eileen R Ridley

Summer Salary 2017
1Ls: $2,700-$3,500/week
2Ls: $2,700-$3,500/week
Post 3Ls: $2,700-$3,500/week
1Ls hired? Yes
Split summers offered? Case by case
Can summers spend time in overseas office? No
Summers 2017: 60
Offers/acceptances 2016:
52 offers, 47 acceptances

Firm Profiles

FOLEY & LARDNER LLP

Fox Rothschild LLP

2000 Market Street, Philadelphia, PA 19103
Tel: 215 299 2000 Fax: 215 299 2150
www.foxrothschild.com

Main areas of work

Corporate; employee benefits and executive compensation; entertainment; financial restructuring and bankruptcy; intellectual property; labor and employment; litigation; real estate; taxation and wealth planning.

Firm profile

Fox Rothschild LLP is a national law firm with over 750 lawyers practicing in 22 offices coast to coast. Our lawyers provide a full range of legal services to public and private companies – from family-run businesses to multinational corporations. We also represent charitable, medical and educational institutions both in the United States and in more than 50 countries worldwide.

Recruitment details

- Number of 1st year associates: 22   • Number of 2nd year associates: 19
- Associate salaries: 1st year: $115,000-$160,000 depending on geographic location
- 2nd year: Non lock step compensation
- Clerking policy: Yes

Law Schools attending for OCIs in 2017:

Berkeley; Cardozo: Chicago; Chicago-Kent; Colorado; Columbia; Cornell; Delaware; Denver; Duquesne; Fordham; GWU; Georgetown; Iowa; Loyola (Chicago); Loyola (Los Angeles); Minnesota; Mitchell Hamline; Nevada; Northwestern; Penn State; Penn; Pittsburgh; Rutgers; Seton Hall; SMU; Temple; Texas; UCLA; UC Hastings; USC; Villanova; Wisconsin

Job Fairs/Consortia attending in 2017: BC/BU NY Recruitment Program; Delaware Minority Job Fair; NJ Law Firm Group Minority Job Fair; Philadelphia Area Minority Job Fair; Minnesota Minority Corporate Conference

Summer details

Summer associate profile:

Our summer program is the foundation of our recruiting efforts. Each summer we invite a diverse group of bright, highly motivated law students to experience the practice of law at Fox Rothschild. Since the majority of our new lawyers come from the pool of second year summer associates who complete our program, we consider the summer program the most important component of the recruiting process.

Summer program components:

Our summer program is designed to expose summer associates to a realistic view of what it is like to practice law at Fox Rothschild. The program provides ongoing interaction with the attorneys on substantive assignments and during varied social events. Summer associates receive work assignments from all departments. We strive to ensure that the assignments given to summer associates are interesting and meaningful, with the results of that work used by our attorneys. Feedback is provided on an assignment-by-assignment basis, as well as through more formal mid-and end-of-summer evaluations. In addition, we encourage all summer associates to provide us with a detailed critique of all aspects of the summer program.

Head Office: Philadelphia, PA
Number of domestic offices: 22
Number of international offices: 0
Partners (US): 470
Associates (US): 224

Main Recruitment Contact:
Natalie Quinn, Associate Recruitment Manager
Recruitment website:
www.foxrothschild.com/careers
Diversity officers: Yesenia Gallegos and Prince Thomas, Diversity Committee Co-Chairs

Summer Salary 2017
1Ls: $2,211-$3,076/week
2Ls: $2,211-$3,076/week
Post 3Ls: N/A
1Ls hired? Yes
Split summers offered? No
Summers 2017: 25
Offers/acceptances 2016:
18 offers, 17 acceptances (2Ls)

Freshfields Bruckhaus Deringer US LLP

601 Lexington Avenue, 31st Floor, New York, NY 10022
Tel: 212 277 4000   Fax: 212 277 4001
www.freshfields.com

Main areas of work

Freshfields' US offices concentrate on corporate and finance transactions, antitrust, tax, litigation and international arbitration, while the firm's US attorneys based in Europe and Asia focus on corporate and securities transactions.

Firm profile

With over 2,500 lawyers in 26 key business centers around the world, Freshfields combines an unrivalled breadth of expertise across practice areas and borders with tremendous growth opportunities within the US practices. This unique balance defines the firm's work style and culture. On one side, there's the friendliness, personal attention and lack of hierarchy one finds in a small firm; on the other, the comprehensive network, breadth of work and resources of an international organization. Freshfields prides itself on being a collegial firm, working and learning together in a cutting edge, global environment.

Recruitment details

- Number of 1st year associates: 19
- Associate salaries: 1st year: $180,000
- Clerking policy: Yes
- Number of 2nd year associates: 17
- 2nd year: $190,000

Law Schools attending for OCIs in 2017:

University of Chicago Law School, Columbia University Law School, Cornell, Duke Law School, Emory University, Fordham University School of Law, George Washington University Law School, Georgetown University Law Center, Harvard Law School, University of Michigan Law School, New York University School of Law, Northwestern University School of Law, University of Pennsylvania Law School, Stanford Law School, Vanderbilt Job Fair, UC Berkeley School of Law, University of Virginia, Yale Law School

Summer details

Summer associate profile:

Freshfields recruits lawyers with many different talents and values individuality. The firm's ability to offer diverse skills locally and across international borders ensures clients have the very best advice possible. Freshfields operates a summer program for US law students in its New York, Washington, DC, Hong Kong, and London offices.

Summer program components:

Freshfields' summer program provides summer associates with exposure to several practice areas. Summer associates get substantive work supported by both formal and informal mentors. Most summer associates spend part of their summer in other Freshfields overseas offices such as London or Hong Kong.

Head Office: New York, NY
Number of domestic offices: 2
Number of international offices: 24
Worldwide revenue: $1.944 billion
Partners (US): 36
Counsel (US): 11
Associates (US): 120
Main Recruitment Contact:
Lesley Slater Stumphauzer
212 230 4674
Hiring Partner: Jerome Ranawake
Recruitment website:
http://www.freshfields.com/en/united_states/careers/

Summer Salary 2017
1Ls: $3,462/week
2Ls: $3,462/week
1Ls hired? Yes
Split summers offered? No
Can summers spend time in overseas office? Yes
Summers 2017: 17
Offers/acceptances 2016:
25 offers (100%), 21 acceptances

Freshfields Bruckhaus Deringer US LLP

Fried, Frank, Harris, Shriver & Jacobson LLP

One New York Plaza, New York, NY 10004
Tel: 212 859 8000   Fax: 212 859 4000
www.friedfrank.com

Main areas of work

Antitrust and competition; bankruptcy and restructuring; corporate (asset management, capital markets, corporate governance, derivatives, environmental, finance, mergers and acquisitions, private acquisitions and private equity); energy and energy enforcement; executive compensation and employee benefits; financial services; intellectual property and technology; international arbitration; international trade and investment; litigation (antitrust litigation, commercial litigation, government contracts, healthcare fraud and compliance, securities and shareholder litigation, securities enforcement and regulation, white collar criminal defense and securities enforcement); pro bono; real estate (corporate; acquisitions, dispositions and related financings; restructuring and financing; leasing; land use, construction and development); tax; trusts and estates; white collar criminal defense.

Firm profile

Fried, Frank, Harris, Shriver & Jacobson LLP is a leading international law firm with offices in New York; Washington, DC; London; and Paris. Our lawyers regularly advise the world's leading corporations and financial institutions on their most critical legal needs and business opportunities.

Recruitment details

- Number of 1st year associates: 60
- Number of 2nd year associates: 52
- Associate salaries: 1st year: $180,000
- 2nd year: $190,000
- Clerking policy: Yes

Law Schools attending for OCIs in 2017:

Boston University, Brooklyn, SUNY Buffalo, Cardozo, University of Chicago, Columbia, Cornell, Duke University, Fordham, Georgetown University, George Washington University, Harvard, Hofstra University, Howard University, University of Michigan, Northwestern University, New York Law, New York University, University of Pennsylvania, Rutgers – Newark, St John's University, University of Virginia, Yale

Summer details

Summer associate profile:

In hiring summer and full time associates, we look for energetic, motivated candidates who demonstrate a high level of intellectual ability and creativity, as well as a strong interest in working in a collegial setting.

Summer program components:

During the program, summer associates receive meaningful work assignments in a variety of practice areas, as well as attend court, client meetings, drafting and negotiation sessions and closings. They are also given significant opportunities to work on a range of pro bono matters. Each summer associate is matched with one partner mentor and two associate mentors, who review and provide feedback on assignments and guide them through the program. Working closely and socializing with partners, counsel and associates, our summer associates leave the program with a clear understanding of what Fried Frank can offer them as a place to begin their legal careers.

Head Office: New York, NY
Number of domestic offices: 2
Number of international offices: 3

Main Recruitment Contact:
Nancy Parker
Hiring Partners: Lisa Bebchick, Mark Hayek and Steven Steinman (NY) Jonathan DeFosse and Michelle Gold (DC)
Recruitment website:
www.friedfrank.com/careers
Diversity officer: Don Smith

Summer Salary 2017
1Ls: $3,750/week
2Ls: $3,750/week
Post 3Ls: $3,750/week
1Ls hired? No
Split summers offered? Case by case
Can summers spend time in overseas office? No
Summers 2017: 68
Offers/acceptances 2016:
67 offers, 61 acceptances

Gibbons P.C.

One Gateway Center, Newark, New Jersey 07102
Tel: 973 596 4500   Fax: 973 596 0545
www.gibbonslaw.com

Main areas of work

The firm's main areas of practice include business and commercial litigation, corporate, criminal defense, employment and labor law, financial restructuring and creditors' rights, government affairs, intellectual property, products liability and real property and environmental.

Firm profile

With more than 200 attorneys, Gibbons is a leading law firm in New Jersey, New York, Pennsylvania and Delaware, ranked among the nation's top 200 firms by *American Lawyer*. Gibbons is one of only 20 law firms nationwide to be named to the *National Law Journal's* inaugural "Midsize Hot List", which recognized firms with fewer than 300 lawyers that have found innovative ways to position themselves and demonstrated creativity and success in recruiting and retaining top talent, developing practice areas, managing operations and generally navigating the economic downturn more effectively than did many larger firms. A 2009 winner of the prestigious Catalyst Award for its innovative Women's Initiative, Gibbons is ranked one of the top 50 firms nationwide for working women by *Working Mother* magazine. The firm has also been recognized among the Best Places to Work in America by the Society for Human Resource Management and Great Place to Work Institute, as well as in New Jersey, New York and Pennsylvania by *NJBIZ*, *Crain's New York Business*, *Philadelphia Business Journal*, and *Central Penn Business Journal*. Gibbons maintains offices in Newark, New Jersey; New York, New York; Trenton, New Jersey; Philadelphia, Pennsylvania; and Wilmington, Delaware.

Head Office:	Newark, NJ
Number of domestic offices:	5
Number of international offices:	0
Partners (US):	140
Associates (US):	65

Main Recruitment Contact: Contact:
Peter J Torcicollo
Hiring Partner: **Peter J Torcicollo**
Recruitment website:
www.gibbonslaw.com
Diversity officer: **Luis J Diaz**

Recruitment details

- Number of 1st year associates: 0
- Number of 2nd year associates: 9
- Associate salaries: 1st year: N/A
- 2nd year: $135,000 + clerkship bonus
- Clerking policy: Yes

Summer details

Summer associate profile:

Since eliminating the firm's Summer Associate Program in 2003, Gibbons has focused on hiring new associates who have completed a judicial clerkship. Fully 70 percent of the attorneys in the business and commercial litigation department served for federal or state judges. These attorneys provide first-hand insight into the preferences and practices of federal and state judges, in addition to a well-developed knowledge of the inner workings of the courts, adding value for the firm's clients.

Gibson, Dunn & Crutcher LLP

333 South Grand Avenue, Los Angeles, CA 90071
Tel: 213 229 7000   Fax: 213 229 7520
Email: lripley@gibsondunn.com
www.gibsondunn.com

Main areas of work

Gibson, Dunn & Crutcher is renowned for both its litigation and transactional work. Major practice groups include antitrust, capital markets, class actions, environmental, electronic discovery, information technology, intellectual property, media and entertainment, mergers and acquisitions, securities, transnational litigation and white-collar defense. The firm is especially known for its appellate work, particularly in the US Supreme Court.

Firm profile

Gibson, Dunn & Crutcher is a full-service global law firm, with over 1,300 lawyers in 20 offices worldwide, including ten offices in major cities throughout the United States and over 190 lawyers in their London, Paris, Munich, Beijing, Brussels, Dubai, Frankfurt, Hong Kong, Singapore and São Paulo offices. The firm is recognized for excellent legal service and its lawyers routinely represent clients in some of the most high-profile litigations and complex transactions in the world.

Recruitment details

- Number of 1st year associates: 75
- Associate salaries: 1st year: $ 180,000
- Clerking policy: Yes
- Number of 2nd year associates: 107
- 2nd year: $190,000

Law Schools attending for OCIs in 2017:

Berkeley, Chicago, Colorado, Columbia, Cornell, Duke, Fordham, George Washington, Georgetown, Harvard, Irvine, Loyola, Michigan, NYU, Northwestern, Pennsylvania, Pepperdine, San Diego, SMU, Stanford, Texas, UCLA, USC, Virginia, Yale

Summer details

Summer associate profile:

Gibson Dunn's summer program is the single largest means through which new lawyers become a part of our firm. Each summer, Gibson Dunn brings together approximately 125 of the most accomplished and ambitious students from the top law schools across the nation, providing them with real involvement in the high quality legal work that our firm does every day. Our summer associates are involved directly in the firm's representation of its clients, maximizing their exposure to the practical aspects of lawyering. In addition to interesting client work, the summer program includes many great social activities giving summer associates the chance to get to know each other and the lawyers of the firm.

Summer program components:

The firm provides significant and substantive training to our select group of summer associates. Each summer associate receives detailed feedback on the projects that they perform plus numerous formal training programs.

Head Office: Los Angeles, CA
Number of domestic offices: 10
Number of international offices: 10
Worldwide revenue: $1,606,500,000
Partners (US): 318
Associates (US): 786

Main Recruitment Contact:
Leslie Ripley, Chief Recruiting Officer
Hiring Partner: Steven E Sletten
Recruitment website:
www.gibsondunn.com
Diversity officer: Zakiyyah Salim-Williams

1Ls hired? Yes
Split summers offered? Yes
Can summers spend time in overseas office? No
Summers 2017: 121
Offers/acceptances 2016:
120 offers, 94 acceptances as of 3/1/17

GIBSON DUNN

Goodwin

www.goodwinlaw.com

Main areas of work

Corporate-based practices: financial industry, intellectual property transactions and strategies, private equity, real estate industry (REITS, real estate capital markets, M&A), tax and technology and life sciences.

Litigation-based practices: business litigation, consumer financial services, financial industry, intellectual property, products liability and mass torts, securities litigation and white-collar defense.

Firm profile

Goodwin is a Global 50 law firm with offices in Boston, Frankfurt, Hong Kong, London, Los Angeles, New York, Paris, San Francisco, Silicon Valley and Washington, DC. Excelling at complex and sophisticated transactional work and precedent-setting, bet-the company litigation, the firm combines in-depth legal knowledge with practical business experience to help clients maximize opportunities, manage risk and move their business forward. The firm hires talented, motivated people committed to excellence, innovation, collaboration and client service and believes that every lawyer and staff member deserves a supportive, meritocratic environment in which people of all backgrounds are given the opportunity to excel and thrive. Through an extensive and longstanding pro bono program, legal staff are encouraged to assist those unable to afford legal representation.

Recruitment details

- Number of 1st year associates: 59
- Associate Salaries: 1st Year: $180,000
- Clerking policy: Yes
- Number of 2nd year associates: 71
- 2nd Year: $190,000

Law Schools attending for OCIs in 2017:

Berkeley, Boston College, Boston University, Brooklyn, Catholic University of America, Columbia, Cornell, Duke, Emory, Fordham, George Washington, Georgetown, Harvard, Howard, Loyola Law School (Los Angeles), McGill, Northeastern, Northwestern, NYU, Santa Clara, Stanford, Suffolk, UC Davis, UC Hastings, UCLA, UNC, University of Chicago, University of Connecticut, University of Michigan, University of Pennsylvania, University of Texas, USC, UVA, Vanderbilt, Washington University in St. Louis, William & Mary, Yale

Summer details

Summer associate profile:

Goodwin hires summer associates with exceptional academic records, demonstrated leadership abilities and excellent written, verbal and interpersonal skills.

Summer program components:

Goodwin's summer program provides summer associates with a realistic work experience mirroring that of a junior associate. We work closely with summer associates to understand their interests and provide opportunities to work on a broad range of assignments. Summer associates are encouraged to observe client meetings, court hearings, depositions, negotiations and attend practice area meetings. We provide leading litigation and business law training programs throughout the summer. Through our adviser program, summer associates are paired with partners and associates to help them integrate.

Largest Office: Boston, MA
Number of domestic offices: 6
Number of international offices: 4
Worldwide revenue: $912,000,000
Partners (US): 311
Counsel (US): 94
Associates (US): 435

Main Recruitment Contact:
Ashley Nelson, Director of Legal Recruitment, Associate & Professional Track Hiring, or see the list of office-based recruiting contacts on our website
Hiring Partner: Kenneth J Gordon, National Hiring Partner
Recruitment website: www.goodwinlaw.com/careers/law-students
Diversity officer: Laura Acosta, Director of Diversity & Inclusion
Summer Salary 2017
1Ls: $3,460/week
2Ls: $3,460/week
Post 3Ls: N/A
1Ls hired? Yes
Split summers offered? No
Can summers spend time in overseas office? Case by case
Summers 2017: 60
Offers/acceptances 2016:
56 offers, 54 acceptances

GOODWIN

Goulston & Storrs

400 Atlantic Avenue, Boston, MA 02110
Tel: 617 482 1776   Fax: 617 574 4112
Email: jsmith@goulstonstorrs.com
www.goulstonstorrs.com

Main areas of work

Real estate, litigation, tax, private clients and trusts, capital markets, bankruptcy, corporate, employment, banking and finance, environmental, intellectual property.

Firm profile

Goulston & Storrs is an Am Law 200 law firm, with offices in Boston, New York and Washington, DC. With nearly 200 lawyers across multiple disciplines, Goulston & Storrs is nationally recognized for its real estate practice, leading-edge corporate, capital markets and finance, litigation, and private client and trust practices. Our lawyers employ a proven team approach that values client outcomes over individual recognition. The firm's dedication to providing prompt, practical legal advice, cost-efficiently and tailored to our clients' business needs, has resulted in Goulston & Storrs being acknowledged for excellence by *Chambers USA*, *BTI's* A-Team for Client Service, *Best Lawyers in America* and other leading industry rankings.

Recruitment details

- Number of 1st year associates: 6
- Number of 2nd year associates: 6
- Associate salaries: 1st year: $180,000

Law Schools attending for OCIs in 2017:

Harvard, Georgetown University, Columbia University, Northeastern University, New York University, Boston College, Boston University, Suffolk University

Summer details

Summer associate profile:

We attract and hire people who: seek a sophisticated and challenging legal practice; are concerned about team success; are willing to work hard.

Summer program components:

As a summer associate, you have a unique opportunity to learn about the legal profession and the Boston area. Expect to live the law firm experience with direct partner and client exposure. Work assignments are substantive and include research and writing assignments, client meetings, conference calls, depositions and attending hearings. Your summer with Goulston & Storrs offers amazing work opportunities throughout several practice areas, assisting the firm's attorneys.

Head Office: **Boston, MA**
Number of domestic offices: **3**
Number of international offices: **0**
Worldwide revenue: **$167,000,000**
Partners (US): **113**
Associates (US): **68**

Main Recruitment Contacts:
Nancy Needle and Jen Smith
Hiring Partner: **Bill Seuch**
Recruitment website:
www.goulstonstorrs.com
Diversity officers: **Kevin O'Flaherty and Matt Epstein**

Summer Salary 2017
1Ls: **$3,400 per week**
2Ls: **$3,400 per week**
1Ls hired? **Yes**
Split summers offered? **Case by case basis**
Can summers spend time in overseas office? **No**
Summers 2017: **7**
Offers/acceptances 2016:
6 offers, 6 acceptances

Greenberg Traurig, LLP

Tel: 212 801 9200 Fax: 212 801 6400
Email: gtrecruiting@gtlaw.com
www.gtlaw.com

Main areas of work

Corporate and securities; litigation; real estate; health and FDA business; intellectual property and technology; global trade and investment; cybersecurity, privacy and crisis management; energy and natural resources; business reorganization and financial restructuring; tax, trusts and estates; government law and policy; public finance; entertainment and media; labor and employment; environmental; global practice group; and business immigration and compliance.

Firm profile

Greenberg Traurig, LLP, celebrating its 50th anniversary in 2017, is a global, multi-practice law firm with approximately 2000 attorneys serving clients from 38 offices in the United States, Latin America, Europe, the Middle East, and Asia. The firm works with clients to address their multi-disciplinary and cross-border needs. Providing associates with the type of client management and business development training previously offered only to partners are key elements to our associate programs.

Recruitment details

- Number of 1st year associates: 72
- Number of 2nd year associates: 22
- Associate salaries: 1st year: $110,000 - $180,000
- 2nd year: N/A

Law Schools attending for OCIs in 2017:

Berkeley; Brooklyn; Chicago-Kent; Columbia; Cornell; Duke; FIU; Fordham; Georgetown; George Washington; Harvard; Loyola; NYU; Northwestern; Notre Dame; Santa Clara; SMU Dedman; Stanford; UC Hastings; UC Irvine; UCLA; Univ of Chicago; Univ of Florida; Univ of Illinois; Univ of Miami; Univ of Michigan; Univ of North Carolina; Univ of Pennsylvania; Univ of Southern California; Univ of Texas; Univ of Virginia; Vanderbilt

Summer details

Summer associate profile:

We recruit students who excel in multiple areas, possessing what we call "3-D" skills (legal, business and leadership), as these are predictors for success in the Greenberg Traurig community.

Summer program components:

We provide summer associates varied professional opportunities to learn about our clients, our attorneys, our staff, our firm and our culture including:

- Day-to-day assignments, with direct shareholder contact
- Dedicated firmwide training and orientation
- Two mentors, one associate and one shareholder
- Mid-summer and end-of-summer review meetings with Summer Program leaders
- A variety of networking events and community outreach programs

An important objective of the program is for summer associates to transition from student to legal practitioner. Our attorneys and attorney recruitment staff help clarify and direct summer associates' decision-making about the start of their legal careers. *The Legal Careers* blog provides an inside glimpse at working at Greenberg Traurig, particularly for summer associates.

Head Office: **Global**
Number of domestic offices: **29**
Number of international offices: **9**
Worldwide revenue: **$1,377,500,000**
Partners (US): **992**
Associates (US): **1051**

Main Recruitment Contact:
Janet McKeegan
Hiring Partner: **Bradford D Kaufman**
Recruitment website:
www.gtlaw.com/Careers/Associates
Diversity officer: **Nikki Lewis Simon**

Summer Salary 2017
1Ls: **N/A**
2Ls: **N/A**
Post 3Ls: **N/A**
1Ls hired? **Yes**
Split summers offered? **CBC**
Can summers spend time in overseas office? **CBC**
Summers 2017: **49**
Offers/acceptances 2016:
47 offers, 42 acceptances

607

Hangley Aronchick Segal Pudlin & Schiller

One Logan Square, 27th Floor, Philadelphia, PA 19103
Tel: 215 568 6200   Fax: 215 568 0300
Email: marketingdept@hangley.com

Main areas of work

Hangley Aronchick Segal Pudlin & Schiller is a multi-faceted law firm that offers specialized legal solutions to a broad range of local, regional, and national clients. The firm is highly regarded nationally for its quality work, innovative strategies, and excellent results. With offices in Philadelphia, Harrisburg, and Norristown, Pennsylvania, and Cherry Hill, New Jersey, Hangley Aronchick offers a suite of diverse legal services, including litigation, business and corporate, insurance coverage, real estate, bankruptcy, education, environmental, family law, and tax and estate planning services.

Firm profile

Hangley Aronchick Segal Pudlin & Schiller is consistently recognized for excellence in legal practice, as well as for its ability to recruit talented attorneys. Founded in 1994, the firm is known for the sophistication of its matters, the roster of its clients and the quality of its work. In the Delaware Valley, the firm is unparalleled in its ability to attract the most highly qualified attorneys, both at the entry level and laterally. The firm includes former Philadelphia City Solicitors; Fellows of the American College of Trial Lawyers, the American College of Bankruptcy, and the American College of Real Estate Lawyers; members of judicial advisory committees; members of the American Law Institute; and adjunct faculty members at area law schools. For further information on the firm's practice areas and outstanding lawyers, readers are invited to visit the firm's website www.hangley.com

Recruitment details

- Number of 1st year associates: 1
- Associate Salaries: 1st Year: $135,000
- Number of 2nd year associates: 1
- Clerking policy: Yes

Summer details

Summer program components:

Hangley Aronchick Segal Pudlin & Schiller does not have a formal summer associate program, though the firm will consider extraordinary candidates for summer employment on occasion.

Head Office: **Philadelphia, PA**
Number of domestic offices: **4**
Number of international offices: **0**

Hiring Partner: **Daniel Segal, Chair of Hiring Committee**
Recruitment website:
www.hangley.com/careers/

HANGLEY
ARONCHICK
SEGAL
PUDLIN
&SCHILLER

Harris, Wiltshire & Grannis LLP

1919 M Street NW, Eighth Floor, Washington, DC 20036
Tel: 202 730 1300   Fax: 202 730 1301
Email: attorneyrecruiting@hwglaw.com
www.hwglaw.com

Main areas of work

Harris, Wiltshire & Grannis is a boutique law firm, meaning we focus on solving fairly specialized legal problems extremely well. We have excellent trial litigators who handle government investigations and criminal defense matters as well as complex civil litigation. We also have an exceptional Supreme Court and appellate litigation group as well as one of the leading legal and government ethics practices. However, the firm started out as a telecom and technology firm and that is still our primary area of practice. We handle just about any kind of matter before the FCC, representing companies both large and small that are involved in all kinds of different technologies, from satellites to wireless phones to undersea cables to the internet.

Firm profile

Work is an integral component of our lives; we gain personal and professional satisfaction from high quality legal advocacy, writing and critical thinking. We enjoy practicing together, working hard and giving our clients the absolute best representation. At the same time, we love our families and our friends and take pleasure in any number of avocations. Harris, Wiltshire & Grannis is a place where smart, dedicated attorneys do work of the highest quality and still live a normal life. Because this is central to the culture of the firm, we have no set billable hours requirement and no aspect of associate compensation is tied to the number of hours billed.

Recruitment details

- Number of 1st year associates: 3
- Number of 2nd year associates: 2
- Associate salaries: 1st year: $178,500
- 2nd year: $189,500
- Clerking policy: Yes

Law Schools attending for OCIs in 2017:

Chicago, Duke, Georgetown, Harvard, Michigan, Stanford, Virginia

Summer details

Summer associate profile:

We seek associates with superlative writing ability and a record of the very highest academic achievement. We will only hire a summer associate that we fully expect to become a superb lawyer and a trusted colleague.

Summer program components:

We treat summer associates like brand new associates. This means that, although summer associates necessarily require a different level of training and supervision, they will be doing the same work associates do, with the same people and under the same conditions. Harris, Wiltshire & Grannis associates are expected to perform as lawyers, not assistant lawyers and we want our summer associates to aim for the same high level of creativity, initiative and skill. Summer associates can expect to work in our telecommunications and technology, criminal defense and litigation, and appellate practices.

Head Office: **Washington, DC**
Number of domestic offices: **2**
Number of international offices: **0**
Partners (US): **32**
Of Counsel (US): **4**
Associates (US): **16**

Main Recruitment Contact:
Jonathan Mirsky
Hiring Partner: **Jonathan Mirsky**
Recruitment website:
www.hwglaw.com/recruiting
Diversity officer: **Brita Strandberg**

Summer Salary 2017
1Ls: **N/A**
2Ls: **$3,350/week**
Post 3Ls: **N/A**
1Ls hired? **No**
Split summers offered? **Yes**
Can summers spend time in overseas office? **N/A**
Summers 2017: **2**
Offers/acceptances 2016:
3 offers, 2 acceptance (1 other summer clerking after graduation)

HWG | HARRIS, WILTSHIRE & GRANNIS LLP

Firm Profiles

Haynes and Boone, LLP

2323 Victory Avenue Suite 700, Dallas, TX 75219
Tel: 214 651 5000
Email: amanda.kelly@haynesboone.com
www.haynesboone.com

Main areas of work

Corporate/securities/M&A, private equity, hedge funds, business litigation (including IP, insurance coverage, environmental, energy, real estate, securities, healthcare and appellate), bankruptcy and restructuring, energy, banking and finance, franchises, intellectual property/technology, labor and employment and real estate.

Firm profile

Haynes and Boone, LLP is an international corporate law firm with offices in Texas, New York, California, Colorado, Washington, DC, London, Shanghai and Mexico City, providing a full spectrum of legal services.

Recruitment details

- Number of 1st year associates: 39
- Associate salaries: 1st year: $180,000
- Clerking policy: Yes

- Number of 2nd year associates: 29

Law Schools attending for OCIs in 2017:

Baylor, Columbia, Cornell, Duke, Fordham, Georgetown, Harvard, Santa Clara, Southern Methodist University, Stanford, UC Berkeley, UC Davis, UC Irvine, UCLA, University of Houston, University of Pennsylvania, USC, University of Texas, University of Virginia, Vanderbilt

Summer details

Summer associate profile:

To sustain what we feel is a blend of culture and sophistication of practice that is unmatched in the market, Haynes and Boone is looking for internally driven law students with a personality that would augment our firm's commitment to teamwork and a long-term approach to the practice of law.

Summer program components:

Our summer associates spend 9-10 weeks (depending on office) with us working in one or two of our practice areas. Each summer associate is given a supervisor who assigns them work and they are able to attend client meetings, negotiations, hearings, etc. Feedback is provided throughout the summer as well as through the mid-clerkship review. Our summer associates also enjoy several social events designed to get to know our attorneys.

Head Office: Dallas, TX
Number of domestic offices: 12
Number of international offices: 3
Worldwide revenue: $375,000,000
Partners (US): 225
Associates (US): 311 (including other attorneys)

Main Recruitment Contact: Amanda Kelly, Manager of Entry-Level Recruiting
Hiring Partner: Eric Williams
Recruitment website: www.haynesboone.com
Diversity officer: Kenya Woodruff, Partner of the Attorney Diversity and Inclusion Committee

Summer Salary 2017
1Ls: $3,462/week
2Ls: $3,462/week
Post 3Ls: $3,462/week
1Ls hired? Yes, in specific offices
Split summers offered? CBC
Can summers spend time in overseas office? No
Summers 2017: 2Ls: 33
Offers/acceptances 2016:
33 offers, 32 acceptances

haynesboone

Hogan Lovells US LLP

555 13th Street, NW, Washington, DC 20004
Tel: 202 637 5600   Fax: 202 637 5910
Email: irena.mcgrath@hoganlovells.com
www.hoganlovells.com

Main areas of work

Working at the intersection of law, business and government, across a wide range of industries, Hogan Lovells US LLP's global practices include corporate; finance; government regulatory; intellectual property, media and technology; litigation, arbitration and employment; and pro bono.

Firm profile

By joining Hogan Lovells, you will become part of a legal practice with a long tradition of excellence. Working as an integrated team, our lawyers provide sophisticated services on a broad spectrum of cutting-edge legal issues. Our unique global platform, collaborative culture and commitment to your professional development, provide an exceptional foundation on which to build a legal career – now and into the future. Hogan Lovells' pioneering US Pro Bono practice began more than 40 years ago when we were the first law firm to establish a separate practice devoted exclusively to providing pro bono legal services. Our culture of inclusion, which respects and values the diversity of all of our people, enhances the quality of Hogan Lovells' workplace and our ability to provide excellent legal services for clients. We prize our friendly, team-oriented environment, which encourages professional development, good associate-partner relations and early client contact.

Recruitment details

- Number of 1st year associates: 58
- Number of 2nd year associates: 51
- Associate salaries: 1st year: Varies by market - in most US offices $180,000
- 2nd year: Varies by market – in most US offices $190,000
- Clerking policy: Yes

Law Schools attending for OCIs in 2017:

American University, Baltimore, Boston College, Boston University, Catholic University, Columbia, Colorado, Cornell, Denver, Duke, Florida, Florida International, Florida State, George Mason, George Washington, Georgetown, Harvard, Howard, Maryland, Miami, Michigan, Minnesota, Northwestern, NYU, Pennsylvania, Stanford, Texas, UC Berkeley, UCLA, USC, UVA, Vanderbilt, Washington & Lee, William & Mary, Yale

Summer details

Summer associate profile:

With guidance from lawyer assignment coordinators/mentors, students do meaningful client work, and participate in training programs designed to develop and enhance legal skills. Summer Associates have opportunities to attend closings, depositions, and legislative and administrative hearings and meet with alumni and clients serving in prominent roles in government and business. In 2017, five US Summer Associates with strong interest in our transnational practices participated in a two-week program in the London office. All US Summer Associates attend a retreat in Washington where firm leaders share insights about Hogan Lovells' pre-eminent practices and strategic plans for the future, our vision and values, and commitment to diversity. Through group dinners and team building exercises, US Summer Associates get to know their colleagues from other offices and make life long connections.

Head Office (US): Washington, DC
Number of domestic offices: 13
Number of international offices: 36
Worldwide revenue: $1.925 billion
Partners (US): 411
Associates (US): 530

Main Recruitment Contact: Irena McGrath, Chief Associate Recruitment Officer
Hiring Partner: Timothy A Lloyd, Esq.
Recruitment website:
http://careers-us.hoganlovells.com/
Diversity officer: Leslie Richards-Yellen

Summer Salary 2017
1Ls: $3,500/week (in most offices)
2Ls: $3,500/week (in most offices)
Post 3Ls: $3,500/week (in most offices)
1Ls hired? Yes (in some offices)
Split summers offered? Case by case
Can summers spend time in overseas office? Case by case
Summers 2017: 126 (111 2Ls, 15 1Ls)
Offers/acceptances 2016:
86 offers, 69 acceptances (to date)

Holland & Knight LLP

701 Brickell Avenue, Suite 3300, Miami, FL 33131
Tel: 305 374 8500   Fax: 305 789 7799
www.hklaw.com

Main areas of work

Holland & Knight advises clients in a broad range of practice areas, including complex commercial litigation, corporate law, intellectual property, private wealth services, mergers and acquisitions, real estate and zoning law, and public policy and regulatory matters. Attorneys work collaboratively across practice groups and teams, drawing upon their depth and breadth of legal experience and industry knowledge to serve clients in the US and abroad.

Firm profile

Holland & Knight is a global firm with more than 1,200 lawyers and other professionals in 24 US offices, as well as London, Bogotá and Mexico City. Recent expansion has helped the firm penetrate new markets and attract sophisticated clients in the US and abroad. With a growing focus on Latin America, the firm leverages more than 30 years of experience in the region to advance client interests, from establishing a business in an emerging economy to expanding an international presence.

Recruitment details

- Number of 1st year associates: 39
- Associate salaries: 1st year: $180,000
- Clerking policy: No
- Number of 2nd year associates: 42
- 2nd year: $190,000

Law Schools attending for OCIs in 2017:

Boston College, Boston University, Columbia University, Duke University, Emory, Florida State University, Fordham University, George Washington University, Georgetown University, Harvard, New York University, Northwestern University, Stanford, University of California, Berkeley – Boalt Hall, University of California - Los Angeles, University of Chicago, University of Florida, University of Michigan, University of Notre Dame, University of Pennsylvania, University of Southern California, University of Virginia, Yale and others

Summer details

Summer associate profile:

Holland & Knight seeks candidates with superior academic credentials and diverse backgrounds who aspire to become leaders in the legal profession and their communities.

Summer program components:

Holland & Knight's Summer Associate Program is structured to provide exposure to many diverse practice areas. Summer associates work on substantive matters and observe conferences, negotiations, oral arguments, closings, depositions, hearings and trials. These experiences provide a broad foundation to assist them in identifying the areas of practice on which they would like to focus as they begin their legal careers.

Head Office: No main office; Managing Partner resident in the Miami office
Number of domestic offices: 24
Number of international offices: 3
Worldwide revenue: $802.9 million
Partners (US): 621
Associates (US): 338

Main Recruitment Contact: Carrie Weintraub, Chief Professional Development & Human Resources Officer, carrie.weintraub@hklaw.com
Hiring Partner: Deborah E Barnard
Recruitment website: www.hklaw.com
Diversity officer: Tiffani G Lee

Summer Salary 2017
1Ls hired? Case by case
Split summers offered? Case by case
Can summers spend time in overseas office? No
Summers 2017: 26
Offers/acceptances 2016:
43 offers, 40 acceptances

Holland & Knight

Hughes Hubbard & Reed LLP

One Battery Park Plaza
Tel: 212 837 6000 Fax: 212 299 6131
www.hugheshubbard.com

Main areas of work

With offices in New York, Washington, DC, Los Angeles, Miami, Jersey City, Kansas City, Tokyo and Paris, Hughes Hubbard offers expertise in a wide-range of practice areas. Our team of more than 350 experienced practitioners works in over 30 specialized practices, from mergers and acquisitions, public offerings, corporate reorganization, real estate and cross-border transactions to general commercial litigation, securities litigation, international trade, anti-corruption and internal investigations, international arbitration and dispute resolution, product liability, antitrust, intellectual property, labor, employee benefits and tax, as well as niche practices such as art law and a credit card practice.

Firm profile

The firm has outstanding diversity scores and consistently receives high marks for its pro bono activities. *The American Lawyer* has consistently recognized Hughes Hubbard on its A-List of the nation's most elite law firms.

Recruitment details

- Number of 1st year associates: 30
- Associate salaries: 1st year: $180,000
- Clerking policy: yes
- Number of 2nd year associates: 26
- 2nd year: $190,000

Law Schools attending for OCIs in 2017:

Brooklyn Law School, Columbia University Law School, Cornell Law School, Duke University School of Law, Fordham University School of Law, George Washington University Law School, Georgetown University Law Center, Harvard Law School, New York University School of Law, Stanford Law School, University of Chicago Law School, University of Michigan Law School, University of Pennsylvania Law School, University of Virginia School of Law, Yale Law School

Summer details

Summer associate profile:

Hughes Hubbard recognizes that a successful recruiting effort is essential to the long-term success of the firm. We are committed to rendering services of the highest professional quality and, to that end, seek lawyers of exceptional ability, integrity and industry. We actively recruit candidates whose academic performance, energy, personality and character suggest that they possess the ability and desire to meet the challenges presented by a demanding practice and are prepared to develop rapidly and assume responsibility early.

Summer program components:

Summer associates work on real problems, not "make-work," and those problems often involve far more than library research. In recent years, for example, summer associates have assisted at depositions, court proceedings and closings. Summer associates participate in a wide variety of client meetings, witness interviews, negotiation sessions and fact-gathering projects and, on some occasions, they have traveled to other offices.

Head Office: New York, NY
Number of domestic offices: 6
Number of international offices: 2
Worldwide revenue: $394,000,000
Partners (US): $2,145,000
Per Lawyer (US): $1,185,000

Main Recruitment Contact: Mr Adrian B Cockerill
Hiring Partner: Mr George A Tsougarakis
Recruitment website:
www.hugheshubbard.com/careers

Summer Salary 2017
1Ls: $3,450
2Ls: $3,450
Post 3Ls: $3,450
1Ls hired? Yes
Split summers offered? No
Can summers spend time in overseas office? Yes
Summers 2017: 22
Offers/acceptances 2016: 21 offers, 21 acceptances

Hughes Hubbard &Reed

Hunton & Williams LLP

2200 Pennsylvania Avenue, NW, Washington, DC 20037
Tel: 202 955 1500   Fax: 202 778 2201
www.hunton.com

Firm profile

Hunton & Williams is the legal advisor of choice for industry leaders on six continents. With more than 750 attorneys practicing from 19 offices across the United States, Europe and Asia, the firm helps clients realize new opportunities and solve complex problems with confidence. Founded in 1901, Hunton & Williams blends more than a century of experience in virtually every key legal discipline with a broad view of current business realities and a forward-looking perspective on emerging issues to provide legal and regulatory advice that will carry its clients well into the 21st century. The firm is regularly named by legal and business publications as among the top law firms for client service and as a place to work.

Recruitment details

- Number of 1st year associates: 29   • Number of 2nd year associates: 28
- Associate salaries: 1st year: $160,000-$180,000 (depending on location)
- Clerking policy: Yes

Law Schools attending for OCIs in 2017:

Columbia University; Cornell University; Duke University; Emory University; Fordham University; Georgetown University; George Washington University; Harvard University; Howard University; New York University; Southern Methodist University; University of California, Berkeley; University of California, Los Angeles; University of Michigan; University of North Carolina; University of Pennsylvania; University of Richmond; University of Southern California; University of Texas; University of Virginia; Vanderbilt University; Washington and Lee University; Washington University in St Louis; College of William and Mary

Summer details

Summer associate profile:

When recruiting summer associates, Hunton & Williams seeks high performing, team oriented and problem-solving law students. In addition to strong academic credentials and excellent written and verbal communication skills, applicants should have a solid record of success and leadership. Prior work experience, professional experience or advanced degrees also are valued.

Summer program components:

Hunton & Williams Summer Program is a focused, ten-week immersion in the real-world practice of law. Rather than simply shadowing experienced associates and partners, participants are actively engaged in practical work and training activities that support the goals of the firm and its clients while fostering professional development. While the program is customized, based on the career goals and interests of each summer associate, it generally includes leadership skills training, career mentoring, business development and client service training, practical experience, client interaction, pro bono opportunities, writing coaching, judicial clerkship counseling, and work projects and experience in the practice areas of interest.

Head Office: **Washington, DC**
Number of domestic offices: **14**
Number of international offices: **5**
Partners (US): **284**
Counsel (US): **92**
Associates (US): **303**

Main Recruitment Contact:
See list of office-based recruiters located on www.huntoncareers.com
Hiring Partners: **Kimberly C MacLeod and Thomas Y Hiner; Judith H Itkin, Partner in Charge of Lawyer Recruiting and Development**
Recruitment website:
www.huntoncareers.com
Diversity co-heads: **A. Todd Brown, Gustavo J. Membiela, Emily Burkhardt Vicente**
Summer Salary 2017
2Ls: **$3,100-$3,500/week**
1Ls hired? **No (Some offices may participate in a 1L diversity program.)**
Split summers offered? **No**
Can summers spend time in overseas office? **No**
Summers 2017: **26**
Offers/acceptances 2016:
28 offers, 24 acceptances

Firm Profiles

Irell & Manella LLP

1800 Avenue of the Stars, Suite 900, Los Angeles, CA 90067
Tel: 310 277 1010   Fax: 310 203 7199
www.irell.com

Main areas of work

Antitrust, appellate, art, bankruptcy reorganization and creditors' rights, class action defense, cyber liability and privacy, debt finance, entertainment litigation, insurance, IP litigation, IP transactions, litigation, media and entertainment transactions, mergers and acquisitions, patent, copyright and trademark, private equity and venture capital, professional liability defense, public offerings and private placements, real estate, securities law and corporate governance, securities litigation and tax.

Firm profile

Irell & Manella is a full service law firm with offices in Los Angeles and Newport Beach, California. Our unique practice and culture offers opportunities for talented law graduates to excel early in their careers. The quality of our work and the flexibility of our organization attract associates with the highest qualifications.

Irell's preeminent reputation brings clients to us from around the country and abroad and allows us to concentrate our physical presence in a single metropolitan area ensuring firm cohesion and a minimum of bureaucracy.

Recruitment details

- Number of 1st year associates: 9
- 1st year associate salary: $180,000
- Clerking policy: Yes
- Number of 2nd year associates: 8
- 2nd year associate salary: $190,000

Law Schools attending for OCIs in 2017:

Law Schools: Berkeley, University of Chicago, Columbia, Duke, Harvard, Michigan, Northwestern, NYU, Stanford, UCLA, UC Irvine, USC, Yale.

Job Fairs & Interview Programs: Lavender Law, Loyola University Chicago Patent Law Interview Program, Los Angeles On Tour Interview Program (OTIP), Penn Regional Interview Program.

Resume collections: Cornell, Georgetown, George Washington, Howard, Loyola (Los Angeles), Notre Dame, Pepperdine, Southwestern, Texas and Vanderbilt.

Summer details

Summer associate profile:

We recruit the top candidates from the top schools. Consideration is given to participation in law school activities, undergraduate record, previous work experience, references and other factors. We look for individuals who are motivated, creative, show leadership, have a strong work ethic and are serious about being a lawyer.

Summer program components:

Our summer program is designed to allow summer associates to explore the various areas of our practice. Summer associates have the opportunity to participate in a mock wrongful death trial that is tried to a jury and presided over by a judge. Each summer associate is assigned a mentor and a work coordinator. Feedback is provided on each project by the assigning attorney and each summer associate has a mid-summer review to deliver additional feedback about his or her progress.

Head Office: Los Angeles, CA
Number of domestic offices: 2
Number of international offices: 0
Partners (US): 45
Associates (US): 55

Main Recruitment Contact:
Edith Gondwe
Hiring Partner: Ellisen Turner
Recruitment website: www.irell.com
Diversity officer: Kyle Kawakami

Summer Salary 2017
1Ls: $3,462/week
2Ls: $3,462/week
Post 3Ls: $3,462/week
1Ls hired? Yes
Split summers offered? Yes – first half of the summer only with a five week minimum
Summers 2017: 12
Offers/acceptances 2016:
19 offers, 11 acceptances. Some offers are outstanding to students who have accepted judicial clerkships.

Firm Profiles

IRELL & MANELLA
LLP

Jackson Walker LLP

2323 Ross Avenue, Ste.600, Dallas, TX 75201
Tel: 214 953 6000 Fax: 214 953 5822
www.jw.com

Main areas of work

Bankruptcy; corporate and securities; energy; ERISA; environmental and legislative; finance; healthcare; intellectual property; labor and employment; litigation; land use; real estate; tax; wealth planning.

Firm profile

Jackson Walker is a Texas-based law firm with a national presence and global reach. With more than 350 attorneys, we're one of the largest firms in the state and we provide comprehensive services in a broad range of practice areas. Our practice now spans the globe and our corporate clients include some of the biggest names in business. We represent approximately 237 of the Fortune 500 companies and 69 of the Fortune 100. But we're also a good fit for smaller companies and our clients include family-owned businesses, local and regional government agencies, individuals and nonprofit groups.

Recruitment details

- Number of 1st year associates: 17
- Associate salaries: 1st year: $180,000
- Number of 2nd year associates: 19
- Clerking policy: Yes

Law Schools attending for OCIs in 2017:

Baylor, Chicago, University of Houston, Notre Dame, St Mary's, Southern Methodist University, South Texas, Texas Southern, University of Texas, University of Virginia, Texas on Tour Interview Program (Duke, Georgetown and Northwestern Universities), SUNBELT Minority Job Fair, Vanderbilt Job Fair

Summer details

Summer associate profile:

Candidates with leadership capabilities, academic excellence, strong interpersonal skills, community involvement and dedicated to practicing over the long term.

Summer program components:

We have a first half of summer program. Summers typically rotate through two practice areas and work on two or three projects at a time. Feedback is provided from the assigning attorney on each project and each summer has both a partner and associate mentor. Summers have the opportunity to attend client meetings, closings, negotiations, depositions, trials and courtroom hearings.

Head Office: Dallas, TX
Number of domestic offices: 7
Worldwide revenue: $246,647,013
Partners (US): 243
Associates (US): 99

Main Recruitment Contact:
Bridgette Stahlman
Hiring Partner: Jim Ryan
Recruitment website:
www.jw.com/careers
Diversity officer: Bruce Ruzinsky

Summer Salary 2017
2Ls: $3,461/week
Post 3Ls: $3,461/week
1Ls hired? Case by case
Split summers offered? Yes
Can summers spend time in overseas office? N/A
Summers 2017: 28
Offers/acceptances 2016:
16 offers, 12 acceptances (2Ls only)

Jenner & Block LLP

353 North Clark Street, Chicago, IL 60654
Tel: 312 222 9350 Fax: 312 527 0484
www.jenner.com

Main areas of work

Appellate and US Supreme Court; communications; complex commercial litigation; content, media and entertainment; copyright; corporate; election law and redistricting; employee benefits and executive compensation; environmental and workplace health and safety law; government contracts; government controversies and public policy litigation; insurance recovery and counseling; international arbitration; media and First Amendment; mergers and acquisitions; patent litigation and counseling; privacy and information governance; private equity, investment funds and SBIC formation; professional responsibility; real estate; restructuring and bankruptcy; securities litigation and enforcement; tax; trademark, advertising, and unfair competition; white collar defense and investigations

Firm profile

Jenner & Block is a firm with global reach, comprised of more than 500 lawyers and offices in Chicago, London, Los Angeles, New York and Washington, DC. Our lawyers are widely recognized for securing significant litigation victories from the trial level through the US Supreme Court as well as producing results in sophisticated and high-profile corporate transactions. We are a firm with a conscience, committed to pro bono and public service, and to creating an unrivaled environment for superior talent. In 2015, *The American Lawyer* named us the number one Pro Bono firm for the sixth time in eight years.

Recruitment details

- Number of 1st year associates: 25
- Associate salaries: 1st year: $180,000
- Clerking policy: Yes
- Number of 2nd year associates: 30
- 2nd year: $190,000

Law Schools attending for OCIs in 2017:

Columbia University, Harvard University, Howard University, New York University, Northwestern University, Stanford University, University of California-Berkeley, University of California-Los Angeles, University of Chicago, University of Illinois, University of Michigan, University of Notre Dame, University of Pennsylvania, University of Southern California, Yale University

Summer details

Summer associate profile:

We seek summer associates who have excelled in law school, and have exceptional oral and written presentation skills, leadership experience, and strong interpersonal skills.

Summer program components:

Summer associates work with our lawyers and firm clients on a wide variety of complex cases and transactions. Among other things, our summer associates attend court hearings and closings, observe depositions and participate in strategy sessions with firm lawyers and clients. We also offer extensive training programs on a wide range of subjects. Summer associates are encouraged to attend department meetings, firmwide monthly associate lunches and weekly lunch-and-learn sessions. All summer associates have mentors and receive feedback from lawyers with whom they have worked.

Head Office: Chicago
Number of domestic offices: 4
Number of international offices: 1
Worldwide revenue: $457,587,742
Partners (US): 213
Associates (US): 221

Main Recruitment Contact: Alexis M Reed, Director of Lateral Partner Recruiting
Hiring Partner: Charlotte L Wager, Chief Talent Officer and Co-Chair of the Hiring Executive Committee
Recruitment website: www.jenner.com/joinus
Diversity officers: Jami de Lou, Associate Director of Talent Development, Diversity & Inclusion; Courtney Dredden, Diversity and Inclusion Manager

Summer Salary 2017
1Ls: N/A
2Ls: $3,077/week
Post 3Ls: $3,077/week
1Ls hired? No
Split summers offered? Yes
Summers 2017: 44 2Ls, 3 3Ls, 2 Pre-Clerks
Offers/acceptances 2016:
27 offers, 25 acceptances; 8 former summer associates will be judicial clerks

Firm Profiles

JENNER&BLOCK

Jones Day

51 Louisiana Avenue, NW, Washington, DC 20001
Tel: 202 879 3939   Fax: 202 629 1700
Email: recruiting@jonesday.com
www.jonesdaycareers.com

Main areas of work

Jones Day's practices cover the spectrum of transactional, litigation, regulatory and tax matters. Core practice areas: corporate/M&A, litigation/trial practice, government regulation, real estate, energy, healthcare, banking/finance, bankruptcy/restructuring, labor and employment, securities litigation, financial institutions, litigation/regulation, antitrust, tax and intellectual property.

Firm profile

The firm is a global legal institution based on a set of core principles and values – the most critical of which are integrity, dedication to the profession and a unity of purpose of and relentless focus on client service that transcends individual interests. Each lawyer is committed to the firm's foundation principles and values, which have a social purpose and permanence and ensure the distinctive quality and value of the legal services they provide their clients. This is one important aspect of what makes Jones Day the client service organization that it is. They function seamlessly across the globe and are truly One Firm Worldwide.

Recruitment details

- Number of 1st year associates: 112   • Number of 2nd year associates: 119
- Associate salaries: 1st year: $160,000-180,000 ($180,000 in Boston, Chicago, Dallas, Houston, Irvine, Los Angeles, New York, San Diego, San Francisco, Silicon Valley, Washington; $160,000 in Atlanta, Cleveland, Columbus, Detroit, Miami, Minneapolis, Pittsburgh)
- 2nd year: Increase is merit based, not lock step
- Clerking policy: Yes

Law Schools attending for OCIs in 2017:

American, Benjamin N. Cardozo, Boston College, Boston University, Case Western, Chicago, Cleveland - Marshall, Columbia, Cornell, Dickinson, Duke, Emory, Florida, Fordham, George Washington, Georgetown, Georgia, Georgia State, Harvard, Houston, Howard, Illinois, Iowa, Michigan, Minnesota, New York University, Northwestern, Notre Dame, Ohio State, Pennsylvania, Pittsburgh, San Diego, SMU, Stanford, Texas, UC- Berkeley, UC-Hastings, UC-Irvine, UCLA, U Miami, USC, Vanderbilt, Virginia, Wisconsin, Yale

Summer details

Summer associate profile:

Jones Day lawyers share certain fundamental principles: exemplary integrity, a selfless dedication to the firm and its clients and a sense of responsibility and initiative that leads one to take ownership of assignments and to complete them at the highest level of quality legal service. Summer associates candidates are evaluated on their fit with this culture.

Summer program components:

Summer associates do real client work in their choice of practice areas. Mentors are assigned to provide one-on-one guidance. Each summer associate will have a formal, mid-summer review. Jones Day's dynamic culture and its global, multidisciplinary practice areas, provide the perfect training ground for summer associates and new lawyers.

Number of domestic offices: **18**
Number of international offices: **26**
Partners (US): **954**
Associates (US): **1381**

Main Recruitment Contact:
Jolie A Blanchard, 202 879 3788
Hiring Partner:
Sharyl A Reisman, 212 326 3405
Recruitment website:
www.jonesdaycareers.com
Diversity coordinator: **Jennifer Shumaker, 202 879 5430**

Summer Salary 2017
1Ls / 2Ls / Post 3Ls: **$13,333/month:** Cleveland, Columbus, Detroit, Miami, Minneapolis, Pittsburgh
$15,000/month: Atlanta, Boston, Chicago, Dallas, Houston, Irvine, Los Angeles, New York, San Diego, San Francisco, Silicon Valley, Washington
1Ls hired? **Varies by office**
Split summers offered? **Varies by office**
Can summers spend time in overseas office? **Case by case**
Summers 2017: **205**
Offers/acceptances 2016:
123 offers, 105 acceptances (some offers still pending at time of publication)

Firm Profiles

K&L Gates LLP

K&L Gates Center, 210 Sixth Avenue, Pittsburgh, PA 15222-2613
Tel: 412 355 6500 Fax: 412 355 6501
www.klgates.com

Firm profile

K&L Gates is a fully integrated global law firm with approximately 2,000 lawyers across five continents. Our broad global platform and deep latticework of relationships across our offices and practices means we can help our clients respond to diverse legal issues and risks through the service of one law firm, with one communication.

In 2017, for the third year in a row, we were recognized as being one of the 10 strongest US law firm brands by legal market research company Acritas. Our commitment to client service and dedication to delivering value to clients has resulted in five straight years on *BTI's* "Client Service 30," placing in the top half for the past three consecutive years. In 2016, K&L Gates was named one of the top 25 corporate law firms in the United States, according to a survey of US general counsel by *Corporate Board Member* magazine and FTI Consulting. In 2015, *The Financial Times* ranked us as a Highly Commended firm in the Compliance and Technology category of its Innovative Lawyers - North America report in recognition of the groundbreaking K&L Gates HUB, in addition to giving the firm a Commended ranking for our Cyber Civil Rights Legal Project.

The industry recognition K&L Gates has garnered over the past five years emanates from the foundation of a global community aligned on behalf of our clients. The people at K&L Gates are committed to working together to create a legacy for each other, the firm, our clients, and the communities we serve. We thrive in an inclusive and socially conscious environment that embraces diversity and takes a holistic approach to the career evolution of all our professionals.

We take pride in constantly striving for innovation, imagination, and an entrepreneurial spirit. We come up with big ideas and then roll up our sleeves to get the job done, guiding our clients through their most complex issues in a variety of industry sectors and across multiple regions of the world. An indication of the firm's collaborative approach to client service is that our top 20 clients used lawyers from an average of 17.7 K&L Gates offices in 2015, and 462 of the firm's 500 largest clients used two or more offices.

We foster an atmosphere in which a great idea can come from anywhere. In 2014, a group of associates conceptualized an idea where the firm would harness its vast network in a massive, global volunteer effort to help those affected by hunger. They pitched the idea to firm management, who immediately approved it and provided resources to execute the program. The K&L Gates Global Day of Service, now an annual effort, was named *The American Lawyer's* 2014 Global Legal Awards "Global Corporate Social Responsibility Initiative of the Year."

Through our diversity and inclusion efforts and our commitment to serving those most in need, we strengthen our firm, enhance our ability to serve the needs of global clients, and make the communities in which we live and work better places. In 2016, K&L Gates was named among Yale Law Women (YLW)'s top 10 Family Friendly Firms. YLW evaluated important family friendliness indicators by collecting data on each firm's policies relating to part-time, parental leave, gender equity, billing requirements, professional development, and pro bono policies. For the seventh consecutive year, the Human Rights Campaign awarded K&L Gates a 100 percent score in the organization's 2017 *Corporate Equality Index* and named the firm a "Top Law Firm for Equality."

Number of domestic offices: **24**
Number of international offices: **22**
Worldwide revenue: **$1,179,139,000**
Partners (US): **629**
Of Counsel (US): **77**
Associates (US): **489**

Main Recruitment Contact: **Roslyn Pitts, Firmwide Director of Talent**
Recruitment website:
www.klgates.com/careers
Diversity officer: **Valerie Jackson, Senior Advisor to the Management Committee and Firmwide Director of Diversity & Inclusion**

Summer Salary 2017
1Ls: **Varies by market**
2Ls: **Varies by market**
Post 3Ls: **Varies by market**
1Ls hired? **Yes**
Split summers offered? **Case by case**
Can summers spend time in overseas office? **No**
Summers 2017: **65**
Offers/acceptances 2016: **69 offers extended, 62 acceptances (2Ls only)**

Recruitment details

- Number of 1st year associates: 63
- Associate salaries: 1st year: varies by market
- 2nd Year: varies by market
- Number of 2nd year associates: 80
- Clerking policy: Yes

Summer details

Summer program components:

As a summer associate, you will learn about our clients, our practices, our lawyers, and our culture. You'll sample projects from different practice areas, working as part of a team and participating in pro bono work that enriches the communities we serve. Through on-the-job experience and a formal training curriculum that includes an intensive writing workshop and practice-specific programs, our summer associates begin to develop the professional skills and competencies that will serve them well throughout their careers. We pair our summer associates with mentors consisting of one partner and at least one associate, who provide guidance on seeking out and completing substantive work assignments, balancing workload demands, dealing with competing projects, integration into the firm's culture, and setting and achieving career goals. You will receive regular formal and informal feedback on your ongoing performance and developmental progress.

Firm Profiles

K&L GATES

Kasowitz Benson Torres LLP

1633 Broadway, New York, New York 10019
Tel: 212 506 1700   Fax: 212 506 1800
www.kasowitz.com

Main areas of work

Kasowitz Benson Torres LLP, one of the largest litigation firms in the country, represents clients in high-stakes lawsuits, with a particular focus on commercial litigation, securities litigation, antitrust litigation, bankruptcy litigation, and white collar defense and litigation. The firm employs a decidedly aggressive approach to litigation and strives to achieve the most favorable results for its clients by focusing from the beginning of each case on preparation for trial. While litigation remains our core focus, the firm also has a strong real estate transactional practice.

Firm profile

Our success in implementing uniquely creative and successful legal strategies across practice areas has brought us clients with exceptionally interesting and challenging work. Such clients include leading companies in the financial services sector, including major hedge funds, private equity firms, and commercial banks, as well as companies in the real estate, high-tech, manufacturing, chemical, automobile, retail, pharmaceutical and telecommunications industries.

Recruitment details

- Number of 1st year associates: 8
- Number of 2nd year associates: 12
- Clerking Policy: Yes
- Associate Salaries 1st year: $180,000
- Associate Salaries: 2nd year: $190,000

Law Schools attending for OCIs in 2017:

Columbia, Cornell, Fordham, Georgetown, NYU, NEBLSA Job Fair, and Penn

Summer details

Summer associate profile:

Strong academic achievement, writing skills, prior work and leadership experience. Outstanding judgment, character and personal skills. Commitment to the practice of law with demonstrated interest in litigation (participation in Moot Court, Law Review and/or other journals preferred).

Summer program components:

Our summer program provides students with quality work assignments and professional experiences reflecting the depth and complexity of our litigation practice. Summer associates learn first-hand about trying cases and drafting legal documents, motions and agreements, and are exposed to courtroom appearances, depositions and client meetings. Our program also provides the opportunity to gain insight into the work and culture of the firm.

Summer associates participate in formal training programs, a partner lunch series and an associate mentor program so that students can get to know our lawyers and our firm. Summer associates receive ongoing feedback from the attorneys with whom they work, as well as formal mid and exit reviews.

Kasowitz hosts social events and coordinates various charitable events throughout the summer which provides summer associates and our attorneys the opportunity to get to know one another in an informal environment.

Head Office: New York, NY
Number of domestic offices: 9
Number of international offices: N/A
Partners: 90
Associates: 125

Main Recruitment contact: Mindy J. Lindenman
Hiring Partner: Aaron H. Marks
Recruitment website:
www.kasowitz.com
Diversity officer: Jennifer Mercado

Summer Salary 2017
2Ls: $3,462/week
Post 3Ls: $3,462/week
1Ls hired? Case-by-case
Split summers offered? Case-by-case
Can summers spend time in overseas office? N/A
Summers 2017: 11
Offers/acceptances 2016: 8 offers/8 acceptances

Firm Profiles

Katten Muchin Rosenman LLP

525 West Monroe Street, Chicago, IL 60661-3693
Tel: 312 902 5200   Fax: 312 902 1061
www.kattenlaw.com

Main areas of work

Corporate, financial services, litigation, real estate, environmental, commercial finance, intellectual property and trusts and estates.

Firm profile

Katten is a full-service law firm with approximately 650 attorneys in locations across the United States and in London and Shanghai. Clients seeking sophisticated, high-value legal services turn to us for counsel locally, nationally and internationally.

Recruitment details

- Number of 1st year associates: 24   • Number of 2nd year associates: 31
- Associate salaries: 1st year: $180,000 (Charlotte: $155,000)
- 2nd Year: $190,000 (Charlotte: $160,000)
- Clerking policy: Yes

Law Schools attending for OCIs in 2017:

Chicago-Kent College of Law, Columbia, Fordham University, Harvard, Howard University, Loyola Law School Los Angeles, Loyola University Chicago School of Law, New York University, Northwestern University, University of California, Los Angeles, University of California at Berkeley, Boalt Hall, The University of Chicago, University of Illinois, University of Michigan, University of North Carolina, University of Pennsylvania, University of Southern California Gould, University of Virginia, Wake Forest University

Summer details

Summer associate profile:

Our summer associate program is our most important recruiting activity. The program offers participants a realistic idea of what life is like for a first year associate. With our diverse client base, summer associates have the opportunity to work in each of our practice areas on a broad spectrum of assignments.

Summer program components:

We provide programs designed specifically for summer associates, including legal writing, negotiation, drafting and trial skills workshops, in addition to presentations introducing the firm's different areas of practice. Summer associates have the opportunity to directly observe lawyers and interact with clients as part of their training experience. We also encourage—and expect—our summer associates to participate in all of the attorney training and development programs presented by the firm and our various departments.

Head Office: Chicago, IL
Number of domestic offices: 11
Number of international offices: 2
Partners (US): 309
Associates (US): 256

Recruitment website:
For recruitment information and contacts, please visit:
www.kattenlaw.com/careers

Summer Salary 2017
Chicago/ Los Angeles/ New York/ Washington, DC:
1Ls/2Ls: $3,461
Post 3Ls: N/A
Charlotte:
1Ls/2Ls: $2,981
Post 3Ls: N/A
1Ls hired? Yes
Split summers offered: Case by case
Can summers spend time in overseas office? No
Summers 2017: 40 (32 2Ls, 8 1Ls)
Offers/acceptances 2016:
34 offers, 26 acceptances

Kilpatrick Townsend & Stockton LLP

1100 Peachtree St. NE, Suite 2800, Atlanta, GA 30309
Tel: 404 815 6500 Fax: 404 815 6555
www.ktrecruits.com

Main areas of work

Mergers and acquisitions, securities, domestic and international tax, employee benefits, financial institutions, global sourcing and technology, government relations, real estate finance and capital markets, real estate investment and development, chemistry and life sciences, patent litigation, trademark and copyright, electronics and software, medical and mechanical devices, bankruptcy and financial restructuring, complex commercial litigation, construction and infrastructure projects, environmental and sustainable development, government enforcement and investigations, insurance recovery, labor and employment, native american affairs.

Firm profile

Kilpatrick Townsend's attorneys fuel progress for innovative businesses of all sizes, types and markets. With more 600 attorneys and professionals in 18 offices, we work together to make businesses smarter, more protected, and more successful. Kilpatrick Townsend had a record-breaking 130 attorneys honored by their peers in The Best Lawyers in America® 2017. The firm garnered national first tier rankings for antitrust law, commercial litigation, construction law, corporate law, employee benefits (ERISA) law, insurance law, Litigation - antitrust, litigation - construction, litigation - ERISA, litigation - intellectual property, Native American law, patent law, real estate law, technology law, and trademark law in *US News – Best Lawyers*® 2017 "Best Law Firms." The firm's 2016 Summer Program was ranked among the nation's top 10 for the second straight year in a row in *The American Lawyer's* Summer Associates Survey.

Recruitment details

- Number of 1st year associates: 16
- Number of 2nd year associates: 11
- Associate salaries: 1st year: $120,000-180,000
- 2nd year: $135,000-195,000
- Clerking policy: yes

Law Schools attending for OCIs in 2017:

Emory University, Santa Clara University, University of North Carolina at Chapel Hill, University of Georgia, Wake Forest University, University of Virginia, George Washington University, Howard University, Duke University, University of California, Los Angeles, Columbia Universtiy, Harvard University, UC Berkeley, Georgetown, Stanford University, New York University.

Summer details

Summer associate profile:

We seek students who have demonstrated academic excellence (top 20%) and possess strong analytical and interpersonal skills. Participation and leadership in extra-curricular activities preferred. Technical backgrounds in engineering and science (eg, Electrical Engineering, Physics, Computer Engineering, Inorganic and Organic Chemistry and advanced degrees in Biological Sciences) are required for patent practices.

Summer program components:

Our Summer Associate Program provides students with the opportunity to do substantive work in a variety of practice areas. Summer Associates can rotate among practice teams with a hiring need for which they have the required technical skills. Summer Associates also participate in three progress evaluations to review attorney feedback on all work product. The Summer Committee members in each office serve as mentors for the course of the program, providing guidance for evaluations, assigning work, and coaching associates as they rotate teams and ensuring a positive work/life balance.

Head Office: **Atlanta, GA**
Number of domestic offices: **15**
Number of international offices: **3**
Worldwide revenue: **$416,404,000**
Partners (US): **238**
Associates (US): **220**

Main Recruitment Contact: **Lori Cates**
Hiring Partner: **Charlie Henn**
Recruitment website:
www.ktrecruits.com
Diversity officer: **Lynda Murray-Blair**

Summer Salary 2017
1Ls: **$2,981 - 3,462/week**
2Ls: **$2,981 - 3,462/week**
Post 3Ls: **$2,981 - 3,462/week**
1Ls hired? **Yes**
Split summers offered? **Yes**
Can summers spend time in overseas office? **No**
Summers 2017: **27**
Offers/acceptances 2016:
22 offers, 16 acceptances, 3 outstanding

KILPATRICK TOWNSEND

Firm Profiles

King & Spalding LLP

1180 Peachtree Street, NE, Atlanta, GA 30309-3521
Tel: 404 572 4600 Fax: 404 572 5100
www.kslaw.com

Main areas of work

Antitrust, appellate, banking and finance, corporate, energy, financial restructuring, government investigations, healthcare, intellectual property, international arbitration, international trade, litigation, pharma/biotech/medical device, real estate, tort and environmental and tax/ERISA.

Firm profile

King & Spalding has over 1000 lawyers in 19 offices across the US, Europe, the Middle East and Asia. King & Spalding combines sophisticated legal practice with a commitment to excellence, collaborative culture, investment in lawyer development, and dedication to community service.

Recruitment details

- Number of 1st year associates: 30   • Number of 2nd year associates: 25
- Associate salaries: 1st year: $155,000 -$180,000 (depending on location)
- Clerking policy: Yes

Law Schools attending for OCIs in 2017:

Columbia, Duke, Emory, Fordham, Georgetown, Georgia State, Harvard, Howard, Mercer, NYU, St Louis, Stanford, University of Alabama, University of California – Berkeley, University of California – Hastings, University of Chicago, University of Florida, University of Georgia, University of Houston, University of Maryland, University of North Carolina, University of Pennsylvania, University of Texas, University of Virginia, Vanderbilt, Yale

Summer details

Summer associate profile:

King & Spalding offers an opportunity to work as part of a team on sophisticated legal matters for top clients in a collaborative environment. We seek candidates who are well-rounded and intellectually curious with a demonstrated record of achievement and who also have diverse life and work experiences and outstanding interpersonal skills. Our summer associates experience what it is like to be a lawyer at King & Spalding and work on challenging matters for real clients. Our summer associates also get to know our lawyers in both professional and social settings.

Summer program components:

Summer associates work on matters in the practice group or groups in which they are interested. Assignment processes vary by office. Some offices have a formal rotation program while in other offices, our summer associates are assigned projects primarily in one practice group in which they are interested. Each summer associate is assigned at least one summer advisor who acts as a mentor.

Training: weekly luncheon seminars, attendance at practice group meetings, and in-house and external training sessions. Summer associates receive a formal mid-summer and end of summer evaluation, as well as ongoing project feedback.

Head Office: **Atlanta, GA**
Number of domestic offices: **9**
Number of international offices: **10**
Worldwide revenue: **$1.058 billion**
Partners (US): **326**
Associates (US): **311**

Main Recruitment Contact:
Michelle Carter
Hiring Partners: **Bobby K. Woo, Jr. (Atlanta); Brad Thompson (Austin); Mark V. Thigpen (Charlotte); Penn C. Huston (Houston); Andrew C. Hruska (New York); Peter A. Stroz (Los Angeles); Donald F. Zimmer, Jr. (San Francisco); Timothy T. Scott (Silicon Valley); Robert K. Hur (Washington, DC)**
Recruitment website:
www.kslaw.com/careers
Diversity officer: **Samuel M Matchett, Partner**

Summer Salary 2017
1Ls: **$3,461/wk (Austin, Houston, New York, San Francisco, Silicon Valley, Washington, DC); $2,980/wk (Atlanta, Charlotte)**
Post 3Ls: **Same as 1Ls**
1Ls hired? **Yes**
Split summers offered? **Yes**
Can summer spend time in an overseas office? **Generally, no**
Summers 2017: **51**
Offers/acceptances 2016:
47 Offers; 33 Acceptances (many acceptances pending due to clerkships)

KING & SPALDING

Kirkland & Ellis LLP

300 North LaSalle, Chicago, IL 60654
Tel: 312 862 2000   Fax: 312 862 2200
Email: info@kirkland.com
www.kirkland.com

Main areas of work

Kirkland's main practice areas are corporate, intellectual property, litigation and re-structuring.

Firm profile

Kirkland & Ellis LLP is a 1,900-attorney law firm representing global clients in private equity, M&A and other complex corporate transactions, litigation and dispute resolution/arbitration, intellectual property, and restructuring matters. The firm has offices in Beijing, Chicago, Hong Kong, Houston, London, Los Angeles, Munich, New York, Palo Alto, San Francisco, Shanghai and Washington, DC. The firm's principal goals are to provide the highest-quality legal services available anywhere; to be an instrumental part of each client's success; and to recruit, retain and advance the brightest legal talent.

Recruitment details

- Number of 1st year associates: 179
- Associate salaries: 1st year: $180,000
- Clerking policy: Yes
- Number of 2nd year associates: 198

Law Schools attending for OCIs in 2017:

Baylor; UC Berkeley; UC Hastings; UCLA; Cardozo; University of Chicago; Columbia; Duke; Fordham; George Washington; Georgetown; Harvard; University of Houston; Howard University; University of Illinois; University of Michigan; New York University; Northwestern University; University of Notre Dame; University of Pennsylvania; USC; Southern Methodist University; Stanford; University of Texas; Tulane; Vanderbilt University; University of Virginia; Washington University; Yale

Summer details

Summer associate profile:

Kirkland looks for candidates who show a record of outstanding academic achievement, evidence of initiative and a desire to assume early responsibility. Kirkland values individuals from diverse social, economic, cultural and personal backgrounds. The firm looks favorably upon law review, moot court and other indicators of intellectual curiosity and drive.

Summer program components:

Kirkland offers summer associates a realistic view of their future as lawyers at the firm. Summer associates are allowed to choose challenging assignments that are of interest to them through Kirkland's open assignment system, including pro bono matters. Each office offers summer associates substantive, practice-specific training, including a mock trial, negotiation workshops and presentations on a variety of topics. Kirkland also hosts ample social events for summer associates to help them get to know our attorneys and their fellow summer associates. By the end of the summer program, summer associates have an understanding of Kirkland's culture and practices, which gives them a strong foundation on which to begin their career at Kirkland.

Head Office: N/A
Number of domestic offices: 7
Number of international offices: 5
Partners (US): 744
Associates (US): 860

Hiring Partners: Elizabeth Deeley, Jason Kanner
Recruitment website:
www.kirkland.com/careers
Diversity officer: Rina Alvarez

Summer Salary 2017
1Ls hired? Some offices
Split summers offered? No
Can summers spend time in overseas office? Yes, the London office has a summer program.
Summers 2017: 230
Offers/acceptances 2016:
145 offers, 119 acceptances

KIRKLAND & ELLIS

Kramer Levin Naftalis & Frankel LLP

1177 Avenue of the Americas, New York, NY 10036
Tel: 212 715 9100   Fax: 212 715 8000
Email: legalrecruiting@kramerlevin.com
www.kramerlevin.com

Main areas of work

Bankruptcy and restructuring; capital markets and M&A; commercial and white collar litigation; employment litigation; finance and banking; immigration; intellectual property; investment funds; real estate; land use and environmental; securitization; tax, employee benefits and individual clients.

Firm profile

Kramer Levin Naftalis & Frankel LLP is a premier, full-service law firm with offices in New York, Silicon Valley and Paris. Firm lawyers are leading practitioners in their respective fields. The firm represents public and private companies - ranging from Global 1000 to middle-market and emerging growth companies - across a broad range of industries, as well as funds, institutions and individuals.

Recruitment details

- Number of 1st year associates: 14
- Associate salaries: 1st year: $180,000
- Clerking policy: Yes
- Number of 2nd year associates: 19
- 2nd year: $190,000

Law Schools attending for OCIs in 2017:

Benjamin N Cardozo, Brooklyn, Columbia University, Fordham University, Georgetown University, Harvard, Hofstra University, New York University School of Law, St John's University, University of California at Berkeley, Boalt Hall School of Law, University of Michigan, University of Pennsylvania, Yale

Summer details

Summer associate profile:

We seek lawyers whose academic achievements, journal writing, and prior work experience demonstrate exceptional ability, motivation and potential for leadership.

Summer program components:

Our summer program offers a realistic experience. We fully involve summer associates in day to day practice and assign work comparable to that given to junior associates. Summer associates participate in our departmental meetings, firmwide events and training programs and are given opportunities to attend court hearings, discovery proceedings, negotiating sessions, closings, pro bono matters and client meetings.

Head Office: **New York, NY**
Number of domestic offices: **2**
Number of international offices: **1**
Worldwide revenue: **$352,000,000**
Partners (US): **98**
Associates (US): **205**

Main Recruitment Contact: **Lauren Tapper, Director of Legal Recruiting**
Hiring Partner: **Kerri Ann Law**
Recruitment website:
www.kramerlevin.com/careers/
Diversity officer: **Lauren Tapper, Director of Diversity**

Summer Salary 2017
1Ls: **$3,750/week**
2Ls: **$3,750/week**
Post 3Ls: **N/A**
1Ls hired? **Yes**
Split summers offered? **Case by case**
Can summers spend time in overseas office? **No**
Summers 2017: **18**
Offers/acceptances 2016:
13 offers, 9 acceptances

KRAMER LEVIN
NAFTALIS & FRANKEL LLP

Latham & Watkins LLP

885 Third Avenue, New York, NY 10022-4834
Tel: 212 906 1200   Fax: 212 751 4864
www.lw.com

Main areas of work

Corporate; environment, land and resources; finance; litigation and trial; tax.

Firm profile

Latham & Watkins' extensive and insightful practices, one-firm culture and global foot-print provide you with virtually limitless opportunities. 2200+ lawyers. 50+ practice groups. 30+ offices. 18 industry teams. 5 departments. Your contribution to our global dynamic will begin right away. Working at Latham means harnessing the power of a fully integrated, global firm. Latham, as a one-firm firm: values integrity and a global perspective; spreads management and leaders throughout the world; has offices in more than 12 countries and lawyers that collectively speak more than 55 languages; and supports every lawyer with exceptional training and world-class resources so we can all work seamlessly with colleagues across the globe. Around the world, Latham lawyers will value your help to address our clients' most important and complex challenges. You will play an essential role in projects that span offices, time zones and teams to ensure the highest-quality result for our clients. Working at Latham means harnessing the power of a fully integrated, global firm. Our culture enables a consistent approach to colleagues, clients and collaborators around the world.

Recruitment details

- Number of 1st year associates: 160
- Associate salaries: 1st year: $170,000
- Number of 2nd year associates: 160
- Clerking policy: Yes

Law Schools attending for OCIs in 2017:

Berkeley, Boston College, Boston University, Chicago, Columbia, Cornell, UC Davis, Duke, Emory, Fordham, George Washington, Georgetown, Harvard, UC Hastings, Houston, Howard, Illinois, UC Irvine, Loyola (LA), Michigan, Northwestern, Notre Dame, NYU, Pennsylvania, SMU, Stanford, Texas, UCLA, USC, USD, Vanderbilt, Virginia, Wash U. (St. Louis), Yale and others

Summer details

Summer associate profile:

Contributing to the firm's success takes more than an incredible legal mind and set of skills. Latham seeks lawyers who are a certain type of professional and, more importantly, a certain type of person. Our core values are: transparency; respect; innovation; and collaboration.

Summer program components:

Our Summer Program gives you a sense of life as a junior associate at Latham — for example, by participating in our Unassigned Program, having an assigned mentor, networking and building relationships, and attending Summer Academy — a highlight of our summer program — where you will join summer associates from across our US, London, Hong Kong, and Singapore offices. Learn more at www.lwcareers.com.

Number of domestic offices: 11
Number of international offices: 20
Worldwide revenue: $2.822 billion (FY2016)
Partners (US): 468
Associates (US): 1,062
Main Recruitment Contact: Debra Clarkson, Director of Global Recruiting
Hiring Partner: Larry Seymour, Global Recruiting Committee Chair
Recruitment website: www.lwcareers.com
Diversity officer: BJ Trach, Diversity Leadership Committee Chair
Summer Salary 2017
1Ls: $3,470/week
2Ls: $3,470/week
Post 3Ls: $3,080/week
1Ls hired? 1L Fellowship Program; others case by case
Split summers offered? Case by case
Can summers spend time in overseas office? Case by case
Summers 2017: 197
Offers/acceptances 2016:
199 offers, 181 acceptances, 10 pending

LATHAM&WATKINS LLP

Linklaters

1345 Avenue of the Americas, New York, NY 10105
Tel: 212 903 9000   Fax: 212 903 9100
www.linklaters.com

Main areas of work

Antitrust/competition, banking, bankruptcy, restructuring and insolvency, capital markets, corporate/M&A, energy and infrastructure/project finance, executive compensation and benefits, financial regulation, international governance and development, investment management, Latin American finance, litigation and arbitration, structured finance and derivatives, tax.

Firm profile

Linklaters LLP is a leading global law firm that has been advising the world's premier companies, financial institutions and governments on their most important and challenging assignments for over 175 years. With more than 2,600 attorneys based in 29 offices in 20 countries, we deliver an outstanding service to our clients anywhere in the world. We boast a strong US practice in New York and Washington, DC, that is reinforced by a global network of US lawyers extending across the world's major business and financial centers, including: Frankfurt, Hong Kong, London, Madrid, Milan, Moscow, Paris, São Paulo, Seoul, Singapore and Tokyo. Our team of US-qualified lawyers delivers integrated advice across multiple legal regimes and market practices, covering transactional, regulatory, disclosure, compliance, litigation and liability management issues globally.

Recruitment details

- Associate salaries: 1st year: $180,000   • 2nd year: $190,000
- Clerking policy: Yes

Law Schools attending for OCIs in 2017:

Brooklyn, Columbia, Cornell, Duke, Fordham, George Washington, Georgetown, Harvard, Michigan, NYU, Penn, UVA

Summer details

Summer associate profile:

We look for people who can make the most of everything Linklaters has to offer: those who will work hard, learn quickly and take responsibility early. You will need analytical intelligence, a high level of attention to detail, creativity, and the people skills required to work well with both colleagues and clients. It is also important to have a genuine interest in business and the financial world, a high level of commercial awareness, and the desire to be part of a global network.

Summer program components:

Linklaters' summer associates typically rotate through two practice divisions and may have the opportunity to spend time in more than one office. Summers are given real responsibility and are expected to participate in pro bono work in addition to working on billable matters.

Along with our dedicated summer associate training program, we encourage our summers to attend training sessions offered to our associates. Each summer associate is assigned a partner and associate mentor and receives two formal appraisals, one at the midpoint and one at the conclusion of the summer.

Number of domestic offices: 2
Number of international offices: 27
Partners (US): 43
Associates (US): 163

Main Recruitment Contact: Jennifer Katz-Hickman
Hiring Partners: Justin Storms and Paul Hessler
Recruitment website: www.linklatersuscareers.com
Diversity Partner: Peter Cohen-Millstein

Summer Salary 2017
1Ls: $3,500/week
2Ls: $3,500/week
Post 3Ls: $3,500/week
1Ls hired? Yes
Split summers offered? No
Can summers spend time in overseas office? Yes
Summers 2017: 26
Offers/acceptances 2016:
15 offers, 14 acceptances (2Ls only)

Firm Profiles

Linklaters

Mayer Brown LLP

www.mayerbrown.com

Firm profile

Mayer Brown is a leading global law firm with offices in 20 cities across the Americas, Asia and Europe. The firm's presence in the world's key business and legal centers enables it to offer clients access to local market knowledge and depth combined with a global reach. The firm's practice areas include: banking and finance; corporate and securities; litigation and dispute resolution; antitrust and competition; US Supreme Court and appellate matters; employment and benefits; environmental; financial services regulatory and enforcement; government and global trade; intellectual property; real estate; tax; restructuring, bankruptcy and insolvency; and wealth management.

Recruitment details

- Number of 1st year associates: 47   • Number of 2nd year associates: 68
- Associate salaries: 1st year: $180,000 plus significant market bonus opportunities
- 2nd year: $190,000 plus significant market bonus opportunities
- Clerking policy: Yes, the firm encourages clerkships, has pre-clerkship summer associate opportunities and pays clerkship bonuses.

Law Schools attending for OCIs in 2017:

Berkeley, Chicago, Columbia, Fordham, Georgetown, Harvard, Houston, Howard, Illinois, Loyola, Michigan, North Carolina, NYU, Northwestern, Penn, Stanford, Texas, Virginia, Wake Forest, Washington & Lee, Yale

Summer details

Summer associate profile:

Mayer Brown seeks to hire associates of exceptional promise from a variety of backgrounds. Because Mayer Brown seeks to hire associates with the potential to become partners at the firm, its hiring standards are rigorous. Above all, Mayer Brown is interested in candidates who share the firm's dedication to providing high-quality legal services and who have demonstrated superior academic ability and personal achievement.

Summer program components:

Summer Associates at Mayer Brown are not assigned to practice areas and there is no formal rotation between groups. The firm's goal is to expose summer associates to as many practices areas and attorneys as possible during the program. Each summer associate is assigned at least two attorney mentors and receives written reviews on every assignment. Each summer associate will attend development meetings with partners at mid-summer and at the end of summer.

Head Office: N/A
Number of domestic offices: 7
Number of international offices: 13
Worldwide revenue: $1.26 billion
Partners (US): 401
Counsel (US): 104
Associates (US): 417

Main Recruitment Contacts:
See www.mayerbrown.com/careers for office specific contacts
Hiring Partner: J Bradley (Brad) Keck
Recruitment website:
www.mayerbrown.com/careers
Diversity officer: Jeremiah DeBerry, Director of Diversity & Inclusion

Summer Salary 2017
1Ls: $3,461/week
2Ls: $3,461/week
Post 3Ls: $3,461/week
1Ls hired? Varies by office
Split summers offered? Case by case, office by office basis
Can summers spend time in overseas office? Atypical
Summers 2017: 60
Offers/acceptances 2016:
187 offers, 56 acceptances

MAYER·BROWN

McDermott Will & Emery LLP

444 West Lake Street
Suite 4000
Chicago, IL 60606-0029
Tel: 312 372 2000   Fax: 312 984 7700
www.mwe.com

Main areas of work

Antitrust and competition, corporate, employee benefits, energy, financial instituations, government strategies, health, intellectual property, private client, state and local tax, trial, U.S. and international tax, white collar and securities defense.

Firm profile

McDermott Will & Emery is an integrated, international law firm with recognized strength in tax, private equity, mergers and acquistions, health care, high-stakes litigation and many other key areas of transactional and regulatory law. We emphasize and foster long-term, industry-focused client relationships with multinational companies, rising entrepreneurial firms, investors and capital providers and many of the world's wealthiest families and individuals. In word and deed, we value integrity, effiency, diversity, pro bono and community service.

Recruitment details

- Number of 1st year associates: 26
- Associate salaries: 1st year: $180,000
- Clerking policy: Yes
- Number of 2nd year associates: 24
- 2nd year: $190,000

Law Schools attending for OCIs in 2017:

American University, Boston College, Boston University, Brooklyn Law School, Columbia, Cornell, Duke, Fordham, George Mason, George Washington, Georgetown University, Harvard, Howard, Illinois, Indiana University, Loyola Chicago, New York Law School, New York University, Northwestern, Santa Clara, Southern Methodist University, Stanford, University of California (Berkeley, Davis, Hastings, Irvine, Los Angeles), University of Chicago, University of Florida, University of Miami, University of Michigan, University of Notre Dame, University of Pennsylvania, University of San Diego, University of Southern California, University of Virginia, William & Mary, Yale.

Summer details

Summer associate profile:

McDermott strives to hire well-rounded candidates who maintain a balance of academic, as well as personal and professional successes. The ideal summer associate candidate is someone who possesses the drive to tackle new challenges and embrace new experiences, takes an active approach to building relationships with attorneys and staff, has a collegial attitude and acts with integrity.

Summer program components:

Our program offers summer associates a realistic introduction to the practice of law and day-to-day life as a McDermott associate. The summer associate program provides meaningful responsibility and feedback that is consistent with a junior associate experience. Summer associates are given the opportunity to accept assignments with many of our practice groups during the summer. This allows summers to experience the type of work they are interested in first-hand and ultimately steer them toward the type of work they enjoy. Our conservative hiring apprach allows students access to a number of substantive assignments and matters. Summer associates receive formal feedback during a mid-summer evaluation and a final review in addition to informal feedback over the course of the summer. Each summer associate is assigned an associate and partner level mentor to provide guidance throughout the summer, explain firm policies, address any questions or concerns and to assist in the transition from law school to life in a law firm.

Head Office: **Chicago, IL**
Number of domestic offices: **10**
Number of international offices: **8 (plus a strategic alliance in Shanghai)**
Worldwide revenue: **$908,692,000**
Partners US: **474**
Associates US: **220**

Main Recruitment Contact: **Erika Gardiner, Non-Partner Legal Recruiting Manager**
Hiring Partner: **Linda Doyle, National Hiring Partner**
Recruitment website: **www.mwe.com/en/careers/unitedstates**
Diversity officer: **Lydia Kelley, Diversity Committee Chair**

Summer Salary 2017
1Ls: **$3,462/week**
2Ls: **$3,462/week**
1Ls hired: **Yes**
Split summer offered: **Yes**
Can summers spend time in overseas offices: **No**
Summers 2017: **41**
Offers/acceptances 2016:
32 offers, 32 acceptances

Firm Profiles

Milbank, Tweed, Hadley & McCloy LLP

28 Liberty Street, New York, NY 10005
Tel: 212 530 5000　Fax: 212 530 5219
www.milbank.com

Main areas of work

Milbank's practice areas include alternative investments, capital markets, corporate, financial restructuring, leveraged finance, litigation (complex commercial, white collar and regulatory, securities and IP), pro bono, project finance, real estate, structured finance, tax, transportation and space finance and, trusts and estates.

Firm profile

Milbank is a premier international law firm handling high-profile cases and complex business transactions. We are a leader in corporate/finance work, including banking, capital markets, project and transportation, finance and M&A. Our litigation group handles complex and high profile civil actions, SEC enforcements and white collar criminal matters. Our financial restructuring attorneys have been involved in every recent major reorganization in the US.

Recruitment details

- Number of 1st year associates: 51 (US), 56 (worldwide)
- Number of 2nd year associates: 48 (US), 64 (worldwide)
- Associate salaries: 1st year: $180,000　　• 2nd year: $190,000
- Clerking policy: Yes

Law Schools attending for OCIs in 2017:

Albany, Berkeley, Boston University, Cardozo, Chicago, Columbia, Cornell Job Fair, Duke, Emory Job Fair, Fordham, Georgetown, George Washington, Harvard, Howard, Lavender Law Job Fair, Loyola Los Angeles (LA), Michigan, Midwest-California-Georgia Recruiting Consortium, New York University, New York Law School, Northwestern, University of Pennsylvania, Stanford, Texas Job Fair, Tulane/Washington University Job Fair, UCI (LA), UCLA (LA), USC (LA), Vanderbilt, Virginia, Yale

Summer details

Summer associate profile:

We are looking for summer associates with diverse backgrounds who demonstrate a high level of intelligence, creativity, leadership, determination and enthusiasm.

Summer program components:

Our program includes a rotation system enabling summers to rotate through several groups. Our comprehensive nine-session training program follows a company's lifecycle from inception to restructuring and includes in-session activities and post-class assignments. Summers are given mentors and receive formal reviews.

Head Office: **New York, NY**
Number of domestic offices: **3**
Number of international offices: **9**
Worldwide revenue: **$855,594,000**
Partners (US): **112**
Counsel (US): **27**
Associates (US): **338**

Main Recruitment Contact: **Ann Bjornstad**
Hiring Partner: **Rod Miller**
Recruitment website:
www.milbank.com/careers
Diversity officer: **Salila Yohn**

Summer Salary 2017
1Ls: **$3,462/week**
2Ls: **$3,462/week**
1Ls hired? **No**
Split summers offered? **No**
Can summers spend time in overseas office? **Yes**
Summers 2017: **84 (72 NY, 8 LA, 4 DC)**
Offers/acceptances 2016:
65 offers, 62 acceptances

Mintz Levin

One Financial Center, Boston, MA 02127
Tel: 617 542 6000   Fax: 617 542 2241
Email: jcarrion@mintz.com
www.mintz.com

Main areas of work

Antitrust; bankruptcy, restructuring and commercial law; communications; consumer product safety, corporate and securities; corporate compliance and investigations; crisis response, risk management and executive protection; employment, labor and benefits; environmental law; health law; immigration; intellectual property; international; litigation; privacy and security; private client; private equity; product risk management and response; project development and finance; public finance; real estate; start-ups; tax; venture capital and emerging companies; white collar defense; government investigations and enforcement.

Firm profile

Mintz Levin is a multidisciplinary firm, characterized by innovation and an entrepreneurial drive that attracts interesting clients, from startups to large public companies, universities, non-profits and family-run businesses. Mintz Levin is dedicated to the continued professional growth of its attorneys at all levels. Incoming associates benefit from a formal orientation program that acclimates them to the Firm. New associates participate in an intensive three-day "base camp" to learn the substantive law of the area of practice in which they will be concentrating. This is followed by a curriculum designed to meet the professional development needs of each attorney at every step of his/her career.

Mintz Levin is proud of its formal mentoring programs that complement the collegiality of our firm. The firm has an extensive associate mentoring program run by a firm-wide mentoring coordinator and on-site mentoring coordinators in each office.

Recruitment details

- Number of 1st year associates: 15
- Number of 2nd year associates: 15
- Associate salaries: 1st year: $180,000
- 2nd year: $190,000
- Clerking policy: Yes (but it depends on the situation)

Law Schools attending for OCIs in 2017:

Boston College Law School, Boston University School of Law, Columbia Law School, Fordham School of Law, Georgetown Law School, Harvard Law School, New York University, Northeastern University School of Law, University of California Los Angeles School of Law, niversity of San Diego School of Law, University of California Berkeley School of Law, University of Southern California Gould School of Law, University of Pennsylvania Law School

Summer details

Summer associate profile:

Summer associates are encouraged to work on assignments from a variety of practice areas. They attend trials, depositions and negotiations. They participate in legal writing workshops, a transactional case study, and a mock trial. Each summer associate is assigned an associate mentor, a member mentor and a writing mentor. Mentors are available for questions, and they facilitate informal feedback on work projects. Through work assignments and social events, our attorneys strive to provide each summer associate with an opportunity to get to know what a career at Mintz has to offer.

Head Office: **Boston, MA**
Number of domestic offices: **7**
Number of international offices: **2**
Worldwide revenue: **$372.5m**
Partners (US): **255**
Associates (US): **190**

Main Recruitment Contact: **Jennifer Carrion**
Hiring Partner: **Bret Leone-Quick**
Recruitment website: **www.mintz.com**
Diversity Officer: **Tyrone Thomas**

Summer Salary 2017
1Ls: **$3,077**
2Ls: **$3,077**
1Ls hired? **Yes**
Split summers offered? **No**
Can summers spend time in overseas office? **No**
Summers 2017: **17**
Offers/acceptances 2016: **9 Offers Extended/8 Offers Accepted**

MINTZ LEVIN
Mintz Levin Cohn Ferris Glovsky and Popeo PC

Firm Profiles

Morgan, Lewis & Bockius LLP

1701 Market Street, Philadelphia, PA 19103-2921
Tel: 215 963 5000   Fax: 215 963 5001
www.morganlewis.com

Main areas of work

At Morgan Lewis, we work around the world and around the clock to respond to the needs of our clients. We provide comprehensive corporate, transactional, litigation and regulatory services that address and anticipate challenges across rapidly changing landscapes. Our international team of lawyers and other specialists support clients across a wide range of industries, including financial services, energy and environmental, healthcare and life sciences, retail and technology

Firm profile

From our 30 offices in the United States, Europe, Asia and the Middle East, we work across all major industries with clients that range from established, global Fortune 100 companies to enterprising startups. Our team comprises more than 2,000 legal professionals including lawyers, patent agents, employee benefits advisors, regulatory scientists and other specialists. We focus on immediate concerns and long-term goals, harnessing our resources from strategic hubs of commerce, law and government around the world. Founded in 1873, we stand on the shoulders of more than 140 years of excellence.

Recruitment details

- Number of 1st year associates: 76
- Number of 2nd year associates: 61
- Associate salaries: 1st year: $160,000-$180,000
- 2nd year: $170,000-$190,000
- Clerking policy: Yes

Law Schools attending for OCIs in 2017:

American, BC, Berkeley, BU, Catholic, Chicago, Columbia, Cornell, Davis, Duke, Fordham, GW, Georgetown, Harvard, Hastings, Houston, Howard, Illinois, Michigan, NYU, Northwestern, Pennsylvania, Rutgers, Santa Clara, Stanford, Southern Methodist, Temple, Texas, UC Irvine, UCLA, USC, USF, UVA, Vanderbilt, Villanova

Summer details

Summer associate profile:

Highly motivated individuals from diverse backgrounds who have a record of outstanding academic achievement, as well as superior writing and analytical skills, a commitment to client service, initiative and an ability to succeed in a challenging, collaborative workplace.

Summer program components:

Our program provides insight into Morgan Lewis, its practices and culture through professional and social experiences. The summer program launches with a multi-day kickoff that brings summer associates from all offices together with firm leaders, other partners and associates. Summer associates have the unique opportunity to tailor their summer experience with the option of either spending the entire summer at the firm or spending a portion of the summer working on-site with a public interest organization. While at the firm, summer associates work on matters typically assigned to first-year associates and participate in a generous mix of training opportunities to hone skills such as legal writing and presentation style. After joining the firm full-time, associates are offered Student Loan Repayment services, an innovative Remote Working Program and a Ramp-Up program, including a reduced hours expectation for six months, for associates returning from an extended leave of absence.

Head Office: **Philadelphia, PA**
Number of domestic offices: **17**
Number of international offices: **13**
Partners (US): **644**
Associates (US): **847**

Main Recruitment Contact: **Lindsay Callantine**
Hiring Partner: **Christina Edling Melendi**
Recruitment website:
www.morganlewis.com
Diversity officer: **Kenneth Imo**

Summer Salary 2017
1Ls: **$3,500/week**
2Ls: **$3,500/week**
1Ls hired? **Case by case**
Split summers offered? **Case by case**
Can summers spend time in overseas office? **No**
Summers 2017: **65**
Offers/acceptances 2016:
57 offers, 53 acceptances

Morgan Lewis

Morrison & Foerster

425 Market Street, San Francisco, CA 94105
Tel: 415 268 7000   Fax: 415 268 7522
Email: fwattorneyrecruiting@mofo.com
www.mofo.com

Main areas of work

Appellate; business restructuring and insolvency; capital markets; clean technology and alternative energy; commercial litigation; emerging companies and venture capital; energy; financial transactions; global risk and crisis management; intellectual property; life sciences; mergers and acquisitions; privacy and data security; private equity; real estate; securities litigation, enforcement and white-collar criminal defense; tax; and technology transactions.

Firm profile

Morrison & Foerster is a global firm of exceptional credentials. With 950 lawyers in 16 offices in key technology and financial centers in the United States, Europe and Asia, the firm advises the world's leading financial institutions, investment banks and technology, telecommunications, life sciences and Fortune 100 companies.

Recruitment details

- Number of 1st year associates: 46
- Associate salaries: 1st year: $180,000
- Clerking policy: Yes
- Number of 2nd year associates: 69
- 2nd year: $190,000

Law Schools attending for OCIs in 2017:

Berkeley, Cardozo, Chicago, Columbia, Cornell, UC Davis, Duke, Fordham, George Washington, Georgetown, Harvard, Howard, McGill, Michigan, Northwestern, New York University, Penn, USD, Santa Clara, Stanford, Texas, UCLA, USC, Virginia, Yale

Summer details

Summer associate profile:

Morrison & Foerster looks for individuals of exceptional intelligence whose academic and other achievements evidence their talent, motivation, energy and creativity.

Summer program components:

The summer program is intended to give summer associates a real sense of what it means to practice at MoFo.

Work is distributed using a central assignment system, taking into account your areas of interest. Typical assignments include writing briefs, motions, contracts and client memoranda, assisting in drafting and negotiation sessions, assisting in depositions and witness preparation and performing due diligence in corporate transactions, as well as pro bono assignments.

A variety of training programs are designed specifically for summer associates, including practice area presentations.

Each summer associate is assigned one or more mentors to help acclimate him or her to the firm. Mentors take their summer associates out to lunch, introduce their summer associates to the lawyers and staff in their practice group and office and act as a sounding board for any questions or concerns summer associates may have throughout the summer.

Largest Office: **San Francisco, CA**
Number of domestic offices: **8**
Number of international offices: **8**
Worldwide revenue: **$945,100,000**
Partners (US): **248**
Associates (US): **394**

Main Recruitment Contact: **Nicole Wanzer**
Hiring Partner: **Craig Martin**
Diversity officer: **Natalie Kernisant**

Summer Salary 2017
1Ls: **$3,462/week**
2Ls: **$3,462/week**
Post 3Ls: **$3,462/week**
1Ls hired? **Yes**
Split summers offered? **Yes, case by case**
Can summers spend time in overseas office? **Yes, case by case**
Summers 2017: **77 (2Ls) + 24 (1Ls)**
Offers/acceptances 2016:
107 offers, 87 acceptances and 5 open

**MORRISON
FOERSTER**

Munger, Tolles & Olson LLP

350 South Grand Avenue, 50th Floor, Los Angeles, CA 90071
Tel: 213 683 9100   Fax: 213 687 3702
www.mto.com

Main areas of work

For over a half a century, attorneys from Munger, Tolles & Olson have been partnering with clients on their most important and complex cases and business deals.
We maintain a national and international practice. Our principal areas of practice
include bet-the-company litigation (from the outset of the case through trial and any
appeals), internal investigations, white collar defense, corporate advice, labor and employment, environmental, real estate, financial restructuring and tax.

Firm profile

Munger Tolles has for decades intentionally maintained low-leverage. We believe our
roughly one-to-one partner-to-associate ratio empowers all of our approximately 200
lawyers to make an impact in the work we do for our clients. We are involved in
some of the highest profile cases in the country and count among our clients Bank of
America, Wells Fargo, LinkedIn, Facebook, the major motion picture studios, Verizon, Intel, KB Home, LG Display, and Berkshire Hathaway.

Recruitment details

- Number of 1st year associates: 6
- Associate salaries: 1st year: $180,000
- Clerking policy: Yes
- Number of 2nd year associates: 7
- 2nd year: $190,000

Law Schools attending for OCIs in 2017:

Berkeley, Chicago, Columbia, Harvard, Howard, Michigan, NYU, Stanford, UCLA,
USC, Yale, Bay Area Diversity Career Fair

Summer associate profile:

Our firm serves as a platform for individuals who want to actively solve their client's
problems. We look for law students who have demonstrated excellence and leadership in their prior pursuits and who bring both leadership, intellectual curiosity, and
a sense of individuality to an already extremely talented and diverse group of lawyers.
Unlike other law firms, where it has become common to expect that young lawyers
will stay only a short time before moving on to other endeavors, we only hire lawyers
we believe have the potential to ultimately join our (one-tier) partnership.

Summer program components:

Our summer program will provide you a realistic idea of what it is like to practice
law at our firm. You will work closely with attorneys in various practice areas, doing
meaningful assignments. Each summer associate is assigned a work coordinator and
social advisor. Your work coordinator will find assignments that are of interest to you
and provide guidance and feedback during the summer. Your summer will include
invitations to attend our weekly lunches, training programs, social events and practice group meetings.

Office:s Los Angeles, CA; San Fran-
cisco, CA; Washington, DC
Number of domestic offices: 3
Number of international offices: 0
Partners (US): 85
Associates (US): 96

Main Recruitment Contact: Kevinn Vil-
lard, 213 683 9242
Hiring Partners: Bethany Kristovich,
Carolyn Luedtke, Gregory Weingart
Recruitment website:
www.mto.com/careers

Summer Salary 2017
1Ls: $3,461/week
2Ls: $3,461/week
Post 3Ls: $3,461/week
1Ls hired? Yes
Split summers offered? Yes
Summers 2017: 15 2Ls, 4 1Ls
(1Ls are not eligible for offers)
Offers 2016: 20 offers

Nixon Peabody LLP

100 Summer Street, Boston, Massachusetts
Tel: 617 345 1000   Fax: 617 345 1300
Email: cfontane@nixonpeabody.com
www.nixonpeabody.com

Main areas of work

Business and finance; litigation and dispute resolution; real estate; intellectual property; private equity and investment funds; M&A; securities, public finance; tax; labor and employment; tax credit finance and syndication; affordable housing; government investigations and white collar defense; estate, trust and financial planning; health services; life sciences; energy; food and beverages; gaming and government relations.

Firm profile

We see the law as a tool to help shape our clients' futures. Our focus is on knowing what is important to our clients now and next so we can foresee obstacles and opportunities in their space and smooth their way. We ensure they are equipped with winning legal strategies as they navigate the exciting and challenging times we live in. The qualities that drive Nixon Peabody are extreme understanding of our clients and their industries, a future-leaning orientation, and a culture that taps collective intelligence to create value for clients. We provide counsel on the full range of corporate transactions, disputes and regulatory challenges.

Recruitment details

- Number of 1st year associates: 20
- Number of 2nd year associates: 27
- Associate salaries: 1st year: $160,000 in metro market offices
- 2nd year: $165,000
- Clerking policy: Yes

Law Schools attending for OCIs in 2017:

Nixon Peabody recruits from top tier law schools throughout the US including UC Berkeley, Cornell, Harvard, University of Michigan, Northwestern, NYU, UCLA and Columbia. In 2017, we expect to conduct interviews at various leading national and regional law schools.

Summer details

Summer associate profile:

We seek candidates with excellent academic credentials, solid research and writing skills, demonstrated leadership ability and sound judgment. We value innovation and collaborative work styles. Prior work experience and diversified outside activities are a plus.

Summer program components:

Our summer program lays the foundation for your career at Nixon Peabody. The program is intended to introduce you to as many opportunities as possible. We believe the more you learn over the summer, the better career choices you will make. You will be exposed to a range of practice areas and take part in billable client work and pro bono projects. In addition to exploring the practice of law, we also encourage our summer associates to get to know the Nixon Peabody attorneys in the cities in which we work. We provide formal and informal mentorship, various group training sessions and substantive feedback through our evaluation process.

Head Office: **Boston, MA**
Number of domestic offices: **12**
Number of international offices: **4**
Partners (US): **325**
Associates (US): **224**

Main Recruitment Contact: **Cristina Fontane**
Hiring Partner: **Stacie Collier**
Recruitment website:
www.nixonpeabody.com/careers
Diversity officers: **Andrew Glincher**

Summer Salary 2017
1Ls: **$3,080/week**
2Ls: **$3,080/week**
Post 3Ls: **N/A**
1Ls hired? **Yes**
Split summers offered? **No**
Can summers spend time in overseas office? **No**
Summers 2017: **18**
Offers/acceptances 2016:
17 offers, 15 acceptances

NIXON PEABODY

Norton Rose Fulbright

1301 McKinney, Suite 5100 Houston, TX 77010
Tel: 713 651 5151 Fax: 713 651 5246
www.nortonrosefulbright.com/US/

Main areas of work

Antitrust and competition; banking and finance; corporate, M&A and securities; dispute resolution and litigation; employment and labor; financial restructuring and insolvency; intellectual property; real estate; regulations and investigations; tax

Firm profile

Norton Rose Fulbright is a global law firm. It provides the world's preeminent corporations and financial institutions with a full business law service. Norton Rose Fulbright has more than 3500 lawyers and other legal staff based in more than 50 cities across Europe, the United States, Canada, Latin America, Asia, Australia, Africa, the Middle East and Central Asia.

Recognized for its industry focus, Norton Rose Fulbright is strong across all the key industry sectors: financial institutions; energy; infrastructure, mining and commodities; transport; technology and innovation; and life sciences and healthcare.

Recruitment details

- Number of 1st year associates: 36
- Number of 2nd year associates: 47
- Associate salaries: 1st year: varies by market-$180,000 (CA, DC, NY, TX offices)
- 2nd year: varies by market
- Clerking policy: Yes

Law Schools attending for OCIs in 2017:

Baylor, Chicago, Columbia, Duke, Fordham, George Washington, Georgetown, Harvard, Houston, Howard, Loyola (CA), NYU, Penn, South Texas, Southern Methodist, The University of Texas, Texas Southern, Texas Tech, UC-Irvine, UCLA, USC, Virginia, Washington University. Job fairs include Lavender Law, Loyola Patent Law Interview Program, Southeastern Minority Job Fair, Vanderbilt Career Fair and Sunbelt Minority Recruitment Program.

Summer details

Summer associate profile:

We recruit motivated, energetic and personable individuals with whom we will enjoy practicing law. Candidates should have high academic achievement, maturity, and initiative. We also value other indicators of likely success at Norton Rose Fulbright, such as demonstrated leadership skills and an entrepreneurial outlook.

Summer program components:

Essential to the long-term success of Norton Rose Fulbright, our summer associate program is the primary source of new legal talent. Our summer associates develop their skills by applying their education to active practice. From proofreading and drafting documents to carrying out legal research and attending meetings, our summer associates work on projects that sharpen their key legal skills. Summer associates participate in significant legal activities, such as client meetings, board meetings, depositions and court appearances. Summer associates also have the opportunity to participate in a variety of legal and business skills workshops and presentations. We offer team building and social activities that are unique to each of the cities in which we work and live. Our lawyers work hard, but they also enjoy spending time with one another and having fun. Summer associates and their families will find a wide selection of sports, cultural, artistic and other activities designed to appeal to a variety of interests.

Head Office: N/A
Number of domestic offices: 11
Number of international offices: 44
Worldwide revenue: $1,737,000,000
Partners (US): 296
Associates (US): 419

Main Recruitment Contact: Jaimee Slovak
Hiring Partner: Doug Wabner
Recruitment website:
www.nortonrosefulbright.com
Diversity Officer: Lisa Genecov

Summer Salary 2017
1Ls: varies by market ($3,500 in CA, DC, NY, TX offices)
2Ls: varies by market ($3,500 in CA, DC, NY, TX offices)
Post 3Ls: varies by market ($3,500 in CA, DC, NY, TX offices)
1Ls hired? Varies by market
Split summers offered? Varies by market
Can summers spend time in overseas office? No
Summers 2017: 31 2Ls; 15 1Ls
Offers/acceptances 2016: 28 acceptances/40 associate offers; 6 pending judicial clerkships

ΛNORTON ROSE FULBRIGHT

Nutter McClennen & Fish LLP

Seaport West, 155 Seaport Blvd, Boston, MA 02210
Tel: 617 439 2000   Fax: 617 310 9000
www.nutter.com

Main areas of work

Business, intellectual property, litigation, real estate and finance, tax and trusts and estates.

Firm profile

Nutter McClennen & Fish LLP has deep roots in Boston and a long-standing reputation for business savvy and pragmatism. Nutter advises clients across a wide range of industries, including life sciences, medical devices, pharmaceuticals, banking and financial services, real estate, energy, and technology. The firm regularly represents major US global corporations and financial institutions, research universities, high technology and emerging companies, investors, developers, foundations, and families that select Nutter for the quality of its lawyers and its depth as a multi-service firm. Nutter was co-founded by Louis D Brandeis, who later became a renowned justice of the US Supreme Court. The founding partners' rich legacy continues to inspire and set an example for the firm. Today Nutter upholds the same standard of focused dedication, innovation, and unwavering commitment to client service that they set over a century ago.

Recruitment details

- Number of 1st year associates: 7
- Number of 2nd year associates: 6
- Associate Salaries: 1st Year: $160,000
- 2nd Year: Not lock step, based on a core competency system
- Clerking policy: Case by case

Law Schools attending for OCIs in 2017:

Boston College, Boston University, Harvard, New England School of Law, Northeastern School of Law, and Suffolk University

Job Fairs: Boston Lawyers Group Job Fair (diversity fair) and Patent Law Interview Program

Summer details

Summer associate profile:

Strong academic record. Intelligent, enthusiastic, confident and results-oriented team players with demonstrated interpersonal and communication skills.

Summer program components:

Our approach to the summer experience at Nutter is to provide our summer associates with as complete and accurate a view of the firm and our practice as possible. Summer associates divide their ten weeks between two departments. For those who desire exposure to other areas, assignment coordinators endeavor to provide them with projects tailored to their individual interests. Each summer associate receives two formal reviews, one at midsummer and the other at the end of the program. These reviews are intended to provide the summer associate with guidance and are based upon written evaluations by supervising attorneys. We expect attorneys to provide individual, ongoing, informal feedback to summer associates and encourage summer associates to solicit feedback directly from attorneys. Each summer associate is assigned mentors, from each department to which he or she is assigned. By the end of the program, our goal is for summer associates to have a thorough understanding of our client-base and the work environment they will encounter as full-time associates.

Head Office: **Boston, MA**
Number of domestic offices: **2**
Number of international offices: **0**
Partners (US): **75**
Counsel (US): **20**
Associates (US): **53**

Main Recruitment Contact: **Donna M. Yergeau, Director of Legal Recruiting**
Hiring Partner: **Christopher H. Lindstrom**
Recruitment website:
www.nutter.com/careers
Diversity officers: **Julia S. Cosentino and David L. Ferrera, Co-Chairs, Diversity and Inclusion Committee**

Summer Salary 2017
1Ls: **$1,500/week**
2Ls: **$3,077/week**
Post 3 Ls: **N/A**
1Ls hired? **Yes**
Split summers offered? **No**
Can summers spend time in overseas office? **No**
Summers 2017: **7**
Offers/acceptances 2016:
7 offers, 6 acceptances

Nutter uncommon law

O'Melveny & Myers LLP

Tel: 213 430 6000   Fax: 213 430 6407
Email: info@omm.com
www.omm.com

Main areas of work

O'Melveny advises industry-leading clients on a full range of cutting-edge litigation, transactional, and regulatory matters. For a complete listing of our client services, please visit www.omm.com.

Firm profile

A global law firm with more than 40 practice and industry groups dedicated to achieving our clients' most important goals, O'Melveny's lawyers work side by side with our clients to help them grow, protect their assets, and navigate complex law and regulation. Regularly recognized for excellence and innovation, we are also committed to cultivating a diverse and inclusive environment and to strengthening our communities through pro bono work, which we treat as equal to billable work. We have an industry-leading talent development program, which includes a career development advisor, an upward review process that helps our partners become better supervisors, and award-winning flexibility options.

Recruitment details

- Number of 1st year associates: 60
- Number of 2nd year associates: 46
- Associate salaries: 1st year: $180,000
- 2nd year: $190,000
- Clerking policy: Yes

Law Schools attending for OCIs in 2017:

Berkeley, Brooklyn, Chapman, Chicago, Columbia, UC Davis, Duke, Fordham, Georgetown, George Washington, Harvard, Hastings, Howard, Lavender Law, Loyola, Michigan, Northwestern, NYU, Penn, Santa Clara, Stanford, Texas, UCI, UCLA, University of Washington, USC, UVA, Yale

Summer details

Summer associate profile:

O'Melveny is looking for summer associates with outstanding academic and personal credentials from diverse backgrounds. We strive to find students with strong interpersonal skills and a desire to work in a collegial atmosphere that values teamwork. In addition to activities like journal work and moot court, we look for a keen interest in O'Melveny's practices, culture, and attorneys.

Summer program components:

Our summer program offers an inside look at what it is like to practice at O'Melveny. During our ten-week program, summer associates work on major cases and transactions, support ongoing pro bono matters, participate in targeted training and development programs, and join in social events to get to know our attorneys. Experiential training includes our Advocacy Institute, Mock Deal Program, and opportunities to accompany O'Melveny lawyers to deal closings, client meetings, depositions, and court appearances. Our work coordination system ensures our summers are exposed to a variety of practice areas, attorneys, and types of work. Mentors, ongoing feedback, and a midsummer review help our summer associates make the most of their experiences.

Head Office: N/A
Number of domestic offices: 7
Number of international offices: 8
Worldwide revenue: $725,000,000
Partners (US): 200
Associates (US): 402

Main Recruitment Contact: Tina Metis, Firmwide Director of Attorney Recruiting
Hiring Partner: Allen Burton, Firmwide Hiring Partner
Recruitment website:
www.omm.com/careers
Diversity officers: Walter Dellinger, Diversity Partner; Mary Ellen Connerty, Director of Diversity and Inclusion

Summer Salary 2017
1Ls: $3,500/week
2Ls: $3,500/week
Post 3Ls: $3,500/week
1Ls hired? Case by case
Split summers offered? Case by case
Can summers spend time in overseas office? No
Summers 2017: 70
Offers/acceptances 2016:
92 offers, 72 acceptances; some offers outstanding due to judicial clerkships

Firm Profiles

Orrick, Herrington & Sutcliffe LLP

51 West 52nd Street, New York, NY 10019
The Orrick Building, 405 Howard Street, San Francisco, CA 94105-2669
Tel: 212 506 5000 (New York)   Tel: 415 773 5700 (San Francisco)
Email: shandley@orrick.com   www.orrick.com

Main areas of work

Tech, energy and infrastructure, finance, corporate, litigation, appellate and intellectual property.

Firm profile

At Orrick, we focus on serving the technology, energy and infrastructure and finance sectors globally. Founded more than 150 years ago in San Francisco, Orrick today has 1,000+ lawyers and offices in 26 markets worldwide, including our newest offices in Houston, TX and Santa Monica, CA. Our clients include 1,600+ high-growth companies, 20% of today's unicorns, public companies, global financial institutions, funds and government entities. We advise them on emerging areas from blockchain technology and cybersecurity to Mexican energy reform and impact finance. We're inspired by opportunities to make an impact with our clients. We're also inspired by our pro bono clients – we have one of the most active pro bono programs of any firm with 92% lawyer participation last year. We value teamwork, transparency and inclusion. To help our associates succeed, we've re-thought the traditional law firm talent model with an approach we call "Agile Working." By agile, we mean responsive, flexible, adaptable, and personalized. This means our associates get early at bats – opportunities for taking on meaningful responsibility and for making a real impact. We also enable each associate to manage and direct his or her career in a personalized way, including a self-paced, merit-based advancement system, flexible work arrangements, and an industry-leading primary caregiver leave program of 22 weeks paid leave and 9 months of job protection. We look forward to talking with you about opportunities at Orrick and learning about what inspires you.

Recruitment details

- Number of 1st year associates: 44
- Associate salaries: 1st year: $165,000-180,000
- Clerking policy: Yes
- Number of 2nd year associates: 33
- 2nd year: $175,000-190,000

Law Schools attended for OCIs in 2017:

Columbia University, Duke University, Fordham University, Georgetown University, George Washington University, Harvard University, McGeorge University, New York University, Santa Clara University, Stanford University, University of California – Berkeley, University of California – Davis, University of California – Hastings, University of California – Los Angeles, University of Chicago, University of Michigan, University of North Carolina, University of Pennsylvania, University of Southern California, University of Texas, University of Virginia, Vanderbilt University

Summer details

Summer associate profile:

We seek out candidates who have diverse backgrounds and interests, and who bring interesting life experiences and perspectives that shape their worldview. We've identified the three qualities our most successful lawyers have in common: grit (determination, perseverance, tenacity and intensity); EQ (the ability to build interpersonal relationships); and teamplay (a propensity to work with others). We believe in having fun while working hard on projects that make a tangible impact on the world, locally and globally.

For more information, please visit us at www.orrick.com, follow us on https://twitter.com/OrrickCareers, get updates with www.Facebook.com/OrrickRecruiting, or see how we're already connected at http://www.linkedin.com/company/orrick-herrington-&-sutcliffe-llp.

Summer program components:

Your first day as a summer associate is the beginning of your Orrick career. Our goal is to immerse you in the firm, introduce you to our clients, engage you in the issues on which we are working and create opportunities for you to start building relationships that we hope will last a lifetime. Our summer associates classes are small – which means focused, and personal attention, practical training, varied assignments spanning across different transactional and litigation practice areas, extensive feedback and hands-on experience with real client matters.

Head Office: New York / San Francisco
Number of domestic offices: 12
Number of international offices: 14
Worldwide revenue: $929,107,673
Partners (US): 287
Associates (US): 379

Main Recruitment Contact: Siobhan Handley
Hiring Partner: Lisa Simpson
Recruitment website: www.orrick.com/careers
Diversity officer: Lorraine McGowen

Summer Salary 2017
1Ls: $3,400/week
2Ls: $3,400/week
Post 3Ls: N/A
1Ls hired? Yes
Split summers offered? Yes, case by case
Can summers spend time in overseas office? No
Summers 2017: 70

Firm Profiles

Patterson Belknap Webb & Tyler LLP

1133 Avenue of the Americas, New York, NY 10036
Tel: 212 336 2000   Fax: 212 336 2222
Email: rlklum@pbwt.com
www.pbwt.com

Main areas of work

Patterson Belknap's practice combines skill in both complex litigation and transactional matters, including corporate, real estate, media and entertainment, intellectual property, sports, art and museum law, employee benefits and tax practices. The firm is regularly recognized in industry publications as a leader in litigation areas including intellectual property and false advertising. In addition, the firm has the leading personal planning and tax-exempt organizations practices in New York City.

Firm profile

Patterson Belknap Webb & Tyler LLP, founded in 1919, is a law firm based in New York City with more than 200 lawyers committed to maintaining its independence, its diversity and its focus of providing superior legal advice and service to clients. The firm delivers a full range of services across more than 20 practice groups in both litigation and commercial law. *The National Law Journal* has included Patterson Belknap on a list of firms which it considers to have "the nimbleness and adaptability that come from lean operations and strong client ties." The firm highly values public service and has consistently ranked at or near the top of *The American Lawyer's* annual pro bono survey.

Recruitment details

- Number of 1st year associates: 2
- Number of 2nd year associates: 10
- Associate salaries: 1st year: $180,000
- 2nd year: $190,000
- Clerking policy: The firm values clerkship experience and actively recruits judicial law clerks.

Program details

Patterson Belknap hires associates directly from judicial clerkships. We will also recruit in August 2017 to hire a select group of 3L law students graduating at the end of the 2018 school year. We look forward to meeting with outstanding law students through both clerkship and 3L recruiting.

Associate profile:

Patterson Belknap looks for smart, collaborative, intellectually curious people who desire early responsibility and are highly motivated to solve complex legal problems.

Head Office: New York, NY
Number of domestic offices: 1
Number of international offices: 0
Worldwide revenue: $185,500
Partners (US): 51
Associates (US): 117

Main Recruitment Contact:
Robin L Klum
Hiring Partners: Robert W Lehrburger and Sarah Zgliniec
Recruitment website: www.pbwt.com
Diversity officers: Peter C Harvey, TJ Tu and Richard R Upton, Co Chairs, Diversity Committee

1Ls hired? No
Summers 2017: 0
Offers/acceptances 2016: N/A

Patterson Belknap Webb & Tyler LLP

Paul Hastings

515 S Flower Street, 25th Floor, Los Angeles, CA 90071
Email: attorneyrecruiting@paulhastings.com
www.paulhastings.com

Firm profile

At Paul Hastings, our purpose is clear - to help our clients and people navigate new paths to growth. With a strong presence throughout Asia, Europe, Latin America and the US, Paul Hastings is recognized as one of the world's most innovative global law firms. In 2015, the firm ranked first on *The American Lawyer's* A-List and Vault's #1 Place to Work.

Main areas of work

We understand the imperative for innovation, efficiency, and breakthrough performance facing today's leading companies - and what it takes to help them succeed.

Our practice areas include: anticorruption and compliance, antitrust and competition, complex commercial litigation, employment, finance and restructuring, global banking and payment systems, intellectual property, investment management, mergers and acquisitions, privacy and data security, private equity, real estate, securities and capital markets, securities litigation, tax, white collar defense and investigations.

Recruitment details

- Number of 1st year associates: 60
- Number of 2nd year associates: 65
- Associate salaries: 1st year: $180,000
- 2nd year: $190,000
- Clerking policy: Yes

Law Schools attending for OCIs in 2017:

Berkeley, University of Chicago, Columbia, Cornell, Duke, Emory, Fordham, Georgia, Georgetown, GW, Harvard, Howard, Michigan, Northwestern, NYU, Penn, Stanford, UC Hastings, University of Houston, UC Irvine, UCLA, USC, University of San Diego, University of Texas, UVA, Vanderbilt, Yale

Summer details

Summer associate profile:

At Paul Hastings, it's smart business to build diverse teams rich in talent, experiences, and creativity. We seek students who exemplify the hallmarks of our successful associates: innovative, strong communication skills, achievement drive, interpersonal savvy, client service excellence and ability to be collaborative team members. Students should be committed to work for a dynamic and entrepreneurial law firm on complex legal matters across practices and offices to help our clients overcome challenges and move their business forward. Law students with outstanding academic credentials, superior writing skills, Law Review, Journal, or Moot Court membership are preferred.

Summer program components:

Our Summer Program serves as a cornerstone for the recruitment of outstanding associates and the future success of our firm. We are fully committed to the professional development and advancement of each summer associate. Summer associates are given substantive and challenging work with a variety of lawyers and a realistic view of practicing law at Paul Hastings. Our summer associates observe and, when possible, assist in trials, hearings, depositions and negotiations, and participate in client meetings and closings. Summer associates can also expect mentoring in a collaborative work environment.

Largest Office: New York, NY
Number of domestic offices: 10
Number of international offices: 11
Worldwide revenue: $1,074,500,000
Partners (US): 246
Counsel (US): 55
Associates (US): 461

Main Recruitment Contact: Cynthia Hasson, Director, Talent Acquisition
Hiring Partners: David Hernand, Teri O'Brien
Recruitment website:
www.paulhastings.com/careers/law-students
Diversity Manager: Karlie Ilaria

Summer Salary 2017
1Ls: $3,500
2Ls: $3,500
Post 3Ls: $3,500
1Ls hired? Yes
Split summers offered? Case by case
Can summers spend time in overseas office? In special cases, we may offer the opportunity to spend two weeks in one of our offices in Asia. The summer associate must have the appropriate language skills.
Summers 2017: 84
Offers 2016: 132

PAUL
HASTINGS

Paul, Weiss, Rifkind, Wharton & Garrison LLP

1285 Avenue of the Americas, New York, NY 10019
Tel: 212 373 3000   Fax: 212 757 3990
Email: lateralhiring@paulweiss.com, summerprogram@paulweiss.com
www.paulweiss.com

Main areas of work

Paul, Weiss is widely recognized as having leading litigation and corporate capabilities, and the firm has developed equally strong practices in the areas of bankruptcy and corporate reorganization, employee benefits and executive compensation, intellectual property, personal representation, real estate and tax law.

Firm profile

Paul, Weiss, Rifkind, Wharton & Garrison LLP is a firm of more than 900 lawyers, with diverse backgrounds, personalities, ideas and interests, who collaborate with clients to help them conquer their most critical legal challenges and business goals. Our long-standing clients include many of the largest publicly and privately held corporations and financial institutions in the United States and throughout the world. We have an unwavering dedication to representing those in need through our pro bono efforts, and have long been a leader in promoting diversity within our firm and the legal profession.

Recruitment details

- Number of 1st year associates: 118
- Associate salaries: 1st year: $180,000
- Clerking policy: Yes
- Number of 2nd year associates: 92
- 2nd year: $190,000

Law Schools attending for OCIs in 2017:

Boston College, Boston University, Berkeley, Brooklyn, Cardozo, Chicago, Columbia, Cornell, Duke, Fordham, Georgetown, George Washington, Harvard, Howard, Lavender Law Job Fair, McGill, Michigan, Northwestern, NYU, Patent Law Job Fair at Loyola, Penn, Stanford, Texas, Toronto, Virginia, Washington University in St. Louis, Yale

Summer details

Summer associate profile:

You should have a strong academic record and life experience and initiative and commitment to excellence in the practice of law.

Summer program components:

The summer associate program at Paul, Weiss is more than just legal training. It's your introduction to the rich variety and depth of life in one of New York's most unique law firms. You'll have the opportunity to shape your summer experience at Paul, Weiss. Choose one department to call your home, or select a variety of work from a number of different practice areas. You'll be mentored by a team of lawyers including associates, counsel and partners. Your mentors will help you make connections with other lawyers at the firm and make informed decisions about the work you choose. You'll receive training in both substantive areas of law and practical legal skills in a mix of highly interactive small group trainings, individual skills development workshops and more traditional classroom style presentations.

Head Office: **New York, NY**
Number of domestic offices: **3**
Number of international offices: **5**
Worldwide revenue: **$1,221,848,220**
Partners (US): **129**
Associates (US): **550**

Main Recruitment Contact:
Pamela N Davidson
Hiring Partners: **Neil Goldman and Catherine Nyarady**
Recruitment website:
www.paulweiss.com/careers
Diversity & Inclusion Director: **Danyale A Price**
Women's Initiative Director: **Anne Weisberg**

Summer Salary 2017
1Ls: **$3,500/week**
2Ls: **$3,500/week**
Post 3Ls: **$3,500/week**
1Ls hired? **Yes**
Split summers offered? **Yes**
Can summers spend time in overseas office? **Yes**
Summers 2017: **131**
Offers/acceptances 2016:
139 offers, 115 acceptances

Paul | Weiss

Firm Profiles

Perkins Coie LLP

1201 Third Avenue, Suite 4900, Seattle, WA 98101-3099
Tel: 206 359 8000   Fax: 206 359 9000
www.perkinscoie.com

Main areas of work

Perkins Coie's practice areas include business; environment, energy and resources; intellectual property; labor and employment; litigation; personal planning; political law; product liability; real estate.

Firm profile

With offices across the United States and in China, Perkins Coie provides a full array of corporate, commercial litigation and intellectual property legal services to clients that span the range of entities in the business world – from Fortune 100 corporations to small, independent start-ups, as well as public and not-for-profit organizations.

Recruitment details

- Number of 1st year associates: 33
- Number of 2nd year associates: 36
- Associate salaries: 1st year: Varies by office
- 2nd year: Varies by office
- Clerking policy: Yes

Law Schools attending for OCIs in 2017:

Arizona State University, Chicago, Columbia, Cornell, Duke, George Washington, Georgetown, Gonzaga, Harvard, Howard, Lewis and Clark, Loyola (Chicago), Loyola (Los Angeles), Michigan, Northwestern, NYU, Penn, Santa Clara, Seattle University, SMU, Stanford, Texas, UC Berkeley, UC Davis, UC Hastings, UC Irvine, UCLA, University of Arizona, University of Illinois, University of Oregon, University of San Diego, University of Washington, USC, Vanderbilt, Virginia, Willamette, Yale

Summer details

Summer associate profile:

Hiring criteria include demonstrated academic excellence, creative problem solving, leadership in and service to the community and dedication to excellence in the legal profession.

Summer program components:

Perkins Coie's summer program provides wide-ranging work opportunities and social events designed to promote interaction among summer associates, attorneys and staff. Supervising attorneys provide informal feedback after each assignment and they submit written, formal evaluations to the office hiring committee. The formal evaluations become part of each summer associate's midsummer and final evaluations. Summer associates have the opportunity for both informal and formal training throughout the program.

Head Office: Seattle, WA
Number of domestic offices: 16
Number of international offices: 3
Worldwide revenue: $781,000,000
Partners (US): 519
Senior Counsel (US): 70
Other Attorneys: (US): 36
Associates (US): 411

Main Recruitment Contact: Michael Gotham, Director of Legal Recruiting and Retention
Recruitment website:
www.perkinscoie.com/careers
Diversity officer: Theresa Cropper

Summer Salary 2017
1Ls: $2,692-$3,462/week
2Ls: $2,692-$3,462/week
Post 3Ls: N/A
1Ls hired? Yes
Split summers offered? Case by case
Can summers spend time in overseas office? No
Summers 2017: 57
Offers/acceptances 2016:
55 offers, 49 acceptances

Firm Profiles

Pillsbury Winthrop Shaw Pittman LLP

1540 Broadway, New York, NY 10036
Tel: 212 858 1000 Fax: 212 858 1500
www.pillsburylaw.com

Main areas of work

Regulatory: Whether working with a startup, a company in growth mode or a market leader, Pillsbury's lawyers help companies limit risk, achieve compliance, defend against investigations, advocate for new laws and challenge restrictions.

Litigation: Pillsbury's litigators handle complex commercial cases, matters of public interest, intellectual property challenges, tax controversies, insurance policyholder disputes, environmental claims, securities class actions, construction disputes and a wide variety of other assignments.

Business: Pillsbury's business teams partner with clients to help find capital, organize new companies, secure patents, purchase real estate, negotiate contracts, challenge competitors, guide investments, protect data, limit liability, outsource support services, minimize taxes, establish policies and expand markets.

Firm profile

Pillsbury is a leading international law firm with a particular focus on the energy and natural resources, financial services, real estate and construction, and technology sectors. The 2017 *Best Lawyers/US News & World Report* survey recognized our lawyers with 80 Tier 1 rankings, and the firm was again named as one of the most innovative law firms by *Financial Times*. Our lawyers are highly regarded for their forward-thinking approach, enthusiasm for collaborating across disciplines and unsurpassed commercial awareness.

Recruitment details

- Number of 1st year associates: 37
- Associate salaries: 1st year: $180,000
- Clerking policy: Yes
- Number of 2nd year associates: 27
- 2nd year: $190,000

Law Schools attending for OCIs in 2017:

University of California, Berkeley; University of California, Davis; University of California, Hastings; University of California, Irvine; University of California, Los Angeles; University of Chicago; Columbia; Cornell; Duke; Fordham; George Washington; Georgetown; Harvard; Hofstra; University of Houston; Howard University; Loyola Law School; University of Michigan; Northwestern; New York University; University of Pennsylvania; Stanford; University of Southern California; University of Texas; University of Virginia

Summer details

Summer associate profile:

Pillsbury seeks energetic, high-performing students who possess sound judgment, determination, common sense, excellent interpersonal skills, the ability to inspire confidence and the drive to produce high quality work and achieve outstanding results.

Summer program components:

Pillsbury's summer associates experience the firm's collaborative style by working side-by-side with attorneys in a variety of practice areas, on industry and client teams and on issue-specific projects. Pillsbury University offers training on everything from legal writing to client service basics to effective networking. Formal reviews supplement the extemporaneous feedback provided to summer associates by our lawyers.

Head Office: New York, NY
Number of domestic offices: 14
Number of international offices: 7
Worldwide revenue: $573,500,000
Partners (US): 309
Associates (US): 180

Main Recruitment Contact: Charles Curtis, Firmwide Director of Attorney Recruiting
Hiring Partner: Mariah Brandt
Recruitment website:
http://careers.pillsburylaw.com/
Diversity officer: Rosa Walker, Director of Diversity and Inclusion

Summer Salary 2017
1Ls: $3,462/week
2Ls: $3,462/week
Post 3Ls: $3,462/week
1Ls hired? No
Split summers offered? Yes, but not preferred
Can summers spend time in overseas office? Case by case
Summers 2017: 39
Offers/acceptances 2016:
41 offers, 34 acceptances

Proskauer Rose

Eleven Times Square, New York, NY 10036-8299
Tel: 212 969 3000   Fax: 212 969 2900
www.proskauer.com

Main areas of work

Private equity; corporate finance and securities; mergers and acquisitions; capital markets; litigation, trials and dispute resolution; corporate defense and investigations; intellectual property; healthcare; labor and employment; employee benefits and executive compensation; real estate; technology, media and telecommunications; privacy and cybersecurity; bankruptcy and restructuring; insurance coverage and recovery; and wealth management. The firm also has significant industry-focused experience across many fields, including financial services, life sciences, sports, media and entertainment, and lodging and gaming.

Firm profile

We are 725+ lawyers serving clients from 13 offices located in the leading financial and business centers in North and South America, Europe and Asia. The world's leading organizations, companies and corporations choose us to be their representatives in their most critical situations. We work with alternative capital providers, major sports leagues, Fortune 500 companies, entertainment industry legends, many of the world's most successful asset managers and other industry-redefining companies which are changing how business is conducted today as well as tomorrow.

Recruitment details

- Number of 1st year associates: 57   • Number of 2nd year associates: 63
- Associate salaries: 1st year: $180,000 (except Boca Raton, New Orleans and Newark)
- 2nd year: $190,000 (except Boca Raton, New Orleans and Newark)
- Clerking policy: Yes

Law Schools attending for OCIs in 2017:

Boston College, Boston University, Columbia, Cornell, Duke, Emory, Fordham, George Washington University, Georgetown, Harvard, Howard, Northwestern, New York University, Rutgers, Stanford, Suffolk, Tulane, University of California (Berkeley, Los Angeles), University of Chicago, University of Connecticut, University of Illinois, University of Michigan, University of Pennsylvania, University of Southern California, University of Texas, University of Virginia, Vanderbilt, Washington University in St Louis, Yale

Summer details

Summer associate profile:

We look for well-rounded students who have demonstrated academic excellence, leadership, community service, intellectual curiosity, maturity and strong motivation to succeed.

Summer program components:

Our summer program is designed to replicate, as closely as possible, the experience of being a lawyer at Proskauer. You will work on complex and challenging legal matters, learn from leaders in the field, and experience our unique culture. Our program features a systematic procedure for review and feedback on all assignments. We take every opportunity to show you first-hand why your work matters and how it will make a difference. You'll also have the chance to up your game in key legal areas through partner-led, interactive training workshops throughout the summer. These workshops get into such areas as corporate negotiation, mergers & acquisitions, mediation and mock trials. Recent cultural and social activities that our summer associates have enjoyed include Major League Baseball games, the Tony Awards, scavenger hunts, cooking classes, private movie screenings and community service team projects, to name a few.

Head Office: New York, NY
Number of domestic offices: 8
Number of international offices: 5
Worldwide revenue: $852,400,000
Partners (US): 217
Associates (US): 384

Main Recruitment Contact:
Caroline K Menes
Hiring Partner: Michael T Mervis
Recruitment website:
www.proskauer.com/careers
Diversity officer: Peter Wilson

Summer Salary 2017
1Ls: $3,462/week (except Boca Raton, New Orleans and Newark)
2Ls: $3,462/week (except Boca Raton, New Orleans and Newark)
Post 3Ls: $3,462/week
1Ls hired? Yes
Split summers offered? Case by case
Can summers spend time in overseas office? No
Summers 2017: 84
Offers/acceptances 2016:
63 offers, 55 acceptances, 3 public interest deferrals

Reed Smith LLP

225 Fifth Avenue, Pittsburgh, PA 15222
Tel: 412 288 3131   Fax: 412 288 3063
www.reedsmith.com

Main areas of work

Reed Smith is a global relationship law firm with more than 1,800 lawyers in 26 offices throughout the United States, Europe, Asia and the Middle East. Its lawyers provide litigation and other dispute-resolution services in multi-jurisdictional and other high-stakes matters; deliver regulatory counsel; and execute the full range of strategic domestic and cross-border transactions. Reed Smith is a preeminent advisor to industries including financial services, life sciences, healthcare, advertising, technology and media, shipping, energy and natural resources, real estate, manufacturing and education.

Firm profile

Reed Smith has been ranked consistently among the top law firms for client service and has been identified as one of the few large firms with a strategic focus on client satisfaction. Reed Smith has grown in large part because of its commitment to delivering high-quality service and developing long-term client relationships. Reed Smith is united by a culture that is defined by core values of quality, integrity, teamwork and respect, performance and innovation and improvement. These are further demonstrated through a firmwide commitment to diversity, pro bono and community support activity and the professional development of the firm's lawyers.

Recruitment details

- Number of 1st year associates: 42
- Associate salaries: 1st year: $130,000-$180,000
- Clerking policy: Yes

Summer details

Summer associate profile:

Reed Smith is looking for summer associates who have a combination of top academics, practical experience and superior analytical and writing skills. The firm values people who are mature and engaging and who demonstrate leadership capabilities and community involvement.

Summer program components:

Reed Smith offers law students first-rate work in a challenging and busy atmosphere where their contributions count from day one. Summer associates will become immersed in law firm life by completing assignments relating to actual client situations. Each assignment presents a fresh opportunity for summer associates to hone their research, writing, judgment, communication and analytical skills.

CareeRS is Reed Smith's competency-based career development program with a focus on role-specific professional training and development, including mentoring, and more developmentally oriented assessments tailored to the needs of associates. The firm offers its summer associates numerous chances to participate in both formal and informal training programs, such as: managing partner's forum, mediation and mergers and acquisitions clinics, law firm economics, cross-cultural training and legal writing. Summer associates also have numerous opportunities to participate in pro bono and community service projects and become acquainted with our Women's Initiative Network and Diversity and Inclusion Committees. Please visit www.reedsmith.com for more information about each of these initiatives.

Head Office: N/A
Number of domestic offices: 15
Number of international offices: 12
Worldwide revenue: $1.123 billion
Partners (US): 514
Associates (US): 449

Main Recruitment Contact:
Kevan Skelton, Global Director of Legal Recruiting
Recruitment website:
www.reedsmith.com
Diversity officer: John Lino, Partner and Director of Global Diversity & Inclusion

Summer Salary 2017
1Ls: $5,208-$6,667 semi-monthly
2Ls: $5,208-$6,667 semi-monthly
1Ls hired? **Case by case**
Split summers offered? **Case by case**
Can summers spend time in overseas office? **No**
Summers 2017: **57 (52 2Ls, 5 1Ls)**
Offers/acceptances 2016: **51 offers, 49 acceptances**

Ropes & Gray LLP

Prudential Tower, 800 Boylston Street, Boston, MA 02119
Tel: 617 951 7000   Fax: 617 951 7050
Email: hiringprogram@ropesgray.com
www.ropesgray.com

Main areas of work

From the boardroom to the courtroom, Ropes & Gray represents the world's leading companies on their most critical matters. On corporate transactional issues, the firm has been recognized as having top-ranked practices in private equity, M&A, finance, investment management, bankruptcy, healthcare, life sciences and intellectual property, among others. The firm also has been cited for its litigation experience and successful track record, including antitrust, appellate, complex business litigation, securities litigation and regulation, government enforcement and white collar criminal defense, IP litigation and privacy and data security.

Firm profile

Ropes & Gray, an international law firm with more than 1,000 attorneys and professionals in 11 offices in the United States, Europe and Asia, provides comprehensive legal services to leading businesses and individuals around the world. Clients benefit from the firm's unwavering standards of integrity, service and responsiveness. The firm is ideally positioned to address its clients' most pressing legal and business issues. In 2016, 1,566 lawyers, paralegals and other Ropes & Gray professionals worldwide logged 134,258 hours toward assisting our pro bono clients. In the US alone, over 850 of our attorneys dedicated 20 or more hours to pro bono legal service.

Recruitment details

- Number of 1st year associates: 126
- Number of 2nd year associates: 112
- Associate salaries: 1st year: $180,000
- 2nd year: $190,000
- Clerking policy: Yes

Law Schools attending for OCIs in 2017:

American, Berkeley, Boston College, Boston University, Brooklyn, Chicago, Columbia, Cornell, Duke, Fordham, George Washington, Georgetown, Harvard, Howard, Illinois, Maryland, Michigan, North Carolina, Northeastern, Northwestern, Notre Dame, NYU, Penn, Santa Clara, Stanford, Suffolk, Texas, UC Davis, UCLA, USC, UVA, Vanderbilt,Washington University in St Louis, Yale

Summer details

Summer associate profile:

Ropes & Gray chooses summer associates based on academic performance, personal skills, motivation, work and leadership experience, practice area interests and the ability to work well in a highly collaborative environment.

Summer program components:

Our goal is to provide summer associates with a realistic sense of what it is like to work at the firm by having them work on actual client matters and by giving them opportunities to get to know our attorneys through a variety of social events, activities and lunches. Our attorneys provide meaningful and timely feedback on work assignments and offer additional perspective through an end-of-summer formal review. Summer associates also benefit from our highly regarded training program, which provides both practice-specific and general soft-skills training designed to support summer associates' professional growth and development.

Head Office: **Boston, MA**
Number of domestic offices: **6**
Number of international offices: **5**
Partners (US): **253**
Associates (US): **779**

Main Recruitment Contact: **Amy Ross**
Hiring Partner: **Peter Erichsen**
Recruitment website:
www.ropesgray.com
Diversity officer: **Lindsay Kendrick**

Summer Salary 2017
1Ls: **N/A**
2Ls: **$3,500/week**
Post 3Ls: **N/A**
1Ls hired? **N/A**
Split summers offered? **Yes**
Can summers spend time in overseas office? **Yes**
Summers 2017: **145**
Offers/acceptances 2016:
144 offers, 137 acceptances

ROPES & GRAY

Schiff Hardin LLP

233 S. Wacker Drive, Suite 6600, Chicago, IL 60606
Tel: 312 258 5500   Fax: 312 258 5600
www.schiffhardin.com

Firm profile

Schiff Hardin was founded in Chicago over 150 years ago and is now a full-service national firm with over 300 attorneys in six offices. Schiff Hardin is recognized for its strong litigation and transactional work and its cutting-edge intellectual property, environmental, and construction practices. Clients range from Fortune 100 corporations to privately held companies, financial institutions, public utilities, government entities, and individuals. Schiff Hardin lawyers embrace several core values: a commitment to excellent work and superior client service, strong team spirit, and a belief that diversity benefits both the firm and its clients. The firm encourages new lawyers to explore different practice areas before they choose a practice group. Schiff's lean staffing and extensive training programs allow associates to take on significant responsibility and have a front-line role early in their careers.

Recruitment details

- Number of 1st year associates: 11
- Associate salaries: 1st year: $180,000
- Clerking policy: Yes
- Number of 2nd year associates: 17
- 2nd year: Tier-based

Law Schools attending for OCIs in 2017:

Chicago, Chicago-Kent, Fordham, Illinois, Indiana, Michigan, Northwestern, Notre Dame. The firm collects resumes at several additional schools and all applicants are welcome to contact the firm at schiffhardin.com

Summer details

Summer associate profile:

Schiff Hardin recruits law students who have a record of leadership and achievement in school, work, and extracurricular and community activities; strong analytical, interpersonal and communication skills; the ability to work independently and on a team; and the drive to gain experience and succeed in a client-service business.

Summer program components:

Schiff Hardin summer associates get a realistic look at what it's like to practice law at the firm. Associate advisors, partner mentors, social events, and weekly meetings integrate summer associates and give them a feel for the firm's culture, practice groups, and management. From day one, summer associates gain experience in the areas of law that interest them by doing real work for real clients. They also learn by observing depositions and trials and attending negotiations and client meetings. Summer associates receive feedback after each assignment and a midsummer review. Finally, summers receive training, including group writing, research and corporate drafting workshops; litigation and communications skills training; business development training; and one-on-one sessions with the firm's writing coach.

Head Office: Chicago, IL
Number of domestic offices: 6
Number of international offices: 0
Partners (US): 82 (IP), 65 (EP)
Associates (US): 87

Hiring Partner: David Blickenstaff
Recruitment website:
www.schiffhardin.com/careers
Diversity officer: Regina Speed-Bost (Diversity Committee Chair)

Summer Salary 2017
1Ls: $3,450/week
2Ls: $3,450/week
Post 3Ls: N/A
1Ls hired? Case by case
Split summers offered? Case by case
Summers 2017: 14
Offers/acceptances 2016:
12 offers, 12 acceptances

Firm Profiles

Schulte Roth & Zabel LLP

919 Third Avenue, New York, NY 10022
Tel: 212 756 2000
Email: recruiting.department@srz.com

Main areas of work

Our specialties include bank regulatory; bankruptcy and creditors' rights litigation; broker-dealer regulatory and enforcement; business reorganization; complex commercial litigation; cybersecurity; distressed debt and claims trading; distressed investing; education law; employment and employee benefits; energy; environmental; finance; financial institutions; hedge funds; individual client services; insurance; intellectual property, sourcing and technology; investment management; litigation; mergers and acquisitions; PIPEs; private equity; real estate; real estate capital markets and REITs; real estate litigation; regulated funds; regulatory and compliance; securities and capital markets; securities enforcement; securities litigation; securitization; shareholder activism; structured finance and derivatives; tax; and white collar defense and government investigations.

Firm profile

Schulte Roth & Zabel is a premier law firm serving the financial services industry from strategically located offices in New York, Washington, DC and London. We take a multidisciplinary approach in our work with a large and impressive array of global and forward-thinking institutional, entrepreneurial and individual clients, from advising clients on investment management, corporate and transactional matters, to providing counsel on regulatory, compliance, enforcement and investigative issues.

Recruitment details

- Number of 1st year associates: 32
- Associate salaries: 1st year: $180,000
- Clerking policy: Yes
- Number of 2nd year associates: 34
- 2nd year: $190,000

Law Schools attending for OCIs in 2017:

Boston College, Boston University, Cardozo, Columbia, Cornell, Duke, Emory, Fordham, George Washington, Georgetown, Harvard, Howard, Michigan, NYU, Penn, Tulane, Virginia, Wash U

Summer details

Summer associate profile:

SRZ hires attorneys who are bright, personable and enthusiastic about early substantive responsibility and client contact. We seek candidates with outstanding academic achievement, high motivation and strong interpersonal skills.

Summer program components:

Our summer associate program allows students to receive substantive assignments from practice groups of their choice during two assigning periods. Summer associates have interaction with our clients, attend meetings and depositions and work on complex projects. Training and feedback are emphasized through regular departmental training sessions, a writing seminar, a corporate negotiation workshop, a trial advocacy program, and a pro bono week. These experiences are all designed to allow students to explore various areas of interest, get immersed in the firm culture and gain first-hand knowledge of what they will see as a junior associate. In addition to our top-notch training programs and hands-on work experience, we offer fun and exciting social activities that allow summer associates to spend time with their associate and partner mentors, develop relationships with our attorneys and get to know everyone outside of the office.

Head Office: **New York**
Number of domestic offices: **2**
Number of international offices: **1**
Partners (US): **89**
Other lawyers (US): **253**

Main Recruitment Contact: **Alissa K Golden**
Hiring Partners: **William H Gussman, Jr, Taleah E Jennings, Jason S Kaplan**
Recruitment website:
www.srz.com/careers
Diversity Officer: **Taleah E Jennings**

Summer Salary 2017
2Ls: **$3,462 per week**
1Ls hired? **No**
Split summers offered? **No**
Can summers spend time in overseas office? **No**
Summers 2017: **38**
Offers/acceptances 2016: **38 offers, 37 acceptances**

Schulte Roth&Zabel

Sedgwick LLP

333 Bush Street, San Francisco, CA 94104
Tel: 415 781 7900   Fax: 415 781 2635
www.sedgwicklaw.com

Main areas of work

Sedgwick attorneys have skillfully managed complex litigation and dispute resolution spanning multiple jurisdictions, from local to international. The firm has been retained in mass tort, class action, multi-district and market share litigation as national or regional trial counsel. We have served as counsel for a broad range of domestic and international companies in industries that include insurance, financial services, retail, pharmaceutical, automotive, media, food and beverage, and medical device manufacturing. Practice areas include product liability, directors and officers liability, retail industry matters, Bermuda Form, business litigation, intellectual property, healthcare, life sciences, real estate, property and casualty coverage, reinsurance, employment, insurance policy drafting/advice, international arbitration, and maritime.

Firm profile

Sedgwick LLP is a resolution-oriented firm. Founded in 1933, Sedgwick has grown into a broad-based international firm of 250 attorneys with 14 offices in the US, London and Bermuda. We have earned a reputation as a top litigation and trial law firm by winning cases and providing clients with sophisticated strategies. A significant number of our attorneys possess successful first-chair jury trial and arbitration experience. Sedgwick attorneys take pride in our longstanding client relationships and in our well-earned reputation for effective and economical representation of some of the world's largest companies. Sedgwick works with clients to assess and manage risks, providing effective solutions through all aspects of government enforcement and compliance initiatives.

Sedgwick also has a strong commitment to inclusion and diversity in the profession based on our belief that attorneys from diverse backgrounds and experiences, working toward a common goal, offer the best opportunity to deliver the superior legal services that our clients expect. We are honored to have been recognized for these efforts, including being named '100 Best Law Firms for Female Attorneys' and '100 Best Law Firm for Minority Attorneys' by Law360 and achieving a perfect score on the 2016 Human Rights Campaign Corporate Equality Index.

Recruitment details

- Number of 1st year associates: 0
- Number of 2nd year associates: 3
- Clerking policy: No

Summer details

Summer program components:

Sedgwick LLP does not have a formal summer program at the moment; however, the firm considers extraordinary candidates on an individual basis for summer associate positions at several of our offices. Participants receive excellent mentoring and training designed to expose them to the key practice areas of the firm. They receive firsthand courtroom experience, challenging 'first year' assignments, continuous evaluation and feedback and the opportunity to get to know the firm's attorneys professionally and socially.

Largest Office: San Francisco, CA
Number of domestic offices: 12
Number of international offices: 2
Partners (US): 121
Associates (US): 129

Main Recruitment Contact: Michele Blay, Director of Attorney Recruiting
Hiring Partner: Steve Di Saia
Recruitment website: www.sedgwicklaw.com/careers/
Diversity officers: Catalina Sugayan, Susan Watson

Summer Salary 2017
1Ls: N/A
2Ls: Varies per office
Post 3Ls: N/A
1Ls hired? No

Firm Profiles

Seward & Kissel LLP

One Battery Park Plaza, New York, NY 10004
Tel: 212 574 1200   Fax: 212 480 8421
www.sewkis.com

Main areas of work

Investment management, corporate finance, global bank and institutional finance, litigation, maritime and transportation finance, capital markets and securities, business transactions, bankruptcy and corporate reorganization, real estate, taxation, trusts and estates, employee benefits, aviation finance, employment law, government enforcement and internal investigations and executive compensation.

Firm profile

Seward & Kissel offers our New York associates the broad experience and training of a large practice in the context of a moderately sized firm. We offer our Washington, DC associates a focused experience concentrating on our investment management, corporate finance and capital markets practices in the context of a small office environment.

Our associates have the opportunity to work on a wide range of challenging and stimulating matters within the practice areas of our particular offices.

Recruitment details

- Number of 1st year associates: 17
- Associate salaries: 1st year: $180,000
- Clerking policy: Case by case
- Number of 2nd year associates: 16
- 2nd year: $190,000

Law Schools attending for OCIs in 2017:

Our New York office participates in the following OCI programs: Albany, American, Boston College, Boston University, Brooklyn, Cardozo, Columbia, Cornell, Duke, Fordham, Georgetown, George Washington, Harvard, Midwest California Consortium, New York University, Tulane/Washington University/Vanderbilt Job Fair, Michigan, University of North Carolina, University of Pennsylvania, University of Virginia, and Vanderbilt

Our Washington, DC office participates in the following OCI programs: Boston College, Boston University, Georgetown, George Washington, University of Virginia, Washington & Lee

Summer details

Summer associate profile:

We rely heavily on our summer program for our hiring needs. The primary goals of the program are to provide summer associates with a realistic, broad-based view of our practice and an opportunity to become acquainted with our attorneys through our informal mentoring program, training sessions and social events.

Summer program components:

Assignments are from our practice areas.

Training: weekly seminars, practice group meetings and in-house training sessions. Feedback is given formally at the middle and end of the summer program.

Head Office: **New York, NY**
Number of domestic offices: **2**
Partners (US): **57**
Counsel (US): **21**
Associates (US): **104**

Main Recruitment Contact:
Royce Wain Akiva
Hiring Partner: **Jack Rigney**
Recruitment website:
www.sewkis.com

Summer Salary 2017
1Ls: **N/A**
2Ls: **$3,461/week**
Post 3Ls: **N/A**
1Ls hired? **No**
Can summers spend time in overseas offices? **N/A**
Summers 2017: **11 (10 in NY, 1 in DC)**
Offers/acceptances 2016:
18 offers, 18 acceptances (16 in NY, 2 in DC)

SEWARD & KISSEL LLP

Shearman & Sterling LLP

599 Lexington Avenue, New York, NY 10022
Tel: 212 848 4000   Fax: 212 848 7179
www.shearman.com

Main areas of work

Anti-corruption and Foreign Corrupt Practices Act, antitrust, capital markets, corporate governance, derivatives and structured products, environmental, executive compensation and employee benefits, finance, financial institutions advisory and financial regulatory, financial restructuring and insolvency, intellectual property, international arbitration, international trade and government relations, investment funds, litigation, mergers and acquisitions, project development and finance, real estate, sports, tax.

Firm profile

Shearman & Sterling LLP is a leading global law firm with approximately 850 lawyers in 20 offices in 13 countries around the world. Founded in 1873, Shearman & Sterling distinguishes itself by the way in which it harnesses the intellectual strength and deep experience of its lawyers across its extensive global footprint. The firm represents many of the world's leading corporations, financial institutions, emerging growth companies, governments and state-owned enterprises.

Recruitment details

- Number of 1st year associates: 62
- Associate salaries: 1st year: $180,000
- Clerking policy: Yes
- Number of 2nd year associates: 42
- 2nd year: $190,000

Law Schools attending for OCIs in 2017:

Shearman & Sterling LLP will be recruiting at the following schools or regional job fairs: American, BC, BU, Cardozo, Chicago, Columbia, Cornell, Duke (including SF regional job fair), Fordham, Georgetown, George Washington, Harvard, Howard, Michigan, NEBLSA job fair, Northwestern, NYU, Osgoode, Penn (including the SF regional job fair), Stanford, Texas, Toronto, Tulane, Washington University, Vanderbilt, UC- Berkeley, UC- Hastings, UCLA, USC, UVA, Yale. In addition, the firm has resume collections at a number of schools

Summer details

Summer associate profile:

We seek candidates who are bright, confident and enthusiastic about the practice of law and bring with them life, work, and educational experiences that will be highly valued by clients and colleagues alike. We also remain strongly committed to diversity and inclusion and overall excellence in our hiring. Finally, we expect that our associates will view collegiality and teamwork as important personal and firm values.

Summer program components:

Summer associates are given the opportunity to rotate through two practice groups. Senior and junior advisors are assigned during each rotation and, depending on the group, summer associates may attend client meetings, court hearings, depositions, or business trips. The firm has a robust training program for summer associates and also hosts a variety of social events.

Head Office: New York, NY
Number of domestic offices: 4
Number of international offices: 16
Worldwide revenue: $912,000,000

Main Recruitment Contact:
Trisha Weiss (Director of Legal Recruiting)
Hiring Partners: John Nathanson, Linda Rappaport
Recruitment website:
www.shearman.com
Diversity officers: John Cannon and Denise Grant, Co-Chairs, Diversity & Inclusion Committee

Summer Salary 2017
1Ls: $3,500/week
2Ls: $3,500/week
Post 3Ls: N/A
1Ls hired? TBD
Split summers offered? No
Can summers spend time in overseas office? Case by case
Summers 2017: 62
Offers/acceptances 2016:
72 offers (100% of 2Ls),
62 acceptances, some offers remain open

SHEARMAN & STERLING LLP

Sheppard, Mullin, Richter & Hampton LLP

333 South Hope Street, 43rd Floor, Los Angeles, CA 90071-1422
Tel: 213 620 1780
www.sheppardmullin.com

Main areas of work

Sheppard Mullin is a full service Global 100 firm. A broad range of practice areas, including counter-cyclical practices, has allowed the firm to succeed through up and down economic cycles. Primary areas include antitrust; business trial; corporate and securities; entertainment, technology and advertising; finance and bankruptcy; government contracts; intellectual property; labor and employment; real estate, land use/natural resources and environment; tax, ERISA and trusts and estates and white collar criminal defense. Clients are in industries ranging from aerospace and banking to entertainment and e-commerce and from real estate and retail to high tech and high fashion.

Firm profile

Founded in Los Angeles in 1927, there are now about 750 attorneys practicing in 15 offices (7 in California, and Chicago, New York, Washington, DC, Shanghai, Beijing, Seoul, Brussels and London). The firm remains a true partnership which governs itself through an elected, representative democracy. Stability is enhanced by skillful administration, excellent cost control and no firm debt. Core values include transparency in financial operations and governance, civility in the daily conduct of its business, advancement and celebration of diversity and inclusiveness and a vigorous pro bono program.

Recruitment details

- Number of 1st year associates: 30
- Associate salaries: 1st year: $180,000
- Clerking policy: Yes
- Number of 2nd year associates: 35
- 2nd year: $190,000

Law Schools attending for OCIs in 2017:

Berkeley, Columbia, Fordham, George Washington, George Mason, Georgetown, Harvard, Hastings, Howard, Loyola (Los Angeles), NYU, Southwestern, Stanford, UC Davis, UC Irvine, UCLA, USC, USD, USF, Virginia, Vanderbilt. Plus 3-4 job fairs (regional and/or diversity)

Summer details

Summer associate profile:

High academic achievement is a precondition to employment. But the firm is interested in more than that: it seeks associates who will succeed over the long term. It looks for associates who have the personal traits needed to become outstanding practicing lawyers: self-awareness, drive to succeed, capacity for hard work and an ability to work well with other people.

Summer program components:

The Summer Program gives students a realistic view of the way the firm practices throughout the year. Assignments include meaningful work on behalf of clients with partners and associates in litigation and/or transactional practice groups. All offices conduct clinical training programs. Pro bono projects are assigned to those who express an interest. Social events offer exposure to the geographic area of the particular office.

Head Office: Los Angeles, CA
Number of domestic offices: 10
Number of international offices: 5 (Shanghai, Beijing, Brussels, London & Seoul)
Worldwide revenue: $607,167,000
Partners (US): 336
Associates (US): 287

Main Recruitment Contact:
Sally Bucklin (Manager of Attorney Hiring)
Hiring Partner: Bess Sully (Chief Human Resources Officer)
Recruitment website:
www.sheppardmullin.com
Diversity officer: Carol Ross-Burnett

Summer Salary 2017
1Ls: N/A
2Ls: $3,462/week
1Ls hired? No
Split summers offered? No
Can summers spend time in overseas office? No
Summers 2017: 33
Offers/acceptances 2016:
28 offers, 28 acceptances

SheppardMullin

Sidley Austin LLP

One South Dearborn, Chicago, IL 60603
Tel: 312 853 7000 Fax: 312 853 7036

787 Seventh Avenue, New York, NY 10019
Tel: 212 839 5300 Fax: 212 839 5599

Main areas of work

Accountants and professional liability; antitrust/competition; banking and financial services; capital markets; communications regulatory; complex commercial litigation; consumer class actions; corporate governance and executive compensation; corporate reorganization and bankruptcy; emerging companies and venture capital; employee benefits and executive compensation; energy; environmental; ERISA litigation; Food, drug and medical device compliance and enforcement; food, drug and medical device regulatory; global finance; government strategies; healthcare; insurance; insurance disputes; intellectual property litigation; international arbitration; international trade; investment funds, advisers and derivatives; labor, employment and immigration; M&A; non-profit institutions; privacy, data security and information law; private equity; products liability; project finance and infrastructure; real estate; securities and derivatives enforcement and regulatory; securities and shareholder litigation; supreme court and appellate; tax; tax controversy; technology and IP transactions; transportation; trusts and estates; white collar: government litigation and investigations.

Firm profile

Sidley provides a broad range of legal services to meet the needs of our diverse client base. The strategic establishment of our offices in the key corporate and financial centers of the world has enabled us to represent a broad range of clients that includes multinational and domestic corporations, banks, funds and financial institutions. With over 1,900 lawyers in 20 offices around the world, talent and teamwork are central to Sidley's successful results for clients in all types of legal matters, from complex transactions to 'bet the company' litigation to cutting-edge regulatory issues.

Recruitment details

- Number of 1st year associates: 117
- Associate salaries: 1st year: $180,000
- Clerking policy: Yes
- Number of 2nd year associates: 135
- 2nd year: $190,000

Law Schools attending for OCIs in 2017:

Berkeley, Chicago, Columbia, Cornell, DePaul, Duke, Fordham, Georgetown, George Washington, Harvard, Howard, Houston, Illinois, Iowa, Chicago – Kent, Loyola, Loyola – LA, Michigan, Minnesota, New York University, Northwestern, Notre Dame, Pennsylvania, Santa Clara, Southern Methodist, Stanford, Texas, Toronto, UCLA, USC, Virginia, Washington University, Wisconsin, Yale

Summer details

Summer associate profile:

Sidley seeks candidates who have demonstrated academic success and possess strong leadership and interpersonal qualities. The firm looks for a diverse group of individuals who are motivated by highly sophisticated legal work practiced in a collegial and supportive environment.

Summer program components:

Sidley's summer associate program is an invaluable window into its practice and firm culture. Participants select projects that interest them and perform legal work under lawyer supervision. An essential component of Sidley's summer program is the opportunity to learn and develop professional skills. Hands-on training includes detailed reviews of each summer associate's work product, as well as more formal training programs such as writing seminars, a mock trial and a mock negotiation exercise. Each summer associate is assigned senior associates and partners to provide guidance and each participant receives a formal review at the midpoint of the summer program.

Head Offices: Chicago, IL; New York, NY
Number of domestic offices: 10
Number of international offices: 10
Worldwide revenue: $1,928,000,000
Partners (US): 586
Other lawyers (US): 988 (includes counsel and associates)

Main Recruitment Contact:
Jennifer L Connelly
Hiring Partners: Anthony J Aiello (CH), Kelly L C Kriebs (LA), John J Kuster (NY) and Rebecca K Wood (DC)
Recruitment website:
www.sidley.com/careers
Diversity officer: Sally L Olson

Summer Salary 2017
1Ls: $3,500/week
2Ls: $3,500/week
Post 3Ls: $3,500/week
Split summers offered? Case by case
Can summers spend time in overseas office? No
Summers 2017: 127
Offers/acceptances 2016:
173 offers, 153 acceptances to date

Firm Profiles

Simpson Thacher & Bartlett LLP

425 Lexington Avenue, New York, NY
Tel: 212 465 2000   Fax: 212 465 2502
Email: attorneyrecruiting@stblaw.com
www.simpsonthacher.com

Main areas of work

Clients in a wide array of industries and in jurisdictions around the world turn to Simpson Thacher to help them address their evolving business challenges. The firm is consistently ranked as one of the world's leading advisors for mergers and acquisitions, capital markets and banking activity, as well as private equity fund formation and investment management. The firm's litigation practice encompasses every type of complex litigation and is recognized as one of the most comprehensive, trial-ready litigation practices in the country.

Simpson Thacher also has leading innovative practices in the areas of antitrust, IP, tax, bankruptcy, real estate, executive compensation and employee benefits, exempt organizations and personal planning. Further, pro bono work is critical to the firm's identity and its record in this area is unparalleled.

Firm profile

Simpson Thacher & Bartlett LLP is one of the world's leading international law firms. The firm was established in 1884 and has more than 900 lawyers globally. Headquartered in New York City, the firm has offices in Beijing, Hong Kong, Houston, London, Los Angeles, Palo Alto, São Paulo, Seoul, Tokyo and Washington, DC. The firm provides coordinated legal advice and transactional capability to clients around the globe. Our focus on client needs is the hallmark of our practice and we value excellence in client service in all respects.

Recruitment details

- Number of 1st year associates: 97
- Associate salaries: 1st year: $180,000
- Clerking policy: Yes
- Number of 2nd year associates: 103
- 2nd year: $190,000

Law Schools attending for OCIs in 2017:

Berkeley, Brooklyn, Cardozo, Chicago, Columbia, Cornell, Davis, Duke, Emory Fordham, George Washington, Georgetown, Harvard, Howard, Michigan, NYU, Northwestern, Notre Dame, Pennsylvania, Santa Clara, St John's, Seton Hall, Stanford, Texas, Tulane, UCLA, USC, Vanderbilt, Virginia, Washington University, Yale

Summer details

Summer associate profile:

The firm looks for candidates with distinguished records of achievement, demonstrated leadership potential, a commitment to excellence and the ability to work cooperatively with clients and colleagues.

Summer program components:

The Simpson Thacher Summer Program is both challenging and satisfying. Summer associates work on assignments from all practice areas side by side with partners and associates on client projects of substantial complexity. Summer associates participate in frequent formal training programs geared to their needs and are also invited to attend other firmwide training programs. Summer associates have partner and associate mentors and are given prompt and specific feedback. At the end of the summer program, summer associates will have a thorough understanding of the firm's work and culture.

Head Office: New York, NY
Number of domestic offices: 5
Number of international offices: 6
Worldwide revenue: $1,301,539,056
Partners (US): 152
Associates (US): 605

Main Recruitment Contacts: Susan Osnato, Chief, Legal Recruiting & Professional Development; Michelle Las, Legal Recruiting Director
Hiring Partners: Nick Goldin, Greg Grogan and Krista Miniutti
Recruitment website:
www.simpsonthacher.com
Diversity officer: Natalia Martín, Director of Diversity

Summer Salary 2017
1Ls: $3,500/week
2Ls: $3,500/week
Post 3Ls: $3,500/week
1Ls hired? Yes
Split summers offered? Yes, case by case
Can summers spend time in overseas office? Yes, subject to need and relevant language skills
Summers 2017: 118
Offers/acceptances 2016:
129 offers, 105 acceptances;
10 open for 2017/2018

Firm Profiles

Skadden, Arps, Slate, Meagher & Flom LLP

4 Times Square, New York, NY 10036
Tel: 212 735 3000 Fax: 212 735 2000
www.skadden.com   Twitter: @skaddenrecruit

Main areas of work

Antitrust, banking, complex litigation and trials, complex mass torts/insurance litigation, corporate finance, corporate restructuring, energy and infrastructure projects, executive compensation and benefits, government enforcement and white collar crime, intellectual property and technology, international arbitration, investment management, mergers and acquisitions, real estate, regulatory, structured finance, tax, trusts and estates.

Firm profile

Skadden attorneys work on bet-the-company issues around the world for leading Fortune 500 corporations, financial institutions, governments and cultural, educational and charitable organizations. Communication and expertise across our offices enable us to provide unparalleled service to our clients. Our attorneys, spread among 22 inter-connected offices around the world, are engaged in more than 60 practice areas, many of which are specialized. We also encourage pro bono work, providing chargeable time credit. With fostering professional growth as a primary goal, our attorney development partners and Training Committee ensure that associates receive appropriate training and mentoring from the start of their careers. Our Diversity Committee promotes cross-cultural appreciation and competency through diversity and inclusion seminars, lunches, and our Facets diversity publication and lecture series. Our widely regarded summer associate program is designed to provide substantive practical skills training, exposure to various practices, as well as a sense of what it is like to be an attorney at Skadden.

Recruitment details

- Number of 1st year associates: 188
- Associate salaries: 1st year: $180,000
- Clerking policy: Yes
- Number of 2nd year associates: 201
- 2nd year: $190,000

Law Schools attending for OCIs in 2017:

Berkeley, Boston University, Brooklyn, Chicago, Columbia, Cornell, Duke, Fordham, Georgetown, George Washington, Harvard, Iowa, Michigan, NYU, Northwestern, Penn, Stanford, Texas, UCLA, USC, Vanderbilt, Virginia, Yale

Summer details

Summer associate profile:

The breadth of our practice and the success it has enjoyed is largely due to the capabilities of our attorneys. We look for candidates who combine intellectual ability with enthusiasm and creativity. Successful candidates display high academic achievement in their law school and undergraduate education. Law Journal and/or Moot Court participation are preferred.

Summer program components:

One of the most comprehensive programs of its kind, our Summer Associate Program (offered in our Boston, Chicago, Houston, Los Angeles, New York, Palo Alto, Washington, DC, Wilmington, London, Hong Kong, Toronto and Tokyo offices) drives our hiring efforts. Summer Associates are assigned to active deals and litigations, providing them with work experiences similar to those of full time associates. For more information visit: www.skadden.com/recruiting.

Head Office: New York, NY
Number of domestic offices: 8
Number of international offices: 14
Partners (US): 297
Counsel (US): 203
Associates (US): 896

Main Recruitment Contact: Carol Lee H Sprague
Hiring Partner: Howard L Ellin
Recruitment website: www.skadden.com/recruiting
Diversity officer: Melique Jones

Summer Salary 2017
1Ls: $3,500
2Ls: $3,500
1Ls hired? Yes – Skadden 1L Scholars Program
Split summers offered? Yes – splits must spend at least 8 weeks with Skadden for first half
Can summers spend time in overseas office? Case by case
Summers 2017: 216
Offers/acceptances 2016:
188 offers, 163 acceptances, 13 offers open for 2018 or later

Snell & Wilmer LLP

One Arizona Center, Phoenix, Arizona 85004
Tel: 602 382 6000   Email: Recruiting@swlaw.com
www.swlaw.com

Main areas of work

Appellate, banking, bankruptcy, business and finance, class action, commercial litigation, construction, election and political law, emerging businesses, employee benefits and executive compensation, environmental and natural resources, estate planning and taxation, financial services and securities, franchise, government investigations/criminal defense and government related litigation, healthcare, intellectual property, international, labor, mergers and acquisitions, municipal finance, professional liability, product liability, professional liability and tort liability, public utilities, legislation and real estate/land use.

Firm profile

Founded in 1938, Snell & Wilmer is a full service business law firm with more than 400 lawyers practicing in nine locations throughout the western United States and in Mexico, including Phoenix and Tucson, Arizona; Los Angeles and Orange County, California; Denver, Colorado; Las Vegas and Reno, Nevada; Salt Lake City, Utah; and Los Cabos, Mexico. The firm represents clients ranging from large, publicly traded corporations to small businesses, individuals and entrepreneurs. Snell & Wilmer and its lawyers have been recognized by clients and peers for exceptional legal skills, ethical and exemplary business practices with various distinguished awards.

Recruitment details

- Number of 1st year associates: 24
- Number of 2nd year associates: 13
- Associate salaries: 1st year: $115,000 - $160,000
- Clerking policy: Yes

Law Schools attending for OCIs in 2017:

Arizona State University; Brigham Young University; Notre Dame; University of Arizona; University of California Irvine; UCLA; University of Colorado; University of Denver; University of Iowa; University of Kansas; University of San Diego; University of Nevada Las Vegas; University of Southern California; University of Utah; Vanderbilt; Virginia; Pepperdine; Loyola Los Angeles; Washington University in St Louis; University of Michigan

Summer details

Summer associate profile:

Snell & Wilmer seeks candidates who not only demonstrate high academic achievement, but also are social, energetic, unique, genuine, motivated, have a sense of humor, and enjoy working with their friends and colleagues and are committed to their communities. We desire diverse individuals who want to resolve new and exciting legal challenges, who enjoy working as part of a team and who will uphold our valued firm culture. In other words, we want great people who will become great lawyers.

Summer program components:

The firm appoints several senior associates to coordinate the program and assign summer associate projects. In addition, each summer associate is assigned a mentor, a partner reader and a reality partner. Summer associate mentors are responsible for making the summer a positive experience for each summer associate. Partner readers provide invaluable feedback on two written assignments a summer associate completes. The "Reality Snell & Wilmer" program matches summer associates with a partner who brings them into other cases and transactions, as needed, to simulate the day-to-day reality of working as an attorney.

Head Office: Phoenix, AZ
Number of domestic offices: 8
Number of international offices: 1
Partners (US): 210
Associates (US): 147

Main Recruitment Contact:
Abigail Raddatz, Director of Attorney Recruiting and Diversity
Hiring Partners: Adam E Lang, Anne M Meyer
Recruitment website: www.swlaw.com/careers
Diversity officers: Greg Gautam and Roxanne Veliz

Summer Salary 2017
1Ls: $2,211-$3,077/week
2Ls: $2,211-$3,077/week
Post 3Ls: $2,211-$3,077/week
1Ls hired? Case-by-case
Split summers offered? Case-by-case
Can summers spend time in overseas office? No
Summers 2017: 23
Offers/acceptances 2016:
29 offers, 26 acceptances

Squire Patton Boggs

4900 Key Tower, 127 Public Square, Cleveland, Ohio 44114
Tel: 216 479 8500　Fax: 216 479 8780
www.squirepattonboggs.com

Main areas of work

Aerospace, defense and government services; automotive; aviation; brands and consumer products; business immigration; chemicals; communications; competition – antitrust; construction and engineering; corporate; data privacy and cybersecurity; energy and natural resources; environmental, safety and health; financial services; government investigations and white collar; healthcare; hospitality and leisure; industrial products; infrastructure; institutional investors; intellectual property and technology; international dispute resolution; international trade; labor and employment; Latin America; life sciences; litigation; media and advertising; pensions; private investment funds; public and infrastructure finance; public policy; real estate; restructuring and insolvency; retail; sports and entertainment; tax credit finance and community development; tax strategy and benefits; transportation, shipping and logistics.

Firm profile

Squire Patton Boggs offers the opportunity to join one of the strongest, most geographically diverse law firms in the world. With 46 offices in 21 countries, our global legal practice is in the markets where our clients do business. We have a team of more than 1,500 lawyers. Our client base spans every type of business, both private and public. We advise a diverse mix of clients, from Fortune 100 and FTSE 100 corporations to emerging companies and from individuals to local and national governments.

Recruitment details

- Number of 1st year associates: 15
- Clerking policy: Yes
- Number of 2nd year associates: 14

Law Schools attending for OCIs in 2017:

American, Arizona, ASU, Case, Cincinnati, Cleveland – Marshall, Colorado, CUA, Denver, George Mason, Georgetown, GW Law, Harvard, Howard, Maryland, Michigan, Ohio State, UNC, UVA

Summer details

Summer associate profile:

Squire Patton Boggs is looking for summer associates with outstanding academic credentials, excellent communication skills, common sense, creativity, a strong work ethic and an ability to cultivate long-term relationships with our clients and colleagues.

Summer program components:

A range of valuable experiences is structured around our three global messages:

Commercial: You will be given the opportunity to work side by side with our partners, attending depositions, hearings, deal negotiations and trials. In addition, you will cover legal writing and research, public speaking, negotiation and advocacy techniques.

Connected: You will be encouraged to attend practice group meetings and associate training programs to build your network of contacts within the business.

Committed: To get real value out of your program you will enjoy a collegial atmosphere with the support of a mentor for the duration of your summer with us.

Founding Office: Cleveland, OH
Number of domestic offices: 17
Number of international offices: 29
Worldwide revenue: $983,100,000
Partners (US): 250
Associates (US): 257
Other Attorneys (US): 164

Main Recruitment Contact:
Crystal L Arnold
Hiring Partner: Aneca E Lasley
Recruitment website:
www.squirepattonboggs.com/careers
Diversity co-chairs: Frederick R Nance, Alethia N Nancoo and Traci H Rollins

Summer Salary 2017
1Ls hired? Yes
Split summers offered? Case by case
Can summers spend time in overseas office? Yes
Summers 2017: 31
Offers/acceptances 2016:
1Ls 4 offers, 3 acceptances
2Ls 17 offers, 15 acceptances

Firm Profiles

Sterne, Kessler, Goldstein & Fox P.L.L.C.

1100 New York Avenue NW, Suite 600, Washington, D.C. 20005
Tel: 202 371 2600   Fax: 202 371 2540
Email: kobrien@skgf.com
www.skgf.com

Main areas of work

Intellectual property.

Firm profile

Sterne, Kessler, Goldstein & Fox is dedicated to the protection, transfer, and enforcement of intellectual property rights. The firm's lawyers have the interdisciplinary background needed to develop, protect, and enforce valuable property rights for its clients. Most of Sterne Kessler's legal professionals hold an advanced level degree, including approximately 55 with a master's degree and over 55 with a doctorate in science or engineering. The firm's team of attorneys, registered patent agents, student associates, and technical specialists include some of the country's most respected practitioners of intellectual property law. The firm was founded in 1978, is based in Washington, DC, and has grown to be one of the largest and highly regarded IP specialty firms in the United States and abroad.

Recruitment details

- Number of 1st year associates: 12
- Associate salaries: 1st year: $180,000
- Clerking policy: Yes
- Number of 2nd year associates: 10
- 2nd year: $190,000

Law Schools attending for OCIs in 2017:

American University College of Law, George Mason University Antonin Scalia Law School, George Washington University School of Law, Loyola University Chicago School of Law (Patent Law Interview "PLI" Program), Howard University School of Law, Catholic University of America Columbus School of Law, University of Baltimore School of Law, University of Maryland School of Law, Georgetown University Law Center

Summer details

Summer associate profile:

Sterne Kessler seeks students with a bachelor's degree in science and/or engineering. All applicants must have at least a 3.0 cumulative GPA in undergraduate, graduate, and law school studies. United States Patent and Trademark Office and/or other industry work experience is a plus. Teamwork, motivation, collaboration, work ethic, and universal respect are core values of the firm.

Summer program components:

Each summer associate is assigned a senior-level and junior associate to help acclimate them to the firm and to answer any questions he/she may have during his/her tenure. Summer associates receive a full week of training in IP prosecution and litigation by experienced practitioners before ever taking an assignment. While hiring decisions lay at the practice group level, summer associates often have the opportunity to work on assignments from attorneys in other practice groups. Summer associates attend weekly practice group lunches where substantive topics are discussed and they participate in other professional development and technical training. Over the past several years, the firm has been consistently rated as a *"best place to work"* based on attorney and staff surveys conducted by *The Washington Post* and *The Washington Business Journal*.

Head Office: **Washington, D.C.**
Number of domestic offices: **1**
Number of international offices: **0**
Worldwide revenue: **WND**
Partners (US): **49**
Associates (US): **87**

Main Recruitment Contact: **Kerrie O'Brien**
Hiring Partner: **Paul Ainsworth**
Recruitment website:
Visit the firm's page on LinkedIn
Diversity officer: **Gaby Longsworth, Chair, Diversity Committee**

Summer Salary 2017
1Ls: **$3,100**
2Ls: **$3,400**
Post 3Ls: **N/A**
1Ls hired? **Yes**
Split summers offered? **CBC**
Can summers spend time in overseas office? **N/A**
Summers 2017: **8**
Offers/acceptances 2016:
4 offers, 4 acceptances

Sterne Kessler Goldstein Fox
ATTORNEYS AT LAW

Firm Profiles

Stroock & Stroock & Lavan LLP

180 Maiden Lane, New York, NY 10038
Tel: 212 806 5400   Fax: 212 806 6006
Email: legalrecruiting@stroock.com
www.stroock.com

Main areas of work

Primary practice areas include real estate; financial restructuring; investment management/private funds; commodities, energy and corporate transactions; insurance; financial services litigation & enforcement; government affairs, goverment contracts & national security; entertainment and intellectual property; personal client services and regulatory support.

Firm profile

Stroock is multi-disciplinary law firm known for 140 years as a market-leading advisor to the financial services and investment communities and for its special focus in financial restructuring, real estate, investment management/private funds and litigation/enforcement.

Recruitment details

- Number of 1st year associates: 14
- Number of 2nd year associates: 14
- Associate salaries: 1st year: $180,000
- 2nd year: $190,000
- Clerking policy: A $50,000 clerkship bonus is provided upon completion of a judicial clerkship with a federal court or state judge in the highest court of that jurisdiction.

Law Schools attending for OCIs in 2017:

New York Office: Boston C, Boston U, Brooklyn, Cardozo, Columbia, Cornell, Fordham, Georgetown, Harvard, Michigan, NEBLSA, NY Law School, NYU, Penn Los Angeles Office: Loyola, UCLA, USC

Summer details

Summer associate profile:

Successful summer associates are self-starters, quickly take ownership of their matters and are able to function at a high level early in their careers. While not a prerequisite, those with prior work experience and those who have held leadership positions typically do well at Stroock.

Summer program components:

The firm's program includes a flexible work assignment system, billable work across different practice areas, extensive training programs, pro bono opportunities, access to Diversity/Affinity Groups' activities and social events. In addition, each summer associate has a partner and an associate mentor, as well as a first-year office mate, which allows summer associates to quickly build relationships with and work alongside Stroock attorneys. Summer associates receive formal feedback at the mid-point and at the end of the summer, as well as when they complete assignments.

Head Office: New York, NY
Number of domestic offices: 4
Number of international offices: 0
Worldwide revenue: $270,700,000
Partners (US): 88
Associates (US): 204

Main Recruitment Contacts:
Halle Schargel and Patty Jeydel
Hiring Partner: Nicole Runyan
Recruitment website:
www.stroock.com
Diversity officer: Yakiry Adal

Summer Salary 2017
1Ls: $3,461/week
2Ls: $3,461/week
Post 3Ls: $3,461/week
1Ls hired? Case by case
Split summers offered? No
Can summers spend time in overseas office? No
Summers 2017: 14
Offers/acceptances 2016:
14 offers, 14 acceptances

STROOCK

Firm Profiles

Sullivan & Cromwell LLP

125 Broad Street, New York, NY 10004
Tel: 212 558 4000   Fax: 212 558 3588
www.sullcrom.com

Main areas of work

Sullivan & Cromwell brings a multidisciplinary approach to providing the fullest and most comprehensive legal advice to our clients. Our global practice includes four main groups: general practice (corporate), litigation, tax and estates and personal.

Our lawyers are trained to be generalists through broad exposure to a wide range of challenging legal matters, many of which have a significant cross-border component. A substantial number of S&C's clients are non-US commercial enterprises and government entities and many of our US clients retain us for international matters. Our lawyers serve our clients through a network of 12 offices in New York, Washington, DC, Los Angeles, Palo Alto, London, Paris, Frankfurt, Tokyo, Hong Kong, Beijing, Melbourne and Sydney.

Firm profile

S&C has the most broadly and deeply trained collection of lawyers in the world. They thrive in our working environment, which is characterized by commitment to clients, leadership, professional development, broad experience, teamwork and commitment to community. Associates at S&C typically acquire leadership skills as lawyers more quickly than they would at other law firms, as they are given early responsibility for managing transactions, counseling clients and representing their interests in dealings with other parties. To supplement this on-the-job experience, we provide comprehensive training programs for associates as well as formal mentoring programs.

Recruitment details

- Number of 1st year associates: 76
- Associate salaries: 1st year: $180,000
- Clerking policy: Yes
- Number of 2nd year associates: 91
- 2nd year: $190,000

Law Schools attending for OCIs in 2017:

S&C interviews at top law schools around the country. Our lawyers are alumni of more than 135 law schools.

Summer details

Summer associate profile:

We are actively seeking people whose intellect, character, motivation and other attributes promise to make them outstanding lawyers.

Summer program components:

Training/Orientation: All summer associates participate in a formal orientation program, as well as a wide variety of training programs and skills workshops.

Advising/Assigning/Evaluations: Summer associates are assigned a partner advisor and an associate advisor, from whom they receive assignments. They are also matched with a junior associate, who is there to help with day-to-day matters at the firm. In addition, each summer associate is assigned to an Associate Development Partner, who oversees the distribution of summer associate assignments.

Events: Every summer, S&C organizes a variety of events, including professional opportunities, social events and charitable events.

Head Office: **New York, NY**
Number of domestic offices: **4**
Number of international offices: **8**
Partners (US): **137**
Associates (US): **454**

Main Recruitment Contact: **Milana L Hogan, Chief Legal Recruiting & Professional Development Officer**
Hiring Partner: **Sergio J Galvis**
Recruitment website:
https://careers.sullcrom.com
Diversity officers: **David Braff and Tracy Richelle High, Partners, Co-Chairs of the Diversity Committee**

Summer Salary 2017
1Ls: **$3,500/week**
2Ls: **$3,500/week**
Post 3Ls: **$3,500/week**
1Ls hired? **Yes**
Split summers offered? **Yes**
Can summers spend time in overseas office? **Yes**
Summers 2017: **134**

SULLIVAN & CROMWELL LLP

Thompson & Knight LLP

1722 Routh Street Suite 1500 Dallas, TX 75201
Tel: 214 969 1700
Fax: 214 969 1751
Email: lauren.mccann@tklaw.com
www.tklaw.com

Main areas of work

Bankruptcy and restructuring; corporate and securities; employment and labor; environmental; finance; government and regulatory; healthcare; intellectual property; oil, gas, and energy; real estate and real estate finance; tax; trial.

Firm profile

Established in 1887, Thompson & Knight is a full-service law firm with more than 300 attorneys that provides legal solutions to clients and communities around the world. The Firm has strong Texas roots, client-focused capabilities on the East and West Coasts, and strategic locations internationally in the Americas, North Africa, and Europe.

Our dedication to clients defines us well. According to *Chambers USA* 2015, Thompson & Knight has *"an enviable client base,"* which includes the four largest US airlines, two of the largest medical device companies in the world, 13 of the 20 largest US oil and gas exploration and production companies, and the largest real estate investment trust in the world, among others.

Our culture – the key reason for our success – emphasizes teamwork and an unparalleled commitment to excellence. Through our collective knowledge, our relationships, our high ethics, our team approach, and our dedication to the community, we make a positive impact on the people we serve. For more information on the firm, please visit our website at www.tklaw.com.

Recruitment details

- Number of 1st year associates: 10
- Associate salaries: 1st year: $180,000
- Clerking policy: yes
- Number of 2nd year associates: 11
- 2nd year: $190,000

Law Schools attending for OCIs in 2017:

Law Schools: Baylor University; Duke University; LSU; South Texas College of Law; Southern Methodist University; Texas Tech University; University of Houston; Harvard University; University of Texas; Tulane University

Job Fairs: Lavender Law Career Fair; Southeastern Minority Job Fair; Sunbelt Minority Recruitment Program; Texas Interview Program; On Tour Job Fair; University of Oklahoma

Summer details

Summer associate profile:

Thompson & Knight's Summer Associate program is our principal source of hiring new Associates. Thompson & Knight has a collegial, team-oriented, and supportive culture. We offer challenging and fulfilling work in an atmosphere of mutual respect and appreciation. Our program provides an unparalleled educational experience and creates lasting relationships between our attorneys and Summer Associates, the future of our firm.

Summer program components:

Summer Associates are assigned two practice areas to clerk in during their clerkship. Our Summer Associate Program is 6-8 weeks for 1L law students and 8-10 weeks for 2L law students. They are also given a Partner and Associate advisor in each section during their time here. The Summer Associates receive a wide range of work and training opportunities.

Head Office: **Dallas, TX**
Number of domestic offices: **6**
Number of international offices: **5**
Worldwide revenue: **$213.4 million**
Partners (US): **152**
Associates (US): **81**

Main Recruitment Contact:
Lauren McCann
Hiring Partner: **Jessica Hammons**
Recruitment website:
www.tklaw.com
Diversity Officer: **Nichole Olajuwon**

Summer Salary 2017
1Ls: **$3,462/week**
2Ls: **$3,462/week**
Post 3Ls: **N/A**
1Ls hired? **Yes**
Split summers offered? **No, 1st half only**
Can summers spend time in overseas office? **No**
Summers 2017: **18**
Offers/acceptances 2016: **8**

Vedder Price

222 North LaSalle Street, Chicago, IL 60601
Tel: 312 609 7500   Fax: 312 609 5005
Email: info@vedderprice.com
www.vedderprice.com

Main areas of work

Corporate, labor and employment, litigation.

Firm profile

Vedder Price is a thriving general-practice law firm with a proud tradition of maintaining long-standing relationships with its clients, many of whom have been with the firm since its founding in 1952. With approximately 300 attorneys and growing, Vedder Price serves clients of all sizes and in virtually all industries from offices in Chicago, New York, Washington, DC, London, San Francisco, Los Angeles and Singapore.

Recruitment details

- Number of 1st year associates: 11
- Associate salaries: 1st year: $180,000
- Clerking policy: No
- Number of 2nd year associates: 6
- 2nd year: $185,000 – $190,000

Law Schools attending for OCIs in 2017:

Brooklyn, Chicago-Kent, Cornell, Fordham, George Washington, Georgetown, Loyola, Northwestern, Notre Dame, University of Chicago, University of Illinois, University of Michigan

Summer details

Summer associate profile:

Vedder Price recruits candidates with strong academic credentials, excellent verbal and written communication skills, initiative and enthusiasm. Ideal candidates have a demonstrated interest in the practice area they are applying for, as evidenced by relevant course work and/or prior work experience. As Summer Associates will interact immediately with senior shareholders and clients, executive presence and maturity are valued.

Summer program components:

Summer Associates are integrated quickly into the practice area they are joining, through substantive work assignments, observation opportunities and training sessions. Summer Associates will work with an assigned associate advisor to receive practical advice and guidance. A firm-wide summer program orientation is hosted in Chicago during the first week of the program for the full summer class to meet each other and engage with Firm Management. There are two formal review sessions, one at mid-summer and the other at the completion of the program, incorporating written attorney feedback regarding each completed project. Social events are frequent, both office-wide and in small groups, to ensure Summer Associates enjoy the collegiality of the firm.

Head Office: **Chicago, IL**
Number of domestic offices: **5**
Number of international offices: **2**
Worldwide revenue: **$239.8 million**
Shareholders (US): **158**
Associates (US): **111**

Main Recruitment Contacts: **Amanda Brummel and Elise Rippe, Managers of Legal Recruiting**
Hiring Shareholder: **Michael J. Waters**
Recruitment website:
www.vedderprice.com/careers
Diversity officer: **Margo Wolf O'Donnell, Shareholder**

Summer Salary 2017
1Ls: **$3,462**
2Ls: **$3,462**
Post 3Ls: **N/A**
1Ls hired? **Yes (Diversity Scholar in the Chicago Office)**
Split summers offered? **No**
Can summers spend time in overseas office? **No**
Summers 2017: **13**
Offers/acceptances 2016: **13 offers, 12 acceptances**

Venable LLP

600 Massachusetts Ave, NW, Washington, DC 20001
Tel: 202 344 4000   Fax: 202 344 8300
www.venable.com

Main areas of work

Government and regulatory affairs, corporate law and business transactions, complex litigation, technology and intellectual property.

Firm profile

Venable is an *American Lawyer* 100 law firm. With almost 700 attorneys in nine offices across the country, we are strategically positioned to advance our clients' business objectives in the US and abroad. Our clients rely on Venable's proven capabilities in all areas of corporate and business law, complex litigation, intellectual property, and regulatory and government affairs. Venable attorneys, many of whom have served in senior corporate, regulatory, prosecutorial, legislative and executive branch positions, understand the needs of their clients.

Recruitment details

- Number of 1st year associates: 35
- Associate salaries: 1st year: $180,000
- Number of 2nd year associates: 34
- Clerking policy: Yes

Law Schools attending for OCIs in 2017:

American University, Benjamin N. Cardozo School of Law, Berkley Law, Brooklyn Law School, Univ. of Baltimore, Catholic University, Cornell, UC Davis, Duke, Fordham, George Mason, Georgetown, George Washington, Harvard, UC Hastings, Howard, UCI Law, Loyola Law School (LA), UCLA, Univ. of Maryland, Univ. of Michigan, New York Law School, NYU, Univ. of Pennsylvania, Univ. of Richmond, Univ. of San Francisco, USC, Stanford, Vanderbilt, UVA, and William & Mary. We will also attend the Southeastern Minority Job Fair, Mid-Atlantic BLSA Job Fair, Western Region BLSA Job Fair, Northeast Region BLSA Job Fair, and Lavender Law Job Fair

Summer details

Summer associate profile:

We consider candidates whose personal and academic achievements demonstrate a commitment to excellence, who act with integrity, and who want to help clients solve problems in a large law firm environment.

Summer program components:

In 2015, Venable's summer associate program was ranked #4 Best Overall Summer Associate Program and #1 Best Prepares for Practice by *Vault*. Our summer associate program is designed to give our summer associates a realistic depiction of everyday life as a junior associate. Each summer associate is assigned a partner mentor and an associate mentor. Summer associates receive real work assignments on behalf of real clients – the same types of assignments our junior associates receive throughout the year. Assignments come from a mix of practice areas, and are supplemented with "take-alongs". Each assignment is reviewed after it is completed and each summer associate receives a formal midsummer and end of summer review by a member of the Hiring Committee. In addition to fun, local events, there are informal dinners, happy hours, and "take a partner to lunch" opportunities to get to know our attorneys. Venable also provides professional development workshops, such as legal writing, communication and time management, to the summer associates during the course of the program.

Head Office: Washington, DC
Number of domestic offices: 9
Worldwide revenue: $498,500,000
Partners (US): 295
Associates (US): 250

Main Recruitment Contact: Ms Kera M Wise, Senior Director of Attorney Recruiting
Hiring Partner: Mr Robert J Bolger, Jr
Recruitment website:
www.venable.com/careers/
Diversity officers: Nora E Garrote, Kathleen S Hardway

Summer Salary 2017
1Ls: N/A
2Ls: $3460/week
Post 3Ls: N/A
1Ls hired? No
Split summers offered? No
Can summers spend time in overseas office? N/A
Summers 2017: 35
Offers/acceptances 2016:
33 offers, 32 acceptances

VENABLE® LLP

Vinson & Elkins LLP

1001 Fannin Street, Suite 2500, Houston, TX 77002-6760
Tel: 713 758 2222 Fax: 713 758 2346
www.velaw.com

Main areas of work

Antitrust; appellate; complex commercial litigation; condemnation; construction; employment, labor and OSHA; energy litigation; energy regulatory; energy transactions / projects; environmental and natural resources; finance; government contracts; government investigations and white collar; intellectual property; international dispute resolution; M&A/capital markets; media and entertainment; private equity; professional liability; real estate; REITs, restructuring and reorganization; securities litigation/regulation; tax – executive compensation and benefits.

Firm profile

Collaborating seamlessly across 16 offices worldwide, Vinson & Elkins LLP provides outstanding client service. Our lawyers are committed to excellence, offering clients experience in handling their transactions, investments, projects and disputes across the globe. Established in Houston in 1917, the firm's time-tested role as trusted advisor has made V&E a go-to law firm for many of the world's leading businesses. We bring competitive strength, insight and know-how to guide our clients through their most complex transactions and litigation.

Recruitment details

- Number of 1st year associates: 57
- Associate salaries: 1st year: $180,000
- Clerking policy: Yes
- Number of 2nd year associates: 37
- 2nd year: $190,000

Law Schools attending for OCIs in 2017:

Columbia, Cornell, Duke, Fordham, George Washington, Georgetown, Harvard, Howard, LSU, Loyola University, Patent Law Program, NYU, Northwestern, South Texas, SMU, Stanford, The University of Texas, Tulane, UC Berkeley, University of Chicago, University of Houston, University of Maryland, University of Michigan, University of Pennsylvania, University of Richmond, UVA, Vanderbilt, Washington University, Washington & Lee, William & Mary, Yale

Summer details

Summer associate profile:

Vinson & Elkins hires talented and highly motivated individuals who desire a sophisticated legal practice.

We look for candidates who take initiative, offer diverse perspectives, are innovative and will enjoy working alongside top lawyers in a friendly and collegial environment.

Summer program components:

V&E's "one firm" mentality offers summer associates the opportunity to work on cross-office projects from a variety of practice areas of interest. As a summer associate, you'll experience hands-on legal training, develop mentoring relationships and get an understanding of what it is like to practice law at Vinson & Elkins.

Head Office: Houston, TX
Number of domestic offices: 8
Number of international offices: 8
Worldwide revenue: $653,901,000
Partners (US): 210
Associates (US): 316

Main Recruitment Contact: Gretchen Rollins, Director of Entry-Level Hiring
Hiring Partner: Doug Bland
Recruitment website:
www.velaw.com/careers
Diversity officer: Renate Wagner, Director of Attorney Communications & Initiatives

Summer Salary 2017
1Ls: $3,462/week
2Ls: $3,462/week
Post 3Ls: $3,462/week
1Ls hired? Yes
Split summers offered? 10 week program, varies by office
Can summers spend time in overseas office? Case by case
Summers 2017: 95
Offers/acceptances 2016:
61 offers, 43 acceptances

Vinson&Elkins LLP

Waller

511 Union Street, Suite 2700, Nashville, TN 37219
Tel: 615 244 6380   Fax: 615 244 6804
www.wallerlaw.com

Main areas of work

Waller is a full-service general practice firm that advises clients across a spectrum of industries including healthcare, financial services, retail, hospitality, automotive, manufacturing, technology, media and entertainment, real estate, telecommunications and utilities. The firm prides itself on providing creative, cost-effective legal services and solutions to our clients, and providing advice and counsel in core legal areas such as corporate, M&A, litigation and dispute resolution, commercial finance, securities, bankruptcy and restructuring, environmental, intellectual property, real estate, tax, regulatory compliance, government investigations and government relations.

Recruitment details

- Number of 1st year associates: 7
- Number of 2nd year associates: 9
- Associate salaries: 1st year: $115,500
- Clerking policy: Yes

Summer details

Summer associate profile:

Waller recruits students who are diverse in thought, background and education, especially those with strong ties to the four Southeastern cities in which we are located. Individuals who have a record of academic excellence and are motivated to learn and be integrated in a collegial environment will excel at Waller.

Summer program components:

Waller's Summer Program is a hybrid of a standard summer program and key elements from our former internship. This model combines the cutting edge mentoring and training afforded by the learning-based modules from our prior Schola2Juris program with the opportunity to engage in live matters and other assignments with attorneys across all practice areas and offices.

Based on completed client matters, the educational modules that comprise Waller's Summer Program offer students firsthand experience with actual assignments and client relationships and provide tremendous insight into the students' future roles as junior and mid-level associates.

During the program, each summer associate will work closely with two mentors, a partner and a senior associate, who will provide structured feedback on each work assignment and throughout the module process. Summer associates are not relegated to one practice group, but are exposed to various projects across the firm's eight core practice areas. Summer associates will complete two different practice-specific projects developed from historical client matters. The module projects are substantive assignments designed to have summer associates follow the lifecycle of a client matter – giving a better overview of an entire project than could typically be gained in a few weeks' observation. In addition, Summer associates will contribute to current client matters and have opportunities to attend depositions, trials, hearings, negotiations and client conferences. Throughout the program, numerous social functions afford opportunities to get to know Waller partners and associates on a personal level.

Head Office: Nashville, TN
Number of domestic offices: 4
Number of international offices: 0
Partners (US): 116
Associates (US): 107

Main Recruitment Contacts:
Bobby Weiss/Michelle Parsons
Hiring Partner: Tera Rica Murdock
Recruitment website:
www.wallerlaw.com/join-us

Summer Salary 2017
1Ls: $1,650/week
2Ls: $2,000/week
1Ls hired? Yes
Split summers offered? Yes
Can summers spend time in overseas office? N/A
Summers 2017: 12
Offers/acceptances 2016:
13 offers, 6 acceptances

Firm Profiles

Weil, Gotshal & Manges LLP

767 Fifth Avenue, New York, NY 10153
Tel: 212 310 8000 Fax: 212 310 8007
www.weil.com

Main areas of work

The firm offers legal counsel in more than two dozen practices areas categorized by the following groups: business finance and restructuring, corporate, litigation and tax.

Firm profile

Founded in 1931, Weil, Gotshal & Manges LLP has been a preeminent provider of legal services for more than 80 years. With approximately 1,100 lawyers in offices on three continents, Weil has been a pioneer in establishing a geographic footprint that has allowed the firm to partner with clients wherever they do business. The firm's four departments, corporate, litigation, business finance and restructuring, and tax, executive compensation and benefits, and more than two dozen practice groups are consistently recognized as leaders in their respective fields. Weil has become a highly visible leader among major law firms for its innovative diversity and pro bono initiatives, the product of a comprehensive and long-term commitment which has ingrained these values into our culture. Our proven, demonstrated experience allows the firm to provide clients with unmatched legal services. Please see www.weil.com for more information, including awards and rankings.

Recruitment details

- Number of 1st year associates: 84
- Associate salaries: 1st year: $180,000
- Clerking policy: Yes
- Number of 2nd year associates: 70
- 2nd year: $190,000

Law Schools attending for OCIs in 2017:

Weil has a diversified approach to its recruiting process. Firm-wide, Weil interviews at over 45 law schools and job fairs and participates in resume collection programs at over 10 other law schools. For a complete list, please visit careers.weil.com

Summer details

Summer associate profile:

Weil's summer associate program provides an exceptional opportunity for outstanding law students from across the nation to explore a career in the practice of law. Weil seeks candidates with exceptional credentials, both in terms of qualifications and character.

Summer program components:

Summer associates may work in a total of one to three departments of their choice. They are assigned to active transactional and litigation matters and attend client meetings, negotiations, depositions and court hearings. This enables them to gain a much clearer idea of their choice of future practice area and obtain a realistic view of what it is like to practice law at the firm. Weil organizes special seminars during the summer to discuss particular fields of specialization and topics of interest to law students and to provide training in such areas as negotiation, litigation and writing skills. The firm assigns both associate and partner mentors whose role is to guide the summer associate throughout his or her summer experience, both personally and professionally. Feedback is a critical element of the summer experience. Assigning attorneys regularly evaluate the summer associate's performance and written product, in much the same way that a senior attorney reviews a junior attorney's work. The summer associate's performance is formally evaluated twice during the summer.

Head Office: New York, NY
Number of domestic offices: 8
Number of international offices: 11
Worldwide revenue: $1.264 billion
Partners (US): 198
Associates (US): 517

Main Recruitment Contact:
Wesley Powell
Hiring Partners: Joshua Amsel and Jackie Cohen
Recruitment website:
careers.weil.com
Diversity officer: Meredith Moore

Summer Salary 2017
1Ls: $3,462/week
2Ls: $3,462/week
Post 3Ls: $3,462/week
1Ls hired? Case by case
Split summers offered? Case by case
Can summers spend time in overseas office? Case by case
Summers 2017: 136 (including 1Ls)
Offers/acceptances 2016:
82 offers, 69 acceptances
(excluding 1Ls & Judicial Clerks)

Firm Profiles

667

White & Case LLP

1221 Avenue of the Americas, New York, NY 10020
Tel: 212 819 8200   Fax: 212 354 8113
www.whitecase.com

Main areas of work

Antitrust, asset finance, banking, capital markets, commercial litigation, financial restructuring and insolvency, intellectual property, international arbitration, mergers and acquisitions, private equity, pro bono, project finance, tax, trade and white collar.

Firm profile

White & Case is a global law firm with longstanding offices in the markets that matter today. Our on-the-ground experience, our cross-border integration and our depth of local, US and English-qualified lawyers help our clients work with confidence in any one market or across many. We guide our clients through difficult issues, bringing our insight and judgment to each situation. Our innovative approaches create original solutions to our clients' most complex domestic and multijurisdictional deals and disputes. By thinking on behalf of our clients every day, we anticipate what they want, provide what they need and build lasting relationships. We do what it takes to help our clients achieve their ambitions.

Recruitment details

- Associate salaries: 1st year: $180k/$174k ($180k in BOS, LA, NY, SV, DC; $174k in MI)
- 2nd year: $190k/$180k ($190k in BOS, LA, NY, SV, DC; $180k in MI)
- Clerking policy: Yes

Law Schools attending for OCIs in 2017:

American, Bay Area Diversity, Berkeley, Boston College, Boston University, Chicago, Columbia, Cornell, Duke, Florida, Fordham, George Washington, Georgetown, Harvard, Howard, Irvine, Loyola, Loyola Patent Fair, McGill, Miami, Michigan, Mid-Atlantic BLSA, Northeast BLSA, Northwestern, Notre Dame, NYU, Penn, Pepperdine, San Francisco IP Job Fair, Stanford, Toronto, UCLA, USC, Vanderbilt, Virginia, Yale

Summer details

Summer associate profile:

We look for highly motivated individuals with excellent academic credentials, significant personal achievements and a strong commitment to the practice of law in a global and diverse law firm. Fluency in any second language is a plus.

Summer program components:

We pride ourselves on giving summer associates real work for real clients with real deadlines. You will have a full curriculum of training programs in addition to getting hands-on experience working side by side with our lawyers. Our assignment coordinators ensure that you receive exposure to a variety of work that is of interest to you, including pro bono matters. In addition to informal discussions, two formal reviews provide timely and meaningful feedback. Mentors are available to you throughout the summer. One of the highlights is the Summer Associate Conference that takes place in the NY office and provides an opportunity for our US summers to meet each other and learn more about the Firm, our people and our culture.

Head office: **New York, NY**
Number of domestic offices: **6**
Number of international offices: **34**
Worldwide revenue: **$1,630,800,000**
Partners (US): **203**
Associates (US): **450**

Main Recruitment Contact:
Beth Johnson
Hiring Partner: **Brenda Dieck**
Recruitment website:
http://uslawcareers.whitecase.com
Diversity officer: **Maja Hazell**

Summer Salary 2017
1Ls: **$3,500/week in LA, NY, SV, DC; $3,346 in MI**
2Ls: **$3,500/week in LA, NY, SV, DC; $3,346 in MI**
Post 3Ls: **$3,500/week in LA, NY, SV, DC; $3,346 in MI**
1Ls hired? **Yes**
Split summers offered? **Yes**
Can summers spend time in overseas office? **Yes**
Summers 2017: **107 (including 1Ls)**
Offers/acceptances 2016:
94 offers, 87 acceptances

WHITE & CASE

Wiley Rein LLP

1776 K Street NW, Washington, DC 20006
Tel: 202 719 7000   Fax: 202 719 7049
www.wileyrein.com

Main areas of work

Government contracts, insurance, international trade, intellectual property, telecom, media and technology, and litigation.

Firm profile

Wiley Rein operates at the intersection of politics, law, government, business, and technological innovation, representing a wide range of clients - from Fortune 500 corporations to trade associations to individuals - in virtually all industries. We believe delivering consistent and successful results is achieved through building true partnerships with our clients. We do this by understanding the industries and economic climate in which they operate and the current and potential legal issues that impact their business. Most importantly, because Wiley Rein remains a Washington, DC-based firm that largely operates out of a single office, we are able to control costs and billing rates in a manner that is nearly impossible in large, multi-office or multi-national law firms. In addition, Wiley Rein generously gives back to the community, providing significant pro bono legal services and charitable contributions to more than 450 local and national organizations every year.

Recruitment details

- Number of 1st year associates: 8
- Associate salaries: 1st year: $180,000
- 2nd year: $190,000
- Clerking policy: Yes
- Number of 2nd year associates: 11

Head Office: Washington, DC	
Number of domestic offices: 1	
Partners (US): 113	
Associates (US): 62	

Main Recruitment Contact:
Janell Mallard, Senior Recruiting & Diversity Manager
Hiring Partner: Rachel A. Alexander
Recruitment website:
www.wileyrein.com/careers.cfm
Diversity officer: Anna Gomez

Summer Salary 2017
1Ls: $3,465/week
2Ls: $3,465/week
Post 3Ls: N/A
1Ls hired? CBC
Split summers offered? No
Summers 2017: 10
Offers/acceptances 2016: 10 offers, 10 acceptances

Law Schools attending for OCIs in 2017:

George Mason University School of Law, The George Washington University Law School, Georgetown University Law Center, Harvard Law School, Howard University School of Law, University of Pennsylvania School of Law, University of Virginia School of Law, Vanderbilt Law School, Washington and Lee University School of Law

Summer details

Summer associate profile:

Wiley Rein's summer associate program is the foundation of our recruiting efforts. We ensure that summer associates experience the excellence and diversity of our firm and we provide opportunities for each student to handle responsibilities typically assumed by first year associates.

Summer program components:

The defining feature of our program is the flexibility of work assignments. We assist students in tailoring their assignments so that they gain significant exposure to a wide variety of practice areas through our interactive database of assignments. In addition, summer associates receive an associate mentor to help integrate them into the firm and our practices. We host an extensive litigation skills training program in addition to other professional development and social events throughout the summer.

Firm Profiles

Willkie Farr & Gallagher LLP

787 Seventh Avenue, New York, NY 10019
Tel: 212 728 8000   Fax: 212 728 8111
www.willkie.com

Main areas of work

Antitrust and competition; asset management; business reorganization and restructuring; communications, media and privacy; commodities and derivatives; corporate and financial services; environmental; energy; health and safety; executive compensation and employee benefits; government relations; insurance; intellectual property; litigation; private clients; real estate and tax.

Firm profile

Willkie Farr & Gallagher LLP was founded more than 125 years ago upon principles that still characterize our practice today. Our founders and memorable colleagues, like Wendell Willkie and Felix Frankfurter, established a strong foundation of integrity, innovation, pragmatism, flexibility and intellectual agility designed to continually meet the ever changing business needs of our clients. We continue our tradition of excellence by keeping nimble, working collaboratively together, with respect and professionalism, and by integrating this philosophy into our client relationships. Our clients not only rely on us for our creativity, skill, leadership, decisiveness and highquality work, but because they know we are solution-oriented and we get the job done effectively and efficiently.

Recruitment details

• Number of 1st year associates: 51
• Associate salaries: 1st year: $180,000
• Clerking policy: Yes

• Number of 2nd year associates: 52
• 2nd year: $190,000

Law Schools attending for OCIs in 2017:

Brooklyn, Columbia University, Cornell, Duke, Emory Fordham University, GWU, Georgetown University, Harvard, Howard University, NYU, Northwestern University, St John's University, Tulane, University of Michigan, University of Pennsylvania, University of Texas, UCLA, UVA, Vanderbilt, Washington University, Yale

Summer details

Summer associate profile:

Willkie seeks motivated individuals who have excelled academically. We are looking for candidates who possess ambition, maturity, strong communication skills and the ability to work collaboratively with others.

Summer program components:

Willkie's summer program is a terrific introduction to the firm. We offer summer associates the opportunity to work side by side with our attorneys in practice areas of their choice. We offer departmental rotations during the course of the summer. In addition, summer associates participate in a presentation skills workshop, mock arbitration and corporate negotiation training seminars and attend department overviews. Summer associates are evaluated twice during the program: once at mid-summer and then at the end of the program. In addition to providing an introduction to life as an associate, we provide a wide array of social events with the goal of helping our sumer associates to get to know one another, our lawyers and the city.

Head Office: **New York, NY**
Number of domestic offices: **3**
Number of international offices: **6**
Partners (US): **140**
Associates (US): **338**

Main Recruitment Contacts:
Christie Bonasera, Associate Director of Legal Recruiting (NY/Houston), Gail McGinley, Associate Director of Legal Personnel & Recruiting, (DC)
Hiring Partners: **Elizabeth J Bower (DC); Rajab Abbas; Sameer Advani, Amelia Cottrell, David C Drewes, A Mark Getachew, Matthew J Guercio, Benjamin McCallen; Carly Saviano; Danielle Scalzo; Angela Olivarez (TX)**
Recruitment website:
www.willkie.com
Diversity officer: **Kim A Walker, Director of Diversity & Inclusion**

Summer Salary 2017
1Ls: **N/A**
2Ls: **$3,462/week**
Post 3Ls: **N/A**
1Ls hired? **Case-by-case**
Split summers offered? **Yes, details by office**
Can summers spend time in overseas office? **Case-by-case**
Summers 2017: **60**
Offers/acceptances 2016:
63 offers, 52 acceptances

WILLKIE FARR & GALLAGHER LLP

WilmerHale

60 State Street, Boston, MA

350 S. Grand Avenue, Suite 2100, Los Angeles, CA

7 World Trade Center, 250 Greenwich Street, New York, NY

950 Page Mill Road, Palo Alto, CA

1875 Pennsylvania Ave, NW, Washington, DC

Main areas of work

Our global practice includes over 600 litigators with unmatched trial, appellate and Supreme Court experience; a preeminent securities law practice with over 130 lawyers; a regulatory practice that includes more than 110 lawyers who have held high-level government positions; an intellectual property practice enriched by the expertise of more than 170 attorneys and technology specialists who hold scientific or technical degrees; more than 200 seasoned corporate transactional lawyers and business counselors; and lawyers who focus on bankruptcy, environmental, labor and employment, private client, real estate and tax matters.

Firm profile

WilmerHale offers unparalleled legal representation across a comprehensive range of practice areas that are critical to the success of our clients. We practice at the very top of the legal profession and offer a cutting-edge blend of capabilities that enables us to handle deals and cases of any size and complexity. With a practice unsurpassed in depth and scope by any other major firm, we have the ability to anticipate obstacles, seize opportunities and get the case resolved or the deal done—and the experience and know-how to prevent it from being undone. Our heritage includes involvement in the foundation of legal aid work early in the 20th century, and today we consistently distinguish ourselves as leaders in pro bono representation. Many of our lawyers have played, and continue to play, prominent roles in public service activities of national and international importance—from counseling US presidents to opposing discrimination and defending human rights around the world. Most importantly, our firm stands for a steadfast commitment to quality and excellence in everything we do—a commitment reflected in the continued success of our clients across the globe and our dedication to the development of our attorneys.

Recruitment details

- Number of 1st year associates: 65
- Number of 2nd year associates: 51
- Associate salaries: 1st year: $180,000
- 2nd year: $190,000
- Clerking policy: Yes. The firm welcomes applications from judicial clerks. Approximately one-third of our recent incoming classes have come to the firm after serving one or more judicial clerkships. We value the experience of clerkships and give credit for clerkships for compensation and seniority purposes. We also pay a competitive bonus to incoming clerks.

Law Schools attending for OCIs in 2017:

University of California-Berkeley, Boston College, Boston University, University of Chicago, Columbia, Cornell, Duke, Fordham, George Washington, Georgetown, Harvard, Howard, Loyola Law School - LA, Michigan, Northwestern, Northeastern, NYU, University of Pennsylvania, Santa Clara, Stanford, Suffolk, University of California-LA (UCLA), University of Colorado-Boulder, University of Denver, University of Southern California (USC), University of Virginia, Yale.

Head Office: Boston, MA and Washington, DC

Number of domestic offices: 7

Number of international offices: 5

Worldwide revenue: $1,130,400,000

Partners (US): 255

Associates (US): 568

Main Recruitment Contacts:

Beth Miller (firmwide)

Karen Rameika (Boston)

Nancy Lam (Denver)

Terri Janezeck (Los Angeles)

Nancy Gray (New York)

Nancy Lam (Palo Alto)

Melissa Grossman (Washington, DC)

Hiring Partners:

Mark Ford (Boston)

Natalie Hanlon Leh & Andy Spielman (Denver)

Randall Lee (Los Angeles)

Erin Sloane & Alan Schoenfeld (New York)

Mark Flanagan (Palo Alto)

Jonathan Paikin (Washington, DC)

Recruitment website:

www.wilmerhalecareers.com

Diversity officer: Nimesh Patel

Firm Profiles

WilmerHale (continued)

1225 17th Street #2600, Denver, CO
www.wilmerhale.com
www.wilmerhalecareers.com

Summer details

Summer associate profile:

We seek to hire an extraordinarily talented and diverse group of students whose academic and personal record of achievement demonstrates a commitment to excellence and who want to practice law at the highest and most demanding levels, while still enjoying lives enriched by public, professional and personal pursuits outside the firm. We have identified six competencies—commitment, confidence, oral communication, problem solving, teamwork and writing—that outline what constitutes outstanding performance at WilmerHale and are used to align our selection criteria and evaluations of candidates and summer associates with our expectations of attorneys. In addition, we seek individuals whose character, intelligence, judgment and training will inspire their colleagues and clients to have confidence in their advice and representation.

Summer program components:

By providing a realistic view of the firm through interesting work assignments, practical training and the opportunity to work and socialize with many of our lawyers, we give summer associates the insight needed to make an informed decision to join the firm after graduation or a clerkship. Summer associates do substantive client work and have the opportunity to try a broad range of practices or focus on a few, depending on their interests. Summer associates also have the opportunity to attend client meetings and trials whenever possible. Our mentors provide guidance and constructive feedback throughout the summer and make themselves available to their mentees as resources in the firm. We have developed training programs specifically for our summer associates designed to assist in their professional development by introducing the practical skills lawyers need and provide a sample of our training programs for our attorneys. Summer training topics include: research skills, leadership, negotiation skills, deposition skills, presentation skills/oral communication skills, legal writing, departmental panels and meetings, case studies and mock trials. In addition, summer associates receive a review of their work and are encouraged to provide feedback about their experience.

Summer Salary 2017
1Ls: $3,500/week
2Ls: $3,500/week
Post 3Ls: N/A
1Ls hired? Yes
Split summers offered? Yes
Can summers spend time in overseas office? Yes
Summers 2017: 77
Offers/acceptances 2016:
80 offers, 57 acceptances, 20 pending

Wilson Sonsini Goodrich & Rosati

650 Page Mill Road, Palo Alto, California, CA 94304-1050
Tel: 650 493 9300   Fax: 650 493 6811
Email: wsgr@wsgr.com   www.wsgr.com

Main areas of work

Corporate governance, corporate finance (private equity, capital markets, venture capital, finance and structured finance, fund services, and restructuring), mergers and acquisitions, litigation (securities and governance litigation, patent litigation, commercial litigation, consumer litigation, Internet law and strategy, white collar, board and internal investigations, government investigations, class action litigation, trade secret litigation, employment litigation, appellate litigation, and arbitration), intellectual property counseling and transactions (technology transactions, patents and innovation, trademarks and copyright, and post-grant review), antitrust counseling and litigation, employee benefits and compensation, export control and sanctions, FCPA and anti-corruption, energy and infrastructure, privacy and data protection, national security/CFIUS, cybersecurity, Federal Trade Commission, real estate, and tax.

Firm profile

Wilson Sonsini Goodrich & Rosati is the premier provider of legal services to technology, life sciences, and other growth enterprises worldwide, as well as the venture firms, private equity firms, and investment banks that finance and advise them. The firm represents clients in a vast array of industries at all stages of development, from venture-backed start-ups to multibillion-dollar global corporations. We are nationally recognized as a leader in the fields of corporate governance and finance, mergers and acquisitions, private equity, securities litigation, intellectual property, and antitrust, among many other areas of law. Over the past 50-plus years, since its inception in Silicon Valley, the firm has established its reputation by having a superior knowledge of its clients' industries, as well as deep and longstanding contacts throughout the technology and life sciences sectors.

Recruitment details

- Number of 1st year associates: 55
- Associate salaries: 1st year: $180,000
- Clerking policy: Yes

- Number of 2nd year associates: 53
- 2nd year: $190,000

Law Schools attending for OCIs in 2017:

Berkeley; Stanford; Boston College; U. Chicago; Boston University; U. Michigan; Columbia; U. Penn; Cornell; U. San Diego; Duke; U. Texas; Fordham; U. Washington; George Mason; UC Davis; George Washington; UC Hastings; Georgetown; UC Irvine; Harvard; UCLA; Loyola; USC; Northwestern; UVA; NYU; Yale; Santa Clara

Summer details

Summer associate profile:

We look for candidates who are enthusiastic about working at our firm and for our client base, and have a solid understanding of what we do and the practices we have. Given our extensive work for technology, life sciences, renewable energy, and other growth companies at all stages of development, we are particularly interested in candidates who want to work for those companies. We are also interested in candidates who have the requisite scientific expertise for one of our intellectual property practices. Depending on the experience, we typically prefer candidates with prior work experience. Given our particular client base and entrepreneurial orientation, work experience for technology, life sciences, renewable energy, or other growth companies is particularly valuable, as is experience starting a company or student organization. We also value experience in management consulting, accounting, paralegal and similar types of backgrounds.

Summer program components:

Our summer program offers law students an opportunity to observe and participate in the work of the leading provider of legal services to technology, life sciences, and other growth enterprises worldwide. Summer at our firm incorporates all the things important to our culture: challenging and varied assignments, direct working relationships with our innovative clients, meeting a wide range of attorneys, a comprehensive training program, and exciting social activities that take advantage of our locations in technology centers around the country.

Head Office: Palo Alto, CA
Number of domestic offices: 11
Number of international offices: 4
Worldwide revenue: $755 million
Partners (US): 203
Associates (US): 464

Main Recruitment Contact: Elizabeth Pond
Hiring Partners: Michael Coke, Maura Rees and Lisa Stimmell
Recruitment website: www.wsgr.com/AttorneyRecruiting
Diversity officer: Chris Boyd

Summer Salary 2017
1Ls: N/A
2Ls: $3,462/week
Post 3Ls: N/A
1Ls hired? No
Split summers offered? Yes, for returning 1Ls only
Can summers spend time in overseas office? On a case-by-case basis
Summers 2017: 56
Offers/acceptances 2016: 54 offers, 42 acceptances

Firm Profiles

Wilson Sonsini Goodrich & Rosati
PROFESSIONAL CORPORATION

Winston & Strawn LLP

35 West Wacker Drive, Chicago, IL 60601
Tel: 312 558 5600   Fax: 312 558 5700
www.winston.com

Main areas of work

Litigation, corporate and financial, intellectual property, labor and employment relations, tax, employee benefits and executive compensation, energy, environmental, government relations and regulatory affairs, healthcare, maritime, real estate, trusts and estates.

Firm profile

Throughout its more than 160 year history, Winston & Strawn LLP has handled many significant, high profile matters for its clients – from antitrust litigation to cross-border mergers, energy transactions to labor negotiations. The firm is a global law firm with more than 875 attorneys across the US, Europe and Asia. The firm's mission is to provide the highest quality legal services to meet the difficult legal challenges of the world's most important companies and organizations. Winston & Strawn is consistently honored by its clients for outstanding legal service.

Recruitment details

- Number of 1st year associates: 51
- Associate salaries: 1st year: $180,000
- Clerking policy: Yes
- Number of 2nd year associates: 47
- 2nd year: $190,000

Law Schools attending for OCIs in 2017:

Please visit the Careers section of winston.com for a list of OCI Schools.

Summer details

Summer associate profile:

Winston & Strawn prefers strong academic performance, participation in law review or other law school publications or competitive endeavors and a good balance of academic and interpersonal skills.

Summer program components:

Summer associates have the opportunity to learn about a wide range of Winston practice areas and the specialized skills each one demands. Individual department presentations allow summer associates to meet lawyers from specific practice groups who detail what they do in their daily practice. The Firm Highlights Lecture Series gives an inside look at some of the most publicized and interesting cases that the firm handled in the past year. In addition, the firm offers a practical training component that provides hands-on experience with activities such as drafting a legal research memorandum, negotiating a deal, drafting an IPO document, taking a deposition and trying a case in a mock trial. Summer associates learn from veteran Winston attorneys with years of experience and insight, who make the law come alive through examples, personal experience and anecdotes. In addition, summer associates have the opportunity to build relationships with attorneys through a variety of social activities throughout the summer.

Head Office: Chicago, IL
Number of domestic offices: 10
Number of international offices: 7
Worldwide revenue: $822,800,000
Partners (US): 356
Associates (US): 447

Main Recruitment Contact: Lisa A McLafferty, Director of Attorney Relations
Hiring Partners: Suzanne Jaffe Bloom, William C O'Neil, Co-Chairs, Hiring Committee
Recruitment website: www.winston.com
Diversity officer: Linda Coberly, Chair, Diversity Committee

Summer Salary 2017
1Ls: $3,461/week
2Ls: $3,461/week
Post 3Ls: N/A
1Ls hired? Yes
Split summers offered? No
Can summers spend time in overseas office? No
Summers 2017: 68
Offers/acceptances 2016:
64 offers, 57 acceptances

Regional Guide

Where to start your practice?
We assess the pros and cons of becoming an attorney in key legal markets across the US:

Alaska & Hawaii

The perks to lawyering in Hawaii are as clear as its sunny blue skies: a tropical climate, Hawaiian shirts in the office, and a laid back atmosphere where you don't have to practice the ancient art of Ho'oponopono (traditional dispute resolution and forgiveness) to feel goodwill toward your coworkers. A legal career in Alaska offers the advantages of mountain views, clear air and moose sauntering through your backyard.

Hawaii

You don't have to practice the ancient art of Ho'oponopono (traditional dispute resolution and forgiveness) to be accepted into the Hawaiian legal community.

HAWAII'S legal market is concentrated in downtown Honolulu, and the courts, government agencies and law firms there tend to be small in size. Local firms that offer summer programs include Carlsmith Ball, Goodsill Anderson Quinn & Stifel, Case Lombardi & Pettit, Starn O'Toole Marcus & Fisher, Damon Key Leong Kupchak Hastert, and the nattily named M4. Ties to the area, whether through family or education, are at a premium when it comes to getting recruited.

The University of Hawaii's prestigious William S. Richardson School of Law is the surest way into a legal career in Honolulu. It offers state-specific courses in Native Hawaiian law, environmental law and Pacific-Asian studies. Places are limited though, and its admission team tends to favor students who are already resident on the islands. Carving out a legal career in Hawaii isn't easy, and some aspiring lawyers hoping for a side of sun often turn to larger hubs like Miami or LA.

Hawaii is best known as a tourist hub, welcoming planeloads of lei-toting visitors all year round thanks to its tropical climate. Its development into a summer-sports paradise has posed some distinct legal challenges, many of which are related to Native Hawaiian rights. Native Hawaiians have protected access to fishing and hunting rights, as well as certain water sources and areas of land. But in a small and densely populated cluster of islands, these rights are increasingly challenged by businesses eager to expand their reach. The Native Hawaiian Legal Corporation provides legal assistance to communities and families whose lands and resources are under threat.

> **On chambers-associate.com...**
>
> • An introduction to Indian Law

Native Hawaiians are also battling for greater recognition by the federal government, or even independence. The state was an independent kingdom until the US illegally overthrew Queen Lili'uokalani in 1893, and now Native Hawaiians comprise only 10% of the islands' populations. Senator Daniel Akaka tried to push through a bill for federal recognition of Native Hawaiians between 2000 and 2010, but efforts to establish nation-to-nation relations have floundered, in part due to Native Hawaiian frustration at the US government's failure to make reparations for its decades of colonialism. In 2016, the US Department of the Interior announced that there would be an administrative procedure that will allow a future unified Native Hawaiian government to enter into a formal government-to-government relationship with the US. However, only time will tell if this actually follows through.

Alaska

Chasing the Northern Lights isn't the only reason lawyers head to America's chilliest state.

The bright lights of Anchorage, which houses 40% of Alaska's population and most of its businesses, shine on a small but lively legal market. The capital isn't the easiest place to live, thanks to inhospitable weather and virtually endless winter nights, but for lawyers who can brave the freeze, there's the advantage of a close-knit community and more winter sports than you can shake a ski-pole at.

While other states wrestle with a dramatic oversupply of law graduates, Alaska has no such trouble. It's the only state without an ABA accredited law school. Seattle University's School of Law, which has long offered its students a summer program on Alaskan legal issues at its satellite campus in Anchorage, is on its way to remedying this: in 2014 it won ABA approval to allow students to spend not only their summers, but their entire third year in Alaska.

Environment, natural resources and regulated industries are big practice areas in Alaska. It's no secret why: the state sits on vast oil reserves and is home to an impressive range of flora and fauna (black bears are often sighted within cities, and the Anchorage area in particular plays host to a lot of mountain goats and wolves). The interests of ecologists, native Alaskans, oil prospectors and the federal government are constantly rubbing up against each other, making for a lot of litigation work, often with a regulatory slant.

There are 13 *Chambers USA*-ranked law firms in Alaska. These include a handful of national names, like K&L Gates as well as Seattle or DC-based outfits that have spread their wings, among them Davis Wright Tremaine, Perkins Coie, Lane Powell, Dorsey & Whitney and Stoel Rives. The bulk of these firms have launched offices in Alaska to take advantage of all the oil and gas work, much of which involves exploration work or issues related to the Trans-Alaska Pipeline System. Big homegrown firms in Alaska include: Birch, Horton, Bittner & Cherot

(which also has a Washington, DC office to serve the state of Alaska in government dealings); Durrell Law Group; Ashburn & Mason; Guess & Rudd; Atkinson, Conway & Gagnon; and Sedor, Wendlandt, Evans & Filippi.

The market might not be the most varied one out there, but if you're a fan of the climate there's a lot to be said for the lifestyle the region can offer. Just make sure you're not going to change your mind: flights to the lower 48 are lengthy and don't come cheap.

"For lawyers who can brave the freeze, there's the advantage of a close-knit community and more winter sports than you can shake a ski-pole at."

Boston & New England

In our associate happiness survey, young Bostonian lawyers were among the happiest and least stressed in the US. They think Boston law firms' reputation for stuffiness can get stuffed...

The Cradle students never want to leave

With a population of around 650,000 and tens of thousands more traveling in from the suburbs each day, Boston is New England's commercial center. To many in the region – whether from New Hampshire, Vermont, Rhode Island, Maine or Connecticut – the capital of Massachusetts is their city. There are over 100 colleges and universities in the Greater Boston area, and students here have access to *"some of the best and brightest professors and are able to study alongside other highly intelligent students,"* enthuses a source at Choate, Hall & Stewart.

The city's reputation for academic excellence means that it's crammed full of students for eight months of the year. In the summer, though, many head home for the holiday, *"and the dynamic totally changes,"* a junior associate at Nutter McClennen & Fish told us. *"The buses and trains suddenly become a lot quieter!"* Of course, *"with such a rich history and culture, the students are often replaced by tourists over the summer."*

All the associates we interviewed from Boston old-timer Choate had grown up and/or studied in New England. At Goodwin Procter, a source in the firm's Boston headquarters observed that *"they seem for each office to hire locally – there's an appreciation for Boston-area schools here."* According to our sources: *"Law students here are encouraged to build up a support network which often includes their peers, professors and members of the legal profession they come into contact with over the course of their studies."* This could go some way to explaining why so many graduates choose to stay in the area.

Boston is a top destination for building up a stonking resume thanks to the number of organizations offering externships and the breadth of pro bono opportunities available to aspiring lawyers. These can be vital in supplementing that all-important BigLaw application, with senior sources at Boston-based firms telling us they're on the lookout for students who've taken advantage of such opportunities. *"Don't be afraid to take on pro bono work during your summer program,"* advised one Beantowner. *"It's a great way to show you're interested in exploring Boston's legal scene."*

Your new social life

Colloquially known as The Hub, Boston has *"all the advantages of a much larger city,"* an associate at Nutter tells us. At the same time, *"it's not as overwhelming as some other cities. It's relatively easy to escape all the hustle and bustle."* Others went on to describe *"an impressive live music scene with plenty of smaller shows to complement the big headliners,"* and mentioned how seriously the city takes its sports teams. And for good reason too: the Bruins lifted the Stanley Cup in 2011 and the Red Sox won the World Series in 2013, so there's some serious sporting clout in this Northeastern state. On the whole, interviewees felt Boston is *"more collegial than most cities. Whenever you go out you're likely to run into people you know, and any new restaurants or bars are discussed in the same circles."*

Boston is an undeniably expensive city, *"but you can still get good value for money,"* our sources insist, adding that *"one of the main advantages is its relative affordability compared to New York. Being able to afford a decent amount of space is a big plus. It's pricey, but living downtown is still doable."* Not that living a little further out is a problem: *"Boston is a very walkable city. You can live a reasonable distance away and still be within a ten to 15-minute bus or subway journey."*

Another bonus? The compact geography of New England means *"it's easy to hop in the car and have an adventure on the weekend, whether it's hiking in New Hampshire, strolling down Rhode Island's beaches or apple-picking in Vermont."*

Regeneration

Boston has long been associated with 'white shoe' firms and their reputation as strait-laced and somewhat stuffy. However, the startup boom has seen a steady stream of tech businesses crop up in the city in recent years, transforming Boston's legal scene into *"a highly creative business culture,"* we hear. In the past, such businesses opted for the lure of Silicon Valley's more established technology and media industry, but now that trendy names like TripAdvisor and ZipCar have set up shop in the city, others are following suit. In turn, Boston has attracted the attention of some of the largest national and international firms, including Skadden, Jones Day and DLA Piper.

Regional Guide

The modern, youthful ethos of hi-tech industry has trickled into many firms in the area. A Boston-based Goodwin Procter associate said that *"while there definitely remain a lot of partners who wouldn't be caught dead in anything besides a suit, there are many others who wear jeans more often than not."* Associates at Cooley chimed in to tell us that their office *"definitely doesn't have this so-called 'Boston attitude.' People don't take themselves too seriously; it's pretty lighthearted."* That's not to say the quality of candidates these firms seek has dropped, though. *"They really are looking for high achievers."*

Associates in Boston told us that the structure of the city's legal market means there's room to cut your teeth on smallish local matters while also gaining exposure to commercial clients of a national and international scale. With a healthy smattering of *Fortune 500* companies, among them Staples and defense giant Raytheon, there's all the usual corporate and commercial litigation work one might expect of a BigLaw firm. This is set to grow in the years ahead, as demonstrated through General Electric's recently-announced plans to relocate its corporate headquarters to Boston. The move *"illustrates the strength and vibrancy of the Greater Boston economy,"* says Choate's chairman John Nadas. *"GE is one of the largest companies in the world. After considering many, many attractive options, GE chose Boston on the announced basis that Boston has the most dynamic and creative ecosystem in the country."* Many firms in Boston also undertake *"a good deal of estate planning and trustee work, much like the smaller firms,"* revealed an associate at Nutter. *"I think it's good that firms have the capacity to address these smaller individual matters."* And then there's the work that arises out of Boston's booming education and healthcare industries.

All in all, interviewees went on to tell us that *"this is a great city for doing interesting work with a little of the pressure taken off you – there's less of a national or global spotlight than in some of the headquarter offices of larger firms in New York."* At the same time, they were keen to note that *"Boston is one of the largest and most competitive legal markets outside New York, but its smaller Bar means that there's a greater sense of community. It's much easier here for juniors to take on leadership roles and be responsible for their own work. From an associate's perspective, that's fantastic for career development."*

Spotlight on Hartford

Hartford, Connecticut isn't just home to one of the largest stone arch bridges in the world: branches of some pretty well-known law firms reside here too, including Axinn Veltrop & Harkrider, Bracewell, Brown Rudnick

and Dechert. Many insurance companies have their headquarters in Hartford – the city's not nicknamed the 'Insurance Capital of the World' for nothing – and it's a ripe place for young lawyers looking to get into insurance law. Plenty of other practices flourish here too. Small in size but big in ambition, fast-growing Axinn is ranked by *Chambers USA* as a top practitioner of general commercial litigation, and its Hartford office hosts the bulk of the firm's IP practice too. At bigger players like Brown Rudnick, it's a more complex operation covering practices as diverse as environmental law, government law and real estate. Associates here frequently work with colleagues from several offices at a time. *"At some point during your first few years, they pay for you to fly to another office and get to know your colleagues there. And if you need to be in another office for whatever reason, you can just call ahead and there'll be a room ready."*

Black coat, white shoes, black hat, Cadillac...

"Boston is a white-washed city," said a Goodwin Procter associate. *"So to improve diversity firms here have to fight against those circumstances as well as the lack of inclusion that's been inherent in the practice of law for so long."* At Choate, 82% of associates and a staggering 96% of partners are white. Likewise, Ropes & Gray is your classic firm where *"most partners are white males."* At the time of our research in 2016, 91% of R&G partners and 77% of its associates were white. All hope's not lost however: both of these firms and many of their peers are active on the diversity front, partly spurred by the demand to more accurately reflect their diverse client base. Check out The Inside View on each for more diversity stats and details on what they're doing to address the issue.

Here to stay

One benefit of legal life in Boston and New England at large is that *"you can build a long-term career here. The typical view of law firm life in places like New York is that you get there and stick it out for as long as you're willing to put up with the lifestyle sacrifices, and then you leave. It's not like that in Boston. Firms aren't used as a stepping stone with a large number of people leaving after three, four or five years. In fact, at most firms throughout the region you'll see as many sixth, seventh, eighth-year associates as you do juniors. The firms try to grow and develop people."* As one Nutter associate told us: *"To me, that makes a lot more sense. I definitely feel that the firm is more invested in me and that I can forge my own career path. You don't feel lost in some big corporate machine here. In fact, we get a lot more attention and exposure to higher quality work than in the larger offices in New York."*

California

'The Governator' Arnie Schwarzenegger's famous proclamation that *"California has the ideas of Athens and the power of Sparta"* might be a touch grandiose, but California still boasts the highest population and highest revenues of any state...

THE distinctive perks of California living are pretty well documented: blissful weather, surfing, a laid back attitude and relentless positivity. As the writer Don DeLillo sourly quipped: *"Californians invented the concept of lifestyle. This alone warrants their doom."* Since it birthed the hippie in the 1960s, the state has increasingly combined its trademark brand of Cali-cool with impressive corporate credentials. California's claim to being a modern-day ancient Greece largely rests on the shoulders of the technological philosophers of Silicon Valley and the bronzed gods of Hollywood. Thanks to these industries, the state's GDP now measures up to that of the world's richest countries: in 2015 it was the sixth highest in the world, with $2.46 trillion to its name – only the United States, China, Japan, Germany and the United Kingdom surpass it.

California cool

Although working in BigLaw is never a picnic, California law firms tend to offer a lighter, brighter lifestyle than their out-of-state counterparts. Our California junior associates tell us that *"instead of the older, stuffy dark-suit atmosphere in New York law firms that you see on TV shows, there's a lighter, brighter feeling here."* In a legacy of the hippies' famed contempt for the neck-tie, Cali-locals like Sheppard Mullin put the casual into dressing business casual – one associate there told us that *"I tend to hide behind my desk in my leggings a lot of the time, and a lot of partners wear jeans every day."* California litigation stalwarts Quinn Emanuel put them to shame in the dress-down stakes, though. Their co-founding partner Bill Urquhart is on record as saying that *"the only dress code we have is that you to have something between your feet and the carpet – and that's because our insurance company requires it!"* The firm's even issued QE-branded flip-flops to summer associates in the past.

Californians are linguistic pioneers, responsible for spreading the 'valley girl' and 'surfer dude' speech pattern stereotypes in the 1980s, and we can blame California for the infiltration of 'like' as a multipurpose conversational filler, as well as other gems like 'hella', 'totally', 'awesome', 'dude', and the underused 'gnarly'. We wouldn't recommend pulling out any of the above words in court, but words like *"relaxed"* frequently come up in our conversations with junior lawyers over the years, many of whom feel that *"people are more laid back here,"* wherever their firm is headquartered. This could be down to all that glorious vitamin D, part and parcel of a *"climate you can enjoy year-round."* Still, even at coastal offices, *"lawyers are really focused on living their professional lives; it's not like we're at the beach every weekend."*

Indeed, don't get carried away with visions of short working days and long evenings spent lazing on the sand. Perhaps this corporate associate in Gibson Dunn's LA office sums up the Cali approach to lawyering best: *"I leave the office around 7pm and work from home all the time. Most of the people I work with are good at not creating extra stress. They're flexible; they're not going to sweat someone's decision to work from home. You're given a lot of freedom when it comes to how and where you get your work done."* Note that the approach itself may be relaxed and flexible, but lawyers are still working those notorious BigLaw hours all the same.

A Tale of Two Cities

California was late to develop compared to other states, which makes sense considering part of its distinctive mythos is that people came there not out of necessity, but for the purposes of self-fulfillment and to put dreams into action. It's been shaped by two successive waves of self-starting, entrepreneurial energy, each of which has its own thriving hub. The first was the flood of movie-makers to Hollywood in the early 20th century. Initially they came to avoid paying Thomas Edison's fees (he had a patent on the movie-making process), as well as for the reliable sunshine and mild climate. As the studios grew through the 1920s and 1930s, writers, directors and technicians flooded in from around the world – with high numbers of displaced Jewish immigrants among their number – to create the world's first and most prolific movie industry.

Today, glamorous Hollywood clients flock to national firms' branches in Century City, the site of a former backlot for 20th Century Fox, for industry-specific services in areas like finance, employment and IP. One associate found the culture in Century City *"more trendy than in our other offices, because when your clients are cool production companies and you've got models and actors coming in, you have a different sort of attitude and interests. It's a very casual, low-key atmosphere."* If it's entertainment-related work that appeals most, check out *Chambers USA's* top-ranked firms in the area, which include Akin Gump, Jenner & Block, Loeb & Loeb, Sheppard Mullin, Munger, Gibson Dunn and Davis Wright Tremaine.

Do robots dream of electric sheep?

The second wave of entrepreneurship shaping California's economy started in the 1940s and 50s, when the then dean of Stanford University encouraged graduates and academics to stay in the area to found businesses (this is how Hewlett-Packard got its start). A growing amount of hi-tech entrepreneurs powered by dreams of stardom on a rather smaller kind of screen stuck around, and the area became known as Silicon Valley. According to one anonymous Cali wit, the recipe for Silicon Valley was *"take one great research university, add venture capital, and shake vigorously."* Hollywood's supremacy is increasingly on the wane, but Silicon Valley goes from strength to strength. The speculation-driven industry is prone to booms and busts, but for now it seems to have seen off both the 2000–01 threat of the dot-com bubble burst and the more recent recession.

Stanford still feeds plenty of its hi-tech expertise into Silicon Valley: its graduates are responsible for eBay, Netflix, LinkedIn and Instagram, each of which got its start with dizzying sums of venture capital investment. The Valley has a reputation for throwing billions around in relaxed style, with megabuck deals sealed on a handshake. Law firms targeting the silicon dollar tend to set up outlets in Palo Alto. The area has a distinctive atmosphere: one White & Case junior based there told us that *"we adopt a Silicon Valley mentality, so we work hard and play hard too. People from our New York office make fun of us and say we shouldn't be dressed in business casual, but if you meet a client in suit and tie here they'll laugh you out the room!"*

> *"People from our New York office make fun of us and say we shouldn't be dressed in business casual."*

Quinn Emanuel's Bill Urquhart reports that there has been *"a literal explosion of new tech companies in various hotspots across the country. For example, there is an area called Silicon Beach in LA which has attracted startups like Snapchat, as well as more established hi-tech companies like Google and big internet game companies like Electronic Arts."* The city's location and Hispanic cultural heritage mean that work often has a Latin American slant. Urqu-

hart also tells us that *"our Los Angeles office provides lawyers the rare opportunity to do exciting work in Southern California where people go to relax, head for the beach and lay under palm trees."* As another BigLaw source based in Los Angeles raved, *"within two hours you can go to the desert, the beach or snow-skiing in the mountains."* This might be true on weekends, but as the US's second largest city, Los Angeles inevitably has a frenetic feel. One source felt that *"the best thing about working here is the diversity and richness of the city's culture, and the worst thing hands down is the traffic."*

Over in San Francisco, California's alternative heritage lives on in the form of health foods, organic farming and various eco movements. The state's environmental policies and targets are the strictest in the US – the city bans all its retailers from handing out plastic bags – and it has been named the greenest city in the US and Canada. In a less concrete (and potentially spurious) legacy, one survey found that 63% of Californians actually have hugged a tree. In any case, the area is a center for environmental law and green businesses like solar energy generation. Like LA, San Francisco is home to growing numbers of hi-tech businesses, including internet oversharers' favorites Instagram, Pinterest and Twitter. There's also plenty of corporate and finance work courtesy of the Financial District, home to the headquarters of national players like Wells Fargo, Gap and Levi Strauss.

San Fran has plenty of work for aspiring lawyers, but a move there comes with a mighty price tag. In its recently published National Rent Report, Real-estate rental website Zumper found that of the one million active, one-bedroom listings it had analyzed, six of the 20 most expensive US cities for renters were in California. San Francisco and its surrounding areas were deemed the most expensive place to set up camp in the entire country, a position that has pushed up prices south of the Golden Gate City to promote the San Jose and Oakland metros to fourth and sixth place respectively. So while those starting salaries at BigLaw firms appear to be very generous, it's worth bearing in mind those dollars won't stretch as far as they could elsewhere, especially when it comes to housing. And if you're looking to buy? Well, San Francisco is one place where that'll be quite the challenge. The city's real estate market has reached dizzying heights; with the average homeowner's annual income standing at a nationwide high of around $160,000. To put this into perspective, the salary required to buy a home in Pittsburgh, Pennsylvania is $32,373.50.

Getting schooled

Of California's law school options, Stanford is arguably the most prestigious – it tends to come in the top three in various US law school rankings – and University of

California Berkeley is not too far behind. Other respectable showings include UCLA, the University of Southern California (Gould), Loyola and Southwestern. Successful Cali-grads have a host of well-established local law firms to choose from: Orrick, Herrington & Sutcliffe, founded and headquartered in San Francisco, is one of the state's largest and oldest firms, while other prestigious California outfits include Morrison & Foerster (MoFo), litigation giant Quinn Emanuel, Gibson Dunn, Wilson Sonsini and Sheppard Mullin.

There are also a host of boutiques catering to California's key industries, such as top-flight IP boutique Finnegan and property specialists Allen Matkins. And many BigLaw firms from across the US have Cali outposts, often in Silicon Valley or nearby San Francisco to profit from the area's surging tech industry. Los Angeles is also a desirable location thanks to its strong links with the Latin America market, while some large firms like Simpson Thacher use a Palo Alto base to extend their business further west. At this ST office one associate told us: *"We're very much Asia-facing on both the litigation and transactional side. We work on a lot of price-fixing issues with Asian companies."* Elsewhere, Orange County increasingly entices firms with its booming property market.

One for the money

California's government has one of the highest debt burdens in the US – partly a function of the state's 'bad debt' fueled housing crisis. The state's individual income tax system is broken down into ten brackets, and the top rate, at 13.3%, is the highest in the entire country. Economic challenges in recent years have included deep cuts at state government level, a surging birth rate that outstripped job levels, continued stagnant demand for housing in parts of SoCal, and a stronger dollar hurting California's tech exports. Still, sectors of California's economy are booming, and the state continues to lure in big businesses. As Bill Urquhart tells us, *"Northern California wasn't hurt by the recession as much as Southern California because of the strength of the tech industry. Construction is a big part of the Southern California economy. That segment of the economy really suffered. That industry has rebounded. Thankfully, I think the recession for the most part appears to be behind us in both Northern and Southern California."* All the signs point to a positive future for the Golden State. Of all US states, California leads the pack when it comes to revenue growth in the agriculture, manufacturing and technology industries. Workers' pockets have been a big beneficiary of this growth: in 2015 Californians' personal income increased by 6.3%, which was faster than any other US state.

Chicago & The Midwest

The Midwest has a knack for birthing top law firms: five of Am Law's top ten are locals (DLA Piper, Baker McKenzie, Jones Day, Sidley Austin, and Kirkland & Ellis), and the region is also the base for other serious national and international players.

MOST of these firms have sprung up in the fertile city ground of Chicago, but Columbus, Cleveland, Cincinnati, Minneapolis and Detroit are also significant legal centers in the Midwest. The region has a lot to offer junior associates, but don't think you can just waltz in unannounced; our BigLaw sources suggested applicants *"have a good explanation for being in the area. Just about everyone here has some kind of familial tie to the state. Firms want you to stay, and if you don't have a clear reason they'll be wondering how long it'll be before you leave for New York or Houston or wherever. That's a generality for Midwest firms. There are out-of-towners, but there's always a link."*

A local link should also set you in good stead in terms of your appreciation of 'Midwestern values,' often a big deal to firms based here – think humility, honesty, unpretentiousness, a hard-working attitude and wholesome Uncle Buck-style family loyalty (minus the urge to imprison miscreant teen boyfriends in the trunk). Lois Casaleggi, senior director of the University of Chicago Law School career services, explains: *"I think the culture inside law firms would be a little different compared to, say, New York. Midwesterners are generally a little more down to earth, friendly and polite. It's just a different vibe. However, the environment is also really hard-working – you're not going to be kicking your feet up."*

Our sources at Midwest firms concurred. Squire Sanders juniors told us that *"our firm's Midwestern in its attitude, meaning that it's much more laid back and low key. That doesn't mean we're not sophisticated or aggressive when we need to be, or capable of pulling off complex deals, but we're also very good-natured and easy to deal with, with no big egos."* An associate at Schiff Hardin felt similarly: *"We value our Midwestern culture, which means we value modesty and humility. We're not looking for showboats – we want people who are motivated to do an excellent job, but who aren't necessarily driven by competition."* Rookie associates felt that the region is a good place to raise children, thanks to relatively low property prices and *"family-oriented"* values that allow for a better work/life balance than in New York.

Illinoise

Home to the world's first skyscraper, a steel-framed high-rise built in 1885, Chicago is an urban jungle to rival any in the world. As America's third-largest city (behind New York and LA), Chicago has a predictably expansive legal market, with a surprisingly big emphasis on tech work. *"When people think about tech, they usually think Silicon Valley, but Chicago has a vibrant tech market that is not always as well known, with companies like Motorola and Groupon, to name just two,"* Casaleggi notes. *"There are a lot of media companies here, old and new. Part of the appeal is that it does a lot of things well. Locally the business community is so diverse and strong, and that feeds into the legal market."* It's a growing industry: the Bureau of Labor Statistics reveals a 2.8% rise in employment in financial activities, part of the larger 23,200 increase in jobs between between November 2015 and 2016. While the average hourly wage of a lawyer in the Chicago area falls just under four dollars below the national average at $61.80, wages have continued to increase steadily between 2016 and 2017 against a decline in the national average.

The city is also home to big media companies like regional television studios, radio corporations, and major newspaper publishers like Tribune and the now-depleted Sun-Times Media, which once housed Conrad Black's vast international media empire and still owns dozens of local newspapers.

Chicago started out as a blue-collar town, shaped by migrants from all over Southern, Eastern and Western Europe. These roots are evident in its most famous culinary inventions: artery-clogging deep dish pizza and the Chicago hot dog, dressed with mustard, onion and celery salt (add ketchup at your peril). The city's high murder rate is no secret with 2016 proving to be a record breaker, racking up 4,368 shooting victims; though there have been strong police attempts to discourage gang violence recently. There's also lots of state money going into beautification projects. Casaleggi tells us that *"being on the lake is such a huge advantage – the water gives the city a different feel and opens up a lot of activities. There are bike paths, running paths, beaches, and you can rent boats. It's a city that is very abundant in green spaces, and there are parks everywhere."* As well as being famously windy, Chicago is also rather chilly, so in winter pedestrians make for the pedways – five miles of underground and overhead walkways that connect the city's downtown.

Charlotte Wager, chief talent officer at Chicago-headquartered firm Jenner & Block, tells us: *"I was struck by Chicago being a modern, metropolitan and sophisticated city with theater, opera, beautiful architecture, museums, parks and the magnificent lakefront, but without some of the stresses that come with living on either coast."* She reports that *"the Chicago legal community is small and close-knit – not necessarily in numbers but in the way it operates – which makes practicing law here all the more enjoyable. It's very supportive."* The Chicago Bar Association is a popular center for lawyerly life in the city, with its wood-burning fireplace, popular lunchroom and full program of social events, including the annual musical comedy revue. The show's been running for more than 90 years, and pun-tastic show titles like 'A Christmas Quarrel,' 'Pay Miserables' and 'The Merry Old Land of Lawz' suggest its wit is evergreen.

Put Your Hands Up 4 Detroit

Defeated by a population decline of more than 60% since its 1950s heyday, Detroit filed the largest-ever municipal bankruptcy case in 2013. But in the past few years the acres of boarded-up and crumbling houses and public buildings have attracted swaths of young professionals and empty-nesters to the city. Value for money and opportunity for investment has proven an attractive lure, and since 2008 the sale of luxury homes has risen by 107%. Detroit now offers a legal scene that stretches beyond foreclosures and bankruptcies, with real estate and emerging company work growing fast. Sarah Staup, director of professional personnel at Detroit-founded Dykema Gossett, tells us: *"We are seeing more and more younger associates living in Detroit. This past recruitment season we had a couple of people who wanted to be here. We wanted to put them in our suburban office* [in Bloomfield Hills] *due to their practice, but they wanted to be down here. Detroit has challenges, but it has growing sectors that are attracting young professionals and art groups."* Part of this is because *"the cost of living is really manageable. If you aspire to own a home, you are able to do that here."* Duane Morris, Foley & Lardner and Pepper Hamilton also have offices in Detroit; elsewhere in Michigan, there's Schiff Hardin and Dykema in Ann Arbor.

Staup goes on to tell us about *"up north, where there's so much natural beauty and all sorts of recreational opportunities. This state is an absolute find for anyone who's into the outdoors. And if you are into sports at all, it's a mecca."* Indeed, in addition to major league teams of the 'big four' variety (baseball, basketball, hockey and football), there's the lake and Michigan's Upper Peninsula, which offer every water-based diversion imaginable. There's also the country's only feather bowling alley in Detroit's Cadieux Cafe. We hear the quirky sport is a niche interest even in its homeland of Belgium.

A sailor went to CCC

The three Cs for a successful legal career in Ohio are Columbus, Cleveland and Cincinnati. Although they don't always boast the same big names as Chicago, each has a bustling legal market. Cleveland, birthplace of Jones Day and Squire Patton Boggs, has suffered from a bad rep in the past. Efforts to renovate the area and bring about an urban renaissance have been ongoing since the 80s, and in spite of ups and downs there are concrete results to suggest that the haters might just be out of touch with the real Cleveland. As one proud associate there said, *"at law school they told us we're one of the biggest legal markets between Chicago and New York."*

The medical center Cleveland Clinic has been ranked as one of the top five hospitals in the US and is widely recognized as a big contributor to Ohio's thriving bioscience industry. The city isn't lagging behind culturally either: a $350 million architectural renovation of the Cleveland Museum of Art was initiated in 2002 with a view toward catering to citizens and tourists, and there's also the Rock n Roll Hall of Fame, designed by top dog of modern architecture I M Pei, on the lakefront, as well as the Playhouse Square, the second-largest performing arts center in the US (right behind the Lincoln Center).

Columbus is the capital of the Buckeye State, and its swing-state politics have attracted an *"unusual number of top political minds,"* says one Ohio State student. Culture is the order of the day in Columbus: the local cuisine is highly revered, and annual music and arts festival ComFest comes highly recommended. Speaking of cuisine, Cincinnati once adopted the moniker 'Porkopolis' for its thriving pork industry in the 19th century – apparently the excess of pork fat that came as a result provided Messrs Procter and Gamble with the means to build a thriving soap business. For the most part, the city's broken free of its porky past and is increasingly a retreat for hipsters setting up microbreweries. Another claim to fame is the Cincinnati Reds, America's first official baseball team.

Money talks

The Midwest has been called America's breadbasket, and indeed its rich soil makes it some of the most lucrative farmland in the world. As well as wheat for your daily loaf, there's soybeans, corn and cattle in abundance. Over the past few years, farmers have been struggling with

Regional Guide

685

drought conditions as well as unexpected torrential rain, both of which have prompted them to ramp up the pressure on the government to maintain crop insurance payments. So-called 'ag-gag' laws are another farming legal battleground: these essentially ban journalists and protesters from filming inside agricultural facilities or taking on jobs with the intention of reporting on their findings.

Industry is the other traditional cornerstone of the Midwestern economy, particularly in Michigan, where the economy is driven by the 'big three' automobile manufacturers that have dominated the home-grown scene for nearly a century: Chrysler, Ford and General Motors. Detroit's dramatic rise and decline has become a lesson in the unreliable fortunes of the American motor industry. When times are good, orders surge. When times are bad, potential customers are thin on the ground, and those that remain are more likely to be tempted by the growing variety of foreign imports.

Barack Obama opted to bail out the motor industry in 2009 by handing Chrysler and General Motors billion-dollar loans. Since then, the industry has made an impressive turnaround. Low replacement rates during the recession mean that the average American car is now a grand old age of 11.5 years, an all-time high. This is good news for manufacturers, because as the economy recovers and household wealth grows, the demand for new vehicles is surging. Sarah Staup feels that *"we have finally turned the corner, and there's a positive horizon ahead – we're used to getting tough economic news in Michigan, so we can recover pretty quickly."*

The Midwest as a whole continues to pull out of the recession, and former industrial centers are forging new identities as their inner city areas regenerate and redevelop. Still, there are plenty of long-term challenges to the region's economy. An aging population, combined with a historical resistance to immigration, means the workforce is shrinking, even as the demand for jobs picks up. Meanwhile, the strong dollar is a threat to Chicago's growing tech expertise, and long-term it's hard to be sure that the recovery of the automobile industry will stay on the road to success. For young lawyers, though, the region offers a wide array of international BigLaw options, combined with low house prices, the promise of a livable work/life balance, and a more low-key way of life.

New York

"It's overwhelmingly awesome. It sucks you in. It's hard to live here then go somewhere else. New Yorkers rule the world."

EVERYONE wants to monkey around in the concrete jungle. *"It's got everything: the best food and the most diverse culture of any city. It's the best city in the world."* Those who crave a spot in the heart of the legal action in Manhattan, though, be warned: the location comes at a hefty premium. Even on a BigLaw starting salary, rents are a stretch: *"$3,000 a month for a shoebox"* makes us question how Carrie could afford those Manolos. In fact, NYC has the highest cost of living of any US city, and the 16th highest in the world. If you've got any cash left after paying rent, two tickets to the movies will typically set you back more than $30; gym membership can be around $100 a month.

For those willing to commute, New York's most populated borough, Brooklyn, is a popular place to look, and rents in the area are on average 20% lower than those of the city center. However, with the average price of property now close to $800,000, it's no longer the budget location it once was. *"Queens or New Jersey are now the most viable options,"* NYC associates tell us. In more extreme cases, we've heard from sources commuting from out of state (usually New Jersey), noting that the favorable position of many BigLaw firms makes the trip relatively smooth. Partners, with a vastly superior budget and often bigger families, *"tend to live on the Upper East or Upper West sides."* of the city. *"There's more open space and the apartments are bigger."*

Gold digga

In May 1792, 24 stockbrokers signed an agreement outside 68 Wall Street (called the Buttonwood Agreement, as the ink was put to paper under a buttonwood tree) that led to the founding of the New York Stock Exchange (NYSE), today the largest stock exchange in the world. Most, if not all, of the trillions of dollars' worth of financial transactions the exchange hosts are conducted electronically these days, in seconds; but beneath the streets in the vaults of the Federal Reserve Bank of New York, 50 feet below sea level, you'll find more gold bullion than in any other gold repository anywhere on the planet. The thousands of tons of gold contained within the vault are worth hundreds of billions of dollars, the vast majority of it owned by central banks of various nations.

The financial services industry employs more than 460,000 people in NYC and accounts for roughly 35% of the city's income. The likes of Goldman Sachs, Morgan Stanley, JPMorgan Chase and Bank of America Merrill Lynch require legions of legal advisers, in pretty much every area of law you can think of, from employment to capital markets, white-collar defense to restructuring and tax. The vast amounts of work provided by banking giants remain a big draw for the largest US and international law firms in Manhattan today, as well as smaller niche players. However, as Bess Sully, chief human resources officer at Sheppard Mullin, points out: *"Not all New York legal work is dictated by Wall Street. While every kind of finance work, from straightforward banking and finance to IPOs and LBOs, is available, other areas such as IP and environmental law are generating a lot of revenue."*

More than 10% of the Fortune 500 is headquartered in the city, including Verizon, Pfizer, American Express and Time Warner. New York has the highest proportion of overseas employers of any US city: one in ten private sector jobs is with a foreign company based in NYC, and post-Brexit vote the city overtook London to become the most popular location for overseas commercial property investors. A large number of foreign law firms, including four of the UK's five magic circle firms (Clifford Chance, Linklaters, Allen & Overy and Freshfields) have offices in New York and DC to serve international clients conducting business in the region, as well as to compete in the US market themselves.

Center of the Earth

For almost as long as the United States of America has existed, New York has stood as its biggest gateway to the rest of the world. More than 12 million immigrants came to the country via Ellis Island between 1892 and 1954 (though most of the island is in fact part of New Jersey), and NYC today is home to more than three million foreign-born migrants. The Big Apple could also be described as America's diversity capital, home as it is to the nation's largest Jewish, African American, Puerto Rican and Italian American populations. As such, it's all the more disappointing that diversity in BigLaw remains an ongoing issue – you can find more information on the subject here. Multinationals like Baker McKenzie and Shearman & Sterling encourage international travel for associates to help address these issues, but as with most firms, there's still a way to go.

Legendary author E.B. White dubbed New York City the 'Capital of the World'. He probably hadn't stopped to consider the future of legal practice as a multinational enterprise when he said this, but would have been right to do so, as there are few better routes into international law than practicing in the Big Apple. *"There's very open communication"* at most global firms, *"time difference aside there's really no issues collaborating with Paris or London. You learn so much more from people with different backgrounds."* Language skills will serve you well if that's a path you want to take (and in NYC generally, as the city is home to speakers of literally hundreds of languages). Associates told us *"coming in with a language is a huge plus, it can come up a lot and get you staffed on cases you wouldn't otherwise,"* though many assured us *"it's not essential. What's most important is having an interest in both US law and working with international clients."*

No city for old men (or Californians)

We asked junior associates if the New York City cliché of insanely long work hours is accurate. Mostly yes, they replied, but it's not just the city's lawyers who could do with some more downtime. *"To be honest, people in other industries have to work just as hard,"* one associate reflected. They were surely thinking of investment bankers – or perhaps over worked bartenders – when they added: *"Being an attorney is probably less extreme than other professions."* Still, one admitted that *"working in this city can be a little crazy; being on call 24 hours a day can be a little wearing. We probably work harder than in other parts of the country."* Others agreed: *"In California this schedule would be insane. But the cut-throat image is overplayed."*

You'd expect to be compensated handsomely for your hard work, and you'd be correct to do so. It's of little surprise that the 2016 associate salary rise extravaganza was ignited in New York City, by hyper-prestigious Cravath, Swaine & Moore. The firm's introduction of a $180,000 starting salary for newcomers took many by surprise, but the cream of NYC BigLaw quickly fell in line. Those outside the traditional institutions often thought *"it was no sure thing we'd match,"* but very many firms did. Even more unexpectedly, the move was also followed in markets like Philadelphia and Texas with far lower living costs, leaving associates there *"pleasantly surprised"* and New Yorkers perhaps feeling a bit shortchanged – as an indicator, living in Houston will save you about 25% of your cash, compared to being in the Big Apple.

"In California this schedule would be insane. But the cut-throat image is overplayed."

While dreams of becoming a lawyer in New York were dashed for many graduates coming into the industry in the days after the recession, the situation seems to have picked up, with firms hiring more summers in the last few years. Luckily for young lawyers, there's a trend toward *"retaining people longer"* in order to make the most of their experience and expertise. As you'd expect, culture and entertainment-wise New York is *"awesome,"* associates confirmed. There's a seemingly infinite number of visitor attractions and things to do in your spare time; among our sources, the Museum of the City of New York came especially highly recommended, as did the NYC Transit Museum, a little off the beaten track in Brooklyn. Fitness freaks will be pleased to know New York *"is a really active city. It's easy to go running, cycling or just for a wander round Central Park with friends."* And if for some reason you tire of the metropolis, *"you can head out to the beach or mountains,"* both of which are accessible via car or New York's decent public transport infrastructure. Most places are reasonably easy to get to via the subway network, and the majority of associates we spoke to for our research reported *"it's a very convenient location when it comes to public transport, most of the major law firms are within a couple of blocks of each other. But the closer you get to Times Square the busier it gets!"* Foodies will be pleased to hear that you're never far from a great restaurant in NYC.

Empire state of mind

Columbia, Cornell and New York University are the holy trinity of law schools in the Empire State, but they're not the be all and end all, and we've interviewed associates at top firms who'd graduated from Fordham, St John's, Cardozo and Brooklyn School of Law among others. Of course, it's perfectly viable to study at one of the country's (or world's) other top legal institutions and make the trip to the Big Apple. While firms in many regions will look for demonstrable commitment to the local area you're applying to work in, that's less important in New York: the prominence of its legal market is reason enough to gravitate there. What's more crucial is being able to explain why you want to work for the particular firm you're interviewing with – *Chambers Associate* profiles will provide an excellent starting guide, but the more research you put in, the better.

As for exit opportunities, where better to look to the future of your legal career than the home of some of BigLaw's biggest clients? More and more associates are heading to in-house positions than ever before, as companies bulk up their internal legal divisions. Baker McKenzie North American managing partner Rick Hammett explains: *"what you're going to see is a range of different opportunities, far more than once upon a time when you'd start at a firm as first year associate then simply move forward. What's going to happen as different providers of legal services grow is that some students will* embrace traditional opportunities, others will find alternative routes into the profession – for instance, as companies develop their in-house departments." If you do fancy sticking it out and grabbing a slice of the equity at your firm one day, it's worth considering that if a firm's hub is in New York there may be more competition than in satellite offices; on the other hand, close proximity to clients means you'll have a leg up for business development.

The final word must go to the associate who described New York as *"overwhelmingly awesome. It sucks you in. It's hard to live here then go somewhere else. New Yorkers rule the world."*

"We are seeing associates with sophisticated knowledge of law firms as businesses. Associates are very attuned now to the footprint of law firms: where the resources are, their national and international reach."
Robert Hays, chairman of King & Spalding

The Pacific Northwest

The Pacific Northwest drips coolness: with its grunge heritage and a techy future, is it patently the place to be for young lawyers?

Lately things, they don't seem the same

Seattle: nestled between the picturesque Puget Sound and Lake Washington, flanked by the Olympic and Cascade Mountains, loomed over by Mount Rainier; for many it's synonymous with its old Hendrix and Cobain days, for some it's still reminiscent of jazzy nights with Ray Charles and Quincy Jones. And while these musical legends left a rich legacy in this culturally complex city – as well as some of their old stuff (the Experience Music Project is worth a trip for Cobain's smashed guitars alone) – the city has now put down its broken guitar, emerged gracefully from the grunge period, and got itself on the straight and narrow. So much so that Starbucks is a staple, and even oozes chicness, provided you find the original branch down at Pike Place Market, where they've been spelling customers' names wrong since 1971.

Believe it: today Seattle is a hub for green industry, a model for sustainable development, one of the fastest-growing cities in the country and a major gateway for trade with Asia thanks to its port, the 8th largest in the US. It is home to massive businesses such as Amazon, Starbucks, Boeing, department store Nordstrom and freight forwarder Expeditors International. For obvious reasons, Microsoft is also based here. Time to put down your skinny mocha and do some serious work...

With the lights out, it's less dangerous

Portland – aka the City of Roses – is Oregon's commercial and cultural epicenter. This verdant haven is home to the country's largest wilderness park within city limits, covering a whopping 5,000 acres. It also plays host to the smallest (Mill Ends Park is no more than a two-foot diameter circle) and the city consistently features among the top 10 greenest cities in the US, if not the world. Among Portland's many pull factors are rose gardens, abundant outdoor activities, liberal values, microbreweries and coffee enthusiasm. If it's falafel off a cart you're after, Portland is where it's at: both US News & World Report and CNN have named it the best place in the world for street food.

But it's not all pretty flowers and culinary delights. Portland is known for attracting big businesses, most notably athletic and footwear manufacturers: adidas, Nike, Columbia Sportswear, Li Ning (China's largest footwear manufacturer), Hi-Tec Sports and Korkers all call Portland home. KinderCare, Laika, The Original Pancake House, The Spaghetti Factory and Leatherman also reside here.

"Will the last person leaving Seattle – turn out the lights."

On April 16, 1971, real estate agents Bob McDonald and Jim Youngren put these words on a billboard near SeaTac International Airport in protest of the phenomenon known locally as the 'Boeing Bust'. The Boeing company had previously established Seattle as a center for aircraft manufacturing, but following the oil crisis and a costly debacle over the Boeing 747, the company suffered and many were forced to leave the area in search of alternative work.

Thankfully the area recovered and underwent a technological revolution as a stream of new software, biotechnology and internet companies led to an economic revival. This began with Microsoft's 1979 move from Albuquerque to nearby Bellevue. Seattle then became home to a number of tech companies, including Amazon, Nintendo of America and T-Mobile USA.

Portland underwent a similar change in the 90s, welcoming computer components manufacturer Intel, which is now one of the area's largest employers. Today Greater Portland is home to more than 1,200 tech companies, which has led to the nickname 'Silicon Forest' in homage to the area's arboreal abundance. Nearby Boise, aka 'The City of Trees' in Idaho, has also seen a rise in technology investment and hi-tech industry in recent years; resident businesses include Hewlett-Packard and Microsoft.

Degrees of knowledge

The Pacific Northwest has a *"somewhat typical legal market in the sense that you'll find practice groups in all traditional legal sectors, including litigation, corporate, real estate and land use, taxation and IP,"* says Paul Danielson, recruiter for BCG Attorney Search. However, the area hasn't escaped the influence of its tech-focused residents. Danielson explains: *"While not on par with the Silicon Valley in terms of relative revenue and the sheer number of tech-based companies, the tech sector's significance to the overall Pacific Northwest economy is what has driven the demand for patent prosecution work historically. While* the demand for patent litigation associates and partners has waned recently due to a rash of hiring in the Pacific Northwest which left firms fully staffed on that front, patent prosecution remains strong in these sectors." With regards to hiring patent litigators though, watch this space, as he explains *"it goes in cycles."*

Danielson further updates us in 2016 confirming that over the past few years *"finance, lending, M&A and litigation have all increased in demand and are very strong at the moment. Litigation is a particularly active market in Seattle right now, so lateral litigation candidates looking to move to Seattle should jump on the opportunity. Taxation work has also ticked up, which is expected at this stage in the market cycle."* He explains this is due to a growth in wealth following the business boom, and then families and businesses responding with tax planning.

"Nearly all openings call for a technical degree in computer science, electronic engineering or physics."

There's an important caveat to consider for all IP-related opportunities in the region, Danielson warns, particularly at midsized and major firms: *"Nearly all openings call for a technical degree in computer science, electronic engineering or physics, as well as direct experience with things like software, programming, wireless communications and microchip technology."*

There are also plenty of other practice areas thriving in the region at the moment. Danielson notes: *"Portland and Seattle have both enjoyed significant and steady population growth due to the attractiveness of the region from a quality-of-life perspective, and this in turn has driven demand for legal services in real estate and land use, as well as litigation positions that emphasize experience with construction disputes, which we see on a relatively regular basis. There is also plenty of transactional work to be had, as many major brands, manufacturers and retailers are headquartered in the area and nearby."*

While most industry sectors in the Pacific Northwest were mangled by the recession, Danielson says that *"employment has generally come back online at a steady pace."* However, *"overall demand is still depressed compared to pre-crash levels. For instance, housing and real estate jobs have come back considerably relative to their recession lows, but if you zoom out a bit they are still slightly below pre-recession levels."*

Livin' La Vida Legal

We'll be blunt: it rains a lot in Seattle. One Perkins Coie associate called it *"the coolest city with the worst weather."* Despite this, Paul Danielson asserts that *"it is often not* as bad as claimed, and many residents prefer it because it contributes to the lush and verdant nature of the local environment." An associate at K&L Gates (Bill Gates' dad gave the firm its current name) agreed: *"If it didn't rain so much, it wouldn't look like this. When the clouds go away, it's beautiful."* Of course, what's *"not as bad as claimed"* for one person might be just plain awful for another. Danielson presents us with an example: *"During my first year of college in the greater Seattle area, there were over 100 days in a row where it rained at some point, often throughout the entire day. That will get to you after a while."*

"You'd be looked at strangely if you wore a suit to work and weren't going to court."

The region's renowned *"relaxed"* and *"quirky"* vibe lends itself an *"informal legal atmosphere,"* our sources agreed. A Perkins Coie associate said: *"When I interviewed in other cities, I got taken to the country club, but that just doesn't happen here. It's a very laid back legal environment. People aren't the mythical figures you see at the New York firms, and you'd be looked at strangely if you wore a suit to work and weren't going to court. There's more of an emphasis on a balanced lifestyle too. We have days when we work late, but it's not as regular as in the other legal markets that I've worked in. I like being able to have a life outside of work."*

While you could argue this comes at a price since, historically, salaries in the region have been on average between 20% and 30% lower than in the major legal markets, Danielson notes: *"We have been seeing a small but potentially significant shift in thinking among many firms towards raising their compensation packages, in part to be competitive for top candidates from other markets, but more likely because the economic and population boom in Portland and Seattle have led to a rapid rise in the cost-of-living, particularly housing."* If this happens, then billable hours or billable rates and bonuses will all have to increase: Perkins Coie recently offered its Seattle associates a two tier billing system – those opting for the higher level can expect to receive payouts in line with the New York market. Another thing to consider is that the Pacific Northwest is now targeted by techies working in the Bay Area trying to avoid San Fran and Silicon Valley's super-high rents, which is in turn causing a rise in Portland house prices. This is unlikely to dip again.

"You also see a relatively low turnover at the associate and partner level, because people simply tend to stay put once they are established."

Major law schools in Portland include Lewis & Clark, the University of Oregon and Willamette, while Seattle has the University of Washington, Seattle University and Gonzaga University. Cooley, Davis Wright Tremaine, DLA Piper, K&L Gates, Stoel Rives, Sedgwick and Perkins Coie all have a big stake in the region's commercial market, though legal work for local businesses and individuals is often performed by *"solid midsized regional firms or local firms"* because it's a smaller market. Getting hired here isn't a walk in the park, Danielson explains: *"Because the Portland and Seattle areas are so desirable in terms of the quality of life, and because the legal markets are smaller relative to major cities like New York, Chicago, Los Angeles and San Francisco, competition for law firm jobs is fierce. You also see a relatively low turnover at the associate and partner level, because people simply tend to stay put once they are established."*

"Aside from the generally positive credentials like a degree from a prestigious law school, top grades and clerkship experience, Pacific Northwest firms place a high degree of emphasis on having local ties and/or extensive familiarity with the region," he continues. *"A part of this is due to the weather – as lush and beautiful as the region is, a number of recruiting coordinators I have met with from Portland and Seattle firms have stories of lateral associates departing within a year or two after discovering the weather did not agree with them."* Our associate sources agreed, with one saying: *"I think employers look for good grades, but also some sort of connection geographically. Firms are looking for people who are going to stay; that's a big part of it."*

"You also see a relatively low turnover at the associate and partner level, because people simply tend to stay put once they are established."

The Southeast

A steadily recovering banking sector, a growing technology industry and relatively low living costs have seen major cities such as Miami, Atlanta and Charlotte become increasingly diverse and vibrant economic centers...

Not-so-small-town America

The three major hubs for those looking to embark upon a legal career in the Southeast are Atlanta, Georgia; Charlotte, North Carolina; and Miami, Florida. Compared to New York, the go-to location for many ambitious young attorneys, these cities are positively deserted, all with populations well below one million. A lower population density has a lot of positives, though, not least the price of real estate and cost of living, both of which are significantly lower than in the great metropolises of Chicago or New York. As one Charlotte-based associate put it: "*Here in the Southeast you can have all the benefits of living in a big city but with that lovely small town feel to it.*" Their smaller size has not stopped these three cities from attracting the attention of many national and multinational companies whose presence helps make local business communities cutting-edge places to work.

City Too Busy To Hate

Atlanta set down roots in 1837 at the intersection of two great railroads. After complete destruction during the Civil War, the city rose from the ashes and, capitalizing on its position as the primary transport hub for the South East, grew into a vibrant cultural and economic center. Excellent rail and highway links enable national businesses here to access markets across the country, while Hartsfield-Jackson Atlanta International airport (the busiest in the world by both passenger volume and aircraft traffic since 1998) opens up the rest of the globe. Atlanta's bustling business community that thrives today is a nod to the city's nickname, coined during the days of the civil rights movement: the City Too Busy To Hate.

Atlanta's transport links have helped its economy become both expansive and very diverse. The city's rail connection remains, as it houses the classification yards of both Norfolk Southern and CSX. Many major companies have their national or international headquarters within the city's metropolitan area, including UPS, Coca-Cola, Delta Air Lines and Home Depot.

Georgia contains the highest concentration of colleges and universities of any of the Southern states, and 28% of African Americans in Atlanta hold a bachelor's degree, second in the US only to DC at 32%. An abundance of bright young graduates has helped the city to build up thriving media and technology sectors. The city is a major television programming center and home to the headquarters of Cox Enterprises, which owns the nation's third largest cable television service and publishes over a dozen major daily and weekly local newspapers. Other notable television channels based here are Cartoon Network and several CNN subsidiaries.

Although Georgia and Atlanta in particular were badly hit by the financial crash and recession, there have been signs of a steady recovery over the past few years. Many of the jobs created recently have been in the highly paid finance and professional services sectors – areas where legal advice is often required, which is good news for lawyers in the area. Many national and international firms view Atlanta as an essential part of their network of domestic offices, with the likes of Jones Day, DLA Piper and Greenberg Traurig all maintaining offices in the city.

Many perceive Southern firms to embody a certain gentility and, as a result, an old-fashioned approach to work. However, we've heard the opposite from associates in Atlanta. "*Our Atlanta office is much more relaxed than the others; it's casual, and you quickly get to know almost everyone in the office,*" said one junior. Compared to the Big Apple, Atlanta's smallish size and less intensive working culture are big selling points to many, but one trade-off is that nights out are not as regular. As a Finnegan associate explained: "*People tend to be a bit older, so they often have a spouse and kids they want to get home to after work. But on weekends we'll invite each other to our kids' birthdays, summer barbecues, that kind of thing.*" On the plus side, the cost of living is lower in Atlanta than the likes of New York, and house prices even fell a couple of years ago, meaning that a BigLaw starting salary of $160,000 stretches even further.

The hornet's nest

Charlotte, North Carolina was first incorporated in 1768. Since then it's grown into a major financial market, second only to New York as a US banking center (in terms of the value of assets held). NCNB is still in residence, although it is now in the form of the national headquarters of Bank of America. Until 2008, homegrown banking giant Wachovia also operated out of Charlotte, but that year it was bought by Wells Fargo, and Wachovia's Charlotte office is now home to the East Coast operations of Wells Fargo. *"The presence of these huge national and international banks brings a sophistication to the legal work you don't get in many other regional locations,"* thought an associate at K&L Gates.

Charlotte also plays host to 13 Fortune 500 companies, including Duke Energy and Sonic Automotive. Other major businesses span a huge range of sectors, from television production (Time Warner Cable and Fox Sports 1) to food and drink (Compass Group USA and Coca-Cola Bottling Co. Consolidated). Charlotte is also home to over 240 companies tied to the energy sector, including Babcock & Wilcox, Siemens Energy and Toshiba, earning it the title 'The New Energy Capital'. *"As a city it's making great strides at bringing in new industries,"* said one associate. *"Lots of companies are relocating here, and the economy is really diversifying. I definitely get the impression it's on the up and up – they're building a new railyard and expanding the airport as well."* With that growth comes an increased need for legal services of many different kinds – good news for local lawyers.

This isn't all that commends a legal career in Charlotte, however; there's also the *"beautiful weather, great travel opportunities and great universities,"* a local source pointed out. The city has all the amenities one might expect: *"Plenty of shows, plays and art museums. And lots of upmarket stores like Armani and Chanel. The restaurants really are fantastic too."* The cost of living is low, with one associate enthusing: *"On a BigLaw starting salary you can live like a king in Charlotte! Join the best athletics club, eat out every night and even afford to drive around in a brand-new BMW!"* Another thought: *"If you work in a regional office here of a firm with a global presence, you get the best of both worlds. It's easy to maintain a work/life balance, and you get to draw upon resources from all across the world."* Our sources were all of the opinion that *"the city is definitely recovering from the hit the banking sector took in 2008. Right now, Charlotte is hiring!"*

Welcome to Miami

Miami was founded in 1896 and grew rapidly. The late 20th century, following the Cuban Revolution and upheaval across the Caribbean and Latin America, saw an influx of wealthy Cubans and others from the region. Today, Miami is a multicultural and colorful international financial and cultural center whose growth has outpaced the national average in the past year. As a result, the city has continued to attract a wide range of businesses and corporations from around the world, and household names like American Airlines, Office Depot and Motorola all have their headquarters here. Miami is very closely intertwined with the Spanish-speaking nations of the Caribbean and Latin America, and it has a very large population of native Spanish speakers, second in size only to El Paso, Texas. Many multinationals have taken advantage of these language skills and ease of access and established their Latin American headquarters in the city, including Western Union, Microsoft and Canon.

As a result, Miami has developed a very diverse professional services industry – perfect for an aspiring attorney seeking a varied and challenging career. According to an associate at Holland & Knight, *"Miami is THE legal city in Florida. The reason is that it's culturally vibrant and very international – especially because of the Spanish-speaking influences."* The city is a thriving trade hub, with the Port of Miami and Miami International Airport some of the busiest ports of entry in the country. Tourism also sucks in money, and one in seven of the world's cruise passengers sets off from Miami.

Putting down roots

Southeastern natives could not speak more highly of the atmosphere and working culture common to firms and offices in the region. As one associate explained: *"We're expected to cope with complex matters and to produce great work, but there's more of a balance. No one's working an 80-hour week like some in New York. I think possibly it's something to do with that traditional Southern hospitality. It's really just an ability to relate to others and to understand where they're coming from."* Also, being based in a smaller urban community means that being an attorney still carries the kind of weight more common a century ago. *"As a lawyer you're a well-respected member of the community. This carries a certain level of prestige though also big expectations."*

This sense of community and pleasant atmosphere often makes it easier for associates to stay at a firm long-term. Employers *"expect you to work hard and put the hours in, but they know family is important and respect that. They allow you to reach your own balance,"* said one associate, while another told us: *"I work with a lot of parents and, say, if their kid had a soccer game then, barring the imminent closing of a major deal, they can get there and log back in later when it suits them."* Our sources felt the emphasis is *"definitely on the long term. They want you to stay and put down roots. The scales tip in favor of people staying put for the seven or eight years it might take to make partner, rather than heading up and out."*

So, you're set on a career in the Southeast. What next?

"You really need to be able to demonstrate a commitment not just to the law and the firm, but to the city you plan to be based in," thought our associate sources. *"Firms here want people to stay, not head off after a few years."* In order to demonstrate you're serious about a certain city, it *"would be best to attend law school in that state – unless, of course, you're at a top-tier firm elsewhere."* One associate urged applicants *"to summer down here at a law firm or intern in another local industry – either is very attractive to firms. Explore other options as well, such as clerking or pro bono work. It will really give you a chance to see what we're all about and why people love it here so much!"*

"On a BigLaw starting salary you can live like a king in Charlotte! Join the best athletics club, eat out every night and even afford to drive around in a brand-new BMW!"

Texas & The South

"In the South there's a greater attention to form and decorum. If you're a jackass around here, you ain't gonna last long."

Everything is bigger in Texas...

...SO they say, and not just with regard to the intimidating food portions. Land in Texas and the South is cheaper than elsewhere, particularly in contrast to Chicago and New York, making the area popular with big families; playgrounds in Texas now bustle with an above-average number of kids. As Karen Sargent of the career services office at Southern Methodist University notes: *"Texas is a great place for young families. There are excellent school districts and lots of ways to get involved with the community. It's bringing people in from all over the world."* For a state that often receives bad press for its conservative values, you may be surprised to learn that San Antonio, Texas's second biggest city, boasted the largest community of gay parents in the US according to a poll conducted back in 2011, with the metropolitan mix of its big cities providing something different to the Southern stereotype.

The state is welcoming to more than just those who want to settle down. *"Houston's a great place to live for young people,"* an associate at Baker Botts in Houston attested. *"You can live close to the office and enjoy a short commute and relatively low cost of living. Generally, younger folks might rent an apartment close in for a bit, then look for a house with a yard and a few bedrooms when they want to start a family."* Already the state's biggest city, Houston has been a popular destination for young attorneys in the past few years. As an associate at Bracewell stipulated: *"I think Houston has garnered a lot more national recognition as a good place to live with a good legal market, since we weathered the recession better than some cities. In the past it might have seemed weird for people to move to Texas if they didn't already have connections with the state, but now it's completely normal."*

Texas has the second largest economy of the United States, cashing in a healthy $1.6 trillion dollars, and an abundance of investment opportunities has bred pretty healthy legal markets. Dallas and Houston are two of the largest markets in the country, with the Dallas/Fort Worth area housing more than 10,000 corporate HQs, more than anywhere else in the States. As such, Texas firms have opened their doors to a flood of lateral hires over the past few years. One Haynes & Boone associate told us: *"There's been a lot of change in the Houston market over the last few years, with many national and international firms opening up here. We've seen people leaving the traditional Texan firms to go to them, so there's been*

more in the way of turnover than normal." Since 2010, Latham & Watkins, Sidley Austin, Quinn Emanuel, Kirkland & Ellis, Arnold & Porter, K&L Gates, Reed Smith, Orrick and Katten Muchin have all launched Houston branches. Longstanding Texan firms are increasingly under pressure to up their game since young associates looking to start their careers now have a lot more choice of where to go.

Houston and Dallas rank among the highest-paying metropolitan areas in the country for lawyers, and most associates in Texas can expect to earn the same as their New York counterparts. Since the state doesn't collect individual income tax, however, the standard BigLaw salary goes a lot further here: according to a recent CNN survey, a salary of $160,000 in Dallas gets you the same buying power as someone raking in $374,772 in New York. Inevitably, the state's social services have suffered from these low tax rates, but for young lawyers they're highly alluring.

But it's not just lawyers that are falling for the Lone Star State; Texas remains a popular destination for tradesmen, professionals, families... anybody in fact. A 2015 Forbes list of America's fastest growing cities put a Texan trio of Houston, Austin and Dallas in the top three (in that order). In a recent survey by the US Census Bureau, the state housed eight of 2015's top 20 US counties when measured by population gain. According to the Texas A&M University Real Estate Center, swelling numbers have pushed Texas' median home price up by 37% in the past decade, topping out at $189,000 in January 2016. Still, living in Texas remains a steal compared to the likes of LA or New York.

Oh my gush!

A thick black soup rained down on Texas and the South in the early 20th century and continues to shape the economic landscape to this day. The oil discoveries of the so-called Gusher Age fueled a meteoric rise in the area's fortunes, and these days a number of high-profile petroleum companies are based in the state, among them ExxonMobil, ConocoPhillips, Valero, Halliburton and Marathon Oil. These Fortune 500s generate not only power but also a healthy check for lawyers, with energy work a huge component of many local firms' business.

The boom time may well be up in this respect, though. Due to an increasing global supply and falling demand there have been huge falls in oil prices of late, falling to a ten-year low of $26.55 on January 20th 2016. Texas produces more than a third of the United States' total oil output, and such disparaging figures posed a huge blow to the sector, losing around a third of its jobs (9,000 direct and indirect jobs) since a price collapse in 2014. In spite of this torrid affair, the picture now looks a little rosier. The OPEC countries agreed to reduce output in 2016, increasing exports from the US oil fields, and prices have recovered a little from their nadir. Then there's President Trump's encouraging attitude toward the energy sector, with the president repeatedly stating his determination to cut regulation and trigger a new energy boom.

Clearly a revived market would be good for lawyers, with more deal-related work, but ongoing fluctuations would also bode well for the state's legal workforce, prompting a rise in bankruptcy, restructuring and employment-related work. Amanda Kelly, manager of attorney recruitment at Haynes and Boone, remains optimistic: *"Despite the downturn in energy prices, the Texas economy is still robust. For law school students the array of jobs available here, coupled with the low cost of living, continues to make Texas very enticing."* Karen Sargent of SMU chimes in to note that *"a number of Northeastern schools are now bringing their students down here to recruit."*

Whatever happens on that front, the energy sector isn't Texas's only pull-factor. As Kelly points out: *"Many people don't realize that Texas is second only to New York in the number of Fortune 1000 company headquarters. Our firm serves 20% of the Fortune 500 corporations in a wide variety of industries, including energy, technology, aviation, transportation and healthcare so we are diversified and staying busy. Right now, for example, real estate has ramped up nicely, and a good amount of our work is coming in from outside Texas, especially on the IP side."* Sargent adds: *"I'd say intellectual property law was originally the rocket docket in East Texas – we have a US patent and trademark office opening in Dallas now, and IP is a big focus of our law school. Obviously energy is big here, but that ebbs and flows with the economy. On the corporate side, we're a center for some of the largest corporations in the country, and that brings in a big deal of M&A work. Law firms are now moving into the Dallas area for IP and transactions, where they'd previously moved to Houston for energy."*

Gone to Texas

The Panic of 1819 saw the first wave of mass migration to Texas. Droves of Americans flocked to the state with crippling debts hard on their heels, leaving only the simple message 'Gone To Texas,' or 'GTT,' fixed to their doors. Today it's lawyers and other corporate workers who are relocating to the Lone Star State en masse: since the millennium, one million more people have moved to Texas from other states than have left, with many seeking out a cheaper way of life and a less regulated climate in which to do business.

As a result, Texas's traditionally resource-fueled economy has become increasingly tech-oriented as the likes of Dell and AT&T plant HQs in the state; many have opened operations in The Silicon Hills of Austin in particular, including Facebook, eBay, Google and Apple. To maintain its competitive edge in a time of fast-developing technology and fickle alliances, certain cities have resorted to facelifts. *"San Antonio, for example, is a very family-oriented city,"* a Jackson Walker associate told us, *"but there's a growing culture of nightlife benefiting from the growing number of tech firms bringing young professionals into the city."*

"Dallas is now drawing in young people who are attracted to the economy and are moving into all the new developments," Karen Sargent tells us. *"They're moving into areas that are becoming heavily populated with young people, and they're having a good time."* The city has been investing in its Arts District and green spaces in particular; Houston is likewise intent on creating a greener, more attractive city, spending more than $6 billion on regeneration projects over the past 15 years. *"Houston has really been developing its downtown area,"* an associate at Baker Botts confirmed. *"Discovery Green park has blossomed into a popular spot, hosting events and music to draw people down at weekends. They've made an effort to make it a really nice place."* And then there's the capital: *"I think Austin is probably the best place to be living in Texas right now,"* said a Baker Botts associate based there. *"It really lives up to its slogan, 'Keep Austin Weird.' There's a great music scene and great food, and it's really lively. I think a lot of it has to do with the University of Texas being here, so it's more collegey."*

Ask a Texan about life in the South and they'll tell you it gets hotter than a honeymoon hotel. Starched collars are bound to wilt in the tropical warmth, but apparently Houston's got an innovative way to beat the summer heat: *"It's really brutal, but we've got an air-conditioned tunnel system downtown – all the offices are connected underground, with restaurants, dry cleaners and so on. It's like a ghost town above ground because you can go straight from your car to the office."*

Law and border

So the South has come a long way to cast off its image as resource-rich and intellect-sparse; it has also largely shifted the racial demographics which dominated up until the 1980s. While it's true that Southern cities were the domain of white men in the days of oil, the past three decades have seen the population become far more diverse.

The 2010 survey showed Houston to have a population that was 43.1% Hispanic, 25.8% white and 23.5% black and a 2012 report named the Houston metropolitan area the most diverse in the US. Its proximity to the Mexican border has often seen the Lone Star try to protect itself from Mexican immigration and influence, historically pushing for insularity in the face of progression. The fact that more restrictive immigration policies (perhaps most memorably focused on the Mexico border) formed an inextricable part of President Trump's campaign will certainly have contributed to his winning 52.6% share of the popular vote in the state. But, like the world-famous TexMex fusion, the cultures have largely come to coexist. With the immigration of Latinos, Asians and African-Americans over the past few decades, the state has become a melting pot of cultures from all corners of the globe.

What can you expect of life as a lawyer in Texas and the South?

Our interviewees in Texas and the South have long been quick to sing the praises of Southern culture, telling us a big part of that is respecting people's personal lives outside of work. *"We have a very family-friendly environment,"* an associate at Jackson Walker said. *"When we have social events we try to involve spouses whenever possible, and I feel like the firm respects my personal time. You're expected to work hard and provide excellent client service, but I definitely feel like the partners and other attorneys want me to enjoy my family time, to be a well-rounded person and get involved with community. The attitude here is that that's the right thing to do."*

According to an associate from Waller: *"In the South there's a greater attention to form and decorum. If you're a jackass around here, you ain't gonna last long."* It's fitting that 'Texas' originates from the word 'tejas', which means 'friends' in the Caddo language. But friendliness doesn't detract from the serious work Southern lawyers do. When we asked Karen Sargent, of SMU, if practicing law in the South was more laid back than in New York, she replied: *"It's more about civility. The attorneys here all know each other and their reputation is on the line at all times. They make sure to maintain civility in the legal profession."*

The emphasis on a life outside of work doesn't necessarily mean you'll have fewer billables in the South. The big local firms in Texas – Haynes and Boone, Baker Botts and Bracewell – all have 2,000 hour billing targets, the same target that DLA Piper in New York, Katten Muchin in Chicago, Irell & Manella in LA, and Hunton & Williams in Richmond all set their associates. (In fact, you can find firms in those high-octane markets with even lower billing targets: Dechert and Epstein juniors, for example, are set 1,950 hours each.) Granted, working for Haynes and Boone or Baker Botts won't be the same as slugging it out at the traditional New York firms, many of which set no targets because it's assumed juniors will fly past them anyway, but it's worth noting that at firms like Haynes and Boone and Bracewell associates aren't compensated on the lockstep scale favored by NYC firms if they fall short of their targets. At Bracewell there's a reduced compensation track, and at Haynes juniors told us they were put on a 'low base' bonus system if they didn't rack up 2,000, though review performance is also taken into account.

Washington, DC

'The City of Magnificent Intentions'

Charles Dickens coined this nickname for the then fledgling capital city of the United States in 1842 during his tour of the nation. It was only in the late 1860s, following the end of the Civil War, that DC really started to turn intentions into reality. The population grew, peaking at over 800,000 after World War Two thanks to a boom in the number of federal government employees. Today there are over 650,000 people living in DC, though the wider Washington metropolitan area has a population of almost six million. The federal government remains at the heart of the district, employing nearly 240,000 people, according to the Bureau of Labor Statistics. Service industries over the years have flocked to the city to assist those who work in government and, as in the case of many law firms, to help with the very workings of government.

The DC economy didn't suffer as much as other places during the recession, largely because of the steady flow of government-related work that needs to be done, recession or no recession. The capital's share of the $700 billion bank bailout and $814billion economic stimulus package deployed to help keep the economy afloat was much larger than the district's size would in theory merit, DC *"is a little insulated,"* NALP's executive director Jim Leipold confirms. *"There is so much regulatory and government work that it is less exposed to the ups and downs in the economy."* As of 2012, 29% of jobs in DC were related to federal government; the only bigger driver of the economy, to the tune of $4.8 billion, is a thriving tourism industry.

Under (a little less) pressure

WHILE a career in Washington, DC carries equivalent prestige to New York, *"the culture is a little more laid back and less intense,"* according to junior associates based here. *"We are a bit more civilized,"* one junior joked, *"and have a better understanding of balance."* One DC-er noticed that their firm *"isn't buttoned up or formal, and it's a more collegial and family-friendly environment than my friends at New York firms experience."* Part of the reason for this could be the government setting, as one junior put it: *"In the government there is a tradition of valuing quality of life."* Compared to the perceived excesses of BigLaw in New York, *"here there's a happy medium. There isn't a need to sit in your office twiddling your thumbs if you are not doing work. The work ethic here is very, very strong, but it's a targeted effort."* Of course, *"there are still the normal pressures exerted by billing and client needs."*

Getting out at a reasonable time means there are more opportunities to sample the area's delights. We've heard from *"young and single"* associates who were anxious that a more *"family-friendly"* environment might limit afterwork frivolities, but thankfully DC has a thriving social scene of bars and clubs. *"Venture away from the Mall and there are great restaurants and bars on the 14th Street corridor,"* one associate advised.

"Within a matter of months I was on the Hill, advocating directly to congressional staff."

"Being close to the political and legal heart of the nation is an exciting prospect," juniors told us. Government-related work can be a big part of DC associates' workload, depending on the firm: one associate told of *"representing local government and regional transport authorities on urban policy issues,"* while another told us that *"within a matter of months I was on the Hill, advocating directly to congressional staff and in meetings with members of Congress."* Being so close to the action can be particularly fruitful come election time – in our latest round of research we talked to associates who'd worked on both Donald Trump's and Hillary Clinton's campaigns.

It's not yet certain how the winner of the race will affect the local legal market, but on current form, Trump's exploits have made lawyers optimistic about the volume of work. Stroock co-managing partner Jeff Keitelman tells us his firm is *"poised for growth coming out of expected changes in the new administration – we have a lot of regulatory practitioners in Washington as well as a good part of our real estate practice,"* while Richard Hays of Alston & Bird reveals *"a lot of our Washington attorneys deal with healthcare public policy, and they've been very busy."*

"Many are instead drawn to DC because of the stability of its economy."

There are certainly places where, as one source put it, *"we talk politics every now and then, but it doesn't overshadow the firm. If you're a corporate lawyer or a litigator here, you can have a completely independent practice."* Increasingly, DC associates have been reporting on *"working for a lot of small businesses and startups."* That can involve *"a significant amount of contracts work from tech clients"* – you might get the chance to draft the terms and conditions for the hottest new app. Admittedly, a proportion of these upstart companies have ties to the government, but many are instead drawn to DC because of the stability of its economy. The shift in startup investment models, from a need for venture capital to more flexible routes such as crowd-funding, has also made it easier for businesses to set up shop outside of the traditional California startup heartlands.

Working for the man

What sort of government-related work do associates do? Here's a snapshot from interviewees at various DC firms:

- *"There's a lot of appellate and Supreme Court work."*
- *"I did the gamut of healthcare public policy."*
- *"30% of what I do is representing foreign governments on the international law side of things."*
- *"We make sure that if an entity is being formed in say, Italy, it's compliant both with local requirements and US securities laws."*
- *"I have been very active in the role of policy interpretation around the health reform bill."*
- *"Our group does anything that would be considered FCC [Federal Communications Commission] work."*
- *"Our clients are mutual funds and hedge fund managers. We basically do filings they have to do. We also act as experts for the enforcement and litigation groups."*
- *"A lot of people do really fascinating work, particularly government-facing enforcement."*
- *"We had a lot of post-Fukushima energy regulation to worry about."*
- *"My work is very DC-based because so many government agencies are here."*
- *"There's a lot of document review in internal investigations, but it's not just simple stuff, you're putting together conclusions."*
- *"After just a year I'm considered a privacy and data securities specialist, recently working on an FTC regulatory enforcement action."*

Getting cozy with the government serves another purpose – it could present a cushy career path should you tire of the thrills and spills of BigLaw. *"Candidly, I don't know if I'll spend the rest of my career at the firm,"* an associate confided, *"I could easily see myself working for the government. I've talked to the chairs of my group and they said that doesn't matter as long as I work hard while I'm here."* Another revealed *"a lot of people leave to go into government. Their mindset goes beyond being a partner at a law firm."* On the flip side, don't worry if you've got your sights set on a big national firm that joining a base other than New York will limit your path to the top. Firms' DC offices are often smaller, so there's less competition for coveted partnership positions, and growing inter-office connectivity is making it less important where you call home.

House of the rising sum

Washington used to be an attractive option for bright, ambitious lawyers who wanted top-notch work but were put off by New York's sky-high rents and apartment prices. As almost all BigLaw firms pay the same $180,000 starting salary in DC as they do the Big Apple, your money will go further due to the lower cost of living. However, the district is less cheap these days. *"Over the last ten years, everything has changed,"* one associate said bluntly. *"There's been a dramatic increase in house prices, and rents – high already – have only climbed higher."* Some hoped that *"with new buildings going up all the time, prices should stabilize soon."* They may be disappointed to learn the effects may be canceled out by continued high buyer demand; while net migration into New York and LA was negative in 2015, DC is only getting busier. The population currently stands at more than 680,000, and the thousands who commute in from neighboring states each day tips it over the million mark on most days.

> *"The only downside is when you're trying to do a conference call and the White House motorcades go off."*

Many who work in the capital commute in from the surrounding suburbs or even further afield from areas like Maryland and Virginia. Once you're in town it's pretty easy to get around on foot. *"Walkability is brilliant,"* enthused one junior. Many lawyers in the district get around by walking or taking the metro as *"DC's roads have a tendency to be too busy at times,"* though we did hear from one who mainly biked. A King & Spalding source this year described their *"hilariously idyllic walk to work: I'm in the background of most of the tourist photos! We also have this crazy amazing rooftop where we watch fireworks on the fourth of July. The only downside is when you're trying to do a conference call and the White House motorcades go off."*

Working close by to the most famous home in the world is a very real possibility, as many BigLaw firms are based within a few blocks. Alston & Bird attorneys based in DC felt they were *"at the heart of everything"* as a result, while associates at Baker McKenzie described theirs as a *"trophy location."* Social occasions could even come with a presidential vibe: at Orrick's office *"the closing event of the summer is always in a swanky hotel with a view of the White House."* Close proximity to the center of US government is a sure-fire way to be ready as soon as a big political or legal change comes into view.

Finally, it's worth giving a mention to DC's law schools. Georgetown University and the George Washington University are the two biggest players and the best options if you've got your heart set on a BigLaw career. Studying locally before going on to practice in DC comes with the advantage of early opportunities to forge government connections, and *"there's a big benefit from having the opportunity to learn from professors on specialty courses. Studying in DC was amazing, you get to see every part of government and other areas of the legal realm."*

"Personally, it's an issue [work/life balance] that's very important to me. We have always been open to working flexibly and I spent 15 years here on a reduced schedule to help balance the needs of my family. We encourage our people to work in the way that is smartest for them within the demands of the job. It's a powerful tool for retaining and attracting the best talent."

- Eve Howard, regional managing partner
at Hogan Lovells

The *Chambers USA* Awards for Excellence 2017

Award 1

Antitrust

Shortlist:

Cleary Gottlieb Steen & Hamilton
Cravath, Swaine & Moore
Davis Polk & Wardwell
Gibson, Dunn & Crutcher
Hausfeld
Paul, Weiss, Rifkind, Wharton & Garrison
Skadden, Arps, Slate, Meagher & Flom
Weil, Gotshal & Manges

Winner: Cleary Gottlieb Steen & Hamilton

Award 2

Bankruptcy

Shortlist:

Davis Polk & Wardwell
Kirkland & Ellis
Klee, Tuchin, Bogdanoff & Stern
Kramer Levin Naftalis & Frankel
Pachulski Stang Ziehl & Jones
Proskauer Rose
Weil, Gotshal & Manges

Winner: Kirkland & Ellis

Award 3

Construction

Shortlist:

Jones Day
Moye, O'Brien, Pickert & Dillon
Peckar & Abramson
Pepper Hamilton
Varela, Lee, Metz & Guarino

Winner: Jones Day

Award 4

Corporate Crime & Government Investigations

Shortlist:

Debevoise & Plimpton
Gibson, Dunn & Crutcher
Kirkland & Ellis
Latham & Watkins
Quinn Emanuel Urquhart & Sullivan
Sullivan & Cromwell

Winner: Sullivan & Cromwell

Award 5

Corporate/M&A

Shortlist:

Baker Botts
Cleary Gottlieb Steen & Hamilton
Cravath, Swaine & Moore
Fenwick & West
Skadden, Arps, Slate, Meagher & Flom
Sullivan & Cromwell
Weil, Gotshal & Manges

Winner: Cravath, Swaine & Moore

Award 6

Employee Benefits & Executive Compensation

Shortlist:

Baker McKenzie
Cleary Gottlieb Steen & Hamilton
Davis Polk & Wardwell
Latham & Watkins
Proskauer Rose
Simpson Thacher & Bartlett

Winner: Davis Polk & Wardwell

Award 7

Energy/Projects: Oil & Gas

Shortlist:

Baker Botts
Bracewell
Caldwell Boudreaux Lefler
Kirkland & Ellis
Latham & Watkins
Vinson & Elkins

Winner: Baker Botts

Award 8

Energy/Projects: Power (including Renewables)

Shortlist:

Balch & Bingham
Chadbourne & Parke
Foley & Lardner
Gibson, Dunn & Crutcher
Latham & Watkins
Orrick, Herrington & Sutcliffe
Spiegel & McDiarmid

Winner: Orrick, Herrington & Sutcliffe

Award 9

Environment

Shortlist:

Arnold & Porter Kaye Scholer
Beveridge & Diamond
Bracewell
Crowell & Moring
Hunton & Williams
Latham & Watkins
Sidley Austin

Winner: Hunton & Williams

Award 10

Finance

Shortlist:

Cahill Gordon & Reindel
Davis Polk & Wardwell
Debevoise & Plimpton
Kirkland & Ellis
Latham & Watkins
Simpson Thacher & Bartlett
Weil, Gotshal & Manges

Winner: Simpson Thacher & Bartlett
Client Service: Debevoise & Plimpton

Award 11

Healthcare

Shortlist:

Baker, Donelson, Bearman, Caldwell & Berkowitz
Bass, Berry & Sims
Dentons
Hogan Lovells
McDermott Will & Emery
Polsinelli
Ropes & Gray

Winner: McDermott Will & Emery

Award 12

Insurance

Shortlist:

Clyde & Co
Covington & Burling
Debevoise & Plimpton
Latham & Watkins
McKool Smith
Reed Smith
Willkie Farr & Gallagher

Winners: Willkie Farr & Gallagher (Insurer)
Covington & Burling LLP (Policyholder)

Award 13

Intellectual Property (including Patent, Copyright & Trademark)

Shortlist:

Cooley
Dorsey & Whitney
Gibson, Dunn & Crutcher
Jones Day
Kirkland & Ellis
Sutton McAughan Deaver

Winner: Gibson, Dunn & Crutcher

Award 14

International Trade

Shortlist:

Akin Gump Strauss Hauer & Feld
Baker McKenzie
Covington & Burling
Sidley Austin
Steptoe & Johnson
White & Case

Winner: Sidley Austin

Award 15

Investment Funds

Shortlist:

Cooley
Dechert
Ropes & Gray
Schulte Roth & Zabel
Sidley Austin
Stradley Ronon Stevens & Young
Willkie Farr & Gallagher

Winner: Willkie Farr & Gallagher
Client Service: Ropes & Gray

Award 16

Labor & Employment

Shortlist:

Jones Day
Gibson, Dunn & Crutcher
Littler Mendelson
Morgan, Lewis & Bockius
Proskauer Rose
Seyfarth Shaw

Winner: Jones Day
Client Service: Morgan, Lewis & Bockius

Award 17

Privacy & Data Security

Shortlist:

Baker & Hostetler
Cooley
Covington & Burling
Hogan Lovells
McDermott Will & Emery
Morrison & Foerster
Ropes & Gray
Venable

Winner: Hogan Lovells

Award 18

Product Liability

Shortlist:

Faegre Baker Daniels
Goldman Ismail Tomaselli Brennan & Baum
Kirkland & Ellis
Quinn Emanuel Urquhart & Sullivan
Reed Smith
Shook, Hardy & Bacon
Tucker Ellis

Winner: Reed Smith
Client Service: Kirkland & Ellis

Award 19

Real Estate

Shortlist:

Cleary Gottlieb Steen & Hamilton
Fried, Frank, Harris, Shriver & Jacobson
Gibson, Dunn & Crutcher
Greenberg Traurig
Holland & Knight
Kirkland & Ellis
Simpson Thacher & Bartlett
Sullivan & Cromwell

Winner: Greenberg Traurig

Award 20

Securities and Financial Services Regulation

Shortlist:

Davis Polk & Wardwell
Debevoise & Plimpton
Gibson, Dunn & Crutcher
King & Spalding
Murphy & McGonigle
Sidley Austin
Skadden, Arps, Slate, Meagher & Flom
Sullivan & Cromwell
WilmerHale

Winner: Skadden, Arps, Slate, Meagher & Flom

Award 21

Tax

Shortlist:

Chamberlain, Hrdlicka, White, Williams & Aughtry
Davis Polk & Wardwell
Latham & Watkins
Morgan, Lewis & Bockius
Simpson Thacher & Bartlett
Skadden, Arps, Slate, Meagher & Flom

Winner: Simpson Thacher & Bartlett

Award 22

Litigation: Business Trial Lawyers (individuals)

Shortlist:

Philip S. Beck - Bartlit Beck Herman Palenchar & Scott
Dane H. Butswinkas - Williams & Connolly
James F. Hurst - Kirkland & Ellis
W. Mark Lanier - The Lanier Law Firm
Randy M. Mastro - Gibson, Dunn & Crutcher
Robert A. Van Nest - Keker Van Nest & Peters
Beth A. Wilkinson - Wilkinson Walsh + Eskovitz

Winner: Randy M. Mastro - Gibson, Dunn & Crutcher

Award 23

Litigation: White Collar Crime & Gov't Investigations (individuals)

Shortlist:

Cristina C. Arguedas - Arguedas, Cassman & Headley
Steven M. Bauer - Latham & Watkins
George S. Canellos - Milbank, Tweed, Hadley & McCloy
David Gerger - Quinn Emanuel Urquhart & Sullivan
Daniel M. Gitner - Lankler Siffert & Wohl
Mark J. MacDougall – Akin Gump Strauss Hauer & Feld
Mark Rochon - Miller & Chevalier Chartered
Reid H. Weingarten - Steptoe & Johnson

Winner: Mark Rochon – Miller & Chevalier

Award 24

Outstanding Contribution to the Legal Profession

F. Joseph Warin
Gibson, Dunn & Crutcher

Award 25

Lifetime Achievement Award

Franci J. Blassberg
Debevoise & Plimpton

Useful Resources

General

American Bar Association (ABA)
Chicago HQ:
321 North Clark Street
Chicago, IL 60654
Phone: 312 988-5000
DC office:
1050 Connecticut Ave. NW
Suite 400
Washington, DC 20036
Phone: 202 662-1000
www.americanbar.org

National Association for Law Placement (NALP)
1220 19th Street NW
Suite 401
Washington, DC 20036-2405
Phone: 202 835-1001
www.nalp.org

National Institute for Trial Advocacy (NITA)
1685 38th Street, Suite 200
Boulder, CO 80301-2735
Phone: 1.800.225.6482

Diversity

Disability:
National Association of Law Students with Disabilities
Contact: via website
www.nalswd.org
LGBT:
National LGBT Bar Association
1875 I Street NW, 11th Floor
Washington, DC 20006
Phone: 202 637-7661
E-mail: info@LGBTbar.org
www.lgbtbar.org

Minorities:
Asian American Legal Defense and Education Fund (AALDEF)
99 Hudson St, 12th Floor
New York, NY 10013
Phone: (212) 966-5932
E-mail: info@aaldef.org
www.aaldef.org

Hispanic National Bar Association (HNBA)
1020 19th Street NW,
Suite 505
Washington, DC 20036
www.hnba.com

Lawyers' Committee for Civil Rights Under Law
1401 New York Avenue, NW,
Suite 400
Washington, DC 20005
Phone: (888) 299-5227
www.lawyerscommittee.org

Minority Corporate Counsel Association (MCCA)
1111 Pennsylvania Avenue, NW
Washington, DC 20004
Phone: (202) 739-5901
www.mcca.com

The NAACP Legal Defense & Educational Fund
40 Rector Street, 5th floor
New York, NY 10006
(212) 965-2200
www.naacpldf.org

National Asian Pacific American Bar Association (NAPABA)
1612 K Street NW, Suite 1400
Washington, DC 20006
Phone: (202) 775-9555
www.napaba.org

National Asian Pacific American Law Student Association (NAPALSA)
Contact: via website
www.napalsa.com

National Bar Association (NBA)
1225 11th Street, NW
Washington, DC 20001
Phone: (302) 842-3900
www.nationalbar.org

National Black Law Students Association (NBLSA)
1225 11th Street NW
Washington, DC 20001-4217
Phone: (202) 618-2572
E-mail: info@nblsa.org
www.nblsa.org

National Latina/o Student Association (NLLSA)
E-mail: info@nllsa.org
www.nllsa.org

Practicing Attorneys for Law Students Program (PALS)
42 West 44th Street
New York, NY 10036
Phone: (212) 730-PALS
E-mail: info@palsprogram.org
www.palsprogram.org

South Asian Bar Association of North America
www.sabanorthamerica.com

Women

Ms.JD
E-mail: staff@ms-jd.org
http://ms-jd.org

National Women's Law Center
11 Dupont Circle, NW, #800
Washington, DC 20036
Phone: (202) 588-5180
E-mail: info@nwlc.org www.nwlc.org

New York Women's Bar Association (NYWBA)
132 East 43rd Street, #716,
The Chrysler Building
New York, NY 10017-4019
Phone: 212-490-8202
E-mail: info@nywba.org
www.nywba.org

Women's Bar Association of the District of Columbia & WBA Foundation
2020 Pennsylvania Avenue, NW
Suite 446
Washington, DC 20006
Phone: 202-639-8880
E-mail: admin@wbadc.org
www.wbadc.org

Pro Bono

American Civil Liberties Union (ACLU)
125 Broad Street, 18th Floor
New York NY 10004
Phone: 212-549-2500
www.aclu.org

Equal Justice Works
1730 M Street NW, Suite 1010
Washington, DC 20036-4511
Phone: (202) 466-3686
www.equaljusticeworks.org

Legal Aid Society
199 Water Street
New York, NY 10038
Phone: (212) 577-3300
www.legal-aid.org

New York Legal Assistance Group (NYLAG)
7 Hanover Square, 18th Floor
New York, NY 10004
Phone: (212) 613-5000
E-mail: volunteer@nylag.org

Pro Bono Institute
1025 Connecticut Avenue, NW
Suite 205
Washington, DC 20036
Phone: (202) 729-6699
www.probonoinst.org

Public Counsel Law Center
610 South Ardmore Avenue
Los Angeles, CA 90005
Phone: (213) 385-2977
www.publiccounsel.org